# CONSTITUTIONAL
# LAW

### TENTH EDITION

## *Jacqueline R.* KANOVITZ

## *Michael I.* KANOVITZ

 LexisNexis®

 anderson publishing
A member of the LexisNexis Group

**John C. Klotter Justice Administration Legal Series**

## Constitutional Law, Tenth Edition

Copyright © 1968, 1971, 1977, 1981, 1985, 1991, 1995, 1999, 2002, 2005
Matthew Bender & Company, Inc., a member of the LexisNexis Group

Phone 877-374-2919
Web Site www.lexisnexis.com/anderson/criminaljustice

LexisNexis and the Knowledge Burst logo are trademarks of Reed Elsevier Properties, Inc.
Anderson Publishing is a registered trademark of Anderson Publishing, a member of the LexisNexis Group

Kanovitz, Jacqueline R.
   Constitutional Law / Jacqueline R. Kanovitz, Michael I. Kanovitz. -- 10th ed.
      p.  cm.
      Includes index.
      ISBN 1-59345-968-8  (softbound : alk. paper)

Cover design by Tin Box Studio, Inc.

EDITOR  Elisabeth Roszmann Ebben
ACQUISITIONS EDITOR  Michael C. Braswell

# Preface

Almost four decades have passed since the first edition of this textbook. During the 1960s and 1970s, the Supreme Court waged a campaign to reform the criminal justice system through the selective incorporation of Bill of Rights safeguards into the Fourteenth Amendment. Having constitutionalized criminal procedure, the Supreme Court then elaborated a set of constitutionally mandated restraints on police behavior. The "goodness" or "badness" of a legal precept, nevertheless, depends on how well it works in practice. This can only be known through empirical validation. So it is with constitutional interpretations. Just as the 1960s and 1970s were periods of reform and tremendous constitutional expansion, the 1980s and 1990s were a time of retrenchment and correction.

Criminal justice became ensconced as a learned profession in the 1960s when Congress recognized that compliance with the Supreme Court's constitutional mandates required better-educated police officers and appropriated funds to establish programs for their higher education. Discerning the need for high-quality learning materials, John Klotter embarked on a career of police scholarship that has spanned more than four decades. I was fortunate enough to be John's co-author since the first edition of this book. After seven editions, John decided to make a transition from working on this textbook to concentrating on keeping his other titles up-to-date. Michael Kanovitz came on board as co-author at that time. Taking what was already a successful formula, yet recognizing the changing needs of our audience, we revised the style and format in the Eighth Edition. The new format has been well received.

We wish to thank the professors, instructors, and police departments who have used our book over the years, especially for their suggestions, comments, and support, and most of all for the opportunity they have given us to engage in the intensive study of the Constitution as it applies to criminal justice personnel. We hope you will be pleased with the Tenth Edition and we welcome your comments.

# John C. Klotter
# Justice Administration Legal Series

**John C. Klotter**, J.D. is a Professor Emeritus and Former Dean of the School of Justice Administration, University of Louisville. Professor Klotter began his association with Anderson Publishing in 1967, serving as Editorial Director of its newly formed Police Publications Advisory Board. In 1968, he co-authored, with Jacqueline Kanovitz, the first edition of *Constitutional Law for Police*, whose title was later changed to *Constitutional Law*. This book was made part of a Justice Administration Legal Series for which Klotter also authored *Criminal Evidence* in 1971 (now in its eighth edition) and later added *Criminal Law* (now in its seventh edition). *Legal Guide for Police: Constitutional Issues*, now in its fifth edition, was first published in 1977.

In honor of Professor Klotter's contribution to the field of criminal justice and his role with Anderson Publishing in serving this discipline, LexisNexis is proud to rename the series the *John C. Klotter Justice Administration Legal Series* with the publication of this tenth edition of *Constitutional Law*, which Klotter and Kanovitz introduced 37 years ago.

# About the Authors

**Jacqueline Kanovitz** is an Emeritus Professor of the Brandeis School of Law where she taught for thirty years and served as Associate Dean for Student Affairs. She also taught at other law schools. She holds a J.D. (summa cum laude) from the University of Louisville School of Law. She is the recipient of numerous awards for teaching and writing excellence and has been a co-author of this textbook since the first edition in 1968.

**Michael Kanovitz** holds a J.D. (cum laude) from Cornell University School of Law. He is a partner in the law firm of Loevy & Loevy in Chicago, Illinois, where he practices federal and state civil rights litigation involving criminal justice and First Amendment issues.

# Table of Contents

## Chapter 3
## Authority to Detain and Arrest; Use of Force                      81

## Chapter 4
## Search and Seizure                                                 157

## Chapter 5
## Eavesdropping and Interception of Communications                   245

## Chapter 6
## Interrogations and Confessions                                     279

## Chapter 7
## Compulsory Self-Incrimination                                      329

Section

## Chapter 8
## Right to Counsel                                                   361

Section

## Chapter 9
## Trial and Punishment                                           389

## Chapter 10
## Federal Criminal and Civil Remedies
## for Unconstitutional Conduct                                   441

# Case Citation Guide

The following list provides an explanation of case citations used in *Constitutional Law*, Eighth Edition, for readers who may be unfamiliar with how court decisions are cited.

U.S.                  *United States Reports*. Published by the United States government, this is the official source of United States Supreme Court decisions. It reports only United States Supreme Court decisions.

S. Ct.                *Supreme Court Reporter*. Published by West Publishing Company, this publication reports United States Supreme Court decisions.

L. Ed./L. Ed. 2d      *United States Reports, Lawyers' Edition, First Series/Second Series*. Published by Lawyers Cooperative Publishing Company, this publication reports United States Supreme Court decisions.

F.2d/F.3d             *Federal Reports, Second Series/Third Series*. Published by West Publishing Company, it reports decisions of the Federal Courts of Appeals.

F. Supp.              *Federal Supplement*. Published by West Publishing Company, this reports decisions of the Federal District Courts.

# Sample Case Citations

Gideon v. Wainwright, 372 U.S. 335 (1963). This case is located in volume 372 of the *United States Reports*, beginning on page 335. It was decided in 1963.

Gideon v. Wainwright, 83 S. Ct. 792 (1963). Gideon v. Wainwright is published in volume 83 of the *Supreme Court Reporter*, beginning on page 792.

Gideon v. Wainwright, 9 L. Ed. 2d 799 (1963). Gideon v. Wainwright is also published in volume 9 of *Supreme Court Reports, Lawyers' Edition*, Second Series, beginning on page 799.

Phillips v. Perry, 106 F.3d 1420 (9th Cir. 1997). This case is located in volume 106 of *Federal Reports*, Third Series, beginning on page 1420. It was decided by the Ninth Circuit Court of Appeals in 1997.

Brockway v. Shepherd, 942 F. Supp. 1012 (M.D. Pa. 1997). This case is located in volume 942 of *Federal Supplement*, beginning on page 1012. It was decided in 1997 by the Federal District Court for the Middle District of Pennsylvania.

# History, Structure, and Content of the United States Constitution   1

*We the People of the United States, in Order to form a more perfect Union, establish Justice, insure domestic Tranquility, provide for the common defence, promote the general Welfare, and secure the Blessings of Liberty to ourselves and our Posterity, do ordain and establish this Constitution for the United States of America.*

Preamble to the United States Constitution

# Chapter Outline

## § 1.1  History of the United States Constitution

The men who met in Philadelphia in 1787 had ample precedent for the notion of a written constitution. Americans had been living under colonial charters for more than 100 years. After declaring their independence, the 13 former colonies immediately began working on constitutions in preparation for statehood. New Hampshire was the first to complete this process.[1] By 1779, all 13 former colonies had constitutions in place. The governments established by these constitutions were patterned after the English parliamentary system. Nearly all provided for a bicameral legislature that was responsible for selecting the governor.

## § 1.2  —Early Steps Toward National Unity

The federal union established by the Constitution of 1789 was not the first attempt at alliance. In 1643, the colonies of Massachusetts, New Plymouth, Connecticut, and New Haven formed a coalition, known as the New England Confederacy, for mutual defense against the Dutch and Indians. The colonists were, nevertheless, apprehensive about establishing a strong central government with sovereign authority over them. Self-interest was necessary to overcome their apprehensions.

The Revolutionary War provided the first major impetus for unification. Coordinating the war effort required something more than 13 independent nations fighting separately toward a common goal. When the First Continental Congress assembled in Philadelphia in 1774, all colonies except Georgia sent delegates.[2] However, the colonists were not yet ready to pledge their permanent allegiance to a sovereign national government. Preparing to wrest power from one sovereign, they were in no hurry to turn it over to another. Consequently, they gave the Continental Congress only powers that were strictly necessary for carrying on the war. The Continental Congress functioned as the instrument of the states, with the states retaining sovereignty.

---

[1]    ERIKSSON, AMERICAN CONSTITUTIONAL HISTORY, ch. 7 (1933).
[2]    EVANS, CASES ON CONSTITUTIONAL LAW, ch. 1 (1933).

## § 1.3 —Articles of Confederation

It soon became apparent that greater centralization was needed. In 1776, a committee was appointed to study this problem. This committee wrote the Articles of Confederation, which went into effect in March of 1781. While the Articles of Confederation set up a national government, the government's powers over domestic affairs were so limited that the government was doomed to fail before it began. Distrustful of a strong central government, the states refused to delegate the vital power to levy taxes, regulate commerce, or pass laws affecting domestic affairs.[3] The Union established under the Articles of Confederation was little more than a loosely joined league of sovereign and independent states. The chief function of the national government was to represent the league of states in foreign affairs.

After the War of Independence was won, the American people were confronted with the realization that the government they had hastily thrown together for the purpose of carrying on the war was too weak to protect their common interests in peacetime. Fortunately, the leaders of this period were reasonable people and were able solve this problem without the power struggles and bloodshed that so often follow a revolution.

## § 1.4 —Drafting the United States Constitution

In February of 1787, the Congress established under the Articles of Confederation adopted a resolution calling for a convention to consider revision. Three months later, 55 delegates, representing every state except Rhode Island, assembled in Philadelphia and selected George Washington as their unanimous choice to preside over the Convention. The session lasted nearly four months.

The most immediate question facing the Convention was whether the Articles of Confederation could be salvaged or whether it was necessary to begin anew. James Madison recommended salvaging the best feature of the Articles of Confederation—the idea of separating the powers of the national government into three branches—and building a new constitution around it. After heated debate and compromise on such issues as the amount and kinds of powers to delegate to the national government, the basis for representation in the national legislature, and the relations between the nation and the states, the Convention ended with a constitution that bore little resemblance to the document the delegates had been assembled to "revise." The proposed Constitution conferred broad powers on the federal government.

---

[3]    ERIKSSON, *supra* note 1.

## § 1.5  —Ratification by the States

Although drafting the Constitution was a monumental task, an even greater one remained. Public sentiment was divided about the wisdom of conferring broad powers on the national government. James Madison, Alexander Hamilton, and John Jay undertook the task of selling the Constitution to the people. In their historic *Federalist Papers*, they argued that a strong central government was necessary to ensure political stability and national security. Their opponents countered that:

1.  Granting the federal government the power to tax was dangerous.
2.  The Constitution lacked a Bill of Rights and the assurance of a fair trial.
3.  Concentrating so much power in the federal government threatened the sovereignty of the states.

The ratification process moved forward in the face of heated debate. On June 21, 1788, New Hampshire became the ninth state to ratify the Constitution. Although ratification by nine states was sufficient to make the Constitution operative in the states that had ratified it, New York and Virginia had to be won over in order to ensure the political future of the new government. On June 25, 1788, Virginia ratified the Constitution by a narrow margin, over the fiery opposition of George Mason and Patrick Henry. On July 2, 1788, the Constitution was declared to have been duly ratified. New York ratified the Constitution less than a month later. North Carolina and Rhode Island remained outside the Union, watching from the sidelines for many months. The passage by Congress of a tariff on foreign imports, including goods imported from North Carolina and Rhode Island, drove them into the union. North Carolina and Rhode Island ratified the Constitution on November 21, 1789, and May 29, 1790, respectively.[4]

On September 13, 1788, the Continental Congress passed a resolution putting the new Constitution into effect. On April 30, 1789, George Washington was inaugurated as the first president of the United States. Within a span of 25 years, the 13 former colonies accomplished two major victories. They won the War of Independence and established a firm and stable government that has endured for more than 200 years.

---

[4]  The dates that the individual states ratified the Constitution are as follows: Delaware—December 7, 1787; Pennsylvania—December 11, 1787; New Jersey—December 18, 1787; Georgia—January 2, 1788; Connecticut—January 9, 1788; Massachusetts—February 6, 1788; Maryland—April 26, 1788; South Carolina—May 23, 1788; New Hampshire—June 21, 1788; Virginia—June 25, 1788; New York—July 26, 1788; North Carolina—November 21, 1789; Rhode Island—May 29, 1790.

## § 1.6   Structure and Content of the Constitution

The United States Constitution is divided into seven parts, called articles. The content of each article is summarized below.[5]

ARTICLE I.     Article I establishes the legislative branch of government. It provides that the legislative powers of the United States shall be vested in Congress, which shall consist of two chambers—the Senate and the House of Representatives. Sections 2 through 7 provide for the number and qualifications of the representatives in each chamber, the method of selecting them, the procedures to be followed in enacting legislation, and the manner of impeachment. Section 8 outlines the powers of Congress in domestic and foreign affairs; sections 9 and 10 impose various limitations on the powers of Congress and of the states.

ARTICLE II.     Article II establishes the executive branch of government. It provides that the executive powers of the United States shall be vested in the President and outlines the President's powers and duties. The remainder of this article deals with the qualifications of the President and Vice President, the manner of election, oath of office, and the method and grounds for removal.

ARTICLE III.     Article III establishes the judicial branch of government. The Supreme Court is the only court expressly created by the Constitution. Article III vests the judicial power of the United States in the Supreme Court "and in such inferior courts as Congress should see fit to establish." It goes on to outline the jurisdiction of the Supreme Court and the lower federal courts. Article III also defines the crime of treason and the proof necessary for a conviction.

ARTICLE IV.     Article IV establishes the duties states owe one another. These duties include the duty to extend full faith and credit to the laws of sister states, to grant the citizens of sister states equal privileges and immunities, and to surrender fleeing felons for interstate extradition. Article IV also provides for the admission of new states, grants Congress plenary power to govern territorial possessions of the United States, and assures each state a republican form of government. Finally, it guarantees the states federal protection against external invasions and internal insurrections.

ARTICLE V.     Article V establishes procedures for amending the Constitution. Constitutional amendments can be proposed in one of two ways— either by a two-thirds vote in both houses of Congress or through a recommendation endorsed by two-thirds of the state legislatures. Once proposed, the amendment must be ratified by the legisla-

---

[5]    The Constitution is reprinted in Part III. You are encouraged to read the full text now and reread the individual sections when they are discussed in later chapters.

tures of three-fourths of the states, or by conventions in three-fourths of the states, in order to become part of the Constitution.

ARTICLE VI.   Article VI contains the "supremacy clause." The supremacy clause provides that the Constitution, laws, and treaties of the United States shall be the supreme law of the land and shall bind state judges, displacing contrary provisions in state constitutions and statutes. Federal and state officials are required to take an oath of office to support the Constitution.

ARTICLE VII.   Article VII has historic importance only. It provides that the Constitution shall go into effect once it is ratified by nine states and shall be operative in the states that ratified it.

## § 1.7 —Separation of the Powers of the National Government

The Framers were apprehensive of concentrated power. They believed that liberty would be more secure if the national government's powers were divided among three separate branches—a bicameral legislature with the power to make laws, an executive with the power to enforce them, and a judiciary with the power to interpret the laws and apply them in individual cases.[6] They accomplished this in the first three articles. These articles distribute the powers of the national government among three branches—Congress, the Presidency, and the Judiciary—and describe the powers allocated to each. This allocation is fixed. The Constitution prohibits one branch from encroaching on the powers delegated to another branch and from turning its powers over to another branch.

Figure 1.1
**Separation of Powers**

Our Constitution divides the powers of the national government among three branches—a bicameral legislature with the power to make laws, an executive with the power to enforce them, and a judiciary with the power to interpret and apply them in individual cases.

---

[6]   THE FEDERALIST No. 47, at 241 (J. Madison) (J. Gideon ed. 1831).

## A. Encroachment on Powers Delegated to a Coordinate Branch

While Congress has the power to enact laws, it may not exercise this power in ways that encroach upon the powers of the President or the judiciary. Because the power to interpret the Constitution belongs to the judiciary, Congress cannot override the Supreme Court's constitutional decisions by statute. A reminder is occasionally needed. In *City of Boerne v. Flores*,[7] Congress, disturbed by a Supreme Court decision that placed a restrictive interpretation on the First Amendment guarantee of freedom of religion, enacted a law that called for a different result. The Supreme Court's reaction was abrupt and to the point. It told Congress in no uncertain terms that it had overstepped its legislative powers and invaded the province of the judiciary. The doctrine of separation of powers prevents Congress from nullifying the Supreme Court's constitutional decisions by statute. A constitutional amendment is the only action that can accomplish this. Amending the Constitution is a cumbersome process. This process has been undertaken successfully only 27 times in American history.

The Supreme Court's statutory interpretations stand on a different footing.[8] Because Congress has the power to enact laws, Congress can change them if it does not like the way they are interpreted. The amended statute will govern the decisions of courts in future cases. However, Congress cannot change the outcome of cases that were previously decided under the statute because the judicial power includes the power to render binding decisions, subject to reversal only by a higher court.[9]

## B. Delegation of Power to Coordinate Branch

The doctrine of separation of powers also prohibits one branch from turning its powers over to another branch. Congress, for example, cannot delegate responsibility for enacting laws to the executive or judicial branches. The nondelegation doctrine stems from the language of Article I, Section 1, which declares that "[a]ll legislative powers herein granted shall be vested in a Congress of the United States." However, the Constitution does not prohibit Congress from seeking assistance from coordinate branches. The volume of regulations needed to run the nation is so mammoth that Congress could not function unless able to legislate in broad terms, leaving discretion to fill in the details to others. Under settled interpretation, Congress does not violate the constitutional separation of powers by delegating rule-making authority to agencies within the executive branch, provided it lays down clear standards to guide the agencies in exercising their delegated authority.

---

[7]     521 U.S. 507, 117 S. Ct. 2157, 138 L. Ed. 2d 624 (1997).

[8]     Engel v. Vitale, 370 U.S. 421, 82 S. Ct. 1261, 8 L. Ed. 2d 601 (1962).

[9]     Plaut v. Spendthrift Farms, Inc., 514 U.S. 211, 115 S. Ct. 1447, 131 L. Ed. 2d 328 (1995).

When Congress enacted the Controlled Substances Act, for example, it delegated authority to the Attorney General to update the controlled substance schedules by adding new drugs found to meet certain statutory criteria. The addition of new drugs automatically caused their manufacture, possession, and distribution to become a federal criminal offense. The Supreme Court, nevertheless, upheld this delegation of authority because the Controlled Substances Act set forth intelligible criteria to guide the Attorney General's exercise of the delegated authority.[10]

Regulations adopted by federal agencies to implement the statutes that Congress enacts are published in the Code of Federal Regulations, which is one of today's most important bodies of law.

## § 1.8 —Division of Power between the National Government and the States

The Constitution also divides power between the national government and the states. Understanding the vertical division of power calls for a brief review of history. With the signing of the Declaration of Independence, the colonies renounced their allegiance to England and Parliament's authority over them, and assumed the status of separate sovereign entities. Each state had its own constitution and functioned autonomously. The states retained their sovereignty and independence under the Articles of Confederation. However, they were forced to yield a portion of it in order to form a federal union. There was no historical precedent for the dual (federal-state) system of government established by the Framers in 1789. It remained for the subsequent course of history to define and redefine the precise nature of the federal union and the relationship between the nation and the states. However, the structural framework was laid out in 1789.

The division of power between the federal government and the states is accomplished through a combination of three sections. The Constitution begins by listing the powers delegated to the federal government. This is accomplished in Article I, Section 8. Article I, Section 10 then withdraws certain powers from the states by prohibiting the states from exercising them. The implication from this scheme is that all powers that have not been delegated to the federal government and that the states are not forbidden to exercise remain in the states, from whence the power originated. This implication was made explicit with the adoption of the Tenth Amendment in 1791, which reads: "The powers not delegated to the United States by the Constitution, nor prohibited by it to the States, are reserved to the States respectively, or to the people."

There are three things to keep in mind about the division of power between the federal government and the states. First, the federal government

---

[10]   Touby v. United States, 500 U.S. 160, 111 S. Ct. 1752, 114 L. Ed. 2d 219 (1991).

is a government of enumerated and limited powers. It can exercise only the powers that have been delegated. These powers are found primarily in Article I, Section 8, which is the focus of the next section. Second, while the federal government is a government of enumerated and limited powers, it is supreme within its sphere of operation. When Congress enacts a law within the scope of its delegated powers, the federal law supersedes and annuls conflicting state laws. This results from the supremacy clause of Article VI, which declares that "[t]his Constitution, and Laws of the United States which shall be made in Pursuance thereof, . . . shall be the supreme Law of the Land, . . . any Thing in the Constitution or Laws of any state to the Contrary notwithstanding." For example, should Congress decided to pass a law reducing the maximum speed on federal highways to 50 miles per hour, this law would supersede and annul state laws permitting a higher speed. Third, all powers that have not been delegated to the federal government and that the states are not prohibited from exercising belong to the states.

The Civil War put to the test whether a state, having once joined the union and surrendered a portion of its sovereignty, could withdraw from the union by a unilateral act of secession. The indestructible nature of the federal union was decided on the battlefield. The union was permanent.

Figure 1.2
**Division of Power between the Federal Government and the States**

> The Constitution divides power between the federal government and the states by: (1) enumerating the powers delegated to the federal government, (2) prohibiting states from exercising certain powers, and (3) providing that "[t]he powers not delegated to the United States by the Constitution, nor prohibited by it to the States, are reserved to the States . . ." The federal government, though a government of enumerated and limited powers, is supreme in its sphere of operation. When Congress enacts legislation within the scope of its delegated powers, its laws prevail over contrary state laws.

## § 1.9 —Powers Granted to the Federal Government

Brevity is a striking feature of the Constitution. The Framers did not clutter the Constitution with unnecessary details that might have rendered it obsolete within a generation or two. Instead, they laid out a broad framework, having faith that courts would interpret the language wisely and in accordance with the evolving needs of society.

Every law enacted by Congress must be based on one or more of its enumerated powers. The powers granted to the federal government are found primarily in Article I, Section 8. The following section provides an overview of the federal government's powers, emphasizing those that are most important.

## A.  *The Power to Levy Taxes and Make Expenditures for the National Defense and General Welfare*

The federal government has the power to tax. This power is essential because no government can survive without a source of revenue. The lack of taxing power was a major weakness of the government established by the Articles of Confederation. Congress occasionally uses this power to accomplish goals that go beyond simply raising revenue.[11] The Harrison Anti-Narcotics Act,[12] for example, imposes an occupational tax on drug dealers and requires them to register with the Internal Revenue Service. Though the tax is small and Congress's main reason for imposing the tax was to force drug dealers to register and identify themselves or face federal prosecution for tax evasion, the Harrison Act has been upheld as a constitutional exercise of the taxing power.[13]

## B.  *The Power to Borrow Money on the Credit of the United States*

The federal government also has the power to borrow money. This power provides an auxiliary source of revenue when taxes are insufficient to cover the government's operating expenses.

## C.  *The Power to Regulate Interstate and Foreign Commerce*

Congress has the power to "regulate Commerce with foreign Nations, and among the several States." Next to the taxing power, this is the most important power granted to the federal government. The commerce clause enables Congress to regulate: (1) channels and instrumentalities used in interstate commerce, such as interstate highways, railroads, trucking concerns, airlines, and telephone and telegraph companies; (2) persons or things involved in interstate commerce; and (3) any commercial activity that has a substantial effect on interstate commerce, including activity that takes place entirely within the confines of a single state.[14] This interpretation gives the federal government vast regulatory powers. In an industrialized society, economic activity that occurs in one state no longer affects that state alone. Waves are felt in other parts of the nation. These waves produce consequences that affect

---

[11]  United States v. Doremus, 249 U.S. 86, 39 S. Ct. 214, 63 L. Ed. 493 (1919); Sonzinsky v. United States, 300 U.S. 506, 57 S. Ct. 554, 81 L. Ed. 772 (1937).

[12]  26 U.S.C. § 4701 *et seq.* (1989).

[13]  Minor v. United States, 396 U.S. 87, 90 S. Ct. 284, 24 L. Ed. 2d 283 (1969).

[14]  United States v. Darby, 312 U.S. 100, 61 S. Ct. 451, 85 L. Ed. 609 (1941); **United States v. Lopez, 514 U.S. 549, 115 S. Ct. 1624, 131 L. Ed. 2d (1995); United States v. Morrison, 529 U.S. 598, 120 S. Ct. 1740, 146 L. Ed. 2d 658 (2000).**

the flow of goods and services across state lines. The vast reach of the commerce clause is illustrated by *Wickard v. Filburn,*[15] in which the Supreme Court held that a farmer who produced wheat to feed his livestock and for personal consumption was subject to penalty under the Agricultural Adjustment Act for exceeding his federal allotment, even though none of his wheat was sold in interstate commerce, or even locally. The Court found that production of wheat for personal consumption had a "substantial effect" on interstate commerce because home-grown wheat competes with wheat in commerce and can produce surpluses and lower the market price.

The commerce clause has been used to prescribe safety standards in transportation and industry, labor legislation, crop restriction programs, antitrust laws, and other economic regulations. However, economic regulations do not exhaust Congress's powers under the commerce clause. Congress has used the commerce clause to enact social legislation such as public accommodation laws, fair housing laws, and laws prohibiting discrimination against the handicapped and the elderly.[16] The commerce clause has also supplied the basis for a large body of federal criminal statutes, including the Mann Act, which makes it a federal crime to transport women across state lines for immoral purposes, the National Motor Vehicle Theft Act, which makes it a crime to transport stolen vehicles in interstate commerce, and the Federal Kidnapping Act, which makes it a crime to kidnap a person and take him or her across state lines. The establishment of federal law enforcement agencies, such as the Federal Bureau of Investigation, also rests in part on the commerce clause.

For a time, the powers of Congress under the commerce clause seemed boundless. Congress, with the Supreme Court's blessing, enacted laws that stretched the commerce clause to its limits. *United States v. Lopez*[17] marked a turning point. The Supreme Court, for the first time in modern history, told Congress that it had gone too far. *Lopez* involved the constitutionality of the federal Gun-Free School Zones Act, which it made it a crime to possess a gun in a school zone. Although this law was predicated on the commerce clause, it did not require proof that the gun or the perpetrators had crossed state lines or that the acts condemned had any other relationship to interstate commerce.

The Court began its analysis by noting that the commerce clause reaches three broad categories of activities: (1) channels and instrumentalities used in interstate commerce, (2) persons or things involved in interstate commerce, and (3) any activity that has a substantial effect on interstate commerce. The

---

[15]   317 U.S. 111, 63 S. Ct. 82, 87 L. Ed. 122 (1942).

[16]   Katzenbach v. McClung, 379 U.S. 294, 85 S. Ct. 377, 13 L. Ed. 2d 290 (1964) (upholding congressional power to ban racial discrimination at restaurants that served food, a substantial portion of which had moved in interstate commerce); Heart of Atlanta Motel, Inc. v. United States, 379 U.S. 241, 85 S. Ct. 348, 13 L. Ed. 2d 258 (1964) (upholding congressional power to ban racial discrimination in hotels because this discrimination had a "disruptive effect . . . on commercial intercourse"); United States v. Darby, *supra* note 14 (upholding congressional power to forbid interstate commerce in goods made by child labor because traffic in such goods encourages "competition . . . injurious to the commerce").

[17]   *Supra* note 14.

government argued that possession of a gun in a school zone fell within the third category because the presence of guns in school zones creates a tense learning environment that can, in turn, affect the nation's economic productivity by producing a less competent body of citizens. The Court was not impressed by this tortured line of reasoning. The scope of the commerce clause, the Court declared, "must be considered in the light of our dual system of government and may not be extended so as to embrace effects upon interstate commerce so indirect and remote that to embrace them, in view of our complex society, would effectually obliterate the distinction between what is national and what is local and create a completely centralized government." Under our federal system, the states have the primary authority for enacting and enforcing criminal laws. Congress may use the commerce clause to make local acts of violence federal crimes only if they are directed at channels or instrumentalities used in interstate commerce or persons or things involved in interstate commerce. Otherwise, regulation of local acts of violence falls within the legislative domain of the states.

In *United States v. Morrison*,[18] the Supreme Court once again rejected an attempt by Congress to regulate local criminal activity under the third category. This category, the Court wrote, may only be used to regulate activities that are economic or commercial in nature; it may not be used to regulate activities that are noncommercial. However, Congress's power under the first two categories is not so limited. Congress, for example, can make it a federal crime for a convicted felon to own a firearm that has previously been shipped in interstate commerce, even though the regulated activity is not commercial, because this regulation is sustainable under the second category. Regulations sustainable under the third category, in contrast, must involve commercial activity.

Figure 1.3.
**Commerce Clause Powers**

> The commerce clause allows Congress to regulate three broad categories of activities: (1) instrumentalities and channels involved in interstate commerce, (2) movement of persons or things across state lines, and (3) any commercial activity that has a substantial effect on interstate commerce.

---

[18]   *Supra* note 14.

## D. *The Power to Establish National Rules Regarding Immigration, Naturalization, and Bankruptcy*

The federal government alone can regulate immigration and naturalization. The states are forbidden to legislate on this subject. The federal government also has exclusive legislative control over bankruptcy laws and the establishment of bankruptcy courts. States, nevertheless, remain free to enact laws dealing with the legal rights of debtors and creditors, so long as they do not conflict with federal bankruptcy laws.[19]

## E. *The Power to Coin Money, Regulate Currency, and Punish Counterfeiting*

Congress has the exclusive power to regulate currency. This includes the power to coin money, designate the medium of exchange, forbid melting, defacing, and counterfeiting, and establish agencies to enforce the currency laws.

## F. *The Power to Establish Post Offices and Post Roads*

Congress also has the power to establish post offices and post roads. This power enables Congress to regulate what can be placed in the mail, to make theft from the mails and use of the mails for illegal purposes federal crimes, and to establish federal agencies to enforce the postal laws.

## G. *The Power to Secure for Authors and Inventors the Exclusive Right to Writings and Discoveries for a Limited Period of Time*

The Constitution grants Congress the power to secure for authors and inventors the exclusive rights to the fruits of their labors. This provision supplies the constitutional basis for federal patent and copyright laws.

## H. *The Power to Establish Judicial Tribunals Inferior to the Supreme Court*

The Supreme Court is the only court expressly created by the Constitution; however, Congress was given the power to establish judicial tribunals inferior to the Supreme Court. In 1789, Congress exercised this

---

[19]    Kesler v. Department of Public Safety, 369 U.S. 153, 82 S. Ct. 807, 7 L. Ed. 2d 641 (1962).

power. The Judiciary Act of 1789 provided for the establishment of 13 district and three circuit courts. While the number of lower federal courts has grown, the basic pattern remains the same today. The federal court system has three tiers. Federal district courts are at the bottom: they function as federal trial courts. Federal criminal trials are held in federal district courts. Federal appeals courts are immediately above the district courts. Federal appeals courts are appellate courts rather than trial courts: they hear appeals from federal district courts. The Supreme Court is the highest court of the land. Very few appeals ever reach the Supreme Court.

## I.   The Power to Make and Enforce Laws Related to Piracies and Felonies Committed on the High Seas and Offenses Against the Laws of Nations

Congress has the power to regulate criminal activity committed on the high seas or committed against United States vessels.

## J.   The Power to Declare War

Congress alone has the power to declare war. The domestic powers of Congress are expanded during wartime, allowing Congress to impose economic controls that would be unconstitutional in peacetime.[20] The Constitution, nevertheless, makes the President Commander-in-Chief of the armed forces. This division of authority has given rise to a peculiar state of affairs. In modern times, successive presidents have claimed authority, as Commander-in-Chief, to send American troops into combat abroad without waiting for Congress to declare war. Congress has declared war only five times; American troops have been deployed in combat operations abroad more than 100 times.[21] Because Congress has never called the President to the task for initiating military operations without congressional approval, the Supreme Court has never had to decide whether the President as Commander-in-Chief has the inherent power to deploy American troops in military actions without consulting Congress.

---

[20]   Johnson v. Maryland, 254 U.S. 51, 41 S. Ct. 16, 65 L. Ed. 2d 126 (1920).

[21]   John Yoo, *The Continuation of Politics by Other Means: The Original Understanding of War Powers*, 84 Cal. L. Rev. 167, 177 (1996).

### K. *The Power to Raise and Support an Army and Navy and Provide for their Regulation*

Congress has the authority to enact draft laws, acquire land for military installations, establish military regulations, and set up military courts. The Uniform Code of Military Justice derives from this power.

### L. *The Power to Organize a Militia and Call the Militia into the Service of the United States When Necessary to Execute Federal Law, Suppress Insurrections, and Repel Invasions*

"Militia" refers to the organization today known as the National Guard. The Constitution divides control of the militia between the federal government and the states. Congress is responsible for organizing and equipping the militia and has the authority to call the militia into federal service when needed to suppress insurrections, repel invasions, and execute the laws of the United States. The states are responsible for training the militia according to standards prescribed by Congress. Enlistment in the state National Guard simultaneously results in enlistment in the Army National Guard. Enlistees retain their status as state Guard members until ordered into active federal duty and again revert to state status when they are relieved from federal service.[22]

### M. *The Power to Govern the District of Columbia and all Federal Enclaves and Establishments*

Congress has exclusive legislative control and oversight of the District of Columbia and federal installations such as military posts, national parks, and federal buildings, even though they are located inside a state.

### N. *The Power to Enact All Laws Necessary and Proper for Carrying into Execution the Specifically Enumerated Powers*

The final clause of Article I, Section 8 grants Congress the power to enact "all Laws which shall be necessary and proper for carrying into execution . . . all other Powers vested by this Constitution in the Government of the United States, or in any Department or Officer thereof . . ." This clause is known as the *necessary and proper clause*. It confers broad discretion on the federal government to select any means that are appropriate to exercise its constitutionally delegated powers. In 1819, a controversy arose about

---

[22] Perprich v. Department of Defense, 496 U.S. 334, 110 S. Ct. 2418, 110 L. Ed. 2d 312 (1990).

whether Congress had the power to establish a national bank.[23] The Supreme Court ruled that Congress had this power, even though no specific language in the Constitution mentioned it; the power existed under the necessary and proper clause. Chief Justice Marshall, who wrote the Court's opinion, proclaimed:

> Let the end be legitimate, let it be within the scope of the Constitution, and all means which are appropriate, which are plainly adapted to that end, which are not prohibited, but consistent with the letter and spirit of the Constitution, are constitutional.

The ends the federal government can pursue are circumscribed by its delegated powers. However, if the ends are constitutional, the federal government can select any means that are appropriate. Because Congress has the power to lay and collect taxes and to borrow money, Congress could establish means for safeguarding federal revenues pending their expenditure. Incorporating a bank was, therefore, appropriate. Marshall's interpretation of the necessary and proper clause forms the basis of the *implied powers doctrine*. The federal government has the implied power to adopt any measures, not prohibited by the Constitution, that are appropriate for carrying its delegated powers into effect.

## § 1.10   —Powers the States Are Forbidden to Exercise

Article I, Section 10 expressly forbids the states from doing five things.[24] States may not:

1.   Enter into treaties, alliances, or confederations.
2.   Coin money, emit bills of credit, or make anything besides gold or silver coin legal tender in payment of debts.
3.   Lay duties on imports or exports without the consent of Congress.
4.   Keep troops or ships of war in times of peace.
5.   Pass bills of attainder, ex post facto laws, or laws impairing the obligations of contract.

The first four restrictions have a common thread. They involve matters in which the existence of a uniform national policy is critical. The federal government has the exclusive power to make treaties, establish currency, regulate foreign commerce, and declare war; the states are prohibited from exercising legislative authority in these areas.

The fifth restriction outlaws three arbitrary practices. States are forbidden to enact *bills of attainder*, *ex post facto* laws, or to impair the obligations of contract. A bill of attainder is a legislative act that brands a person a crim-

---

[23]   McCulloch v. Maryland, 17 U.S. (4 Wheat.) 316, 4 L. Ed. 579 (1918).

[24]   U.S. Const., art. I, § 10.

inal without a trial.[25] Legislatures cannot declare individuals criminals and impose sanctions on them. Only a court can do this.

States are also forbidden to enact ex post facto laws. Ex post facto means "after the fact." This clause protects an accused from being disadvantaged by changes made in the law after a crime is committed. Laws that: (1) change the elements of a crime or make conduct, innocent when done, criminal,[26] (2) increase the punishment,[27] or (3) alter rules of evidence and require less evidence to convict, cannot be applied to crimes completed before they were enacted.[28] The same holds true for laws that change sentencing guidelines and credit for good behavior.[29] However, the accused enjoys no ex post facto protection against mere changes in procedural rules, even when they work to his or her disadvantage. In *California Department of Corrections v. Morales,*[30] the Supreme Court rejected an *ex post facto* challenge to a prison regulation decreasing the frequency of parole hearings because the change was procedural and presented little risk of prolonging the duration of a prisoner's confinement.

The restrictions discussed above are found in the text of the Constitution. Certain other restrictions are implicit from the nature of federalism. The principle that a state may not tax an agency of the federal government is an example. Permitting the states to tax an agency of the federal government runs counter to federalism because it permits the states to exert control over the operations of the federal government.

However, the most far-reaching restrictions on state power did not become part of the Constitution until after the Civil War. These restrictions are contained in the Fourteenth Amendment and are discussed in §§ 1.15 and 1.16 of this Chapter.

## § 1.11  —Sovereign Powers Retained by the States

Believing that diffusion of power affords maximum security for individual liberty, the framers of our Constitution delegated specific powers to the federal government and provided that all powers not so delegated would be reserved to the governments of the states and the American people. The powers retained by the states are called *police powers.* These powers are ascer-

---

[25]   Landgraf v. USI Film Products, 511 U.S. 244, 114 S. Ct. 1483, 128 L. Ed. 2d 229 (1994).

[26]   Calder v. Bull, 3 Dall. 386, 390, 1 L. Ed. 648 (1798). Article I, Section 9, Paragraph 1 contains an identical ex post facto clause applicable to the federal government.

[27]   California Department of Corrections v. Morales, 514 U.S. 499, 115 S. Ct. 1597, 131 L. Ed. 2d 588 (1995); Johnson v. United States, 529 U.S. 695, 120 S. Ct. 1795, 146 L. Ed. 2d 727 (2000).

[28]   Carmell v. Texas, 529 U.S. 513, 120 S. Ct. 1620, 146 L. Ed. 2d 577 (2000) (retroactive application of statute authorizing conviction for certain sexual offenses on the victim's testimony alone, where corroborating evidence was previously required, violated the ex post facto clause); Stogner v. California, 539 U.S. 607, 123 S. Ct. 2446, 156 L. Ed. 2d 544 (2003) (statute authorizing criminal prosecutions after prior limitations period for the offense had expired violated ex post facto clause).

[29]   Lynce v. Mathis, 519 U.S. 433, 117 S. Ct. 891, 137 L. Ed. 2d 63 (1997); Miller v. Florida, 482 U.S. 423, 107 S. Ct. 2446, 96 L. Ed. 2d 351 (1987).

[30]   *Supra* note 27.

tained through constitutional mathematics. Before the adoption of the Constitution, sovereignty resided in the states. The states surrendered a portion of their sovereignty when they formed a federal union. The powers retained by the states are determined by subtracting from their original sovereignty, the powers they delegated to the federal government (Art. 1, § 8) and the powers the Constitution forbids them to exercise (Art. 1, § 10). This method of fixing the boundaries of federal and state power is set forth in the Tenth Amendment, which reads: "The powers not delegated to the United States by the Constitution, nor prohibited by it to the States, are reserved to the States respectively, and to the people."

In making this division of power, the Framers assumed that the powers retained by the states would be greater than those delegated to the federal government. James Madison made this point in the *Federalist Papers* where he described the balance of power as follows:

> The powers delegated by the proposed Constitution to the Federal Government, are few and defined. Those which are to remain in the State Governments are numerous and indefinite. The former will be exercised principally on external objects, as war, peace, negotiation, and foreign commerce. . . . The powers reserved to the several States will extend to all the objects, which, in the ordinary course of affairs, concern the lives, liberties and properties of the people; and the internal order, improvement, and prosperity of the State.[31]

James Madison's description of the federal/state balance of power, though accurate in 1798, is no longer accurate today. The balance of power has shifted in favor of the federal government as a result of judicial interpretations placed on the scope of the delegated powers. Article I, Section 8 describes the powers delegated to the federal government in broad, general language. The elasticity of the language allows it to be stretched. Since the states hold the residual of power (i.e., all powers that have not been delegated to the federal government), the powers retained by the states pivot on the interpretation of the delegated powers. Expansive interpretations of the powers delegated to the federal government have steadily constricted the powers retained by the states. However, the tide has now turned and efforts to restore a more balanced system of federalism are now in progress.

The federal government's powers are mainly over the American people. It may not employ these powers to regulate the actions of state governments in ways that infringe on their sovereignty.[32] This limitation is implicit in fed-

---

[31]   THE FEDERALIST No. 45, at 313 (J. Cooke ed. 1961).

[32]   *See, e.g.,* New York v. United States, 505 U.S. 144, 112 S. Ct. 2408, 120 L. Ed. 2d 120 (1992); **Printz v. United States, 521 U.S. 98, 117 S. Ct. 2365, 138 L. Ed. 2d 914 (1997)** (holding unconstitutional federal legislation requiring local officials to assist in background checks for gun purchases); Alden v. Maine, 527 U.S. 706, 119 S. Ct. 2240, 144 L. Ed. 2d 636 (1999) (holding that congress may not impose monetary obligations on state governments to pay damages to private parties for violating their rights under federal laws enacted under the commerce clause); Kimel v. Florida Board of Regents, 528 U.S. 62, 120 S. Ct 631, 145 L. Ed. 2d 522 (2000) (same).

eralism. The states are not political subdivisions of the federal government; they are separate sovereign entities. Accordingly, Congress may not force state governments to enact particular laws,[33] to administer federal programs,[34] to enforce federal statutes,[35] or to compensate individuals for violating their rights under federal laws enacted under the Article I powers of Congress.[36] In *Printz v. United States*,[37] the Supreme Court struck down a provisions of the Brady Handgun Violence Prevention Act that required state law enforcement officers to conduct background checks on prospective handgun purchasers. The Court stated that requiring state law enforcement officers to administer federal programs is "fundamentally incompatible with our constitutional system of dual sovereignty."

The reader should not infer that the federal government is powerless to regulate the actions of state governments. The Fourteenth Amendment, which was adopted immediately after the Civil War, placed certain restrictions on state governments and authorized the federal government to enforce the restrictions by appropriate legislation. The federal government's Fourteenth Amendment powers include the power to prohibit state governments from discriminating on the basis of race, religion, gender, or national origin and from denying persons rights protected by the Bill of Rights.[38] These restrictions are discussed in later sections.

## § 1.12  The Bill of Rights

During the ratification debates, there was a strong push for a bill of rights. Delegates to the state conventions wanted assurance that the liberty of the people would be secure.[39] The Federalists, though originally disputing the need for a bill of rights, eventually capitulated and agreed to make the framing of a bill of rights the first order of business when the new Congress met. During the first session of Congress, James Madison introduced 20 amendments culled from the hundreds that had been proposed. Of these, 12 were approved by Congress and 10 were ratified by the states. The first 10 amendments went into effect in November of 1791.

---

[33]  New York v. United States, *supra* note 32.
[34]  **Printz v. United States**, *supra* note 32.
[35]  *Id.*
[36]  Alden v. Maine, *supra* note 32 (Congress may not impose monetary obligations on state governments to pay damages for violating federal laws enacted under the commerce clause); Kimel v. Florida Board of Regents, *supra* note 32 (same).
[37]  *Supra* note 32.
[38]  *See, e.g.,* Title VII of the Civil Rights Act of 1964, 42 U.S.C. § 2000e *et seq.*, covered in § 11.7 *infra*, making it an unlawful employment practice to discriminate based on race, color, religion, gender, or national origin; 42 U.S.C. § 1983, covered in Chapter 10, creating a federal civil cause of action against persons who act under color of state law in depriving citizens of their federal constitutional and statutory rights *See also* Nevada Department of Human Resources, et al. v. Hibbs, 538 U.S. 721, 123 S. Ct. 1972, 155 L. Ed. 2d 953 (2003) (holding that state employees may recover damages against their government employer for violating their rights under federal laws enacted under the Fourteenth Amendment).
[39]  ERIKSSON, *supra* note 1, at 220.

The first 10 Amendments to the Constitution, or more appropriately, the first eight, are called the Bill of Rights. Before discussing the content of the Bill of Rights, two observations are in order. First, the Bill of Rights is not a declaration of the rights that citizens have against each other. It is a declaration of rights that the American people have against their government. Second, the government against which the Bill of Rights is addressed is the federal government. This is apparent from the wording. The First Amendment begins "*Congress* shall make no law respecting the establishment of religion . . ." In an early case, Supreme Court ruled that the Bill of Rights does not bind the states.[40]

Figure 1.4 below shows the rights protected by the first eight Amendments. Review the text of the Bill of Rights in Appendix I and carefully study the material below.

Figure 1.4
**Content of the Bill of Rights**

| Amendment | Rights Protected |
|---|---|
| First Amendment | **Freedom of speech**[41]<br>**Freedom of the press**[42]<br>**Right to assemble**[43]<br>**Right to petition Congress for a redress of grievances**[44] |
| Second Amendment | Right to keep and bear arms[45] |
| Third Amendment | *Protection against involuntary quartering of soldiers in private homes |
| Fourth Amendment | **Protection against unreasonable searches and seizures**[46]<br>**Protection against the issuance of warrants without probable cause, supported by an oath or affirmation, particularly describing the place to be searched or the persons or things to be seized**[47] |
| Fifth Amendment | Right to be indicted by a grand jury before being tried for a capital or otherwise infamous crime[48]<br>**Protection against double jeopardy (i.e., against being tried more than once for the same offense)**[49]<br>**Protection against compulsory self-incrimination**[50] |

---

[40]   Barron v. Mayor and City Council of Baltimore, 32 U.S. (7 Pet.) 243, 8 L. Ed. 672 (1833).
[41]   Gitlow v. New York, 268 U.S. 652, 666, 45 S. Ct. 625, 630, 69 L. Ed. 1138 (1925); Stromberg v. California, 283 U.S. 359, 51 S. Ct. 532, 75 L. Ed. 1117 (1931).
[42]   Near v. Minnesota, 283 U.S. 697, 701, 51 S. Ct. 625, 626, 75 L. Ed. 1357 (1931).
[43]   DeJonge v. Oregon, 299 U.S. 353, 57 S. Ct. 255, 81 L. Ed. 278 (1937).
[44]   *Id.*
[45]   Presser v. Illinois, 116 U.S. 252, 6 S. Ct. 580, 29 L. Ed. 2d 615 (1886).
[46]   **Mapp v. Ohio, 367 U.S. 643, 81 S. Ct. 1684, 6 L. Ed. 2d 1081 (1961)**.
[47]   *Id.*
[48]   Hurtado v. California, 332 U.S. 46, 67 S. Ct. 1672, 91 L. Ed. 1903 (1947).
[49]   Benton v. Maryland, 395 U.S. 784, 89 S. Ct. 2056, 23 L. Ed. 2d 707 (1969).
[50]   Malloy v. Hogan, 378 U.S. 1, 84 S. Ct. 1489, 12 L. Ed. 2d 653 (1964).

Figure 1.4, *continued*

| Amendment | Rights Protected |
|---|---|
| Fifth Amendment | Protection against deprivation of life, liberty, or property without due process of law[51]<br>**Right to just compensation when private property is taken for a public use**[52] |
| Sixth Amendment | **Right to a speedy criminal trial**[53]<br>**Right to a public criminal trial**[54]<br>**Right to a jury trial in criminal cases**[55]<br>**Right to be informed of the nature and grounds of a criminal accusation**<br>**Right to confront and cross-examine prosecution witnesses**[56]<br>**Right to compulsory legal process to compel attendance of defense witness**[57]<br>**Right to the assistance of counsel in criminal cases**[58] |
| Seventh Amendment | Right to a jury trial in civil cases when the amount in controversy exceeds $20[59] |
| Eighth Amendment | **Protection against excessive bail**[60]<br>**Protection against excessive fines**[61]<br>**Protection against cruel and unusual punishment**[62] |

Boldface type means that the Supreme Court has determined that this protection is incorporated into the Fourteenth Amendment and that the states must comply with federal constitutional standards.

Regular type means that the Supreme Court has decided that this protection is not incorporated into the Fourteenth Amendment.

An asterisk [*] means that the Supreme Court has not yet decided this question.

The most important Bill of Rights guarantees are found in the First, Fourth, Fifth, Sixth, and Eighth Amendments. The First Amendment guarantees freedom of speech. The Fourth, Fifth, Sixth, and Eighth Amendments curb the authority of the police to detain, interrogate, arrest, and search people suspected of crimes and establish procedural safeguards that apply dur-

---

[51]  This provision applied, and continues to apply, only to the federal government and agents exercising federal authority. However, this fact ceased to be consequential after the passage of the Fourteenth Amendment. The Fourteenth Amendment contains an identical limitation applicable to state governments. The Fifth and Fourteenth Amendment due process clauses have received the same interpretation. The meaning of the due process clause is discussed in §§ 1.14 - 1.15 *infra*.

[52]  Fiske v. State of Kansas, 274 U.S. 380, 47 S. Ct. 655, 71 L. Ed. 1108 (1927).

[53]  Klopfer v. North Carolina, 386 U.S. 213, 87 S. Ct. 988, 18 L. Ed. 2d 1 (1967).

[54]  In re Oliver, 333 U.S. 257, 68 S. Ct. 499, 92 L. Ed. 682 (1948).

[55]  Duncan v. Louisiana, 391 U.S. 145, 149, 88 S. Ct. 1444, 1447, 20 L. Ed. 2d 491 (1968).

[56]  Pointer v. Texas, 380 U.S. 400, 85 S. Ct. 1065, 13 L. Ed. 2d 923 (1965).

[57]  Washington v. Texas, 388 U.S. 14, 87 S. Ct. 120, 13 L. Ed. 2d 923 (1965).

[58]  **Gideon v. Wainwright, 372 U.S. 335, 83 S. Ct. 792, 9 L. Ed. 2d 799 (1963)**.

[59]  Minneapolis & St. Louis R. Co. v. Bombolis, 241 U.S. 211, 36 S. Ct. 595, 60 L. Ed. 961 (1916).

[60]  Schilb v. Kuebel, 404 U.S. 357, 365, 92 S. Ct. 479, 484-85, 30 L. Ed. 2d 502 (1971) (by implication).

[61]  Tate v. Short, 401 U.S. 395, 91 S. Ct. 668, 28 L. Ed. 2d 130 (1971) (by implication).

[62]  Louisiana ex rel. Francis v. Resweber, 329 U.S. 459, 67 S. Ct. 374, 91 L. Ed. 422 (1947); Furman v. Georgia, 408 U.S. 238, 257, 92 S. Ct. 2726, 2736, 33 L. Ed. 2d 346, 360 (1972).

ing criminal trials. Because these Amendments are given in-depth treatment in later chapters, they will not be discussed here.

The Second, Third, and Seventh Amendment have limited importance. The Second Amendment provides: "A well regulated Militia, being necessary to the security of a free state, the right of the people to keep and bear Arms, shall not be infringed." This Amendment was largely ignored until the recent gun control controversy when opponents of gun control legislation began using it to argue that prohibiting ownership of guns violates the Second Amendment right to bear arms. This argument has not been favorably received by the courts because it ignores the first clause of the Second Amendment. Properly read, the Second Amendment protects the right to bear arms only when they are kept to fulfill militia obligations, not when they are used for hunting, recreation, self-protection, or other purposes.[63]

The Third Amendment condemns the quartering of soldiers in private homes without the owner's consent. This Amendment has generated no litigation because the U.S. government does not engage in this practice. The Seventh Amendment guarantees the right to trial by jury in civil cases in which the amount in controversy exceeds $20. This language is straight-forward and requires no explanation.

The Ninth and Tenth Amendments, technically speaking, are not part of the Bill of Rights because they do not establish individual rights. The Ninth Amendment states: "The enumeration of the Constitution, of certain rights, shall not be construed to deny or disparage others retained by the people." What this language means remains a constitutional mystery. The argument is occasionally made that the Ninth Amendment authorizes the Supreme Court to recognize constitutional rights beyond those mentioned in the Bill of Rights. The Supreme Court has not been comfortable with this interpretation and has never adopted it. Conferring authority on courts to recognize constitutional rights that lack textual support would open a Pandora's box. For this reason, the Supreme Court has never relied on the Ninth Amendment as the sole basis for any constitutional decision.

The Tenth Amendment deals with federalism and was discussed in §1.11.


## § 1.13   —Applying the Bill of Rights to the States through the Fourteenth Amendment

The Bill of Rights constituted a declaration of rights that the American people had against the federal government. Americans had no protection against arbitrary acts of state governments until almost a century later. The Fourteenth Amendment, ratified in 1868, contained a mechanism that was

---

[63]   United States v. Miller, 307 U.S. 174, 178, 59 S. Ct. 816, 818, 83 L. Ed. 1206 (1938); Love v. Peppersack, 47 F.3d 120 (4th Cir. 1995); Gillespie v. City of Indianapolis, 185 F.3d 693 (7th Cir. 1999). *But see* United States v. Emerson, 270 F.3d 203 (5th Cir. 2001), *cert. denied*, Emerson v. United States, 536 U.S. 907, 122 S. Ct. 2362, 153 L. Ed. 2d 184 (2002).

used to impose the Bill of Rights guarantees on the states. That mechanism was the *due process clause.*

The Fourteenth Amendment forbids the states to "deprive any person of life, liberty or property without *due process of law.*" The phrase without *due process of law* means "without the process that is due under the law."[64] Restated, the Fourteenth Amendment forbids the states from depriving people of life, liberty, or property without affording them the process due them under the law. Where did the Supreme Court look to determine what process was due? You guessed it—the Bill of Rights.

The central guarantees contained in the Bill of Rights have gradually been absorbed into the Fourteenth Amendment due process clause and made binding on state governments through an approach known as *selective incorporation.* Under this approach, rights deemed fundamental to the American system of justice are regarded as components of due process that states are forbidden to deny.[65] Most provisions found in the Bill of Rights have been incorporated. The standard used to decide whether to incorporated a particular right is whether the right is fundamental to the American justice system.[66] Figure 1.5 shows the current incorporation status of each of the rights guaranteed by the Bill of Rights. Notice that all but five rights have been incorporated.

Incorporation into the Fourteenth Amendment means that states must give constitutional protection that is at least as great as that given by federal government. Federal standards become the minimum protection states must give, although they remain free to give greater protection under state constitutions.[67]

Figure 1.5
**Overview of the Fourteenth Amendment**

> The Fourteenth Amendment: (1) makes most of the Bill of Rights applicable to the states; (2) prevents the states from depriving people of life, liberty, or property without procedural and substantive due process; (3) prohibits the states from treating people differently because of race, gender, or national origin except in the most extraordinary circumstances; and (4) gives Congress power to pass legislation enforcing these restrictions.

---

[64]  In re Winship, 379 U.S. 358, 90 S. Ct. 1068, 25 L. Ed. 2d 368 (1979).
[65]  Duncan v. Louisiana, 391 U.S. 145, 148-149, 88 S. Ct. 1444, 1446-1447, 20 L. Ed. 2d 491 (1968).
[66]  *Id.*
[67]  Cooper v. California, 386 U.S. 58, 87 S. Ct. 788, 17 L. Ed. 2d 730 (1967).

# § 1.14   The Fourteenth Amendment as a Limitation on State Power

The Civil War altered the relationship between the national government, the states, and the American people. Before the Civil War, the American people viewed the states as the watchdogs of their liberty and feared the federal government. The fact that the Bill of Rights was directed only at the federal government shows this. The Civil War changed things. After the Civil War, the states were viewed as the menace and the federal government as the protector. Demand for federal protection against oppressive acts of state governments led to the passage of the Fourteenth Amendment.

The Fourteenth Amendment reads:

> No State shall make or enforce any law which shall abridge the privileges or immunities of citizens of the United States; nor shall any State deprive any person of life, liberty, or property, without due process of law; nor deny to any person within its jurisdiction the equal protection of the laws.

We previously saw how the Fourteenth Amendment served as the vehicle for imposing the central guarantees of the Bill of Rights on the states. However, the importance of the Fourteenth Amendment goes far beyond this. Before delving into its contents, there are two things you need to keep in mind. Both stem from the first three words. The Fourteenth Amendment begins "[n]o state shall . . ." First, the Fourteenth Amendment is addressed to the states. It regulates the conduct of states; it does not regulate the conduct of the federal government or private citizens. Second, the Fourteenth Amendment is phrased in the negative. It forbids the states to take arbitrary action; it does not require them to take helpful action. This point was made tragically clear in *DeShaney v. Winnebago County Department of Social Services*.[68] The plaintiff, Joshua DeShaney, was a four-year-old boy who suffered permanent brain damage due to his father's beatings. The defendants were social workers, employed by the state, who allegedly knew that Joshua was being abused, but took no steps to remove him from his father's home. Joshua claimed that their failure to protect him from his father's violence deprived him of liberty without due process in violation of the Fourteenth Amendment. The Supreme Court disagreed, ruling that:

> . . . [N]othing in the language of the Due Process Clause itself requires the State to protect the life, liberty, and property of its citizens against invasion by private actors. The Clause is phrased as a limitation on the State's power to act, not as a guarantee of certain minimal levels of safety and security. It forbids the State itself to deprive individuals of life, liberty, or property without "due process of law," but its language cannot fairly be extended to impose an affirmative obligation on the State to ensure that those interests do not come to harm through other means.

---

[68]   **489 U.S. 189, 109 S. Ct. 998, 103 L. Ed. 2d 249 (1989).**

*DeShaney's* message, while disturbing, represents a correct interpretation of the Fourteenth Amendment. The Fourteenth Amendment forbids the states from engaging in oppressive action; it does not require them to take helpful action.

## § 1.15  —Due Process of Law

The Fourteenth Amendment due process clause reads "[n]o State shall . . . deprive any person of life, liberty, or property, without due process of law . . ."[69] This clause provides two kinds of protection—one procedural and the other substantive. *Procedural due process* requires states to use fair procedures in reaching decisions that deprive a person of life, liberty, or property. *Substantive due process* requires them to have an adequate justification or, in other words, a good enough reason for the deprivation. Procedural and substantive due process work together to prevent arbitrary deprivations of life, liberty, and property. Suppose, for example, that a state child welfare agency wants to remove a child from a parent's home. Since the right to the care and custody of one's children is part of the liberty protected by the due process clause,[70] the state cannot take this right away without establishing an adequate justification (substantive due process) and providing notice and a hearing (procedural due process). The strength of the justification required to satisfy the demands of substantive due process varies with the importance of the rights at stake. The state cannot interfere with rights that qualify as "fundamental rights," such as the right of parents to raise their children, without establishing a "compelling reason."

### A.  Procedural Due Process

Suppose when you go home tonight, you discover that your furniture and possessions are gone and you are informed that a judge awarded them to your landlord for nonpayment of rent. How would you feel? You would probably feel that this was unfair. You should have been notified that legal proceedings affecting your property were taking place and allowed to appear and present your side of the story. Your sense of injustice is due to a lack of procedural due process.

Procedural due process requires the government to give notice and a hearing before depriving a person of life, liberty, or property. This requirement is not limited to criminal proceedings. It applies whenever the government

---

[69]  The Fifth Amendment contains an identical clause that is binding on the federal government and is interpreted in the same way. Consequently, federal and state officers are subject to the same constitutional limitation on their authority.

[70]  Troxel v. Granville, 530 U.S. 57, 120 S. Ct. 2054, 147 L. Ed. 2d 49 (2000); Stanley v. Illinois, 405 U.S. 645, 92 S. Ct. 1208, 31 L. Ed. 2d 551 (1972).

takes action that deprives a person of any of the three interests mentioned in the Fourteenth Amendment. Procedural due process, for example, is required before the government can condemn a person's property as unfit for habitation, suspend a student from public school, revoke a person's probation,[71] or fire a tenured government employee [72] because each of these actions deprive the person effected of property or liberty.

The procedures necessary to satisfy due process vary with the importance of the right at stake; (2) the extent to which the additional safeguards would reduce the risk of an erroneous decision; and (3) the increased fiscal or administrative burden on the government of providing them.[73] Maximum procedural protection is required at criminal trials because the harm likely to flow from an erroneous decision is the greatest. When the government accuses a person of a crime and threatens to take away his or her life or liberty, the Constitution insists on a broad array of procedural safeguards. These safeguards include the right to notice of the charges;[74] to be tried before an impartial tribunal;[75] to cross-examine prosecution witnesses;[76] to testify and compel attendance of defense witnesses;[77] to be represented by counsel of his or her choice[78] or to an attorney furnished by the government (if the accused cannot afford private counsel);[79] to be assisted by experts, such as psychiatrists;[80] and to be set free unless the government proves guilt beyond a reasonable doubt.[81]

## B. *Substantive Due Process*

The due process clause does more than guarantee fair procedures. It also has a substantive component.[82] Substantive due process is a concept that is difficult to explain, especially given the space limitations of this chapter. The two main areas where this concept is applied are: (1) affording protection for "fundamental rights"[83] and (2) providing a remedy for egregious misconduct by public officials.[84]

---

[71] Young v. Harper, 520 U.S. 143, 117 S. Ct. 1148, 137 L. Ed. 2d 270 (1997); Morissey v. Brewer, 408 U.S. 471, 92 S. Ct. 2593, 33 L. Ed. 2d 484 (1972).

[72] Gilbert v. Homar, 520 U.S. 924, 117 S. Ct. 1807, 138 L. Ed. 2d 120 (1997); Cleveland Bd. of Education v. Loudermill, 470 U.S. 532, 105 S. Ct. 1487, 84 L. Ed. 2d 494 (1985).

[73] Cafeteria & Restaurant Workers Union v. McElroy, 367 U.S. 886, 895, 81 S. Ct. 1743, 1748, 6 L. Ed. 2d 1230 (1961). *Id.*

[74] U.S. Const., amend. VI.

[75] *Id.*

[76] *Id.*

[77] *Id.*

[78] *Id.*

[79] **Gideon v. Wainwright, 372 U.S. 335, 83 S. Ct. 792, 9 L. Ed. 2d 799 (1963)**.

[80] Ake v. Oklahoma, 470 U.S. 68, 105 S. Ct. 1087, 84 L. Ed. 2d 53 (1985).

[81] In re Winship, 397 U.S. 358, 90 S. Ct. 1068, 25 L. Ed. 2d 368 (1970).

[82] Planned Parenthood of Southeastern Pennsylvania v. Casey, 505 U.S. 833, 112 S. Ct. 2791, 120 L. Ed. 2d 674 (1992).

[83] See authorities cited in notes 85 - 93 *infra.*

[84] County of Sacramento v. Lewis, 523 U.S. 833, 118 S. Ct. 1708, 140 L. Ed. 2d 1043 (1998).

## 1. Protection of Fundamental Rights

Some rights are so fundamental to the liberty of free citizens that they cannot be denied without a compelling reason. These rights are called "fundamental rights." The label of a fundamental right has been reserved for important choices that are central to an individual's self-concept, dignity, and autonomy. Rights recognized as fundamental include the right to marry,[85] to have children,[86] to direct their upbringing and education,[87] to enjoy privacy,[88] to practice birth control,[89] to terminate unwanted pregnancies,[90] to make health-care decisions,[91] and to forego life-sustaining treatment.[92] Once a right is recognized as fundamental, the government cannot encroach on it without a *compelling reason*. The Supreme Court has explained that "'[a]t the heart of liberty is the right to define one's own concept of existence, of meaning, of the universe, and of the mystery of human life. Beliefs about these matters could not define the attributes of personhood were they formed under compulsion of the State.'"[93]

---

[85]   *See, e.g.,* Loving v. Virginia, 388 U.S. 1, 87 S. Ct. 1817, 18 L. Ed. 2d 1010 (1967) (invalidating law prohibiting marriage between persons of different races); Cleveland Board of Education v. LaFleur, 414 U.S. 632, 639-640, 94 S. Ct. 791, 39 L. Ed. 2d 52 (1974) ("This Court has long recognized that freedom of personal choice in matters of marriage and family life is one of the liberties protected by the Due Process Clause of the Fourteenth Amendment.").

[86]   *See, e.g.,* Skinner v. Oklahoma ex rel. Williamson, 316 U.S. 535, 62 S. Ct. 1110, 86 L. Ed. 1655 (1942) (invalidating law requiring sterilization of felons after third conviction of an offense involving 'moral turpitude').

[87]   *See, e.g.,* Troxel v. Granville, *supra* note 70 (overturning court order granting visiting rights to grandparent as a violation of a parent's fundamental rights "to make decisions concerning the care, custody, and control of their children"); Meyer v. Nebraska, 262 U.S. 390, 43 S. Ct. 625, 67 L. Ed. 1042 (1923) (invalidating law prohibiting teaching of foreign language to students below the eighth grade as undue interference with fundamental right of parents to make decisions about the education of their children); Pierce v. Society of Sisters, 268 U.S. 510, 45 S. Ct. 571, 69 L. Ed. 1070 (1925) (invalidating law requiring parents to educate their children in public schools as undue interference with fundamental right of parents to make decisions about the education of their children).

[88]   *See, e.g.,* Griswold v. Connecticut, 381 U.S. 479, 85 S. Ct. 1678, 14 L. Ed. 2d 510 (1965) (recognizing right of married couples to privacy in use of contraception).

[89]   *See, e.g., Id.*; Eisenstadt v. Baird, 268 U.S. 510, 92 S. Ct. 1029, 31 L. Ed. 2d 349 (1972) (invaliding law prohibiting sale of contraceptives to unmarried persons).

[90]   *See, e.g.,* Roe v. Wade, 410 U.S. 113, 93 S. Ct. 705, 35 L. Ed. 2d 147 (1973) (upholding right of women to terminate an unwanted pregnancy); Carey v. Population Services International, 431 U.S. 678, 97 S. Ct. 2010, 52 L. Ed. 2d 675 (1977) ("[T]he Constitution protects individual decisions in matters of childbearing from unjustified intrusion by the State.").

[91]   *See, e.g.,* Washington v. Harper, 494 U.S. 210, 110 S. Ct. 1028, 108 L. Ed. 2d 178 (1990) (recognizing a substantive due process right to avoid unwanted administration of antipsychotic drugs). Substantive due process also protects the right to bodily security and integrity. *See, e.g.,* Rochin v. California, 342 U.S. 165, 72 S. Ct. 205, 96 L. Ed. 183 (1952) (holding that government may not pump a suspect's stomach to retrieve evidence).

[92]   *See, e.g.,* Cruzan v. Director, Mo. Dept. of Health, 497 U.S. 261, 278, 110 S. Ct. 2841, 2851, 111 L. Ed. 2d 224 (1990) (recognizing right of competent adults to refuse unwanted lifesaving medical treatment). *But see* Washington v. Glucksberg, 521 U.S. 702, 117 S. Ct. 2258, 138 L. Ed. 2d 772 (1997) (right to assistance in committing suicide is not a fundamental right).

[93]   Planned Parenthood of Southeastern Pennsylvania v. Casey, *supra* note 82.

Having said this, the Supreme Court, nevertheless, in *Bowers v. Hardwick*[94] declined to recognize the right to be a practising homosexual as a fundamental right. The majority upheld a state statute criminalizing sodomy. Four Justices dissented, arguing:

> Only the most willful blindness could obscure the fact that sexual intimacy is "a sensitive, key relationship of human existence, central to family life, community welfare, and the development of human personality." The fact that individuals define themselves in a significant way through their intimate sexual relationships with others suggests, in a Nation as diverse as ours, that there may be many "right" ways of conducting those relationships, and that much of the richness of a relationship will come from the freedom an individual has to choose the form and nature of these intensely personal bonds.[95]

The position taken in *Bowers v. Hardwick* was abandoned 17 years later in *Lawrence v. Texas*.[96] Police responded to a hoax call that a weapons disturbance was taking place in John Lawrence's apartment. They burst into the apartment and found Lawrence having consensual sex with another adult male. Lawrence was arrested for engaging in "deviant sexual intercourse," which was defined under Texas law as having "anal or oral sex with a member of the same sex."[97]

The Supreme Court set his conviction aside, holding that there are certain spheres of life "where the government should not be a dominant presence." Private sexual conduct behind closed doors is one of those sphere. This case did not involve sex with a minor, public conduct, prostitution, or "whether the government must give formal recognition to any relationship that homosexual persons seek to enter." Rather, it involved private sexual conduct between two consenting adult homosexuals. "The State," the court declared, "cannot demean their existence or control their destiny by making their private sexual conduct a crime. Their right to liberty under the Due Process Clause gives them the full right to engage in their conduct without intervention of the government."[98]

*Lawrence v. Texas* is constitutionally important, not only because it invalidates sodomy laws, but because it undercuts the most powerful argument justifying discrimination against gays and lesbians, namely that their behavior is immoral and illegal.[99] Sodomy laws, though rarely enforced,

[94]   478 U.S. 186, 106 S. Ct. 2841, 92 L. Ed. 2d 140 (1986) (substantive due process does not protect the right to engage in homosexual sodomy).
[95]   *Id.* at 478 U.S. at 205, 106 S. Ct. at 2851.
[96]   **539 U.S. 558, 156 L. Ed. 2d 508, 123 S. Ct. 2472 (2003).**
[97]   Before 1960, all 50 states outlawed sodomy. **Lawrence v. Texas**, *supra* note 96. At the time of *Bowers*, more than half the states had repealed their sodomy laws. *Id.* By 2003, when *Lawrence v. Texas* was decided, only 13 states—Alabama, Florida, Idaho, Kansas, Louisiana, Mississippi, Missouri, Oklahoma, North Carolina, South Carolina, Texas, Utah, and Virginia—made sodomy a crime. *Id.* Of these, only four states—Texas, Kansas, Oklahoma, and Missouri—criminalized sodomy only when both partners were of the same sex. *Id.*
[98]   *Id.* 123 S. Ct. at 2484.
[99]   *Id.* 123 S. Ct. at 2482 ("When homosexual conduct is made criminal by the law of the State, that declaration in and of itself is an invitation to subject homosexual persons to discrimination both in the public and in the private spheres.").

demean the lives of homosexuals by branding them criminals. Although the Court could have overturned the Texas statute on equal protection grounds because it made sodomy a crime only when both partners were of the same sex, the Court went further than expected and seized the occasion to deliver a strong statement that moral disapproval of homosexual conduct does not justify legal intolerance and that gay and lesbian persons are entitled to the government's respect.[100] *Lawrence v. Texas* has been hailed as the *Brown v. Board of Education* of the gay community. It is likely to have far-reaching effects in the future.

### 2. Egregious Misconduct by Public Officials

Providing a remedy for egregious misconduct committed by public officials that is not otherwise prohibited by the Constitution is the second area where courts use substantive due process. The Supreme Court has established a high threshold for when such misconduct violates substantive due process. The conduct must be so outrageous that it shocks the conscience.[101] Abusing official authority to extort sexual favors is an example. While nothing in the Constitution prohibits public officials from using their position to extort sexual favors, this abuse of authority is so egregious that it shocks the conscience. It therefore violates substantive due process and exposes the official to federal criminal and civil liability.[102]

## § 1.16 —Equal Protection of the Laws

The Fourteenth Amendment contains another equally important safeguard, located in the equal protection clause. This clause forbids a state to "deny any person within its jurisdiction the equal protection of the laws."[103] The equal protection clause was included to protect former slaves against unfair treatment at the hands of state governments, a purpose that was not realized until almost a century later. In 1896, the Supreme Court handed down *Plessy v. Ferguson*,[104] in which it held that state-mandated racial segregation

---

[100] *Id.* 123 S. Ct. at 2484. ("The petitioners are entitled to respect for their private lives. The State cannot demean their existence or control their destiny by making their private sexual conduct a crime. Their right to liberty under the Due Process Clause gives them the full right to engage in their conduct without intervention of the government. 'It is a promise of the Constitution that there is a realm of personal liberty which the government may not enter.' The Texas statute furthers no legitimate state interest which can justify its intrusion into the personal and private life of the individual.").

[101] County of Sacramento v. Lewis, *supra* note 84.

[102] United States v. Lanier, 520 U.S. 259, 117 S. Ct. 1219, 137 L. Ed. 2d 432 (1997) (judge sexually assaulted women in his chamber); Rogers v. City of Little Rock, Ark., 152 F.3d 790 (8th Cir. 1998) (police officer intimidated motorist into having sex). *See also* § 10.15 *infra.*

[103] The Fourteenth Amendment applies only to state governments. However, the Fifth Amendment due process clause has been interpreted as imposing identical limitations on the federal government. *See, e.g.,* Adarand Constructors, Inc. v. Pena, 515 U.S. 200, 115 S. Ct. 2097, 132 L. Ed. 2d 158 (1995); Bolling v. Sharpe, 347 U.S. 497, 74 S. Ct. 693, 98 L. Ed. 884 (1954).

[104] 163 U.S. 537, 16 S. Ct. 1138, 41 L. Ed. 256 (1896).

satisfied the equal protection clause, provided that equal facilities were available to members of both races. *Plessy* established the doctrine of "separate but equal." After this, segregation codes flourished, infesting every avenue of American life, from restrooms, drinking fountains, telephone booths, hospitals, and prisons, to the books used by children in segregated public schools.[105] Justice Harlan alone dissented in *Plessy*, sounding what would become the Supreme Court's position in 1954. Justice Harlan wrote:

> . . . [I]n view of the Constitution, in the eye of the law, there is in this country no superior, dominant, ruling class of citizens. There is no caste here. Our Constitution is color-blind, and neither knows nor tolerates classes among citizens. In respect of civil rights, all citizens are equal before the law. The humblest is the peer of the most powerful. The law regards man as man and takes no account of his surroundings or his color when his civil rights as guaranteed by the supreme law of the land are involved.

The national conscience was reawakened in 1954, when the Supreme Court handed down the landmark decision of *Brown v. Board of Education*,[106] in which it announced that the "separate but equal" doctrine no longer satisfied the Constitution in the field of public education. It soon became apparent that *Brown v. Board of Education* was not limited to public education. *Brown v. Board of Education* ended the era of government-imposed barriers to racial equality.

Protection against unequal legal treatment at the hands of the government is a right that all Americans enjoy, not just members of racial minorities. The meaning of the equal protection clause can be summarized in one sentence. *The government must treat all persons who are similarly situated alike.* This does not mean that the governments is barred from making distinctions. Drawing lines is an unavoidable aspect of legislating. Welfare programs, for example, cannot operate without income eligibility requirements. Income eligibility requirements result in citizens with different incomes being treated differently. However, statutory distinctions do not offend the equal protection clause unless they are *arbitrary*.

Making blue eyes a requirement to receive welfare is an example of an arbitrary distinction. Fortunately, regulations like this are rare because legislatures generally have some purpose in mind for making a distinction. Whether a distinction can survive can equal protection challenge depends on the standard used to test its constitutionality. Courts use three different standards, called *levels of scrutiny—low, intermediate, and strict scrutiny.*

Statutes that distinguish between classes of citizens for reasons besides race, color, religion, national origin, or gender are tested by the lowest standard, called rational relationship review. Courts defer to the legislature

---

[105]   Woodward, The Strange Career of Jim Crow 83-86 (1965).
[106]   347 U.S. 483, 74 S. Ct. 686, 98 L. Ed. 873 (1954).

and will uphold the statute unless the challenger proves that the distinction has *no rational relationship to any legitimate government purpose.*[107]

Classifications based on gender are subject to *intermediate-level scrutiny* which means that courts examine them more closely. For a gender-based distinction to survive, the government provide an *exceedingly persuasive justification* for treating men and women different. Virginia Military Institute's (VMI) all-male admissions policy, for example, was held unconstitutional because the Military Institute was unable to do this.[108] This policy could have withstood rational relationship review because VMI had many legitimate reasons for wanting to remain an all-male school. However, gender-based distinctions require a stronger justification. VMI lost because it was unable to establish an exceedingly persuasive reason for refusing to accept qualified women into its program. Governments may not deny qualified women an opportunity to aspire based on stereotyping assumptions about their abilities and talents.

Race, creed, color, religion, and national origin are known as *suspect classes.* Differences in treatment that turn on these factor are subject to the most rigorous review standard, called *strict scrutiny.* A *compelling government interest* is necessary to satisfy strict scrutiny.[109] Because a *compelling government interest* is harder to establish than a *legitimate purpose* (low-level scrutiny) or an *exceedingly persuasive reason* (intermediate scrutiny), distinctions based on race, creed, color, religion, or national origin rarely survive a constitutional challenge.

While strict scrutiny has traditionally been used to invalidate laws that discriminate *against* members of suspect classes, the same analysis applies to laws that treat them more favorably.[110] Affirmative action programs were once thought to represent "benign discrimination" because their purpose is to raise the economic status of disadvantaged minorities, not to discriminate. However, whenever the government gives preferential treatment to members of one race, unequal treatment of members of the other race results. Consequently, affirmative action programs that make distinctions based on race are subject to strict scrutiny and are unconstitutional unless they advance a compelling government interest.[111]

---

[107] Heller v. Doe, 509 U.S. 312, 113 S. Ct. 2637, 125 L. Ed. 2d 257 (1993) (Legislative classifications that do not involve race, creed, color, religion, national origin, or gender violate equal protection only if the disparity of treatment is not rationally related to any legitimate government purpose.); Kimel v. Florida Board of Regents, 528 U.S. 62, 120 S. Ct. 631, 145 L. Ed. 2d 522 (2000) (age-based distinctions violate the equal protection clause only when there is no rational relationship between the disparity in treatment and any legitimate state interest).

[108] United States v. Virginia, 518 U.S. 515, 116 S. Ct 2264, 135 L. Ed. 2d 735 (1996). *See also* Tuan Anh Nguyen v. Immigration and Naturalization Service, 533 U.S. 53, 121 S. Ct. 2053, 150 L. Ed. 2d 115 (2001).

[109] Shaw v. Hunt, 517 U.S. 899, 116 S. Ct. 1894, 135 L. Ed. 2d 207 (1996); Adarand Constructors, Inc. v. Pena, *supra* note 103; Richmond v. J.A. Croson Co., 488 U.S. 469, 491, 109 S. Ct. 706, 720, 102 L. Ed. 2d 854 (1989).

[110] See cases *supra* note 109.

[111] *Id.*

The Supreme Court has not yet decided which review standard applies to distinctions based on sexual orientation. Most courts use the lowest standard. In 1993, former President Clinton instituted the "don't ask/don't tell" policy; this policy was later codified by Congress.[112] As a result of this policy, the armed forces no longer ask recruits to disclose their sexual orientation when they enter the military. However, the policy continues to treat voluntary admission of homosexuality and engaging in homosexual conduct as grounds for discharge. Lower federal courts, applying rational relationship review, have generally upheld the policy on the grounds that it furthers the military's legitimate interest in reducing friction in the armed services.[113] The Supreme Court's recent decision in *Lawrence v. Texas*,[114] holding that private homosexual conduct between consenting adults cannot be made as a crime, means that courts may need to rethink this matter.[115]

Police officers are bound by the equal protection clause in their dealings with members of the public. The perception that police inappropriately consider race and ethnicity in making enforcement interventions, a practice known as "racial profiling," has emerged as one of the most critical issues facing law enforcement. Taking a person's race or ethnicity into account in making enforcement decisions is unconstitutional[116] unless police are seek-

---

[112] Department of Defense Directives 1332.14 and 1332.30, 32 C.F.R. § 41, App. A (1992); (codified at 10 U.S.C. § 654 (1994)). This policy is commonly referred to as "Don't Ask, Don't Tell."

[113] Holmes v. California National Guard, 124 F.3d 1126 (9th Cir. 1997), *cert. denied*, 525 U.S. 1067, 119 S. Ct. 794, 142 L. Ed. 2d 657 (1999) (military has legitimate interest in discharging service members who engage in homosexual conduct to maintain efficiency in the armed services); Richenberg v. Perry, 97 F.3d 256 (8th Cir. 1996) (same); Philips v. Perry, 106 F.3d 1420 (9th Cir. 1997) (same).

[114] *Supra* note 96.

[115] *See, e.g.,* Quinn v. Nassau County Police Dep't, 53 F. Supp. 2d 347 (E.D.N.Y. 1999) (government agencies violate a homosexual employee's right of equal protection when they treat that person differently from the way they would treat a heterosexual employee in the same situation, based solely upon the employee's sexual orientation).

[116] *See, e.g.,* **Alexis v. McDonald's Restaurant of Massachusetts, Inc., 67 F.3d 341 (1st Cir. 1995)** (complaint that officer credited restaurant manager's assertion that she had caused a disturbance, ignored her request to inquire of other customers about what happened, forcibly removed her from the restaurant, even though she asked to be allowed to walk out on her own, handcuffed her, dragged her to a police car, and made racially disparaging remarks, stated a claim for denial of equal protection); Hardy v. Emery, 241 F. Supp. 2d 38 (D. Me. 2003) (black participants in apartment complex altercation with whites stated claim for denial of equal protection against police officer sent to deal with altercation where complaint alleged that officer chose to credit the account of a white male on the scene and ignored their attempts to get him to listen to their version of the events, used excessive and unnecessary force in arresting them, and made racially pejorative remarks); Flowers v. Fiore, 239 F. Supp. 2d 173 (D.R.I. 2003) (selective enforcement of motor vehicle laws on the basis of race, a practice known as racial profiling, violates equal protection); Carrasca v. Pomeroy, 313 F.3d 823 (3d Cir. 2002) (complaint that officer singled out plaintiffs, rather than other similarly situated non-Hispanic swimmers, for enforcement of the swimming hours regulations, and used racially pejorative language, stated claim for damages for selective enforcement); State v. Soto, 324 N.J. Super. 66, 734 A.2d 350 (1996) (unrebutted statistical evidence of disproportionate traffic stops against African American motorists established *de facto* policy of targeting blacks for investigation, violating the equal protection clause and requiring suppression of all evidence seized during stop). Selective enforcement is covered in greater detail in § 10.16 *infra*.

ing to apprehend a specific suspect sought in connection with a particular unlawful incident who has been described, in part, by race or ethnicity.[117]

While the Fourteenth Amendment only prohibits discriminatory enforcement by state officials, the Fifth Amendment due process clause imposes comparable restrictions on federal officials, and divers federal, state, and local statutes prohibit discrimination by private individuals.

## § 1.17 Adjudication of Constitutional Questions

The Constitution is not self-defining. Determining what the Constitution demands in different contexts requires an ongoing process of interpretation. The Supreme Court is the ultimate authority on what the Constitution means. The Supreme Court's decisions interpreting the Constitution become the law of the land, establishing standards that are binding on police officers.

Most of the Supreme Court's criminal justice decisions stem from appeals brought by state prisoners. Nonlawyers are often curious about how a prisoner's case gets to the Supreme Court. This section examines how constitutional issues reach the Supreme Court.

Federalism results in a dual system of federal and state courts. Within each system, there are two types of courts—trial courts and appeals courts. Trial courts determine the facts, apply the law to the facts, and reach verdicts. Appeals courts do not retry facts. Their function is to review the trial judge's rulings on questions of law to determine if they were correct. Appeals courts have the power to reverse criminal verdicts only if the verdict resulted from incorrect rulings on questions of constitutional or statutory law, or rules of evidence.

Understanding how cases reach the Supreme Court requires a brief sketch of state judicial systems. Most states have three levels of courts. The trial courts are at the bottom. This is where criminal prosecutions take place. Directly above the trial courts are middle-level appeals courts. Their function is to hear cases that are appealed from trial courts. Appeal to middle-level appeals courts generally exists as a matter of right. The highest state court, often called the supreme court, is at the top of the judicial pyramid. Two levels of appeals courts exist to ensure that everyone has an opportunity to have a higher court review trial court rulings on questions of law and decide whether the rulings were correct. Middle-level appeals courts perform this function. Review at the highest level—the supreme court level—is normally discretionary. State supreme courts generally have discretion whether to hear a particular appeal. This allows the state's highest court to

---

[117] *See, e.g.,* Farm Labor Org. Comm. v. Ohio State Highway Patrol, 308 F.3d 523 (6th Cir. 2002); United States v. Montero-Camargo, 208 F.3d 1122 (9th Cir. 2000). *See also* Lorie Fridell et al., *Racially Biased Policing: A Principled Response.* (Police Executive Research Forum, 2001), available at http://police-forum.mn-8.net/.

control its docket and hear only cases that raise issues of special importance to the legal system.

This is also how it works with the United States Supreme Court. The Supreme Court has discretion whether to hear a particular appeal. Requests to the Supreme Court for discretionary review are instituted by filing a petition for a writ of certiorari. If at least four members of the Supreme Court vote to hear the case, the petition will be granted and the appeal will be allowed; if less than four are interested, the petition will be denied and the appeal will be dismissed. Each term (which begins the first Monday of each October and usually continues through June), the Supreme Court receives thousands of petitions seeking discretionary (certiorari) review. The Supreme Court usually hears about 150 appeals per term. The remaining petitions for discretionary review are rejected. Denial of certiorari does not mean that the Supreme Court agrees with the legal principles that were applied by the court below. This is a mistake commonly made in news reports. The only meaning that can be attributed to the Supreme Court's denial of certiorari is that less than four Supreme Court justices were interested in hearing the appeal.

Constitutional issues raised by state prisoners generally reach the Supreme Court through one of two routes: direct review and habeas corpus review.

**Direct review.** Criminal prosecutions for state crimes are tried in state courts. If the trial results in a conviction, the defendant can petition the United States Supreme Court for direct review after he or she receives a final judgment from the highest state court available.[118] In other words, a defendant seeking direct review must go up the state appellate ladder to the highest court available before petitioning the Supreme Court to have his or her case heard on direct review. State prisoners cannot ask the Supreme Court to review claimed violations of state law; their appeals must involve a substantial federal question.

**Habeas corpus review.** Constitutional errors are not always discovered in time to seek direct review. Federal law gives state prisoners a post-conviction remedy called habeas corpus.[119] Habeas corpus is a remedy that has obtaining release from unlawful confinement as its goal. A state prisoner commences this action by filing a petition in federal court, alleging that he or she is being detained in prison in violation of his or her constitutional rights and requests the issuance of a writ of habeas corpus. A writ of habeas corpus directs the party having custody, usually the warden, to produce the prisoner in court, so that the court can inquire into the matter.[120] The writ of habeas corpus enables state prisoners to have a federal judge review the constitutionality of their state court convictions. Federal habeas corpus involves a collateral attack on a state court judgment. The reason it is called a collateral attack is that the courts of one jurisdiction (federal) are exercising review powers over a case decided by the courts of another jurisdiction (state).

---

[118]   28 U.S.C. § 1257.
[119]   28 U.S.C. § 2241.
[120]   28 U.S.C. § 2254(a).

Federal habeas corpus is a common path that state prisoners travel on their road to the Supreme Court. A petition is filed in a federal district court.[121] If the prisoner's claim is denied by the federal district court, the prisoner appeals to the United States Court of Appeals and, from there, petitions the Supreme Court for discretionary (certiorari) review.

In recent years, the number of state prisoners filing habeas corpus petitions in federal courts has increased exponentially, growing from 127 in 1941 to 12,000 in 1990.[122] The flood of habeas corpus petitions from state prisoners became so heavy that lower federal courts were having difficulty managing their other dockets. In 1996, Congress restricted the availability of habeas corpus review, eliminating second and successive habeas corpus petitions[123] and review of claims previously litigated in a state court unless the state court decision is contrary to clearly established constitutional standards.[124] These new procedural changes will make it more difficult for state prisoners to make their way to the Supreme Court.

## § 1.18    Federal Remedies for Constitutional Abuses

Why are students in training to become law enforcement officers required to study the United States Constitution?

There are three reasons. First, all citizens should have a basic knowledge of the Constitution because preservation of our constitutional liberties depends on an informed citizenry. Second, police officers are regularly required to make decisions with constitutional implications. The decision to detain a suspect for investigation, make an arrest, conduct a frisk, use force, search for evidence, and interrogate a suspect are some of the many decisions police routinely make that are regulated by the Constitution. Professionalism means taking constitutional rights seriously. In the words of the late Justice Brandeis:

> Our government is the potent, the omnipresent teacher. For good or for ill, it teaches the whole people by its example. . . . If the government becomes a lawbreaker, it breeds contempt for law. . . . To declare that in the administration of the criminal law the end justifies the means—to declare that the government may commit crimes in order to secure the conviction of a private criminal—would bring terrible retribution. Against that pernicious doctrine this court should resolutely set its face.[125]

---

[121]   United States district courts are the federal court system's trial courts. They have both criminal and civil jurisdiction. There are a total of 94 federal judicial districts—at least one for each state, the District of Columbia, and Puerto Rico. The 94 judicial districts are organized into 12 regional circuits, each of which has a United States Court of Appeals. The United States Courts of Appeals hear appeals from the district courts located within their circuits.

[122]   Withrow v. Williams, 507 U.S. 680, 697, 113 S. Ct. 1745, 123 L. Ed. 2d 407 (1993) (O'Connor, J., concurring).

[123]   28 U.S.C. § 2254 and 2255.

[124]   28 U.S.C. §§ 2254 (d).

[125]   **Olmstead v. United States, 277 U.S. 438, 468, 48 S. Ct. 564, 72 L. Ed. 944 (1928)** (Brandeis, J., dissenting).

Finally, constitutional violations carry serious consequences for the person whose rights are violated, for the criminal justice system, and for the officer personally. Constitutional misconduct can lead to:

1.   Exclusion of evidence procured in violation of the Constitution.
2.   Reversal of criminal convictions.
3.   Disciplinary action.
4.   Civil liability.
5.   Criminal prosecution.

These sanctions are covered in later chapters. We briefly mention them here to underscore the importance of the material that follows. Thus, it is extremely important that police officers "know the rules" and obey them.

## § 1.19   Summary

The Constitution of the United States is the highest law of the land. It contains seven articles. The first three articles apportion the powers of the national government among three branches (legislative, executive, and judicial) and describe the powers of each. The separation of powers among the three branches is permanently fixed. Encroachment and delegation are forbidden.

The apportionment of power between the national government and the states is accomplished by: (1) delegating a broad range of powers to the federal government (Article I, Section 8); (2) expressly prohibiting the exercise of specified powers by the states (Article I, Section 10); and (3) declaring that all powers not expressly delegated to the federal government, nor forbidden to the states, belong to the states (Tenth Amendment). The powers retained by the states depend on interpretation of the scope of the powers delegated to the federal government. Generous interpretations have resulted in a gradual shift in the federal/state balance of power. The federal government today has far greater power than the states. Expansive interpretation of the commerce clause has been the single most important factor. The commerce clause allows the federal government to regulate any activity—national, state, or local—that has a substantial direct or indirect effect on interstate commerce. When Congress enacts legislation within the scope of its delegated powers, federal law nullifies contrary state law. This results from the supremacy clause, which makes the Constitution and laws of the United States the supreme law of the land, superseding contrary state law. However, our Constitution requires a distinction between matters that are truly national and matters that are truly local. The federal government may not regulate matters that are truly local.

The Constitution establishes a process for amendment. There are now 26 Amendments. The first 10, known as the Bill of Rights, were adopted in 1791, two years after the Constitution was ratified. The Bill of Rights addresses many aspects of criminal procedure that are discussed in later chapters.

Although the Bill of Rights originally limited only the federal government, the most important safeguards have been incorporated into the Fourteenth Amendment and are now binding on state governments as well.

The Fourteenth Amendment contains the due process and equal protection clauses. The due process clause provides two kinds of protection—one procedural and the other substantive. Procedural due process requires fair procedures before the government may take away a citizen's life, liberty, or property. Substantive due process prohibits: (1) arbitrary restrictions on "fundamental rights" and (2) conscience-shocking behaviour by public officials. The equal protection clause prohibits state governments from making arbitrary distinctions between classes of citizens

The Supreme Court has discretion whether or not to hear an appeal. Criminal appeals generally reach the Supreme Court through one of two routes—direct review and habeas corpus review. Direct review requires the aggrieved party to take his or her case to the highest state court available before petitioning the Supreme Court for certiorari (discretionary) review. Habeas corpus review is a post-conviction remedy. The prisoner brings an action in federal court, challenging the constitutionality of his or her state court conviction and resulting confinement.

Violating constitutional rights can lead to five different sanctions: (1) exclusion of evidence procured in violation of the Constitution, (2) reversal of a criminal conviction, (3) disciplinary action, (4) civil liability and, in extreme cases, (5) criminal prosecution.

# Freedom of Speech                    2

*Congress shall make no law . . . abridging the freedom of speech, or of the press; or the right of the people peaceably to assemble, and to petition the Government for a redress of grievances.*

*First Amendment*

# Chapter Outline

## § 2.1  Historical Background

Many portions of the Bill of Rights have origins that go back to the Magna Charta or descend from time-honored English traditions. This is not the case with the First Amendment.[1] The First Amendment was adopted in response to abuses of the Crown. The union of church and state provided a hospitable climate for religious and political repression. Censorship was first practiced to prevent the spread of unorthodox religious ideas. In 1585, the Court of the Star Chamber issued a decree prohibiting books from being printed unless they were reviewed and licensed by the Archbishop.[2] Licensing laws ended in 1694, only to be succeeded by seditious libel laws.[3] The crime of seditious libel consisted of criticizing public officials. During the heyday of these laws, a person could be punished for this crime if he or she read libelous material, heard it read and laughed at it, or repeated it to another.[4]

The framing of a Bill of Rights was the first order of business facing the Congress that met after the ratification of the Constitution. The foundation for a strong central government had been laid. Now restraints were needed to prevent the repressive English experience from being repeated. In specifying the rights of the American people against the federal government, freedom of speech was mentioned first. This was no coincidence. The Framers had the vision to realize that without freedom of speech, political rights would not be secure. In the First Amendment, they placed freedom of speech outside the

---

[1]  BRYANT, THE BILL OF RIGHTS 81 (1965).

[2]  *Id.* at 98-100.

[3]  *Id.* at 94.

[4]  *Id.* at 114.

federal government's control. With the adoption of the Fourteenth Amendment, which prohibits states from depriving citizens of liberty without due process of law, the freedoms guaranteed by the First Amendment applied to state governments as well.[5]

The United States has experienced more than two centuries of political stability. When viewed against the background of world history, this is remarkable. The First Amendment has played a singularly important role. When citizens can openly criticize their government, changes come about through orderly political processes. When grievances exist, they must be aired, if not through the channels of public debate, then by riots in the streets. The First Amendment functions as a safety valve through which the pressures and frustrations of a heterogeneous society can be ventilated and defused. Professor Emerson has identified another function that free speech serves in a democratic society:

> [F]reedom of expression is an essential process for advancing knowledge and discovering truth. An individual who seeks knowledge and truth must hear all sides of the question, consider all alternatives, test his judgment by exposing it to opposition, and make full use of different minds. . . . The reasons which make open discussion essential for an intelligent individual judgment likewise make it imperative for rational social judgment.[6]

## § 2.2 Overview of Constitutional Protection for Speech and Expressive Conduct

The First Amendment directs that "Congress shall make no law . . . abridging the freedom of speech . . ." Although Congress alone is mentioned, the First Amendment binds all branches and levels of government.[7] The initial inquiry in First Amendment analysis is whether "speech" is involved. In most cases, the answer is obvious. However, written and spoken words are not the only forms of speech protected by the First Amendment. The boundaries of "speech" are explored in § 2.3.

The determination that "speech" is involved begins the constitutional inquiry. It means that the controversy will be decided under the First Amendment. However, it does not ordain the outcome. The right to speak is not absolute. A society in which the government was powerless to restrain citizens from speaking at any time and place, about any subject, however loudly they please, would be an insufferable place to live. The First Amendment does not strip the government of power to regulate speech; it prohibits the government from "abridging freedom of speech." Deciding when a restriction "abridges freedom of speech" is what First Amendment jurisprudence is about; this determination calls for complex value judgments.

---

5   Gitlow v. New York, 268 U.S. 652, 45 S. Ct. 625, 69 L. Ed. 1138 (1925).
6   EMERSON, THE SYSTEM OF FREEDOM OF EXPRESSION 6-7 (1969).
7   *Id.*

The Framers were primarily concerned with protection against censorship. They wanted to ensure that the choice of ideas that could be expressed would remain in the hands of the people. Consequently, in deciding whether freedom of speech has been abridged, an important distinction exists between government interventions that are directed at a speaker's *message* (e.g., arresting a person for expressing offensive ideas) and those that are directed at a speaker's *conduct* (e.g., arresting a person for using a loudspeaker in a residential neighborhood after dark)[8] The First Amendment embodies the belief that a free marketplace of ideas is essential to informed decisionmaking and individual self-development.[9] The following passage from *Cohen v. California*[10] explains these assumptions:

> The constitutional right of free expression is powerful medicine in a society as diverse and populous as ours. It is designed and intended to remove governmental restraints from the arena of public discussion, putting the decision as to what views shall be voiced largely into the hands of each of us, in the hope that use of such freedom will ultimately produce a more capable citizenry and more perfect polity and in the belief that no other approach would comport with the premise of individual dignity and choice upon which our political system rests.

Accordingly, the First Amendment sharply curtails the government's ability to impose content-based restrictions on speech. Punishing citizens for *what* they say is, with rare exception, unconstitutional unless their speech falls within a small category of topics that have been written out of the First Amendment. These topics are discussed in §§ 2.5-2.11.

A violation of the First Amendment is less likely when restrictions on speech are targeted at features besides the message. Free speech can have annoying side effects. Bullhorns are loud, billboards are unsightly, and parades interrupt traffic. These effects flow from a speaker's conduct. The balance of Chapter 2 deals with the government's ability to regulate conduct that is intertwined with speech. Figure 2.1 contains a flow chart showing the main concepts that will be discussed in this chapter.

## § 2.3  Is Speech Involved?

When a citizen claims that his or her First Amendment rights have been abridged, the court's first consideration is whether speech is involved.

The First Amendment meaning of "speech" cannot be looked up in a dictionary. Dictionaries record standard usages. A broader meaning is necessary to fulfill the purpose of the First Amendment. The essence of free speech is

---

[8]   Grayned v. City of Rockford, 408 U.S. 104, 92 S. Ct. 2294, 33 L. Ed. 2d 222 (1972).
[9]   Whitney v. California, 274 U.S. 357, 375-376, 47 S. Ct. 641, 648, 71 L. Ed. 1095 (1927) (Brandeis, J., concurring).
[10]  403 U.S. 15, 24, 91 S. Ct. 1780, 1787-1788, 29 L. Ed. 2d 284, 293 (1971).

Figure 2.1
**Overview of the First Amendment**

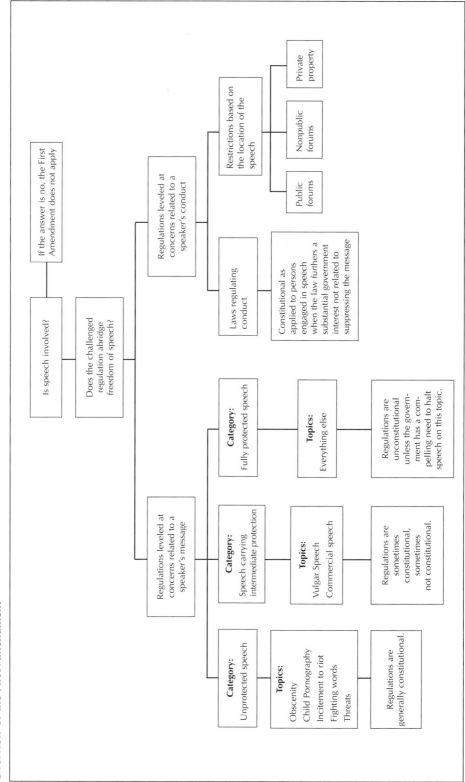

the right to share one's beliefs with others. However, because it is necessary to receive information to form beliefs in order to share them, the First Amendment protects this right as well.[11] There are an infinite variety of techniques for sharing beliefs. A partial list includes: making speeches; participating in parades,[12] marches, pickets, and other public demonstrations;[13] displaying signs and placards; distributing literature, pamphlets, and other written materials; writing letters;[14] soliciting membership in organizations, signatures on petitions, and contributions for causes;[15] broadcasting via radio, television, or cable;[16] communicating over the Internet;[17] filing public interest litigation;[18] participating in politically motivated business boycotts;[19] and engaging in artistic forms of expression such as dance, music, and painting.[20] All of these activities constitute "speech" within the meaning of the First Amendment.

Figure 2.2
**First Amendment Concept of Speech**

---

The First Amendment concept of speech includes the right to:

1.  receive information,
2.  hold beliefs,
3.  communicate them to others,
4.  engage in ideological silence, and
5.  engage in symbolic speech.

---

Speech also includes the freedom not to speak or, in other words, to remain silent. Forcing citizens to voice public adherence to ideas they find unacceptable is repugnant to the First Amendment.[21] In *West Virginia State Board of Education v. Barnette*,[22] the Supreme Court struck down a state statute requiring schoolchildren to pledge allegiance to the American flag, declaring:

---

[11]   Lamont v. Postmaster General, 381 U.S. 301, 85 S. Ct. 1493, 14 L. Ed. 2d 398 (1965).

[12]   Hurley v. Irish-American Gay, Lesbian and Bisexual Group of Boston, 515 U.S. 557, 115 S. Ct. 2338, 132 L. Ed. 2d 487 (1995).

[13]   Thornhill v. Alabama, 310 U.S. 88, 60 S. Ct. 736, 84 L. Ed. 1093 (1940); Edwards v. South Carolina, 372 U.S. 229, 83 S. Ct. 680, 9 L. Ed. 2d 697 (1963).

[14]   Procunier v. Martinez, 416 U.S. 396, 94 S. Ct. 1800, 40 L. Ed. 2d 224 (1974).

[15]   **International Soc. for Krishna Consciousness, Inc. v. Lee, 505 U.S. 672, 112 S. Ct. 2701, 120 L. Ed. 2d 541 (1992)**; Thomas v. Collins, 323 U.S. 516, 65 S. Ct. 315, 89 L. Ed. 430 (1945).

[16]   Turner Broadcasting System, Inc. v. FCC, 512 U.S. 622, 114 S. Ct. 2445, 129 L. Ed. 2d 497 (1994).

[17]   Reno v. American Civil Liberties Union, 521 U.S. 844, 117 S. Ct. 2329, 138 L. Ed. 2d 874 (1997).

[18]   NAACP v. Button, 371 U.S. 415, 83 S. Ct. 347, 9 L. Ed. 2d 405 (1960).

[19]   NAACP v. Claiborne Hardware Co., 458 U.S. 886, 102 S. Ct. 3409, 73 L. Ed. 2d 1215 (1982).

[20]   Ward v. Rock Against Racism, 491 U.S. 781, 109 S. Ct. 2746, 105 L. Ed. 2d 661 (1989); Schad v. Mount Ephraim, 452 U.S. 61, 101 S. Ct. 2176, 68 L. Ed. 2d 671 (1981).

[21]   West Virginia State Board of Education v. Barnette, 319 U.S. 624, 63 S. Ct. 1178, 87 L. Ed. 1628 (1943); Wooley v. Maynard, 430 U.S. 705, 97 S. Ct. 1428, 51 L. Ed. 2d 752 (1977).

[22]   West Virginia State Board of Education v. Barnette, *supra* note 21.

If there is any fixed star in our constitutional constellation, it is that no official, high or petty, can prescribe what shall be orthodox in politics, national-
ism, religion, or other matters of opinion or force citizens to confess by word
or act their faith therein. If there are any circumstances which permit of an
exception, they do not now occur to us.[23]

Speech also includes mute conduct like displaying a red flag,[24] wearing a
black armband,[25] staging a sit-in demonstration,[26] wearing a Nazi uniform,[27]
and burning a cross at a Ku Klux Klan rally.[28] These acts constitute speech
because they communicate a message. Mute conduct performed for the sake
of communicating a message that is likely to be understood by those who view
it is called **symbolic speech**.[29]

## § 2.4 First Amendment Distinction between a Speaker's Message and the Conduct Associated with Communicating It

Some mediums of expression, such as writing a newspaper editorial, have
only one ingredient—the message. Others, such as marching, picketing, and
handbilling, have two. The second ingredient is public conduct. A large group
of people marching down a city street, broadcasting their message over a bullhorn may interrupt traffic, hinder pedestrians, obstruct entrances to buildings,
and cause distracting noise. The First Amendment distinguishes between a
speaker's message and his or her conduct. While the message has almost
absolute protection under the First Amendment, the speaker's conduct does not.

In *United States v. O'Brien*,[30] the Supreme Court established the controlling test for when laws prohibiting conduct may be enforced against people
engaged in speech. O'Brien burned his draft card during an anti-war demonstration to express his opposition to the war. He was prosecuted under a federal statute that made deliberate destruction of draft cards a crime. He argued
that the statute could not be applied to him because he destroyed his draft card
as a symbolic substitute for words. The Supreme Court rejected this defense,
holding that laws prohibiting conduct may be applied to persons engaged in
speech *when they further a substantial government interest that is unrelated to
suppressing the message that accompanies the conduct*. Because the govern-

---

[23]   *Id.* at 642, 63 S. Ct. at 1187, 87 L. Ed. at 1639.
[24]   Stromberg v. California, 283 U.S. 359, 51 S. Ct. 532, 75 L. Ed. 1117 (1931).
[25]   Tinker v. Des Moines Independent School Dist., 393 U.S. 503, 89 S. Ct. 733, 21 L. Ed. 2d 731 (1969).
[26]   Brown v. Louisiana, 383 U.S. 131, 86 S. Ct. 719, 15 L. Ed. 2d 637 (1966).
[27]   National Socialist Party of America v. Skokie, 432 U.S. 43, 97 S. Ct. 2205, 53 L. Ed. 2d 96 (1977).
[28]   **Virginia v. Black, 538 U.S. 343, 123 S. Ct. 1536, 155 L. Ed. 2d 535 (2003)**; Brandenburg v. Ohio, 395 U.S. 444, 89 S. Ct. 1827, 23 L. Ed. 2d 430 (1969).
[29]   **Texas v. Johnson, 491 U.S. 397, 109 S. Ct. 2533, 105 L. Ed. 2d 342 (1989)**.
[30]   391 U.S. 367, 88 S. Ct. 1673, 20 L. Ed. 2d 672 (1968).

ment had a legitimate reason for requiring preservation of draft cards—a reason that had nothing to do with stifling political dissent—O'Brien's conviction was valid.

The holding in *United States v. O'Brien* has broad application for police. It means that police are free to apply the general laws of the community (i.e., noise, traffic, trespass, disorderly conduct, breach of the peace, etc.) to persons engaged in speech because these laws advance important community interests that are unrelated to suppressing the speaker's message. If the law says it is illegal to use artificial sound amplification equipment, obstruct traffic, block entrances to public buildings, or engage in other disruptive acts, police may arrest people who perform these acts, even when they are engaged in speech-related activity.

In *Clark v. Community for Creative Non-Violence*,[31] the Supreme Court upheld the constitutionality of applying a park regulation prohibiting sleeping in a public park to a group that wanted to hold a sleep-in to protest the plight of the nation's homeless. In *Barnes v. Glen Theatre, Inc.*,[32] the Court ruled that a general prohibition on public nudity could be applied to nude erotic dancers in adult entertainment establishments. In both cases, the focus of the government's regulatory concern was the speaker's conduct, not the message.

The reverse was true in *Schacht v. United States*.[33] In *Schacht*, the Supreme Court struck down a federal statute prohibiting the wearing of military uniforms in dramatic productions under circumstances tending to discredit the armed forces. While this statute ostensibly regulated conduct (wearing military uniforms in dramatic productions), the government's real concern was the message (depicting the armed forces in an unfavorable light). Because the statute's regulatory focus was on the message, the statute was unconstitutional under the *O'Brien* test.

A similar result was reached in *Texas v. Johnson*,[34] which involved a state statute that made it a crime to desecrate an American flag. The defendant was arrested under this statute for burning an American flag during a protest demonstration. The Supreme Court pointed out that the government's only interest in how Americans treat flags that are their own property is promoting respect for national symbols. Because this interest is inextricably linked to the message that accompanies the act of flag desecration, the Texas statute was unconstitutional under the *O'Brien* test. The Court cautioned: "We do not consecrate the flag by punishing for its desecration, for in doing so we dilute the freedom that this cherished emblem represents."

---

[31] 468 U.S. 288, 104 S. Ct. 3065, 82 L. Ed. 2d 221 (1984).
[32] 501 U.S. 560, 111 S. Ct. 2456, 115 L. Ed. 2d 504 (1991).
[33] 398 U.S. 58, 90 S. Ct. 1555, 26 L. Ed. 2d 44 (1970).
[34] *Supra* note 29. This decision infuriated Congress, which retaliated by enacting a federal flag desecration statute. The federal statute was sufficiently different from the statute struck down in *Texas v. Johnson* to give the Supreme Court an opportunity to reconsider. In *United States v. Eichman*, 496 U.S. 310, 110 S. Ct. 2404, 110 L. Ed. 2d 287 (1990), the Supreme Court reconsidered, but refused to back down. The First Amendment prohibits the government from making disrespectful treatment of the flag a crime.

The previous discussion in no way exhausts the range of activities that are considered "speech." The determination that "speech" is involved leads to the next question. Does the challenged restriction abridge freedom of speech? As previously noted, the answer often hinges on whether the restriction is directed at the speaker's message or at some other feature.[35]

Figure 2.3
**Expressive Conduct**

> The general laws of the community (i.e., trespass, breach of the peace, disorderly conduct, blocking the public passage, etc.) may be applied to people engaged in **expressive conduct** when they further important government interests that are unrelated to suppressing the speaker's message.

## § 2.5  Punishing Speech Because of the Message

The First Amendment sharply limits the government's power to punish people for what they say or for the language they use to say it. Subject to a small number of exceptions that will be discussed shortly, restrictions on speech because of the ideas, viewpoint, or message are unconstitutional unless the restriction is necessary to further a *compelling government interest*.[36] A compelling interest means an interest of paramount importance. In *Linmark Associates, Inc. v. Township of Willingboro*,[37] the Supreme Court struck down an ordinance outlawing the use of "for sale" and "sold" signs in residential neighborhoods. The ordinance had been enacted in order to stem the tide of panic selling in newly integrated neighborhoods. The Supreme Court chastised the legislature for suppressing truthful information out of fear of the public's reaction. The choice "between the dangers of suppressing information, and the dangers of its misuse if it is freely available," the Court stated, "is one the First Amendment has already made for us."[38] In *Brown v. Hartlage*,[39] the Court held that a political candidate's First Amendment rights were violated when he was prosecuted under an election corruption statute for making a questionable campaign promise. Mr. Justice Brennan wrote:

---

[35]  Simon & Schuster, Inc. v. New York Crime Victims Bd., 502 U.S. 105, 112 S. Ct. 501, 116 L. Ed. 2d 476 (1991); Burson v. Freeman, 504 U.S. 191, 112 S. Ct. 1846, 119 L. Ed. 2d 5 (1992); R.A.V. v. City of St. Paul, 505 U.S. 377, 112 S. Ct. 2538, 120 L. Ed. 2d 305 (1992); Republican Party of Minnesota v. White, 536 U.S. 765, 122 S. Ct. 2528, 153 L. Ed. 2d 694 (2002).

[36]  *See* cases *supra* note 35.

[37]  431 U.S. 85, 97 S. Ct. 1614, 52 L. Ed. 2d 155 (1977).

[38]  456 U.S. 45, 102 S. Ct. 1523, 71 L. Ed. 2d 732 (1982). *See also* Republican Party of Minnesota v. White, *supra* note 35 (judicial ethics rule prohibiting candidates for judicial election from announcing their views on disputed legal or political issues violated First Amendment because it prohibited speech on basis of content).

[39]  Brown v. Hartlage, *supra* note 38, 456 U.S. at 60, 102 S. Ct. at 1532.

[The First] Amendment embodies our trust in the free exchange of ideas as the means by which the people are to choose between good ideas and bad, and between candidates for political office. The State's fear that voters might make an ill-advised choice does not provide the State with a compelling justification for limiting speech. It is not the function of government to "select which issues are worth discussing or debating," . . . in the course of a political campaign.

The belief that truth is most likely to emerge through an unfettered exchange of ideas is central to the First Amendment. The First Amendment protects expression even of the most loathsome ideas on the theory that ideas, once expressed, can be openly debated and that the truth will emerge from this process.[40]

## A. Topics That Have Diminished or No Free Speech Protection

Although free speech generally means freedom to speak on any matter, a small number of speech topics have been written out of the First Amendment. They include: (1) **obscenity** and **child pornography**;[41] (2) **fighting words**;[42] (3) threats;[43] and (4) incitement to riot.[44] The Supreme Court has explained that "such utterances are no essential part of any exposition of ideas, and are of such slight social value as steps toward discovery of truth that any benefit derived from them is outweighed by society's interest in order and morality."[45] Speech that lacks First Amendment protection is proscribable. This means that citizens may be arrested for what they say if their speech lacks constitutional protection. However, the converse is also true. They may not be arrested for what they say if their speech is protected.[46] Consequently, careful attention must be paid to the boundaries of the unprotected speech categories. Speech that enjoys First Amendment protection may not be considered as a factor in making an arrest decision. The speaker's conduct, however, may always be considered.

---

[40] Abrams v. United States, 250 U.S. 616, 630, 40 S. Ct. 17, 22, 63 L. Ed. 1173 (1919) (Holmes, J., dissenting).

[41] See § 2.6.

[42] See § 2.7 *infra*.

[43] See § 2.8 *infra*.

[44] See § 2.9 *infra*.

[45] Chaplinsky v. New Hampshire, 315 U.S. 568, 572, 62 S. Ct. 766, 769, 86 L. Ed. 1031 (1942).

[46] **Norwell v. City of Cincinnati, 414 U.S. 14, 94 S. Ct. 187, 38 L. Ed. 2d 170 (1973)**; Gooding v. Wilson, 405 U.S. 518, 521-522, 92 S. Ct. 1103, 1105-1106, 31 L. Ed. 2d 408 (1972).

# § 2.6  —Obscenity and Child Pornography

In 1957, the Supreme Court ruled that obscenity lacks First Amendment protection[47] and then struggled for the next 15 years to agree on a constitutional definition. The contemporary test was announced in *Miller v. California*.[48] Under the *Miller* test, three findings must be made before a work can be branded obscene and denied First Amendment protection on this basis. The fact finder must determine that the work:

1.  appeals to prurient interests;
2.  depicts "hard-core" sexual acts, previously defined by applicable state law, in a patently offensive way; and
3.  lacks serious literary, artistic, political, scientific, or other value.

A "prurient interest" is not the same thing as a normal, wholesome interest in sex.[49] Works that do no more than evoke a normal, wholesome interest in sex are not obscene. Prurient connotes an abnormal, voyeuristic, shameful, or degrading interest in sex. In addition, the work must depict "hard-core"sexual acts, previously defined in the state's obscenity law, in a patently offensive way. These acts may include: patently offensive verbal or visual depictions of ultimate sexual acts (normal or perverted, real or simulated); masturbation; lewd exhibition of genitals; sadomasochistic sexual behavior; violent sex; bestiality; and sexual perversions.[50] Finally, the work, considered as a whole, must lack serious literary, political, scientific, artistic, or other value. Works that have serious literary or other value are not obscene even though they contain isolated objectionable pictures or passages.

Figure 2.4
**Constitutional Test for Obscenity**

To be considered obscene in the constitutional sense, a literary work must:

1.  appeal to prurient interests;
2.  depict hard-core sexual acts previously defined by state law in a patently offensive way; and
3.  lack serious literary, artistic, political, scientific, or other value.

---

[47]  Roth v. United States, 354 U.S. 476, 77 S. Ct. 1304, 1 L. Ed. 2d 1498 (1957), overruled, Miller v. California, 413 U.S. 15, 93 S. Ct. 2607, 37 L. Ed. 2d 419 (1973).
[48]  *Supra* note 47.
[49]  Brockett v. Spokane Arcades, Inc., 472 U.S. 491, 105 S. Ct. 2794, 86 L. Ed. 2d 394 (1985).
[50]  Ward v. Illinois, 431 U.S. 767, 97 S. Ct. 2085, 52 L. Ed. 2d 738 (1977).

The *Miller* test was developed as a general test of obscenity. No attention was given to the special interest of children. Studies show that exploiting children by using them to produce **child pornography** can cause permanent psychological damage. Because the *Miller* test was not formulated with this problem in mind, states are free to use a different standard to regulate child pornography. However, departure from *Miller* is allowed only for works that visually depict *real* children engaged in sexual activity, not adults posing as children or computer-generated images.[51] States are also free to use a different standard in laws that regulate the sale of sexually explicit materials to minors.[52]

The line between obscene and nonobscene is not so sharp that police can instantly recognize on which side of the line certain works fall. Because obscene materials are not stripped of First Amendment protection until after they have been adjudicated obscene in a legal action, special procedures have been developed for obscenity searches and seizures. These procedures are designed to minimize the risk that innocent works will be seized. They differ from standard procedure in the following ways.

First, police must obtain a preliminary determination from a magistrate that there is probable cause to believe that a particular work is obscene before they may seize it.[53] Police, in short, must always procure a search warrant. Undercover purchases are exempt from this requirement because they do not involve a seizure.[54] Undercover purchases are a convenient way to acquire evidence needed to support an application for a search warrant.

Second, a much higher degree of specificity is needed in the affidavit for an obscenity search warrant. Ideally, the judge should view the material personally. When this is not feasible, the officer must prepare a highly detailed affidavit to compensate for the lack of a personal viewing.[55] The amount of detail needed is illustrated in the sample affidavit in Figure 2.5.

---

[51]  New York v. Ferber, 458 U.S. 747, 102 S. Ct. 3348, 73 L. Ed. 2d 1113 (1982) (because of the State's interest in protecting the children exploited by the production process, pornography depicting actual children may be proscribed whether or not the images are obscene under *Miller*); Ashcroft v. Free Speech Coalition, 535 U.S. 234, 122 S. Ct. 1389, 152 L. Ed. 2d 403 (2002) (child pornography produced through the use of youthful-looking adults or computer-imaging technology may be banned only if the work is obscene under the *Miller* test).

[52]  Denver Area Educ'l Telecommunications Consortium, Inc. v. FCC, 518 U.S. 727, 116 S. Ct. 2374, 125 L. Ed. 2d 888 (1997); Ginsberg v. New York, 390 U.S. 629, 88 S. Ct. 1274, 20 L. Ed. 2d 195 (1968); FCC v. Pacifica Foundation, 438 U.S. 726, 98 S. Ct. 3026, 57 L. Ed. 2d 1073 (1978). *See also* Bethel School District v. Fraser, 478 U.S. 675, 106 S. Ct. 3159, 92 L. Ed. 2d 549 (1986).

[53]  Roaden v. Kentucky, 413 U.S. 496, 93 S. Ct. 2796, 37 L. Ed. 2d 757 (1973); Walter v. United States, 447 U.S. 649, 100 S. Ct. 2395, 65 L. Ed. 2d 410 (1983).

[54]  Maryland v. Macon, 472 U.S. 463, 105 S. Ct. 2778, 86 L. Ed. 2d 370 (1985).

[55]  Roaden v. Kentucky, *supra* note 53; Heller v. New York, 413 U.S. 483, 93 S. Ct. 2789, 37 L. Ed. 2d 745 (1973), *cert. denied sub. nom.*, Buckley v. New York, 418 U.S. 944, 94 S. Ct. 3231, 41 L. Ed. 2d 1175 (1974).

Figure 2.5
**Sample Affidavit for an Obscenity Search Warrant**

The affidavit below was upheld as legally sufficient in *New York v. P.J. Video, Inc.,* 475 U.S. 868, 878 106 S. Ct. 1610, 89 L. Ed. 2d 871 (1986).

"I, I.M. VIRTUOUS, being duly sworn, deposes and says:

I am presently a Confidential Criminal Investigator assigned to the Hope County District Attorney's Office and prior to this, was a detective with the State of Confusion Police Department for approximately 25 years.

On September 26th, 1998 I rented and viewed the videotape movie "CALIFORNIA VALLEY GIRLS" in a viewing booth at Sex Frolics, an adult entertainment establishment located at 6900 Smut Road. The viewing of "CALIFORNIA VALLEY GIRLS" began at 12:00 Noon and lasted until 1:33 P.M.

The content and character of the above mentioned video movie is as follows: Six white females, approximately 18 to 25 years of age, are unemployed and attempt to make a living by becoming prostitutes. The first scene is a bedroom scene where two females are involved in lovemaking, fondling, and cunnilingus. The second scene depicts a white male and a white female having intercourse in the back of a van. The third scene is a house scene where six girls, all white females, are introduced to the art of lovemaking. One male, approximately 35 years of age, is teaching the girls the art of fellatio with each one of them performing this act on him. The next scene is a bedroom scene in a home where a husband and wife, and the wife's friend, perform various sexual acts which include intercourse, fellatio, anal intercourse, and cunnilingus. The movie ends with some lesbianism where the wife performs cunnilingus on the friend while the latter performs fellatio on the husband and they engage in intercourse and anal intercourse.

    Third, the requirement that search warrants particularly describe the "things to be seized" is strictly applied to search warrants authorizing the seizure of literary materials. General language authorizing seizure of "all obscene publications" found at a particular location is unconstitutional because it delegates to the executing officer authority to make on-the-spot determinations whether particular works are obscene. This determination is one that must be made by a judge.[56]

    Finally, police officers may not seize all copies of items described in their search warrant. Their mission is to obtain evidence for use at trial; one or two copies are enough for this purpose. Police may not halt sales by seizing all copies of a work until after the work has been found obscene in an adversarial criminal proceeding.[57]

---

[56] Marcus v. Search Warrant, 367 U.S. 717, 81 S. Ct. 1708, 6 L. Ed. 2d 1127 (1961); A Quantity of Copies of Books v. Kansas, 378 U.S. 205, 84 S. Ct. 1723, 12 L. Ed. 2d 809 (1964).

[57] Marcus v. Search Warrant, *supra* note 56; Heller v. New York, *supra* note 55; Fort Wayne Books, Inc. v. Indiana, 489 U.S. 46, 109 S. Ct. 916, 103 L. Ed. 2d 34 (1989).

## § 2.7 —Fighting Words

In *Chaplinsky v. New Hampshire*,[58] a man was arrested for calling the city marshal "a God damned racketeer" and a "damned Fascist" in a face-to-face encounter. Prior to *Chaplinsky*, the Court had observed that a "resort to epithets or personal abuse is not in any proper sense communication of information safeguarded by the Constitution . . ."[59] In *Chaplinsky*, the Supreme Court officially excluded "fighting words" from the protection of the First Amendment.

The scope of this exclusion was refined in later cases. This exclusion is not concerned with provocative ideas. Ideas are not stripped of First Amendment protection because they move others to anger.[60] Marching in Nazi uniforms with swastikas, for example, though deeply offensive, is symbolic speech that is protected by the First Amendment because this conduct communicates a message about the marchers' beliefs.[61] Speech that communicates a message is protected by the First Amendment, even when the message is provocative.[62] "Fighting words" are used for a different purpose. Their purpose is solely to inflict injury.

There is no judicially established list of words that, when spoken, always constitute "fighting words." Whether language constitutes "fighting words" requires an examination both of the words and the context. A person may be arrested for using "fighting words" only if the person's language is:

1. Personally abusive or insulting.
2. Spoken in a face-to-face encounter under circumstances likely to provoke the other person into making an immediate violent response.[63]

Whether the second element is present calls for consideration of the factual context, including the time and place of the communication, the characteristics of the parties, their proximity, and other factors. Personally abusive remarks

---

[58]   315 U.S. 568, 62 S. Ct. 766, 86 L. Ed. 1031 (1942).

[59]   Cantwell v. Connecticut, 310 U.S. 296, 60 S. Ct. 900, 84 L. Ed. 1221 (1940) (dicta).

[60]   Edwards v. South Carolina, 372 U.S. 229, 83 S. Ct. 680, 9 L. Ed. 2d 697 (1963); Cox v. Louisiana, 379 U.S. 536, 85 S. Ct. 453, 13 L. Ed. 2d 471 (1965); Street v. New York, 394 U.S. 576, 89 S. Ct. 1354, 22 L. Ed. 2d 572 (1969); Bachellar v. Maryland, 397 U.S. 564, 90 S. Ct. 1312, 25 L. Ed. 2d 570 (1970); Forsyth County v. Nationalist Movement, 505 U.S. 123, 112 S. Ct. 2395, 120 L. Ed. 2d 101 (1992).

[61]   National Socialist Party of America v. Skokie, *supra* note 27. *See also* R.A.V. v. City of St. Paul, 505 U.S. 377, 395, 112 S. Ct. 2538, 120 L. Ed. 2d 305 (1992) (invalidating statute making it an offense to display symbols, such as burning crosses and swastikas, known to arouse anger in others on the basis of race, creed, religion, or gender); Brandenburg v. Ohio, *supra* note 28 (overturning conviction for burning a cross at a Ku Klux Klan rally); Sons of Confederate Veterans, Inc. ex rel. Griffin v. Commissioner of Virginia Dept. of Motor Vehicles, 288 F.3d 610 (4th Cir. 2002) (invalidating statute which prohibited use of Confederate flag on specialty license plates); Church of American Knights of Ku Klux Klan v. Kerik, 232 F. Supp. 2d 205 (S.D.N.Y. 2002) (invalidating statute prohibiting wearing of masks at public gathering).

[62]   Terminiello v. Chicago, 337 U.S. 1, 4, 69 S. Ct. 894, 895, 93 L. Ed. 1131 (1949).

[63]   Lewis v. City of New Orleans, 415 U.S. 130, 94 S. Ct. 970, 39 L. Ed. 2d 214 (1974); Gooding v. Wilson, 405 U.S. 518, 92 S. Ct. 1103, 31 L. Ed. 2d 408 (1972); City of Houston v. Hill, 482 U.S. 451, 107 S. Ct. 2502, 96 L. Ed. 2d 398, *cert. denied*, 483 U.S. 1001, 107 S. Ct. 3222, 97 L. Ed. 2d 729 (1987); **Sandul v. Larion, 119 F.3d 1250 (6th Cir. 1997)**. *See also* Allen T. McGlynn, *The Constitutional Ramifications of Calling a Police Officer an "Asshole,"* 16 S. Ill. U. L.J. 741 (1992).

made by a feeble old lady or a person passing by in a car, for example, would not constitute "fighting words," because the second element is lacking.

The "fighting words" exclusion has a narrow application when the target of the verbal abuse is a police officer because police officers are trained not to respond in physical ways.[64] Accordingly, making profane gestures[65] or calling a police officer an "ass"[66] is not enough to justify an arrest for using "fighting words." While the Supreme Court has stopped short of saying the "fighting words" exclusion can never apply when the object of verbal abuse is a police officer, the indignities must go far beyond what an ordinary person would be expected to endure.[67] In *Lewis v. City of New Orleans*,[68] the Supreme Court overturned the conviction of a woman who hurled a litany of four-letter words at a police officer when he asked her husband for his driver's license. The officer arrested the woman under an ordinance making it a crime to "curse or revile or to use . . . opprobrious language toward or with reference to any member of the city police while in the actual performance of his duty." The Supreme Court declared the ordinance unconstitutional because it made cursing at a police officer a crime without regard to whether the words were likely to provoke an immediate violent response. The Court commented that this likelihood is reduced when abusive language is addressed to a police officer because they are trained not to respond in physical ways. The Supreme Court repeated this observation in *City of Houston v. Hill*,[69] this time noting that "freedom of individuals verbally to oppose or challenge police actions without thereby risking arrest is one of the principal characteristics by which we distinguish a free nation from a police state." Consequently, police officers should think twice about arresting citizens who insult them unless their abusive language is accompanied by provocative gestures like making a fist or spitting.

## § 2.8  —Threats

Threats are another class of speech that receive no protection under the First Amendment.[70] However, before a person can be punished for making a threat, a genuine threat must be made. A threat, for purposes of the First Amendment, requires communication of a serious expression of intent to commit an act of unlawful violence.[71] In *Watts v. United States*,[72] a young man took the floor at an anti-war rally and said:

---

[64]   See authorities *supra* note 63.

[65]   *See, e.g.*, Brockway v. Shepherd, 942 F. Supp. 1012 (M.D. Pa. 1997).

[66]   *See, e.g.*, **Buffkins v. City of Omaha, 922 F.2d 465 (8th Cir. 1990)**; Sweatt v. Bailey, 876 F. Supp. 1371 (M.D. Ala. 1995).

[67]   In the Matter of M.A.H. and J.L.W., 572 N.W.2d 752 (Minn. App. 1997).

[68]   *Supra* note 63.

[69]   *Supra* note 63.

[70]   Watts v. United States, 394 U.S. 705, 89 S. Ct. 1399, 22 L. Ed. 2d 664 (1969); Virginia v. Black, *supra* note 28.

[71]   **Virginia v. Black**, *supra* note 28.

[72]   *Supra* note 70.

They always holler at us to get an education. And now I have already received my draft classification as 1-A and I have got to report for my physical this Monday morning. I am not going. If they ever make me carry a rifle, the first man to get in my sights is L.B.J. They are not going to make me kill my black brothers.

The "L.B.J." the young man was referring to was Lyndon Baines Johnson, then President of the United States. Watts was indicted and convicted under a federal statute making it a crime to "knowingly and willfully . . . [make] any threat to take the life of or to inflict bodily harm upon the President . . ." The Supreme Court overturned Watts' conviction on the grounds that his statement, interpreted in context, amounted to nothing more than "a kind of very crude offensive method of stating political opposition to the President."

As *Watts v. United States* indicates, whether language constitutes a threat or a statement of political beliefs often depends on the context. The act of burning a cross, for example, can have multiple meanings.[73] Cross-burning can be used to deliver a threat, such as when a cross is burned on someone's lawn, and when used in this manner is not protected by the First Amendment.[74] On the other hand, cross-burning can also be performed as a symbolic statement of shared white supremacist ideological beliefs, such as when the cross-burning occurs as part of a ritual ceremony at a Ku Klux Klan rally. The second meaning, though deeply offensive, is nevertheless protected by the First Amendment.[75] In *Virginia v. Black*,[76] the Supreme Court struck down a statute that made cross-burning prima facie evidence of an intent to intimidate. This statute was unconstitutional because it ignored the factual context necessary to distinguish between the different types of cross-burnings.

# § 2.9 —Incitement to Riot

Inflammatory speech at the right time and place can incite action. Establishing the point at which speech advocating violence or other unlawful acts loses First Amendment protection was one of the Supreme Court's major concerns during the first half of the twentieth century. In a case decided in 1919, the Supreme Court adopted the "clear and present danger" test as the boundary indicator. *Schenck v. United States*,[77] the case that adopted this test, arose from the conviction of a Socialist Party leader for obstructing World War I

---

[73] **Virginia v. Black**, *supra* note 28. *See also* generally, Jennifer E. Rothman, *Freedom of Speech and True Threats*, 25 HARV. J. L. & PUB. POL'Y 283 (2001); John T. Nockleby, Note, *Hate Speech in Context: the Case of Verbal Threats*, 42 BUFF. 653 (1994).

[74] **Virginia v. Black**, *supra* note 28 (cross-burning with intent to intimidate is not protected by the First Amendment) ; United States v. J.H.H., 22 F.3d 821 (8th Cir. 1994) (upholding conviction for cross-burning with intent to intimidate where three boys ignited a cross in the middle of the night in an African-American family's yard).

[75] **Virginia v. Black**, *supra* note 28.

[76] *Id.*

[77] 249 U.S. 47, 39 S. Ct. 247, 63 L. Ed. 470 (1919).

military recruiting efforts by mailing circulars urging young men who had been called up for service to resist the draft. The Supreme Court affirmed his conviction, writing:

> We admit that in many places and in ordinary times the defendants, in saying all that was said in the circular, would have been within their constitutional rights. But the character of every act depends upon the circumstances in which it is done. . . . The question in every case is whether the words used are used in such circumstances and are of such a nature to create a clear and present danger that they will bring about the substantive evils that Congress has a right to prevent.[78]

The clear and present danger test proved too malleable. In the years that followed, the Supreme Court held that advocating the doctrine of the necessity of the violent overthrow of the government was so inherently dangerous to society that advocacy of this doctrine in any form could be prohibited.[79] Justices Holmes and Brandeis opposed this application, taking the position that advocacy of even the most alarming ideas should be protected by the First Amendment, unless the speech posed a clear and present danger of immediate unlawful action. In a famous dissenting opinion, they argued:

> Fear of serious injury cannot alone justify suppression of free speech and assembly. Men feared witches and burnt women. It is the function of speech to free men from the bondage of irrational fears. To justify suppression of free speech there must be reasonable ground to fear that serious evil will result if free speech is practiced. There must be reasonable ground to believe that the danger apprehended is imminent. There must be reasonable ground to believe that the evil to be prevented is a serious one. . . . [E]ven advocacy of violation [of the law], however reprehensible morally, is not a justification for denying free speech where . . . there is nothing to indicate that the advocacy would be immediately acted on . . .

> Those who won American independence by revolution were not cowards. They did not fear political change. They did not exalt order at the cost of liberty. To courageous, self-reliant men, with confidence in the power of free and fearless reasoning applied through the processes of popular government, no danger flowing from speech could be deemed clear and present, unless the incidence of the evil apprehended is so imminent that it may befall before there is an opportunity for full discussion. If there is time to expose through discussion the falsehoods and fallacies, to avert the evil by the processes of education, the remedy to be applied is more speech, not enforced silence. Only an emergency can justify repression.[80]

---

[78] *Id.* at 52, 39 S. Ct. at 249.

[79] Abrams v. United States, 250 U.S. 616, 40 S. Ct. 17, 63 L. Ed. 1173 (1919); Gitlow v. New York, 268 U.S. 652, 45 S. Ct. 625, 69 L. Ed. 1138 (1925).

[80] Whitney v. California, 274 U.S. 357, 376-377, 47 S. Ct. 641, 649-649, 71 L. Ed. 1095 (1927), overruled, **Brandenburg v. Ohio, 395 U.S. 444, 89 S. Ct. 1827, 23 L. Ed. 2d 430 (1969)**.

## A. Brandenburg *Test*

The position taken by Justices Holmes and Brandeis was accepted by the Supreme Court 40 years later in *Brandenburg v. Ohio*[81] and has been the law ever since. Brandenburg, a Ku Klux Klan leader, was convicted under an Ohio statute that made it a crime to advocate "the duty, necessity, or propriety of crime, sabotage, violence, or unlawful methods of terrorism as a means of accomplishing . . . political reform . . ." His conviction stemmed from a speech he delivered at a Ku Klux Klan rally on a farm outside Cincinnati, Ohio. A local television reporter, who had been invited to witness the rally, filmed the event and later broadcast portions of the footage, in which Brandenburg asserted that "if our President, our Congress, our Supreme Court, continues to suppress the white, Caucasian race, it's possible that there might have to be some revengeance [sic] taken." Brandenburg further stated that "the nigger should be returned to Africa, the Jew returned to Israel." The Supreme Court overturned Brandenburg's conviction, holding that advocacy of violence or other unlawful action can be made a crime only when the advocacy is "both directed toward inciting or producing imminent lawless action, and likely to incite or produce such action."

The Supreme Court applied the *Brandenburg* test in *Hess v. Indiana*,[82] involving the disorderly conduct conviction of an anti-war demonstrator for shouting "We'll take the f——ing street later!" while the police were attempting to move a crowd of demonstrators off the street so that vehicles could pass. The Supreme Court set the conviction aside because the unlawful action urged ("We'll take the f——ing street later) was to occur at some indefinite time in the future. Speech advocating unlawful action in the future is fully protected by the First Amendment.

Figure 2.6
**Incitement to Riot**

> Speech advocating violence loses First Amendment protection only when it is:
>
> 1.   directed toward inciting imminent lawless action, and
> 2.   an outbreak seems imminent.

## B. Premature Fears

Speech may not be suppressed out of premature fears of what might occur if the speech is allowed.[83] On April 30, 1992, the day after verdicts of acquittal were announced in a highly publicized trial of several Los Angeles police officers accused of the racially motivated beating of a black motorist, a num-

---

[81]   *Supra* note 80.
[82]   414 U.S. 105, 94 S. Ct. 326, 38 L. Ed. 2d 303 (1973).
[83]   Collins v. Jordan, 110 F.3d 1363 (9th Cir. 1996).

ber of demonstrations occurred in various parts of San Francisco. Most were peaceful, but a few were not. That evening, the mayor of San Francisco declared a local emergency and imposed a 9:00 P.M. curfew. The next day, he and the chief of police decided to ban all demonstrations, peaceful or otherwise, effective May 1, 1992, and to arrest all demonstrators who refused to obey dispersal orders. Later that day, local authorities became aware that a demonstration was planned for the BART (Bay Area Rapid Transit) Plaza area. Police went to the scene, issued dispersal orders, and began arresting people. A federal court ruled that imposing a ban on demonstrating before the demonstrators have done anything illegal is unconstitutional. The court stated:

> The law is clear that First Amendment activity may not be banned simply because prior similar activity led to or involved instances of violence. There are sound reasons for this rule. Demonstrations can be expected when the government acts in highly controversial ways, or other events occur that excite or arouse the passions of the citizenry. The more controversial the occurrence, the more likely people are to demonstrate. Some of these demonstrations may become violent. The courts have held that the proper response to potential and actual violence is for the government to ensure an adequate police presence, and to arrest those who actually engage in such conduct, rather than to suppress legitimate First Amendment conduct as a prophylactic measure.

The court stressed the importance of allowing citizens to express their frustrations with recent events by engaging in spontaneous protest. Banning demonstrations because others have or might abuse the privilege deprives innocent individuals of their First Amendment rights. The court, nevertheless, left open the question of whether a city, confronted with widespread violence beyond the capabilities of the police, might in rare instances impose a time-limited ban on all demonstrations. The court found it unnecessary to address this question because it concluded that this point had not been reached in San Francisco at the time the mayor imposed the ban in controversy.

The Ohio Supreme Court expressed a similar view in setting aside an injunction that prohibited two groups with opposing viewpoints from simultaneously picketing outside the home of a Nazi war criminal whose conviction had been overturned by the Israeli Supreme Court.[84] The Coalition for Jewish Concerns was picketing to show their opposition, while the Ku Klux Klan was picketing to show their support. Picketing had been peaceful, but local authorities were concerned. The Ohio Supreme Court overturned the ban on simultaneous picketing, holding that prohibiting speech is not a constitutionally acceptable means of averting a feared disturbance.

---

[84]    City of Seven Hills v. Aryan Nations, 76 Ohio St. 3d 304, 667 N.E.2d 942 (1996).

## C. Hostile Reception

Police intervention is justified when an outbreak appears imminent, but the response permitted depends on whether the speaker[85] or the audience[86] is responsible. When the threat of an outbreak stems from a hostile reaction to an unpopular speaker's views, peacekeeping efforts must be directed at the audience, not the speaker.[87] In *Cox v. Louisiana*,[88] 2,000 African American university students assembled a few blocks from the courthouse in Baton Rouge to protest segregation. They walked in an orderly fashion, obeying traffic laws, until they reached the courthouse, where they pledged allegiance to the flag, prayed briefly, sang two "freedom songs," and listened to a speech delivered by Cox, their leader. A crowd of 100 to 300 spectators gathered on the sidewalk to watch. There was some angry muttering and jeering, but the protesters did not respond and the police presence at the scene was adequate to maintain order. At the end of his speech, Cox urged the demonstrators to go uptown and "sit in" at various segregated lunch counters. The sheriff, worried about the crowd's reaction, took a bullhorn and ordered the demonstrators to go home. When the order was ignored, the police arrested Cox for causing a breach of the peace. The Supreme Court reversed Cox's conviction, holding that the First Amendment does not allow the police to arrest a speaker because a hostile audience threatens to react with violence.[89] Police, instead, have a constitutional duty to maintain order so that the speech can continue.[90] Accordingly, peacekeeping efforts must be directed at the hecklers.

However, miscalculations occasionally occur about the strength of the peacekeeping force needed to maintain order. Halting speech should never be considered, except as a last resort. Police would be justified in asking demonstrators to suspend their activity in the face of an uncontrollable crowd reaction. If their request is refused, they may take the demonstrators into custody for their own protection, but may not arrest them for the disorderly conduct of spectators who are hostile to them.[91]

---

[85] Feiner v. New York, 340 U.S. 315, 71 S. Ct. 303, 95 L. Ed. 295 (1951).
[86] Cox v. Louisiana, 379 U.S. 536, 85 S. Ct. 453, 13 L. Ed. 2d 471 (1965).
[87] Forsyth County v. Nationalist Movement, 505 U.S. 123, 112 S. Ct. 2395, 120 L. Ed. 2d 101 (1992); Gregory v. City of Chicago, 394 U.S. 111, 89 S. Ct. 946, 22 L. Ed. 2d 134 (1969); Cox v. Louisiana, *supra* note 86.
[88] *Supra* note 86.
[89] See cases *supra* note 87.
[90] Glasson v. City of Louisville, 518 F.2d 899, 906 (6th Cir. 1975).
[91] Gregory v. City of Chicago, *supra* note 87; Wright v. Georgia, 373 U.S. 284, 293, 83 S. Ct. 1240, 1246, 10 L. Ed. 2d 349 (1963) ("the possibility of disorder by others cannot justify exclusion of persons from a place if they otherwise have a constitutional right . . . to be present).

## § 2.10   —Hate Speech

**Hate speech** refers to speech that expresses loathing for others because of their race, creed, color, religion, sexual orientation, or other characteristic that makes them vulnerable.[92] Freedom to engage in hate speech is one of the most troubling issues in First Amendment jurisprudence.[93] While some argue that society would be better served by excluding hate speech from the scope of constitutionally protected expression, this is not the way the First Amendment is interpreted. The First Amendment protects the right to preach racism, sexism, anti-Semitism, homophobia, xenophobia, and other bigotries. In *R.A.V. v. City of St. Paul*,[94] the Supreme Court overturned a hate speech ordinance that made it a crime to display symbols that were likely to arouse anger, resentment, or alarm based on race, color, ethnicity, or religion. The Court has specifically upheld the right of National Socialist Party members to march through Jewish neighborhoods in Nazi uniforms;[95] the right of private organizers of a St. Patrick's Day parade to exclude gays and lesbians;[96] and the right of Ku Klux Klan members to deliver hate speeches and burn crosses at Klan rallies.[97]

Bigotry, nevertheless, is protected only as long as it remains an expressed belief. People have the right to march, carry banners, and deliver speeches about racial superiority and inferiority as long as they like, because they are expressing their views. However, the First Amendment confers absolutely no protection on hate-motivated conduct.[98] Once a person goes beyond expressing his or her beliefs and acts on them, the person may be punished.[99] States, for example, can make it a crime to assault another person because of the person's race, religion, or sexual orientation. States are also free to take bigoted motives into account by providing enhanced punishment for defendants who select their victims because of their race, religion, sexual orientation, or other distinguishing characteristics.[100] An offender whose sentence is increased under a statute providing enhanced punishment for hate crimes is not punished for his or her *beliefs*; he or she is punished for his or her *conduct*. Moreover, hate speech itself is punishable when it is accompanied by threatening words

---

[92]   Kathleen E. Mahoney, *Hate Speech: Affirmation or Contradiction of Freedom of Expression*, 1996 U. ILL. L. REV. 789 (1996).

[93]   Richard A. Glenn & Otis H. Stephens, *Campus Hate Speech and Equal Protection: Competing Constitutional Values*, 6 WIDENER J. PUB. L. 349, 352 (1997).

[94]   *Supra* note 61.

[95]   National Socialist Party of America v. Skokie, *supra* note 27.

[96]   Hurley v. Irish-American Gay, Lesbian and Bisexual Group of Boston, *supra* note 12.

[97]   **Virginia v. Black**, *supra* note 28.

[98]   United States v. McDermott, 971 F. Supp. 939 (E.D. Pa. 1997) (upholding a conviction for burning a cross with the intent to threaten African Americans who witnessed it).

[99]   *See* authorities *supra* note 98 and *infra* note 100.

[100]  Wisconsin v. Mitchell, 508 U.S. 476, 113 S. Ct. 2194, 124 L. Ed. 2d 436 (1993) (upholding statute providing enhanced sentence for defendants who intentionally selected their victim based on victim's race); People v. Nitz, 285 Ill. App. 3d 364, 674 N.E.2d 802 (1996) (upholding conviction of hate crime offense, based on defendant's racially motivated harassment of his neighbor).

or gestures, such as burning a cross in someone's yard with the intent to intimidate them,[101] or when it is used in circumstances that constitute fighting words,[102] because neither of these categories of speech is protected by the First Amendment.

## § 2.11  —Crude and Vulgar Speech

Under traditional First Amendment analysis, speech was either fully protected by the First Amendment or had no protection at all. There was nothing in-between. This scheme left no place for crude, profane, or **vulgar speech**. Vulgar speech contributes so little to the exchange of ideas that full protection seemed wrong. At the same time, it is not so harmful that complete withdrawal of First Amendment protection seemed proper, either. As a result, the Supreme Court had difficulty locating a place within the First Amendment for vulgar speech. The status has unfolded gradually through a series of cases.

*Cohen v. California*[103] was the first case in the series. Cohen was arrested for breach of the peace when he appeared in a courtroom wearing a jacket with the message "F—— the Draft!" displayed across the front. The Supreme Court ruled that Cohen's language, while vulgar, was protected by the First Amendment because in a society as diverse as ours, the government has "no right to cleanse public debate to the point where it is grammatically palatable to the most squeamish among us." Ever since *Cohen*, it has been illegal for police to arrest citizens for using vulgar language in public.[104]

In *Bethel School District v. Fraser*,[105] decided 15 years later, the Supreme Court refused to extend the same protection to students in public schools. The Court distinguished *Cohen* on the grounds that schools have a mission to inculcate values and teach the boundaries of socially appropriate behavior. *Cohen* was again distinguished in *FCC v. Pacifica Foundation*,[106] where the Court upheld the government's authority to prohibit radio stations from airing programs with vulgar language during hours when children were likely to be listening.

---

[101] **Virginia v. Black**, *supra* note 28 (holding that states may ban cross burning carried out with intent to intimidate, but finding statute unconstitutional because it made cross burning prima facie evidence of this intent).

[102] *See, e.g.*, In re John, 201 Ariz. 424, 36 P.3d 772 (2001) (Juvenile's racially hostile outburst—"fuck you, you goddamn nigger"—constituted fighting words that were not constitutionally protected speech. Court observed that "few words convey such an inflammatory message of racial hatred and bigotry as the term 'nigger'"); In re Spivey, 345 N.C. 404, 480 S.E.2d 693, 699 (1997) (affirming removal of a district attorney from office for using the derogatory and abusive racial epithet nigger; observing that "[n]o fact is more generally known than that a white man who calls a black man a nigger within his hearing will hurt and anger the black man and often provoke him to confront the white man and retaliate").

[103] 403 U.S. 15, 91 S. Ct. 1780, 29 L. Ed. 2d 284 (1971).

[104] Brooks v. N.C. Department of Corrections, 984 F. Supp. 940 (E.D.N.C. 1997); United States v. McDermott, *supra* note 98.

[105] 478 U.S. 675, 106 S. Ct. 3159, 92 L. Ed. 2d 549 (1986). *See also* Hazelwood School District v. Kuhlmeier, 484 U.S. 260, 108 S. Ct. 562, 98 L. Ed. 2d 592 (1988).

[106] 438 U.S. 726, 98 S. Ct. 3026, 57 L. Ed. 2d 1073 (1978).

Finally, in *Young v. American Mini Theaters, Inc.*,[107] the Supreme Court made a clean break with the traditional notion that speech must be either fully protected or unprotected. Upholding the constitutionality of a zoning ordinance that restricted the location of adult movie theaters, the Court wrote:

> . . . [E]ven though we recognize that the First Amendment will not tolerate the total suppression of erotic materials that have some arguably artistic value, it is manifest that society's interest in protecting this type of expression is of . . . different, and lesser, magnitude than the interest in untrammeled political debate. . . . Whether political oratory or philosophical discussion moves us to applaud or to despise what is said, every schoolchild can understand why our duty to defend the right to speak remains the same. But few of us would march our sons and daughters off to war to preserve the citizen's right to see "Specified Sexual Activities" exhibited in the theaters of our choice. Even though the First Amendment protects communication in this area from total suppression, we hold that the State may legitimately use the content of these materials as the basis for placing them in a different classification from other motion pictures.

As a result of *Young* and subsequent cases, there are now three categories of speech: (1) fully protected, (2) unprotected, and (3) speech that is protected in some contexts, but not in others. Vulgar speech occupies the middle category.

## § 2.12 —Commercial Speech

**Commercial speech** refers to speech calculated to stir up interest in a commercial transaction. The Supreme Court has explained that there are "commonsense differences between speech that does 'no more than propose a commercial transaction'" and speech that expresses a viewpoint and invites dialogue, and these differences justify "a different degree of protection."[108] Accordingly, commercial speech has also been placed in the middle category. Reduced protection for commercial speech allows the government to do such things as protect consumers from misleading and deceptive advertising;[109] require sellers to warn consumers of health hazards from their product;[110] and prevent overly aggressive advertising.[111] Content controls like these would be unconstitutional if the government tried to impose them on fully protected speech.

---

[107] 427 U.S. 50, 96 S. Ct. 2440, 49 L. Ed. 2d 310 (1976).

[108] Virginia State Board of Pharmacy v. Virginia Citizens Consumer Council Inc., 425 U.S. 748, 771 n. 24, 196 S. Ct. 1817, 1830 n. 24, 48 L. Ed. 2d 346 (1976); Central Hudson Gas & Elec. Corp. v. Public Serv. Comm'n of N.Y., 447 U. S. 557, 566, 100 S. Ct. 2343, 65 L. Ed. 2d 341 (1980) (commercial speech may be regulated if asserted governmental interest is substantial; regulation directly advances that interest; and regulation is not more extensive than is necessary to serve that interest).

[109] Liquormat, Inc. v. Rhode Island, 517 U.S. 484, 116 S. Ct. 1495, 134 L. Ed. 2d 711 (1996); Florida Bar v. Went For It, Inc., 515 U.S. 618, 115 S. Ct. 2371, 132 L. Ed. 2d 541 (1995).

[110] Virginia State Board of Pharmacy v. Virginia Citizens Consumer Council, Inc., *supra* note 108.

[111] Florida Bar v. Went For It, Inc., *supra* note 109.

## § 2.13  Restraints on Speech Based on Considerations Other Than the Message

We are now ready to consider the government's power to regulate a speaker's conduct. Some speech dissemination techniques involve a large component of public conduct. Handbilling, parading, picketing, and marching are examples. Freedom of speech would have little value for many in our society if it did not carry at least some right to use public spaces to engage in activities like these. For people championing poorly funded causes, streets, parks, and sidewalks are often the only locations available for reaching a sizable audience. There are, nevertheless, competing nonspeech claims on use of these facilities.

What would a day in the life of the community be like if First Amendment activities like handbilling, marching, parading, and picketing were immune from regulation? The following is a grisly sketch. After being kept awake all night the clamor of sound trucks and the blasts of bullhorns, Jane leaves for work. As she walks down the street, she is accosted by people who want financial contributions, signatures on petitions, and ideological support. Jane finally makes it to her car and, after removing the handbills, begins inching her way to work. Traffic is slow because of the need to stop at intersections to wait for parades and marches to pass. Traffic eventually clears. Jane picks up speed and crashes into an oncoming vehicle that is blocked from view by a cluster of billboards. Noise, congestion, delays, safety hazards, and intrusions on privacy would result if a speaker's conduct shared the same protection as the message.

Fortunately, the First Amendment does not require this.[112] A different approach is used to evaluate the constitutionality of placing restrictions on a speaker's conduct. How does a court decide whether local governments can prohibit individuals from using loudspeakers after dark?[113] Soliciting contributions on public streets?[114] Holding parades during rush hour? Or erecting giant billboards?[115] The answer is through an approach called *forum analysis*.

---

[112] See § 2.4 *supra*.

[113] Kovacs v. Cooper, 336 U.S. 77, 69 S. Ct. 448, 93 L. Ed. 513 (1949) (upholding ordinance prohibiting use of sound trucks emitting "loud and raucous" noise in residential neighborhoods).

[114] **International Soc. for Krishna Consciousness, Inc. v. Lee, 505 U.S. 672, 112 S. Ct. 2701, 120 L. Ed. 2d 541 (1992)** (upholding ban on solicitation of contributions in airport terminals). See § 2.15 *infra*.

[115] Metromedia, Inc. v. San Diego, 453 U.S. 490, 101 S. Ct. 2882, 69 L. Ed. 2d 800 (1981) (upholding ban on offsite billboard advertising).

Figure 2.7
**Government's Power to Limit First Amendment Activity on Government Property**

| Type of property | Criteria for inclusion | Illustrations | Validity of restrictions on speech |
|---|---|---|---|
| Nonpublic forums | Government's business property | Office buildings, military bases, police stations, jails, municipal airports, etc. | Restrictions are valid if they are: (1) neutral as to viewpoint and (2) reasonable in light of the purpose the particular facility serves. |
| Public forums | | | |
| Traditional | Long-standing history and tradition of First Amendment use by members of the public | Streets, sidewalks, parks | (1) A compelling government interest is necessary to justify forbidding speech in a public forum; (2) A substantial government interest is necessary to justify restricting the time, place, or manner of speech use. |
| By designation | Earmarked by government for First Amendment uses | Municipal auditoriums, meeting halls | |

# § 2.14   Free Speech Access to Government Property: Public Forums and Nonpublic Forums

Our Constitution does not guarantee unrestricted access to government property for speech-related purposes simply because the government owns it.[116] The government's ability to restrict speech depends on the nature of the location and the disruption that the activity in question might cause. Consider the disruption that would result if citizens had a right to pass out literature, solicit contributions, and hold rallies in places like firehouses, police stations, and jails.[117]

The Supreme Court has adopted a "forum-based" approach to assessing restrictions on the speech use of government property. The Court first classifies the location as being either a **public forum** or a **nonpublic forum**, and then tests the restriction, using the legal standards that have been established for forums of that type.

## A. Criteria Used to Determine Forum Status

Public forums receive maximum protection under the First Amendment. Speech may be restricted only for weighty reasons. The status of being a public forum can be acquired either by tradition or designation. Public streets, sidewalks, and parks—locations that have a long history of use by members of the public to hold assemblies, distribute literature, and discuss public affairs—are called **traditional public forums**.[118] The status of a public forum can also be acquired through the government's deliberate decision to set a particular facility aside for speech uses by members of the public. Facilities like municipal auditoriums and public meeting halls that acquire their public forum status this way are called **public forums by designation**.[119] All other

---

[116] Cornelius v. NAACP Legal Defense & Ed. Fund, Inc., 473 U.S. 788, 800, 105 S. Ct. 3439, 3448, 87 L. Ed. 2d 567 (1985) (Observing that "[n]othing in the Constitution requires the Government freely to grant access to all who wish to exercise their right to free speech on every type of Government property without regard to the nature of the property or to the disruption that might be caused by the speaker's activities." ).

[117] United States v. Kokinda, 497 U.S. 720, 110 S. Ct. 3115, 111 L. Ed. 2d 571 (1990) (handbilling may be prohibited on postal sidewalk constructed for traffic between postal parking lot and post office building); Jones v. Watson, 106 F.3d 774 (7th Cir. 1997) (public libraries are not appropriate places for giving speeches or engaging in any other conduct that would disrupt the quiet and peaceful library environment); Greer v. Spock, 424 U.S. 828, 96 S. Ct. 1211, 47 L. Ed. 2d 505 (1976) (military bases may be declared off-limits to First Amendment uses by members of the public).

[118] Hague v. CIO, 307 U.S. 496, 515, 59 S. Ct. 954, 964, 83 L. Ed. 1423 (1939); **United States v. Grace, 461 U. S. 171, 103 S. Ct. 1702, 75 L. Ed. 2d 736 (1983)**.

[119] Southeastern Promotions, Limited v. Conrad, 420 U.S. 546, 95 S. Ct. 1239, 43 L. Ed. 2d 448 (1975) (municipal theater); Widmar v. Vincent, 454 U.S. 263, 102 S. Ct. 269, 70 L. Ed. 2d 440 (1981) (public university meeting place).

property—schools, office buildings, military installations, police stations, post offices, municipal airports, etc.—are nonpublic forums.[120] This is the property the government uses to conduct its official business.

## B. *Control Over Speech in Nonpublic Forums*

The government enjoys maximum control over speech in nonpublic forums because its role resembles that of a private owner.[121] Restrictions on speech are valid if they are: (1) reasonable and (2) neutral as to viewpoint.[122]

A restriction's reasonableness is evaluated in light of the forum's physical characteristics and use. The government may restrict speech activity that is incompatible with the orderly conduct of its business. A regulation prohibiting members of the public from distributing handbills in the lobbies of government buildings, for example, would be reasonable, but one prohibiting the wearing of campaign buttons would not because the latter activity does not interfere with the conduct of the government's business.[123]

Restrictions on speech in nonpublic forums must also be neutral as to viewpoint.[124] The government may not practice favoritism in making resource allocation decisions. School boards, for example, though not required to make school facilities available to *any* group for after-hours use, may not grant access only to groups whose viewpoint they favor.[125] Discriminating against would-be speakers based on viewpoint constitutes censorship, a practice forbidden by the First Amendment.

## C. *Control Over Speech in Public Forums*

The government's power to restrict speech in public forums is more limited. The Supreme Court has stressed the importance of public forums to citizens championing poorly funded causes. For those who cannot afford

---

[120]  United States v. Kokinda, *supra* note 117 (sidewalks entirely on Postal Service's property in front of post office); Jones v. North Carolina Prisoners' Labor Union, 433 U.S. 119, 97 S. Ct. 2532, 53 L. Ed. 2d 629 (1977) (prison); Lehman v. City of Shaker Heights, 418 U.S. 298, 94 S. Ct. 2714, 41 L. Ed. 2d 770 (1974) (advertising space on vehicles of a city transit system); Greer v. Spock, *supra* note 117 (1976) (military base).

[121]  Free speech access to private property is discussed in § 2.16 *infra*.

[122]  **International Soc. for Krishna Consciousness, Inc. v. Lee**, *supra* note 114.

[123]  United States v. Kokinda, *supra* note 117 (upholding ban on leafleting in pedestrian walkway connecting post office building with its parking lot); **International Soc. for Krishna Consciousness, Inc. v. Lee**, *supra* note 114 (upholding ban on soliciting funds inside municipal airport terminal); Members of City Council of Los Angeles v. Taxpayers for Vincent, 466 U.S. 789, 810-811, 104 S. Ct. 2118, 2131-2132, 80 L. Ed. 2d 772 (1984) (upholding ban on attaching signs and posters to municipal lampposts and fire hydrants); Lehman v. City of Shaker Heights, *supra* note 120 (upholding municipal transit authority policy against selling advertising space on buses to persons wanting to use the space for political advertisements).

[124]  Lamb's Chapel v. Center Maracas Union Free School District, 508 U.S. 384, 113 S. Ct. 2141, 124 L. Ed. 2d 352 (1993) (after-hours access to public school property may not be withheld based on viewpoint); Rosenberger v. Rector and Visitors of Univ. of Va., 515 U.S. 819, 115 S. Ct. 2510, 132 L. Ed. 2d 700 (1995) (public university's student activities funds may not be disbursed based on viewpoint considerations).

[125]  See authorities *supra* note 124.

newspaper advertisements, television time, or billboards, streets, sidewalks, and parks offer the only opportunity for making contact with a large audience. However, these facilities also serve important nonspeech uses. Local governments are unavoidably forced to mediate between conflicting demands on the use of outdoor public spaces.

When a restriction on speech access to a public forum is challenged, the court will balance the restriction's impact on speech against the strength of the government's regulatory interest.[126] The government bears a heavy burden to justify restrictions that prevent would-be speakers from reaching their intended audience. Restrictions that foreclose meaningful access to a public forum are sustainable only when they advance a *compelling government interest*.[127] Restrictions that have only a minor impact on speech, on the other hand, will be sustained when they further a *substantial government interest*.[128] Because a substantial interest is easier to establish than a compelling one, restrictions that have only a minor impact on speech stand a greater chance of being upheld.

Suppose a municipality enacts two ordinances—one that makes it illegal to distribute handbills on any public street or sidewalk and another that makes it illegal to hold noisy demonstrations in front of schools during class hours. While both ordinances restrict speech in a public forum, a city-wide ban on handbilling forecloses access to an entire medium of expression that is vital to groups with limited funds and for which no alternative exists that can reach as many people as cheaply. Regulations that deny meaningful access to a public forum are sustainable only when they advance a compelling interest. Prohibiting handbilling will reduce litter, but reducing litter is scarcely a compelling reason to abolish speech. Consequently, the first ordinance is unconstitutional.[129]

The second ordinance illustrates what courts call a "time, place, or manner" restriction. Time, place, or manner restrictions limit the time, place, or manner in which public forums may be used for speech, but leave ample alternatives available for reaching the intended audience. The second ordinance will not prevent anyone's voice from being heard, because a group desiring to

---

[126] *See, e.g.*, Ward v. Rock Against Racism, 491 U.S. 781, 791, 109 S. Ct. 2746, 2753-2754, 105 L. Ed. 2d 661 (1989); City of Ladue v. Gilleo, 512 U.S. 43, 114 S. Ct. 2038, 2045-2047, 129 L. Ed. 2d 36 (1994).

[127] *See, e.g.*, City of Ladue v. Gilleo, *supra* note 126 (city ordinance banning display of yard signs on residential property violated First Amendment because it closed off a "unique and important" mode of expression for which there is "no practical substitute").

[128] *See, e.g.*, Ward v. Rock Against Racism, *supra* note 126 (municipal noise regulation requiring performers to use sound system and sound technician provided by city to ensure that music performances did not disturb surrounding residents, did not violate free speech rights of performance).

[129] Schneider v. State, 308 U.S. 147, 60 S. Ct. 146, 84 L. Ed. 155 (1939) (invalidating ordinance banning handbilling on city streets; commenting that cities can save street-cleaning costs without banning handbilling by enforcing anti-litter laws against persons who drop handbills on street); McIntyre v. Ohio Elections Comm'n, 514 U.S. 334, 115 S. Ct. 1511, 131 L. Ed. 2d 426 (1995) (striking down law banning distribution of anonymous campaign literature); Watchtower Bible & Tract Society of N.Y., Inc. v. Village of Stratton, 536 U.S. 150, 122 S. Ct. 2080, 153 L. Ed. 2d 205 (2002) (invalidating ordinance making it a misdemeanor to engage in door-to-door canvassing for any cause without first registering with the mayor and receiving a permit).

hold a noisy demonstration in front of a school can wait until classes are over, use a quieter medium like handbilling, or select a different location. Because time, place, and manner restrictions do not foreclose speech, the government's burden of justification is lower. A *substantial government interest* will suffice to sustain them. Maintaining an environment conducive to learning provides ample justification for imposing a time-limited restriction on holding noisy demonstrations in front of schools.[130]

# § 2.15 —Protecting the Community from Nuisances Linked to Speech

Now that we have explored the approach courts use to evaluate restrictions on speech access to government property, we are ready to discuss the outcomes they have reached.

## A. Anti-Noise Ordinances

Free speech can be raucous and rowdy. The Supreme Court has upheld the constitutionality of noise control measures regulating bullhorns, sound amplification equipment, loud music, and other noises that are likely to disturb people in the area.[131]

---

[130]  Grayned v. City of Rockford, 408 U.S. 104, 116, 92 S. Ct. 2294, 2303, 33 L. Ed. 2d 222 (1972) (upholding ban on picketing in front of schools during class hours). *See also* City of Los Angeles v. Alameda Books, Inc., 535 U.S. 425, 122 S. Ct. 1728, 152 L. Ed. 2d 670 (2002) (ordinance barring more than one adult entertainment business in same building analyzed as time, place, and manner regulation of speech because it did not ban adult entertainment establishments altogether; upheld based on substantial government interest in reducing crime).

[131]  *See, e.g.*, Madsen v. Women's Health Center, Inc., 512 U.S. 753, 114 S. Ct. 2516, 129 L. Ed. 2d 593 (1994) (upholding a court injunction limiting use of sound amplification equipment in front of abortion clinic); Grayned v. City of Rockford, *supra* note 130 (upholding ordinance prohibiting picketing in front of schools during class hours); Ward v. Rock Against Racism, *supra* note 126 (upholding ordinance regulating sound equipment that could be used in outdoor municipal bandstand); Kovacs v. Cooper, *supra* note 113 (upholding ordinance prohibiting use of sound trucks emitting "loud and raucous" noise in residential neighborhoods); Housing Works, Inc. v. Kerik, 283 F.3d 471 (2d Cir. 2002) (upholding ordinance banning the use of amplified sound on the steps, sidewalks, and plaza area directly in front of New York City Hall); Sharkey's, Inc. v. City of Waukesha, 265 F. Supp. 2d 984 (E.D. Wis. 2003) (upholding noise ordinances that prohibited bars from having "unreasonably" loud noises tending to cause a disturbance in the area, or noises "tending to unreasonably disturb" persons in the area); Holland v. City of Tacoma, 954 P.2d 290 (Wash. App. 1998) (upholding ordinance that prohibited playing automobile sound equipment at volume that could be heard more than 50 feet from car).

## B. Ordinances Protecting Residential Privacy and Tranquility

Home is the place where individuals retreat to escape the stresses of their daily lives. Recognizing that individuals are a captive audience inside their home, the Court has given local governments broad authority to protect their right to be left alone, including placing restrictions on door-to-door solicitation[132] and residential picketing.[133]

## C. Anti-Litter Laws

Anti-litter laws are constitutional. However, enforcement efforts must be directed at the people who drop handbills and produce litter, not against those who distribute them.[134] Handbilling cannot be made illegal in order to control litter.

## D. Interference with Ingress and Egress to and from Buildings and Traffic

A large group of people conducting a free speech gathering on a public street or sidewalk are likely to obstruct entrances to buildings and interfere with traffic. Laws prohibiting obstruction of the public passage are constitutional and may be applied to persons engaged in speech.[135]

Deliberate obstruction of ingress and egress is a tactic sometimes used by anti-abortion protesters to prevent women from seeking services at abortion clinics.[136] A federal law known as the Freedom of Access to Clinic Entrances Act ("FACE")[137] makes this conduct a crime. Many states have adopted similar statutes. In *Hill v. Colorado*,[138] the Supreme Court upheld a state statute requiring anti-abortion protesters to stay eight feet away from individuals who were within 100 feet from the entrance to abortion clinic as being a reasonable time, place, and manner restriction on speech.

---

[132] Beard v. City of Alexandria, 341 U.S. 622, 71 S. Ct. 920, 95 L. Ed. 1233 (1951) (upholding ordinance allowing residents to prohibit uninvited canvassers from entering their property by posting a "No Solicitation" sign). *But see* Watchtower Bible & Tract Society of N.Y., Inc. v. Village of Stratton, *supra* note 129 (village ordinance making it a misdemeanor to go upon private property to promote any cause without first registering with the mayor and receiving a permit held unconstitutional for violating pamphleteer's First Amendment right to remain anonymous).

[133] Frisby v. Schultz, 487 U.S. 474, 108 S. Ct. 2495, 101 L. Ed. 2d 420 (1988) (upholding ordinance banning "picketing before or about the residence or dwelling of any individual").

[134] Schneider v. State, *supra* note 129.

[135] Cameron v. Johnson, 390 U.S. 611, 88 S. Ct. 1335, 20 L. Ed. 2d 182 (1968).

[136] Madsen v. Women's Health Center, Inc., 512 U.S. 753, 114 S. Ct. 2516, 129 L. Ed. 2d 593 (1994); Schenck v. Pro-Choice Network New York, 519 U.S. 357, 117 S. Ct. 855, 137 L. Ed. 2d 1 (1997); Cox v. Louisiana, 379 U.S. 536, 553-555, 85 S. Ct. 453, 463-465, 13 L. Ed. 2d 471 (1965).

[137] 18 U.S.C. § 248.

[138] 53 U.S. 703, 120 S. Ct. 240, 147 L. Ed. 2d 597 (2000)

### E. Restrictions on Face-to-Face Solicitation

Downtown business districts in most large metropolitan areas are overrun by homeless panhandlers.[139] Because the statement "Sir, can you spare some change?"involves speech, restrictions on **panhandling** require analysis under the First Amendment.[140] The Supreme Court has not yet considered a panhandling case, but many lower courts have. Ordinances that prohibit all forms of panhandling any place in the city have uniformly been held invalid because they go too far.[141] Measures that totally foreclose a speaker's ability to gain access to a public forum are valid only when they advance a compelling government interest.[142] Although it is annoying to be approached by a panhandler, protecting citizens from petty annoyances that they can readily avoid on their own does not furnish a compelling reason to abolish speech.[143] Less global solutions are needed. Rather than banning all panhandling, municipalities must concentrate on aggressive and unacceptable conduct associated with panhandling and panhandling in inconvenient locations.

Aggressive panhandling is not protected by the First Amendment. Panhandlers who harass, touch, block, threaten, or otherwise intimidate persons to extract money from them may be charged with disorderly conduct, assault, or under special statutes dealing with aggressive panhandling.[144] Local governments may also outlaw conduct associated with panhandling that poses a safety hazard, such as walking up to motorists stopped at a traffic light,[145] and also objectionable nonspeech conduct associated with panhandling,[146] such as sleeping in parks[147]or sitting or lying on the sidewalk.[148]

Panhandlers often frequent places like train, bus, and subway stations,[149] airport terminals,[150] and lobbies of government office buildings.[151] Local governments can outlaw all forms of panhandling in these locations because they are nonpublic forums. Restrictions on speech in nonpublic forums are only

---

[139] For comprehensive treatment of this issue, see Robert C. Ellickson, *Controlling Chronic Misconduct in City Spaces: Of Panhandlers, Skid Rows, and Public-Space Zoning*, 105 YALE L.J. 1165 (1996).

[140] **International Soc. for Krishna Consciousness v. Lee**, *supra* note 114.

[141] **Loper v. New York City Police Department, 999 F.2d 699 (2d Cir. 1993)** (striking down ordinance prohibiting all begging on a public street); Benefit v. City of Cambridge, 424 Mass. 918, 679 N.E.2d 184 (1997) (same); Ledford v. State, 652 So. 2d 1254 (Fla. Dist. Ct. App. 1995) (same).

[142] See § 2.14 (C).

[143] See authorities *supra* note 141.

[144] Douchette v. City of Santa Monica, 955 F. Supp. 1192 (C.D. Cal. 1997) (upholding ordinance outlawing aggressive begging).

[145] *Id.*

[146] United States v. O'Brien, *supra* note 30 (First Amendment permits the government to regulate conduct associated with speech when the government's regulatory focus is on the conduct, not the message).

[147] Clark v. Community for Creative Non-Violence, *supra* note 31.

[148] Roulette v. City of Seattle, 97 F.3d 300 (9th Cir. 1996) (upholding ordinance prohibiting sitting or lying on sidewalks in commercial areas).

[149] Young v. New York City Transit Authority, 903 F.2d 146 (2d Cir.), *cert. denied*, 498 U.S. 984, 111 S. Ct. 516, 112 L. Ed. 2d 528 (1990) (upholding ban against begging in municipal subway system).

[150] **International Soc. for Krishna Consciousness v. Lee**, *supra* note 114.

[151] United States v. Kokinda, *supra* note 117.

required to be reasonable.[152] This requirement is satisfied because panhandling in these locations, even when nonaggressive, adds to congestion, slows traffic, and intrudes on people who are in a hurry.

To summarize, local governments may regulate aggressive panhandling and nonspeech conduct associated with panhandling in public forums and may outlaw panhandling altogether in nonpublic forums.

## F.  Signs and Billboards

Although billboards are a form of speech, they take up space, obstruct views, distract motorists, and pose other problems that legitimately call for regulation."[153] As a result, the Court has upheld restrictions on the size, location, and physical characteristics of billboards.[154] The Court has also upheld laws prohibiting attachment of signs to fire hydrants, telephone posts, and other roadside fixtures.[155] However, residential lawn signs stand on a different footing. The Supreme Court has twice struck down ordinances banning residential lawn signs on the grounds that the government's interest in avoiding visual clutter does not outweigh a homeowner's right to take advantage of this "unique and important" mode of expression for which there is "no practical substitute."[156] Lower courts have also been solicitous of the right of homeowners to place signs in their yards.[157]

## G.  Permit Regulations

All communities require permits for large-scale parades, marches, and demonstrations. Advance notice is needed for orderly scheduling, effective resource allocation, and adequate policing. Requiring a permit is the only practical way to obtain these advantages. The First Amendment, nevertheless, is hostile toward laws that require citizens to obtain advance permission from

---

[152]  See authorities *supra* note 117.

[153]  City of Ladue v. Gilleo, *supra* note 126.

[154]  Metromedia, Inc. v. San Diego, 453 U.S. 490, 101 S. Ct. 2882, 69 L. Ed. 2d 800 (1981) (upholding ban on offsite billboard advertising as valid means of furthering city's interest in traffic safety and aesthetics).

[155]  Members of City Council of Los Angeles v. Taxpayers for Vincent, 466 U.S. 789, 104 S. Ct. 2118, 80 L. Ed. 2d 772 (1984).

[156]  City of Ladue v. Gilleo, *supra* note 126 (invalidating ordinance banning all residential signs); Linmark Associates, Inc. v. Township of Willingboro, 431 U.S. 85, 97 S. Ct. 1614, 52 L. Ed. 2d 155 (1977) (invalidating law prohibiting homeowners from placing "For Sale" or "Sold" signs on their property).

[157]  Arlington County Republican Comm'n v. Arlington County, 983 F.2d 587 (4th Cir. 1993) (invalidating ordinance limiting homeowners to two signs); Whitton v. City of Gladstone, Mo., 54 F.3d 1400 (8th Cir. 1995) (invalidating ordinance imposing time limits on political signs).

a public official before exercising their right to free speech.[158] Laws that require advance permission create a danger that permission will be denied to groups whose appearance, lifestyles, or views are unacceptable. Consequently, permit laws are constitutional only if they incorporate adequate safeguards to ensure that censorship is not practiced. To be constitutional, they must: (1) contain clear, narrow, objective standards for permit officials to follow, (2) not impose unreasonably long advance notice requirements; and (3) not allow discretion to vary the fee.

Delegation of broad discretion is fatal to permit laws because discretion creates a danger of censorship. For permit laws to be constitutional, discretion must be limited to matters of resource allocation and scheduling. The Supreme Court has consistently invalidated laws that allow discretion to consider factors such as the speaker's moral character, the subject matter of the gathering, the gathering's anticipated effect on the peace, safety, decency, morals, or good order of the community, and the likelihood of riots.[159] Considerations like these leave permit officials with nothing beyond their own opinions to guide their decisionmaking. The right to engage in free speech cannot be left to the unfettered discretion of a permit official.

Second, permit ordinances may not impose unreasonably long advance notice requirements. Long waiting periods stifle speech that is reactive to late-breaking events and discourage some citizens from applying.[160] An ordinance requiring 30 days advance notice, for example, would have silenced groups who wanted to hold a rally to protest the Bush Administration's threatened military action in Iraq because the invasion was already in progress by then.

Finally, although a nominal fee may be charged to defray the cost of administration,[161] the fee must be set in accordance with a content-neutral fee

---

[158]   Watchtower Bible & Tract Society of N.Y., Inc. v. Village of Stratton, *supra* note 129 (invalidating village ordinance making it a misdemeanor to go upon private property to promote any cause without first registering with the mayor and receiving a permit); Shuttlesworth v. City of Birmingham, 394 U.S. 147, 89 S. Ct. 935, 22 L. Ed. 2d 162 (1969).

[159]   Shuttlesworth v. City of Birmingham, *supra* note 158 (invalidating ordinance vesting discretion to refuse a permit when required by "public welfare, peace, safety, health, decency, good order, morals or convenience"); Hague v. C.I.O., 307 U.S. 496, 59 S. Ct. 954, 83 L. Ed. 1423 (1939) (invalidating ordinance vesting discretion to refuse a permit when necessary to prevent "riots, disturbances or disorderly assemblage"); Staub v. Baxley, 355 U.S. 313, 78 S. Ct. 277, 2 L. Ed. 2d 302 (1958) (invalidating ordinance vesting discretion to refuse a permit to applicants who are "not of good character" or who are "canvassing for a project not free from fraud"). *But see* Thomas v. City of Park District, 534 U.S. 316, 122 S. Ct. 775, 151 L. Ed. 2d 783 (2002) (upholding ordinance requiring permit to hold a large-scale outdoor gathering where permit could be denied only when the application was incomplete or contained material misrepresentations, the applicant has damaged park property on prior occasions and has not paid for the damage, a permit has been granted to an earlier applicant for the same time and place, or the intended use would present an unreasonable danger to the health or safety of park users).

[160]   *See, e.g.,* Church of the American Knights of the Ku Klux Klan v. City of Gary, 334 F.3d 676 (7th Cir. 2003) (invalidating ordinance requiring applications for permits to hold public rally to be submitted 45 days in advance); Grossman v. City of Portland, 33 F.3d 1200 (9th Cir. 1993) (permit ordinance requiring seven-day wait before making use of public park unconstitutional as applied to small gathering of six to eight protesters).

[161]   Cox v. New Hampshire, 312 U.S. 569, 61 S. Ct. 762, 85 L. Ed. 1049 (1941).

schedule.[162] Moreover, the fee may not include the cost of maintaining order because this would make unpopular groups responsible for the cost of keeping spectators who are hostile to them in line.[163]

## § 2.16 —Free Speech Access to Private Property

The First Amendment reads *"Congress* shall make no law . . . abridging the freedom of speech . . ."* This language reaches only the government. Private parties are not affected by the First Amendment.[164] They are not required to allow speech on their premises and, if they decide to allow some speech, are free to pick and choose.

A controversy existed at one time about whether corporate malls and shopping centers had an obligation to permit First Amendment activity on their premises. Civil libertarians argued that shopping center streets and sidewalks were "functionally" indistinguishable from streets and sidewalks in downtown business districts and that the First Amendment should therefore apply. The Supreme Court briefly entertained this argument,[165] but later discarded it.[166] In *Lloyd v. Tanner*,[167] the Supreme Court held that even though the streets, sidewalks, and parking areas in modern shopping centers serve a purpose similar to facilities in downtown business districts, the First Amendment is inapplicable because these locations are privately owned. Shopping center proprietors are, therefore, under no First Amendment obligation to allow picketing, handbilling, solicitation, or other similar activities on their premises. However, police officers should never arrest peaceful First Amendment actors simply because they are on private property. Their presence becomes a criminal trespass only if they remain after being asked to leave by the owner.

The fact that there is no First Amendment right of access to privately owned property does not mean that state law cannot create such a right. Some states have statutes requiring shopping malls to allow picketing and handbilling on their premises; these statutes are a valid exercise of police power.[168]

---

[162]   Center for Auto Safety, Inc. v. Athey, 37 F.3d 139, 145 (4th Cir. 1994), *cert. denied*, 514 U.S. 1036, 115 S. Ct. 1401, 131 L. Ed. 2d 289 (1995); Coalition for the Abolition of Marijuana Prohibition v. City of Atlanta, 219 F.3d 1301 (11th Cir. 2000).

[163]   *See, e.g.*, Forsyth County v. Nationalist Movement, 505 U.S. 123, 112 S. Ct. 2395, 120 L. Ed. 2d 101 (1992); Church of the American Knights of the Ku Klux Klan v. City of Gary, *supra* note 160 (conditioning permit to hold rally on white supremist group's payment of stiff permit fee to cover costs of police protection to rein in the hecklers violated First Amendment).

[164]   *See generally*, Weinstein, *Symposium: Free Speech and Community: A Brief Introduction to Free Speech Doctrine*, 29 ARIZ. ST. L.J. 461 (1997).

[165]   Amalgamated Food Employees Local v. Logan Valley Plaza, 391 U.S. 308, 88 S. Ct. 1601, 20 L. Ed. 2d 603 (1968).

[166]   Lloyd v. Tanner, 107 U.S. 551, 92 S. Ct. 2219, 33 L. Ed. 2d 131 (1976); Central Hardware Co. v. NLRB, 407 U.S. 539, 92 S. Ct. 2238, 33 L. Ed. 2d 122 (1976); Hudgens v. NLRB, 424 U.S. 507, 96 S. Ct. 1029, 47 L. Ed. 2d 196 (1975).

[167]   *Supra* note 166.

[168]   Pruneyard Shopping Center v. Robins, 447 U.S. 74, 100 S. Ct. 2035, 64 L. Ed. 2d 741 (1980).

## § 2.17 —Need for Precision in Regulating Speech

In *Gooding v. Wilson*,[169] a group of anti-war protesters deliberately obstructed the entrance to an army induction center to prevent inductees from entering. When an officer attempted to remove the protesters, the defendant, who was part of the group, angrily remonstrated: "White son of a bitch, I'll kill you." "You son of a bitch, I'll choke you to death." "You son of a bitch, if you ever put your hands on me again, I'll cut you all to pieces." Threats like this, as you recall, are not protected by the First Amendment. The officer arrested the defendant under a statute prohibiting the use of "opprobrious words or abusive language." It may come as a surprise that the Supreme Court overturned the conviction.

What did the officer do wrong? The answer is nothing. The problem was in the statute. Criminal laws, particularly those designed for application to people engaged in speech, must contain narrow, clear, and precise standards to guide arrest decisions.[170] This requirement serves two equally important purposes.[171] The first is fair notice.[172] Citizens are entitled to know in advance when their behavior will subject them to arrest. The Constitution therefore requires criminal laws to define the prohibited conduct with sufficient clarity that ordinary citizens would understand what they are forbidden to do.[173] Fair notice is particularly important for laws that apply to speech. Cautious citizens faced with laws of uncertain meaning will often choose to forgo exercising their First Amendment rights rather than risk arrest. Vague laws cause self-censorship and silence more speech than the legislature intended.

Clear standards are also necessary to guide police officers in making arrest decisions.[174] In a "nation of laws and not of men," legislatures may not delegate standardless discretion to police officers to arrest whomever they please.[175] Laws that lack clear standards lend themselves to arbitrary and discriminatory applications. As a result, courts sometimes allow persons to attack the constitutionality of the statute under which they were arrested, even though their own conduct was not protected by the First Amendment and would have subjected them to arrest under a properly drawn law.[176]

---

[169]   405 U.S. 518, 92 S. Ct. 1103, 31 L. Ed. 2d 408 (1972).

[170]   City of Houston v. Hill, 482 U.S. 451, 107 S. Ct. 2502, 96 L. Ed. 2d 398 (1987); Kolender v. Lawson, 461 U.S. 352, 357, 103 S. Ct. 1855, 1858, 75 L. Ed. 2d 903 (1983); Grayned v. City of Rockford, 408 U.S. 104, 92 S. Ct. 2294, 33 L. Ed. 2d 222 (1972); Gooding v. Wilson, *supra* note 46.

[171]   Kolender v. Lawson, *supra* note 170.

[172]   See authorities *supra* note 170.

[173]   *Id.*

[174]   *Id.*

[175]   Grayned v. City of Rockford, *supra* note 170 (vague laws are constitutionally objectionable because they "impermissibly delegate basic policy matters to policemen, judges, and juries for resolution on an ad hoc and subjective basis . . .").

[176]   Gooding v. Wilson, *supra* note 169; Brockett v. Spokane Arcades, Inc., 472 U.S. 491, 503, 105 S. Ct. 2794, 2801, 86 L. Ed. 2d 394 (1985); New York v. Ferber, 458 U.S. 747, 772, 102 S. Ct. 3348, 3362, 73 L. Ed. 2d 1113 (1982); Smith v. Goguen, 415 U.S. 566, 582, 94 S. Ct. 1242, 1251, 39 L. Ed. 2d 605 (1974).

Police, therefore, need to pay attention to the statutes they invoke in a speech context. Opportunities often exist to choose between several statutes. Police should always prefer statutes that contain precise, narrow, and objective criteria over statutes that confer broad discretion and invite subjective judgments.

There are three varieties of statutes that police should never use in a speech context, even when the speaker's conduct is not protected by the First Amendment. They are described below.

## A. Statutes Authorizing Arrests for "Disturbing," "Annoying," or "Offensive" Conduct

In *Coates v. City of Cincinnati*,[177] the Court invalidated an ordinance that made it unlawful for "three or more persons to assemble . . . on any sidewalks, and there conduct themselves in a manner annoying to persons passing by." Laws that make arrest decisions turn on an officer's assessment of whether others were offended or annoyed by the arrestee's conduct are unconstitutional for three different reasons.[178] First, they fail to give ordinary citizens adequate notice of the conduct to be avoided because virtually any conduct might annoy at least some people in the vicinity. Second, they vest too much discretion in the police to decide whether the statute has been violated. How is an officer to know whether people passing by were annoyed by the arrestee's conduct? The best an officer can do to gauge the reactions of others is to consider his or her own reaction. A statute that, read literally, makes it a crime to annoy a police officer comes dangerously close to a police state. Finally, these statutes cover speech protected by the First Amendment. Speech does not cease to have protection because it offends or annoys another person.[179] For these reasons, statutes authorizing arrest for offensive or annoying conduct should never be used to arrest people engaged in speech, even when their speech is not protected by the First Amendment.

---

[177] 402 U.S. 611, 91 S. Ct. 1686, 29 L. Ed. 2d 214 (1971).

[178] Cordova v. Reno, 920 F. Supp. 135 (D. Nev. 1997) (invalidating ordinance creating criminal liability for behavior that has the tendency to annoy, insult, or disturb any person passing by).

[179] Forsyth County, Ga. v. The Nationalist Movement, *supra* note 163 (invalidating parade permit ordinance authorizing administrator to establish the permit fee based on the estimated cost of policing the event because the ordinance required the administrator to speculate about public reaction to the message in order to estimate the cost of maintaining order); Smith v. Goguen, 415 U.S. 566, 582, 94 S. Ct. 1242, 1251, 39 L. Ed. 2d 605 (1974) (invalidating statute making it a crime to treat the United States flag "contemptuously" because it left police free to make arrests based on their own views about how flags should be treated).

## B. *Statutes Authorizing Arrests for Refusal to Obey a Police Officer's Order to Move On*

Statutes authorizing police to arrest for disobeying an order to "move on" should also be used with extreme caution. Such statutes are constitutional only when they specify the conditions under which such orders may be issued.[180] Legislatures may not invest police officers with standardless discretion to issue orders to move on and arrest those who disobey.

*Shuttlesworth v. City of Birmingham*[181] is the leading case on point. Shuttlesworth, a civil rights activist, and several of his companions were standing outside a department store during a protest boycott when a police officer approached them and told them to move on. The others left, but Shuttlesworth stayed behind. When he questioned the officer's authority to order him to leave, he was arrested under an ordinance that made it an offense to "stand . . . upon any street or sidewalk of the city after having been requested by any police officer to move on." The Supreme Court reversed Shuttlesworth's conviction, declaring that legislatures may not delegate to police officers the authority to arrest those who disobey their orders to disperse without furnishing objective criteria for when such orders may be issued. The following observations made by Mr. Justice Black in a different case explain the reason. Mr. Justice Black wrote:

> [U]nder our democratic system of government, lawmaking is not entrusted to the moment-to-moment judgment of the policeman on his beat. Laws, that is valid laws, are to be made by representatives chosen to make laws for the future, not by police officers whose duty it is to enforce laws already enacted and to make arrests only for conduct already made criminal. . . . To let a policeman's command become equivalent to a criminal statute comes dangerously near making our government one of men rather than of laws.[182]

Statutes making the failure to obey a police order to move grounds for arrest are not objectionable when they detail the circumstances under which police have the authority to issue such an order. Had the Birmingham ordinance made it an offense to "obstruct the free passage upon any public street and remain after having been requested by an officer to move on," the unconstitutional discretion would have been eliminated.[183] The right to stand on the street no longer depends on an officer's whim because the statute now requires the officer to observe overt acts declared unlawful in the statute before issuing an order, the violation of which becomes grounds for arrest.

---

[180]  Shuttlesworth v. City of Birmingham, 382 U.S. 87, 86 S. Ct. 211, 15 L. Ed. 2d 176 (1965); Chicago v. Morales, 527 U.S. 41, 119 S. Ct. 1849, 144 L. Ed. 2d 67 (1999).

[181]  *Supra* note 180.

[182]  Gregory v. City of Chicago, 394 U.S. 111, 120, 89 S. Ct. 946, 951, 22 L. Ed. 2d 134 (1969).

[183]  Boos v. Barry, 485 U.S. 312, 108 S. Ct. 1157, 99 L. Ed. 2d 333 (1988) (upholding ordinance prohibiting persons from congregating within 500 feet of the embassy and not dispersing when ordered to do so).

The point of this discussion is that law enforcement officers have no inherent power to issue arrest-triggering orders, and legislators may not confer this power on them. However, because law enforcement officers lack the ability to judge whether the laws they enforce are constitutional, the following rule of thumb will help prevent problems: *If First Amendment actors are in a place where they have a legal right to be and are conducting themselves in a peaceful and lawful manner, an officer cannot make their conduct a crime by ordering them to disperse and arresting them if they refuse.*

## C.  Statutes Authorizing Arrests for "Loitering"

The typical loitering statute makes it a crime to "wander, idle, or stroll around from place to place without any apparent purpose." Statutes such as this have been before the Supreme Court on a number of occasions and have uniformly been found unconstitutional.[184] The problem with loitering statutes is that they include within their sweep large amounts of harmless behavior, without providing adequate guidance to police to enable them to distinguish guilty conduct from innocent conduct. Enforcement decisions are left to an officer's unfettered discretion. Loitering statutes like the one above are too lacking in standards to be enforced at all, in any context.[185] This principle is so well-established that police officers who make arrests for "loitering" run the risk of being sued.

## § 2.18  Summary

The First Amendment prohibits the police from abridging freedom of speech. Speech encompasses a variety of mediums, including parades, pickets, protest demonstrations, and symbolic speech. A critical distinction exists between interventions directed at a speaker's message and those directed at his or her conduct.

## A.  First Amendment Protection for a Speaker's Message

Police may not arrest people solely for what they say or for the language they use to say it unless their speech lacks First Amendment protection. The following speech categories have been excluded from the realm of protected speech.

---

[184]  Chicago v. Morales, *supra* note 180; Kolender v. Lawson, *supra* note 170; Papachristou v. City of Jacksonville, 405 U.S. 156, 92 S. Ct. 839, 31 L. Ed. 2d 110 (1972). However, loitering statutes have been upheld as constitutional when the statute requires proof of some other overt act or criminal intent in addition to loitering. *See, e.g.,* People v. Superior Court, 46 Cal. 3d 381, 758 P.2d 1046, 250 Cal. Rptr. 515 (1988) (loitering to solicit lewd or unlawful act).

[185]  *See* cases *supra* note 184.

- **Obscenity.** Obscenity refers to materials that appeal to prurient interests, depict hard-core sexual acts in a patently offensive manner, and lack serious literary, artistic, political, scientific, or other value. Police officers are not allowed to make this decision; it must be made by a judge. Police may not seize allegedly obscene materials unless a judge has issued a search warrant.

- **Child pornography.** Child pornography refers to materials that visually depict real children engaged in sexual acts. In order to protect children from exploitation, states may outlaw production and distribution of child pornography, whether or not the materials are obscene.

- **Fighting words.** "Fighting words" are derogatory or abusive remarks spoken to another in a face-to-face encounter under circumstances likely to provoke the other into making an immediate violent response. The fighting words exclusion has a narrow application when the target of verbal abuse is a trained police officer.

- **Threats.** A threat, for purposes of the First Amendment, requires communication of a serious expression of intent to commit an act of unlawful violence

- **Incitement to riot.** Speech advocating violence or other unlawful action ceases to be protected by the First Amendment only if the speech is both directed toward inciting imminent lawless action and is likely to produce such action. A hostile audience reception does not furnish grounds for arresting people engaged in orderly protest.

## B. First Amendment Protection for a Speaker's Conduct

Conduct and speech are often intertwined. However, the First Amendment does not confer the same protection on a speaker's conduct as on the message. General laws prohibiting conduct may be applied to people engaged in speech when they serve a substantial government interest that is not related to suppressing the speaker's message.

The government's authority to restrict speech on government property depends on whether the location is a public forum or a nonpublic forum. Restrictions on speech access to nonpublic forums, such as schools, police stations, military installations, and government buildings, need only be reasonable and neutral as to viewpoint. Restrictions on speech access to public forums, such as streets, parks, sidewalks, and municipal auditoriums, in contrast, require a significant government interest and, in some instances, a compelling government interest to be valid. The First Amendment does not guarantee a right of speech access to privately owned property, including shopping centers and malls.

Laws that require a permit to hold a parade, march, or demonstration must: (1) contain clear, narrow, objective standards for permit officials to follow, (2) not impose unreasonably long advance notice requirements; and (3) not allow discretion to vary the fee.

Criminal laws that are capable of being applied to speech must contain clear, precise, and objective standards to guide arrest decisions. In policing open-air speech gatherings, an officer must keep several things in mind. First, speakers may not be arrested for inciting a breach of the peace unless they urge imminent lawless action. Urging unlawful action down the road is not enough. Second, police may not arrest an unpopular speaker for a hostile audience reaction. Their duty is to protect the speaker's right to speak.

# Authority to Detain
# and Arrest; Use of Force     3

*The right of the people to be secure in their persons . . . against unreasonable . . . seizures, shall not be violated, and no Warrants shall issue, but upon probable cause, supported by Oath or affirmation, and particularly describing the persons . . . to be seized.*

Fourth Amendment

# Chapter Outline

Affidavit
Arrest
Arrest warrant
Common law
Exigent circumstances
Felony
Fresh pursuit
Hot pursuit
Investigatory detention
Investigatory stop

Misdemeanor
Pretextual traffic stop
Probable cause
Reasonable grounds
Reasonable suspicion
Seizure
Show of legal authority
*Terry* stop
Voluntary encounter

# § 3.1 Introduction

During a routine day, an officer may pull a car over to advise the driver that her tire is dangerously low, ask three men loitering in front of a liquor store what they are doing there, arrest a shoplifter, and fire warning shots at a dangerous criminal. The Fourth Amendment guarantees citizens the right to go about their business free of unreasonable interference by the police. Because the concern is with *unreasonable* interference, the Fourth Amendment does not treat all police interventions alike. Developing workable principles for when citizens may be detained for questioning, arrested, or forcibly subdued requires a trade-off between society's need for effective law enforcement and the need of its members for freedom from unwarranted interference with their liberty. This chapter explores the balance that has been struck.

A police officer's authority to detain citizens against their will is regulated by three layers of legal principles—the Fourth Amendment to the United States Constitution, state constitutions, and state arrest laws. The Fourth Amendment guarantees the "right of the people to be secure in their persons . . . against *unreasonable . . . seizures . . .*" Whenever a police officer detains a suspect for investigation, makes an arrest, or uses force to bring a suspect under control, the suspect is seized and the officer's conduct must conform to Fourth Amendment standards of reasonableness. However, the Fourth Amendment is not the only rule police officers must obey. All states have constitutional and statutory provisions covering these matters as well. A police officer's actions must comply with state constitutions and arrest laws, as well as the Fourth Amendment. The primary focus of this chapter is on the Fourth Amendment. Students will receive in-depth instruction in the arrest laws of their state as part of their police department training programs.

Figure 3.1
**Legal Restrictions on Arrest Authority**

In order to be lawful, an arrest must comply with:

1. Fourth Amendment standards,
2. State constitutional standards, and
3. State arrest laws.

## § 3.2   Overview of the Fourth Amendment

An **arrest** results in a deprivation of liberty that carries serious consequences. It can damage important relationships, disrupt the ability to earn a living, and destroy a person's reputation in the community. As a result, common law judges wisely decided at an early date that arrest decisions should not be left to the unfettered discretion of the police. They established safeguards to reduce the likelihood of false arrests. In the case of an arrest for a **misdemeanor**, the **common law** required a prior judicial determination that the arrest was justified, unless the offense was committed in the officer's presence.[1] This is the origin of the modern **arrest warrant**. A warrant was not required to arrest for a **felony** because delaying action might jeopardize the public safety. Protection against arbitrary arrests was provided through the requirement that the officer have **probable cause** to believe that a felony had been committed and that the person to be arrested had committed it.[2] These concepts helped shape the Fourth Amendment and play a central role in contemporary arrest law.[3]

### A.  Historical Purpose of the Fourth Amendment

General warrants and writs of assistance were the historic evil that led to the Fourth Amendment's adoption. These instruments conferred blanket authority on British customs officials to decide whom to search, where to search, and what to search for.[4] Armed with these dreaded instruments, customs officials could enter anyone's home without grounds for believing they

---

[1]    10 HALSBURY'S LAWS OF ENGLAND 344-345 (3d ed. 1955); 4 W. BLACKSTONE, COMMENTARIES * 292; 1 J. STEPHEN, A HISTORY OF THE CRIMINAL LAW OF ENGLAND 193 (1883).

[2]    *See* sources *supra* note 1.

[3]    Henry v. United States, 361 U.S. 98, 100, 80 S. Ct. 168, 170, 4 L. Ed. 2d 134 (1959).

[4]    Barbara C. Salken, *The General Warrant of the Twentieth Century? A Fourth Amendment Solution to Unchecked Discretion to Arrest for Traffic Offenses*, 62 TEMP. L. REV. 221 (1989).

had committed a crime or that contraband would be found there.[5] Hatred of this practice was one of the driving forces behind the American Revolution.[6] The purpose of the Fourth Amendment is announced in the first clause:

> **The right of the people to be secure in their persons**, houses, papers, and effects, **against unreasonable** searches and **seizures, shall not be violated** . . .

## B. *Overview of Fourth Amendment Detention and Arrest Provisions*

The Fourth Amendment recognizes two classes of seizures: **investigatory stops** and **arrests**. Neither is mentioned in the language of the Fourth Amendment. The crucial term is **seizure**. The Fourth Amendment states that "[t]he right of the people to be secure in their persons . . . against unreasonable . . . seizures shall not be violated."

A seizure occurs when a suspect submits to a police officer's show of legal authority or the officer gains actual physical control over him or her.[7] When an officer activates lights and siren and stops a vehicle, the motorist has been seized through submission to the officer's **show of legal authority** (i.e., activating the lights and siren). When an officer takes a person from his or her home to the police station at gunpoint, the person is also seized. Seizures are classified as investigatory stops or arrests according to their duration and intrusiveness. Investigatory stops are limited seizures made for the purpose of conducting a brief investigation.[8] Pulling a vehicle over to check the registration because the vehicle matches the description of a stolen car is an example. Because investigatory stops are shorter and less intrusive than arrests, they are permitted on a lower degree of suspicion.[9] The degree of suspicion needed for an investigatory stop is known as **reasonable suspicion**.[10] When the police restrain a suspect's liberty beyond the degree allowed for an investigatory stop, the seizure automatically becomes an arrest and triggers the full protection of the Fourth Amendment. Arrests can occur either because an officer intends to make an arrest or because a seizure lasts too long or is too intrusive to qualify as a limited seizure.[11] Taking a suspect to the police station at gunpoint, for example, is so intrusive that it constitutes an arrest, whether or not the officer intended this consequence.

---

[5]    Steagald v. United States, 451 U.S. 204, 220, 101 S. Ct. 1642, 1651, 68 L. Ed. 2d 38 (1981).

[6]    *Id.* at 494 U.S. at 266, 110 S. Ct. at 1056.

[7]    California v. Hodari D., 499 U.S. 621, 111 S. Ct. 1547, 113 L. Ed. 2d 690 (1991); United States v. Mendenhall, 446 U.S. 544, 100 S. Ct. 1870, 64 L. Ed. 2d 497 (1980).

[8]    Terry v. Ohio, 392 U.S. 1, 88 S. Ct. 1868, 20 L. Ed. 2d 889 (1968).

[9]    *Id.*

[10]    United States v. Cortez, 449 U.S. 411, 101 S. Ct. 690, 66 L. Ed. 2d 621 (1981).

[11]    Kaupp v. Texas, 538 U.S. 626, 123 S. Ct. 1843, 155 L. Ed. 2d 814 (2002); Dunaway v. New York, 442 U.S. 200, 209, 99 S. Ct. 2248, 2255, 60 L. Ed. 2d 824 (1979); Brown v. Illinois, 422 U.S. 590, 95 S. Ct. 2254, 45 L. Ed. 2d 416 (1975).

The Fourth Amendment is violated only when the seizure is *unreasonable*. A seizure may be considered *unreasonable* for any of the following reasons: (1) the officer lacked adequate grounds for the seizure; (2) the officer failed to procure a warrant in a situation in which one was required; or (3) the officer used excessive force to effect the seizure.

The Fourth Amendment requires grounds for a seizure. The officer must be aware of facts that support the degree of suspicion needed for the type of seizure that was made. A higher degree of suspicion is needed for an arrest than for an investigatory stop because it is more intrusive. If the officer lacks adequate grounds to justify the seizure, the seizure will violate the Fourth Amendment.[12]

The Fourth Amendment also regulates the method of effecting a seizure. The police, for example, are required to obtain an arrest warrant before they may enter a private residence to arrest someone inside.[13] Even though the police have probable cause to make the arrest, if they arrest a suspect inside his or her home without a warrant, the arrest is unconstitutional—not because they lacked grounds, but because they used the wrong method. An arrest warrant was necessary. Finally, the Fourth Amendment regulates the degree of force that may be used to effect a seizure. The force permitted varies with the seriousness of the offense and whether the officer's safety or the safety of others appears to be at risk.[14]

## C. Consequences of an Unconstitutional Arrest or Detention for Investigation

Fourth Amendment violations have serious consequences—for the person whose constitutional rights are violated, the criminal justice system, and the officer personally. A false arrest can destroy an innocent person's reputation. It can also hamper the prosecution of a guilty person. Procuring evidence of the crime is one of the main purposes of a criminal investigation. This purpose can be defeated if the suspect's arrest violates the Fourth Amendment. If the arrest is unconstitutional, any search that follows is unauthorized, and physical evidence or incriminating statements obtained as a result are inadmissible as evidence.[15] While an unconstitutional arrest does not bar the government from trying a person,[16] if the only evidence that the state has to convict an armed robbery suspect is a gun, stocking, and large roll of bills taken from him during a search incident to an unconstitutional arrest, the offender will go free. Consequently, police officers must be able to recognize when their conduct involves a seizure, whether the seizure constitutes an investigatory stop or an

---

[12]   Beck v. Ohio, 379 U.S. 89, 85 S. Ct. 223, 13 L. Ed. 2d 142 (1964).

[13]   *See* § 3.15 *infra*.

[14]   *See* § 3.16 *infra*.

[15]   The impact of an unconstitutional arrest on the admission of evidence is covered in Chapter 4.

[16]   *See, e.g.*, State v. Crews, 445 U.S. 463, 100 S. Ct. 1244, 63 L. Ed. 2d 537 (1980).

arrest, and whether they have grounds for taking this action. The police also have a personal stake in complying with the Fourth Amendment. Violating a suspect's Fourth Amendment rights can lead to a civil lawsuit and, if the violation is intentional, to criminal prosecution as well.[17]

Figure 3.2
**Consequences of an Unconstitutional Seizure**

An unconstitutional seizure can:

1. Ruin an innocent person's reputation.
2. Destroy admissibility of evidence.
3. Lead to a civil suit and, in rare cases, criminal prosecution of the officer.

## § 3.3 Crossing the Boundary of the Fourth Amendment

Police encounters with suspects range from contacts in which the suspect's cooperation is voluntary to full-blown arrests. Students must learn to recognize and distinguish among three kinds of interactions—**voluntary encounters**, **investigatory stops**,[18] and **arrests**. Figure 3.3 summarizes the descriptive characteristics and Fourth Amendment relevance of each. Because investigatory stops and arrests are both subcategories of seizures, the concept of a seizure must be understood first.

Voluntary encounters are not regulated by the Fourth Amendment. The police have a "free zone" for investigative work—a zone in which they are at liberty to approach members of the public and ask questions or request other forms of assistance, even though they are acting on nothing more than a hunch. The critical characteristic of the "free zone" is that the suspect's compliance with the officer's request is voluntary and consensual. The officer has not done or said anything that would convey the message that compliance is required. The moment this changes and the atmosphere becomes overbearing, threatening, or oppressive, the transition to a seizure is in progress. A seizure occurs when a suspect's freedom of movement is restricted and the suspect is brought under an officer's control, either through submission to the officer's show of legal authority or physical restraint. Seizure is a critical point in Fourth Amendment jurisprudence. Once a seizure occurs, the officer's conduct will be examined for compliance with the Fourth Amendment.

---

[17] A police officer's civil and criminal liability for violating constitutional rights is covered in Chapter 11.
[18] "Investigatory stops" are also called "investigatory detentions," "Terry stops," and sometimes "stop and frisks."

Figure 3.3
**Types of Investigatory Encounters and Suspicion Needed to Initiate**

| Type of Encounter | Free Zone | Fourth Amendment Threshold | Encounters Regulated by the Fourth Amendment | |
| --- | --- | --- | --- | --- |
| | Voluntary Encounter | Seizure | Investigatory Stop | Arrest |
| **Descriptive Characteristics** | The police ask the suspect to cooperate in the investigation, such as answer questions, consent to a search, take a Breathalyzer test, etc. without restraining the suspect's freedom of movement or indicating, in any manner, that compliance is mandatory. | A seizure occurs when a suspect's freedom of movement is restricted and the suspect is brought under the officer's control, either by a. submission to a show of legal authority, or b. physical restraint. The Fourth Amendment kicks in at this point. | Seizure of limited scope and duration. | Seizure effected with intent to make an arrest or that exceeds the boundaries of an investigatory stop. |
| **Suspicion Needed to Initiate** | None. | | Officer must have a reasonable suspicion that the suspect is involved in criminal activity. | Officer must have probable cause to believe that the suspect has committed or is committing a crime. |

## § 3.4  —"Free Zone" for Investigative Work

Under the Fourth Amendment, as well as under other provisions of the Bill of Rights, people who voluntarily cooperate with the police have no standing to complain that their constitutional rights have been violated. The police do not need probable cause, reasonable suspicion, or any other grounds to initiate a voluntary encounter. Investigative encounters conducted without a seizure are not regulated by the Fourth Amendment. Police officers are free to ask suspects for any form of voluntary assistance—identification,[19] answers to questions,[20] permission to search their luggage,[21] consent to take a Breathalyzer test, etc.—provided they do not restrict the suspect's freedom of movement or communicate through words or conduct that compliance with their request is mandatory.[22] It goes without saying that the suspect has a corresponding right to refuse the officer's request. However, the important point is that officers do not need grounds to ask. Evidence is always admissible when a suspect furnishes it voluntarily.

Figure 3.4
**Characteristics of a Voluntary Encounter**

> Voluntary police/suspect encounters are not regulated by the Fourth Amendment. Encounters are considered voluntary only if the police do not:
>
> 1.  restrict the suspect's freedom of movement, or
> 2.  communicate through words, conduct, or gestures that compliance with their request is mandatory.
>
> No grounds for suspicion are needed to initiate a voluntary encounter. However, the suspect has a corresponding right to refuse to cooperate.

## 3.5  —"Seizure" Defined

Because seizures trigger the Fourth Amendment, knowing when conduct involves a seizure must become an automatic reflex. Otherwise, violations of the Fourth Amendment will be inevitable. We have invented a crook named Sticky-Fingered Sam to illustrate concepts in this chapter. The assertion that Officer Blake "seized" Sticky-Fingered Sam evokes the image of Officer Blake grabbing Sam. This is one way Officer Blake can seize Sam. However, he can also seize him without laying a hand on him. Suppose Officer Blake, while patrolling a residential neighborhood late at night, sees Sam lugging a

---

[19]  INS v. Delgado, 466 U.S. 210, 104 S. Ct. 1758, 80 L. Ed. 2d 247 (1984).

[20]  Florida v. Rodriguez, 469 U.S. 1, 105 S. Ct. 308, 83 L. Ed. 2d 165 (1984).

[21]  **United States v. Drayton, 536 U.S. 194, 122 S. Ct. 2105, 153 L. Ed. 2d 242 (2002)**; Florida v. Bostick, 501 U.S. 429, 111 S. Ct. 2382, 115 L. Ed. 2d 389 (1991); Florida v. Royer, 460 U.S. 491, 103 S. Ct. 1319, 1326, 75 L. Ed. 2d 229 (1983).

[22]  **United States v. Drayton,** *supra* note 21; Florida v. Bostick, *supra* note 21; Dunaway v. New York, *supra* note 11.

stereo down the street. He gets out of his patrol car and, with one hand resting on his revolver, stands in front of Sam and says in an authoritative tone of voice, "Hey bud! Put that stereo down, show me some identification, and tell me where you got that stereo." Sam stops, puts the stereo down, and answers Officer Blake's questions. Sam has been seized.

In order to effect a seizure, the police must gain control over the suspect. Control can be gained either through: (1) physical restraint or (2) the suspect's submission to a show of legal authority.[23] Sticky-Fingered Sam was seized in the second way. Officer Blake made a show of legal authority when, standing with his hand on his gun, he directed Sam to put the stereo down and explain where he got it. Sam complied, not because he wanted to, but because he understood from Officer Blake's words and conduct that he had no choice. Officer Blake brought Sam under his control psychologically. Interactions with a suspect do not have to involve physical contact or a trip to the police station in order to constitute a seizure.[24]

Figure 3.5
**Definition of a Seizure**

> A suspect is seized when he or she is deprived of freedom of movement and brought under a police officer's control either through:
>
> 1.   submission to a show of legal authority, or
> 2.   physical restraint.

Because submission to a show of legal authority is one way suspects can be seized, police officers must be able to recognize when conduct amounts to a show of legal authority. An objective standard is used to make this determination. Courts are not concerned with whether the officer actually intended to restrict the suspect's freedom of movement or with whether the suspect subjectively believed that the officer had this intent. Some citizens are so intimidated by the police that they never feel free to refuse an officer's request, no matter how politely they are asked. Whether an officer's conduct amounts to a show of legal authority depends on how a reasonable person in the suspect's position would have assessed the situation.[25] If the officer's words and conduct would have conveyed the message to a reasonable person that he or she was not free to terminate the encounter and leave, a suspect who complies with an officer's request is seized.

Police interactions with a suspect can start off as voluntary, but then change. It is often necessary for courts to pinpoint the exact moment during an encounter when a suspect was seized. The reason is that evidence procured from a suspect without a seizure is always admissible, whereas evidence pro-

---

[23]   **California v. Hodari D.,** *supra* note 7; United States v. Mendenhall, *supra* note 7.
[24]   **Terry v. Ohio,** *supra* note 8.
[25]   **United States v. Drayton,** *supra* note 21; Florida v. Bostick, *supra* note 21; **California v. Hodari D.,** *supra* note 7; INS v. Delgado, *supra* note 19; United States v. Mendenhall, *supra* note 7.

cured after a seizure may or may not be. Admissibility will turn on whether the officer had grounds for the seizure.[26] Grounds must exist at the time the officer makes the seizure; a seizure cannot be justified by what an officer learns afterwards. Consequently, courts are regularly called upon to decide whether the police became aware of facts that gave them grounds to make the seizure before or after they made it. This makes it imperative for officers to be able to recognize when they are on the verge of making a seizure and not cross this line until they have constitutional grounds to proceed.

## A. Submission to a Show of Legal Authority

The consensual aspects of an encounter vanish once a police officer's conduct conveys the message that the suspect is not free to leave. Such conduct is called a *show of legal authority*. A seizure based on submission to a show of legal authority can occur even though the suspect submits without protest. Below are two hypothetical police/suspect encounters. The first is voluntary; the second is a seizure.

> *Encounter 1.* A narcotics detective observes a nervous young man pull out a roll of $100 bills at a Miami airport ticket counter and pay cash for a one-way ticket to New York. Acting on a hunch that he is a drug courier, she approaches him, shows her badge, and says, "Do you mind if I ask you a few questions about the purpose of your travel and the contents of your attaché case?" The young man answers the questions without putting up a protest.[27]

Even though the detective identified herself as a narcotics agent before requesting an interview, this encounter is consensual because she asked permission. A request for permission conveys the message that the suspect is free to decline. Incriminating information procured in response to an approach like this is always admissible.

> *Encounter 2.* The detective, after observing the ticket purchase, approaches the young man, shows her badge, and says in a commanding voice: "I have a hunch you're a drug courier. Pick up your bags and follow me. I'm taking you to the security office for questioning." The young man does as he is told.[28]

The second interaction constitutes a seizure. The detective did not ask for the young man's cooperation, she ordered him to follow her. Because a reasonable person who is advised that he is under suspicion and told that he must

---

[26]  *See, e.g.*, Brown v. Illinois, *supra* note 11; Wong Sun v. United States, 371 U.S. 471, 83 S. Ct. 407, 9 L. Ed. 2d 441 (1963). The Fourth Amendment exclusionary rule is discussed in Chapter 4.

[27]  *See, e.g.*, **United States v. Drayton,** *supra* note 21 (Police did not "seize" bus passengers when, as part of a routine drug and weapons interdiction effort, they boarded a bus at a rest stop and began asking passengers at random for permission to search their luggage); Florida v. Bostick, *supra* note 21 (same).

[28]  These facts are taken from Florida v. Royer, *supra* note 21. The court held that a traveller was seized when detectives told him he was suspected of being a drug courier and had to accompany them to the airport security office for questioning.

accompany a police officer to another location does not feel free to refuse, the young man's submission resulted in a seizure.[29]

Application of the "free to leave" test is fact-specific. It requires consideration of all the circumstances surrounding an encounter, viewed from the perspective of a reasonable person in the suspect's position.[30] Courts have identified the following factors, among others, as relevant: the time and place of the encounter; the number of uniformed officers present; whether the officers speak in an authoritative tone of voice or use overbearing or threatening language; whether they touch the suspect, surround him, or obstruct his path of exit; whether they draw a weapon; whether they tell the suspect that he or she is suspected of a crime; and whether the suspect is alone with the police during the encounter or whether others are present.[31] The perception of not being free to leave must arise from the behavior of the police and not from the fact that the encounter takes place on a bus[32] or at another location where it would be inconvenient for the suspect to leave.[33] While an encounter can be voluntary without the suspect being told that he or she is free to leave,[34] it is wise to inform the suspect because this dispels any possible confusion over the matter.[35]

Below are three examples of seizures. In all three cases, the actions of the police convey the message that the suspect is not free to ignore their request and go about his or her business.

- An officer activates a siren and pursues the suspect's car. The suspect pulls over.[36]

- Police pound on the suspect's door, shouting "Open up! This is the police." The suspect opens the door.[37]

- Five police officers exit squad cars and surround the suspect, while one questions him. The suspect answers.[38]

---

[29]  *Id.*

[30]  Michigan v. Chesternut, 486 U.S. 567, 108 S. Ct. 1975, 100 L. Ed. 2d 565 (1988).

[31]  For a discussion of the factors relevant to free-to-leave analysis, *See, e.g.*, Florida v. Bostick, *supra* note 21, 501 U.S. at 434-435, 111 S. Ct. at 2386-2387; United States v. Watson, 423 U.S. 411, 424, 96 S. Ct. 820, 828, 46 L. Ed. 2d 598 (1976).

[32]  **United States v. Drayton,** *supra* note 21 (bus passenger not seized where officer spoke in non-threatening tone of voice, did not block passenger's path to exit, and said nothing that would lead passenger to believe that he was required to answer officer's question).

[33]  INS v. Delgado, *supra* note 19.

[34]  *See, e.g.*, **United States v. Drayton,** *supra* note 21 (no seizure, despite officer's failure to advise suspect of his right to refuse cooperation, where circumstances surrounding encounter indicated that consent was voluntary).

[35]  *Id.*

[36]  Stopping a moving vehicle by making a show of legal authority is always a seizure. *See* § 3.10 *infra.*

[37]  United States v. Jerez, 108 F.3d 684 (7th Cir. 1997) (seizure occurred when police banged on door, announced their presence, and ordered occupants to open it); United States v. Saari, 272 F.3d 804 (6th Cir. 2001) (seizure occurred when officers positioned themselves in front of the only exit from defendant's apartment with their guns drawn and knocked forcefully, announcing that they were the police and ordering defendant to come outside).

[38]  *See, e.g.*, United States v. Alarcon-Gonzalez, 73 F.3d 289 (10th Cir. 1996) (seizure occurred when suspect was surrounded on all sides by uniformed police officers); United States v. Packer, 15 F.3d 654 (7th Cir. 1994) (seizure occurred when two police officers parked their cars on either side of the suspect's vehicle and shined a "take down" light through his window).

The following interventions also involve seizures: terminating a suspect's movement by putting up barricades or roadblocks;[39] halting a suspect's flight by drawing a weapon or firing a warning shot;[40] surrounding a suspect on all sides;[41] stopping a suspect through an order to halt or freeze;[42] grabbing,[43] frisking,[44] or putting handcuffs on a suspect;[45] making a suspect get into a squad car; retaining possession of a suspect's car keys, driver's license, airline tickets, or other objects that prevent the suspect from leaving;[46] and psychologically immobilizing a suspect by telling him or her that he or she is suspected of a crime.[47] Whenever a suspect answers questions, produces identification, allows the police to search his or her possessions, pulls over to the shoulder of the road, or submits to any other infringement on his or her liberty in response to a show of legal authority, the suspect has been seized.

## B. Physical Restraint

Most people submit to a police officer's show of legal authority without putting up resistance.[48] When a suspect resists, he or she must be brought under physical control in order for the seizure to be complete.[49] Pursuing a suspect, shouting "you're under arrest," "stop in the name of the law," "halt," or "freeze" is not a seizure if the suspect continues to flee.[50] Until the suspect is captured, there is no seizure.

This principle was applied *California v. Hodari D.*,[51] in which a juvenile who was standing on a street corner ran when he saw an approaching unmarked police car. The officers got out of the car and pursued him on foot,

---

[39] Brower v. County of Inyo, 489 U.S. 593, 599, 109 S. Ct. 1378, 1382-83, 103 L. Ed. 2d 628 (1989) (suspect seized when his car crashed into an impassable tractor-trailer barricade deliberately placed across the highway by the police to capture him).

[40] United States v. Mendenhall, *see* note 7 (opinion of Stewart, J.) ("Examples of circumstances that might indicate a seizure, even where the person did not attempt to leave, would be the threatening presence of several officers, the display of a weapon by an officer, some physical touching of the person of the citizen, or the use of language or tone of voice indicating that compliance with the officer's request might be compelled.").

[41] *See* cases *supra* note 38.

[42] United States v. Mendenhall, *supra* note 7.

[43] Sibron v. State, 392 U.S. 40, 88 S. Ct. 1889, 20 L. Ed. 2d 917 (1968) (suspect seized when police officer grabbed him by the collar).

[44] **Terry v. Ohio,** *supra* note 8.

[45] United States v. Wilson, 2 F.2d 226 (7th Cir. 1993).

[46] *See, e.g.* Florida v. Royer, *supra* note 21 (airline traveler seized when officers took and retained his airline ticket, identification, and baggage claim check, and asked him to accompany them to the security office). *See also* United States v. Chan-Jimenez, 125 F.3d 1324 (10th Cir. 1997); United States v. Sanchez, 89 F.3d 715 (10th Cir. 1996).

[47] United States v. White, 890 F.2d 1413 (8th Cir. 1989) (suspect seized when an officer told him he had been stopped because he exhibited characteristics displayed by drug couriers).

[48] Albright v. Oliver, 510 U.S 266, 114 S. Ct. 807, 127 L. Ed. 2d 114 (1994) (suspect seized when he voluntarily surrendered to authorities after learning of outstanding warrant for his arrest).

[49] Brower v. County of Inyo, *supra* note 39 (suspect seized when his car crashed into a tractor-trailer barricade placed across the highway by police in order to capture him).

[50] **California v. Hodari D.,** *supra* note 7.

[51] *Id.*

yelling at him to stop. The youth discarded a rock of crack cocaine seconds before the officers tackled him. The Supreme Court held that, even though the officers lacked grounds for seizing the youth when they began the chase, the crack cocaine was not subject to suppression because the youth was not seized until he was captured. By then, he had already discarded the cocaine. The discarded cocaine was admissible because it was not the fruit of an unconstitutional seizure. *California v. Hodari D.* stands for the proposition that evidence discarded by a suspect while being pursued by the police is not subject to suppression, even if the police lack grounds for seizing the suspect when they start the chase.

Police, nevertheless, should not knowingly place themselves in a position in which they are forced to rely on *California v. Hodari D.* Chasing a suspect when the officer lacks grounds to capture him or her has a happy ending only if the suspect discards the contraband during the chase. This happens only by chance. If the suspect still has the contraband in his or her possession when he or she is seized, an illegal chase will end in an unconstitutional capture, the evidence will be suppressed, and the officer is likely to be sued. Police take this risk when they chase people without having constitutional grounds to capture them.

## § 3.6 —Fourth Amendment Grounds for a Lawful Seizure

The determination that the suspect was seized leads to the next stage of Fourth Amendment analysis. Did the police have constitutional grounds?

A police officer's constitutional authority to interfere with a suspect's liberty depends on the degree of suspicion concerning the suspect's guilt. Increasingly intrusive interventions are allowed as the degree of suspicion grows. Figure 3.6 shows the relationship between degrees of suspicion and responses permitted by the Constitution.

Figure 3.6
**Degrees of Suspicion and Response Permitted by the Constitution**

| Degree of Suspicion | Response Permitted by the Constitution |
|---|---|
| Hunch | Interactions with the suspect must be consensual |
| Reasonable suspicion that the suspect is involved in criminal activity | Suspect may be seized and detained for a brief investigation |
| Probable cause to believe that the suspect is guilty | Suspect may be arrested |
| Proof beyond a reasonable doubt | Suspect may be convicted of the crime and punished. |

There are four relevant degrees of suspicion. Figure 3.6 lists them in ascending order. A hunch is the lowest degree of suspicion. Each successively higher degree requires either more or stronger evidence of guilt. When police have nothing more than a raw hunch that the suspect is involved in criminal activity, they may investigate, but their encounter with the suspect must be consensual—the suspect may not be seized. When police have evidence that justifies a reasonable suspicion of criminal activity, they may conduct an investigatory detention. An **investigatory detention** is a limited seizure made for the purpose of investigating the circumstances that aroused the officer's reasonable suspicion. Investigatory detentions must be brief because evidence that forms the basis for a reasonable suspicion does not justify a prolonged detention. Probable cause is the next level of suspicion. Once the police know of enough facts to warrant a reasonable person in *believing*, not just *suspecting*, that a particular individual is guilty of a crime, they have probable cause to make an arrest. However, in order to obtain a conviction and deprive a person of his or her liberty over an extended period, there must be a higher degree of certainty yet. The government must present evidence that establishes guilt beyond a reasonable doubt.

## A. *Comparison of Reasonable Suspicion and Probable Cause*

Reasonable suspicion and probable cause both involve assessments of a suspect's probable guilt. Rational people make assessments based on the strength of the evidence. The evidence on which police officers act comes from a variety of sources. These sources include personal observation, physical evidence found at the crime scene, information supplied by other law enforcement agencies or contained in police records, and reports from citizens and informants.[52] Based on this pool of information, the police draw inferences and make assessments about the suspect's probable guilt. The probability increases as the information pointing to this conclusion mounts. The level of suspicion rises accordingly. Probable cause and reasonable suspicion represent different points on an evidentiary continuum, rather than discrete concepts.

## B. *Process Used to Evaluate the Existence of Reasonable Suspicion/Probable Cause*

Judges consider the same sources of information for reasonable suspicion and probable cause determinations. The only difference is the amount of evidence needed to satisfy the two standards. Judges also use this same evaluation process.[53] The process consists of identifying the facts and circumstances known to the officer at the time of the action and then weighing them to decide whether they were sufficient to satisfy the relevant standard.

---

[52] United States v. Cortez, 449 U.S. 411, 101 S. Ct. 690, 66 L. Ed. 2d 621 (1981).
[53] Ornelas v. United States, 517 U.S. 690, 116 S. Ct. 1657, 134 L. Ed. 2d 911 (1996).

Figure 3.7
**Procedure Used to Evaluate Whether Constitutional Grounds
Existed for the Action Taken**

> In order to determine whether the officer had constitutional grounds (i.e., reasonable suspicion/probable cause) for the action taken, courts:
>
> 1. identify all the facts and circumstances known to the officer at the time the action was taken,
> 2. weigh the facts in combination, and
> 3. evaluate their implications from the perspective of a trained police officer.

How do judges weigh facts to decide whether they are sufficient to satisfy the relevant standard? First, they view the facts and circumstances known to the officer in combination. In other words, they look at the whole picture. Second, they view them in the way that a trained police officer would view them. Even though each fact, standing by itself, may be innocent, when the facts are viewed in combination through the eyes of an experienced police officer, they may present an entirely different picture. Suppose an officer sees two men standing on a street corner, talking. This behavior is perfectly innocent. Suppose that the time is 1:00 in the morning. This behavior is still innocent. There is nothing particularly unusual about two men conversing at a street corner at 1:00 A.M. Now add one more fact. The site of the rendezvous is a neighborhood in which there have been numerous arrests for drug trafficking. Now there is something worth looking into.

This is where decisions get tough. A hunch does not justify a seizure; interactions with the suspect must remain voluntary. Reasonable suspicion, on the other hand, does justify a seizure; the officer may stop and detain the suspect for a brief investigation. Although different degrees of suspicion carry vastly different legal consequences, there are, unfortunately, no hard-edged boundaries between them. Consequently, deciding when the required level of suspicion exists often presents a difficult judgment call. On the facts just given, the Supreme Court ruled that the officer's observations justified a hunch, but not reasonable suspicion.[54] Why did the Supreme Court find that these facts justified only a hunch?

Reasonable suspicion requires that an officer observe behavior that is out of the ordinary in ways that are suggestive of criminal activity. In this case, the officer cannot point to anything unusual about the actions of these men that justifies suspecting them of anything. The facts that aroused the officer's suspicion were associated with the neighborhood and the time of day. Suspicion that develops solely because of the surrounding circumstances and would apply to any person who happened to be standing there is a hunch, not a reasonable suspicion. Had the officer seen one man take out a bundle of money and hand it to the other, the officer's suspicion would now be grounded on facts associated with the conduct of these men that would justify a reasonable suspicion that they had engaged in a drug transaction.

---

[54]    Brown v. Texas, 443 U.S. 47, 99 S. Ct. 2637, 61 L. Ed. 2d 357 (1979).

## C. Inferences and Assumptions from Known Facts and Circumstances

The officer's reasonable suspicion in the fact situation above derives from two elements: (1) the things the officer observed, and (2) the officer's assumptions and deductions about their meaning. The officer knew four things: (1) the neighborhood was frequented by drug users; (2) drug transactions normally take place in the early morning hours; (3) it was 1:00 A.M.; and (4) a large sum of money changed hands between these two men. From these facts, the officer drew an inference that the men might be engaged in a narcotics transaction.

When behavior is observed, inferences are made about its meaning. Three people on a street corner who see a man pushing a screaming and fighting seven-year-old into a car may see three different things. One may see a beleaguered father harassed by an ill-tempered child; the second an abusive father; and the third a kidnapper. All three witnessed the same sequence of events, but each drew a different inference. Where did their different inferences originate?

Sensory input is meaningless until the observer interprets it. When an event is observed, the information is processed through the lens of the observer's prior experience, and inferences and assumptions are added. These mental additions come from the observer's prior life experiences. The inferences and assumptions that are added bind the pieces of information together and shape their meaning to the observer. Interpretation of sensory input in light of prior experience is a normal part of the human mental process and explains why these three observers saw three different things.

Police officers are trained observers. They are sometimes able to see patterns that are suggestive of criminal activity in ordinary behavior that others without their experience would be unlikely to see. An untrained observer noticing a loose arm panel in the backseat of a car, for example, would be likely to interpret this as a sign of wear and tear. However, a trained narcotics detective who has searched many cars will see another possibility. To the detective, loose panels in the backseats of cars also raise the possibility that drugs may be secreted there.[55]

The Supreme Court has repeatedly emphasized that law enforcement officers are expected to rely on their prior experience in drawing inferences and using them to assess the probability of criminal activity.[56] In evaluating whether the officer had reasonable suspicion or probable cause, courts look at the facts the way a trained police officer would.[57] However, the ultimate deci-

---

[55]   Ornelas v. United States, *supra* note 53.
[56]   United States v. Arvizu, 534 U. S. 266, 122 S. Ct. 744, 151 L. Ed. 2d 740 (2002); Ornelas v. United States, *supra* note 53; United States v. Sokolow, 490 U.S. 1, 109 S. Ct. 1581, 104 L. Ed. 2d 1 (1989); Florida v. Royer, *supra* note 21; United States v. Cortez, *supra* note 52.
[57]   *See* cases *supra* note 56.

sion of whether the facts known to the officer, along with the inferences that arise from the officer's experience, are sufficient to satisfy the relevant standard, rests with the court. The officer's subjective belief that grounds exist has no bearing on this matter.[58]

## § 3.7  Investigatory Stops

Today, seizures are classified as *limited* or *full*. This has not always been the case. Prior to *Terry v. Ohio*,[59] the Fourth Amendment universe was black and white. No degree of suspicion was required for an officer to approach a suspect and attempt to strike up a voluntary investigative encounter, but as soon as the encounter ceased being voluntary, the suspect was seized. There was only one class of seizures and one constitutionally recognized justification. Whenever the police detained a suspect against his or her will, even momentarily, the seizure constituted an arrest for which probable cause was necessary.[60] The same level of suspicion was needed to stop a vehicle on the highway for a two-minute registration check as to take a suspect under formal arrest to the police station for booking and fingerprinting.

Probable cause is an exacting standard. To have probable cause for an arrest, the officer must possess information that would justify a reasonably cautious person in believing that the person arrested had committed a crime.[61] This standard hampered effective law enforcement in cases in which an officer's on-the-spot observations prompted a reasonable suspicion of criminal activity, but not probable cause for an arrest.

This predicament is common in law enforcement. A patrol officer on the beat receives a radio dispatch that a liquor store three blocks away has just been robbed. En route to the robbery scene, the officer sees a man running down the street with a bag in his hand, constantly looking back to see whether anyone is following him. The man's dress and running style indicate that he is not jogging for exercise. Although the officer has a sound basis for a reasonable suspicion, he does not have probable cause to make an arrest.

Before *Terry v. Ohio*, officers in this situation faced an impossible choice—let the person run by or make an unconstitutional arrest. The stakes grew higher after *Mapp v. Ohio*,[62] in which the Supreme Court held that evidence procured in violation of the Fourth Amendment is inadmissible. If the police detained this man for investigation and found a gun and a roll of money in his possession, the gun and the money were the product of an unconstitutional arrest, made without probable cause, and could not be used as evidence.

---

[58]   The constitutionally required levels of suspicion needed for investigatory stops and arrests are discussed in greater depth in §§ 3.8 and 3.13 *infra*.

[59]   **392 U.S. 1, 88 S. Ct. 1868, 20 L. Ed. 2d 889 (1968).**

[60]   Dunaway v. New York, 442 U.S. 200, 99 S. Ct. 2248, 60 L. Ed. 2d 824 (1979).

[61]   Carroll v. United States, 267 U.S. 132, 45 S. Ct. 280, 69 L. Ed. 543 (1925); Beck v. Ohio, 379 U.S. 89, 85 S. Ct. 223, 13 L. Ed. 2d 142 (1964).

[62]   **367 U.S. 643, 81 S. Ct. 1684, 6 L. Ed. 2d 1081 (1961).**

Whether the police should have the power to detain a citizen for investigation when they lacked probable cause to arrest him or her was hotly debated for many decades. In *Terry v. Ohio*,[63] decided in 1968, the Supreme Court spoke. The police would be entrusted with this power, but the scope and duration of the intrusion would be proportionately limited.

## A. Terry v. Ohio

The facts of *Terry v. Ohio*[64] are similar to thousands of other cases in which the police observe behavior that arouses a reasonable suspicion that criminal activity is afoot, but not probable cause for an arrest. While patrolling in downtown Cleveland, a police officer observed three men gazing through a store window, studying what was going on inside. The men walked a short distance, turned back, gazed through the store window again, and then assembled for a conference. They repeated this ritual five or six times. Suspecting them of casing the store in preparation for a robbery, the officer approached them, identified himself, and directed them to recite their names. When they mumbled something inaudible, the officer grabbed one of them (Terry), spun him around, and held him while patting down his exterior clothing. Feeling a pistol in the left breast pocket, the officer ordered Terry to remove his overcoat, reached in, and retrieved a .38-caliber revolver. Terry was indicted for carrying a concealed weapon. His attorney moved to suppress the revolver on the grounds that the Fourth Amendment does not allow police officers to conduct a weapons frisk unless they have probable cause for an arrest.

The issue in *Terry v. Ohio* centered on the constitutionality of the weapons frisk. However, because the constitutionality of the weapons frisk depended on the constitutionality of stopping Terry for questioning without probable cause to arrest him, the Supreme Court was forced to decide both questions.

Concerning the constitutionality of the stop, the Supreme Court ruled that the police may briefly detain a person for questioning when his or her conduct creates a reasonable suspicion that he or she is involved in criminal activity. The reasonable suspicion standard is less demanding than probable cause for an arrest. Having granted authority to detain on reasonable suspicion, the Supreme Court went on to rule that:

> When an officer is justified in believing that the individual whose suspicious behavior he is investigating at close range is armed and presently dangerous to the officer or to others, . . . the officer [has] the power to take necessary measures to determine whether the person is in fact carrying a weapon and to neutralize the threat of physical harm.

---

[63]  *Supra* note 59.
[64]  *Id.*

*Terry v. Ohio* established two rules that are of central importance to police officers. First, police officers may detain a person for investigation when his or her conduct arouses an officer's reasonable suspicion that he or she is involved in criminal activity. Second, an officer who is justified in detaining a person for investigation may conduct a protective weapons search (i.e., frisk) if, in addition, the officer has a reasonable suspicion that the detainee may be armed or dangerous. *Terry v. Ohio* did not establish the permissible scope and duration of an investigatory stop, however. This remained for later cases.

## B. *Purpose of a* Terry *Investigatory Stop*

The purpose of a *Terry* **stop** is to enable the police to investigate the circumstances that prompted the stop in order to confirm or dispel their suspicion within a relatively short period.[65] If the investigation confirms the suspicion, police now have probable cause for an arrest and can proceed to the next stage. However, if additional facts needed to establish probable cause are not forthcoming after a brief investigation, police must let the suspect go. The police may not detain suspects indefinitely on nothing more than reasonable suspicion of involvement in criminal activity.[66]

Figure 3.8
**Purpose of a *Terry* Stop**

> The purpose of a *Terry* stop is to enable the police to investigate the circumstances that prompted the stop in order to confirm or dispel their suspicion within a relatively short period.

## C. *Constitutional Requirements for Making a Lawful* Terry *Investigatory Stop*

There are three constitutional requirements for a lawful *Terry* stop. First, police must have reasonable suspicion to make the stop. Second, they must conduct the business of the stop as expeditiously as possible to avoid prolonging the period of involuntary detention. Finally, they must stay within the investigative boundaries allowed for *Terry* stops. These boundaries are narrower than those for an arrest. Failure to comply with any of these three requirements violates the Fourth Amendment.

---

[65]   Florida v. Royer, *supra* note 21; United States v. Brignoni-Ponce, 422 U.S. 873, 880, 95 S. Ct. 2574, 2580, 45 L. Ed. 2d 607 (1975).

[66]   Florida v. Royer, *supra* note 21, 460 U.S. at 709-710, 103 S. Ct. at 2646.

Figure 3.9
**Requirements for a Constitutional *Terry* Investigatory Stop**

There are three requirements for a lawful *Terry* stop. Police must:

1. have reasonable suspicion to make the stop;
2. conduct the business of the stop as expeditiously as possible to avoid pro-longing the period of involuntary detention;
3. stay within the investigative boundaries allowed for *Terry* stops.

## D. Location of a Terry Investigatory Stop

Although the detention in *Terry* involved a pedestrian standing on a street corner, investigatory stops are not limited to any particular geographic location. They may be made on highways, in airport terminals, on buses,[67] inside buildings, or anywhere a police officer observes facts that arouse his or her reasonable suspicion that criminal activity is afoot.[68] Homes, however, enjoy special protection under the Fourth Amendment.[69] Police may not make a non-consensual entry into a private residence to conduct a *Terry* investigation unless there is an urgent need for immediate action.[70]

## E. Suspected Criminal Activity for Which a Terry Investigatory Stop May Be Made

*Terry* stops are typically made in response to on-the-spot observations that lead an officer to reasonably believe that criminal activity is in progress. The observation of three men casing a store provided the impetus for the stop in *Terry v. Ohio*. However, the suspicion that prompts the stop can also relate to past criminal activity. An officer, for example, may come into contact with a person who matches the description of a suspect wanted by the police for a previous crime and need to detain the person while looking into this matter.[71] In short, *Terry* stops may be made whenever the police have a reasonable suspicion that the person detained has committed, is committing, or is about to commit a crime.

---

[67]    *See, e.g.,* **United States v. Drayton,** *supra* note 21; Florida v. Bostick, *supra* note 21.

[68]    Florida v. Royer, *supra* note 21; **Place v. United States, 462 U.S. 696, 103 S. Ct. 2637, 77 L. Ed. 2d 110 (1983)**; United States v. Mendenhall, *supra* note 7.

[69]    *See, e.g.,* Silverman v. United States, 365 U.S. 505, 81 S. Ct. 679, 5 L. Ed. 2d 734 (1961) ("At the very core [of the Fourth Amendment] stands the right of a man to retreat into his own home and there be free from unreasonable governmental intrusion."). Special Fourth Amendment protection for the sanctity of the home is covered in § 3.15 *infra*.

[70]    *See, e.g.,* Alto v. City of Chicago, 863 F. Supp. 658 (N.D. Ill. 1994) (hot pursuit of suspect fleeing from the scene of a Terry stop); Harbin v. City of Alexandria, 712 F. Supp. 67, 71-72 (E.D. Va. 1989) (same).

[71]    United States v. Hensley, 469 U.S. 221, 105 S. Ct. 675, 83 L. Ed. 2d 604 (1985).

## F. Relevance of the Officer's Intent

Police need not intend to make a *Terry* stop in order to be held responsible for making one. *Terry* stops are seizures. Whenever a person submits to an officer's show of legal authority or is physically restrained, the person is seized. If the seizure is brief and limited in scope, the court will characterize the encounter as a *Terry* stop and move on to the next question. Did the officer have the requisite degree of suspicion?

## § 3.8 —Reasonable Suspicion

### A. Definition of Reasonable Suspicion

The Supreme Court has provided the following test for reasonable suspicion:

> The officer must be able to point to specific and articulable facts which, taken together with rational inferences from those facts, provide a particularized and objective basis for suspecting the detainee of criminal activity.[72]

On an evidentiary spectrum (see Figure 3.6), reasonable suspicion lies somewhere between a hunch and probable cause for an arrest. In order to satisfy this standard, the officer must be capable of verbalizing and explaining with particularity why he or she suspected the detainee of involvement in criminal activity. Further, his or her reasons must be based on objective facts and circumstances that would warrant a reasonable police officer in reaching this conclusion. The Fourth Amendment does not allow suspects to be involuntarily detained on a mere hunch.[73] The difference between a hunch and reasonable suspicion is that reasonable suspicion must be based on objective facts related to the detainee's *behavior* that suggest involvement in criminal activity—*not* unexplainable, gut reactions.

The facts of *Terry v. Ohio*[74] provide a textbook illustration of the application of the reasonable suspicion standard. The officer in *Terry* watched three men repeatedly go through the ritual of peering into a store window, walking a short distance, conferring, turning back, and peering into the store window again. The implications that arise from this behavior are unmistakable. The grounds for the officer's suspicion in *Terry* can readily be put into words and explained. The Supreme Court held that a police officer may detain a person for investigation when "he observes *unusual conduct* which leads him reasonably to conclude in light of his experience that criminal activity may be afoot."

---

[72]    *See* authorities *supra* note 56.

[73]    *Id.*

[74]    *Supra* note 59.

Figure 3.10
**Grounds for Reasonable Suspicion of Involvement in Criminal Activity**

---

In order to satisfy the reasonable suspicion standard, the officer must possess an objective and particularized basis for suspecting the detainee of committing, having committed, or being about to commit a crime. To satisfy this standard, the officer must be able to:

1.  point to behavior of the detainee that is different from what one might ordinarily expect of an innocent person in the vicinity, and
2.  be able to explain why the detainee's behavior suggests the possibility of criminal activity.

---

In *Brown v. Texas*,[75] in contrast, the officers acted on a hunch. Two police officers cruising an area with a high incidence of drug trafficking observed Brown and another man walking away from one another in an alley. They got out of the patrol car, detained Brown, and demanded identification and an explanation for his presence. When he refused to comply, they frisked him. The Supreme Court held that the officers lacked reasonable suspicion for a stop and frisk because Brown's behavior—walking in a high-crime area, protesting an illegal detention, and refusing to provide identification—were as consistent with innocent conduct as with guilty conduct.

In order to have an objective basis for reasonable suspicion, police must be able to point to something specific about the detainee's *behavior* that caused them to associate it with criminal activity. It must be different from the behavior one would ordinarily expect of an innocent person in the vicinity.[76] In *Reid v. Georgia*,[77] a drug enforcement agent stopped a traveler in the Atlanta airport based on the fact that: (1) he arrived from a city that was a principal point of origin for cocaine sold elsewhere in the country; (2) in the early hours of the morning, when law enforcement activity tends to be lax; (3) with no luggage other than a shoulder bag; and (4) occasionally looked back over his shoulder as he walked toward the concourse. The Supreme Court ruled that the observed behaviors did not provide grounds for a reasonable suspicion that the individual was a drug courier because they "describe a very large category of presumably innocent travelers, who would be subject to virtually random seizures were the Court to conclude that as little foundation as there was in this case could justify a seizure."[78]

None of the following behaviors, standing alone, are enough to provide reasonable suspicion. Nevertheless, they are capable of adding background, color, and context, and may be considered as part of the totality of facts and circumstances in evaluating whether such suspicion is present.[79]

---

[75]   443 U.S. 47, 99 S. Ct. 2637, 61 L. Ed. 2d 357 (1979).

[76]   *Id.*

[77]   448 U.S. 438, 100 S. Ct. 2752, 65 L. Ed. 2d 890 (1980).

[78]   *Id.*

[79]   **Illinois v. Wardlow, 528 U.S. 119, 120 S. Ct. 673, 145 L. Ed. 2d 570 (2000)** (presence in an area with a high incidence of drug trafficking, coupled with sudden flight upon spotting a patrol car, provided reasonable suspicion for *Terry* stop).

1. The person is spotted in a high-crime area or an area with a high frequency of drug-related arrests.[80]
2. The person has a criminal record[81] or is in the company of others who have criminal records.[82]
3. The person attempts to avoid contact with the officer or flees.[83]
4. The person gives suspicious, inconsistent, or false answers to routine questions.[84]
5. The person is of a particular race or ethnicity. Race and ethnicity are unique. These factors may legitimately be considered *only* when they match the description of the offender or fit the facts of a known offense.[85]
6. The person appears abnormally nervous and fidgety or fails to make eye contact with the officer.[86]

## B. Rational Deductions and Inferences that Arise from an Officer's Prior Experience

Police officers have special expertise and training that sometimes enables them to spot criminal activity in conduct that would seem innocent to an untrained observer.[87] Recognizing this, courts examine the facts that prompted the stop through the eyes of a trained police officer. *Ornelas v. United States*[88] shows how a veteran narcotics detective's observations, combined with his prior experience in apprehending drug traffickers and a quick check of police records, created a reasonable suspicion justifying an investigatory stop. The officer, an experienced narcotics detective, observed a 1981 two-door Oldsmobile with a California license plate pull into a motel parking lot in downtown Milwaukee at 4:00 A.M. This incident attracted his attention because: (1) California was a "source state" for drugs; (2) older-model General Motors cars were popular with drug couriers; and (3) Milwaukee was an unlikely winter vacation spot for a California visitor. His suspicion aroused,

---

[80]   *Id.*

[81]   *See, e.g.*, United States v. Childs, 256 F.3d 559 (7th Cir. 2001) (though reasonable suspicion cannot be based solely on suspect's prior criminal record, criminal record may be considered in conjunction with other information in forming a reasonable suspicion); United States v. McRae, 81 F.3d 1528 (10th Cir. 1996) (criminal record, nervous behavior and implausible travel plans deemed sufficient to establish reasonable suspicion).

[82]   *See* cases *supra* note 81.

[83]   *See, e.g.*, United States v. Arvizu, *supra* note 56 (ignoring sighted police officer); **Illinois v. Wardlow**, *supra* note 79 (flight).

[84]   *See, e.g.*, United States v. Gonzales, 328 F.3d 755 (5th Cir. 2003); United States v. Valles, 292 F.3d 678 (10th Cir. 2002); United States v. Zubia-Melendez, 263 F.3d 1155 (10th Cir. 2001); United States v. Acuna Ramirez, 64 Fed. Appx. 683 (10th Cir. 2003).

[85]   *See, e.g.*, United States v. Waldon, 206 F.3d 597 (6th Cir. 2000); United States v. Ruiz, 961 F. Supp. 1524 (D. Utah 1997).

[86]   United States v. Arvizu, *supra* note 56; United States v. Linkous, 285 F.3d 716 (8th Cir. 2002).

[87]   *See, e.g.*, United States v. Arvizu, *supra* note 56; Ornelas v. United States, *supra* note 53; United States v. Sokolow, *supra* note 56; United States v. Brignoni-Ponce, *supra* note 65.

[88]   *Supra* note 53.

the detective radioed the registration number to his dispatcher, obtained the owner's name, and ran the name through the Narcotics and Dangerous Drugs Information System (NADDIS), a federal database of known and suspected drug traffickers. The NADDIS report identified the vehicle's owner as a heroin dealer from California. These facts, viewed in combination through the eyes of an experienced narcotics detective, provided a particularized and objective basis for suspecting the vehicle's owner of being in Milwaukee on drug business and detaining him for investigation.

Law enforcement agencies have developed an investigative tool called the "drug courier profile," which is used to identify candidates to approach for investigation on suspicion of transporting drugs. The drug courier profile consists of a list of behavioral characteristics commonly seen in persons engaged in drug trafficking. The characteristics, which have been distilled from the collective experience of law enforcement agencies, generally include the following: the suspect is generally between the ages of 20 and 30; travels to or from a major source city; has made numerous trips to or from this destination before; remains in the destination city only a short time; purchases an airline ticket shortly before the time for departure; uses a false name on the ticket; pays cash for the ticket; carries little or no luggage or, at most, a carry-on bag; travels in the early morning, when law enforcement is likely to be lax; appears nervous; walks hurriedly, constantly scanning the environment in a manner that suggests he or she is trying to detect and avoid contact with the police; makes a telephone call immediately after deplaning; uses public transportation; and gives a false explanation about the reason for the trip.[89]

The Supreme Court has reviewed several cases in which detainees were selected for investigatory stops because their observable characteristics matched some of the drug courier profile characteristics.[90] In *United States v. Sokolow*,[91] Sokolow was detained for investigation at Honolulu International Airport after a return trip from Miami, based on the officer's knowledge of the following facts: (1) Sokolow paid $2,100 for two round-trip tickets from a roll of $20 bills; (2) he traveled under a name that did not match his name in the telephone directory; (3) he flew from Honolulu to Miami, a source city for illicit drugs; (4) he stayed in Miami for only 48 hours, even though a round-trip flight from Honolulu to Miami takes 20 hours; (5) he appeared nervous during his trip; and (6) he checked none of his luggage. The Supreme Court ruled that, while none of these facts by themselves were indicative of wrongdoing, when viewed in combination through the eyes of an experienced narcotics officer, they provided a reasonable basis for suspecting Sokolow of being a drug courier.

---

[89]   4 Wayne R. LaFave, Search and Seizure: A Treatise on the Fourth Amendment § 9.4(E) (3d ed. 1996); Kimberly J. Winbush, *Propriety of Stop and Search By Law Enforcement Officers Based Solely on Drug Courier Profile*, 37 A.L.R. 5th 1 (1996).

[90]   United States v. Sokolow, *supra* note 56; Florida v. Royer, *supra* note 21.

[91]   *Supra* note 56.

The reader should not jump to the conclusion that exhibiting characteristics that match those found in the drug courier profile automatically provides grounds for an investigatory stop.[92] Whether it does or does not depends on whether the characteristics the officer has observed sufficiently distinguish the suspect's behavior from that of an ordinary traveler.[93] Some of the characteristics in the drug courier profile, like arriving from a source city late at night with only carry-on luggage and appearing nervous, are too widespread and common to form the basis for a reasonable suspicion of criminal activity.[94] The fact that Sokolow paid cash for his ticket, traveled under an assumed name, and stayed in Miami for a period suspiciously short as compared to the travel time were the characteristics that distinguished Sokolow's behavior from the behavior of an ordinary traveler. Reliance on drug courier profiles does not eliminate the need to observe atypical behavior that suggests involvement in criminal activity.

## C. Information Furnished by Members of the Public

Reports received from members of the public can vary greatly in reliability. They can be fabricated or stem from rumors as well as from firsthand knowledge. Consequently, police may not act on information the public supplies as the sole basis for a *Terry* stop unless they have reason to believe that it is reliable.[95] They are required to consider both the tipster's "credibility" and "basis of knowledge" in making this determination. A tip from a known informant who has given accurate leads in the past can stand on its own in supplying reasonable suspicion.[96] However, a proven track record is not always necessary. The fact that the informant is known to the police and the police can track him or her down and hold him or her accountable if the report is later shown to have been fabricated also lends credibility to a report.[97]

---

[92]   *See, e.g.,* Reid v. Georgia, *supra* note 77; State v. Young, 569 N.W.2d 84 (Wis. Ct. App. 1997).

[93]   *See, e.g.,* United States v. Barrett, 976 F. Supp. 1105 (N.D. Ohio 1997) (fact that bus passenger paid cash for ticket and that his call back number was to an answering machine with a woman's voice did not provide articulable grounds for a reasonable suspicion).

[94]   Reid v. Georgia, *supra* note 77.

[95]   Adams v. Williams, 407 U.S. 143, 92 S. Ct. 1921, 32 L. Ed. 2d 612 (1972); Alabama v. White, 496 U.S. 325, 110 S. Ct. 2412, 110 L. Ed. 2d 301 (1990); **Florida v. J.L., 529 U.S. 266, 120 S. Ct. 1375, 146 L. Ed. 2d 245 (2000).**

[96]   Adams v. Williams, *supra* note 95.

[97]   *Id.*

Figure 3.11
**Information Furnished by Members of the Public**

> The police may not act on information received from members of the public as the sole basis for a *Terry* stop unless they have reason to believe that the tip is reliable. Police should consider both the tipster's credibility and basis for knowledge in making this determination. Information received from: (1) known police informants and (2) citizens who identify themselves and report matters of which they have personal knowledge, can stand on it own in providing reasonable suspicion. Tips received from anonymous callers, in contrast, must be corroborated through independent police work.

Police are also required to consider the tipster's basis for knowledge. If a person calls the police and says, "This is Mary Smith. I live in Apartment 3 at 218 Brook Street. I have heard a rumor that Jack Green, the man who lives directly above me, is a dope peddler," the police must corroborate this information before acting on it because the caller has not demonstrated an adequate basis for knowledge of the facts reported. On the other hand, if the same person calls and reports, "This is Mary Smith. I live in Apartment 3 at 218 Brook Street. Two minutes ago, I saw a heavy-set man wearing a black leather jacket and green pants go upstairs and enter Apartment 13. I just heard gunfire, screaming, and saw this man run down the stairs, get into a 1996 white Chevrolet, and head west on Brook Street," the police may act on this information.

A recent Utah case illustrates application of the reasonable suspicion standard to reports received from citizens who identify themselves and report matters of which they have personal knowledge.[98] A fast-food restaurant worker noticed a customer drinking a can of beer while waiting for his order at a drive-through window. He immediately telephoned the police and reported what he saw, along with his own telephone number and location, a description of the vehicle's make, model, and license plate number, and the direction it turned when it left the restaurant. This information was dispatched over the police radio and the suspect was stopped a few blocks away. The stop was upheld even though the officer who made it knew nothing about the suspect's behavior beyond what the caller reported. When a caller identifies him or herself, gives a detailed account of a criminal activity he or she has observed, and provides a description sufficient to enable the police to identify the subject, the information can stand on its own in providing reasonable suspicion for a *Terry* stop.[99]

Anonymous tips, in contrast, have relatively low reliability because the tipster's credibility and basis for knowledge are largely unknown. It would be frightening to think that citizens could be detained for investigation because a

---

[98] City of St. George v. Carter, 945 P.2d 165 (Utah 1997).

[99] *See, e.g.,* United States v. Quarles, 330 F.3d 650 (4th Cir. 2003) (Information provided by 911 caller, to the effect that defendant was wanted by government on firearms charges, was sufficiently reliable to provide police with reasonable suspicion for a *Terry* stop, where caller gave enough information to be identified later, arranged for police to meet with him after the phone call, and gave specific information, which included a wealth of detail and indicated personal knowledge of the defendant); City of St. George v. Carter, *supra* note 98; State v. Florida, 692 So. 2d 216 (Fla. Dist. Ct. App. 1997); Jones v. State, 949 S.W.2d 509 (Tex. Ct. App. 1997).

prankster or someone who harbors a grudge makes an anonymous phone call to the police. Consequently, when a tip carries a low degree of reliability, police must corroborate it through independent police work before using it to make a *Terry* stop.[100] Corroboration was found in *Alabama v. White*,[101] where police received an anonymous tip that a woman named White would leave a particular apartment building in a described vehicle at a certain time, that she would be going to a particular motel, and that she would be in possession of cocaine. Officers immediately proceeded to the apartment building where they saw a woman get into the described vehicle at the designated time, and followed her as she proceeded along the most direct route to the motel. They stopped her just short of the motel, and arrested her after discovering drugs in her car. Though characterizing this as a close case, the Supreme Court concluded that this tip had been corroborated as reliable before the stop was made. The caller's ability to predict White's future behavior was the controlling consideration. The general public would have had no way of knowing that White would leave her apartment building at a certain time, get into a particular car, and drive to a particular motel. The uncanny accuracy and detail with which the caller predicted White's future movements demonstrated a special familiarity with her private affairs. Because only a small number of people would be likely to know this information, the police could infer that the caller was someone in whom White had confided and could regard the anonymous tip as being reliable.

An anonymous tip's reliability can also be corroborated through observations made at the scene of the stop. In one case,[102] an officer responding to a radio bulletin relaying an anonymous report that a black male had just fired a pistol at a particular location, immediately went to the location and observed a black male who matched the tipster's description, in a crouched position, peeking around the corner a short distance from the spot where the shot was allegedly fired. When the officer made eye contact with him, the man jerked back as if he was trying to hide. The court ruled that this behavior sufficiently corroborated the anonymous tip to furnish the basis for a *Terry* stop.

In *Florida v. J.L.*,[103] in contrast, there was no corroboration. Police received an anonymous tip that a young African American man in a plaid shirt, standing at a bus stop, was carrying a concealed gun. When police arrived at the bus stop, they saw three African American men; one was wearing a plaid shirt. Although the police had no reason, apart from the tip, to suspect the man wearing a plaid shirt of anything, they frisked him and found a gun. The Supreme Court ruled that an uncorroborated anonymous tip does not provide reasonable suspicion for a *Terry* stop. The anonymous caller's ability to provide an accurate description of the subject's appearance and present location provided nothing from which police could conclude that the caller was honest or that his assertion that the subject had a concealed gun was reliable. Anyone

---

[100] Alabama v. White, *supra* note 95; **Florida v. J.L.,** *supra* note 95.
[101] *Supra* note 95.
[102] United States v. Sims, 296 F.3d 284 (4th Cir. 2002).
[103] *Supra* note 95.

who observed the man standing on the street corner could just as well have placed this call. Additional information is necessary to verify the reliability of an anonymous tip and the police did not obtain any. The police, accordingly, lacked reasonable suspicion to perform a frisk. The Court refused to adopt a lower standard for frisks based on anonymous concealed weapons tips because this would enable pranksters and people harboring a grudge to set in motion intrusive police searches.

## D. Information Transmitted Through Official Law Enforcement Channels

Suppose Officer Blake receives a radio dispatch advising her to "be on the lookout for the driver of a dilapidated green Mazda van with license plate number G6207, believed to be carrying stolen property." The dispatcher follows the customary practice of not reporting the facts that support the requested action. Two minutes later, Officer Blake sees a green van that matches the dispatcher's description and pulls it over. Did Officer Blake have a reasonable suspicion to make the stop?

The answer is no, not personally, because Officer Blake was not informed of the underlying facts that supported the requested action and observed nothing suspicious at the scene. However, this does not mean that the stop was unconstitutional. The Supreme Court has ruled that an officer who makes an investigatory stop or arrest at the direction of another officer need not be informed of the factual basis for the requested action.[104] Requiring police bulletins to communicate the facts supporting a requested action would hamper prompt investigation of criminal activity. Officers who receive official communications must be able to act swiftly and do not have time to conduct a detailed investigation.

However, grounds for the action must exist somewhere. If the officer making the investigatory stop or arrest lacks grounds to support it, the constitutionality of the action will depend on whether the officer or agency requesting the action had such grounds.[105] When a radio dispatch or other communication is supported by adequate grounds, any authorized officer may implement the action without being advised of the factual foundation behind it. This principle was applied in *United States v. Hensley*,[106] in which officers from the Covington, Kentucky, police department stopped a person based on a teletyped communication from a neighboring police department stating that he was wanted in connection with an armed robbery, but disclosing no further details. The

---

[104] United States v. Hensley, 469 U.S. 221, 105 S. Ct. 675, 83 L. Ed. 2d 604 (1985) (holding that a police officer may, in detaining and questioning an individual, rely on a bulletin posted by another police department, as long as the department that posted the bulletin possessed reasonable suspicion to justify the stop). *See also* generally, 4 WAYNE R. LAFAVE, SEARCH AND SEIZURE: A TREATISE ON THE FOURTH AMENDMENT § 9.4(i), at 233-235 (1996).

[105] Whiteley v. Warden, 401 U.S. 560, 91 S. Ct. 1031, 28 L. Ed. 2d 306 (1971).

[106] *Supra* note 104.

Supreme Court, after determining that the department requesting the action had reasonable suspicion to make the stop, held that the stop was constitutional.

A somewhat related problem arises when information needed to support an action is divided between several officers engaged in a common investigation. Suppose that the Officer X, who requests an action, is aware of facts 1 and 2, and that Officer Y, who implements the action, learns of fact 3 when he arrives at the scene. Suppose further that neither officer's separate information will support the action, but that their combined information will. Is the action constitutional?

The Supreme Court has not yet addressed this question. Had Officer X shared facts 1 and 2 with Officer Y, this problem would not arise because Officer Y would now be in possession of all the facts needed to support the action. The problem arises only when the information is not shared. Lower courts are divided on whether the focus should be on the collective knowledge or the separate knowledge of officers acting together, in determining whether grounds existed. In some jurisdictions, X's knowledge will be imputed to Y, even if it is not shared, and the action will be treated as constitutional if X and Y's combined information is sufficient to support the action.[107] In other jurisdictions, uncommunicated information held by other officers working on an investigation will not be imputed to the acting officer.[108] The action will be treated as constitutional only if the officer directing the action (X) or the officer taking it (Y) individually knew of enough facts to support it.

## § 3.9  —Scope and Duration of Investigatory Stops

The authority of the police to interfere with a suspect's liberty is directly related to their degree of certainty about the suspect's guilt. Police are more restricted in what they can do during *Terry* stops than during arrests because stops are allowed on a lower degree of suspicion. Limitations on police authority are necessary to maintain the required alignment between the level of suspicion and degree of intrusiveness. When the police overstep the boundaries of a *Terry* stop, the stop automatically escalates into an arrest, resulting in a violation of the detainee's Fourth Amendment rights—unless the police have developed probable cause in the meantime.[109] This is why police must understand and stay within the boundaries allowed for *Terry* stops until they have probable cause for an arrest. This section explores those boundaries. However, before discussing the boundaries, the purpose of the stop needs to be explained.

---

[107]  *See, e.g.*, United States v. Edwards, 885 F.2d 377 (7th Cir. 1989) (imputing knowledge of one arresting officer to another when officers act together in making arrest); Johnson v. State, 660 So. 2d 648 (Fla. 1995) (imputing knowledge of an outstanding arrest warrant to an arresting officer who was unaware of its existence and otherwise lacked probable cause for the arrest); State v. Soukharith, 253 Neb. 310, 570 N.W.2d 344 (1997) (reasonable suspicion should be applied to the collective knowledge of officers engaged in a common investigation).

[108]  *See, e.g.*, United States v. Morgan, 997 F.2d 433 (8th Cir. 1993); United States v. Shareef, 100 F.3d 1491 (10th Cir. 1996); United States v. Conner, 948 F. Supp. 821 (N.D. Iowa 1996).

[109]  *See, e.g.*, Florida v. Royer, *supra* note 21.

## A. *Purpose of a* Terry *Stop*

The purpose of a *Terry* stop is to enable the police to investigate the underlying suspicion as quickly as possible. If the suspicion is confirmed, the police now have probable cause for an arrest and may move to the next stage. However, if police do not develop grounds for an arrest within a relatively short period, they must release the detainee, even though their investigation remains incomplete. The Fourth Amendment does not allow police to detain citizens for lengthy periods on a mere suspicion of criminal activity.

All activities during *Terry* stops must be directed toward one of two goals: (1) securing the officer's safety, when precautions are necessary; and (2) investigating the underlying suspicion as quickly as possible.

Figure 3.12
**Actions Authorized During a *Terry* Stop**

All police actions undertaken during a *Terry* stop must be directed at one of the following two purposes:

1. Securing the officer's safety, when precautions are necessary.
2. Investigating the underlying suspicion as quickly as possible.

## B. *Procedures Appropriate During* Terry *Stops*

Requesting identification and questioning are the two most common procedures performed during *Terry* stops. Because of the comparatively non-threatening nature of the typical encounter, *Miranda*[110] warnings are not required unless use of arrest-like force becomes necessary.[111] When arrest-like force becomes necessary, so do *Miranda* warnings.[112] Police should avoid premature administration of *Miranda* warnings during *Terry* stops because some courts view this as evidence that the encounter has escalated into an arrest, leading to a violation of the Fourth Amendment unless probable cause for arrest has already arisen.[113]

Although police may question *Terry* detainees about the suspected criminal activity, they may not treat their refusal to answer as grounds for arrest because this would violate the Fifth Amendment privilege against self-incrimination.[114] However, police may arrest detainees for refusing to dis-

---

[110] Miranda v. Arizona, 384 U.S. 436, 86 S. Ct. 1602, 16 L. Ed. 2d 694 (1966).

[111] Berkemer v. McCarty, 468 U.S. 420, 439-40, 104 S. Ct. 3138, 82 L. Ed. 2d 317 (1984) (stating that there is no right to *Miranda* warnings during a routine *Terry* stop).

[112] *See, e.g.*, United States v. Perdue, 8 F.3d 1455, 1466 (10th Cir. 1993) (*Miranda* warnings necessary where detainee was stopped on an isolated, rural road at gunpoint, ordered to lie face-down on the ground, and interrogated with guns still drawn.).

[113] *See, e.g.*, United States v. Obasa, 15 F.3d 603 (6th Cir. 1994); State v. Wilkenson, 118 Ohio Misc. 2d 10, 769 N.E.2d 430 (Ohio Com. Pl. 2001).

[114] Terry v. Ohio, *supra* note 59 (White, J. concurring); Kolender v. Lawson, 461 U.S. 352, 103 S. Ct. 1855, 1860, 75 L. Ed. 2d 903 (1983) (Brennan, J. concurring).

close their name if local statutes authorize this because a name is rarely self-incriminating.[115]

Police may pursue the following lines of inquiry in addition to questioning when they are relevant to furthering their investigation or to legitimate safety concerns:[116]

1. Communicate with others to verify the detainee's explanation.
2. Run a check of police records, automobile registration records, or other records.[117]
3. Transport the detainee a short distance to a nearby crime scene for a show-up identification.[118]
4. Fingerprint the detainee at scene of the stop.[119]
5. Bring a narcotics detection dog to the stop site to perform a sniff test of the detainee's luggage, vehicle, or other property.[120]
6. Request permission to conduct a search, administer a Breathalyzer test, or perform other procedures designed to further the investigation, keeping in mind that these procedures are allowed during *Terry* stops only when conducted with permission.[121]

Figure 3.13
**Investigative Activity Appropriate During *Terry* Stops**

After a lawful *Terry* stop, the police may always:

1. ask for identification, and
2. question the detainee about the circumstances that aroused their reasonable suspicion.

Police may, in addition, pursue the following lines of inquiry when they are relevant to furthering their investigation or to legitimate safety concerns:

3. Communicate with others to verify the suspect's explanation;
4. Run checks of police records, etc.;
5. Fingerprint the suspect at the stop location or ask the suspect to appear on his or her own at the police station;
6. Bring a drug detection dog to the stop location to perform a sniff test;
7. Transport the detainee a short distance to a fresh crime scene for a show-up identification; and
8. Ask for permission to search or perform another procedure designed to confirm or dispel the suspicion.

---

[115] Hiibel v. Sixth Judicial Dist. Court, ___ U.S. ___, 124 S. Ct. 2451, 159 L. Ed. 2d 292 (2004).

[116] United States v. Sharpe, 470 U.S. 675, 682, 105 S. Ct. 1568, 1573, 84 L. Ed. 2d 605 (1985).

[117] United States v. Hensley, *supra* note 104; United States v. Finke, 85 F.3d 1275 (7th Cir. 1996); United States v. Shareef, *supra* note 108.

[118] People v. Brown, 277 Ill. App. 3d 989, 661 N.E.2d 533 (Ill. Ct. App. 1996); People v. Rowe, 236 A.D.2d 637, 654 N.Y.S.2d 787 (1997).

[119] **Hayes v. Florida, 470 U.S. 811, 817, 105 S. Ct. 1643, 1647, 84 L. Ed. 2d 705 (1985).**

[120] **United States v. Place, 462 U.S. 696, 103 S. Ct. 2637, 77 L. Ed. 2d 110 (1983).**

[121] Schneckloth v. Bustamonte, 412 U.S. 218, 93 S. Ct. 2041, 36 L. Ed. 2d 854 (1973).

## C. Authority to Conduct Protective Weapons Searches

The authority to frisk detainees for weapons does not arise as an automatic incident of a *Terry* stop. This authority exists only when the police can point to facts and circumstances that justify a reasonable suspicion that the detainee is armed and dangerous.[122] Reasonable suspicion, for example, is present when the crime for which the stop is made is one for which the suspect is likely to be carrying a weapon[123] or reaches for something that could be a weapon.[124] Traditional "totality of circumstances" analysis is used to evaluate whether grounds exist for a protective weapons search.[125]

*Terry* searches have only one legitimate object—weapons. Officers may not search for nondangerous contraband during a *Terry* stop.[126] Searching for objects besides weapons is permitted only when the police have a search warrant, probable cause for an arrest, or obtain consent. When an officer's search goes beyond what is necessary to determine whether the suspect is armed, the search ceases to be valid under *Terry* and the fruits of the search are inadmissible.[127] If a weapon is found during a lawful *Terry* pat-down, the officer may remove it and hold on to it until the investigation is completed, at which time the officer must return the weapon to the detainee if his or her possession is lawful.[128]

---

[122] **Terry v. Ohio**, *supra* note 59.

[123] *See, e.g.*, **Terry v. Ohio**, *supra* note 59, 392 U.S. at 33, 88 S. Ct. 1868 (Harlan, J., concurring) (stating that when officer suspects a crime of violence, the same information that will support an investigatory stop will, without more, support a frisk); United States v. Jackson, 300 F.3d 740 (7th Cir. 2002) (reasonable suspicion that detainee is engaged in drug-related activity and knowledge that he had been armed in the past supplied grounds for frisk); United States v. Sinclair, 983 F.2d 598 (4th Cir. 1993) (frisk of suspected drug dealer proper, given they fact that they frequently carry weapons). *See also* 4 WAYNE R. LAFAVE, SEARCH AND SEIZURE: A TREATISE ON THE FOURTH AMENDMENT § 9.5 (3d ed. 1996) ("Lower courts have been inclined to view the right to frisk as being "automatic" whenever the suspect has been stopped upon the suspicion that he has committed, was committing, or was about to commit a type of crime for which the offender would likely be armed, whether the weapon would be used to actually commit the crime, to escape if the scheme went awry, or for protection against the victim or others involved. This includes such suspected offenses as robbery, burglary, rape, assault with weapons, homicide, and dealing in large quantities of narcotics.").

[124] *See, e.g.*, United States v. Mitchell, 951 F.2d 1291 (D.C. Cir. 1991) (frisk justified where officer observed defendant "moving both his hands under his coat in a manner suggesting that he was hiding a gun"); United States v. Flippin, 924 F.2d 163 (9th Cir. 1991) (frisk justified where defendant grabbed her makeup bag when officer turned his back); United States v. Lane, 909 F.2d 895 (6th Cir. 1990) (frisk justified where defendant "twice attempted to reach into his coat pocket").

[125] *See, e.g.*, United States v. Brown, 188 F.3d 860 (7th Cir. 1999) (officer had articulable grounds for reasonable suspicion that person subjected to traffic stop might be armed and dangerous, sufficient to justify his decision to conduct an initial pat-down search; circumstances included officer's knowledge of FBI surveillance of the vehicle as a possible part of a large-scale drug operation, the smell of marijuana smoke from the car, detainee's unusually nervous demeanor, including his failure to make eye contact, and his glancing back to the vehicle, where the other occupants rolled down the tinted windows during the traffic stop, and the fact that the stop occurred in a high-crime area where there was gang and drug activity and had been recent shootings); United States v. Menard, 95 F.3d 9 (8th Cir. 1996) (officer justified in conducting pat-down after arresting defendant's companion for gun-possession where encounter occurred on a relatively deserted highway in the early hours of the morning).

[126] **Terry v. Ohio**, *supra* note 59, 392 U.S. at 26, 88 S. Ct. at 1882.

[127] Minnesota v. Dickerson, 508 U.S. 366, 113 S. Ct. 2130, 124 L. Ed. 2d 334 (1993).

[128] **Terry v. Ohio**, *supra* note 59.

*Terry* searches have precisely defined boundaries. Officers are limited to patting down the suspect's outer clothing. Reaching inside the detainee's pockets or requiring the detainee to empty them is allowed only if the officer feels an object that might be a weapon and cannot make a conclusive determination through touch alone. After an object is ruled out as being a weapon, an officer may not continue touching it to try to figure out what it is. *Terry* search authority is exhausted once the officer is satisfied that the detainee is unarmed.[129]

While an officer may not search for objects other than weapons, if, while patting down the suspect's outer clothing, the officer feels an object that he or she immediately recognizes as contraband, the officer may seize it, even though he or she knows it is not a weapon. This rule is called the "plain feel" doctrine. The "plain feel" doctrine applies only when the identity of the object is immediately apparent to the officer from its shape and the way it feels. An officer may not seize an object that is unmistakably not a weapon, if determining its identity requires further manipulation. The reason for this fine line is that when the incriminating nature of an object is immediately apparent to the officer from its shape and the way it feels, seizing it does not invade the suspect's privacy beyond the degree that is already authorized. When making this determination requires further manipulation, an additional invasion of privacy is necessary and the additional invasion is not allowed.

The Supreme Court applied the "plain-feel" doctrine in *Minnesota v. Dickerson*,[130] in which an officer conducting a lawful pat-down search felt a lump inside the suspect's pocket that he knew was not a weapon. He continued squeezing and manipulating it until deciding it might be crack cocaine, at which point he removed it. The officer was right. However, the cocaine was inadmissible because it was discovered by the officer while overstepping the bounds of his *Terry* search authority. Once the officer determined that the lump was not a weapon, he lacked the authority to continue touching it.

### D. *Procedures Prohibited During* Terry *Stops*

Two procedures are never permitted during *Terry* stops—searching a detainee for anything other than a weapon and taking a detainee to the police station for *any* purpose.[131] Although both are a standard part of normal arrest routine, *Terry* stops are not arrests. They are limited seizures. Searching a detainee for evidence and taking him or her to the police station too closely resemble an arrest to be allowed on reasonable suspicion.

---

[129]   *Id.*

[130]   *Supra* note 127.

[131]   *See, e.g.*, Minnesota v. Dickerson, *supra* note 127 (police may not search *Terry* detainees for anything besides weapons); Kaupp v. Texas, 538 U.S. 626, 123 S. Ct. 1843, 155 L. Ed. 2d 814 (2002) (suspect was arrested within the meaning of the Fourth Amendment when he was awakened in his bedroom at three in the morning by three police officers, one of whom stated, "we need to go and talk," and was taken from his home in handcuffs, without shoes, in his underwear to the police station for questioning); **Hayes v. Florida,** *supra* note 119 (taking a suspect to the police station against his will for questioning is "sufficiently like arres[t] to invoke the traditional rule that arrests may constitutionally be made only on probable cause").

In addition to these specific restrictions, there is an overriding general limitation. Police must avoid any action that is more intrusive than necessary to safely accomplish the business of the stop. The Supreme Court has expressed this limitation by stating that officers must use the *least intrusive methods reasonably available* to verify or dispel the underlying suspicion within a relatively short period.[132] Forcible restraints are the most common violation of this restriction. Police may not draw weapons, use handcuffs, place *Terry* detainees in squad cars, or force them to lie prostrate on the ground unless they have legitimate concerns for their safety.[133] Using forcible restraints when they are not necessary transforms an investigative stop, valid on reasonable suspicion, into a de facto arrest that requires probable cause.[134]

Figure 3.14
**Actions Prohibited During *Terry* Stops**

The following actions are prohibited during *Terry* stops:

1. Taking the detainee to the police station.
2. Searching the detainee for anything other than a weapon.
3. Displaying weapons, using handcuffs, placing detainees in squad cars, etc. when these precautions are not necessary for safety.
4. Moving the detainee to a second location when the move is not necessary to further the investigation or for safety.
5. Investigating matters beyond the scope of the stop for which the officer lacks reasonable suspicion.

Investigatory stops should generally not extend beyond the place where they are first effected. Police are not allowed to move a *Terry* detainee to a second location unless the move is necessary to further their investigation[135] or for safety.[136] Police, for example, may take the detainee to a nearby crime scene for a show-up identification,[137] but not to a second location for fingerprinting

---

[132] Florida v. Royer, *supra* note 21.

[133] *See, e.g.*, Baker v. Monroe Township, 50 F.3d 1186 (3d Cir. 1995); United States v. Glenna, 878 F.2d 967 (7th Cir. 1989).

[134] Unwarranted use of coercive restraints resulted in an unconstitutional arrest in the following cases: United States v. Del Vizo, 918 F.2d 821 (9th Cir. 1990) (drawing weapon, handcuffing, and ordering detainee to lie prone); United States v. Richardson, 949 F.2d 851 (6th Cir. 1991) (locking detainee in the backseat of squad car while interrogating companion); United States. v. Ramires, 172 F. Supp. 2d 1208 (D. Neb. 2001) (handcuffing detainee and making him lie on the ground); United States v. Edwards, 67 F. Supp. 2d 1205 (D. Colo. 1999) (handcuffing detainee and placing him in backseat of squad car); State v. Wilkenson, *supra* note 113 (locking detainee in the backseat of squad car and administering "*Miranda*" warnings").

[135] *See* 4 WAYNE LAFAVE, SEARCH AND SEIZURE § 9.2(g) (3d ed. 1996).

[136] United States v. Pino, 855 F.2d 357 (6th Cir. 1988) (proper to take suspect, stopped on freeway off-ramp, to area underneath overpass to get out of rain and for safety); United States v. Richards, 500 F.2d 1025 (9th Cir. 1974) (proper to take detainee, stopped on airport runway, into terminal, where it was easier to talk and phone could be used).

[137] *See, e.g.*, United States v. Lewis, 486 A.2d 729, 734 (D.C. 1985); Commonwealth v. Williams, 422 Mass. 111, 661 N.E.2d 617, 623 (1996). *But see* State v. Solano, 187 Ariz. 512, 930 P.2d 1315 (Ariz. Ct. App. 1996) (transporting *Terry* detainee to crime scene for questioning converted the stop into an arrest when officer knew witnesses had already left).

or questioning because these procedures can be performed at the stop location.[138] The move, accordingly, is unnecessary. In *Florida v. Royer*,[139] the Supreme Court ruled that a *Terry* stop, lawful when made, was transformed into an unconstitutional arrest when the police required the detainee to accompany them from the airport concourse where he was stopped to the security office for questioning. This procedure was more intrusive than necessary because the detainee could have been questioned at the place where the stop took place.

The guiding principle for police to follow during *Terry* stops is *do nothing that is more intrusive than necessary to accomplish the purpose of the stop, having due regard for safety.*

## E. Permissible Duration of a Terry Stop

*Terry* stops must be brief. Most last only a few minutes. While the Supreme Court has declined to set a maximum time,[140] it has suggested that 90 minutes is generally too long,[141] unless the detainee's behavior is responsible for the delay.[142] However, any detention lasts too long if it lasts longer than necessary.[143] Once a stop is made, the officer must proceed expeditiously in conducting the investigation. A 30-minute detention is acceptable if this amount of time is necessary to complete the investigation,[144] whereas a 15-minute detention is too long if it is not.[145]

Unnecessary delay in completing the investigation carries a stiff penalty—the stop escalates into a de facto arrest. In *United States v. Place*,[146] police officers failed to arrange to have a narcotics detection dog present to perform a "sniff test," even though they knew several hours in advance that the detainee would be arriving at LaGuardia on a particular flight, carrying luggage believed to contain narcotics. The detainee was kept waiting until the narcotics detection dog arrived. The Supreme Court held that the detention violated the Fourth Amendment because the police prolonged it unnecessarily. The clear message is that police must conduct *Terry* investigations as expeditiously as possible. When officers know beforehand that a particular person will be stopped and that special arrangements will be needed to conduct the investigation, the arrangements must be made in advance.

---

[138]  **Hayes v. Florida**, *supra* note 119 (fingerprinting); State v. Solano, *supra* note 137 (questioning).

[139]  *Supra* note 21.

[140]  United States v. Sharpe, 470 U.S. 675, 105 S. Ct. 1568, 84 L. Ed. 2d 605 (1985).

[141]  This limitation stems from **United States v. Place, 462 U.S. 696, 103 S. Ct. 2637, 77 L. Ed. 2d 110 (1983)**. While the Court upheld a 16-hour border detention of a suspected drug smuggler in United States v. Montoya De Hernandez, 473 U.S. 531, 105 S. Ct. 3304, 87 L. Ed. 2d 381 (1985), border detentions occupy a special class. The Court emphasized that this ruling did not apply to domestic law enforcement.

[142]  United States v. Sharpe, *supra* note 140.

[143]  *Id.*

[144]  *Id.*

[145]  Munafo v. State, 105 Md. App. 662, 671, 660 A.2d 1068 (1995).

[146]  *Supra* note 141.

Investigative activity during *Terry* stops must be confined to the suspicion that justified it. Police may not prolong a suspect's involuntary detention to check out "hunches" about unrelated criminal activity.[147] Once they have concluded their investigation, they must either arrest the detainee or let him or her go. Continued detention violates the Fourth Amendment unless police acquire reasonable suspicion of unrelated criminal activity during the stop or the detainee consents.[148] Police, for example, may not detain a motorist stopped for a traffic violation to await the arrival of a drug detection dog, unless observations during the stop create reasonable suspicion that the motorist is transporting drugs or the motorist consents.[149]

A few states have enacted statutes limiting the duration of *Terry* stops. In Arkansas, for example, an officer must complete the business of the stop within 15 minutes. At the end of 15 minutes, officers must let the detainee go unless they have probable cause to arrest him or her.[150] Students should check the statutes of their state to determine whether there are time limits on *Terry* stops.

Figure 3.15
**Duration of a *Terry* Stop**

---

A *Terry* stop must be:

1. brief—90 minutes probably being the outer limit;
2. conducted efficiently so the period of involuntary detention lasts no longer than necessary;
3. confined to investigating the suspicion that prompted the stop, unless: (1) reasonable suspicion of unrelated criminal activity develops during the stop or (2) the detainee consents to an extension.

---

## § 3.10  Traffic and Vehicle Stops

### A. *Constitutional Authority to Stop Motorists*

Stopping a motorist is *always* a seizure, whether the officer's purpose is to make an arrest, issue a traffic citation, investigate a non-traffic offense, or simply to check the motorist's license and vehicle registration.[151] The requirements of the Fourth Amendment do not change when a pedestrian enters a motor vehicle. Police officers are held to the same Fourth Amendment standards. This

---

[147] United States v. Valadez, 267 F.3d 395 (5th Cir. 2001); United States v. Wood, 106 F.3d 942 (10th Cir. 1997); United States v. Restrepo, 890 F. Supp. 180 (E.D.N.Y. 1995).

[148] United States v. Sanchez-Valderuten, 11 F.3d 985 (10th Cir. 1993).

[149] Graham v. State, 119 Md. App. 444, 705 A.2d 82 (1997); Simmons v. State, 223 Ga. App. 781, 479 S.E.2d 123 (1996).

[150] ARK. CODE ANN. § 16-81-204(b) (15 minutes). *See also* GUAN CODE ANN. § 30.30 (15 minutes); NEV. REV. ST. § ST 171.123(4) (60 minutes).

[151] United States v. Martinez-Fuerte, 428 U.S. 543, 96 S. Ct. 3074, 49 L. Ed. 2d 1116 (1976); United States v. Brignoni-Ponce, *supra* note 65; Delaware v. Prouse, 440 U.S. 648, 99 S. Ct. 1391, 59 L. Ed. 2d 660 (1979).

means that they need probable cause to make a traffic arrest or issue a traffic citation and reasonable suspicion to stop a motorist for investigation.

Contrary to popular belief, police do not have the authority to stop motorists at random and demand to see their drivers' license and vehicle registration.[152] Police must have grounds to suspect a motorist of wrongdoing before the stop is made.[153] The Fourth Amendment demands individualized suspicion. Suspicion that some motorists are driving under the influence of alcohol or without a license, though undoubtedly correct, does not supply grounds for stopping a particular motorist. Police must have grounds to suspect the motorist who is stopped.

## B. Special Rules for Checkpoint Stops

However, an exception exists for stops made at a fixed checkpoint.[154] Individualized suspicion of wrongdoing plays no role in such stops. The Fourth Amendment, instead, imposes the following requirements.

First, checkpoint programs must serve a special need that goes beyond the general need to control crime.[155] Protecting the national borders against entry of illegal aliens;[156] promoting highway safety by checking drivers' licenses, vehicle registrations, and safety equipment;[157] performing sobriety checks;[158] and intercepting dangerous criminals traveling along a particular route[159] are examples of the types of special needs that justify a checkpoint. However, checkpoints may not be used to investigate whether motorists are guilty of ordinary criminal wrongdoing. For example, police may not use checkpoints to investigate whether vehicle occupants are committing drug crimes.[160] While

---

[152] Delaware v. Prouse, *supra* note 151.

[153] *See, e.g.*, United States v. Brignoni-Ponce, *supra* note 65 (random stops by border patrol officer to check for the presence of illegal aliens are unconstitutional).

[154] *See, e.g.*, Illinois v. Lister, 124 U.S. 885, 124 S. Ct. 885, 157 L. Ed. 2d 843 (2004); United States v. Martinez-Fuerte, *supra* note 151.

[155] Indianapolis v. Edmond, 531 U.S. 32, 121 S. Ct. 447, 148 L. Ed. 2d 333 (2000).

[156] United States v. Martinez-Fuerte, *supra* note 151.

[157] Delaware v. Prouse, *supra* note 151; Mullinax v. State, 327 Ark. 41, 938 S.W.2d 801 (1997); State v. Williams, 85 Wash. App. 271, 932 P.2d 665 (1997).

[158] Michigan Department of State Police v. Sitz, 496 U.S. 444, 450, 110 S. Ct. 2481, 2485, 110 L. Ed. 2d 412, 420 (1990).

[159] *See, e.g.*, United States v. O'Mara, 963 F.2d 1288 (9th Cir. 1992); United States v. Harper, 617 F.2d 35 (4th Cir. 1980); State v. Gascon, 119 Idaho 932, 812 P.2d 239 (1991). *See also* Illinois v. Lister, *supra* note 154 (upholding brief checkpoint stop at which highway police sought information about recent fatal hit-and-run accident on that highway).

[160] Indianapolis v. Edmond, *supra* note 155. In *Indianapolis v. Edmond*, the city of Indianapolis began operating a drug interdiction checkpoint. During the stop, a narcotics detection dog would be walked around the vehicle to sniff for the presence of drugs. The Supreme Court found this practice unconstitutional, stating that "[w]hen law enforcement authorities pursue . . . general crime control purposes at checkpoints such as here, . . . stops can only be justified by some quantum of individualized suspicion." The Court did not address whether drug interdiction operations may be performed at checkpoints established for some other valid purpose, such as performing sobriety checks. Nevertheless, it would be surprising if the Supreme Court found this practice constitutional. To do so would violate the rule that police may not prolong a motorist's involuntary detention to investigate matters that are unrelated to the purpose of the stop.

drug trafficking is a serious social problem, it does not pose the type of *immediate* threat to the public safety that justifies tying up traffic and inconveniencing motorists. Individualized suspicion of wrongdoing is necessary before a vehicle may be stopped to investigate whether the occupants are committing an ordinary crime.

Figure 3.16
**Fourth Amendment Requirements for Checkpoint Stops**

Checkpoint programs must comply with the following requirements in order to satisfy the Fourth Amendment. They must:

1.  further a special need beyond the normal need to control crime;
2.  be authorized by a supervisory-level police department official;
3.  be operated under systematic procedures that eliminate discretion in selecting which vehicles to stop; and
4.  be conducted so as to avoid unnecessary fear, danger, and inconvenience to motorists.

Second, the checkpoint must be properly authorized. The decision to conduct a checkpoint and the site selection must be made by supervisory-level officials, not by officers operating in the field.[161]

Third, checkpoints must be operated under standardized procedures that eliminate discretion in deciding which vehicles to stop.[162]

Finally, operations must be conducted so as to avoid unnecessary fear, danger, and inconvenience to motorists.[163] There must be signs warning motorists that they are approaching a checkpoint. The site must be illuminated and police control visible so that motorists will not be placed in fear that they are being ambushed. Routine interactions should rarely last longer than a few minutes. If reasonable suspicion is aroused, the motorist may be referred to a second location for a *Terry* investigation.[164] Otherwise, the motorist must be allowed to go on once routine interactions are over. Vehicles stopped at checkpoints may not be searched unless the motorist consents or police acquire probable cause for an arrest.[165]

---

[161]   *See, e.g.*, People v. Fullwiley, 710 N.E.2d 491 (Ill. Ct. App. 1999); State v. Downey, 945 S.W.2d 102 (Tenn. 1997); State v. Park, 810 P.2d 456 (Utah Ct. App. 1991).

[162]   *See, e.g.*, Brown v. Texas, *supra* note 54; People v. Fullwiley, *supra* note 161; State v. Manos, 516 S.E.2d 548 (Ga. Ct. App. 1999).

[163]   *See, e.g.*, United States v. Martinez-Fuerte, *supra* note 151; Mullinax v. State, 327 Ark. 41, 938 S.W.2d 801 (1997).

[164]   State v. Eggleston, 109 Ohio App. 3d 217, 671 N.E.2d 1325 (1996).

[165]   United States v. Ortiz, 422 U.S. 891, 95 S. Ct. 2585, 45 L. Ed. 2d 623 (1975).

## § 3.11 —Pretextual Traffic Stops

A **pretextual traffic stop** is a traffic stop made for an observed traffic violation in which the officer's real motive is to check out a hunch about unrelated criminal activity. Pretextual stops are widely used in drug interdiction. An officer who has a hunch that a motorist is transporting drugs, but lacks grounds for an investigatory stop, will follow the vehicle until the motorist commits a minor traffic violation and then pull the vehicle over for a chance to look inside the passenger compartment.

This practice acquired legitimacy in *Whren v. United States.*[166] Two plainclothes police officers patrolling a neighborhood known for drug traffic noticed a truck with a temporary license plate paused at a stop sign. When the officers headed toward the truck, the driver turned without signaling. The police followed the truck and pulled the driver over. Upon approaching the vehicle, they saw two plastic bags in the passenger compartment containing a substance that looked like crack cocaine. They seized the bags and arrested the occupants. The question before the Court was whether stopping a motorist for an observed traffic violation offends the Fourth Amendment if the officer's real reason is to check out a hunch about unrelated criminal activity. The Court ruled that the Fourth Amendment requires adequate grounds for a traffic stop, but if grounds exist, the officer's subjective motives for making the stop are irrelevant. Subjective motives play no role in Fourth Amendment analysis.

*Whren* significantly expanded the investigative authority of the police because virtually any motorist, if followed long enough, is likely to drive a mile or two above the speed limit or commit some other minor traffic infraction. Consequently, police now have the authority to stop motorists when they have reasonable suspicion that the motorist is engaged in criminal activity and also when they do not, if they observe the motorist commit a minor traffic violation.

Traffic stops have become a major tool in the war on drugs. This makes familiarity with the Fourth Amendment rules for conducting traffic stops a must for effective police work.

### A. Grounds for a Traffic Stop

Because a pretextual traffic stop involves a seizure, police must have grounds for the underlying stop. Otherwise evidence uncovered during the stop will be suppressed.[167] Most traffic stops are based on an observed traffic or equipment violation. An officer who observes a traffic or equipment violation, however minor, has probable cause to stop the vehicle. Vehicle stops may also be based on reasonable suspicion of a violation. However, a suspicion is

---

[166]   **517 U.S. 806, 116 S. Ct. 1769, 135 L. Ed. 2d 89 (1996).**
[167]   Wong Sun v. United States, 371 U.S. 471, 83 S. Ct. 407, 9 L. Ed. 2d 441 (1963).

not *reasonable* if it is based on a mistake of law, such as an erroneous belief that motorists must have a license plate in the front as well as the rear of their vehicle, and the resulting stop violates the Fourth Amendment.[168]

In a pretextual traffic stop, the traffic violation serves an important but limited function. It justifies stopping the motorist and provides an opportunity to look inside the passenger compartment. But this is all. The officer must stick to administering the traffic violation unless reasonable suspicion of unrelated criminal activity surfaces during the stop.

## B. Safety Precautions During Traffic Stops

A large percentage of police shootings occur during routine traffic stops.[169] The Fourth Amendment allows police officers to take precautions for their safety. After making a lawful traffic stop, they may take the following precautions as a matter of normal operating procedure: (1) order the motorist and passengers to step out of the vehicle and remain outside during the stop,[170] (2) ask them whether they have loaded guns or weapons in the vehicle,[171] (3) visually look inside the vehicle and shine a flashlight around the interior,[172] and (4) run a criminal records check.[173] These precautions may be taken as a matter of course without any degree of suspicion. Frisking the occupants and searching the passenger compartment for weapons, on the other hand, involve a greater intrusion on privacy and are not permitted unless police have reasonable suspicion that the occupants are armed and dangerous.[174]

Figure 3.17
**Precautions for Safety during Traffic Stops**

Officers who make a valid traffic stop may take the following precautions for their safety, as a matter of course: (1) order the motorist and passengers to remain outside of the vehicle, (2) ask them whether they have guns or weapons, (3) visually look inside the vehicle and shine a flashlight around the interior, and (4) run a criminal records check. Frisking the occupants and searching the passenger compartment for weapons require reasonable suspicion that the occupants may be armed and dangerous.

---

[168] *See, e.g.,* United States v. Twilley, 222 F.3d 1092 (9th Cir. 2000); United States v. Lopez-Soto, 205 F.3d 1101 (9th Cir. 2000); United States v. Mariscal, 285 F.3d 1127 (9th Cir. 2002).

[169] In 1999 alone, 6,048 officers were assaulted and eight were killed while enforcing traffic laws. *See* United States v. Holt, 264 F.3d 1215 (110th Cir. 2001) (citing Federal Bureau of Investigation, *Uniform Crime Reports: Law Enforcement Officers Killed and Assaulted* 82, 28 (1999)).

[170] Pennsylvania v. Mimms, 434 U.S. 106, 98 S. Ct. 330, 54 L. Ed. 2d 331 (1977) (driver); Maryland v. Wilson, 519 U.S. 408, 117 S. Ct. 882, 137 L. Ed. 2d 41 (1997) (passenger).

[171] United States v. Holt, 264 F.3d 1215, 1221 (10th Cir. 2001) (en banc).

[172] *Id.;* United States v. Beatty, 170 F.3d 811 (8th Cir. 1999); United States v. Weatherspoon, 82 F.3d 697 (6th Cir. 1996).

[173] United States v. Purcell, 236 F.3d 1274 (11th Cir. 2001) (upholding computer check for criminal history and inquiry whether motorist has weapons in vehicle as a reasonable precaution for officer's safety).

[174] For a discussion of a police officer's weapon search authority during a traffic stop, *see* § 4.10 *infra.*

## C. Scope and Duration of Traffic Stops

Traffic stops more closely resemble *Terry* stops than custodial arrests.[175] Like *Terry* stops, they must be brief, minimally intrusive, and last no longer than necessary to effect the purpose of the stop.[176] During the stop, an officer may request the driver's license, vehicle registration, and insurance papers, run a computer check on them, run a criminal records check, check for outstanding warrants, and ask a few general questions about the driver's destination and travel plans.[177] After this, the officer must complete the business of the stop and issue a citation or warning. Further involuntary detention beyond this point is unconstitutional unless reasonable suspicion of unrelated criminal activity arises during the stop.[178]

Whether police may inquire into drug activity during a routine traffic stop is an unsettled question.[179] The issue generally comes up as follows: An officer, while waiting for the results of a computer records check, asks the motorist whether he or she is transporting drugs and for permission to search the trunk. The motorist, taken off guard, consents. The search turns up drugs that the motorist seeks to suppress, claiming that his Fourth Amendment rights were violated when the officer questioned him about matters beyond the scope of the stop. A majority of courts would reject this argument on the theory that the Fourth Amendment is concerned with the duration of the stop, not with the questions asked during it, and that unrelated questions do not violate the Fourth Amendment unless they prolong the duration of the stop.[180] In these

---

[175] **Berkemer v. McCarty,** *supra* note 111 (noting similarity between a routine traffic stop and a *Terry* stop); United States v. Walker, 933 F.2d 812 (10th Cir. 1991); United States v. Wood, *supra* note 147; People v. Hood, 265 Ill. App. 3d 232, 202 Ill. Dec. 618, 638 N.E.2d 264 (1994).

[176] United States v. Holt, *supra* note 171; United States v. Jones, 234 F.3d 234 (5th Cir. 2000)

[177] United States v. Holt, *supra* note 171; United States v. Jones, *supra* note 176; United States v. Purcell, *supra* note 173; United States v. Linkous, 285 F.3d 716 (8th Cir. 2002); United States v. Mendoza-Carrillo, 107 F. Supp. 2d 1098 (D. S. D. 2000).

[178] *See, e.g.*, United States v. Jones, *supra* note 176 (though initial stop of defendants' vehicle was valid, their continued involuntary detention, after completion of computer check on drivers' licenses and vehicle rental papers, for three additional minutes, violated Fourth Amendment); United States v. West, 219 F.3d 1171, 1176 (10th Cir. 2000) (A driver must be permitted to proceed after a routine traffic stop if a license and registration check reveal no reason to detain the driver further unless the officer has reasonable suspicion of other crimes or the driver voluntarily consents to further questioning.").

[179] *See, e.g.*, United States v. Purcell, *supra* note 173 (Consent to search given while officer was waiting for completion of computer check was valid; questioning about subjects unrelated to the purpose of the stop does not violate the Fourth Amendment as long as it does not affect the duration of the stop); United States v. Shabazz, 993 F.2d 431 (5th Cir. 1993) (police questioning about matters unrelated to the purpose of the traffic stop does not violate the Fourth Amendment if it does not prolong the duration of the stop); United States v. Childs, 277 F.3d 947 (7th Cir. 2002) (where police stopped vehicle for cracked windshield and observed seatbelt violation by passenger, officer's question to passenger as to whether he was carrying marijuana did not turn reasonable detention into unreasonable detention where the question was asked while the driver was being processed and did not extend the duration of the stop). *But see* United States v. Jones, *supra* note 176 (holding that questions asked during traffic stop must be reasonably related in scope to the circumstances that justified the stop). For a general discussion of this topic, *see* Amy L. Vazquez, *Do You Have Any Drugs, Weapons, or Dead Bodies in Your Car?" What Questions Can a Police Officer Ask during a Traffic Stop?* 76 TUL. L. REV. 211 (2001).

[180] *See* authorities *supra* note 179.

jurisdictions, police are free to use the time spent waiting for the results of the computer check to inquire into drug activity because this is "dead time." However, a better time exists for conducting this inquiry.

### D. De-escalation from Traffic Stop into a Voluntary Investigative Encounter

Police are free to inquire into drug activity once the traffic stop has been brought to a conclusion. Just as consensual encounters can escalate into seizures, seizures can de-escalate into consensual encounters.[181] De-escalation can occur without the motorist being expressly told that he or she is free to leave. In *Ohio v. Robinette*,[182] an officer, while handing the motorist's license back, said: "One question before you get gone: are you carrying any illegal contraband in your car? Any weapons of any kind, drugs, anything like that?" When Robinette replied "no," the officer asked for and received permission to search his car. The search turned up narcotics, which Robinette sought to suppress on the grounds that his consent was the product of an illegal detention. The Supreme Court disagreed, holding that formal notice that the motorist is legally free to go is not required for a traffic stop to end and a voluntary investigative encounter to take place. However, two things are necessary.[183] The officer must: (1) conclude the business of the stop and return the motorist's license and registration because, without them, the motorist is not free to go, and (2) conduct post-stop interactions with the motorist in a nonauthoritarian and nonthreatening manner.[184]

---

[181]   *See, e.g.*, United States v. Werking, 915 F.2d 1404 (10th Cir. 1990) (investigative detention ended and encounter became consensual when police returned motorist's license and papers); United States v. Carrate, 122 F.3d 666 (8th Cir. 1997) (same); People v. Easley, 288 Ill. App. 3d 487, 680 N.E.2d 776 (1997) (same).

[182]   519 U.S. 33, 117 S. Ct. 417, 136 L. Ed. 2d 347 (1996). Post-traffic stop dialogues like the one in *Robinette* have become exceedingly common. The officer who conducted the *Robinette* stop testified in a separate case that, in one year alone, he had asked almost 800 motorists for permission to search their vehicle. *See* State v. Retherford, 93 Ohio App. 3d 586, 639 N.E.2d 498 (1994), discussed in LEWIS R. KATZ & PAUL C. GIANELLI, OHIO ARREST, SEARCH & SEIZURE § 16.7 (2002 ed.).

[183]   James A. Brown, *Miles of Asphalt and the Evolving Rule of Law: Are We There Yet? A Survey of Traffic Stops and Drug Interdiction in the Tenth Circuit*, 1-MAY J. KAN. B. A. 21, 22 (2002) ("[A] traffic stop on the highway that begins as a seizure may, in some circumstances, de-escalate into a consensual encounter when the officer returns his driver's license or other documentation. On the other hand, even if the officer returns the license or other documentation, the encounter may remain a detention if the officer communicates to the driver that he is not free to go by some show of authority, such as the displaying of a weapon, use of a commanding tone of voice, physical touching of the driver, or leaning on the vehicle.").

[184]   *See, e.g*, United States v. West, *supra* note 178 (A traffic stop may become a consensual encounter, requiring no reasonable suspicion, if the officer returns the license and registration and asks questions without further constraining the driver by an overbearing show of authority); United States v. Walker, *supra* note 175 (traffic stop cannot become consensual until motorist's license and papers are returned); United States v. Gregory, 79 F.3d 973 (10th Cir. 1996) (traffic stop had not yet ended when office leaned on motorist's car when he asked about drugs because a reasonable person would not feel free to leave while an officer is leaning on his car).

## E. Fourth Amendment Search Authority During Traffic Stops

The Fourth Amendment search authority of the police during traffic stops depends on whether they make an arrest or issue a traffic citation. Police have automatic authority to conduct a search whenever they make a lawful custodial arrest.[185] The crime for which the arrest is made does not matter. Police have Fourth Amendment authority to conduct a search whenever they make an arrest for any offense, including a minor, fine-only traffic violation.[186] That the arrest was made as a pretext to conduct a search does not render a search unreasonable under the Fourth Amendment.[187] Thus, an officer who has a hunch that a motorist is engaged in transporting drugs, may, without violating the Fourth Amendment, follow the motorist until the motorist commits a minor, fine-only traffic violation, arrest the motorist, and search the motorist and passenger compartment for drugs. However, police need to check state law before acting on this because states are free, as a matter of their own law, to impose greater restrictions than the Fourth Amendment requires. In some jurisdictions, police have no authority to make an arrest for a traffic violation that carries a fine only.

Issuance of a traffic citation, in contrast, carries no search authority. Police may not conduct a search incident to a traffic citation, even when they have probable cause to make an arrest, but decide to ticket the motorist instead.[188]

Figure 3.18
**Search Authority during a Traffic Stop**

Traffic arrests, even for minor, fine-only traffic violations, carry the authority to search the motorist and passenger compartment of the vehicle for drugs, weapons, and evidence of any crime. Traffic citations, in contrast, carry no search authority.

---

[185]  New York v. Belton, 453 U.S. 454, 101 S. Ct. 2860, 69 L. Ed. 2d 768 (1981) (officer who makes a law-ful custodial arrest of the occupant of an automobile may, as a contemporaneous incident of that arrest, search the passenger compartment of the automobile and all containers inside); **United States v. Robinson, 414 U.S. 218, 94 S. Ct. 467, 38 L. Ed. 2d 427 (1973)** (motorist's person may be searched after valid traffic arrest).

[186]  Atwater v. City of Lago Vista, 532 U.S. 318, 121 S. Ct. 1536, 149 L. Ed. 2d 549 (2001) (Fourth Amend-ment not violated by arrest and jailing of motorist for committing a minor, fine-only traffic violation, such as a seat-belt violation); McNair v. Coffey, 279 F.3d 463 (7th Cir. 2002) (arrest for failing to pay parking fine did not violate Fourth Amendment).

[187]  Arkansas v. Sullivan, 532 U.S. 769, 121 S. Ct. 1876, 149 L. Ed. 2d 994 (2001) (arrest for minor, fine-only traffic violation does not violate Fourth Amendment, even when arrest is made as a pretext to search for drugs).

[188]  Knowles v. Iowa, 525 U.S. 113, 119 S. Ct. 484, 142 L. Ed. 2d 492 (1998).

## F. Racial Targeting

Recent studies show that African American and Hispanic motorists are more likely to be targeted for pretextual traffic stops and treated differently during them than members of other demographic groups.[189] This problem, often referred to as *racial profiling*, has received considerable media attention and is the focus of numerous lawsuits.[190] The constitutional basis for attacking racial profiling is the Fourteenth Amendment equal protection clause, not the Fourth Amendment.[191]

---

[189] Blacks and Hispanics, for example, are more likely, after being stopped for a traffic violation, to be asked to step out of their vehicle, questioned about drugs, frisked, searched, or asked for consent to search than members of other demographic groups. *See, e.g.*, State v. Soto, 324 N.J. Super. 66, 734 A.2d 350 (1996) (statistical evidence that blacks were 4.85 times more likely than whites to be stopped for traffic violations established prima facie case of racially discriminatory enforcement); Interim Report of the State Police Review Team Regarding Allegations of Racial Profiling ("Interim Report"), released in April of 1999, http://www.state.nj.us/lps/intm_419.pdf (concluding that the problem of disparate treatment during traffic stops is real and not imagined). Although racial profiling is generally associated with enforcement of traffic laws, the problem of racially biased policing goes much deeper. *See, e.g.*, Anderson v. Corneyo, 284 F. Supp. 2d 1008 (N.D. Ill. 2003) (class action challenging disproportionate targeting of African American women for pat-down and strip searches by customs officials following their arrival on international flights); Hardy v. Emery, 241 F. Supp. 2d 38 (D. Me. 2003) (complaint by black participants in apartment complex altercation with whites, alleging that officer called to the scene chose to credit the accounts of the white participants and repeatedly ignored their attempts to get him to listen to their version of events; used the term "nigger bitch" and other foul language when interacting with them; allowed the white participants to employ provocative language without arresting them while arresting black participants for similar language; and used excessive force on them, stated claim for denial of equal protection); Carrasca v. Pomeroy, 313 F. 3d 823 (3d Cir. 2002) (complaint that officer singled out plaintiffs who were Hispanic, rather than other similarly situated non-Hispanics, for enforcement of the swimming hours regulations, stated claim for selective enforcement); Roman v. City of Reading, 257 F. Supp. 2d 799 (E.D. Pa. 2003) (allegation that police officers refused to investigate shooting incident due to fact that victim was African American stated claim for denial of equal protection.) Racially biased policing is covered in greater detail in § 10.16 *infra*. A wealth of literature can be found on the Department of Justice (http://www.usdoj.gov), the U.S. Commission on Civil Rights (http://www.usccr.gov), the American Civil Liberties Union (http://www.aclu.org); and the Police Executive Research Forum (http://policeforum.mn-8.net) web sites. *See, e.g.*, U.S. Dept. J., *A Resource Guide on Racial Profiling Data Collection Systems: Promising Practices and Lessons Learned*, http://www.ncjrs.org/pdffiles1/bja/184768.pdf; David A. Harris, *Driving While Black: Racial Profiling on Our Nation's Highways*, http:// www.aclu.org/profiling/report/index.html; U.S. Dept. J., *Civil Rights, Guidance Regarding the Use of Race by Federal Law Enforcement Agencies* (June, 2003), http://www.usdoj.gov/crt/split/documents/guidance_on_race.htm; U.S. Dept. J., Fact Sheet on Racial Profiling (June 17, 2003), http://www.usdoj.gov/opa/pr/2003/June/racial_profiling_fact_sheet.pdf; Lorie Fridell et al., *Racially Biased Policing: A Principled Response* (Police Executive Research Forum, 2001), http://policeforum.mn-8.net; Interim Report of the State Police Review Team Regarding Allegations of Racial Profiling ("Interim Report"), released in April of 1999, http://www.state.nj.us/lps/intm_419.pdf.

[190] *See, e.g.*, State v. Soto, *supra* note 189; Farm Labor Org. Comm. v. Ohio State Highway Patrol, 308 F.3d 523 (6th Cir. 2002); Chavez v. Illinois State Police, 251 F.3d 612 (7th Cir. 2001); Bingham v. City of Manhattan Beach, 341 F.3d 939 (9th Cir. 2003); Marshall v. Columbia Lea Regional Hosp., 345 F.3d 1157 (10th Cir. 2003); White v. Williams, 179 F. Supp. 2d 405 (D. N.J. 2002).

[191] **Whren v. United States**, *supra* note 166 (holding that, while purposeful racial discrimination can violate the equal protection clause, it cannot render a search or seizure unreasonable under the Fourth Amendment).

Although racial profiling suits have enjoyed some success in the courts, litigation is not an effective technique for addressing this problem. The public perception that police engage in racially biased policing leads to hostility, mistrust, and resentment, and drives a wedge into the relationship between the police and the minority community.[192] Professor David A. Harris writes:

> Pretextual traffic stops aggravate years of accumulated feelings of injustice, resulting in deepening distrust and cynicism by African-Americans about police and the entire criminal justice system. But the problem goes deeper. If upstanding citizens are treated like criminals by the police, they will not trust those same officers as investigators of crimes or as witnesses in court.[193]

Racial profiling is an unfair practice that must end. More than 20 states and hundreds of local governments across the nation have enacted legislation condemning this practice.[194] The typical statute contains a policy statement declaring racial profiling illegal,[195] provides for the collection and analysis of data on traffic stops to determine the nature and extent of the problem and to monitor compliance,[196] establishes training programs to teach police how to avoid racial profiling,[197] and puts mechanisms in place to strengthen police accountability.[198]

---

[192]   *See, e.g.*, MINN. ST. ANN. § 626.8471 (1) ("The legislature finds that the reality or public perception of racial profiling alienates people from police, hinders community policing efforts, and causes law enforcement to lose credibility and trust among the people law enforcement is sworn to protect and serve."); U.S. Dept. J., *A Resource Guide on Racial Profiling Data Collection Systems: Promising Practices and Lessons Learned, supra* note 189 at 3 ("When law enforcement practices are perceived to be biased, unfair, or disrespectful, communities of color are less willing to trust and confide in police officers, report crimes, participate in problem-solving activities, be witnesses at trials, or serve on juries.").

[193]   Harris, *The Stories, the Statistics, and the Law: Why "Driving While Black" Matters*, 84 MN. L. REV. 265, 268-269 (1999). The Police Executive Research Forum cautions: "There are grave dangers in neglecting to take the issue of biased policing seriously and respond with effective initiatives. Societal division on racial grounds will leach the vigor from quality-of-life initatives, regardless of how well-intended and well-funded. If a substantial part of the population comes to view the justice system as unjust, they are less likely to be cooperative with police, withholding participation in community problem-solving and demonstrating their disaffection in a variety of ways. The loss of moral authority could do permanent injury to the legal system, and deprive all of society of the protection of the law." Lorie Fridell et al., *Racially Biased Policing: A Principled Response, supra* note 189, at 6.

[194]   See, e.g, Arizona, (ARIZ. STAT. § 12-12-1401 *et seq.*); California (WEST'S ANN. CAL. PENAL CODE § 13519.4); Colorado (COLO. REV. STAT. § 24-31-309); Connecticut (CONN. GEN. STAT. § 54-11); Kentucky (K.R.S. § 15A.19); Minnesota (MINN. STAT. ANN. § 626.8471); Missouri (MO. REV. STAT. § 590.650); Nebraska (NEB. REV. STAT. § 20-501 *et seq.*); Nevada (WEST'S NEV. REV. ST. § 289.820); Rhode Island (R.I. STAT. § 31-21.1-2 *et seq.*); West Virginia (W. VA. CODE § 30-29-19).

[195]   *See* authorities *supra* note 194.

[196]   *See, e.g.*, Colorado (COLO. REV. STAT. § 42-4-115); Louisiana (LSA-R.S. 32:398.10); Maryland (MD. CODE. ANN., TRANSP. § 25-113); Minnesota (MINN. STAT. ANN. § 626.8471(5)), Nebraska (NEB. REV. STAT. § 20-504); North Carolina (N.C. GEN. STAT. § 114-10); Tennessee (TENN. CODE. ANN. § 38-1-402); Texas (VERNON'S ANN. TEXAS CODE CRIM PRO. ARTS. 2.131, 2132 (b)); Washington (WASH. REV. CODE ANN. § 43.43.480(1)).

[197]   *See, e.g.*, California (WEST'S ANN. CAL. PENAL CODE § 13519.4); Missouri (MO. REV. STAT. § 590.050); Minnesota Oklahoma (OKLA. STAT. tit 22, § 34.5); Texas (TEX. OCC. CODE ANN. § 1701.253); Washington (WASH. REV. CODE ANN. § 43.43.490).

[198]   *See, e.g.*, Minnesota (MINN. STAT. ANN. § 626.9517 (providing for installation of automatically activated video cameras on all police vehicles to record traffic stops and monitor compliance with anti-racial profiling policies); Oklahoma (OKLA. STAT. tit. 22, § 34.4 (2002) (authorizing victims of racial profiling to file a complaint with Human Rights Commission or district attorney for the county in which the stop or arrest occurred).

Police departments must take decisive action to address this problem. Providing police officers with concrete guidance as to when they may take a person's race, ethnicity, or national origin into account in making routine enforcement decisions (i.e., decisions on whom to stop, detain, question, frisk, search, request permission to search, etc.) is a starting point. Racial profiling rests on the erroneous assumption that African Americans and Hispanics are more likely than whites to be involved in drug activity. This assumption becomes a self-fulfilling prophecy, as the following passage explains:

> Because police will look for drug crimes among black drivers, they will find it disproportionately among black drivers. More black drivers will be arrested, prosecuted, convicted, and jailed, thereby reinforcing the idea that blacks constitute the majority of drug offenders. This will provide a continuing motive and justification for stopping more black drivers as a rational way of using resources to catch the most criminals. At the same time, because police will focus on black drivers, white drivers will receive less attention, and the drug dealers and possessors among them will be apprehended in proportionately smaller numbers than their presence in the population would predict.[199]

Police departments must end this vicious cycle by making it clear that generalized racial and ethnic stereotypes have no place in routine law enforcement. The Department of Justice, Police Execution Research Forum, and other highly respected organizations have arrived at the same conclusion—that race and ethnicity should not be considered, to any extent, in making policing decisions unless these factors are part of a specific suspect description.[200] Accordingly, police departments should adopt the following policy as part of their standard operating procedure:

> Officers may not consider race or ethnicity to *any* degree in selecting individuals to subject to routine investigatory activities or in making other law enforcement decisions unless they are acting on trustworthy, locally relevant information that links a person or persons of particular race or ethnicity to a particular crime or other unlawful incident. This prohibition applies even where the use of race or ethnicity might otherwise be lawful.

This guideline allows officers to consider race or ethnicity in making enforcement decisions only when they have specific, trustworthy information to be on the lookout for a specific individual or individuals who are connected to a particular unlawful incident and who are identified in part by race or ethnicity.

---

[199] Harris, *The Stories, the Statistics, and the Law: Why "Driving While Black" Matters*, 84 MN. L. R. 265, 297 (1999).

[200] *See* U.S. Dept. J., *Civil Rights, Guidance Regarding the Use of Race by Federal Law Enforcement Agencies* (June, 2003), *supra* note 189; Lorie Fridell *et al.*, *Racially Biased Policing: A Principled Response*, *supra* note 189; New Jersey Attorney General's "Interim Report," *supra* note 189.

## § 3.12 Requirements for a Constitutional Arrest

### A. Arrest Defined

Prior to *Terry v. Ohio*, defining "arrest" was simple. "Arrest" and "seizure" were one and the same. Whenever the police detained a person against his or her will, even momentarily, the person was seized, the encounter was an arrest, and probable cause was necessary.[201] *Terry v. Ohio* carved out an exception to the probable cause requirement for brief, limited seizures conducted for investigation.

One consequence of *Terry* is that defining an arrest has ceased to be simple. There are now two kinds of arrests—formal and de facto. Formal arrests are intentional. The officer intends to make an arrest, generally announces this intent to the suspect, and the suspect either submits or is brought under the officer's control. Thus, a formal arrest has two ingredients—an intent to make an arrest combined with a seizure. Merely saying "you're under arrest," without bringing the suspect under control, is insufficient to constitute an arrest because the suspect has not yet been seized.[202]

De facto arrests, in contrast, are unintentional. They arise by operation of law when police exceed the boundaries allowed for a *Terry* stop. These boundaries were explored in § 3.9. When a stop lasts too long or is too intrusive to be justified on reasonable suspicion, the seizure automatically escalates into an arrest and probable cause becomes necessary.[203]

### B. Probable Cause for an Arrest

The Fourth Amendment requires probable cause for an arrest. Probable cause is a commonsense concept that deals with the probability that the person to be arrested is guilty of a crime.[204] An officer has probable cause to make an arrest when he or she is aware of facts and circumstances that create a fair probability of guilt.[205]

---

[201] Dunaway v. New York, 442 U.S. 200, 99 S. Ct. 2248, 60 L. Ed. 2d 824 (1979).

[202] *See* § 3.5(B) *supra*.

[203] *See* § 3.9 *supra*.

[204] United States v. Cortez, *supra* note 10; Maryland v. Pringle, 540 U.S. 366, 124 S. Ct. 795, 157 L. Ed. 2d 769 (2003).

[205] Illinois v. Gates, 462 U.S. 213, 103 S. Ct. 2317, 76 L. Ed. 2d 527 (1983); Draper v. United States, 358 U.S. 307, 79 S. Ct. 329, 3 L. Ed. 2d 327 (1959); Brinegar v. United States, 338 U.S. 160, 69 S. Ct. 1302, 93 L. Ed. 1879 (1949); Maryland v. Pringle, *supra* note 204.

## C. Procedures for Determining Whether Probable Cause Exists for an Arrest

With investigatory stops, police officers must decide on the spot whether they have enough evidence to justify this action. With arrests, they have an alternative. They can apply for an arrest warrant and have a magistrate decide this question for them. An officer applies for an arrest warrant by preparing a sworn **affidavit** detailing the results of the investigation. The magistrate reviews the officer's affidavit and determines whether the facts set forth establish probable cause for an arrest. Although the same probable cause standard applies whether the arrest is made with or without a warrant, there are important reasons for having a magistrate decide this question when time permits. Before discussing them, we will briefly outline when the Fourth Amendment requires a warrant.

## D. Fourth Amendment Requirement of an Arrest Warrant

The first clause of the Fourth Amendment guarantees citizens the right to be free from unreasonable searches and seizures; the second clause states that "no Warrant shall issue, but upon probable cause." It is unclear whether the Framers intended these clauses to be connected, making arrests unreasonable unless carried out under a warrant issued upon probable cause. However, the Supreme Court has read them separately.[206] Under settled interpretation, an arrest warrant is necessary only when an arrest is made *inside a private dwelling*.[207] In all other cases, an arrest warrant is optional, even when an officer has time to obtain one.[208]

## E. Advantages of an Arrest Warrant

There are several reasons police officers should develop the habit of applying for arrest warrants whenever they have time, even when a warrant is not necessary. First, because magistrates are neutral and have more experience in making probable cause determinations, putting this decision in a magistrate's hands reduces the risk of mistakes. Because of this, the Supreme Court has expressed a strong preference for actions taken under a warrant.[209]

Second, a magistrate's determination of probable cause carries a presumption of correctness.[210] As a result of this presumption, a magistrate's

---

[206]   United States v. Watson, 423 U.S. 411, 96 S. Ct. 820, 46 L. Ed. 2d 598 (1976).

[207]   Kirk v. Louisiana, 122 S. Ct. 2458, 153 L. Ed. 2d 599 (2002); Payton v. New York, 445 U.S. 573, 100 S. Ct. 1371, 63 L. Ed. 2d 639 (1980). This restriction is discussed in § 3.15 *infra*.

[208]   United States v. Watson, *supra* note 206. However, state statutes occasionally impose more stringent warrant requirements. *See infra* §§ 3.17-3.18.

[209]   Illinois v. Gates, *supra* note 205.

[210]   *Id.*

determination will be set aside only if the officer who applied for the warrant: (1) deliberately or recklessly included false information in the affidavit,[211] or (2) failed to provide enough facts in the affidavit to enable the magistrate to make an independent determination of probable cause.[212] Both of these deficiencies are within the officer's control. If the officer's affidavit truthfully recounts the facts, and recounts enough facts to enable a magistrate to make an independent decision, the magistrate's decision that probable cause exists for the arrest is final and cannot be challenged.

The warrant arms the officer with an "insurance policy." The "insurance policy" is important for two reasons. First, because the admissibility of evidence seized during an arrest turns on the constitutionality of the arrest itself, admissibility has now been guaranteed. A police officer's determination of probable cause carries no presumption of correctness. If the constitutionality of the arrest is later challenged, the judge will make an independent determination. If probable cause is found to be lacking, evidence seized during the arrest will be suppressed.

Finally, an arrest warrant protects an officer against civil liability.[213] An officer who makes an arrest under a facially valid warrant cannot be sued for making an unconstitutional arrest unless the officer: (1) deliberately or recklessly falsified information in his or her affidavit,[214] or (2) prepared an affidavit that fell so far short of establishing probable cause that the decision to apply for a warrant reflected gross incompetence.[215]

What are the drawbacks of applying for an arrest warrant, assuming there is time to obtain one? There are none. If the magistrate refuses to issue a warrant, this does not mean that the officer's investigative efforts have been for naught. A magistrate's refusal to issue a warrant means that the officer needs to gather more evidence to satisfy the probable cause standard. An officer is fortunate to learn this beforehand because the officer has been spared the consequences of making an unconstitutional arrest. Consequently, police officers have nothing to lose and everything to gain from seeking a judicial determination of probable cause in advance. Uncertainties in the application of the probable cause standard make advance confirmation the most prudent course of action.

---

[211] Franks v. Delaware, 438 U.S. 154, 98 S. Ct. 2674, 57 L. Ed. 2d 667 (1978).

[212] Illinois v. Gates, *supra* note 205, 462 U.S. at 239, 103 S. Ct. at 2332 ("Sufficient information must be provided to the magistrate to allow that official to determine probable cause; his action cannot be a mere ratification of the bare conclusions of others."); Whiteley v. Warden, 401 U.S. 560, 91 S. Ct. 1031, 28 L. Ed. 2d 306 (1971).

[213] Malley v. Briggs, 475 U.S. 335, 106 S. Ct. 1092, 89 L. Ed. 271 (1986).

[214] Franks v. Delaware, *supra* note 211.

[215] Malley v. Briggs, *supra* note 213.

Figure 3.19
**Advantages of an Arrest Warrant**

Arrests made under the authority of a warrant carry two advantages over arrests without a warrant. A facially valid warrant:

1. ensures admissibility of evidence seized during a search incident to the arrest, and
2. protects the officer against liability in a civil suit.

However, both advantages are lost if the officer:

1. deliberately or recklessly falsifies information in his or her affidavit in support of the warrant, or
2. fails to include enough information to enable the magistrate to make an independent determination that probable cause exists for the arrest.

### F. Prompt Judicial Review of Warrantless Arrests

While a police officer's determination of probable cause will support an arrest, it does not provide legal justification for incarcerating the arrestee for more than a short period. Arrested persons may not be deprived of their liberty for any extended period without a judicial determination that probable cause existed for their arrest. When the arrest is made without a warrant, such that this determination was not made in advance, the arrestee is entitled to a prompt judicial determination of probable cause after the arrest. The purpose of a post-arrest judicial determination is to prevent lengthy unconstitutional confinements. Consequently, this procedure is required only for persons who are: (1) arrested without a warrant, and (2) not released on bail.[216] Absent extraordinary circumstances, a post-arrest probable cause determination must be made within 48 hours of a warrantless arrest.[217] The Fourth Amendment does not require an adversarial hearing in which the arrestee is represented by counsel and has a right to put on evidence. Post-arrest judicial review procedures need not be any more elaborate than the procedures that would have been used to decide whether to issue a warrant in advance of the arrest.

## § 3.13    —Probable Cause

To be lawful, an arrest must be based on probable cause. For probable cause to exit, the officer must be aware of facts sufficient to create a fair probability that the person to be arrested committed a crime.[218] Probable cause and reasonable suspicion are identical in all ways but one. Probable cause requires

---

[216] Gerstein v. Pugh, 420 U.S. 103, 95 S. Ct. 854, 43 L. Ed. 2d 54 (1975); City of Riverside v. McLaughlin, 500 U.S. 44, 111 S. Ct. 1661, 114 L. Ed. 2d 49 (1991); Atwater v. City of Lago Vista, 532 U.S. 318, 121 S. Ct. 1536, 149 L. Ed. 2d 549 (2001).

[217] See authorities supra note 216.

[218] Beck v. Ohio, 379 U.S. 89, 85 S. Ct. 223, 13 L. Ed. 2d 142 (1964).

a higher probability of guilt, and thus requires more evidence or more reliable evidence. Consequently, earlier discussions of reasonable suspicion are also relevant here.[219]

The Fourth Amendment requires probable cause for four different purposes. Probable cause must exist to: (1) obtain an arrest warrant, (2) make an arrest without a warrant, (3) obtain a search warrant, and (4) conduct some searches without a warrant. The difference between probable cause for an arrest and probable cause for a search is what the officer must have probable cause to believe. To secure an arrest warrant or make an arrest without a warrant, the officer must have probable cause to believe that the person to be arrested committed an offense. To obtain a search warrant, an officer must have probable cause to believe that the evidence sought will be found at the location to be searched. However, the amount of supporting evidence needed to satisfy the four probable cause standards is the same. Consequently, courts regularly rely on cases from one context as authority in the other. Having pointed this out, it will not be necessary to repeat the same information in Chapter 4.

Probable cause may be based on evidence from a variety of sources other than the officer's personal observations. These sources include physical evidence found at the scene; information supplied by other law enforcement officers or agencies, or in police records; reports received from eyewitnesses, victims, and informants; and rational inferences drawn from the officer's prior experience.[220] Determinations of probable cause are case-specific. Each case turns on its own unique combination of facts. No two cases are ever exactly alike. Knowing when evidence is sufficient to establish probable cause for an arrest requires experience and sound professional judgment. There is no better way to acquire this judgment than routinely applying for arrest warrants and observing when a magistrate will issue one.

Officers occasionally observe the commission of a crime with their own eyes, but this is rare. In most cases, probable cause derives from a combination of mutually reinforcing facts. In evaluating whether the officer's evidence is sufficient to satisfy the probable cause standard, the magistrate will identify all the facts and circumstances known to the officer at time of the action, view them in combination, and evaluate their evidentiary significance in the way a trained police officer would. A single piece of evidence, weak on its own, can be reinforced when other evidence points to the same conclusion.

Investigations are often initiated by information received from members of the public. In determining the weight that should be given to such information in assessing probable cause for an arrest, the officer must consider the information provider's trustworthiness and basis for knowledge. When information comes from the victim or an eyewitness, veracity and basis for knowledge may be assumed.[221] When the information comes from an anonymous

---

[219]  See § 3.6 supra.

[220]  Id.

[221]  United States v. Armstrong, 16 F.3d 289 (8th Cir. 1993); Buggs v. State, 693 So. 2d 57 (Fla. Dist. Ct. App. 1997); Anderson v. State, 932 S.W.2d 502 (Tex. Crim. App. 1996) (en banc); Belton v. State, 900 S.W.2d 886 (Tex. Ct. App. 1995).

informant, veracity and basis for knowledge must be corroborated, either by confirming details that are not easily obtainable, or through independent police work.[222]

In *Illinois v. Gates*,[223] police received an anonymous letter accusing Lance Gates and his wife of trafficking in drugs and predicting that, in early May, Gates' wife would drive from Chicago to Florida, leave their car there to be loaded with drugs, and Gates would fly to Florida a few days later, pick up their car, and drive it back to Chicago. Gates was arrested on his return from the predicted itinerary. The Supreme Court held that the police were justified in considering the anonymous tip reliable because it contained a large number of details that were not easily obtainable. From the informant's ability to predict the Gates' future travel plans in precise and accurate detail, police could infer that the informant acquired the information directly from Gates or his wife and that the information was therefore reliable.

Suppose that police receive a tip from an anonymous caller who reports that a woman who lives at 1105 Brook Street, named Mary Wanna, is a drug dealer. Officers confirm that Mary Wanna resides at that location and further learn that Mary Wanna has a criminal record for drug trafficking. Have the police corroborated enough details to have probable cause for an arrest?

This situation is readily distinguishable from *Illinois v. Gates*. The details the police have corroborated are easily obtainable. Corroboration of easily obtainable details gives no assurance that an anonymous caller is trustworthy or that the information provided is reliable.[224] The caller could be playing a prank on Mary Wanna, seeking revenge, or reporting a rumor. When an anonymous tip lacks indicia of reliability, it must be corroborated through independent police work.

Probable cause depends entirely on the facts of each case. The hazards of assessing when evidence is sufficient to satisfy this standard can be removed by applying for an arrest warrant.

## § 3.14  —Requirements for a Valid Arrest Warrant

The Fourth Amendment warrant clause reads that "no Warrants shall issue, but upon probable cause, supported by Oath or affirmation, and particularly describing . . . the persons . . . to be seized." This language establishes three requirements for the issuance of an arrest warrant: (1) a judicial officer, normally a magistrate, must determine that probable cause exists for the arrest; (2) this determination must be supported by information given under oath; and (3) the warrant must contain a particularized description of the person to be seized. As previously noted, an arrest warrant insulates the fruits of

---

[222]  Illinois v. Gates, *supra* note 205.
[223]  *Id.*
[224]  Parish v. State, 939 S.W.2d 201 (Tex. Ct. App. 1997).

an arrest from suppression and the officer from civil suit.[225] However, to perform these functions, it must be issued in conformity with the three requirements listed above.[226] A warrant that fails to satisfy these requirements is subject to challenge.

Figure 3.20
**Fourth Amendment Requirements for a Valid Arrest Warrant**

> The Fourth Amendment warrant clause imposes three requirements for a constitutional arrest warrant:
>
> 1. The magistrate must make an independent determination that probable cause exists for the arrest.
> 2. The magistrate's determination must be supported by information given under oath.
> 3. The warrant must contain a particularized description of the person to be arrested.

## A. Determination of Probable Cause by a Magistrate

The Fourth Amendment divides responsibility for the issuance of a warrant between the magistrate and the officer who applies for the warrant. The magistrate is responsible for deciding whether probable cause exists for an arrest or search. However, because the magistrate lacks independent knowledge of the underlying facts, the Fourth Amendment places responsibility for supplying this information on the applicant. A police officer begins the warrant process by preparing a sworn written statement, called an affidavit, in which the officer sets forth the facts on which his or her application is made. The magistrate reviews the officer's affidavit and decides whether the facts stated in it are sufficient. In making this decision, the magistrate considers both the content of the information and the reliability of the officer's sources.

## B. Supported by Oath or Affirmation

The Fourth Amendment requires that the magistrate's probable cause determination be based on information given under oath. An oath is required to ensure that the information on which the magistrate acts is trustworthy. Magistrates normally rely exclusively on the information contained in the officer's sworn affidavit; they rarely take oral testimony or call other witnesses. This means that the validity of the warrant will hinge on whether the officer's affidavit contains enough information to enable the magistrate to make an independent determination of probable cause.[227] On a scale of one to 10, of the

---

[225]  *See* § 3.12(E) *supra.*
[225]  *Id.*
[227]  Aguilar v. Texas, 378 U.S. 108, 111, 84 S. Ct. 1509, 1512, 12 L. Ed. 2d 723 (1964).

skills needed to be a police investigator, knowing how to prepare a constitutionally sufficient affidavit rates a "10."

To support the issuance of a warrant, the officer's affidavit must contain a detailed account of the facts uncovered by the investigation, the source of these facts, and any other information that the magistrate will need to evaluate the reliability of the officer's sources. If the officer has observed a particular matter with his or her own eyes, the officer should say so. If the officer heard about it from a third party, he or she should identify the third party and then explain the third party's basis for knowledge and the officer's reasons for believing that the third party's information is reliable. This is particularly important when the existence of probable cause depends on information supplied by a police informant.[228] Courts consider police informants disreputable and their information suspect.[229] Consequently, special attention must be given to providing information that will enable the magistrate to evaluate an informant's credibility and basis of knowledge.

Below are two sample affidavits. The first is constitutionally deficient.

Figure 3.21
**Sample Affidavit I**

> I, Officer Susan Blake, based on information received from reliable persons, do solemnly swear that sometime between 8:00 and 10:00 p.m. on October 27, 2004, Sam Wanna (alias Sticky-Fingered Sam) did unlawfully break into and enter a home owned by Vicki Royce, located at 406 Meadow Lane in Euphoria County, and did then and there steal property worth in excess of $12,000.
>
> /s/ Susan Blake
> Affiant
>
> Subscribed and sworn to before me this 29th day of October, 2004.
>
> /s/ Betty Hitchcock
> Clerk, Associate Division
> Circuit Court of Euphoria County

This affidavit is constitutionally deficient because it sets forth Officer Blake's *conclusion* that Sticky-Fingered Sam committed a burglary, but discloses none of the underlying facts that lead Officer Blake to reach this conclusion.[230] It is impossible for a magistrate to make an independent determination of probable cause from an affidavit like this. All the magistrate can do is act as a rubber stamp. Issuance of a warrant on an affidavit that is devoid of facts violates the Fourth Amendment. A competent magistrate will not issue a warrant and, if a magistrate issues one, it will not insulate evidence from suppression[231]

---

[228]  Illinois v. Gates, *supra* note 205; Spinelli v. United States, 393 U.S. 410, 89 S. Ct. 584, 21 L. Ed. 2d 637 (1969); Aguilar v. Texas, 378 U.S. 108, 84 S. Ct. 1509, 12 L. Ed. 2d 723 (1964).

[229]  People v. Kurland, 28 Cal. 3d 376, 168 Cal. Rptr. 667, 618 P.2d 213 (1980).

[230]  Whiteley v. Warden, 401 U.S. 560, 91 S. Ct. 1031, 28 L. Ed. 2d 306 (1971).

[231]  United States v. Leon, 468 U.S. 897, 914, 104 S. Ct. 3405, 3416, 82 L. Ed. 2d 677 (1984).

or the officer from civil liability.[232] When a warrant is issued on an insufficient affidavit, the problem cannot be cured through testimony that the officer knew more facts than were included in the affidavit.[233] It is therefore imperative that officers learn how to prepare a constitutionally sufficient affidavit.

The affidavit below shows the details that Officer Blake should have put in her application for a warrant.

Figure 3.22
**Sample Affidavit II**

---

Comes now Susan Blake, being first duly sworn and upon oath, does state:

I am a Euphoria County Police Detective. The date of this Affidavit In Support of an Application for an Arrest Warrant is October 29, 2004. I have been employed as a Euphoria Police Officer for the past seven years. During this period, I have participated in more than 150 arrests for burglary, larceny, and armed robbery.

Sometime between 8:00 p.m. and 10:00 p.m. on October 27, 2004, a burglary occurred at the home of Vicki Royce at 406 Meadow Lane. The burglary was discovered at 10:15 p.m. when Vicki Royce returned home. The property stolen during the burglary included a large Indian Head coin collection stored in a maroon and gold case, jewelry, and sterling silver place settings. I was given a detailed description of the stolen property when I interviewed Vicki Royce at her residence after the burglary was discovered.

While I was there, Alan Polk, a neighbor who lives at 408 Meadow Lane, saw my squad car and came over. He stated that he was out walking his dog about 9:20 p.m. that evening and that he saw a man leave Vicki Royce's house, get into a maroon or rust-colored "K-car type" station wagon, and drive off. He described the man as white, bald, approximately 5'9", of medium build, and in his early fifties.

On the morning of October 28, 2004, Officer Dave Fox of the Euphoria County Police Department received a telephone call from a woman who stated that she wished to remain anonymous. This individual informed Officer Fox that a man named Sam M. Wanna, who lives in a rented house at 721 Preston Street, invited her into his home the previous evening shortly before midnight, and offered to sell her some Indian Head coins, jewelry, and silverware.

I ran a criminal records check and learned that Sam M. Wanna (alias Sticky-Fingered Sam) has three convictions for burglary (1989, 1995, 1999) and one for check forgery (1992). The criminal records show that Sam Wanna is 48 years old, 5'10", and weighs 170 pounds.

I went to 721 Preston Street and saw a maroon Chrysler station wagon parked in front, bearing an in-state license plate, number 256-JRV. I ran a vehicle registration check and verified that this vehicle is registered to Sam M. Wanna.

As a result of this information, it is my belief that Sam M. Wanna burglarized Vicki Royce's home on October 27, 2004.

/s/ Susan Blake
     Affiant

Subscribed and sworn to before me this 29th day of October, 2004.

/s/ Betty Hitchcock
Clerk, Associate Division
Circuit Court of Euphoria County

---

[232] Malley v. Briggs, *supra* note 213.

[233] Whiteley v. Warden, Wyoming State Penitentiary, *supra* note 230.

This affidavit is sufficient to enable a magistrate to make an independent determination of whether probable cause exists for an arrest. If the magistrate issues a warrant, the existence of probable cause will be conclusively established unless Officer Blake recklessly or deliberately falsified the facts on which the magistrate's determination was based.[234]

Notice the certification above Betty Hitchcock's signature, at the bottom of Officer Blake's affidavit. The certification recites that the information in the Officer Blake's affidavit was subscribed and sworn (i.e., given under oath), as required by the Fourth Amendment. Officers should make certain that their affidavit contains a signed certification like this one, or the warrant will not be issued in conformity with the Fourth Amendment and the arrest will be unconstitutional.

## C. The Person to be Seized Must be Particularly Described

The Fourth Amendment also requires that arrest warrants "particularly describ[e] the . . . persons . . . to be seized." This requirement can be satisfied either by designating the arrestee by name or providing some other combination of characteristics that are sufficient to identify him or her.[235]

Figure 3.23
**Particularized Description of the Person to be Arrested**

---

In order to satisfy the Fourth Amendment requirement of a particularized description of the person to be arrested, the face of the warrant must designate the intended arrestee either by:

1.   his or her actual name, or
2.   if his or her actual name is unknown, some other name or description that identifies him or her with reasonable certainty.

---

The usual method of describing an arrestee is by name. Minor discrepancies in spelling do not destroy a warrant's validity; however, when the arrestee's name is the only identifying information on the face of the warrant, the name that appears must be similar to the arrestee's real name. A warrant for the arrest of "Sam Cook" confers no authority to arrest "Sam Wanna" if he has never been known by this name, even though Sam Wanna was the person intended, but the officer was mistaken about his name.[236] When police have probable cause to arrest a person, but are uncertain of his or her real name, the

---

[234]   **United States v. King, 227 F.3d 732 (6th Cir. 2000).** This case contains an unusually clear discussion of what an affidavit must contain in order to satisfy the probable cause requirement.
[235]   West v. Cabell, 153 U.S. 78, 85, 14 S. Ct. 752, 753, 38 L. Ed. 643 (1894).
[236]   *Id.*

warrant must describe the intended arrestee by a cluster of characteristics that are sufficient to identify him or her. These characteristics may include traits like his or her occupation, age, date of birth, physical appearance, place of residence, aliases, nicknames, the vehicle the person drives, distinguishing features like scars or limps, and so forth.[237]

The combination of characteristics used to describe the arrestee must be sufficient to identify him or her with reasonable certainty. Police may not select an arbitrary name, like "John Doe," and use it as the sole means of identification.[238] A warrant for the arrest of "John Doe," without more, does not contain a particularized description of anyone.[239] To satisfy the Fourth Amendment, the description on the face of the warrant must leave little doubt about the identity of the party intended.[240] A warrant for the arrest of "John Doe, alias Sticky-Fingered Sam, who lives at 721 Preston Street and drives a maroon Chrysler station wagon" would be sufficient.[241]

The opposite problem arises when the name on the face of the warrant is correct, but the police arrest the wrong person. Suppose, for example, that a warrant is issued for the arrest of "Sam Wanna (alias Sticky-Fingered Sam)" and police, by mistake, arrest his cousin George who looks a great deal like Sam. Have the police violated George's Fourth Amendment rights?

The answer, astonishingly, is "no." The warrant for Sam Wanna's arrest was issued in conformity with the Fourth Amendment. The defect was in the execution. The police arrested the wrong person. The Fourth Amendment offers little solace to victims of mistaken identity. A warrant issued in conformity with the Fourth Amendment provides probable cause to arrest any person whom the police reasonably believe is the person named in the warrant.[242] The police, therefore, had probable cause to arrest George, and his Fourth Amendment rights were not violated.

[237] People v. Montoya, 255 Cal. App. 2d 137, 63 Cal. Rptr. 73 (1967).
[238] Powe v. City of Chicago, 664 F.2d 639 (7th Cir. 1981).
[239] United States v. Doe, 703 F.2d 745 (3d Cir. 1983).
[240] People v. Simmons, 210 Ill. App. 3d 692, 569 N.E.2d 591 (1991).
[241] United States v. Espinosa, 827 F.2d 604, *cert. denied*, 485 U.S. 968, 108 S. Ct. 1243, 99 L. Ed. 2d 441 (1987) (description of arrestee by physical appearance, place of residence, and vehicle he drives is sufficient to satisfy the Fourth Amendment); United States v. Ferrone, 438 F.2d 381, 389 (3d Cir. 1971) (description of arrestee as "John Doe, a white male with black wavy hair and stocky build observed using the telephone in Apartment 4-C, 1806 Patricia Lane, East McKeesport, Pennsylvania" is sufficient to satisfy the Fourth Amendment).
[242] Baker v. McCollan, 443 U.S. 137, 99 S. Ct. 2689, 61 L. Ed. 2d 433 (1979); Hill v. California, 401 U.S. 797, 91 S. Ct. 1106, 28 L. Ed. 2d 484 (1971).

## D. Form and Content of the Warrant

Arrest warrants are short, one-page documents. Below is a sample warrant for Sticky-Fingered Sam's arrest.

Figure 3.24
**Sample Arrest Warrant**

---

The State of Confusion
To any Sheriff, Constable, Marshal, or Police Officer of the State of Confusion:
     It appearing that there are reasonable grounds for believing that Sam M. Wanna (alias Sticky-Fingered Sam) committed the offense of burglary in the County of Euphoria on October 27, 2004, you are therefore commanded, forthwith, to arrest Sam M. Wanna, and bring him before some magistrate of Euphoria, to be dealt with according to law.

          Given under my hand the 29th day of October, 2004
          Betty Bright,
          Justice of the Peace for Euphoria County

---

The form and content of arrest warrants are prescribed by statute. State statutes typically impose the following seven requirements and sometimes additional requirements.[243] The arrest warrant must:

1. Be issued in the name of the state or a municipality.
2. Contain the date and the county or municipality where it was issued.
3. Designate the officer or class of officers who are directed to execute it. The usual practice, as shown in the sample arrest warrant, is to designate all peace officers in the state so that any of them can execute it.
4. Name or otherwise identify the person to be arrested.
5. Command that this person be arrested and brought before the nearest accessible court for an initial appearance.
6. Describe the offense charged in general terms sufficient to apprise the arrested person of the nature of the charges.
7. Be signed by the judge of the court who issued it.

Examine the sample arrest warrant above and identify the place in it where each of these requirements is satisfied.

---

[243] *See, e.g.,* IOWA CODE ANN. § 804.2 (West 1994); MONT. CODE ANN. § 46-6-214 (1991); OKLA. STAT. ANN. § 2203 (West 1996).

## E. Proper Execution

A warrant must also be properly executed in order for an arrest to be valid. The requirements for proper execution include the following:

1. The party executing the warrant must be the specific officer or member of the class of officers to whom the warrant is directed.
2. The warrant must be executed within the territorial jurisdiction of the magistrate who issued it.[244]
3. The officer must either serve the warrant or advise the arrestee that a warrant has been issued. The common law required arresting officers to have the warrant in their possession at the time of the arrest so that they could show it on demand. While a person who has been arrested unquestionably has a right to see the warrant, the modern trend is toward allowing greater flexibility in the timing. The Federal Rules of Criminal Procedure[245] and many state codes[246] provide that the arresting officer need not have the warrant in his or her possession at the time of the arrest, but must, upon request, show the warrant to the defendant as soon as practicable.

Special requirements exist when the arrest requires a nonconsensual entry into a private dwelling. The requirements for making an arrest inside a private dwelling are covered in § 3.15.

## § 3.15 —Arrests Inside a Private Residence

While probable cause is enough to authorize an arrest in a public place, it is not enough to authorize entry into a private dwelling to arrest someone inside. Fear of warrantless intrusions by British customs officials searching for goods imported in violation of British law was the catalyst that led to the Fourth Amendment's adoption.[247] This concern is reflected in the language of the Fourth Amendment, which declares that: "the right of the people to be secure in their . . . houses . . . shall not be violated." The Supreme Court has established a firm and inflexible rule concerning arrests inside private dwellings. Absent consent or **exigent circumstances**, police may not enter a private dwelling to arrest someone inside unless a magistrate issues a warrant.[248]

---

[244] *See* § 3.18 *infra*.

[245] FED. R. CRIM. P. 4(d)(3).

[246] *See, e.g.*, ARIZ. REV. STAT. ANN. § 13-3887 (1989).

[247] United States v. United States District Court, 407 U.S. 297, 92 S. Ct. 2125, 32 L. Ed. 2d 752 (1972).

[248] Kirk v. Louisiana, *supra* note 207; **Payton v. New York, 445 U.S. 573, 100 S. Ct. 1371, 63 L. Ed. 2d 639 (1980).**

Figure 3.25
**Requirements for Making an Arrest Inside a Private Dwelling**

|  | Type of Warrant | Procedure for Execution | Excuse for Noncompliance |
|---|---|---|---|
| Arrestee's residence | Arrest warrant | Knock-and-announce | Consent to enter given by person with authority<br>Hot pursuit of a suspect wanted for a felony |
| Third party's residence | Arrest warrant & search warrant | Knock-and-announce | Danger to officer's safety<br>Danger to a third party<br>Risk of the suspect's escape<br>Risk of destruction of evidence |

## A. *Type of Warrant Required*

The Fourth Amendment makes provisions for two kinds of warrant—arrest and search. The type of warrant needed to make an arrest inside a private residence depends on who resides there. When the person to be arrested resides on the premises, police are only required to have an arrest warrant. When the residence belongs to someone else, police must also have a search warrant because they may have to search the person's home in order to find the suspect.[249] Thus, when police officers come to B's house to arrest A, who does not reside there, they must come armed with two warrants—a search warrant authorizing them to search B's residence, and an arrest warrant authorizing them to arrest A.[250] If A and B both reside on the premises, an arrest warrant will suffice. In a society in which people frequently move in with friends or family for prolonged periods, deciding whether a suspect "resides" at a particular location or is simply visiting can be problematic. When in doubt about this matter, officers should come equipped with both warrants.

## B. *Locations Covered by the Warrant Requirement*

The police are required to obtain a warrant only when the arrest is made inside a private dwelling. They do not have to procure a warrant to make an arrest in a public place or inside a commercial establishment. Dwellings, for purposes of the Fourth Amendment, include hotel and motel rooms and temporary residences, as well as permanent residences.[251]

Fourth Amendment protection against warrantless arrests starts on the other side of the front door. Police do not need a warrant to arrest people who are standing in their yard, on their front porch, or even in an open doorway,

---

[249] Steagald v. United States, 451 U.S. 204, 101 S. Ct. 1642, 68 L. Ed. 2d 38 (1981).

[250] *Id.*

[251] Hoffa v. United States, 385 U.S. 293, 87 S. Ct. 408, 17 L. Ed. 2d 374 (1966); Stoner v. California, 376 U.S. 483, 84 S. Ct. 889, 11 L. Ed. 2d 856 (1964).

because people who stand in a place visible to the public have a reduced expectation of privacy.[252]

Moreover, because the purpose of requiring a warrant is to protect the sanctity of the home, it is not a violation of the Fourth Amendment to use a noncoercive subterfuge to lure suspects out of their home so that they can be arrested without a warrant outside.[253] People who voluntarily leave the confines of their home expose themselves to arrest without a warrant.

### C. "Knock and Announce" Requirement[254]

Police are required to knock and announce their identity and purpose before attempting a forcible entry into a private dwelling.[255] This requirement can be traced to the early common law and has withstood the test of time because it makes good sense. Knocking and announcing before resorting to force avoids unnecessary destruction of property and protects officers from being shot by panicked homeowners who mistake them for thieves. Accordingly, police officers generally must do two things before they can force their way into a private residence to arrest someone inside: (1) secure the appropriate warrant or warrants, and (2) knock and announce their presence.

### D. Exceptions that Excuse Compliance with the Warrant and/or Knock and Announce Requirements

There are three exceptions that excuse both the need for a warrant or for knocking: (1) consent, (2) **hot pursuit**, and (3) exigent circumstances. However, police must still have probable cause to believe that the person to be arrested committed an offense and a reasonable belief that the person will be found inside.[256]

**Consent.** Police officers do not need an arrest warrant to walk up to a person's front door, ring the bell, and ask for permission to enter. Permission given by someone with authority eliminates the need for a warrant. To have authority, the person must live on the premises.[257] Any person of sufficient age

---

[252]   United States v. Santana, 427 U.S. 38, 96 S. Ct. 2406, 49 L. Ed. 2d 300 (1976) (open doorway); Dyer v. State, 680 So. 2d 612 (Fla. Dist. Ct. App. 1996) (yard).

[253]   Alvarez v. Montgomery County, Maryland, 963 F. Supp. 495 (D. Md. 1997); United States v. Vasiliav-itchious, 919 F. Supp. 1113 (N.D. Ill. 1996).

[254]   The procedures described in this section apply to execution of both arrest and search warrants.

[255]   United States v. Banks, 124 U. S. 521, 124 S. Ct. 521, 157 L. Ed. 2d 343 (2003); United States v. Ramirez, 523 U.S. 65, 118 S. Ct. 992, 140 L. Ed. 2d 191 (1998); Richards v. Wisconsin, 520 U.S. 385, 117 S. Ct. 1416, 137 L. Ed. 2d 615 (1997); Wilson v. Arkansas, 514 U.S. 927, 115 S. Ct. 1914, 131 L. Ed. 2d 976 (1995).

[256]   **Payton v. New York,** *supra* note 248.

[257]   United States v. Matlock, 415 U.S. 164, 94 S. Ct. 988, 39 L. Ed. 2d 242 (1974); Illinois v. Rodriguez, 497 U.S. 177, 110 S. Ct. 2793, 111 L. Ed. 2d 148 (1990); Humphrey v. State, 327 Ark. 753, 940 S.W.2d 860 (1997).

who resides on the premises can give valid consent. Hotel clerks,[258] landlords,[259] nonresident caretakers,[260] and occasional babysitters[261] lack authority to give police permission to enter because they do not reside on the premises.

Consent is effective only if it is given voluntarily. Consent given in response to an ordinary knock on the door and a nonauthoritarian request for permission to enter is considered voluntary;[262] consent procured by pounding on the door and shouting "open in the name of the law" is not.[263] Police do not have to advise the person answering the door that he or she has the right to withhold consent in order for consent to be voluntary.[264] Nor do police have to reveal their true identity.[265] People who invite a police officer into their home expose themselves to a warrantless arrest, even though they are mistaken as to their visitor's identity. However, consent is not voluntary when entrance is gained under a false assertion that police have a warrant because the occupant is misled into believing that he or she has no authority to resist the entry.[266]

**Exigent circumstances.** Police officers are not required to obtain a warrant or to knock and announce their presence before making a nonconsensual entry when they are confronted with exigent circumstances.[267] For exigent circumstances to exist, the officer must have reasonable suspicion that complying with one or both of these requirements will: (1) endanger the lives or safety of the officer, the suspect, or a third party; (2) enable the suspect to escape; or (3) lead to the destruction of evidence.[268] The exigent circumstances exception only applies to arrests for serious offenses.[269] Whether police are

---

[258] Stoner v. California, 376 U.S. 483, 84 S. Ct. 889, 11 L. Ed. 2d 856 (1964).

[259] United States v. Elliott, 50 F.3d 180 (2d Cir. 1995).

[260] Peterson v. People, 939 P.2d 824 (Colo. 1997) (en banc).

[261] People v. Walter, 890 P.2d 240 (Colo. Ct. App. 1994).

[262] United States v. Vaneaton, 49 F.3d 1423 (9th Cir. 1995), *cert. denied*, 516 U.S. 1176, 116 S. Ct. 1271, 134 L. Ed. 2d 218 (1996).

[263] United States v. Conner, 127 F.3d 663 (8th Cir. 1997).

[264] **United States v. Drayton,** *supra* note 21; Ohio v. Robinette, *supra* note 182; Schneckloth v. Bustamonte, *supra* note 121.

[265] Lewis v. United States, 385 U.S. 206, 87 S. Ct. 424, 17 L. Ed. 2d 312 (1966) (consent valid even though officer gained entry by pretending to be a drug buyer); United States v. Bramble, 103 F.3d 1475 (9th Cir. 1996) (consent valid even though officer gained entry by pretending to respond to advertisement); State v. Johnston, 84 Wis. 2d 794, 518 N.W.2d 759 (1994) (consent valid even though officer gained entry by posing as invited party guest); People v. Catania, 140 Mich. App. 755, 366 N.W.2d 38 (1985) (consent valid even though officer gained entry by posing as a motorist experiencing car trouble who needed to make a phone call).

[266] Bumper v. North Carolina, 391 U.S. 543, 88 S. Ct. 1788, 20 L. Ed. 2d 787 (1968) (Fourth Amendment violated when consent to enter was obtained only after officer falsely asserted that he had a warrant); Truelove v. Hung 67 F. Supp. 2d 569 (D.S.C. 1999) (Fourth amendment violated where police gained entry into home under a forged custody order issued by nonexistent court).

[267] United States v. Santana, *supra* note 252; Griffin v. City of Clanton, 932 F. Supp. 1359 (M.D. Ala. 1996) (third party's home).

[268] United States v. Banks, *supra* note 255; Richards v. Wisconsin, 520 U.S. 385, 117 S. Ct. 1416, 137 L. Ed. 2d 615 (1997).

[269] United States v. Banks, *supra* note 255; Welsh v. Wisconsin, 466 U.S. 740, 104 S. Ct. 2091, 80 L. Ed. 2d 732 (1984).

confronted with exigent circumstances must be decided on a case-by-case basis. States may not categorically exclude drug offense arrests from the knock-and-announce requirement on the theory that suspected drug offenders, if forewarned, will invariably destroy evidence.[270]

**Hot pursuit.** Police are also allowed to enter a private residence, without a warrant and without knocking, when they are in continuous hot pursuit of a suspected felon, encountered in a public place, who flees and takes refuge inside.[271] Suspects are not allowed to thwart an otherwise proper arrest that has been set in motion in a public place by retreating into their home. Police may follow them inside and arrest them.

The Supreme Court announced this ruling in *United States v. Santana*.[272] Police went to a known stash house to arrest a suspect who had earlier sold drugs to an undercover officer. They were within 15 feet of the house when they recognized the suspect standing in the entranceway of her home. When they displayed their identification and shouted "police," she retreated inside. They followed her through the open door and arrested her. The Supreme Court ruled that when the police undertake to make a lawful arrest without a warrant in a public place and the suspect flees into his or her home, the police may follow and make the arrest inside. The Court treated the suspect's entranceway as a public place, for purposes of this rule, because she was as visible to the public while standing there as she would have been if she had been standing on a public street.

The hot pursuit exception, like the exigent circumstances exception, only applies to serious crimes. Police may not pursue suspects into their home to arrest them for a minor offense, such as drunk driving.[273] When a petty offender manages to flee and takes sanctuary inside his or her home, officers must stop at the threshold, turn around, and get an arrest warrant.

The Supreme Court has not yet decided whether police may enter a private residence in hot pursuit of a *Terry* suspect, but lower courts generally allow this.[274]

---

[270] Richards v. Wisconsin, *supra* note 268.

[271] United States v. Santana, *supra* note 252 (suspect may not defeat a felony arrest set in motion in a public place by fleeing into her house).

[272] *Id.*

[273] Welsh v. Wisconsin, *supra* note 269 (hot pursuit exception to warrant requirement does not apply to DUI arrest).

[274] *See, e.g.*, Harbin v. City of Alexandria, 712 F. Supp. 67 (E.D. Va. 1989) (*Terry* stop need not end when suspect walks from porch into house), *aff'd*, 908 F.2d 967 (4th Cir. 1990); Hopkins v. State, 661 So. 2d 774 (Ala. Ct. App. 1994).

Figure 3.26
**Fourth Amendment Restrictions on Force**

---

The Fourth Amendment regulates the force that can be used in making an arrest or other seizure. The officer may use no more force than necessary to:

1.　protect self or others from danger,
2.　overcome resistance, or
3.　prevent escape.

Further limitations exist for deadly force. Deadly force is allowed only if:

1.　the suspect threatens the officer with a weapon, or
2.　the officer has probable cause to believe that the suspect committed a crime involving serious bodily harm and that his or her escape will endanger the public.

---

## § 3.16　Use of Force in Making an Arrest or Other Seizure

Our Constitution accepts that force is sometimes necessary to maintain law and order, but requires that its use be *reasonable*. Use of force is regulated by three separate provisions of the Constitution—the Fourth, Eighth, and Fourteenth Amendments. Each is active during a different phase of the criminal process and each imposes a different standard. The Fourth Amendment, which prohibits *unreasonable seizures*, regulates the use of force during arrests and investigatory stops. The Fourth Amendment imposes a standard of objective reasonableness.[275] The Eighth Amendment, which bans *cruel* and unusual punishment, regulates the use of force on offenders who have been convicted and are serving a prison sentence. It prohibits the use of force for malicious or sadistic reasons.[276] The Fourteenth Amendment, which prohibits the taking of life or liberty without due process, regulates the use of force during the period between arrest and conviction.[277] Thus, the Constitution prohibits the use of unnecessary force on persons who are in the custody of the law continuously from the time of their initial seizure until they have completed their sentence.

This section covers Fourth Amendment limitations on the use of force.

---

[275]　**Graham v. Connor, 490 U.S. 386, 109 S. Ct. 1865, 104 L. Ed. 2d 443 (1989)**.
[276]　Hope v. Pelzer, 536 U.S. 730, 122 S. Ct. 2508, 153 L. Ed. 2d 666 (2002) (handcuffing a prisoner to a hitching post in the hot sun for an extended period violates the Eighth Amendment because it involves wanton and malicious infliction of pain).
[277]　**Graham v. Connor**, *supra* note 275.

## A. *Fourth Amendment Requirement of Objectivity/Reasonableness*

The Fourth Amendment limits the force police may use to effect an arrest or investigatory stop.[278] The standard imposed by the Fourth Amendment is objective reasonableness. Police must have a legitimate reason for using force, and the force employed must be reasonable in degree.

## B. *Appropriate Justifications for Using Force*

There are only three legitimate reasons for using force: (1) for self-protection or protection of others from physical harm; (2) to overcome resistance; or (3) to prevent escape.[279] All other uses of force are illegitimate. Police, for example, are not justified in using their nightsticks on people who "mouth off" at them.[280] Further, although force may be justified to overcome resistance, once a suspect has been subdued, the force must cease.[281] Striking, hitting, or kicking suspects after they have been brought under control violates the Fourth Amendment[282] and can result in criminal prosecution.[283]

## C. *Degree of Force Authorized*

In addition to an appropriate reason for using force, the force used must be reasonable in degree. Courts assess the reasonableness of an officer's use of force from the perspective of a reasonable officer on the scene. Force is excessive if it exceeds what a reasonable officer on the scene would have deemed necessary to manage the situation at hand. The severity of the crime, whether the suspect posed an immediate threat to the safety of the officer or others, actively resisted arrest, or attempted to flee are the principal considerations.[284] The Supreme Court has cautioned that appropriate allowance should be made "for the fact that police officers are often forced to make split-second judgments—in circumstances that are tense, uncertain, and rapidly evolving—about the amount of force that is necessary in a particular situation."[285] Lower courts have interpreted this to mean that courts should limit their focus to the exact moment when the force was used.[286] The issue is not whether the offi-

---

[278]   *Id.*; **Tennessee v. Garner, 471 U.S. 1, 105 S. Ct. 1694, 85 L. Ed. 2d 1 (1985)**.

[279]   *See* cases *supra* note 278.

[280]   Stewart v. Bailey, 876 F. Supp. 1571 (N.D. Ala. 1996).

[281]   Ellis v. Wynalda, 999 F.2d 243 (7th Cir. 1993).

[282]   Frazell v. Flanigan, 102 F.3d 877 (7th Cir. 1996); Rambo v. Daley, 68 F.3d 203 (7th Cir. 1995).

[283]   Criminal prosecution for excessive force is covered in Chapter 10.

[284]   **Graham v. Connor**, *supra* note 275.

[285]   *Id.*, 490 U.S. at 396, 109 S. Ct. at 1872.

[286]   *See, e.g.*, Carter v. Buscher, 973 F.2d 1328 (7th Cir. 1992); Schultz v. Long, 44 F.3d 643 (8th Cir. 1995); Forrett v. Richardson, 112 F.3d 416 (9th Cir. 1997).

cer's earlier management contributed to the need for force or whether alternative strategies existed; the issue is whether the officer made a reasonable split-second judgment at this exact moment.[287]

## D. Limitations on the Use of Deadly Force

The Fourth Amendment imposes additional limitations on the use of deadly force—force likely to cause death or seriously bodily injury. Society's interest in effective law enforcement does not always justify taking a human life in order to prevent a suspect from escaping. In some circumstances, the Fourth Amendment requires that police officers allow a suspect to escape rather than kill him or her. Deadly force may be used only when the officer has probable cause to believe that such force is necessary for self-protection or protection of others from immediate, serious bodily harm.[288]

This has not always been the rule. The common law allowed police to use all necessary force, including deadly force, to effect an arrest for any felony. In *Tennessee v. Garner*,[289] the Supreme Court decided that the value of human life must also be considered in determining whether deadly force is reasonable. The decision arose out of the tragic death of a 15-year-old youth who had burglarized a house. The officer interrupted the burglary and chased the youth until cornering him against a six-foot chain-link fence. The officer observed the youth with a flashlight, determined that he was unarmed, and ordered him to stop. The youth disobeyed and began climbing the fence. The officer shot the youth in the back of the head to prevent him from escaping. A purse with $10 was found beside the youth's body.

The Supreme Court, horrified by the boy's senseless death, wrote:

> The use of deadly force to prevent the escape of all felony suspects, whatever the circumstances, is constitutionally unreasonable. It is not better that all felony suspects die than that they escape. Where the suspect poses no immediate threat to the officer and no threat to others, the harm resulting from failing to apprehend him does not justify the use of deadly force to do so. . . . A police officer may not seize an unarmed, non-dangerous suspect by shooting him dead.[290]

To justify using deadly force, an officer must have reasonable cause to believe that such force is necessary for self-protection or protection of others from death or immediate, serious bodily harm. This standard is generally satisfied only if: (1) the person threatens the officer or someone else with a weapon, or (2) the officer has probable cause to believe that the suspect committed a crime involving serious bodily harm and that his or her escape will

[287] *See* cases *supra* note 286.
[288] **Tennessee v. Garner**, *supra* note 278.
[289] *Id.*
[290] *Id.*

endanger the public. A warning must be given ("stop or I'll shoot"), when practicable, before resorting to deadly force.[291]

Perception of *immediate* danger is generally required for deadly force to be reasonable.[292] In a recent case, a federal court held that police, who were conducting surveillance of a cabin where a suspect was holed up, violated his Fourth Amendment rights when they fired a fatal shot, without warning, as he ran toward the cabin. Although the suspect had exchanged fire with the police the previous day, at the time he was shot, he posed no threat of immediate danger to anyone.[293] The court stated:

> Law enforcement officials may not kill suspects who do not pose an immediate threat to their safety or to the safety of others simply because they are armed. . . . A desire to prevent an armed suspect from entering the place he is residing because it may be difficult to persuade him to reemerge is insufficient cause to kill him. Other means exist for bringing the offender to justice, even if additional time and effort are required. When Horiuchi shot Harris, without any warning, as he was retreating toward an area of safety, he acted in a patently unreasonable manner . . .

On the other hand, courts uphold the use of deadly force when suspects reach for objects that an officer reasonably, but mistakenly, believes is a weapon.[294]

## § 3.17  State Arrest Laws

The Fourth Amendment establishes the *minimum* requirements for a constitutional arrest. However, states remain free, as a matter of local law, to impose more stringent requirements.[295] Violations of state requirements generally have the same consequences as violations of the Fourth Amendment. This means that detaining suspects for investigation longer than state law allows, or failing to obtain a warrant when state law requires one, will result in suppression of evidence, even if the arrest satisfies the Fourth Amendment. Compliance with state arrest laws is more important today than in former times. The Supreme Court's gradual retrenchment from the liberal Fourth Amendment jurisprudence of the Warren and Burger Courts has created a situation in which state law often affords greater protection than the Fourth Amendment. This shift has led defense attorneys to scrutinize for state law violations more carefully than they once did.

---

[291]  *Id.* at 11-12, 105 S. Ct. at 1701
[292]  Schultz v. Long, 44 F.3d 643 (8th Cir. 1995).
[293]  Harris v. Roderick, 126 F.3d 1189 (9th Cir. 1997).
[294]  Reese v. Anderson, 926 F.2d 494 (5th Cir. 1991).
[295]  Oregon v. Hass, 420 U.S. 714, 95 S. Ct. 1215, 43 L. Ed. 2d 570 (1975).

Because arrest laws vary from state to state, only a cursory examination is possible. Each student is responsible for determining whether the laws of his or her state impose special restrictions on a police officer's arrest authority.

## A. *Distinctions Between Authority to Arrest for Felonies and Misdemeanors*

All states have statutes defining the conditions under which arrests are authorized.[296] We will recap the Fourth Amendment standard to use it for comparison. An officer must have probable cause to believe that a person committed an offense to have Fourth Amendment authority to make an arrest. The only time a warrant is necessary is when police contemplate making the arrest inside a private residence.

State law generally gives police the same authority to arrest for a felony as the Fourth Amendment. Although state statutes sometimes use the phrase **"reasonable grounds"** instead of "probable cause," this difference is semantic.[297] However, a real difference exists with respect to authority to arrest for a misdemeanor. In most states, a warrant is necessary unless the misdemeanor is committed *in the officer's presence.*[298] If the misdemeanor is committed outside the officer's presence, the officer must procure an arrest warrant. The distinction between felony and misdemeanor arrests is not required by the Fourth Amendment;[299] it is a legacy of the common law.[300]

The statute below codifies the common law.

> (1) A peace officer may make an arrest:
>     (a) In obedience to a warrant; or
>     (b) Without a warrant when a felony is committed in his presence; or
>     (c) Without a warrant when he has probable cause to believe that the person being arrested has committed a felony; or
>     (d) Without a warrant when a misdemeanor . . . has been committed in his presence . . .[301]

---

[296]  *See, e.g.*, KY. REV. STAT. § 431.005(1)

[297]  *See, e.g.*, Draper v. United States, 358 U.S. 307, 310 n. 3, 79 S. Ct. 329, 331 n. 3, 3 L. Ed. 2d 327 (1959).

[298]  *See generally*, William A. Schroeder, *Warrantless Misdemeanor Arrests and the Fourth Amendment*, 58 MO. L. REV. 771 (1993).

[299]  Welsh v. Wisconsin, 466 U.S. 740, 756, 104 S. Ct. 2091, 80 L. Ed. 2d 732 (1984) (White, J., dissenting) ("[T]he requirement that a misdemeanor must have occurred in the officer's presence to justify a warrantless arrest is not grounded in the Fourth Amendment"); Atwater v. City of Lago Vista, 533 U.S. 924, 121 S. Ct. 2540, 150 L. Ed. 2d 709 (2001) (Fourth Amendment authority to make warrantless arrests for misdemeanors is not restricted to cases of breaches of the peace); Field v. City of South Houston, 922 F.2d 1183 (5th Cir. 1991).

[300]  10 HALSBURY'S LAWS OF ENGLAND 344-345 (3d ed. 1955); 4 W. BLACKSTONE, COMMENTARIES * 292; 1 J. STEPHEN, A HISTORY OF THE CRIMINAL LAW OF ENGLAND 193 (1883).

[301]  KY. REV. STAT. § 431.005(1).

This statute is modeled on the common law. Under subsection (1)(a), peace officers may arrest for any offense when they have an arrest warrant. When they do not have a warrant, their arrest authority depends on whether the offense is a felony or a misdemeanor. If the offense is a misdemeanor, subsection (d) controls; they may arrest without a warrant only if the misdemeanor is committed in their presence. If the offense is a felony, subsection (c) controls; they may arrest without a warrant based on probable cause alone. Subsection (b) is redundant because, when a felony is committed in the officer's presence, the officer invariably has probable cause to believe the person committed a felony and, thus, already has authority to arrest under subsection (c).

A growing number of states are now moving toward a unified standard that grants arrest authority to the full extent allowed under the Fourth Amendment.[302] In Illinois, for example, "[a]ny law enforcement officer may make an arrest without a warrant if the officer has probable cause to believe that the person has committed or is committing any crime, . . . even if the crime was not committed in the presence of the officer."[303] A unified standard based on the Fourth Amendment is simpler and offers fewer opportunities for mistakes. The officer does not have to make an on-the-spot judgment about whether the crime is a felony or misdemeanor, or whether the offense took place in his or her presence.

A few states take an intermediate position, authorizing warrantless arrests for misdemeanors not committed in the officer's presence when the officer is confronted with exigent circumstances.[304] In Nebraska, for example, police have the authority to make a warrantless arrest for a misdemeanor when the offender is likely to flee, destroy or conceal evidence, cause injury to self or others, or cause damage to property unless apprehended immediately.[305] Another variation is to authorize warrantless arrests for designated misdemeanors or classes of misdemeanors.[306]

## B. Determining Whether an Offense is a Misdemeanor or a Felony

Whether an offense is classified as a felony or misdemeanor turns on the punishment. Offenses punishable by death or a prison term (usually of one year or more) are classified as felonies, while those punishable by a jail sentence (usually of less than one year) or a fine are misdemeanors. Remembering the classification for every offense is difficult. Consequently, in jurisdictions that distinguish between felonies and misdemeanors for purposes of arrest authority, officers should procure a warrant whenever they are in doubt.

---

[302]  *See, e.g.*, COLO. REV. STAT. § 16-3-102

[303]  ILL. COMP. STAT. § 5.112A-26(2)

[304]  *See, e.g.*, NEB. REV. STAT. § 29-404.02(2); WYO. STAT. ANN. § 7-2-103(4).

[305]  NEB. REV. STAT. § 29-404.02(2).

[306]  MD. ANN. CODE art. 27, § 594B (d)(e).

### C. Meaning of "In the Officer's Presence"

For a misdemeanor to be committed "in the officer's presence," the officer must be aware that it is taking place while it is still in progress. The officer need not observe the misdemeanor from the beginning to end, but a misdemeanor is not committed in an officer's presence if it is completed before the officer arrives. It is not necessary that an officer actually *see* the misdemeanor for it to occur in his or her presence. It is enough that the officer is aware that it is taking place through any of the senses—sight, touch, hearing, smell, or taste. The first three illustrations below satisfy this requirement. We will let you decide for yourself whether the fourth one does.

1.  Officer Blake answers a 911 domestic disturbance call. While waiting for the door to be opened, she hears a man shouting "I'll kill you, you bitch!" the sound of struggling, and a woman screaming "Please, don't hit me again!"[307]

2.  While conducting a traffic stop, Officer Blake smells alcohol on the driver's breath and marijuana smoke in the passenger compartment.

3.  A government informant agrees to wear a radio transmitter concealed under his clothing while making a drug purchase. Officer Blake electronically monitors the transaction from a squad car several blocks away.[308]

4.  Officer Blake, walking a beat, rounds a corner where she spots Sticky-Fingered Sam, standing beside a puddle of liquid, zipping up his trousers. Was Sam's offense of public urination committed in Officer Blake's presence?[309]

When arrest authority derives from the commission of a misdemeanor in the officer's presence, the arrest must be made on the spot or in hot pursuit. If the arrest is not made until later, a warrant is necessary. As an illustration, suppose that Officer Blake sees Sticky-Fingered Sam steal a bike and ride away. Several hours later, she spots Sam on foot. If she works in a jurisdiction that requires a warrant to arrest for misdemeanors not committed in an officer's presence and bike theft is a misdemeanor, she would lack the authority to arrest Sam unless she has procured an arrest warrant in the meantime.

---

[307] State v. Bryant, 678 S.W.2d 480 (1984).
[308] *See, e.g.*, Carranza v. State, 266 Ga. 263, 467 S.E.2d 315 (1996).
[309] United States v. Williams, 754 F.2d 1001 (D.C. Cir. 1985).

## § 3.18 —Territorial Limits on a Police Officer's Arrest Authority

State and local police officers have territorial limits on their arrest authority—both intrastate (within the state) and interstate (between states).

### A. Intrastate Territorial Limits

In the absence of a statute, a police officer lacks the authority to take official action outside the boundaries of the government unit in which he or she holds appointment.[310] However, many states today have statutes authorizing statewide service of arrest warrants.[311] A warrant issued by a magistrate in one part of the state can also have an indirect effect in other parts of the state. Suppose, for example, that Sticky-Fingered Sam is stopped for a traffic violation in County A and the officer learns from a computer check that County B has an outstanding warrant for Sam's arrest on a felony charge. Knowledge that County B has issued a warrant for Sam's arrest provides probable cause to believe that Sam committed a felony and, thus, furnishes grounds for making a warrantless arrest in County A.[312]

**Fresh pursuit** is an important exception to the rule that police lack the authority to make an arrest outside their territorial jurisdiction. Fresh pursuit refers to the immediate, uninterrupted pursuit of a person who is trying to avoid apprehension. Under the common law and the statutes of most states, police are allowed to enter other parts of the state in order to make an arrest when they are in fresh pursuit. The common law limited this privilege to felony arrests. For misdemeanors and traffic violations, the chase had to end at the district or county line.[313] Although a few states retain this limitation, a growing number of states now authorize statewide fresh pursuit for all offenses.[314] The Delaware statute below is typical:

> Any peace officer of a duly organized county, municipality, town, interstate bridge or university peace unit . . . may carry out fresh pursuit of any person anywhere within this State, regardless of the original territorial jurisdiction of such officer, in order to arrest such person pursued, when there are reasonable grounds to suspect that a felony, misdemeanor, or violation of the Motor Vehicle Code has been committed in this State by such person.[315]

---

[310]  State v. Masat, 239 Neb. 849, 479 N.W.2d 131 (1992).

[311]  *See, e.g.*, N.J. STAT. ANN. § 39:5-28.

[312]  People v. Gouker, 665 P.2d 113 (Colo. 1983) (en banc).

[313]  *See, e.g.*, State v. Stahl, 838 P.2d 1193 (Wyo. 1992).

[314]  *See, e.g.*, DEL. CODE ANN. tit. 11, § 1935.

[315]  *Id.*

If Sticky-Fingered Sam lives in Delaware, Officer Blake may pursue him across district or county lines and chase him throughout the state to arrest him for any offense. While investigatory stops are rarely mentioned in fresh pursuit statutes, fresh pursuit statutes are generally interpreted to cover them as well.[316]

## B. Interstate Territorial Limits

Each state is a sovereign political entity. Authority conferred by state law ends at the state line. Police officers do not carry their authority with them when they enter a second state. This limitation stems from the nature of our federal union. Under our federal system, no state can confer authority effective in another state. Before a police officer can take official action in another state, the state in which the action is taken must grant this authority.

Interstate cooperation within the law enforcement community is on the increase. Most states provide for issuance of "fugitive arrest warrants," directing the arrest of persons found inside the state who are wanted elsewhere so they can be returned for trial.[317] Most states also have *inter*state fresh pursuit statutes, authorizing out-of-state police officers to enter the state in fresh pursuit to make an arrest for a felony.[318] The Delaware statute below, which authorizes interstate fresh pursuit for *any* offense, is broader than most.

> Any member of a duly organized state, county, or municipal peace unit of another state of the United States who enters this State in fresh pursuit, and continues within this State in such fresh pursuit, of a person in order to arrest the person on the ground that the person is believed to have committed a felony, a misdemeanor or a violation of the motor vehicle code in such other state, shall have the same authority to arrest and hold such person in custody, as has any member of any duly organized state, county or municipal peace unit of this State, to arrest . . .[319]

Application of the fresh pursuit doctrine has become increasingly common as means of rapid transportation have improved. To understand the exact territorial limits of their arrest authority, officers must be familiar with the fresh pursuit statutes of all neighboring states, as well as their own.

An officer who makes an extraterritorial arrest not authorized by the laws of the jurisdiction in which the arrest is made has the same authority as a private citizen.[320] State laws vary on the circumstances in which citizens may make an arrest, but whatever authority a citizen has can generally be claimed by an out-of-state police officer.[321]

---

[316] People v. Pollard, 216 Ill. App. 3d 591, 575 N.E.2d 970 (1991).

[317] *See, e.g.,* CAL. PENAL CODE § 1551; NEB. REV. STAT. at § 29-409.

[318] *See, e.g.,* TEX. CODE CRIM. P. ANN. art. 14.051.

[319] DEL. CODE ANN. tit. 11, § 1932(a).

[320] Stevenson v. State, 287 Md. 504, 413 A.2d 1340 (1980).

[321] *Id.*

## 3.19    Summary and Practical Suggestions

The Fourth Amendment prohibits unreasonable seizures of persons. A seizure occurs when a person submits to a police officer's show of legal authority or the officer gains actual physical control over him or her. Police officers do not need any grounds to approach members of the public and ask for their voluntary cooperation in resolving the officer's suspicion of them. To determine whether the suspect's cooperation was voluntary or resulted from a seizure, the court inquires into whether a reasonable person in the suspect's position would have believed that he or she was free to disregard the officer's request and leave. If a reasonable person would not have felt free to leave, a suspect who cooperates is seized.

Seizures are broken down into two categories—investigatory stops and arrests. Under *Terry v. Ohio*, an officer is permitted to detain a person for investigation when the officer is aware of specific, articulable facts that, in light of the officer's prior experience, would warrant a reasonable police officer in suspecting that the person detained is committing, has committed, or is about to commit a crime. Once the stop is made, the officer may conduct a weapons frisk if, in addition to the grounds for the stop, the officer has a reasonable suspicion that the detainee may be armed and dangerous. An officer may not search a detainee for objects other than weapons, but may seize nondangerous contraband when it is in plain view or is detected through plain "feel" or touch without overstepping the boundaries of a *Terry* pat-down search. The officer must proceed with the investigation expeditiously in order to avoid unnecessarily prolonging the period of involuntary detention. *Miranda* warnings are not necessary unless the encounter becomes a custodial arrest.

There is no bright line separating *Terry* stops from custodial arrests. Factors that courts consider in determining when a stop, made on a reasonable suspicion, has escalated into an arrest, for which probable cause is necessary, include the duration of the detention, the diligence with which the officers pursue the investigation, and the scope and intrusiveness of the detention. If the detention lasts too long or is too intrusive to be allowed on reasonable suspicion, the encounter becomes a de facto arrest. During *Terry* stops, police officers are not allowed to conduct evidentiary searches, take detainees to a police station, or perform any acts that are more intrusive than necessary to conduct the investigation or for safety and security. As a general rule, the stop may not last longer than 90 minutes.

An arrest occurs when an officer: (1) seizes a suspect and formally announces that he is under arrest, or (2) exceeds the parameters of a *Terry* stop. To justify an arrest, police officers must have probable cause to believe the person has committed or is committing a crime. Probable cause for an arrest may be based on a variety of sources besides the officer's own observations. These sources include physical evidence found at the scene; information supplied by other law enforcement officers or agencies, or in police records; reports received from victims, eyewitnesses, and informants; and rational inferences drawn from the officer's prior experience. The facts and circumstances known to the officer are considered in combination and evaluated from the perspective of a trained police officer. Probable cause exists when the facts and circumstances known to the officer at the moment of arrest are sufficient to establish a fair probability that the suspect is guilty of a crime.

The same standard is also used to evaluate whether probable cause exists for the issuance of an arrest warrant. Absent exigent circumstances or hot pursuit, police officers must obtain an arrest warrant before making a nonconsensual entry into a private dwelling to arrest someone inside. When the dwelling belongs to someone else, the Fourth Amendment also requires a search warrant. A majority of states, by statute, also require police officers to obtain an arrest warrant in order to arrest for a misdemeanor, unless the misdemeanor is committed in the officer's presence.

The preferable method of making an arrest is under the authority of a warrant, even when one is not required. A properly issued arrest warrant ensures the admissibility of evidence seized during the arrest and immunizes the arresting officer from liability for making an unconstitutional arrest. However, these advantages will be lost if the officer deliberately or recklessly misstates facts in the affidavit, or if the affidavit fails to contain enough information about the underlying facts to enable the magistrate to make an independent determination of probable cause. Persons arrested without a warrant are entitled to a post-arrest judicial review of grounds for their arrest no later than 48 hours after the arrest unless they have already been released on bail.

Traffic stops involve seizures and require probable cause or reasonable suspicion unless they are made at a fixed checkpoint. Evidence of drugs uncovered during a pretextual traffic stop is admissible if police have grounds for the underlying stop and do not exceed the limits on scope and duration, which are similar to *Terry* stops.

When police officers have grounds for a seizure, they may use force to effect the seizure, if necessary. However, the force used must be reasonable under the circumstances. Deadly force—force likely to cause death or serious bodily harm—may be used only if the suspect threatens the officer or someone else with a weapon or the officer has probable cause to believe that the suspect committed a crime involving the infliction or threatened infliction of serious injury and will be a threat to the community if he or she escapes. Whenever feasible, the officer must give the suspect some warning ("stop or I'll shoot") before resorting to deadly force.

# Search and Seizure 4

*The right of the people to be secure in their persons, houses, papers, and effects, against unreasonable searches and seizures, shall not be violated, and no Warrants shall issue, but upon probable cause, supported by Oath or affirmation, and particularly describing the place to be searched, and the persons or things to be seized.*

Fourth Amendment

# Chapter Outline

# § 4.1  Overview of the Law of Search and Seizure

The Fourth Amendment regulates three activities in addition to those covered in Chapter 3: (1) searching persons for evidence, (2) searching places and things for evidence, and (3) seizing evidence. These three activities are grouped together into a single category called "search and seizure" law. The work that police officers do often requires them to coordinate the rules covered in Chapter 3 with those covered in Chapter 4. Gathering evidence is usually necessary to develop probable cause for an arrest. Further evidence-gathering generally occurs during an arrest and often afterward to develop the case for trial. The same Fourth Amendment language that regulates **investigatory detentions** and **arrests** also regulates searches and seizures. It should, therefore, come as no surprise that the requirements in both contexts are similar.

We will begin this chapter by examining a recent police investigation known as the "Curious Case of the Artless Art Thief." What makes this case unique is that Inspector Clueso's compliance with the Fourth Amendment was, for once in his career, impeccable.

## THE CURIOUS CASE OF THE ARTLESS ART THIEF

### Prologue

Several summers ago, a collection of famous works of art, on loan from the Louvre museum in Paris, was on tour in the United States and exhibited in various local museums. While these works were on display at the Whosville Art Institute, a brazen burglary took place. The burglar broke in under cover of night and stole two paintings—Leonardo da Vinci's *Mona Lisa* and Marcell du Chump's *Nude Descending a Fireman's Pole*. There were no witnesses and the only physical evidence recovered by the Whosville Police Department (WPD) at the crime scene was a single left-handed white glove bearing the monogram SS.

### The Investigation

The WPD's finest, Inspector Clueso, surmised that the glove belonged to none other than Sticky-Fingered Sam, Whosville's most infamous criminal. Glove in hand, Clueso headed straight to the local magistrate, Judge Stickler, and requested a warrant to search Sam's home. After reviewing the evidence, Stickler denied the warrant, exclaiming with exasperation:

"You dunce, you should know by now that a glove bearing the initials SS is not enough evidence to establish probable cause to believe that the stolen works of art will be found in Sam's house. You had no business asking for a search warrant on such meager evidence. It shows a complete disregard for the rights of the citizens who elected me."

Undaunted, Clueso set up surveillance outside Sam's home. He waited on the street outside Sam's house each morning, followed Sam to his office, waited outside, and then followed Sam home again. In the evenings, when Sam took his garbage out to the curb, Clueso rummaged through the cans, looking for incriminating materials. He also put in a requisition for a pair of Super-Spy X-Ray Binoculars, explaining that he needed the equipment to look through Sam's walls. His request was denied with advice that he "could get in big trouble for using a device like that without a search warrant."

After one week, Clueso had observed nothing unusual, but his garbage rummaging had turned up several art magazines and a receipt for one pair of gloves. Once again Clueso applied for a search warrant and once again was told against that his evidence was not sufficient to satisfy the Fourth Amendment.

Feeling like a failure, Clueso sank into a depression and was unable to work for several weeks. However, on the first night that he returned to work, Clueso hit what he thought would be a pay dirt—a right-handed white glove, discarded in Sam's garbage, bearing the initials SS. This time Stickler agreed that there was probable cause, but not the kind for which Sam had hoped. The matching glove, considered in combination with Sam's criminal record, established probable cause to believe that Sam committed the theft, allowing for issuance of an arrest warrant, but not a search warrant. A search warrant, Stickler explained, required probable cause to believe that the stolen paintings would be found in Sam's home. Because the burglary had happened almost a month before and Clueso had not kept Sam's house under observation for much of this period, it was just as probable that Sam had already disposed of the paintings. As a result, no search warrant would be issued.

A big break in the case came several months later. Fortunately for Clueso, Sam loved art more than his privacy and installed a large display window facing the street to let in the northern light. As Clueso drove by Sam's house one day, he saw a painting of a woman resembling the *Mona Lisa*, clearly visible through the window. Believing that he now had enough evidence to support a search warrant, but was afraid to let the painting out of his sight, he rang Sam's doorbell and introduced himself as Joe, a world-renowned art critic. He told Sam that he couldn't help but notice the dazzling painting he saw through the window, and asked whether he could come in to admire it up closer. Flattered, Sam agreed, and took Clueso into his living room.

Once inside, Clueso could see that the painting looked very much like the *Mona Lisa*, but could not be sure. The famous smile on the painting was all wrong and the paint appeared to be wet. Either this was a common reproduction of the famous painting or Sam had been altering it to suit his own sense of aesthetics. To solve this mystery, Clueso took the painting from the wall and sniffed around the smile. Sure enough, the paint was wet. Confident that the painting was authentic, Clueso placed Sam under arrest. He then scanned the room and looked inside a closet near where Sam was standing, but the du Chump painting was nowhere to be seen. However, he spotted a set of finger paints, which he seized.

When advised of these developments, Judge Stickler hastily issued a warrant to search Sam's home for "Du Chump's *Nude Descending a Fireman's Pole*, tools used in connection with the theft, and any other items evidencing Sam's responsibility." Armed with the search warrant, Clueso returned to Sam's home and, this time, looked in every room and closet. He found the *Nude Descending a Fireman's Pole* unharmed behind the bureau in Sam's bedroom. As he moved the bureau, he dislodged a plastic sandwich bag containing what appeared to be several ounces of marijuana that was wedged behind it and seized that as well. Sam's motion to suppress the evidence taken from his home was denied and he was convicted of two counts of grand theft, one count of willful destruction of property, and one count of possession of a controlled substance. Sam's conviction was upheld on appeal.

### Epilogue

Clueso was promoted to head of the WPD, Sam finished out his sentence, and the investigation has been hailed as a resounding success.

## Analysis of the Investigation

Inspector (now Chief) Clueso's investigation fully complied with the Fourth Amendment. "Privacy" and "property" are the centerpieces of Fourth Amendment search and seizure law. A **search** occurs when police intrude on a suspect's **reasonable expectation of privacy**. A seizure occurs when they interfere with a suspect's possessory rights in property. As with **seizures of persons**, searches and seizures of property are graded according to invasiveness. Some evidence-gathering is not regulated by the Fourth Amendment because there is no interference with the suspect's privacy or property rights. Other evidence-gathering involves an intrusion, but the intrusion is sufficiently brief and limited as to call for less stringent regulation. Finally, some intrusions are sufficiently serious as to constitute full-blown searches or seizures. Clueso's investigation contains examples of each, as well as a host of other concepts that will be covered in this chapter.

> A search occurs when police intrude on a suspect's reasonable expectation of privacy. A seizure occurs when they interfere with a suspect's possessory rights in property.

## A. Nonsearch Activity

Investigative activity that does not interfere with interests protected by the Fourth Amendment constitutes a "free zone" for police work. In detention and arrest law, this zone is defined in terms of the suspect's freedom to go about his or her business. In search and seizure law, it is defined in terms of the suspect's privacy and property rights. Police operate in the free zone as long as their investigative activity does not infringe on any of these three interests.

Investigative activity that infringes on a suspect's *reasonable expectation of privacy* results in a search. A search can occur either because police make a trespassory entry into a constitutionally protected location or because they use high-tech surveillance devices that invade privacy.[1] Inspector Clueso was careful not to perform a search until he developed Fourth Amendment grounds. The initial stages of his investigation were conducted on the public streets. He was standing on the street when he saw what appeared to be the stolen *Mona Lisa* through Sam's front window where it was visible to anyone who looked. Suspects have no reasonable expectation of privacy in matters they knowingly expose to the public. Consequently, police surveillance of activities exposed to public view is not a search. This also explains why rummaging through Sam's garbage container was not a search. Once Sam placed the garbage container on the curb for collection, he no longer had any reasonable expectation of privacy in the contents. Just as the public could see the

---

[1]    **Katz v. United States, 389 U.S. 347, 88 S. Ct. 507, 19 L. Ed. 2d 576 (1967).**

*Mona Lisa* through Sam's undraped window, so vagabonds, children, and snooping neighbors could have picked through his garbage. Consequently, Clueso was free to rummage through it as well.[2]

Clueso also avoided **seizing** evidence before he developed grounds. A seizure occurs when police interfere with a suspect's property rights.[3] Removing items from Sam's garbage container was not a seizure because Sam deliberately abandoned his property rights in objects he discarded as trash.

## B. Consent Searches and Seizures

Sam's house is a location that is protected by the Fourth Amendment. A physical entry into a constitutionally protected location constitutes a search[4] and normally requires a **search warrant**.[5] However, consent voluntarily given by someone who resides on the premises eliminates the need for a warrant. Clueso's misrepresentation of his police identity did not destroy the voluntariness of Sam's consent.[6] Accordingly, his entry into Sam's home did not violate the Fourth Amendment.

## C. Brief, Limited Searches and Seizures

When Inspector Clueso removed the *Mona Lisa*-like painting from Sam's wall, he interfered with Sam's property rights because he had only been given permission to *look* at the painting. Removing it from the wall was, therefore, a seizure. Probable cause to believe that property is connected to a crime is necessary before police may seize it for use as evidence.[7] Because Inspector Clueso had not yet developed this degree of certainty, he would have violated Sam's Fourth Amendment rights had he put the painting under his arm and left with it. However, Clueso removed the painting for a lesser purpose—to examine it to determine whether it was stolen. Police are allowed to perform brief, limited seizures for investigation when they have a reasonable suspicion that property is connected to criminal activity.[8] This authority is based on the principles announced in *Terry v. Ohio*[9] and is governed by the same standard. Clueso's reasonable suspicion that the painting was the stolen *Mona Lisa* justified his removing it from Sam's wall for a closer examination. Once satisfied that it was the real thing, Inspector Clueso now had probable cause to seize it as evidence.

[2]  **California v. Greenwood, 486 U.S. 35, 108 S. Ct. 1625, 100 L. Ed. 2d 30 (1988)**.
[3]  Maryland v. Macon, 472 U.S. 463, 105 S. Ct. 2778, 86 L. Ed. 2d 370 (1985).
[4]  **Katz v. United States**, *supra* note 1.
[5]  Carroll v. United States, 267 U.S. 132, 45 S. Ct. 280, 69 L. Ed. 543 (1925).
[6]  Lewis v United States, 385 U.S. 206, 17 L. Ed. 2d 312, 87 S. Ct. 424 (1966).
[7]  Warden v. Hayden, 387 U.S. 294, 87 S. Ct. 1642, 18 L. Ed. 2d 782 (1967).
[8]  **United States v. Place, 462 U.S. 696, 103 S. Ct. 2637, 77 L. Ed. 2d 110 (1983)**.
[9]  **392 U.S. 1, 88 S. Ct. 1868, 20 L. Ed. 2d 889 (1968)**.

### D. Full Searches and Seizures

Searches for criminal evidence are called **full searches**. Unlike arrests, in which a warrant is usually optional, full searches *always* require a search warrant unless an established exception to the warrant requirement applies. However, a number of exceptions exist and consent is one of them. Sam's consent was, nevertheless, limited. He invited Clueso into his living room to look at his painting. When Clueso developed probable cause to believe that the painting on the wall was the stolen *Mona Lisa* and placed Sam under arrest, however, a second exception became applicable. Clueso was entitled to perform a search incident to the arrest.

Searches incident to arrest, and indeed all searches, have defined boundaries. An arrest only justifies a search of the arrestee's person and the area under his or her immediate control, which is defined as the area within arm's reach. Consequently, it was necessary for Clueso to get a search warrant before he could search the rest of Sam's home. Judge Stickler, who had previously refused to grant a search warrant because Clueso's evidence failed to establish probable cause to believe that the stolen works of art were still in Sam's home, was now willing to do so. Discovery of the stolen *Mona Lisa* created probable cause to believe that the du Chump painting was probably still there, too.

The search warrant only authorized the seizure of the du Chump painting and articles related to the theft. Police, nevertheless, are not required to ignore criminal evidence and **contraband** discovered in plain view during an authorized search, even when they are not listed in the warrant.[10] The **plain view exception** to the warrant requirement supplied the basis for Clueso's seizure of the marijuana.[11]

Now that the *Curious Case of the Artless Art Thief* has been solved, we are ready to explore the law of search and seizure.

## § 4.2 —Definition of a Search

Every Fourth Amendment analysis begins with the basic question "Did the conduct of the police constitute a "search" or a "seizure?" If the answer is "no," no further Fourth Amendment inquiry is necessary. As you learned in Chapter 3, there is a free zone in which police are able to investigate without having to worry about the Fourth Amendment. In fact, the Fourth Amendment covers only two activities—searches and seizures. As long as the police avoid doing either, their activity is not regulated by the Fourth Amendment.

The Fourth Amendment restricts the search authority of the police to protect privacy. General warrants and writs of assistance, which authorized British customs officials to enter private homes and rummage through their contents in search of smuggled goods or anything else incriminating, without

---

[10]    Coolidge v. New Hampshire, 403 U.S. 443, 467, 91 S. Ct. 2022, 2038, 29 L. Ed. 2d 564 (1971).
[11]    The plain view doctrine is discussed in § 4.4.

grounds for believing that anything incriminating would be found, made the colonists acutely aware of this need.[12] Concern for privacy is also the controlling consideration in determining whether there has been a search. The Supreme Court defines a search as police activity that intrudes upon a citizen's reasonable expectation of privacy. However, this has not always been the case.

## A. *Fourth Amendment Interpretation from* Olmstead *to* Katz

The Supreme Court originally interpreted the term "search" to require a physical intrusion into a constitutionally protected location. Persons, houses, papers, and effects are the four subjects mentioned in the Constitution. This interpretation was adequate to protect the privacy of citizens for the first 200 years of American history. However, as technology became more sophisticated, the government acquired the ability to monitor private activities without a physical trespass. Technology created new ways to communicate, eliminating the need to conduct private business face-to-face behind closed doors. Invention of the telephone made it possible to communicate at a distance. While parties to telephone conversations intend their communications to be private, the conversation can easily be intercepted without physically entering either party's home. The telephone was just the beginning of the new technology. Developments in police surveillance technologies created new ways for the government to snoop. The traditional concept of a search as involving a physical intrusion into a constitutionally protected location was no longer capable of protecting citizens' full range of privacy expectations.

The Supreme Court's first encounter with the impact of the new technologies on Fourth Amendment analysis occurred in *Olmstead v. United States*.[13] Olmstead, a bootlegger, was convicted of violating the National Prohibition Act based on evidence obtained by tapping his telephone line from a junction box located on a public street. The Supreme Court stood by the traditional interpretation, holding that Olmstead's Fourth Amendment rights were not violated because the police listened to his conversation without trespassing on any property that belonged to him.

*Olmstead* remained the Supreme Court's official position until the 1967 case of *Katz v. United States*,[14] which marked the beginning of modern Fourth Amendment jurisprudence. Katz, a bookie, was convicted of transmitting wagering information based on evidence overheard by FBI agents who attached a recording device to the exterior of a public telephone booth Katz regularly used to conduct his business. The conduct of the police did not violate the Fourth Amendment under traditional analysis because the recording device did not penetrate the wall of the booth. As a result, there was no phys-

---

[12]   James Otis, *Against the Writs of Assistance* (1761) in 1 ORATORS OF AMERICA 23-28 (G. Carlton Lee ed., 1900).

[13]   **277 U.S. 438, 48 S. Ct. 564, 72 L. Ed. 944 (1928)**.

[14]   **Katz v. United States**, *supra* note 1.

ical intrusion into a constitutionally protected location. The Supreme Court, nevertheless, ruled that a person who occupies a telephone booth, shuts the door, and pays the toll has a reasonable expectation that his telephone conversation is private and that this expectation is entitled to Fourth Amendment protection. The Court declared:

> . . . the Fourth Amendment protects people, not places. What a person knowingly exposes to the public, even in his own home or office, is not a subject of Fourth Amendment protection. But what he seeks to preserve as private, even in an area accessible to the public, may be constitutionally protected.

*Katz* redefined the term *search*. A search occurs whenever the police intrude on a suspect's reasonable expectation of privacy. This definition does not withdraw the protection that previously existed against physical intrusions into constitutionally protected locations.[15] The Supreme Court's goal in *Katz* was to make the Fourth Amendment responsive to changes in surveillance technology that made it possible for the police to invade privacy without committing a physical trespass.

## B. Search Defined

We are now ready to formulate a working definition of the term *search*. A search occurs whenever police invade a suspect's reasonable expectation of privacy. An invasion can occur either because the police: (1) physically intrude into a constitutionally protected location (i.e., a location in which the suspect has a reasonable expectation of privacy),[16] or (2) use advanced surveillance technologies to spy on activities that citizens reasonably expect are private.[17]

---

A search occurs whenever police invade a suspect's reasonable expectation of privacy, either by physically intruding into a constitutionally protected location or using advanced surveillance technologies to spy on activities that citizens reasonably expect are private.

---

### 1. Physical Intrusion into a Constitutionally Protected Location

The most common way a search occurs is by physically intruding into a constitutionally protected location. The Fourth Amendment mentions four subjects—persons, houses, papers, and effects—as having constitutional protection. These subjects have been interpreted expansively as denoting broad general categories.

---

[15]   Soldal v. Cook County, Illinois, 506 U.S. 56, 113 S. Ct. 538, 121 L. Ed. 2d 450 (1992).
[16]   Silverman v. United States, 365 U.S. 505, 81 S. Ct. 679, 5 L. Ed. 2d 734 (1961).
[17]   **Katz v. United States,** *supra* note 1.

**Persons.** The term *persons*, for search purposes, encompasses those parts of a suspect's body and clothing that are not exposed to the public, such as private parts of the anatomy, biological materials, and pockets and undergarments. Examining private parts of a suspect's body[18] or clothing[19] for evidence constitutes a search and requires Fourth Amendment search authority. Searches of clothing and personal belongings are covered in §§ 4.6 to 4.9. Highly intrusive body searches, such as strip searches and body cavity searches, and the taking of blood and urine samples, are subject to special rules that are covered in Chapter 7.

**Houses.** *Houses* includes homes and their surrounding buffer zone known as the **curtilage**, apartments, hotel rooms, private offices and warehouses, telephone booths, and even fixtures like file cabinets and lockers. In fact, this term has been defined to include any location, structure, or fixture in which there is a reasonable expectation of privacy.[20] Shopping malls and retail establishments, in contrast, are constitutionally protected locations only during hours when they are closed to the public. Searches of protected premises are covered in §§ 4.13 to 4.16.

**Papers and personal effects.** *Papers* encompasses letters, journals, records, films, and other private documents. *Personal effects* encompasses handbags, briefcases, packages, luggage and other closed **containers**, and vehicles, among other things. Searches involving papers and effects are discussed at various points in this chapter.

Police may not physically enter a suspect's home,[21] reach into his or her pocket,[22] look inside his or her luggage,[23] or intrude into any other location in which the suspect has a reasonable expectation of privacy without a recognized source of Fourth Amendment search authority.

### 2. Technological Invasions of Privacy

Today, a search can also occur through technological invasions of privacy. *Olmstead* and *Katz* both involved intrusions into the privacy of telephone conversations. In *Katz*, the Supreme Court held that a person who enters a public telephone booth and closes the door, shutting out the world, has a reasonable expectation that the conversation will be private and that this expectation is protected by the Fourth Amendment. Telecommunication surveillance is now regulated by a federal statute. Six months after *Katz*, Congress enacted the Omnibus Crime Control and Safe Streets Act of 1968,[24] which brought law enforcement use of wiretapping and other interception devices under judicial control by requiring prior court authorization.

---

[18]   **Schmerber v. California, 384 U.S. 757, 86 S. Ct. 1826, 16 L. Ed. 2d 908 (1966)**.

[19]   Minnesota v. Dickerson, 508 U.S. 366, 113 S. Ct. 2130, 124 L. Ed. 2d 334 (1993).

[20]   Maryland v. Macon, *supra* note 3.

[21]   **Payton v. New York, 445 U.S. 573, 100 S. Ct. 1371, 63 L. Ed. 2d 639 (1980)**.

[22]   Minnesota v. Dickerson, *supra* note 19.

[23]   **United States v. Place**, *supra* note 8.

[24]   18 U.S.C. §§ 2510-2520 (West 1997).

Despite the promise held out in *Katz* that citizens would enjoy broad protection against the government's secret monitoring of their comings and goings, this has not turned out to be the case. Technological advances since *Katz* have furnished the police with sophisticated devices that enable them to obtain much of the same information that once required a physical trespass and the Supreme Court has given police considerable latitude to use the tools of modern science to fight crime.[25] Practically speaking, there are only two limitations on surreptitious surveillance of matters other than communications. First, surveillance devices must be employed from a location where the officer has a right to be. Second, police may not use special surveillance equipment that is not generally available to the public to spy on activities inside a residence.[26] Had Inspector Clueso used Super-Spy X-Ray Specs to monitor activities inside Sam's home, such use would have constituted a search and a search warrant would have been necessary.

Constitutional and statutory limitations on wiretapping and other technological invasions of privacy are covered in greater depth in Chapter 5.

Figure 4.1
**Nonsearch Investigative Activity**

---

The Fourth Amendment does not treat the following activities as searches:

1. Searches and seizures performed by private parties without government complicity;
2. Searches and seizures of abandoned property;
3. Investigation of matters exposed to public view; and
4. Canine inspections to detect for the presence of narcotics

---

## C. Nonsearches

A search, as we have seen, is defined as police activity that invades a suspect's reasonable expectation of privacy. This definition has two components: (1) police activity and (2) an invasion of a suspect's reasonable expectation of privacy. If either of these components is missing, there is no search and the Fourth Amendment does not apply.

---

[25] *See, e.g.*, United States v. Knotts, 460 U.S. 276, 103 S. Ct. 1081, 75 L. Ed. 2d 55 (1983) (approving use of electronic tracking devices to monitor location and movement of suspect's vehicle); California v. Ciraolo, 476 U.S. 27, 106 S. Ct. 1809, 90 L. Ed. 2d 210 (1986) (permitting aerial surveillance and photographing of suspect's backyard).

[26] **Kyllo v. United States, 533 U.S. 27, 121 S. Ct. 2038, 150 L. Ed. 2d 94 (2001)** (use of thermal imaging device to detect whether amount of heat emanating from suspect's home was consistent with presence of high-intensity lamps used in marijuana growth constitutes search).

## 1. Private-Party Searches

Our Constitution operates as a limitation only on the actions of the government. Searches conducted by private parties without police complicity are not regulated by the Fourth Amendment. As a result, police may use evidence that private parties turn over to them without worrying about how they got it.[27] Furthermore, police activity that would normally be a search is not a search if it merely duplicates the activity that a private party has previously performed. Suppose an airline traveler inadvertently leaves her travel bag on an airplane and an airline employee opens it to determine the owner's identity. Upon discovering a vial of cocaine, the employee closes the bag and hands it over to the police. Although it would normally be a search for police to open a travel bag and look inside, it is not a search after a private party has opened it and viewed the contents, because the owner's reasonable expectation of privacy has already been compromised.[28] However, police activity becomes a search when it exceeds the previous exploratory activity and invades privacy interests that have not yet been invaded. If an apartment maintenance worker discovers a vial of cocaine while fixing a leaking faucet and turns it over to the police, police may not re-enter the apartment and search it in its entirety. Unlike the travel bag, which was fully examined before being turned over to the police, a person's apartment contains countless other possessions that have not been viewed. The occupant's reasonable expectation of privacy in the unviewed objects is still intact.[29] Consequently, a police investigation following a private-party search is not considered a search only if it goes no farther than the private-party search.

## 2. Police Investigations Conducted without Invading Privacy

The Fourth Amendment does not apply to police investigations that are conducted without intruding on a suspect's reasonable expectation of privacy. Because suspects lack a reasonable expectation of privacy in matters exposed to public view and abandoned property, police surveillance of these matters falls outside the Fourth Amendment.

**Matters exposed to public view.** Police are allowed to make the same observations that any member of the public could make. Anything that can be seen or heard by members of the public from a vantage point where the officer is lawfully present is said to be in "open view."[30] Police surveillance of matters in "open view" is not a search because no reasonable expectation of privacy is recognized in such matters. If there is an undraped window, a knothole in a fence, or a garbage can on the sidewalk, police are free to take a look.

---

[27]   United States v. Jacobsen, 466 U.S. 107, 104 S. Ct. 1652, 80 L. Ed. 2d 85 (1984). However, if the police affirmatively encourage a private search and the private individual acts to assist the police rather than for independent reasons, the search must satisfy the Fourth Amendment. *See, e.g.*, United States v. Jarrett, 338 F.3d 339 (4th Cir. 2003); Dawson v. State, 106 S.W.3d 388 (Tex. Ct. App. 2003).

[28]   United States v. Jacobsen, *supra* note 27.

[29]   *See, e.g.*, Walter v. United States, 447 U.S. 649, 100 S. Ct. 2395, 65 L. Ed. 2d 410 (1980); United States v. Runyan, 275 F.3d 449 (5th Cir. 2001); United States v. Allen, 106 F.3d 695 (6th Cir. 1997).

[30]   *See generally*, 1 WAYNE R. LAFAVE, SEARCH & SEIZURE § 2.2 (3d ed. 1996).

The fact that it takes extraordinary measures to reach a vantage point from which a view is possible does not prevent the matter from being in "open view." Even if an officer has to climb 20 flights of stairs to reach the outdoor fire escape of a public building so that he or she can climb up to the rooftop garden that overlooks the defendant's backyard, the backyard is still considered to be in open view. What matters is that the officer is standing in a place where he or she has a right to be when he or she observes things that any member of the public standing in that place could have observed.[31] Police, moreover, are free to use flashlights, binoculars, telescopes, or any other device in general public use to enhance their sensory capabilities.[32] In *California v. Ciraolo*,[33] police officers, acting on an anonymous tip, flew a helicopter over the defendant's backyard, which was shielded from street-level observation by a 10-foot-high fence, and observed marijuana plants growing below. The Supreme Court held that the aerial surveillance was not a search because any member of the public flying in this airspace who glanced down could have seen everything the officers observed.

The same principle applies to evidence detected through the sense of hearing or smell. Police officers are allowed to use any of their natural senses when lawfully present at the vantage point where their senses are used.[34] Thus, it is not a search for police to listen with the naked ear to goings-on inside a motel room from an adjoining room or from a common hallway,[35] or to sniff the exterior of a car parked on a public street for the odor of drugs.[36]

The Supreme Court has extended this principle to inspections by trained drug detection dogs. In *United States v. Place*,[37] the Supreme Court ruled that the use of trained drug detection dogs to sniff luggage is not a search because this procedure does not require opening the luggage and exposing the contents to public view. Trained dogs function as little more than an extension of the officer's own senses. Drug detection dogs are now being used to perform inspections at airports, bus terminals, train stations, and elsewhere.[38] It is not

---

[31]   *Id.*

[32]   United States v. Dunn, 480 U.S. 294, 107 S. Ct. 1134, 94 L. Ed. 2d 326 (1987); Texas v. Brown, 460 U.S. 730, 103 S. Ct. 1535, 75 L. Ed. 2d 502 (1983); United States v. Lee, 274 U.S. 559, 47 S. Ct. 746, 71 L. Ed. 1202 (1927).

[33]   *Supra* note 25.

[34]   *See, e.g.,* LAFAVE, *supra* note 30 ("As a general proposition, it is fair to say that when a law enforcement officer is able to detect something by utilization of one or more of his senses while lawfully present at the vantage point where those senses are used, that detection does not constitute a "search" within the meaning of the Fourth Amendment.").

[35]   United States v. Jackson, 588 F.2d 1046 (5th Cir. 1979); United States v. Agapito, 477 F. Supp. 706 (S.D.N.Y. 1979).

[36]   United States v. Marlar, 828 F. Supp. 415 (N.D. Miss. 1993) (canine inspection of motel room door opening onto public sidewalk and parking lot did not constitute a search); Jennings v. Joshua Independent School District, 877 F.2d 313 (5th Cir. 1989) (use of trained dogs to sniff cars parked on public parking lots does not constitute Fourth Amendment search), *cert. denied*, 496 U.S. 935, 110 S. Ct. 3212, 110 L. Ed. 2d 660 (1990).

[37]   *Supra* note 8.

[38]   Kenneth R. Vallentin, *Dogs Are a Prosecutor's Best Friend: Canine Search and Seizure Law*, PROSECUTOR 31 (October 1997)

a search for an officer to walk a drug detection dog down a public street, through a parking lot, airport terminal, train station, hotel corridor, or any other location where the officer has a right to be.[39] Dogs may be used to sniff the exterior surface of checked luggage, parked cars, lockers, and any other object to which the police have a lawful right of access.[40]

Police, nevertheless, do not have the right to touch and feel everything they are free to look at or smell. Exploratory touching involves a greater invasion of privacy. In *Bond v. United States*,[41] a border patrol agent boarded a bus to check the immigration status of the passengers. As he walked forward to exit the bus after completing the check, he squeezed the soft luggage passengers had placed in the overhead storage bins to feel for the presence of contraband objects. He felt a brick-like object in the defendant's luggage that turned out to be a brick of methamphetamine. The Supreme Court ruled that the border patrol agent's tactile examination of the defendant's luggage to determine the contents constituted a search. Although bus passengers who store luggage in overhead storage bins expect that other passengers may move or shove it to make room for their own, they do not expect that others will touch their luggage in the exploratory manner in which the border patrol agent did. As a result, the border patrol agent's tactile examination of the defendant's luggage constituted a search.

**Abandoned property.** A person who abandons property voluntarily relinquishes any reasonable expectation of privacy in that property. This explains why rummaging through the contents of garbage cans that have been placed on the curb for collection is not a search.[42]

Figure 4.2
**Essentials for a Lawful Search**

> For a search to be lawful, the officer must:
>
> 1.  act under a recognized source of search authority, and
> 2.  confine the search activity to authorized search boundaries.
>
> Grounds for search authority and search boundaries vary with the purpose of the search.

---

[39] *See, e.g.*, Commonwealth v. Welch, 420 Mass. 646, 651 N.E.2d 392 (1995) (lockers in fire department's common room); United States v. Friend, 50 F.3d 548 (8th Cir. 1995) (car parked on private property but not within curtilage); United States v. Roby, 122 F.3d 1120 (8th Cir. 1997) (common corridor of a motel); United States v. Marlar, *supra* note 36 (outside motel room door); United States v. Lingenfelter, 997 F.2d 632 (9th Cir. 1993) (exterior of commercial warehouse); United States v. Colyer, 878 F.2d 469 (D.C. Cir. 1989) (Amtrak sleeper car); Scott v. State, 927 P.2d 1066 (Okla. Crim. App. 1996) (luggage checked with bus company).

[40] **United States v. Place**, *supra* note 8, 462 U.S. at 707, 103 S. Ct. at 2644; United States v. Jacobson, *supra* note 27, 466 U.S. at 123, 104 S. Ct. at 1661-1662; *See also* cases *supra* note 39.

[41] **529 U.S. 334, 120 S. Ct. 1462, 146 L. Ed. 2d 365 (2000)**.

[42] **California v. Greenwood**, *supra* note 2.

# § 4.3 —Sources of Search Authority

Whenever police perform an act that the Fourth Amendment treats as a search, they must have search authority. What is necessary to have search authority varies with the purpose of the search. The three main purposes for searching are to gather evidence, to disarm suspects for self-protection, and to make an inventory of property that the police have impounded. The first kind of search is called a **full search**, the second a **limited weapons search** or **frisk**, and the third an **inventory search**.

Rummaging through a citizen's property in search of anything that might be incriminatory is a general search, the evil against which the Fourth Amendment is directed.[43] Accordingly, in order for a search to be valid, police must: (1) have search authority, and (2) confine their search to the authorized search boundaries.[44] Each ground for search authority has rules delineating the boundaries of the search. Descriptions of search boundaries have two features: **scope** (i.e., the locations that may be searched) and **intensity** (i.e., the thoroughness with which these locations may be searched). However, there is one overriding limitation that governs all searches: *The scope and intensity of a search may never be greater than necessary to locate the objects for which an officer has search authority.*

Figure 4.3
**Categories of Searches**

| Category | Purpose of Search | Grounds for Conducting |
|---|---|---|
| Full Search | Gather evidence | Search warrant or recognized exception to warrant requirement |
| Limited Weapons Search | Disarm suspect to protect officer's safety | Reasonable suspicion that a lawfully detained suspect is armed and dangerous |
| Inventory Search | Catalogue property that police have taken into custody | Authority to impound and adherence to police department regulations governing conduct of inventory searches |

---

[43]  **Payton v. New York**, *supra* note 21.

[44]  **Chimel v. California, 395 U.S. 752, 89 S. Ct. 2034, 23 L. Ed. 2d 685 (1969); Arizona v. Hicks, 480 U.S. 321, 107 S. Ct. 1149, 94 L. Ed. 2d 347 (1987).**

## A. *Full Searches*

Searches conducted to gather criminal evidence are called full searches. When the purpose of the search is to gather evidence, the Fourth Amendment always requires either a search warrant or a recognized exception to the warrant requirement.[45]

Figure 4.4
**Probable Cause for a Search Warrant**

---

In order to secure a search warrant, an officer must possess facts sufficient to warrant a person of reasonable caution in believing three things:

1.  That a crime has been (or is being) committed;
2.  That specific objects associated with the crime exist; and
3.  That they will be found in the place to be searched.

---

### 1. Searches Under the Authority of a Warrant

The Supreme Court has expressed a strong preference for searches and seizures to be conducted under the authority of a warrant, because a warrant places the decision of whether there is probable cause for the search in the hands of a neutral and detached judge.[46] Fourth Amendment search and seizure analysis starts with the presumption that a search warrant is necessary and then carves out an abundance of exceptions that cut deep inroads into the general rule. Nevertheless, even when an exception applies, it is good policy to obtain a warrant, if possible, because a search warrant carries at least two advantages. First, a facially valid search warrant shields the officer from civil and criminal liability.[47] Second, judges take a more lenient view at suppression hearings of whether grounds existed for the search if the officer has taken the precaution of obtaining a warrant.[48]

The Fourth Amendment provides that 'no Warrants shall issue, but upon probable cause, supported by Oath or affirmation." Probable cause for a search warrant is similar to probable cause for an **arrest warrant**. It requires the same level of certainty, which is more than a hunch or even a reasonable suspicion, but less than proof beyond a reasonable doubt.[49] The facts upon which **probable cause for a search** are based may be gathered from the same sources and must have the same degree of reliability as those supporting **probable cause to arrest**.[50] The major difference is what the officer must have probable cause to believe. Probable cause for a search warrant requires facts sufficient to justify a person of reasonable caution in believing three things:

---

[45]   **Flippo v. West Virginia, 528 U.S. 11, 120 S. Ct. 7, 145 L. Ed. 2d 16 (1999)**.
[46]   **Payton v. New York**, *supra* note 21.
[47]   Malley v. Briggs, 475 U.S. 335, 106 S. Ct. 1092, 89 L. Ed. 2d 271 (1986).
[48]   *Id.*
[49]   Illinois v. Gates, 462 U.S. 213, 103 S. Ct. 2317, 76 L. Ed. 2d 257 (1983).
[50]   *Id.*

(1) that criminal activity has taken place, (2) that specific objects associated with that crime exist, and (3) that they will be found at the place to be searched. Courts do not insist on direct evidence that the objects of the search are located at the place to be searched; it is enough that they are probably there.[51] Courts, for example, will assume that the gun used to commit a crime and the clothing worn during its commission are probably at the suspect's home, absent evidence to the contrary.[52]

A second difference is the freshness of the information needed to support an application for a search warrant.[53] Unlike facts that support probable cause to believe that a suspect has committed a crime, facts supporting probable cause to believe that items of evidence will be found at a given location can grow stale. If the information is too old, it may have little value in showing that the evidence is still present at the place for which the warrant is sought. This explains why Judge Stickler, although willing to issue an arrest warrant once the second glove was found, refused to issue a search warrant. By the time Clueso developed probable cause to believe that Sam had stolen the paintings, several weeks had passed and Sam could have sold or removed them in the meantime. Consequently, even though Clueso now had enough evidence for an arrest, the passage of time prevented him from making the showing required to obtain a search warrant.

Finally, the Fourth Amendment requires that search warrants contain a particularized description of the place to be searched and the things to be seized. The purpose is to guard against general searches. The warrant's description of the place to be searched limits the search to locations for which police have demonstrated probable cause to believe that the objects of the search are located, and the description of the things to be seized limits the intensity of the search to activity no greater than necessary to locate those objects. These two limitations combine to prevent indiscriminate rummaging through a citizen's private belongings.

### a. Scope of a Search Under a Warrant

The warrant's description of the place to be searched defines the permissible **scope of the search**. Although warrants are usually issued for searches of homes and businesses, they can also be issued for searches of vehicles, containers, and even people. Search authority under a warrant extends only to the locations described in it. If a warrant is issued to search Sam's kitchen, police may not search the bedroom, garage, or the cabana behind his pool. However, descriptions like this are rare. It is more common to describe the premises to be searched by address. When the premises are described by address, search

---

[51]    United States v. Hernandez, 80 F.3d 1253 (9th Cir. 1996).

[52]    State v. Smith, 868 S.W.2d 561 (Tenn. 1993).

[53]    E.g., State v. Padavich, 536 N.W.2d 743 (Iowa 1995).

authority extends to the residence, the yard, and all structures within the **curtilage**.[54] According to many courts, search authority also extends to the owner's vehicles that are parked within the curtilage.[55]

### b. Intensity of a Search Under a Warrant

The warrant's description of the premises to be searched grants authority to enter. Once inside, the **intensity** of the search—whether the officer may look inside closets, open drawers or containers, read mail, etc.—is controlled by the warrant's description of the objects to be seized. Police may only look in places that are potential repositories of the objects for which they have search authority.[56] If the police secure a warrant to search Sam's home for a stolen pink baby elephant named Cha Cha, they may look in the basement and walk through all the rooms, but they may not open envelopes or look inside drawers, behind furniture, or under beds, because it would be impossible for a stolen elephant to be hidden there. Looking in places where Cha Cha could not possibly be violates the Fourth Amendment. On the other hand, when a search warrant is issued for small, easily concealed objects such as money or drugs, which can be hidden almost anywhere, police may meticulously go over every square inch of the premises with a fine-tooth comb.

Figure 4.5
**Warrant Requirement for Evidentiary Searches**

A search warrant is necessary to conduct a full search, except when:

1. police obtain consent from someone who has authority to give it.
2. the search is conducted as an incident to a lawful custodial arrest.
3. police have probable cause to believe that a motor vehicle contains property they may lawfully seize.
4. police are confronted with exigent circumstances that require immediate warrantless action.

### 2. Full Searches Conducted Under an Exception to the Warrant Requirement

The Supreme Court has expressed a strong preference that searches be conducted under the authority of a warrant because the decision of whether probable cause exists is made by a neutral and detached magistrate in a calm atmosphere rather than a hurried decision by an officer on the scene.[57] How-

---

[54] United States v. Gorman, 104 F.3d 272 (9th Cir. 1996).

[55] *See, e.g.*, United States v. Gottschalk, 915 F.2d 1459 (10th Cir. 1990) (search of car in driveway); United States v. Asselin, 775 F.2d 445 (1st Cir. 1985) (search of car next to carport); United States v. Napoli, 530 F.2d 1198 (5th Cir. 1976) (search of camper in driveway).

[56] *See, e.g.*, **United States v. Weinbender, 109 F.3d 1327 (8th Cir. 1997)**; People v. Llanos, 288 Ill. App. 3d 592, 681 N.E.2d 598 (1997).

[57] United States v. Ventresca, 380 U.S. 102, 85 S. Ct. 741, 13 L. Ed. 2d 684 (1965); United States v. Jeffers, 342 U.S. 48, 72 S. Ct. 93, 96 L. Ed. 59 (1951).

ever, search warrants are necessary only for full searches. Even then, four exceptions exist. Full searches are permitted without a warrant: (1) with consent, (2) as an incident to a lawful arrest, (3) when police have probable cause to believe a motor vehicle contains evidence that is subject to seizure, and (4) when exigent circumstances are present. Each of these exceptions is briefly described below and in greater detail later in this chapter. Pay close attention to what is necessary to have search authority under each of the exceptions and the scope and intensity of search activity that is permitted.

### a. Consent to Search

A warrant is not necessary to search a person or his or her property if the person consents. Third parties can give an effective consent only if they have joint access to, control over, or a reasonable expectation of privacy in the property to be searched.[58] In the case of a residence, they must be an occupant, such as a spouse, roommate, or adult child who lives on the premises. The consent, moreover, generally extends only to the areas shared in common, such as the living room, dining room, kitchen, and bathrooms. Police may not act on a third party's consent to search another adult occupant's separate bedroom or personal belongings, such as a desk, computer, or handbag in which there are strong privacy interests, without determining whether the consent-giver has a lawful right of access to them as well.[59]

Actual authority is not required for consent to be valid. It is enough that police reasonably believe that the consent-giver has such authority. In *Illinois v. Rodriguez*,[60] police received consent to search the suspect's apartment from

---

[58]  See, e. g., United States v. Matlock, 415 U.S. 164, 94 S. Ct. 988, 39 L. Ed. 2d 242 (1974) ("voluntary consent of any joint occupant of a residence to search the premises jointly occupied is valid against the co-occupant, permitting evidence discovered in the search to be used against him at a criminal trial"); United States v. Hylton, 349 F.3d 781 (4th Cir. 2003) (consent given by defendant's girlfriend to search apartment and bedroom that she shared with defendant valid); United States v. Padilla, 242 F.3d 378 (8th Cir. 2000) (operator of vehicle, whether or not owner, may give valid consent to search). Although oral consent is legally sufficient, it is customary to have the person sign a "Permission to Search" form something like the following: "I, Charles T Brown, do hereby voluntarily authorize L. Jones, of the Whosville Police Department, with such assistance as he/she deems proper, to search _____ (description). I am giving this written permission freely and voluntarily, without any threats or promises having been made to me, and after having been informed that I have the right to refuse to permit this search."

[59]  See WAYNE R. LaFAVE, SEARCH & SEIZURE § 8.3 (f) (3d. ed. 1996). See also United States v. Davis, 332 F.3d 1163 (9th Cir. 2003) (Police could not rely on apparent authority to consent where tenant told the police that the bedroom belonged to her roommate and that the gym bag found under the bed belonged to her roommate's boyfriend); United States. v. Melgar, 227 F.3d 1038 (7th Cir. 2000) (consent to search a closed container is not valid when police have positive information that the consenting party does not have common authority over it, such as a locked briefcase with someone else's initials on it); Krise v. State, 746 N.E.2d 957 (Ind. 2001) (defendant's housemate lacked authority to consent to warrantless search of defendant's purse, even though the purse was found in a bathroom they both shared); State v. Friedel, 714 N.E.2d 1231 (Ind. Ct. App. 1999) (driver's authority to consent to the search of his vehicle did not extend to a passenger's purse); People v. Goforth, 564 N.W.2d 526 (Mich. App. 1997) (mother's consent to search son's bedroom valid when police officer reasonably believed that mother had common authority over the room and the right to enter it).

[60]  497 U.S. 177, 110 S. Ct. 2793, 111 L. Ed.2d 148 (1990).

a woman who referred to the apartment as "our[s]," unlocked the door with her own key, and gave the police permission to enter. The woman had no actual authority to consent because she had moved out of the apartment a month before, taking her clothing with her. The Court, nevertheless, held that the search was valid because the police reasonably believed that she was the suspect's roommate. The Fourth Amendment only requires the police to act reasonably in determining whether the person giving permission has a legally valid basis to consent, not that they be right. This does not mean that police may rely on consent given under ambiguous circumstances without making an inquiry or that they may accept clearly erroneous assertions of authority. Police, for example, may not search a suspect's room in reliance on a landlord's or hotel clerk's consent because the person giving consent is not an occupant and, once the police inquire into the consent-giver's relationship to the premises, as they should when the relationship is unclear, they understand this.[61]

The permissible scope, intensity, and duration of a consensual search are measured by the consent that has been given. Consent may be limited, and when the limits are clearly stated, police must comply with them. However, when permission is given in general terms, as is more common, the permissible scope of the search is determined based on what the typical reasonable person would have understood by the exchange between the officer and the suspect.[62] The express object of the search is the most important consideration. General consent to search a vehicle for drugs, for example, would reasonably permit the police to examine both the passenger compartment and trunk and to look in all containers in which the express object of the search could fit.[63]

Consent to search must be voluntary in order to be effective. However, the Fourth Amendment does not require police officers to advise people of their right to refuse when asking for permission to search.[64]

### b. Search Incident to a Lawful Arrest

A lawful custodial arrest carries automatic authority to search the arrestee and everything under his or her immediate control for weapons and evidence, whether or not the officer has grounds to believe that either will be found.[65]

---

[61] *See, e.g.*, Chapman v. United States, 365 U.S. 610, 81 S. Ct. 776, 5 L. Ed. 2d 828 (1961) (Fourth Amendment violated where police searched rented premises, without a warrant, in the tenant's absence based on landlord's consent); Stoner v. California, 376 U.S. 483, 84 S. Ct. 889, 11 L. Ed. 2d 856 (1964) (hotel clerk has no authority to permit the police to search a hotel guest's room).

[62] Florida v. Jimeno, 500 U.S. 248, 111 S. Ct. 1801, 114 L. Ed. 2d 297 (1991) (permission to search automobile for narcotics carries authority to open any closed containers that might contain the object of the search unless the permission is qualified); United States v. Anderson, 114 F.3d 1059 (10th Cir. 1997) (permission to "scout around" vehicle authorized full search, including looking underneath); *but see* United States v. Cleave, 129 N.M. 355, 9 P.3d 157 (2000) (permission to "inspect" car trunk for drugs did not authorize performance of inspection by trained narcotics detection dog).

[63] *See* authorities *supra* note 62.

[64] United States v. Drayton, 536 U.S. 194, 122 S. Ct. 2105, 153 L. Ed. 2d 242 (2002); Schneckloth v. Bustamonte, 412 U.S. 218, 93 S. Ct. 2041, 36 L. Ed. 2d 854 (1973); Ohio v. Robinette, 519 U.S. 33, 117 S. Ct. 417, 136 L. Ed. 2d 347 (1996).

[65] United States v. Robinson, 414 U.S. 218, 94 S. Ct. 467, 38 L. Ed. 2d 427 (1973); Chimel v. California, *supra* note 44.

The arrest itself provides all the justification that is needed. A search incident to arrest is not restricted in the same ways as a pat-down search.[66] Being a full search, it can be more intensive. Officers may require arrested persons to remove their overcoats, turn their pockets inside out, examine the contents of their wallets, and even read their private documents.

### c. Vehicle Search Based on Probable Cause To Believe that the Vehicle Contains Criminal Evidence or Contraband

Police may conduct a warrantless search of a vehicle whenever they have probable cause to believe that the vehicle contains contraband or evidence of criminal activity.[67] This exception to the warrant requirement exists because of the ease with which motor vehicles can be moved. Within the time it takes to return with a search warrant, the vehicle may be gone. Accordingly, a search warrant is not necessary when officers have probable cause to believe that the vehicle contains evidence that they may lawfully seize. The scope of the search is coextensive with the entire vehicle and all containers inside. The police, nevertheless, may only look inside areas and containers in which the object of their search could fit. For example, they may not look inside the glove compartment when searching for a stolen television.

### d. Exigent Circumstances and Hot Pursuit

Police are allowed to enter private property without a search warrant when they are confronted with exigent circumstances that create an urgent need for immediate action.[68] The three main circumstances that fall within this exception are hot pursuit of a fleeing suspect, threats to safety, and threatened destruction of evidence.[69]

Exigent circumstances searches are limited, both in scope and intensity, to action immediately necessary to address the exigency that justified the entry.[70] For example, if the exigency concerns destruction of evidence, police may

---

[66] See, e.g., **United States v. Robinson**, *supra* note 65 (upholding search of a crumpled pack of cigarettes found in the pocket of person arrested for a traffic violation).

[67] Maryland v. Dyson, 527 U.S. 465, 119 S. Ct. 2013, 144 L. Ed. 2d 442 (1999); California v. Acevedo, 500 U.S. 566, 111 S. Ct. 1982, 114 L. Ed. 2d 619 (1991); **United States v. Ross, 456 U.S. 798, 102 S. Ct. 2157, 72 L. Ed. 2d 472 (1982)**.

[68] Segura v. United States, 468 U.S. 796, 104 S. Ct. 3380, 82 L. Ed. 2d 599 (1984); United States v. Santa, 236 F.3d 662 (11th Cir. 2000) (exigent circumstances exception applies when "the inevitable delay incident to obtaining a warrant must give way to an urgent need for immediate action").

[69] United States v. Santa, *supra* note 68 (exigent circumstances include danger of flight or escape; danger of harm to police officers or the general public; risk of loss, destruction, removal, or concealment of evidence; and "hot pursuit" of a fleeing suspect); Ingram v. City of Columbus, 185 F.3d 579 (6th Cir. 1999) (same). Exigent circumstances searches are covered in § 4.16.

[70] Segura v. United States, *supra* note 68 (when police have probable cause to believe that a drug operation is being conducted inside an apartment, they may enter to secure the premises and prevent removal or destruction of evidence while applying for warrant); Illinois v. McArthur, 531 U.S. 326, 121 S. Ct. 946, 148 L. Ed. 2d 838 (2001) (where police have probable cause to believe that drugs are located inside a dwelling and good reason to fear that residents will destroy the evidence before they return with a warrant, they may seal off the premises and prevent residents from entering, pending issuance of a search warrant).

enter for the sake of securing the premises to prevent people inside from destroying or removing the evidence while applying for a search warrant, but must postpone the search until a warrant is obtained.[71]

## B. Limited Weapons Searches: Frisks and Protective Sweeps

The traditional Fourth Amendment requirements of probable cause and a search warrant apply only to searches conducted to obtain evidence, known as **full searches**. Searches conducted for other reasons, such as to disarm a suspect or to prepare an inventory of property impounded for safekeeping, are governed by different Fourth Amendment standards.

Police may perform a **limited weapons search** or **frisk** when they have reason to believe that a person whom they have lawfully detained for investigation may be armed and dangerous.[72] The purpose of a frisk is to disarm the suspect so that police can conduct the investigation without fear for their safety. Weapons frisks are limited searches. They are limited both in the objects for which police may search and in their scope and intensity. Police may search only for weapons and are limited to patting down the suspect's outer clothing. If the detention involves a vehicle, they are limited to performing a cursory visual inspection of areas and receptacles inside the passenger compartment that are capable of housing a weapon.[73]

**Protective sweeps** are another type of limited search. When police make an arrest inside a residence, they are allowed to perform a cursory visual inspection of closets and other spaces immediately adjoining the place of arrest in which cohorts who pose a danger to the officers might be hiding.[74]

## C. Inventory Searches

An **impoundment** occurs when police take custody of property for reasons other than use as evidence. Vehicles and personal belongings taken from arrestees before placing them in a detention facility are the articles most often impounded.[75] The Fourth Amendment permits the warrantless search of all lawfully impounded property.[76] The reason traditional Fourth Amendment requirements do not apply is that the search is not investigatory. The purpose of the search is to protect the owner's property while it is in police custody and to pro-

---

[71]　*See* cases *supra* note 70.

[72]　**Terry v. Ohio**, *supra* note 9. *Terry* stops are covered in §§ 3.7-3.9.

[73]　*Terry* pat-down searches are discussed in greater detail in § 4.7.

[74]　Protective sweeps are covered in greater detail in § 4.15.

[75]　South Dakota v. Opperman, 428 U.S. 364, 96 S. Ct. 3092, 49 L. Ed. 2d 1000 (1976) (inventory search of abandoned automobile impounded by police); Illinois v. Lafayette, 462 U.S. 640, 103 S. Ct. 2605, 77 L. Ed. 2d 65 (1983) (inventory search of contents of arrestee's shoulder bag before placing arrestee in detention facility); Florida v. Wells, 495 U.S. 1, 110 S. Ct. 1632, 109 L. Ed. 2d 1 (1990).

[76]　*See* cases *supra* note 75.

tect the police department against false claims of lost or stolen property. The Fourth Amendment is satisfied if police have legal authority for the impoundment and conduct the search according to standard operating procedures.[77]

## § 4.4  Fourth Amendment Requirements for Seizing Property

So far this chapter has discussed only searches. However, the Fourth Amendment also regulates seizures. Although it is common to use the phrase "search and seizure" as if the two are inseparable, this is not the case. There can be searches without seizures and seizures without searches.[78] The Fourth Amendment provides separate requirements for each.

There are at least four different reasons police seize property: (1) to use the property as evidence, (2) to detain the property while conducting a brief investigation into its ownership or content, (3) to prevent the property from being moved while applying for a search warrant, and (4) to impound property for safekeeping. As with searches, Fourth Amendment requirements vary with the reason for the seizure. Each ground for seizure has its own set of rules. We will start by defining the term *seizure* as applied to things.

> A seizure, in the Fourth Amendment sense, occurs when police commit a meaningful interference with a person's possessory interest in property.

### A.  Seizure Defined

Under property law, the possessor of property has the exclusive right to use it and the absolute right to exclude others from doing so. Even the slightest touching violates the possessor's property rights, when done without permission. However, Fourth Amendment protection is not this broad. A seizure in the Fourth Amendment sense occurs only when police *commit a meaningful interference with a person's possessory interest in property*.[79] This definition has two key phrases—"meaningful interference" and "possessory interest in property." Both must be understood in order to grasp the concept of a seizure. The following example will help explain.

---

[77]  Inventory searches are discussed in greater detail in §§ 4.8 and 4.12. There are other reasons for searching other than the ones covered in this chapter. Each has its own set of rules. For example, routine searches made at the national borders to collect duties and prevent introduction of contraband do not require any level of suspicion. *See, e.g.*, United States v. Flores-Montano, 124 U.S. 1582, 124 S. Ct. 1582, 158 L. Ed.2d 311 (2004).

[78]  *See, e.g.*, Zurcher v. Stanford Daily, 436 U.S. 547, 98 S. Ct. 1970, 56 L. Ed. 2d 525 (1978); United States v. Jacobsen, *supra* note 27. Taking suspect's briefcase from his custody and detaining it for several hours without opening it is an example of a seizure without a search because there is an intrusion on possessory rights, but not on privacy. Conversely, requiring a suspect to open his briefcase so police can look inside, without taking the briefcase from the suspect's custody, is an example of a search without a seizure because there is an intrusion on the suspect's privacy, but not on his possessory rights.

[79]  Maryland v. Macon, *supra* note 3.

## Duffel Trouble for Officer Caesar

Ralph Riefer (the second stupidest drug dealer in Whosville history) recently placed an anonymous telephone call to the Whosville Police Department to report a theft. Riefer told police that Mary Wanna (the stupidest drug dealer in Whosville) had just stolen a duffel bag full of his "personal stash" and was planning to smuggle it across the border into Mexico. Officer Caesar, who took the call, believed it was a practical joke and asked the caller to identify himself. When Riefer refused, Caesar told him that he could do nothing without more information, "What do you want me to do, arrest every woman in Whosville carrying a duffel bag?"

"No, you idiot," Riefer replied, "just look at the name tag on the duffel. If it says 'Ralph Riefer,' that's the one." Riefer then hung up quickly, hoping that the call would not be traced, but he was too late.

Caesar sent a car down to Riefer's house to determine whether the call was a joke, but decided in the meantime to check Whosville Air's next flight to Mexico, just in case Riefer was telling the truth. Sure enough, when he arrived at the airport, Caesar observed three women in line at the check-in counter, each traveling with a duffel bag.

The first woman had already checked her bag with the ticket agent, so Caesar stepped behind the counter, checked the tag, and determined that the bag did not belong to Riefer. The second woman had her duffel strapped to her back with a name tag dangling from it. Caesar snuck up, flipped it over, and read it without her noticing. Again, not Riefer's bag.

The third woman, who had been watching Caesar the whole time, clutched her bag tightly to her chest as he approached. Caesar politely asked her if he could examine the name tag on her luggage, but she refused. Caesar did not bother her further. Instead, he headed straight to the airport security office to telephone his superior for instructions. The superior instructed Caesar to keep the woman under observation and to see if she checked in under the name "Mary Wanna." In the meantime, the third woman became nervous, tossed her duffel in a nearby garbage can and headed out of the airport. When Caesar returned, he found the duffel, opened it, and located Riefer's stash. The duffel bag and the stash were admitted into evidence against Mary and Ralph and both were convicted of drug offenses.

Caesar touched all three bags, but none of his acts amounted to a meaningful interference with possessory rights, each for a different reason.

### 1. Touching or Moving Property While the Owner Is Not Around

Caesar did not interfere with the first owner's possessory rights because the bag was not in her possession when he touched it. She had already relinquished possession to the airline and had no intention of reclaiming her bag until she reached her destination. Touching or moving luggage while the owner is not around is not a seizure if the acts of the police do not damage the luggage, delay its arrival, or interfere with the owner's travel plans.[80]

### 2. Touching or Moving Property in the Owner's Presence without Depriving the Owner of Possession

Caesar touched the second duffel bag while the owner was carrying it. However, the touching did not constitute a *meaningful* interference with the second owner's possessory rights because he did not deprive the owner of possession and control of her bag.[81] The Supreme Court has decided two cases in which the police handled an owner's property in the owner's presence. In one case, the police detained a traveler's luggage for 90 minutes. The Court found that this was a seizure because the owner was denied access to his luggage and was prevented from taking it with him.[82] Depriving a traveler of his right to take his luggage with him, even for a few minutes, constitutes a meaningful interference with possession. In the second case, the police turned stereo equipment around to examine the serial numbers to determine whether it was stolen, also in the owner's presence. The Court held that this handling was not a seizure.[83] Putting these cases together, the following principle emerges: To constitute a meaningful interference with possession, the police must deprive the suspect of possession of his or her property—by taking it away, detaining it, or preventing the suspect from retrieving it.

### 3. Abandoned Property

Caesar did not seize the third duffel bag when he fished it out of the garbage can because Mary abandoned her property rights when she threw it there. Tossing something in the garbage is an unequivocal act of abandonment. A person who abandons property is in no position to complain of a seizure.[84] Consequently, Caesar was justified in retrieving the bag. Had Mary simply left it unattended on a chair and walked away, this would not support a conclusion

---

[80]   *See, e.g.*, United States v. Johnson, 990 F.2d 1129 (9th Cir. 1993) (removing traveler's luggage from airline luggage cart and subjecting it to canine inspection to detect for odor of narcotics is not a seizure when procedure is completed prior to time the luggage is scheduled to be placed on airplane). *See also* WAYNE R. LAFAVE, SEARCH & SEIZURE § 9.7(e) (3d ed. 1996) (no seizure occurs when an airline or bus passenger's luggage is moved slightly to facilitate a canine inspection, at a time when the luggage is outside the passenger's immediate presence, if the investigation does not delay the journey of the passenger or the luggage).

[81]   *See, e.g.*, **Arizona v. Hicks**, *supra* note 44 (1987) (turning stereo equipment around to examine serial number to determine whether it was stolen was not a seizure); **United States v. McIver, 186 F.3d 1119 (9th Cir. 1999)** (placement of small electronic tracking device on undercarriage of suspect's vehicle did not constitute a seizure because it did not damage the vehicle or deprive the owner of dominion or control over it).

[82]   **United States v. Place**, *supra* note 8 (removing luggage from passenger's custody and detaining it for investigation constitutes a seizure).

[83]   **Arizona v. Hicks**, *supra* note 44.

[84]   Stansbury v. State, 684 A.2d 823 (Md. 1996).

of abandonment because it is common for travelers to lay things down and later come back for them.

Denying ownership is another way property can be abandoned. Had Caesar approached Mary as she stood a few feet away from the bag, asked Mary if the bag was hers, and had she denied ownership, this, too, would have been treated as an abandonment.[85]

Figure 4.6
**Fourth Amendment Requirements for Seizing Property**

| Purpose of the Seizure | Fourth Amendment Requirements |
| --- | --- |
| Use the object as evidence | Probable cause to associate the object with a crime and either a search warrant describing it or a plain view discovery. |
| Detain the object for investigation | Reasonable suspicion that the object is or contains criminal evidence or contraband. |
| Prevent the object from being moved while applying for a search warrant | Probable cause to obtain a search warrant coupled with the risk that the object will be moved unless the police seize it now. |
| Impound the property | Legal authority to impound. |

## B. Seizure of Property for Use as Evidence

The requirements for seizing property vary with the purpose. Figure 4.6 shows the four main purposes for seizing property and summarizes the requirements for each. In order to seize property for use as evidence, the officer must have probable cause to believe that the property is connected to a crime.[86] The purpose of this requirement is to guard against excessively speculative seizures. Otherwise, officers conducting a lawful search would seize everything that looked even a little suspicious.[87] The officer must, in addition, either have a search warrant authorizing the seizure or discover the item in plain view.[88] More will be said about the second requirement shortly. We must first consider the kinds of objects police are permitted to seize as evidence.

> There are four categories of objects police may seize as evidence: fruits of a crime, instrumentalities of its commission, other evidence of its commission, and contraband.

---

[85]　United States v. Leshuk, 65 F.3d 1105 (4th Cir. 1995).

[86]　**Arizona v. Hicks**, *supra* note 44; United States v. Wick, 52 F. Supp. 2d 1310 (D.N.M. 1999).

[87]　United States v. Wick, *supra* note 86 (storage locker rental agreement could not be seized because officer lacked probable cause to believe that it was an incriminating document).

[88]　*See* § 4.4(B)(3) *infra*.

## 1. Objects that May Be Seized as Evidence: The Requirement of Probable Cause

There are four categories of items that police may seize as evidence: (1) **fruits of a crime**, such as stolen money or goods; (2) the **instrumentalities used to commit crime**, such as weapons; (3) contraband, a category that includes anything that it is a crime to possess, such as an unregistered gun or narcotics; and (4) "**mere evidence**," a catch-all phrase that includes any other objects that link a suspect to a crime or provide evidence of its commission, such as a mask worn by a bank robber, a shoe that matches footprints found at the crime scene, or a receipt for the purchase of the murder weapon.[89]

A police officer must be able to make a reasoned determination that the object he or she is viewing falls into one of these four categories before he or she may seize it without a search warrant and, to some extent, even when the officer has one.[90] Police officers' experience and training generally enable them to recognize fruits, instrumentalities, and contraband without much difficulty.[91] Cash in unusual quantities or packaged in particular ways sends up a "red flag" that it is probably the fruits of a crime.[92] Police officers do not have to know what the crime was or who committed it in order to have probable cause to treat bundles of $100 bills crammed into a briefcase as **seizable evidence**. Experience also helps police officers to recognize instrumentalities of a crime and contraband. In *Texas v. Brown*,[93] for example, the Supreme Court held that a police officer had probable cause to seize a balloon knotted a half-inch from the tip, even though he could not see what was inside, because the officer knew from prior experience that balloons knotted this way are often used to transport drugs. Based on similar reasoning, a Maryland court held that police officers investigating a recent burglary had probable cause to seize a crowbar in the possession of the man they arrested, even though they were not yet unaware of the means used to gain entry, because a crowbar is a burglar's "stock in trade."[94]

## 2. Requirement of a Search Warrant

As in the case of searches, the Supreme Court has expressed a strong preference for seizures under the authority of a warrant because a warrant protects against mistaken seizures.[95] An officer is not forced to decide on the spot

---

[89] Warden v. Hayden, *supra* note 7; Zurcher v. Stanford Daily, *supra* note 78. Rule 41(b) of the Federal Rules of Criminal Procedure provides that "[a] warrant may be issued under this rule to search for and seize any (1) property that constitutes evidence of the commission of a criminal offense; or (2) contraband, the fruits of crime, or things otherwise criminally possessed; or (3) property designed or intended for use or which is or has been used as the means of committing a criminal offense . . ."

[90] *See, e.g.,* **Arizona v. Hicks**, *supra* note 44; Warden v. Hayden, *supra* note 7.

[91] *See, e.g.,* United States v. Padilla, 819 F.2d 952 (10th Cir. 1987).

[92] United States v. Bono, 946 F. Supp. 972 (M.D. Fla. 1996).

[93] 460 U.S. 738, 103 S. Ct. 1535, 75 L. Ed. 2d 502 (1983).

[94] Williams v. State, 342 Md. 724, 679 A.2d 1106 (1996).

[95] *See, e.g.,* Coolidge v. New Hampshire, *supra* note 10.

whether an object that comes into view constitutes the fruits, instrumentalities, or other evidence of a crime or contraband because the judge has already decided this. The listing of an object in a search warrant carries a judicial finding that there is probable cause to believe that the object is properly subject to seizure. All the officer has to do is locate it. Moreover, a warrant prevents officers from conducting overly broad searches because the warrant limits the intensity of the search to places where the objects listed in the warrant could fit. Finally, the particularized description that search warrants must contain reduces the danger of mistaken seizures of the wrong property.[96]

Figure 4.7
**Authority to Seize Evidence in Plain View**

Police may seize evidence, without a warrant, if they discover it and develop probable cause to believe that it is connected to criminal activity without exceeding the boundaries of their lawful search authority. Evidence is considered to be in plain view only if:

1. the initial intrusion that brings the officer in contact with the evidence is lawful;
2. it is immediately apparent to the officer that the object observed is criminal evidence or contraband; and
3. the officer is able to gain physical access to seize it without violating the Fourth Amendment.

### 3. Plain View Exception to the Warrant Requirement

The only time police are allowed to seize objects for use as evidence without a search warrant describing them is when the plain view exception to the warrant requirement applies. This exception allows the police to seize criminal evidence that comes into plain view within the confines of a lawful search. The Supreme Court has explained that once an officer is lawfully in a position to view an object, the owner's privacy interest in that object is lost and it would be a needless inconvenience and sometimes even dangerous to require the officer to obtain a search warrant, to say nothing of the risk that the object might be removed or destroyed in the meantime.[97] The plain view exception originally applied only to objects discovered by accident. The thinking was that if the officer knew of the object's existence in advance, he or she should obtain a warrant. This limitation was abandoned in *Horton v. California*.[98] Consequently, even though plain-view discoveries normally occur by chance, chance discovery is no longer necessary.

The plain view exception has three requirements that are designed to ensure that police do not abuse this exception to conduct exploratory searches. A warrantless seizure is justified only if: (1) the initial intrusion that brings the

---

[96]   The requirements for a valid search warrant are covered in § 4.5.
[97]   Arizona v. Hicks, *supra* note 44; Coolidge v. New Hampshire, *supra* note 10; **United States v. Weinbender**, *supra* note 56.
[98]   496 U.S. 128, 110 S. Ct. 2301, 110 L. Ed. 2d 112 (1990).

officer in contact with the evidence is lawful; (2) it is immediately apparent to the officer that the object observed constitutes criminal evidence or contraband; and (3) the officer is able to gain physical access to the object to seize it without violating the Fourth Amendment.[99]

### a. The Initial Intrusion that Brings the Officer in Contact with the Evidence Must Be Lawful

For criminal evidence to be considered to be in "plain view," the initial intrusion that brings the officer in contact with the evidence must be lawful. In other words, there must be a lawful discovery. This requirement is satisfied when police discover criminal evidence or contraband in a public place, when they discover it while executing a search warrant to search for other objects, and also when they discover it while conducting a lawful search under *any* of the numerous exceptions to the warrant requirement. For example, if a police officer discovers marijuana in a glove compartment while inventorying the contents of an impounded vehicle, the marijuana is considered in "plain view" and the officer may seize it as evidence. The plain view rule is not limited to items that can be seen. It also applies to objects recognized through the sense of touch. For example, if an officer, while conducting a lawful *Terry* pat-down search to determine whether a suspect is armed, feels an object that he or she instantly recognizes as contraband from its shape and the way it feels, the officer may seize it.[100]

The converse is also true. Anything an officer discovers while exceeding his or her lawful search authority is the fruit of an illegal search and will be suppressed. For example, if the police discover a marijuana garden inside a broom closet while executing a search warrant to search Sam's home for "Cha Cha, a pink baby elephant," the evidence will be suppressed because the officer had no business looking inside a broom closet when searching for an elephant.

### b. The Object's Criminal Nature Must Be Immediately Apparent

The second requirement causes the most trouble, because officers instinctively tend to examine things that look suspicious. However, the plain view exception does not allow this. To satisfy the "immediately apparent" requirement, the officer must have probable cause to associate the object with criminal activity (i.e., must have probable cause to believe that it constitutes the

---

[99] Minnesota v. Dickerson, *supra* note 19 ("[i]f police are lawfully in a position from which they view an object, if its incriminating character is immediately apparent, and if the officers have a lawful right of access to the object, they may seize it without a warrant. If, however, the police lack probable cause to believe that an object in plain view is contraband without conducting some further search of the object—i.e., if its incriminating character is not immediately apparent—the plain-view doctrine cannot justify its seizure.").

[100] Minnesota v. Dickerson, *supra* note 19; **State v. Wilson, 112 N.C. App. 777, 437 S.E.2d 387 (1993)**.

fruits, instrumentalities, or other evidence of a crime or contraband), and must be able to do this with no additional exploratory activity beyond that which is authorized.[101]

"Immediately apparent" is a rigorous requirement that courts take very seriously. Moving a suspicious object as little as one inch to make a closer examination is not allowed, if this action is unrelated to the justification that brought the officer in contact with it.[102] The officer must develop probable cause to believe that the object viewed is criminal evidence or contraband without exceeding lawful search boundaries.

In *Arizona v. Hicks*,[103] a bullet fired through the floor of the defendant's apartment struck and injured the occupant of the apartment below. The police entered the defendant's apartment to search for the shooter, weapons, and additional victims. Upon entering the apartment, a police officer saw two sets of expensive-looking stereo equipment in the "squalid and otherwise ill-appointed four-room apartment." Suspecting that the equipment might have been stolen, the officer moved a turntable in order to view its serial number. A computer check of the serial number revealed that the equipment was, in fact, stolen. The Supreme Court ruled that the plain view doctrine did not apply because police had to move the turntable and examine the serial number in order to develop probable cause to believe that the stereo was stolen and this action had no relationship to the reason they were on the premises. If police need to feel, touch, or conduct further exploration beyond viewing what is already visible in order to determine whether the object is subject to seizure, then its incriminating nature is not immediately apparent and the plain view doctrine does not apply.

A similar problem arises when police read ledgers, journals, or similar writings that come into view during a search, but are not listed in the search warrant. In *United States v. Silva*,[104] police obtained a warrant authorizing them to search the home of a bank robbery suspect for a gun, a holster, ammunition, certain items of clothing, business suits, ties, ski masks, and a pair of wide-rimmed sunglasses. In the course of the search, an officer came across a brown satchel, opened it, and emptied the contents onto the floor. The satchel contained a pair of wide-rimmed sunglasses and a yellow spiral notebook. The officer leafed through the notebook page by page, looking for stolen currency. What she found was a five-page letter. The top page began "Dearest Samantha" and directed "Samantha" to destroy the letter upon reading it. Suspicion aroused, the officer read the entire letter and on page four discovered a paragraph that read: "I'll never allow my family to become street people. Not as long as I have a gun and there is a bank. This letter is written on the eve of such an event."

---

[101] Minnesota v. Dickerson, *supra* note 19; **Arizona v. Hicks**, *supra* note 44; Coolidge v. New Hampshire, *supra* note 10; **State v. Wilson**, *supra* note 100.

[102] Arizona v. Hicks, *supra* note 44.

[103] *Id.*

[104] 714 F. Supp. 693 (S.D.N.Y. 1999)

The court suppressed the letter, holding that, even though the officer was authorized to look inside the satchel because it was large enough to contain some of the items listed in the warrant, she exceeded her search authority when she read the letter because its incriminating content was not immediately apparent and, indeed, was not discovered until the fourth page. While executing a search warrant, police may not examine writings they come across that are not described in the warrant beyond glancing at what is plainly visible.[105]

### c. *The Officer Must Be Able to Gain Physical Access to the Object without Violating the Fourth Amendment*

Police occasionally observe property that they have probable cause to seize, but lack present authority to do so because gaining access requires crossing the threshold of a constitutionally protected location. This happened when Clueso saw what he thought was the stolen *Mona Lisa* through Sam's living room window. Crossing the threshold of Sam's home to gain access to the painting would have constituted a search and, at that point, none of the exceptions to the warrant requirement applied. Consequently, it was necessary for Sam to obtain a search warrant or consent to enter.[106]

> Objects recognized as criminal evidence or contraband may be seized without a search warrant only if the officer is able to gain physical access to them without violating the Fourth Amendment. If a physical intrusion into a constitutionally protected location is necessary to gain access, the officer must obtain a search warrant or consent to enter.

## C. *Brief, Limited Seizures*

Police sometimes have suspicions about property, but lack a search warrant or the authority to seize it under the plain view doctrine. They may, nevertheless, be able to detain the property and prevent it from being moved so that they can conduct a brief investigation into its contents or hold it while they apply for a search warrant. Preventing a person from moving his or her property is a meaningful interference with possessory rights and, therefore, constitutes a seizure.[107] However, the Fourth Amendment imposes less rigorous requirements for brief, limited seizures.

Brief, limited seizures are generally used to detain closed **containers** such as briefcases, suitcases, and mailed parcels. Seizable evidence is sometimes located inside containers like these. Containers are personal effects—one of

---

[105] United States v. Maude, 481 F.2d 1062 (D.C. Cir. 1973).

[106] Illinois v. Andreas, 463 U.S. 765, 103 S. Ct. 3319, 77 L. Ed. 2d 1003 (1983) (for plain view doctrine to operate, not only must the officer be lawfully located in a place from which the object can be plainly seen, but he or she must also have a lawful right of access to the object itself); Horton v. California, *supra* note 98 (same).

[107] **United States v. Place,** *supra* note 8.

the four categories protected under the Fourth Amendment. Suspects have both privacy and property rights in containers owned by them. Opening a closed container and examining the contents intrudes on a suspect's reasonable expectation of privacy and, therefore, always constitutes a search. Consequently, police need a search warrant or a warrant clause exception that permits them to open a closed container before they may look inside. However, when an officer suspects that a movable container houses seizable evidence, the officer may be able to take less aggressive action, such as detaining the container while applying for a search warrant or while conducting a brief investigation.

### 1. Seizure Pending Issuance of a Search Warrant

Police may seize a container while applying for a search warrant to examine the contents whenever they have probable cause to believe that the container houses seizable evidence and there is a risk that the container may be moved while they are applying for the search warrant.[108] This exception rests on exigent circumstances. For example, suppose that police learn that Sam has left a package with $10,000,000 worth of stolen diamonds with UPS for delivery to his "French connection," and that the plane containing the package is about to take off for Paris. Even though police have no warrant, exigent circumstances justify seizing it from UPS. This preserves the status quo, pending application for a search warrant. Once the container has been secured, police must obtain a warrant before they may look inside.[109]

### 2. Brief, Limited Seizures for Investigation

If the police only have a reasonable suspicion that the container houses seizable evidence, they cannot obtain a search warrant because a search warrant requires probable cause. However, reasonable suspicion is enough to seize a container for a brief investigation.[110] Investigatory detentions of property are based on the principles established in *Terry v. Ohio*[111] and are governed by the same standards.[112] For example, if police spot a woman in an airport who matches a drug courier profile, they may temporarily detain her for investigation and also her luggage.[113] However, because reasonable suspicion does not confer authority to open closed containers, investigatory detentions of containers are of little use to the police unless they can confirm their suspicion without looking inside.

---

[108]  United States v. Chadwick, 433 U.S. 1, 97 S. Ct. 2476, 53 L. Ed. 2d 538 (1977).

[109]  United States v. Van Leeuen, 397 U. S. 294, 90 S. Ct. 1029, 25 L. Ed. 2d 282 (1970).

[110]  **United States v. Place**, *supra* note 8.

[111]  *Supra* note 72.

[112]  **United States v. Place**, *supra* note 8 (removing luggage from passenger's custody and detaining it for investigation constitutes seizure; suppression required because 90-minute detention went beyond police authority to detain luggage reasonably suspected to contain narcotics for brief investigation).

[113]  *Id.*

The chief application of this exception occurs in narcotics work. As you learned previously, sniff examinations performed by trained drug detection dogs are not regarded as searches.[114] Consequently, when police have reasonable suspicion that there are drugs in a traveler's luggage, they may seize the luggage from the traveler's custody and detain it briefly to subject it to a canine examination. Because no search is involved, the only requirement necessary to perform this procedure is grounds for an investigatory detention (i.e., reasonable suspicion that the luggage contains drugs). If the dog detects drugs, the officer will then have probable cause for a lengthier seizure, pending application for a search warrant.

However, no degree of suspicion is necessary to perform this procedure if police are in a position to gain access to a container without seizing it.[115] Police do not need reasonable suspicion to perform canine examinations of containers not then in the owner's possession, such as checked luggage,[116] cars parked on a street, or packages in the control of the postal service[117] when they are able to perform the examination expeditiously because there is no interference with possession.

## D. Seizures of Vehicles and Personal Belongings for Impoundment

Conventional Fourth Amendment requirements do not apply when property is seized for a noninvestigative reason, such as to **impound** it (i.e., take custody for safekeeping).[118] Vehicles and an arrested person's clothing are the two articles most often impounded. Statutes generally give police authority to impound vehicles when they are abandoned, illegally parked, not drivable, or when no one

---

[114] See § 4.2(C)(2) supra.

[115] See, e.g. United States v. Harvey, 961 F.2d 1361 (8th Cir. 1992), cert. denied, 506 U.S. 883, 113 S. Ct. 238, 121 L. Ed. 2d 173 (1992) (removal of luggage from overhead rack of bus while travelers were inside station is not a seizure); United States v. Brown, 884 F.2d 1309 (9th Cir. 1989) (brief detention of airline passenger's luggage to subject it to canine inspection, after checked but before delivered to cargo hold, does not constitute a "seizure" if does not delay arrival or otherwise interfere with passenger's travel); See also authorities supra notes 34, 36, 39, and 80.

[116] See cases supra notes 36, 39, 80, and 115.

[117] See, e.g., United States v. Vasquez, 213 F.3d 425 (8th Cir. 2000) (officers' actions in subjecting package to dog sniff as it sat at the rear of a delivery truck did not constitute a meaningful interference with suspect's possessory interest, requiring reasonable suspicion); United States v. Terriques, 319 F.3d 1051 (8th Cir. 2003) (mailed package was not detained for Fourth Amendment purposes when postal clerk sorting incoming mail briefly observed factors about the package that he believed suggested possible drug trafficking and handed the package to postal inspectors; however, seizure occurred when postal authorities thereafter removed package from the stream of mail); United States v. Quiroz, 57 F. Supp. 2d 805 (D. Minn. 1999) (reasonable suspicion not required to subject mail to canine examination when it does not delay probability of timely delivery).

[118] Florida v. White, 526 U.S. 559, 119 S. Ct. 1555, 143 L. Ed. 2d 748 (1999) (vehicle forfeitable as contraband); Florida v. Wells, supra note 75 (driver arrested and taken to jail); South Dakota v. Opperman, supra note 75 (abandoned automobile); Colorado v. Bertine, 479 U.S. 367, 107 S. Ct. 738, 93 L. Ed. 2d 739 (1987) (driver arrested and taken to jail); United States v. Gordon, 23 F. Supp. 2d 79 (D. Me. 1998) (car parked four feet away from curb).

is available to take charge of them after a driver's arrest.[119] Clothing and other articles in an arrested person's possession at the time of arrest are generally impounded before the person is placed in a detention facility, in order to prevent articles posing a security risk from being introduced into the facility.[120]

Once property is impounded, a search will be conducted to produce an inventory. The Fourth Amendment regulates inventory searches, but not by the same standards that are used for evidentiary searches, because the purpose of the search is to protect the owner's property while in police custody and to deter false claims of loss or theft.[121] The Fourth Amendment requirements for inventory searches are designed to ensure that they are used for this purpose and not as a subterfuge to search for evidence. For the search to be valid, (1) there must be a law or police department regulation authorizing the impoundment, (2) the impoundment must be made in good faith and not as a pretext to search for evidence, and (3) the search must be conducted according to standardized operating procedures establishing clear guidelines for where, when, and how such searches are to be conducted.[122]

## § 4.5   —The Fourth Amendment Search Warrant

Much has been made of the fact that a search warrant is generally necessary to search for or seize evidence. Little, however, has been said of the search warrant itself. Before proceeding further, we will pause to examine what a search warrant looks like, how one is obtained, and what is necessary for proper execution. Because Fourth Amendment requirements for an arrest warrant (§§ 3.14-3.15) also apply, for the most part, to search warrants, the following explanation focuses on the differences.

### A.  Applying for a Search Warrant

The mechanics of applying for search and arrest warrants are similar. For both, the officer must submit an affidavit under oath to a magistrate setting forth facts showing probable cause.[123] The facts must be true to the best of the officer's knowledge[124] and must be sufficiently detailed to enable the magistrate to make an independent determination of probable cause.[125] The main dif-

---

[119]  *See* cases *supra* note 118.

[120]  Illinois v. Lafayette, *supra* note 75 (1983) (inventory search of contents of arrestee's shoulder bag before placing arrestee in a detention facility).

[121]  *Id.*

[122]  Colorado v. Bertine, *supra* note 118 (in the absence of showing that police, who followed standardized caretaking procedures, acted in bad faith for the sole purpose of investigation in conducting inventory search of defendant's van, evidence discovered during search was admissible. Reasonable police regulations relating to inventory procedures administered in good faith satisfy Fourth Amendment).

[123]  Illinois v. Gates, *supra* note 49.

[124]  Malley v. Briggs, *supra* note 47.

[125]  Illinois v. Gates, *supra* note 49.

ference is what the facts in the affidavit must show. For a search warrant, the facts must establish probable cause to believe that: (1) a specific offense has been committed;[126] (2) the items the officer seeks constitute evidence of that offense; and (3) the items are located at the place to be searched.[127]

To satisfy the second requirement, the officer must identify particular items he or she wishes to seize and explain why it is reasonable to believe that these items constitute evidence of a crime. When authority is sought to search for the **fruits** or **instrumentalities of a crime** or **contraband**, the connection is generally self-evident and simply describing the object in the application is generally enough.[128] For example, if the application establishes probable cause to believe that Mary Wanna is dealing in drugs from her home, it will be easy for the judge to see why a balance scale could be an instrumentality of that crime.[129] However, if police wish to search for and seize **mere evidence**, such as "one black overcoat" (allegedly worn by the perpetrator of the crime) they should be sure to include in the application the facts that lead them to believe that the item furnishes evidence of the crime—for example, the fact that an eyewitness saw the perpetrator fleeing the scene of the crime while wearing such a coat.

To satisfy the last requirement, the affidavit must set forth facts supporting a belief that the objects described are *now* at the place to be searched.[130] Facts establishing probable cause to search can grow stale with the passage of time because, even though the police had probable cause to believe that the objects were there a month ago, they may not be there now. The staleness of the facts in Clueso's affidavit was one of the reasons Judge Stickler initially refused to issue a search warrant. If a significant amount of time passes between the facts relied on to establish probable cause and the application for a search warrant, police must include facts showing why they believe the objects described are still at the location. For example, had Clueso kept Sam's house under observation for the entire month, and had Stickler been informed of that fact, the passage of time would not have precluded issuance of the search warrant.

## B. Contents and Form of the Search Warrant

The Fourth Amendment requires that search warrants "*particularly describe*" the place to be searched and the things to be seized. The purpose of this requirement is to ensure that police do not seize the wrong property and that they search only in locations where there is probable cause to believe that the objects of their search will be found.

---

[126] Zurcher v. Stanford Daily, *supra* note 78 (it is not necessary that the owner or possessor of the premises to be searched be suspected of involvement in the crime for a search warrant to be issued).
[127] *See* Figure 4.4 *supra*.
[128] *See* Warden v. Hayden, *supra* note 7.
[129] United States v. Jones, 543 F.2d 627 (8th Cir.), *cert. denied*, 429 U.S. 1051, 97 S. Ct. 763, 50 L. Ed. 2d 767 (1976).
[130] Sgro v. United States, 287 U.S. 206, 53 S. Ct. 138, 77 L. Ed. 2d 260 (1932).

## 1. Particular Description of the Place to be Searched

Oftentimes a search warrant will be executed by a person other than the one who knows the facts of the case and who swore to them in the application. Accordingly, the search warrant must describe the place to be searched with sufficient particularity to allow an executing officer who is unfamiliar with the facts to locate and identify it with reasonable certainty.[131] If a warrant is issued to search premises, a street address will suffice unless the building is subdivided into units—in which case the unit number must also be included.[132] If a warrant is issued to search a vehicle, reference to the vehicle's make and license number, or make and owner is sufficient, but other facts, such as color, model, model year, or vehicle identification number (VIN), should be included, if this information is known.

## 2. Particular Description of the Things to be Seized

The Fourth Amendment requires a particularized description of the items to be seized for two reasons—to avoid seizures of the wrong property and to prevent indiscriminate rummaging.[133] The more precisely an object is described, the more limited the search of the premises is likely to be. Accordingly, the warrant must describe the objects of the search with sufficient particularity to avoid misidentification and to prevent the police from invading privacy to any greater extent than necessary.[134]

Whether a particular warrant description is adequate to accomplish these purposes varies with the nature of the object, the ease of describing it, the amount of detail known to the police, and the risk of misidentification.[135] For example, a warrant authorizing a search for "drug paraphernalia" in a tobacco shop should contain a fairly specific description of what items are considered "paraphernalia." Otherwise, the executing officers could end up seizing tobacco pipes even though there is no probable cause to believe that they are associated with the use of illegal drugs.

Even when the risk of seizing innocent items is low, as, for example, when a warrant authorizes the seizure of drug paraphernalia from a record store, the warrant's description must be as specific as the circumstances of the case per-

---

[131] Steele v. United States, 267 U.S. 498, 45 S. Ct. 414, 69 L. Ed. 757 (1925); **United States v. King, 227 F.3d 732 (6th Cir. 2000)**.

[132] Maryland v. Garrison, 480 U.S. 79, 107 S. Ct. 1013, 94 L. Ed. 2d 72 (1987).

[133] Coolidge v. New Hampshire, *supra* note 10; Marron v. United States, 275 U.S. 192, 48 S. Ct. 74, 72 L. Ed. 231 (1927); State v. Lefort, 248 Kan. 332, 806 P.2d 986 (1991); People v. Bennett, 171 Misc. 2d 264, 653 N.Y.S.2d 835 (1996).

[134] *See* cases *supra* note 133.

[135] *See, e.g.*, United States v. Ford, 184 F.3d 566 (6th Cir. 1984) ("Degree of specificity required in a search warrant depends on what information is reasonably available to the police in the case; thus, a general description may suffice when the police could supply no better information, but fail when a narrower description was available.") *See also* Marcus v. Search Warrant, 367 U.S. 717, 81 S. Ct. 1708, 6 L. Ed. 2d 1127 (1961) (a higher degree of particularity is required when the items to be seized carry the protection of the First Amendment).

mit.[136] Failure to do so violates the Fourth Amendment because it leads to overly broad searches and unnecessary invasions of privacy.[137] For example, a warrant issued to search a robbery suspect's home for "weapons used in the robbery" would violate the particularity requirement if the police knew that the weapon used was a machine gun because "weapons" is a category that includes everything from missiles with multiple warheads to tiny razor blades. Failure to describe the weapon sought as a machine gun will result in unnecessary intrusions on privacy because it allows police to look inside places a "weapon" would fit, but a machine gun would not.

### 3. The "Facially Valid" Warrant

A warrant that appears to contain a particularized description of the place to be searched and the items to be seized is said to be "**facially valid**."[138] Even though the description turns out to be less precise than it had appeared and the warrant is held invalid, evidence seized under it will not be suppressed as long as the executing officer reasonably failed to appreciate the warrant's deficiency.[139] *Maryland v. Garrison*[140] is an illustrative case. Police obtained and executed a search warrant for premises known as "2036 Park Avenue, third floor apartment" and learned later that the third floor was divided into two apartments and that they had searched the wrong unit. The Supreme Court, nevertheless, upheld the admissibility of the evidence, despite the warrant's invalidity, because the executing officers were excusably ignorant that there were two separate units on the third floor.

Whether the executing officer should have recognized the warrant's defects depends on a number of considerations, including the degree to which the officer participated in the investigation and preparation of the affidavit. For example, a description of items to be seized as "women's jewelry" could seem perfectly adequate to an officer who is unfamiliar with the case, but overly broad to an officer who is intimately familiar and knows that only a small portion of the jewelry likely to be found on the premises will be relevant. Likewise, an officer who prepared the affidavit might review the list of items in the warrant and understand that extraneous items have been included. Thus, the reasonableness of the officer's reliance on a defective warrant must be determined on a case-by-case basis.[141]

[136] United States v. Ford, *supra* note 135 (failure to limit broad descriptive terms renders search warrant invalid when further descriptive information is available to the police); State v. Schrager, 472 So. 2d 896 (Fla. Dist. Ct. App. 1985).
[137] United States v. Guidry, 199 F.3d 1150 (10th Cir. 1999); United States v. Robertson, 21 F.3d 1030 (10th Cir. 1994).
[138] United States v. Wood, 6 F. Supp. 2d 1213 (D. Kan. 1998).
[139] United States v. Leon, 468 U.S. 897, 104 S. Ct. 3405, 82 L. Ed. 2d 677 (1984).
[140] 480 U.S. 79, 107 S. Ct. 1013, 94 L. Ed. 2d 72 (1987).
[141] *See, e.g.*, People v. Bradford, 15 Cal. 4th 1229, 939 P.2d 259 (1997).

However, reliance on a warrant that fails to give *any* description of the place to be searched or the items to be seized is never reasonable.[142] The search warrant in Figure 4.8 is facially invalid because it completely fails to list any of the items for which it is issued.

Figure 4.8
**Sample Search Warrant/Without Item Listing**

To any Sheriff, Constable, Marshal, or Police Officer of the State of Confusion:

You are hereby authorized and directed to search the following premises located: 2443 Morris Avenue, Apartment/Room # 7, IN THE COUNTY OF WHADYASAY, STATE OF CONFUSION.
This search warrant must be executed between 6:00 a.m. and 9:00 p.m.
This search warrant must be executed not more than 10 days after the date of issuance.
The search warrant and any property seized must be returned and delivered without any unnecessary delay.

Given under my hand this 13th Day of May 2004
/s/ Betty Bright
Justice of the Peace, Whadyasay County

## C. Requirements for Executing the Warrant

The procedure for executing search warrants is similar to the procedure for executing arrest warrants. In both cases, only the persons to whom the search warrant is addressed may execute it;[143] the warrant must be presented upon execution; and officers must knock and announce their presence before making a forcible entry unless compliance will jeopardize their safety or risk destruction of evidence. However, there are two important differences.

---

[142] Groh v. Ramirez, ___ U.S.___, 124 S. Ct. 1284, 157 L. Ed. 2d 1068 (2004) (Fourth Amendment, by its terms, requires particularity in the warrant. A search warrant that utterly fails to describe the persons or things to be seized is invalid on its face, notwithstanding that requisite particularized description was provided in search warrant application).

[143] Hanlon v. Berger, 526 U.S. 808, 119 S. Ct 1706, 143 L. Ed. 2d 978 (1999) (police may not take reporters, photographers, or other third parties whose presence is not necessary with them during execution of search warrant because this leads to unnecessary invasion of privacy); Wilson v. Layne, 526 U.S. 603, 119 S. Ct. 1692, 143 L. Ed. 2d 818 (1999) (same).

First, search warrants must be executed within a reasonably short time after their issuance.[144] This is in contrast to arrest warrants, which can remain valid for a long time—even years. Once facts make it reasonable to believe that a given person is guilty of a crime, the reasonableness of that belief will not change over time. The same is not true of search warrants, which require probable cause to believe that the objects described in the warrant are located at the place to be searched. Even though there is probable cause to believe that the objects are there when the warrant is issued, this probability weakens with the passage of time. Delay in executing a search warrant violates the Fourth Amendment if the probable cause that supported its issuance no longer exists when it is executed.

Second, after completing the search, the executing officer must prepare an inventory of the property seized, give the owner a copy, and return the warrant, together with a copy of the inventory, to the judge who issued it.[145] Although failure to make a timely return will rarely invalidate an otherwise lawful search, it can cause other problems because the prosecutor is required to *authenticate* objects offered into evidence (i.e., establish that they are what they purport to be and have not been tampered with). A timely return is important because the longer the police wait, the more difficult it will be for the prosecutor to establish authenticity.

We have just completed a condensed tour of the main principles governing search and seizure law. Police are called upon to apply these principles in three primary settings: searches involving people, searches involving vehicles, and searches involving premises. Examining the rules a second time in the settings police apply them will solidify them. The rules need to be instantly accessible because most searches are conducted without a warrant, forcing police officers to make on-the-spot decisions about the scope of their authority. Their decisions need to be correct because the admissibility of evidence can be destroyed if police overstep the boundaries of their lawful search authority.[146]

---

[144] Statutes and court rules often require that search warrants be executed or returned within a specified period after their issuance. Federal search warrants, for example, must command the officer to execute the warrant within a specified time no longer than 10 days. *See* FED. R. CRIM. P. 41 However, execution within the time specified in the warrant does not ensure compliance with the Fourth Amendment. Delay in execution will violate the Fourth Amendment if the probable cause that supported the issuance of the warrant no longer exists at the time of execution. *See, e.g.*, United States v. Grant, 108 F. Supp. 2d 1172 (D. Kan. 2000) (finding violation of Fourth Amendment where search warrant, issued on an affidavit showing a single sale of rock cocaine at the address to be searched, was executed six and one-half months later). State v. Nelson, 817 So. 2d 158 (La. App. 2002) (validity of the warrant depends upon whether the probable cause recited in the affidavit continues until the time of execution of the warrant.). *See also* 2 WAYNE R. LAFAVE, SEARCH AND SEIZURE § 3.7(a) at p. 342 (1996) ("Absent additional facts tending to show otherwise, a one-shot type of crime, such as a single instance of possession or sale of some form of contraband, will support a finding of probable cause only for a few days at best.").

[145] *See* Berger v. New York, 388 U.S. 41, 87 S. Ct. 1873, 18 L. Ed. 2d 1040 (1967).

[146] The requirements for the plain view doctrine are discussed in § 4.4(B).

## § 4.6　Searches Involving People and Personal Items

Although search warrants may be issued to search people,[147] most such searches are conducted without a warrant. *Terry* pat-down searches and searches incident to custodial arrests are the two most common grounds for searching people.

We begin with the following example.

### Operation Grab 'n' Sniff

The Whosville PD recently implemented Operation "Grab 'n' Sniff" at the Whosville international airport. The operation involves placing trained dogs in the baggage handling area to detect illegal drugs. As soon as the bags from an arriving flight are unloaded, Whosville officers separate out bags that appear suspicious and present them for a canine examination.[148] Usually, the dogs detect nothing and the bags are returned to the airline for standard handling. When a dog detects something, police officers seize the bag and proceed to the magistrate for a warrant to search the bag and a second warrant to arrest the owner.

Last week, Officer Caesar of the Whosville PD separated out a Gucci gym bag that looked suspicious and subjected it to a canine examination. Sure enough, the dog detected something. The name tag on the bag showed that it was owned by Bugsy Boss. Recognizing the name as the head of Whosville's biggest crime syndicate, Caesar decided that instead of following the standard procedure, he would place the bag back on the carousel and arrest Boss when he claimed it. That way, Caesar reasoned, Boss would not be able to extricate himself from the situation with expensive attorneys. Caesar returned the Gucci bag to the airline and staked out the baggage claim area, but Boss was nowhere to be seen.

A young man named Tom Thug, also familiar to Caesar because of a prior armed robbery conviction, retrieved the Gucci bag. Caesar watched as Tom headed outside, made eye contact with Boss, placed the bag on the curb beside him, and returned to the baggage claim area. Suspecting Tom of being an accomplice, Caesar radioed for a second officer to arrest Boss while he kept Tom under surveillance.

Officer Fromkin, responding to the call, placed Boss under arrest and handcuffed him. He then opened the Gucci bag and methodically searched the contents, retrieving two rocks of crack cocaine. Disappointed with this meager find, he proceeded to rummage through Boss's pockets and wallet where he found a note titled "Things to do today." The note read: "1. Buy milk, 2. Bribe Mayor Kruger re: road contract, 3. Blackmail jurors in RICO trial." There were check marks next to "2" and "3." Because the note dealt with matters unrelated to Boss's arrest, Fromkin put it back in Boss's wallet and returned it to him.

Meanwhile, Caesar watched Tom remove two more bags from the carousel. As he carried them from the airport, Caesar approached Tom and asked if he

---

[147]　*See, e.g.*, Ybarra v. Illinois, 444 U.S. 85, 88, 100 S. Ct. 338, 340, 62 L. Ed. 2d 238, 243 (1979).

[148]　It is not a search or a seizure to expose luggage and other packages to a canine inspection while they are outside the owner's immediate custody and control. *See* cases *supra* notes 34, 36, 39, 80, and 115.

would answer a few questions. "I'm too busy," Tom replied, and kept walking. Caesar said, "Not so fast buddy! WPD—let me see some identification." As Tom reached for his wallet, Caesar noticed a strange bulge underneath his coat and proceeded to pat him down for weapons. The bulge was bumpy but pliable and clearly not a weapon. As Caesar poked, squeezed, lifted, and pushed on the bulge, he heard a "clinking" sound like glasses tapping each other. As a result, Caesar was able to conclude that the bulge was a baggie containing several glass vials of the kind used to package illegal drugs. At that point, Caesar reached into the breast pocket of Tom's sportcoat and removed a bag full of glass vials containing crack, just as he had expected, and immediately placed Tom under arrest.

The Boss, Tom, the plastic bag, and the three pieces of luggage were transported to the Whosville police station. Upon arrival, Caesar searched the remaining two bags and made a huge bust—he found several kilograms of crack cocaine. At the arraignment the next day, the judge denied bail for Boss (due to his prior record), but ruled that Tom had been illegally arrested and released him.

After the arraignment, Caesar placed Boss in a lockup, exchanged his street clothes for an orange jumpsuit, and searched his pockets and his wallet again. Coming across the "things to do" note, he read it and set it aside for use as evidence. He then looked through the Gucci bag where he discovered a bound ledger book that Officer Fromkin had missed and thumbed through it to determine whether it contained anything incriminating. Sure enough, it contained vast records of drug transactions, bribery, and corrupt dealings. After completing the inventory, Caesar took the ledger and the "things to do" note to the evidence room, and the rest of Boss's belongings to the property room for safekeeping. At the trial, the judge suppressed everything except the two rocks of crack cocaine recovered from Boss's Gucci bag at the scene of his arrest and the "things to do" note. As you read the materials that follow, try to figure out why the rest of the evidence is inadmissible.

## § 4.7 —The *Terry* Search Revisited

A number of searches were performed in Operation Grab 'n' Sniff—some legal, some illegal. We will begin our analysis with Officer Caesar's *Terry* search of Tom. Although the search began properly, it quickly went awry. As a result, all the evidence against Tom had to be suppressed.

### A. Required Grounds

Police perform weapons frisks when they have reasonable concerns for their safety during investigative encounters. Although this practice is longstanding, the Supreme Court never had occasion to rule on its constitutionality until 1968 in the landmark case of *Terry v. Ohio*,[149] discussed in Chapter 3. The Court acknowledged the need for police officers to take precautions for

---

[149] *Supra* note 9.

their safety, then went on to discuss the justification for the search and its limitations. The Court laid down two requirements for protective weapons searches. First, the officer must have an adequate reason to initiate the encounter. The usual reason is to check out suspicious circumstances. That is why Officer Caesar initiated his encounter with Tom. The circumstances surrounding the encounter must arouse "reasonable suspicion" for the stop to be valid.[150] The canine alert in response to Boss's luggage, Caesar's observation that Tom appeared to be working with Boss, and his knowledge that both had previously been involved in criminal activity provided ample justification for initiating the stop.

However, the fact that a stop is lawful does not automatically justify a weapons frisk.[151] A frisk is permitted only if the officer has reasonable suspicion that the detainee is carrying a weapon or could be dangerous.[152] The crime under investigation, knowledge of the detainee's criminal past, weapon-like bulges in the detainee's clothing, hostile behavior, furtive gestures, and the late hour or secluded location of the stop are some of the many factors that might justify a frisk. Caesar's observation of the bulge in Tom's jacket,[153] combined with his knowledge of Tom's prior armed robbery conviction,[154] provided a basis for believing that he might be armed.

## B. Permissible Scope

The scope of a *Terry* weapons search extends to the detainee's person[155] and any unlocked containers within grabbing distance that the officer has reason to believe might contain a weapon.[156] Officer Caesar would not have been justified in searching the luggage Tom was carrying for a weapon because the bags were probably locked, rendering any weapons that might be inside inaccessible. Also, the chance of there being weapons inside was slim because the bags had previously cleared airport security.

## C. Permissible Intensity

Officer Caesar's search went bad, not because he lacked grounds for frisking Tom, but because he exceeded the **intensity** permitted for this kind of search. A *Terry* weapons search is limited to activity necessary to determine

---

[150]  *Id.*

[151]  *Id.*; State v. Garland, 270 N.J. Super. 31, 636 A.2d 541 (1994).

[152]  **Terry v. Ohio,** *supra* note 9; **Florida v. J.L., 529 U.S. 266, 120 S. Ct. 1375, 146 L. Ed. 2d 254 (2000).**

[153]  Pennsylvania v. Mimms, 434 U.S. 106, 98 S. Ct. 330, 54 L. Ed. 2d 331 (1977).

[154]  *See* Adams v. Williams, 406 U.S. 143, 92 S. Ct. 1921, 32 L. Ed. 2d 612 (1972).

[155]  **Terry v. Ohio,** *supra* note 9.

[156]  United States v. Flippin, 924 F.2d 163 (9th Cir. 1991) (officer justified in looking inside makeup bag when suspect grabbed it after he turned away); State v. Ortiz, 67 Haw. 181, 683 P.2d 822 (1984) (officer justified in looking inside knapsack when detainee made quick grab for it after stating that it was empty).

whether the suspect is armed. When the search is directed at the suspect's person, the intensity is limited to patting down the suspect's outer clothing.[157] When there is authority to search a container, the intensity is limited to a cursory visual inspection of the contents—just enough to determine whether there is a weapon inside.[158]

Once Officer Caesar determined that the bulge under Tom's coat was not a weapon, he reached the limits of his *Terry* search authority. When he continued to poke, squeeze, and push the bulge, he was no longer searching for weapons, but was trying to determine other things about the object. Because these acts were not necessary to rule the object out as being a weapon, Caesar's continued tactile examination exceeded the boundaries of his *Terry* search authority and resulted in the suppression of the glass vials of cocaine he removed from Sam's pocket.[159]

Figure 4.9
**Requirements for a "Plain Feel" Seizure During a *Terry* Stop**

| |
|---|
| 1. Police feel an object in the course of a weapons pat-down. |
| 2. They immediately recognize the object as "feeling" something like a specific kind of contraband. |
| 3. Other circumstances surrounding the encounter reinforce the belief that the object is what it feels like. |

## D. Seizure of Evidence in "Plain Feel" during a Terry Pat-Down Search

Although police officers may not initiate a pat-down search solely because they suspect that a detainee has contraband on his or her person, they may seize it if they discover it in the course of a lawful pat-down search. The **plain view** doctrine has an analogue known as the "plain feel" doctrine, which applies to *Terry* searches. If an officer feels an object during a lawful pat-down search and its contours and mass make it immediately apparent that the object is contraband, the officer may to seize it without a warrant.[160] "Immediately apparent" means that the officer must develop probable cause to believe that the object felt is contraband without exceeding the boundaries of his or her *Terry* search authority. Once the officer rules the object out as being a weapon, his or her *Terry* search authority is spent. The officer's continued manipulation of an object to determine its identity, such as Officer Caesar's, violates the Fourth Amendment.

Police are seldom able to develop probable cause to believe that an unseen object is contraband solely from the light touch that is permissible during a

---

[157]  **Terry v. Ohio,** *supra* note 9.
[158]  Michigan v. Long, 463 U.S. 1032, 103 S. Ct. 3469, 77 L. Ed. 2d 1201 (1983).
[159]  Minnesota v. Dickerson, *supra* note 19; **State v. Wilson, 112 N.C. App. 777, 437 S.E.2d 387 (1993).**
[160]  *See* cases *supra* note 159.

pat-down search. What feels like a rock of crack cocaine could be just a rock;[161] a "one-hitter" pipe could be a pen; and a film canister might actually contain only film.[162] However, police officers are allowed to take other information into account.[163] For example, if an officer feels what he or she believes could be a rock of crack cocaine in a suspect's shirt pocket during a pat-down search, this alone does not provide probable cause to seize it.[164] However, if the officer also observes a glass tube and a box of Brillo pads on the front seat of the suspect's car, which he or she knows from prior experience are often used to smoke crack, the officer would then have grounds to seize it.[165]

## § 4.8 —Search Following a Custodial Arrest

Bugsy Boss and Tom Thug were both arrested and searched. The Boss search derived from a lawful arrest and was conducted in a proper manner, producing evidence that could be used in his trial. Tom's arrest, in contrast, was illegal because it derived from a *Terry* search violation. The unconstitutional arrest tainted the search that followed. Tom was released because there was no evidence that could be used against him.

### A. *Required Grounds*

The majority of searches conducted by the police are made after an arrest. Whenever a custodial arrest is made, there is always some danger that the arrestee might try to gain access to a weapon, escape, or destroy evidence. Although the need to disarm suspects before taking them into custody and to preserve evidence supplies the justification for this exception to the warrant requirement, the right to perform a search incident to an arrest does not vary with the nature of the crime or the probability that the search will turn up weapons or evidence.[166] The Supreme Court has explained that the potential dangers lurking in every custodial arrest make it reasonable to perform a search without requiring the police to calculate the probability that the person arrested actually possesses weapons or destructible evidence. Consequently, a lawful arrest for any offense provides all the justification needed to perform a search incident to an arrest.[167] However, there must be a full-fledged custodial arrest.

---

[161] *Id.*

[162] State v. Bridges, 963 S.W.2d 487 (Tenn. 1997); Campbell v. State, 864 S.W.2d 223 (Tex. Ct. App. 1993).

[163] Illinois v. Gates, *supra* note 49; Taylor v. People, 454 Mich. 580, 564 N.W.2d 24 (1997). *See also* United States v. Chhien, 266 F.3d 1 (1st Cir. 2001) ("[E]ven though an officer may not seize an object during a *Terry* frisk unless he or she has probable cause to believe that it is contraband, nothing prevents an officer from inquiring into the nature of an object that he feels is suspicious.").

[164] Minnesota v. Dickerson, *supra* note 19.

[165] State v. Wilson, *supra* note 159; People v. Mitchell, 65 Ill. 2d 211, 650 N.E.2d 1014 (1995).

[166] United States v. Robinson, *supra* note 65.

[167] *Id.*

The authority to search for evidence does not arise when the police issue a traffic citation, even if they have probable cause to make an arrest, but decide to ticket the motorist instead.[168]

It goes without saying that the arrest must be legal. If the arrest is made without probable cause or the probable cause derives from tainted evidence, the search that follows is not authorized, and the evidence will be suppressed.[169] That is why the judge suppressed the cocaine that Officer Caesar discovered in Tom's luggage after he placed Tom under arrest. Tom's arrest was illegal because the probable cause for his arrest derived from a *Terry* search violation.

Figure 4.10
**Authority to Search Incident to an Arrest**

Authority to search incident to an arrest:

* Arises whenever police make a lawful arrest for any offense
* Extends to the arrestee's person and everything within the area under his or her immediate control
* Encompasses weapons, contraband, and evidence of any crime, including crimes other than the one for which the arrest was made
* May be as intensive as necessary to discover even the smallest item of evidence
* Must, except for the suspect's clothing, be exercised at the time and place of the arrest

## B. Permissible Scope

Search authority incident to an arrest is broader than *Terry* search authority because the purposes it serves are broader. The authority exists to protect the officer's safety and to prevent the arrestee from destroying evidence.[170] The search boundaries have been contoured in light of these purposes. Search authority extends to the arrestee's person and everything within the area under his or his or her immediate control, but not beyond.[171]

The "immediate control" test was established in *Chimel v. California*.[172] In *Chimel*, the defendant was arrested in his home for the burglary of a coin shop. After his arrest, police conducted a warrantless search of his entire home and discovered some of the stolen coins in a drawer in his bedroom. The Supreme Court ruled that the search the police conducted vastly exceeded their search authority and proceeded to discuss the scope of a warrantless search incident to an arrest. The Court explained that "[a] gun on a table or in a drawer in front of one who is arrested can be as dangerous to the arresting officer as one concealed in the clothing of the person arrested." Consequently, the search may

---

[168]   Knowles v. Iowa, 525 U.S. 113, 119 S. Ct. 484, 142 L. Ed. 2d 492 (1998).

[169]   Wong Sun v. United States, 371 U.S. 471, 83 S. Ct. 407, 9 L. Ed. 2d 441 (1963).

[170]   United States v. Robinson, *supra* note 65.

[171]   Chimel v. California, *supra* note 44.

[172]   *Id.*

extend beyond the suspect's person to everything within the area under the suspect's immediate control. The Court then defined this area as the area from within which the suspect might reach to gain possession of a weapon or destroy evidence. Consequently, after placing a suspect under arrest, the arresting officer may search the suspect's person and everything within grabbing distance.[173] However, an arrest does not provide an occasion to search for evidence in other places. If a more extensive search is needed, police may take reasonable steps to secure the premises, but must then apply for a search warrant.[174]

## C. Permissible Intensity

Searches incident to arrest are allowed to be more intensive than *Terry* searches because the lawful objects of the search include criminal evidence, as well as weapons. The search may be as intensive as necessary to discover even the smallest piece of evidence.[175]

After placing a person under arrest, the arresting officer may examine everything in the suspect's pockets, wallet or purse, inspect receipts, read private papers, examine the contents of packages he is carrying—in short, meticulously go over everything on the suspect's person or within arm's reach, in search of evidence of *any* crime, not just the crime for which the arrest is made.[176]

Officer Fromkin's search of Bugsy Boss and his gym bag at the scene of the arrest was no broader than the law allows. In fact, it was narrower because he could have seized the "things to do" note. Since police are permitted to read writings discovered while conducting a search incident to an arrest, when Officer Fromkin read the references to blackmail and bribery, he had the authority to seize the note. The fact that the note furnished evidence of an unrelated crime is of no consequence because police, when conducting a search incident to arrest, are not limited to searching for evidence of the crime for which the arrest is made.

---

[173] United States v. Johnson, 16 F.3d 69 (5th Cir. 1994) (briefcase was not within area under suspect's "immediate control" where, at the time of his arrest, the suspect was seated at his desk about approximately eight feet away from the chair on which his briefcase was lying and four officers were present in the room); United States v. Perea, 986 F.2d 633 (2d Cir. 1993) (search of duffel bag located in trunk of cab in which suspect was riding at time of his arrest could not be justified as search incident to arrest because a trunk is not within a passenger's reach).

[174] *See* cases *supra* note 70.

[175] **United States v. Robinson**, *supra* note 65.

[176] **United States v. Robinson**, *supra* note 65 (upholding seizure of heroin capsules discovered while examining contents of cigarette pack after motorist's arrest for driving with a revoked license); United States v. Armstrong, 16 F.3d 289 (8th Cir. 1994) (wallet); United States v. Phillips 607 F.2d 808 (8th Cir. 1979) (wallet); Corrasco v. State, 712 S.W.2d 120 (Tex. Crim. App. 1986) (handbag); State v. Smith, 119 Wash. 2d 675, 835 P.2d 1025 (1992) (knapsack); *See also* WAYNE R. LAFAVE, 3 SEARCH & SEIZURE § 5.3 (3d. ed. 1996).

### D. Timing of Searches Incident to an Arrest

A search incident to an arrest must take place roughly contemporaneously with the arrest because the justification for the search ceases to exist once police have secured control over the arrestee and he or she is no longer able to reach for weapons or destroy evidence.[177] Courts disagree whether the time for searching the area under the suspect's immediate control expires as soon as the police have gained control of the suspect or whether they may subdue the suspect first and then perform the search.[178] For example, if police arrest a person inside a room, handcuff him, and take him downstairs, may they now go back upstairs and search the objects that were within his reach at the time of the arrest?[179] The prevailing view is that a search of the area under the suspect's immediate control is timely so long as it is roughly contemporaneous with and an integral part of the arrest process, even though it occurs after the suspect has been handcuffed and led away.[180] However, if the search is delayed beyond this point, a search warrant will generally be necessary.

The one exception to this rule relates to searches involving an arrested person's clothing, wallet, or handbag. Such searches may be performed either at the scene of the arrest, when the suspect arrives at the place of detention, or at both places.[181] The Supreme Court has not been troubled even by substantial delays in searching these objects. In *United States v. Edwards*,[182] for example, police searched the defendant's clothing at the police station hours after his arrest for attempting to break and enter a post office. The arrest was made at 11:00 P.M. and the defendant was taken to jail. An investigation of the burglary scene after the defendant's arrest revealed that the attempted entry had been made through a wooden window, which had been pried up, leaving paint chips on the window sill. The next morning, the defendant's shirt, trousers and other articles of clothing were taken from him and tested for paint chips. A positive match was found. The Supreme Court upheld the delayed search, stating:

---

[177] *See, e.g.*, United States v. Vasey, 834 F.2d 782 (9th Cir. 1987) (search of passenger compartment of arrestee's automobile 30 to 45 minutes after he was arrested, handcuffed, and placed in the rear of police car lacked "contemporaneity" needed for search incident to arrest).

[178] *Compare* In re Sealed Case, 153 F.3d 759 (D.C. Cir. 1997) (gun and drugs found on chair in arrestee's bedroom, next to where he was standing when arrested, could be searched after arrestee was handcuffed and taken downstairs because they were located in area under defendant's immediate control at time of arrest) *with* State v. Canas, 597 N.W.2d 488 (Iowa 1999) (where police pulled defendant outside and handcuffed and arrested him when he opened motel room door, entering room and searching bag on night stand was not permissible under *Chimel*).

[179] United States v. Hudson, 100 F.3d 1409 (9th Cir. 1996) (search qualified as incident to arrest where police arrested the defendant in his bedroom, handcuffed him, and removed him from the house, and about three minutes later, one of the officers returned to the bedroom in which the defendant had been found and conducted a search, resulting in the discovery of a gun and drug paraphernalia).

[180] *See, e.g.*, United States v. Abdul-Saboor, 85 F.3d 664 (D.C. Cir. 1996) (trial courts should focus on "whether the arrest and search are so separated in time or by intervening events that they cannot fairly be said to have been incident to the former"); United States v. McLaughlin, 170 F.3d 889 (9th Cir. 1998) (search of vehicle commenced five minutes after defendant was arrested and removed from scene qualified as search incident to arrest, inasmuch as arrest, completion of paperwork, and initial search were part of one continuous series of events closely connected in time); *See also* cases *supra* notes 178 and 179.

[181] United States v. Edwards, 415 U.S. 800, 94 S. Ct. 1234, 39 L. Ed. 2d 771 (1974).

[182] *Id.*

. . . [O]nce the accused is lawfully arrested and is in custody, the effects in his possession at the place of detention that were subject to search at the time and place of his arrest may lawfully be searched and seized without a warrant even though a substantial period of time has elapsed between the arrest and subsequent administrative processing, on the one hand, and the taking of the property for use as evidence, on the other. This is true where the clothing or effects are immediately seized upon arrival at the jail, held under the defendant's name in the "property room" of the jail, and at a later time searched and taken for use at the subsequent criminal trial. The result is the same where the property is not physically taken from the defendant until sometime after his incarceration.

The Supreme Court has never explained why a warrantless search of the suspect's clothing performed at the station house qualifies as a search incident to an arrest, even though it occurs hours later. Perhaps it is because a thorough examination of the suspect's clothing at the scene of the arrest would be embarrassing, inconvenient, and impracticable, or because an inventory search of the suspect's clothing will take place, in any event, before the arrestee is booked into jail.

The *Edwards* exception is limited to the clothing the defendant is wearing and his or her wallet or handbag.[183] It does not apply to briefcases, suitcases, packages, or other possessions taken from the defendant at the time of arrest.[184] Police may not wait until they get to the police station to search belongings like these. Once police have reduced luggage, briefcases, and packages to their exclusive control, and there is no longer any danger that the arrestee might gain access to them to seize a weapon or destroy evidence, a search of that property is no longer an incident of the arrest and requires a search warrant.[185] Consequently, while the search of Boss's wallet at the police station was sustainable as an incident to his arrest, rendering the things-to-do

---

[183] *See, e.g.*, United States v. Phillips, 607 F.2d 808 (8th Cir. 1979) (upholding search of defendant's wallet at police station as valid search incident to arrest); State v. Wade, 215 Wis. 2d 684, 573 N.W.2d 228 (1997) (allowing delayed search at the police station of a female arrestee's purse); Curd v. City Court of Judsonia, Arkansas, 141 F.3d 839 (8th Cir. 1998) (same).

[184] Warrantless searches of luggage or other property seized at the time of an arrest cannot be justified as incident to that arrest if the search is remote in time or place from the arrest. *See, e.g.*, United States v. Chadwick, *supra* note 108 (station house search of 200-pound footlocker more than an hour after suspect's arrest too remote in time and place for warrantless search incident to arrest); United States v. $639,558 in U.S. Currency, 955 F.2d 712 (D.C. Cir. 1992) (warrantless search of luggage at police station 30 minutes after arrest did not qualify as search incident to arrest); United States v. Schleis, 582 F.2d 1166 (8th Cir. 1978) (en banc) (search of briefcase at station house not valid search incident to arrest); Preston v. State, 784 A.2d 601 (Md. App. 2001) (Warrantless search of defendant's automobile was not valid as a search incident to arrest, as it was not "essentially contemporaneous" with the arrest, where defendant was arrested just after he arrived at his place of employment and alighted from his car, and the search occurred at a police garage at least two or three hours later.).

[185] *See* cases *supra* 184.

note admissible, the search of his Gucci bag was not. However, station house searches can sometimes be justified under a different exception to the warrant requirement—the **inventory search** exception.[186]

## E. *Inventory Searches Incident to Booking an Arrestee into Jail*

When a person is arrested at a place other than his or her home, belongings in his or her possession at the time of arrest will be bundled up and take to the police station unless there is someone present who can take charge of them.[187] During routine booking procedures incident to incarceration, the suspect's clothing and other belongings will be impounded and an inventory search will be performed. The purpose of an inventory search is not to discover evidence. The purpose is to secure valuables and protect the police department against false claims of loss or theft, and to prevent weapons and contraband from being introduced into the jail community.[188] The search should not be performed until it is determined that the suspect will not be released on bail because, until then, it is premature.[189] If the inventory search is conducted properly, evidence that comes to light during the search will be admissible under the plain view rule.[190] Evidence missed during a search incident to an arrest is sometimes discovered in this manner.

An inventory search must be conducted in conformity with the police department's standard operating procedures concerning the time, place, and manner for conducting such searches, in order to satisfy the Fourth Amendment.[191] The purpose of this requirement is to ensure that police do not use inventory searches as a ruse to search for evidence. For example, if the department's standard operating procedures do not provide for opening closed containers and inventorying their contents separately, but instead require them to be securely taped and sealed and placed into a locker, opening and searching them will violate the Fourth Amendment and evidence uncovered will be inadmissible.[192]

The permissible intensity of an inventory search also differs from a search incident to arrest because police are performing an administrative and caretaking function, not looking for evidence. Accordingly, police may not examine the articles they are inventorying to any greater extent than necessary to

---

[186]   State v. Paturzzio, 292 N.J. Super. 542, 679 A.2d 199 (App. Div. 1996) (upholding inventory search of satchel brought by arrestee to police station); State v. Gelvin, 318 N.W.2d 302 (N.D.), *cert. denied*, 459 U.S. 987, 103 S. Ct. 341, 74 L. Ed. 2d 383 (1982) (upholding inventory search of wallet of person brought to police station for detoxification).

[187]   United States v. Perea, 986 F.2d 633 (2d Cir. 1993).

[188]   Inventory searches are discussed in § 4.3 *supra* and 4.12 *infra*.

[189]   United States v. Mills, 472 F.2d 1231 (D.C. Cir. 1972).

[190]   Illinois v. Lafayette, *supra* note 75; South Dakota v. Opperman, *supra* note 75 (inventory searches satisfy Fourth Amendment when they are part of routine police practice and are not conducted as a pretext for evidentiary search).

[191]   *See* cases *supra* note 190.

[192]   Colorado v. Bertine, *supra* note 118; Florida v. Wells, *supra* note 75.

describe them on an inventory.[193] A superficial examination is generally enough. Caesar's reading of Boss's ledger book, for example, exceeded the permissible intensity of an inventory search because reading the contents was not necessary to describe it on an inventory. Because the reading occurred too late to qualify as a search incident to arrest and was too intensive for an inventory search, the ledger book cannot be used as evidence.

### F.  Searches Preceding an Arrest

Police occasionally do things out of sequence, such as searching the suspect before placing him or her under arrest. This is not a problem when probable cause for arrest already exists. When grounds for arrest are present, a search conducted immediately prior to an arrest is considered contemporaneous with that arrest, and constitutes a valid search. However, the fruits of a search cannot supply grounds for the arrest that follows. If the police do not have grounds when they start the search, the search and subsequent arrest are both illegal.[194]

## § 4.9  Vehicle Searches

Although it is a wise practice to obtain a search warrant when feasible, for obvious reasons, this is often not feasible in the case of motor vehicle searches. As a result, most motor vehicle searches are conducted without a warrant. There are four theories, in addition to consent, for searching motor vehicles without a warrant: (1) vehicular limited weapons searches, (2) searches incident to the arrest of a motorist or passenger, (3) searches based on probable cause to believe that the vehicle contains criminal evidence or contraband (referred to as the "motor vehicle exception"), and (4) inventory searches. Officers need a strong grasp of these theories because there is rarely time to ponder when the need to search arises.

The four theories can operate in a chain-reaction fashion, with one theory triggering another. An officer develops grounds for conducting a vehicular limited weapons search during a *Terry* or traffic stop and, while conducting the search, comes across drugs or contraband. The officer places the motorist under arrest, conducts a more intensive search (allowed as an incident to arrest), and finds additional drugs or contraband. This discovery gives the officer probable cause to believe that there may be more evidence in areas not yet searched and enlarges the scope of the officer's search authority by trig-

---

[193]  United States v. Khoury, 901 F.2d 948 (11th Cir. 1990) (reading contents of notebook during inventory search not permitted because it does not further purposes of inventory search)

[194]  Smith v. Ohio, 494 U.S. 541, 110 S. Ct. 1288, 108 L. Ed. 2d 464 (1990) (warrantless search of suspect's bag could not be justified as a search incident to a lawful arrest when the suspect was not arrested on drug charges until after drug paraphernalia was found in bag).

gering the third exception. The officer performs a highly intensive search based on probable cause to believe that the vehicle contains criminal evidence. When this search is completed, because the motorist has been arrested and there is no one to take charge of the vehicle, it is towed to the police impound lot where it is searched a fourth time, under the inventory search exception.

In studying the four theories for searching motor vehicles without a warrant, pay close attention to the grounds for search authority and areas that can be searched, because they vary markedly from theory to theory. Consider the following example.

## A Mid-Summer's Nightmare

Back before the rock group The Thankless Incarnates broke up, Mary Wanna and Ralph Riefer decided to spend a whole summer following the band. Although Ralph's parents told him to "get a haircut and earn some money for once," Ralph convinced them he could make a killing going from concert to concert selling knickknacks and trinkets to the other Incarnate Heads in the parking lot during each show. Ralph's parents finally gave up and agreed to lend him the family's baby blue Volkswagen Bug so that he could at least travel in style. Due to a series of mishaps that Ralph would later describe to his lawyer as "an unforeseeable bummer," Ralph and Mary got arrested and spent the last part of the summer behind bars.

As Ralph and Mary wound their way through Whosville, they were stopped by Officer Bobby Weird, who was acting on a tip from the WPD's most reliable informant that a "major drug dealer named Ray V. Gravy would be passing through town in a blue VW Bug, carrying a large stash of marijuana in the trunk." The informant also told Weird that Gravy was "usually heavily armed, uses numerous aliases, and often travels with girlfriends." Weird felt confident that Ralph was the suspect he'd been waiting for since he'd been watching the highway all week and this was the first Bug he'd seen.

Weird pulled Ralph over with his siren and lights and approached the vehicle with his hand on his holster. Rich from the sales of thousands of counterfeit Incarnate sweatshirts and trinkets, Ralph offered Weird a roll of twenties and a free Thankless Incarnate key chain if he'd just let them go, saying: "Look, we're in a hurry to get to a concert. I don't know what I did, but I'm sure this is enough to pay the fine."

Weird pushed the money aside, ordered Ralph to get out of the car, and patted him down for weapons. He found none and proceeded to search the interior of the passenger compartment. He found a flat envelope under the driver's seat, pulled it out, opened it, and found a few fliers advertising "Ralph's Thankless Knock-Off-Knickknacks: We cut out the band's share and pass the savings on to you." He put the fliers in his pocket and continued the search.

As it turns out, Ralph had expanded the business model during the course of the trip, and Weird found two large bags of marijuana in the glove compartment and a large roll of $20 bills in the console. While this was going on,

Mary was sitting in the front passenger seat, shaking and crying and clutching her handbag. After searching the passenger compartment, Weird grabbed Mary's handbag from her and looked inside. At first glance all he saw was some make-up, change, and a crumpled pack of cigarettes. However, when he opened the cigarettes he found a vial of cocaine. He then placed Ralph and Mary under arrest, handcuffed them, and put them in the squad car. Weird also took the keys from Ralph and opened the trunk, where he found some scales and other materials used in connection with drug distribution but, to his surprise, no drugs or counterfeit goods.

Officer Weird had Ralph's Bug towed to the impound lot where the contents of the vehicle were inventoried. The only items found were miscellaneous trash, spare change, and the like. Later that same day, the real Ray V. Gravy passed through Whosville in a beaten-up, blue VW Bug and he, too, was arrested.

Weird was puzzled by the fact that no more drugs or goods were discovered in Ralph's car and was concerned that the couple would get off light unless more evidence was found. Two days later, it came to Weird like a flash; he had been looking in the wrong places. Luckily, Ralph's father had not yet been able to travel to Whosville to pick up the car, so Weird jumped on the chance and used some tools to take out the steering wheel hub, door panels, the dash board, and back seat. Sure enough, Weird found 30 pounds of marijuana, a case of counterfeit glow-in-the-dark Thankless Incarnate action figures, and nearly $37,000 in cash (mostly $20 bills).

Ralph was charged with possession of marijuana with intent to distribute, possession of counterfeit goods, and attempted bribery of a police officer; Mary was charged with possession of a vial of cocaine. The judge denied all of their motions to suppress and both of them are now serving sentences in the Whosville jail.

Figure 4.11
**Vehicle Limited Weapons Search**

- The sole object of the search is weapons
- The officer must have reasonable suspicion that weapons are located inside a lawfully stopped vehicle
- The scope of the search is confined to the passenger compartment
- The intensity is limited to a cursory visual inspection of areas (and containers) inside the passenger compartment in which a weapon would fit

## § 4.10 —Search of Vehicles Pursuant to a Detention or Arrest

*Terry* weapons searches of vehicles and searches incident to the arrest of a vehicle occupant share one feature. The area that can be searched is limited to the passenger compartment. However, that is where the similarity ends. There are significant differences in the lawful objects of the search and the intensity of search activity permitted.

## A. Terry *Searches of Vehicles*

### 1. Grounds for Search Authority

A limited weapons search, as the name suggests, is a search that is strictly limited to weapons that could be used against the officer. An officer who makes a lawful *Terry* or traffic stop may take the precaution of ordering the driver and passengers to step out of the vehicle, as a matter of course, with no additional grounds beyond those necessary for a stop.[195] However, an officer must possess reasonable suspicion to search the vehicle for weapons.[196] When reasonable suspicion exists, the search may be performed even though the driver and passengers have been ordered to step out of the vehicle because they will have access to the weapons once they are permitted to re-enter.[197]

### 2. Scope and Intensity

The scope of a vehicle protective weapons search is limited to the passenger compartment.[198] The trunk is off-limits because a locked trunk is not a place from which the occupants can gain immediate access to a weapon. The intensity of the search is limited to a cursory visual inspection of areas within the passenger compartment in which a weapon could fit.[199] These areas include the floors, dashboard, seats, area under the seats, glove compartment, console, storage compartments, rear window ledge, and all containers inside the passenger compartment in which a weapon could fit. A cursory visual inspection of these areas is all that is permitted.[200] If criminal evidence or contraband is discovered by the police while searching within these confines, they may seize it under the plain view rule.[201]

Officer Weird cannot be faulted for his decision to stop Ralph's car, frisk him, and perform a vehicular weapons search. He had received a tip from a reliable informant that a heavily armed drug dealer would be passing through Whosville and he had every reason to believe that Ralph was the suspect he had been waiting for.[202] Ralph's car matched the informant's description in every detail; he was traveling with a woman companion, as Gravy normally did; and, because traffic rarely passes through Whosville, Officer Weird was

---

[195] Pennsylvania v. Mimms, *supra* note 153 (driver); Maryland v. Wilson, 519 U.S. 408, 117 S. Ct. 882, 137 L. Ed. 2d 41 (1998) (passenger).

[196] Michigan v. Long, *supra* note 158.

[197] *Id.*

[198] *Id.*

[199] *Id.*

[200] *Id.*

[201] The plain view doctrine is discussed in § 4.4(B)(3) *supra*.

[202] United States v. Taylor, 162 F.3d 12 (1st Cir. 1998) (detailed tip from reliable informant that occupants of automobile were in possession of crack cocaine and weapons exhibited sufficient indicia of reliability to justify investigatory stop of automobile).

reasonable in concluding that Ralph was the suspect he'd been waiting for and that Ralph was armed and dangerous.[203]

However, Officer Weird twice overstepped the boundaries of a *Terry* vehicular weapons search. The first time was when he felt a flat envelope under the front seat. Because Officer Weird knew that the envelope was not a weapon and did not contain a weapon, he had no authority to open it, much less read the contents.[204] Once an officer rules an object out as being a weapon, the officer lacks further authority to touch or examine it unless the officer has probable cause to believe that the object felt is contraband.[205] This, of course, was not the case with the flat envelope. The second time Weird exceeded the boundaries of a vehicular weapons search was when he examined the crumpled cigarette pack in Mary's handbag.[206] This, too, was not a place in which a weapon would fit.

Even though Officer Weird exceeded the boundaries of a vehicular weapons search, he did not violate the Fourth Amendment because he had probable cause to arrest Ralph before the search began. Ralph had attempted to bribe him and attempting to bribe a police officer is a crime. Accordingly, the search Weird performed needs to be analyzed under the search incident to arrest exception to the warrant requirement. We turn now to an examination of this exception.

Figure 4.12
**Vehicle Search Incident to the Arrest of an Occupant**

- Objects of the search include weapons, contraband, and evidence of any crime
- The officer must make a lawful custodial arrest of the driver or a passenger
- The scope of the search extends to the entire passenger compartment and all containers located inside, without regard for ownership
- The intensity may be as thorough as necessary to find every item of evidence, however small
- The search must be conducted substantially contemporaneously with the arrest

---

[203] United States v. Perrin, 45 F.3d 869, 873 (4th Cir. 1995) (noting that "it is certainly reasonable for an officer to believe that a person engaged in selling crack cocaine may be carrying a weapon for protection").

[204] Minnesota v. Dickerson, *supra* note 19.

[205] The "plain feel" doctrine is discussed in § 4.4(B)(3).

[206] Commonwealth v. Silva, 318 N.E.2d 895 (Mass. 1974) (police exceeded constitutional limits of *Terry* vehicular weapons search when they opened small pouch that weighed no more than two ounces found under the front seat of car; the contents were not in plain view because it required unzipping the pouch to discover the narcotics inside; because it was inconceivable that the pouch could have contained a weapon, unzipping it and examining the contents was clearly a search for evidence rather than a protective weapons search).

## B. Vehicle Searches Incident to the Custodial Arrest of an Occupant

### 1. Grounds for Search Authority

When a police officer makes a lawful custodial arrest of a motor vehicle occupant, either the driver or a passenger, the Fourth Amendment allows the officer to perform a vehicle search incident to the arrest.[207] This authority is not limited to cases in which the suspect is still seated in the vehicle. It also applies when the suspect has just exited, but is still in close proximity when approached by the police.[208] The Supreme Court has explained that the arrest of a person standing next to a vehicle "presents identical concerns regarding officer safety and the destruction of evidence as the arrest of one who is inside the vehicle."[209] Consequently, police may perform a vehicle search when they arrest a recent occupant if the person is still in close proximity to the vehicle, both temporally and spatially, when they initiate contact. The arrest can be for any offense, including a traffic violation or a misdemeanor, and may even be made as a pretext to conduct a search.[210] The search is valid as long as the arrest is lawful.[211] The issuance of a traffic citation, in contrast, does not confer authority to search for evidence, although protective weapons searches are permitted in an appropriate case.[212]

### 2. Scope and Intensity of the Search

As was noted in § 4.8, searches incident to an arrest cannot extend beyond the area under the suspect's immediate control. In the case of arrests involving the occupant of a motor vehicle, this area always includes the entire passenger compartment and everything inside.[213] The Supreme Court adopted this position because it furnishes a clear standard that is easy for police to apply. Accordingly, whenever the police arrest a motor vehicle occupant, they are

---

[207] New York v. Belton, 453 U.S. 454, 101 S. Ct. 2860, 69 L. Ed. 2d 768 (1981). *See also* Maryland v. Pringle, 504 U.S. 366, 124 S. Ct. 795, 157 L. Ed. 2d 769 (2003) (discovery of a substantial quantity of drugs and money in glove compartment and behind backseat arm rest creates probable cause to arrest the passengers, as well as the driver if none of them claim it, on the reasonable assumption that they are engaged in a common enterprise).

[208] Thornton v. United States, ___ U.S. ___, 124 S. Ct. 2127, 158 L. Ed. 2d 905 (2004) (police may search the passenger compartment not only when the suspect is arrested while in the car, but also when he or she has exited, but is still in close proximity, both temporally and spatially, when police initiate contact). *But see* State v. Robb, 605 N.W.2d 96 (Minn. 2000) (offering arrestee access to his vehicle as a courtesy cannot be used to justify search of vehicle).

[209] Thornton v. United States, *supra* note 208.

[210] Knowles v. Iowa, *supra* note 168.

[211] Atwater v. City of Lago Vista, 532 U.S. 318, 121 S. Ct. 2540, 149 L. Ed. 2d 549 (2001) (arrest for seat belt violation); Arkansas v. Sullivan, 532 U.S. 769, 121 S. Ct. 1876, 149 L. Ed. 2d 994 (2001) (arrest for speeding and improperly tinted windshield).

[212] New York v. Belton, *supra* note 207.

[213] *Id.*

allowed to search the entire passenger compartment (i.e., seats, floor, glove compartments, consoles, etc.) and all the contents (i.e., luggage, boxes, bags, briefcases, jackets, handbags, etc.).[214] However, they may not search the engine area or the trunk[215] unless the trunk is accessible without exiting the passenger compartment,[216] or rip up upholstery, remove dashboards, or take out door panels because objects hidden in places like these are not accessible to persons seated inside the vehicle.[217] The search of the passenger compartment may otherwise be as thorough as necessary to discover even the smallest piece of evidence.

### 3. Timing of the Search

The timing of a search incident to a motorist's arrest must be roughly contemporaneous with the arrest and generally before either the arrestee or the vehicle have been moved from the scene.[218]

### 4. Further Analysis of "A Mid-Summer's Nightmare"

Because Officer Weird had probable cause to arrest Ralph for attempted bribery before his search began, he was not restricted to performing a protective weapons search. He could search the entire passenger compartment for contraband and evidence of any crime, as well as for weapons. Accordingly, Weird did not exceed his search authority when he retrieved the envelope from under the driver's seat and read the contents.[219]

Mary's handbag, nevertheless, raises special considerations. In *Wyoming v. Houghton*,[220] the Supreme Court considered whether, when police have probable cause to search a vehicle, their search authority extends to the personal belongings of passengers whom police have no reason to suspect of anything. In the *Houghton* case, a highway patrol officer stopped a car for speeding. During the stop, the officer noticed a syringe in the driver's pocket. When asked about the syringe, the driver admitted that he used it to take

---

[214] New York v. Belton, *supra* note 207 (jacket on backseat of car deemed to be within the driver's control); United States v. Richardson, 121 F.3d 1051 (7th Cir. 1977) (shaving bag located in backseat of passenger compartment deemed to be under the driver's immediate control); United States v. McCrady, 774 F.2d 868 (8th Cir. 1985) (search of locked glove compartment and envelope after car owner's arrest qualified as search incident to arrest).

[215] United States v. Perea, *supra* note 187 (search of duffel bag located in trunk of cab in which suspect was riding at time of arrest could not be justified as search incident to arrest).

[216] United States v. Pino, 855 F.2d 357 (6th Cir. 1988) (station wagon), *cert. denied*, 493 U.S. 1090, 110 S. Ct. 1160, 107 L. Ed. 2d 1063 (1990); United States v. Russell, 670 F.2d 323 (D.C. Cir.) (hatchback), *cert. denied*, 457 U.S. 1108, 102 S. Ct. 2909, 73 L. Ed. 2d 1317 (1982).

[217] *See* WAYNE R. LAFAVE & JEROLD H. ISRAEL, CRIMINAL PROCEDURE §§ 3.7 (1984) (the "passenger compartment" means the area that is reachable without exiting the vehicle and without dismantling parts of the car).

[218] United States v. Vasey, 834 F.2d 782 (9th Cir. 1987) (search conducted between 30 and 45 minutes after defendant was arrested, handcuffed, and placed in rear of police vehicle lacked "contemporaneity" required for search incident to arrest.

[219] United States v. McCrady, *supra* note 214.

[220] **526 U.S. 295, 119 S. Ct. 1297, 143 L. Ed. 2d 408 (1999).**

drugs, giving the officer probable cause to search the vehicle. During the search, the officer spotted a handbag on the back seat. He searched it even though he knew that it belonged to a passenger, and arrested her when he found drugs found inside. The Supreme Court upheld the search even though the officer lacked probable cause to suspect the woman of anything before looking in her handbag. The Court stated that, when police have probable cause to search a vehicle, requiring them to determine the ownership of belongings found inside before searching them would encourage drivers to stash their contraband in passengers' belongings or have passengers claim ownership in order to thwart the search. This would impair the effectiveness of law enforcement. Accordingly, when police have probable cause to search a vehicle, they may search all containers found inside that are capable of housing the object of their search, without concern for ownership.

Although *Houghton* involved a vehicle search conducted under the motor vehicle exception, courts have applied the Supreme Court's reasoning to searches of motor vehicles incident to an arrest.[221] As one court explained:

> When police stop a car with multiple passengers and arrest one of them, the need for the police to discover either hidden weapons that could be turned upon them or evidence that could be destroyed is no less acute than when the police stop a vehicle and arrest its sole occupant. Indeed, because of the number of people involved, the need may be even greater. Given that third-party ownership of an item within a car's passenger compartment would not necessarily prevent an arrestee from gaining access to it, third-party ownership of an item should not bar police from searching that item in the same manner as if it were owned by the arrestee.[222]

Consequently, when police arrest a motor vehicle occupant, they may search all belongings found inside the passenger compartment without concern for their ownership. Weird was justified in searching Mary's handbag even though he lacked probable cause to suspect her of anything.

However, Officer Weird cannot rely on this exception to justify his search of Ralph's trunk or the search he conducted two days later.[223] Authority to search vehicle trunks or to search a vehicle at a time and place remote from the scene of an arrest can derive only from the exceptions covered in the next two sections.

---

[221] *See, e.g.*, People v. Morales,799 N.E.2d 986 (Ill. Ct. App. 2003) (holding that police had authority to search passenger's jacket found on backseat incident to driver's arrest); State v. Ray, 260 Neb. 868, 620 N.W.2d 83 (2000) (holding that warrantless search incident to driver's arrest extended to knapsack in passenger compartment that belonged to passenger); State v. Tognotti, 663 N.W.2d 642 (N.D. 2003) (holding that arresting officer could search the contents of a nonarrested occupant's purse); State v. Pallone, 236 Wis. 2d 162, 188, 613 N.W.2d 568 (2000) (holding that the warrantless search of a passenger's duffel bag was valid search incident to arrest of driver).

[222] People v. Morales, *supra* note 221. However, the rule allowing police to search a nonarrested passenger's personal belongings does not extend to the clothing they are wearing. *See, e.g.*, State v. Tognotti, *supra* note 221.

[223] *See* authorities cited in notes 215 and 218 *supra*.

Figure 4.13
**Vehicle Searches Based on Probable Cause ("Automobile Exception")**

---

- The officer must have probable cause to believe that the vehicle contains criminal evidence or contraband
- The scope of the search extends to the entire vehicle, from motor compartment to trunk and all the contents
- The intensity is limited to search activity necessary to find the objects the officer has probable cause to believe are hidden in the vehicle

---

# § 4.11 —Search of Vehicles Based on Probable Cause ("Automobile Exception")

## A. Grounds for Search Authority

The third exception, known as the "automobile exception," permits police to search motor vehicles without a warrant whenever they have probable cause to believe that the vehicle contains evidence that they may lawfully seize (i.e., criminal evidence or contraband).[224] This exception is based on the ready mobility of motor vehicles, which creates a risk that they might be gone by the time the police return with a search warrant,[225] and on the owner's reduced expectations of privacy, because a vehicle's interior compartment is exposed to anyone who looks.[226]

This is the broadest of the four exceptions relating to motor vehicles. Police do not need a search warrant to search a vehicle stopped on the highway, parked on a curb, or encountered elsewhere[227] if they have probable cause to believe that the vehicle contains criminal evidence or contraband, even if they have time to obtain a warrant.[228] A few states, nevertheless, use an older, more restrictive version that requires exigent circumstances as well probable cause.[229]

---

[224] Pennsylvania v. Labron, 518 U.S. 938, 116 S. Ct. 2485, 135 L. Ed. 2d 1031 (1996); California v. Acevedo, *supra* note 67.

[225] Carroll v. United States, 267 U.S. 132, 151, 45 S. Ct. 280, 284, 69 L. Ed. 543 (1925) ("A necessary difference [exists] between a search of a store, dwelling house or other structure in respect of which a proper official warrant readily may be obtained, and a search of a ship, motor boat, wagon or automobile, for contraband goods, where it is not practicable to secure a warrant because the vehicle can be quickly moved out of the locality or jurisdiction in which the warrant must be sought.")

[226] Cardwell v. Lewis, 417 U.S. 583, 94 S. Ct. 2464, 41 L. Ed. 2d 325 (1974) (noting that vehicles often contain personal effects, which are in plain view); Cady v. Dombrowski, 413 U.S. 433, 93 S. Ct. 2523, 37 L. Ed. 2d 706 (1973) (explaining that use of automobiles is highly regulated, bringing law enforcement in contact with persons in their vehicles where contraband may be in plain view).

[227] Cardwell v. Lewis, *supra* note 226; State v. Colvin, 123 N.J. 428, 433, 437, 587 A.2d 1278 (1991). However, the automobile exception does not apply to vehicles parked on residential property. *See, e.g.,* State v. LeJeune, 576 S.E.2d 888 (Ga. 2003) (holding that automobile exception does not apply where the suspect's car is legally parked in his residential parking space).

[228] Maryland v. Dyson, 527 U.S. 465, 467, 119 S. Ct. 2013, 144 L. Ed. 2d 442 (1999); Pennsylvania v. Labron, 518 U.S. 938, 940, 116 S. Ct. 2485, 135 L. Ed. 2d 1031 (1996).

[229] *See, e.g.,* State v. Cooke, 751 A.2d 92 (N.J. 2000); State v. Coleman, 2 P.3d 399 (Or. Ct. App. 2000); Fletcher v. State, 990 P.2d 192 (Nev. 1999).

## B. Scope and Intensity

When a vehicle search is supported by probable cause, the search authority of the police extends to the entire vehicle from bumper to bumper.[230] Police may search the vehicle as thoroughly as if they had a search warrant,[231] even to the point of removing structural parts.[232] Their search authority also extends to containers within the vehicle.[233] They may open any container capable of housing the object of their search, including containers known to belong to third parties whom police have no reason to suspect of anything.[234] However, their search authority does not extend to the vehicle occupants. Police may not search them or the clothing they are wearing unless they have probable cause to believe that the objects of the search are, in fact, located on their persons.[235]

As is true of all searches, the permissible intensity of a vehicle search is controlled by the object. The search may be no broader than necessary to locate the objects for which the police have search authority. For example, if the police have probable cause to believe that drugs are hidden *somewhere* in the vehicle, they may search the entire vehicle from engine compartment to trunk and everything inside in which drugs could fit. On the other hand, if the only thing they have probable cause to believe is that there is a briefcase containing drugs in the trunk, they are limited to opening the trunk and looking inside the briefcase.[236]

## C. Timing of the Search

Unlike searches incident to an arrest, there is no contemporaneousness requirement for searches conducted under the automobile exception.[237] Requiring police to stop everything and conduct an immediate search at the

---

[230] United States v. Ross, *supra* note 67 ("If probable cause justifies the search of a lawfully stopped vehicle, it justifies the search of every part of the vehicle and its contents that may conceal the object of the search.").

[231] *Id.*

[232] *See, e.g.*, Carroll v. United States, *supra* note 225 (upholstery); Ornelas v. United States, 517 U.S. 690, 116 S. Ct. 1657, 134 L. Ed. 2d 911 (1996) (side door panel); Cardwell v. Lewis, *supra* note 226 (paint sample); United States v. Zucco, 860 F. Supp. 363 (E.D. Tex. 1994) (wall paneling in recreational vehicle).

[233] United States v. Ross, *supra* note 67.

[234] **Wyoming v. Houghton**, *supra* note 220 (upholding search of a passenger's purse based on fact that police had probable cause to believe that the driver was a drug user and had controlled substances somewhere in his car, even though the police had no reason to suspect the passenger of anything).

[235] Ybarra v. Illinois, 444 U.S. 85, 91, 100 S. Ct. 338, 62 L. Ed. 2d 238 (1979) (warrant authorizing search of tavern and bartender did not carry authority to search customers present on the premises at the time of the search); United States v. Di Re, 332 U.S. 581, 68 S. Ct. 222, 92 L. Ed. 210 (1948) (probable cause to search a car did not justify a body search of a passenger).

[236] California v. Acevedo, *supra* note 67; United States v. Ross, *supra* note 67.

[237] *See, e.g.*, United States v. Johns, 469 U.S. 478, 105 S. Ct. 881, 83 L. Ed. 2d 890 (1985) (upholding warrantless search of packages three days after their seizure from vehicle); Florida v. Meyers, 466 U.S. 380, 104 S. Ct. 1852, 80 L. Ed. 2d 381 (1984) (per curiam) (upholding warrantless search of automobile at police impound lot conducted approximately eight hours after initial search); Chambers v. Maroney, 399 U.S. 42, 90 S. Ct. 1975, 26 L. Ed. 2d 419 (1970) (explaining that whenever the police could have searched vehicle without a warrant earlier at the scene, had they so chosen, they may search it at the police station later); United States v. Gastiaburo, 16 F.3d 582, 586 (4th Cir. 1994) ("[T]he justification to conduct a warrantless search under the automobile exception does not disappear merely because the car has been immobilized and impounded.").

roadside whenever they have probable cause to believe that a vehicle contains evidence subject to seizure would impede efficient and thorough criminal investigations. Probable cause to believe that a vehicle contains evidence subject to seizure does not vanish with the passage of time, at least not as long as the vehicle remains continuously under police control.[238] Consequently, any search that could be conducted at the roadside without a warrant may be delayed and conducted without a warrant after the vehicle reaches the police impoundment lot.[239]

## D. Further Analysis of "A Mid-Summer's Nightmare"

Officer Weird's search of the passenger compartment at the scene of the stop gave him reason to believe that there was more criminal evidence and contraband as yet undiscovered. It was obvious from the fliers that Ralph was a traveling peddler who sold counterfeit wares. The two bags of marijuana and large wad of $20 bills found in the passenger compartment suggested that Ralph was peddling drugs as well. These discoveries supplied probable cause to believe that there were counterfeit trinkets and drugs in other parts of the vehicle, triggering the automobile exception and broadening Officer Weird's search authority.[240] Weird was no longer restricted to searching the passenger compartment. He could now search the car from bumper to bumper, including the trunk.

Officer Weird's superficial roadside search did not exhaust his search authority under the automobile exception because he remained convinced, despite this search, that there were undiscovered drugs and counterfeit goods elsewhere in the vehicle.[241] Search authority under the automobile exception does not have to be exercised at the scene of the stop.[242] When police have probable cause to believe that a vehicle contains criminal evidence or contraband, they may seize it and search it later at a more convenient location.[243]

---

[238] Michigan v. Thomas, 458 U.S. 259, 102 S. Ct. 3079, 73 L. Ed. 2d 750 (1982) (per curiam) (the justification to conduct a warrantless search under the automobile exception does not disappear merely because the vehicle is immobilized and impounded); United States v. Henderson, 241 F.3d 638 (9th Cir. 2000) (authority to search defendant's rental car, under automobile exception to warrant requirement, did not evanesce because officers decided to impound vehicle and search it later). *But see,* United States v. Brookins, 228 F. Supp. 2d 732 (E.D. Va. 2002) (although police officers had probable cause to search vehicle at time of suspect's arrest, probable cause no longer existed where suspect was allowed to leave scene and vehicle was found parked at his residence 15 minutes later, because the suspect could have disposed of the contraband in the meantime).

[239] *See* authorities *supra* note 237.

[240] Myles v. State, 946 S.W.2d 630 (Tex. Ct. App. 1997) (discovery of marijuana in interior of vehicle stopped for traffic violation provided probable cause for more thorough search of entire vehicle, including inside of spare tire); United States v. Bullock, 94 F.3d 896 (4th Cir. 1996) (discovery of wad of money, two cellular telephones, and a beeper, combined with the motorist's nervous behavior, attempts to conceal console, and incredible explanation of his trip, provided probable cause to believe vehicle contained contraband and justified search under the automobile exception).

[241] *See* authorities *supra* note 237.

[242] *Id.*

[243] Michigan v. Thomas, *supra* note 238.

The fact that two days elapsed between the seizure of Ralph's car and the second search is also not a problem because, as mentioned above, searches under the automobile exception do not have occur simultaneously with the seizure.[244] Courts have upheld searches under the automobile exception even in the face of substantial delays.[245] In one case, police searched a hidden compartment behind the radio in the dashboard for drugs more than a month after the vehicle was impounded.[246] The court upheld the search notwithstanding the delay.

The scope and intensity of searches under the automobile exception are also different from searches conducted as an incident to an arrest. When the police have probable cause to search a motor vehicle, they may search any location where the objects of their search could be hidden, even if it requires disassembling parts of the vehicle.[247] Officer Weird was, accordingly, justified in looking inside the steering wheel column and behind the dashboard, and removing the door panels and backseat because they are locations where drug dealers sometimes hide drugs and that could also serve as hiding places for counterfeit trinkets.

Figure 4.14
**Vehicle Inventory Search**

- The purpose of the search is to secure the owner's valuables and protect the police department against liability for loss and theft
- Police must have legal authority to impound the vehicle
- The decision to impound must be made in good faith and not as a pretext to search for evidence
- Police must follow standard procedures for inventorying the contents of impounded vehicles
- The scope of the search is governed by these procedures
- The intensity is limited to activity necessary to catalog and safeguard the items

---

[244] *See, e.g.,* United States v. Gastiaburo, *supra* note 237 (warrantless search of hidden compartment behind radio in dashboard conducted 38 days after vehicle was impounded upheld as valid search under automobile exception); Bayless v. City of Frankfort, 981 F. Supp. 1161 (S.D. Ind. 1997) (warrantless search of vehicle more than four months after impoundment upheld as valid search under automobile exception).

[245] *See* cases *supra* note 244.

[246] United States v. Gastiaburo, *supra* note 237.

[247] *See, e.g.,* United States v. McSween, 53 F.3d 684 (5th Cir. 1995) (suspect's four prior arrests on narcotics charges and smell of odor of burned marijuana provided probable cause to search entire vehicle, including under the hood, where officer found marijuana in hole in fire wall); United States v. Zucco, 71 F.3d 188 (5th Cir. 1995) (proper to remove door panel after canine alert created probable cause to search vehicle for drugs); United States v. Gastiaburo, *supra* note 237 (upholding search of hidden compartment behind radio in console of car); United States v. Anderson, 114 F.3d 1059 (10th Cir. 1997) (upholding search of gas tank); *See also* authorities *supra* note 232.

# § 4.12   —Inventory Searches of Impounded Vehicles

## A. *Grounds for Search Authority*

The first requirement for a lawful inventory search is a lawful impound-ment.[248] Legal authority to impound vehicles exists for a variety of reasons, including illegal parking, unpaid traffic tickets, abandonment, mechanical failures, disablement due to accident, and the arrest or other incapacitation of the driver.[249] The decision to impound must also be made in a good faith. The police, for example, may not impound a vehicle after a driver's arrest purely for the opportunity to conduct an inventory search, when other licensed dri-vers are present who are capable of taking charge of it.[250] Evidence that comes to light during an inventory search will be suppressed unless police both have legal authority to impound the vehicle and act in good faith in making the decision to impound.[251]

Once a vehicle has been impounded, an inventory search will follow. Inventory searches are exempt from conventional Fourth Amendment require-ments because police are performing a caretaking function.[252] To be sustain-able as an inventory search, the search must be conducted in accordance with "standardized criteria" specifying where, when, and how inventory searches are to be conducted (i.e., whether the search is to be conducted at the scene before the vehicle is released to a third-party towing company or when it reaches the impoundment lot, what parts of the vehicle may be searched, whether police may open closed containers, etc.).[253] Standardized procedures are necessary to ensure that inventory searches are used for their intended pur-poses and not as a ruse to search for evidence.[254] It is up to each individual police department to formulate inventory search procedures. Once policies and procedures have been put into place, they must be routinely followed in order for the search to be upheld under the inventory search exception.

---

[248]   The requirements for a lawful impoundment—that there be a law or regulation providing for impound-ment under the circumstances and that police officers make a good faith choice among the alterna-tives—are explained in § 4.4.

[249]   United States v. Foreman, 993 F. Supp. 186 (S.D.N.Y. 1998).

[250]   Yaws v. State, 38 S.W.3d 720 (Tex. Ct. App. 2001); State v. Lark, 748 A.2d 1103 (N.J. 2000); Butler v. Com, 525 S.E.2d 58 (Va. Ct. App. 2000); Philips v. State, 167 Ga. App. 260, 305 S.E.2d 918 (1983).

[251]   United States v. Cooley, 119 F. Supp. 2d 824 (N.D. Ind. 2000).

[252]   South Dakota v. Opperman, *supra* note 75; Colorado v. Bertine, *supra* note 118.

[253]   *See, e.g.*, California v. Bertine, *supra* note 118 (police may not open locked containers in impounded vehicles unless inventory procedures mandate opening of all such containers).

[254]   South Dakota v. Opperman, *supra* note 75 (emphasizing standardized procedures as means of curbing abuses); United States v. Thompson, 29 F.3d 62, 65 (2d Cir. 1994) (fruits of inventory searches will be suppressed when the searching officers act in bad faith solely for the purpose of investigation); United States v. Prescott, 599 F.2d 103 (5th Cir. 1979) (inventories used as pretext for investigatory search are unlawful).

## B. Scope and Intensity of Inventory Searches

All search activity performed during an inventory search must be geared toward one or more of the following purposes: (1) safeguarding valuables inside the vehicle; (2) protecting law enforcement agencies against unjustified claims of loss or damage; or (3) locating potentially hazardous articles like weapons and flammables.[255] Police, for example, are not allowed to open and read journals, diaries, and planners, search cellular phones for telephone numbers, or listen to tapes during an inventory search because this activity advances none of the purposes for which inventory searches may be conducted.[256] Police, in addition, are not allowed dismantle parts of the vehicle, such as removing steering wheel hubs and door panels, because the police department is not responsible for safeguarding valuables stored in places like these.[257] A noted authority on the law of search and seizure writes:[258]

> The inventory must be reasonably related to its purpose, which is the protection of the car owner from loss, and the police or other custodian from liability or unjust claim. It extends to the open areas of the vehicles, including areas under seats, and other places where property is ordinarily kept, e.g., glove compartments and trunks. It does not permit a search of hidden places, certainly not the removal of car parts in an effort to locate contraband or other property. The owner having no legitimate claim for protection of property so hidden, the police could have no legitimate interest in seeking it out.

## C. Inventory Exception and the Inevitable Discovery Rule

Standard operating procedures for conducting inventory searches are important for a second reason. Their existence can salvage evidence from suppression under a doctrine known as the inevitable discovery rule. As will be explained in § 4.17, evidence that comes to light by unlawful means may nonetheless be used at trial if it would inevitably have been revealed in some other lawful way.[259] Consequently, even though an earlier vehicle search is

---

[255] WAYNE R. LAFAVE, SEARCH & SEIZURE § 7.4 (3d ed. 1996).

[256] United States v. Flores, 122 F. Supp. 2d 491 (S.D.N.Y. 2000) (suppressing evidence gained by reading planner and searching cellular telephone for numbers); United States v. Chan, 830 F. Supp. 531 (N.D. Cal. 1993) (suppressing evidence gained by warrantless activation of pager); State v. Jewell, 338 So. 2d 633 (La. 1976) (suppressing evidence gained from inspecting contents of Excedrin bottle); Crowley v. State, 25 Md. App. 417, 334 A.2d 557 (1975) (suppressing LSD capsules found in can of mechanics' cleansing soap).

[257] United States v. Best, 135 F.3d 1223 (8th Cir. 1998) (suppressing drugs discovered while shining flashlight to look inside door panel to find out what was obstructing front window from rolling down); United States v. Lugo, 978 F.2d 631 (10th Cir. 1992) (searching behind door panels does not qualify as standard inventorying procedure or serve the purpose of protecting the car and its contents); People v. Rutovic, 193 Colo. 397, 566 P.2d 705 (1977) (looking inside zipped seat covers impermissible during inventory search); Fields v. State, 382 So. 2d 1098 (Miss. 1980) (vacuuming car cannot be justified as inventory search).

[258] LAFAVE, *supra* at p. 255.

[259] Nix v. Williams, 467 U.S. 431, 104 S. Ct. 2501, 81 L. Ed. 2d 377 (1984).

unlawful, the evidence uncovered can be used if it would, in any event, have been discovered during a routine inventory search.[260]

### D. Final Analysis of "A Mid-Summer's Nightmare"

The search Officer Weird performed at the police impoundment lot was not sustainable as an inventory search because Weird's purpose was not to safeguard Ralph's property or to protect the WPD from liability. He was looking for evidence. His search, moreover, exceeded the scope and intensity allowed for an inventory search. The search, nevertheless, was sustainable under the automobile exception because he had probable cause to believe that drugs and other incriminating evidence were hidden somewhere in the vehicle. Police officers do not need to have a particular exception in mind when they conduct a warrantless search. The search is valid if it can be sustained under any exception to the warrant requirement.

## § 4.13 Search of Protected Premises

When police officers cross the threshold of a home in search of evidence, the values protected by the Fourth Amendment are most at risk. Accordingly, it is at this point that the Fourth Amendment affords maximum protection. A search warrant is required so that the decision to invade a resident's privacy will be made only after proper consideration and the boundaries for the search will be established in advance. Unlike searches of people and vehicles, in which warrants are more the exception than the rule, the only two circumstances in which police officers may search protected premises without a warrant are when they enter with the consent of an occupant and when they are confronted with a grave emergency.

Consider this last example as you examine the rules for premises searches.

---

### A Final "Tail"

Something evil has been taking place in Officer Goodfellow's neighborhood. One by one, his neighbors' pets have vanished. In the once-peaceful suburb where cats and dogs roamed freely, people are now frightened and lock their animals up with them at night. Still, the disappearances continue.

---

[260] *See, e.g.*, United States v. Kimes, 246 F.3d 800 (6th Cir. 2001) (applying inevitable discovery rule); United States v. Blaze, 143 F.3d 585 (10th Cir. 1998) (evidence unlawfully seized from briefcase inside trunk admissible under theory of inevitable discovery because it would have been inevitably discovered in a subsequent inventory search); United States v. Haro-Salcedo, 107 F.3d 769 (10th Cir. 1997) (cocaine seized from trunk during overly broad search incident to arrest admissible under inevitable discovery doctrine, when police officers lawfully impounded vehicle after defendant's arrest, police department procedures mandated inventory search to secure personal items found in defendant's seized vehicle, and proper inventory search would have uncovered cocaine in trunk of vehicle).

The first disappearance occurred at about the same time that a strange old woman, Mrs. Metzger, moved into the neighborhood. Metzger purchased the largest lot in the neighborhood, known as "the Farm." The lot consists of three acres surrounded by a hog wire fence. Located inside are a main house, a separate three-car garage, and a dilapidated barn situated at the far rear in an area overgrown with weeds and brush.

The neighbors first put two-and-two together when they learned that Mrs. Metzger had started her own sausage company and was running it out of the barn and garage. Metzger Sausages were rumored to have a "curiously gamey flavor," unlike any other brand on the market. Time and time again a pet would disappear early in the evening, and the sausage trucks would pull up to the barn the next morning.

Neighbors called various government offices to report the atrocities, but little attention was paid to them. They ultimately persuaded an inspector from the county's Board of Food Safety to conduct a surprise search. The inspector went to Mrs. Metzger's home, demanded to see the sausage production facilities in the barn and garage, pronounced the facilities "safe," left, and reported that he did not see anything unusual. So the neighbors turned to Officer Goodfellow and begged him to stop the carnage.

Goodfellow agreed. That night, he hopped over the fence, flashlight in hand, and began examining the barn. Immediately outside the barn door he found two animal collars, one with the name "Fido" on it, the other "Boogums." He entered the barn through an unlocked door, inspected the machinery and found what looked like cat hair near one of the grinders. He took the hair with him.

Goodfellow proceeded to the garage. Using his flashlight, he could see more machinery through the windows and a car parked in a far corner of the building. Unfortunately, the doors were locked and he could not enter. Leaving, Goodfellow noticed some garbage cans outside the garage. Out of curiosity, he opened one, and found something that sent a chill down his spine—a shoe box filled with animal collars. Too scared to look further without backup, Goodfellow grabbed the box and headed straight to the local magistrate, seeking a warrant to search the entire estate and an arrest warrant for Mrs. Metzger. The magistrate refused both, saying: "Just because you found some animal collars doesn't mean that there is probable cause to believe that Mrs. Metzger committed a crime or that evidence of a crime will be found on her property. I'm sorry, but you need to do some more police work."

The next evening, Goodfellow made the rounds of the neighborhood, knocking on doors and asking if anyone could identify the Fido and Boogums' collars. Goodfellow finally felt that he had probable cause when Jason P. Thomas, a neighbor for many years whom Goodfellow knew to be trustworthy, told him that "Fido" and "Boogums" were two of the pets that had disappeared from the neighborhood within the last week. But before Goodfellow could get back to the magistrate, a frightened young girl came running up to him, screaming "Please save Snowball! She didn't come back tonight." Eerily, at that same moment, they heard the low hum of machinery coming from Mrs. Metzger's place and the lights in the garage came on.

Believing that Snowball had only a few minutes left, Goodfellow ran into the garage to save her. He burst through the door screaming "Stop! You're under arrest." As soon as Mrs. Metzger saw him, she dropped a white fluffy cat to the floor and ran into the main house. Goodfellow chased her inside, and began a systematic search, looking in rooms, closets, and under beds in an effort to find her, bending down to pick up pet collars as he made his way. When he opened the door to the basement, approximately 50 animals, cats and dogs, came running out. Mrs. Metzger came out behind them and asked that she be allowed to speak to a lawyer.

As it turns out, all of the neighborhood's pets were unharmed. Mrs. Metzger, a zoophile, simply wanted them all to herself. She received a suspended sentence and is currently undergoing counseling.

In the sections that follow, we will explore whether Mrs. Metzger's Fourth Amendment rights were violated by the warrantless incursions onto her property. Because her property was used as a business as well as a residence, we will analyze the Fourth Amendment protection for each.

## § 4.14 —Premises Protected by the Fourth Amendment

While a literal reading of the Fourth Amendment would suggest that "houses" are the only premises protected by the Fourth Amendment because they are the only ones mentioned, this is not the case.[261] The term "house" has never been interpreted this narrowly.[262] The Fourth Amendment protects any location, including business premises, for which there exists a reasonable expectation of privacy.[263]

> The Fourth Amendment protects any location for which there exists a reasonable expectation of privacy.

### A. Fourth Amendment Protection for Business Premises

Fourth Amendment protection for business premises turns on whether they are open to the public, such as retail establishments, or closed to the public, such as private offices and warehouses.[264] Police do not need a search warrant to enter any business premises that members of the public are invited to enter because their entry does not infringe on any reasonable expectation of

---

[261] New York v. Harris, 495 U.S. 14, 110 S. Ct. 1640, 109 L. Ed. 2d 13 (1990).
[262] *See, e.g.,* **Katz v. United States,** *supra* note 1 (public telephone booth); WAYNE R. LAFAVE, 1 SEARCH & SEIZURE § 2.1[d] (3d ed. 1996).
[263] **Katz v. United States,** *supra* note 1.
[264] **Maryland v. Macon,** *supra* note 3 (it is not a search for an officer to enter an adult bookstore and examine merchandise displayed for sale).

privacy.[265] However, they may enter only during business hours and may go only into areas that are members of the public are invited to enter.[266] Officers acting on a tip on that the defendant is running an illegal bingo hall, for example, are free to enter while a bingo game is in progress, but not to sneak into back offices or to force their way into the establishment during hours when the business is closed.[267]

## B. Fourth Amendment Protection of Residences

The Fourth Amendment affords maximum protection for homes because the home is the place where expectations of privacy are the greatest.[268] Police may not make a warrantless entry into a home—absent consent or exigent circumstances.[269] Homes, for Fourth Amendment purposes, include any structure occupied as a dwelling, such as a house, apartment, mobile home, or even a tent. The structure need not be a permanent residence. Hotel rooms, motel rooms, railway sleeping cars, and bedrooms occupied by overnight guests are also treated as homes for Fourth Amendment purposes.[270] Entry into someone's home is always considered a search and police must have search authority.

## C. Outdoor Spaces: Areas within the Curtilage and "Open Fields"

Outdoor spaces surrounding a home are classified into two categories—areas within the curtilage and open fields. The curtilage refers to the area immediately surrounding the home that is regularly used for family purposes and carries the same protection as the home.[271] The rest of the land is classified as an open field and carries no Fourth Amendment protection. The phrase "open field" is misleading because the area need not be open or a field in any literal sense; it can be woods, a condominium parking area, or even a lake.[272] Police do not need a search warrant to enter an open field because there is no reasonable expectation of privacy in outdoor activities that take place beyond the curtilage. Accordingly, entering an open field is not a search, even though it may be a trespass under property law.

---

[265]  *Id.*

[266]  *Id.*

[267]  State v. Foreman, 662 N.E.2d 929 (Ind. 1996).

[268]  **Payton v. United States**, *supra* note 21 ["The Fourth Amendment protects the individual's privacy in a number of settings, but in none is the zone of privacy more clearly defined than when bounded by the unambiguous physical dimensions of an individual's home—a zone that finds its route in clear and specific constitutional terms. . . . [T]he Fourth Amendment has drawn a firm line at the entrance to the home."]; Lewis v. United States, *supra* note 6.

[269]  Donovan v. Dewey, 452 U.S. 594, 101 S. Ct. 2534, 69 L. Ed. 2d 262 (1981).

[270]  Roberts v. State, 599 N.E.2d 595 (Ind. 1993).

[271]  United States v. Dunn, *supra* note 32.

[272]  *See, e.g.,* State v. Matthews, 805 S.W.2d 776 (Tenn. Crim. App. 1990) (apartment complex parking lot). *See also* 1 WAYNE R. LaFAVE, SEARCH & SEIZURE § 2.4 (3d ed. 1996).

Whether a particular area is within the curtilage depends on four factors: Its proximity to the home, whether the area is included within an enclosure surrounding the home, whether it is used for family purposes, and the steps taken by the resident to protect the area from observation by persons passing by.[273] No single factor is determinative, but they each inform a court's decision as to whether the outlying area is so intertwined with the residents' "home life" that it should be considered part of the home for Fourth Amendment purposes. Professor Klotter has noted the following about the curtilage:

> The curtilage has been defined as the open space situated within a common enclosure and belonging to the dwelling house. It has also been defined as the space that is necessary and convenient and is habitually used for family purposes, including a yard, a garden, or even a field that is near and used in connection with the dwelling. It is often difficult to define the area included within the curtilage, but certainly the yard around the house is included and protected under the Fourth Amendment and the state provisions.[274]

Although the curtilage concept does not apply to business establishments,[275] the grounds surrounding a business establishment are entitled to similar protection when special precautions are taken to keep members of the public from entering, such as by putting up a tall fence with a locked gate.[276] Police may not climb over tall fences with locked gates to enter the grounds surrounding a business establishment unless they have search authority.[277]

## D. Analysis of "A Final 'Tail'"

Officer Goodfellow violated the Fourth Amendment when he entered Mrs. Metzger's curtilage in search of evidence. The more difficult question is determining the curtilage's boundaries. Mrs. Metzger's garage was within the curtilage both because of its proximity to her home and because garages are commonly used for domestic purposes, even though hers was being used partly for business. Consequently, Goodfellow performed a search when he walked up to her garage, shined a flashlight to look inside, and retrieved a shoe box full of pet collars from a garbage can just outside. The fact that the shoe box had been placed in a garbage can did not destroy Fourth Amendment protection because until a garbage can is placed outside the curtilage for collection, its contents cannot be said to have been abandoned.[278] The garbage can is just another container that is being used for domestic purposes.

---

[273] United States v. Dunn, *supra* note 32.

[274] KLOTTER & KANOVITZ, CONSTITUTIONAL LAW 259 (7th Ed. 1994).

[275] Dow Chemical Co. v. United States, 476 U.S. 227, 106 S. Ct. 1819, 90 L. Ed. 2d 226 (1986) (noting that a lesser expectation of privacy exists in lands surrounding commercial buildings).

[276] *See, e.g.*, United States v. Oliver, 686 F.2d 356 (5th Cir. 1982); Pearl Meadows Mushroom Farms v. Inc. v. Nelson, 723 F. Supp. 432 (N.D. Cal. 1989); United States v. F.M.C. Corp., 428 F. Supp. 615 (D.C.N.Y. 1977).

[277] *See* authorities *supra* note 276.

[278] California v. Greenwood, *supra* note 2.

The pet collars found near the barn stand on a different footing because the barn was situated in an "open field." The reason the land around the barn was an open field was its distance from Mrs. Metzger's house, its dilapidated condition, which suggested that the barn was not being put to domestic use, and the fact that it was actually being used for business.[279] Had the barn been closer or used for domestic purposes, its characterization would have been more difficult.

### E. Outbuildings

Even though the barn was situated in an "open field," and Goodfellow was free to walk around outside, his warrantless entry constituted a search because the barn itself is entitled to the same privacy protection as any other closed building used for business.[280] Police may not enter closed buildings used for business without exigent circumstances, consent, or a warrant.[281]

This does not mean that barns and outbuildings situated in an open field enjoy the same privacy protection as structures located inside the curtilage. If a barn is situated in an open field, police are free to walk up, peer through the windows, and use a flashlight to illuminate the interior.[282] Police are not allowed to do this for buildings that lay within the curtilage because they have no right to enter the curtilage to search for evidence without a search warrant.

## § 4.15 —Entry and Search of Premises Under a Warrant

### A. Search of Premises for Evidence

Most of the problems encountered in "A Final Tail" would have been avoided if the police had obtained a search warrant. A search under the authority of a search warrant extends to the entire premises covered by the warrant. When the premises are described by street number, search authority also extends to the curtilage, other structures within the curtilage and also, according to most courts, to vehicles belonging to the owners that are parked on the premises.[283]

The permissible intensity of a premises search is controlled by the warrant's description of the items to be seized. Officers may explore any place where objects described in their warrant could fit. When the objects sought are small, police may look under beds, in drawers and closets, and even in the

---

[279] United States v. Dunn, *supra* note 32 (holding that a barn located 60 yards from the dwelling that was used to manufacture drugs lay outside curtilage).

[280] Fite v. State, 873 P.2d 293 (Okla. Crim. App. 1993).

[281] *Id.*

[282] United States v. Dunn, *supra* note 32.

[283] *See, e.g.*, United States v. Gottschalk, 915 F.2d 1459 (10th Cir. 1990); United States v. Asselin, 775 F.2d 445 (1st Cir. 1985); United States v. Napoli, 530 F.2d 1198 (5th Cir. 1976).

pockets of the clothing hanging inside.[284] They do not need a particularized reason to believe that the objects of their search are located in a specific drawer or a specific pocket. The fact that there is probable cause to believe that listed items are somewhere on the premises supports searching any locations where the objects could be hidden.

Police may ordinarily assume that all personal property that they find while executing a search warrant is the property of a resident and, hence, searchable. Whether a search warrant confers authority to search property that police actually *know* belongs to a non-resident or visitor is a question on which courts disagree. In *Wyoming v. Houghton*,[285] the Supreme Court ruled that where police have probable cause to search a vehicle, they may search any package within the vehicle that is capable of containing the object of their search, without consideration of ownership. Whether this ruling will be applied to searches of protected premises under the authority of a warrant remains to be seen.[286] Until this matter is settled, police executing a search warrant should not search personal property known to belong to third parties for objects listed in the warrant unless they have probable cause to believe that the third party is connected to the crime or that the objects of the search will be found among that person's belongings.

## B. *Detention of Persons on the Premises While Executing a Search Warrant*

The issuance of a search warrant carries the implied authority to detain the occupants of the premises while the search is in progress.[287] This intrusion is necessary to prevent flight in the event that incriminating evidence is found. Authority to detain rests on the principles announced in *Terry v. Ohio*.[288] Because a search warrant embodies a magistrate's determination that there is probable cause to believe that a crime has been committed and that evidence relating to that crime will be found on the premises, the issuance of a search

---

[284] United States v. Lucas, 932 F.2d 1210 (8th Cir. 1991) (a search warrant that sufficiently describes the premises to be searched justifies a search of all personal effects that might contain items described in warrant).

[285] *Supra* note 220.

[286] *Compare* United States v. Vogl, 7 Fed. Appx. 810 (10th Cir. 2001) (declining to extend the Court's *Houghton* automobile search analysis to a premises search) *with* State v. Reid, 77 P.3d 1134 (Or. App. 2003) (warrant confers authority to search all items that could contain articles of the sort identified in the warrant except those that are in the actual physical possession of a person not subject to the warrant). *See also* generally WAYNE R. LaFAVE, 2 SEARCH & SEIZURE § 4.10 (b) (3d ed 1996); Zachary H. Johnson, *Personal Container Searches Incident to Execution of Search Warrants: Special Protection for Guests?* 75 TEMP. L. REV. (2002); Diane L. Schmauder, *Propriety of Search of Nonoccupant Visitor's Belongings Pursuant to Warrant Issued for Another's Premises*, 51 A.L.R.5TH 375 (1997).

[287] Michigan v. Summers, 452 U.S. 692, 101 S. Ct. 2587, 69 L. Ed. 2d 640 (1981); United States v. Fullwood, 86 F.3d 17 (2d Cir. 1996) (police officers arriving at defendant's residence to execute search warrant could require defendant, who was outside the residence and entering a vehicle, to reenter his home and could detain him while they conducted search).

[288] *Supra* note 9.

warrant casts suspicion on all who regularly occupy the premises and justifies detaining them.[289] However, a search warrant does not carry the implied authority to detain others, like visitors or customers, who are coincidentally present.[290] Detention of nonoccupants is justified only when police have reasonable suspicion that they are connected to the crime.[291]

## C. Search of Persons on the Premises While Executing a Search Warrant

Searching persons found on the premises involves a greater intrusion on privacy than simply detaining them. In *Ybarra v. Illinois*,[292] the Supreme Court ruled that a search warrant authorizing the search of a tavern and its bartender for narcotics did not confer authority to search customers present at the tavern when the warrant was executed. The Supreme Court stated:

> . . .[A] search or seizure of a person must be supported by probable cause particularized to that person. This requirement cannot be undercut or avoided by simply pointing to the fact that coincidentally there exists probable cause to . . . search the premises where the person may happen to be.[293]

Thus, while a search warrant carries the authority to search property found on the premises for objects described in the warrant, it does not carry the authority to search persons.[294] Police may search individuals present on the premises only if they have probable cause to believe that they have objects described in the warrant secreted on their persons.[295] A noted authority on the

---

[289]  Michigan v. Summers, *supra* note 287.

[290]  Hummel-Jones v. Strope, 25 F.3d 647 (8th Cir. 1994) ("*Summers* did not announce a per se rule authorizing . . . detention of anyone found on any premises being searched subject to a warrant, regardless of the circumstances, but simply permits the temporary detention of those residents of a house rendered suspect by a contraband warrant for that house.").

[291]  Hummel-Jones v. Strope, *supra* note 290 (detention of patients in clinic waiting room of birthing clinic pursuant to warrant based on suspected practicing of medicine without a license violated Fourth Amendment because they had no connection to the crime for which the warrant was issued); State v. Crane, 19 P.3d 1100 (Wash. Ct. App. 2001) (individual's entry into area that police officer had been ordered to secure while awaiting search warrant, without more, does not give rise to reasonable suspicion justifying such individual's detention); Proferes v. State, 13 P.3d 955 (Nev. 2000) (seizing persons who knock on door during execution of warrant to search residence violates the Fourth Amendment unless police have reasonable suspicion, based on objective information, that they are connected to crime for which warrant was issued); *but see* United States v. Bohannon, 225 F.3d 615 (6th Cir. 2000) (officers could reasonably infer that man who drove down long driveway while they were executing warrant to search for drugs was either drug distributor or customer because his quick exit from car and rapid approach to residence indicated apparent familiarity; police were, therefore, justified in detaining him).

[292]  444 U.S. 85, 100 S. Ct. 338, 62 L. Ed. 2d 238 (1979) (mere propinquity does not give rise to probable cause to search visitors).

[293]  *Id.*

[294]  *Id.*

[295]  Hummel-Jones v. Strope, *supra* note 290 (warrant to search medical establishment for records and tools of unauthorized practice of medicine cannot reasonably be relied upon to authorize the nonconsensual search of innocent patients who are present).

law of search and seizure[296] writes that the "requisite probable cause is most likely to be deemed present if the person searched lives at the place searched, was implicated by the search warrant affidavit in the crimes under investigation, had engaged in suspicious or incriminating conduct, or was found in the immediate proximity of contraband in open view."[297]

### 1. Search of Persons Listed in the Warrant

If police have advance knowledge that persons likely to be in possession of items listed in the warrant could be present on the premises during an authorized search, they should apply for a search warrant naming them and expressly authorizing police to search them. While courts may, under limited circumstances, issue a warrant to search "all persons present" at a particular location, such broad search authority is suspect. Such a warrant is valid only if there is probable cause to believe that all persons present at that location at the time of the search are likely to be involved in the crime and have evidence of the crime on their persons.[298] This situation generally exists only when the location is a crack house.[299] It did not exist in the *Ybarra* case because public taverns are likely to have at least some innocent patrons present.[300]

### 2. *Terry* Search of Persons on the Premises

A search warrant does not carry automatic authority to perform a pat-down search.[301] Reasonable suspicion remains necessary.[302] Unless the nature of the suspected crime supports a reasonable belief that all persons present are likely to be armed—such as when the premises are a mob safe house—police must have particularized reasons for suspecting the people who are frisked.

---

[296]  3 WAYNE R. LAFAVE, LAW OF SEARCH & SEIZURE § 6.6(a) (3d ed. 1996).

[297]  *See, e.g.*, United States v. Khounsavanh, 113 F.3d 279 (1st Cir. 1997) (police had probable cause to search occupants after informant made controlled purchase of drugs from them and they attempted to flee when police entered apartment to execute search warrant); State v. Farrell, 242 Neb. 877, 497 N.W.2d 17 (1993) ("it was reasonable for the officers to believe that defendant was concealing evidence on his person," as he whispered to his wife "I've got it" and then asked to use the bathroom); Patton v. State, 148 Ga. App. 793, 252 S.E.2d 678 (1979) (police had probable cause to search person seated beside table with marijuana when he surreptitiously put hand in pocket).

[298]  State v. Prior, 617 N.W.2d 260 (Iowa 2000); 2 WAYNE R. LAFAVE, SEARCH & SEIZURE § 4.5(e) (3d ed. 1996).

[299]  *See, e.g.*, State v. Allard, 674 A.2d 921 (Me. 1996).

[300]  United States v. Guadarrama, 128 F. Supp. 2d 1202 (E.D. Wis. 2001).

[301]  Ybarra v. Illinois, *supra* note 292 (pat-down search of tavern patrons impermissible in absence of reasonable suspicion that they were involved in criminal activity or were armed or dangerous); In re J.V., 762 A.2d 376 (Pa. Super. 2000) (mere presence during execution of drug warrant does not provide reasonable suspicion for a *Terry* search).

[302]  United States v. Bohannon, 225 F.3d 615 (6th Cir. 2000) (frisk justified where person acted very nervous and twice ignored officer's request to keep hands out of his pocket while police were executing search warrant at residence suspected of being laboratory for illegal drug operations).

## D. *Search of Premises Pursuant to an Arrest Warrant*

As was explained in Chapter 3, absent exigent circumstances or hot pursuit, police officers may not enter private premises to effect an arrest unless they first obtain an arrest warrant.[303] If the arrestee is believed to be present in another person's home, the officers must, in addition, obtain a search warrant for that person's home.[304] Both warrants carry the authority to search the premises to the degree necessary to locate the suspect. This does not mean looking in kitchen cabinets and bureau drawers. When officers enter to make an arrest, they are restricted to performing a cursory visual inspection of places where a person could hide.[305]

Once the suspect is found and placed under arrest, two new grounds for search authority arise. Police are entitled to perform a **protective sweep** and a search incident to the arrest.

### 1. Protective Sweeps

A protective sweep consists of a cursory visual inspection of closets and other spaces *immediately adjoining* the place of arrest in which accomplices and others who pose a danger to the officers could be hiding.[306] Authority to conduct a protective sweep arises as an automatic incident to an in-home arrest and does not depend on probable cause or reasonable suspicion that potential attackers are, in fact, hiding in the area to be swept.[307] However, such a belief is necessary in order to conduct a broader sweep.[308] Protective sweeps may last no longer than necessary to dispel any suspicion of danger, and in any event no longer than it takes to complete the arrest and depart from the premises.

### 2. Search Incident to an In-House Arrest

An arrest does not justify a full-blown search of the arrestee's entire home. The scope of the search is limited to the arrestee's person and the area under his or her immediate control (defined as "the area from within which he might gain possession of a weapon or destructible evidence").[309] One court paraphrased the test, defining the area under the arrestee's control as the area "conceivably accessible to the arrestee—assuming that he was neither an acrobat [nor] a Houdini."[310] If the police want to search a larger area, they may take

---

[303]  *See* § 3.15 *supra*.

[304]  *Id.*

[305]  Maryland v. Buie, 494 U.S. 325, 110 S. Ct. 1093, 108 L. Ed. 2d 276 (1990).

[306]  *Id.*

[307]  *Id.*

[308]  *Id.*; In re Sealed Case, 153 F.3d 759 (D.C. Cir. 1997) (protective sweep could extend to small bedroom located between the bedroom where arrest was made and top of the stairs because it was a space from which an attack could be launched).

[309]  Chimel v. California, *supra* note 44.

[310]  United States v. Lyons, 706 F.2d 321 (D.C. Cir. 1983).

reasonable precautions to secure the premises to prevent removal or destruction of evidence, but must then apply for a search warrant.[311]

## § 4.16  —Entry and Search of Premises without a Warrant

There are only two justifications for searching protected premises without a search warrant: exigent circumstances and consent.[312]

Figure 4.15
**Exigent Circumstances Exception**

---

The exigent circumstances exception authorizes the police to make a warrantless entry when:

1. they have probable cause to believe that life or property is in imminent danger or that a serious crime is in progress.
2. they have probable cause to believe that evidence will be destroyed or removed unless they act immediately; or
3. they are in hot pursuit of a felon who flees and takes refuge inside.

---

### A. Grounds for Warrantless Entry

Films and television programs regularly portray police officers bursting through the door in the nick of time to save a victim, but never show them waiting nervously outside the magistrate's door for a search warrant. That is because the Fourth Amendment excuses the police from obtaining a warrant when they are confronted with an emergency that requires immediate action. There are an endless number of emergencies that can justify an immediate warrantless entry. Fires,[313] shootings,[314] domestic violence reports,[315] screams,[316] hot pursuit of dangerous criminals,[317] the belief that a burglary is

---

[311]  *See* authorities *supra* note 70.

[312]  **Payton v. New York**, *supra* note 21; Steagald v. United States, 451 U.S. 204, 101 S. Ct. 1642, 68 L. Ed. 2d 38 (1981).

[313]  State v. Loh, 275 Mont. 460, 914 P.2d 592 (1996) (exigent circumstances of apparent fire and the possibility that individuals were still inside justified warrantless entry).

[314]  People v. Dixon, 721 N.Y.S.2d 402 (N.Y.A.D. 2001) (entry justified where made in response to radio transmission that a man had just killed his wife and was alone with their baby in the apartment).

[315]  Fletcher v. Town of Clinton, 196 F.3d 41 (1st Cir. 1999) (officer who, responding to domestic disturbance report, was informed by neighbors that shouting had ended right before his arrival, was justified in concluding that someone inside might have been injured and in need of medical care or protection; police may enter dwelling without warrant to render emergency aid and assistance to persons whom they reasonably believe to be in distress).

[316]  United States v. Barone, 330 F.2d 543 (2d Cir. 1964) (screams coming from inside apartment); United States v. Gillenwaters, 890 F.2d 679 (4th Cir. 1989) (call from stab victim requesting help).

[317]  Warden v. Hayden, *supra* note 7.

in progress,[318] concerns for the safety of children[319] or colleagues inside,[320] and fears that evidence is about to be destroyed[321] are just a few.

Exigent means urgent. The exigent circumstances exception to the warrant requirement deals with urgent circumstances in which there is no time to obtain a warrant.[322] There are three broad categories of cases that come within this exception. Failure to obtain a warrant before entering a residence is excused when police reasonably believe that: (1) lives or property are in imminent danger or that a serious crime is in progress;[323] (2) evidence will be destroyed or moved if they postpone taking action until a search warrant can be obtained;[324] or (3) they are in hot pursuit of a felon who flees and takes refuge inside.[325]

## B. Exigent Circumstances and the Plain View Exception

Discovery of incriminating evidence while on the premises generally provides the context in which questions about the exigent circumstances exception arise. Two police officers, patrolling a residential neighborhood in the

---

[318] In re Sealed Case, *supra* note 308.

[319] State v. Peterson, 543 S.E.2d 692 (Ga. 2001) (entry for the purposes of making sure children left without adult supervision were safe).

[320] People v. Lee, 723 N.Y.S.2d 833 (N.Y. City Crim. Ct. 2001) (police justified in entering prostitute's apartment without search warrant when an undercover officer working with the vice squad unit failed to emerge after prearranged 20-minute period inside and his team members became concerned that his life might be in danger).

[321] Illinois v. McArthur, *supra* note 70; United States v. Rivera, 248 F.3d 677 (7th Cir. 2001) (warrantless search of defendant's residence was justified by exigent circumstances, where at moment of entry, agents had reason to believe that evidence might be destroyed or removed before a warrant could be secured; agents observed defendant transport packages containing marijuana to his residence, other individuals continuously entered defendant's residence and left with small packages that agents presumed to be narcotics).

[322] *See, e.g.,* In re Sealed Case, *supra* note 308 ("[t]he test for exigent circumstances is whether police had an 'urgent need' or 'an immediate major crisis in the performance of duty afford[ing] neither time nor opportunity to apply to a magistrate.'").

[323] *See, e.g.,* Arizona v. Hicks, *supra* note 44 (exigent circumstances justified entry to search for person who fired a shot through the floor, injuring man in apartment below); Michigan v. Tyler, 436 U.S. 499, 509, 98 S. Ct. 1942, 56 L. Ed. 2d 486 (1978) (burning building presents exigency of sufficient proportions to render warrantless entry reasonable); Mincey v. Arizona, 437 U.S. 385, 392, 98 S. Ct. 2408, 57 L. Ed. 2d 290 (1978) (recognizing that need to protect or preserve life or avoid serious injury justifies warrantless entry); Minnesota v. Olson, 495 U.S. 91, 100, 110 S. Ct. 1684, 109 L. Ed. 2d 85 (1990) (recognizing that warrantless entry may be justified by the risk of danger to the police or to other persons inside or outside the dwelling); In re Sealed Case, *supra* note 308 (warrantless entry justified where officers, while patrolling residential neighborhood, observed what they reasonably thought was burglary in progress).

[324] Because of the ease with which narcotics can be destroyed, cases invoking this exception frequently involve narcotics busts. *See, e.g.,* Illinois v. McArthur, *supra* note 70.

[325] Warden v. Hayden, *supra* note 7 (warrantless search for suspect and weapons reasonable where delay posed grave danger); Welsh v. Wisconsin, 466 U.S. 740, 748, 104 S. Ct. 2091, 80 L. Ed. 2d 732 (1984) (exigent circumstances do not justify warrantless entry to search for nondangerous suspect). *See also* Richards v. Wisconsin, 520 U.S. 385, 395, 117 S. Ct. 1416, 137 L. Ed. 2d 615 (1997) (no need to "knock and announce" when executing a search warrant where officers reasonably suspect that evidence might be destroyed).

early hours of the morning, see a man run up a path leading to a dark residence, strike the main door with his shoulder, force it open, and enter without turning on the lights. Believing that a burglary is in progress and that lives and property are in danger, the police stop the car, follow the man into the house and, guess what? It turns out that the man was entering his own house, but the police, while on the premises investigating, see a large quantity of marijuana in plain view.

This scenario requires the court to determine whether the entry was justified by exigent circumstances,[326] because if the initial intrusion that brings the police in contact with the evidence is lawful, they immediately recognize its incriminating nature, and they are able to gain physical access to it without violating the Fourth Amendment, they may seize it under the plain view exception.[327]

## C. Search Activity Permitted Under the Exigent Circumstances Exception

When an entry is made under the exigent circumstances exception, search authority is limited to actions immediately necessary to address the exigency that justified the entry.[328] As to what the police may do once inside, one authority writes:

> [T]his must be assessed upon a case-by-case basis, taking into account the type of emergency which appeared to be present. . . . The officer's post-entry conduct must be carefully limited to achieving the objective which justified the entry.[329]

For example, if the entry is made to render emergency assistance, the officer may do no more than is reasonably necessary to ascertain whether someone is in need of assistance and provide it.[330] When the entry is to prevent destruction of evidence, the police may perform a cursory visual inspection of rooms, closets, and other locations in which persons who might destroy the evidence could hide.[331] If the evidence sought is discovered in plain view while the police are performing a cursory visual inspection, the police may seize it under the plain view doctrine. If no evidence is discovered, the police may secure the premises, but must then apply for a search warrant.[332]

While on the premises, police may not investigate unrelated hunches; they must stick to addressing the exigency that justified their entry. In *Arizona v. Hicks*,[333] a bullet was fired through the floor of the defendant's apartment,

---

[326] The facts recited in the previous paragraph are from In re Sealed Case, *supra* note 308. The court held that warrantless action was justified.

[327] The plain view exception to the warrant requirement is discussed in § 3.4.

[328] Mincey v. Arizona, *supra* note 323 (search activity while on the premises is " 'strictly circumscribed by the exigencies which justify its initiation.' ").

[329] 3 WAYNE R. LAFAVE, SEARCH & SEIZURE § 6.6(a) (3d ed. 1996).

[330] *Id.*

[331] Mincey v. Arizona, *supra* note 323; Illinois v. McArthur, *supra* note 70; **Arizona v. Hicks**, *supra* note 44.

[332] *See* authorities *supra* note 331.

[333] *Supra* note 44.

striking and injuring a man in the apartment below. The police entered the defendant's apartment and, while searching for the shooter and the weapon, noticed some very expensive stereo equipment that seemed out of place. Acting on a hunch that the equipment was stolen, they turned the stereo around and read the serial numbers to a radio operator who confirmed that it was stolen. The Supreme Court held that, while the initial entry was justified by exigent circumstances, turning the stereo around to read the serial numbers resulted in an additional search unrelated to the exigency that justified the entry and violated the Fourth Amendment.

## D. Entry to Prevent Destruction of Evidence

Police tend to overuse the excuse that they entered without a warrant in order to prevent destruction of evidence. This exception is actually very narrow. Police may enter a person's home without a warrant to prevent destruction of evidence only if they have: (1) probable cause to secure a search warrant *and* (2) an objectively reasonable belief that there are persons inside who will destroy the evidence if they do not act right now.[334] When both conditions are present, police may enter for the limited purpose of securing the premises while they apply for a search warrant, but must postpone the search until after a warrant is obtained.[335] Entry even for this limited purpose is not permitted if the risk of destruction can be adequately controlled by conducting a perimeter stakeout (i.e., sealing off the premises and preventing anyone from entering).[336]

## E. Analysis of "A Final 'Tail'"

"A Final Tail" contains two examples of the exigent circumstances exception. The first occurred when Officer Goodfellow burst into Mrs. Metzger's garage and the second when he pursued her into her home. Officer Goodfellow was justified in bursting into Mrs. Metzger's garage without a warrant because he had probable cause to believe that Snowball was inside and, at the

---

[334] *See, e.g.*, Illinois v. McArthur, *supra* note 70 (after defendant's wife informed police that defendant had illegal drugs inside their home, police justified in preventing defendant from entering his residence without an officer until a search warrant was obtained); United States v. Lewis, 231 F.3d 238 (6th Cir. 2000) (belief that drug evidence inside house was in danger of imminent destruction not justified when informant had indicated that there would be drug transaction outside the house and gave no indication that anyone would be in the house at time of transaction, and officers had no other indication that someone was inside house at the time).

[335] *See* authorities *supra* note 331.

[336] Illinois v. McArthur, *supra* note 70 (when police have probable cause to believe there are illegal drugs inside residence and reason to fear evidence will be destroyed, they may seal off residence and refuse to allow occupants to enter, unless accompanied by a police officer, until a warrant can be obtained); Mincey v. Arizona, *supra* note 323 (exigent circumstances do not justify search where police guard at door could prevent loss of evidence).

moment of entry, he had reason to believe that Snowball was about to be destroyed. He had just confirmed that the pet collars found the previous day belonged to cats that had mysteriously disappeared; moments later, he learned that Snowball had disappeared, too; Goodfellow had previously seen the grinding machines inside Mrs. Metzger's barn and garage; and now he heard them start up and begin humming. In his mind, there was only one explanation that could account for this bizarre sequence of events. Snowball was about to be ground up and would be no more by the time he returned with a search warrant. Snowball was more than just a pet;[337] he was evidence of criminal activity. Consequently, Goodfellow was justified in rushing in to prevent what he believed was the imminent destruction of evidence.

Mrs. Metzger's retreat into her home to avoid arrest provided the second occasion for applying the exigent circumstances exception. This time the exception was concerned with hot pursuit. Mrs. Metzger could not defeat Officer Goodfellow's attempt to make a lawful arrest by fleeing and taking refuge inside her home. He was entitled to follow her and search for her inside.[338] Officer Goodfellow did a marvelous job of complying with the Fourth Amendment. Unfortunately, few medals are given for capturing little old ladies who love animals.

## F. Consent

Consent affords the second and only other justification for entering protected premises without a search warrant. Actual consent is necessary to enter a home or its curtilage, but implied consent is enough to justify the warrantless inspections of business premises to determine compliance with government regulations.

### 1. Actual Consent

Police are always free to walk up to a suspect's door, ring the bell, and ask for permission to enter. A warrantless entry is justified when police receive knowing, voluntary, and intelligent consent[339] from someone who has authority.[340]

The person answering the door does not have to be informed of the right to refuse in order for the consent to be voluntary.[341] Concealment of police

---

[337] Suss v. American Society for the Prevention of Cruelty to Animals, 823 F. Supp. 181 (S.D.N.Y. 1993) (recognizing that exigent circumstances exception may, in limited situations, allow warrantless action to protect animals against cruelty).

[338] *See* authorities *supra* 317.

[339] Schneckloth v. Bustamonte, *supra* note 64; United States v. Conner, 127 F.3d 663 (8th Cir. 1997) (unconstitutional search occurs when officers gain physical access to a motel room after an occupant opens the door in response to a demand issued under color of authority).

[340] Illinois v. Rodriguez, *supra* note 60. *See also* §§ 3.15(D), 4.3(A)(2)(a) *supra*.

[341] Schneckloth v. Bustamonte, *supra* note 64.

identity does not destroy the effectiveness of the consent.[342] However, there are limits on how far police may go to secure admission. Police may not misrepresent that they have a warrant[343] or threaten to obtain one when they lack grounds.[344] Generally speaking, only a person who occupies the premises can give an effective consent.[345]

Once police gain entry, the boundaries of the search will be determined by the consent that has been given.[346] Police may only look in places and for things for which they have been given permission to search.[347] The consenter also controls the duration of the search. He or she can limit the duration at the outset[348] or ask police to leave at any time.[349] However, after the police discover incriminating evidence, it is generally too late, because at this point other warrant exceptions generally arise.

### 2. Implied Consent—Statutory Authority and Administrative Searches

The Fourth Amendment permits warrantless inspections of business premises to determine compliance with government regulations.[350] This exception to the warrant requirement is often said to rely on implied consent. The warrantless inspection performed by the official from the Board of Food Safety is an example. When Mrs. Metzger began producing sausages, she knew that food service is a heavily regulated industry and that the regulations often include periodic, unannounced inspections. By going into this business, she impliedly consented to abide by the regulations and was in no position to claim that her Fourth Amendment rights were violated when an official from the Board of Food Safety arrived and demanded to inspect her sausage production facilities.

---

[342] Lewis v. United States, *supra* note 6.

[343] Bumper v. North Carolina, 391 U.S. 543, 88 S. Ct. 1788, 20 L. Ed. 2d 797 (1968).

[344] State v. Apodaca, 839 P.2d 352 (Wash. 1992); Orhorhaghe v. INS, 38 F.3d 488 (9th Cir. 1994) (agent represented to alien that he had authority to enter without a warrant).

[345] Illinois v. Rodriguez, *supra* note 60. *See also* § 4.3(A)(2)(a) *supra*.

[346] United States v. Dichiarinte, 445 F.2d 126 (7th Cir. 1971) (police exceeded consent to search for narcotics when they read through defendant's personal papers).

[347] *Id.*

[348] State v. Douglass, 123 Wis. 2d 13, 365 N.W.2d 580 (1985).

[349] *See, e.g.*, State v. Mer, 441 N.W.2d 762 (Iowa 1989); Mason v. Pullman, 557 F.2d 426 (5th Cir. 1977); United States v. Million-Rodriguez, 759 F.2d 1558 (11th Cir. 1985).

[350] Donovan v. Dewey, 452 U.S. 594, 101 S. Ct. 2534, 69 L. Ed. 2d 262 (1981) (upholding warrantless inspections by federal mine inspectors of underground mines to ensure compliance with health and safety standards); United States v. Biswell, 406 U.S. 311, 92 S. Ct. 1593, 32 L. Ed. 2d 87 (1972) (upholding warrantless inspection of premises of licensed gun dealers to determine compliance with the Gun Control Act).

# § 4.17  The Exclusionary Rule

The exclusionary rule is a criminal defendant's remedy for police violations of his or her constitutional (Fourth, Fifth, or Sixth Amendment) rights. This remedy entitles the criminal defendant to have all evidence obtained as a result of the violation excluded from his or her trial. The remedy serves two purposes: to undo the damage that the defendant has suffered by preventing illegally seized evidence from being used against him or her,[351] and to discourage police from future violations by depriving them of the fruits of their transgressions.[352]

> The exclusion of evidence is a criminal defendant's remedy for police violations of his or her constitutional rights.

## A. History of the Exclusionary Rule

The exclusionary rule has been attacked ever since its recognition, but no one has ever summarized the frustration that many feel about the rule better than Justice (then Judge) Cardozo did in his opinion in *People v. Defore*,[353] when he lamented: "The criminal is to go free because the constable has blundered."

In recent years, the Supreme Court has attempted to balance the costs to criminal justice inherent in allowing the guilty to "go free" against the benefits of discouraging police violations of the Constitution. In the process, it has reshaped the rule and created many exceptions to it. As you read through the following materials, ask whether it is still the case today that the criminal who would otherwise have been convicted "goes free" simply because "the constable has blundered."

### 1. Recognition and Framing of the Rule

The Supreme Court first announced the exclusionary rule in *Weeks v. United States*.[354] In that case, a federal marshal working with state police entered Weeks' house without a warrant and seized his private papers—some of which showed that he was guilty of running an illegal lottery. Prior to trial, Weeks moved unsuccessfully to have the prosecution return the papers to him to prevent the prosecution from using them. The Supreme Court overturned the conviction, but not because Weeks had a constitutional right to suppress evidence seized in violation of the Fourth Amendment. Reversal was required because the defendant had a constitutional right to the return of his property, which was violated when the prosecution refused to give it back.[355]

---

[351]  **Mapp v. Ohio, 367 U.S. 643, 81 S. Ct. 1684, 6 L. Ed. 2d 1081 (1961)**.
[352]  Wong Sun v. United States, 371 U.S. 471, 83 S. Ct. 407, 9 L. Ed. 2d 441 (1963).
[353]  242 N.Y. 13, 150 N.E. 585 (1926).
[354]  232 U.S. 383, 34 S. Ct. 341, 58 L. Ed. 652 (1914).
[355]  *Id.*

It was not until the Court's later decisions that it came to regard suppression itself as the proper remedy for an illegal search and seizure.[356] However, the rule lost its characterization as a constitutional right and became simply a judicially created remedy for the illegal search and seizure, which judges could apply or refuse to apply, depending on whether or not it would achieve the goals of deterrence in a given case.[357] Although the prevailing view now is that the rule is not a constitutional right, but a judicially created remedy,[358] both views continue to shape the rule and its exceptions.

## 2. Application of the Rule to the States

When it was first recognized by the Supreme Court, the exclusionary rule applied only to evidence seized by federal officials.[359] The Court did not apply it to the states.[360]

It was not until almost 50 years after *Weeks* that the Supreme Court finally made the exclusionary rule binding on the states in the now-famous case of *Mapp v. Ohio*.[361] The facts of the case were particularly egregious, and they highlighted the need for a requirement that tainted evidence be suppressed in order to curb illegal police activity.

Mapp involved a prosecution for the possession of obscene materials. Police officers initially sought entrance to Mapp's home after learning that an unnamed person, wanted for questioning in connection with a recent bombing, might be hiding inside, and that Mapp also had a large amount of revolutionary literature in her home. Mapp refused to admit them without a warrant, so the officers left and returned three hours later with a fake warrant. When Mapp demanded to see it, a scuffle ensued, in which Mapp was forcibly subdued and placed under arrest. Police officers proceeded to scour the home. The obscene materials for which Mapp was eventually charged were uncovered during that search in a locked trunk in her basement.

Faced with such facts, the Supreme Court acknowledged that a mandatory exclusionary rule was essential to the Fourth Amendment:

> The ignoble shortcut to conviction left open to the State tends to destroy the entire system of constitutional restraints on which the liberties of the people rest. Having once recognized that the right to privacy embodied in the Fourth Amendment is enforceable against the States, and that the right to be secure against rude invasions of privacy by state officers is, therefore, constitutional in origin, we can no longer permit that right to remain an empty promise. Because it is enforceable in the same manner and to like effect as other basic

---

[356]   Silverthorn Lumber Co. v. United States, 251 U.S. 385, 40 S. Ct. 182, 64 L. Ed. 319 (1920).

[357]   United States v. Leon, *supra* note 139.

[358]   Arizona v. Evans, 514 U.S. 1, 115 S. Ct. 1185, 131 L. Ed. 2d 34 (1995).

[359]   Wolf v. Colorado, 338 U.S. 25, 69 S. Ct. 1359, 93 L. Ed. 1782 (1949).

[360]   *Id.*

[361]   *Supra* note 351.

rights secured by the Due Process Clause, we can no longer permit it to be revocable at the whim of any police officer who, in the name of law enforcement itself, chooses to suspend its enjoyment.[362]

Since *Mapp v. Ohio*, suppression of illegally obtained evidence has been required in both federal and state courts as a matter of Fourth Amendment law.

## B. Scope of the Rule

The defendant's right to suppression includes not only evidence uncovered during an illegal search or seizure, but also any other evidence that police discover as a result of it.[363] This is known as the "fruit of the poisonous tree doctrine," or the *Wong Sun* doctrine—after the case in which it was recognized. The recognition of the fruit of the poisonous tree doctrine means that illegal police activity can have far-ranging effects on a prosecution. Once police obtain evidence by violating the Fourth Amendment, the prosecution will not only lose the benefit of that evidence; it will bear the burden of showing that all other evidence that it seeks to introduce was acquired from a source untainted by the illegal evidence-gathering activity.[364]

## C. Standing to Assert the Rule

The exclusionary rule is a remedy for criminal defendants whose Fourth Amendment rights have been violated. Because it is a remedy (rather than a general prohibition on the use of illegally obtained evidence), only a defendant whose rights were violated when police obtained the evidence can demand suppression.[365] If the illegally obtained evidence is offered against another person, whose rights were not violated, then there is no constitutional injury to remedy. Accordingly, a person whose rights were not violated has no standing to complain if tainted evidence is admitted against him or her.

Suppose, for example, that police break into Mary Wanna's home without a warrant or probable cause, looking for evidence of drug trafficking. While inside, they find five kilograms of cocaine and a photograph of her brother Sam cultivating a marijuana garden in his basement. Based on the photograph, police obtain a warrant for Sam's home. They seize the plants and a photograph depicting Mary assisting Sam in his basement operation. Mary is charged on both cocaine and marijuana counts. She will "walk" on both counts

---

[362] *Id.*

[363] Wong Sun v. United States, *supra* note 352.

[364] Murray v. United States, 487 U.S. 533, 108 S. Ct. 2529, 101 L. Ed. 2d 472 (1988).

[365] Rakas v. Illinois, 439 U.S. 128, 99 S. Ct. 421, 58 L. Ed. 2d (1978); Minnesota v. Carter, 525 U.S. 83, 119 S. Ct. 469, 142 L. Ed. 2d 373 (1998) (capacity to claim protection of Fourth Amendment depends on whether the person who claims it has a reasonable expectation of privacy in the place invaded; a person present in another's apartment for a few hours to package cocaine lacks a reasonable expectation of privacy in the premises).

because all the evidence against her derives either directly (the cocaine) or indirectly (the photographs linking her to Sam's marijuana operations) from the illegal search of her home. Sam, on the other hand, is going to jail because the police did not violate *his* Fourth Amendment rights and he has no standing to complain that police acquired probable cause for his search warrant and some of the evidence used against him by violating his sister Mary's rights.

## D. Exceptions to the Rule

Because the Supreme Court has come to regard the exclusionary rule as a judge-made remedy, rather than a constitutional right, it has recognized a number of exceptions based on whether the rule will have a deterrent effect in a given situation and whether suppression is otherwise an appropriate remedy.

Figure 4.16
**Exceptions to the Exclusionary Rule**

Suppression is not required:

1. if the same evidence inevitably would have been discovered through lawful means;
2. if the officer acted in objective good faith;
3. if the evidence is offered for the limited purpose of impeaching (i.e., discrediting) the defendant's own testimony;
4. if the evidence is offered in a proceeding other than the defendant's criminal trial.

### 1. Inevitable Discovery/Independent Source Exception

Because the exclusionary rule is designed to undo the effects of a Fourth Amendment violation and to discourage future violations, the Supreme Court has determined that suppression is not required in cases in which the police obtain no advantage from their unlawful conduct. Accordingly, illegally obtained evidence will be admitted if the prosecution can show that the same evidence inevitably would have found its way into the hands of the police through lawful means in the absence of the illegal discovery. The reasoning behind this exception is that the government should not be better off as a result of unlawful activity, but neither should it be worse off.[366]

The inevitable discovery exception often works in conjunction with the inventory search exception to wash out earlier errors committed by the police. For example, if the police perform an overly broad motor vehicle search after arresting a motorist, but the same evidence inevitably would have been discovered during a routine inventory search, the evidence is admissible because the police did not reap any advantage from their wrongdoing.[367]

---

[366]   *See* Nix v. Williams, *supra* 259.

[367]   United States v. George, 971 F.2d 1113 (4th Cir. 1992) (government must prove that it would have found same evidence under the police department's standard inventory procedures).

## 2. Good Faith Exception

The exclusionary rule cannot deter all violations of the Fourth Amendment because, no matter how hard police try to avoid them, accidental violations will occur. Because the exclusionary rule applies only when it will deter illegal conduct, the rule does not apply when the officer who violated the Fourth Amendment acted in good faith.

In order to act in good faith, two elements are needed. First, the violation of the Fourth Amendment must be unintentional—the officer must believe that he or she is acting in compliance with the Fourth Amendment. Second, the officer's belief must be objectively reasonable. For example, in the case of *Arizona v. Evans*,[368] police officers made a routine traffic stop and ran a computer check on the driver's name. The computer reported that there was an outstanding warrant for the driver's arrest, so the officers took him into custody. In the course of doing so, they discovered marijuana on his person and in his car. As it turned out, the arrest was illegal because the warrant had been quashed 17 days earlier. The database simply failed to reflect this. The defendant argued that the marijuana should be suppressed as the fruit of an illegal arrest and search.

The Supreme Court disagreed, finding that the officers had acted in objective good faith. They did not intend an illegal arrest. Moreover, it was reasonable, indeed inescapable, for them to rely on computer reports in discharging their daily responsibilities. Suppression under the circumstances, the Court pointed out, would not reduce the number of illegal arrests; thus, the exclusionary rule should not apply. Likewise, in *Illinois v. Krull*,[369] the Supreme Court ruled that if police officers relied in good faith on an administrative search statute that was later determined to be unconstitutional, the evidence they obtained is admissible. The *Krull* court noted that, as long as the statute is not unconstitutional on its face, it is reasonable for officers to rely on it.

The most important application of the good faith doctrine, however, is the exception for reliance on a facially valid warrant that is later determined to be defective.[370] The Court recognized this exception in *United States v. Leon*.[371] In *Leon*, police officers investigating suspected drug dealing made out an affidavit stating the facts that they felt supported probable cause to believe that there was contraband in Leon's home. The magistrate reviewed the affidavit, found probable cause, and issued the warrant. At a later suppression hearing, however, the trial court determined that the magistrate was incorrect—the facts in the affidavit did not support a finding of probable cause and suppressed the evidence. In reviewing that decision, the Supreme Court accepted that probable cause was lacking but held that evidence should not be sup-

---

[368] *Supra* note 358.
[369] 475 U.S. 868, 107 S. Ct. 1160, 94 L. Ed. 2d 364 (1987).
[370] United States v. Leon, 468 U.S. 897, 104 S. Ct. 3405, 82 L. Ed. 2d 677 (1984); Massachusetts v. Sheppard, 468 U.S. 981, 104 S. Ct. 3424, 82 L. Ed. 2d 737 (1984).
[371] United States v. Leon, *supra* note 370.

pressed when it is seized under a search warrant that the executing officers reasonably believe is valid.

The *Leon* Court listed four situations in which police officers cannot claim that they acted in objective good faith: (1) when the magistrate was misled by information in the affidavit that the affiant knew or should have known was false; (2) when the magistrate has wholly abandoned his or her judicial role; (3) when the affidavit is so lacking in indicia of probable cause as to render official belief in its existence entirely unreasonable; and (4) when the warrant is so facially deficient—in failing to particularize the place to be searched or the things to be seized—that the executing officers cannot reasonably presume it to be valid.[372]

The lesson of *Leon* is that police officers do not have to be perfect, but that they must act in good faith and they must reasonably follow the proper procedures for obtaining and executing a search warrant. First, officers must never execute a warrant if they actually believe that it is invalid. Second, their determination that the warrant is valid must be reasonable under the circumstances. This means: (1) officers must reasonably believe that the facts are sufficient to justify the magistrate in finding probable cause; (2) they must reasonably believe that the magistrate considered the affidavit rather than just "rubber-stamping" it; and (3) the warrant itself must appear sufficient in form.

### 3. Impeachment

The exclusionary rule prevents the prosecution from offering illegally obtained evidence to prove its case. However, if the defendant takes the witness stand and commits perjury, the prosecution may offer the evidence for the limited purpose of impeaching (i.e., discrediting) the defendant's own **testimony**.[373] Impeachment consists of offering evidence that contradicts the defendant's testimony for the sake of showing that the defendant is lying. The exception for impeachment is narrow because it applies only if the defendant takes the stand and gives contradictory testimony at the trial and, as is explained in later chapters, the defendant is not required to testify.

---

[372] *See, e.g., Id.*; United States v. Ninety-Two Thousand Four Hundred Twenty-Two Dollars and Fifty-Seven Cents, 307 F.3d 137 (3d Cir. 2002) (to come within exceptions to good faith exception to exclusionary rule applicable when a search warrant is based on affidavit so lacking in indicia of probable cause or so lacking in requisite particularity as to render official belief in its existence unreasonable, party seeking suppression must show that the magistrate judge's error was so obvious that a law enforcement officer, without legal training, should have realized, upon reading the warrant, that it was invalid); Hester v. State, 551 N.E.2d 1187 (Ind. Ct. App. 1990) (search warrant to search for "any and all property which may have been stolen" from a described residence on a specified date was so facially deficient that "good faith" exception to the exclusionary rule did not apply).

[373] Walder v. United States, 347 U.S. 62, 74 S. Ct. 354, 98 L. Ed. 503 (1954) (permitting the prosecutor to introduce into evidence heroin obtained through an illegal search to undermine the credibility of the defendant's claim that he had never possessed narcotics).

### 4. Use Outside Criminal Trials

The only kind of proceeding in which the exclusionary rule applies is a criminal trial.[374] The Supreme Court has repeatedly declined to extend the rule to other proceedings. Thus, for example, illegally obtained evidence can be offered in grand jury proceedings,[375] parole hearings,[376] civil trials,[377] and even administrative hearings for deportation.[378] The Court limits the exclusionary rule to the criminal trial because it believes that suppression in other contexts serves no deterrent effect. Its reasoning is that when police intentionally violate the Fourth Amendment, they do so in order to obtain evidence for a conviction, not to convince a grand jury that a criminal should be prosecuted, or an immigration official that an alien should be deported. Because the Court believes that the Fourth Amendment's deterrent policy would not be served under these circumstances, it refuses to apply the rule.

## § 4.18　Summary and Practical Suggestions

The Fourth Amendment prohibits unreasonable searches and seizures. A search occurs whenever police invade a suspect's reasonable expectation of privacy, either by physically intruding into a constitutionally protected location (i.e., persons, houses, papers, and effects) or committing a technological invasion of privacy. A seizure occurs when police commit a meaningful interference with a suspect's possessory interest in property. Minor interferences with possession do not trigger Fourth Amendment protection.

The Fourth Amendment generally requires a search warrant before police may search for or seize property for use as evidence. A search warrant protects against general searches by interposing between a citizen and the police the disinterested determination of a neutral, detached magistrate that there is probable cause for the search and by specifying where the police may search or what they may search for. The warrant's description of the place to be searched limits the scope of the search to locations where the police have demonstrated probable cause to believe that the objects of the search are likely to be found. The description of the things to be seized limits the intensity of the search activity to that necessary to uncover the items listed in the warrant. Police are allowed to search for evidence without a warrant in four situations: consent, searches incident to a lawful arrest, exigent circumstances, and vehicle searches. The Fourth Amendment also allows warrantless limited weapons searches and inventory searches.

---

[374]　Pennsylvania Board of Probation and Parole v. Scott, 524 U.S. 357, 118 S. Ct. 2014, 141 L. Ed. 2d. 344 (1998).

[375]　United States v. Calandra, 414 U.S. 338, 94 S. Ct. 613, 38 L. Ed. 2d 561 (1974).

[376]　Pennsylvania Board of Probation and Parole v. Scott, *supra* note 374.

[377]　United States v. Janis, 428 U.S. 433, 96 S. Ct. 3021, 49 L. Ed. 2d 1046 (1976).

[378]　INS v. Lopez-Mendoza, 468 U.S. 1032, 104 S. Ct. 3479, 82 L. Ed. 2d 778 (1984).

Property may be seized for various reasons, the most common being to use it as evidence. When the purpose of the seizure is to obtain criminal evidence, the Fourth Amendment requires probable cause to believe that the property is connected to a crime and either a search warrant describing it or discovery in plain view. There are four general categories of articles that may be seized: fruits of crime, instrumentalities of crime, contraband, and "mere evidence." The "plain view" doctrine allows police to seize evidence without a warrant when they discover it in plain view while conducting a lawful search for some other article and immediately develop probable cause to believe that it constitutes the fruits, instruments, or evidence of a crime or contraband. Brief, limited seizures are permitted on a lesser showing. When the police have probable cause to believe that a container houses criminal evidence or contraband, they may seize it without a warrant, but must obtain a warrant before opening and searching it. Police may act on reasonable suspicion in seizing containers for the purpose of subjecting them to a canine examination for illegal drugs, but the period of detention must be brief. Finally, police may impound property without a warrant under various circumstances unrelated to the discovery of evidence.

When evidence is obtained in violation of these requirements, the exclusionary rule applies. Under this rule, a person whose Fourth Amendment rights have been violated can move to have all resulting evidence excluded from his or her criminal trial. There are several exceptions to this rule, the most important of which allows admission of evidence obtained in violation of the Fourth Amendment so long as the officer made a good faith mistake.

# Eavesdropping and Interception of Communications 5

*The Congress makes the following findings: There has been extensive wiretapping carried on without legal sanctions, and without the consent of any of the parties to the conversation. Electronic, mechanical, and other intercepting devices are being used to overhear oral conversations made in private, without the consent of any of the parties to such communications. . . . To safeguard the privacy of innocent persons, the interception of wire or oral communications . . . should be allowed only when authorized by a court [and] with assurances that the interception is justified and that the information obtained thereby will not be misused.*

Congressional Findings,
Omnibus Crime Control
and Safe Streets Act of 1968

# Chapter Outline

## § 5.1  Introduction to the Laws Governing Eavesdropping and the Use of Interception Devices

This chapter discusses the constitutional and statutory rules that apply when the government engages in clandestine forms of surveillance to develop evidence of crimes. The bulk of this chapter deals with **eavesdropping** and **interception**.

*Eavesdropping* is an ancient form of investigation that relies on normal powers of hearing. It gets its name from medieval English laws that made it a crime to stand beneath the eaves of a house in order to overhear conversations inside.[1] *Interception* refers to listening with the aid of a device. Interception devices were introduced in the early part of the twentieth century and have become increasingly sophisticated. A noted authority on the law of search and seizure writes:

> Tiny microphones can be secreted behind a picture or built into a coat button. Highly directive microphones known as "parabolic microphones" are capable of eavesdropping on a conversation taking place in an office on the opposite side of a busy street or on a park bench or outdoor restaurant terrace hundreds of feet away. Laser beams can pick sound waves off closed windows. A small, continuously operating transmitter can be placed beneath the fender of an automobile and its signal picked up by a receiver in another car or in a fixed plant. A special gun developed for American military authorities can shoot a small dart containing a wireless radio microphone into a tree, window pane, awning or any other object near the subject of investigation.[2]

---

[1]    4 BLACKSTONE, COMMENTARIES, ch. 13, § 5.

[2]    WAYNE R. LaFAVE, SEARCH AND SEIZURE § 2.2 (3d ed. 1996).

Interception devices are generally more sensitive than the human ear, can record communications and transmit them great distances and, above all, are less conspicuous than a human listener. These features enable them to be used without the parties knowing, or even having reason to suspect, that their conversation is being monitored. As a result, the use of interception devices is regulated by constitutional and statutory controls that do not exist when the police listen with their ears alone. Suspects enjoy scant constitutional protection against eavesdropping. This is because people who speak loudly enough for others within earshot to hear have no reason to expect that no one is listening.[3] The absence of a **reasonable expectation of privacy** means that Fourth Amendment protection is unavailable.[4] However, people who take precautions to protect their privacy do have such an expectation. The surreptitious use of an interception device to monitor conversations that the parties reasonably assume are private generally leads to a **search** and triggers the need for Fourth Amendment procedural safeguards.[5] Congress provided these safeguards in Title III of the Omnibus Crime Control and Safe Streets Act of 1968.[6] However, we are jumping ahead of ourselves. We will start by considering Fourth Amendment protection for conversations.

## § 5.2   Fourth Amendment Protection of Communications

### A.  Historical Development

Our Founding Fathers were acutely aware of the importance of privacy. In the Fourth Amendment, they protected "the right of the people to be secure in their persons, houses, papers, and effects, against unreasonable searches and seizures." However, they did not have telephones and had no way to anticipate future technological developments. As a result, they listed only persons, houses, papers, and effects as being entitled to Fourth Amendment protection.

The question of Fourth Amendment protection for telephone conversations first reached the Supreme Court in the 1928 case of *Olmstead v. United States*.[7] Olmstead was convicted of conspiring to violate the National Prohibition Act based on evidence obtained by tapping his telephone line from a junction box located on the public street. The tap was conducted without probable cause or a search warrant. The Court, nevertheless, rejected Olmstead's claim that his Fourth Amendment rights were violated based on a mechanical, literal reading of the Fourth Amendment. A "search," the Court declared, requires a physical intrusion into a constitutionally protected location and a "seizure,"

---

[3]    United States v. Ramirez, 112 F.3d 849 (7th Cir. 1997).
[4]    **Katz v. United States, 389 U.S. 347, 88 S. Ct. 507, 19 L. Ed. 2d 576 (1967).**
[5]    *Id.*
[6]    18 U.S.C. § 2510 *et seq.*
[7]    **277 U.S. 438, 48 S. Ct. 564, 72 L. Ed. 944 (1928).**

the taking of tangible property. Olmstead's Fourth Amendment rights were not violated by the tapping of his telephone because government agents never set foot on his property or took anything tangible; his telephone conversations were "acquired" through their sense of hearing only.

Justice Brandeis dissented, arguing that technological advances had made it necessary to reconceptualize the notion of a search.

> . . . [I]n the application of a Constitution, our contemplation cannot be only of what has been, but of what may be. The progress of science in furnishing the government with means of espionage is not likely to stop with wire tapping. Ways may some day be developed by which the government, without removing papers from secret drawers, can reproduce them in court, and by which it will be enabled to expose to a jury the most intimate occurrences of the home. Advances in the psychic and related sciences may bring means of exploring unexpressed beliefs, thoughts and emotions. . . . Can it be that the Constitution affords no protection against such invasions of individual security?[8]

Brandeis's critique of the *Olmstead* majority decision grew more compelling as time passed.[9] Twenty years later, George Orwell published his famous novel, *1984*, depicting a world in which Brandeis's prophecy came true:

> BIG BROTHER IS WATCHING YOU, the caption said. . . . You had to live—did live, from habit that became instinct—in the assumption that every sound you made was overheard, and, except in darkness, every movement scrutinized.[10]

In *Katz v. United States*,[11] the Supreme Court recognized that it had taken the wrong direction and embarked upon a new course. Katz, a bookie, was convicted of illegal wagering based on evidence obtained by attaching a tape recorder to the exterior of a public telephone booth that he regularly used for wagering calls. Because the listening device did not penetrate the walls of the phone booth, the interception would not have been considered a search under *Olmstead*. The Supreme Court ignored this fact, declaring:

> . . . the Fourth Amendment protects people, not places. What a person knowingly exposes to the public, even in his own home or office, is not a subject of Fourth Amendment protection. But what he seeks to preserve as private, even in an area accessible to the public, may be constitutionally protected.[12]

---

[8]   *Id.* at 474, 48 S. Ct. at 474.

[9]   *See, e.g.*, Michael Froomkin, *The Death of Privacy*, 52 STAN. L. R. 1461 (2000) (describing the vast range of privacy-destroying technologies now available to the government).

[10]  George Orwell, *1984* (1949).

[11]  *Supra* note 4.

[12]  *Id.* at 351, 88 S. Ct. at 511. *See also* David A. Sullivan, Note, *A Bright Line in the Sky? Toward a New Fourth Amendment Search Standard for Advancing Surveillance Technology*, 44 ARIZ. L. REV. 967 (2002) (tracing the Supreme Court's subsequent applications of the *Katz* test in cases involving clandestine government surveillance).

Whether the secret recording of Katz's telephone constituted a search depended on whether he had a "reasonable expectation" that his conversation was private. The Court had no trouble concluding that a person who enters a telephone booth, closes the door, and pays the toll to place a call has a right to expect privacy. The presence of the concealed tape recorder violated the privacy on which Katz justifiably relied in placing the call, and resulted in a search.

The Court then turned its attention to whether the search was conducted according to Fourth Amendment standards. Even though the police had probable cause to believe that Katz was using the phone booth to conduct illegal gambling operations, this was not enough to justify surreptitiously monitoring his phone calls. The prior approval of a judge was necessary.

The need for prior approval by a judge left Congress with two choices. It could either put a stop to the government's use of wiretapping and electronic surveillance in criminal investigations or place their use under court supervision. Congress chose the latter course and in the following year enacted Title III of the Omnibus Crime Control and Safe Streets Act of 1968,[13] which establishes procedures for obtaining judicial authorization to use wiretapping and electronic surveillance in criminal investigations. Congress, nevertheless, did not want to restrict government surveillance practices to any greater extent than necessary. Consequently, Title III requires judicial authorization only in cases in which the Fourth Amendment would treat the surveillance as a search. This requires an examination of Fourth Amendment protection for communications.

Figure 5.1
**Regulation of Communication Surveillance**

|  | Distinguishing Characteristics | Governing Legal Provisions |
|---|---|---|
| Eavesdropping: | Police use their ordinary powers of hearing. | Fourth Amendment. |
| Interception: | Police listen with a device. | Fourth Amendment and Title III. |

## B. Overview of Fourth Amendment Protection for Communications

The Fourth Amendment protects conversations only when they take place under circumstances that give rise to a reasonable expectation of privacy. This leads to different treatment for eavesdropping and interception of communications with a device.

---

[13]    18 U.S.C. § 2510 *et seq.*

## 1. Eavesdropping

The Fourth Amendment places almost no constraints on eavesdropping, because in order to fall prey, the suspect must speak loudly enough for others within earshot to hear. People who knowingly expose their conversation to the ears of others have no legitimate expectation of privacy and their conversation, accordingly, is not protected by the Fourth Amendment.[14] Consequently, no interception order is necessary to eavesdrop.

## 2. Interception of Conversations with a Device

Device listening poses a greater threat to privacy than eavesdropping because a human eavesdropper has to be present. This creates the possibility of discovery, but more importantly, the parties can protect their privacy by choosing a more secure environment or speaking in a whisper. These precautions are ineffective against interception devices because the listener is out of sight. As a result, the parties have no reason to expect that anyone is listening. The secret use of an interception device to monitor conversations that both parties reasonably assume are private, therefore, results in a search and requires judicial approval in advance.[15] Title III of the Omnibus Crime Control and Safe Streets Acts of 1968,[16] which will be discussed shortly,[17] establishes a statutory procedure for obtaining that approval.

## 3. Interception by or with the Consent of a Participant

The situation is different when one of the parties to the intercepted conversation is working with the government. The typical scenario involves an undercover police agent or informant who engages the suspect in an incriminating conversation while secretly recording or transmitting it. The law gives no protection to a wrongdoer whose trusted accomplice turns out to be a police undercover agent or informant.[18] At some point in life, most people

---

[14]  *See, e.g.*, United States v. Burns, 624 F.2d 95 (10th Cir.) *cert. denied*, 449 U.S. 954, 101 S. Ct. 361, 66 L. Ed. 2d 219 (1980) (no reasonable expectation of privacy existed in conversation audible in adjoining hotel room); United States v. Jackson, 588 F.2d 1046 (5th Cir. 1979) (same).

[15]  **United States v. Katz,** *supra* note 4; United States v. McIntyre, 582 F.2d 1221 (9th Cir. 1978) (leaving briefcase containing a concealed microphone and transmitter in the assistant chief of police's office to monitor his conversations resulted in a search).

[16]  18 U.S.C. § 2510 *et seq.*

[17]  See *infra* §§ 5.4-5.6.

[18]  United States v. White, 401 U.S. 745, 91 S. Ct. 1122, 28 L. Ed. 2d 453 (1971) (individuals take the risk that their conversations will be reported to authorities); Hoffa v. United States, 385 U.S. 293, 302, 87 S. Ct. 408, 17 L. Ed. 2d 374 (1966) ("The risk of being overheard by an eavesdropper or betrayed by an informer or deceived as to the identity of one with whom one deals is probably inherent in the conditions of human society"); Lopez v. United States, 373 U.S. 427, 83 S. Ct. 1381, 10 L. Ed. 2d 462 (1963) (one contemplating illegal activities assumes the risk that his companions may be reporting to the police and, therefore, has no reasonable expectation of privacy protected by the Fourth Amendment in the conversations he knowingly exposes to them); On Lee v. United States, 343 U.S. 747, 72 S. Ct. 967, 96 L. Ed. 1270 (1952); **United States v. Longoria, 177 F.3d 1179 (10th Cir. 1999)** (concluding that defendant "had no reasonable expectation that the person in whose presence he conducts conversations will not reveal those conversations to others. He assumed the risk that the informant would reveal his incriminating statements to law enforcement.").

learn that people they trust sometimes betray them. When they voluntarily disclose incriminating information, they appreciate the risk that the other may report what was said to the authorities. Because the other party could have gone to the police and reported what was said from memory, the betrayed party is no worse off if the conversation is secretly recorded or transmitted so that the police can listen to it directly.[19] The betrayed party's misfortune stems from misplaced trust and not from the violation of any justifiable expectation of privacy. Because there can be no justifiable expectation that the other party to the conversation will keep it secret. The Fourth Amendment is not violated when a conversation is intercepted by someone who is a party to it.[20]

Figure 5.2
**Eavesdropping**

> Eavesdropping is not a search when the police: (1) listen with their ears alone (2) in a location where they are lawfully present.

## § 5.3 —Eavesdropping

You learned in Chapter 4 that it is not a search for an officer to take notice of anything that can be observed by members of the public from a vantage point where the officer is lawfully present.[21] The same holds true for anything that can be overheard.[22] This explains why eavesdropping is not a search. Suspects who speak loud enough for others lawfully present to hear them lack a reasonable expectation that their conversation is private.[23] Consequently, the Fourth Amendment is not violated when officers: (1) listen with their ears alone (i.e., without the use of any device or apparatus), (2) from a vantage point where they are lawfully present.

The fact that it takes a great deal of effort to hear makes no difference. In one case, narcotics detectives rented a hotel room adjoining the suspect's. To hear the conversations in the next room, they had to lie prone on the floor and press their ears against a three-quarter inch crack at the bottom of the connecting door. The court declined to find a search because the officers were able to overhear the conversation using their ears alone from a place where they were lawfully present.[24]

---

[19]    See cases *supra* note 18.

[20]    *Id. See also* § 5.6(1) *infra.*

[21]    See § 4.2.

[22]    WAYNE R. LaFAVE, I SEARCH & SEIZURE § 2.2 (3d ed. 1996).

[23]    **United States v. Longoria,** *supra* note 18 (conversations that a person knowingly exposes to the public are not a subject of Fourth Amendment protection); United States v. Burns, *supra* note 14 (same); United States v. Jackson, *supra* note 14 (same).

[24]    United States v. Jackson, *supra* note 14.

## A. Listening with the Unaided Ear

Police do not need the prior authorization of a judge to listen to anything that can be overheard without using an artificial aid. Moreover, anything that can be overheard may be secretly recorded.[25] It is not a search or an interception to secretly record conversations that are actually overheard because, when a recorder is used for this purpose, it is not being used to listen.[26] It is being used to obtain reliable evidence of matters heard independently. However, an entirely different situation exists when a tape recorder is used to monitor conversations that have not been heard independently. This happened in *Katz v. United States*.[27] Government agents secretly installed a tape recorder on top of a public phone booth in order to monitor Katz's calls. Because the government's access to the words Katz spoke into the phone derived exclusively from the recording device, a search resulted and a search warrant was necessary.

Suspects have occasionally argued that the secret recording of their conversation constituted a search, even though the conversation was heard by the party who recorded it, because they deliberately spoke in a foreign language that the listener could not understand.[28] Courts have roundly rejected this argument, pointing out that in our increasingly multilingual society, no one can ever be sure that others within earshot do not understand the language they are speaking. Because suspects who expose their conversation to the ears of others take this risk, the secret recording of conversations heard independently does not intrude on any justifiable expectation of privacy, even if the listener who records them does not understand the content.[29]

Police should use an ordinary cassette-type recorder with a standard microphone to record conversations that are audible to them because a more sensitive device might pick up matters that were not audible. Should this happen, the tape recorder will be treated as an interception device, making compliance with Title III necessary.

---

[25]   People v. Siripongs, 45 Cal. 3d 548, 745 P. 2d 1301 (1988), *cert. denied*, 488 U.S. 1019, 109 S. Ct. 820, 102 L. Ed. 2d 810 (1989) (no Fourth Amendment violation where officer standing beside prisoner as he talked on the phone secretly recorded what he said); John Doe, Trader Number One, 722 F. Supp. 419 (N.D. Ill. 1989) (suspect had no reasonable expectation of privacy in conversation audible to FBI agent standing a few feet away who secretly recorded it).

[26]   See cases *supra* note 25.

[27]   *Supra* note 4.

[28]   **United States v. Longoria**, *supra* note 18 (suspect did not have a reasonable expectation of privacy in clearly audible conversation spoken in a government informant's presence, even though conversation was in a foreign language that the informant did not understand; one exposing conversations to others necessarily assumes the risk that his conversation will be overheard and understood or recorded); People v. Siripongs, *supra* note 25 (prisoner did not have a constitutionally reasonable expectation of privacy in conversation spoken in Thai within earshot of a prison guard).

[29]   See authorities *supra* note 18.

## B. Lawful Presence

Lawful presence is also necessary. The important location is the location where the officer is standing when the conversation is overheard, not the location where it occurs.[30] Officers are free to eavesdrop in any location that is accessible to members of the public.[31] For example, they may eavesdrop on conversations occurring inside a dwelling if they are able to hear them without entering the **curtilage**.[32] They are also free to listen to conversations in the suspect's apartment or hotel room while standing in a common hallway[33] or in an adjoining unit.[34]

Although consent or a warrant is necessary to enter a dwelling,[35] once inside, police are free to listen to anything that catches their attention.[36] They may even listen to messages being left on a suspect's answering machine.[37]

# § 5.4 Title III of the Omnibus Crime Control and Safe Streets Act of 1968

## A. Overview of Title III

Authority to engage in wiretapping and electronic surveillance is crucial in the investigation of some crimes. In the year 2000, wiretap orders were issued in 479 federal investigations and 711 state investigations, resulting in 3,411 arrests and 736 convictions.[38] Drug offenses accounted for the greatest number of wiretaps, followed by racketeering, gambling, homicide and assault, kidnapping, extortion, larceny and theft, and bribery.[39] Commenting on the importance of wiretapping and electronic surveillance, a district attorney involved in a successful drug investigation stated: "[w]ithout the wiretap,

---

[30] United States v. Curran, 498 F.2d 30 (9th Cir. 1974).

[31] United States v. Brown, 169 F.3d 89 (lst Cir. 1999) (hotel lobby); United States v. Hawkins, 139 F.3d 29 (1st Cir. 1998) (en banc) (basement of multi-unit apartment building); United States v. Jackson, *supra* note 14 (adjoining hotel room); United States v. Marlar, 828 F. Supp. 415 (N.D. Mo. 1993) (outside motel room door); United States v. Whaley, 779 F.2d 585 (11th Cir. 1986) (neighboring residence); United States v. Llanes, 398 F.2d 880 (2d Cir. 1968) (common hallway outside suspect's apartment).

[32] United States v. Acosta, 965 F.2d 1248 (3d Cir. 1992); United States v. Sewell, 942 F.2d 1209 (7th Cir. 1991); United States v. Penco, 612 F.2d 19 (2d Cir. 1979); Brown v. United States, 627 A.2d 499 (D.C. Ct. App. 1993).

[33] United States v. Llanes, *supra* note 31.

[34] United States v. Jackson, *supra* note 14.

[35] See § 3.15.

[36] People v. Sloss, 34 Cal. App. 3d 74 (1973).

[37] United States v. Upton, 763 F. Supp. 232 (S.D. Ohio 1991) (listening to messages left on answering machine while executing search warrant did not violate Fourth Amendment).

[38] Paula J. Casey, *Regulating Federal Prosecutors: Why McCade Should be Repealed,* 19 GA. ST. U. L.R. 395 (2002).

[39] *Id.*

the head of this distribution organization and his chief co-conspirators would not have been convicted. Conventional investigative techniques would have only resulted in the conviction of the organization's 'mules.'[40]

Since 1968, wiretapping and electronic surveillance have been regulated by Title III of the Omnibus Crime Control and Safe Streets Act.[41] Enactment was made necessary by the holding in *Katz v. United States*,[42] requiring prior judicial approval to use interception devices in criminal investigations. Title III establishes standards and procedures that apply in federal investigations and a blueprint for enactment of state wiretap laws.[43] The Act originally applied only to wire and oral communications. However, changes in communications technology made amendment necessary. In 1986, Congress enacted the Electronic Communications Privacy Act (ECPA),[44] bringing wireless and cellular communications,[45] and computer data transmissions[46] under Title III's protection. The USA Patriot Act,[47] enacted after the September 11, 2001, terrorist attacks, expanded the federal government's wiretape and electronic surveillance authority.

---

[40]  *Id.*

[41]  18 U.S.C. § 2510 *et seq.*

[42]  *Supra* note 4.

[43]  Title III actually does far more than this. It outlaws the use of interception devices by private citizens unless they are a party to the intercepted communication or one of the parties consents and also prohibits law enforcement uses except in accordance with the statute. 18 U.S.C. § 2511(1). In addition, it regulates the manufacture, possession, and sale of interception devices and provides for confiscation of illegal devices. 18 U.S.C. §§ 2512, 2513. However, these aspects of Title III are beyond the scope of this chapter.

[44]  Electronic Communications Privacy Act of 1986, PUB. L. 99-508, 100 STAT. 1848 (1986) (codified at 18 U.S.C. §§2510-22, 2701- 09, 3121-27). Because of various changes instituted by the 1986 Act and by subsequent amendments, decisions rendered under earlier versions of Title III should always be checked against the language of the current provisions. In some instances, amendments have overridden interpretations placed on former statutory language.

[45]  18 U.S.C. § 2510(1).

[46]  18 U.S.C. § 2510(14).

[47]  PUB. L. NO. 107-56, 115 STAT. 272 (2001). Law enforcement and intelligence officials were hopelessly unprepared for the 9/11 attacks. Fragmentation of authority, lack of coordination and information sharing, inadequate skills in analyzing intelligence, inadequate resources, and other factors all contributed to weaknesses in the system that hampered the authorities in gathering and utilizing information that might have prevented the attacks. See Michael T. McCarthy, *USA Patriot Act,* 39 HARV. J. LEGIS. 435 (2002). The USA Patriot Act was hastily enacted and signed into law six weeks after the attacks. It is a sweeping piece of legislation that spans more than 342 pages and makes changes to more than 15 different federal statutes. The changes include expanding the wiretapping and surveillance authority of federal law enforcement and intelligence officials, removing barriers that prevented information sharing between them (particularly in relationship to foreign intelligence matters); increasing authority to detain and deport aliens suspected of terrorist ties; tightening control over money-laundering activities by adding financial disclosure and reporting requirements; authorizing seizure of assets belonging to terrorist organizations; creating new federal terrorism-related crimes and increasing the penalty for others, etc. Comprehensive coverage of the USA Patriot Act is beyond the scope of this chapter. For a summary of the changes made to Title III and related laws dealing with the government's surveillance powers, see American Civil Liberties Union v. U.S. Dept. of Justice, 265 F. Supp. 2d 20 (D.D.C. 2003); Mary W.S. Wong, *Electronic Surveillance and Privacy in the United States After September 11, 2001: The USA Patriot Act*, 2002 SING J. LEGA. STUD. 214 (2002); Charles Doyle, *The USA PATRIOT Act: A Legal Analysis*, a report prepared by the Congressional Research Service, 15 April 2002, available online at http://www.fas.org/irp/crs/RL31377.pdf.

If one had to summarize what law enforcement officials need to know about Title III in a single sentence, it would be this: the Act prohibits the government from intercepting wire, oral, and electronic communications with a device unless a judge issues an interception order or one of the parties consents.[48] Violations carry serious consequences. The Act imposes civil and criminal penalties on violators,[49] creates a damage remedy for those whose rights are violated,[50] and makes illegally obtained evidence and derivative evidence inadmissible in both state and federal courts.[51]

Title III is not the only statute concerned with protecting the privacy of communications. Communications surveillance in national security cases is regulated by a separate statute known as the Foreign Intelligence Surveillance Act,[52] which is covered in § 5.7. There is also a maze of federal statutes that deal with protection for stored communications, as well as transaction and subscriber information. Finally, the District of Columbia and every state except Arkansas, Mississippi, South Carolina, South Dakota, Virginia, Vermont, and Washington have adopted surveillance laws that apply to state and local law enforcement agencies.[53] These laws generally follow the federal statute, although states have the option to adopt more restrictive legislation.[54]

---

Interception occurs when an electronic, mechanical, or other device is used to acquire the contents of a protected communication

---

## B. Interception

Title III's coverage is limited to interception of communications with a device. Eavesdropping is not covered because Congress did not want to hinder law enforcement to a greater extent than the Fourth Amendment makes necessary. The definition of "interception" is central to the coverage of Title III. An interception occurs when (1) an electronic, mechanical, or other device

---

[48]   18 U.S.C. § 2511.

[49]   18 U.S.C. § 2511(4), (5).

[50]   18 U.S.C. § 2520.

[51]   18 U.S.C. §§ 2515, 2518(9).

[52]   50 U.S.C. § 1801 *et seq.*

[53]   See Susan L. Kopecky, *Dealing with Intercepted Communications: Title III of the Omnibus Crime Control and Safe Streets Act in Civil Litigation*, 12 REV. LITIG. 441 (1993). *See also, generally,* Stacy L. Mills, *He Wouldn't Listen to Me Before, But Now . . .: Interspousal Wiretapping and an Analysis of State Wiretapping Statutes*, 37 BRANDEIS L.J. 415, 429 (1998) (discussing differences among state wiretapping statutes generally); Report of the Director of the Administrative Office of the United States Courts, *Applications for Orders Authorizing or Approving the Interception of Wire, Oral, or Electronic Communications* at 6 (1998); 51 Carol N. Bast, *What's Bugging You? Inconsistencies and Irrationalities of the Law of Eavesdropping*, 47 DEPAUL L. REV. 837, 851 (1998).

[54]   *See, e.g.,* Commonwealth v. Barboza 54 Mass. App. Ct. 99, 763 N.E.2d. 547, 553 (2002) ("Although a state wiretap statute may adopt standards more stringent than the requirements of federal law, thus excluding from state courts evidence that would be admissible in federal courts, a state may not adopt standards that are less restrictive and would thereby allow evidence in state court that would be inadmissible in federal court.").

is used to (2) acquire access to the contents (3) of a protected communication.[55] Study this definition carefully because every word is meaningful.

### 1. Electronic, Mechanical, or Other Device

Title III does not contain a list of prohibited devices. The device does not have to be unusual, technologically sophisticated, or specially designed for spying activity. It can be a parabolic microphone that picks up conversations miles away, an electronic "bug," wiretapping apparatus, a concealed, unattended tape-recorder, or some other device.[56] The nature of the device does not matter. What matters is how it is used.[57] If a device is used to obtain access to the contents of a protected communication that the officer is not otherwise in a position to hear, the device constitutes an interception device and its use is regulated by Title III. A garden-variety extension phone, for example, constitutes an interception device when it is used by a police officer to listen to a telephone conversation without the knowledge or consent of either party.[58]

### 2. Acquire Access to the Contents

Title III only regulates the use of devices that provide access to the *contents* of a communication. It does not regulate the use of devices that provide access to other information, such as the telephone numbers dialed to or from a particular phone.[59] Moreover, not only must the device yield access to the contents of the communication, it must do so in "real-time." An interception requires a contemporaneous acquisition, one that occurs while the message is being transmitted.[60] The major impact of this limitation is on e-mail and voice mail. To constitute an "interception" under Title III, access must be acquired during transmission—before the message reaches its destination and is stored

---

[55]    *See* 18 U.S.C. § 2510(4) defining interception as "the aural or other acquisition of the contents of any wire, electronic, or oral communication through the use of any electronic, mechanical, or other device."

[56]    *See, e.g.*, Malpas v. State, 16 Md. App. 69, 695 A.2d 588 (1997) (parabolic microphone); United States v. Lucht, 18 F.3d 541 (8th Cir. 1993) (electronic bug); State v. Denman, 100 F.3d 399 (5th Cir. 1996) (wiretap apparatus); United States v. McIntyre, *supra* note 15 (concealed microphone and transmitter).

[57]    18 U.S.C. § 2510(5) defines an interception device as "any device or apparatus which can be used to intercept a wire, oral, or electronic communication. . . ." other than a hearing aid or similar device used to correct subnormal hearing.

[58]    *See, e.g.*, In re State Police Litigation, 888 F. Supp. 1235 (D. Conn. 1995) (telephone extension used without the consent of either party constitutes an interception device); United States v. Murdock, 63 F.3d 1391 (6th Cir. 1995) (recorder connected to extension phone that was automatically activated when the extension phone handset was lifted constituted an interception device).

[59]    United States v. New York Tel. Co., 434 U.S. 159, 98 S. Ct. 364, 54 L. Ed. 2d 376 (1977).

[60]    *See, e.g.*, Steve Jackson Games, Inc. v. U.S. Secret Service, 36 F.3d 457 (5th Cir. 1994) (seizure of e-mail from electronic storage before they have been retrieved and read by the recipient is not an interception under Title III); United States v. Steiger, 318 F.3d 1039 (11th Cir. 2003) (acquisition through hacking of information stored on computer hard drive does not involve an interception); Konop v. Hawaiian Airlines, Inc, 302 F.3d 868 (9th Cir. 2002) (for electronic communications to be intercepted within the meaning of the Wiretap Act, acquisition must occur while they are being transmitted, not while they are in storage).

on the intended recipient's server or in other storage.[61] Access to stored communications is regulated by a separate federal statute—the Stored Wire and Electronic Communications and Transactional Records Act.[62] Stored communications receive less privacy protection, making it easier for law enforcement officials to gain access to them.[63]

### 3. Protected Communications

Title III protects three categories of communications: wire, electronic, and oral.[64]

#### a. "Wire Communications"

**"Wire communications"** involve the transmission of human voice messages over a public communications networks or, in other words, telephone conversations.[65] While the term "wire communication" accurately described land-line telephone systems, the only kind that existed in 1968, the Act has since been amended to include cordless and cellular telephone systems.[66] Interoffice telephone and private intercom systems are not covered because they are not public communications networks.

#### b. "Electronic Communications"

**"Electronic communications"** involve the transmission of sounds (other than of the human voice), signs, signals, text, images, and other kinds of data

---

[61] See authorities *supra* note 60. Voicemail messages are subject to the same limitation; access must be acquired during transmission to constitute an interception. United States v. Moriarty, 962 F. Supp. 217, 220 (D. Mass.1997) (listening to stored voicemail messages is not interception because this form of access does not take place while information is in transmission);

[62] Stored Wire & Electronic Communications & Transactional Records Access, 18 U.S.C.A. § 2701 *et seq.*

[63] 18 U.S.C. § 2703(a). The government does not have to comply with the cumbersome procedures of Title III to obtain access to stored wire and electronic communications. Access can be obtained under an ordinary search warrant and, in the case of electronic communications held in storage for more than 180 days, by a subpoena or a court order issued on a mere showing that the information is relevant to a criminal case. Section 2703 further provides for government access to subscriber information and transactional records, also through a subpoena or court order issued on a showing that the information is relevant to a criminal case.

[64] Electronic Communications Privacy Act of 1986, *supra* note 44.

[65] 18 U.S.C. § 2510 (1) defines a wire communication as "any aural transfer made in whole or in part through the use of facilities for the transmission of communications by the aid of wire, cable, or other like connection between the point of origin and the point of reception (including the use of such connection in a switching station) furnished or operated by any person engaged in providing or operating such facilities for the transmission of interstate or foreign communications or communications affecting interstate or foreign commerce."

[66] Communications Assistance for Law Enforcement Act, 108 STAT. 4279, 4290, P.L. 103-414, § 202(a)(1) (1996).

over wire, radio, electromagnetic, photoelectronic or photooptical systems.[67] Electronic mail, telegrams, faxes, computer data transmissions, and display pager messages are examples of electronic communications covered by Title III.

### c. "Oral Communications"

**"Oral communications"** are the "old-fashioned" kind, the kind that travel by sound waves. They typically take the form of face-to-face conversations and sound waves that escape into the room when a person talks on the telephone.[68] Title III incorporates the *Katz* test into its definition of an oral communication. Oral communications are covered only when they are uttered with "an expectation that such communication is not subject to interception under circumstances justifying such expectation"[69] or, in other words, with a reasonable expectation of privacy.[70] The reason that proof of such an expectation is necessary for protection of oral communications, but not for wire and electronic communications, is that parties to wire and electronic communications naturally assume that their conversation will not be intercepted, but parties to oral communications may or may not make this assumption, or their assumption may not be reasonable. The nature of the location, the presence and proximity of others, and how loudly a person speaks are some of the factors that can affect whether freedom from interception is expected and whether such expectation is reasonable.[71] Courts, for example, routinely deny protection for oral communications when: (1) the user of the interception device is close

---

[67]  18 U.S.C. § 2510(12). Electronic communications are generally regulated in same manner as wire and oral communications, but electronic communications receive less protection in three ways. First, any U.S. attorneys may seek judicial authorization to intercept electronic communications. § 2516(3) Second, authorization may be sought in the investigation of *any* federal felony. § 2516(3). Finally, and most important of all, Title III's statutory exclusion does not apply to electronic communications. § 2515.

[68]  *See, e.g.*, United States v. Levine, 690 F. Supp. 1165 (E.D.N.Y. 1988); People v. Siripongs, *supra* note 25.

[69]  18 U.S.C. § 2510(2) defines an oral communication as a "communication uttered by a person exhibiting an expectation that such communication is not subject to interception under circumstances justifying such expectation."

[70]  **Katz v. United States**, *supra* note 4.

[71]  *See, e.g.*, Kee v. City of Rowlett, 247 F.3d 206, 212 (5th Cir. 2001) (conversation between father and grandmother occurring during outdoor grave site service for murdered children not protected against interception accomplished by placing electronic surveillance microphone in funeral urn); Hornberger v. American Broadcasting Companies, Inc., 351 N.J. Super. 577, 799 A.2d 566 (2002) ("Courts have identified several factors relevant to evaluating the existence of a reasonable expectation of privacy in oral communications made in publicly accessible places. These factors include: (1) the volume of the communication or conversation; (2) the proximity or potential of other individuals to overhear the conversation; (3) the potential for communications to be reported; (4) the affirmative actions taken by the speakers to shield their privacy; (5) the need for technological enhancements to hear the communications; and (6) the place or location of the oral communications as it relates to the subjective expectations of the individuals who are communicating."); United States v. Carroll, 337 F. Supp. 1260 (D.D.C. 1971) (conversation in hotel room not protected against interception by Title III where it could be heard in adjoining room, by the unassisted ear, and was recorded by using a cassette-type recorder with a standard microphone no more sensitive than the human ear); United States v. Burns, 624 F.2d 95 (10th Cir. 1980) ("Legitimate privacy expectations cannot be separated from a conversation's context. Bedroom whispers in the middle of a large house on a large, private tract of land carry quite different expectations of privacy, reasonably speaking, than does a boisterous conversation occurring in a crowded supermarket or subway.")

enough to the speaker to be within normal hearing distance, (2) notice has been given that the conversation will be monitored, or (3) the conversation takes place in a highly controlled police environment where monitoring is common.

### d. User of the Interception Device Is
### Within Normal Hearing Distance

Earlier in this chapter you learned that it is not a violation of the Fourth Amendment for officers to secretly record conversations audible without the aid of a device because a suspect has no legitimate expectation of privacy in conversations that others are in a position to hear.[72] The same is true under Title III. In *People v. Siripongs*,[73] a correctional officer, standing next to a prisoner as he talked on the telephone, secretly recorded the words he spoke into the mouthpiece. The court rejected the argument that this constituted the interception of a wire communication, because only one side of the telephone conversation was recorded. The words the prisoner spoke into the receiver also lacked protection as an oral communication, because a person who makes a phone call with a correctional officer standing three feet away has no justifiable expectation of noninterception.

### e. Interception Where Notice Has Been Given
### that the Conversation Will Be Monitored

Title III does not protect conversations when notice is given that the conversation will be monitored, because notice dispels any reasonable expectation of noninterception. Notice can be actual, such as where a sign is posted near the telephone stating that calls are monitored,[74] or implied, such as when parties carry on a conversation while standing next to a visible "hot" microphone, intercom box, or running tape recorder.[75]

### f. Interception in Highly Controlled Police Environments Where
### Monitoring Is Commonly Practiced

Title III also provides no protection for conversations that take place in highly controlled police environments like jails, squad cars, prisons, and police stations, where official surveillance is common—so common, in fact, that one court remarked that anyone "who expects privacy under the circumstances of prison visiting is, if not actually foolish, exceptionally naive."[76]

---

[72]  See §§ 5.2(B)(3), 5.3(A) *supra*.

[73]  *Supra* note 25.

[74]  *See, e.g.*, People v. Santos, 26 Cal. App. 3d 397 (1972).

[75]  *See, e.g.*, State v. Owens, 643 N.W.2d 735 (S.D. 2002); Ex parte Graves, 853 S.W. 2d 701 (Tex. Ct. App. 1993).

[76]  United States v. Harrelson, 754 F.2d 1153, 1170 (5th Cir. 1985). *See also* United States v. Clark, 22 F.3d 799 (8th Cir. 1994) (no constitutionally protected expectation of privacy exists in the backseat of police car); United States v. McKinnon, 985 F.2d 525 (11th Cir.), *cert. denied*, 510 U.S. 843, 114 S. Ct. 130, 126 L. Ed. 2d 94 (1993) (same); People v. Riel, 22 Cal. 4th 1153, 998 P. 2d 969, 96 Cal. Rptr. 1 (2000) (no constitutionally protected expectation of privacy exists in a jail visitors' room).

Because privacy is not expected, no interception order is necessary to secretly monitor conversations among inmates or between inmates and visitors.[77] However, a justifiable expectation of non-interception can be created by giving assurances that privacy will be respected. Illustrative is a case in which a detective, whose office was located in the same building as the jail, left a concealed tape-recorder running after telling the arrestee and his wife that they could use his office to converse in private, excusing himself, and shutting the door behind him."[78] The court held that the secret recording of the conversation violated Title III because the detective had lulled the parties into believing that their conversation would not be intercepted.

## § 5.5  —Procedural Requirements for Intercepting Protected Communications

Title III was enacted in response to the Supreme Court's ruling in *Katz*[79] that police must secure prior judicial authorization to engage in wiretapping and other forms of interception. In keeping with this, Title III makes it illegal to intercept protected communications with a device without an **interception order**[80] unless there is an emergency[81] or one of the parties consents.[82] Title III establishes a comprehensive regulatory scheme for issuance and supervision of interception orders. It specifies the crimes for which interception orders may be sought,[83] who may authorize the making of an application and who may apply for one,[84] the information the application must contain,[85] the findings the judge must make before issuing an order,[86] the order's form and contents,[87] how orders are to be executed,[88] when information obtained from intercepted communications may be disclosed and to whom,[89] and a host of other issues. The procedures incorporate the requirements of the Fourth Amendment and, in some instances, go beyond them, imposing restrictions

---

[77]  See cases *supra* note 76.
[78]  North v. Superior Court, 8 Cal. 3d 301, 502 P.2d 1305 (1972).
[79]  **Katz v. United States**, *supra* note 4.
[80]  18 U.S.C. § 2511.
[81]  18 U.S.C. § 2518(7).
[82]  18 U.S.C. § 2511(2)(c).
[83]  18 U.S.C. § 2516(1).
[84]  18 U.S.C. § 2516.
[85]  18 U.S.C. § 2518(1).
[86]  18 U.S.C. § 2518(3).
[87]  18 U.S.C. § 2518(4).
[88]  18 U.S.C. § 2518(5).
[89]  18 U.S.C. § 2517.

that are not applicable to conventional search warrants. If an interception is conducted in violation of these procedures, the prosecutor is not permitted to use that evidence to establish that defendant's guilt.[90]

## A. Crimes for Which Interception Orders Can Be Obtained

Interceptions are more intrusive than traditional investigative techniques and, consequently, may only be used when important law enforcement interests are at stake. Federal officials may seek interception orders only for serious crimes such as espionage, sabotage, terrorism, treason, murder, kidnapping, robbery, extortion, counterfeiting, dealing in drugs, and crimes dangerous to life, limb, or property.[91] Moreover, the government may not resort to this method of investigation unless traditional investigative techniques have been tried and failed, appear unlikely to succeed, or are too dangerous to try.[92]

## B. Authorization to Apply for an Interception Order

The decision to apply for an interception order is not left to criminal investigators. Congress wanted authority and responsibility for this decision to be in the hands of politically accountable government officials. In federal investigations, applications for an order to intercept wire and oral communications must be reviewed and approved by the United States Attorney General or another designated ranking official within the Justice Department before they may be submitted to a judge.[93] In state investigations, responsibility for mak-

---

[90] Actually, this overstates what Title III does. The Title III exclusionary rule, which is found in 18 U.S.C. § 2515, applies only to wire and oral communications. Section 2515 reads:

> "Whenever any wire or oral communication has been intercepted, no part of the contents of such communication and no evidence derived therefrom may be received in evidence in any trial, hearing, or other proceeding in or before any court, grand jury, department, officer, agency, regulatory body, legislative committee, or other authority of the United States, a State, or a political subdivision thereof if the disclosure of that information would be in violation of this chapter."

Electronic communications are admissible despite violation of Title III.

[91] 18 U.S.C. § 2516(1). State wiretap statutes may authorize issuance of interception orders for the following crimes: murder, kidnapping, gambling, robbery, bribery, extortion, or dealing in narcotic drugs, marihuana or other dangerous drugs, or other crime dangerous to life, limb, or property, and punishable by imprisonment for more than one year. 18 U.S.C. § 2516(2).

[92] 18 U.S.C. § 2518(3)(c).The traditional investigative techniques that judges consider in reviewing the necessity requirement include: (1) standard visual and aural surveillance; (2) questioning and interrogation of witnesses or participants; (3) use of search warrants; (4) infiltration of conspiratorial groups by undercover agents or informants; and (5) use of pen registers and trap-and-trace devices. *See* United States v. Ramirez-Encarnacion, 291 F.3d 1219 (10th Cir. 2002).

[93] 18 U.S.C. § 2516(1). Authorization requirements for interception of electronic communications are not as stringent. 18 U.S.C. § 2516(3) provides that "any attorney for the government" may apply for court authorization for interception of electronic communications in connection with the investigation of "any federal felony."

ing the application rests with the principal prosecuting officer of the state or political subdivision.[94]

> Prosecutors, not the police, are primarily responsible for applying for and overseeing implementation of interception orders.

## C. Form and Contents of Interception Orders

Interception orders are a specialized kind of search warrant. They authorize law enforcement officials to search for and seize conversations. Consequently, they must comply with the Fourth Amendment directive that "no Warrants shall issue, but upon probable cause, . . . particularly describing the place to be searched, and the persons or things to be seized." The court may issue an interception order only if it finds probable cause to believe that: (1) a person is committing a crime for which an interception order may be issued; (2) the targeted facilities are being used in connection with that crime; and (3) an interception will produce communications relevant to that crime.[95] The contents of an interception order are similar to those of a traditional search warrant. The order must identify the person, if known, whose communications will be intercepted and contain a particularized description of the types of communications that may be intercepted and the facilities from which, or place where, interception is authorized.[96]

## D. Duration of Interception Orders

Interception orders are required to specify a period during which they remain in effect. Unlike conventional searches, which rarely take longer than a few hours, ongoing interception operations sometimes continue for days or even months.[97] As a way of preserving judicial oversight, Title III limits the duration for which interception orders may be approved to 30 days, subject to any number of additional extensions.[98] Each extension requires a fresh application with the same showing required for the initial application.[99] This enables the judge to monitor the progress and evaluate the need for continued interception. Interception orders terminate upon attainment of the authorized objective or expiration of the period specified in them, whichever occurs first.[100]

---

[94]  18 U.S.C. § 2516(2).
[95]  18 U.S.C. § 2518(3).
[96]  18 U.S.C. § 2518(4).
[97]  Congressional findings, Omnibus Crime Control and Safe Streets Act of 1968, § 801.
[98]  18 U.S.C. § 2518(5).
[99]  Id.
[100]  Id.

## E. Access and Assistance in Placing the Interception Device

Most interceptions are accomplished either through wiretapping or "bugging." Bugging is performed by installing a small microphone or recorder in the room to be bugged. For the operation to be effective, the equipment must be installed without the suspect's knowledge. This generally requires a covert entry. An order granting authority to conduct interception surveillance at a described location confers implied authority to secretly enter for the sake of installing and servicing the necessary equipment.[101] A separate warrant is unnecessary. A judge who issues an interception order may, in addition, direct landlords, custodians, and others to furnish information, facilities, or technical assistance necessary to accomplish the interception without discovery.[102]

The logistics of wiretapping used to be much simpler. All police had to do was to attach a pair of alligator clips to a telephone line and put on a set of earphones.[103] Today, telephone companies use digital transmissions that have to pass through complex decoding equipment at the carrier's central office before they become intelligible to the human ear.[104] Consequently, there is no convenient way to intercept a telephone conversation other than at the carrier's central office. A judge issuing an interception order may direct providers of wire or electronic communication services to furnish information, facilities, and technical assistance necessary to accomplish the interception.[105] Logistics are less likely to be a problem in the future because the Communications Assistance for Law Enforcement Act, or CALEA,[106] enacted in 1994, requires telecommunications companies to engineer their facilities in ways that provide easy access to law enforcement agencies operating under proper legal authority.

When the subject of the operation is itinerant, or purposely changes locations or uses different telephone booths to thwart detection, the judge can authorize a "roving wiretap"—an interception order that authorizes surveillance of any phone that the subject may use, instead of a specific facility or location.[107] Roving wiretap warrants were developed partly in response to the increased use of cellular telephones. Suspects frequently change cellular phones to elude interception. CALEA requires cellular providers to engineer systems capable of accommodating roving wiretaps.[108]

---

[101]  Dalia v. United States, 441 U.S. 238, 99 S. Ct. 1682, 60 L. Ed. 2d 177 (1979).

[102]  18 U.S.C. § 2518(4).

[103]  Andrew H. Hull, *The Digital Dilemma: Requiring Private Carriers' Assistance to Reach Out and Tap Someone in the Information Age—An Analysis of the Digital Telephone Act*, 37 SANTA CLARA L. REV. 117, 131 (1996).

[104]  *Id.* at 132.

[105]  18 U.S.C. § 2518(4).

[106]  47 U.S.C. § 1001 *et seq.*

[107]  18 U.S.C. § 2518(11); United States v. Hermanek, 289 F.3d 1076 (9th Cir. 2002).

[108]  47 U.S.C. § 1002(d).

## F. Duty to Minimize Interceptions of Conversations Beyond the Scope of the Order

Interception orders are required to specify the kinds of communications that may be intercepted. During the surveillance, it is inevitable that police will find themselves listening to communications that have nothing to do with the reasons for the interception order. Some of the conversations will be truly innocent: a crime boss still calls his mother on Sunday, and drug dealers have been known to send out for pizza. Indeed many, if not most, communications intercepted during ongoing operations have nothing to do with the crimes under investigation. The Federal Bureau of Investigation reported that in listening to more than 1.3 million conversations using wiretaps and bugs, only 15 percent contained incriminating information.[109] To complicate matters, criminals engaged in organized crime often converse in code. This can make differentiating truly innocent conversations from seemingly innocent conversations challenging.

The Fourth Amendment prohibits general searches. Even criminal suspects have a right to keep their private lives private. Herein lies the dilemma. With searches involving tangible objects, the requirement that police limit their search to areas and containers capable of housing the object of the search keeps the intrusiveness of the search within bounds. However, with interception orders, there is no way to tell whether a given communication contains information relating to the crimes listed in the order other than to intercept the communication and listen.

While recognizing that interception of innocent communications is unavoidable, Title III nevertheless requires investigators to conduct their operations in a manner designed to minimize intrusions into communications that are beyond the scope of the order.[110] Normally, the prosecutor in charge of the investigation will issue protocols for officers to follow regarding proper minimization. The usual practice is to monitor every communication for a couple of minutes to determine whether the conversation concerns crimes specified in the interception order.[111] Once satisfied that the call is irrelevant or after listening for a couple of minutes without anything materializing, the officer must stop listening.[112] If the officer overhears a conversation about an unrelated crime during the first few minutes, the officer may continue listening, but should notify the prosecutor immediately afterward so that the prosecutor can bring this matter to the attention of the judge who issued the order and seek the judge's approval.[113] Only if the judge finds that the government was fol-

---

[109]    David Burnham, *The F.B.I.*, THE NATION, Aug. 11, 1997, at 11.

[110]    18 U.S.C. § 2518(5).

[111]    *See, e.g.*, United States v. Abascal, 564 F.2d 821 (9th Cir. 1977); United States v. Chavez, 533 F.2d 491 (8th Cir. 1976); United States v. Scott, 516 F.2d 751 (D.C. Cir. 1975); United States v. Borrayo-Gutierrez, 119 F. Supp. 2d 1168 (D. Colo. 2000).

[112]    See cases *supra* note 111.

[113]    18 U.S.C. § 2517(5).

lowing the minimization procedures when it stumbled across evidence of an unrelated crime will the government be permitted to use this evidence in a judicial proceeding.[114]

## G. Return of Recordings to the Court

Intercepted communications should be recorded in a manner that protects them from editing or alteration.[115] As soon as the surveillance ends, the tapes must be returned to the judge who issued the order, to be sealed pending trial. The purpose of sealing is to prevent the tapes from being tampered with. The presence of the seal or a satisfactory explanation for its absence is necessary for the tapes to be admitted into evidence. Despite the ease of compliance, lack of timely sealing is one of the most common reasons evidence obtained through an authorized interception is refused admission into evidence.

## H. Limitations on Disclosure and Use of Intercepted Communications

Title III imposes a tight lid on the use and disclosure of communications intercepted under a judicial interception order. The information may be used and disclosed for only one of three purposes. The first is to further a criminal investigation. Criminal investigators may use information intercepted under a judicial interception order to perform their official duties and may disclose the information to other criminal investigators when the information is appropriate to the latter's duties.[116] Officers who are informed of the communication are bound by the same restrictions as those who intercepted it. The second purpose concerns national security. When the contents of an intercepted communication relate to foreign intelligence or counterintelligence, the communication may be disclosed to other federal law enforcement, intelligence, immigration, national defense, and national security officers to assist them in performing their duties.[117] The final purpose is to further a criminal prosecution. Officers may disclose information while giving testimony in court and the recordings may be introduced as evidence.[118] No other use or disclosure is permitted. Thus, while it would be appropriate for an officer to share information about a large drug buy with a DEA agent, sharing it with a local news reporter violates Title III.

---

[114]   *Id. See also* State v. Gerena, 653 F. Supp. 974 (D. Conn. 1987).

[115]   18 U.S.C. § 2518(8)(a); United States v. Ojeda Rios, 495 U.S. 257, 110 S. Ct. 1845, 109 L. Ed. 2d 224 (1990); United States v. Hermanek, 289 F.3d 1076 (9th Cir. 2002); United States v. Santarpio, 540 F.2d 503 (1st Cir. 1976).

[116]   18 U.S.C. § 2517(1)(2).

[117]   18 U.S.C. § 2517(6). This provision was added as part of the USA Patriot Act, *supra* note 47, to promote closer working relationships between criminal investigators, immigration authorities, and the intelligence community. Lack of information-sharing hampered efforts to gather and utilize information that might have prevented the 9/11/01 terrorist attacks.

[118]   18 U.S.C. § 2517(3).

Restrictions on use and disclosure apply only to communications intercepted under a judicial interception order. There are no restrictions on the use and disclosure of communications overheard without mechanical aids or with the consent of a party.[119]

Figure 5.3
**Restrictions on the Use and Disclosure of Intercepted Communications**

| Communication protected | Permissible uses | Permissible disclosures |
| --- | --- | --- |
| Wire, oral, or electronic communications obtained as a result of an authorized interception. | May only be used to further a police investigation or as evidence in a judicial proceeding. | May only be disclosed to other law enforcement personnel, the prosecutor, or in court. |
| Communications intercepted with the consent of a party, or overheard through normal listening. | No restrictions on use. | No restrictions on disclosure. |

# § 5.6 —Exceptions to the Requirement of an Interception Order

There are a limited number of situations in which interceptions are lawful without prior judicial authorization. Consent and emergency surveillance are the two most important.

### 1. Interception by or with the Consent of a Party to the Communication

Title III provides that no interception order is necessary "for a person acting under color of law to intercept a wire, oral, or electronic communication, where such person is a party to the communication or one of the parties to the communication has given prior consent to such interception."[120] This section permits police officers to intercept communications without an interception order when they are a party to the communication or someone who is a party consents. A common application of this exception occurs in police undercover work when a police undercover agent, wired for sound, engages the suspect in an incriminating conversation while secretly recording or transmitting it.[121] Title III does not require an interception order in this situation.

---

[119] This is because neither Title III nor the Fourth Amendment applies to such communications. See § 5.2(B)(c) *supra*.
[120] 18 U.S.C. § 2511(2)(C).
[121] *See, e.g.,* **United States v. Longoria**, *supra* note 18.

Title III also permits police to monitor communications, without an interception order, when someone who is a participant consents.[122] Consent may be implied as well as expressed. Implied consent arises when the surrounding circumstances indicate that a person has received notice that communication facilities are monitored, but uses them anyway. Jails and prisons, for example, typically have a standard policy of monitoring inmate phone calls. The purpose of this policy is to protect institutional security. Inmates who use the phone with notice of this policy impliedly consent to the interception of their conversation.[123] This is true even though they have no choice and would be denied use of the phone if they did not consent.[124] Notice is also found when monitoring policies are disclosed in prison handbooks and orientation lectures, signs are posted above phones, or beeper warnings are given.[125]

### 2. The Emergency Exception

Emergency situations occasionally arise in which police must act promptly or risk losing critical evidence. Anticipating this, Congress included a provision that allows police, under limited circumstances, to commence intercepting before a judge issues an interception order and to apply for an order afterward. This provision is patterned on the "exigent circumstances" exception to the Fourth Amendment warrant requirement, which permits the police to take action without a search warrant when they are confronted with an emergency that requires prompt action. For the emergency surveillance provision to apply, the following four conditions are necessary.[126]

First, the police must be confronted with an emergency that involves: (1) immediate danger of death or serious physical injury to a person, (2) conspiratorial activity threatening national security, or (3) conspiratorial activity characteristic of organized crime.

Second, grounds must exist for believing that an interception order would have been granted had the authorities had time to apply for one.

Third, authorization to initiate emergency surveillance must be obtained from a high-ranking official within the Justice Department in federal investigations and from the principal prosecuting attorney of the state or political subdivision in state investigations.

---

[122] Although consent of one party is sufficient under Title III, officers should check state law before taking action. Statutes in a number of states make it illegal to use a device to listen to or record a conversation unless all of the parties consent. *See, e.g.*, ILL. REV. STAT., Ch. 38, par. 14-2(a) (1991).

[123] *See, e.g.*, **United States v. Willoughby**, 860 F.2d 15 (2d Cir. 1988); United States v. Amen, 831 F.2d 373 (2d Cir. 1987); Griggs-Ryan v. Smith, 904 F.2d 112 (1st Cir. 1990).

[124] *See, e.g.*, United States v. Horr, 963 F.2d 1124 (8th Cir. 1992).

[125] *See, e.g.*, **United States v. Willoughby**, *supra* note 123; United States v. Vesta, 649 F. Supp. 974 (S.D.N.Y. 1986).

[126] 18 U.S.C. § 2518(7).

Finally, application must be made to a judge for an order approving the interception within 48 hours after emergency interception surveillance has begun. If the order is denied, the interception must terminate immediately.

The emergency surveillance provision has not been widely used. The Justice Department has invoked it sparingly, in life-threatening situations only.[127]

## § 5.7   Foreign Intelligence Surveillance Act

There is a second federal statute that deals with wiretapping and electronic surveillance—the Foreign Intelligence Surveillance Act, better known as FISA. This statute regulates domestic surveillance conducted for national security purposes.[128] There has been a sharp increase in the number of applications for FISA surveillance orders since September 11, 2001.[129] As a result, we decided to include a new section on this statute.

### A.  Overview of the Foreign Intelligence Surveillance Act

The Foreign Intelligence Surveillance Act establishes a special statutory procedure for government surveillance performed for the purpose of gathering **foreign intelligence information**.[130] A special secret court—the Foreign Intelligence Surveillance Court (FISC)—is created to oversee this process.[131] The FISC is composed of 11 federal district court judges, selected by the Chief Justice of the U.S. Supreme Court, to hear applications for orders autho-

---

[127]   Clifford S. Fishman, *Interception of Communications in Exigent Circumstances: The Fourth Amendment, Federal Legislation, and the United States Department of Justice*, 22 GA. L. REV. 1, 47 (1987).

[128]   50 U.S.C. § 1801 *et seq*. The Foreign Intelligence Surveillance Act, as originally enacted, covered only electronic surveillance warrants, but it was amended in 1994 to cover physical searches. See 50 U.S.C. §§ 1821-1829. The provisions regarding physical search warrants are similar to those for electronic surveillance orders and are beyond the scope of this chapter. For a discussion of the Foreign Intelligence Surveillance Act, *see generally* Alison A. Bradley, Comment, *Extremism in the Defense of Liberty? The Foreign Intelligence Surveillance Act and the Significance of the USA Patriot Act*, 77 TUL. L. REV. 465 (2002); William Michael, *A Window on Terrorism: The Foreign Intelligence Surveillance Act*, 58 NOV BENCH & B. MINN 23 (2001).

[129]   *FBI's Use of Wiretaps, Secret Searches Jumps Probes of Terrorism, Spying Lead to Record Number of Special Warrants. Senators Want to Broaden Uses*, BEACON JOURNAL (AKRON) May 2, 2003 at A3.

[130]   Foreign intelligence information includes information that relates to actual or potential attacks, hostile acts, and clandestine intelligence activities of foreign powers or their agents, international terrorism, and information with respect to foreign powers that relates to our national defense or security, or conduct of foreign affairs. 50 U.S.C. § 1801 (e).

[131]   50 U.S.C. § 1803. The FISA court operates in extreme secrecy and the opportunities for review of its decisions are limited. *See, e.g.*, United States v. Rahman, 861 F. Supp. 247 (S.D.N.Y. 1994) (upholding admission of wiretap evidence obtained under a FISA surveillance order in the prosecution of Omar Ahmad Ali Abdel Rahman over the defendant's objection that the government had misused its FISA surveillance authority. The court stated that once the reviewing court finds that an authorized executive branch official has certified that the purpose of the investigation was to gather intelligence information, and "his certification is supported by probable cause to believe that the target is an agent of a foreign power as defined in the statute, and that the location is one being or to be used by the target, and it appears from the application as a whole that the certification is not clearly erroneous, the task of that court is at an end. . . . A reviewing court is not to 'second-guess' the certification.")

rizing electronic surveillance and physical searches in national security cases.[132] The court's proceedings are secret, records of the proceedings are sealed after the application is heard, and the subject never learns of the surveillance unless criminal charges are later brought.

## B. Authorized Targets of FISA Surveillance Orders

FISA surveillance orders may be issued only when the target of the surveillance is a foreign power or agent of a foreign power,[133] terms that include international terrorist organizations and their members.[134] FISA orders cannot be obtained to conduct surveillance of groups and individuals engaged in purely domestic terrorism who have no ties to foreign powers. Authorization must, instead, be sought under the tougher requirements of Title III.

## C. Procedures for Obtaining FISA Surveillance Authority

All applications for FISA surveillance orders must be personally approved by the Attorney General.[135] The application must state facts warranting a belief that the target of the surveillance is a foreign power or agent of a foreign power, describe the manner in which the order will be implemented, and contain the certification of a senior national security official, typically the Director of the FBI, that the information sought is foreign intelligence information and that the information cannot "be obtained by normal investigative techniques."[136] The FISC judge is required to approve the application if, based on the facts established in the application, there is probable cause to believe that the target of the surveillance is a foreign power or agent of a foreign power and all necessary certifications are attached.[137] Judicial scrutiny of FISA applications is minimal. Of the thousands of applications for FISA orders made since 1978, only one has ever been denied.[138]

## D. Use of FISA to Gather Evidence for a Criminal Prosecution

Title III surveillance orders, which are used in regular criminal investigations, are the full equivalent of a Fourth Amendment search warrant. Issuance requires probable cause to believe that the target of the surveillance is com-

---

[132] 50 U.S.C. § 1803.

[133] 50 U.S.C. § 1805 (a)(3)(A).

[134] 50 U.S.C. §§ 1801 (a)(4), (b)(2)(C), (c).

[135] 50 U.S.C. § 1804 (a)(7).

[136] 50 U.S.C. §§ 1804 (a)(4)(7), 1801(h).

[137] 50 U.S.C. § 1805.

[138] See, e.g., David B. Kopel & Joseph Olson, *Preventing a Reign of Terror: Civil Liberties Implications of Terrorism Legislation*, 21 OKLA. CITY U. L. REV. 247, 311 (1996); William F. Zieske, *Demystifying the USA Patriot Act*, 92 ILL. B.J. 82, 86 (2004)

mitting a crime for which an interception order may be issued, that the targeted facilities are being used in connection with that crime, and that an interception will produce relevant evidence.[139] FISA surveillance orders, in contrast, are issued on a mere showing of probable cause to believe that the target of the surveillance is a foreign power or agent of a foreign power.[140] The government is not required to establish probable cause to believe that the target is involved in criminal activity.

This reduced showing comes at a price. FISA orders may be issued only when gathering **foreign intelligence** is a *significant purpose* of the investigation.[141] Prior to the USA Patriot Act amendments,[142] gathering foreign intelligence had to be the *"primary* purpose" of the investigation.[143] If the government's primary purpose was to gather evidence for a criminal prosecution, even for a crime related to foreign intelligence, the government had to satisfy the more stringent requirements of Title III.

This has now been changed. The USA Patriot Act,[144] adopted in the aftermath of the September 11, 2001, attacks, reduced the showing needed for FISA surveillance authority from the "primary purpose" to a "significant purpose."[145] This change allows the government to use FISA to gather evidence for a criminal prosecution—without establishing probable cause to believe that a crime has been committed—as long as collecting foreign intelligence is also a *significant purpose* of the investigation.[146] However, the crime under investigation must be a foreign intelligence crime (such as spying, espionage, sabotage, political assassination, terrorists acts committed by or on behalf of a foreign power, etc.).[147] FISA orders may not be used to investigate ordinary crimes like narcotics offenses and bank robbery.[148] If the government wants to use electronic surveillance to investigate an ordinary crime, it must apply for a Title III surveillance order.

The Patriot Act also seeks to foster closer working relationships between federal intelligence agents, prosecutors, and law enforcement officers. Federal officers conducting FISA investigations are now expressly permitted to share

---

[139]  18 U.S.C. § 2518(3).
[140]  50 U.S.C. § 1805 (a)(3)(A).
[141]  50 U.S.C. § 1804 (a)(7)(B). Foreign intelligence is defined as information that relates to actual or potential attacks or other grave hostile acts of foreign powers or their agents, clandestine spying activity, sabotage, and international terrorism, or that relates to the national defense and security of the United States and the conduct of foreign affairs. 50 U.S.C. § 1801(e).
[142]  *Supra* note 47.
[143]  *See, e.g.,* United States v. Duggan, 743 F.2d 59 (2d Cir. 1984); United States v. Pelton, 835 F.2d 1067 (4th Cir. 1987), *cert. denied,* 486 U.S. 1010, 108 S. Ct. 1741, 100 L. Ed. 2d 204 (1988); United States v. Badia, 827 F.2d 1458 (11th Cir. 1987), *cert. denied,* 485 U.S. 937, 108 S. Ct. 1115, 99 L. Ed. 2d 275 (1988).
[144]  *Supra* note 47.
[145]  50 U.S.C. § 1804 (a)(7)(B).
[146]  *Id.*
[147]  In re Sealed Case, 310 F.3d 717 (Foreign Int. Surv. Ct. Rev. 2002).
[148]  *Id.*

information with federal and state law enforcement officials and officials in other federal agencies to coordinate efforts to investigate and protect against threats to our national security.[149]

---

FISA electronic surveillance orders:

- Must be approved by the Foreign Intelligence Surveillance Court
- May be used only to monitor foreign powers or their agents, including members of international terrorist organizations
- May be obtained only when collecting foreign intelligence information is a significant purpose of the investigation

---

## § 5.8  Technologically Assisted Surveillance of Matters Other Than Communications

Advances in police surveillance technology have outfitted the police with powerful tools to fight crime. Video surveillance cameras equipped with wide-angle lenses, night vision capabilities, and supermagnification powers are now being installed at intersections to catch traffic violators, deter street crimes, and increase personal security.[150] Face recognition technology can enable the police to determine whether a known criminal or terrorist is present in a large, crowded area, such as a football stadium.[151] Beeper technology makes it possible to track the movement of a suspect's vehicle without the need for maintaining visual contact, which might alert the suspect that he or she is being trailed.[152] Thermal

---

[149]   50 U.S.C. § 1806 (k)(1).

[150]   *See, e.g.*, Christopher Slobogin, Symposium, *Public Privacy: Camera Surveillance of Public Places and the Right to Anonymity*, 72 MISS. L. J. 213 (2002); Christopher Slobogin, *Technologically Assisted Physical Surveillance: The American Bar Association's Tentative Draft Standards*, 10 HARV. J. L. & TECH. 383, 406 (1997); Andrew W. J. Tarr, Recent Development, *Picture It: Red Light Cameras Abide by the Law of the Land*, 80 N.C. L. Rev. 1879 (2002); Christopher S. Milligan, Note, *Facial Recognition Technology, Video Surveillance, and Privacy*, 9 S. CAL. INTERDISC. L. J. 295, 301 (1999). Video surveillance is covered in § 5.8 (A), below.

[151]   Facial recognition technology uses facial recognition software and video surveillance cameras. The cameras scan the faces of everyone present at that location and a computer then checks the scanned images for matches against a central database of known criminals or terrorists. *See, e.g.*, Christopher Benjamin, *Shot Spotter and Faceit: The Tools of Mass Monitoring*, 2002 UCLA J. LAW & TECH. 2 (2002); Quentin Burrows, *Scowl Because You're on Candid Camera: Privacy and Video Surveillance*, 31 VAL. U. L. REV. 1079 (1997); Christopher S. Milligan, *supra* note 150.

[152]   A beeper is a small, concealable tracking device that police attach to a vehicle or other object within a suspect's control. The device is then monitored by remote to track the movements of the object to which it is attached. *See, e.g.*, Michael Froomkin, *The Death of Privacy*, 52 STAN. L. REV. 1461 (2000); Richard S. Julie, *High-Tech Surveillance Tools and the Fourth Amendment: Reasonable Expectation of Privacy in the Technological Age*, 37 AM. CRIM. L. REV. 127 (2000). Beeper surveillance is discussed in § 5.8 (B). *See also* notes 155, 157, 167 *infra*.

imaging devices can enable the police to determine whether a person is growing marijuana inside his or her home without physically entering.[153] These are just some of the many police surveillance technologies currently in use.

Title III does not regulate the use of surveillance devices that register information other than communications. However, police must still comply with the Fourth Amendment. The Supreme Court summarized Fourth Amendment restrictions on the surreptitious use of police surveillance devices in *Katz v. United States* when it observed:

> What a person knowingly exposes to the public, even in his own home or office, is not a subject of Fourth Amendment protection. But what he seeks to preserve as private, even in an area accessible to the public, may be constitutionally protected.[154]

Accordingly, police do not need a search warrant to use surveillance devices to monitor activities in full public view.[155] However, they do need a warrant to make a covert entry into a constitutionally protected location to install equipment[156] or to use equipment not generally available to the public to monitor activities inside a private home.[157] In *Kyllo v. United States*,[158] the Supreme Court ruled that use of a thermal-imaging device to determine

---

[153] Indoor marijuana gardens require heat lamps that produce substantial amounts of heat. Thermal imaging devices create a picture based on heat emissions, much like a camera creates a picture based on light. When directed at a building suspected of being used to grow marijuana, the device can confirm those suspicions by detecting an abnormal heating pattern suggestive of a marijuana growing operation. *See, e.g.*, Jonathan Todd Laba, *If You Can't Stand the Heat, Get Out of the Drug Business: Thermal Imagers, Emerging Technologies, and the Fourth Amendment*, 84 CALIF. L. REV. 1437 (1996) (describing technology and function of thermal imaging devices and their current uses in law enforcement).

[154] Katz v. United States, *supra* note 4.

[155] Dow Chem. Co. v. United States, 476 U.S. 227, 106 S. Ct. 1819, 90 L. Ed. 2d 226 (1986) (warrant not required for aerial surveillance); United States v. Knotts, 460 U.S. 267, 103 S. Ct. 1081, 75 L. Ed. 2d 55 (1983) (warrant not required to place beeper device in cargo scheduled for pickup by suspect's truck in order to track the truck's movements in public); United States v. Jackson, 213 F.3d 1269 (10th Cir. 2000) (warrant not required to install video surveillance camera on telephone pole outside defendant's residence); **United States v. McIver, 186 F.3d 1119 (9th Cir. 1999), *cert. denied*, 528 U.S. 1177, 120 S. Ct. 1210, 145 L. Ed. 2d 1111 (2000)** (warrant not required to install motion-activated video cameras near marijuana plants growing in national forest nor to install magnetic tracking device on undercarriage of suspect's vehicle while it was parked outside the curtilage); Osborne v. State, 44 P.3d 523 (Nev. 2002) (warrant not required to attach electronic beeper device to bumper of defendant's truck).

[156] United States v. Jackson, *supra* note 155; United States v. Mesa-Rincon, 911 F.2d 1433 (10th Cir. 1990) (authorizing installation of a silent video camera inside a warehouse believed to house counterfeiting operation); United States v. Torres, 751 F.2d 875 (7th Cir. 1984), *cert. denied*, 470 U.S. 1087, 105 S. Ct. 1853, 85 L. Ed. 2d 150 (1985); United States v. Williams, 124 F.3d 411 (3d Cir. 1997) (authorizing video surveillance of office believed to be headquarters of gambling operation).

[157] **Kyllo v. United States, 533 U.S. 27, 121 S. Ct. 2038, 150 L. Ed. 2d 94 (2001)** ("[O]btaining by sense-enhancing technology any information regarding the interior of the home that could not otherwise have been obtained without physical 'intrusion into a constitutionally protected area' * * * constitutes a search—at least where (as here) the technology in question is not in general public use."); United States v. Karo, 468 U.S. 705, 104 S. Ct. 3296, 82 L. Ed. 2d 530 (1984) (beeper monitoring of cannister that suspect took into his home constituted search).

[158] *Supra* note 157. *See also* generally, David A. Sullivan, Note, *A Bright Line in the Sky? Toward a New Fourth Amendment Search Standard for Advancing Surveillance Technology*, 44 ARIZ. L. REV. 967 (2002).

whether heat emissions from a private home were consistent with the presence of high-intensity lamps used in indoor marijuana cultivation constituted a search for which a warrant was necessary. Though *Kyllo* has received varying interpretations, the most widely accepted is that when police use surveillance devices not generally available to the public to gather information about private activities inside a home, the observer's conduct is a search and a search warrant is necessary.

## A. Video Surveillance

The Fourth Amendment does not regulate video surveillance of activities in full public view. For example, police do not need a search warrant to install video surveillance cameras on a telephone post outside a suspect's home,[159] in a public park,[160] or in any other location where the equipment is used to capture activities exposed to public view.[161] When used in this manner, the equipment merely allows the police to do more efficiently what they could already do using only their own senses. Accordingly, the Fourth Amendment is not implicated. However, a search warrant is necessary to perform video surveillance in locations in which suspects have a reasonable expectation of privacy,[162] such as hotel rooms[163] and private homes and offices.[164] Although silent video surveillance is not covered by Title III, courts have looked to the Act for guidance in fashioning video surveillance warrants on the theory that Title III codifies Fourth Amendment procedural protections.[165]

---

[159] United States v. Jackson, *supra* note 155.

[160] **United States v. McIver**, *supra* note 155 (warrantless video surveillance of marijuana garden in National Forest did not violate the Fourth Amendment).

[161] *See, e.g.*, Hudspeth v. State, 349 Ark. 315, 78 S.W.3d 99 (2002) (suspect lacked reasonable expectation of privacy in methamphetamine laboratory operations captured on video surveillance cameras where activities occurred in an open field); People v. Wemette, 285 A.D.2d 729, 728 N.Y.S.2d 805 (2001) (suspect lacked reasonable expectation of privacy in activities occurring on his open front porch that were captured on video surveillance camers); Cowles v. State, 23 P.3d 1168 (Alaska 2001) (warrantless video surveillance of box office did not violate box officer manager's Fourth Amendment rights where her activities were observable by members of public through the ticket window and by coemployees circulating through the office); State v. Augafa, 92 Hawai'i 454, 992 P.2d 723 (Haw. Ct. App. 1999) (no reasonable expectation of privacy existed in drug transaction captured on video surveillance camera installed on public sidewalk); State v. McLellan, 144 N.H. 602, 744 A.2d 611 (1999) (school custodian's Fourth Amendment rights not violated by warrantless video surveillance of classroom because classroom was accessible to other staff members and students).

[162] *See, e.g.*, Cowles v. State, 23 P.3d 1168 (Alaska 2001) (Fourth Amendment violated by warrantless video surveillance of public restroom stalls).

[163] United States v. Nerber, 222 F.3d 597 (9th Cir. 2000) (suspect had reasonable expectation of privacy in hotel room rented by government informant for suspect's use); United States v. Shabazz, 883 F. Supp. 422 (D. Minn. 1995) (same).

[164] United States v. Taketa, 923 F.2d 665 (9th Cir. 1991) (warrantless warrant video surveillance of employee's private office constituted search).

[165] *See, e.g.* United States v. Williams, 124 F.3d 411 (3d Cir. 1997); United States v. Falls, 34 F.3d 674, 680 (8th Cir. 1994); United States v. Mesa-Rincon, 911 F.2d 1433, 1437 (10th Cir. 1990); United States v. Torres, 751 F.2d 875 (7th Cir. 1984).

## B. Tracking Devices ("Beepers")

Beepers are small radio transmitters that can be hidden in or on vehicles or other objects whose movements police want to track. They send out radio signals that enable the police, with the aid of a ground-based or satellite receiver, to monitor the device's location and movements for a range of up to several miles.[166] Beeper monitoring of a suspect's vehicle as it travels from one location to another involves neither a search nor a seizure.[167] There is no search because the beeper reveals nothing that police could not readily observe using the own senses.[168] There is no seizure because the presence of the beeper does not interfere with the suspect's possession or use of his vehicle.[169] Accordingly, police do not need a search warrant to perform beeper surveillance of a suspect's vehicle, provided they can attach the beeper without entering the suspect's curtilage.

However, police must procure a search warrant to engage in beeper surveillance of the movement of objects inside a suspect's home.[170] In *United States v. Karo*,[171] police concealed a beeper inside a can of ether that the suspect purchased from a police informant and used to extract cocaine in an operation conducted out of his home. The Supreme Court ruled that use of a beeper to monitor the movements of objects inside a private home constitutes a search for which a warrant is necessary.

## C. Pen Registers and Trap-and-Trace Devices

Pen registers and trap-and-trace devices are recording devices attached to a telephone line that perform a function different from a wiretap. They identify the source and destination of all calls made to (pen registers) or from (trap-and-trace devices) a particular telephone, much like a secret Caller ID. For many years there were no constitutional or statutory controls on the use of these devices.[172] In 1986, Congress enacted the Electronic Communications

---

[166] *See* authorities *supra* notes 152, 155.

[167] United States v. Knotts, *supra* note 155 (warrant not required to place beeper device in cargo scheduled for pickup by suspect's truck to monitor the truck's movements; motorists traveling on public thoroughfares have no reasonable expectation of privacy in their movements from one place to another); **United States v. McIver**, *supra* note 155 (warrant not required to install magnetic tracking device on undercarriage of suspect's vehicle while parked outside the curtilage); Osbourne v. State, 44 P.3d 523 (Nev. 2002) (warrant not required to attach electronic beeper device to bumper of defendant's truck).

[168] *See* authorities *supra* note 167.

[169] **United States v. McIver**, *supra* note 155.

[170] United States v. Karo, *supra* note 157.

[171] *Id.*

[172] Fourth Amendment protection is unavailable for dialing information because telephone companies use this information for billing and other purposes. Records maintained by businesses are not private and, therefore, carry no Fourth Amendment protection. Smith v. Maryland, 442 U.S. 735, 99 S. Ct. 2577, 61 L. Ed. 2d 220 (1979). Title III protection is also unavailable because pen registers and trap-and-trace devices do not provide access to the *contents* of the communication. Thus, for many years there were no legal controls on use of pen registers and trap-and-trace devices.

Privacy Act (ECPA),[173] which made it illegal to install pen registers and trap-and-trace devices without court approval. However, the requirements for court approval are negligible. Judges are required to approve an application, on no additional findings, if the government certifies that the information likely to be obtained from the installation and use is relevant to an ongoing criminal investigation.[174] Pen register and trap-and-trace orders may also be issued to capture source and addressee information for computer conversations, such as e-mail.[175]

## § 5.9 Summary and Practical Suggestions

Legal controls on listening vary depending on whether the police listen with the naked ear or with the aid of a device. Police are free to use their normal powers of hearing whenever they are lawfully present at the location where the hearing takes place. People who speak in a tone loud enough for others within earshot to hear lack a reasonable expectation of privacy and, consequently, have no Fourth Amendment protection. Eavesdropping becomes a search only if the officer is not lawfully present when the listening occurs.

Listening with a device, in contrast, almost always involves a search because the parties have no reason to expect that others would go to this extreme to eavesdrop on them. In *Katz v. United States,* the Supreme Court ruled that the Fourth Amendment requires a search warrant before police may intercept private communications with a device. A year later, Congress enacted Title III of the Omnibus Crime Control and Safe Streets Act, which provided the procedural safeguards that *Katz* mandated.

Title III makes it illegal for police to intercept wire, electronic, or oral communications with a device unless a judge issues an interception order, there is an emergency, or a party to the intercepted communication consents. Interception orders are a specialized kind of search warrant. The decision to apply for one must be approved by a designated high-ranking prosecutorial official. Orders are available only for the investigation of serious crimes such as espionage, sabotage, treason, kidnapping, extortion, murder, robbery, counterfeiting, and dealing in drugs. They may be sought only after normal investigative procedures have been tried and failed or appear unlikely to succeed. In executing the order, efforts must be made to minimize interception of innocent conversations. The order terminates on the attainment of the authorized objective or 30 days from issuance, whichever comes first, but the court may grant extensions. There are restrictions on the use and disclosure of information obtained under an interception order. The information may only be used for law enforcement purposes and may be disclosed only to another law enforcement officer when appropriate to the other's duties or when giving testimony in court.

---

[173] 18 U.S.C. § 3121 *et seq.*
[174] 18 U.S.C. § 3122.
[175] 18 U.S.C. § 3121, 3123.

The Foreign Intelligence Surveillance Act establishes a separate statutory procedure for regulating wiretapping and electronic surveillance conducted for foreign intelligence purposes. FISA surveillance orders, which are issued on a more relaxed probable cause standard, may be obtained only when collecting foreign intelligence information is a significant purpose of the investigation and may be used only to monitor foreign powers or their agents.

Title III does not regulate use of video surveillance, tracking, or other devices that record information other than communications. However, police must still comply with the Fourth Amendment.

# Interrogations and Confessions 6

# Chapter Outline

# § 6.1 Introduction

The law of **interrogations** and confessions is not set out in any single article or amendment to the Constitution. The restrictions come from five constitutional provisions, combined with federal and state statutes requiring prompt **arraignment** of suspects in **custody**. The five constitutional provisions that bear on the admissibility of confessions are the Fourth Amendment exclusionary rule, the Fifth Amendment privilege against self-incrimination, the Sixth Amendment right to counsel, and the Fifth and Fourteenth Amendment due process clauses.

Constitutional restrictions on the admission of confessions are designed to ensure that confessions are voluntary and trustworthy. Coerced statements are considered unreliable. However, even if this were not so, restrictions on admission serve to discourage police officers from engaging in practices that our society does not tolerate.

## A. Five Requirements for Admissibility

Admission of a confession may be challenged on at least five different grounds. The first stems from the Fifth and Fourteenth Amendment due process clauses. It is a violation of due process for a court to admit into evidence a confession that is not a product of the defendant's free will and voluntary choice.[1] Coerced confessions are considered untrustworthy because an innocent person may give in to pressure in order to gain relief.

Figure 6.1

**Legal Hurdles That Confessions Must Pass in Order to be Admissible as Evidence**

> Confessions that fail to satisfy any of the following requirements are inadmissible as evidence of guilt.
>
> 1. The due process free and voluntary rule,
> 2. The Fourth Amendment exclusionary rule,
> 3. The Fifth Amendment privilege against self-incrimination, and
> 4. The Sixth Amendment right to counsel.
>
> Confessions may also be suppressed for violating federal and state delay-in-arraignment statutes.

The second requirement stems from the Fourth Amendment exclusionary rule, which is covered in Chapter 4. The Fourth Amendment exclusionary rule applies to confessions as well as to physical evidence. Police are aware that people tend to confess when the "cat is out of the bag." To reduce the temptation to force the cat out of the bag illegally, the Fourth Amendment requires suppression of confessions that are causally related to an illegal *Terry* stop, **arrest**, or **seizure** of property, even if the confession was voluntary and its reliability is not in question.[2]

The third requirement, known as the *McNabb-Mallory* delay-in-arraignment rule,[3] is based on federal and state statutes that require suspects to be taken before a magistrate for arraignment "without undue delay" after the arrest. The period between arrest and arraignment is inherently coercive, because the suspect is generally held incommunicado, without counsel or access to the outside world. Concerns for the voluntariness of confessions given during this period prompted the Supreme Court to adopt the *McNabb-Mallory* rule, which requires suppression of confessions given during the interval between a suspect's arrest and arraignment if police officers were guilty of unnecessary delay in taking the arrestee before a magistrate.

The fourth requirement, known as the *Miranda* rule,[4] is grounded in the Fifth Amendment privilege against self-incrimination.[5] This requirement applies to confessions elicited during police **custodial interrogations**. Confessions given by suspects while in police custody will be suppressed unless the prosecution proves that the suspect was warned of his or her *Miranda* rights and voluntarily waived them before making the statement.

---

[1]    *See* § 6.2 *infra.*

[2]    *See* § 6.3 *infra.*

[3]    *See* § 6.5 *infra.*

[4]    Miranda v. Arizona, 384 U.S. 436, 86 S. Ct. 1602, 16 L. Ed. 2d 694 (1966).

[5]    *See* §§ 6.6-6.8 *infra.*

The fifth requirement stems from the Sixth Amendment right to counsel.[6] After **formal charges** have been filed, police officers are forbidden to contact the accused to discuss the pending charges unless counsel is present or the accused has chosen not to be represented. The accused, nevertheless, remains free to initiate contact with the police.

Confessions provide powerful evidence of guilt and are often necessary for a conviction. However, they are easily contaminated. Violation of the rules discussed in this chapter will result in suppression. Consequently, police officers must be thoroughly versed in the law of interrogations and confessions. Although restrictions on police interrogations are designed to protect the accused, compliance serves the interests of society by producing confessions that can be used as evidence.

## B. Legally Relevant Phases in the Development of a Criminal Case

Police questioning may take place at different stages in the development of a criminal case, with the tone varying from inquisitive to accusatory. The legal requirements that police officers must observe are not the same across the entire spectrum of questioning situations. Although confessions must pass five legal hurdles in order to be admissible, all five do not materialize the instant a police officer asks a question. The requirements in effect during police questioning vary with the stage when questions are asked and the tone of the questioning. In developing an overview of the law of interrogations and confessions, it is useful to break down the development of criminal cases into three phases and focus on the legal requirements that police officers must observe during each stage. This will lead to a clearer understanding of what police officers are required to do, and when they are required to do it, in order to preserve the admissibility of confessions. The timeline at the top of Figure 6.2 identifies three legally relevant phases in the development of a criminal case. The first phase (noncustodial **investigative questioning**) spans the period between the unfolding of a hunch and the time when a suspect is placed under formal arrest or taken into custody. The tone of questioning is inquisitive during the first phase, but becomes accusatory once the case enters the second phase. The second phase (**custodial interrogation**) begins when the suspect is placed under formal arrest or is taken into custody and continues until formal charges have been made. Once formal charges are filed, the case enters the third phase, which continues until the trial. The five legal requirements discussed in this chapter are shown along the left-hand margin of Figure 6.2. The shaded areas show the periods during which each of them is in effect.

---

[6]   See § 6.9 infra.

Figure 6.2
**Timeline in the Development of a Criminal Case Showing the Periods During Which Each of the Five Hurdles Operates**

| Timeline | Phase I: Noncustodial Investigative Questioning of Suspects Who Are Not in Custody | | Phase II: Interrogation of Suspects Who Are in Custody | Phase III: Interrogation of Defendants After Formal Charges Have Been Filed |
|---|---|---|---|---|
| | Consensual encounter | Investigatory detentions and traffic stops | | |
| Due process free and voluntary rule | | ▓ | ▓ | ▓ |
| Fourth Amendment exclusionary rule | | ▓ | ▓ | |
| McNabb-Mallory rule | | | ▓ | |
| Miranda rule | | | ▓ | |
| Sixth Amendment right to counsel | | | | ▓ |

The typical criminal case begins when an officer develops a hunch that a person has committed, is committing, or is about to commit a crime, and decides to investigate further. The officer approaches the suspect, introduces him or herself, and asks whether the suspect would be willing to answer some questions. As long as a reasonable person in the suspect's position would feel free to decline the interview, terminate the encounter, and go about his or her business, the investigative encounter is consensual, and none of the five requirements applies. In Chapter 3, we used the phrase "free zone" to describe police activity that is not regulated by the Constitution.[7] The "free zone" concept applies here as well. Incriminating statements elicited during consensual investigative encounters will always be admissible.

However, investigative encounters are not always consensual. This is true of investigatory detentions and traffic stops. Although the suspect has not yet been arrested or taken into custody, investigatory detentions and traffic stops are not consensual because the suspect has been seized. Statements made during these encounters are capable of being contaminated because two of the five legal requirements—the due process free and voluntary rule and the Fourth Amendment exclusionary rule—are in effect.

The second phase, the *custodial interrogation phase*, begins when police officers place a suspect under formal arrest or take a suspect into custody. Once the investigation enters this phase, the tone of the questioning changes. The questioning is no longer inquisitive; it becomes accusatory. The mere fact of being in police custody puts pressure, both internal and external, on a suspect. As a result, restrictions on police questioning tighten and, as Figure 6.2 shows, four of the five requirements are now in effect.

At some point after the arrest, formal charges will be filed. When this happens, the suspect becomes an accused and the Sixth Amendment right to counsel attaches. The now case enters the third phase—the *prosecutorial* stage—and obtaining an admissible confession now becomes extremely difficult.

## § 6.2 The Free and Voluntary Rule

At early common law, confessions were admissible as evidence of guilt even when they were tortured from suspects. As time passed, judges came to appreciate that coerced confessions are not reliable. Everyone has a breaking point. When exposed to extreme pressure, even an innocent person may confess. This insight led to the adoption, both in England and the United States, of the rule that confessions must be voluntary in order to be admissible as evidence of guilt. This requirement is incorporated into the Fifth and Fourteenth Amendment due process clauses. Suppression of coerced confessions serves three main purposes. It (1) protects against convictions based on unreliable evidence; (2) preserves a suspect's freedom of choice; and (3) deters police from engaging in interrogation practices our society does not tolerate.

---

[7]    For the characteristics of a voluntary investigative encounter, *see* Chapter 3, §§ 3.3-3.5.

Figure 6.3
**Due Process Free and Voluntary Requirement**

> Confessions are not voluntary and will be suppressed when: (1) an agent of the government exerts pressures that (2) overcome a suspect's free will and cause the suspect to make a statement that he or she would not otherwise have made.

## A. The Two-Part Test of "Voluntariness"

A confession is involuntary under the due process clause if it results from coercive pressures exerted by an agent of the government that overcome the suspect's free will and induce the suspect to make a statement that he or she would not otherwise have made.[8] The due process test of voluntariness has two components—the first is concerned with the source of the pressure and the second with its impact on the suspect.

The government must be responsible for the pressures that cause a suspect to confess in order for a confession to be involuntary in a constitutional sense. This is because our Constitution only regulates the actions of the government. Suppose that Sticky-Fingered Sam suffers a head injury in an auto accident that temporarily incapacitates the "lying" center of his brain. For a few (poorly-timed) moments, Sam is unable to speak anything but the truth. When the police reach the accident scene, Sam confesses to all of his past crimes. Although Sam's confession was not a product of his free will, his confession satisfies the due process test of voluntariness because the police did nothing improper to induce the confession.

The Supreme Court used this reasoning in a case in which a chronic schizophrenic suffering from auditory hallucinations walked into a police station and confessed to murdering a young girl.[9] The Supreme Court refused to suppress the confession, despite psychiatric testimony that the deranged man believed that God's voice had ordered him to confess, because the confession was obtained without improper police conduct. Improper police conduct is necessary for a confession to be involuntary in a due process sense.

## B. Factors Considered in Determining Voluntariness

Some police misconduct, such as beating confessions out of suspects or putting a gun to their head, is so obviously coercive that confessions extracted by these means are involuntary as a matter of law.[10] When pressures to confess

---

[8]   Nix v. Williams, 467 U.S. 431, 104 S. Ct. 2501, 81 L. Ed. 2d 377 (1984); Colorado v. Connelly, 479 U.S. 157, 107 S. Ct. 515, 93 L. Ed. 2d 473 (1986).

[9]   Colorado v. Connelly, *supra* note 8.

[10]  Beecher v. Alabama, 389 U.S. 35, 88 S. Ct. 189, 19 L. Ed. 2d 35 (1967) (statement obtained after police held a gun to suspect's head and threatened to kill him if he did not tell the truth); Payne v. Arkansas, 356 U.S. 560, 78 S. Ct. 844, 2 L. Ed. 2d 975 (1958) (statement obtained after police threatened to turn the suspect over to an angry lynch mob); Brown v. Mississippi, 297 U.S. 278, 56 S. Ct. 461, 80 L. Ed. 682 (1936) (statement obtained after police whipped suspect).

are less extreme, questions of voluntariness are resolved by examining the totality of circumstances surrounding the confession, with emphasis on: (1) the pressures exerted by the police; (2) the suspect's degree of susceptibility; and (3) the conditions under which the interrogation took place.[11]

Figure 6.4
**Factors Relevant to Voluntariness**

> Beating and torturing suspects render confessions involuntary as a matter of law. When the pressures are not this extreme, courts determine voluntariness by examining the totality of circumstances surrounding the making of the confession, with emphasis on:
>
> 1.　the pressures exerted by the police;
> 2.　the suspect's degree of susceptibility; and
> 3.　the conditions under which the interrogation took place.

**Pressures exerted by the police.** Courts first examine the methods used by the police to elicit the confession. No methods are more revolting than torture. Force and brutality render a confession involuntary as a matter of law. While instances of "beating" confessions out of suspects are rare in modern times, they are unfortunately not rare enough. The following is an unnerving account of testimony given by a defendant in an Illinois case concerning the circumstances surrounding his confession.[12] The defendant testified that, following his arrest, he was taken to an interrogation room where he was interrogated for six hours with his wrists handcuffed behind his back. When he persisted in denying knowledge of the crime, one of the detectives put a chrome .45 caliber automatic gun in his mouth and told him that he would blow off his head because he knew that the defendant was lying. The defendant further testified that the detective struck him in the stomach with a flashlight three or four times and, when he fell out of the chair, stomped on him and hit him with the flashlight. When he continued denying knowledge of the crime, the detective put a plastic bag over his head while another officer kicked him. Thereafter, three officers took him to another room and again placed a plastic bag over his head, this time for about two minutes. At this point, the defendant confessed.

---

[11]　**Arizona v. Fulminante, 499 U.S. 279, 285-286, 111 S. Ct. 1246, 113 L. Ed. 2d 302 (1991)**; Schneckloth v. Bustamonte, 412 U.S. 218, 93 S. Ct. 2041, 36 L. Ed. 2d 854 (1973).

[12]　People v. Banks, 549 N.E.2d 766 (Ill. 1989). Cases like *People v. Banks* are not unique. On January 11, 2003, two days before leaving office, Illinois governor George Ryan pardoned four inmates on death row who were convicted on the basis of confessions tortured from them through tactics similar to those used in the *Banks* case. *See* James Webb, *Illinois Governor Pardons Four Inmates Condemned to Death*, COURIER JOURNAL A7 (Jan. 11, 2003). On the following day, Governor Ryan commuted all 167 remaining Illinois death sentences to prison terms, stating: "The facts that I have seen in reviewing each and every one of these cases raised questions not only about the innocence of people on death row, but about the fairness of the death penalty as a whole." Jodi Wilgoren, *Illinois Governor Cleans Out Death Row*, COURIER JOURNAL A1 (Jan. 12, 2003).

Although the officers denied these incidents, their testimony was not convincing. A physician who examined the defendant found lacerations on both wrists, multiple scrapes and scratches on his chest and abdomen, bruises on both legs and upper thighs, swollen muscles, and a lump under the skin in his lower rib cage. Confessions procured through tactics like these are involuntary as a matter of law.

Physical force is not the only misconduct that can render a confession involuntary. Coercion may take other forms, such as threats, false promises, trickery, deceit, and even psychological coercion.[13] Threats, such as the threat to turn the suspect over to an angry lynch mob[14] arrest innocent members of the suspect's family, or take the suspect's children away can often be as effective in overcoming a suspect's free will as force.[15] False promises can also have this effect. Promising a suspect that, by confessing, he or she will avoid prosecution or receive a lighter sentence or some other form of leniency, will render a confession involuntary if police lack the intent or authority to deliver.[16] However, it is not improper to tell a suspect that the prosecutor will be informed of his or her cooperation.[17] Nor is it improper to inform the suspect that he or she faces jail time or to refer to the maximum penalty he or she could receive.[18] Police officers are allowed to make truthful representations about the suspect's legal predicament.

If the court determines that the police used improper interrogation tactics, it will next consider whether the suspect's will was overborne. The suspect's degree of susceptibility is the central focus of this inquiry.

**Suspect's degree of susceptibility.** People vary in the degree and types of pressure they can withstand. The suspect's background, education, intellect, prior experience with the criminal justice system, physical and mental condition, ability to cope with stress, and other traits will be examined to decide whether the suspect's free will was overcome by the stresses that were placed on him or her.[19]

**Conditions under which the interrogation took place.** The details of the interrogation are the last consideration. Because a suspect's capacity to resist pressures can be eroded by factors, such as the location of the interrogation;

---

[13] *See, e.g.*, Rogers v. Richmond, 365 U.S. 534, 81 S. Ct. 735, 5 L. Ed. 2d 760 (1961) (invalidating confession made in response to bogus threat to arrest suspect's ailing wife); Lynum v. Illinois, 372 U.S. 528, 83 S. Ct. 917, 9 L. Ed. 2d 922 (1963) (invalidating confession made in response to bogus threat to take away suspect's children); Spano v. New York, 360 U.S. 315, 79 S. Ct. 1202, 3 L. Ed. 2d 1265 (1959) (invalidating confession where officer lied to childhood friend that he would lose his job and this would create a family hardship if suspect did not cooperate).

[14] Payne v. Arkansas, *supra* note 10.

[15] Rogers v. Richmond, 365 U.S. 534, 81 S. Ct. 735, 5 L. Ed. 2d 760 (1961).

[16] *See, e.g.*, United States v. LeBrun, 306 F.3d 545 (8th Cir. 2002); State v. Sturgill, 469 S.E.2d 557 (N.C. Ct. App. 1996). However, vague assurances that cooperation is in the suspect's best interest are not considered improper. *See, e.g.*, United States v. Ruggles, 70 F.3d 262, 265 (2d Cir. 1995); United States v. Nash, 910 F.2d 749, 752-753 (11th Cir. 1990); Collins v. State, 509 N.E.2d 827, 830 (Ind. 1987).

[17] United States v. Westbrook, 125 F.3d 996 (7th Cir. 1997).

[18] United States v. Braxton, 112 F.3d 777 (4th Cir. 1997) (telling a suspect "if you don't come clean, you can get five years" is not improperly coercive).

[19] *See, e.g.*, **Arizona v. Fulminante**, *supra* note 11 (below-average intelligence, fourth-grade education, poor coping skills).

the length, intensity, and frequency of the interrogation sessions; food and sleep deprivation; the intimidating presence of large numbers of police officers; and other factors endemic to the interrogation setting, these factors will be examined as well.[20]

## C. Procedures for Determining the Voluntariness of a Confession

The question of whether a confession is voluntary is one that the judge must decide before admitting the confession into evidence. The judge may not admit it and leave this question to the jury, with instructions to disregard the confession if the jury finds it involuntary.[21] It is unrealistic to expect lay jurors to disregard a confession once they have heard it. Consequently, when the voluntariness of a confession is challenged, the judge must hold a hearing outside the presence of the jury and take testimony about the circumstances surrounding the making of the confession.[22]

The burden of proof at the voluntariness hearing is on the government. To secure admission, the government must prove that the defendant confessed of his or her own free will. In *Lego v. Twomey*,[23] the defendant argued, without success, that the government should be required to prove this fact "beyond a reasonable doubt." The Court disagreed, holding that, while the government must establish guilt beyond a reasonable doubt, the Constitution does not require this degree of certainty to secure the admission of a confession. The Court adopted a "preponderance of the evidence" standard; the government must establish that it is more probable than not that the defendant confessed of his or her own free will. If the evidence at the suppression hearing is equally weighted, the government will lose because its burden of proof has not been carried.

Summarizing, involuntary confessions—confessions that are a product of police misconduct that overbears a suspect's free will—are inadmissible. Voluntariness is determined by examining the methods police used to elicit the confession, the suspect's degree of susceptibility, and the conditions under which the interrogation took place. The government bears the burden of proving by a preponderance of the evidence (i.e., that it is more probable than not) that the defendant confessed of his or her own free will.

---

[20]   Mincey v. Arizona, 437 U.S. 385, 98 S. Ct. 2408, 57 L. Ed. 2d 290 (1978) (statement obtained from suspect under sedation in intensive care unit); Greenwald v. Wisconsin, 390 U.S. 519, 88 S. Ct. 1152, 20 L. Ed. 2d 77 (1968) (statement obtained from suspect interrogated nonstop for more than 18 hours without food or sleep); Reck v. Pate, 367 U.S. 433, 81 S. Ct. 1541, 6 L. Ed. 2d 948 (1961) (statement obtained after depriving suspect of adequate food, sleep, and contact with family); Malinski v. New York, 324 U.S. 401, 65 S. Ct. 781, 89 L. Ed. 1029 (1945) (statement obtained after forcing suspect to remain naked).

[21]   Jackson v. Denno, 378 U.S. 368, 84 S. Ct. 1774, 12 L. Ed. 2d 908 (1964).

[22]   This position is codified in **18 U.S.C.A. § 3501(a)**.

[23]   404 U.S. 477, 489, 92 S. Ct. 619, 626, 30 L. Ed. 2d 618 (1972).

## § 6.3  The Fourth Amendment Exclusionary Rule

The second ground for challenging the admissibility of a confession stems from the Fourth Amendment exclusionary rule. The Fourth Amendment exclusionary rule applies to confessions as well as to physical evidence. If the police illegally search a suspect's car, find stolen property, and the suspect, confronted with the stolen property, immediately confesses, the confession will be suppressed, even if it is otherwise voluntary. The same holds true for confessions precipitated by an unconstitutional arrest or **investigatory stop**. Moreover, when a confession is tainted by police misconduct, the taint generally carries over and destroys the admissibility of **derivative evidence** discovered as a result of the confession.

This branch of the Fourth Amendment exclusionary rule is known as the "fruit of the poisonous tree" doctrine. The fruit of the poisonous tree doctrine derives from the case of *Wong Sun v. United States*.[24] The facts of *Wong Sun* are complicated, but the relevant facts for our purposes are as follows. Federal agents, engaged in drug detection, barged into Blackie Toy's apartment, handcuffed him, and placed him under arrest, without probable cause or a warrant. Toy made incriminating statements at the scene of his arrest, in which he implicated both himself and another person, Johnny Yee. The agents then went to Yee's home, arrested him, and found heroin in his possession, which Yee told the police he got from Toy and another person named Wong Sun. The police next arrested Wong Sun. Wong Sun was released on his own recognizance and several days later voluntarily returned to the police station and confessed. The Supreme Court dealt with Blackie Toy's and Wong Sun's situations separately. Concerning Blackie Toy, the Supreme Court ruled that the incriminating statements made by Toy at the scene of his arrest and the heroin found in Johnny Yee's bedroom, which would not have been discovered without Toy's confession, were the fruits of Toy's unconstitutional arrest and were not admissible against Toy.

Figure 6.5
**Fourth Amendment Exclusionary Rule**

> The Fourth Amendment exclusionary rule requires suppression of confessions that are: (1) causally connected (2) to a violation of the suspect's Fourth Amendment rights (i.e., illegal *Terry* stop, arrest, or search). Further, when a confession is tainted beyond use, derivative evidence that would not have been discovered without the confession will also be suppressed.

The Court, nevertheless, declined to hold that a suspect whose Fourth Amendment rights have been violated can never give an admissible confession. Rather, the question turns on whether the violation of the defendant's Fourth Amendment *caused* the confession or whether there was a break in the

---

[24]   371 U.S. 471, 83 S. Ct. 407, 9 L. Ed. 2d 441 (1963).

causal chain. A causal connection is presumed and the burden is on the government to prove that the taint was no longer present at the time of the confession. Courts consider three factors in deciding this: (1) the length of time between the violation and the confession, (2) the presence of intervening circumstances, and (3) the purpose and flagrancy of the violation.[25]

**Length of time.** The length of time between the Fourth Amendment violation and the confession is the first consideration. When the confession occurs at the scene or shortly thereafter, there is no break in the causal chain and suppression is required.[26] Blackie Toy's confession in *Wong Sun*, which occurred when the police barged into his home, was suppressed for this reason. When the confession occurs hours or days later, the remaining two factors will be examined.[27]

**Presence of intervening circumstances.** The passage of time alone is not enough to break the causal chain. There must be intervening circumstances that show that the suspect's decision to confess was an independent act of free will. Consulting with an attorney and voluntarily returning after being released from police custody are the two circumstances most often relied on to show this.[28] In *Wong Sun*, the Supreme Court admitted Wong Sun's confession, which was given several days after his illegal arrest, because he returned to the police station on his own after being released. This showed that his decision to confess was a thought-out and considered act, and not a panicked reaction to an illegal arrest. Administration of *Miranda* warnings, in contrast, are not sufficient to break the causal chain.[29] The Supreme Court has reviewed several cases in which suspects confessed at the police station following an unconstitutional arrest, having received *Miranda* warnings in the meanintime;[30] in only one case did the Court find a break in the causal chain and it was for reasons other than administration of *Miranda* warnings.[31]

**Purpose and flagrancy of the violation.** The purpose and flagrancy of the violation is the last consideration. This factor is tied to the policy behind the exclusionary rule, which is to discourage police from violating the Fourth Amendment by taking away the incentive.[32] *New York v. Harris*[33] is one of the few cases in which a confession given at the police station following an illegal arrest was admitted. The police in that case had probable cause to make the arrest, but arrested Harris inside his home, without a warrant, in violation of

---

[25] Kaupp v. Texas, 538 U.S. 626, 123 S. Ct. 1843, 155 L. Ed. 2d 814 (2003); New York v. Harris, 495 U.S. 14, 110 S. Ct. 1640, 109 L. Ed. 2d 13 (1990); Taylor v. Alabama, 457 U.S. 687, 102 S. Ct. 2664, 73 L. Ed. 2d 314 (1982); Dunaway v. New York, 442 U.S. 200, 99 S. Ct. 2248, 60 L. Ed. 2d 824 (1979); Brown v. Illinois, 422 U.S. 590, 95 S. Ct. 2254, 45 L. Ed. 2d 416 (1975).

[26] Wong Sun v. United States, *supra* note 24, 371 U.S. at 484-488, 83 S. Ct. at 416.

[27] *See* cases *supra* note 25.

[28] Wong Sun v. United States, *supra* note 24; United States v. Patino, 862 F.2d 128 (7th Cir. 1988).

[29] *See* authorities, *supra* note 25; State v. Ford, 30 S.W.3d 378 (Tenn. Crim. App. 2000).

[30] *See* authorities *supra* note 25.

[31] New York v. Harris, *supra* note 25.

[32] *See, e.g.*, United States v. Leon, 468 U.S. 897, 906, 104 S. Ct. 3405, 3411, 82 L. Ed. 2d 677 (1984).

[33] *Supra* note 25.

the *Payton* rule.[34] The Court reasoned that, because the police had probable cause for the arrest and could have arrested Harris lawfully had they waited for him to come outside, their violation ended once he was removed from his home and he was lawfully in custody when he later confessed. That the police violation of the Fourth Amendment did not enable them to obtain a confession that they could not have obtained lawfully was the basis for the holding. Suppressing a confession where the police did not profit from their wrong would not serve the deterrent purpose of the exclusionary rule.

On the other hand, when a suspect confesses at the police following an arrest made without probable cause, the police violation of the suspect's Fourth Amendment rights is the reason the suspect is in custody. The police now have obtained a confession that they could not have obtained lawfully. Allowing them to keep it would encourage future violations. Accordingly, confessions given at the police station following an illegal arrest will be suppressed unless there are intervening circumstances sufficient to break the causal chain.[35]

The three factors used to determine causation—length of time between the violation and the confession, the presence of intervening circumstances, and the purpose and flagrancy of the police misconduct—admittedly do not yield a high degree of predictability. However, the lack of predictability will not prevent police from properly discharging their duties because causation analysis takes place after the Fourth Amendment violation has occurred. Police officers do not need to know in advance how long the effects of their Fourth Amendment violation will linger in order to properly discharge the responsibilities of their job.

## § 6.4  Overview of the Rules Governing Custodial Interrogation

At this point, two grounds for suppression have been discussed. First, confessions are inadmissible unless they are a product of the suspect's own free will. Second, they are inadmissible if a police violation of the suspect's Fourth Amendment rights *caused* the suspect to confess. Notice in Figure 6.2 that both grounds carry over and continue to provide the basis for challenging confessions made during the second and third phases of a criminal case. Notice further that confessions made during the second phase are vulnerable to challenge on two additional grounds: the *McNabb-Mallory* rule and the *Miranda* rule.

These requirements were developed to counterbalance the pressures that arise from the fact of being in police custody. Once a suspect is arrested or taken into custody, the tone of the questioning changes. The questions are no longer inquisitive; they are now accusatory. Moreover, once in custody, sus-

---

[34]  **Payton v. New York, 445 U.S. 573, 100 S. Ct. 1371, 63 L. Ed. 2d 639 (1980)**, discussed in § 3.15, requires an arrest warrant before the police may enter a suspect's home to arrest him or her.

[35]  *See* Taylor v. Alabama, *supra* note 25; Dunaway v. New York, *supra* note 25; Brown v. Illinois, *supra* note 25.

pects find themselves in strange surroundings, often behind closed doors, and experience interrogation methods that may be new to them, but with which their interrogators have considerable expertise and experience. Most important, the suspect is alone, without an advocate or even an impartial witness. As a result, the atmosphere is inherently coercive, even when police interrogation methods are not. Consequently, there are fewer guarantees that confessions elicited during police custodial interrogations will be a product of the suspect's free will and voluntary choice. To counteract this danger, the Supreme Court has imposed two additional safeguards that become effective once the suspect is arrested or taken into custody—the *McNabb-Mallory* rule and the *Miranda* requirement.

The *McNabb-Mallory* rule seeks to alleviate the pressured atmosphere of a police custodial interrogation by requiring the police to present the arrested person to a magistrate promptly after the arrest. Presentment to a magistrate reassures the suspect that the outside world is aware that he or she is in police custody and that the police are accountable to the courts. This procedure also reinforces protection for an arrested person's constitutional rights. The magistrate will inform the person of his or her constitutional rights and confirm that he or she understands them and knows that he or she is free to exercise them. The *McNabb-Mallory* rule enforces compliance with this requirement by suppressing confessions obtained during a period of unnecessary delay in presenting the arrested person to a magistrate.

It is also at this point that the *Miranda* rule goes into effect. The *Miranda* rule requires the police to issue a detailed set of warnings—"you have the right to remain silent, anything you say can and will be used against you, you have a right to an attorney, and one will be appointed for you if you cannot afford one"—before initiating a custodial interrogation and to cease the interrogation if the suspect at any time thereafter expresses a desire to exercise his or her rights. Failure to give the required warnings or to cease interrogation if the suspect invokes his or her rights will result in the suppression of any resulting confession.

## § 6.5  The *McNabb-Mallory* Delay in Arraignment Rule

Rule 5(a) of the Federal Rules of Criminal Procedure and the procedural rules of most, if not all, states, direct police officers to take arrested persons before the nearest available magistrate, commissioner, or other committing officer for an arraignment "without unnecessary delay" following an arrest. The purpose of requiring a prompt arraignment is to protect people who are under arrest from pressures to confess before they have seen a magistrate. In the period before the *McNabb-Mallory* rule, police ignored this requirement because statutes requiring a prompt arraignment contained no penalties for their violation.

## A. *Statement and Discussion of the* McNabb-Mallory *Rule*

The Supreme Court cured this problem in *McNabb v. United States*.[36] The Court announced that confessions obtained in violation of Rule 5(a) of the Federal Rules of Criminal Procedure (the federal prompt arraignment statute) were inadmissible in federal criminal trials, even if the confession was voluntary.

The Supreme Court reaffirmed this position in *Mallory v. United States*.[37] Mallory, a rape suspect, was arrested between 2:00 and 2:30 P.M. the day after the rape and taken to police headquarters, where he was questioned for about 30 minutes before agreeing to submit to a polygraph test. The polygraph operator was not located until later that evening. Mallory was detained at police headquarters for four hours while the police waited for the polygraph operator to arrive, even though several magistrates were available in the immediate vicinity. The polygraph questioning began at around 8:00 P.M. Approximately 90 minutes into the interview, Mallory stated that he "might" have done it. At this point, the police made their first attempt to reach a United States Commissioner, but when they were unsuccessful, asked Mallory to repeat his confession, which he agreed to do. Between 11:30 P.M. and 12:30 A.M., Mallory dictated his confession to a typist. Mallory was not brought before a United States Commissioner until the next morning. His confession was admitted despite the delay in taking him before a magistrate. He was found guilty and sentenced to death. The Supreme Court reversed his conviction, declaring "[w]e cannot sanction this extended delay, resulting in a confession, without subordinating the general rule of prompt arraignment to the discretion of arresting officers . . ."

## B. *Determining Whether a Delay in Arraignment Is "Unnecessary"*

The *McNabb-Mallory* rule does not impose a fixed period within which arrestees must be taken before a committing magistrate for an arraignment. The question is whether the police obtained the confession during a period of "unnecessary delay." Each case is evaluated on its own facts. Delays due to causes beyond the government's control, such as lack of an available magistrate,[38] the distance that needs to be traveled,[39] transportation problems,[40] mechanical breakdowns, hazardous weather conditions, and the like, do not

---

[36]  318 U.S. 332, 63 S. Ct. 608, 87 L. Ed. 819 (1943), *reh'g denied*, 319 U.S. 784, 63 S. Ct. 1322, 87 L. Ed. 1727 (1943).

[37]  354 U.S. 449, 77 S. Ct. 1356, 1 L. Ed. 2d 1479 (1957).

[38]  United States v. Gorel, 622 F.2d 100 (5th Cir. 1979).

[39]  United States v. McCormick, 468 F.2d 68 (10th Cir. 1972).

[40]  United States v. Odom, 526 F.2d 339 (5th Cir. 1976).

constitute "unnecessary delays," and therefore do not place confessions at risk. The same holds true for delays needed to complete booking,[41] to sober prisoners up,[42] or to provide necessary medical treatment.[43]

Figure 6.6
**McNabb-Mallory Rule**

> The *McNabb-Mallory* or "delay in arraignment" rule requires suppression of confessions obtained during a period of unnecessary delay in presenting the suspect to a magistrate for arraignment.

## C. Current Status of the McNabb-Mallory Rule in Federal Courts

In 1968, Congress passed § 3501 of the Omnibus Crime Control and Safe Streets Act,[44] which took much of the former sting out of the *McNabb-Mallory* rule. Section 3501 requires federal judges to admit confessions found to be voluntary, but allows them to consider a number of factors in making this determination, one of which is "the time elapsing between arrest and arraignment of the defendant." Thus, federal courts may no longer automatically exclude confessions because of unnecessary delay in taking the arrestee before a committing magistrate for arraignment.[45] A confession may be excluded only if the judge decides it was not voluntary. The judge may consider unnecessary delay in presentment as a factor in deciding this, but if, after examining the circumstances surrounding a confession, the judge decides that the confession was voluntary despite the delay, it must be admitted.[46] Subsec-

---

[41] United States v. Rubio, 709 F.2d 146 (2d Cir. 1983); United States v. Johnson, 467 F.2d 630 (2d Cir. 1972).

[42] United States v. Christopher, 956 F.2d 536 (6th Cir. 1991) *cert. denied*, 505 U.S. 1207, 112 S. Ct. 2999, 120 L. Ed. 2d 875 (1992); United States v. Bear Killer, 534 F.2d 1253 (8th Cir. 1976).

[43] United States v. Isom, 588 F.2d 858 (2d Cir. 1978).

[44] **Omnibus Crime Control and Safe Streets Act, 18 U.S.C. § 3501.** This statute is reproduced in Part II. Subsection (a) of 18 U.S.C. § 3501 makes voluntariness the sole test of admissibility of confessions in federal criminal prosecutions. Subsection (b) requires the court to consider a number of factors in determining voluntariness, one of which is the time elapsing between arrest and arraignment. Subsection (c) provides that a confession made while a defendant is in custody may not be treated as inadmissible solely because of delay in bringing the person before a magistrate if (1) the confession is found by the judge to be voluntary.

[45] *See, e.g.*, United States v. Christopher, *supra* note 42, (holding confession admissible, but commenting that courts must be alert to possibility that delay was used for purpose of conducting improperly coercive interrogation); United States v. Mayes, 552 F.2d 729 (6th Cir. 1977); United States v. Clarke, 110 F.3d 612 (8th Cir. 1997). *See also* Timothy M. Hall, Annotation, *Construction and Application of Provision of Omnibus Crime Control and Safe Streets Act of 1968, as Amended (§ 18 U.S.C.A. 3501(c)), that Defendant's Confession Shall Not Be Inadmissible in Evidence in Federal Criminal Prosecution Solely Because of Delay in Presentment before Magistrate*, 124 A.L.R. FED. 263 (1995, updated January, 2000).

[46] Section 3501 also tried to overturn the *Miranda* rule by requiring judges to admit unwarned confessions if they found them to be voluntary. The Supreme Court declared this portion of the statute unconstitutional in *Dickerson v. United States*, 530 U.S. 28, 120 S. Ct. 2326, 147 L. Ed. 2d 405 (2000).

tion (c) of the 1968 law further restricts the judge's discretion to exclude confessions because of delay in presentment by making the first six hours after an arrest on federal charges a "safe harbor" period. Confessions procured during the first six hours after an arrest on federal charges may not be suppressed as involuntary solely because of delay in taking the defendant before a magistrate, regardless of the reason for the delay. Unnecessary delay in presentment may be considered as a factor relevant to voluntariness only for confessions procured beyond the six-hour safe harbor period.

### D. *Status of the* McNabb-Mallory *Rule in State Courts*

The *McNabb-Mallory* rule was not a constitutional doctrine. It was promulgated by the Supreme Court under its authority to establish rules for the federal courts.[47] The ruling was never binding on state courts,[48] although many adopted it voluntarily. However, few states today adhere to the *McNabb-Mallory* rule in its original form.[49] Most follow the federal practice of treating delay as a factor bearing on voluntariness, which is the focal point of the admissibility inquiry.[50]

Consequently, while the *McNabb-Mallory* rule has not disappeared from confession law, its importance has been greatly diminished. Unnecessary delay in arraignment no longer provides automatic grounds for suppressing confessions as it once did. It has become a factor that judges consider in deciding whether a confession is voluntary. This change does not mean that police officers can ignore rules requiring a prompt arraignment. When police officers deliberately flaut procedures established to protect criminal defendants in order to buy time to interrogate them, it sends a message to judges that the confession needs to be examined carefully for other evidence of overreaching.

---

[47]  United States v. Alvarez-Sanchez, 511 U.S. 350, 114 S. Ct. 1599, 128 L. Ed. 2d 319 (1994).

[48]  Culombe v. Connecticut, 367 U.S. 568, 600-601, 81 S. Ct. 1860, 1877-1878, 6 L. Ed. 2d 1037 (1961).

[49]  *See, e.g.*, Williams v. State, 75 Md. 404, 825 A.2d 1078 (2003) (holding that delay in taking an arrested person before a magistrate remains a factor to be considered, along with any others, in determining voluntariness, but adding that deliberate and unnecessary delay must be given "very heavy weight in determining whether a resulting confession is voluntary, because that violation creates its own aura of suspicion"); Rhiney v. State, 935 P.2d 828 (Alaska Ct. App. 1997); Landrum v. State, 328 Ark. 361, 944 S.W.2d 101 (1997); People v. Cipriano, 431 Mich. 315, 429 N.W.2d 781 (1987). *See also generally* Romuldo P. Eclavea, Annotation, *Admissibility of Confession or Other Statement Made by Defendant as Affected by Delay in Arraignment—Modern State Cases*, 28 A.L.R. 4TH 1121 (1984, updated February, 2003).

[50]  *See* cases *supra* note 49.

## § 6.6  Protection for the Fifth Amendment Privilege against Self-Incrimination during Police Interrogations: The *Miranda* Rule

In 1966, the Supreme Court handed down the most famous of all criminal justice decisions—*Miranda v. Arizona*.[51] The decision was based on the Fifth Amendment privilege against self-incrimination, which the Court extended to police custodial interrogations. After surveying police interrogation manuals recommending strategies designed to capitalize on the isolated surroundings of a custodial interrogation to break down and overcome resistance to confess, the Court concluded that station house interrogations were inherently coercive and that special procedures were needed to ensure that suspects in police custody are aware of their constitutional rights and that the police respect their decision to exercise them. The Court laid out the procedures that the police henceforth would be required to follow in order to obtain an admissible confession during a police custodial interrogation. The *Miranda* decision was so controversial and unpopular that Congress immediately took steps to overturn it by enacting a statute, 18 U.S.C. § 3501, requiring judges to admit unwarned confessions that were found to have been voluntarily given. This statute was ignored by police and prosecutors on the assumption that it was unconstitutional, an assumption that was later borne out.[52] Although many predicted that *Miranda* would make it impossible for the police to obtain legitimate confessions, this has not turned out to be the case. The police have managed to live comfortably with *Miranda* for almost 40 years.

Figure 6.7
**Statement of the *Miranda* Rule**

The *Miranda* rule is activated whenever police interrogate a suspect who is then in custody. To procure an admissible confession, police must:

1.  warn the suspect of his or her Fifth Amendment rights;
2.  secure a knowing, intelligent, and voluntary waiver before initiating questioning; and
3.  cease interrogation if the suspect anytime thereafter manifests a desire to remain silent or to consult with an attorney.

### A. *Overview of the* Miranda *Rule*

There are two aspects of the *Miranda* rule that police officers must commit to memory—*when it applies* and *what it requires*. *Miranda* procedural safeguards must be observed only when the police **interrogate** a suspect who is then in police **custody**. Prior to initiating a custodial interrogation, the officer must warn the suspect: (1) that he or she has the right to remain silent,

---

[51]  **384 U.S. 436, 86 S. Ct. 1602, 16 L. Ed. 2d 694 (1966).**
[52]  Dickerson v. United States, *supra* note 46.

(2) that anything he or she says can be used against him or her in a court of law, and (3) that he or she has the right to the presence of an attorney, and (4) that one will be appointed if he or she cannot afford one.[53] The officer must then make sure that the suspect understands these rights and determine whether he or she wishes to exercise them before proceeding with questioning.[54] Unless the prosecution can demonstrate that the required warnings were given and that the suspect made a voluntary and intelligent waiver of his or her *Miranda* rights, statements made during the custodial interrogation will be suppressed.[55]

## § 6.7 —Custodial Interrogation Defined

Two factors combine to determine when warnings are necessary. These factors are *custody* and *interrogation*. *Miranda* safeguards are necessary only when police interrogate a suspect who is then in custody. They are not required in any other situation.[56] For example, warnings do not have to be given to grand jury witnesses, even when they are the focus of the investigation, because grand jury proceedings do not have the coercive atmosphere of a police custodial interrogation.[57] Custodial interrogations are unique. Being questioned in police custody, with no one else around, brings into play feelings of fear, isolation, and vulnerability that place suspects at a psychological disadvantage, making it difficult for them to resist the pressure to confess. *Miranda* warnings were developed to neutralize the inherently coercive atmosphere of a police custodial interrogation.

### A. Custody Defined

Figure 6.8
**Definition of Custodial Interrogation**

---

*Miranda* safeguards must be observed whenever police interrogate a suspect who is then in custody.

1. *Custody* requires a formal arrest or a restraint of the suspect's freedom of action to the degree associated with a formal arrest.
2. An *interrogation* occurs when the police ask investigative questions or engage in other words or actions they should know are reasonably likely to elicit an incriminating response from the suspect.

---

[53] *Supra* note 51 at 467-474, 479, 86 S. Ct. at 1624-1628, 1630.

[54] *Id.*, at 475, 86 S. Ct. at 1628.

[55] Exclusion of the unwarned confession is a criminal defendant's sole remedy for *Miranda* violations. Failure to administer *Miranda* warnings does not furnish a basis for awarding damages in a civil action. Chavez v. Martinez, 538 U.S. 760, 123 S. Ct. 1994, 155 L. Ed. 2d 984 (2003) (plurality opinion).

[56] Minnesota v. Murphy, 465 U.S. 420, 104 S. Ct. 1136, 79 L. Ed. 2d 409 (1984) ("The mere fact that an investigation has focused on a suspect does not trigger the need for *Miranda* warnings in noncustodial settings. . . .").

[57] United States v. Washington, 431 U.S. 181, 97 S. Ct. 1814, 52 L. Ed. 2d 238 (1977); United States v. Mandujano, 425 U.S. 564, 96 S. Ct. 1768, 48 L. Ed. 2d 212 (1976); United States v. Wong, 431 U.S. 174, 97 S. Ct. 1823, 52 L. Ed. 2d 231 (1977).

A custodial interrogation has two components: *custody* and *interrogation*. When both are present, warnings are necessary whether the suspected offense is a felony or a misdemeanor.[58]

### 1. Objective Nature of the Inquiry

Custody requires either a formal arrest or a restraint of a suspect's freedom of action to the "degree associated with a formal arrest."[59] Courts use an objective test to decide whether the suspect's freedom of action was restrained to this degree. They examine the circumstances surrounding the encounter and ask how a reasonable person in the suspect's position would have perceived the situation.[60] A suspect is in custody whenever the objective circumstances of an encounter are such that a reasonable person would perceive the situation as tantamount to an arrest.[61] When the circumstances surrounding an interrogation have the coercive atmosphere of an arrest, *Miranda* safeguards are necessary.[62] The officer's intent to make or not to make an arrest has no bearing on this question unless it is communicated to the suspect, because, without communication, it has no influence on how a reasonable person would assess the situation.[63]

Questioning does not have to occur at the police station for a suspect to be in custody and the converse is also true.[64] Custody, for example, was not present in *Oregon v. Mathiason*,[65] where a suspect received a communication that the

---

[58]　Berkemer v. McCarty, 468 U.S. 420, 104 S. Ct. 3138, 82 L. Ed. 2d 317 (1984).

[59]　Thompson v. Keohane, 511 U.S. 318, 116 S. Ct. 457, 133 L. Ed. 2d 383 (1995); Stansbury v. California, 511 U.S. 318, 114 S. Ct. 1526, 128 L. Ed. 2d 293 (1994).

[60]　Stansbury v. California, *supra* note 59; Yarborough v. Alvarado, ___ U.S. ___, 124 S. Ct. 2140, 158 L. Ed. 2d 311 (2004) (whether a suspect is in custody for warning purposes calls for objective inquiry into how a reasonable person would have experienced the encounter; the suspect's individual characteristics, such as youthful age and lack of prior experience with the criminal justice system are not relevant).

[61]　*See* cases *supra* note 59.

[62]　Stansbury v. California, *supra* note 59. Students should not confuse the *Miranda* test for when a suspect is in "custody" with the Fourth Amendment test for when a suspect is "seized." "Seizure" and "custody" are not congruent concepts. The "free to leave" test is used to determine when a suspect is seized. A suspect is seized when a reasonable person under the circumstances of the encounter would believe that he or she is no longer free to leave. At this point, the suspect acquires Fourth Amendment protection. If the seizure was effected without reasonable suspicion, statements made during the encounter will be suppressed under the Fourth Amendment exclusionary rule. *See* § 6.3 *supra*. *Miranda* protection requires more than an objectively reasonable belief that one is not free to leave. A person is in custody for *Miranda* warning purposes only if the objective circumstances of the encounter are such that a reasonable person would experience the encounter as tantamount to an arrest. Accordingly, suspects can be seized in a Fourth Amendment sense without necessarily being in custody for *Miranda* purposes. This explains why suspects are generally not entitled to *Miranda* warnings during traffic stops and *Terry* stops. They are "seized," but they are not "in custody." Accordingly, warnings are not necessary. *See* § 6.7 (A)(3) *infra*.

[63]　Stansbury v. California, *supra* note 59.

[64]　*Id.*

[65]　429 U.S. 492, 97 S. Ct. 711, 50 L. Ed. 2d 714 (1977). *But see* United States v. LeBrun, 306 F.3d 545 (8th Cir. 2002) (suspect was in custody during police station interview, even though he was told that he was not under arrest, where police drove him there under a false pretense and interrogated him in a highly coercive way); United States v. Wauneka, 770 F.2d 1434 (9th Cir. 1985) (custody found where suspect was brought to station by police, questioning was accusatory, suspect was without transportation to leave, and officers never offered an opportunity to leave); Commonwealth v. Magee, 423 Mass. 381, 668 N.E.2d 339 (1996) (questioning was custodial for *Miranda* purposes even though suspect voluntarily came to police station on her own, where suspect was questioned in closed room at police station by three officers for more than seven hours and was never told she could leave).

police wanted to talk to him, he went to the police station on his own and, after being told that he was not under arrest and could leave at any time, confessed to a burglary and was allowed to leave without hindrance. The suspect was not in custody because his presence at the police station was at all times voluntary.

## 2. Custody Indicators

While there is no infallible checklist for when a suspect is in custody, a number of factors can contribute to the coercive atmosphere of an arrest, including:[66] (1) prolonged questioning; (2) isolated surroundings; (3) the threatening presence of several police officers; (4) weapon displays; (5) physical touching; (6) a hostile demeanor; (7) an intimidating tone of voice or language; (8) restrictions on movements, handcuffs, and other forms of restraint; and (9) making accusations.[67] This list is not exhaustive and all of the factors need not be present; they are mentioned simply as things to watch for. Deciding whether a suspect is in custody can be a tricky call.[68] In making this assessment, the officer should consider whether he or she would feel intimidated, vulnerable, and under pressure to answer if he or she was in the suspect's position. If the answer is "yes," *Miranda* warnings should be given. If the answer is "perhaps," *Miranda* warnings should also be given. It is better to give warnings when they are not required than to ignore them when they are necessary.

---

[66] For Supreme Court decisions finding questioning custodial, *see, e.g.*, New York v. Quarles, 467 U.S. 649, 104 S. Ct. 2626, 81 L. Ed. 2d 550 (1984) (suspect surrounded by four police officers and handcuffed); Orozco v. Texas, 394 U.S. 324, 89 S. Ct. 1095, 22 L. Ed. 2d 311 (1969) (suspect awakened in middle of the night by four police officers who entered his bedroom); Mathis v. United States, 391 U.S. 1, 88 S. Ct. 1503, 20 L. Ed. 2d 381 (1968) (suspect questioned while incarcerated in jail for unrelated offense). For Supreme Court decisions finding questioning noncustodial, *see, e.g.*, **Berkemer v. McCarty**, *supra* note 58 (motorist detained for routine traffic stop).

[67] For cases containing a good general discussion of factors bearing on "custody," *see, e.g.*, United States v. Kim, 292 F.3d 969 (9th Cir. 2002) (suspect was in custody for *Miranda* purposes where police, while executing search warrant, locked door to shop with her inside, deliberately isolating her from her husband, before conducting lengthy interrogation session); United States v. Johnson, 64 F.3d 1120, 1126 (8th Cir. 1995), *cert. denied*, 516 U.S. 1139, 116 S. Ct. 971, 133 L. Ed. 2d 891 (1996) (defendant was in custody for *Miranda* purposes where he was ordered out of his vehicle at gunpoint, handcuffed, placed in the back of a patrol car, and questioned by detectives); United States v. Smith, 3 F.3d 1088, 1097-1098 (7th Cir. 1993), *cert. denied*, 510 U.S. 1061, 114 S. Ct. 733, 126 L. Ed. 2d 696 (1994) (defendant was in custody for *Miranda* purposes where police stopped the cab in which defendant was riding and frisked and handcuffed him and surrounded him while he was questioned); State v. Rucker, 821 A.2d 439 (Md. 2003) (defendant was not "in custody" for *Miranda* purposes when he made incriminating statement during investigatory stop in public parking lot, detention was brief, no weapons were drawn, and defendant was not handcuffed or physically restrained until after he admitted having cocaine).

[68] Oregon v. Elstad, 470 U.S. 298, 105 S. Ct. 1285, 84 L. Ed. 2d 222 (1985).

### 3. Suspect's Awareness that He or She Is Speaking with a Police Officer

Custodial interrogation requires an awareness that the interrogator is a police officer because, without it, the interview lacks the coercive atmosphere that makes *Miranda* warnings necessary.[69] In *Illinois v. Perkins*,[70] a police undercover agent, posing as an inmate, was placed in a jail cell with a suspect who made incriminating statements, implicating himself in the crime the agent was investigating. The suspect asserted that his Fifth Amendment rights were violated because the undercover agent questioned him without reading him his rights. The Court ruled against him, holding that the *Miranda* rule "was not meant to protect suspects from boasting about their criminal activities in front of persons whom they believe to be their cellmate."[71]

### 4. Traffic Stops, *Terry* Stops, and the *Miranda* Rule

Have you ever been stopped for a traffic violation? If you have, did the officer administer *Miranda* warnings? Our bet is that the officer did not, because *Miranda* warnings need not be given during routine traffic stops. The Supreme Court has held that roadside questioning during routine traffic stops does not involve custody.[72] Go back and review the custody indicators on page 300. How many of these factors are generally present during the typical traffic stop? The answer is "None of them." Traffic stops occur on a public street, generally with other people around, there is no prolonged questioning, the period of detention is brief, and the police do not draw weapons or use handcuffs. In fact, motorists are generally treated courteously. Because the typical traffic stop lacks the atmosphere of an arrest, *Miranda* warnings are unnecessary.[73]

---

[69] Illinois v. Perkins, 496 U.S. 292, 110 S. Ct. 2394, 110 L. Ed. 2d 243 (1990) (*Miranda* warnings are not required when the defendant is unaware that his or her interrogator is a police officer).

[70] *Id.*

[71] In *Illinois v. Perkins*, the suspect had not yet been formally charged with the offense the undercover agent was investigating. The rules concerning undercover questioning by jailhouse plants change once formal charges are initiated and the suspect becomes an accused. Police may not approach an accused who has retained or requested appointment of counsel to discuss the pending charges unless his attorney is present. This limitation derives from the Sixth Amendment right to counsel, which attaches once formal charges are initiated. Sixth Amendment restrictions on police-initiated interrogations of persons under formal charges apply to surreptitious interrogations by police undercover agents. *See* § 6.9(B) *infra*.

[72] Berkemer v. McCarty, *supra* note 58 (holding that roadside questioning of a motorist detained for a routine traffic stop does not constitute a "custodial interrogation"). Traffic stops are discussed in Chapter 3, §§ 3.10-3.11.

[73] *See, e.g.*, Berkemer v. McCarty, *supra* note 58; United States v. Jones, 187 F.3d 210 (1st Cir. 1999) (*Terry* stop not custodial where it occurred on public highway, only one officer questioned each of the defendants, no physical restraints were used, the stop was brief, and the questions asked were few and specifically directed to the justification for making the stop); United States v. Burns, 37 F.3d 276 (7th Cir. 1994) (questioning noncustodial when suspect was detained for 10 minutes, without handcuffs or physical restraints, while two law enforcement officers searched premises). *Terry* stops are discussed in §§ 3.7-3.9.

The same is true for many *Terry* stops. The term "custody" does not include temporary detentions for investigation in which the officer asks a moderate number of questions to determine a person's identity and to obtain information confirming or dispelling the officer's suspicions.[74] Given the comparatively nonthreatening character and limited scope and duration of *Terry* stops, detainees are not in custody for *Miranda* purposes unless their freedom of action is curtailed in a significant way. Drawing weapons, using handcuffs, ordering detainees to lie face-down on the ground, and placing them in squad cars, while permitted during *Terry* stops when the situation warrants their use,[75] render a *Terry* detainee in custody and make *Miranda* safeguards necessary.[76] As one court tersely put it, "Police officers must make a choice—if they are going to take highly intrusive steps to protect themselves from danger, they must similarly provide protection to their suspects by advising them of their constitutional rights."[77]

## B. Interrogation Defined

Interrogation is the second component. *Miranda* procedural safeguards come into play only when a person in custody is subjected to an interrogation. Suspects sometimes blurt out incriminating statements before the police have time to Mirandize them. While being taken into custody, they may say things like "How did you find me so quickly?" "Did Joe blow the whistle on me?" or "Why are you arresting both of us when I did it?"[78] Spontaneous, unsolicited statements are not affected by the *Miranda* rule because they are not the product of an interrogation.[79]

---

[74] **Berkemer v. McCarty**, *supra* note 58.

[75] *See, e.g.*, United States. v. Perdue, 8 F.3d 1544 (10th Cir. 1993); United States v. Clemons, 201 F. Supp. 2d 142 (D.D.C. 2002).

[76] *See, e.g.*, United States v. Foster, 70 Fed. Appx. 415 (9th Cir. 2003) (Defendant was in custody during *Terry* stop, requiring suppression of his statements made in absence of *Miranda* warning where he was (1) stopped by a combined unit of four armed federal and local officers on a remote rural highway, (2) had three police and Border Patrol vehicles positioned in single file behind him; (3) was accused by the officers of engaging in the trafficking of illegal narcotics; (4) was informed that the officers had discovered a large quantity of illegal drugs nearby and that they believed he was in the area to pick it up; (4) had his driver's license and car registration seized; and (5) was pressured by the officers to be "honest" and to confess that the marijuana belonged to him); United States v. Perdue, 8 F.3d 1455 (10th Cir. 1993) (officers who draw weapons and force detainees to the ground while conducting *Terry* stop create a custodial situation in which *Miranda* warnings are required); United States v. Clemons, 201 F. Supp. 2d 142 (D.D.C. 2002) (*Terry* detainee was in custody for *Miranda* purposes when he was removed from vehicle, handcuffed, and forced to lie on the ground); State v. Morgan, 254 Wis. 2d 602, 648 N.W.2d 23 (2002) (*Terry* detainee was in custody for *Miranda* purposes where police drew weapons, four officers were present, suspect was frisked and handcuffed, and the questioning occurred while suspect was detained in squad car).

[77] United States v. Perdue, *supra* note 75.

[78] United States v. Crowder, 62 F.3d 782 (6th Cir. 1995); United States v. Montano, 613 F.2d 147 (6th Cir. 1980); United States v. Gonzalez, 954 F. Supp. 48 (D. Conn. 1997).

[79] *See, e.g.*, **Miranda v. Arizona**, *supra* note 51, 384 U.S. at 478, 86 S. Ct. at 1630; United States v. Hawkins, 102 F.3d 973 (8th Cir. 1996); United States v. Hayes, 120 F.3d 739 (8th Cir. 1997); United States v. Sherwood, 98 F.3d 402 (9th Cir. 1996). However, police must administer warnings before asking follow-up questions if the answers are likely to be incriminating. *See, e.g.*, State v. Walton, 41 S.W.3d 75 (Tenn. 2001).

The basic test for what constitutes an interrogation was established in *Rhode Island v. Innis.*[80] The term *interrogation* includes both express questioning and any other words or actions that police should know are reasonably likely to elicit an incriminating response from the suspect.[81]

### 1. Express Questioning

Interrogations usually take the form of express questions, but express questions do not invariably involve an interrogation. "Would you like to make a phone call?" is an example. To constitute an interrogation, the officer must have reason to expect that the question is likely to elicit an incriminating response from the suspect.[82] Small talk about matters unrelated to the investigation and questions asked for administrative purposes are not treated as interrogations. For example, if Officer Quizzard, while driving Mary Wanna to the police station during a heavy snowstorm, attempts to make small talk by saying, "What do you think about this weather?" and she replies "Terrible! You caught me with two kilos because I haven't made a sale for the last two days," her unwarned statement is admissible because it is not the product of an interrogation.[83] The same is true for routine booking questions covering matters such as name, address, height, weight, eye color, date of birth, age, and the like.[84] Routine booking questions may be asked without administering *Miranda* warnings because they are not designed to elicit an incriminating response.[85] However, questions like how much alcohol a person arrested for drunk driving has consumed are not booking questions.[86] Police may not ask investigative questions, even during the booking process, without administering *Miranda* warnings.

---

[80]   **446 U.S. 291, 100 S. Ct. 1682, 64 L. Ed. 2d 297 (1980)** ("[T]he term "interrogation" under *Miranda* refers not only to express questioning but also to any words or actions on the part of the police (other than those normally attendant to arrest and custody) that the police should know are reasonably likely to elicit an incriminating response from the suspect.").

[81]   **Pennsylvania v. Muniz, 496 U.S. 582, 601, 110 S. Ct. 2638, 2650, 110 L. Ed. 2d 528 (1990)**; Rhode Island v. Innis, *supra* note 80.

[82]   **Pennsylvania v. Muniz,** *supra* note 81; State v. Griffin, 814 A.2d 1003 (Me. 2003) ("Even in a custodial situation, an officer may, without giving *Miranda* warnings, ask questions designed to identify the suspect, check her identification and resolve any health or safety concerns regarding the suspect or others.").

[83]   *See, e.g.,* State v. Tucker, 81 Ohio St. 3d 431, 692 N.E.2d 171 (1998).

[84]   *See, e.g.,* **Pennsylvania v. Muniz,** *supra* note 81; Vasquez v. Filion, 210 F. Supp. 2d 194 (E.D.N.Y. 2002); Colon v. State, 568 S.E.2d 811 (Ga. Ct. App. 2002).

[85]   Pennsylvania v. Muniz, *supra* note 81.

[86]   State v. Chrisicos, 813 A.2d 513 (N.H. 2002) (booking officer's question how much alcohol defendant arrested for drunk driving had consumed was not routine booking question, but was instead designed to elicit incriminating statement).

## 2. Functional Equivalent of Express Questioning

The definition of interrogation also includes words or actions that are the "functional equivalent" of an express question. "Functional equivalent" covers maneuvers designed to trick suspects into confessing. The test for whether something is the "functional equivalent" of an express question is whether the police knew or should have known that their actions were reasonably likely to elicit an incriminating response from the suspect.[87] Any knowledge that police have about a suspect's unusual susceptibility to a particular form of persuasion is taken into consideration in deciding this.

In *Rhode Island v. Innis*,[88] two police officers, while transporting an armed robbery suspect to the police station, held a conversation between themselves concerning the missing shotgun. One of the officers mentioned to the other that there was a school for handicapped children near the vicinity of the robbery and said "God forbid one of the children should find the gun and hurt herself." The suspect, who was listening in the back seat, interrupted the conversation and told the officers to turn the squad car around and go back to the robbery scene so he could show them where the gun was located.

Were these officers engaged in the functional equivalent of express questioning? This depends on whether the officers should have anticipated that their actions were reasonably likely to elicit an incriminating response from the suspect. Had the officers known that the suspect was unusually susceptible to the theme of their conversation and staged this conversation to provoke an incriminating response, their actions would have constituted an interrogation. However, the Supreme Court did not read the facts this way. The Court viewed the conversation as "offhand remarks" between two police officers for which no response from the suspect was expected. Viewed this way, the police were not responsible for the suspect's unforeseen response.

However, the Supreme Court reached the opposite conclusion in a case in which the use of an identical strategy was deliberate. Police, knowing of the murder suspect's deep religious convictions, told him that the victim's missing body deserved a "Christian" burial. This statement prompted the suspect to tell the officers where the body was located.[89] The Supreme Court held that the statement was the product of a police interrogation.

Telling suspects who are in custody that they have been implicated by someone else, identified by eyewitnesses, or that their alibi was not confirmed are illustrations of actions that are functional equivalents of express question-

---

[87]  **Rhode Island v. Innis**, *supra* note 80.

[88]  *Id.*

[89]  Brewer v. Williams, 430 U.S. 387, 97 S. Ct. 1232, 51 L. Ed. 2d 424 (1977) (decided under the Sixth Amendment right to counsel).

ing.[90] Statements like these are intended to elicit incriminating responses. In one case, in which an elderly man who was severely beaten and stabbed died on the way to the hospital, police officers told the son, whom they suspected of murdering him, that his father had lived long enough to tell the police that he did it.[91] The son then admitted to the acts, explaining that he had performed them in a blacked-out state. "[I]t wasn't me, it was like another Marty Tankleff that killed them." The son's unwarned confession was certainly the product of an interrogation. The confession was, nevertheless, held to be admissible because one ingredient was missing. The missing ingredient was custody. The son had come to the police station voluntarily and was not in custody when he made the statement. Custody and interrogation are both necessary before *Miranda* warnings are required.

### 3. Public Safety Exception

Police officers may dispense with *Miranda* safeguards before interrogating a suspect in custody when they are confronted with an emergency that requires immediate action to protect the public safety or their own safety.[92] This is known as the "public safety" exception. The Supreme Court articulated the public safety exception in a case in which two police officers on patrol encountered a woman who stated that she had just been raped by a man with a gun, and that he had gone into a nearby grocery store. The police entered the store and saw a man fitting the suspect's description approaching the checkout counter. When the suspect saw the police, he dropped his items and fled into the aisles. After the suspect was apprehended and frisked, the police discovered an empty shoulder holster, and before warning the suspect of his *Miranda*

---

[90]  *See, e.g.*, Drury v. State, 368 Md. 331, 793 A.2d 567 (2002) (officers engaged in functional equivalent of an interrogation when they confronted suspect with physical evidence of the crime and told him that they were going to send the evidence to be examined for fingerprints); United States v. Orso, 266 F.3d 1030 (9th Cir. 2001) (suspect subjected to the functional equivalent of an interrogation when officer engaged in detailed discussion of the evidence and witnesses against the suspect and penalties for the crime of which she was suspected, going so far as to make up some of the evidence); United States v. Collins, 43 Fed. Appx. 99 (9th Cir. 2002) (defendant's statement "I've heard enough, you got me," in response to playing of incriminating audiotape was inadmissible because defendant was subjected to functional equivalent of an interrogation); United States v. Guerra, 237 F. Supp. 2d 795 (E.D. Mich. 2003) (*Miranda* violated where police told defendant that his accomplice had confessed and invited him to discuss the case after defendant had invoked his right to remain silent); State v. Brown, 592 So. 2d 308 (Fla. Dist. Ct. App. 1991) (confessions obtained in violation of *Miranda*, where, after defendant clearly invoked his rights, officer informed defendant that victim named him as suspect, that three witnesses placed him at scene of crime, that his girlfriend implicated him in burglary, and that he had been seen in possession of items stolen in burglary, causing defendant to state later that he wanted to tell "the truth" or "his side of the story.") *But see* White v. State, 374 Md. 232, 821 A.2d 459 (2003) (conduct of police in providing defendant with statement of charges, after he had invoked his *Miranda* rights, was not the functional equivalent of an interrogation where notification of the charges was a routine part of the booking process.).

[91]  Tankleff v. Senkowski, 993 F. Supp. 151 (E.D.N.Y. 1997).

[92]  New York v. Quarles, *supra* note 66.

rights, asked him where the gun was. The suspect pointed to some empty cartons and said "The gun is over there." The officers retrieved a loaded .38-caliber revolver from one of the cartons.

The suspect was later prosecuted for possession of a weapon and moved to suppress his unwarned statement and the weapon discovered as a result of it. The Supreme Court ruled that *Miranda* warnings may be delayed temporarily when police officers are confronted with an immediate need for answers to questions in a situation posing a threat to the public safety or to the officer's safety. The Court was careful to limit this exception in order to prevent abuse. Warnings may be delayed without violating the *Miranda* rule only when the officer's perception of danger is "objectively reasonable."[93] Further, police are restricted to asking questions necessary to address the immediate danger.[94] They may ask an unwarned suspect "Where is the gun?" but not "Who owns it?" "Where did you buy it?" or "Do you have a license for it?" Investigative questions such as these may not be asked until after *Miranda* warnings have been administered.

### 4. Non-Police Interrogators

Private detectives and security officers are not bound by the *Miranda* rule[95] because the rule is based on the Fifth Amendment and, like other portions of the Bill of Rights,[96] reaches only the actions of the government.[97] Although the *Miranda* rule applies only to government interrogators, the interrogator does not have to be a police officer. Government officials employed in other capacities are required to administer warnings when they conduct custodial interviews seeking information that could later be used against the person in a criminal prosecution.[98] Prison psychiatrists, for example, are required to

---

[93]    *Id.* at 659 n. 8, 104 S. Ct. at 2633 n. 8; **Benson v. State, 698 So. 2d 333 (Fla. Dist. Ct. App. 1997)** (warnings unnecessary when police need to ask questions to address what they reasonably believe is a life-threatening emergency); United States v. Reyes, 249 F. Supp. 2d 277 (S.D.N.Y. 2003) (asking suspect about to be searched about the possible presence of objects that could pose a danger to the officer comes within the public safety exception only when officer has some genuine, particularized reason for believing that dangerous, undetected objects might exist).

[94]    United States v. Simpson, 974 F.2d 845, 845 (7th Cir. 1992).

[95]    United States v. Garlock, 19 F.3d 441 (8th Cir. 1994); United States v. Antonelli, 434 F.2d 335 (2d Cir. 1970); United States v. Birnstihl, 441 F.2d 368 (9th Cir. 1971); United States v. Bolden, 461 F.2d 998 (8th Cir. 1972) (per curiam); United States v. Casteel, 476 F.2d 152 (10th Cir. 1973); Woods v. City of Tucson, 128 Ariz. 477, 626 P.2d 1109 (1981); State v. Brooks, 862 P.2d 57 (N.M. Ct. App. 1992).

[96]    *See, e.g.,* Burdeau v. McDowell, 256 U.S. 465, 475, 41 S. Ct. 574, 576, 65 L. Ed. 1048 (1921) (Fourth Amendment provides no protection against private searches).

[97]    *See* cases *supra* note 95.

[98]    *See, e.g.,* Mathis v. United States, *supra* note 66 (*Miranda* violated by IRS civil investigator's failure warn inmate before questioning him about matters that could lead to a criminal prosecution); Estelle v. Smith, 451 U.S. 454, 101 S. Ct. 1866, 68 L. Ed. 2d 359 (1981) (unwarned statement made to psychiatrist during court-ordered psychiatric evaluation inadmissible); State v. Bankes, 57 P.3d 284 (Wash. Ct. App. 2002) (same). *See also* 2 WAYNE R. LaFAVE ET AL., CRIMINAL PROCEDURE § 6.10(C), at 622-624 (2d ed. 1999) (custodial questioning by any government employee comes within *Miranda* whenever prosecution of the defendant being questioned is among the purposes, definite or contingent, for which the information is elicited; this is generally the case whenever the government questioner's duties include investigation or reporting of crimes).

administer *Miranda* warnings before eliciting information from prison inmates when the information is intended for use at the trial, but not when seeking information that will be used for diagnosis or treatment.[99]

Summarizing, the *Miranda* rule applies only during custodial interrogations. A custodial interrogation has two ingredients: custody and interrogation. Custody requires a formal arrest or a restraint of the suspect's liberty to the degree usually associated with a formal arrest. The latter is determined from the vantage point of a reasonable person in the suspect's shoes. An interrogation includes not only express questions, but any words or actions on the part of the police that they should know are reasonably likely to elicit an incriminating response from the suspect. Volunteered statements are not subject to *Miranda* warnings because they are not elicited through interrogation. To constitute an interrogation, the questions must be asked for the sake of eliciting an incriminating response; routine booking questions are not considered interrogations and, consequently, do not have to be preceded by warnings. Undercover questioning is also not covered by the *Miranda* rule because the suspect must be aware that he or she is speaking with a police officer in order for the interview to have the coercive atmosphere of a police custodial interrogation, which makes warnings necessary. Police officers may temporarily postpone giving *Miranda* warnings before interrogating a suspect when they are confronted with an emergency that requires immediate action to protect their own safety or the safety of the public.

## § 6.8 —Procedural Requirements for Custodial Interrogations: *Miranda* Warnings and Waivers

The *Miranda* warnings are the best-known aspect of this Supreme Court opinion, but they are only part of the steps necessary to obtain an admissible statement. *Miranda* established a complete set of rules that remain in effect throughout the interrogation.[100] These rules are summarized below.

Once *Miranda* warnings have been administered, the officer must give the suspect an opportunity to exercise his or her rights and must respect the suspect's decision to do so. Questioning may lawfully begin only if the suspect makes a knowing, intelligent, and voluntary waiver of *Miranda* rights. Despite an initial waiver, the suspect remains free to change his or her mind and stop the questioning at any time. If at any point during the interview the suspect

---

[99] Estelle v. Smith, *supra* note 98 (interrogation conducted by a court-appointed competency psychiatrist at the county jail implicates *Miranda* rights).

[100] In a recent case, four Justices on the Supreme Court took the position that the rules established in *Miranda* do not function as a direct restraint on the police, but operate instead purely as a limitation on the admissibility of evidence. According to them, the administration of *Miranda* warnings is optional and police do not have to give them unless they want to use the confession as evidence, but not if they want to use it for leads or other purposes. *See* Chavez v. Martinez, *supra* note 55. *See generally* Steven D. Clymer, *Are the Police Free to Disregard Miranda?* 112 YALE L.J. 447 (2002). Had a majority agreed, the *Miranda* rule would have all but passed into history.

expresses a desire to speak with an attorney, all questioning must cease and may not resume until counsel is available, unless the suspect—not the police—reopens the dialogue. If the suspect invokes the right to remain silent, questioning must also cease and may not resume unless the suspect reopens the dialogue. However, police may initiate questioning about an unrelated crime after a sufficient waiting period.

Violation of *Miranda* rules at any point in an interview will make statements obtained thereafter inadmissible. Consequently, police officers must be able to recognize when they may start questioning and when they must stop.

## A. *The Requirement to Warn the Suspect*

### 1. Required Content of *Miranda* Warnings

Anyone who regularly watches television or attends movies can probably recite from memory the *Miranda* warnings scripted by Chief Justice Warren:

> [You have] the right to remain silent, anything [you say] can and will be used against [you] in court. [You have] the right to consult with a lawyer and to have the lawyer with [you] during [questioning]. [If you are unable to afford] a lawyer, one will be appointed to represent [you].[101]

Four "warnings" or explanations are necessary. The suspect must be warned that:

1.  He or she has the right to remain silent;
2.  Anything he or she says can and will be used against him or her in a court of law;
3.  He or she has the right to have an attorney present during interrogation; and
4.  If he or she cannot afford an attorney, one will be appointed for him or her.[102]

Although police departments equip officers with *Miranda* script copies to carry with them and read at appropriate times, in the haste and confusion surrounding an arrest, they sometimes use their own wording. When this happens, a court must decide whether the officer's wording was legally sufficient. While departures from the Supreme Court's carefully scripted language are not fatal if the warnings given are adequate to advise the suspect of his or her rights,[103] deviations should be avoided because they engender needless controversy.

---

[101]  **Miranda v. Arizona**, *supra* note 51.

[102]  *Id.*

[103]  Duckworth v. Eagan, 492 U.S. 195, 109 S. Ct. 2875, 106 L. Ed. 2d 166 (1989); California v. Prysock, 453 U.S. 355, 101 S. Ct. 2806, 69 L. Ed. 2d 696 (1981) (per curiam).

## 2. Frequency of Warnings

*Miranda* warnings are required on three occasions. First, warnings are always necessary before interrogating a suspect for the first time. The prevailing practice is to administer the first set of warnings immediately after the arrest. The reason is that police officers sometimes inadvertently elicit incriminating statements without being aware that they are engaged in an interrogation. The notion of an interrogation is not limited to formal interrogation sessions. An officer is engaged in an interrogation, for *Miranda* purposes, any time the officer asks a question, even a casual one, that the officer should know is reasonably likely to elicit an incriminating response. Saying to Sticky-Fingered Sam, "You look familiar. Weren't you the guy I stopped on Primrose Avenue about two months ago for questioning in connection with a burglary?" constitutes an interrogation. Consequently, to avoid slip-ups, police should issue the first set of *Miranda* warnings immediately after the arrest. Second, *Miranda* warnings can lose their efficacy and grow stale with the passage of time. To avoid controversies about whether earlier warnings had grown stale, police should issue a fresh set of *Miranda* warnings each time they initiate a new interrogation. Finally, warnings should be given before resuming interrogation of a suspect who initiates dialogue with the police after invoking *Miranda* rights.[104]

## B. The Necessity of Waiver Before Continuing with Custodial Interrogation

In order for statements made during custodial interrogations to be admitted as evidence, the prosecution must prove that the accused made a knowing, voluntary, and intelligent waiver of his or her *Miranda* rights before giving the statement.[105] It is up to the police to make sure that this evidence is available. If a suspect, after being advised of his or her *Miranda* rights, indicates a willingness to talk, the police should ask him or her to sign a written "advice of rights and waiver" form similar to the one below.

---

[104] The rules concerning resumption of interrogation when the suspect seeks further communication with police after invoking *Miranda* rights are discussed below.

[105] Withrow v. Williams, 507 U.S. 680, 113 S. Ct. 1745, 127 L. Ed. 2d 407 (1993); North Carolina v. Butler, 441 U.S. 369, 99 S. Ct. 1755, 60 L. Ed. 2d 286 (1979); Tague v. Louisiana, 444 U.S. 469, 100 S. Ct. 652, 62 L. Ed. 2d 622 (1980).

Figure 6.9
**Advice of Rights and Waiver**

> Prior to any questioning, I was advised that I have the right to remain silent, that whatever I say can or will be used against me in a court of law, that I have a right to speak with a lawyer and have a lawyer present during questioning, and that, if I cannot afford a lawyer, one will be appointed for me. I was further advised that, even if I sign this waiver, I have the right to stop the interview and refuse to answer further questions or ask to speak with an attorney at any time I so desire. I fully understand my rights. I am willing to answer questions and make a statement. I do not wish to consult with a lawyer or to have a lawyer present.

While written waivers are not required, they are desirable because they aid the prosecution in proving that a confession was obtained properly. A suspect's oral statement that he or she understands his or her rights, does not wish to speak with a lawyer, and is willing to talk, while equally sufficient in a legal sense, is more difficult to prove.[106]

An explicit waiver of *Miranda* rights it is not always necessary. A waiver may sometimes be inferred from conduct. For example, a suspect's participation in answering questions, after being warned of his or her *Miranda* rights, and asked whether he or she understands them is generally sufficient to support the finding of a waiver.[107] However, this is as far as courts are willing to go in inferring a waiver from silence. Proof that the officer administered warnings and that the suspect thereafter answered questions is not enough to show that a suspect understood his or her rights and intended to forego them.[108] If there is any doubt about a suspect's understanding of his or her rights or willingness to waive them, police should clarify these matters before asking any questions.

## C. *Police Duties When a Suspect Invokes* Miranda *Rights after Waiving Them*

A suspect's waiver of *Miranda* rights is not a blanket authorization for police officers to continue an interrogation until they obtain all the information they need from the suspect. The suspect's waiver merely allows questioning to begin. However, the suspect remains free to change his or her mind at any time. If the suspect expresses a desire to invoke his or her right to remain silent or to speak with an attorney at any point in the interview, questioning must cease immediately.

---

[106] *See, e.g.*, United States v. Gaines, 295 F.3d 293, 298 (2d Cir. 2002) (declining to suppress defendant's statement, even though defendant did not sign form acknowledging that he received *Miranda* warnings, where arresting officer testified, *inter alia*, that he read warnings to defendant from a form and that defendant verbally acknowledged his understanding of each right).

[107] North Carolina v. Butler, *supra* note 105; United States v. Frankson, 83 F.3d 79 (4th Cir. 1996); United States v. Barahona, 990 F.2d 412 (8th Cir. 1993).

[108] Tague v. Louisiana, *supra* note 105.

However, once a suspect makes an initial waiver, the burden is on the suspect to make known to his interrogators that he has changed his mind and now wants to exercise his rights.[109] Accordingly, police are at liberty to continue questioning a suspect who has waived his or her *Miranda* rights until the suspect makes a clear request to speak with a lawyer[110] or to end further questioning.[111] Ambiguous or equivocal statements such as "maybe I should talk to a lawyer," do not constitute a sufficiently clear request for an attorney to obligate the police to stop questioning.[112] Although it is good practice to clarify whether a suspect who makes an ambiguous request wants to speak to an attorney, this is not necessary. Police may ignore an ambiguous request and continue interrogating.

## D. Resumption of Questioning After Miranda Rights Have Been Invoked

Once the suspect makes a clear request to speak with an attorney or to remain silent, the questioning must cease immediately.[113] If the police persist and the suspect gives in, a subsequent statement will not be admissible.[114] This restriction is designed to prevent police from badgering suspects into waiving their previously invoked *Miranda* rights.

---

[109] **Davis v. United States, 512 U.S. 452, 114 S. Ct. 2351, 129 L. Ed. 2d 362 (1994).**

[110] *Id.*

[111] Medina v. Singletary, 59 F.3d 1095, 1100 (11th Cir. 1995).

[112] **Davis v. United States,** *supra* note 109. The problem of what constitutes a sufficiently clear request for an attorney to require the police to stop questioning was raised in the prosecution of accused sniper Lee Boyd Malvo. Commonwealth v. Malvo, 2003 WL 21033418 (Va. Cir. Ct. 2003). The court ruled that Malvo's question, "Do I get to talk to my attorneys?" was not a sufficiently clear and unambiguous request for counsel to bar further questioning. *See also* Clark v. Murphy, 317 F.3d 1038 (9th Cir. 2003) ("I think I would like to talk to a lawyer" and "should I be telling you, or should I talk to an attorney?" not unambiguous requests for counsel); Sofar v. Cockrell, 300 F.3d 588 (5th Cir. 2002) (asking officer during interrogation whether he should get attorney, how he could get one, and how long it would take to have attorney appointed considered too ambiguous to constitute assertion of right, and thus did not preclude admission of incriminating statements made afterward); United States v. Mendoza-Cecelia, 963 F.2d 1467, 1472 (11th Cir. 1992 ) ("I don't know if I need a lawyer, maybe I should have one, but I don't know if it would do me any good at this point." treated as ambiguous request); Poyner v. Murray, 964 F.2d 1404, 1410 (4th Cir. 1992) ("Didn't you tell me I had the right to an attorney?" treated as ambiguous request); Lord v. Duckworth, 29 F.3d 1216, 1220 (7th Cir. 1994) ("I can't afford a lawyer, but is there any way I can get one?" treated as ambiguous request). *But see* Com. v. Barros, 779 N.E.2d 693 (Mass. App. Ct. 2002) ("I don't think I want to talk to you anymore without a lawyer" constitutes unambiguous assertion of right to counsel).

[113] Edwards v. Arizona, 451 U.S. 477, 101 S. Ct. 1880, 68 L. Ed. 2d 378 (1981).

[114] *Id.*

### 1. Resuming Questioning After a Suspect Has Invoked the Right to Counsel

After a suspect invokes the right to counsel, questioning may resume in only two instances—if the suspect reopens the dialogue or counsel is present.[115] This rule was announced in *Edwards v. Arizona*.[116] Edwards was questioned by the police until he said that he wanted an attorney. Questioning then ceased, but police came to the jail the following day and, after stating that they wanted to talk to Edwards and again informing of his *Miranda* rights, obtained a confession from him. The Supreme Court ruled that after a suspect expresses a desire to deal with the police only through counsel, no waiver of this right will be recognized during a police-initiated contact. Accordingly, police officers may not interrogate a suspect who has invoked the right to counsel without an attorney being present unless the suspect, without police prodding, reopens the dialogue.

To reopen the dialogue, the suspect must initiate further communications with the police in a manner that shows a willingness and desire to engage in a generalized discussion of the case. Breaking the silence with a statement like "What time is it?" or "May I have a drink of water?" does not indicate a desire to resume discussion of the crime and, consequently, does not authorize resumption of questioning. The clearest example of reopening the dialogue would be the case in which a suspect, who previously invoked the right to counsel, sends a message that he or she has changed his or her mind and now wants to tell his or her side of the story. However, this degree of clarity rarely exists and courts do not insist on it. Asking a question like "What is going to happen to me now?" after invoking the right to counsel, allows the police to explore whether the suspect wants to resume a generalized discussion of the crime.[117] However, in order to avoid misunderstandings, police officers must issue a fresh set of *Miranda* warnings. Only if the suspect willingly participates after manifesting a desire to resume the discussion and receiving fresh a fresh set of *Miranda* warnings will the suspect be considered to have reopened the dialogue.

### 2. Resuming Questioning After a Suspect Has Invoked the Right to Remain Silent

After a suspect has invoked the right to remain silent, questioning must also cease. Police may not initiate contact to question the suspect about the same offense after the right to remain silent has been invoked; the only way

---

[115] *Id.*

[116] *Id.*

[117] Oregon v. Bradshaw, 462 U.S. 1039, 103 S. Ct. 2830, 77 L. Ed. 2d 405 (1983) (plurality opinion); Clayton v. Gibson, 199 F.3d 1162 (10th Cir. 1999) ("I have something I want to get off my chest" sufficient to reopen dialogue); Vann v. Small, 187 F.3d 650 (9th 1999) ("What is going to happen to me? What do you think I should do?" authorizes police to explore whether suspect wants to reopen dialogue); United States v. Michaud, 268 F.3d 728 (9th Cir. 2001) (Police were justified in inquiring whether defendant wished to re-open dialogue where county detective informed police that defendant's cellmate had told him, in the defendant's presence, that defendant wanted to speak to someone "about a murder.").

questioning may resume is if the suspect reopens the dialogue. Police, never-theless, may contact the suspect for questioning about an unrelated offense after waiting a sufficient period of time.[118] This option does not exist after a suspect has invoked the right to counsel. Once a suspect expresses a desire to deal with police only through counsel, the police may not question the suspect, even about an unrelated offense, during a police-initiated contact, until coun-sel is present.[119]

To summarize, *Miranda* warnings should be given each time a suspect is subjected to a custodial interrogation. Questioning may not begin unless the suspect makes a knowing, voluntary, and intelligent waiver of his or her *Miranda* rights. Ideally, the waiver should be in writing, but a suspect's express oral statement to this effect will also suffice. In certain situations, courts will infer an intent to waive *Miranda* rights from a suspect's conduct, but to avoid a misunderstanding, the officer should clarify whether the suspect wants to speak with an attorney or wants to remain silent before initiating questioning. Once *Miranda* rights have been waived, officers may begin questioning and may continue questioning unless or until the suspect makes a clear request for an attorney or expresses a clear desire to end the questioning. If the suspect, either before or during questioning, makes a clear request for an attorney, questioning must stop immediately and may not resume unless the suspect renews the dialogue or counsel is present. Questioning must also stop any time the suspect invokes his or her right to remain silent. The suspect may not be questioned about the same offense after invoking the right to remain silent unless the suspect initiates further discussion. However, the police may initi-ate questioning about an unrelated offense, after waiting a sufficient period.

## § 6.9 The Sixth Amendment Right to Counsel during Interrogations Conducted After the Commencement of Adversary Judicial Proceedings

The Sixth Amendment provides that "[i]n all criminal prosecutions, the *accused* shall enjoy the right . . . to have the assistance of counsel for his defense." Upon the lodging of formal charges, the suspect officially becomes an "accused" and the case enters the third phase. The system has now become fully adversarial and restrictions on engaging the accused at a time when coun-sel is not present tighten. Figure 6.10 summarizes the restrictions that go into effect when the case enters the third phase.

---

[118] Michigan v. Mosley, 423 U.S. 96, 96 S. Ct. 321, 46 L. Ed. 2d 313 (1975).
[119] Edwards v. Arizona, *supra* note 113; Arizona v. Robertson, 486 U.S. 675, 108 S. Ct. 2093, 100 L. Ed. 2d 704 (1988).

Figure 6.10
**Sixth Amendment Restrictions on Police Questioning**

- The Sixth Amendment right to counsel attaches simultaneously with the initiation of adversary criminal proceedings.
- After adversary criminal proceedings are initiated, the police are precluded from attempting to elicit incriminating statements concerning the charges at a time when counsel is not present unless the defendant gives a valid waiver of the right to counsel.
- This restriction applies only when the defendant is questioned about the charges. It does not apply when the questions relate to other uncharged criminal activity.
- A criminal defendant who has not yet retained or requested counsel may give a valid waiver. Administration of *Miranda* warnings is sufficient to support a waiver of the Sixth Amendment right to counsel.
- A defendant who has previously retained or requested appointment of counsel is incapable of giving a valid waiver in a contact that the police initiate.

## A. *Attachment of the Sixth Amendment Right to Counsel*

The Sixth Amendment right to counsel attaches when adversary judicial proceedings are commenced.[120] This generally occurs at the earliest of any of the following four events: (1) an **arraignment** (i.e., the defendant's first appearance before a committing magistrate); (2) a **grand jury indictment**; (3) an **information** (i.e., a formal complaint filed by a prosecutor); or (4) a **preliminary hearing** (i.e., a hearing at which the judge finds that there is enough evidence to bind the accused for trial).[121] Criminal prosecutions are not commenced by issuance of an arrest warrant[122] or the making of an arrest.[123] Although police have the authority to conduct investigations and make arrests, only judges, prosecutors, and grand juries can initiate a criminal prosecution.

The most common way criminal prosecutions are initiated is at arraignments and preliminary hearings held after the police make an arrest. However, other sequences are possible. The prosecutor, for example, can convene a grand jury and seek an indictment without waiting for the police. If an indictment is returned, the judge will issue a warrant for the accused's arrest. When a prosecution is initiated in this manner, the Sixth Amendment right to counsel will already have attached at the time of arrest and there will be no *Miranda* phase.

---

[120] *See, e.g.*, Moran v. Burbine, 475 U.S. 412, 106 S. Ct. 1135, 89 L. Ed. 2d 410 (1986) (The Sixth Amendment, "[b]y its very terms . . . becomes applicable only when the government's role shifts from investigation to accusation. For it is only then that the assistance of one versed in the 'intricacies . . . of law' is needed to assure that the prosecution's case encounters 'the crucible of meaningful adversarial testing.'"); Kirby v. Illinois, 406 U.S. 682, 92 S. Ct. 1877, 32 L. Ed. 2d 411 (1972) (The right to counsel attaches only when "the government has committed itself to prosecute, [for it is] only then that the adverse positions of government and defendant have solidified.").

[121] *See* cases note 120 *supra*.

[122] *See, e.g.*, United States v. D'Anjou, 16 F.3d 604, 608 (4th Cir.), *cert. denied*, 512 U.S. 1242, 114 S. Ct. 2754, 129 L. Ed. 2d 871 (1994).

[123] *See, e.g.*, United States v. Langley, 848 F.2d 152, 153 (11th Cir. 1988).

## B. Policy Behind Sixth Amendment Restrictions on Questioning

Once formal charges are filed, the Sixth Amendment entitles the defendant to the assistance and presence of counsel whenever the police deliberately attempt to elicit incriminating information about the charges. The purpose of this restriction is to prevent the police from undermining the ability of defense counsel to mount an effective defense. After a defendant confesses, mounting an effective defense is no longer possible. The best counsel can do is to try to work out a plea bargain. Consequently, after formal charges are filed, the Sixth Amendment makes it difficult for the police to elicit an admissible confession at a time when counsel is not present.

## C. The Deliberate Elicitation Standard

The restrictions imposed by the Sixth Amendment right to counsel on police questioning can be summarized in one sentence. After a formal accusation has been made—and a person who had previously been just a "suspect" has become an "accused," police are forbidden to *deliberately elicit* incriminating statements pertaining to the charges at a time when counsel is not present unless the defendant gives a valid waiver.[124]

The Sixth Amendment right to counsel has a broader application than the *Miranda* rule. The *Miranda* rule applies only during custodial interrogations.[125] The Supreme Court has explicitly declined to read the custodial interrogation standard into the Sixth Amendment.[126] The standard used in Sixth Amendment cases is *deliberate elicitation*.[127] Protection of the Sixth Amendment right to counsel is triggered whenever the government deliberately

---

[124] *See, e.g.*, Fellers v. United States, 540 U.S. 519, 124 S. Ct. 1019, 157 L. Ed. 2d 1016 (2004) ("An accused is denied the basic protections of the Sixth Amendment 'when there [is] used against him at his trial evidence of his own incriminating words, which federal agents . . . deliberately elicited from him after he had been indicted and in the absence of his counsel.'"); Michigan v. Jackson, cited below (Police violate a defendant's Sixth Amendment right to counsel when they "deliberately elicit information from [from him] following indictment under circumstances where counsel is absent and the right to counsel is not waived."); **Kuhlmann v. Wilson, 477 U.S. 436, 106 S. Ct. 2616, 91 L. Ed. 2d 364 (1986)** ("[O]nce a defendant's Sixth Amendment right to counsel has attached, he is denied that right when federal agents 'deliberately elicit' incriminating statements from him in the absence of his lawyer."); **Michigan v. Jackson, 475 U.S. 625, 106 S. Ct. 1404, 89 L. Ed. 2d 631 (1986)** (The arraignment signals "the initiation of adversary judicial proceedings" and thus the attachment of the Sixth Amendment; thereafter, government efforts to elicit information from the accused, including interrogation, represent "critical stages" at which the Sixth Amendment applies.").

[125] *See* § 6.7 *supra*.

[126] *See, e.g.*, Fellers v. United States, *supra* note 124 (noting that "we have expressly distinguished [the deliberate elicitation] standard from the Fifth Amendment custodial-interrogation standard]; **Michigan v. Jackson**, *supra* note 124 (noting that "the Sixth Amendment provides a right to counsel . . . even when there is no interrogation and no Fifth Amendment applicability"); **Rhode Island v. Innis**, *supra* note 80 (stating that "[t]he definitions of 'interrogation' under the Fifth and Sixth Amendments, if indeed the term 'interrogation' is even apt in the Sixth Amendment context, are not necessarily interchangeable").

[127] *See* authorities *supra* note 124.

attempts to elicit incriminating information pertaining to the charges, whether the defendant is in custody, the questioning constitutes an interrogation, or the defendant even knows that the questioner is a police officer.[128]

The deliberate elicitation standard was first announced in *Massiah v. United States*.[129] Massiah and a co-defendant were indicted, one of the events that initiates a criminal prosecution. After the indictment, the co-defendant consented to become a government informant and permitted federal agents to install a listening device in his car. He later engaged Massiah in a lengthy conversation that was secretly recorded and used against Massiah at his trial. The Supreme Court held that Massiah was denied the basic protections of the Sixth Amendment when, after his indictment, the government deliberately elicited incriminating statements from him in the absence of counsel. This has come to be known as the *Massiah* rule. The *Massiah* rule is violated whenever, after formal charges are lodged, the police deliberately elicit incriminating statements from a defendant at a time when counsel is not present, whether their approach is direct or indirect through police undercover agents and paid informants.

Active elicitation or prompting is necessary to violate the deliberate elicitation standard. No violation was found in a case in which the police planted an inmate-informant in the defendant's cell for the purpose of learning the identity of his accomplices.[130] The informant was instructed to "keep his ears open" for names, but not to ask any questions. He did as instructed and, in the course of time, the defendant made incriminating statements that were introduced into evidence. The Supreme Court held that the Sixth Amendment right to counsel is not violated by placing a government informant in close proximity to a criminal defendant if the informant takes no action deliberately designed to elicit incriminating information, and merely served as a willing listener.

Restrictions on undercover questioning go into effect only after formal charges are lodged. Police are free to elicit confessions using undercover agents and informants during the *Miranda* (Fifth Amendment) phase because there is no custodial interrogation unless the suspect is aware that the questioner is a police officer. In *Illinois v. Perkins*,[131] the police planted an undercover police officer in the jail cell of a man who was suspected of murder, but had not yet been charged with this crime. The officer posed as a fellow inmate and engaged him in a conversation in which he gave a detailed description of the murder. The suspect sought suppression, claiming that his *Miranda* rights were violated when an undercover police officer questioned him without read-

---

[128] *See, e.g.,* Fellers v. United States, *supra* note 124 (officers violated Sixth Amendment by deliberately eliciting information from defendant during post-indictment visit to his home absent counsel or waiver of counsel, regardless of whether officers' conduct constituted an "interrogation"); United States v. Henry, 447 U.S. 264, 100 S. Ct. 2183, 65 L. Ed. 2d 115 (1980) (defendant's Sixth Amendment right to counsel was violated when paid informant, planted in a cellblock with him, "deliberately elicited" incriminating statements concerning the pending charges, even the defendant was unaware that the questioner was a police informant).

[129] 377 U.S. 201, 84 S. Ct. 1199, 12 L. Ed. 2d 246 (1964) (Sixth Amendment right to counsel was violated when informant working for police elicited incriminating statements subsequent to indictment).

[130] Kuhlmann v. Wilson, 477 U.S. 436, 106 S. Ct. 2616, 91 L. Ed. 2d 364 (1986).

[131] *Supra* note 69.

ing him his *Miranda* rights. The Supreme Court held that *Miranda* warnings were not required because a cellblock conversation between a suspect and a person whom he believes to be fellow inmate lacks the coercive atmosphere of a police custodial interrogation. A suspect must be aware that he is speaking with a police officer for questioning to come within the *Miranda* rule.

### D. *Offense-Specific Nature of the Sixth Amendment Right to Counsel*

The Sixth Amendment right to counsel is offense-specific, meaning that it applies only when police question a defendant under formal charges about *that* offense.[132] It does not apply when their questions relate to uncharged criminal activity.[133] The Supreme Court explained that the police have the right, if not the responsibility, to investigate unsolved crimes and that to restrict the police when they question a suspect about one crime simply because he or she is under formal charges for another "would unnecessarily frustrate the public's interest in the investigation of criminal activities. . . ." Consequently, when the police question a suspect under formal charges about uncharged criminal activity, the Sixth Amendment right to counsel has no application.[134]

In *Texas v. Cobb,*[135] the Supreme Court was asked to carve out an exception for crimes that are closely related factually. The police received a report that a home was burglarized and that a woman and child who occupied the home were missing. Acting on an anonymous tip that Cobb who lived across the street was involved in the burglary, the police questioned him about the events. Cobb gave a written confession to the burglary, but denied knowledge of the disappearances. He was subsequently indicted for the burglary and an attorney was appointed to represent him. While he was out on bail, Cobb admitted to his father that he had killed the missing woman and child and his father contacted the police. Cobb was arrested, taken into custody, given *Miranda* warnings, and confessed to the murders. He later sought suppression, claiming that the police violated his Sixth Amendment right to counsel. His theory was that when the Sixth Amendment right to counsel attaches, it attaches not only for the charged offense (i.e., the burglary), but also for other uncharged offenses that are "closely related factually" (i.e., the murders). The Supreme Court found this argument unpersuasive and reaffirmed that when a person under formal charges for one offense is questioned about a separate uncharged offense, the Sixth Amendment right to counsel has no application.

---

[132]    McNeil v. Wisconsin, 501 U.S. 171, 111 S. Ct. 2204, 115 L. Ed. 2d 158 (1991); Texas v. Cobb, 532 U.S. 162, 121 S. Ct. 1335, 149 L. Ed. 2d 321 (2001) (same).

[133]    *See* cases *supra* note 132.

[134]    *Id.* The *Miranda* rule will, nevertheless, apply if the suspect is questioned about uncharged criminal activity while in jail awaiting trial on other charges. *See, e.g.,* Mathis v. United States, *supra* note 66 (*Miranda* rule applies when police question a suspect about a crime that he has not yet been charged with while he is incarcerated in jail awaiting trial for different crime).

[135]    *Supra* note 132.

Because Cobb had not yet been charged with the murders when he confessed to them, his only right was the right to *Miranda* warnings, and he received them. His confession was, therefore, admissible as evidence.

### E. *Waiver of the Sixth Amendment Right to Counsel*

The Sixth Amendment right to counsel does not bar questioning in the absence of counsel if the defendant waives this right. However, the police have only a limited window of opportunity to obtain a valid waiver, because once an accused retains counsel or requests the appointment of counsel, which generally occurs at the arraignment, the accused is incapable of giving a valid waiver during a police-initiated contact. The Supreme Court announced this rule in *Michigan v. Jackson.*[136] Jackson requested appointment of counsel at his arraignment, but before he had an opportunity to consult with his attorney, the police contacted him and advised him of his *Miranda* rights. He waived his rights and gave a confession. The Supreme Court held that Jackson's waiver was invalid because he had previously requested appointment of counsel at his arraignment. Once a defendant requests appointment of counsel or retains counsel, the police are incapable of obtaining a valid waiver of the Sixth Amendment right to counsel from the defendant during a contact that they initiate.[137] The inability of defendants who have previously invoked their Sixth Amendment right to counsel to waive it and give an admissible statement during a contact that the police initiate is designed to protect them from being overreached.

However, defendants are capable of giving a valid waiver before they have invoked the right to counsel (i.e., retained or requested counsel) and, even afterward, during a contact that they initiate.[138] If Sticky-Fingered Sam, after being indicted for burglary and retaining an attorney, presents himself at the police station and announces that he has come to confess, police may take his statement after advising him of his *Miranda* rights. Because *Miranda* warnings inform the defendant of his right to counsel, the Supreme Court has held that a valid *Miranda* waiver will also validly waive the Sixth Amendment right to counsel.[139]

Because the Sixth Amendment right to counsel and the *Miranda* (Fifth Amendment) right to counsel both require suppression of incriminating statements obtained at a time when counsel is not present unless the person gives a valid waiver of the right to counsel, it is easy to confuse them. There are, to be sure, similarities, but the differences are more pronounced. Figure 6.11 highlights the key differences.

---

[136]  *Supra* note 125.

[137]  *Id.*

[138]  Patterson v. Illinois, 487 U.S. 285, 108 S. Ct. 2389, 101 L. Ed. 2d 261 (1988) (rejecting argument that police are completely barred from initiating investigative encounters outside counsel's presence after adversary judicial proceedings are commenced).

[139]  *Id.*

Figure 6.11
**Differences between the Sixth Amendment Right to Counsel
and the *Miranda* (Fifth Amendment) Right**

- The *Miranda* right to counsel applies before formal charges are lodged, the Sixth Amendment right to counsel afterward.
- The *Miranda* right to counsel is available only during custodial interrogations. The Sixth Amendment right to counsel applies whenever the police deliberately elicit incriminating information concerning pending criminal charges, whether the defendant is in custody or even aware that the questioner is a police officer.
- The Sixth Amendment right to counsel is offense-specific; it applies only when a defendant under formal charges is questioned about *that* offense. The *Miranda* rule is not offense-specific; it applies whenever a suspect in custody is interrogated about *any* uncharged criminal activity, not just the crime for which the arrest was made.
- Both rights to counsel may be waived and the procedures for obtaining a valid waiver are the same. However, a valid waiver of the Sixth Amendment right to counsel cannot be given during a police-initiated interrogation if the defendant has already retained counsel or requested the court to appoint counsel.

To summarize, the Sixth Amendment right to counsel attaches (becomes operative) once formal charges are filed. Attachment of the Sixth Amendment right to counsel brings heightened restrictions on police questioning. However, the heightened restrictions apply only when questioning concerns the charges. Once adversary judicial proceedings are commenced, the Sixth Amendment entitles the defendant to the presence and assistance of counsel whenever the government deliberately elicits incriminating information about the charges, whether the defendant is in custody or even knows that the questioner is a police officer. Like *Miranda* rights, the Sixth Amendment right to counsel can be waived. However, a defendant is incapable of giving a valid waiver of the Sixth Amendment right to counsel during a police-initiated investigative encounter after the defendant has retained counsel or requested the court to appoint counsel.

## § 6.10 Use of Inadmissible Confession for Impeachment

Confessions must be freely and voluntarily given, not caused by a violation of the accused's Fourth Amendment rights, and not obtained in violation of the *Miranda* rule or the Sixth Amendment right to counsel in order to be admissible as evidence of guilt. However, confessions that fail these requirements are not entirely useless. They can be used for a limited purpose—impeachment.[140]

---

[140] Harris v. New York, 401 U.S. 222, 91 S. Ct. 643, 28 L. Ed. 2d 1 (1971) (holding that voluntary, unwarned statements, though inadmissible as evidence of guilt, may be used to impeach a defendant's inconsistent trial testimony); Michigan v. Harvey, 494 U.S. 344, 110 S. Ct. 1176, 108 L. Ed. 2d 293 (1990) (holding that voluntary statements obtained in violation of the Sixth Amendment right to counsel may be used for impeachment).

Impeachment involves an attack on a witness's credibility. One way to attack a witness's credibility is to show that the witness previously made statements that are inconsistent with his or her trial testimony. If the accused takes the witness stand and tells the jurors a story different from the one he or she previously told the police, the prosecution may, during cross-examination, use an inadmissible confession as impeachment evidence. In *Walder v. United States*,[141] the Supreme Court explained that "it is one thing to say that the Government cannot make an affirmative use of evidence unlawfully obtained. It is quite another to say that the defendant can turn the illegal method by which evidence in the Government's possession was obtained to his own advantage, and provide himself with a shield against contradiction of his untruths."[142] However, even this use is prohibited if the confession was not voluntary.[143] Involuntary confessions are considered too unreliable to be used for any purpose, including impeachment.

Figure 6.12
**Impeachment Use of Inadmissible Confessions**

---

An inadmissible confession may be used for impeachment only if:

1. the defendant takes the stand and testifies in his or her own behalf.
2. he or she tells the jurors a story different from the one he or she told the police, and
3. the confession was freely and voluntarily given.

When a confession is admitted for impeachment purposes, the jurors may consider it for the sake of evaluating the trustworthiness of the defendant's trial testimony, but not as evidence of guilt.

---

When a confession has been contaminated so that it can be used only for impeachment, its benefits are greatly reduced. A confession can be the most powerful piece of evidence that is put before a jury. When a confession is introduced as substantive evidence of guilt, the impact on the defense is devastating. However, only an admissible confession (i.e., one obtained in conformity with the requirements discussed in this chapter) may be introduced as evidence of guilt. The prosecution's potential gains from a contaminated confession are meager by comparison. First, it is the defense, not the prosecution, that controls whether an inadmissible confession can be introduced as impeachment evidence. The defense can thwart impeachment use by having the accused not testify, a right the accused enjoys under the Fifth Amendment. This generally happens in cases in which an accused has previously given an inadmissible confession because the accused now has little to gain and much to lose by testifying. Second, even if the accused takes the witness stand and tells the jurors a different story from the one he or she told the police, when a

---

[141] 347 U.S. 62, 74 S. Ct. 354, 98 L. Ed. 503 (1954).
[142] *Id.* 347 U.S. at 65, 74 S. Ct. at 356.
[143] Harris v. New York, *supra* note 140; Michigan v. Harvey, *supra* note 140.

confession is used on cross-examination as impeachment evidence, the jurors may consider it for only one purpose—to evaluate whether the accused's trial testimony is trustworthy. The jurors will be instructed that they may not consider the confession as evidence of guilt.

## § 6.11　Restrictions on the Use of Derivative Evidence

Statements given in response to an interrogation are often instrumental in uncovering other evidence. The suspect, for example, may tell the police the location of physical evidence, such as the murder weapon or drugs, or identify potential prosecution witnesses. The initial statement may also prompt the suspect to give a subsequent statement in which further damaging disclosures are made. Evidence that derives from a confession is called "derivative evidence." Derivative evidence is generally treated the same as the confession. When a confession is obtained in compliance with all applicable legal requirements, the evidence is admissible. On the other hand, when a confession is tainted by illegal police practices, the taint generally carries over and destroys the admissibility of derivative evidence.[144]

The rule requiring suppression of derivative evidence is known as the "fruit of the poisonous tree" doctrine. The fruit of the poisonous tree doctrine was developed to destroy the incentive for police to violate the Constitution by taking away all gains.[145] Suppose Sticky-Fingered Sam is arrested on burglary charges and taken to the police station, where he is deprived of food and sleep for two days until he finally confesses. Sam admits to the crime, tells the police where he hid the stolen property, and names Joe as his accomplice. Several hours later, Sam, believing his goose is cooked, gives a second confession, this time in writing. The police locate the stolen property where Sam said it was hidden, prevail on Joe to testify, and offer the stolen property, Joe's testimony, and Sam's second confession into evidence. None of it can be used because it was discovered through a violation of the due process free and voluntary requirement.[146] Allowing police to benefit from coercive interrogation practices would operate as an incentive to continue them. Consequently, when police use coercion to obtain a confession, courts will invoke the poisonous tree doctrine and suppress the fruits along with the confession.[147] The same

---

[144]　Nardone v. United States, 308 U.S. 338, 60 S. Ct. 2663, 84 L. Ed. 307 (1939); Wong Sun v. United States, *supra* note 24. *See also generally*, Yale Kamisar, *On the "Fruits" of Miranda Violations, Coerced Confessions, and Compelled Testimony*, 93 MICH. L. REV. 929 (1995).

[145]　*See* authorities *supra* note 144.

[146]　*See, e.g.*, Clewis v. Texas, 386 U.S. 707, 87 S. Ct. 1338, 18 L. Ed. 2d 423 (1967).

[147]　*Id.*

generally also holds true for the fruits of confessions obtained in violation of the Fourth Amendment search and seizure clause[148] and the Sixth Amendment right to counsel.[149]

Figure 6.13
**Restrictions on Admission of Derivative Evidence**

1.   Violations of the due process free and voluntary requirement, the Fourth Amendment search and seizure clause, and the Sixth Amendment right to counsel require suppression of derivative evidence.
2.   *Miranda* warning violations do not require suppression of derivative evidence, if the confession is voluntarily given and the violation is not deliberate.

However, the Supreme Court does not consider *Miranda* warning violations to be as serious as other violations. The prosecution is barred from introducing the unwarned statement in its case-in-chief, but not from using derivative evidence discovered as a result of the statement.[150] This position has been justified on the grounds that noncoercive *Miranda* violations do not violate a suspect's Fifth Amendment privilege against self-incrimination, but only prophylactic measures laid down to safeguard the privilege.[151]

This does not mean that police can deliberately violate a suspect's *Miranda* rights for the purpose of obtaining derivative evidence.[152] In *Missouri v. Seibert*,[153] Seibert was arrested for starting a fire that killed a mentally ill teenager staying in her home. She was questioned at the police station, without *Miranda* warnings, for 30 to 40 minutes until she confessed. The officer

---

[148]   *See, e.g.*, Wong Sun v. United States, *supra* note 24 (physical evidence derived from confession procured in violation of suspect's Fourth Amendment rights inadmissible); Brown v. Illinois, *supra* note 25 (subsequent confession suppressed where police violation of suspect's Fourth Amendment rights caused suspect's initial confession).

[149]   *See, e.g.*, Brewer v. Williams, *supra* note 89; Nix v. Williams, *supra* note 8; United States v. Wade, 388 U.S. 218, 87 S. Ct. 1926, 18 L. Ed. 2d 1149 (1967) (same); United States v. Johnson, 196 F. Supp. 2d 795 (N.D. Iowa 2002).

[150]   *See, e.g.*, United States v. Patane, ___ U.S. ___, 124 S. Ct. 2620, ___ L. Ed. 2d ___ (2004) (admitting physical evidence, the existence and location of which were divulged during an unwarned interrogation); Michigan v. Tucker, 417 U.S. 433, 94 S. Ct. 2357, 41 L. Ed. 2d 182 (1990) (admitting testimony of witness whose identity was discovered as a result of an unwarned custodial interrogation); Oregon v. Elstad, *supra* note 68 (admitting a warned confession given at the police station that followed an earlier unwarned confession given at the scene of the arrest). *But see* **Missouri v. Seibert**, ___ **U.S.** ___, **124 S. Ct. 2601**, ___ **L. Ed. 2d** ___ **(2004)** (deliberately interrogating a suspect about the same matters twice, the first time without *Miranda* warnings and the second time after warnings are administered as part of a calculated strategy to undermine the exercise of *Miranda* rights requires suppression of both confessions).

[151]   *See, e.g.*, Oregon v. Elstad, *supra* note 68; Michigan v. Tucker. *supra* note 150; Dickerson v. United States, *supra* note 46.

[152]   **Missouri v. Seibert**, *supra* note 150; United States v. Faulkingham, 295 F.3d 85 (1st Cir. 2002) (expressing view that suppression is required when police deliberately fail to give *Miranda* warnings in the hopes of obtaining admissible derivative or impeachment evidence or leads). *See also generally*, Charles D. Weisselberg, *Deterring Police From Deliberately Violating Miranda: In The Stationhouse After Dickerson*, 99 MICH. L. REV. 1121 (2001).

[153]   *Supra* note 150.

then administered warnings, obtained a written waiver, turned on the tape recorder, and had her repeat the confession. He testified, with unusual honesty, at the suppression hearing that he made a conscious decision to question first without warnings and that this was an interrogation technique that he had been taught. The Supreme Court suppressed the warned statement, declining to follow a prior holding that voluntary warned statements are not rendered inadmissible because they constitute the fruits of an earlier unwarned statement.[154] The case that had applied this rule involved a good faith failure to administer warnings, not a manipulative failure, as here. The deliberate failure to give *Miranda* warnings until after a suspect confesses deprives—and, indeed, is *intended* to deprive—the warnings of their effectiveness. Police cannot magically transform inadmissible confessions into admissible ones by withholding warnings until after the suspect confesses, administering them, and then asking the suspect to repeat the confession. Deliberate violations of the *Miranda* rule are unlikely to yield usable derivative evidence of any kind.[155]

## § 6.12 Restrictions on the Use of Confessions Given by Accomplices

This section begins with another story about Sticky-Fingered Sam. Sam pulled off a big "after hours" bank robbery by working a deal with Tillie Teller to share half the loot in exchange for keys to the bank vault. Unfortunately for Sam, his driver's license fell out while stuffing money into his pockets and the police quickly caught up with him. Sam was taken to the police station, where he was subjected to coercive interrogation methods. He confessed and named Tillie as his accomplice. Tillie is now facing trial. May she object to the prosecutor's introduction of Sam's confession as evidence against her?

This question raises a problem that prosecutors encounter when they try to introduce one accomplice's confession as evidence against another. There are two constitutional objections Tillie might raise—one valid and the other invalid. The most obvious objection—that the police violated Sam's constitu-

---

[154] *Oregon v. Elstad, supra* note 68, was the case involved.

[155] The Supreme Court has yet to address whether deliberate violations of the *Miranda* rule require suppression of physical fruits and leads discovered through the unwarned statement. Lower courts are split on this question, but the better cases have held that suppression is required. *See, e.g.,* United States v. Faulkingham, 295 F.3d 85 (1st Cir. 2002) (recognizing that "fruit of the poisonous tree" doctrine requires suppression when officers deliberately fail to give accused required *Miranda* warnings to obtain derivative evidence). *See also generally,* Yale Kamisar, *On the "Fruits" of Miranda Violations, Coerced Confessions, and Compelled Testimony,* 93 Mich. L. Rev. 929, 933 (1995) ("Unless the courts bar the use of the often-valuable evidence derived from an inadmissible confession, as well as the confession itself, there will remain a strong incentive to resort to forbidden interrogation methods."); David A. Wollin, *Policing the Police: Should Miranda Violations Bear Fruit?,* 53 Ohio St. L.J. 805, 843-848 (1992) ("Police officers seeking physical evidence are not likely to view the loss of an unwarned confession as particularly great when weighed against the opportunity to recover highly probative nontestimonial evidence, such as a murder weapon or narcotics."); Steven D. Clymer, *Are Police Free to Disregard Miranda?* 112 Yale L.J. 447 (2002). Decisions admitting this evidence in the face of a deliberate violation will need to be reconsidered in light of **Missouri v. Seibert**.

tional rights to obtain the confession—is not valid. The problem is *lack of standing*. Only a person whose constitutional rights have been violated has standing to challenge the admissibility of evidence on the grounds that it was unconstitutionally obtained.[156] That the confession was coerced is an objection that only Sam can raise.

However, Tillie has a valid objection to the prosecutor's introduction of Sam's confession against her. The Sixth Amendment confrontation clause guarantees that "[i]n all criminal prosecutions, the accused shall enjoy the right . . . to be confronted with the witnesses against him."[157] The purpose of this guarantee is to enable an accused to challenge the credibility of prosecution witnesses and expose inaccuracies in their testimony.

An accused's Sixth Amendment right to confront prosecution witnesses bars the government from using an out-of-court statement given by one accomplice, implicating another, as evidence against the latter unless the government can prevail on the accomplice who gave the statement to appear at the trial.[158] This means that Sam's confession cannot be introduced as evidence against Tillie unless Sam is willing to testify. Unfortunately for the prosecution, Sam can invoke the Fifth Amendment and refuse to testify because his testimony is self-incriminatory. Consequently, a prosecutor who wants to use one accomplice's confession as evidence against another is generally forced to grant immunity or work out some other deal in exchange for this testimony.

## § 6.13   The Requirement of Corroboration of Valid Confessions

In order to secure a conviction, the prosecution must prove that a crime was committed and that the defendant was the person who committed it. Under early English common law, the defendant's confession could be used to establish both elements. This practice increased the danger that an innocent person might be convicted—even of a crime that never happened. To combat this danger, most American jurisdictions adopted the rule that in order to secure a conviction based on a confession, the prosecution must produce some evidence independent of the confession that the crime was committed by someone or, in other words, that there was in fact a crime.[159] The independent proof requirement is known as the **corpus delicti** rule.

The phrase corpus delicti means the "body of the crime" (i.e., the fact that the crime charged was committed by someone). In the case of an unlawful

---

[156] Alderman v. United States, 394 U.S. 165, 89 S. Ct. 961, 22 L. Ed. 2d 176 (1969).

[157] The Sixth Amendment confrontation clause applies to the states through the Fourteenth Amendment. Pointer v. Texas, 380 U.S. 400, 85 S. Ct. 1065, 13 L. Ed. 2d 923 (1965).

[158] Lilly v. Virginia, 527 U.S. 116, 119 S. Ct. 1887, 144 L. Ed. 2d 117 (1999) (admission of nontestifying accomplice's confession violated defendant's confrontation clause rights).

[159] For a general discussion of the corroboration requirement, *see* Thomas A. Mullen, *Rule Without Reason: Requiring Independent Proof of the Corpus Delicti as a Condition of Admitting an Extrajudicial Confession*, 27 U.S.F. L. REV. 385 (1993) (recommending elimination of corpus delicti rule).

homicide, for example, the prosecution would have to prove that a person is dead, and that his or her death was caused by a crime, before a confession given by the accused may be introduced as evidence. Courts differ on the amount of proof necessary to satisfy the foundation required by the corpus delicti rule. However, the modern tendency is to minimize this requirement by establishing a low threshold of proof.[160] The corpus delicti requirement is generally stated as demanding "some evidence" or "slight evidence," independent of the defendant's confession, that the confessed crime was committed.[161]

The corpus delicti requirement made sense when no safeguards existed against the admission of confessions secured by coercion. The danger that innocent people might be coerced into confessing to crimes that were never committed was real. However, with *Miranda* safeguards and the due process free and voluntary requirement, the legal situation has changed. With these changes, the original purpose of the corpus delicti requirement no longer exists[162] and some have expressed misgivings about whether this requirement should be retained.[163] Requiring the prosecution to present independent evidence that the confessed crime was in fact committed before introducing a confession rarely accomplishes anything other than allowing the guilty to go free.[164]

## § 6.14  Summary and Practical Suggestions

A confession must pass at least four, and in some jurisdictions five, legal hurdles before it will be received as evidence of guilt. Voluntary confessions that fail some of these requirements may be used as impeachment evidence (i.e., to attack the credibility of the accused's trial testimony if he or she takes the witness stand and tells the jurors a different story from the one he or she told the police). However, this use is relatively unimportant. Consequently, students need a solid grounding in the requirements for a valid confession and the phases in the development of a criminal case when each applies.

**Due process free and voluntary requirement.** When a confession is offered as evidence, the government bears the burden of proving by a preponderance of the evidence that the confession was given voluntarily. A confession is considered involuntary under the due process clause when: (1) an agent of the government applies improper pressures that (2) overcome the suspect's free will. Voluntariness is determined by examining the totality of circumstances under which the confession was given, with emphasis on: (1) the interrogation methods used by the police; (2) the suspect's degree of susceptibility; and (3) the conditions under which the interrogation took place.

---

[160]  *Id.* at 390-391.
[161]  State v. Van Hook, 39 Ohio St. 3d 256, 261-262, 530 N.E.2d 883, 888-889 (1988); Thomas A. Mullen, *supra* note 159, at 390-391.
[162]  Willoughby v. State, 552 N.E.2d 462, 466 (Ind. 1990).
[163]  Thomas A. Mullen, *supra* note 159.
[164]  State v. Thompson, 560 N.W.2d 535 (N.D. 1997) (confession insufficient to sustain conviction for sexual contact with young child when there was no independent evidence establishing the corpus delicti).

**Fourth Amendment exclusionary rule.** Confessions that are causally related to a police violation of the suspect's Fourth Amendment rights (i.e., unconstitutional investigatory stop, arrest, or search) are inadmissible, even if voluntary. Courts consider the following three factors in deciding whether a causal relationship exists: the length of time between the violation and the confession, the presence of intervening circumstances, and the purpose and flagrancy of the violation.

*McNabb-Mallory* **rule.** The *McNabb-Mallory* rule was developed to enforce compliance with the federal prompt arraignment statute. As originally formulated, the rule required automatic suppression of confessions obtained during a period of unnecessary delay in taking the arrested person before a magistrate for arraignment, even if otherwise voluntary. Congress modified the *McNabb-Mallory* rule in the 1968 Omnibus Crime Control and Safe Streets Act. The 1968 Act requires federal judges to admit confessions found to be voluntary, but allows them to consider a number of factors in making this decision, including unnecessary delay in taking the suspect to a magistrate. The first six hours after an arrest on federal charges, nevertheless, is a "safe harbor" period and delays during this period may not be considered. The *McNabb-Mallory* rule was based on the Supreme Court's supervisory powers over the administration of criminal justice in the federal courts and was never binding on binding on state courts. Most states follow the federal approach of treating an unnecessary delay in arraignment as a factor bearing on voluntariness, but not automatic grounds for suppression.

**Fifth Amendment/***Miranda*** rule.** The *Miranda* rule, which is grounded in the Fifth Amendment privilege against self-incrimination, was developed to counteract the coercive atmosphere of a police custodial interrogation. *Miranda* warnings must be administered whenever the police: (1) interrogate a suspect; (2) who is then in custody; (3) about an offense with which he or she has not yet been charged. (If the suspect has already been charged with the offense, police must observe Sixth Amendment right to counsel procedures, which are summarized below.) A suspect is considered "in custody" whenever the objective circumstances surrounding the encounter are such that a reasonable person would assess the situation as equivalent to an arrest. The suspect must be aware that the questioner is a police officer for custody to exist. An interrogation occurs when police ask questions or engage in other words or actions that they should know are reasonably likely to elicit an incriminating response from the suspect. Unless confronted with an emergency requiring immediate action to protect the public safety or their own safety, police must warn the suspect and obtain an intelligent and voluntary waiver before initiating questioning. If the suspect, either before or during the questioning, clearly expresses a desire to speak with an attorney or to remain silent, questioning must stop immediately and may resume only under narrowly defined circumstances. Failure to comply with *Miranda* requirements results in suppression of the confession, but not derivative evidence unless police are guilty of coercion.

**Sixth Amendment right to counsel.** The Sixth Amendment right to counsel attaches upon the initiation of adversary criminal proceedings by way of a preliminary hearing, indictment, information, or arraignment. Attachment of the Sixth Amendment right to counsel brings heightened restrictions designed to prevent the police from unfairly compromising a defendant's right to effective representation at trial. After formal charges are lodged, police may not deliberately elicit incriminating statements from the accused at a time when counsel is not present unless the defendant gives a valid waiver of the right to counsel. However, this restriction applies only when questioning relates to the charges; it does not apply when the police question an accused about other, uncharged criminal activity. Neither custody nor interrogation are necessary for questioning after the initiation of a criminal prosecution to violate the Sixth Amendment. Administration of *Miranda* warnings is sufficient to apprise the defendant of his or her rights and will support a valid waiver of the Sixth Amendment right to counsel. However, once a defendant has retained counsel or requested appointment of counsel during an arraignment or similar proceeding, the defendant is no longer capable of giving a valid waiver during a police-initiated contact.

# Compulsory Self-Incrimination 7

*No person . . . shall be compelled in any criminal case to be a witness against himself . . .*

Fifth Amendment, 1791

# Chapter Outline

# § 7.1  Introduction

Governments need the power to compel citizens to testify and produce evidence. Without this power, there could be no trials unless all citizens with relevant evidence were willing to come forward voluntarily. However, our Constitution limits the government's authority to turn these powers on the accused. The terrifying practices of the Court of the Star Chamber, in which suspects were interrogated in secret for hours until they confessed, were still fresh in memory when our nation was founded. The Framers of the Constitution made the choice to establish an accusatorial system—a system in which the government carries the burden of proving its charges against the accused through evidence secured through its own independent investigation. An accusatorial system protects autonomy and dignity by limiting the government's power to force citizens to disclose information that implicates them in criminal activity. The self-incrimination clause of the Fifth Amendment is the cornerstone of this protection. It provides that no "person . . . shall be compelled in any criminal case to be a witness against himself."

However, it would be inaccurate to say that the Constitution establishes a purely accusatorial system. There are many acts that suspects can be compelled to perform that can appropriately be described as self-incriminatory.

Our Constitution makes a critical distinction between forcing suspects to share their knowledge of their criminal activity and forcing them to aid the government in building a case against them in other ways.

Figure 7.1
**Constitutional Restrictions on Compulsory Self-Incrimination**

| Constitutional provision | Type of incriminating evidence | Scope of restriction |
|---|---|---|
| Fifth Amendment | Testimony | The government is prohibited from compelling suspects to disclose knowledge of their criminal activity. |
| Fourth Amendment | Physical evidence | The government may compel suspects to permit use of their body to produce evidence when it has grounds for the initial seizure and for any further invasion of privacy or bodily integrity that the compelled production of the evidence entails. |

Suspects have a monopoly on many forms of evidence that are essential to establishing their guilt. Suppose Veronica Victim is found dead in her apartment, shot in the head with her own gun. Forensic analysis reveals that there are two sets of fingerprints on the gun and that it was fired twice, but the bullet in Veronica Victim's head is the only one found in her apartment. Investigators take samples from a trail of blood leading away from her apartment. A lab report establishes that the blood belongs to someone else. Based on this, police surmise that Victim shot her assailant, who then grabbed her gun and killed her. A woman living in the apartment next door, Nosie Neighbor, reports seeing a heavy-set, well-dressed man in his early thirties, about six feet tall, leave Victim's apartment at about the time of death. Victim's ex-husband, Stephan Bullette, matches this description and is known to have made previous threats on Victim's life.

Unless Bullette can be compelled to cooperate, the police will probably be unable to solve this crime. The police would like to compel Bullette to assist them in the following ways: (1) answer questions about his relationship with Victim and his activities at the time of the crime; (2) appear before Neighbor in a lineup; (3) provide fingerprints for comparison; (4) provide a blood sample for forensic analysis; (5) submit to an examination of his body to determine whether he was shot and, if he was; (6) undergo surgery to have the bullet removed for ballistics testing. The first form of compulsory assistance involves **testimony** and is regulated by the Fifth Amendment. The remaining five involve **physical evidence**[1] and are regulated by the Fourth Amendment.

## A. *Fifth Amendment Protection against Testimonial Self-Incrimination*

The Fifth Amendment is the only provision in the Constitution that explicitly addresses the subject of compulsory **self-incrimination**. Its concern is limited to compelled testimony. The Fifth Amendment declares that "[n]o person . . . shall be compelled in any criminal case to be a **witness** against himself." A witness is a person who testifies. Although the Fifth Amendment speaks of compulsion in a criminal case, this language has not been interpreted literally. A person is considered to be a "witness against himself in a criminal case" whenever he is compelled to disclose information that could later be used against him in a criminal case, no matter where or when the compulsion takes place.[2]

The Fifth Amendment has a narrow sphere of operation—compelled testimony—but provides absolute protection within this sphere. The government may not compel Bullette to disclose knowledge of his own criminal activities, whether inside or outside a courtroom. However, the Fifth Amendment gives Bullette absolutely no protection against being forced to assist the government in other ways. This has been the settled interpretation of the Fifth Amendment going back to 1910, when the Supreme Court declared:

> . . . [T]he prohibition of compelling a man in a criminal court to be a witness against himself is a prohibition of the use of physical or moral compulsion to extort communications from him, not an exclusion of his body as evidence when it may be material.[3]

## B. *Fourth Amendment Protection against Bodily Self-Incrimination*

The source of constitutional protection for Bullette's body is the Fourth Amendment, not the Fifth. The Fourth Amendment protects that "[t]he right of the people to be secure in their persons . . . against unreasonable searches and seizures." Bullette's right to security in his person reaches three interests he has in his body. The first is his interest in his freedom of movement. In order to use Bullette's body as a source of evidence, the police must gain physical

---

[1]    Physical evidence includes all forms of evidence that do not involve testimony.

[2]    Garner v. United States, 424 U.S. 648, 96 S. Ct. 1178, 47 L. Ed. 2d 370 (1976) (on income tax returns); Lefkowitz v. Turley, 414 U.S. 70, 94 S. Ct. 316, 38 L. Ed. 2d 274 (1973) (in any legal proceeding, civil or criminal, formal or informal); **Miranda v. Arizona, 384 U.S. 436, 86 S. Ct. 1602, 16 L. Ed. 2d 694** (1966) (during custodial interrogations).

[3]    Holt v. United States, 218 U.S. 245, 31 S. Ct. 2, 53 L. Ed. 1021 (1910).

control over him. Consequently, evidence obtained from Bullette's body without his consent will be suppressed unless the police have constitutional grounds for seizing and detaining him long enough to obtain the evidence.

Bullette also has an interest in bodily privacy. This interest does not reach the parts of his body that are exposed to public view,[4] such as his voice, handwriting, physical appearance, and fingerprints,[5] but it does reach the parts that are not. Examining Bullette's nude body for evidence of a bullet wound will intrude on his privacy. Finally, Bullette has an interest in his bodily integrity. Drawing blood and performing surgery to retrieve the bullet will intrude on this interest.[6] When the police perform procedures that invade a suspect's privacy or bodily integrity, they must satisfy two sets of Fourth Amendment requirements. They must have grounds for the initial seizure and also for any further invasion of privacy or bodily integrity that compulsory production of the evidence entails.

## § 7.2 Fifth Amendment Protection against Testimonial Self-Incrimination

The Fifth Amendment privilege against self-incrimination was adopted as a direct response to the horrors that took place in the Court of the Star Chamber in early seventeenth-century England. The accused could be placed under oath and forced to reveal knowledge of his own criminal activities on pain of being thrown into prison for perjury if he lied and for contempt of court if he remained silent.[7] The text of the Fifth Amendment self-incrimination clause, which applies to the states through its incorporation in the Fourteenth Amendment,[8] reads: "[n]o person . . . shall be compelled in any criminal case to be a witness against himself." While this language seems to be limited to compulsion exerted during criminal trials, this is not the way it has been interpreted. A person is compelled to be a witness against him or herself in a criminal case whenever he or she is compelled to disclose information to the government that might later be used against him or her in a criminal case. Fifth Amendment protection is available in all legal proceedings, judicial or administrative, formal or informal, criminal or civil.[9] Moreover, protection is not limited to legal proceedings. The Fifth Amendment also applies outside the courtroom. In Chapter 6, you saw an important out-of-court application of the Fifth Amendment—its application during police **custodial interrogations**.[10]

---

[4]   **Katz v. United States, 389 U.S. 347, 88 S. Ct. 507, 19 L. Ed. 2d 576 (1967).**
[5]   United States v. Dionisio, 410 U.S. 1, 93 S. Ct. 764, 35 L. Ed. 2d 67 (1973).
[6]   **Schmerber v. California, 384 U.S. 757, 86 S. Ct. 1826, 16 L. Ed. 2d 908 (1966).**
[7]   Murphy v. Waterfront Comm'n of New York Harbor, 378 U.S. 52, 84 S. Ct. 1594, 12 L. Ed. 2d 678 (1964); Doe v. United States, 487 U.S. 201, 108 S. Ct. 2341, 101 L. Ed. 2d 184 (1988); **Pennsylvania v. Muniz, 496 U.S. 582, 110 S. Ct. 2638, 110 L. Ed. 2d 528 (1990).**
[8]   Malloy v. Hogan, 378 U.S. 1, 84 S. Ct. 1489, 12 L. Ed. 2d 653 (1963).
[9]   Lefkowitz v. Turley, *supra* note 2; Maness v. Meyers, 419 U.S. 449, 95 S. Ct. 584, 42 L. Ed. 2d 574 (1975).
[10]  *See* §§ 6.8-6.11.

The Fifth Amendment affords two different forms of protection: (1) the right to remain silent, and (2) the **privilege** not to answer self-incriminating questions. The right to remain silent involves a complete exemption of the citizen's normal duty to give testimony. This protection is available in only two settings—during police custodial interrogations and at a defendant's criminal trial. Suspects in police custody have an absolute right to remain silent. They do not have to answer any police questions, even questions that lack incriminating potential.[11] If the suspect invokes the right to remain silent, questioning must cease. Defendants also enjoy the right to remain silent (i.e., not to testify) at their criminal trial.[12] If they decide to excise this right, the prosecution may not call them as a witness.

Figure 7.2
**Degrees of Fifth Amendment Protection**

| |
|---|
| 1. Suspects have the right to remain silent during custodial interrogations.<br>2. Criminal defendants have a right to remain silent at their criminal trial.<br>3. In all other legal contexts, citizens have a right not to answer specific questions that might tend to incriminate them. |

In no other proceedings do citizens enjoy the right to remain silent. They are, however, privileged not to reveal incriminating information.[13] The difference between these two forms of protection is illustrated by the following example. Suppose Bullette receives a subpoena to appear before a grand jury, which is investigating whether he should be indicted for murdering Victim. Bullette has no choice about whether to testify.[14] If subpoenaed, he must appear and make himself available for questioning. However, if asked a question that calls for a self-incriminating response, he may invoke the Fifth Amendment and refuse to answer.[15] To be regarded as incriminating, the answer need not exhibit guilt outright. A witness is privileged not to answer questions if the answer could provide a link in a chain of facts evidencing his guilt.[16] "Did you ever threaten Victoria Victim's life?" "Did you see her the night she died?" or "Did you know she owned a gun?" are examples of questions that call for answers that "tend to incriminate." If Bullette is asked questions like these while testifying before the grand jury, he may invoke the Fifth Amendment and refuse to answer. Furthermore, Bullette does not have to explain what it is about the answer that would be incriminating. If witnesses had to do this, they would be compelled to surrender the very protection that the privilege guarantees. The

---

[11]   Miranda v. Arizona, *supra* note 2. The *Miranda* rule is covered in §§ 6.8-6.11.
[12]   Murphy v. Waterfront Comm., *supra* note 7; Malloy v. Hogan, *supra* note 8.
[13]   Hoffman v. United States, 341 U.S. 479, 71 S. Ct. 814, 95 L. Ed. 1118 (1951).
[14]   United States v. Dionisio, *supra* note 5.
[15]   *Id.*
[16]   Hoffman v. United States, *supra* note 13.

judge is required to sustain a claim of privilege unless it is perfectly clear, considering the implications of the question and the setting in which it is asked, that the answer could not possibly be incriminating.[17]

Having provided this introduction, we are now ready to get into the nitty-gritty of the Fifth Amendment.

# § 7.3 —Prerequisites for Application of the Fifth Amendment

The most efficient way to analyze the Fifth Amendment is to break the language down into components. The text prohibits the government from: (1) *compelling* a person (2) to be a *witness* (3) *against himself in a criminal case*. Three elements must coalesce in order to activate protection: (1) compulsion, (2) testimony, and (3) self-incrimination.

## A. *Testimony*

The Fifth Amendment's concern is limited to testimony. It provides no protection against compelled production of other forms of evidence.[18] When witnesses testify, they communicate information. Testimony, for Fifth Amendment purposes, includes any behavior that, implicitly or explicitly, makes a statement or communicates information.[19] Compulsion to speak does not invariably involve testimony. Suspects in lineups, for example, are sometimes required to repeat words spoken by the perpetrator to determine whether their voice characteristics are recognizable. Voice characteristics may be the only way a culprit who puts a gun in someone's back and demands "your money or your life" can be identified. Compulsion to repeat words spoken by a perpetrator does not involve testimony because the suspect is not being compelled to communicate anything he or she knows. The compulsion, instead, relates to voice characteristics.[20] Compulsion to exhibit physical characteristics involves physical evidence and suspects must look to the Fourth Amendment for any protection that may be available.[21]

---

[17]   *Id.*

[18]   **Schmerber v. California**, *supra* note 6.

[19]   *See, e.g.*, Doe v. United States, *supra* note 7 ("[I]n order to be testimonial, an accused's communication must, explicitly or implicitly, relate a factual assertion or disclose information. Only then is a person compelled to be a 'witness' against himself."); **Pennsylvania v. Muniz**, *supra* note 7 (same).

[20]   United States v. Dionisio, *supra* note 5.

[21]   *See* § 7.7 *infra.*

Figure 7.3
**Prerequisites for Application of the Fifth Amendment**

> Testimony, compulsion, and self-incrimination are necessary for the Fifth Amendment to apply.
>
> 1. Testimony encompasses any behavior that explicitly or implicitly makes a statement or discloses information.
> 2. Compulsion occurs when a person is threatened with a serious consequence unless he makes a statement or discloses information.
> 3. A disclosure is self-incriminating when it exposes the maker to a risk of criminal prosecution.

## B. *Compulsion*

Compulsion occurs when the government threatens serious consequences unless a person makes a statement or discloses information. The normal manner in which our legal system compels testimony is by issuing a subpoena. A **subpoena (ad testificatum)** is a court order to appear and testify, on penalty of being held in **contempt** of court and fined or imprisoned. However, the threatened harm can take any form as long as it is serious. Suppose that a police officer is summoned to appear before a disciplinary board where he is accused of having taken a bribe and told that he will be fired unless he makes a full disclosure. He capitulates and admits to wrongdoing. The officer is protected under the Fifth Amendment against the use of his statement in a criminal prosecution because the statement was compelled.[22]

Compulsion also has a temporal dimension. The relevant time for evaluating whether a person has been compelled to incriminate him or herself in violation of the Fifth Amendment is when the statement is made originally. The Fifth Amendment prohibits the government from compelling individuals to *make* incriminating statements, not from using incriminating statements they previously made *voluntarily*. As a result, a person who voluntarily prepares incriminating records, journals, or other documents cannot claim Fifth Amendment protection for the contents. When the government is aware of the existence and location of an incriminating writing, it may seize it under a search warrant and use it as evidence.[23]

---

[22] *See, e.g.*, Garrity v. New Jersey, 385 U.S. 493, 87 S. Ct. 616, 17 L. Ed. 2d 562 (1967) (testimony compelled where police officer was given choice between incriminating himself or losing his job); Uniformed Sanitation Men Ass'n, Inc. v. Commissioner of Sanitation of City of New York, 392 U.S. 280, 88 S. Ct. 1917, 20 L. Ed. 2d 1089 (1968) (same); Spevack v. Klein, 385 U.S. 511, 87 S. Ct. 625, 17 L. Ed. 2d 574 (1967) (testimony compelled where attorney was given choice between incriminating himself or disbarment).

[23] **United States v. Hubbell, 530 U.S. 27, 20 S. Ct. 2037, 147 L. Ed. 2d 24 (2000)**; Fisher v. United States, 425 U.S. 391, 96 S. Ct. 1569, 48 L. Ed. 2d 39 (1976); Packwood v. Senate Select Committee On Ethics, 510 U.S. 1319, 114 S. Ct. 1036, 127 L. Ed. 2d 530 (1994); Couch v. United States, 409 U.S. 322, 93 S. Ct. 611, 34 L. Ed. 2d 548 (1973); United States v. Moody, 977 F.2d 1425 (11th Cir. 1992) (personal writings); State v. Barrett, 401 N.W.2d 184 (Iowa 1987) (journal); State v. Andrei, 574 A.2d 295 (Me. 1990) (diary).

When the government does not know the location, it will have to use a subpoena (duces tecum) to obtain it. A **subpoena (duces tecum)** is an order, issued by a court or legislative body, that commands the person named in it to appear and produce designated books, papers, records, or other items. Even though voluntarily prepared writings lack Fifth Amendment protection, a person faced with a subpoena to turn over incriminating documents to the government may, in some instances, be able to assert the privilege because the act of production has incriminating communicative aspects in its own right. Compliance with a subpoena tacitly admits that the documents exist, that they are in the producing party's possession, and that they are the ones sought by the subpoena. In cases in which these admissions are incriminating, compliance with the subpoena may be resisted under the Fifth Amendment.[24]

## C. Self-Incrimination

Fifth Amendment protection is available only for disclosures that are self-incriminating. To be incriminating, they must do more than reveal criminal activity. *They must create a risk of the person's being convicted of the crimes revealed.*[25] The government is permitted to compel disclosure of information that lacks this potential. People under **arrest**, for example, may be compelled to furnish biographical information (i.e., name, address, Social Security number, etc.) needed for booking because this information is not incriminating.[26]

Even when disclosures relate to criminal activity, they may be compelled if they do not expose the person to a risk of conviction.[27] This risk is removed if the person has already been tried for the crime because the double jeopardy clause will bar reprosecution.[28] Suppose that Sticky-Fingered Sam commits a burglary and stores the stolen property at his sister Mary Wanna's house. Mary Wanna is guilty of aiding and abetting. However, she can be forced to testify against Sam if she has already been tried, even though her testimony will require disclosure of her own criminal activity, because her testimony is no longer incriminating. The double jeopardy clause has removed the risk of reconviction and Fifth Amendment protection along with it.

---

[24]   *See, e.g.,* **United States v. Hubbell,** *supra* note 23 (recognizing that the act of producing self-incriminatory documents in response to a subpoena has communicative aspects of its own, apart from the contents of the documents produced); Fisher v. United States, *supra* note 23 (same). *See also* generally Lance Cole, *The Fifth Amendment And Compelled Production of Personal Documents After* United States v. Hubbell—*New Protection For Private Papers?* 29 AM. J. CRIM. L. 123 (2002): Thomas Kiefer Wedeles, Note, *Fishing for Clarity in a Post-*Hubbell *World: The Need For a Bright-line Rule in The Self-incrimination Clause's Act of Production Doctrine,* 56 VAND. L. REV. 613 (2003).

[25]   Kastigar v. United States, 406 U.S. 441, 92 S. Ct. 1653, 32 L. Ed. 2d 212 (1972).

[26]   *See, e.g.,* **Pennsylvania v. Muniz,** *supra* note 7.

[27]   Kastigar v. United States, *supra* note 25.

[28]   In re Keijam, 226 Conn. 497, 628 A.2d 562 (1993). *See also,* In re Grand Jury Subpoena to Doe, 41 F. Supp. 2d 616 (W.D. Va. 1999) (a witness may not invoke the privilege against self-incrimination when prosecution is barred by such legal barriers as the statute of limitations, the doctrine of double jeopardy, or grants of immunity); Ex parte Moore, 804 So. 2d 245 (Ala. Civ. App. 2001) (same).

Nevertheless, the most common way in which claims of privilege are over-ridden is through grants of immunity.[29] Grants of immunity are used when the government needs the testimony of a "small fish" to convict a "big fish." Two forms of immunity are available—absolute and use. **Absolute immunity** (also called transactional immunity) bars the government from prosecuting the witness for crimes revealed through compelled testimony.[30] Because the government is barred from prosecuting, the testimony is no longer incriminating.

The government, nevertheless, is not required to grant absolute immunity in order to compel testimony. The Fifth Amendment is satisfied if the government grants the witness immunity from the government's use of the testimony and its fruits in any prosecution it later brings.[31] This level is called **use immunity**, or **use, including derivative use**, **immunity**. The reason use immunity is adequate to satisfy the Constitution is that it grants legal protection equivalent to the "fruit of the poisonous tree" remedy given for evidence procured in violation of constitutional rights. By providing this remedy in advance, the government removes the witness's objection to testifying, while retaining the right to prosecute. If the government later decides to prosecute after granting use immunity, it will be required to prove that all evidence it seeks to introduce was derived independently of the compelled testimony.[32]

When the same criminal act is punishable under both state and federal law, grants of immunity given by either jurisdiction will bind the other to the extent of use immunity.[33] While the other jurisdiction remains free to prosecute, it must establish that the evidence it plans to introduce was obtained through its own independent investigation and not, directly or indirectly, from the previously immunized testimony.[34]

Grants of immunity must be recommended by the prosecutor and approved by the judge. Police lack authority to promise suspects that they will receive immunity if they cooperate.[35] Confessions induced by false promises of immunity are considered involuntary and cannot be used as evidence.[36]

---

[29]  Kastigar v. United States, *supra* note 25.
[30]  *Id.*
[31]  *Id.*
[32]  *Id.*
[33]  Murphy v. Waterfront Comm., *supra* note 7.
[34]  Kastigar v. United States, *supra* note 25.
[35]  Jackson v. State, 562 So. 2d 1373 (Ala. Crim. App. 1990).
[36]  *See* § 6.4 *supra.*

## § 7.4 —Rules for Invoking and Waiving Fifth Amendment Protection

### A. *Invoking the Fifth Amendment*

Criminal defendants have the right to remain silent at their trial. They invoke this right by not taking the witness stand. A defendant's decision not to testify is final; the prosecutor is not permitted to call the defendant as a witness. The decision not to testify is a difficult choice for defendants, because jurors tend to speculate about why they failed to take the stand and deny the charges. The Fifth Amendment prohibits the prosecutor from capitalizing on this tendency. In a leading case, the prosecutor, during closing arguments, told the jurors that the defendant was the only person who could provide information relating to the victim's murder, and yet he had "not seen fit to take the stand and deny or explain."[37] The Supreme Court reversed the conviction, holding that the prosecutor's comment impermissibly infringed on the defendant's Fifth Amendment right to remain silent. Adverse comments on a defendant's failure to testify penalize the exercise of a constitutional right and make assertion costly. When a defendant chooses to remain silent, the prosecution is prohibited from drawing attention to this choice by arguing to the jurors that it furnishes evidence of guilt. Even so, the danger remains that jurors may draw adverse inferences on their own. Consequently, the judge must, on request, instruct the jurors that they may not infer guilt from a defendant's silence.[38]

Other witnesses are required to testify, but are privileged not to answer questions that call for an incriminating response. The privilege against self-incrimination is not self-executing. A witness who desires its protection must expressly invoke it. This puts the judge on notice that the witness considers the answer incriminating. If the witness voluntarily answers the question without invoking the privilege, the answer will not be considered "compelled."[39] Witnesses invoke the privilege by stating in response to a specific question: "I refuse to answer on the grounds that it might incriminate me." When a witness invokes the privilege, the judge must determine whether a truthful answer would, in fact, have this tendency. Because the judge has no way of knowing what the witness's answer would be, the judge must rule on the witness's claim of privilege based on the incriminating potential of the question. When the incriminating potential is unclear, the judge faces a dilemma. The Supreme

---

[37] Griffin v. California, 380 U.S. 609, 85 S. Ct. 1229, 14 L. Ed. 2d 106 (1965).

[38] Carter v. Kentucky, 405 U.S. 288, 101 S. Ct. 1112, 67 L. Ed. 2d 241 (1981).

[39] *See, e.g.*, United States v. Monia, 317 U.S. 424, 63 S. Ct. 409, 87 L. Ed. 376 (1943); Johnson v. United States, 318 U.S. 189, 63 S. Ct. 549, 87 L. Ed. 704 (1943). *See also* Minnesota v. Murphy, 465 U.S. 420, 104 S. Ct. 1136, 79 L. Ed. 2d 409 (1984) (defendant's failure to assert the privilege against self-incrimination during meeting with probation officer left him in no position to complain that his statement admitting commission of rape and murder was compelled); Garner v. United States, 424 U.S. 648, 96 S. Ct. 1178, 47 L. Ed. 2d 370 (1976) (failure to claim privilege against self-incrimination before disclosing incriminating information on a federal tax return forfeited the right to object to use of information in a criminal prosecution on the grounds that it was compelled).

Court has indicated that claims of privilege should be honored unless there is no rational basis for believing that a truthful answer to the question could be incriminating.[40] If the judge erroneously instructs the witness to answer, the witness's testimony has been compelled and cannot be used against him or her in subsequent criminal proceedings.

## B. *Waiver of the Privilege*

A waiver occurs when a person who has a Fifth Amendment privilege voluntarily testifies without invoking it. Under *Miranda*, a valid waiver requires a warning that the person is not required to answer, that his or her answers can and will be used against him or her, and that he or she has a right to consult with an attorney. However, the Supreme Court has declined to impose a similar requirement in other in other contexts.[41] Judges, nevertheless, generally take extreme precautions to ensure that the decision of a criminal defendant to waive the protection of the Fifth Amendment is made intelligently and with full knowledge of the consequences.

## C. *Scope of the Waiver*

Criminal defendants who take the witness stand waive the privilege, but only concerning the matters about which they have testified.[42] They cannot waive the privilege for the sake of putting forth their version of the facts and then invoke it to block cross-examination. A contrary rule would give them an unfair advantage. However, they retain the right to invoke the privilege if they are cross-examined about matters beyond the scope of their testimony.[43] If Bullette takes the witness stand and limits his testimony to the fact that he was at a bar, drinking with friends, when Victim was killed, he may be cross-examined about his alibi, but not about whether he hated Victim, knew she owned a gun, or threatened her life, because he did not testify about these matters. This strikes a fair balance between the interests of the defendant and the government. A defendant is permitted to limit the subjects he or she is willing to discuss, but not to distort the truth.

---

[40]  Maness v. Meyers, *supra* note 9.

[41]  *See, e.g.*, Minnesota v. Murphy, *supra* note 39 (probation officers not required to administer warnings before asking questions that call for incriminating response); United States v. Washington, 431 U.S. 181, 97 S. Ct. 1814, 52 L. Ed. 2d 238 (1977) (judges not required to issue warnings to witnesses called to testify before grand juries investigating them).

[42]  Mitchell v. United States, 526 U.S. 314, 119 S. Ct. 1307, 143 L. Ed. 2d 424 (1999); Brown v. United States, 356 U.S. 148, 78 S. Ct. 622, 2 L. Ed. 2d 589 (1958).

[43]  *See* authorities *supra* note 42.

## § 7.5 —Protection against Adverse Consequences from Exercising the Privilege against Self-Incrimination

When people invoke the Fifth Amendment, the natural tendency is to think that they have something to hide. The Fifth Amendment prohibits the government from capitalizing on this tendency in criminal cases,[44] including sentencing proceedings.[45] Neither the prosecutor nor the judge is allowed to call attention to the fact that the defendant failed to take the witness stand and deny the charges at his trial or to suggest that it furnishes evidence of guilt.[46] Allowing jurors to draw a negative inference from a defendant's failure to testify would discourage exercise of the Fifth Amendment privilege out of fear that silence would be equally incriminating. For the same reasons, the jurors are not allowed to be told that the defendant invoked the Fifth Amendment when questioned by the police.[47]

While the Fifth Amendment precludes drawing an adverse inference from the defendant's silence during criminal trials and sentencing proceedings, it does not prohibit doing so in civil cases, parole revocation hearings, police disciplinary actions and, indeed, in all other proceedings in which the privilege against self-incrimination applies.[48] Although the Fifth Amendment guarantees witnesses the right to invoke the privilege in these proceedings, it does not guarantee that their decision to do so will be cost-free. Chapter 11 considers the consequences of invoking the privilege in police disciplinary proceedings.

## § 7.6 —Self-Reporting Laws and the Fifth Amendment

Each year, millions of Americans are compelled, on penalty of criminal prosecution, to fill out a report to the federal government, detailing their year's economic activity. The report is a 1040 income tax return. What protection does the Fifth Amendment confer on citizens like Sticky-Fingered Sam, whose income derives exclusively from crime?

---

[44] Griffin v. California, *supra* note 37 (prosecutor may not comment on defendant's failure to testify); Carter v. Kentucky, *supra* note 38 (upon defendant's request, court must charge jury that no adverse inference may be drawn from defendant's failure to testify).

[45] Mitchell v. United States, *supra* note 42.

[46] Griffin v. California, *supra* note 37.

[47] Doyle v. Ohio, 426 U.S. 610, 96 S. Ct. 2240, 42 L. Ed. 2d 91 (1976).

[48] *See, e.g.,* Baxter v. Palmigiano, 425 U.S. 308, 96 S. Ct. 1551, 47 L. Ed. 2d 810 (1976) (Noting that "the prevailing rule [is] that the Fifth Amendment does not forbid adverse inferences against parties to civil actions when they refuse to testify in response to probative evidence against them"; holding that adverse inferences may be drawn from prisoner's silence in prison disciplinary proceedings); United States v. Stein, 233 F.3d 6 (1st Cir. 2000) (bar discipline proceeding); United States v. Serafino, 82 F.3d 515 (1st Cir. 1996) (civil tort action).

Whether the Fifth Amendment privileges citizens not to file government reports that could draw attention to their criminal activity depends on the government's regulatory purpose in requiring the report. Citizens are not excused from complying with reporting statutes like the Internal Revenue Code, which serve a regulatory purpose that is unrelated to discovering criminal activity. Sam must file a federal income tax return and pay his taxes just like the rest of us.[49] He may, however, refuse to answer specific questions on the form that could incriminate him, such as the nature of his occupation or the source of his income.[50] Income tax laws, sales tax laws, occupational tax laws, and hit-and-run motorist statutes are examples of some of the many statutes with reporting requirements that serve a legitimate regulatory purpose.[51] The Fifth Amendment provides no defense for failing to comply with statutes like these.

People engaged in criminal activity, on the other hand, do not have to comply with statutes that are enacted purely for the sake of entrapping them. Suppose that Congress enacts a statute that imposes a special tax on income from the sale of stolen property. Taxpayers subject to this "tax" are required, on penalty of criminal prosecution, to file a tax return, disclosing their name, Social Security number, and source of income. The purpose of this so-called tax law is not to raise revenue. Its purpose is to force people who traffic in stolen property to identify themselves to the government. Citizens may ignore reporting statutes that (1) apply to a highly select group engaged in criminal activity and (2) require them to report information that could, and probably will, lead to their prosecution.[52] Laws with these characteristics are not legitimate regulatory measures. The Fifth Amendment provides a complete defense against prosecution for violating them.

## § 7.7   Fourth Amendment Protection against Bodily Self-Incrimination

Information stored in memory is not the only thing that can incriminate a person. The person's appearance, fingerprints, footprints, breath, blood, hair, saliva, and other biological characteristics can be just as incriminating. However, the Fifth Amendment does not protect suspects from compulsory self-incrimination through evidence that derives from their body because this evidence is physical, not testimonial.

---

[49]   Garner v. United States, 424 U.S. 648, 96 S. Ct. 1178, 47 L. Ed. 2d 370 (1975); United States v. Sullivan, 274 U.S. 259, 47 S. Ct. 607, 71 L. Ed. 1037 (1927).

[50]   Garner v. United States, *supra* note 49.

[51]   California v. Byers, 402 U.S. 424, 91 S. Ct. 1535, 29 L. Ed. 2d 748 (1983) (hit-and-run motorist statute); United States v. Sullivan, *supra* note 49 (federal income tax).

[52]   Marchetti v. United States, 390 U.S. 39, 88 S. Ct. 697, 19 L. Ed. 2d 889 (1968) (invalidating statute requiring gamblers to register with the Internal Revenue Service); Grosso v. United States, 390 U.S. 62, 88 S. Ct. 709, 19 L. Ed. 2d 906 (1968) (invalidating statute imposing an excise tax on gambling); Haynes v. United States, 390 U.S. 85, 88 S. Ct. 722, 19 L. Ed. 2d 923 (1968) (invalidating statute requiring registration of firearms, used to prosecute persons engaged in criminal activity); Leary v. United States, 395 U.S. 6, 89 S. Ct. 1532, 23 L. Ed. 2d 57 (1969) (invalidating statute requiring persons trafficking in marijuana to register and pay an occupational tax).

The constitutional distinction between compelled testimony and compulsory production of **physical evidence** was dramatically illustrated during the O.J. Simpson murder trial when Simpson was forced to try on a glove found at the murder scene in front of the jury. Had the glove fit, the effect could have been almost as devastating as a confession. The Fifth Amendment gave Simpson no protection against being forced to try on the glove because he was being compelled to exhibit physical characteristics (i.e., the size of his hand), not to reveal his thoughts. Simpson, on the other hand, did not take the witness stand and the prosecution did not call him because the Fifth Amendment protected him from being forced to testify.

The Framers relegated protection for the suspect's body to the Fourth Amendment, which guarantees "(t)he right of the people to be secure in their persons . . . , against unreasonable searches and seizures . . ." The right to security in one's person encompasses interests that people have in their bodies—(1) freedom of movement; (2) bodily privacy; and (3) bodily integrity. Concentrating on these three interests is the key to understanding Fourth Amendment protection against compulsory production of physical evidence. Freedom of movement is always implicated when the police perform procedures that require use of the suspect's body. This means that the police always need grounds for a seizure. Whether they need grounds beyond this depends on whether the procedures subsequently performed invade the suspect's privacy or bodily integrity. When police perform procedures that invade privacy or bodily integrity, they must have separate grounds for the second invasion as well.

For the sake of clarity of analysis, it is useful to group evidence obtained through police procedures that make use of a suspect's body into two categories: (1) **appearance evidence** and (2) **bodily evidence**.

## A. Appearance Evidence

**Appearance evidence** refers to evidence that derives from body characteristics that are routinely displayed to the public.[53] Compulsory submission to photographing, lineups, fingerprinting, handwriting and voice samples, and field sobriety tests[54] are examples of such procedures.[55] Because a person's physical appearance, voice, handwriting, fingerprints, and body coordination are external characteristics that are exposed to public view, neither privacy nor bodily integrity is invaded when the police compel a suspect to allow his or

---

[53]  United States v. Dionisio, *supra* note 5 (voice exemplar); United States v. Mara, 410 U.S. 19, 93 S. Ct. 774, 35 L. Ed. 2d 99 (1973) (handwriting exemplar); United States v. Wade, 388 U.S. 218, 87 S. Ct. 1926, 18 L. Ed. 2d 1149 (1967) (compulsion to repeat the perpetrator's words during a lineup); **Pennsylvania v. Muniz**, *supra* note 7 (field sobriety test).

[54]  Field sobriety tests are based on the relationship between intoxication and loss of coordination. Tests for sobriety include such things as having the suspect walk heel-to-toe, stand on one foot, or touch the tip of the nose with his or her finger.

[55]  *See* authorities note 53.

her body to be used to produce this evidence. Only one interest is implicated—the suspect's interest in freedom of movement. Police must gain physical control over the suspect to perform these procedures.

> Because only one interest is implicated, the rule for when police may compel suspects to participate in appearance evidence procedures is easy to remember: *Police are permitted to compel participation whenever they have constitutional grounds to seize the suspect and detain him or her long enough to perform the procedure.*

### B. Bodily Evidence

**Bodily evidence** refers to physical evidence obtained by searching areas of a suspect's body not normally exposed to the public, penetrating the body surface, or removing biological[56] or foreign substances.[57] In the hypothetical posed at the beginning of this chapter, searching Bullette's naked body for evidence of a gunshot wound,[58] taking a blood sample for analysis,[59] and surgically removing the bullet[60] are examples of bodily evidence. These procedures implicate two interests. The police must restrain Bullette's freedom of movement (the first invasion) long enough to perform a highly intrusive procedure (the second invasion). When procedures performed on a suspect's body intrude upon the suspect's privacy or bodily integrity, having grounds for the initial seizure is not enough. *There must be separate grounds for the second invasion.*

## § 7.8 —Requirements for Appearance Evidence

The most common procedures involving appearance evidence are: (1) station house lineups; (2) showup identifications at the crime scene; (3) photographing, measuring, fingerprinting, and taking handwriting and voice exemplars; and (4) field sobriety tests. These procedures invade the suspect's interest in freedom of movement and, consequently, require grounds for a seizure, but this is all. Because a person's physical appearance, fingerprints, footprints, handwriting, voice, body coordination, and manner of walking are outwardly manifested traits exposed to public view, there is no privacy interest in them. As a result, a lawful arrest is the only constitutional requirement necessary to compel participation.[61] The *Miranda* rule does not apply to

---

[56] **Schmerber v. California**, *supra* note 6; Skinner v. Railway Labor Executives' Ass'n, 489 U.S. 602, 109 S. Ct. 1402, 103 L. Ed. 2d 639 (1989).
[57] Cupp v. Murphy, 412 U.S. 291, 93 S. Ct. 2000, 36 L. Ed. 2d 900 (1973).
[58] Bell v. Wolfish, 441 U.S. 520, 99 S. Ct. 1861, 60 L. Ed. 2d 447 (1979).
[59] **Schmerber v. California**, *supra* note 6.
[60] Winston v. Lee, 470 U.S. 753, 105 S. Ct. 1611, 84 L. Ed. 2d 662 (1985).
[61] *See* cases *supra* note 53.

compulsory production of appearance evidence because this rule applies only to custodial interrogation.[62]

Figure 7.4
**Appearance Evidence**

> Appearance evidence refers to evidence that can be taken from a suspect's body without: (1) searching areas not normally exposed to the public, (2) penetrating the surface, or (3) removing biological or foreign materials. The main examples include:
>
> 1.  Station house lineups.
> 2.  Showup identifications at the crime scene.
> 3.  Photographs, fingerprints, footprints, body measurements, and voice and handwriting exemplars.
> 4.  Field sobriety tests.
>
> These procedures are considered routine incidents of a lawful arrest and require no justification beyond grounds for arrest.

## A. Compulsory Production of Appearance Evidence During Terry Stops

*Terry* stops are required to be brief and minimally intrusive. Consequently, appearance evidence procedures that are intrusive or time-consuming are beyond their scope. In addition, there is a hard and fast rule about taking *Terry* detainees to the police station. Police are not allowed to take *Terry* detainees to the police station without their consent for lineups, photographing, fingerprinting, or for any other procedure.[63] However, nonintrusive procedures, such as fingerprinting and photographing, can be performed at the stop location when this can be done expeditiously.[64] Moving a *Terry* detainee to a second

---

[62] Williams v. State, 257 Ga. App. 54, 570 S.E.2d 362 (Ga. Ct. App. 2002) (*Miranda* warnings not required before taking blood sample for DNA testing); State v. Harmon, 952 P.2d 402 (Idaho Ct. App. 1998) (same, blood-alcohol test); Com. v. Cameron, 44 Mass. App. Ct. 912, 689 N.E.2d 1365 (1998) (same, field sobriety test); State v. Lee, 184 Ariz. 230, 908 P.2d 44 (1995) (same, Breathalyzer test); State v. Acosta, 951 S.W.2d 291 (Tex. Ct. App. 1997) (same, asking suspect to count backward as test for intoxication).

[63] *See, e.g.,* Hayes v. Florida, 470 U.S. 811, 105 S. Ct. 1643, 84 L. Ed. 2d 705 (1985); Dunaway v. New York, 442 U.S. 200, 99 S. Ct. 2248, 60 L. Ed. 2d 824 (1979); 4 W. LAFAVE, TREATISE ON SEARCH & SEIZURE § 9.2 (f) (g) (3d ed. 1996).

[64] *See, e.g.,* Hayes v. Florida, *supra* note 63; People v. Green, 298 Ill. App. 3d 1054, 233 Ill. Dec. 389, 700 N.E.2d 1097 (1998) (photographing suspect at stop location permissible during lawful *Terry* stop); State v. Eastman, 691 A.2d 179 (Me. 1997) (administering field sobriety test permissible during *Terry* stop).

location is always a risky venture. The only time this is allowed is when the movement is to a nearby crime scene for a showup identification, but even here the preferred procedure is to bring the witnesses to the stop location.[65]

## B. Special Statutory Procedures for Obtaining Nontestimonial Identification Evidence

In some jurisdictions, an alternative statutory procedure exists for obtaining appearance evidence.[66] The judge is given authority, upon the request of a prosecutor, to enter an order (commonly called a "nontestimonial identification order") directing a suspect to appear at a particular place and time to undergo a covered procedure. The covered procedures generally include lineups; photographing; fingerprinting; foot printing; measurements; handwriting and voice exemplars; and hair, blood, urine, semen, and saliva samples.[67] The court-ordered alternative is particularly attractive because judges have the authority to issue nontestimonial identification orders on a showing lower than **probable cause for arrest**, a showing that resembles **reasonable suspicion**.[68] This enables nontestimonial identification orders to be used as an investigative tool to obtain identification evidence from suspects for whom probable cause for arrest is lacking. Once reasonable suspicion exists, the prosecutor can seek a court order compelling the suspect to appear for a lineup or other covered procedure to gather additional evidence needed to establish probable cause for an arrest.

Court orders to appear are enforced through contempt sanctions. The failure to appear in response to a court order is punishable as contempt of court.

## C. Consequences of Violating the Fourth Amendment

An illegal arrest taints appearance evidence. If the police arrest Sticky-Fingered Sam without probable cause and obtain a positive match between his fingerprints and the ones found at the crime scene, and then place him in a

---

[65]    *See, e.g.*, People v. Ross, 317 Ill. App. 3d 26, 739 N.E.2d 50 (2000) (officers conducting a field investigation immediately after the commission of a crime permitted to transport suspect a short distance to a nearby crime scene for a showup identification where witnesses are available who can confirm or deny that police have apprehended the right person); Commonwealth v. Barros, 425 Mass. 572, 682 N.E.2d 849 (1997) (same); State v. Lund, 853 P.2d 1379 (Wash. Ct. App. 1993) (same).

[66]    *See, e.g.* ALASKA R. CT. 16(c)(1)-(2); ARIZ. REV. STAT. ANN. § 13-3905; COLO. R. CRIM. P. 41.1; IDAHO CODE ANN. § 19-625;, IOWA CODE § 810.1 *et seq.*; NEB. REV. STAT. §§ 29-3301 *et seq.*; N.C. GEN. STAT. § 15A-271 *et seq.*; UTAH CODE ANN. §§ 77-8-1 *et seq.*; VERMONT R. CRIM. P. 41. *See also* 4 W. LAFAVE, TREATISE ON SEARCH & SEIZURE § 9.7(b), at 327 (3d ed.1996).

[67]    *See, e.g.*, N.C. GEN. STAT. § 15A-271 (1999); VERMONT R. CRIM. P. 41.1.

[68]    *See, e.g.*, In re Nontestimonial Identification Order Directed to R.H., 171 Vt. 227, 762 A.2d 1239 (2000) (upholding nontestimonial identification order, issued on reasonable suspicion, requiring suspect to submit to collection of saliva for DNA comparison); Bousman v. Iowa Dist. Court, 630 N.W. 2d 789 (Iowa 2001) (nontestimonial identification orders do not violate Fourth Amendment because their issuance is based on reasonable suspicion, rather than probable cause).

lineup where he is identified by the victim, the fingerprint match and lineup identification will be suppressed as the tainted fruits of the poisonous tree.[69] However, there are limits as to how far the taint will go and how long it will last. Photographs and fingerprints are commonly taken as a routine part of the booking process and are retained as a permanent part of the police files, available for use on future occasions in the investigation of unrelated crimes. If police illegally arrest Sam, take his mug shot, and put it in the mug shot book and months or years later the victim of a different offense identifies him from his mug shot, suppression is not required because the use of a mug shot to obtain an identification in the investigation of an unrelated offense months or years later is sufficiently removed from the illegal arrest to be purged of the taint.[70]

## § 7.9 —Requirements for Bodily Evidence

A lawful arrest carries the authority to conduct a full search of the arrestee's person for weapons, evidence of crime, and contraband.[71] Police officers may search the arrestee's outer clothing, and go through his or her pockets and wallet, simply by virtue of making a lawful custodial arrest. Probable cause to believe that incriminating evidence will be found is unnecessary.[72] However, the search authority that accompanies a lawful arrest does not automatically extend to: (1) searching parts of a suspect's body that are not normally exposed to the public; (2) searching below the body's surface; or (3) removing bodily fluids, tissues, or residues. Physical evidence obtained by invading a suspect's privacy or bodily integrity is called *bodily evidence.* Examples include:

---

[69]   *See, e.g.,* Hayes v. Florida, 470 U.S. 811, 105 S. Ct. 1643, 84 L. Ed. 2d 705 (1985) (suppressing fingerprints obtained during illegal detention); Davis v. Mississippi, 394 U.S. 721, 89 S. Ct. 1394, 22 L. Ed. 2d 676 (1969) (same); United States v. Crews, 445 U.S. 463, 100 S. Ct. 1244, 63 L. Ed. 2d 537 (1980) (suppressing pretrial identification through use of photograph taken during illegal detention); United States. v. Guevara-Martinez, 262 F.3d 751 (8th Cir. 2001) (suppressing fingerprints obtained during unlawful stop); United States v. Fisher, 702 F.2d 372 (2d Cir. 1982) (suppressing eyewitness identification made after illegal arrest); In re T.L.L., 729 A.2d 334 (D.C. 1999) (suppressing eyewitness identification that was product of illegal detention); State v. Rolle, 265 N.J. Super. 482, 627 A.2d 1157 (1993) (suppressing lineup identification that derived from illegal arrest); United States v. Perez, 732 F. Supp. 347, 352 (E.D.N.Y. 1990) (suppressing photograph obtained after illegal detention).

[70]   *See, e.g.,* United States v. Beckwith, 22 F. Supp. 2d 1270 (D. Utah 1998) (routine taking of photograph after illegal arrest does not preclude its use for identification in connection with unrelated offense); People v. McInnis, 6 Cal. 3d 821, 100 Cal. Rptr. 618, 494 P.2d 690 (1972) (photograph taken during routine booking procedures following an illegal arrest may later be used in connection with investigation of an unrelated charge); Paulson v. State, 257 So. 2d 303 (Fla. Dist. Ct. App. 1972) (fingerprints routinely taken after illegal arrest may be used in a subsequent prosecution for another crime). *See also* WAYNE R. LAFAVE, 3 SEARCH AND SEIZURE § 11.4 (g) (3d ed. 1996).

[71]   United States v. Robinson, 414 U.S. 218, 94 S. Ct. 467, 38 L. Ed. 2d 427 (1973); United States v. Edwards, 415 U.S. 800, 94 S. Ct. 1234, 39 L. Ed. 2d 771 (1974). *See also generally,* WAYNE R. LAFAVE, 3 SEARCH AND SEIZURE § 5.3 (3d ed. 1996).

[72]   *See* authorities *supra* note 71.

- Removing incriminating residue from the body's surface
- Taking X-rays
- Performing strip searches and body cavity searches
- Taking body tissue and fluids for forensic analysis
- Reaching inside a suspect's mouth or pumping a suspect's stomach to recover evidence

Intrusive procedures like these normally require additional justification beyond grounds for arrest.[73]

Figure 7.5
**Bodily Evidence Defined**

Bodily evidence refers to evidence taken from a suspect's body by: (1) searching parts not normally exposed to the public; (2) penetrating the body's surface; or (3) taking biological or foreign materials. Examples include:

- Removing incriminating residues from the body's surface
- Taking X-rays
- Conducting strip searches and body cavity searches
- Taking body tissue and fluids for forensic analysis
- Reaching into a suspect's mouth or pumping his or her stomach to recover evidence

Intrusive bodily searches are generally allowed only when: (1) the government's need for the evidence exceeds the intrusion into the suspect's privacy or bodily integrity necessary to retrieve it; (2) there is a clear indication that the desired evidence will be found; (3) a search warrant is obtained (or is excused due to exigent circumstances); and (4) the procedure used to retrieve the evidence is reasonable and is performed in a reasonable manner.

## A. *The Framework for Evaluating Compelled Production of Bodily Evidence:* **Schmerber v. California**

The modern framework for evaluating when highly invasive bodily searches may be performed to retrieve evidence was established in *Schmerber v. California*.[74] Schmerber was convicted of driving while intoxicated based on the chemical analysis of a blood sample taken from his body without his consent. The blood was drawn by a physician, at the direction of the police, while Schmerber was in the hospital, where he had been taken from the scene of the accident following his arrest for drunk driving. Schmerber objected to this evidence on the grounds that drawing blood without his consent violated his Fifth Amendment privilege against self-incrimination and Fourth Amendment right

---

[73] *See, e.g.*, Illinois v. Lafayette, 462 U.S. 640, 103 S. Ct. 2605, 77 L. Ed. 2d 65 (1983); Fuller v. M.G. Jewelry, 950 F.2d 1437 (9th Cir. 1991); Mary Beth G. v. City of Chicago, 723 F.2d 1263 (7th Cir. 1983).
[74] 384 U.S. 757, 86 S. Ct. 1826, 16 L. Ed. 2d 908 (1966).

to be free from unreasonable searches and seizures. The Supreme Court made short shrift of his first claim. Because the evidence taken from Schmerber's body was physical, not testimonial, the Fifth Amendment privilege against self-incrimination did not apply. Schmerber's Fourth Amendment claim raised a more serious question.

After establishing that drawing blood from a suspect's body without consent constitutes a search, the Court established a framework for evaluating when searches below the body surface satisfy Fourth Amendment standards of reasonableness. Four factors must be considered: (1) the reasonableness of compelling the suspect to submit to the procedure, (2) the probability that the desired evidence will be found, (3) whether a search warrant is obtained, and (4) whether the procedure is reasonable and is performed in a reasonable manner.

The first factor—the reasonableness of compelling the suspect to submit to the procedure—is determined by balancing the government's need for the evidence against the invasiveness of the procedure required to obtain it. The government's need for the evidence must be greater than the medical risk and pain for forced submission to be considered reasonable. Second, invasive bodily searches are not allowed on a mere chance that evidence will be found; there must be a "clear indication" that the desired evidence is present. Third, police must obtain a search warrant before forcing a suspect to submit to the procedure unless the evidence will be destroyed as a result of the delay needed to obtain a warrant. Finally, the procedure performed to retrieve the evidence must be reasonable and must be performed in a reasonable manner.

Applying these factors, the Supreme Court concluded that drawing Schmerber's blood for chemical analysis was reasonable under the circumstances of this case, even though this procedure was performed without a warrant. The smell of alcohol on Schmerber's breath, as well as his bloodshot eyes, provided a clear indication that he was intoxicated. Consequently, there was a high probability that a blood-alcohol test would be successful in recovering evidence. Second, drawing blood is a routine medical procedure that carries no threat to health and almost no pain. The government's need for the evidence, therefore, outweighed the invasion of Schmerber's bodily integrity required to obtain the evidence. Third, though a search warrant is normally required before forcing a suspect to undergo a medical procedure, none was required here because the percentage of alcohol in the blood begins to diminish shortly after drinking stops. Delaying the search to obtain a warrant would have resulted in the destruction of this evidence. Finally, because the blood extraction was performed in a hospital setting by a trained professional, the procedure was reasonable and was performed in a reasonable manner. That drawing blood is a routine medical procedure that carries no risk and almost no pain was pivotal to the decision. The Court warned that this decision should not be understood as applying to highly invasive and dangerous procedures.[75]

---

[75]    *Id.* at 772, 86 S. Ct. at 1836.

## B. Surgical Intrusions to Recover Evidence

Nine years later, the Supreme Court was asked to decide whether a suspect could be compelled to undergo surgery. In *Winston v. Lee,*[76] a prosecutor sought a court order to compel a suspect who was shot during a robbery to undergo surgery to remove a bullet lodged in his collarbone so the prosecutor could use it as evidence. Using the approach outlined in *Schmerber*, the Court ruled against the government. The surgical procedure for which the authorization was sought was far more painful, dangerous, and invasive than the blood extraction authorized in *Schmerber*, while the evidence was less necessary because the prosecutor already had ample evidence to secure a conviction.[77] This being the case, forced surgery was constitutionally unreasonable. However, the general tone of the opinion makes it doubtful that the government's need for evidence could ever be great enough to force a suspect to undergo surgery under general anesthesia, putting his or her life at risk.

# § 7.10   —Necessity of a Search Warrant to Explore for Bodily Evidence

*Schmerber* and *Winston* both involved searches that intruded below the body's surface. In *Schmerber*, the intrusion resulted from insertion of a needle to draw blood, while in *Winston* the intrusion resulted from performing surgery. In discussing the need for a search warrant before performing searches that penetrate the surface of the body, the *Schmerber* Court wrote:

> Search warrants are ordinarily required for searches of dwellings, and absent an emergency, no less could be required where intrusions into the human body are concerned . . . The importance of informed, detached and deliberate determinations of the issue whether or not to invade another's body in search of evidence is indisputable and great.

Although the quoted language stresses the fact that the contemplated procedure—drawing blood—intruded into the body, courts have not treated this as a limiting factor. Police should generally obtain a search warrant before compelling suspects to undergo procedures on their bodies that involve any of the following: (1) penetrating the body's surface; (2) taking saliva,[78] urine,[79] semen, or pubic hair samples,[80] or other bodily tissues or fluids; (3) manually

---

[76]   470 U.S. 753, 105 S. Ct. 1611, 84 L. Ed. 2d 662 (1985).

[77]   *Id.* at 765-766, 105 S. Ct. at 1619-1620.

[78]   United States v. Nicolosi, 885 F. Supp. 50 (E.D.N.Y. 1995); State v. Ostroski, 201 Conn. 534, 518 A.2d 915 (1986).

[79]   **National Treasury Employees Union v. Von Raab, 489 U.S. 656, 109 S. Ct. 1384, 103 L. Ed. 2d 685 (1989)** (requiring a person to provide a urine sample involves a search); United States v. Edmo, 140 F.3d 1289 (9th Cir. 1998) (search warrant required unless evidence will be destroyed by delay).

[80]   State v. Towne, 158 Vt. 607, 615 A.2d 484 (1992).

inspecting rectal or genital cavities;[81] (4) severe pain or discomfort; (5) risks to health; or (6) intense humiliation.[82] On the other hand, courts have not insisted on a search warrant before performing unobtrusive procedures like "the placing of the arrestee's hands under an ultraviolet lamp; examining the arrestee's arms to determine the age of burn marks; swabbing the arrestee's hands with a chemical substance; taking scrapings from under the arrestee's fingernails; [or] taking a small sample of hair from the arrestee's head."[83]

Figure 7.6
**Bodily Evidence Procedures for Which a Search Warrant Is Necessary**

Unless confronted with an emergency in which the delay could cause evidence to be destroyed, the officer should obtain a search warrant before performing or arranging for the performance of procedures that:

1.   involve taking bodily tissues or fluids,
2.   penetrate the surface of the body,
3.   require examination of rectal or genital cavities,
4.   involve significant pain or physical discomfort,
5.   are dangerous to health, or
6.   are extremely degrading or humiliating.

When a search warrant is required, searching without a warrant violates the Fourth Amendment unless the search falls within the narrow class of exceptions covered in Chapter 4. One of the exceptions deals with exigent circumstances. This exception allows the police to conduct a warrantless search to preserve evidence when they have grounds for a search and probable cause to believe that the evidence will be destroyed if they delay action to obtain a warrant.[84] Courts have applied the exigent circumstances exception to the following three situations: (1) taking blood, breath, or urine samples to perform tests for alcohol intoxication; (2) swabbing residues left on the skin; and (3) reaching into a suspect's mouth to prevent evidence from being swallowed. The exigent circumstances exception eliminates the need for a search warrant, but not the three other requirements laid down in *Schmerber*, which must still be satisfied.

## A. Testing for Alcohol Intoxication

Because the percentage of alcohol in the blood begins to decrease rapidly once drinking stops, police officers need to take immediate action to preserve this evidence once they make an alcohol-related arrest. The exigent circum-

[81]   Rodriques v. Furtado, 950 F.2d 805 (1st Cir. 1991); Fuller v. M.G. Jewelry, *supra* note 73; State v. Fontenot, 383 So. 2d 365 (La. 1980); People v. More, 738 N.Y.S.2d 667, 764 N.E.2d 967 (N.Y. 2002).
[82]   State v. Williams, 15 Kan. App. 2d 656, 815 P.2d 569 (1991).
[83]   3 WAYNE R. LAFAVE, SEARCH & SEIZURE § 5.3 (3d ed. 1996)
[84]   Michigan v. Tyler, 436 U.S. 499, 98 S. Ct. 1942, 56 L. Ed. 2d 486 (1978); Ker v. California, 374 U.S. 23, 83 S. Ct. 1623, 10 L. Ed. 2d 726 (1963).

stances exception formed the basis for the Supreme Court's holding in *Schmerber*, allowing blood to be drawn without a search warrant for alcohol testing. Breathalyzer tests and chemical analysis of urine are alternative procedures for measuring the presence of alcohol in the body and, consequently, may also be performed without a search warrant.

Students should not conclude that a warrant is never necessary before blood is drawn for chemical analysis. The properties for which the blood will be tested determines whether a warrant is necessary. When the properties are stable and do not change over time, such as DNA or blood type, there are no exigent circumstances and a warrant must be obtained before blood may be drawn.[85]

## B. Swabbing Incriminating Residue on the Skin

Many crimes leave incriminating residue on the perpetrator's skin. Firing a gun leaves microscopic chemical residue; physical contact with the victim may leave biological tissue and fiber residue. Residue evidence must be taken as soon as police officers are aware of its existence, because residue can be washed off, wiped off, and disappears naturally in the normal course of living. Techniques for obtaining residue evidence are even less intrusive than for drawing blood. Residue can be removed by rubbing a cotton swab over the suspect's skin where the residue is located and sending the specimen to a laboratory for analysis. In *Cupp v. Murphy*,[86] the police, while questioning the murder victim's husband, noticed debris under his fingernails that looked like dried blood and asked for permission to take a scraping. When the suspect refused, put his hands in his pockets, and started abrading his fingernails against coins and keys, the officers grabbed him and took the scraping without his consent. A lab analysis of the scraping revealed traces of his wife's blood. The Supreme Court held that the police were justified in taking the scraping without a warrant because they had probable cause to believe that Cupp had murdered his wife and was in the process of destroying evidence and were, therefore, confronted with exigent circumstances.

## C. Reaching Inside a Suspect's Mouth to Prevent Evidence from Being Swallowed

Suspects in narcotics investigations sometimes try to swallow evidence to prevent discovery. With the suspect chomping on evidence, there is no time to get a warrant. Because a suspect's mouth is not considered a "sacred orifice,"[87] police may use reasonable force it pry it open.[88] When this fails, officers some-

---

[85]  McBride v. State, 840 S.W.2d 111 (Tex. Ct. App. 1992).
[86]  412 U.S. 291, 93 S. Ct. 2000, 36 L. Ed. 2d 900 (1973).
[87]  People v. Johnson, 231 Cal. App. 3d 1, 15, 282 Cal. Rptr. 114, 122 (1991).
[88]  *See, e.g.*, State v. Strong, 493 N.W.2d 834 (Iowa 1992).

times try to prevent swallowing through a maneuver called a "chokehold," which consists of grabbing the suspect by the throat and applying pressure. While this maneuver is effective to prevent swallowing, it also cuts off breathing and, as a result, some courts consider it too dangerous to be used.[89]

When a suspect succeeds in swallowing evidence, stomach pumping is sometimes tried as a last resort. In *Rochin v. California*,[90] the Supreme Court found this practice unconstitutional. However, *Rochin* was decided before *Schmerber* and it is unlikely that it would be decided the same way today. Stomach pumping is not life-threatening and causes no lasting trauma or pain. As a result, most courts consider stomach pumping to be a constitutionally acceptable means of recovering evidence when performed in a hospital setting by a trained physician.[91]

## § 7.11 —Strip Searches and Body Cavity Searches

Strip and body cavity searches involve substantial invasions of privacy. While there are no universally accepted definitions for these terms, **strip searches** involve compulsory disrobing followed by a visual inspection of the nude body while **manual body cavity searches** involve touching or probing of rectal or genital cavities.[92] Words are incapable of capturing the extremely degrading quality of these searches.[93] In a recent case, the court described the pre-incarceration search routine at a particular detention facility.[94] Newly arriving detainees are required to remove all their clothing. An intake officer

---

[89] *See, e.g.*, Merriweather v. State, 228 Ga. App. 246, 491 S.E.2d 467 (1997) (allowed); People v. Fulkman, 235 Cal. App. 3d 555, 286 Cal. Rptr. 728 (1992) (allowed); State v. Tapp, 353 So. 2d 265 (La. 1977) (not allowed).

[90] 342 U.S. 165, 72 S. Ct. 205, 96 L. Ed. 183 (1952).

[91] *See, e.g.*, Hendrix v. State, 843 So. 2d 1003 (Fla. Dist. Ct. App. 2003); Lewis v. State, 56 S.W.3d 617 (Tex. Ct. App. 2001); Beck v. State, 216 Ga. App. 532, 455 S.E.2d 110 (1995); State v. Strong, 493 N.W.2d 834 (Iowa 1992); Oviedo v. State 767 S.W.2d 214 (Tex. Ct. App. 1989). *But see* Williams v. Payne 73 F. Supp. 2d 785 (E.D. Mich. 1999) (forcible stomach pumping to retrieve evidence violates Fourth Amendment).

[92] *See, e.g.*, Roberts v. State of Rhode Island, 239 F.3d 107, 108 (1st Cir. 2001); Sarnicola v. County of Westchester, 229 F. Supp. 2d 259 (S.D.N.Y. 2002) (noting that "case law reveals stark and significant discrepancies in the definitions of terms such as 'strip search' and 'body cavity search'" and concluding that "[i]t is obvious that there is a pressing need for clarity and uniformity in the terminology used to describe strip searches, so that courts and officials share an understanding of what is permissible under the Fourth Amendment."). Some states have statutes defining strip and body cavity searches and establishing criteria for when these intrusive bodily searches are justified. *See, e.g.*, WA. STAT. §10.79.070 *et seq.* defining "strip search" as having "a person remove or arrange some or all of his or her clothing so as to permit an inspection of the genitals, buttocks, anus, or undergarments of the person or breasts of a female person" and "body cavity search" as "touching or probing the stomach or rectum of a person or the vagina of a female person."

[93] *See, e.g.*, Mary Beth G. v. City of Chicago, *supra* note 73 at 1272 (7th Cir. 1983) (describing strip and body cavity searches entailing inspection of anal and/or genital areas as "demeaning, dehumanizing, undignified, humiliating, embarrassing, repulsive, degrading, and extremely intrusive of one's personal privacy.").

[94] *See, e.g.*, Rhode Island Department of Corrections Policy & Procedure 9.14-1 Part III.B.2. (dated January 27, 1997), *quoted in* Roberts v. State of Rhode Island, *supra* note 92. *See also* Murcia v. County of Orange, 226 F. Supp. 2d 489 (S.D.N.Y. 2002).

then looks inside their ears, mouth, and nostrils, runs his fingers through their hair, has them lift their penises and testicles to provide a clear view of their groin area, and then has them bend over and spread their rectum to provide a clear view of this area. Female detainees are required to lift their breasts and bend forward while spreading the cheeks of the buttocks to facilitate visual inspection of their vaginal and anal cavities.

Strip and body cavity searches are not routine searches; they require additional justification beyond grounds for arrest.[95] The Supreme Court has, unfortunately, provided limited guidance as to what exactly is needed.[96] The prevailing view is that strip searches require reasonable suspicion that the search will turn up evidence of drugs, weapons, or contraband[97] and that manual body cavity searches that involve an intrusion into the body require compliance with the requirements set forth in *Schmerber*.[98]

Figure 7.7

**Legal Standards for Conducting Strip and Body Cavity Searches**

| Strip search | Manual body cavity search |
|---|---|
| Police must have reasonable suspicion that a strip search will turn up evidence of drugs, weapons, or contraband. | Police must comply with the requirements established in *Schmerber*. |

---

[95]  *See, e.g.*, United States v. Ford, 232 F. Supp. 2d 625 (E.D. Va. 2002) (authority to conduct a body cavity search is not an automatic incident of lawful custodial arrest); Fuller v. M.G. Jewelry, *supra* note 73 (search incident to arrest does not extend to a strip search or body cavity search); Mary Beth G. v. City of Chicago, *supra* note 73 (same); State v. Bullock, 661 So. 2d 1074 (La. Dist. Ct. App. 1995) (body cavity search exceeded the scope of a search incident to an arrest).

[96]  Bell v. Wolfish, 441 U.S. 520, 99 S. Ct. 1861, 60 L. Ed. 2d 447 (1979) (holding that the reasonableness of a strip search must be determined by balancing the need for the particular search against the invasion of personal rights that the search entails; the factors to be considered include the scope of the particular intrusion, the justification for initiating it, and the place and manner in which it is conducted).

[97]  *See, e.g.*, Swain v. Spinney, 117 F.3d 1 (1st Cir. 1997) (stating that a strip search, at minimum, requires at least reasonable suspicion that an arrestee is concealing drugs, weapons, or contraband); Foote v. Spiegel, 118 F.3d 1416 (10th Cir. 1997) (same); Sarnicola v. County of Westchester, *supra* note 92 (same). Justification beyond reasonable suspicion is required in a few jurisdictions. In Massachusetts, for example, "(b)efore police may command removal of an arrested person's last layer of clothing, they must have probable cause to believe that they will find a weapon, contraband, or the fruits or instrumentalities of criminal activity that they could not reasonably expect to discover without forcing the arrested person to discard all of his or her clothing."

[98]  *See, e.g.*, United States v. Oyekan, 786 F.2d 832 (8th Cir. 1986) (stating that "a body cavity search must be conducted consistently with the *Schmerber* factors"); Giles v. Ackerman, 746 F.2d 614 (9th Cir. 1984) (stating that Schmerber "implies that intrusions into the arrestee's body, including body cavity searches . . . are not authorized by arrest alone"); People v. Moore, 738 N.Y.S.2d 667 (N.Y. 2002) (manual body cavity searches must be conducted consistent with *Schmerber* requirements); Moss v. Com., 516 S.E.2d 246 (Va. App. 1999) (same)

## A. Strip Searches

The most common occasion for a strip search is when an arrestee is booked into a detention facility. The purpose of the search is to protect jail security needs. Blanket strip search policies were at one time the norm. However, such policies have been declared unconstitutional in virtually every recent case in which this issue has been raised.[99] Strip searches may not be performed on everyone booked into a detention facility, regardless of the nature of the crime or other individualized factors. Police must have a reasonable suspicion that drugs, weapons, or contraband will, in fact, be found.[100] Such suspicion is automatically present when an arrest is made for a violent crime or one in which possession of a weapon is likely,[101] but rarely in other cases and certainly not when an arrest is made for a misdemeanor or a traffic violation.[102] When the nature of the offense does not warrant reasonable suspicion that the person has drugs, weapons, or contraband concealed on his or her person, a strip search is unconstitutional unless police have some other basis for such suspicion.[103]

---

[99] See, e.g., Wilson v. Jones, 251 F.3d 1340 (11th Cir. 2001) (jail policy requiring search of all arrestees violates Fourth Amendment); Brown v. City of Boston, 154 F. Supp. 2d 131 (D. Mass. 2001) (concern for jail security does not justify blanket policy of strip searching all arrestees admitted to jail, regardless of crimes with which they are charged or other individual factors); Murcia v. County of Orange, 226 F. Supp. 2d 489 (S.D.N.Y. 2002) (blanket policy of strip-searching all newly arrested detainees before placement in correctional facility without individualized reasonable suspicion that the person searched has drugs, weapons, or contraband secreted on his or her person violates the Fourth Amendment). See also generally, John H. Derrick, Fourth Amendment as Prohibiting Strip Searches of Arrestees or Pretrial Detainees, 78 A.L.R. FED. 201 (1986)

[100] See, e.g., Swain v. Spinney, 117 F.3d 1 (1st Cir. 1997) (a particularized reasonable belief that arrestee is secreting contraband required before officer may conduct strip search); Foote v. Spiegel, 118 F.3d 1416 (10th Cir. 1997) (same); Sarnicola v. County of Westchester, supra note 92 (same).

[101] See, e.g., Brown v. City of Boston, supra note 99; Roberts v. State of Rhode Island, supra note 94 (stating that reasonable suspicion for strip search is present when the arrest is for a violent felony).

[102] See, e.g., Wilson v. Jones, 251 F.3d 1340 (11th Cir. 2001) (strip search of woman arrested for drunk driving unconstitutional); Roberts v. Rhode Island, supra note 94 at 112 (1st Cir. 2001) (strip search of person arrested for minor offense unconstitutional); Kelly v. Foti, 77 F.3d 819 (5th Cir. 1996) (arrest for making illegal turn and lack of driver's license does not create a reasonable suspicion that arrestee is hiding weapons or contraband so as to justify a strip search); Masters v. Crouch, 872 F.2d 1248 (6th Cir. 1989) (strip search of individuals arrested for nonviolent minor offense violates Fourth Amendment unless there are individualized factors that create reasonable suspicion that they are carrying weapons or contraband); Brown v. City of Boston, supra note 99 (strip search not justified after arrest for crimes like operating a motor vehicle while under the influence of alcohol, violating a municipal ordinance requiring a peddler's license, or petty larceny growing out of failure to return a video game); Murcia v. County of Orange, supra note 99 (strip searches of individuals charged with misdemeanors or other minor offenses are lawful only when officers have some other basis for reasonable suspicion that they are have drugs, weapons, or contraband hidden on their body); People v. Jennings, 97 A.D.2d 644, 747 N.Y.S.2d 235 (2002) (same).

[103] See, e.g., State v. Pena, 869 P.2d 932 (Utah 1994) (strip search supported by reasonable suspicion that defendant was carrying drugs when officer knew that arrestee had previously been arrested for drug offense and observed him with his hands in his pants as though attempting to conceal something); State v. Armstead, 832 So. 2d 389 (La. Dist. Ct. App. 2002) (strip search justified where officer observed a person give suspect money in exchange for a small object and defendant then stuck something down the back of her pants); People v. Taylor, 294 A.D.2d 825, 741 N.Y.S.2d 822 (2002) (defendant lawfully strip-searched at station after officer discovered crack pipe in his pocket and observed him moving legs and torso in a suspicious way). But see Swain v. Spinney, 117 F.3d 1 (1st Cir. 1997) (the fact that the

When authority exists to conduct a strip search, care must be taken to protect the person's privacy. The search must be conducted by an officer of the same gender in a location where the search cannot be observed by others.[104]

### B. Body Cavity Searches

There are few things more degrading than being forced to submit to a rectal or genital examination by someone searching for evidence. Because rectal and genital cavity searches intrude inside the body, most courts apply the requirements laid down in *Schmerber*.[105] To justify a body cavity search, there must be a clear indication that evidence will be found and the officer must obtain a search warrant.[106] Courts have rejected application of the exigent circumstances exception to manual body cavity searches because objects hidden inside rectal or genital cavities are not in danger of being destroyed.[107] Police can prevent destruction by keeping the arrestee under observation until a search warrant is obtained. Rectal and genital cavity searches must be performed under sanitary conditions by a medical professional, not a police officer.[108]

## § 7.12 Summary and Practical Suggestions

Constitutional restrictions on the government's power to compel suspects to provide assistance in building a case against them depend on whether the government is seeking physical evidence or testimony.

Compulsion to provide incriminating testimony is regulated by the Fifth Amendment, which bars the government from compelling defendants to take the witness stand at their criminal trial and from introducing previously com-

---

plaintiff dropped a baggie of marijuana at the scene of the crime did not justify a strip search); People v. Jennings, *supra* note 102 (strip search of defendant conducted incident to his arrest for the unlawful possession of marijuana unjustified where search was based on nothing more than discovery of bag of marijuana in vehicle in which the defendant was a passenger).

[104] *See, e.g.*, Farmer v. Perrill, 288 F.3d 1254 (10th Cir. 2002) (strip search of motorist detained for a minor traffic offense, conducted in lobby area in view of 10 to 12 persons, violated Fourth Amendment); Johnson v. State, 613 So. 2d 554 (Fla. Dist. Ct. App. 1993) (roadside strip search performed in public view unconstitutional).

[105] *See* authorities *supra* note 98.

[106] *Id.*; *see also*, United States v. Ford, *supra* note 95; Amaechi v. West, 87 F. Supp. 2d 556 (E.D. Va. 2000); Rodriques v. Furtado, *supra* note 81; State v. Clark, 65 Haw. 488, 654 P.2d 355 (1982); State v. Fontenot, *supra* note 81; People v. More, 738 N.Y.S.2d 667, 764 N.E.2d 967 (N.Y. 2002); Lewis v. State, 56 S.W.3d 626 (Tex. Ct. App. 2001); Hughes v. Com., 1 Va.App. 447, 524 S.E.2d 155 (Va. Ct. App. 2000); Moss v. Com., 516 S.E.2d 246 (Va. Ct. App. 1999).

[107] *See, e.g.*, State v. Clark, *supra* note 106; Fuller v. M.G. Jewelry, *supra* note 73; State v. Fontenot, *supra* note 81.

[108] *See, e.g.*, Rodriques v. Furtado, *supra* note 81; United States v. Ford, *supra* note 95 (officer's search of suspect's anal cavity on side of public highway in broad daylight, following a traffic stop, violated Fourth Amendment).

pelled self-incriminating statements as evidence against them. Protection of the Fifth Amendment privilege against self-incrimination may be invoked in all legal proceedings, whether judicial or administrative, criminal or civil, or formal or informal, and also during police custodial interrogations. The Fifth Amendment provides two forms of protection: (1) the right to remain silent, and (2) the privilege not to answer incriminating questions. The right to remain silent involves a complete exemption from a citizen's normal duty to give testimony. This protection is available in only two contexts—during police custodial interrogations and at the defendant's criminal trial. In all other contexts, citizens are privileged to not answer incriminating questions, but are not privileged to refuse to testify.

Three factors are necessary to activate the protection of the Fifth Amendment: (1) testimony, (2) compulsion, and (3) self-incrimination. Testimony encompasses any behavior that explicitly or implicitly makes a statement or discloses information. Compulsion occurs when the government threatens a serious consequence unless the person makes a statement. Self-incrimination requires that the statement subject the maker to a risk of criminal prosecution. This risk can be removed by granting immunity. Witnesses who have been granted immunity from the government's use of their testimony may not invoke the Fifth Amendment because the testimony is no longer self-incriminating.

The Fifth Amendment provides no protection against compulsory self-incrimination through evidence that derives from a suspect's body because this evidence is physical, not testimonial. The source of protection for a suspect's body is the Fourth Amendment, which confers protection on a suspect's (1) freedom of movement, (2) bodily privacy, and (3) bodily integrity.

Evidence that derives from body characteristics that are exposed to the public is called *appearance evidence*. Station house lineups, showups at the crime scene, photographing, measurements, fingerprinting, handwriting and voice samples, and field sobriety tests are the main examples of police procedures that yield appearance evidence. Because these procedures do not invade a suspect's privacy or bodily integrity, they may be performed whenever police have constitutional grounds to seize a suspect and detain him or her long enough to perform the procedure.

Evidence obtained by searching a suspect's private parts, penetrating inside the body, or removing biological or other substances from the body is called *bodily evidence*. Searches for bodily evidence are generally allowed only when: (1) the government's need for the evidence outweighs the bodily intrusion required to obtain it, (2) there is a clear indication that the desired evidence will be found, (3) the police obtain a search warrant (or are confronted with exigent circumstances that excuse the need for obtaining one), and (4) the procedure used to retrieve the evidence is medically reasonable and is performed in a medically reasonable manner. Unless confronted with exigent circumstances, police should obtain a search warrant before compelling suspects to undergo any procedure that involves penetrating the body surface, taking blood, saliva, urine, public hair, semen or other tissue samples, or that involves severe discomfort or risk to health. Strip and manual body cavity searches require justification beyond grounds for arrest. The former requires reasonable suspicion to believe that the search will turn up evidence, while the latter requires compliance with the four requirements listed above.

# Right to Counsel 8

*In all criminal prosecutions, the accused shall enjoy the right . . . to have the Assistance of Counsel for his defense.*

Sixth Amendment, 1791

# Chapter Outline

## Key Terms and Concepts

| | |
|---|---|
| Accused | Interrogation |
| Appointed counsel | Lineup |
| Arraignment | Photographic identification |
| Confrontation | Prosecution |
| Critical stage | Retained counsel |
| Indictment | Showup |
| Information | Suspect |

# § 8.1 Overview of the Sixth Amendment Right to Counsel

The Sixth Amendment right to counsel represents a departure from the English common law rather than an adoption of it. It was not until 1836 that persons accused of felonies acquired the right to counsel in England.[1] Counsel was less important during early common law England because criminal cases were prosecuted by the victim, not the state.[2] Consequently, the **accused** and accuser stood on relatively equal footing, reducing the need for professional assistance.

However, since colonial times, crimes in the United States have been prosecuted by highly trained professionals who represent the government.[3] The advent of this system created the need for defendants to hire lawyers to do battle for them. This was the background against which the Framers adopted the Sixth Amendment, which guarantees that "[i]n all criminal prosecutions, the accused shall enjoy the right . . . to have the Assistance of Counsel for his defense."[4]

---

[1] Powell v. Alabama, 287 U.S. 45, 68, 53 S. Ct. 55, 64, 77 L. Ed. 2d 158 (1932) (stating that the common law, as it existed in England at the time the U.S. Constitution was adopted, generally denied counsel to felony defendants); Adam D. Young, *An Analysis of the Sixth Amendment Right to Counsel as it Applies to Suspended Sentences and Probation: Do Argersinger and Scott Blow a Flat Note on Gideon's Trumpet?*, 107 DICK. L. R. 699 (2003) (stating that, while the English common law recognized the right to counsel for individuals charged with treason, misdemeanor offenses, and in civil litigation, there was no right to counsel for individuals accused of felonies until 1836).

[2] Powell v. Alabama, *supra* note 1.

[3] *Id.*; United States v. Ash, 413 U.S. 300, 93 S. Ct. 2568, 37 L. Ed. 2d 919 (1973).

[4] U.S. CONST. AMEND. VI (1971).

The Sixth Amendment right to counsel performs two functions vital to our adversarial system of criminal justice. First and foremost, counsel is necessary to avoid unjust convictions. The average layperson lacks the legal skills needed to put forth an effective defense. This places uncounseled defendants at risk of being convicted, even though innocent. The Supreme Court has stressed the importance of legal assistance to avoiding unjust convictions:

> The right to be heard would be, in many cases, of little avail if it did not comprehend the right to be heard by counsel. Even the intelligent and educated layman has small and sometimes no skill in the science of law. If charged with crime, he is incapable, generally, of determining for himself whether the indictment is good or bad. He is unfamiliar with the rules of evidence. Left without the aid of counsel he may be put on trial without a proper charge, and convicted upon incompetent evidence, or evidence irrelevant to the issue or otherwise inadmissible. He lacks both the skill and knowledge adequately to prepare his defense, even though he have a perfect one. He requires the guiding hand of counsel at every step in the proceedings against him. *Without it, though he be not guilty, he faces the danger of conviction because he does not know how to establish his innocence.*[5]

The right to counsel is so important to the fair administration of justice that counsel must be made available, free of charge, to defendants who cannot afford to hire an attorney on their own and ineffective assistance of counsel renders a conviction vulnerable to challenge.

The right to counsel also performs a second function. Representation is necessary for effective assertion of a criminal defendant's other constitutional rights. Protections like the right to remain silent during custodial interrogations and to have the fruits of an illegal arrest, search, or seizure suppressed are basic to our adversarial system of criminal justice, but the average defendant is not sufficiently familiar with the Court's decisions to claim them. Without the guiding hand of counsel to assist defendants in asserting their constitutional rights, the Court's decisions would have little practical application. Because important rights may be lost during stages of the criminal process other than the trial, the right to counsel is no longer just a "trial right." It is also available in a variety of pretrial and post-trial contexts.[6]

## § 8.2 —The Indigent Person's Right to Appointed Counsel

At common law and throughout most of the Sixth Amendment's history, assistance of counsel was available only to defendants who could afford an attorney. The Sixth Amendment right to counsel was interpreted to mean only that the government could not deny defendants who had the means to hire a

---

[5]  Powell v. Alabama, *supra* note 1 (emphasis added).

[6]  *See* § 8.3 *infra*.

lawyer the ability to do so. It imposed no obligation on the government to furnish counsel to defendants who lacked the means. This interpretation seems unjust by modern standards. If, as the founders believed,[7] assistance of counsel is necessary to assure a fair trial, then it followed that those who could not afford a lawyer were being convicted, imprisoned, and even executed unfairly.

*Powell v. Alabama*[8] was the first case to recognize the right of an indigent criminal defendant to court-appointed counsel. In *Powell*, nine indigent and illiterate African-American youths were charged with raping two white girls. They were tried in a racially tense environment in which the state militia had to be called in to protect them from an angry mob waiting outside the courthouse. The youths were tried without the aid of counsel. Eight of the nine were convicted and sentenced to death.

The Supreme Court set aside their convictions, holding that they were denied the right to **appointed counsel**. The source of this right was not the Sixth Amendment right to counsel. *Powell* involved a state court conviction and, at the time it was decided, the safeguards contained in the Bill of Rights were not binding on the states. The Supreme Court located the right of state criminal defendants to court-appointed counsel in the due process clause of the Fourteenth Amendment, which guarantees a fair trial. The Court reasoned that placing illiterate youths on trial for their life without affording them the help of a lawyer rendered the trial fundamentally unfair, violating the Fourteenth Amendment prohibition against depriving citizens of "life . . . without due process of law." *Powell v. Alabama* was an exceedingly narrow ruling, as the following passage reveals:

> We are of opinion that, under the circumstances . . . counsel was so vital and imperative that the failure of the trial court to make an effective appointment of counsel was . . . a denial of due process within the meaning of the Fourteenth Amendment. Whether this would be so in other criminal prosecutions, or under other circumstances, we need not determine. All that it is necessary now to decide . . . is that in a capital case, where the defendant is unable to employ counsel, and is incapable adequately of making his own defense because of ignorance, feeble-mindedness, illiteracy, or the like, it is the duty of the court, whether requested or not, to assign counsel for him as a necessary requisite of due process of law.[9]

*Powell* gave state criminal defendants facing serious charges the right to court-appointed counsel if they were illiterate or otherwise at a disadvantage in defending themselves. Predicated on the due process right to a fair trial, *Powell* required proof of special circumstances that caused the failure to provide court-appointed counsel to result in an unfair trial. Six years later, the Supreme Court conferred a broader right to counsel on indigent criminal defendants facing federal criminal charges, a right that derived from the Sixth

---

[7] Powell v. Alabama, *supra* note 1.

[8] *Id.*

[9] *Id.*

Amendment, and did not depend on proof that they were illiterate or otherwise handicapped in defending themselves.[10] The Sixth Amendment right to court-appointed counsel was available to any federal criminal defendant facing serious charges who lacked the means to hire a lawyer.[11]

The law stood at this point for the next 25 years. Federal courts had to provide counsel for any criminal defendant facing serious charges who lacked the means to hire an attorney,[12] while state courts had to provide counsel only for defendants who, because of "special circumstances," were incapable of receiving a fair trial without representation by counsel.[13]

In the celebrated case of *Gideon v. Wainwright*,[14] the Supreme Court erased the distinction between federal and state prosecutions. Gideon was charged by the state of Florida with a felony that carried a five-year sentence. He demanded that the trial court appoint an attorney for him, his only reason being that he could not afford one. The court denied Gideon's demand, explaining that because he was not illiterate or otherwise hindered from representing himself, he was not entitled to appointment of counsel. Gideon was convicted and eventually brought a habeas corpus petition challenging the constitutionality of his imprisonment on the basis that he was denied the Sixth Amendment right to court-appointed counsel. The Supreme Court agreed, ruling that court-appointed counsel must henceforth be furnished to state criminal defendants facing felony charges who lack the means to hire a lawyer on their own.[15]

The Sixth Amendment today entitles indigent defendants in state criminal prosecutions to representation at the state's expense before they may be sentenced to prison, whether the crime is a felony or a misdemeanor. However, the Supreme Court has carved out an exception for misdemeanor prosecutions in which a fine alone is imposed. The Sixth Amendment does not require appointment of counsel for indigent state criminal defendants charged with a misdemeanor unless they are actually sentenced to prison.[16] This exception is based on practical considerations. The cost of providing court-appointed counsel in cases in which a fine alone is imposed would be too burdensome on the government.

Once the right to appointment of trial counsel became firmly established, a period of rapid expansion followed. Indigent criminal defendants today have the right to have counsel appointed to represent them during all critical pretrial stages,[17] post-trial sentencing proceedings,[18] and the first appeal of a conviction or sentence.[19] The right to counsel during these stages is covered in the next section.

[10] Johnson v. Zerbst, 304 U.S. 458, 58 S. Ct. 1019, 82 L. Ed. 1462 (1938).
[11] *Id.*
[12] *Id.*; Argersinger v. Hamlin, 407 U.S. 321, 92 S. Ct. 2006, 32 L. Ed. 2d 530 (1972).
[13] Betts v. Brady, 316 U.S. 455, 62 S. Ct. 1252, 86 L. Ed. 1595
[14] **372 U.S. 335, 83 S. Ct. 792, 9 L. Ed. 2d 799 (1963).**
[15] *Id.*
[16] Scott v. Illinois, 440 U.S. 367, 99 S. Ct. 1158, 59 L. Ed. 2d 383 (1979); Argersinger v. Hamlin, *supra* note 12; Alabama v. Shelton, ___ U.S.___, 122 S. Ct. 1764, 152 L. Ed.2d 888 (2002) (suspended sentence may not be imposed on an unrepresented indigent defendant because the sentences may end up in an actual deprivation of liberty in the future.).
[17] United States v. Wade, 388 U.S. 218, 87 S. Ct. 1926, 18 L. Ed. 2d 1149 (1967).
[18] Mempa v. Rhay, 389 U.S. 128, 88 S. Ct. 254, 19 L. Ed. 2d 336 (1967).
[19] Douglass v. California, 372 U.S. 363, 83 S. Ct. 814, 9 L. Ed. 2d 811 (1963).

## § 8.3 —The Right to Assistance of Counsel in Pre- and Post-Trial Proceedings: Critical Stages of the Prosecution and Criminal Appeals

The purpose of the Sixth Amendment right to counsel is to protect the accused from being forced to do battle with the government alone.[20] When the Sixth Amendment was adopted, the trial itself was the only phase at which there was an adversarial confrontation between the government and the accused. There were few, if any, pretrial judicial proceedings, and no police force to engage the defendant in interrogations or other investigative procedures.[21] As a result, the Sixth Amendment right to assistance of counsel was originally viewed as applying only at trial.[22]

In modern times, there are a number of pretrial events, hearings, and investigative encounters, during which the accused is subjected to an adversary confrontation with the prosecutor (or the police). Some of these events can have a serious negative effect on the outcome of the trial if the defendant is forced to proceed without assistance of counsel. The defendant, for example, has a Fifth Amendment right to remain silent (i.e., not to testify) at his or her trial. This right plays an important role in defense strategy. Nevertheless, as the Supreme Court recognized in *Miranda v. Arizona*,[23] the defendant can be deprived of the benefits of this right as a result of incriminating statements made during a police **interrogation**. If the defendant confesses while being interrogated by the police, his or her goose may be cooked. This is just one example of how the presence of counsel during pretrial encounters between the accused and representatives of the government can affect the outcome of the trial.

Changes in criminal procedure made it necessary for the Supreme Court to extend the Sixth Amendment right to counsel into the pretrial period. "**Critical stage**" is a phrase coined by the Supreme Court to describe pretrial events in which the accused has the right to have counsel present.[24] A pretrial event must have the following characteristics in order to be treated as a "critical stage." First, the event must take place after the government has initiated **prosecution**.[25] Initiation of prosecution is the point at which the suspect officially becomes an "accused" and the Sixth Amendment right to counsel attaches.[26] Second, the event must involve "**confrontation**" between the government and the accused or, in other words, an adversarial encounter in which the government's representative and the accused are both present.[27] The government is entitled to investigate and prepare for trial without having defense counsel

---

[20]   United States v. Wade, *supra* note 17.
[21]   *Id.*
[22]   *Id.*
[23]   **384 U.S. 436, 86 S. Ct. 1602, 16 L. Ed. 2d 694 (1966)**.
[24]   Kirby v. Illinois, 406 U.S. 682, 92 S. Ct. 1877, 32 L. Ed. 2d 411 (1972).
[25]   *Id.* Determining when a prosecution is commenced is covered in § 6.9(A) and § 8.10(A).
[26]   *See* §§ 6.9(A) and § 8.10(A).
[27]   United States v. Ash, *supra* note 3.

looking over its shoulder. Defense attorneys have no right to be present during witness interviews, crime lab tests, and other procedures that do not require the presence of the accused. A contrary rule would hamper the prosecution's investigation and trial preparation and the presence of defense counsel is, for this reason, not allowed.[28] Finally, the encounter must be of such a nature that important rights might be lost or a fair trial jeopardized if the defendant is forced to proceed without counsel being present.[29]

The Supreme Court has recognized the following pretrial judicial proceedings as critical stages: (1) preliminary hearings, (2) bail hearings, and (3) arraignments.[30] All three proceedings involve confrontations between the government and the accused, occurring after the initiation of prosecution, in which the absence of counsel might detract from the accused's ability to receive a fair trial. During these proceedings, the defendant may waive defenses,[31] make admissible statements,[32] and even plead guilty. As a result, the accused is entitled to have counsel present during these proceedings. The Supreme Court also considers interrogations,[33] lineups,[34] and showups[35] to be critical stage events when they take place after the initiation of prosecution. Interrogations were covered in Chapter 6. Lineups and showups are discussed later in this chapter.

## A. Post-Trial Rights to Counsel

The Sixth Amendment right to counsel continues to apply, even after the trial, to post-conviction sentencing proceedings[36] and the first appeal of a conviction or sentence.[37] Although the Sixth Amendment right does not extend to subsequent appeals or habeas corpus proceedings,[38] persons convicted of a crime have always been entitled to retain counsel to represent them in these proceedings as a matter of due process.

---

[28] *Id.*

[29] *Id.*

[30] *See, e.g.,* Iowa v. Tovar, 541 U.S. 77, 124 S. Ct. 1379, 158 L. Ed. 2d 209 (2004); Coleman v. Alabama, 399 U.S. 1, 90 S. Ct. 1999, 26 L. Ed. 2d 387 (1970); McMann v. Richardson, 397 U.S. 759, 90 S. Ct. 1441, 25 L. Ed. 2d 682 (1965). The defendant also enjoys the right to counsel during court-ordered psychiatric exams to determine competency to stand trial. Estelle v. Smith, 451 U.S. 454, 101 S. Ct. 1866, 68 L. Ed. 2d 359 (1981).

[31] *See* Hamilton v. Alabama, 368 U.S. 52, 82 S. Ct. 157, 7 L. Ed. 2d 114 (1961) (insanity defense).

[32] *See* White v. Maryland, 373 U.S. 59, 83 S. Ct. 1050, 10 L. Ed. 2d 193 (1963).

[33] **Michigan v. Jackson, 475 U.S. 625, 106 S. Ct. 1404, 89 L. Ed. 2d 631 (1986);** Maine v. Moulton, 474 U.S. 159, 106 S. Ct. 477, 88 L. Ed. 2d 481 (1985).

[34] United States v. Wade, *supra* note 17.

[35] Moore v. Illinois, 434 U.S. 220, 98 S. Ct. 458, 54 L. Ed. 2d 424 (1973).

[36] Mempa v. Rhay, *supra* note 18.

[37] Douglass v. California, *supra* note 19.

[38] *Id.*

## § 8.4 —The Defendant's Right to Self-Representation

In addition to the right to assistance of counsel and to have counsel appointed if the accused cannot afford a lawyer, the Sixth Amendment guarantees yet a third right: the right to waive assistance of counsel and represent oneself at trial.[39] In striking contrast to the *Gideon* case, the Supreme Court, in *Faretta v. California*,[40] set aside a conviction not because the defendant was denied appointed counsel, but because he was convicted after the trial court forced him to accept a public defender:

> There can be no blinking the fact that the right of an accused to conduct his own defense seems to cut against the grain of this Court's holdings that the Constitution requires that no accused can be convicted and imprisoned unless he has been accorded the right to counsel. For it surely is true that the basic thesis of those decisions is that the help of a lawyer is essential to assure the defendant a fair trial. . . . [But] it is not inconceivable that . . . the defendant might present his case more effectively by conducting his own defense. . . . The defendant, not the lawyer or the State, will bear the personal consequences of a conviction. It is the defendant, therefore, who must be free personally to decide . . . .[41]

Two conditions are necessary before a judge will accept a waiver of the right to counsel: (1) The defendant must be mentally competent to make this decision, and (2) the waiver must be knowingly, voluntarily, and intelligently made.[42] The standard for competence to waive the right to counsel is low. Possession of a minimal understanding of the nature of the proceedings is all that is necessary.[43] Once competence is determined, the judge must advise the defendant of his or her right to counsel and caution him or her of the dangers and disadvantages of waiving this right, in order to ensure that the decision to forego counsel is knowingly and intelligently made.[44]

If a competent defendant makes an informed choice to waive the right to counsel and represent him or herself, the judge must honor this choice and may not force unwanted representation on the defendant, even in a death penalty case.[45] The trial judge may, nevertheless, appoint standby counsel to

---

[39] Faretta v. California, 422 U.S. 806, 95 S. Ct. 2525, 45 L. Ed. 2d 562 (1975). However, the Sixth Amendment right to self-representation is a trial right. Criminal defendants do not have the constitutional right to conduct their own appeals, although courts sometimes exercise their discretion in permitting them to do so. Martinez v. Court of Appeals of California, Fourth Appellate Dist., 528 U.S. 152, 120 S. Ct. 684, 145 L. Ed. 2d 597 (2000).

[40] *Supra* note 39.

[41] *Id.*

[42] Faretta v. California, *supra* note 39; Martinez v. Court of Appeals of California, *supra* note 39; Godinez v. Moran, 509 U.S. 389, 113 S. Ct. 2680, 125 L. Ed. 2d 321 (1993).

[43] Godinez v. Moran, *supra* note 42.

[44] *Id.*

[45] Faretta v. California, *supra* note 39; Sherwood v. State, 717 N.E.2d 131 (Ind. 1999) (Sixth Amendment rights violated when judge forced representation on defendant who was competent to stand trial).

function as a legal advisor during the trial, but does not have to take this action.[46] The right to engage in self-representation is a double-edged sword. A defendant who elects to forego counsel cannot complain of inadequate representation if displeased with the outcome.

## § 8.5 —Ineffective Assistance of Counsel

The mere presence of counsel is not always sufficient to assure that the adversary process will produce a just conviction. The defendant may be in no better position, and the legitimacy of the conviction no more certain, if his or her appointed counsel is incompetent, than if he or she was denied access to counsel outright. Accordingly, the Supreme Court has established minimum standards that counsel must meet in order for a conviction to be upheld.

The requirement that counsel render adequate assistance developed in the context of representation by appointed counsel. After *Gideon v. Wainwright*,[47] both state and federal governments had an affirmative duty to appoint counsel to represent indigents. Failing to do so would result in convictions being set aside. Because verdicts based on incompetent representation are just as suspect as those obtained without any representation at all, in its later decisions the Court made clear that the government did not satisfy its Sixth Amendment duty unless appointed counsel gave reasonably competent assistance to the defendant.[48] Accordingly, the Court held that inadequate representation by appointed counsel, or "ineffective assistance of counsel," would require setting aside the conviction.[49]

Even though the government is not responsible for ineffective assistance when the defendant hires his or her own lawyer, ineffective representation by **retained counsel** still provides grounds for challenging a conviction. The Court made this clear in the case of *Cuyler v. Sullivan*,[50] in which Sullivan was made the "fall guy" by his own lawyer. Sullivan was charged in a Mafia-style murder along with two other men. "Friends" of his co-defendants retained counsel to represent all three of them. Sullivan's case came to trial first. Sullivan's attorney failed to put on evidence at the close of the prosecution's case and he was convicted. His co-defendants were both acquitted. Sullivan subsequently brought a habeas corpus petition based on ineffective assistance of counsel. The Supreme Court granted the petition, rejecting the state's argument that because Sullivan had retained counsel, he could not complain if he received inadequate representation. The Court stated:

---

[46]    McKaskle v. Wiggins, 465 U.S. 168, 104 S. Ct. 944, 79 L. Ed. 2d 122 (1984); Faretta v. California, *supra* note 39.

[47]    **Gideon v. Wainwright**, *supra* note 14.

[48]    McMann v. Richardson, *supra* note 30.

[49]    *Id.*

[50]    446 U.S. 335, 100 S. Ct. 1708, 64 L. Ed. 2d 33 (1980).

The vital guarantee of the Sixth Amendment would stand for little if the often uninformed decision to retain a particular lawyer could reduce or forfeit the defendant's entitlement to constitutional protection. Since the State's conduct of a criminal trial itself implicates the State in the defendant's conviction, we see no basis for drawing a distinction between retained and appointed counsel that would deny equal justice to defendants who have to choose their own lawyers.

Defendants may challenge the adequacy of the assistance rendered in their case when appealing a conviction and, in more limited circumstances, in a collateral habeas corpus claim for ineffective assistance of counsel.[51] Nevertheless, of the numerous claims lodged each year alleging ineffective assistance of counsel, few are found meritorious. An ineffective assistance of counsel claim has two components. The defendant must first convince the court that counsel's performance was inadequate. However, adequate representation is not a demanding standard. Assistance by counsel satisfies the standard, even though it falls below the average rendered by defense lawyers, as long as it is not so poor that counsel ceased to play a active role in the adversary process or provided assistance so inadequate as to undermine confidence in the verdict.[52] Most assistance provided by counsel satisfies this standard.[53] Second, the defendant must also show that he or she was prejudiced by the inadequate representation. To establish this, the defendant must convince the court that there is a reasonable probability the results of the proceedings would have been different (i.e., that he or she would have been acquitted or received a lesser sentence), had the representation been adequate.[54] When the evidence against a defendant is overwhelming, doing this is next to impossible. Claims of ineffective assistance have been sustained only in the most egregious cases, such as where counsel represents co-defendants with conflicting interests, making effective representation of both impossible,[55] fails to seek suppression of clearly illegal and prejudicial evidence,[56] or fails to present clearly exculpatory evidence.[57]

---

[51]　E.g., United States v. Booker, 981 F.2d 289 (7th Cir. 1992).

[52]　*See* Strickland v. Washington, 466 U.S. 668, 689, 104 S. Ct. 2052, 2052, 80 L. Ed. 2d 674 (1984) ("Judicial scrutiny of counsel's performance must be highly deferential. It is all too tempting for a defendant to second-guess counsel's assistance after conviction or adverse sentence, and it is all too easy for a court, examining counsel's defense after it has proved unsuccessful, to conclude that a particular act or omission of counsel's was unreasonable. . . . [A] court must indulge a strong presumption that counsel's conduct falls within the wide range of reasonable professional assistance; that is, the defendant must overcome the presumption that, under the circumstances, the challenged action "might be considered sound trial strategy."); United States v. Cronic, 466 U.S. 648, 104 S. Ct. 2039, 80 L. Ed. 2d 657 (1984).

[53]　*See, e.g.*, Mickens v. Taylor, 535 U.S. 162, 122 S. Ct. 1237, 152 L. Ed. 2d 291 (2002); Bell v. Cone, 535 U.S. 685, 122 S. Ct. 1843, 152 L. Ed. 2d 914 (2002); Roe v. Flores-Ortega, 528 U.S. 470, 120 S. Ct. 1029, 145 L. Ed. 2d 985 (2000).

[54]　Strickland v. Washington, *supra* note 52.

[55]　*See, e.g.*, Cuyler v. Sullivan, *supra* note 50.

[56]　*See, e.g.*, Tomlin v. Myers, 30 F.3d 1235 (9th Cir. 1994).

[57]　*See, e.g.*, Wiggins v. Smith, 539 U.S. 510, 123 S. Ct. 2527, 156 L. Ed. 2d 471 (2003) (failure to investigate and present mitigating evidence of defendant's dysfunctional background during death penalty sentencing proceedings violated defendant's Sixth Amendment right to counsel).

# § 8.6  Sixth Amendment Restrictions on the Conduct of the Police

The Sixth Amendment right to counsel automatically attaches with the initiation of prosecution and brings with it restrictions on police interactions with the defendant.[58] These restrictions can be summarized as follows. First, all investigatory contacts with the defendant occurring after prosecution has been initiated must be conducted with due regard for the defendant's Sixth Amendment right to counsel. Police must, before enlisting the defendant's participation in questioning, lineups, showups, or other investigatory procedures, either secure a knowing, voluntary, and intelligent waiver of the Sixth Amendment right to counsel or wait until counsel is present.[59] If the defendant desires a lawyer but is unable to afford one, police must see to it that one is provided. Second, police must refrain from improper interference with the attorney-client relationship. Failure to observe these restrictions will lead to suppression of evidence.[60]

## A.  Investigatory Interactions with Defendants After Prosecution Has Been Commenced

After a criminal prosecution has been initiated, all subsequent contacts with the defendant must be conducted with due regard for the defendant's Sixth Amendment right to counsel. Compliance requires knowledge of the rules concerning warnings and waivers and the responsibility for seeing that counsel is provided.

### 1.  Warning and Waiver of the Sixth Amendment Right to Counsel

Whenever police question the defendant or conduct a lineup or showup after prosecution has been initiated, they must secure a valid waiver of the defendant's Sixth Amendment right to counsel or wait until counsel is present.[61] A court will not find a valid waiver of the right to counsel unless the defendant: (1) knew that he or she had the right to have counsel present during the proceeding (and to appointment of counsel if he or she could not afford a lawyer); (2) understood the possible consequences of participating without a lawyer; and (3) made the decision to forego this right without being pressured by the police.[62] In order to obtain a valid waiver of the Sixth Amendment right to counsel, police should follow *Miranda* procedures.[63]

---

[58]  Attachment of the Sixth Amendment right to counsel is discussed in §§ 6.9(A) and 8.10(A).

[59]  United States v. Wade, *supra* note 17; Patterson v. Illinois, 487 U.S. 285, 108 S. Ct. 2389, 101 L. Ed. 2d 261 (1988).

[60]  *See, e.g.*, United States v. Wade, *supra* note 17.

[61]  *See* cases *supra* note 59.

[62]  Patterson v. Illinois, *supra* note 59.

[63]  *Id.*

Extra precautions should be taken when obtaining a waiver from a juvenile to ensure that the juvenile understands the warning and the consequences of participating without an attorney.[64] Some states have statutes detailing the procedures that must be followed when obtaining a waiver from a juvenile. When no such statute exists, the best practice is to have the juvenile's parents or guardian present when police administer warnings and obtain waivers.[65] If a parent or guardian cannot be located, police should secure counsel to assist the juvenile in deciding whether to waive counsel.

The procedures outlined above will not produce a valid waiver of the Sixth Amendment right to counsel if the defendant has already retained a lawyer or has asked the court to appoint one. The reason is that once a prosecution has been initiated and the defendant has obtained or requested counsel to represent him or her, there can be no valid waiver of the Sixth Amendment right to counsel during a police-initiated contact.[66] The policy behind this rule is to prevent the police from subverting the protection provided by the Sixth Amendment by sneaking around behind counsel's back. Police may not contact a defendant who is under formal charges and who has retained or requested a lawyer unless his or her attorney is present.

## 2. Police Responsibility to Provide Counsel

If the defendant, having been warned of his or her Sixth Amendment right to counsel, expresses a wish to have counsel present during a critical stage event, the police must respect this wish. Police department procedures specify what officers must do to secure appointed counsel for defendants who lack the means to hire a lawyer on their own. Indigent criminal defendants are not entitled to counsel of their choice.[67] Representation is usually provided by a public defender. If the defendant has the means to retain a lawyer, police must wait for the defendant's counsel of choice to arrive before starting the procedure.[68] However, the police do not have to wait forever. If the lawyer the defendant retains fails to arrive after a reasonable waiting period or if urgent circumstances require immediate action, police may secure appointed counsel to provide temporary representation and go on with the procedure.[69]

## 3. Participation by Counsel

The degree to which the police must allow defense counsel to play an active role in pretrial procedures they are entitled to attend varies with the procedure. With lineups and showups, counsel is present to observe whether the

---

[64]   *See* Fare v. C., 442 U.S. 707, 99 S. Ct. 2560, 621 L. Ed. 2d 197 (1979).
[65]   *Id.*
[66]   **Michigan v. Jackson,** *supra* note 33.
[67]   United States v. Wheat, 406 U.S. 153, 108 S. Ct. 153, 100 L. Ed. 2d 140 (1988).
[68]   *Id.*
[69]   United States v. Wade, *supra* note 17; *see also* United States v. Clark, 346 F. Supp. 428 (E.D. Pa. 1972).

identification procedure conforms to constitutional standards so that objections can be raised about witness identification testimony at the trial if the procedure is conducted improperly.[70] The police do not have to comply with counsel's objections about the manner in which the lineup or showup is being conducted. However, if a slight modification will satisfy counsel's objections and avert a later challenge at trial, it would be wise to comply.[71]

Suspects are also entitled to have counsel present during police custodial interrogations. The purpose for counsel's presence during an interrogation is to ensure that the suspect understands his or her rights and that the police do not engage in overreaching behavior. The police must allow the suspect to consult with his or her lawyer in private. The lawyer is entitled to call the shots on the suspect's degree of participation in the interrogation. The lawyer has the right to object to particular questions and to instruct the suspect not to answer, and the police must "grin and bear it."[72]

## B. Improper Interference with the Attorney-Client Relationship

Confidentiality is of utmost importance in the attorney-client relationship and is essential for effective assistance of counsel. Police must refrain from improper intrusions into the attorney-client relationship, such as surreptitiously monitoring or tape recording private conversations between them,[73] intercepting telephone calls,[74] or prevailing on counsel to betray his or her client.[75] Conduct such as this, occurring after the Sixth Amendment right to

---

[70] United States v. Wade, *supra* note 17; Goodwin v. Superior Court, 90 Cal. App. 4th 215, 108 Cal. Rptr. 2d 553 (2001) ("[T]he right to counsel at a lineup is a limited one. Thus, the attorney 'may not insist law enforcement officials hear his objection to procedures employed, nor may he compel them to adjust their lineup to his views of what is appropriate. At most, defense counsel is merely present at the lineup to silently observe and to later recall his observations for purposes of cross-examination or to act in the capacity of a witness. . . .' ").

[71] Stovall v. Denno, 388 U.S. 263, 87 S. Ct. 1951, 18 L. Ed. 2d 1199 (1967).

[72] *See, e.g.*, People v. Settles, 46 N.Y.2d 154 (1978).

[73] *See, e.g.*, **State v. Quattlebaum, 338 S.C. 441, 527 S.E.2d 105 (2001)** (government's clandestine videotaping of defendant's conversation with his attorney violated defendant's Sixth Amendment right to counsel, requiring reversal of his conviction), Wilson v. Superior Court of Los Angeles County, 70 Cal. App. 3d 751, 139 Cal. Rptr. 61 (2d Dist. 1997) (suppressing evidence obtained through surreptitious recording of conversation between defendant and his attorney while they were conferring in a private conference room at the police station); Shillinger v. Haworth, 70 F.3d 1132 (10th Cir. 1995) (reversing conviction where deputy sheriff eavesdropped on inmate's conversation with attorney and divulged contents to prosecutor).

[74] *See, e.g.*, Tucker v. Randall, 948 F. 2d 388 (7th Cir. 1991) (surreptitious recording of inmate's telephone conversations with attorney violated Sixth Amendment); State v. Pecard, 196 Ariz. 371, 998 P.2d 453 (2000) (same).

[75] *See, e.g.*, United States v. DiDomenico, 78 F.3d 294 (7th Cir. 1996) (offering inducement to counsel to betray client).

counsel has attached, will lead to suppression of evidence[76] and, in rare cases, dismissal of the criminal charges.[77]

Having discussed the right to counsel in this chapter and its application to interrogations in Chapter 6, we will now consider its application to pretrial identification procedures. However, the Sixth Amendment is not the only constitutional provision that applies. The rest of this chapter discusses the various constitutional provisions that regulate pretrial identification.

## § 8.7 Pretrial Identification Procedures

Pretrial identification procedures are used for two main purposes: to verify that the police have apprehended the right person and to generate evidence for use at trial. Police use three separate procedures: (1) **photographic identifications** (the witness is shown a photograph of the suspect, either alone or as part of a photospread); (2) **showups** (the witness views a lone suspect ); and (3) **lineups** (the witness views the suspect, along with others who possess similar physical characteristics, to determine whether the witness can identify the suspect). Each procedure fulfills a different law enforcement need. Figure 8.1 shows the main use for each. Photographic identifications are mainly used to narrow the focus of an investigation when the witness and the police are uncertain of the offender's identity. Showups are used when swift action is required to confirm that the police have apprehended the "right person." Lineups are used to confirm that the police have apprehended the "right person" when swift action is not required. All three procedures, when conducted in conformity with the Constitution, generate evidence that can be admitted at trial. A positive eyewitness identification made shortly after the crime furnishes convincing evidence of guilt.

---

[76] *See, e.g.*, Wilson v. Superior Court of Los Angeles County, *supra* note 73.

[77] **State v. Quattlebaum**, *supra* note 73 (reversing conviction and disqualifying solicitor's office from prosecuting defendant at his new trial where deputy solicitor participated in clandestine videotaping of defendant's conversation with his attorney); United States v. Marshank, 777 F. Supp. 1507 (N.D. Cal. 1991) (dismissing indictment where federal agents used defendant's attorney as a government informant to aid the government in building its case against defendant); United States v. Orman, 417 F. Supp. 1126 (D. Colo. 1976) (dismissing indictment where police interferred with the right to counsel by eavesdropping on conversation between defendant and counsel); State v. Cory, 62 Wash. 2d 371, 382 P.2d 1019 (1963) (same). *But see* Weatherford v. Bursey, 429 U.S. 545, 97 S. Ct. 837, 51 L. Ed. 2d 2130 (1977).

Figure 8.1
**Main Use of Each Identification Procedure**

| Identification Procedure | Main Use in Law Enforcement |
| --- | --- |
| Photographic Identification | Used to narrow the focus of an investigation in cases in which the witness and the police are uncertain of the offender's identity |
| Showup identification | Used when swift action is necessary to confirm that the police have apprehended the right person. |
| Lineup Identification | Used when swift action is not necessary to confirm that the police have apprehended the right person. |

Despite the faith jurors place in eyewitness testimony, extensive published research reveals that eyewitnesses often make mistakes and that their mistakes have sent many an innocent person to prison. A noted researcher writes that "mistaken eyewitness identification is the single largest source of wrongful convictions."[78] Recognizing this, the Supreme Court has crafted several constitutional doctrines designed to minimize the risk of police-induced mistaken identifications. Depending on the circumstances, admission of pretrial identification testimony may be challenged under four separate constitutional provisions—the Fifth and Fourteenth Amendment due process clauses, the Sixth Amendment right to counsel, and the Fourth Amendment search and seizure clause. The Fourth Amendment search and seizure clause and the Fifth and Fourteenth Amendment due process clauses apply to all three pretrial identification procedures regardless of when they occur, while the Sixth Amendment right to counsel applies only to lineups and showups, and is further limited to those conducted after a prosecution has been initiated. Figure 8.2 summarizes the requirements laid down by each provision.

---

[78] *See, e.g.*, Gary L. Wells & Eric P. Seelau, *Eyewitness Identification: Psychological Research and Legal Policy on Lineups*, 1 PSYCHOL., PUB. POL'Y, & L. 765, 765 (1995). *See also* UNITED STATES DEPARTMENT OF JUSTICE OFFICE OF RESEARCH PROGRAMS, EYEWITNESS EVIDENCE: A GUIDE FOR LAW ENFORCEMENT (Oct. 1999); Donald P. Judges, *Two Cheers for the Department of Justice's Eyewitness Evidence: A Guide for Law Enforcement*, 53 A.R.L.R. 231 (2000); ELIZABETH F. LOFTUS, EYEWITNESS TESTIMONY (1996 ed.); GARY L. WELLS & ELIZABETH F. LOFTUS, EYEWITNESS TESTIMONY: PSYCHOLOGICAL PERSPECTIVE (Cambridge University Press 1987); Mark Hansen, *Second Look at the Line-Up*, 87 A.B.A.J. 20 (Dec. 2001) (stating that faulty eyewitness identification is the leading cause of wrongful convictions).

Figure 8.2
**Constitutional Requirements for Pretrial Identification**

| Procedure | Fourth Amendment Requirements | Due Process Requirements | Sixth Amendment Requirements |
|---|---|---|---|
| Photographic identification | Photograph must be acquired without violating suspect's Fourth Amendment rights. | Police must: (1) select an identification procedure that is appropriate under the circumstances and (2) avoid unnecessary suggestiveness in conducting the procedure. | The Sixth Amendment is inapplicable. |
| Showup | Police must have constitutional grounds to seize the suspect. This procedure is permitted after investigatory detentions and arrests. | Same as above. | The Sixth Amendment applies only to showups conducted after initiation of prosecution. Before conducting a critical stage showup, police must either obtain a waiver of the right to counsel, (2) secure appointed counsel, or (3) wait for retained counsel to arrive. |
| Lineup | Police must have constitutional grounds to make an arrest. This procedure is not allowed after an investigatory detention. A valid arrest is necessary. | Same as above. | Same as above. |

# § 8.8 —Fourth Amendment Requirements for Pretrial Identification

Evidence of a positive pretrial identification will be suppressed if it derives from an illegal arrest or detention.[79] This is rarely a problem with photo identifications, because police do not have to seize the suspect to show his or her photograph to a witness. The only way the Fourth Amendment can affect the admissibility of a photographic identification is if police make a bogus arrest in order to take a suspect's photograph. Evidence of a positive identification made from a photograph acquired in this fashion would be suppressed.[80]

Fourth Amendment issues are much more common with lineups and showups because police must acquire physical control over the suspect in order to perform the procedure. If a suspect is arrested or detained in violation

---

[79]　See § 7.7 *supra.*
[80]　See United States v. Crews, 445 U.S. 463, 100 S. Ct. 1244, 63 L. Ed. 2d 537 (1980).

of the Fourth Amendment, evidence of a positive pretrial identification will be suppressed under the "fruit of the poisonous tree" doctrine.[81] A lawful arrest, on the other hand, carries the authority to compel participation in lineups and showups as a matter of course.[82] As explained in Chapter 7, appearance evidence procedures like lineups and showups infringe on only one constitutionally protected interest of the suspect—the interest in freedom of movement.[83] Probable cause for an arrest provides all the constitutional justification needed to interfere with this interest. Accordingly, police may, as a matter of course, compel suspects to participate in showups or lineups whenever they have probable cause to arrest them.[84] The scope of an investigatory stop is more limited. While showups are permitted during *Terry* stops,[85] lineups are not because police are not permitted to take *Terry* detainees to the police station.[86] Because lineups are conducted at the station house, they are beyond the scope of a *Terry* stop.

A witness who makes a pretrial identification that is inadmissible on Fourth Amendment grounds will be permitted to make a courtroom identification during the trial only if the court finds that the witness's ability to make the courtroom identification resulted from independent recollections of the perpetrator acquired at the time of the crime and not from having observed him or her during the tainted pretrial identification procedure.[87]

## § 8.9    —Due Process Requirements for Pretrial Identification Procedures

Of the three constitutional provisions that apply to pretrial identifications, the due process clause is far and above the most important. The due process clause prohibits courts from convicting a defendant on the basis of unreliable evidence.[88] Experimental memory research has demonstrated that the memory of eyewitnesses is capable of being altered and changed through exposure to

---

[81]  *Id.*

[82]  *See, e.g.*, Kirby v. Illinois, *supra* note 24 (admitting evidence obtained in showup conducted after lawful arrest); United States v. Fisher, 702 F.2d 372 (2d Cir. 1982) (suppressing evidence of showup conducted pursuant to an illegal arrest); Goodwin v. Superior Court, *supra* note 70 (a suspect whom police have probable cause to arrest has no Fourth or Fifth Amendment right to refrain from participating in a lineup).

[83]  § 7.7-7.8 *supra*.

[84]  *See* cases *supra* note 82.

[85]  Dempsey v. Town of Brighton, 749 F. Supp. 1215 (W.D.N.Y. 1990), *aff'd*, Curenton v. Town of Brighton, 940 F.2d 648 (2d Cir. 1991), *cert. denied*, Dempsey v. Town of Brighton, 502 U.S. 925, 112 S. Ct. 338, 116 L. Ed. 2d 278 (1991).

[86]  **Hayes v. Florida, 470 U.S. 811, 105 S. Ct. 1643, 84 L. Ed. 2d 705 (1985).** This limitation is discussed in § 3.9(D).

[87]  United States v. Crews, *supra* note 80.

[88]  Neil v. Biggers, 409 U.S. 188, 93 S. Ct. 375, 34 L. Ed. 2d 401 (1972); Manson v. Brathwaite, 432 U.S. 98, 97 S. Ct. 2243, 53 L. Ed. 2d 140 (1970); Simmons v. United States, 390 U.S. 377, 88 S. Ct. 967, 19 L. Ed. 2d 1247 (1968); Stovall v. Denno, *supra* note 71; **United States v. Downs, 230 F.3d 272 (7th Cir. 2000).**

suggestive influences after an event is witnessed.[89] To reduce the risk of wrongful convictions, the due process clause prohibits admission of testimony concerning a pretrial identification obtained under circumstances that are so unnecessarily suggestive as to create a substantial risk of misidentification.[90]

Courts use a two-part test to determine whether an out-of-court identification is admissible.[91] They first consider whether the police used an unnecessarily suggestive procedure to obtain the identification. If the procedure was not unnecessarily suggestive, the inquiry stops here. If it was, the court then examines the surrounding circumstances to determine whether the unnecessary suggestiveness created a substantial risk of misidentification. Because people who have sharp and clear memories of an event are less susceptible to suggestion, courts consider the following five factors in assessing this risk: (1) whether the witness had an adequate opportunity to view the suspect at the time of the crime, (2) the witness's degree of attention, (3) the accuracy of the witness's prior description of the suspect, (4) the level of certainty exhibited at the time of the identification, and (5) the length of time between the crime and the identification.[92] The greater the witness's observation time and degree of attention, the more accurate the witness's prior description, the higher the witness's level of certainty, and the shorter the interval between the crime and the identification, the more likely it is that a court will admit evidence of a positive eyewitness identification despite use of an unnecessarily suggestive identification procedure.[93] Police, nevertheless, should strive to make their procedures as accurate and reliable as possible.

---

[89]  WELLS & LOFTUS, EYEWITNESS TESTIMONY: PSYCHOLOGICAL PERSPECTIVES (Cambridge, 1984).

[90]  *See* cases *supra* note 88.

[91]  *Id.*

[92]  *Id.*

[93]  *See, e.g.*, **United States v. Downs**, *supra* note 88 (line-up in which the defendant was only person without a moustache was unduly suggestive, but bank teller's identification was sufficiently reliable to be admitted notwithstanding where teller had been very close to robber and had paid strict attention to him, expressed certainty when she saw him, line-up was held only five days after robbery, and teller had seen only one man in lineup before seeing the defendant); State v. Gross, 776 N.E.2d 1061 (Ohio 2002) (circumstances of showup identification of capital murder defendant by two witnesses, in which witnesses, sitting in separate police cars, identified defendant as he stood with his hands behind his back between two officers, although suggestive, were not so suggestive as to create very substantial likelihood of irreparable misidentification, where both witnesses had time to view defendant during commission of crimes, focused their attention on him, described him prior to showup identification, were confident in their respective identifications, and made the identification mere hours after witnessing the crime); State v. Meyers, 153 Ohio App. 3d 547, 795 N.E.2d 77 (2003) (identification procedure was sufficiently reliable to allow admission of alleged rape victim's identification of defendant as her assailant, even though alleged victim was presented with a second photograph array that included defendant after she failed to identify defendant as her assailant in first photograph array; alleged victim got good look at assailant, had high degree of attention while observing assailant, provided detective with complete description of assailant shortly after incident, and rated her level of certainty as a seven out of ten upon identifying defendant from second photograph array, and length of time between attack and identification of defendant was six weeks). *But see* Wise v. Commonwealth, 6 Va. App. 178, 367 S.E.2d 197 (1988) (showing Virginia bank employees single bank surveillance photo depicting defendant as robber of Maryland bank five months after the Virginia robbery tainted employees' subsequent identifications of defendant from photographic array where employees were unable, prior to seeing the single photograph, to describe robber's facial features or to identify him in earlier photographic identification array).

## A. *Choosing the Proper Procedure for Identification*

Unnecessary suggestiveness can be introduced in one of two ways—either by selecting an inappropriate witness identification procedure (i.e., one that is unnecessarily suggestive under the circumstances) or conducting an appropriate procedure in an unnecessarily suggestive way.

Challenges based on choice of procedures generally involve showups. Showups are the most inherently suggestive of the three identification procedures because only one person is presented for identification, that person is in police custody, and the clear implication is that the police think "he's the one." As a general rule, showups should be used only when police have a strong need for a quick confirmation that they have apprehended the right person.[94] The ideal case is one in which the showup takes place close in time to the crime and the public safety would be threatened if the perpetrator were to remain at large.

Suppose that Veronica Victim reports that she has just been robbed at gunpoint by a four-foot tall white man with long green hair and an artificial leg, wearing a T-shirt that reads "Kiss the Chef." Police dispatch a car to her residence. En route, they spot a man matching the description hobbling at his best speed away from her neighborhood and apprehend him. This is a proper case for a showup. First, swift action is necessary because of the violent nature of the crime and Veronica's report that the perpetrator was armed. A photographic identification would delay confirmation while a dangerous criminal remains at large. Moreover, the risk that a showup will induce a misidentification is negligible because the showup occurred close in time to the crime, the victim furnished a detailed description of a perpetrator who had unique identifying characteristics, the suspect was apprehended near the scene of the crime, and his unique appearance matched the victim's description of him. A quick viewing in the immediate aftermath of a crime is justified by the need to determine whether the person detained is the right person while the perpetrator's image is still fresh in the victim's memory. Rapid identification enables the police to focus their investigation, enhances the reliability of the identification, and minimizes the risk that innocent persons will be unjustly detained.

Suppose instead that Mrs. Lucy Marbles calls to report that she just discovered that her prized 24-carat gold lawn flamingo is missing. "I kept it in my front yard for years," she says, "and no one ever took it. What's the world coming to?!" After racking her brain for a few days, she calls again, this time

---

[94]   *See, e.g.,* Fite v. State, 60 S.W. 3d 314 (Tex. Ct. App. 2001) (showup proper where police picked up suspect who fit the victim's description of man who, moments before, had forced his way into her home, threatened her life, and spent 20 minutes rummaging through her belongings); State v. Mansfield, 343 S.C. 66, 538 S.E.2d 257 (2000) (showup proper where eyewitness observed the defendant trying break into neighbor's home and had an opportunity to get a good look at him, and showup occurred within minutes after he fled the scene). *But see* Ex parte Appleton, 828 So. 2d 894 (Ala. 2001) (showup improper where witness was unable to see robber's face at the time of the crime because it was covered with a mask and there was no urgency); In re Duane F., 764 N.Y.S.2d 434 (2003) (Precinct house showup at which witness identified juvenile was unduly suggestive where showup did not take place near the crime scene nor did it result from the culmination of an unbroken chain of fast-paced events).

to report that she knows who has taken it. She believes it was taken by a man who briefly came to her door a week ago and offered to pave her driveway "for cheap." Her description of the man, a five-foot-four white male with a mustache, matches many of the usual suspects known to local police, including Sticky-Fingered Sam. Under these circumstances, it would be inappropriate to use a showup identification. First, there is no urgency. The crime is not a violent one, the public safety is not at risk, and the police have no special need to know whether Sam is the perpetrator right now. They know where Sam lives and can pick him up anytime they want. Because there is no rush, a photographic identification will serve the needs of law enforcement equally well. Moreover, there is a substantial risk that a showup will induce a mistaken identification. Mrs. Marbles viewed the perpetrator briefly a week before and had no reason to focus attention on his appearance because she was unaware of the theft at that time. Memories of the facial characteristics of strangers observed momentarily during a chance encounter tend to fade rapidly. The fact that the police think Sam is the perpetrator may prompt Mrs. Marbles to mistakenly "remember" him. These considerations make the use of a showup identification a poor choice on these facts.

### B. Avoiding Suggestive Measures During Identification Procedures

Unnecessary suggestiveness can also be introduced by the way in which a procedure is conducted. Police must avoid saying or doing things that might influence the witness's decision. While it is rare for police to point out a suspect and say "We've caught our man. He's the one," their conduct can say this as loudly as their language. *Foster v. California* [95] is an illustrative case. Police first placed the suspect in a police station lineup along with two other men, both of whom were a half a foot shorter. The suspect was the only one wearing a leather jacket, a characteristic that played prominently in the witness's description of the robber. When the lineup did not lead to a positive identification, police arranged a one-on-one confrontation between the witness and the defendant. The witness continued to be uncertain. A week later, the police arranged a second lineup, in which there were five participants. The suspect was the only person in the second lineup who had also participated in the first lineup. This time the witness made a positive identification. The Supreme Court threw the identification testimony out, stating:

> The suggestive elements in this identification procedure made it all but inevitable that David would identify petitioner whether or not he was in fact "the man." In effect, the police repeatedly said to the witness, "This is the man." This procedure so undermined the reliability of the eyewitness identification as to violate due process.

---

[95]    394 U.S. 440, 89 S. Ct. 1127, 22 L. Ed. 2d 402 (1969).

## 1. Conducting Photographic Identification Procedures

The United States Department of Justice recently promulgated a series of guidelines for handling eyewitness evidence. Many of the Justice Department's recommendations have been incorporated into the discussions that follow.[96]

When conducting a photographic identification, police should prepare a photospread that includes at least five photographs in addition to the suspect's. The suspect's photograph should be reasonably contemporary. The photographs of the fillers—i.e., non-suspects—should match the witness's description of the criminal rather than the person whom the police suspect of the crime. However, the fillers should not so closely resemble the suspect that even people familiar with the suspect might have difficulty distinguishing the two. The photospread should include only one photograph of the suspect. Repeatedly showing the suspect's picture increases the risk of misidentification by reinforcing that suspect's image in the witness's mind. It also contains an implied suggestion that the police think that person whose picture is being repeatedly shown is the perpetrator.[97]

Before starting the procedure, the investigator should caution the witness that the person who committed the crime may or may not be in the photospread, thus eliminating pressure on the witness to select someone. If there are multiple eyewitnesses, officers should conduct separate identifications to prevent them from influencing each other.[98] It goes without saying that police should avoid saying anything during the procedure that might influence the witness's decision.

There are rare occasions when showing a single photograph is permitted.[99] A Maryland court, for example, ruled that an out-of-court identification made

---

[96] In 1999, the United States Department of Justice published a research report titled UNITED STATES DEPARTMENT OF JUSTICE OFFICE OF RESEARCH PROGRAMS, EYEWITNESS EVIDENCE: A GUIDE FOR LAW ENFORCEMENT (Oct. 1999). This document can be obtained free of charge from the Office of Justice Programs at http://www.ojp.usdoj.gov. The Justice Department's EYEWITNESS EVIDENCE GUIDE offers valuable recommendations for interviewing eyewitnesses and conducting witness identifications. For favorable commentary, see Donald P. Judges, *Two Cheers for the Department of Justice's Eyewitness Evidence: a Guide for Law Enforcement*, 53 ARK. L. REV. 231 (2000). THE EYEWITNESS EVIDENCE GUIDE'S recommendations for conducting photographic identifications are found at pp. 39-40 of the Guide.

[97] *Id.*

[98] *See, e.g.*, United States v. Bagley, 772 F. 2d 482 (9th Cir. 1985) (photographic display was unnecessarily suggestive where one witness looked over another's shoulder as she was viewing the pictures and saw her select Bagley's mug shot. The court stated: "A joint confrontation is a disapproved identification procedure. Clearly, the better procedure is to keep witnesses apart when they view photographic spreads."). *But see* United States v. Bowman, 215 F.3d 951 (9th Cir. 2000) (allowing witnesses to attend line-up as group and to write down their observations on written form did not create substantial likelihood of misidentification where they were instructed not to talk to one another, not to let anyone see their choices, and not to make comments or gestures as they viewed lineups, and where law enforcement officer remained in room to ensure that these instructions were carried out).

[99] United States v. Lumpkin, 192 F.3d 280 (2d Cir. 1999) (suppressing pretrial identification made from single photograph, but finding that officers had independently reliable bases upon which to make in-court identification); Hyppolite v. State, 774 N.E.2d 584 (Ind. Ct. App. 2002) (while exhibiting a single photograph to a crime witness for identification is normally an unnecessarily suggestive procedure, an exception is sometimes made when the crime witness is an investigating police officer).

by a crime victim who was shown only one photograph was sufficiently reliable to be admissible because the victim had been in his assailant's presence for more than four hours and had escaped shortly before viewing the photograph.[100] In addition, another factor was present. There was an outstanding warrant for the arrest on unrelated charges of the person shown in the photograph and the police wanted to know whether the victim could identify him and provide information on his whereabouts. Consequently, the police had a legitimate law enforcement purpose for showing only one photograph.

### 2. Lineups

Lineups have been described as "the most useful and least questionable witness identification procedure."[101] They are more reliable than photographic identifications and less suggestive than one-man showups and, consequently, should be employed whenever feasible.

However, the reliability of a lineup depends on how it is conducted.[102] Police must avoid making the suspect conspicuous. A suspect can be made conspicuous either by selecting stand-ins whose age, race, physique, etc. bear no resemblance to the victim's description of the perpetrator[103] or by presenting the suspect in a way that draws attention, such as by having only the suspect wear the distinctive clothing worn by the perpetrator.[104] However, presenting the suspect in ways that draw attention may occasionally be unavoidable. Suppose that a bank is robbed by a bearded man, and the next day several eyewitnesses identify Sticky-Fingered Sam from a photo array of known bearded bank robbers. Police arrest Sam and place him in a lineup with other bearded men to see whether the witnesses will identify him. Unfortunately, Sam shaved his beard before his arrest and he is the only person in the

---

[100]  Smith v. State, 6 Md. App. 59, 250 A.2d 285 (1969), *cert. denied,* 397 U.S. 1057, 90 S. Ct. 1402, 25 L. Ed. 2d 674 (1970).

[101]  WAYNE LAFAVE, JEROLD H. ISRAEL, & NANCY KING, CRIMINAL PROCEDURE § 7.3(c) (2d ed. 1999).

[102]  The Justice Department's recommendations for conducting to lineups are similar to its recommendations for photographic identifications. *See* UNITED STATES DEPARTMENT OF JUSTICE OFFICE OF RESEARCH PROGRAMS, *supra* note 96 at 40-42.

[103]  Frazier v. New York, 187 F. Supp. 2d 102 (S.D.N.Y. 2002) (lineup unnecessarily suggestive where hairstyle was the only consistent, distinctive feature in victim's descriptions of perpetrator, defendant was only participant in the lineup whose dreadlocks hairstyle matched the description, and police could have disguised this feature by making participants wear hats); Solomon v. Smith, 645 F.2d 1179, 1183 (2d Cir. 1981) (lineup unnecessarily suggestive where victim described assailant as 5'7" tall and weighing 145 pounds and a lineup was held in which the defendant, who was 5'6" tall and weighed 130 pounds, was the only person near that description—all but one of the other participants being four to six inches taller than the defendant and the remaining participant, though only two inches taller than the defendant, being 65 pounds (i.e., 50%) heavier; **United States v. Downs**, *supra* note 88 (lineup unnecessarily suggestive where bank robbery suspect was only participant who had no facial hair).

[104]  Raheem v. Kelly, 257 F.3d 122 (2d Cir. 2001) (lineup unnecessarily suggestive where defendant was the only participant who appeared in black leather coat, a characteristic that featured prominently in witness's description of suspect. The court stated that a "lineup is unduly suggestive as to a given defendant if he meets the description of the perpetrator previously given by the witness and the other lineup participants plainly do not."); Bell v. State, 847 So. 2d 880 (Miss. Ct. App. 2002) (photographic identification was impermissibly suggestive, where defendant's photograph was the only one in which a person was depicted with long hair, in an orange jumpsuit, and with shackles or handcuffs).

lineup with an artificial beard. Forcing Sam to wear an artificial beard is permissible, even though it is likely to draw attention to him, because Sam created the situation that made it necessary to alter his appearance.

Police do not have to go to extraordinary lengths to find stand-ins who look like the suspect.[105] They are only required to make a reasonable effort. Police, for example, would have no excuse for assembling a lineup in which the suspect is the only African American when this feature is part of the witness's description of the perpetrator. However, if the suspect has a unique identifying characteristic, such as a star-shaped birthmark or tattoo on his cheek, police do not have to find stand-ins with a similar characteristic. They nevertheless should try to conceal this characteristic by requiring all lineup participants to wear a bandage covering this part of their face.

## C. Consequences of an Unduly Suggestive Identification

Testimony about an out-of-court identification will be suppressed if the pretrial identification procedure is so unnecessarily suggestive that it creates a substantial likelihood of a mistaken identification.[106] A witness who has been exposed to such a procedure will, in addition, be barred from making an identification in the courtroom during the trial unless the judge concludes that the witness's testimony stems from independent recollection acquired at the time of the crime and not from having observed the accused at the suggestive pretrial identification procedure.[107] The amount of time the witness was in the presence of the defendant; the distance between them; the lighting conditions; the witness's degree of attention to the defendant; the accuracy of any prior description of the perpetrator by the witness; the witness's level of certainty at the pretrial identification; and the length of time between the crime and the tainted identification are among the factors the judge will consider in deciding this.[108] However, even if the judge permits the witness to make an identification in the courtroom during the trial, defense counsel can argue to the jury why it should distrust this testimony. Thus, no matter what the judge decides, an unnecessarily suggestive pretrial identification can weaken the prosecution's case.

---

[105] *See, e.g.*, United States v. Traeger, 289 F.3d 461 (7th Cir. 2002) (lineup not *unnecessarily* suggestive, even though bank robbery suspect's mammoth 6 feet, 5-inch height, 350-pound weight made him stand out from other participants because finding five or six other men who approximated suspect's size very difficult); Roldan v. Artuz, 78 F. Supp. 2d 260 (S.D.N.Y. 2000); Taylor v. Kuhlmann, 36 F. Supp. 2d 534 (E.D.N.Y. 1999); United States v. Shakur, 560 F. Supp. 353 (S.D.N.Y. 1983).

[106] Neil v. Biggers, *supra* note 88; Stovall v. Denno, *supra* note 71.

[107] United States v. Lumpkin, *supra* note 99 (finding that investigating officers had independently reliable basis upon which to make in-court identifications where officers had unobstructed view of the suspect selling crack cocaine during daylight on two occasions, and immediately recognized him on the second occasion); Hyppolite v. State, *supra* note 99.

[108] *See* cases *supra* notes 106, 107.

## § 8.10 —Right to Counsel during Pretrial Identification Procedures

Attendance of counsel during pretrial identification procedures is desirable so that counsel can observe whether the procedure was properly conducted and gather ammunition for an attack on the admission of witness identification testimony at the trial if it was not. However, the Sixth Amendment only guarantees the right to counsel during "critical stages" of a criminal proceedings. Lineups and showups conducted after the initiation of a prosecution are considered critical stages for purpose of the right to counsel,[109] but photographic identifications are not.[110] This is because photographic identification sessions do not involve an adversarial confrontation. Equally important, the presence of defense counsel is not necessary for effective challenge based on suggestiveness because the photo display can be reconstructed for counsel's benefit afterward.[111] Lineups and showups, in contrast, cannot be reconstructed in the same way. As a result, suggestive influences may never come to light unless defense counsel is present as an observer. Thus, criminal defendants have a Sixth Amendment right to have counsel present during critical stage lineups and showups (i.e., those conducted *after* initiation of prosecution), but not during photographic identification sessions.[112]

### A. Determining Whether Prosecution Has Commenced

The prosecution commences, for Sixth Amendment purposes, as soon as the government commits itself to prosecute.[113] The Supreme Court has identified the following actions as indicating this commitment: (1) the **arraignment** of the defendant pursuant to an arrest warrant or on charges filed in the form of a criminal complaint; (2) the filing of an **information** by the prosecutor; and (3) the return of a grand jury **indictment**.[114] Although the prosecution certainly is commenced by the time any of the above events takes place, some

---

[109] United States v. Wade, *supra* note 17; Moore v. Illinois, 434 U.S. 220, 98 S. Ct. 458, 54 L. Ed. 2d 424 (1977) (defendants have no constitutional right to the presence of counsel during identification procedures conducted before prosecution is initiated).

[110] United States v. Ash, *supra* note 3.

[111] *Id.*

[112] United States v. Wade, *supra* note 17; United States v. Ash, *supra* note 3.

[113] United States v. Wade, *supra* note 17.

[114] Kirby v. Illinois, *supra* note 24 (pre-indictment showup not critical stage); In re Groban, 352 U.S. 330, 77 S. Ct. 510, 1 L. Ed. 2d 376 (1957).

states hold that the government commits itself to prosecute at earlier stages[115]—even at the time the suspect is booked.[116] Accordingly, officers should familiarize themselves with the rules in their jurisdiction.

### B. Consequences of Failing to Provide Counsel

If police officers conduct a showup or lineup after prosecution is initiated without obtaining a waiver or providing counsel, the results can be devastating to the prosecution. First, evidence of the pretrial identification will be excluded from trial, regardless of whether there was undue suggestiveness.[117] Second, any witness who participates in the illegal pretrial identification is presumptively incompetent to identify the accused at trial. In accordance with the "fruit of the poisonous tree" doctrine,[118] the prosecution must show by clear and convincing evidence that the in-court identification has a sufficient basis in the witness's observation of the accused other than at the pretrial identification.[119] If the prosecution cannot meet this burden, and there are no other witnesses to identify the accused or other evidence proving his or her identity as the perpetrator, the result will be a complete acquittal.

## § 8.11 Summary and Practical Suggestions

The Sixth Amendment guarantees those accused of crime the assistance of counsel for their defense. The right to assistance of counsel includes the right to retain counsel of one's own choosing, to have counsel appointed, or to engage in self-representation.

The right to counsel applies prior to trial during several critical stages, including the preliminary hearing, bail hearing, arraignment, and certain investigative procedures—including interrogations, lineups, and showups occurring after the initiation of the prosecution. Generally, prosecution begins on the earliest of several events: arraignment of the defendant pursuant to an arrest warrant or on charges filed in the form of a criminal complaint, the filing of an information by the prosecutor, or the return of a grand jury indictment. State courts, however, sometimes recognize earlier points of initiation.

---

[115] *See* United States v. Zelker, 468 F.2d 159, 163 (2d Cir. 1972), *cert. denied*, 411 U.S. 939, 93 S. Ct. 1892, 36 L. Ed. 2d 401 (1973) (right attached upon issuance of arrest warrant under New York penal law); Cannistraci v. Smith, 470 F. Supp. 586, 592 n.16 (S.D.N.Y. 1979) (right attached after arrest and booking); United States v. Cuyler, 439 F. Supp. 1173, 1180-1181 (E.D. Pa. 1977), *aff'd*, 582 F.2d 1278 (3d Cir. 1978) (right attached upon issuance of arrest warrant under Pennsylvania law); People v. Hinton, 23 Ill. App. 3d 369, 372, 319 N.E.2d 313, 316 (1974) (right attached upon filing of complaint and issuance of arrest warrant); Commonwealth v. Richman, 458 Pa. 167, 170, 320 A.2d 351, 353 (1974) (right attached upon filing of complaint and issuance of arrest warrant).

[116] *See* Cannistraci v. Smith, *supra* note 115.

[117] United States v. Wade, *supra* note 17; *see also* cases *supra* note 115.

[118] Wong Sun v. United States, 371 U.S. 471, 83 S. Ct. 407, 9 L. Ed. 2d 444 (1963).

[119] *See* United States v. Wade, *supra* note 17.

When police officers conduct pretrial identification procedures, they are bound not only by the Sixth Amendment right to counsel, but also by the due process clause and the Fourth Amendment. The Fourth Amendment requires that police officers have proper grounds before forcing the suspect to participate in an identification procedure. If police have probable cause to support an arrest, they can conduct either a lineup or a showup. If there is only reasonable suspicion for a detention, they may still conduct a showup. The due process clause requires that officers avoid conduct that unduly suggests whom the witness should identify. In addition to the Fourth Amendment and due process requirements, if a showup or lineup takes place after the prosecution has been initiated, police officers must comply with Sixth Amendment warning and waiver requirements. Valid waivers require that the officer warn the accused of his or her rights and of the consequences of a waiver. *Miranda* warnings will suffice. In addition to respecting the accused's decision to have counsel, police officers must refrain from interfering with the attorney-client relationship.

# Trial and Punishment 9

*[No] person [shall] be subject for the same offense to be twice put in jeopardy of life or limb . . .*

Fifth Amendment, 1791

*In all criminal prosecutions, the accused shall enjoy the right to a speedy and public trial, by an impartial jury . . . and to be informed of the nature and cause of the accusation [and] to be confronted with the witnesses against him . . .*

Sixth Amendment, 1791

*Excessive bail shall not be required, nor excessive fines imposed, nor cruel and unusual punishments inflicted.*

Eighth Amendment, 1791

# Chapter Outline

## § 9.1 Overview of Constitutional Safeguards during the Trial and Punishment Phases of a Criminal Case

An inscription on the walls of the Department of Justice reads: "The United States wins its points when justice is done its citizens in the courts." This sentiment is echoed throughout the Constitution, but is especially apparent in the constitutional provisions covered in this chapter: the double jeopardy clause of the Fifth Amendment, which prohibits the government from placing an accused person twice in jeopardy of conviction or punishment for the same offense, the Fifth and Fourteenth Amendment due process clauses, the Sixth Amendment guarantee of a fair trial, and the Eighth Amendment prohibition against cruel and inhuman punishment. Citizens have not always enjoyed these rights. There was a time in the Western world when people accused of crime could be condemned without a trial and subjected to barbaric, torturous punishments. The first major triumph in the evolution of the Anglo-American criminal justice system occurred at Runnymede, England, in 1215, when King John was forced to capitulate to the demands of insurgent barons and signed the historic document known as the Magna Charta. The Magna Charta guaranteed that no free man would be condemned to death or sent to prison "except by the legal judgment of his peers or by the law of the land."[1]

---

[1]  MAGNA CHARTA, ch. 39, reprinted in R. PERRY & J. COOPER, SOURCES OF OUR LIBERTIES 17 (1959).

This phrase is the precursor of the due process clause enshrined in the Fifth and Fourteenth Amendments to the United States Constitution. However, the Framers were not content to rely on the general assurance of due process to perpetuate the numerous procedural safeguards that, over the centuries, had come to be associated with a fair trial. In the Bill of Rights, they laid out what would be required. This chapter examines the safeguards that the Framers incorporated to fortify the integrity of the trial process and to ensure that criminal punishments would be administered with respect for human dignity.

## § 9.2 The Fifth Amendment Double Jeopardy Prohibition

The double jeopardy clause of the Fifth Amendment mandates that no person shall "be subject for the same offense to be twice put in jeopardy of life or limb . . ." This clause prohibits the government from twice prosecuting or punishing a criminal defendant for the same offense.[2] Although double jeopardy is not mentioned in the Magna Charta, the seeds were already sown[3] and this protection was fully entrenched in the English legal system by the colonial period.[4]

### A. Reasons for Prohibiting Double Jeopardy

The prohibition of double jeopardy reflects society's judgment that a person who has stood trial for an offense should be able to put this ordeal behind him or her and go on to other things. A criminal trial is a heavy strain, both personal and financial. An acquittal would not end the defendant's ordeal if he or she could be retried.[5] Even a conviction would not have this effect because the government could retry the defendant in the hopes of obtaining a more severe punishment. The double jeopardy safeguard prevents the government from using its vast resources to imprison innocent people by repeatedly trying them until they are too worn out, psychologically and financially, to put forth an adequate defense.[6]

### B. Scope of the Prohibition against Double Jeopardy

The double jeopardy clause imposes two closely related restraints. First, it prevents the government from retrying a criminal defendant for the same

---

[2]    Benton v. Maryland, 395 U.S. 784, 89 S. Ct. 2056, 23 L. Ed. 2d 707 (1969).

[3]    Bartkus v. Illinois, 359 U.S. 121, 79 S. Ct. 676, 3 L. Ed. 2d 684 (1959) (Black, J., dissenting).

[4]    J.A. Sigler, Double Jeopardy 22 (1969).

[5]    Green v. United States, 355 U.S. 184, 78 S. Ct. 221, 2 L. Ed. 2d 199 (1957).

[6]    Id.

offense following an acquittal or conviction.[7] Second, it prevents the government from imposing multiple punishments for the same offense.[8] If a defendant is convicted, the sentence imposed fixes the punishment and may not thereafter be augmented or changed. Moreover, the power to prosecute may be lost if the government has previously "punished" the defendant for the same offense in some other way, such as by seizing his or her property as a penalty.[9]

Although the double jeopardy clause seems straightforward, it is actually complex. There are two sources of difficulty. The first is the meaning of "same offense." Suppose a masked man enters a federally insured bank, takes a gun from his pocket, points it at the teller, demands that she fill a bag with cash, and speeds away in his car. During this period, our masked bandit has committed at least four separate crimes in addition to the bank robbery. The other crimes were carrying a concealed weapon, making a terroristic threat, reckless endangerment of the lives of other persons present in the bank, and speeding. The double jeopardy clause bars a second prosecution only when it is brought for the "same offense." The number of offenses determines how many times a defendant can be tried. How many "offenses" did our masked bandit commit—one or five?[10]

A second problem is with the meaning of "punishment." When do government-imposed sanctions amount to "punishment?" Suppose Mary Wanna and Thrifty Penny are convicted of operating a multi-million dollar drug ring and each is sentenced to five years in the penitentiary. Thrifty Penny is in a hurry to "pay her debt to society" so that she can get out and spend the millions she amassed from her drug business. Mary is indifferent because she has already blown her share. Suppose further that, while in prison, the government confiscates all of Penny's drug money. Since Penny suffered a second burden that Mary did not, does this mean that she has been punished twice for the same offense?[11] Both questions call upon courts to make difficult choices.

## § 9.3 —Prohibition of Multiple Prosecutions for the Same Offense

Three conditions are necessary for a defendant to have double jeopardy protection against a second prosecution. First, an earlier prosecution must progress to the point of jeopardy attachment. Second, a subsequent prosecution must involve the same offense. Finally, both prosecutions must be brought

---

[7]　Fong Foo v. United States, 369 U.S. 141, 82 S. Ct. 671, 7 L. Ed. 2d 629 (1962).

[8]　United States v. DiFrancesco, 449 U.S. 117, 101 S. Ct. 426, 66 L. Ed. 2d 328 (1980); North Carolina v. Pearce, 395 U.S. 711, 89 S. Ct. 2072, 23 L. Ed. 2d 656 (1969).

[9]　See, e.g., Department of Revenue of Montana v. Kurth Ranch, 511 U.S. 767, 114 S. Ct. 1937, 128 L. Ed. 2d 767 (1994); United States v. Bajakajian, 524 U.S. 321, 118 S. Ct. 2028, 141 L. Ed. 2d 314 (1998); United States v. Halper, 490 U.S. 435, 109 S. Ct. 1892, 104 L. Ed. 2d 487 (1989).

[10]　United States v. Dixon, 509 U.S. 688, 704, 113 S. Ct. 2849, 2860, 125 L. Ed. 2d 556 (1993); Ashe v. Swenson, 397 U.S. 436, 90 S. Ct. 1189, 25 L. Ed. 2d 469 (1970).

[11]　See United States v. Ursery, 518 U.S. 267, 116 S. Ct. 2135, 135 L. Ed. 2d 549 (1996).

by the same government entity. Because the federal government and the states are separate **sovereign** entities, each is separately empowered to prosecute for violations of its laws.[12]

Figure 9.1
**Conditions Necessary for Double Jeopardy Protection Against Reprosecution**

---

Three conditions are necessary to acquire double jeopardy protection against reprosecution:

1.   An earlier prosecution must progress to the point of jeopardy attachment;
2.   The subsequent prosecution must involve the same offense; and
3.   Both prosecutions must be brought by the same government entity.

---

## A.  Did Jeopardy "Attach" in the Prior Proceedings?

Because the Fifth Amendment prohibits the government from placing a criminal defendant twice in jeopardy for the same offense, a defendant is not protected from reprosecution unless he or she has already once before been placed in jeopardy of a conviction for this offense. If an earlier prosecution is scuttled before this point is reached, the government is free to start over.

The jeopardy attachment point is the point at which it is too late for the government to turn back and retain the right to prosecute. There are a number of points in a criminal case that could have been selected. The earliest is when formal charges are filed. However, selecting this point is undesirable because it would force the government to try everyone it charges, whether or not it then has enough evidence, or be barred from trying them later. This position would benefit no one and is the reason for Supreme Court's rejection. None of the steps preliminary to placing a defendant on trial constitute jeopardy. A defendant who is released after being arrested or who otherwise succeeds in having charges against him or her dismissed without a trial acquires no constitutional protection against being forced to face them again later.[13]

The latest point for the attachment of jeopardy is when a jury (or judge) returns a verdict on the charges. Selection of this point would mean that the government could reprosecute a defendant as many times as necessary to have the charges resolved on the merits. The English common law selected this point.[14] However, the U.S. Supreme Court has opted for an earlier attachment point. When a defendant is tried before a jury, jeopardy attaches as soon as the jury has been empaneled and sworn.[15] In non-jury trials, jeopardy attaches

---

[12]   United States v. Lanza, 260 U.S. 377, 43 S. Ct. 141, 67 L. Ed. 314 (1922); Bartkus v. Illinois, 359 U.S. 121, 79 S. Ct. 676, 3 L. Ed. 2d 684 (1959).

[13]   Serfass v. United States, 420 U.S. 377, 95 S. Ct. 1055, 43 L. Ed. 2d 265 (1975); Collins v. Loisel, 262 U.S. 426, 43 S. Ct. 618, 67 L. Ed. 1062 (1922); Bassing v. Cady, 208 U.S. 386, 28 S. Ct. 392, 52 L. Ed. 540 (1908).

[14]   Note, *Double Jeopardy: The Reprosecution Problem*, 77 HARV. L. REV. 1272, 1273 (1964).

[15]   Illinois v. Somerville, 410 U.S. 458, 93 S. Ct. 1066, 35 L. Ed. 2d 425 (1973); Downum v. United States, 372 U.S. 734, 83 S. Ct. 1033, 10 L. Ed. 2d 100 (1963); Crist v. Bretz, 437 U.S. 28, 98 S. Ct. 2156, 57 L. Ed. 2d 24 (1978).

when the first witness is sworn and the judge has begun hearing testimony.[16] The American attachment rule reflects the judgment that, once a trial has started, the defendant has a valued right to have the charges resolved by the first **tribunal** chosen so that his or her ordeal can be brought to a close. This means that, once the trial begins, it will normally be the government's one and only shot at establishing the defendant's guilt. However, the Supreme Court has recognized three situations in which the defendant's interest in having his or her ordeal end with one trial will be subordinated to society's interest in pressing forward until a verdict is reached. When any of the following exceptions apply, the defendant can be retried for the same offense despite the fact that the first trial progressed beyond the jeopardy attachment point.

## 1. Retrial After an Early Termination Requested by the Defendant

The first exception arises when the defendant requests a mistrial. A defendant who requests an early termination cannot object to being retried because this request operates as a deliberate election to forego the valued right to have the charges resolved by the first tribunal.[17] However, it will not be treated as an election if the need for making the request is caused by the prosecutor's deliberate commission of a prejudicial error to force the defendant into aborting a trial that is going poorly for the government.[18] A defense request made under these circumstances operates as a bar to retrial.

## 2. Retrial After an Early Termination Based on "Manifest Necessity"

Forcing a defendant to undergo a second trial that he or she has not solicited frustrates the defendant's interest in having his or her ordeal ended with one trial. On the other hand, freeing a defendant whenever his or her first trial progresses beyond the jeopardy attachment point but ends without a verdict, regardless of the underlying reason, makes too light of society's stake in criminal prosecutions. In *United States v. Perez*,[19] the Supreme Court struck a compromise. Under the *Perez* doctrine, retrial is permissible despite the absence of a defense request for a mistrial whenever, taking all the circumstances into account, there is a "manifest necessity" for ending the first trial prematurely.

Jury "deadlock" is the most common situation calling for application of the *Perez* principle.[20] In most jurisdictions, the jurors' verdict must be unanimous. This is true for both acquittals and convictions. When the jury is unable

---

[16]    Serfass v. United States, *supra* note 13.
[17]    United States v. Dinitz, 424 U.S. 600, 96 S. Ct. 1075, 47 L. Ed. 2d 267 (1976); United States v. Scott, 437 U.S. 82, 98 S. Ct. 2187, 57 L. Ed. 2d 65 (1978).
[18]    Oregon v. Kennedy, 456 U.S. 667, 102 S. Ct. 2083, 72 L. Ed. 2d 416 (1982).
[19]    22 U.S. (9 Wheat.) 579, 6 L. Ed. 165 (1824).
[20]    Logan v. United States, 144 U.S. 263, 12 S. Ct. 617, 36 L. Ed. 429 (1892); Richardson v. United States, 468 U.S. 317, 104 S. Ct. 3081, 82 L. Ed. 2d 242 (1984).

to reach a verdict, there is no choice but to end the trial. Because a hung jury does not constitute an acquittal, the defendant may be retried. The *Perez* doctrine also allows retrial when supervening events like wars make it impossible to complete the first trial[21] and when the judge,[22] a juror,[23] or the accused[24] becomes too ill to continue. The Supreme Court has refused to establish rigid criteria for what constitutes a "manifest necessity" for bringing a criminal trial to a premature close, choosing instead to resolve each case on its facts.

### 3. Retrial After the Successful Appeal of a Conviction

A defendant who is acquitted of the charges at his or her trial gains absolute constitutional immunity against reprosecution for the same offense.[25] It makes no difference that the acquittal resulted from trial errors prejudicial to the prosecution or that the prosecutor later discovers evidence that conclusively demonstrates the defendant's guilt.[26] An acquittal is final and ends the defendant's ordeal, regardless of the underlying reasons.

A conviction has the same constitutional finality—that is, if the defendant is willing to acquiesce in the outcome. However, if the defendant appeals and secures a reversal,[27] the defendant can be retried unless the conviction is reversed because the prosecutor failed to prove the defendant's guilt beyond a reasonable doubt. A reversal on this ground means that the defendant should have been acquitted and is the legal equivalent of an acquittal.[28] However, if the conviction is reversed for any other reason, such as that the judge erred in admitting a coerced confession or illegally seized evidence, the defendant can be retried. Appeals courts, as the Supreme Court has recognized, would scarcely be as solicitous of a defendant's constitutional rights if the reversal of a conviction meant that the defendant could not be retried.[29] Retrying a defendant after a successful appeal does not violate double jeopardy because this is the very relief that a defendant requests when he or she brings a criminal appeal.

---

[21]   Wade v. Hunter, 336 U.S. 684, 69 S. Ct. 834, 93 L. Ed. 974 (1949).

[22]   Freeman v. United States, 237 F. 815 (2d Cir. 1916).

[23]   United States v. Potash, 118 F.2d 54 (2d Cir.), *cert. denied*, 313 U.S. 584, 61 S. Ct. 1103, 85 L. Ed. 1540 (1941).

[24]   United States v. Stein, 140 F. Supp. 761 (S.D.N.Y. 1956).

[25]   Fong Foo v. United States, *supra* note 7; Green v. United States, *supra* note 5; Kemper v. United States, 195 U.S. 100, 24 S. Ct. 797, 49 L. Ed. 114 (1904); United States v. Ball, 163 U.S. 662, 16 S. Ct. 1192, 41 L. Ed. 300 (1896).

[26]   *See* authorities *supra* note 25.

[27]   United States v. Tateo, 377 U.S. 463, 84 S. Ct. 1587, 12 L. Ed. 2d 448 (1964); Sattazahn v. Pennsylvania, 537 U.S. 101, 123 S. Ct. 732, 154 L. Ed. 2d 588 (2003) (A defendant who is convicted of murder and sentenced to life imprisonment is not protected by the double jeopardy clause against imposition of a death sentence if he succeeds in having his conviction set aside on appeal and is convicted again on retrial).

[28]   Burks v. United States, 437 U.S. 1, 98 S. Ct. 2141, 57 L. Ed. 2d 1 (1978).

[29]   United States v. Tateo, *supra* note 27.

## B. Does the Subsequent Prosecution Involve the "Same Offense"?

When new charges, different from previous ones, are brought against a defendant who has already once before been placed in jeopardy, the court must decide whether the new charges represent the "same offense" or a different one. Only if the new charges represent the "same offense" will the second prosecution be foreclosed.

Deciding when new charges brought under a different section of the penal code represent the "same offense" is the most difficult question in double jeopardy law. When the Constitution was adopted, the number of crimes was relatively small and each crime covered a broad spectrum of conduct. Consequently, there were few opportunities for a prosecutor, displeased with the outcome of the first trial, to indict the defendant under a different section of the penal code and start all over again. This is no longer true. Modern criminal codes are replete with instances of overlapping and duplicating statutes dealing with slightly different aspects of the same underlying conduct.

Faced with the problem of determining when charges brought under different sections of the penal code represent the "same offense," courts have taken one of two approaches.[30] The first, and most widely used approach, is called the *Blockburger*[31] or **"same elements"** test. As you probably already know, legislatures define crimes by the acts that must be performed, the required mental state, and the consequences. These are the **elements** of the crime. The "same elements" test determines whether charges brought under different sections of the penal code represent the same offense by making a textual comparison of the elements the prosecutor must prove in order to obtain a conviction under each statute. Crimes defined under different sections of the penal code are considered different offenses and separate prosecutions may be brought under each as long as each statute requires proof of at least one distinct element.[32] If the statutory crime charged at the second trial requires proof of at least one new element, it will be considered a separate offense and the second prosecution may go forward, even though it is based on the same underlying criminal conduct as the first and the variations in the statutory charges are slight.[33] The hypothetical bank robber mentioned earlier

---

[30] For a discussion of these approaches, *see* Kirchheimer, *The Act, The Offense, and Double Jeopardy*, 58 YALE L.J. 513 (1949); Thomas, *The Prohibition of Successive Prosecutions for the Same Offense in Search of a Definition*, 71 IOWA L. REV. 323 (1986); Note, *Twice in Jeopardy*, 75 YALE L. REV. 262 (1965).

[31] Blockburger v. United States, 284 U.S. 299, 304, 52 S. Ct. 180, 182, 76 L. Ed. 306 (1932).

[32] United States v. Dixon, *supra* note 10; Carter v. United States, 530 U.S. 225, 120 S. Ct. 2159, 147 L. Ed. 2d 203 (2000) (finding that offense of taking and carrying away, with intent to steal anything of value exceeding $1,000 belonging to a bank was an offense distinct from taking from the person or presence of another, by force, violence, or intimidation, anything of value belonging to a bank, because the former offense contained three elements not included in latter offense, namely, specific intent to steal, asportation, and valuation exceeding $1,000. The fact that the two statutory offenses were similar and arose out of the same underlying conduct does not make them the same offense).

[33] *See* cases *supra* note 32.

in the chapter committed five distinct, same-element-test offenses—bank robbery, carrying a concealed weapon, making a terroristic threat, reckless endangerment, and speeding—and, consequently, may be tried five separate times. The "same elements" test provides scant protection against successive prosecutions for the same underlying conduct.[34] It nevertheless satisfies the Fifth Amendment and is the test used by federal courts and a majority of state courts.[35]

The second approach, known as the "**same transaction**" test, focuses on the underlying conduct to determine the number of times a defendant can be tried. Under this approach, all criminal charges that derive from the same underlying conduct must be joined for prosecution in a single trial.[36] The prosecutor cannot hold some of the charges in reserve to start over again if disappointed with the outcome of the first trial because the prosecutor is barred from bringing multiple prosecutions for the same criminal conduct.

### C. Is the Same Governmental Entity Prosecuting?

The double jeopardy prohibition applies only when both prosecutions are brought by the same government entity. It does not prevent separate prosecutions by different sovereign entities when the offense is a crime against the laws of each. Bank robbery is a classic example. Robbing a federally insured bank (a category that today includes virtually all banks) is a federal crime; robbing a bank located within the jurisdiction of the state is a state crime. Thus, our bank robber can be prosecuted for the same bank robbery by the federal government and the state in which the bank is located without violating the double jeopardy clause.[37] The same is true for crimes that cross state lines; all states whose laws are violated are permitted to prosecute.[38]

## § 9.4 —Prohibition of Multiple Punishments for the Same Offense

There is a second aspect to double jeopardy—the prohibition against multiple punishments for the same offense. This aspect has come before the Court repeatedly as states have undertaken increasingly aggressive measures to deal with criminals who are not deterred by traditional forms of punishment. These

---

[34]   Two doctrines, the included offense doctrine and collateral estoppel, block retrial in limited situations. *See* Brown v. Ohio, 432 U.S. 161, 97 S. Ct. 2221, 53 L. Ed. 2d 187 (1977) (recognizing included offense doctrine); Ashe v. Swenson, 397 U.S. 436, 90 S. Ct. 1189, 25 L. Ed. 2d 469 (1970) (applying collateral estoppel). Discussion of these doctrines is beyond the scope of this book.

[35]   United States v. Dixon, *supra* note 10.

[36]   For cases following this approach, *see* Neal v. State, 55 Cal. 2d 11, 357 P.2d 839 (1960), *cert. denied*, 365 U.S. 823, 81 S. Ct. 708, 5 L. Ed. 2d 700 (1961); State v. Corning, 289 Minn. 354, 184 N.W.2d 603 (1971); State v. Brown, 262 Or. 442, 497 P.2d 1191 (1972).

[37]   United States v. Lanza, *supra* note 12; Bartkus v. Illinois, *supra* note 12.

[38]   Heath v. Alabama, 474 U.S. 82, 106 S. Ct. 433, 88 L. Ed. 2d 387 (1985).

aggressive measures take a variety of forms, including laws authorizing confiscation of money and property gained from criminal activity;[39] "Megan's" laws, requiring convicted sexual offenders to register with the local police when they move into a community;[40] sexual predator laws, requiring involuntary civil commitment of habitual sexual offenders upon completion of their criminal sentences;[41] and laws imposing enhanced sentences on habitual offenders.[42] Because these laws impose burdens beyond the criminal punishment the offender has already received, they raise the question of what constitutes "punishment" for double jeopardy purposes.

Whether burdens like these constitute a punishment is not determined from the offender's point of view.[43] From the offender's point of view, any burden that accrues because of the commission of a crime looks like a punishment. The double jeopardy clause is not offended by imposition of civil penalties in addition to criminal punishments. Whether a statute imposes a civil penalty or exacts a criminal punishment depends on the legislature's purpose. If the purpose is to further a nonpunitive goal and the legislature characterizes the remedy as civil, the Supreme Court will normally accept this characterization unless the statute is so obviously punitive as to negate the legislature's avowed purpose.[44]

Laws requiring involuntary commitment of habitual sex offenders after they complete their sentence and "Megan's" laws, requiring registration of convicted sex offenders, for example, impose civil remedies, not criminal, because their purpose is to protect the community from future crimes, not to punish sex offenders for their past crimes.[45] Forfeiture laws authorizing the government to seize money and property gained from, or used in connection with, criminal activity are also treated as civil when the forfeiture is limited to "guilty property"[46] (i.e., profits gained from illegal activity, **instrumentalities**

---

[39]   United States v. Ursery, *supra* note 11.

[40]   McAllister, *The Constitutionality of Kansas Laws Targeting Sex Offenders*, 36 W.B.N. L.J. 419, 436 (1997) ("sexual offender registration laws which exist in every state generally have not been successfully challenged on constitutional grounds").

[41]   Selig v. Yount, 531 U.S. 250, 121 S. Ct. 727, 148 L. Ed. 2d 734 (2001) (state court's determination that sexual predator statute was civil rather than criminal precluded inmate's double jeopardy challenge because there is no constitutional protection against successive civil and criminal remedies; involuntary civil commitment following completion of criminal sentence was justified by state's interest in protecting public from dangerous individuals with untreatable mental conditions); Kansas v. Hendricks, 521 U.S. 346, 117 S. Ct. 2072, 138 L. Ed. 2d 501 (1997) (involuntary civil commitment of habitual sexual offenders following completion of their prison sentence does not violate double jeopardy clause).

[42]   Monge v. California, 524 U.S. 721, 118 S. Ct. 2246, 141 L. Ed. 2d 615 (1998) (laws imposing enhanced sentences on repeat offenders do not violate double jeopardy protection against multiple punishments for the same offense because the sentence enhancement is not imposed as additional punishment for the previous offense, but as a stiffened penalty for the present offense, which is regarded as more serious by virtue of its repetition).

[43]   Department of Revenue of Mont. v. Kurth Ranch, 511 U.S. 767, 114 S. Ct. 1937, 128 L. Ed. 2d 767 (1994).

[44]   Seling v. Young, *supra* note 41

[45]   *See* authorities *supra* notes 41 and 42.

[46]   United States v. Ursery, *supra* note 11.

used to commit a crime, and **contraband**).[47] Forfeiture of "guilty property" serves the nonpunitive goal of preventing offenders from committing future crimes by depriving them of the means to commit them.

Most jurisdictions also have statutes imposing enhanced sentences, often as much as double, on repeat offenders. The Supreme Court has also sustained these laws, over double jeopardy challenge, on the grounds that they do not punish the offender a second time for past crimes; the enhanced punishment is imposed for the present crime, which is considered a more aggravated offense due to its repetition.[48]

## § 9.5 Sixth Amendment and Due Process Requirements for Fair Trials

We will now take up consideration of the constitutional requirements for a fair trial. Most are found in the Sixth Amendment. You are already familiar with one of the most important provisions for ensuring a fair trial—the Sixth Amendment right to assistance of counsel. As explained in Chapter 8, the right to counsel is essential to protect innocent people from being convicted because they lack the legal skill and knowledge needed to defend themselves. This chapter investigates other provisions that are also essential to a fair trial, including the guarantee of a speedy and public trial; the requirement that the tribunal be fair and impartial; the right to trial by jury; and the right to confront and cross-examine adverse witnesses.

## § 9.6 —Speedy Trial

The Sixth Amendment guarantees defendants, in both state and federal prosecutions, the right to a speedy trial.[49] Delays in the administration of justice jeopardize several interests. First, for those unable to obtain release on bail, delays result in a loss of freedom, a consequence that is particularly tragic for defendants who are later acquitted.[50] Even for defendants who are able to afford bail, time spent waiting for trial is emotionally and financially taxing. Outstanding criminal charges can damage a person's reputation, curtail employment opportunities, disrupt important relationships, and cause intense anxiety.[51] Most important of all, when the wheels of justice turn too slowly, the integrity of the proceedings may be compromised. Time has a dulling effect

---

[47]    United States v. Bajakajian, 524 U.S. 321, 118 S. Ct. 2028, 141 L. Ed. 2d 314 (1998).

[48]    *See* Monge v. California, *supra* note 42; *see also* United States v. Watts, 519 U.S. 148, 117 S. Ct. 633, 136 L. Ed. 2d 554 (1997); Witte v. United States, 515 U.S. 389, 115 S. Ct. 2199, 132 L. Ed. 2d 351 (1995).

[49]    Klopfer v. North Carolina, 386 U.S. 213, 87 S. Ct. 988, 18 L. Ed. 2d 1 (1967).

[50]    Barker v. Wingo, 407 U.S. 514, 92 S. Ct. 2182, 33 L. Ed. 2d 101 (1972).

[51]    *Id.*; Smith v. Hooey, 393 U.S. 374, 89 S. Ct. 575, 21 L. Ed. 2d 607 (1972); Klopfer v. North Carolina, *supra* note 49.

on memory. Key defense witnesses, in addition, may die or disappear.[52] The problem is particularly serious for defendants who are incarcerated during this period. The Supreme Court has noted:[53]

> . . ."[T]he possibilities that long delay will impair the ability of an accused to defend himself" are markedly increased when the accused is incarcerated. . . . Confined in a prison, . . . his ability to confer with potential defense witnesses, or even to keep track of their whereabouts, is obviously impaired. And, while "evidence and witnesses disappear, memories fade, and events lose their perspective," a man isolated in prison is powerless to exert his own investigative efforts to mitigate these erosive effects of the passage of time.[54]

Although the speedy trial guarantee is intended to protect the accused, society also suffers when justice is delayed. The testimony of prosecution witnesses is subject to the same time hazards; they, too, can die, disappear, or forget, depriving the government of crucial evidence.[55] In *Barker v. Wingo*,[56] the Supreme Court elaborated on the consequences of tardy justice:

> . . . [T]here is a societal interest in providing a speedy trial which exists separate from, and at times in opposition to, the interests of the accused. The inability of courts to provide a prompt trial has contributed to a large backlog of cases in urban courts which, among other things, enables defendants to negotiate more effectively for pleas of guilty to lesser offenses and otherwise manipulate the system. In addition, persons released on bond for lengthy periods awaiting trial have an opportunity to commit other crimes. . . . Moreover, the longer an accused is free awaiting trial, the more tempting becomes his opportunity to jump bail and escape. Finally, delay between arrest and punishment may have a detrimental effect on rehabilitation.

When all the costs of delay are taken into account, it becomes apparent that the maxim that "justice delayed is justice denied" rings true for everyone.

## A. *Attachment of the Right to a Speedy Trial*

Criminal trials represent the culmination of a process that begins with the commission of a crime and proceeds through discovery of the crime, investigation, the defendant's arrest, indictment, arraignment, and beyond. It is necessary to select a point to mark the start of the period in which the government must bring the accused to trial or lose the right to prosecute—i.e., the point at

---

[52] *See* authorities *supra* note 51.

[53] Smith v. Hooey, *supra* note 51.

[54] *Id.* at 379-380, 89 S. Ct. at 578.

[55] Dickey v. Florida, 398 U.S. 30, 42, 90 S. Ct. 1564, 1571, 26 L. Ed. 2d 26 (1970) (Brennan, J., concurring); *see also* Ponzi v. Fessenden, 258 U.S. 254, 264, 42 S. Ct. 309, 312, 66 L. Ed. 2d 607 (1922).

[56] *Supra* note 50.

which the right to a speedy trial attaches. In *United States v. Marion*,[57] the Supreme Court ruled that the Sixth Amendment guarantee of a speedy trial starts to run only after the prosecutorial phase commences. By conferring the right to a speedy trial on an "accused," the drafters manifested an intent to exclude pre-accusatory delays from consideration in determining whether the right to a speedy trial has been denied. As with the right to counsel, the suspect stands "accused" only after the government decides to prosecute by obtaining an indictment or filing formal charges. Delays before a suspect has been charged with a crime are not taken into account in determining whether a speedy trial has been denied.

The interests of both the accused and the public are also better served by granting authorities ample time to investigate crimes before they make formal charges. The prosecution benefits because it will not lose the right to prosecute if is slow to learn of the crime or to develop the case. Likewise, the would-be defendant benefits because the prosecution will conduct a more thorough examination before lodging formal charges, making it less likely that innocent persons will be accused. Moreover, criminal defendants already have other legal protection against delays in charging them. First, for most crimes there are **statutes of limitation** that require that criminal charges be made within a fixed number of years after the crime has been committed. If the delay exceeds the period of limitation, prosecution will be barred. Second, the due process clause provides a further basis for relief in cases in which the prosecution deliberately delays filing charges in order to obtain a tactical advantage over the defendant or does so with knowledge of an appreciable risk that the delay will cripple the defendant's ability to put forth an adequate defense.[58]

Even though the right to a speedy trial has attached, the prosecution[59] or defense[60] can stop the clock by having the charges dismissed. If the prosecution subsequently reinstates the charges, the period in between will be excluded from Sixth Amendment computation. Only the period during which a defendant bears the status of an accused is taken into account in determining whether a speedy trial has been denied.

## B. Determining Whether the Right Has Been Denied

There is no set period in which a trial must take place after prosecution has begun. Rather, in determining whether the right to a speedy trial has been denied, the Supreme Court balances four factors:[61] (1) the length of the delay; (2) the reasons for the delay; (3) whether the defendant asserted his or her right to a speedy trial or sat idly by; and (4) whether the delay prejudiced the defendant's case.

---

[57] 404 U.S. 307, 92 S. Ct. 455, 30 L. Ed. 2d 468 (1971); *see also* United States v. MacDonald, 456 U.S. 1, 102 S. Ct. 1497, 71 L. Ed. 2d 696 (1982).

[58] United States v. Lovasco, 431 U.S. 783, 97 S. Ct. 2044, 52 L. Ed. 2d 752 (1977) (dicta).

[59] United States v. MacDonald, *supra* note 57.

[60] United States v. Loud Hawk, 474 U.S. 302, 106 S. Ct. 648, 88 L. Ed. 2d 640 (1986).

[61] Barker v. Wingo, *supra* note 50.

There is only one remedy for deprivation of the right to a speedy trial—permanent dismissal of the charges. The government cannot compensate the accused for unconstitutional delay by proceeding with the trial and subtracting the period of unconstitutional delay from the sentence imposed.[62] Freeing defendants without trial even though they may be guilty is a serious action. Consequently, the finding that delay has denied the defendant a speedy trial is reserved only for the most extraordinary cases.

## 1. Length of Delay

The first factor, duration of the delay, operates as a red flag signaling the need to inquire into the other three factors. An inquiry is necessary only when the delay is long enough to be presumptively prejudicial.[63] What constitutes a presumptively prejudicial delay varies with the nature of the case. A presumptively prejudicial delay in the case of an ordinary street crime, for example, would be less than for a tax evasion case, both because less time is needed to prepare for trial and because eyewitness testimony, the kind used to prove street crimes, grows stale more rapidly than documentary evidence, the kind typically presented in a tax evasion case.[64] Although the Constitution does not set an absolute time limit, some jurisdictions have adopted statutes requiring automatic dismissal of charges against non-violent offenders who are incarcerated while awaiting trial unless the trial is brought within a relatively short, fixed period.[65]

## 2. Reasons for Delay

The second factor in speedy trial analysis focuses on allocating responsibility for the delay. The Sixth Amendment does not protect an accused against delays that he or she has requested or for which he or she is responsible.[66] An accused cannot complain of delays resulting from the government's inability to locate him or her while a fugitive from justice;[67] of trial postponements caused by his or her own illness[68] or due to defense motions seasonably acted upon;[69] or for periods during which he or she was mentally incompetent to stand trial.[70] The only delays relevant for Sixth Amendment purposes are those attributable to the government.

---

[62]　Strunk v. United States, 412 U.S. 434, 93 S. Ct. 2260, 37 L. Ed. 2d 56 (1973).

[63]　Barker v. Wingo, *supra* note 50.

[64]　*Id.*

[65]　*See* United States v. West, 504 F.2d 253 (D.C. Cir. 1974).

[66]　Dickey v. Florida, *supra* note 55 (Brennan, J., concurring); United States v. Loud Hawk, *supra* note 60; United States v. Lustman, 258 F.2d 475 (2d Cir.), *cert. denied*, 358 U.S. 880, 79 S. Ct. 118, 3 L. Ed. 2d 109 (1958); United States v. Ferguson, 498 F.2d 1001 (D.C. Cir.), *cert. denied*, 419 U.S. 900, 95 S. Ct. 183, 42 L. Ed. 2d 145 (1974).

[67]　United States v. Simmons, 338 F.2d 804 (2d Cir. 1964), *cert. denied*, 380 U.S. 983, 85 S. Ct. 1352, 14 L. Ed. 2d 276 (1965).

[68]　Joy v. United States, 416 F.2d 962 (9th Cir. 1969).

[69]　United States v. Jones, 524 F.2d 834 (D.C. Cir. 1975).

[70]　United States v. Cartano, 420 F.2d 362 (1st Cir.), *cert. denied*, 397 U.S. 1054, 90 S. Ct. 1398, 25 L. Ed. 2d 671 (1970); Nickens v. United States, 323 F.2d 808 (D.C. Cir. 1963), *cert. denied*, 379 U.S. 905, 85 S. Ct. 198, 13 L. Ed. 2d 178 (1964); United States v. Lustman, *supra* note 66.

However, some reasons for prosecutorial delay are dealt with more harshly than others. When the delay results from reasons beyond the government's control, such as the inability to locate a crucial prosecution witness, an appropriate delay may be excused. Deliberate delays interjected in order to impair the defense, in contrast, are weighed heavily against the government.[71] Even negligent delays can, at times, work a speedy trial violation. For example, in *Doggett v. United States*,[72] the authorities did nothing to search for the defendant for six years due to an erroneous assumption that he was out of the country. Had they made an effort to locate him, they could have discovered his whereabouts in minutes, because he was living and working openly under his own name. Characterizing this delay as extraordinary, the Supreme Court ruled that Doggett had been denied his right to a speedy trial.

### 3. Defendant's Assertion of Rights

Prior to *Barker v. Wingo*, a majority of federal courts adhered to the so-called "demand-waiver" rule. This rule required the court to disregard any delays occurring before the accused demanded that his case be docketed for trial.[73] The defendant's silence in the face of delay was regarded as an automatic waiver. The *Barker* Court acknowledged that the defendant's timely assertion of his rights was "one of the factors to be considered," and that the "failure to assert the right" would "make it difficult for a defendant to prove that he was denied a speedy trial," but declined to treat this factor as automatic grounds for rejecting a claim. A defendant, for example, cannot be faulted with delay in making a demand when he or she is unaware that charges against him or her are outstanding.[74] Even when the defendant is aware of the charges, the impact of not demanding a speedy trial varies with the facts. The failure, for example, would be weighed more heavily against a defendant who, on the advice of his or her attorney, makes a strategic decision to acquiesce in the delay, hoping that the government will abandon the prosecution, than against one who is uncounseled and whose failure to make a timely demand for trial is caused by ignorance.

### 4. Prejudice to Defendant

Whether the defendant was damaged by the delay is the last and most important factor. This factor is evaluated in light of the interests that the constitutional guarantee of a speedy trial protects. Accordingly, delays are more serious for defendants who are subjected to oppressive pretrial confinements than for those who are free on bail.[75] However, even for defendants who are

---

[71]   Barker v. Wingo, *supra* note 50. *See also* United States v. Loud Hawk, *supra* note 60.
[72]   505 U.S. 647, 112 S. Ct. 2628, 120 L. Ed. 2d 520 (1992).
[73]   Barker v. Wingo, *supra* note 50.
[74]   Doggett v. United States, *supra* note 72.
[75]   Petition of Provoo, 17 F.R.D. 183 (D. Md.), *aff'd sub nom.*, United States v. Provoo, 350 U.S. 857, 76 S. Ct. 101, 100 L. Ed. 761 (1955); United States ex rel. Von Cseh v. Fay, 313 F.2d 620 (2d Cir. 1963).

free on bail, delay can be harmful because job opportunities may be fore-closed, important relationships may be strained, and anxieties over the future can be immobilizing. However, the most serious damage is that which occurs to a defendant's ability to defend. Defendants who are able to demonstrate that crucial defense witnesses have died, disappeared, or forgotten important facts during an extended delay for which the government is responsible have a strong basis for claiming they were denied their constitutional right to a speedy trial.

## § 9.7 —Public Trial

The Sixth Amendment also guarantees the right to a public trial. Having criminal trials open to the public is a strong American tradition. Distrust of secret trials can be traced back to the excesses and abuses of the English Court of Star Chamber, known for its secretive, arbitrary, and oppressive inquisi-tions.[76] Although Star Chamber-like proceedings are a thing of the past, the constitutional guarantee of a public trial is claimed to be important for the fol-lowing three reasons: (1) witnesses are more likely to tell the truth when they are required to testify in front of an audience; (2) unknown persons with information about the crime may learn about the trial and come forward; and (3) public trials afford citizens an opportunity to observe the operation of their judicial system and evaluate whether courts are discharging their constitu-tional responsibility to administer justice.[77] Of these three justifications, the last is the most important. Open trials enhance "both the basic fairness of the criminal trial and the appearance of fairness so essential to public confidence in the system."[78]

The guarantee of a public trial applies both to the actual trial and to ancil-lary pretrial proceedings, such as **voir dire** examinations of potential jurors[79] and hearings on motions to suppress illegally seized evidence.[80] However, it does not apply to **grand jury** proceedings, which have always been conducted in secret.[81] Secrecy is important in grand jury proceedings to protect the rep-utation of innocent people in the event that the evidence presented is insuffi-cient to return an indictment.[82]

---

[76] In re Oliver, 333 U.S. 257, 68 S. Ct. 499, 92 L. Ed. 682, 690-692 (1948).

[77] *See* Gannett Co. v. DePasquale, 443 U.S. 368, 99 S. Ct. 2898, 61 L. Ed. 2d 608 (1979); Globe News-paper Co. v. Superior Court, 457 U.S. 596, 102 S. Ct. 2613, 73 L. Ed. 2d 248 (1982); United States v. Kobli, 172 F.2d 919 (3d Cir. 1949); State v. Schmit, 273 Minn. 78, 139 N.W.2d 800 (1966); People v. Jelke, 308 N.Y. 56, 123 N.E.2d 769 (1954).

[78] Press-Enterprise Co. v. Superior Court, 464 U.S. 501, 508, 104 S. Ct. 819, 823, 78 L. Ed. 2d 629 (1984).

[79] *Id.*

[80] Waller v. Georgia, 467 U.S. 39, 104 S. Ct. 2210, 81 L. Ed. 2d 31 (1984).

[81] *See* FED. R. CRIM. P. 6; *see also* Douglas Oil Co. v. Petrol Stops, Etc., 441 U.S. 211, 222, 99 S. Ct. 1167, 1674, 60 L. Ed. 2d 156 (1979).

[82] United States v. Procter & Gamble Co., 356 U.S. 677, 681-682, n.6, 78 S.Ct. 983, 986, 2 L. Ed. 2d 1077 (1958).

Although the Supreme Court has vigorously protected a criminal defendant's right to a public trial, this right is not absolute. Occasions may arise when a judge considers it necessary to exclude members of the public from the courtroom. Before taking this action, the judge must make findings that this action is necessary to advance an overriding interest and that there are no reasonable alternatives to protect this interest.[83] Closure, for example, is allowed when a child witness is called to testify about matters too embarrassing or frightening to discuss in public.[84] Even here, the judge must make case-specific findings that, because of the sensitive nature of the testimony and the child's age, closure is necessary to protect the child's physical and psychological well-being.

The right to a public trial is a two-way street. Not only does the defendant have a right to a public trial, members of the public and the press have a corresponding right to attend. Their right is grounded in the common law and the First Amendment. Even when a defendant asks the judge to clear the courtroom, the judge must consider the interest of the public and press in ruling on the motion. In *Richmond Newspapers, Inc. v. Virginia*,[85] the Supreme Court ruled that members of the public and press may be excluded from the courtroom at the defendant's request only when this action is necessary to protect the defendant's right to a fair trial.

## § 9.8 —Confrontation of Adverse Witnesses

The Sixth Amendment also guarantees an accused the right to confront witnesses who testify against him or her in open court. A courtroom confrontation enhances the reliability of testimony in several ways.[86] First, testimony in court is given under oath and on penalty of perjury. Second, jurors have an opportunity to observe the witness's demeanor and decide whether the witness is telling the truth. Finally, and most important of all, testimony given in open court is subject to cross-examination. Cross-examination has been described as the "greatest legal engine ever invented for discovery of truth."[87] The witness may have had an inadequate opportunity to observe the matters about which he or she testifies, his or her memory may be faulty or language imprecise, or he or she may not be telling the truth. Cross-examination gives the accused an opportunity to challenge a witness's veracity and expose weaknesses in his or her testimony. Cross-examination is so central to the right of confrontation that the Supreme Court has often spoken of the Sixth Amendment as guaranteeing the "right to confront and cross-examine" adverse wit-

---

[83]   Waller v. Georgia, *supra* note 80; Press-Enterprise Co. v. Superior Court, *supra* note 78.

[84]   Globe Newspaper Co. v. Superior Court, *supra* note 77 (decided under First Amendment).

[85]   448 U.S. 555, 100 S. Ct. 2814, 65 L. Ed. 2d 973 (1980); *see also* Globe Newspaper Co. v. Superior Court, *supra* note 77.

[86]   Chambers v. Mississippi, 410 U.S. 284, 93 S. Ct. 1038, 35 L. Ed. 2d 297 (1973); Maryland v. Craig, 497 U.S. 836, 845-846, 110 S. Ct. 3157, 3165, 111 L. Ed. 2d 666 (1990).

[87]   California v. Green, 399 U.S. 149, 90 S. Ct. 1930, 26 L. Ed. 2d 489 (1970).

nesses as if both terms appeared in the Constitution.[88] Because the confrontation clause provides a fundamental mechanism for ensuring the reliability of the evidence offered against an accused, it is regarded as an integral part of due process and is binding on the states.[89]

Historically, the right to confront adverse witnesses meant the right to confront them face-to-face. While a defendant could forfeit this right by not showing up for trial[90] or by being so disruptive that it was necessary to remove him or her from the courtroom, this right could not otherwise be denied.[91] However, the Supreme Court has since carved out an exception for child sex abuse trials.[92] Putative child sexual abuse victims may be permitted to testify via one-way, closed-circuit television if the judge determines that facing the accused in the courtroom would cause severe trauma and impair the child's ability to testify.

## § 9.9 —Fair and Impartial Tribunal

Few rights are more important than the right to be tried before an impartial tribunal. The Sixth Amendment guarantees the right to an impartial jury, but impartiality is also an ingredient of due process of law and applies in bench trials as well. There are many potentially biasing influences. The trier of fact (the judge or jury) may harbor racial or religious prejudice against the defendant; they may stand to gain, in some way, from his or her conviction; they may have past ties that cause them to believe the defendant is capable of diabolical deeds; or they may harbor animosity toward the defendant because of things they have heard or read about the case. Each of these influences can be corrupting.

Figure 9.2
**Elements of an Impartial Tribunal**

The judge sitting as a trier of fact or the members of the jury panel must:

1. not have a stake in the outcome of the case;
2. not bear any personal animosity toward the specific defendant;
3. be able to set aside any general prejudice toward a class to which the defendant belongs;
4. be able to set aside any preconceived notions about the proper outcome of the case and be able to render a verdict based solely on the evidence presented at trial.

---

[88]   Chambers v. Mississippi, *supra* note 86.
[89]   Pointer v. Texas, 380 U.S. 400, 85 S. Ct. 1065, 13 L. Ed. 2d 923 (1965).
[90]   Taylor v. United States, 414 U.S. 17, 94 S. Ct. 194, 38 L. Ed. 2d 174 (1973).
[91]   Illinois v. Allen, 397 U.S. 337, 90 S. Ct. 1057, 25 L. Ed. 2d 353 (1970).
[92]   Maryland v. Craig, *supra* note 86.

An obviously biasing influence exists when the judge or a juror has a financial stake in the outcome. In *Tumey v. Ohio*,[93] the Supreme Court set aside a conviction because the judge who tried the case was paid from the fines and costs levied against persons found guilty, rather than out of the general funds, which is the normal way judges are compensated. This method of compensation created an incentive to resolve doubtful cases in favor of fee-generating guilty verdicts.

In *Mayberry v. Pennsylvania*,[94] the judge who tried the case harbored animosity toward the defendant for reasons that were richly deserved. The defendant, who insisted on representing himself, showed contemptuous disdain for the judge's authority. When he disagreed with a ruling, he would hurl insults at the judge, calling him names like "hatchet man for the state," "dirty sonofabitch," and "tyrannical old dog." His conduct eventually became so insufferable that he had to be gagged in order for the trial to proceed. After the jury returned a verdict, the judge held the defendant in contempt of court and sentenced him to between 11 and 22 years in prison. The Supreme Court set the contempt conviction aside. Characterizing the defendant's trial demeanor as "a shock to those raised in the Western tradition," the Court ruled that a judge who has been the target of repeated vitriolic attacks must turn the trial of contempt charges over to another judge who does not bear the "sting of . . . slanderous remarks."[95] A defendant is entitled to be tried before an impartial tribunal even when the defendant is responsible for the animosity of which he or she complains.

Special precautions may be necessary to avoid prejudice during jury trials that would not be required during a bench trial, because jurors may be swayed by influences that would not sway a judge. The defendant, for example, may not be forced to stand trial in prison clothing because compelling a defendant to dress in this manner furthers no policy of importance to the government and could be taken by jurors as an indication of guilt.[96] This does not mean that a defendant is entitled to have the courtroom purified of everything from which jurors might infer guilt. Some practices, like the presence of armed guards in the courtroom, are necessary for security. When a practice is necessary for security, the defendant cannot complain that it may create an unfavorable impression in the minds of the jurors.[97]

Finally, and most importantly, a fair trial means that the defendant's guilt must be determined on the basis of testimony developed in open court, and not on preconceived notions and prejudices.[98] Of course, a panel of jurors that is totally free of prejudice is a goal that is rarely, if ever, reached. All human beings are prejudiced, at least on some level, about some issues. To ferret out

---

[93]   273 U.S. 510, 47 S. Ct. 437, 71 L. Ed. 749 (1927); *see also* Ward v. Village of Monroeville, 409 U.S. 57, 93 S. Ct. 80, 34 L. Ed. 2d 267 (1972).

[94]   400 U.S. 455, 91 S. Ct. 499, 27 L. Ed. 2d 532 (1971).

[95]   *Id.*

[96]   Estelle v. Williams, 425 U.S. 501, 96 S. Ct. 1691, 48 L. Ed. 2d 126 (1976).

[97]   Holbrook v. Flynn, 475 U.S. 560, 106 S. Ct. 1340, 89 L. Ed. 2d 525 (1986).

[98]   Parker v. Gladden, 385 U.S. 363, 87 S. Ct. 468, 17 L. Ed. 2d 420 (1966).

the worst prejudices, defense counsel is permitted to conduct a voir dire examination of prospective jurors during the jury selection process to determine whether they have "disqualifying attitudes" about the case. If so, the potential juror will be "struck" from the panel. What constitutes a disqualifying attitude depends on the issues involved in the case. A prospective juror's admission that he favors the death penalty and would automatically vote to impose it if the defendant is found guilty would be a disqualifying attitude in a death penalty case because it would prevent the juror from considering mitigating factors in imposing the sentence.[99] The same attitude, however, would not disqualify the juror from sitting in a non-capital trial, even though this attitude may indicate a bent in favor of conviction.

## § 9.10 —Pretrial Publicity

A fair and impartial tribunal is one that reaches its decision solely from the evidence presented at the trial, rather than from information learned elsewhere. The rules of evidence, which are designed to filter reliable facts from unsubstantiated rumors, would mean little if the jurors came to the trial already knowing the "correct outcome" based on things they read in the newspaper.

There is usually no problem assembling a jury panel that will make its decision based solely on the evidence presented at trial because members of the jury usually have no independent knowledge of the case. To help ensure that no one with independent knowledge finds his or her way onto the jury, trial counsel will be allowed to examine prospective jurors to learn whether they know the defendant or the victim, or have some other connection to the case that might provide a source of independent knowledge. If a potential juror indicates having preconceived notions about the case that could affect his or her decision, the judge will excuse the juror so that another, without a connection to the case, can be selected.

However, in this day of mass media, some cases are of such intense public interest that it may be impossible to find a juror who has not heard of the case before being selected to sit on the jury. Mr. Justice Frankfurter summarized this problem when he questioned:

> How can fallible men and women reach a disinterested verdict based exclusively on what they heard in court when, before they entered the jury box, their minds were saturated by press and radio for months preceding by matters designed to establish the guilt of the accused?[100]

---

[99]   Morgan v. Illinois, 504 U.S. 719, 112 S. Ct. 2222, 119 L. Ed. 2d 492 (1992).

[100]   Irvin v. Dowd, 366 U.S. 717, 729-730, 81 S. Ct. 1639, 1646, 6 L. Ed. 2d 751, 760 (1961) (Frankfurter, J., concurring). *See also generally,* Robert Hardaway & Douglas B. Tumminello, *Pretrial Publicity in Criminal Cases of National Notoriety: Constructing a Remedy for the Remediless Wrong,* 46 AM. U. L. REV. 39 (1996).

The problem is illustrated by the trial of Dr. Sam Sheppard, in which the nation was drawn into rumors that he had murdered his wife in their suburban Cleveland home. Dr. Sheppard was not even charged in the killing before a Cleveland newspaper had proclaimed his guilt on the front page and began demanding "justice." During the weeks and months before the trial, headlines were saturated with stories of Sheppard's lack of cooperation, his refusal to take a lie detector test, his secret love affairs, interviews with "bombshell witnesses," and other prejudicial disclosures. The courtroom was packed with reporters throughout the trial. The reporters often commented on the evidence right in front of the jury. The state appeals court described the trial as "a 'Roman holiday' for the news media" while the Supreme Court called it a "carnival atmosphere."[101] Sheppard spent 10 years in prison before the U.S. Supreme Court declared that he had received an unfair trial and ordered that he be released. Although he was acquitted at the new trial, he and his family were ruined.

## A. Constitutional Standards for Choosing an Impartial Jury When There Has Been Significant Pretrial Publicity

In a nation in which most citizens either read the newspaper or own radios or televisions, the facts associated with names like O.J. Simpson and Scott Peterson are likely to come to the attention of virtually every person qualified for jury service. If media exposure to some of the facts of the case was enough to disqualify prospective jurors, selecting a constitutionally acceptable jury would be impossible except in routine cases. However, the due process standard for impartiality does not require that the prospective juror be unfamiliar with the case, or even that the juror hold no "preconceived notion as to the guilt or innocence of the accused."[102] Rather, the test is whether the "juror can lay aside his impression or opinion and render a verdict based on evidence presented in court."[103]

During their voir dire examination, prospective jurors will be asked if they are familiar with the case and, if so, whether they believe that they can decide the defendant's guilt based solely on the evidence. A juror's affirmation that he or she can make an unbiased determination does not conclusively establish this fact. The defendant can still attempt to show that the panel was biased. For example, in *Irvin v. Dowd*,[104] the entire community was flooded with prejudicial media reports during the six months prior to the trial. Ninety percent of those questioned expressed uncertainty about whether they could render an impartial verdict based on the evidence developed at the trial and eight of the 12 jurors who were eventually selected to sit in the case admitted to having

---

[101] Sheppard v. Maxwell, 384 U.S. 333, 86 S. Ct. 1507, 16 L. Ed. 2d 600, 608 (1966).

[102] Irvin v. Dowd, *supra* note 100. *See also* Murphy v. Florida, 421 U.S. 794, 95 S. Ct. 2031, 44 L. Ed. 2d 589 (1975).

[103] Rideau v. Louisiana, 373 U.S. 723, 83 S. Ct. 1417, 10 L. Ed. 2d 663 (1963); Irvin v. Dowd, *supra* note 100. *But see* Patton v. Yount, 467 U.S. 1025, 104 S. Ct. 2885, 81 L. Ed. 2d 847 (1984).

[104] *Supra* note 100.

preconceived notions about the defendant's guilt. However, because they stated that they could put their beliefs aside and act impartially, the trial court allowed them to sit in the case. The Supreme Court was skeptical about their ability to do this and reversed the conviction, stating, "[w]here so many, so many times, admitted prejudice, such a statement of impartiality [by the jurors actually selected] can be given little weight."[105]

Courts consider the following factors in deciding whether a panel that has been exposed to prejudicial media coverage was able to render an impartial verdict:

## 1. Prejudicial Nature of the Publicity

Factual news reports containing a straightforward, unemotional account of unfolding events are far less likely to deprive prospective jurors of the ability to act impartially than are editorialized indictments. However, even factual reports can compromise the fairness of the proceedings if the reports lead to disclosure of incriminating evidence that is later ruled inadmissible.[106] Reports about inadmissible confessions are particularly likely to cause damage, because people usually remember confessions. In *Rideau v. Louisiana*,[107] the accused confessed to the details of a brutal rape-murder during a televised interview from jail. The Supreme Court set his conviction aside on the grounds that it was impossible for the accused to receive a fair trial after the entire community had seen him confess on television.

## 2. Extent of Publicity

The extent of the publicity is also important.[108] Adverse publicity must normally be pervasive before an accused can complain of being denied a fair trial.

## 3. Proximity to Time of Trial

The length of time between the damaging disclosures and the trial is a third consideration.[109] Memories tend to fade with time. Consequently, the chances of finding an impartial jury improve as the interval between the damaging disclosures and the trial grows.[110] Jury exposure to contaminating news stories during the trial are the most dangerous, but are also the easiest to prevent.[111] The judge can order the jurors not to read, watch, or listen to any reports, or may even **sequester** them in order to prevent all contact with the outside world while the trial is in progress.

---

[105]   *Id.*
[106]   Rideau v. Louisiana, *supra* note 103.
[107]   *Id.*
[108]   *See* Sheppard v. Maxwell, *supra* note 101.
[109]   Patton v. Yount, *supra* note 103.
[110]   *Id.*
[111]   United States v. Concepcion Cueto, 515 F.2d 160 (1st Cir. 1975); United States v. Bowe, 360 F.2d 1 (2d Cir. 1966), *cert. denied*, 385 U.S. 961, 87 S. Ct. 401, 17 L. Ed. 2d 306 (1967).

### 4. Attitudes Revealed on Voir Dire Examination

Prospective jurors are subject to **voir dire** examination. The attitudes they reveal on voir dire are likely to mirror the sentiments of the community. In *Murphy v. Florida*,[112] the Supreme Court observed:

> The length to which the trial judge must go in order to select jurors who appear to be impartial is . . . [a] factor relevant in evaluating those jurors' assurances of impartiality. In a community where most veniremen will admit to a disqualifying prejudice, the reliability of the others' protestations may be drawn into question; for it is then more probable that they are part of a community deeply hostile to the accused, and more likely that they may unwittingly have been influenced by it.[113]

## B. Methods of Counteracting Media Contamination After It Has Taken Place

Once a community has been exposed to media contamination, there are several precautions a trial judge can take in an attempt to preserve the accused's right to a fair and impartial trial. First, special efforts can be made in the jury selection process to identify and eliminate prospective jurors who hold fixed opinions about the defendant's guilt by asking probing questions on voir dire. However, as *Irvin v. Dowd* shows, once a community has been thoroughly saturated, probing voir dire examinations may not be enough to prevent the damage from seeping into the jury box. A second alternative is to postpone the trial until the case has lost its notoriety. Although delay has antiseptic value, this method of securing a fair trial has serious drawbacks: repairing damage to one constitutional right is achieved at the cost of injury to another. By the time the case has lost its notoriety, it may no longer be possible to afford the accused a speedy criminal trial. In the tradeoff, the accused has been forced to give up his or her right to a speedy trial in order to obtain an impartial jury, both of which are his or her constitutional due.

Changing the venue of the trial to a different community may afford an alternative to delay.[114] However, this solution will work only if the publicity has been localized. No community is so remote that a name such as O.J. Simpson is unknown. For cases in which contaminating disclosures have been plastered across the front pages of newspapers all over the country, finding a constitutionally acceptable jury may be next to impossible.

---

[112] 421 U.S. 794, 95 S. Ct. 2031, 44 L. Ed. 2d 589 (1975).
[113] *Id.* at 803-804, 95 S. Ct. at 2037. *But see* Patton v. Yount, *supra* note 103.
[114] Groppi v. Wisconsin, 400 U.S. 505, 91 S. Ct. 490, 27 L. Ed. 2d 571 (1971). *See also* Sheppard v. Maxwell, *supra* note 101.

None of the methods for trying to undo damage after it has occurred are entirely satisfactory. Their efficacy is incapable of being measured, and their use is often accompanied by added costs, delays, or the sacrifice of other constitutional rights.

## C. *Proactive Measures Designed to Avert Media Contamination of Criminal Trials*

During the 1970s, criminal trial judges began experimenting with more aggressive measures for protecting the accused's right to a fair trial. The traditional approaches focused on reducing damage after it happened. The newer approaches were bolder—they attempted to keep inflammatory information out of print. The media's response was to claim the protection of the First Amendment.

### 1. Restraining Publication: Media Gag Orders

Media "gag orders" were one of the first approaches to be tried. Trial judges in high-profile cases would enter orders directing media representatives to refrain from reporting specified details that posed a threat to the fairness of the proceedings. This approach was reviewed in *Nebraska Press Association v. Stuart.*[115] A few days after the accused was arrested in a small, rural community for murdering six members of the same family, the trial judge issued an order prohibiting representatives of the media from publishing information about the existence and contents of confessions, inculpatory statements, or other "strongly implicative" details. The Supreme Court unanimously ruled that the First Amendment prevents trial judges from restraining publication of news reports about what transpires in open court. Criminal trials are public events and what goes on in the court room is public property. The Justices, nevertheless, split on whether the First Amendment prevents trial judges from restraining publication of damaging information learned from other sources, such as from attorneys or the police. Three took the position that media gag orders are always unconstitutional while the remainder stopped just short of this. However, the gist of this case is that of all the various methods for controlling prejudicial pretrial publicity, ordering media representatives to refrain from publishing lawfully gathered information is the least acceptable.

### 2. Preventing Media Access to Newsworthy Information: Closure Orders

After *Nebraska Press Association*, criminal trial judges switched to "closure orders." Trial judges would close the proceedings to media representatives and members of the public when testimony and arguments were being

---

[115]    427 U.S. 539, 96 S. Ct. 2791, 49 L. Ed. 2d 683 (1976).

presented that the judge did not want reported. The use of closure orders set the stage for a second round of constitutional litigation. The issue was no longer whether criminal trial judges could restrain publication of lawfully gathered information, but whether they could prevent the media from learning the facts in the first place.

*Gannett Co. v. DePasquale*[116] was the first closure case to reach the U.S. Supreme Court. The trial judge, at the request of both the prosecutor and the accused, closed the court during arguments on a pretrial motion to suppress evidence alleged to have been illegally seized. The Supreme Court upheld the closure order, noting that the purpose of a pretrial suppression hearing is to eliminate inadmissible evidence so that jurors will not be made aware of its existence at the trial. This purpose could be defeated if the outcome of a pretrial suppression hearing were carried in the news. The rule that emerges from *Gannett Co. v. DePasquale* and subsequent cases[117] is that trial judges may close specified portions of criminal proceedings if, but only if: (1) there is a substantial probability that publicity from open proceedings will compromise the accused's right to a fair trial, and (2) alternatives short of closure would be inadequate to protect this right. An order clearing the courtroom for the duration of the trial, for example, would violate the First Amendment because publicity about what happens at the trial has no potential to compromise the integrity of the proceedings because it discloses nothing the jurors have not already heard.[118] The real threat is that jurors (actual or potential) will read about damaging information that was not introduced at the trial or comments on evidence that was introduced. This danger can be managed, at least in part, by excluding media from pretrial suppression hearings, admonishing the jurors not to read news articles or to listen to radio or television reports about the case and, if necessary, by sequestering them during the trial.

### 3. Controlling the Release of Information to the Media

Although media gag orders violate the First Amendment, there is nothing wrong with ordering prosecutors, defense attorneys, prospective witnesses, and police officers to refrain from discussing specific aspects of a case with the media.[119] The American Bar Association (ABA) has promulgated a set of guidelines governing pretrial release of information by lawyers, prosecutors, judges, and law enforcement officers.[120] Disclosure of the following matters carries a "substantial likelihood of prejudicing criminal proceedings" and, therefore, should be avoided:

---

[116] 443 U.S. 368, 99 S. Ct. 2898, 61 L. Ed. 2d 608 (1979).

[117] *See* Press-Enterprise Co. (II) v. Superior Court, 478 U.S. 1, 106 S. Ct. 2735, 92 L. Ed. 2d 1 (1986).

[118] 448 U.S. 555, 100 S. Ct. 2814, 65 L. Ed. 2d 973 (1980).

[119] *See* Sheppard v. Maxwell, *supra* note 101.

[120] **ABA STANDARDS FOR CRIMINAL JUSTICE, FAIR TRIAL AND FREE PRESS §§ 8-1.1, 8-2.1 (1992).** The ABA Standards are reproduced in Part II.

1. a suspect's prior criminal record;
2. a suspect's character or reputation;
3. opinions about the suspect's guilt, the merits of the case, or the strength of the government's evidence;
4. the existence or contents of confessions or inculpatory statements, or a suspect's refusal to make a statement;
5. the outcome of examinations or laboratory tests or the suspect's refusal to cooperate;
6. the identity, expected testimony, criminal records, or credibility of prospective witnesses;
7. the possibility of a plea bargain, guilty plea, or other disposition; and
8. any other information that the officer knows or has reason to know would be inadmissible as evidence in a trial.

The following matters, on the other hand, are considered appropriate subjects for public comment:

1. the accused's name, age, residence, occupation, and family status;
2. the identity of the victim (if release of this information is not otherwise prohibited by law);
3. information necessary to aid in a suspect's apprehension or to warn the public of dangers;
4. requests for assistance from the public in obtaining evidence;
5. general information about the investigation, including its length and scope, and the identity of the investigating officers;
6. the facts and circumstances surrounding the arrest, including its time and place, and the identity of the arresting officer;
7. the general nature of the charges against the defendant, with an accompanying explanation that the charges are merely accusations and that the defendant is presumed innocent until proven guilty;
8. the scheduling or results of any judicial proceeding; and
9. any information contained in a public record.

The ABA guidelines also address the propriety of granting media representatives access to persons in police custody. While police are not required to take special precautions to shield persons in custody from news cameras, they should not pose them for picture-taking sessions or make them available for press conferences unless they consent after being informed of their right to refuse and to confer with counsel in making this decision.

The ABA standards are binding on lawyers, who can be disciplined for violating them.[121] The standards can become effective against police officers through a different route, by encouraging police professional organizations and departments to adopt them in codes of professional responsibility and departmental regulations. Law enforcement agencies would do well to study the ABA standards. Because the First Amendment limits the power of judges to halt publication of damaging information once it finds its way into the

---

[121]   Gentile v. State Bar of Nevada, 501 U.S. 1030, 111 S. Ct. 2720, 115 L. Ed. 2d 888 (1991).

hands of the media, prosecutors, attorneys, and law enforcement agencies must be careful about releasing information. There is no First Amendment duty to grant media representatives access to crime information that is not available to the general public.[122] If law enforcement agencies restrict press releases along the lines contained in the ABA standards, this will go a long way toward protecting the right of the accused to a fair trial.

## § 9.11  —Trial by Jury

Trial by jury is an ancient and venerable institution. In 1215, the Magna Charta proclaimed that no free man could be condemned to death or sent to prison except by the legal judgment of his peers.[123] While the Magna Charta laid the foundation for the jury, there is little evidence of the existence of a jury concept even remotely resembling the modern jury until the fourteenth century.[124] For a while, the jury method of determining guilt existed in competition with several older, barbaric methods, such as "trial by ordeal" and "trial by battle."[125] Gradually, the older methods fell into disuse and the jury method emerged as the sole procedure. By the time the United States was settled, the institution of trial before a panel of 12 laymen, known as a **petit jury**, had a tradition dating back several centuries.

Figure 9.3
**Constitutional Right to Trial by Jury**

| Constitutional entitlement | Required number of jurors | Selection process | Need for unanimity |
|---|---|---|---|
| Only for offenses carrying a penalty of six months or more in jail. | Twelve in federal courts; no fewer than six in state courts. | Jury venires must be drawn from a source that is fairly representative of the community. Peremptory strikes may not be used to exclude potential jurors solely because of their race or gender. | Required in federal trials, but not in state trials unless the jury is comprised of only six persons. |

---

[122] The Florida Star v. BJF, 491 U.S. 524, 109 S. Ct. 2603, 105 L. Ed. 2d 445 (1989); Houchins v. KQED, Inc., 438 U.S. 1, 98 S. Ct. 2588, 57 L. Ed. 2d 553 (1979).

[123] MAGNA CHARTA, ch. 39, reprinted in R. PERRY & J. COOPER, SOURCES OF OUR LIBERTIES 17 (1959).

[124] 1 F. POLLOCK & R. MAITLAND, THE HISTORY OF ENGLISH LAW BEFORE THE TIME OF EDWARD I, 173 n. 3 (2d ed. 1909); 2 J. STORY, COMMENTARIES ON THE CONSTITUTION OF THE UNITED STATES, 540-541 (4th ed. 1873); Frankfurter and Corcoran, *Petty Federal Offenses and the Constitutional Guaranty of Trial by Jury*, 39 HARV. L. REV. 917, 923 (1926).

[125] Wells, *The Origin of the Petty Jury*, 27 L.Q. REV. 347, 357 (1911); *see also* CORNISH, THE JURY 10-12 (1968).

William Blackstone, writing in 1768, hailed the jury principle as the "glory of English law" and "the most transcendent privilege which any subject can enjoy or wish for."[126] While Blackstone's praise seems lavish by modern standards, his words reflect eighteenth-century sentiments. Those who drafted our Constitution held the jury principle in such high esteem that they took double precautions to ensure its preservation. In Article III, section 2 of the original Constitution, they declared that "[t]he Trial of all Crimes, except in Cases of Impeachment, shall be by Jury . . ." When the Bill of Rights was added two years later, they repeated in the Sixth Amendment that "[i]n all criminal prosecutions, the accused shall enjoy the right to . . . trial, by an impartial jury . . ."

The jury system offers at least three advantages over other methods of determining guilt. First, it gives citizens an opportunity to participate and, through shared participation, to evaluate the workings of the criminal justice system. Second, it imparts humanizing qualities and the community's sense of justice into the guilt-determining process. Finally, it enhances public confidence in criminal verdicts. In *Duncan v. Louisiana*,[127] the Supreme Court observed:

> A right to jury trial is granted to criminal defendants in order to prevent oppression by the Government. Those who wrote our constitutions knew from history and experience that it was necessary to protect against unfounded criminal charges brought to eliminate enemies and against judges too responsive to the voice of higher authority. The framers of the constitution strove to create an independent judiciary but insisted upon further protection against arbitrary action. Providing an accused with the right to be tried by a jury of his peers gave him an inestimable safeguard against the corrupt or overzealous prosecutor and against the complacent, biased, or eccentric judge. If the defendant preferred the common-sense judgment of a jury to the more tutored but perhaps less sympathetic reaction of the single judge, he was to have it . . .[128]

The Sixth Amendment right to trial by jury is deemed a fundamental right that constitutes an integral part of due process of law. Accordingly, states are required to provide jury trials in all cases in which this right is available in federal court.[129]

## A. *Proceedings in Which a Jury Trial Is Available*

The English common law recognized limited instances in which defendants did not enjoy the right to trial by jury. Defendants, for example, were not entitled to a jury trial in criminal prosecutions brought for "petty offenses."[130]

---

[126]   3 W. Blackstone, Commentaries 379.

[127]   391 U.S. 145, 88 S. Ct. 1444, 20 L. Ed. 2d 491 (1968).

[128]   *Id.* at 155-156, 88 S. Ct. at 1451 (footnote omitted).

[129]   *Id.*

[130]   Frankfurter & Corcoran, *Petty Federal Offenses and the Constitutional Guaranty of Trial by Jury*, 39 Harv. L. Rev. 917, 934 (1926).

Although the Sixth Amendment uses sweeping language, proclaiming that the accused shall enjoy the right to trial by jury in "all criminal prosecutions," the Supreme Court has consistently interpreted this language as perpetuating the historic distinction between petty and serious offenses.[131] The only dispute has been about where to draw the line.

The Supreme Court early on rejected the felony-misdemeanor distinction as the proper boundary marker because some misdemeanors carry substantial penalties, as well as significant stigma.[132] This matter was finally settled in *Baldwin v. New York*,[133] in which the Supreme Court ruled that the maximum punishment authorized by the legislature is the best indicator of the seriousness of an offense. The Court drew the line at six months in prison. Where the maximum punishment authorized by the legislature does not exceed six months in prison, the advantages of speedy, inexpensive nonjury trials outweigh the hardship to the defendant of being tried by a judge. The offense is, therefore, petty and there is no constitutional right to a jury trial.[134] The Supreme Court, conversely, has made the right to trial by jury available in criminal contempt cases, even though no such right was recognized under the common law.[135] Six months is the maximum sentence that a judge may impose for criminal contempt without empaneling a jury.[136]

There are several other proceedings in which the right to trial by jury is not available. There is no right to trial by jury in (1) proceedings before a military tribunal,[137] (2) juvenile court proceedings,[138] and (3) sentencing proceedings.[139] However, in capital punishment sentencing, the defendant is entitled to have a jury determine the existence or nonexistence of aggravating circumstances before the death penalty may be imposed.[140]

---

[131] Baldwin v. New York, 399 U.S. 66, 90 S. Ct. 1886, 26 L. Ed. 2d 437 (1970); Frank v. United States, 395 U.S. 147, 89 S. Ct. 1503, 23 L. Ed. 2d 162 (1969); Cheff v. Schnackenberg, 384 U.S. 373, 86 S. Ct. 1523, 16 L. Ed. 2d 629 (1966) (plurality opinion); District of Columbia v. Clawans, 300 U.S. 617, 57 S. Ct. 660, 81 L. Ed. 843 (1937); Callan v. Wilson, 127 U.S. 540, 8 S. Ct. 1301, 32 L. Ed. 223 (1888).

[132] Callan v. Wilson, *supra* note 131.

[133] *Supra* note 131.

[134] Baldwin v. New York, *supra* note 131; Blanton v. City of North Las Vegas, 489 U.S. 538, 109 S. Ct. 1289, 103 L. Ed. 2d 550 (1989) (driving under the influence (DUI) for first-time offenders was a petty offense where the maximum punishment was six months' imprisonment, even though conviction also carried a mandatory fine of between $200 and $1000, automatic loss of driver's license for 90 days, and compulsory attendance in alcohol abuse education course); Lewis v. United States, 518 U.S. 322, 116 S. Ct. 2163, 135 L. Ed. 2d 590 (1996) (offense carrying maximum authorized prison term of six months was a petty offense for which defendant was not entitled to jury trial, even though he was charged with multiple counts in single proceeding so that aggregate maximum prison term exceeded six months).

[135] Bloom v. Illinois, 391 U.S. 194, 88 S. Ct. 1477, 20 L. Ed. 2d 522 (1968).

[136] Taylor v. Hayes, 418 U.S. 488, 94 S. Ct. 2697, 41 L. Ed. 2d 897 (1974) (contempt of court is a petty offense that may be tried without jury when the sentence actually imposed does not exceed six months); Frank v. United States, *supra* note 131.

[137] Ex parte Milligan, 71 U.S. (4 Wall.) 2, 122, 18 L. Ed. 281, 296 (1886). *See also* Dennis, *Jury Trial and the Federal Constitution*, 6 COLUM. L. REV. 423 (1906).

[138] McKeiver v. Pennsylvania, 403 U.S. 528, 91 S. Ct. 1976, 29 L. Ed. 2d 647 (1971).

[139] Libretti v. United States, 516 U.S. 29, 116 S. Ct. 356, 133 L. Ed. 2d 271 (1995).

[140] Ring v. Arizona, 1536 U.S. 584, 22 S. Ct. 2428, 153 L. Ed. 2d 556 (2002).

The government may not chill assertion of the right to trial by jury by authorizing juries to impose the death penalty, while making life imprisonment the maximum sentence that can be imposed by a judge.[141] The natural tendency of such a provision would be to discourage defendants from asserting their constitutional right to be tried by a jury.

## B. Required Number of Jurors

The common law trial jury (**petit jury**) consisted of a body of 12 individuals selected at random from the community, whose function was to hear evidence presented in open court and to render a unanimous verdict.[142] This pattern continues to exist today in the federal courts and in most states.

However, at least five states—Florida, Louisiana, South Carolina, Texas, and Utah—provide for less than 12-member juries in the trial of felony cases and at least eight states provided for them in the trial of misdemeanor cases.[143] Once the U.S. Supreme Court decided in *Duncan v. Louisiana*[144] that the Sixth Amendment right to trial by jury was binding on the states, it was forced to determine whether the Constitution mandates a 12-person jury in state criminal prosecutions, as existed under the common law and is required in federal courts. This question came before the Court in *Williams v. Florida*,[145] in which a felony conviction was returned by a six-person jury. The Court determined that the number "12" was not an immutable corollary of the Sixth Amendment right to a jury trial. Justice White, who wrote the majority opinion, stated that the relevant inquiry was not whether a particular feature was buttressed by centuries of tradition, but whether it was critical to the jury's constitutional role. Having cast the inquiry in this form, Justice White concluded:

> [T]he essential feature of a jury obviously lies in the interposition between the accused and his accuser of the commonsense judgment of a group of laymen, and in the community participation and shared responsibility that results [sic] from that group's determination of guilt or innocence. The performance of this role is not a function of the particular number of the body that makes up the jury. To be sure, the number should probably be large enough to promote group deliberation, free from outside attempts at intimidation, and to provide a fair possibility for obtaining a representative cross-section of the community. But we find little reason to think that these goals are in any meaningful sense less likely to be achieved when the jury numbers six, than when it numbers 12. . . . And, certainly the reliability of the jury as a factfinder hardly seems likely to be a function of its size.[146]

---

[141] United States v. Jackson, 390 U.S. 570, 88 S. Ct. 1209, 20 L. Ed. 2d 138 (1968). *But see* Corbitt v. New Jersey, 439 U.S. 212, 99 S. Ct. 492, 58 L. Ed. 2d 466 (1980).

[142] 1 W. HOLDSWORTH, A. HISTORY OF ENGLISH LAW 325 (1927).

[143] Williams v. Florida, 399 U.S. 78, 99 n. 45, 90 S. Ct. 1893, 1905, n. 45, 26 L. Ed. 2d 446, 459, n. 45 (1970).

[144] 391 U.S. 145, 88 S. Ct. 1444, 20 L. Ed. 2d 491 (1968).

[145] *Supra* note 143.

[146] *Id.*

A six-member jury, however, is the minimum constitutionally acceptable size. In *Ballew v. Georgia*,[147] the Supreme Court ruled that a state criminal defendant was deprived of his Sixth and Fourteenth Amendment rights when he was tried before a five-member jury for a non-petty offense. A five-member panel, the Court stated, was too small to achieve the broad-based representation with diverse points of view that the constitutional right to a jury trial is designed to ensure.

## C. Requirement of Unanimity

Under the common law, a jury's verdict had to be unanimous in order to obtain either a conviction or an acquittal. If the jurors could not agree, a mistrial would be declared and the accused remained subject to retrial. The requirement of unanimous verdicts in criminal cases was firmly entrenched in Anglo-American jurisprudence when the Constitution was drafted and continues to be the prevailing practice today. Some states, however, depart from this requirement. In Louisiana and Oregon, for example, a ten-to-two vote is sufficient to render a verdict in non-capital felony cases,[148] although unanimity continues to be required in capital cases.[149] Several other jurisdictions have dispensed with the need for unanimity in misdemeanor trials. These experiments were undertaken in an effort to reduce the costs and delays accompanying frequent mistrials resulting from hung juries.[150]

In *Apodaca v. Oregon*,[151] the Supreme Court decided that the Sixth Amendment requires a unanimous verdict in order to convict in a federal criminal proceeding, but can be satisfied by less in a state trial. The Oregon statute upheld in *Apodaca* provided for a 12-member panel, but permitted conviction on a vote of only 10. In *Burch v. Louisiana*,[152] the Supreme Court was asked to decide whether states could combine less-than-unanimous verdicts with a substantial reduction in the jury's size. The statute under review in *Burch* authorized five-to-six verdicts for certain non-petty misdemeanor offenses. The Court balked, finding this departure from the common law pattern too extreme to be acceptable under the Sixth Amendment. If states elect to cut the jury's size in half, the verdict must be unanimous.

## D. Racial/Gender Composition of the Jury

The Sixth Amendment expressly requires that the jury be comprised of persons drawn from the "State and district wherein the crime shall have been

---

[147]   435 U.S. 223, 98 S. Ct. 1029, 55 L. Ed. 2d 234 (1978).
[148]   LA. CODE CRIM. PROC. ANN. art. 782; OR. REV. STAT. ANN. § 136.450.
[149]   *Id.*
[150]   Comment, *Should Jury Verdicts Be Unanimous in Criminal Cases?* 47 OR. L. REV. 417 (1968).
[151]   406 U.S. 404, 92 S. Ct. 1628, 32 L. Ed. 2d 184 (1972).
[152]   441 U.S. 130, 99 S. Ct. 1623, 60 L. Ed. 2d 96 (1979).

committed." Although a defendant can ask for a change in venue when necessary to obtain a fair trial, the petit jury must be drawn from a source that is fairly representative of the community in which case is eventually tried.[153]

## 1. Composition of the Jury Venire

The **jury venire** (the group or panel from which the trial jury will be selected) must be drawn from a fair cross-section of the community. Systematic exclusion of any distinctive group violates the right to trial by jury.[154] The reason was explained in *Peters v. Kiff*:[155]

> . . . Illegal and unconstitutional jury selection procedures cast doubt on the integrity of the whole judicial process. They create the appearance of bias in the decision of individual cases, and they increase the risk of actual bias as well. . . . [T]he exclusion from jury service of a substantial and identifiable class of citizens has a potential impact that is too subtle and too pervasive to admit of confinement to particular issues or particular cases. . . .

> . . . [W]e are unwilling to make the assumption that the exclusion of Negroes has relevance only for issues involving race. When any large and identifiable segment of the community is excluded from jury service, the effect is to remove from the jury room qualities of human nature and varieties of human experience, the range of which is unknown and perhaps unknowable. It is not necessary to assume that the excluded group will consistently vote as a class in order to conclude . . . that their exclusion deprives the jury of a perspective on human events that may have unsuspected importance in any case that may be presented.

The Sixth Amendment is violated whenever members of any distinctive group are systematically excluded from jury service.[156]

## 2. Prosecution's Use of Peremptory Challenges

Not only does the accused have a right to have the jury selected in a nonarbitrary manner, potential jurors themselves have a right, grounded in the equal protection clause of the Fourteenth Amendment, to be free of race and gender-

---

[153] Taylor v. Louisiana, 419 U.S. 522, 95 S. Ct. 692, 42 L. Ed. 2d 690 (1975).
[154] *Id.*
[155] 407 U.S. 493, 92 S. Ct. 2163, 33 L. Ed. 2d 83 (1972).
[156] *Id.* The criteria for being considered a "distinctive group" is articulated in United States v. Raszkiewicz, 169 F.3d 459 (7th Cir. 1999). There must be: (1) qualities that define a group, (2) a similarity of attitudes, beliefs, or experiences, and (3) a community of interest among the members. African-Americans, Peters v. Kiff, *supra* note 155, women, Taylor v. Louisiana, *supra* note 153, Hispanics, United States v. Lara, 181 F.3d 183, 192 n.1 (1st Cir. 1999), and Jews, United States v. Gelb, 881 F.2d 1155, 1161 (2d Cir. 1989) qualify under these criteria, but blue-collar workers, Anaya v. Hansen, 781 F.2d 1 (1st Cir. 1986), college students, United States v. Fletcher, 965 F.2d 781 (9th Cir. 1992), and persons under or over a particular age, Brewer v. Nix, 963 F.2d 1111 (8th Cir. 1992), do not.

based discrimination.[157] Equal protection challenges to jury selection generally involve discriminatory exercises of **peremptory challenges**.[158] Both sides in a criminal case are allowed to strike a certain number of jurors without cause (i.e., without having to show that the potential juror is biased). These are called peremptory challenges. Although the prosecutor need not have any particular reason for using a peremptory challenge, peremptory challenges may not be used to exclude potential jurors solely because of their race or gender.[159]

### E.  Waiver of the Right to Jury Trial

Under the common law of England, trial by jury was required for all serious offenses. The defendant could not waive a jury and be tried by a judge.[160] Although "consent" was technically required, the defendant could be tortured into submission.[161] Even after torture was no longer practiced, the accused had no choice as to the mode of trial. Jury trials were the only type available.

In modern times, all jurisdictions offer bench trials as an alternative to jury trials. Still, the ability to waive a jury trial is often restricted. The right to waive a jury trial and be tried by a judge is often conditioned upon the approval of the court, the prosecutor, or both. These restrictions do not violate a defendant's constitutional rights because the only constitutional right a defendant has concerning the method of trial is the right to trial by jury.[162]

## § 9.12   —Preservation and Disclosure of Evidence Favorable to the Defense

The prosecutor occupies a unique position in our adversarial system of criminal justice. Several decades ago, the Supreme Court observed:

> The United States Attorney is the representative not of an ordinary party to a controversy, but of a sovereignty whose obligation to govern impartially is as compelling as its obligation to govern at all; and whose interest, therefore, in a criminal prosecution is not that it shall win a case, but that justice shall be done. As such, he is, in a peculiar and very definite sense the servant of the law, the twofold aim of which is that guilt shall not escape or innocence suffer. He may prosecute with earnestness and vigor—indeed, he should do so.

---

[157] Batson v. Kentucky, 476 U.S. 79, 106 S. Ct. 1712, 90 L. Ed. 2d 69 (1986) (race); *see also* J.E.B. v. Alabama, 511 U.S. 127, 114 S. Ct. 1419, 128 L. Ed. 2d 89 (1994) (gender), Powers v. Ohio, 499 U.S. 400, 111 S. Ct. 1364, 113 L. Ed. 2d 411 (1991).

[158] *See* cases *supra* note 157.

[159] *Id.*

[160] Singer v. United States, 380 U.S. 24, 85 S. Ct. 783, 13 L. Ed. 2d 630, 633-634 (1965) (defendant's only constitutional right concerning method of trial is to an impartial trial by jury).

[161] *Id.*

[162] Note, *Constitutional Law: Criminal Procedure: Waiver of Jury Trial: Singer v. United States, 308 U.S. 24 (1965)*, 51 CORNELL L. REV. 339, 342-343 (1966).

But, while he may strike hard blows, he is not at liberty to strike foul ones. It is as much his duty to refrain from improper methods calculated to produce a wrongful conviction as it is to use every legitimate means to bring about a just one.[163]

This observation marked the beginning of a line of cases that eventually developed into two constitutional duties imposed on the prosecution and, indirectly, the police. The first duty is to disclose to the accused any evidence within the government's possession or knowledge that is favorable to the accused and material to guilt or punishment. The second duty is to preserve evidence that might be expected to play a significant role in the defense. Both obligations are grounded on the fundamental fairness implicit in due process, rather than on specific language found in the Constitution.

Figure 9.4

**Comparison of Police Obligations to Preserve and Disclose Exculpatory Evidence**

| Evidence that must be preserved | Evidence that must be disclosed |
|---|---|
| Police have a duty to preserve physical evidence that: <br> 1. has an exculpatory value that is apparent to the police; and <br> 2. is of a type the defense cannot obtain by other means. | Police have a duty to make sure that the prosecutor is aware of all evidence known to the police or anyone under their control that may help to: <br> 1. show that the defendant is innocent; <br> 2. counter the prosecution's version of the events; or <br> 3. challenge the credibility of key prosecution witnesses. |

## A. The Requirements for Disclosure of Exculpatory Information

The prosecution's obligation to disclose exculpatory information evolved from cases in which the prosecutor had either knowingly used false testimony[164] or allowed false testimony to go uncorrected.[165] When this happened, the Supreme Court had little trouble concluding that use of perjured testimony denied the defendant due process. However, in *Brady v. Maryland*,[166] the Supreme Court took a broad leap and transformed what had begun as a narrow doctrine concerned with the use of perjured testimony into a broad obligation to disclose all evidence within the government's possession or control favorable to the accused that is material to guilt or punishment.

---

[163]   Berger v. United States, 295 U.S. 78, 88, 55 S. Ct. 629, 633, 79 L. Ed. 1314, 1321 (1935).

[164]   Mooney v. Holohan, 294 U.S. 103, 55 S. Ct. 340, 79 L. Ed. 791 (1935).

[165]   Alcorta v. Texas, 355 U.S. 28, 78 S. Ct. 103, 2 L. Ed. 2d 9 (1957).

[166]   373 U.S. 83, 83 S. Ct. 1194, 10 L. Ed. 2d 215 (1963).

In *Brady*, the prosecutor failed to disclose that one of Brady's accomplices had confessed to the killing for which Brady was charged, even though his attorney made a formal request for any such statements. Brady was sentenced to death, but the Supreme Court reversed, announcing what has become known as the *Brady* rule:

> [T]he suppression by the prosecution of evidence favorable to an accused upon request violates due process where the evidence is material either to guilt or to punishment, irrespective of the good faith or bad faith of the prosecution. The principle . . . is not punishment of society for misdeeds of a prosecutor but avoidance of an unfair trial to the accused. . . . A prosecution that withholds evidence on demand of an accused which, if made available, would tend to exculpate him or reduce the penalty helps shape . . . a proceeding that does not comport with standards of justice, even though, as in the present case, his action is not "the result of guile . . ."[167]

The duty established in *Brady* does not depend upon proof that the prosecutor acted in bad faith. The rule is premised on recognition that whenever the government withholds evidence that could change the outcome of a case, the integrity of the verdict is compromised. The *Brady* rule recently surfaced in the Timothy McVeigh case. McVeigh's bombing of the Oklahoma City federal building resulted in 168 deaths. Shortly before his scheduled execution, the FBI discovered 3,135 pages of documents that McVeigh's lawyers had never seen. Characterizing the FBI's conduct as "deplorable," the federal judge reviewed the materials, but fortunately found nothing in them that would have changed the outcome.[168] Had the evidence of McVeigh's guilt been less clear, the FBI's blunder could have cost the Justice Department a conviction that took millions of dollars and years to obtain.

### 1. Types of Evidence that Must Be Disclosed

The constitutional duty to disclose extends to evidence that is favorable to the accused and material either to guilt or to punishment. It is impossible to formulate a comprehensive list of evidence that must always be disclosed because this list varies with the nature of the crime, the background (including criminal histories) of government witnesses, the prosecution's theory of the case, and other factors. Favorable evidence includes evidence that may help establish the defendant's innocence, counter the prosecution's version of

---

[167] *Id.* at 87-88, 83 S. Ct. 1196-1197.

[168] Neil A. Lewis & David Johnston, *Cleanup That Made a Mess: Putting Together Story on McVeigh Files, Government, So Far, Finds No Culprit,* Seattle Times at A3 (May 13, 2001); Editorial, *The Final Verdict. McVeigh's Fate Weighed Reasonably. Is the Story Finished?* Akron Beacon Journal, at A14, June 10, 2001. McVeigh was executed June 11, 2001, almost one month after his first execution was scheduled. McVeigh's execution was the first federal execution in 38 years.

the events, or impeach the credibility of key prosecution witnesses.[169] Certainly, a defendant is entitled to know whether someone else has confessed to the crime, whether a key prosecution witness has a criminal record or received a promise of leniency,[170] or whether there are documented errors on police crime laboratory reports[171] or negative results that indicate that the accused may not be guilty.[172] In *Barbee v. Warden*,[173] the prosecutor introduced the defendant's revolver into evidence without informing the defense that the police had run ballistics and fingerprint tests on the revolver and had learned that it was not the weapon used in the crime. The prosecutor failed to inform the defense because the prosecutor was unaware of the test results. The Fourth Circuit reversed the defendant's conviction, holding that the prosecutor was responsible for disclosing this information to the defense because it was in the hands of the police.

## 2. Scope of the Disclosure Obligation

The Supreme Court has consistently broadened the scope of the prosecutor's disclosure obligations. Today, it is settled law that the prosecutor is responsible for disclosing all evidence known to anyone assisting the prosecutor, including the police,[174] when the evidence is both favorable to the defense and material to guilt or punishment, regardless of whether the defense has specifically requested disclosure.[175]

---

[169] Stickler v. Green, 527 U.S. 263, 119 S. Ct. 1936, 144 L. Ed. 2d 286 (1999) ("[T]he duty to disclose . . . is applicable even though there has been no request by the accused and . . . encompasses impeachment evidence as well as exculpatory evidence. Such evidence is material 'if there is a reasonable probability that, had the evidence been disclosed to the defense, the result of the proceeding would have been different.' Moreover, the rule encompasses evidence 'known only to police investigators and not to the prosecutor.' In order to comply with *Brady*, therefore, 'the individual prosecutor has a duty to learn of any favorable evidence known to the others acting on the government's behalf in this case, including the police.'"); **People v. Wright, 86 N.Y.2d 591, 658 N.E.2d 1009, 635 N.Y.S.2d 136 (1995)**. *See also* generally R. Michael Cassidy, *Toward a More Independent Grand Jury: Recasting and Enforcing the Prosecutor's Duty to Disclose Exculpatory Evidence,* 13 GEO. J. LEGAL ETHICS 361, fn 33 (2000) ("Stated simply, the prosecution must disclose to the defense prior to trial any 'information known to or available to them which may develop doubt about the government's narrative.' The *Brady* line of cases has established a broad definition of constitutionally exculpatory evidence, including evidence which would impeach a government witness (such as prior inconsistent statements or inconsistent identification), evidence which would show bias on the part of a government witness (such as promises, rewards, or inducements), evidence which would cast doubt on any essential element of the crime charged, or evidence which would suggest that someone other than the defendant committed the crime. Exculpatory evidence includes not only documents or testimony admissible in evidence, but also inadmissible materials which, if defense counsel had access to them, might lead to admissible evidence.").

[170] Giglio v. United States, 405 U.S. 150, 92 S. Ct. 763, 31 L. Ed. 2d 104 (1972) (due process violated by failure to disclose promise of leniency given to key prosecution witness in exchange for testimony); United States v. Bagley, 473 U.S. 667, 105 S. Ct. 3375, 87 L. Ed. 2d 481 (1975): **People v. Wright,** *supra* note 169.

[171] United States v. Sebring, 44 M.J. 805 (1996).

[172] **Kyles v. Whitley, 514 U.S. 419, 115 S. Ct. 1555, 131 L. Ed. 2d 490 (1995)**.

[173] 331 F.2d 842 (4th Cir. 1964).

[174] *Id.; see also* Giglio v. United States, *supra* note 170.

[175] **Kyles v. Whitley,** *supra* note 172. However, a reversal is required only when there is a reasonable probability that the defendant's conviction or sentence would have been different had the evidence been disclosed; the focal point is whether the absence of the evidence deprived the defendant of a fair trial. *See, e.g.*, Stickler v. Greene, *supra* note 169.

Normally, the prosecutor will contact police to learn whether any exculpatory information is known to the department. However, when the police know of information favorable to the defense, they should advise the prosecutor of its existence without waiting to be asked. Sometimes a harried prosecutor may neglect to ask for the police file. Police can botch a prosecution by not taking the initiative to ensure that the prosecutor is aware of *Brady* material.

In *Kyles v. Whitley*,[176] the prosecution at a murder trial argued that the killer drove to the lot where the murder occurred, killed the victim, and drove off in the victim's car, leaving his own behind. The prosecutor showed the jury a blurry photo of the cars in the parking lot, which the prosecutor claimed substantiated this fact. However, he failed to disclose that the police had recorded the license plate numbers of all the cars in the parking lot when they took the photo, and that the defendant's car was not among them. The reason the prosecutor failed to disclose this information was that the police did not tell him. The government's argument that prosecutors are not accountable for information known to the police, but not to them, fell on deaf ears. The Court held that prosecutors have a duty to find out whether the police have uncovered *Brady* material. Knowledge of information in the hands of the police will be imputed to the prosecutor for the sake of determining whether the government has discharged its *Brady* responsibilities. A contrary rule, the Court stated, would "substitute the police for the prosecutor, and even for the courts themselves, as the final arbiters of the government's obligation to ensure fair trials."[177]

## B. Police Responsibility to Preserve Evidence

Police are also under a second, closely related duty—the duty to preserve evidence favorable to the defense. This duty was first recognized in *California v. Trombetta*.[178] The prosecutor in *Trombetta* was unable to comply with a *Brady* request to produce a breath sample taken from the defendant at the time of his drunk driving arrest because the police, acting under the department's

---

[176] *Supra* note 172 ("The prosecution has the duty to learn of any evidence known to others acting on the government's behalf, including police, and to disclose this information to the defense. Failure to disclose is not excused because the prosecutor was unaware of the information.").

[177] *Id.* at 514 U.S. at 438, 115 S. Ct. at 1568, 131 L. Ed. 2d at 509. However, federal prosecutors are not accountable under *Brady* for information possessed by state officials and vice versa. *See, e.g.*, United States v. Beers, 189 F.3d 1297 (10th Cir. 1999) (holding that a state's knowledge and possession of potential impeachment evidence cannot be imputed to a federal prosecutor for purposes of establishing a *Brady* violation). The same is true for information possessed by private third parties. *See, e.g.*, United States v. Levitt, 198 F.3d 259 (10th Cir. 1999) (prosecutor not guilty of *Brady* violation in failing to disclose personal medical records of key government witness where the records were not in the government's possession and the prosecutor had no knowledge of them). Even for information in the government's possession, the prosecutor is not accountable if the person who knows of the information is employed in a different office that does not regularly work with the prosecutor's office. Imputing knowledge of all information within the government's possession, regardless of who knows it, would impose an unreasonable burden on prosecutors. *See, e.g.*, United States v. Avellino, 136 F.3d 249 (2d Cir.1998).

[178] 467 U.S. 479, 104 S. Ct. 2528, 81 L. Ed. 2d 413 (1984).

normal procedures, had destroyed it after receiving a positive result on the Intoxilyzer test. The Supreme Court ruled that police have a constitutional duty to preserve evidence only when the evidence (1) possesses an exculpatory value that is apparent before it is destroyed and (2) is of such a nature that it cannot be replaced by other reasonable available means. Neither requirement was satisfied here. The breath sample that tested positive for intoxication had no apparent exculpatory value because Intoxilyzer® tests are highly accurate, making it unlikely that a second test would have yielded a different result, and the defendant could challenge the result without the sample by hiring an expert to testify about the margin of error on Intoxilyzer® tests.

Four years later, in *Arizona v. Youngblood*,[179] the Court narrowed the *Trombetta* test, holding that destruction of potentially useful evidence constitutes a deprivation of due process only when the evidence is destroyed in bad faith or, in other words, when the police act with a conscious intent to suppress exculpatory evidence. In *Arizona v. Youngblood*, police failed to refrigerate a semen sample taken from a child sexual molestation victim. The tests run on the sample were inconclusive because the sample was left unrefrigerated for too long. The defendant argued that he was mistakenly identified, that the semen sample, if preserved, would have proven this, and that as a result, he was denied due process. The Court began its analysis by noting that "[w]henever potentially exculpatory evidence is permanently lost, courts face the treacherous task of divining the import of materials whose contents are unknown and, very often, disputed.'" Limiting constitutional relief to cases in which evidence is destroyed in bad faith is necessary to keep the duty of the police to preserve evidence within bounds by confining it to cases in which the interests of justice most clearly require a remedy. In the present case, the semen sample was destroyed before the investigation had focused on a particular suspect and at a time when the police had no way of knowing whether it would inculpate or exculpate the person they eventually charged. Consequently, the most that could be said about the conduct of the police is that they were careless in their handling of the semen sample, but there was nothing to suggest that they acted in bad faith.[180] As a result, the defendant had no remedy for the loss of this evidence.

---

[179] 488 U.S. 51, 109 S. Ct. 333, 102 L. Ed. 2d 281 (1988). *Arizona v. Youngblood* had a startling postscript. Youngblood was released from prison 15 years later when DNA testing, not available at the time the case was tried, established that he did not commit the crime for which he was convicted. The failure of the police to refrigerate the semen sample caused a miscarriage of justice, even though it did not violate Youngblood's constitutional rights. *DNA Evidence Frees Tucson Man Convicted in Sex Case 15 Years Ago*, COURIER JOURNAL at A10 (Aug. 11, 2000).

[180] Illinois v. Fisher, 540 U.S. 544, 124 S. Ct. 1200, 157 L. Ed.2d 1060 (2004) (Where the most that can be said about destroyed evidence is that it *might have been* useful to the defense, a showing of bad faith is necessary even when there was a defense request for it before it was destroyed).

## § 9.13  Eighth Amendment Requirements for Punishment

The Eighth Amendment, which applies to the states through the Fourteenth Amendment, prohibits excessive fines and "cruel and unusual punishments." Humane punishment has not always been practiced. There was a time in England when a person convicted of crime could be burned at the stake, boiled in oil, or have his or her hands or ears cut off. Blackstone, in his *Commentaries on the Law of England*, published in 1769, reported that for the crime of treason an Englishman might be dragged to the gallows, hanged, cut down, disemboweled while still living and, finally, put to death by decapitation and quartering.[181] Public hangings, floggings, and cropping of ears were still being practice when our Constitution was adopted.[182] Thomas Jefferson, one of the most enlightened thinkers of his day, advocated castrating men found guilty of rape, polygamy, or sodomy, and mutilating the faces of women found guilty of similar crimes.[183] These recommendations, though barbaric by modern standards, were not particularly radical when they were proposed. In deciding a whether punishment is cruel and unusual, should a court consider opinions prevalent when the Constitution was adopted or enlightened modern opinion?

To ask this question is to answer it. The Court has repeatedly emphasized the Eighth Amendment's "expansive and vital character"[184] and its capacity for evolutionary growth.[185] The constitutional definition of "cruelty" embodies "contemporary standards of decency,"[186] and changes as "public opinion becomes enlightened."[187] Should the time come when enlightened public opinion has advanced to a point at which the death penalty is no longer acceptable to a majority of Americans, these attitudes will work their way into the Eighth Amendment, and the death penalty will be prohibited. Nevertheless, as of this writing, that time has not yet arrived.

## § 9.14  —Constitutionally Acceptable Punishments

The Eighth Amendment limits the kinds of punishments that may be imposed to fines, prison terms, and executions carried out in a humane fashion. Other kinds of punishment are certainly unusual in modern times and, when they involve unnecessary physical pain, humiliation, or degradation, are also cruel.

---

[181]  Robinson v. California, 370 U.S. 660, 82 S. Ct. 1417, 8 L. Ed. 2d 758 (1962).

[182]  4 W. BLACKSTONE, COMMENTARIES 92.

[183]  Mr. Justice Brennan traced the history of the Eighth Amendment in his concurring opinion in Furman v. Georgia, 408 U.S. 238, 257, 92 S. Ct. 2726, 2736, 33 L. Ed. 2d 346, 360 (1972).

[184]  VAN DEN HAAG, PUNISHING CRIMINALS 193-194 (1975).

[185]  Weems v. United States, 217 U.S. 349, 377, 30 S. Ct. 544, 553, 54 L. Ed. 793, 802 (1910); Trop v. Dulles, 356 U.S. 86, 78 S. Ct. 590, 2 L. Ed. 2d 630 (1958).

[186]  Hudson v. McMillian, 503 U.S. 1, 112 S. Ct. 995, 117 L. Ed. 2d 156 (1992).

[187]  Weems v. United States, *supra* note 185.

Perpetual surveillance[188] and forfeiture of citizenship,[189] for example, have both been held constitutionally unacceptable. So has conditioning suspension of a convicted sex offender's sentence on his agreement to undergo castration.[190]

Even ordinary punishments (i.e., fines, incarceration, and death) violate the Eighth Amendment if they are disproportionately severe to the crime for which they are imposed. The Supreme Court has observed that "[i]t is a precept of justice that punishments for crime should be graduated and proportioned to [the] offense [charged]."[191] This precept is rooted in the language of the Eight Amendment, which declares that "excessive fines [shall not be] imposed."[192] The proportionality limitation has also been applied to the death penalty. This penalty may be imposed only when the underlying offense involves the taking of a human life;[193] it may not be imposed for nonhomicidal crimes such as rape.[194] For a brief period, the Supreme Court attempted to apply the proportionality principle to the length of prison sentences,[195] but eventually abandoned this effort,[196] explaining:

> . . . [T]he "seriousness" of an offense or pattern of offenses in modern society is not a line, but a plane. Once the death penalty and other punishments different in kind from fine or imprisonment have been put to one side, there remains little in the way of objective standards for judging whether or not a life sentence imposed . . . for . . . felony convictions not involving "violence" violates the cruel-and-unusual punishment prohibition of the Eighth Amendment. . . . Whatever views may be entertained regarding severity of punishment, whether one believes in its efficacy or its futility, . . . these are peculiarly questions of legislative policy.[197]

## § 9.15 —The Death Penalty

The death penalty has been the center of a storm of controversy for many years. There are conflicting views about the morality of putting a fellow human being to death, conflicting evidence about the effectiveness of this punishment in deterring violent crimes, and the omnipresent spectre of discover-

---

[188]  *Id.*

[189]  Trop v. Dulles, *supra* note 185.

[190]  State v. Brown, 284 S.C. 407, 326 S.E.2d 410 (1985) (physical castration); People v. Gauntlett, 134 Mich. App. 737, 352 N.W.2d 310 (1984) (mandatory use of sex drive suppressant).

[191]  Weems v. United States, *supra* note 185, 217 U.S. at 367, 30 S. Ct. at 549.

[192]  *See, e.g.*, United States v. Bajakajian, *supra* note 47 (invalidating forfeiture of more than $300,000 in traveler's possession for failure to report it to customs officials as an excessive fine).

[193]  Coker v. Georgia, 433 U.S. 584, 97 S. Ct. 2861, 53 L. Ed. 2d 982 (1977).

[194]  *Id.*

[195]  Solem v. Helm, 463 U.S. 277, 103 S. Ct. 3001, 77 L. Ed. 2d 637 (1983).

[196]  Harmelin v. Michigan, 501 U.S. 957, 111 S. Ct. 268, 115 L. Ed. 2d 836 (1991); Ewing v. California, 538 U.S. 11, 123 S. Ct. 1179, 155 L. Ed. 2d 108 (2003) (noting that "federal courts should be reluctant to review legislatively mandated terms of imprisonment" and that "outside the context of capital punishment, successful challenges to the proportionality of particular sentences have been exceedingly rare").

[197]  Rommel v. Estelle, 445 U.S. 263, 283 n. 27, 100 S. Ct. 1133, 1143-1144 n. 27, 63 L. Ed. 2d 381 (1980).

ing, after the fact, that an innocent person has been executed.[198] However, the most serious and statistically best supported indictment of the death penalty is socioeconomic. It has been documented, time and again, that the death penalty is imposed disproportionately on racial minorities and the poor.

None of these issues is likely to be resolved soon. For now, the Supreme Court has chosen to err on the side of allowing the death penalty, but has limited the crimes for which the death penalty may be imposed, and has developed special procedures designed to ensure, to the greatest extent possible, that the decision to impose this penalty will be based on appropriate considerations and not motivated by passion or prejudice.

Figure 9.5
**Requirements for Death Penalty Sentencing Laws**

To be constitutional, death penalty sentencing laws must incorporate all six of the following safeguards:

1. The death penalty may be imposed only for crimes that involve the taking of a human life;
2. The sentencer must have the discretion to decide whether the death penalty is appropriate;
3. Sentencing discretion must be channeled by establishing statutory aggravating factors that must be present to warrant imposition of the death penalty;
4. Defendants must be afforded an unrestricted opportunity to offer evidence that might convince the tribunal to show compassion and withhold the death penalty;
5. The trial must be conducted in two phases, with the sentencing phase kept separate from the guilt phase; and
6. The death penalty may not be imposed on offenders who are under the age of 16 at the time of the crime, mentally retarded, or criminally insane.

---

[198] Recent DNA exonerations of large numbers of death row prisoners have raised fresh concerns about the death penalty. Support for the death penalty has reached a new low. *See, e.g.*, Carol S. Steiker, *Things Fall Apart, but the Center Holds: the Supreme Court and the Death Penalty*, 77 N.Y.U. L. REV. 1475 (2002) ("Public opinion polling data has shown dramatic drops in public support for capital punishment, documenting a rapid descent from a high of 80% in favor in 1994 to a low of 65% in favor in 2001, the lowest level of support in nineteen years.") On January 11, 2003, two days before leaving office, Illinois governor George Ryan pardoned four inmates on death row, *see* James Webb, *Illinois Governor Pardons Four Inmates Condemned to Death*, COURIER JOURNAL at A7 (Jan. 11, 2003), and on the following day, commuted the 167 remaining death sentences to prison terms, stating: "The facts that I have seen in reviewing each and every one of these cases raised questions not only about the innocence of people on death row, but about the fairness of the death penalty as a whole." *See* Jodi Wilgoren, *Illinois Governor Cleans Out Death Row*, COURIER JOURNAL at A1 (Jan. 12, 2003). In 2002, a maverick federal court judge declared the death penalty unconstitutional. The judge stated that "[w]e now know, in a way almost unthinkable even a decade ago, that our system of criminal justice, for all its protections, is sufficiently fallible that innocent people are convicted of capital crimes with some frequency." The likelihood that a substantial number of innocent people were being put to death made the death penalty constitutionally unacceptable. United States v. Quinones, 196 F. Supp. 2d 416, 420 (S.D.N.Y. 2002); United States v. Quinones, 205 F. Supp. 2d 256 (S.D.N.Y. 2002). This decision was reversed on appeal, the court stating: "The argument that innocent people may be executed—in small or large numbers—is not new; it has been central to the centuries-old debate over both the wisdom and the constitutionality of capital punishment, and binding precedents of the Supreme Court prevent us from finding capital punishment unconstitutional based solely on a statistical or theoretical possibility that a defendant might be innocent." United States v. Quinones 313 F.3d 49 (2d Cir. 2002).

　　Most countries in the European Union have abolished the death penalty and a widespread national debate about the fairness of the death penalty is heating up again in the United States. This is an area of the law that may hold surprises in the future.

## A. *Crimes for Which the Death Penalty May Be Imposed*

As mentioned above, the death penalty may only be imposed for crimes that involve the taking of a human life.[199] The Supreme Court has invalidated state statutes that authorize imposition of the death penalty for crimes such as rape.[200] Unless a human life is taken, the death penalty is ipso facto unconstitutionally cruel punishment.

## B. *Procedures Required for Death-Eligible Crimes*

Even when a human life is taken, the defendant may not be sentenced to death in an impersonal, mechanical fashion. The tribunal must have the discretion to decide whether the circumstances surrounding this particular homicide were heinous enough to warrant the death penalty and also whether the accused's age, background, character, or other traits make it appropriate to show mercy and spare him or her. This has not always been the law.

The Supreme Court's death penalty reforms began when it handed down the landmark case of *Furman v. Georgia*.[201] *Furman* invalidated capital punishment laws around the nation. The Court was disenchanted with the capital punishment sentencing procedures in use at that time. These procedures conferred unguided discretion on sentencing bodies to decide whether to impose the death penalty. The result was random and unequal justice, with the death penalty being imposed almost exclusively on minorities and the poor. The *Furman* Court ruled that unguided discretion to impose the death penalty was constitutionally unacceptable.

*Furman* resulted in a moratorium on the executions of death row prisoners. Chaos ensued as legislatures around the nation met for the purpose of remodeling their capital punishment laws. Because broad and unguided sentencing discretion had led to the death penalty's downfall, it was clear that this feature had to be removed from capital punishment sentencing procedures if the death penalty was to be salvaged. Legislatures took two different approaches. Some retained sentencing discretion but provided standards to guide the sentencing body in its decision to impose the death penalty, while others eliminated sentencing discretion entirely, making death the mandatory punishment for specified crimes. No one knew what the Supreme Court's reaction to the new approaches would be.

In 1976, the Supreme Court issued a number of opinions regarding the states' post-*Furman* capital punishment sentencing procedures.[202] It carefully

---

[199]   **Coker v. Georgia**, *supra* note 193.

[200]   *Id.*

[201]   408 U.S. 238, 92 S. Ct. 2726, 33 L. Ed. 2d 346 (1972).

[202]   Gregg v. Georgia, 428 U.S. 153, 96 S. Ct. 2909, 49 L. Ed. 2d 859 (1976); Proffitt v. Florida, 428 U.S. 242, 96 S. Ct. 2960, 49 L. Ed. 2d 913 (1976); Jurek v. Texas, 428 U.S. 262, 96 S. Ct. 2950, 49 L. Ed. 2d 929 (1976); Woodson v. North Carolina, 428 U.S. 280, 96 S. Ct. 2978, 49 L. Ed. 2d 944 (1976); Roberts v. Louisiana, 428 U.S. 325, 96 S. Ct. 3001, 49 L. Ed. 2d 974 (1976).

selected the cases for review so that it could discuss all the various "do's and don'ts" of capital punishment sentencing. The following summarizes the law of capital punishment sentencing as it has evolved since 1976.

### 1. The Tribunal Must Have Discretion to Determine Whether the Death Penalty Is Appropriate

When a person's life is at stake, the Eighth Amendment demands individualized sentencing discretion.[203] Mandatory death penalty laws are unconstitutional because they treat "all persons convicted of a designated offense, not as uniquely individual human beings, but as members of a faceless, undifferentiated mass to be subjected to the blind infliction of the [death] penalty."[204] This treatment is incompatible with the Eighth Amendment's mandate of respect for human dignity. Thus, legislatures may not make death a mandatory punishment for any crime, even for the deliberate slaying of a police officer.[205]

### 2. Sentencing Discretion Must Be Channeled by Establishing Statutory Aggravating Factors that Must Be Present to Warrant Imposition of the Death Penalty

Although sentencing discretion is essential, the Supreme Court recognized in *Furman v. Georgia* that unguided sentencing discretion leads to arbitrary and unequal applications of the death penalty. To minimize this risk, death penalty sentencing laws must incorporate concrete, clear, and objective guidelines that focus the sentencer's attention on factors accompanying the taking of a human life that make the death penalty appropriate, and distinguish them from other cases involving the taking of a human life for which death is not an appropriate penalty.[206] These factors are called **aggravating circumstances** or aggravating factors.[207] The function of statutory aggravating factors is to "narrow the class of persons eligible for the death penalty and . . . reasonably justify the imposition of a more severe sentence on certain offenders found guilty of the same crime."[208] Unless the sentencer finds the existence of one or more aggravating factors, the death penalty may not be imposed.

Aggravating factors must be specific enough to guide the tribunal's discretion. Aggravating factors typically mentioned in death penalty sentencing statutes include the fact that the killing was accompanied by rape, performed for hire, or the victim was a police officer. In *Godfrey v. Georgia*,[209] the

---

[203] Woodson v. North Carolina, *supra* note 202.

[204] *Id.*, *supra* note 202, 428 U.S. at 304, 96 S. Ct. at 2991, 49 L. Ed. 2d at 961.

[205] Roberts v. Louisiana, 431 U.S. 633, 97 S. Ct. 1993, 52 L. Ed. 2d 637 (1977); *see also* Sumner v. Shuman, 483 U.S. 66, 107 S. Ct. 2716, 97 L. Ed. 2d 56 (1987).

[206] Gregg v. Georgia, *supra* note 202.

[207] Lockett v. Ohio, 438 U.S. 586, 89 S. Ct. 2954, 57 L. Ed. 2d 973 (1978); Eddings v. Oklahoma, 455 U.S. 104, 102 S. Ct. 869, 71 L. Ed. 2d 1 (1982); Richmond v. Lewis, 506 U.S. 40, 113 S. Ct. 528, 121 L. Ed. 2d 411 (1992); Tuilaepa v. California, 512 U.S. 967, 114 S. Ct. 2630, 129 L. Ed. 2d 750 (1994).

[208] Zant v. Stephens, 462 U.S. 862, 103 S. Ct. 2733, 2742-2743, 77 L. Ed. 2d 235 (1983).

[209] 446 U.S. 420, 100 S. Ct. 1759, 64 L. Ed. 2d 398 (1980).

Supreme Court ruled that a statute authorizing imposition of the death penalty upon a finding that the murder "was outrageously or wantonly vile, horrible or inhuman in that it involved . . . depravity of mind, or an aggravated battery to the victim" did not furnish an adequate standard for differentiating between murderers who deserved to die and those who should be spared, because these factors normally accompany every intentional homicide. The statute failed to furnish the type of concrete differentiating standards the Constitution demands before a person convicted of homicide can be put to death.

### 3. Defendants Facing the Death Penalty Must Be Afforded an Unrestricted Opportunity to Offer Evidence that Might Convince the Tribunal to Show Mercy

The fact that the tribunal finds an aggravating circumstance does not mean that it must impose the death penalty; it means that the tribunal has the authority to do so. However, mercy still remains an option. To this end, sentencing procedures must afford the accused an opportunity to establish the existence of factors that make him or her deserving of mercy. These factors are sometimes called mitigating factors or circumstances. **Mitigating circumstances** include such things as the defendant's age, good character, lack of a criminal record, subaverage intellectual functioning, abusive childhood, or any other factor that might influence the tribunal to show mercy and spare him or her.[210]

In *Lockett v. Ohio*,[211] the Supreme Court struck down a death penalty statute that required the sentencing body, upon finding that the murder was accompanied by an aggravating circumstance, to impose the death penalty unless it found that the victim had provoked the offense, the crime resulted from duress, or the accused was suffering from mental illness. The Court ruled that this statute unduly limited the sentencer's discretion to show compassion. For a death sentence to be valid under the Eighth Amendment, the sentencer must be permitted to hear and consider all possible mitigating evidence that the accused elects to offer in the hopes of escaping the death penalty.

### 4. The Tribunal's Consideration of Guilt and Sentencing Must Be Kept Separate

In *Gregg v. Georgia*,[212] the Supreme Court approved Georgia's approach to capital sentencing, and that approach has become the prototype for the laws of other jurisdictions. Not only did the Georgia approach list aggravating and mitigating circumstances, it employed a bifurcated proceeding. The trial was divided into two phases—a guilt phase and a separate sentencing phase. Dur-

---

[210] Lockett v. Ohio, 438 U.S. 586, 89 S. Ct. 2954, 57 L. Ed. 2d 973 (1978); Buchanan v. Angelone, 522 U.S. 269, 118 S. Ct. 757, 139 L. Ed. 2d 702 (1998); Penry v. Johnson, 532 U.S. 782, 121 S. Ct. 1910, 150 L. Ed. 2d 9 (2001).

[211] *Supra* note 210.

[212] *Supra* note 202.

ing the first phase, the issue before the tribunal is whether the accused committed the crime. If the guilt phase results in a conviction, the trial enters a second phase, during which the tribunal hears testimony bearing on the appropriateness of the death penalty. Separating the sentencing phase from the guilt phase is constitutionally necessary because much evidence relevant to fixing the appropriate punishment, such as the accused's character and prior criminal record, is irrelevant to his or her guilt of the crimes for which he or she is on trial, and would be highly prejudicial if introduced at the guilt phase of the trial.

### 5. Offenders Who are Ineligible for the Death Penalty

Death is a penalty that is reserved for the most blameworthy. As a result, it may not be imposed on three classes of offenders—children, the mentally retarded, and the criminally insane. Offenders who are under the age of 16 at the time they commit a crime that would be a capital offense if committed by an adult are ineligible for the death penalty.[213] While the Constitution does not prohibit executing minors who are over age 16 at the time of the crime, jurors must be allowed to consider their youthfulness as a potential mitigating factor, should they wish to show mercy.[214] Because mentally retarded offenders also possess diminished ability to understand and process information, to engage in logical reasoning, to learn from their mistakes, and to control their impulses, they, too, possess diminished moral culpability and are ineligible for the death penalty.[215] The criminally insane are the third category. Civilized societies have from time immemorial recoiled from executing the criminally insane, a moral taboo that has been incorporated into the Eighth Amendment.[216]

---

[213] Thomas v. Oklahoma, 487 U.S. 815, 108 S. Ct. 2687, 101 L. Ed. 2d 702 (1988).

[214] Stanford v. Kentucky, 492 U.S. 361, 109 S. Ct. 2969, 106 L. Ed. 2d 306 (1989).

[215] Atkins v. Virginia, 536 U.S. 304, 122 S. Ct. 2242, 153 L. Ed. 2d 335 (2002), *overruling* Penry v. Lynaugh, 492 U.S. 302, 109 S. Ct. 2934, 106 L. Ed. 2d 256 (1989). The *Atkins* Court left to the states the task of developing criteria for deciding which offenders will be spared the death penalty because of mental retardation, although it approvingly cited the widely accepted clinical definition. This definition requires (1) significantly subaverage intellectual functioning and (2) significant limitations in adaptive skills, such as communication, self-care, and self-direction, manifested before the age of 18. This definition has been incorporated into a number of state statutes prohibiting the execution of the mentally retarded. *See, e.g.,* Ariz. Rev. Stat. § 13-703.02(J)(2) (2001); Ark. Code Ann. § 5-4-618 (Michie 1993); Colo. Rev. Stat. § 18-1.3-1101(2) (2002); Conn. Gen. Stat. § 1-1g (2001); Fla. Stat. Ann. § 921.137(1) (West 2002); Ga. Code Ann. § 17-7-131(a)(3) (1997); Ind. Code § 35-36-9-2 (1998); Kan. Stat. Ann. § 21-4623(e) (1995); Mo. Rev. Stat. § 565.030(6) (2001); N.Y. Crim. Proc. Law § 400.27(12)(e) (McKinney 2002); S.D. Codified Laws § 23A-27A-26.2 (Michie 2002). "Significantly subaverage intellecutal functioning" is generally defined as having an IQ of 70 or below. *See, e.g.,* Ky. Rev. Stat. Ann. § 532.130(2) (Michie 1999); Neb. Rev. Stat. § 28-105.01(3) (2000); N.M. Stat. Ann. § 31-20A-2.1(A) (Michie 2000); N.C. Gen. Stat. § 15A-2005(a)(1)(a)(2001); Tenn. Code. Ann. § 39-13-203(a) (1997); Wash. Rev. Code § 10.95.030(2)(a)(2002).

[216] Ford v. Wainwright, 477 U.S. 399, 106 S. Ct. 2595, 91 L. Ed. 2d 335 (1986).

## C. Lingering Problems of Unfairness in the Application of the Death Penalty

The Supreme Court's sentencing reforms were an attempt to eliminate arbitrary sentencing discretion by focusing the sentencer's attention on factors that would give them a rational basis for making distinctions between offenders, separating those who deserved the death penalty from those who deserved to be spared. These reforms have not achieved all that was hoped for them. It remains true today that racial minorities and the poor are much more likely than others to receive the death penalty. The Supreme Court has acknowledged and lamented this fact. Still, it holds that the death penalty is constitutional.

In *McCleskey v. Kemp*,[217] McCleskey, an African-American man sentenced to death by a Georgia jury for killing a white police officer during a robbery, used statistical evidence to drive home how little the Supreme Court's reforms had genuinely accomplished. McCleskey's statistics showed that African-American defendants charged with killing white victims were four times more likely than anyone else to receive the death penalty. McCleskey contended that these statistics demonstrated that racial considerations continued to play a role in Georgia's capital punishment sentencing and that, as a consequence, the Georgia system still violated the Eighth Amendment. This was a serious challenge—a challenge that, as the Court recognized, went to the legitimacy of permitting juries in a multiracial society to decide who will receive the death penalty. A sharply divided Supreme Court (5-4) voted to affirm McCleskey's sentence in an opinion that admitted with sadness that the current system is still imperfect, but apologized that it was the best the Supreme Court could do. Mr. Justice Powell, who wrote the majority opinion, proclaimed that there can be "no perfect procedure for deciding in which cases governmental authority should be used to impose death."[218]

## § 9.16 —Requirements for the Treatment of Prisoners

Eighth Amendment protection does not end when a sentence is imposed. Prisoners have a right to be free from cruel and inhumane treatment during their confinement.[219] However, courts take the realities of prison life into account in applying the Eighth Amendment. Harsh conditions and rough dis-

---

[217] 481 U.S. 279, 107 S. Ct. 1756, 95 L. Ed. 2d 262 (1987).

[218] *Id.* at 313, 107 S. Ct. at 1778.

[219] *See, e.g.*, Hope v. Pelzer, 536 U.S. 730, 122 S. Ct. 2508, 153 L. Ed. 2d 666 (2002) (inmate's complaint alleging that he was handcuffed to hitching post for seven hours without regular water or bathroom breaks as punishment for disruptive behavior that had long since ended stated claim under the Eighth Amendment); Overton v. Mazzetta, 539 U.S. 126, 123 S. Ct. 2162, 156 L. Ed. 2d 162 (2003) (two-year ban on visitations for inmates serving sentences for substance abuse offenses did not violate Eighth Amendment ban on cruel and unusual punishment because it did not deprive them of basic necessities or entail gratuitous infliction of wanton and unnecessary pain).

ciplinary treatment reach Eighth Amendment proportions only when they lack penological justification and involve wanton and unnecessary infliction of pain.[220] Despite this low standard, correctional officers and officials are sued more often than any other criminal justice professionals. This does not mean they are less competent. Prisoners, who have years on their hands with little else to do, file thousands of lawsuits each year claiming that their Eighth Amendment rights have been violated.[221]

## A.  Sadistic Use of Force Against Inmates

Prisons house a violent and antisocial population. Force is often necessary to maintain prison security and order. The Eighth Amendment does not condemn the use of force, including deadly force, when correctional officers have a good faith belief that force is necessary. The Eighth Amendment standard that applies inside prisons is less demanding than the Fourth Amendment standard that governs the use of force in making an arrest.[222] The Fourth Amendment insists that a police officer's use of force be objectively reasonable.[223] An officer who uses more force than a reasonable police officer on the scene would have considered necessary violates the Fourth Amendment.

Figure 9.6
**Eighth Amendment Standards for Treatment of Prisoners**

| Conduct regulated by the Eighth Amendment | Mental state necessary to incur liability |
|---|---|
| 1.  Application of physical force | Sadistic intent to injure the prisoner |
| 2.  Failure to attend to a prisoner's basic human needs | Deliberate indifference in the face of awareness that a prisoner's basic human needs are not being met |

The Eighth Amendment, in contrast, is concerned with a prison official's mental state. An Eighth Amendment excessive force claim requires proof that physical force was applied maliciously and sadistically for the sake of inflicting injury, rather than out of a good faith belief that it was necessary to main-

---

[220]  *See, e.g.,* Hope v. Pelzer, *supra* note 219; Farmer v. Brennan, 511 U.S. 825, S. Ct. 1970, 128 L. Ed. 2d 811 (1994); Estelle v. Gamble, 429 U.S. 97, 104 S. Ct. 285, 50 L. Ed. 2d 251 (1976).

[221]  In 1995, inmates filed nearly 40,000 federal civil lawsuits—19 percent of the entire federal civil docket. Margo Schlanger, *Inmate Litigation*, 116 HARV L. R. 1555, 1558 (2003) Inmate lawsuits were placing such a heavy strain on the federal courts that in 1996 Congress found it necessary to enact a statute to relieve this burden. The new law, titled *Prison Litigation Reform Act of 1996*, prevents inmates, among other things, from filing lawsuits *in forma pauperis* (i.e., without paying filing fees). *See* 28 U.S.C. § 1915.

[222]  Fourth Amendment restrictions on the use of force are covered in § 3.16.

[223]  *Id.*

tain or restore order. The Supreme Court cases of *Hudson v. McMillian*[224] and *Whitley v. Albers*[225] show the difference between sadistic and good faith applications of force. In the first case, prison guards gratuitously punched an inmate in the mouth, eyes, chest, and stomach on the way to the penitentiary's administrative lockdown. The Supreme Court held that this conduct violated the Eight Amendment, even though the inmate was not seriously injured, because the punches were administered in anger and served no penological purpose. Physical abuse of prisoners that serves no penological purpose violates the Eighth Amendment. In the second case, an inmate who was not one of the rioters was shot when correctional officers rushed in with guns to quell a cellblock disturbance. The Supreme Court declined to consider whether the guards' conduct conformed to professional standards, even though they failed to consider alternatives or to fire warning shots. The prisoner's Eighth Amendment rights were not violated because the force was used in the good faith belief that it was necessary. The guards, therefore, lacked the requisite state of mind to be charged with inflicting cruel and unusual punishment.

## B. Deliberate Indifference to an Inmate's Basic Human Needs

Correctional officials also have a constitutional duty to provide for an inmate's "basic human needs." This duty arises because the government, by incarcerating a person, has stripped the person of the ability to provide for his or her own basic needs.[226] The Eighth Amendment, therefore, imposes a corresponding duty on the government.

A prisoner's "basic human needs" are sparse. Prisoners have a constitutional entitlement to minimally decent conditions of habitation,[227] safety from

---

[224] 503 U.S. 1, 112 S. Ct. 995, 117 L. Ed. 2d 156 (1992) (holding that correctional officers' use of excessive force against an inmate may constitute cruel and unusual punishment even if the inmate does not sustain any serious physical injury). *See also* Hope v. Pelzer, *supra* note 219 (Inmate's Eighth Amendment rights were violated when he was handcuffed to a hitching post and exposed to the heat of the sun, thirst, taunting, and deprivation of bathroom breaks for a 7-hour period as punishment for disruptive behavior. Because the prisoner had already been subued, this treatment amounted to gratuitous infliction of "wanton and unnecessary" pain.); Despain v. Uphoff, 264 F.3d 965 (10th Cir. 2001) (allegation that prison guard discharged pepper spray in inmate's face as a sadistic prank stated Eighth Amendment claim).

[225] Whitley v. Albers, 475 U.S. 312, 106 S. Ct. 1078, 89 L. Ed. 2d 251 (1986).

[226] **DeShaney v. Winnebago County Dep't of Soc. Servs., 489 U.S. 189, 109 S. Ct. 998, 103 L. Ed. 2d 249 (1989)** (explaining that " when the State takes a person into its custody and holds him there against his will, the Constitution imposes upon it a corresponding duty to assume some responsibility for his safety and general well-being").

[227] Hutto v. Finney, 437 U.S. 678, 98 S. Ct. 2565, 57 L. Ed. 2d 522 (1978) (lengthy punitive confinement of a prisoner in filthy, overcrowded eight-by-ten-foot cells where violence was rampant and where the prisoner was served a diet limited to a paste called "gruel" violated the Eighth Amendment); Helling v. McKinney, 509 U.S. 25, 113 S. Ct. 2475, 125 L. Ed. 2d 22 (1993) (housing nonsmoker in cell with inmate who smoked five packs of cigarettes per day violated the Eighth Amendment); Gates v. Collier, 501 F.2d 1291 (5th Cir. 1974) (threat to personal safety by exposed electrical wiring, deficient fire-fighting measures, and housing inmates with others who had serious contagious diseases violated Eighth Amendment); Phelps v. Kapnolas, 308 F.3d 180 (2d Cir. 2002) (complaint stating that inmate was placed on nutrionally inadequate diet for 14 days as punishment for throwing a bowl of cereal stated claim under the Eighth Amendment).

attack, care for serious medical needs,[228] and little more. They are not entitled to education, entertainment, or any of the other amenities of life that people who are not incarcerated enjoy.[229] The harshness of prison life has penological value It reinforces the deterrent goal of criminal punishment.

Failure to provide for an inmate's basic human needs constitutes cruel and unusual punishment only when it is accompanied by a particular culpable mental state described as "deliberate indifference." This mental state requires proof that prison officials actually knew of and disregarded an excessive risk to an inmate's health or safety.[230]

## § 9.17  Summary and Practical Suggestions

This chapter examined a variety of constitutional safeguards that strengthen the integrity of the trial process and ensure that punishments will be administered with respect for human dignity. These safeguards include the Fifth Amendment prohibition of double jeopardy, Sixth Amendment right to a speedy and public trial before an impartial jury, the Sixth Amendment right to confront adverse witnesses, and the Eighth Amendment ban on cruel and unusual punishments.

### A.  Double Jeopardy

The double jeopardy clause prevents the government from trying or punishing an accused person more than once for the same offense. Three conditions must combine in order to have protection against reprosecution: (1) an earlier prosecution must have progressed at least to the point of jeopardy attachment; (2) the subsequent prosecution must have involved the "same offense"; and (3) both prosecutions must have been brought by the same government entity.

In jury trials, jeopardy attaches, so as to bar reprosecution for the same offense, when the jury is empaneled, and in bench trials when the first witness has been sworn and the judge begins taking testimony. Nevertheless, there are three instances in which an accused can be retried for the same offense even though the first trial has proceeded beyond the jeopardy attachment point. Retrial is permissible when: (1) the defense requests the declaration of a mistrial; (2) factors beyond either side's control—such as a deadlocked jury—prevent a verdict from being reached; and (3) the defendant is convicted, appeals, and the conviction is reversed.

---

[228]  Estelle v. Gamble, 429 U.S. 97, 97 S. Ct. 285, 50 L. Ed. 2d 251 (1976) (Eighth Amendment violated by deliberate indifference to a prisoner's known, serious medical needs); Wilson v. Seiter, 501 U.S. 305, 111 S. Ct. 2321, 115 L. Ed. 2d 271 (1991).

[229]  Rhodes v. Chapman, 452 U.S. 337, 349, 101 S. Ct. 2392, 2400, 69 L. Ed. 2d 59 (1981) (the Constitution "does not mandate comfortable prisons").

[230]  *See* authorities *supra* note 220.

When new charges that are slightly different from the previous ones are brought against a defendant who has once before been tried for the same underlying conduct, the court must decide whether the new charges represent the "same offense." Two tests are used to determine whether prosecutions brought under different sections of the penal code involve the "same offense." The *Blockburger* ("same elements") test, which is followed in federal courts and most state courts, allows reprosecution if both crimes have at least one distinct element. The less prevalent test, known as the "same transaction" test, bars multiple prosecutions for crimes that were committed as part of the same underlying criminal transaction.

## B. Speedy Trial

The Sixth Amendment guarantees the right to a speedy trial. This right attaches when formal charges are filed. Courts consider the following four factors in evaluating whether the right to a speedy trial has been denied: (1) the length of the delay; (2) the reasons for the delay; (3) whether the defendant made a timely assertion of his or her rights; and (4) whether he or she was prejudiced by the delay.

## C. Jury Trial

The Sixth Amendment guarantees the right to a jury trial. This right is available only for serious offenses (i.e., offenses punishable by at least six months in prison). Although the prevailing pattern is to use a 12-person jury and to require a unanimous verdict, neither feature is required in state criminal prosecutions.

## D. Fair and Impartial Trial

The Sixth Amendment and the due process clause work together to ensure that the accused receives a fair trial. There are numerous factors that go into the making of a fair trial. They include the right to have a trial that is open to the public, to confront and cross-examine adverse witness, to be tried by an impartial tribunal, and to receive disclosure of all exculpatory evidence in the possession of the police or the prosecutor that is favorable to the defendant and material to guilt or punishment.

### E. Cruel and Unusual Punishment

The Eighth Amendment limits the types of punishments that may be imposed to fines, prison terms, and executions carried out in a humane fashion. Death is the most severe penalty that any society can impose. There are six different Eighth Amendment restrictions surrounding the imposition of the death penalty: (1) the death penalty may only be imposed for a crime that involves the taking of a human life; (2) legislatures cannot require that the death penalty be imposed as a matter of course, even for the most heinous crimes—discretion to impose this sentence is necessary; (3) the discretion must be channeled by establishing statutory aggravating factors that must be present to warrant imposition of the death penalty; (4) defendants must be afforded an unrestricted opportunity to convince the tribunal that they deserve mercy; (5) guilt and sentencing phases of a capital punishment case must be conducted separately; and (6) the death penalty may not be imposed on children, the mentally retarded, or the criminally insane.

The Eighth Amendment imposes two restrictions on prison officials. They must: (1) refrain from unnecessary and sadistic applications of force, and (2) provide for an inmate's "basic human needs." "Basic human needs" fall into three categories: (1) minimally decent conditions of habitation, (2) safety from attack, and (3) care for serious medical needs. Correctional officials are liable for failing to provide for an inmate's basic needs only when they are actually aware that these needs are not being met and act with deliberate indifference.

# Federal Criminal and Civil Remedies for Unconstitutional Conduct    10

*When government officials abuse their offices, actions for damages may offer the only realistic avenue for vindication of constitutional guarantees. On the other hand, permitting damages suits against government officials can entail substantial social costs, including the risk that fear of personal monetary liability and harassing litigation will unduly inhibit officials in the discharge of their duties. Our cases have accommodated these conflicting concerns by generally providing government officials performing discretionary functions with a qualified immunity, shielding them from civil damages liability as long as their actions could reasonably have been thought consistent with the rights they are alleged to have violated. . . . Whether an official protected by qualified immunity may be held personally liable for an allegedly unlawful official action generally turns on the "objective legal reasonableness" of the action, assessed in light of the legal rules that were clearly established at the time it was taken.*

*Anderson v. Creighton*, 483 U.S. 635, 639,
107 S. Ct. 3034, 3038, 97 L. Ed. 2d 523 (1987)

# Chapter Outline

## § 10.1  Introduction

This chapter discusses two federal civil rights laws that have existed since the Reconstruction era. They were enacted to hold state officials accountable for violating federal constitutional rights. After the Civil War, there was a breakdown of law and order. Reports were received in Congress that African-American citizens were being brutalized by white terrorist organizations, and that state and local officials were unwilling to prosecute.[1] Congress responded by enacting the two statutes that are the focus of this chapter. The first one—42 U.S.C. § 1983—creates a civil remedy and the second one—18 U.S.C. § 242—creates a criminal remedy.

## § 10.2  Civil Liability for Unconstitutional Conduct (42 U.S.C. § 1983)

Title 42 U.S.C. § 1983[2] is one of the most widely used of all federal statutes. It imposes civil liability on persons who act "under color of any

---

[1]  United States Commission on Civil Rights, *Law Enforcement: A Report of Equal Protection in the South* 6-10 (1965).

[2]  Section 1983 reads as follows:

> Every person who, under color of any statute, ordinance, regulation, custom, or usage, of any State or Territory or the District of Columbia, subjects, or causes to be subjected, any citizen of the United States or other person within the jurisdiction thereof to the deprivation of any rights, privileges, or immunities secured by the Constitution and laws, shall be liable to the party injured in an action at law, suit in equity, or other proper proceeding for redress, except that in any action brought against a judicial officer for an act or omission taken in such officer's judicial capacity, injunctive relief shall not be granted unless a declaratory decree was violated or declaratory relief was unavailable. For the purposes of this section, any Act of Congress applicable exclusively to the District of Columbia shall be considered to be a statute of the District of Columbia.

[state] statute, ordinance, regulation, custom, or usage" in depriving another of "rights, privileges, or immunities secured by the Constitution and laws" of the United States.[3] The reason § 1983 reaches only persons who act **under color of state law** is that it was enacted by Congress under its power to enforce the Fourteenth Amendment.[4] The Fourteenth Amendment provides that no state shall deprive any person of certain rights. Accordingly, statutes enacted under this amendment can only reach persons who exercise state authority. Section 1983 does not replace civil damages remedies available under state law. Citizens whose constitutional rights are violated generally have a choice between bringing a federal cause of action under § 1983 or a state cause of action under a common law tort theory. Claims brought under § 1983 are constitutional **tort** claims. We emphasize their tort nature because many principles that are now part of § 1983 jurisprudence stem neither from the language of § 1983 nor the Constitution. They have been imported from the common law of torts.[5]

We will begin by briefly outlining the procedural stages of a § 1983 damage suit and develop the chapter around this outline. A plaintiff commences a § 1983 action by filing a complaint alleging that the defendant (1) acted under color of state law in (2) depriving the plaintiff of a certain constitutional right, and asks the court to award damages. The defendant's attorney will respond by filing an answer, along with various pretrial motions, the most important of which is a **motion for dismissal** based on **qualified immunity**. Under the **common law**, police officers were immune from liability for violating constitutional rights if a reasonable officer could have believed that the conduct was lawful. This immunity was called "qualified" because it was available only if the officer's conduct was objectively reasonable. This defense has been assimilated into § 1983. Officers are immune from suit if (1) the constitutional right they are charged with violating was not clearly established at the time they acted, or if (2) a reasonable public official, on these facts, could have believed that his or her conduct conformed to that standard.[6]

Qualified immunity is the first issue that arises in a § 1983 lawsuit.[7] This issue is legal, not factual. A judge ruling on a qualified immunity defense is not concerned with whether the officer committed the acts alleged in the complaint. This will be determined at the trial, assuming one is necessary. The purpose of the qualified immunity hearing is to dispose of claims without a trial where the officer would be immune from liability even if the acts alleged in the complaint happened. Accordingly, the judge must decide whether the con-

---

[3] For a general discussion of § 1983, *see* John R. Williams, *Beyond Police Misconduct and False Arrest: Expanding the Scope of 42 U.S.C. § 1983 Litigation*, 8 SUFFOLK J. TRIAL & APP. ADVOC. 39 (2003); Connuck, *Constitutional Law: The Viability of Section 1983 Actions in Response to Police Misconduct*, 1990 ANN. SURV. AM. L. 747 (1992); Note, *Defending Section 1983 Police Misconduct Actions in the 1990s*, 39 FED. B. NEWS & J. 212 (1992).

[4] District of Columbia v. Carter, 409 U.S. 418, 93 S. Ct. 602, 34 L. Ed. 2d 613 (1973).

[5] The influence of the common law on the interpretation of § 1983 is discussed in § 10.3.

[6] Harlow v. Fitzgerald, 457 U.S. 800, 102 S. Ct. 2727, 73 L. Ed. 2d 396 (1982); Anderson v. Creighton, 483 U.S. 635, 107 S. Ct. 3034, 97 L. Ed. 2d 523 (1987).

[7] Qualified immunity is discussed in § 10.4.

stitutional right the officer is charged with violating was clearly established and, if so, whether the conduct alleged in the complaint was objectively reasonable in light of that standard. If the judge rules against the officer at the qualified immunity hearing, the case will be docketed for trial.

The function of the trial will be to determine whether the acts alleged in the plaintiff's complaint actually happened. The defendant will have an opportunity to cross-examine the plaintiff's witnesses and to put on evidence. There will be two main issues at the trial. These issues derive from the language of § 1983. In order to recover damages, the plaintiff will be required to establish that: (1) the defendant acted under color of state law[8] in (2) depriving him or her of rights secured by the U.S. Constitution.[9] Establishing the second element will require proof that the defendant acted with a culpable mental state.[10] Section 1983 does not specify the mental state that a police officer must possess in order to deprive a person of a constitutional right. The reason is that the required mental state varies with the underlying constitutional violation alleged as a basis for recovery. However, a mental state beyond ordinary negligence is generally necessary.

## § 10.3   —Influence of Common Law Tort Principles

Section 1983 contains a total of two sentences. Developing a comprehensive legal framework for the constitutional liability of public officials in two sentences is, obviously, impossible. Consequently, the Supreme Court is frequently forced to look beyond the text of § 1983 for guidance in matters the statute fails to cover. The source most often relied on is the common law of torts. In *Monroe v. Pape*,[11] the Supreme Court commented that § 1983 must be "read against the background of tort liability that makes a man responsible for the natural consequences of his acts." What the Supreme Court meant is that § 1983 creates a constitutional tort action, and the particulars that the statute fails to cover should be supplied by using common law tort principles. In a recent case, the Court has explained:

> . . . [O]ver the centuries the common law of torts has developed a set of rules to implement the principle that a person should be compensated fairly for injuries caused by the violation of his legal rights. These rules, defining the elements of damages and the prerequisites for their recovery, provide the appropriate starting point for the inquiry under § 1983 as well.[12]

---

[8]   The meaning of the phrase "under color of state law" is discussed in § 10.7.

[9]   The rights, for violation of which § 1983 provides a remedy, are covered in § 10.8 and §§ 10.14-10.16.

[10]   The mental element required for § 1983 claims is covered in § 10.9.

[11]   365 U.S. 167, 81 S. Ct. 473, 5 L. Ed. 2d 492 (1961), *overruled in part*, Monell v. Department of Social Services, 436 U.S. 658, 98 S. Ct. 2018, 56 L. Ed. 2d 611 (1978).

[12]   Heck v. Humphrey, 512 U.S. 477, 114 S. Ct. 2364, 129 L. Ed. 2d 383 (1994).

However, reliance on tort principles does not mean that every wrong committed by a police officer gives rise to a § 1983 damages claim.[13] The language of § 1983 makes it clear that the conduct must violate a right secured by the Constitution or laws of the United States. Consequently, while there is considerable overlap between common law tort liability and constitutional liability under § 1983, the two theories are not the same.

Facts enrich understanding of legal principles. Therefore, we will use the following hypothetical to explore the main issues that arise in a § 1983 damage suit.

## The Frank Smith Incident

Officer Frank Smith was hired by the Cityville Police Department without a background check. This was contrary to the Cityville Police Department's normal hiring practices. However, Police Chief Bob Baker, who was in charge of the Department's hiring decisions, decided that this would be a waste of time because he had known the Smith family since Smith was a toddler. Had Chief Baker performed a background check, he would have learned that Frank Smith had three convictions for aggravated assault and battery while he was away at college.

The following incident occurred two months after Smith was hired. Jill Brown was driving home in the early hours of the morning, after visiting her mother, when she observed a police checkpoint directly ahead. Figuring that she would have to produce her license, she looked down, noticed she had left her handbag at her mother's, and made a U-turn, intending to go back. Officer Smith, who had just gotten off duty and was heading home, saw Ms. Brown's car approach the checkpoint, make a U-turn, and pick up speed headed in the opposite direction. He became suspicious, put on his siren, and gave chase. After overtaking and stopping Ms. Brown's vehicle, Officer Smith got out of his squad car and, with his hand resting on his revolver, walked over to her vehicle. He twice ordered Ms. Brown to get out of her car. When she failed to respond, Officer Smith used an "arm bar" technique, jerking her from the car and spinning her to the ground. The impact caused severe injury to her knee. She has undergone several surgeries and will require a knee replacement. Smith's partner, Officer Michael Daniels, was sitting in the patrol car when this incident happened and saw it.

Ms. Brown was cited for making an illegal turn. She pleaded guilty, paid a $50 fine, and has filed suit under 42 U.S.C. § 1983 against Officers Smith and Daniels, Police Chief Bob Baker, the Cityville Police Department, and Cityville. In her complaint she alleged that Officer Smith acted under color of state law in depriving her of her Fourth Amendment right to be free from use of excessive force during an arrest; that Officer Daniels failed to protect her against Officer Smith's unconstitutional acts; that Police Chief Baker was liable both as Officer Smith's supervisor and for negligence in hiring him; and that Cityville and the Cityville Police Department were liable as his employers.

---

[13]    Baker v. McCollan, 443 U.S. 137, 99 S. Ct. 2689, 61 L. Ed. 2d 433 (1980).

## § 10.4  —Qualified Immunity

Qualified immunity is the first issue that arises in a § 1983 lawsuit.[14] Public officials sometimes make mistakes. If they could be sued for damages every time they made an error in judgment, public officials would be inhibited from taking decisive action. Recognizing this, common law judges developed the concept of *official immunity*.

Figure 10.1
**Qualified Immunity**

---

Police are immune from liability for violating a constitutional right:

1.  if the right they are charged with violating was not clearly established at the time they acted, or
2.  if a reasonable public official, confronted with these facts, could have believed that his or her conduct conformed to that standard.

These determinations are made before the trial.

---

Two forms of immunity are recognized under the common law—*absolute* and *qualified*. **Absolute immunity** is all-inclusive; it provides a defense against liability, even for acts motivated by malice.[15] This degree of immunity is conferred only on judges, legislators, and prosecutors,[16] because it exceeds the degree of immunity that most public officials need in order to engage in the fearless exercise of their official authority.[17] **Qualified immunity**, in contrast, affords a defense only for conduct that a reasonable public official would have believed was lawful.[18] This degree of immunity is ample for most public officials and is the degree that is bestowed on police officers.[19]

The legal standard used to evaluate a police officer's qualified immunity defense was established in *Harlow v. Fitzgerald*,[20] in which the Court announced that police officers are immune as long as their conduct "does not violate clearly established . . . constitutional rights of which a reasonable person would have known." This standard gives an officer two chances to avoid liability. Officers are immune from liability if: (1) the constitutional right they are charged with violating was not clearly established when they acted, or

---

[14]  *See* cases *supra* note 6.

[15]  Hafer v. Melo, 502 U.S. 21, 112 S. Ct. 358, 116 L. Ed. 2d 301 (1991).

[16]  Mireles v. Waco, 502 U.S. 9, 112 S. Ct. 286, 116 L. Ed. 2d 9 (1991) (judges); Imbler v. Pachtman, 424 U.S. 409, 96 S. Ct. 984, 47 L. Ed. 2d 128 (1976) (prosecutors); Tenney v. Brandhove, 341 U.S. 367, 71 S. Ct. 783, 95 L. Ed. 1019 (1951) (legislators).

[17]  Hafer v. Melo, *supra* note 15.

[18]  Harlow v. Fitzgerald, *supra* note 6. The qualified immunity doctrine is supported by two rationales: (1) the injustice of holding public officials liable in cases in which a reasonable public official would not have appreciated the unlawfulness of the conduct, and (2) fear that the threat of personal liability will deter officials from decisive action.

[19]  Pierson v. Ray, 386 U.S. 547, 87 S. Ct. 1213, 18 L. Ed. 2d 288 (1967); Harlow v. Fitzgerald, *supra* note 6.

[20]  *Supra* note 6.

(2) if a reasonable police officer, confronted with these facts, could have believed that his or her conduct conformed to the previously established constitutional standard.

## A. First Prong of the Qualified Immunity Standard

The first prong of the qualified immunity standard requires the court to determine whether the constitutional right the officer is charged with violating was clearly established.[21] This calls for a discussion as to what it takes for a constitutional right to be "clearly established." The right to be free from unreasonable searches, for example, is "clearly established" in the Fourth Amendment, but this level of abstraction is useless because it fails to provide concrete guidance in individual cases. Police are entitled to more particularized notice before liability can be imposed. The test for when a constitutional right has been established with sufficient clarity that a police officer can be held liable for violating it is whether, based on the current state of the law, a reasonable police officer should have known that the right existed, that it applied to this situation, and that his or her conduct violated it.[22]

Figure 10.2
**Test for When Constitutional Rights are Clearly Established**

> The test for when a constitutional right has been established with sufficient clarity that a police officer can be held liable for violating it is whether, based on the current state of the law, a reasonable police officer should have been aware that the right existed, applied to the present situation, and that his or her conduct violated it.

The qualified immunity standard takes into account the fact that officers are called upon to apply imprecise constitutional standards like probable cause and reasonable suspicion in an infinite variety of factual situations.[23] Generally, the only way imprecise constitutional standards can provide concrete guidance is if there is an authoritative precedent applying the constitutional standard to a case with materially similar facts and declaring this precise conduct unlawful.[24] An authoritative precedent means a case decided by the U.S.

---

[21] **Wilson v. Layne, 526 U.S. 603, 119 S. Ct. 1692, 143 L. Ed. 2d 818 (1999)**; United States. v. Lanier, 520 U.S. 259, 117 S. Ct. 1219, 137 L. Ed. 2d 432 (1997).

[22] Anderson v. Creighton, *supra* note 6.

[23] **Graham v. Connor, 490 U.S. 386, 396-97, 109 S. Ct. 1865, 104 L. Ed. 2d 443 (1989)** (noting that qualified immunity takes into account "the fact that police officers are often forced to make split-second judgments—in circumstances that are tense, uncertain, and rapidly evolving—about the amount of force that is necessary in a particular situation"); Wagner v. Bay City, Tex., 227 F.3d 316 (5th Cir. 2000) (observing that "courts must be careful not to engage in second-guessing police officers in situations in which they have to make split-second, on-the-scene decisions while confronted with violent individuals").

[24] Wilson v. Layne, *supra* note 21; Varrone v. Bilotti, 123 F.3d 75, 79 (2d Cir. 1997); Donovan v. City of Milwaukee, 17 F.3d 944, 952 (7th Cir. 1994); Baptiste v. J.C. Penney Co., 147 F.3d 1252, 1257 (10th Cir. 1998).

Supreme Court, a court in the officer's own circuit, or a strong consensus of decisions from other jurisdictions.

This view of what is necessary for a constitutional right to be clearly established finds support in *Wilson v. Layne*,[25] in which the Supreme Court held that police were immune from liability for inviting media representatives to accompany them during the execution of a search warrant where the only case on point declaring this conduct unconstitutional was a federal court of appeals ruling from another circuit that was decided only five weeks before the events that gave rise to this suit. The Court stated that "(t)his scant body of case law was not enough to provide fair notice to the police that allowing media representations to accompany them into private homes when executing a search warrant violated the Fourth Amendment."

The one instance in which courts have not insisted on this degree of case law specificity is when the challenged conduct constitutes such an obvious abuse of authority that no reasonable public official could have believed that it was lawful.[26] *United States v. Lanier*,[27] in which a state court judge sexually assaulted a number of women who came to his chamber on official business was such a case. The Court rejected the judge's argument that he could not be held liable because there was no authoritative precedent declaring this exact conduct unlawful. Qualified immunity is unavailable in a case like this, in which the unlawfulness of the defendant's conduct should have been clear to any public official.[28]

## B. Second Prong of the Qualified Immunity Standard

Even when a constitutional right is clearly established, qualified immunity is still available if the officer's conduct was objectively reasonable in light of that standard or, in other words, if a reasonable police officer, confronted with

---

[25]  *Supra* note 21.

[26]  *See, e.g.*, United States v. Lanier, *supra* note 21 (holding that the precise conduct need not have previously have been held unlawful for qualified immunity to be denied in cases in which the conduct constitutes a clear and obvious abuse of authority); Amaechi v. West, 237 F.3d 356 (4th Cir. 2001) (denying qualified immunity despite lack of factually similar case declaring digital penetration of female genetalia during pat-down search unlawful); Vinyard v. Wilson, 311 F.3d 1340 (11th Cir. 2002) (denying qualified immunity despite lack of factually similar case involving use of pepper spray on arrestee who was subdued, handcuffed and not resisting); Lee v. Ferraro, 284 F.3d 1188 (11th Cir. 2002) (denying qualified immunity despite lack of factually similar case involving slamming arrestee's head on car trunk after he was handcuffed and subdued); Priester v. City of Riviera Beach, Florida, 208 F.3d 919 (11th Cir. 2000) (denying qualified immunity despite lack of similar precedent where officer unleashed unprovoked attack by police dog). *See also* generally, Barbara E. Armacost, *Qualified Immunity: Ignorance Excused*, 51 VAND. L. REV. 583, 634-75 (1998).

[27]  *Supra* note 21.

[28]  *Id.*

these facts, could have believed that he or she was complying with that standard.[29] The second prong of the qualified immunity standard takes into account that police officers are often forced to make split-second decisions in tense and rapidly evolving situations and affords them a margin for reasonable mistakes. For example, a police officer who makes an arrest without probable cause is immune from liability under the second prong if a reasonable officer, based on the information this officer possessed, could have believed that probable cause existed.[30]

Putting both prongs of the qualified immunity standard together, police officers are immune from suit under § 1983 unless their conduct amounts to a clear violation of a clearly established constitutional right. If the officer's qualified immunity defense is rejected, the case will go to trial. The function of the trial will be to hear opposing testimony, sort out the facts, and determine whether the complaint made against the officer is well-founded.

## C. Application of the Qualified Immunity Standard to Officer Smith

Officer Smith is not entitled to qualified immunity because the constitutional right he is charged with violating—the right to be free from the use of excessive force during an arrest—was clearly established at the time he acted and the conduct alleged in Ms. Brown's complaint constituted a clear violation of the previously established standard. In *Graham v. Connor*,[31] decided more than a decade ago, the Supreme Court ruled that use of excessive force in making an arrest violates the Fourth Amendment and then went on to establish guidelines for when force is permissible. The degree of force that may be used varies according to "the severity of the crime at issue, whether the suspect poses an immediate threat to the safety of the officers or others, and whether he is actively resisting arrest or attempting to evade arrest by flight."[32] Because Ms. Brown was arrested for a minor traffic violation, made no threatening gestures, and did not attempt to resist arrest or flee, no reasonable police officer could have believed that the force Officer Smith used was necessary. Accordingly, qualified immunity will be denied and the case will be docketed for trial.[33]

---

[29]  Saucier v. Katz, 533 U.S. 194, 121 S. Ct. 2151, 150 L. Ed. 2d 272 (2001) (police officer not liable for using excessive force as long as a reasonable officer could have made the same mistake under the particular circumstances); Anderson v. Creighton, *supra* note 6; Hunter v. Bryant, 502 U.S. 224, 112 S. Ct 534, 116 L. Ed. 2d 589 (1991).

[30]  Hunter v. Bryant, *supra* note 29.

[31]  **490 U.S. 386, 109 S. Ct. 1865, 104 L. Ed. 2d 443 (1989).** Fourth Amendment excessive force claims are discussed in § 3.16.

[32]  *Id.*

[33]  *See, e.g.*, Secot v. City of Sterling Heights, 985 F. Supp. 715 (E.D. Mich. 1997); Brown v. Bryan County, 67 F.3d 1174 (5th Cir. 1995); DeFour-Dowell v. Cogger, 969 F. Supp. 1107 (N.D. Ill. 1997).

## § 10.5 —Other Grounds for Pretrial Dismissal

Although qualified immunity is the most important defense, others are available. Two deal with the impact of a criminal conviction on a § 1983 claimant's right to recover damages. A criminal conviction will get an officer off the hook for constitutional violations that underlie it in two situations: (1) where the § 1983 plaintiff argued the same constitutional violation unsuccessfully at his or her criminal trial, and (2) where a judgment in the plaintiff's favor would call the validity of his or her prior criminal conviction into question.

### A. Claims Previously Raised Unsuccessfully during the Trial

Section 1983 actions cannot be brought to recover damages for constitutional violations that the claimant previously raised unsuccessfully at his or her criminal trial.[34] The reason is that the claimant has already had his or her day in court on this issue. When a matter has already been litigated and decided, the claimant is barred from raising the same issue in a subsequent legal proceeding involving the same party. This preclusion stems from a doctrine known as **collateral estoppel**. The purpose of the collateral estoppel doctrine is to prevent one party from harassing another by repeatedly raising the same claim in successive legal proceedings.

The typical fact pattern that triggers this doctrine arises as follows. During his criminal trial, Sticky-Fingered Sam claims that he was the victim of an illegal search and seizure, a coerced confession, or another constitutional violation, and moves to suppress the evidence. The trial judge holds a hearing and rules against Sam. Sam is convicted and thereafter files a § 1983 suit seeking damages for the same alleged constitutional violation. Sam has already had his day in court on this issue. He cannot raise the same claim in a § 1983 damage suit.

### B. Damage Claims That Call Into Question the Validity of an Outstanding Criminal Conviction

Section § 1983 cannot be used to challenge the constitutionality of a criminal conviction. Federal habeas corpus is the remedy that Congress designed for this purpose. Accordingly, plaintiffs who have been convicted of an offense are precluded from bringing a § 1983 action where a judgment in their favor would call the validity of their criminal conviction into question. This limitation was announced in *Heck v. Humphrey*,[35] in which a prisoner serving a sentence for killing his wife sought damages against the police for allegedly destroying exculpatory evidence. The Court ruled that damage claims that

---

[34]   Allen v. McCurry, 449 U.S. 90, 101 S. Ct. 411, 66 L. Ed. 2d 308 (1980).
[35]   512 U.S. 477, 114 S. Ct. 2364, 129 L. Ed. 2d 383 (1994).

impugn the validity of a criminal conviction cannot be brought while the conviction remains outstanding. The plaintiff must succeed in having the conviction reversed on appeal, expunged by executive order, or otherwise declared invalid before bringing such an action.

This limitation applies only to claims, success on the merits of which would necessarily imply that the plaintiff's conviction was invalid, such as that the police destroyed exculpatory evidence,[36] counsel was ineffective,[37] or the judge was biased.[38] Jill Brown's claim for excessive force, in contrast, does not have this effect because there can be a valid conviction even though excessive force was used in making an arrest.[39] Consequently, she is free to bring this claim, even though her criminal conviction is still outstanding.

## § 10.6  —Elements of a § 1983 Claim

When her case goes to trial, Ms. Brown will have to prove that Officer Smith: (1) acted under color of state law in (2) depriving her of a right secured by the Constitution or laws of the United States. These elements come straight out of the text of § 1983.

Figure 10.3
**Elements of a 42 U.S.C. § 1983 Claim**

In order to maintain a § 1983 action:

1. the conduct must have been committed by the officer while acting under color of state law; and
2. it must deprive the plaintiff of rights secured by the Constitution or laws of the United States.

## § 10.7  —"Under Color of State Law"

Police officers are not just police officers. They are also private citizens. It is often necessary for courts to determine in which capacity the officer acted because § 1983 provides a remedy only for wrongs committed under color of the officer's legal authority. When a police officer acts as a private citizen, the plaintiff must seek other avenues of redress.

The definition of "under color of state law" was established in *Monroe v. Pape*.[40] Thirteen members of the Chicago police department, who were sued for searching the plaintiffs' home without probable cause or a search warrant,

---

[36]  *Id.*
[37]  Stephenson v. Reno, 28 F.3d 26 (5th Cir. 1994)
[38]  Edwards v. Balisok, 520 U.S. 641, 117 S. Ct. 1584, 137 L. Ed. 2d 906 (1997).
[39]  *See, e.g.,* Jackson v. Suffolk County Homicide Bureau, 135 F.3d 254 (2d Cir. 1998); Nelson v. Jashurek, 109 F.3d 142 (3d Cir. 1997); Robinson v. Doe, 272 F.3d 921 (7th Cir. 2001); Smithart v. Towery, 79 F.3d 951 (9th Cir. 1996).
[40]  *Supra* note 11.

argued that they were not acting under color of state law because state law did not authorize them to commit the wrongs for which they were sued. The Supreme Court rejected this narrow reading. To restrict the phrase "under color of state law" to conduct that a police office has authority under state law to perform would render § 1983 meaningless because state law rarely authorizes police to violate federal constitutional rights. "Color" means an *appearance* or *pretense*. When the government issues police officers a uniform and badge, it creates an appearance of authority for their actions. This appearance continues even when they abuse their authority. "Under color of state law" refers to the "*misuse of power, possessed by virtue of state law and made possible only because the wrongdoer is clothed with the authority of state law.*"

The fact that an individual is a police officer does not mean that his or her every action is under color of state law. The relationship between the officer's status as a police officer and the wrong for which he or she is sued determines whether the officer acted under color of law or as a private citizen.[41] To be considered "under color of law," the acts must relate to the performance of the officer's professional duties or be made possible through misuse of his or her official authority.

Figure 10.4
**Definition of "Under Color of State Law"**

> Action under color of state law refers to the misuse of power, possessed by virtue of state law and made possible only because the wrongdoer is clothed with the authority of state law. To be acting under color of state law, the misconduct for which the officer is sued must:
>
> 1.  relate to the performance of the officer's professional duties, or
> 2.  be made possible through misuse of the officer's official authority.

## A. *Performance of Official Duties*

Whenever a police officer investigates criminal activity, makes an arrest, conducts a search, or performs any other police function, the officer acts "under color of state law."[42] The fact that the officer is on or off duty, or in or out of uniform, is not controlling. [43] It is the nature of the act performed, not the clothing of the actor or even the status of being on duty, or off duty, that

---

[41]   Martinez v. Colon, 54 F.3d 980 (1st Cir.), *cert. denied*, 516 U.S. 987, 116 S. Ct. 515, 133 L. Ed. 2d 423 (1995).

[42]   Monroe v. Pape, *supra* note 11.

[43]   Concerning the § 1983 liability of off-duty police officers, *see generally* Kean, *Municipal Liability for Off-duty Police Misconduct under Section 1983: The "Under Color of Law" Requirement*, 79 B.U. L. Rev. 195 (1999); Libby, *When Off-Duty State Officials Act Under Color of State Law For Purposes of Section 1983*, 22 Mem. St. U. L. Rev. 725 (1992); Miller, *Off Duty, Off the Wall, But Not Off the Hook: Section 1983 Liability for the Private Misconduct of Public Officials*, 30 Akron L. Rev. 325 (1997).

determines the "under color" status of an officer's conduct. For example, action under color of law was found where an officer became involved in an altercation with a motorist that resulted in the latter's death, even though he was off-duty, out-of-uniform, and driving his own vehicle, because under local law the officer had the authority to take official action twenty-four hours a day and was acting in an official capacity when he committed the acts for which he was sued.[44] A similar result was reached in a case in which an off-duty police officer, who was having a drink at a local tavern when a fight broke out, intervened in an attempt to restore order, drew his service revolver and shot three men, killing two of them. The court treated officer's conduct as under color of his legal authority because he was attempting to use the powers granted him by the state when he committed the wrong for which he was sued.[45]

Based on this line of cases, Jill Brown will have no trouble establishing that Officer Smith was acting under color of state law when he grabbed her by the wrist and spun her to the ground, even though he was off-duty at the time.

## B.  Misuse of Official Authority

When officers engage in misconduct for purely personal reasons, their wrongs are treated as the actions of a private individual unless the authority reposed in them by the state makes the wrongdoing possible. Breaking into a home and committing a robbery, for example, are the actions of a private individual, even if the officer is in uniform and on-duty, because the wrongs are accomplished without misuse of official authority.[46] They are acts that any thug could have performed. However, the result would be otherwise if the offi-

---

[44]   Revene v. Charles County Commissioners, 882 F.2d 870 (4th Cir. 1983).

[45]   Stengel v. Belcher, 522 F.2d 438, 441 (6th Cir. 1975) (off-duty police officer having a drink in a bar, acted under color of state law when he shot and killed two men and paralyzed another while intervening in barroom brawl, although he was out of uniform, where police department regulations required officers to carry pistol and mace at all times and to take action to maintain the peace 24 hours a day).

[46]   See, e.g., Almand v. DeKalb County, 103 F.3d 1510 (11th Cir. 1997) (police officer's forcible entry into apartment and commission of rape was a private act and not attributable to power possessed by virtue of state law); Van Ort v. Estate of Stanewich, 92 F.3d 831 (9th Cir. 1997) (off-duty officer who wore mask and used gun to enter victims' home, committing assault and attempted robbery, did not act under color of state law); Roe v. Humke, 128 F.3d 1213 (8th Cir. 1997) (sexual assault of 11-year-old girl by police officer whose duties were to provide security and conduct programs for local school was not "under color of law" where, at the time of the assault, officer was off-duty, driving his own vehicle, not in uniform, not carrying a weapon and "was not engaged in or pretending to engage in acts required of him as part of his official duties as a police officer"); Haines v. Fisher, 82 F.3d 1503 (10th Cir. 1996) (police officers in uniform were not acting under color of law in faking a robbery as a prank); Treiber v. Rompala, No. 01 C 5049, 2002 U.S. Dist. LEXIS 12650 (N.D. Ill. July 9, 2002) ("Even acts committed while a police officer is on duty are not committed under color of state law unless they are in some way related to the performance of police duties.").

cer gained entry under the pretense of conducting law enforcement business, because the officer's misuse of his official authority has now made the wrong-doing possible.[47]

## C. Personal Pursuits

Action under color of law is absent when an officer commits wrongs for personal reasons, with no pretense of exercising official authority. Shooting an acquaintance during an argument over a personal matter[48] or harassing a fellow officer about his sexual orientation[49] are both committed in a private capacity, even if the officer is in uniform, on duty, or uses a service revolver, because these acts have no relationship to the officer's official duties and are committed without any pretense of legal authority.[50]

# § 10.8  —Deprivation of Constitutional Rights

As the second element of her claim, Jill Brown will have to prove that Officer Smith deprived her of a right secured by the Constitution. The past several decades have witnessed a tremendous growth in § 1983 claims. This growth corresponds to the federalization of Bill of Rights safeguards and the burgeoning case law that followed. When the Supreme Court announces a new constitutional rule, it enlarges the decisional base on which § 1983 claims can be brought.

---

[47]   **Johnson v. Cannon, 947 F. Supp. 1567 (M.D. Fla. 1996)** (officer acted under color of state law when he threatened to arrest motorist stopped for traffic violation unless she submitted to his sexual advances); Rogers v. City of Little Rock, Ark.,152 F.3d 790 (8th Cir. 1998) (officer acted under color of state law when he pulled over a woman, followed her home so she could get proof of insurance, and raped her); Crews v. United States, 160 F.2d 746 (5th Cir. 1947) (officer acted under color of state law when he took a man into custody under the pretext of arresting him, drove him to a bridge, and forced him to leap to his death because he obtained physical control over his victim through misuse of his legal authority); Romero v. City of Clanton, 220 F. Supp. 2d 1313 (M.D. Ala. 2002) (officer acting under color of state law when he used his position as a police officer to detain plaintiff, and then made sexual advances).

[48]   Gibson v. City of Chicago, 910 F.2d 1510 (7th Cir. 1990). *See also* Delcambre v. Delcambre, 635 F.2d 407 (5th Cir. 1981) (police chief not acting under color of state law, even though he was on duty and at the police station, when he assaulted his sister-in-law during personal argument over family matter); Bonsignore v. City of New York, 683 F.2d 635 (2d Cir. 1982) (off-duty police officer not acting under color of state law when he used his service revolver to shoot his wife and commit suicide); Johnson v. Hackett, 284 F. Supp. 933 (D.C. Pa. 1968) (on-duty officer not acting under color of law when he called a group of African Americans racially derogatory names and offered to fight, without undertaking any law enforcement action); Lyons v. Adams, 257 F. Supp. 2d 1125 (N.D. Ill. 2003) (off-duty police officer was not acting under "color of state law" when he beat up a bar patron during an altercation in the bar's parking lot prompted by the officer's calling the man a faggot where the officer was wearing street clothing, did not identify himself as a police officer, or did not take or purport to take any official action.).

[49]   Martinez v. Colon, *supra* note 41 (officer not acting under color of state law when he accidentally shot fellow officer while harassing him about his sexual orientation, even though shooting occurred in the police station while both were on duty).

[50]   *See* authorities *supra* note 46.

However, a constitutional violation does not invariably occur every time a citizen is wronged. In *Baker v. McCollan*,[51] a man was arrested under a warrant intended for his brother and detained in jail for three days until the mistake was cleared up. He brought suit under § 1983. The United States Court of Appeals sustained his claim based on the elements of the common law tort of false imprisonment. The Supreme Court reversed, stressing that § 1983 provides a remedy only for constitutional violations. When an action is brought under § 1983, the court must locate a constitutional source for the claim. Although the plaintiff had a valid tort claim, he did not have a constitutional claim under § 1983 because interference with a citizen's liberty must be more serious than occurred here in order for honest mistakes made by public officials to violate the Constitution.

## § 10.9 —Mental State

Section 1983 does not mention the mental state an officer must possess in order to incur liability. The reason is that the mental state is part of the plaintiff's proof that the officer *deprived* him or her of a constitutional right.[52] Each constitutional violation has its own associated mental state. Mental states run the gamut from intentional misconduct to behavior that is objectively unreasonable. The language of the Constitution is the key factor in determining the required mental state. The Fourth Amendment, for example, forbids *unreasonable* searches and seizures, while the Eight Amendment condemns *cruel* and unusual punishment. Cruel behavior is not the same as unreasonable behavior and consequently involves a different mental state.

Similar conduct may implicate different constitutional provisions, depending on the actor's mental state. Take excessive force, for example. When excessive force is used to make an arrest, the plaintiff's claim arises from the Fourth Amendment right to be free from *unreasonable* seizures and requires proof that the officer used more force than a reasonable police officer would have considered necessary.[53] However, when the same force is used on a prison inmate, the claim derives from the Eighth Amendment prohibition against *cruel* and usual punishment and requires proof that the officer applied force with a malicious and sadistic intent to cause harm.[54] Because Jill Brown's claim derives from the Fourth Amendment, she will have to convince a jury that Officer Smith's use of force was objectively unreasonable,[55] but this will not be difficult because she was arrested for a minor traffic violation and put up no resistance. Consequently, no reasonable police officer would have believed that using an arm bar technique to jerk her from her car was necessary.

---

[51]   443 U.S. 137, 99 S. Ct. 2689, 61 L. Ed. 2d 433 (1980).

[52]   **Graham v. Connor, 490 U.S. 386, 109 S. Ct. 1865, 104 L. Ed. 2d 443 (1989)**; Whitley v. Albers, 475 U.S. 312, 106 S. Ct. 1078, 89 L. Ed. 2d 251 (1986); Village of Arlington Heights v. Metropolitan Housing Dev. Corp., 429 U.S. 252, 97 S. Ct. 555, 50 L. Ed. 2d 450 (1977).

[53]   **Graham v. Connor**, *supra* note 52.

[54]   Whitley v. Albers, *supra* note 52.

[55]   **Graham v. Connor**, *supra* note 52.

## § 10.10   —Liability of Municipalities, Supervisory Personnel, and State Governments

Jill Brown also sued Officer Daniels, Chief Baker, Cityville, and the Cityville Police Department. When a police officer violates constitutional rights, the standard practice is to sue the officer's supervisors, the chief of police, the police department, and the governmental body that employs the officer, along with the officer. This section explores the § 1983 liability of third parties.

### A. *Municipal Liability Under § 1983*

The common law imposes vicarious liability (i.e., liability without fault) on employers for wrongs committed by their employees under a doctrine called *respondeat superior. Respondeat superior* is a Latin phrase that means "let the master respond." The justification for vicarious liability is that employers reap the benefits of an employee's services and must take the bitter along with the sweet.

However, this theory of liability is not available in § 1983 actions.[56] The reason stems from the statutory language. Section 1983 imposes liability only on persons who "*subject or cause [another] to be subjected* to a deprivation of their constitutional rights." The terms *subject* and *cause* require personal fault. While municipalities are considered persons under § 1983, they are liable only for constitutional violations they themselves have caused.[57] The municipality's own policies or customs must be responsible for a police officer's unconstitutional conduct in order for liability to be imposed.

To constitute a municipal policy, the policy must have the approval of an official policymaker.[58] Such policies can arise in one of three ways: (1) formal promulgation, (2) a decision made by the city's official policymaker for this particular occasion, or (3) inaction in the face of a known risk that violation of constitutional rights is almost certain to result from this decision.

---

[56]   Monell v. Department of Social Services, 436 U.S. 658, 98 S. Ct. 2018, 56 L. Ed. 2d 11 (1978).
[57]   *Id.*
[58]   *See, e.g.*, Pembaur v. City of Cincinnati, 475 U.S. 469, 106 S. Ct. 1292, 89 L. Ed. 2d 452 (1986); Lytle v. Doyle, 326 F.3d 463 (4th Cir. 2003).

Figure 10.5
**Liability of Municipal Entities**

---

A municipality can be held liable under § 1983 for a rank-and-file police officer's deprivation of a constitutional right only if its own official policies or customs were responsible for causing the deprivation. Liability attaches when the officer's unconstitutional action:

1. Results from execution of a formal written policy, such as an ordinance, regulation, or written policy statement;
2. Is taken at the direction of a city official who has final authority to set policy on the matter; or
3. Is a predictable consequence of the conscious choice of the city's responsible policymaker to take no action in the face of a known risk that deprivation of constitutional rights is almost certain to result.

---

Municipal policies are ordinarily contained in written policies, ordinances, or regulations. If a municipality or municipal agency, such as a police department, adopts a formal, written policy approving an unconstitutional practice, and a police officer acts under this policy, the entity promulgating it is liable.

Municipal policy is also established when a city official, who has final authority to set policy on a particular matter, directs an officer to take unconstitutional action and the officer carries out the order. In *Pembaur v. City of Cincinnati*,[59] the county prosecutor, who was the official policymaker for advising law enforcement officers on legal matters, advised a deputy sheriff, who had been refused entrance to the plaintiff's place of business to serve legal process, that it was legal to "go in and get [them]." The police, at the deputy sheriff's request, obtained an axe and broke down the door. The Supreme Court held that the county was liable for the constitutional deprivation that resulted from this advice.

Finally, municipal policy sufficient to impose liability exists when the city's responsible policymaker makes a conscious choice to do nothing in the face of a known risk that deprivation of constitutional rights is almost certain to result from the decision. Failure to a address a known problem that is extremely likely to result in the violation of constitutional rights is tantamount to adopting a policy of deliberate indifference to the constitutional rights of citizens. This theory of liability was first enunciated in *City of Canton v. Harris*,[60] in which an arrestee who failed to receive needed medical treatment sued the city for damages under § 1983 on the theory that the city's failure to train police officers to recognize when medical treatment was necessary was responsible for the violation of her constitutional rights. The Supreme Court agreed that municipalities can be sued for the unconstitutional acts of poorly

---

[59]  *Supra* note 58 (defining a "policy" as "a deliberate choice to follow a course of action . . . made from among various alternatives by the official or officials responsible for establishing final policy with respect to the subject matter in question").

[60]  489 U.S. 378, 109 S. Ct. 1197, 103 L. Ed. 2d 412 (1989).

trained police officers, but only when the "need for more or different training is so obvious and the inadequacy so likely to result in violation of constitutional rights, that the policymakers of the city can reasonably be said to have been deliberately indifferent to the need."[61] This standard of liability has since been applied to constitutional violations caused by the failure to train, discipline, and supervise police officers, a well as to lax hiring procedures.[62]

In order to charge a municipality with pursuing a policy of deliberate indifference to the constitutional rights of citizens, the plaintiff must demonstrate that the municipality's official policymaker was on notice that violation of constitutional rights was almost certain to result from pursuing a particular course of action or inaction and made a deliberate decision to ignore the risk. Only then can a municipality be said to have adopted an official policy of indifference. A single incident of unconstitutional conduct is not enough to put the city on notice that corrective measures are necessary.[63] However, a widespread pattern of constitutional violations is enough.[64] An official policy of deliberate indifference will be inferred when repeated complaints of constitutional violations are not addressed. In *Beck v. City of Pittsburgh*,[65] the police department was held liable for a police officer's use of excessive force where the department failed to investigate or take meaningful action on similar complaints of misconduct.

Neither Cityville nor the Cityville Police Department is legally responsible for Officer Smith's use of excessive force in the present case because the force was not authorized by their formal written policies or by anyone with final authority to set policy. Their only fault consists of not performing a background check before hiring Smith, but the failure to perform an adequate background check on one occasion is not enough to establish a policy of making lax hiring decisions.[66] Because Jill Brown cannot link Officer Smith's misconduct to any official policy or custom for which Cityville or the Cityville Police Department is responsible, she cannot hold either liable under § 1983.

---

[61]   *Id.*

[62]   Board of County Comm'rs of Bryan County v. Brown, 520 U.S. 397, 117 S. Ct. 1382, 137 L. Ed. 2d 626 (1997) (negligent hiring); Beck v. City of Pittsburgh, 89 F.3d 966, 971 (3d Cir. 1996) *cert. denied*, 519 U.S. 1151, 117 S. Ct. 1086, 137 L. Ed. 2d 219 (1997) (negligent failure to investigate charges against police officers); Davis v. City of Ellensburg, 869 F.2d 1230, 1235 (9th Cir. 1989) (negligent supervision); Benavides v. County of Wilson, 955 F.2d 968, 972 (5th Cir.), *cert. denied*, 506 U.S. 824, 113 S. Ct. 79, 121 L. Ed. 2d 43 (1992) (negligent hiring).

[63]   Board of County Comm'rs of Bryan County v. Brown, *supra* note 62; Oklahoma City v. Tuttle, 471 U.S. 808, 105 S. Ct. 2427, 85 L. Ed. 2d 791 (1985).

[64]   Vann v. City of New York, 72 F.3d 1040 (2d Cir. 1995).

[65]   *Supra* note 62.

[66]   Board of County Comm'rs of Bryan County v. Brown, *supra* note 62.

## B. Section 1983 Liability of Supervisory Personnel

Jill Brown sued Police Chief Bob Baker on the theory that he was Officer Smith's supervisor. The standard for supervisory liability is similar to municipal liability.[67] Jill Brown cannot base liability solely on Police Chief Baker's supervisory capacity or the fact that he was the head of the police department; personal fault is necessary.[68] A supervisor is liable for a subordinate's violation of constitutional rights only if he or she: (1) authorizes or directs a subordinate to take unconstitutional action; (2) is present and fails to intervene; or (3) fails to train, supervise, or discipline subordinates under circumstances that make violation of constitutional rights a predictable consequence.[69]

Jill Brown's suit against Chief Baker will fail because none of these grounds are present. Chief Baker did not direct Officer Smith to take unconstitutional action, was not present when it happened, and was unaware of Officer Smith's violent propensities when he hired him.[70] Consequently, Jill Brown cannot hold Chief Baker liable for Officer Smith's violation of her constitutional rights.

## C. Liability for Failing to Intervene and Stop Constitutional Violations Committed by Fellow Officers

The theory underlying Jill Brown's suit against Officer Daniels was that he failed to intervene to stop Officer Smith's violence. Police officers are liable under § 1983 if they witness comrades committing acts of brutality and do nothing to protect the victim.[71] However, liability attaches only if the officer had a realistic opportunity to intervene.[72] Police officers who stand by and passively watch their comrades commit lawless acts of violence, when they could have stopped them, share their responsibility. However, Jill Brown's suit on this theory will not succeed because the assault happened too quickly for Officer Daniels to do anything.

---

[67] *See generally*, Kinports, *The Buck Does Not Stop Here: Supervisory Liability in Section 1983 Cases*, 97 U. ILL. L. REV. 147 (1997).

[68] Blache Rd. Corp. v. Bensalem Township, 57 F.3d 253, 263 (3d Cir. 1995); Gagan v. Norton, 35 F.3d 1473, 1476 (10th Cir. 1994).

[69] *See, e.g.*, Shehee v. Luttrell, 199 F.3d 295 (6th Cir. 1999); Sanchez v. Alvarado, 101 F.3d 223, 227 (1st Cir. 1996); Rode v. Dellarciprete, 845 F.2d 1195, 1207 (3d Cir. 1988); Gutierrez-Rodriguez v. Cartagena, 882 F.2d 553 (1st Cir. 1989) (upholding a jury verdict holding a supervisor liable when there had been 10 complaints against the officer and the supervisor took no action to formally investigate or discipline the officer).

[70] Board of County Comm'rs of Bryan County v. Brown, *supra* note 62.

[71] Gaudreault v. Municipality of Salem, Mass., 923 F.2d 203, 207 n. 3 (1st Cir. 1990), *cert. denied*, 500 U.S. 956, 111 S. Ct. 2266, 114 L. Ed. 2d 718 (1991); Cabral v. Sullivan, 757 F. Supp. 107, 108 n. 2 (D. Mass. 1991).

[72] Yang v. Hardin, 37 F.3d 282 (7th Cir. 1994); Martinez v. Colon, *supra* note 41; Gaudreault v. Municipality of Salem, Mass., *supra* note 71.

### D. Section 1983 Liability of State Governments and State Agencies

State governments cannot be sued for damages under § 1983 because the Eleventh Amendment grants them immunity from suit in a federal court.[73] However, a state government's Eleventh Amendment immunity does not filter down to state government employees. Their § 1983 liability is no different from a municipal employee's.

## § 10.11 —Liability of Federal Law Enforcement Personnel

Federal law enforcement agents cannot be sued under § 1983 because they act under color of federal authority, not state law. Nevertheless, they are just as accountable for their unconstitutional conduct as state and local officers. Their liability arises directly under the Constitution. In *Bivens v. Six Unknown Named Agents of the Federal Bureau of Narcotics*,[74] the Supreme Court ruled that federal courts have jurisdiction to entertain damage claims against federal agents directly under the Constitution without the aid of legislation. *Bivens* constitutional tort claims are identical to § 1983 suits in all respects; they can be brought for the same constitutional violations and are subject to the same defenses.[75]

## § 10.12 —Liability of Private Individuals

The under-color-of-law requirement does not limit § 1983's reach to public officials. Private parties are considered to act under color of state law when they: (1) act in concert with police; (2) act under state compulsion or with significant state encouragement; or (3) perform a public function.[76]

Figure 10.6
**Conduct of Private Parties as Action Under Color of State Law**

| Action under color of state law is present when private parties: |
| --- |
| 1. Act in concert with police, |
| 2. Act under state compulsion or with significant state encouragement, or |
| 3. Perform a public function. |

---

[73]  Will v. Michigan Dept. of State Police, 491 U.S. 58, 109 S. Ct. 2304, 105 L. Ed. 2d 45 (1989).
[74]  403 U.S. 388, 91 S. Ct. 1999, 29 L. Ed. 2d 619 (1971).
[75]  Mitchell v. Forsyth, 472 U.S. 511, 105 S. Ct. 2806, 86 L. Ed. 2d 411 (1985).
[76]  Lugar v. Edmonson Oil Co., 457 U.S. 922, 102 S. Ct. 2744, 73 L. Ed. 2d 482 (1982).

## A. Concerted Action Theory

Private parties can be sued under § 1983 when they act in concert with police in depriving a person of a constitutional right.[77] However, liability under this theory requires substantial assistance. Merely reporting suspected criminal activity to police is not enough to incur liability.[78]

## B. State Coercion or Encouragement Theory

Action under color of state law is also present when private parties act under government compulsion or with significant government encouragement. For example, during the era when racial segregation was widely practiced, restaurant, motel, and hotel proprietors could be sued under § 1983 for discriminatory denial of service in jurisdictions where segregation was required by state law.[79] Because proprietors in these jurisdictions were acting under government compulsion, their denial of service was considered to be action under color of state law.

## C. Public Function Theory

Private parties also act under color of law when they perform a public function (i.e., a function that has traditionally been performed exclusively by the government).[80] Operating a prison is an example. When a private company contracts with the government to run its prisons, the company acts under color of state law and its employees are liable to suit under § 1983 for violating the constitutional rights of prisoners.[81] In jurisdictions where private detectives and security officers hold commissions from the state, wear police uniforms, carry guns, and are vested with the same powers as a regular police officer, they are subject to same § 1983 liability based on the public function theory.[82] Many jurisdictions have statutes authorizing merchants to detain persons sus-

---

[77]  United States v. Price, 383 U.S. 787, 86 S. Ct. 1152, 16 L. Ed. 2d 276 (1966); Lugar v. Edmondson Oil Co., *supra* note 76; Tower v. Glover, 467 U.S. 914, 104 S. Ct. 2820, 81 L. Ed. 2d 758 (1984).

[78]  *See, e.g.,* Cruz v. Donnelly, 727 F.2d 79 (3d Cir. 1984); Smith v. Brookshire Bros., Inc., 519 F.2d 93, 94 (5th Cir. 1975).

[79]  Peterson v. City of Greenville, 373 U.S. 244, 83 S. Ct. 1119, 10 L. Ed. 2d 323 (1963); Adickes v. S.H. Kress & Co., 398 U.S. 144, 170, 90 S. Ct. 1598, 1615, 26 L. Ed. 2d 142 (1970).

[80]  Evans v. Newton, 382 U.S. 296, 86 S. Ct. 486, 15 L. Ed. 2d 373 (1966).

[81]  Richardson v. McKnight, 521 U.S. 399, 117 S. Ct. 2100, 138 L. Ed. 2d 540 (1997).

[82]  Griffin v. Maryland, 378 U.S. 130, 84 S. Ct. 1770, 12 L. Ed. 2d 754 (1964); Williams v. United States, 341 U.S. 97, 71 S. Ct. 576, 95 L. Ed. 2d 774 (1951); Chiles v. Crooks, 708 F. Supp. 127, 131 (D.S.C. 1989); Temple v. S.O. Albert, 719 F. Supp. 265 (S.D.N.Y. 1989).

pected of shoplifting. However, courts do not consider merchants to be performing a public function when they detain suspected shoplifters because they are acting to further their own economic self-interest.[83]

## § 10.13   Criminal Responsibility for Unconstitutional Conduct (18 U.S.C. § 242)

Title 18 U.S.C. § 242[84] is the criminal counterpart of 42 U.S.C. § 1983. It confers authority on the federal government to prosecute police officers who willfully deprive citizens of their constitutional rights. In 1994, Congress amended § 242 by stiffening the penalties to include the death penalty if the victim's life is taken.

Figure 10.7
**Elements Necessary for a Conviction Under 18 U.S.C. § 242**

A conviction under 18 U.S.C. § 242 requires proof that the officer:

1.  Acted under color of law;
2.  Possessed a willful intent; and
3.  Violated a constitutional right that had
4.  Previously been made specific through judicial decisions.

The language of § 242 parallels § 1983, with the following differences.[85] First, § 242 is a criminal statute. This means that the Justice Department, rather than the injured party, has control of the litigation, and that fines, imprisonment and, in rare cases, the death penalty, will be imposed if the charges are substantiated. Second, § 242 extends to actions taken "under color of law," and not just "under color of *state* law." Accordingly, § 242 can be used to prosecute fed-

---

[83]   White v. Scrivner Corp., 594 F.2d 140 (5th Cir. 1979).

[84]   Section 242 provides:

> Whoever, under color of any law, statute, ordinance, regulation, or custom, willfully subjects any person in any State, Territory, Commonwealth, Possession, or District to the deprivation of any rights, privileges, or immunities secured or protected by the Constitution or laws of the United States, or to different punishments, pains, or penalties, on account of such person being an alien, or by reason of his color, or race, than are prescribed for the punishment of citizens, shall be fined under this title or imprisoned not more than one year, or both; and if bodily injury results from the acts committed in violation of this section or if such acts include the use, attempted use, or threatened use of a dangerous weapon, explosives, or fire, shall be fined under this title or imprisoned not more than ten years, or both; and if death results from the acts committed in violation of this section or if such acts include kidnapping or an attempt to kidnap, aggravated sexual abuse, or an attempt to commit aggravated sexual abuse, or an attempt to kill, shall be fined under this title, or imprisoned for any term of years or for life, or both, or may be sentenced to death.

[85]   For a discussion of § 242, *see generally* Lawrence, *Civil Rights and Criminal Wrongs: The Mens Rea of Federal Civil Rights Crimes*, 67 Tul. L. Rev. 2113 (1993); Hess, Comment, *Good Cop-Bad Cop: Reassessing the Legal Remedies for Police Misconduct*, 1993 Utah L. Rev. 149 (1993).

eral as well as state law enforcement officials. Finally, § 242 incorporates a mental state requirement. Conduct is made criminal only when it is performed with a willful intent to deprive a person of a constitutional right.

To obtain a conviction under § 242, the prosecutor must prove four elements: (1) the accused acted under color of law in (2) willfully subjecting a person (3) to the deprivation of a federal constitutional or statutory right that (4) had previously been made specific through judicial decisions.

## A. *Action Under Color of Law*

The phrase "under color of law" has the same meaning in § 242 as it does in § 1983.[86] It refers to the misuse of power made possible only because the wrongdoer is clothed with official authority. Section 242 can be used to prosecute police officers both for crimes that relate to performance of their official duties and those made possible through misuse of their official authority. Ordinary crimes like extortion, rape, and robbery become federal criminal offenses when a police officer commits them under color of his or her legal authority.[87]

## B. *Willful Intent*

Section 242 has a mental state requirement. To obtain a conviction under § 242, the prosecution must prove that the defendant possessed a "willful intent" to deprive a person of a constitutional right. The meaning of this phrase was established in *Screws v. United States*.[88] The *Screws* case grew out of the prosecution of three Georgia law enforcement officers for bludgeoning an African American prisoner to death with a blackjack. The indictment charged them with acting under color of state law in willfully depriving the deceased of his Fourteenth Amendment right not to be deprived of life without due process of law. The defendants challenged the statute's constitutionality by contending that 18 U.S.C. § 242 lacked an ascertainable standard of guilt. Depriving a person of a constitutional right, they argued, was a standard too vague to provide fair notice of the conduct made criminal. The Supreme Court salvaged the constitutionality of § 242 by focusing on the willful intent requirement. A "willful intent," the Court stated, required proof that the defendant possessed a specific intent to deprive a person of constitutional right that *had been made definite and specific through court decisions*. Because no one could not be prosecuted under § 242 unless the right they were charged with violating had previously been made definite and specific, the statute was not unconstitutionally vague.

---

[86]   The meaning of "under color of law" was discussed in § 10.7.

[87]   United States v. Lanier, *supra* note 21 (rape); United States v. Runnels, 93 F.3d 390 (7th Cir. 1996) (theft committed while executing a search warrant); United States v. Giordano, 260 F. Supp. 2d 477 (D. Conn. 2002) (sexual abuse of two minor children).

[88]   325 U.S. 91, 105, 65 S. Ct. 1031, 1037, 89 L. Ed. 1495 (1945).

Having sustained the statute's constitutionality, the Court proceeded to explain the meaning of "specific intent." In one sentence, the Court asserted that the defendant must act with a "purpose" to deprive a person of a constitutional right, while in the next sentence the Court stated that the defendant need not be aware of the constitutional nature of the right violated. The Court then reconciled these seemingly inconsistent statements by explaining that the defendant must intentionally bring about a result that, based on authoritative decisions, violates the Constitution, whether or not the defendant is aware of the particular provision in the Constitution that makes the conduct illegal. A defendant harbors a "willful intent" to deprive a person of a constitutional right when he or she deliberately, as opposed to accidentally, brings about a result that is forbidden by the Constitution, even though the defendant is not thinking in constitutional terms. The mental state necessary to incur criminal liability for making an unconstitutional arrest, for example, would be satisfied by proof that an officer took a person into custody, fully aware that probable cause was lacking. An officer who acts with this state of mind has a specific intent to deprive the person of a Fourth Amendment right, even if the officer has never heard of the Fourth Amendment.[89] An officer who deliberately uses excessive force, fully aware that this degree of force is unnecessary, also has a willful intent to deprive the person of a constitutional right.[90]

## C. *Constitutional Rights Made Specific by Judicial Decisions*

Police officers cannot can be held criminally accountable under § 242 unless the constitutional right they are charged with violating has previously been made specific through judicial decisions. The "made specific" requirement under § 242 serves the same purposes as the qualified immunity standard in § 1983 cases.[91] Both requirements are designed to ensure that public officials are given fair notice that their conduct will subject them to liability.[92] Moreover, the identical test is used in both contexts.[93] The test is whether, based on the current state of the law, a reasonable public official should have known that the right existed, that it applied to this situation, and that his or her conduct violated it.

While a Supreme Court precedent "on all fours" declaring this exact conduct unconstitutional will unquestionably satisfy this requirement, this degree of case law clarity is not necessary. In *United States v. Lanier*,[94] the Supreme Court recognized that general constitutional rules identified in earlier cases

---

[89]   *See generally*, Note, *Criminal Law: Criminal Deprivation of Another's Constitutional Rights: The Mens Rea Requirement*, 28 Okla. L. Rev. 845 (1975).

[90]   United States v. Koon, 34 F.3d 1416 (9th Cir. 1994); United States v. Bradley, 196 F.3d 762 (7th Cir. 1999).

[91]   United States v. Lanier, *supra* note 21.

[92]   *See generally*, Barbara E. Armacost, *supra* note 26.

[93]   United States v. Lanier, *supra* note 21. The test for when a constitutional right is "clearly established" was covered in § 10.4 (B).

[94]   *Supra* note 21.

may sometimes apply with obvious clarity to the conduct in question, even though this exact conduct has never previously been held unconstitutional. Lanier, the defendant in this case, was a state court judge who was prosecuted for sexually assaulting five court employees and litigants who came to his chamber on official business. The indictment charged him with violating their Fourteenth Amendment substantive due process right to "bodily integrity." Despite a long line of Supreme Court cases recognizing this right, the judge argued that he could not be prosecuted for violating it because the Supreme Court had never applied the right to a case exactly like to his. The Supreme Court ruled against him, holding that general statements of the law are not inherently incapable of giving fair warning. The judge did not need a matching precedent to appreciate that forcing himself on unwilling court employees and litigants violated their right to bodily integrity. When official behavior is so far off the mark that it constitutes an obvious abuse of power, the defendant is in no position to complain that he or she lacked notice of the illegality.

## D. Patterns of Enforcement

The Justice Department is highly selective in choosing cases for prosecution under § 242.[95] Of the thousands of police misconduct claims brought to its attention each year, only a small percentage are accepted for prosecution.[96] Recently, the percentage has been less than two percent.[97] Most involve police brutality, corruption, or violence.[98] The Justice Department's policy of abstaining from bringing § 242 prosecutions unless local authorities are unable or unwilling to prosecute[99] is one reason, but not the main reason, so few federal prosecutions are brought. The main reason is the difficulty of establishing the existence of a willful intent. As a result, prosecutions are brought only for the most serious crimes and with the strongest evidence.[100]

---

[95] See, e.g., Hoffman, The Feds, Lies, and Videotape: The Need for An Effective Federal Role in Controlling Police Abuse in Urban America, 66 S. CAL. L. REV. 1453 (1993); Gest, Making a Federal Case of It, U.S. NEWS & WORLD REP., May 11, 1992; Saul, Not a Federal Case, NEWSDAY, March 31, 1991, at 5.

[96] Jacobi, Prosecuting Police Misconduct, 2000 WIS. L.R. 789, 810-811 (2000); Colbert, Bifurcation of Civil Rights Defendants: Undermining Monell in Police Brutality Cases, 44 HASTINGS L.J. 499 fn.4 (1993).

[97] HUMAN RIGHTS WATCH, SHIELDED FROM JUSTICE: POLICE BRUTALITY AND ACCOUNTABILITY IN THE UNITED STATES 95 (1998), available at http://www.hrw.org/reports98/police/toc.htm; TRAC REPORTS, CIVIL RIGHTS ENFORCEMENT BY BUSH ADMINISTRATION LAGS (2004), available at http://trac.syr.edu/traceports/civright/107/.

[98] The better-known cases brought under § 242 include Screws v. United States, 325 U.S. 91, 65 S. Ct. 1031, 89 L. Ed. 1495 (1945); Williams v. United States, 341 U.S. 97, 71 S. Ct. 756, 95 L. Ed. 774 (1951); United States v. Lester, 363 F.2d 68 (6th Cir. 1966), cert. denied, 385 U.S. 1002, 875 S. Ct. 705, 17 L. Ed. 2d 542 (1967); United States v. Ramey, 336 F.2d 512 (4th Cir. 1964), cert. denied, 379 U.S. 972, 85 S. Ct. 649, 13 L. Ed. 2d 564 (1965); Lynch v. United States, 189 F.2d 476 (5th Cir.), cert. denied, 342 U.S. 831, 72 S. Ct. 50, 96 L. Ed. 629 (1951); Catlette v. United States, 132 F.2d 902 (4th Cir. 1943); United States v. Shafer, 384 F. Supp. 496 (N.D. Ohio 1974).

[99] Freivogel, Justice Dept. to Probe King Case, Bush Says, ST. LOUIS POST DISPATCH, May 1, 1992 at 1A.

[100] See, e.g., United States v. Volpe, 224 F.3d 72 (2d Cir. 2000) (prosecution for viciously forcing broomstick into rectum of prisoner in police custody); (United States v. Webb, 214 F.3d 952 (9th Cir. 2000) (sexual assault); United States v. Lanier, 201 F.3d 842 (6th Cir. 2000) (sexual assault); United States v. Livoti, 196 F.3d 322 (2d Cir. 1999) (choking youth to death); United States v. Bradley, 196 F.3d 762 (7th Cir. 1999) (firing shots into vehicle of motorist being pursued for traffic violation, resulting in motorist's death).

## § 10.14   Rights Protected by the Fourteenth Amendment

A police officer's constitutional accountability extends beyond the rights discussed in earlier chapters. Many cases involve rights protected by the Fourteenth Amendment due process and equal protection clauses. Because these provisions were given only cursory treatment in earlier chapters, we will discuss them now.

## § 10.15   —Substantive Due Process

Substantive due process[101] is a theory for holding government officials liable for serious misconduct that is not addressed by any of the more specific provisions of the Constitution.[102] Recovery requires proof that the defendant (1) engaged in culpable action[103] (2) that is so outrageous that it shocks the conscience.[104]

### A. Culpable Action

Substantive due process claims must be predicated on culpable action or, in other words, on something an officer *did*, not something he or she failed to do. This interpretation stems from *DeShaney v. Winnebago County Department of Social Services*,[105] in which the Supreme Court held that the Fourth Amendment imposes no duty on government officials to come to the aid of members of the public. The ruling grew out of a suit brought by a four-year-old boy, Joshua DeShaney, who was so savagely beaten by his father that he suffered permanent brain damage and had to be institutionalized. He sued the social workers assigned to his case, claiming that their failure to remove him from his father's custody, in the face of strong evidence that he was being abused, deprived him of his rights under the Fourteenth Amendment. The Supreme Court denied Joshua's claim, explaining that the Fourteenth Amendment is phrased as a limitation on the power of the states to act; the states themselves are forbidden to deprive individuals of life, liberty, or property.

---

[101] Substantive due process is briefly discussed in § 1.15 *supra*.

[102] If the underlying behavior is already addressed by another, more specific provision of the Constitution, that Amendment, rather than the more generalized notion of substantive due process, must be used to analyze the claim. *See, e.g.*, Graham v. Connor, 523 U.S. 833, 118 S. Ct. 1708, 140 L. Ed. 2d 1043 (1998); County of Sacramento v. Lewis, 523 U.S. 833, 846, 118 S. Ct. 1708, 140 L. Ed. 2d 1043 (1998).

[103] DeShaney v. Winnebago County Dep't of Soc. Servs., 489 U.S. 189, 109 S. Ct. 998, 103 L. Ed. 2d 249 (1989). *See also generally*, Eaton & Wells, *Government Inaction as a Constitutional Tort: DeShaney and Its Aftermath*, 66 WASH. L. REV. 107 (1991).

[104] County of Sacramento v. Lewis, *supra* note 102; Collins v. City of Harker Heights, 503 U.S. 115, 112 S. Ct. 1061, 117 L. Ed. 2d 261 (1992).

[105] *Supra* note 103.

However, the Fourteenth Amendment does not impose an affirmative duty on the states to ensure that these interests do not come to harm through other means.

Relying on *De Shaney*, courts have held that police have no constitutional duty to protect members of the public from harm, even when they are aware of the danger. This interpretation shields police from liability for failing to respond to 911 calls[106] or to provide other forms of police protection.[107] In one case, police actually witnessed a woman being pulled from her car, sexually assaulted, and robbed, and ignored her cries for help.[108] The court denied her claim in reliance on *DeShaney*.

However, there are three situations in which a police officer's failure to protect members of the public can serve as the basis for a § 1983 claim.

*Discriminatory denial of police protection.* Even though police have no constitutional duty to provide protective services,[109] selective denial of police protection based on a person's race, religion, ethnicity, gender, or sexual orientation is a violation of equal protection.[110] In *Roman v. City of Reading*,[111] a black man whose car was struck by a "hail of bullets" had difficulty getting the police to respond or to investigate. He sued, claiming that the police treated him differently from the way they treated others because he was black. He speculated that the police assumed from the nature of the crime that he was either a drug dealer or a pimp and decided not to investigate. The court ruled that the man's complaint stated a cause of action for denial of equal protection.

---

[106]  *See, e.g.*, Brown v. Commonwealth of Pennsylvania, Dept. of Health Emergency Medical Services Training Institute, 318 F.3d 473 (3d Cir. 2003) (no cause of action existed for delay in responding to 911 emergency call, resulting in infant's death from choking); Hendon v. DeKalb County, 417 S.E.2d 705 (Ga. Ct. App. 1992) (government not liable to stroke victim for failure to respond to 911 call).

[107]  *See, e.g.*, Schieber v. City of Philadelphia, 320 F.3d 409 (3d Cir. 2003) (no liability existed to murdered woman's estate for refusing to forcibly enter her apartment after neighbor reported hearing screams from inside); Hernandez v. City of Goshen, Indiana, 324 F.3d 535 (7th Cir. 2003) (police not liable for failing to prevent workplace shooting spree after being notified by plant manager that angry worker had threatened to return with a gun); Gonzales v. City of Castle Rock, 307 F.3d 1258 (10th Cir. 2002) (police not liable to mother of murdered children for failing to enforce a restraining order against her estranged husband); Windle v. City of Marion, Inc., 321 F.3d 658 (7th Cir. 2003) (no liability existed where police heard cellular phone conversation over their police scanner between student and middle school teacher who was sexually molesting her, but did nothing for six months); Leidy v. Borough of Glenolden, 277 F. Supp. 2d 547 (E.D. Pa. 2003) (police not liable for murder and rape committed by parolee after they failed to arrest him when he came to police station to surrender under a bench warrant issued for a parole violation).

[108]  Jones v. City of Philadelphia, 185 F. Supp. 2d 413 (E.D. Pa. 2001).

[109]  DeShaney v. Winnegago County Dep't of Soc. Servs., *supra* note 103.

[110]  *Id.* ("[t]he State may not . . . selectively deny its protective services to certain disfavored minorities without violating the Equal Protection Clause."); Sinthasomphone v. City of Milwaukee, 785 F. Supp. 1343 (E.D. Wis. 1992); Eckert v. Town of Silverthorne, 25 Fed. Appx. 679 (10th Cir. 2001) ("There is no general constitutional right to police protection, but if the state provides police protection, it is prohibited, under the equal protection clause, from irrational discrimination in providing such protection."); Neighborhood Action Coalition v. Canton, 882 F.2d 1012 (6th Cir. 1989) (finding basis for § 1983 claim because "[t]he [Fourteenth] Amendment is violated when a police department fails to respond to calls from a neighborhood because of the racial make-up of the neighborhood"); Roman v. City of Reading, 257 F. Supp. 2d 799 (E.D. Pa. 2003) (allegation that city police officers refused to adequately respond to and investigate shooting incident due to fact that victim was African American stated claim against city for violation of equal protection).

[111]  *Supra* note 110.

The Milwaukee Police Department settled an equal protection claim with the estate of one of serial killer Jeffrey Dahmer's victims.[112] Konerak Sinthasomphone, a 14-year-old Asian boy, escaped from Dahmer's apartment and ran into the street where two black women spotted him, wandering around in dazed state, naked and bleeding. They called the police. Shortly thereafter, Dahmer arrived on the scene looking for the boy. The women tried to protect the boy from Dahmer. The police, when they arrived, spoke only to Dahmer, who was white, like them. They accepted his explanation that the boy was his 19-year-old lover who had drank too much and had wandered out without clothing, ignoring the black women's protests that the naked boy was only a child, that he had been abused, and that he was trying to escape from his abuser. The officers even threatened to arrest the black women for interfering. They then assisted Dahmer in taking the boy back to his apartment where he was murdered shortly after they left. The boy's estate alleged that the police department had a longstanding custom of discriminating against racial minorities, that the defendant officers were products of this culture, and that it caused them to accept Dahmer's explanation without performing an adequate investigation and to ignore the black women's concerns. The police department settled the case for $850,000 after the court upheld the complaint as stating a cause of action for denial of equal protection.

*Duty to protect persons in custody.* When the police take a person into custody, they incur a substantive due process duty to look out for the person's safety and general well-being.[113] The basis for this duty is that police have, by their prior conduct, restricted the person's ability to care for him or herself. The duties owed to persons in custody include protecting them from violence at the hands of strangers and fellow officers,[114] and securing prompt attention for known, serious medical needs.[115] Serious does not mean minor lacerations or scraped knees.[116] The condition must be life-threatening, extremely painful, or likely to be exacerbated if left untreated. Moreover, it is not enough that the police should have been aware of the condition; they must actually be aware of the condition and its seriousness before liability will be imposed.[117]

---

[112]   Sinthasomphone v. City of Milwaukee, *supra* note 110.

[113]   *See, e.g.,* Estelle v. Gamble, 429 U.S. 97, 97 S. Ct. 285, 50 L. Ed. 2d 251 (1976) (state has duty to provide adequate medical care to incarcerated prisoners); Youngberg v. Romeo, 457 U.S. 307, 102 S. Ct. 2452, 73 L. Ed. 2d 28 (1982) (state must provide involuntarily committed mental patients with services necessary to ensure their "reasonable safety").

[114]   *See, e.g.,* **Yang v. Hardin**, *supra* note 72. *See also* authorities *supra* note 71.

[115]   *See, e.g.,* Haywood v. Ball, 586 F.2d 996 (4th Cir. 1978); El-Uri v. City of Chicago, 186 F. Supp. 2d 844 (N.D. Ill. 2002); Tagstrom v. Pottebaum, 668 F. Supp. 1269 (N.D. Iowa 1987).

[116]   *See, e.g.,* Wesson v. Oglesby, 910 F.2d 278, 284 (5th Cir. 1990) (holding that an inmate's swollen and bleeding wrists from handcuffing did not constitute serious medical need); Martin v. Gentile, 849 F.2d 863, 871 (4th Cir. 1988) (cut over one eye, bruises on shoulders and elbows, and a quarter-inch piece of glass did not constitute serious medical conditions); Davis v. Jones, 936 F.2d 971 (7th Cir. 1991) (scraped elbow and shallow one-inch cut in temple sustained during arrest were not serious medical conditions).

[117]   *See, e.g.,* Watkins v. City of Battle Creek, 273 F.3d 682 (6th Cir. 2001); Carr v. Tatangelo, 338 F.3d 1259 (11th Cir. 2003).

*Liability based on prior actions that place a person in a position of danger.* Liability for failure to protect also exists when the prior actions of the police increase a person's vulnerability to danger beyond the level that would have existed had they left the person alone.[118] This is called the "state-created danger" theory. *Kneipp v. City of Philadelphia*[119] is an example of the kind of behavior that triggers liability under this theory. Joseph Kneipp was trying to help his wife Samantha home from a bar where she had been drinking. She was visibly intoxicated, smelled of urine, and was unable to walk without assistance. Less than a block from their home, a quarrel developed between the couple because Samantha wanted to drink more rather than go home. Officer Tedder stopped the couple for causing a disturbance, but told Joseph he could go ahead because a babysitter was waiting for him at his house. Joseph left, assuming that Officer Tedder would take charge of his wife. Officer Tedder, instead, sent Samantha home unescorted. Samantha never made it. She was discovered several hours later at the bottom of an embankment, unconscious and brain damaged as a result of hypothermia from exposure to the cold. The court held that Samantha's complaint stated a cause of action for violation of her right to substantive due process because Officer Tedder, by separating her from caretaker and sending him home, and then abandoning her on a cold night in an intoxicated state, increased her risk of danger.

## B. High Degree of Culpability

Substantive due process only reaches police misconduct that lies at the extreme end of the fault spectrum. The conduct must be so egregious that it shocks the conscience.[120] In situations that call for split-second judgment with no opportunity for reflection, such as during a high-speed chase, only an actual intent to cause harm can satisfy this standard.[121] On the other, when there is no

---

[118]   *See, e.g.,* Wood v. Ostrander, 879 F.2d 583 (9th Cir. 1989), *cert. denied,* 498 U.S. 938, 111 S. Ct. 341, 112 L. Ed. 2d 305 (1990) (liability existed to female passenger, left stranded in dangerous neighborhood late at night after police arrested driver, who was raped by unknown man with whom she accepted ride); Reed v. Gardner, 986 F.2d 1122, 1127 (7th Cir.), *cert. denied,* 510 U.S. 947, 114 S. Ct. 389, 126 L. Ed. 2d 337 (1993) (allegations that officer arrested sober driver and left a drunken passenger to drive home on his own were sufficient to allege a due process violation under the state-created danger doctrine when the drunken passenger later struck and killed a pedestrian); Estate of Sinthasomphone v. City of Milwaukee, 838 F. Supp. 1320 (E.D. Wis. 1993) (police liable to estate of murdered child for returning him to custody of serial killer after the child escaped and was found naked and injured in street).

[119]   95 F.3d 1199 (3d Cir. 1996).

[120]   County of Sacramento v. Lewis, *supra* note 102 (holding that police are not liable under § 1983 for causing death of motorcycle passenger in high-speed police chase).

[121]   *See, e.g., id.* (holding that "high-speed chases with no intent to harm suspects physically or to worsen their legal plight do not give rise to liability under the Fourteenth Amendment"); Bublitz v. Cottey, 327 F.3d 485 (7th Cir. 2003) (police officers' actions in using tire-deflation device to stop a fleeing robbery suspect, which subsequently caused an accident injuring an innocent driver and killing the driver's wife and child, did not rise to the level of a substantive due process violation, when there was no intent on the part of the officers to cause harm to the family during the course of the high-speed chase.); Claybrook v. Birchwell, 199 F.3d 350 (6th Cir. 2000) (holding that an injured bystander in a police shootout must prove that police acted "maliciously and sadistically for the very purpose of causing harm").

emergency and police have an opportunity to consider alternatives, as Officer Tedder did in *Kneipp v. City of Philadelphia*, deliberate indifference to a known risk of serious harm will suffice to impose liability.[122]

## § 10.16   —Equal Protection of the Laws

The equal protection clause prohibits a state from "deny[ing] any person within its jurisdiction the equal protection of the laws." This is one of the most important provisions in the Constitution. It requires police to treat all persons who are similarly situated alike. Deliberately treating one person differently from the way an officer would treat others in the same situation is a violation of equal protection if the reason is: (1) the person's membership in a protected class;[123] (2) a desire to punish the person for exercising a constitutional right;[124] or (3) a malicious intent to injure the person out of spite.[125]

Figure 10.8
**Equal Protection of the Laws**

It is a violation of equal protection for police to deliberately treat one person differently from the way they would treat another person in the same situation if the reason is:

1.  the person's membership in a protected class;
2.  a desire to punish the person for exercising a constitutional right; or
3.  a malicious intent to injure the person out of spite.

---

[122]  *See, e.g.*, Schieber v. City of Philadelphia, *supra* note 107; Bukowski v. City of Akron, 326 F.3d 702 (6th Cir. 2003) ("(The guiding principle seems to be that a deliberate-indifference standard is appropriate in "settings [that] provide the opportunity for reflection and unhurried judgments."); Carter v. Simpson, 328 F.3d 948 (7th Cir. 2003) ("In situations where actual deliberation is possible, conduct by a governmental official that is 'deliberately indifferent' may in certain circumstances shock the conscience, giving rise to a cognizable substantive due process violation; in emergency situations, however, conduct shocks the conscience only if there was intent to cause harm.").

[123]  *See, e.g.*, United States v. Armstrong, 517 U.S. 456, 116 S. Ct. 1480, 134 L. Ed. 2d 687 (1996); Yick Wo v. Hopkins, 118 U.S. 356, 6 S. Ct. 1064, 30 L. Ed. 220 (1886); Futenick v. Sumpter Township, 78 F.2d 1051 (6th Cir. 1996); **Alexis v. McDonald's Restaurant of Massachusetts, Inc., 67 F.2d 341 (1st Cir. 1995)**; Humphrey v. Demitri, 931 F. Supp. 571 (N.D. Ill. 1996).

[124]  *See, e.g.*, Dixon v. Dist. of Columbia, 394 F.2d 966, 968 (D.C. Cir.1968) (upholding dismissal of prosecution for traffic offense brought in retaliation for the defendant's filing misconduct charge against the arresting police officers); United States v. Steele, 461 F.2d 1148 (9th Cir. 1972) (finding denial of equal protection where defendant who protested census as an invasion of privacy was the only person prosecuted for refusing to answer census questions, even though others also failed to comply with the law.

[125]  *See, e.g.*, Village of Willowbrook v. Olech, 528 U.S. 562, 120 S. Ct. 1073, 145 L. Ed. 2d 1060 (2000); DeMuria v. Hawkes, 328 F.3d 704 (2d Cir. 2003); Shipp v. McMahon, 234 F.3d 907 (5th Cir. 2000); Esmail v. Macrane, 53 F.3d 176 (7th Cir. 1995).

## A. *Membership in a Protected Class*

People of every race, ethnicity, religion, sexual orientation, and gender are equal in the eyes of the law and are entitled to be treated equally.[126] The police, unfortunately, do not always live up to this ideal. **Racial profiling** (i.e., the practice of inappropriately considering race and ethnicity in deciding whom to approach as a suspect, stop, detain, arrest, search, use force against, etc.) is one of the most troubling issues in contemporary law enforcement. Nothing poisons race relations more than discriminatory law enforcement.[127] Discriminatory enforcement fosters deep resentment, fear, and distrust of police, but the poison goes deeper:

> People who see the criminal justice system as fundamentally unfair will be less likely to cooperate with police, to testify as witnesses, to serve on juries, and to convict guilty defendants when they do serve. In addition, people who have lost respect for the law's legitimacy are more likely to break the law themselves. . . . Finally, the perception and reality of a fundamentally unfair criminal justice system contribute to broader racial divisions in society. If we cannot believe that our nation's law enforcement officers will enforce the law in a racially neutral manner, then we will be left with a society where members of the minority community always view the actions of any police officer with great suspicion. . . .[128]

Police departments around the nation have begun to address the problem.[129] Efforts include adopting formal policies banning racial profiling, eliminating ticket quotas, requiring police officers to note the race of all drivers they stop, creating computer databases to track this information, installing

[126] United States v. Avery, 137 F.3d 343 (6th Cir. 1997) (race); Balistreri v. Pacifica Police Depart., 901 F.2d 696 (9th Cir. 1989) (gender); Smith v. Gilpin County, Colorado, 949 F. Supp. 1498 (D. Colo. 1997) (race); Estate of Sinthasomphone v. City of Milwaukee, 838 F. Supp. 1320 (E.D. Wis. 1993) (ethnicity and sexual orientation).

[127] *See generally*, DAVID COLE, NO EQUAL JUSTICE: RACE AND CLASS IN THE AMERICAN CRIMINAL JUSTICE SYSTEM (1999); RANDALL KENNEDY, RACE, CRIME, AND THE LAW x-xi (1997) ("[N]othing has poisoned race relations more than racially discriminatory policing pursuant to which blacks are watched, questioned, and detained more than others. . . . [T]he race line in policing creates cycles of resentment."); Erik Luna, *The New Data: Over-Representation of Minorities in The Criminal Justice System: Race, Crime, and Institutional Design*, 66 LAW & CONTEMPORARY PROBLEMS 183 (2003) ("Minorities are gravely over-represented in every stage of the criminal process—from pedestrian and automobile stops, to searches and seizures, to arrests and convictions, to incarceration and capital punishment."); David A. Harris, *The Stories, The Statistics, and the Law: Why "Driving While Black" Matters*, 84 MINN. L. REV. 265 (1999); David A. Harris, *"Driving While Black" and All Other Traffic Offenses: The Supreme Court and Pretextual Traffic Stops*, 87 J. CRIM. L. & CRIMINOLOGY 544, 559-71 (1997); Angela J. Davis, Race, Cops, and Traffic Stops, 51 U. MIAMI L. REV. 425, 431-32 nn. 41-51 (1997).

[128] **Martinez v. United States, 92 F. Supp. 2d 780 (N.D. Ill. 2000).**

[129] *See, e.g.*, Barbara Boyer & Thomas J. Gibbons Jr., *Police Keep Tabs on Racial Profiling: Philadelphia Requires Officer's Payroll Number, Computerized Records*, BEACON JOURNAL A2 (Feb. 9, 2001); Megan Woolhouse, *Racial Profiling Isn't Just a Big-City Issue, Blacks Say*, COURIER JOURNAL, A1 (March 7, 2001).

video cameras on police cars, aggressively recruiting minorities for the police force, stepping up diversity training, and creating citizen review boards to monitor racial profiling complaints.[130]

## B. Punishment for Exercising a Constitutional Right

Equal protection is also violated when police single a person out for different treatment to punish the person for exercising a constitutional right.[131] Arresting a person to retaliate against him or her for filing a police misconduct complaint is an example.[132]

## C. Malicious Intent to Injure

Finally, equal protection is violated when the police single persons out for different treatment out of a malicious intent to injure them.[133] In *Benigni v. City of Hemet*,[134] the police deliberately waged an orchestrated campaign of harassment against the owner of a local bar. They entered his establishment five or six times a night to check identifications, ticketed patrons as soon as their parking meters expired, and followed them around when they left the establishment, waiting for them to commit a traffic violation. These actions eventually forced the owner to close down and sell his business at a loss. The court held that the plaintiff's equal protection rights were violated because the police deliberately harassed him for malicious and spiteful reasons.

## § 10.17   Summary

In order to recover damages against a police officer under § 1983, the plaintiff must prove that the officer deprived him or her of rights secured by the Constitution or laws of the United States while acting under color of state law. A large percentage of § 1983 claims are dismissed before trial under the doctrine of qualified immunity. Qualified immunity protects police officers from § 1983 liability unless their conduct violates a clearly established constitutional right of which a reasonable police officer should have known. This standard gives an officer two chances to avoid liability. Officers are immune from liability if: (1) the constitutional right they are charged with violating was not clearly established when they acted, or (2) if a reasonable police offi-

---

[130]   *See, e.g.*, Martinez v. United States, *supra* 128.
[131]   *See* authorities *supra* note 124.
[132]   *Id.*
[133]   *See* authorities *supra* note 125.
[134]   879 F.2d 473 (9th Cir. 1989).

cer, confronted with these facts, could have believed that his or her conduct conformed to that standard. An officer will be forced to undergo trial only if the alleged conduct amounts to a clear violation of a clearly established constitutional right.

To recover damages at the trial, the plaintiff will have to prove that the officer (1) acted under color of state law in (2) depriving him or her of a right protected by the Constitution or laws of the United States.

**Action under color of state law**. Action under color of state law refers to the misuse of power, possessed by virtue of state law and made possible only because the wrongdoer is clothed with the authority of state law. Action under color of state law is present when a police officer's misconduct arises out of the performance of professional duties or is made possible through misuse of official authority. It is lacking when an officer engages in misconduct for personal reasons with no pretense of exercising official authority. For wrongs committed in a private capacity, the plaintiff must pursue a remedy under state tort law, not under § 1983.

**Deprivation of the plaintiff's constitutional rights**. The plaintiff must also establish that the officer deprived him or her of a right secured by the Constitution or laws of the United States. Most claims brought under § 1983 are grounded either in the Bill of Rights or the Fourteenth Amendment. Proof of a constitutional violation requires evidence that the officer acted with a culpable mental state. The culpable mental state varies with the constitutional violation alleged as the basis for recovery. Fourth Amendment claims require proof that the officer's conduct was objectively unreasonable. Fourteenth Amendment due process claims require conscience-shocking conduct. Equal protection claims require proof that the conduct was motivated by deliberate discrimination based on: (1) the plaintiff's membership in a socially disfavored group; (2) the exercise of a constitutional right; or (3) spiteful reasons.

When a police officer violates constitutional rights, the standard practice is to sue the municipality and police department that employs the officer and his or her supervisors, along with the officer. Liability under § 1983 requires personal fault. A municipality can be held liable for the unconstitutional acts of a rank-and-file police officer only when its own official policies or customs caused the violation to occur. The official policy or custom that caused the deprivation can stem from: (1) formal written policies sanctioning unconstitutional practices; (2) decisions made by high-ranking municipal officials with final policymaking authority, directing unconstitutional action; or (3) a conscious choice by the city's official policymaker to do nothing in the face of a known risk that violation of constitutional rights is almost certain to result from the decision. The third theory is used to hold municipalities liable for the unconstitutional acts of rank-and-file police officers when a pattern of abuses has placed the city on notice of the need for more or different training, discipline, or supervision and no corrective action takes place. Supervisory liability under § 1983 is similar to municipal liability.

Section 1983 damage suits cannot be brought against state government because of their Eleventh Amendment immunity or against federal law enforcement officers because they act under color of federal law, not state law. The Supreme Court has, nevertheless, fashioned an equivalent federal common law remedy against federal agents. Private individuals are liable to suit under § 1983 when they: (1) act in concert with state officials; (2) perform a public function; or (3) act under state compulsion or with significant state encouragement.

Police officers who willfully deprive citizens of their constitutional rights while acting under color of law are subject to criminal prosecution under 18 U.S.C. § 242. Section 242 differs from § 1983 in three respects: (1) it is a criminal statute; (2) it reaches conduct committed under color of federal law, as well as under state law; and (3) a conviction requires proof that the officer acted with a willful intent to deprive a person of a constitutional right.

# Constitutional and Civil Rights in the Government Workplace     11

Twentieth Century America has a right to demand for itself, and the obligation to secure for its citizens, law enforcement personnel whose conduct is
above and beyond reproach. The police officer is expected to conduct himself lawfully and properly to bring honor and respect to the law which he
is sworn and bound to uphold. He who fails to so comport brings upon the
law grave shadows of public distrust. We demand from our law enforcement officers, and properly so, adherence to demanding standards which
are higher than those applied in many other professions. It is a standard
which demands more than forbearance from overt and indictable illegal
conduct. It demands that in both an officer's private and official lives he
do nothing to bring dishonor upon his noble calling and in no way contribute to a weakening of the public confidence and trust.

*Cerceo v. Darby*, 281 A.2d 251, 255 (Pa. 1971)

# Chapter Outline

## § 11.1  Introduction

Courts have long struggled to determine the level of constitutional protection appropriate in government workplaces. In 1892, Supreme Court Justice Oliver Wendell Holmes, then on the Massachusetts Supreme Court, wrote that a police officer "may have a constitutional right to talk politics, but he has no constitutional right to be a policeman."[1] What Justice Holmes meant is that police officers relinquish all their constitutional rights as a citizen when they accept public employment.

While this is no longer true today, the constitutional rights studied in earlier chapters often have a narrower application in the government workplace. Government agencies, like private businesses, have service obligations to perform. Consequently, public employees retain constitutional rights only to the extent that their exercise is compatible with the government's fulfillment of its service responsibilities. Even so, public employees still have more constitutional protection than employees in the private sector who have no protection at all because the Constitution binds only the actions of the government.

This chapter examines the constitutional rights of police officers in personnel disputes and also their federal protection against employment discrimination. We will begin with the sad tale of Larry Lovermore, a former patrol officer with the Whosville Police Department, who learned the material in this chapter the hard way—through experience.

---

[1]  McAuliffe v. Mayor of New Bedford, 155 Mass. 216, 29 N.E. 517 (1892).

## The Larry Lovermore Incident

Larry Lovermore's downfall began the morning he was told he was one of two finalists on the list of candidates for promotion to sergeant. Lovermore immediately dashed off the following e-mail message to a young female trainee: "Now that I am about to be promoted to sergeant, will you sleep with me?" He meant it as a joke, but the young woman took it seriously. After she complained to Lovermore's supervisor, the supervisor decided to search Lovermore's locker for evidence of job-related misconduct and found a stack of X-rated magazines. As a result of this incident, Lovermore's name was summarily removed from the list of candidates. Believing his constitutional rights had been violated, Lovermore wrote a letter to the Whosville *Inquirer* and the local television station. In his letter, Lovermore summarized what happened, complained of his "unconstitutional and illegal treatment," and stated that there had been "widespread discontent in the Whosville Police Department ever since Police Chief Clueso had taken over." Lovermore's story appeared on the front page of the Whosville *Inquirer* the next morning because nothing more important happened in Whosville the day before. That afternoon, Lovermore received a short e-mail message from Police Chief Clueso—"You're fired!"

Lovermore has filed suit against Police Chief Clueso and the Whosville Police Department under 42 U.S.C. § 1983. In his complaint, Lovermore alleged that he was terminated in retaliation for exercising his right to freedom of speech, that his Fourth Amendment rights were violated by the locker search, and that the removal of his name from the candidate list and subsequent termination, both without a hearing, denied him procedural due process in violation of the Fourteenth Amendment.[2] These issues will be discussed in the sections that follow.

## § 11.2  First Amendment Protection for Work-Related Speech

Had Larry been an ordinary citizen, his letter to the editor criticizing Police Chief Clueso's management of the Whosville Police Department would have been protected by the First Amendment.[3] However, the government has a different interest in restricting speech when the speaker is an employee. Government agencies have service obligations to perform and hire employees to assist them. When an employee's speech is disruptive, the government must be able to remove the employee to maintain workplace efficiency.[4] As one court has aptly observed:

---

[2]    This hypothetical is based on the facts of Olive v. City of Scottsdale, 969 F. Supp. 564 (D. Ariz. 1996).

[3]    *See* § 2.4 *supra*.

[4]    Waters v. Churchill, 511 U.S. 661, 114 S. Ct. 1878, 128 L. Ed. 2d 686 (1994).

A police officer is primarily a public servant, with a myriad of attendant responsibilities. In that role, he cannot always act and speak as he pleases. This does not mean, however, that he loses all semblance of a private citizen just because he happens to have a government job. He maintains the freedom to speak out on matters of public concern, where such speech outweighs the police department's interests in satisfying the public's expectations.[5]

Figure 11.1
**First Amendment Protection for Work-Related Speech**

A police officer is entitled to First Amendment protection for work-related speech only if:

1.  the speech addresses a matter of public concern, and
2.  the officer's interest in speaking outweighs the department's interest in suppressing the speech to promote workplace efficiency.

Courts use a two-part test to determine whether an officer is entitled to First Amendment protection for work-related speech.[6] The court first determines whether the officer's speech addressed a matter of "public concern." If it did not, the inquiry is over, because the First Amendment does not protect speech that relates to an officer's private interests as an employee.[7] If the speech addressed a matter of public concern, the court then balances the officer's interest in speaking out on this matter against the department's interest in suppressing the speech to promote workplace efficiency.[8] The officer will be entitled to First Amendment protection only if the court concludes that officer's interest outweighed the interest of his or her department.[9]

## A. Did the Officer's Speech Relate to a Matter of Public Concern?

Larry Lovermore's first hurdle will be to convince the court that his letter to the Whosville *Inquirer* addressed a matter of "public concern." "Public concern" has been defined broadly as speech that relates to any "matter of political, social or other concern to the community."[10] Public employees have no

---

[5]   Glass v. Dachel, 27 F.3d 733 (7th Cir. 1993).

[6]   The groundwork for the current approach was laid in Pickering v. Board of Education, 391 U.S. 563, 88 S. Ct. 1731, 20 L. Ed. 2d 811 (1968). *See also* **Connick v. Myers, 461 U.S. 138, 103 S. Ct. 1684, 75 L. Ed. 2d 708 (1983)**; Rankin v. McPherson, 483 U.S. 378, 107 S. Ct. 2891, 97 L. Ed. 2d 315 (1987); Waters v. Churchill, 511 U.S. 661, 114 S. Ct. 1878, 128 L. Ed. 2d 686 (1994).

[7]   **Connick v. Myers**, *supra* note 6.

[8]   *Id.* Although the employee has the burden of showing that the speech is on a matter of public concern, courts generally require the employer to establish that the action it took in retaliation was justified by the need to promote workplace efficiency. Rankin v. McPherson, *supra* note 6, 483 U.S. at 388, 107 S. Ct. at 2899; **Connick v. Myers**, *supra* note 6, 461 U.S. at 149, 103 S. Ct. at 1691.

[9]   *Id.* First Amendment protection for work-related speech does not vary with the status of the employee. Police trainees who have not completed their probationary period have the same First Amendment protection as permanent employees. Rankin v. McPherson, *supra* note 6.

[10]  **Connick v. Myers**, *supra* note 6.

First Amendment protection when their speech pertains to work assignments, personnel actions, grievances, or other matters that concern only them.[11]

Whether an officer's speech addresses a matter of public or private concern is determined from the content, form, and context of the speech and the employee's motivation for speaking.[12] In *Connick v. Myers*,[13] an assistant district attorney was dismissed for circulating a questionnaire soliciting the views of fellow staff members on office transfer policies, the need for a grievance committee, and confidence in department supervisors, after receiving notice of a scheduled transfer. The Supreme Court affirmed her dismissal on the grounds that her questionnaire did not address a matter of public concern.

The Court reached this conclusion by examining the content, form, and context of the speech and the assistant district attorney's motivation for speaking. Her questionnaire dealt largely with internal office affairs about which persons outside the department would have scant interest. Even more important, her speech arose in the context of an ongoing dispute with her supervisors regarding her transfer. The point of her speech was not that her supervisors were failing to discharge their responsibilities to the public; she was complaining about the way they had treated her. Her questionnaire was prepared to gather ammunition to contest her own transfer.

Figure 11.2
**Meaning of Speech on a Matter of "Public Concern"**

> A government employee's workplace speech involves a matter of public concern only when:
>
> 1. the topic would be of some interest to people outside the department; and
> 2. the employee is motivated to address this topic in order to further interests that go beyond his or her own.

The Supreme Court's analysis in *Connick v. Myers* points to the factors that courts consider in deciding whether a government employee's speech relates to a matter of public concern. Foremost are: (1) the subject matter of the speech, and (2) the employee's motive for speaking. To satisfy the "public concern" element, the subject matter must possess some interest to people outside the department, and the employee must be motivated to speak, at least in part, to promote interests that go beyond his or her own.

---

[11] Rankin v. McPherson, *supra* note 6 (explaining that government employers, no less than private employers, need the ability to manage the internal affairs of their department).

[12] **Connick v. Myers**, *supra* note 6; Rankin v. McPherson, *supra* note 6.

[13] *Supra* note 6.

## 1. Subject Matter of the Speech

The subject matter of the speech is the most important consideration. To be a matter of "public concern," the speech must relate to a matter of political, social, or other concern to the community.[14] Many things that happen in a police department interest the public; many things do not. Workplace topics run the gamut from concerns about possible wrongdoing and breaches of the public trust to discussions of work assignments and whether to repair or replace older patrol cars. Whether a particular topic involves a matter of public concern is not always easy to decide. The employee's choice of forums may aid in this determination, particularly in a close case, because it suggests how the employee viewed the matter.[15] If the matter is addressed in an internal report, interoffice memorandum, or during a private conference, the chances of its being treated as an internal office affair are increased because the employee's choice of forums indicates that the employee viewed it this way. In *Steinberg v. Thomas*,[16] a staff attorney was fired for criticizing his supervisor's management style during a staff meeting. Seizing on this fact, the court ruled that the attorney's speech involved an internal office affair, but added that it would have reached the same result had it viewed the speech as involving a matter of public concern, because criticizing a supervisor's management style in front of coworkers is so likely to impair harmonious working relationships that the adverse effects of such speech outweigh the benefits.

---

[14]   Mandell v. County of Suffolk, 316 F.3d 368 (2d Cir. 2003) (testimony before public safety committee criticizing department's approach to fighting organized crime, resistance to change, and systemic racism and anti-Semitism involved a matter of public concern); Oladeine v. City of Birmingham, 230 F.3d 1275 (11th Cir. 2000) (charge that police chief tampered with public records to cover up criminal conduct of mayor's daughter involved a matter of public concern); Dill v. City of Edmond, Okla., 155 F.3d 1193 (10th Cir. 1998) (charge that exculpatory evidence was withheld in a murder case involved a matter of public concern); Cooper v. Smith, 89 F.3d 761, 765 (11th Cir. 1996) (corruption in police department is a matter of public concern); Glass v. Dachel, *supra* note 5 (private comments to fellow officer about superior's possible involvement in removal of property from department's property room and questioning whether department's investigation would be adequate involved matters of public concern); Biggs v. Village of Dupo, 892 F.2d 1298 (7th Cir. 1990) (discussion of inadequate police funding involved a matter of public concern); Sook v. Brown, 865 F.2d 887, 893 (7th Cir. 1989) (high-ranking official's misuse of county time and tax dollars on non-work activities is a matter of public concern); Manhattan Beach Police Officers Ass'n, Inc. v. City of Manhattan Beach, 881 F.2d 816 (9th Cir. 1989) (letters by police officers to local newspapers criticizing the city for understaffing the police department involved a matter of public concern); Wagner v. City of Holyoke, 241 F. Supp. 2d 78 (D. Mass. 2003) (speech that discloses racial discrimination and corruption within department relates to a matter of public concern). *But see* City of San Diego v. Roe, ___ U.S. ___, 125 S. Ct. 521, 2004 U.S. LEXIS 8165 (December 6, 2004) (sale of sexually explicit video on eBay, depicting officer ripping off his police uniform and masturbating after issuing a traffic citation was not speech on a matter of public concern); Pereira v. Commissioner of Social Services, 432 Mass. 251, 733 N.E.2d 112 (2000) (racist joke told by speaker at testimonial dinner for retiring members of city council did not constitute speech on a matter of public concern and, thus, was not protected by First Amendment).

[15]   Barkoo v. Melby, 901 F.2d 613, 618 (7th Cir. 1990); Gonzalez v. City of Chicago, 239 F.3d 939 (7th Cir. 2001) (officer who completed routine report as part of his regular job duties did not speak on a matter of public concern even though the report contained information of interest to the public).

[16]   659 F. Supp. 789 (D. Colo. 1987).

## 2. Officer's Motivation for Speaking

The officer's motive for speaking is the second most important consideration. To be addressing a matter of public concern, the officer must be motivated to speak to further interests that go beyond his or her own.[17] When the point of the speech is purely to further the officer's own interests as an employee, the officer is not addressing a matter of *public* concern; the officer is addressing a matter that concerns him or her personally. This was a key factor in the Supreme Court's analysis in *Connick v. Myers*, discussed above. The assistant district attorney's speech did not involve a matter of public concern because that was not the point of her speech. She was not speaking about the office transfer policy because of the way it affected the public or others in her department; she was speaking about the office transfer policy solely out of concern for the way it had affected *her*.

Speech on a matter that would otherwise be of public concern is not protected by the First Amendment if the sole purpose of the speech is to further the officer's private interests as an employee. Consider sexual harassment, for example. Sexual harassment in a government agency can be a matter of serious public concern because it affects how well the agency performs its public responsibilities. However, no First Amendment protection attaches when an officer makes charges of sexual harassment in an employee grievance because the topic is not being addressed as a matter that concerns the public.[18] The officer is seeking redress for a wrong that concerns only him or her.

Airing private grievances in a public forum does not convert them into matters of public concern. In *McEvoy v. Shoemaker*,[19] McEvoy, a police offi-

---

[17]   Gardetto v. Mason, 100 F.3d 803, 812 (10th Cir. 1997) ("In deciding how to classify particular speech, courts focus on the motive of the speaker and attempt to determine whether the speech was calculated to redress personal grievances or whether it had a broader public purpose."); Callaway v. Hafeman, 832 F.2d 414, 417, 42 Ed. Law. Rep. 723 (7th Cir. 1987) (courts must look at the point of the speech: was the employee's point to bring wrongdoing to light or to raise other issues of public concern because they are of public concern, or was the point to further some purely private interest?); Johnson v. Hill, 74 F.3d 1087 (11th Cir. 1996) (a public employee's speech is not protected by the First Amendment when the speech is motivated solely by private concerns); Arndt v. Koby, 309 F.3d 1247 (10th Cir. 2002) (public response to media criticism of officer's management of JonBenet Ramsey murder investigation was not speech on matter of public concern because officer's purpose was to salvage her own personal reputation and good name); Gros v. The Port Washington Police Dist., 944 F. Supp. 1072 (E.D.N.Y. 1996) (officer's speech involving his own promotion not matter of public concern).

[18]   Gustafson v. Jones, 290 F.3d 895 (7th Cir. 2002) ("[M]otive matters to the extent that even speech on a subject that would otherwise be of interest to the public will not be protected if the expression addresses only the personal effect upon the employee, or if the only point of the speech was to further some purely private interest."); Wallscetti v. Fox, 258 F.3d 662 (7th Cir. 2001) (former county employee's harassment complaints about her supervisors did not address issue of public concern where content consisted of complaining of her supervisors' hostility toward her); Smith v. Fruin, 28 F.3d 646, 650 (7th Cir. 1994), *cert. denied*, 513 U.S. 1083, 115 S. Ct. 735, 130 L. Ed. 2d 638 (1995) (if speech pertains to a matter that would interest the public, but the expression addresses only the personal effect of that issue on the employee, the speech is not about a matter that concerns the public); Callaway v. Hafeman, 832 F.2d 414, 42 Ed. Law Rep. 723 (7th Cir. 1987) ("While instances of sexual harassment in government agencies are inherently matters of public concern, the *Connick* test requires courts to look at the point of the speech in question. Was it the employee's point to bring wrongdoing to light? Or to raise other issues of public concern, because they are of public concern? Or was the point to further some purely private interest?").

[19]   882 F.2d 463 (10th Cir. 1989).

cer who was passed up for a promotion, wrote a nine-page letter to the city council complaining of the "mismanagement," "inequities," "internal politicking," and "favoritism" that took place in police department promotions. Although his letter began with the statement that the sentiments he was about to express were "commonly held viewpoints" and that he was "speaking for others," the main focus of his letter was that he had been treated unfairly. The letter resulted in his dismissal and he sued, claiming that he was dismissed in retaliation for exercising his First Amendment rights. The court denied McEvoy's claim on the grounds that his speech did not address a matter of public concern. McEvoy's motive for writing "was not to disclose 'malfeasance on the part of government officials in the conduct of their official duties,' but instead to air his frustration at not having received a promotion." He was, therefore, speaking as a disgruntled employee about a matter that concerned him personally.

The same can be said for Lovermore's letter to the Whosville *Inquirer*. Except for his comment about rank-and-file discontent with Police Chief Clueso's management, everything in Lovermore's letter was about his own "illegal and unconstitutional" treatment. While his comment on the discontent arguably touched on a matter of public concern, it will be read in the context in which it was written—the context of a disgruntled police officer complaining about the way he was treated. Lovermore's remarks about Clueso's management were added to bolster his claim of mistreatment. Because Lovermore's purpose in writing this letter was to air a personal grievance, his letter will be treated as the speech of an employee on a matter of private concern, for which there is no First Amendment protection.

## B.  Balancing the Department's Interest in Workplace Efficiency against the Officer's Interest in Speaking

Many problems that occur inside a police department qualify as matters of public concern because they affect the quality of police protection and ultimately the public safety. However, this does not mean that a police officer is always on safe ground in bringing such matters to the attention of the public. To prevail on a First Amendment retaliation claim, the officer's interest in addressing the matter must outweigh the department's interest in suppressing the speech to promote workplace efficiency.[20]

Figure 11.3
**First Amendment Protection for Work-Related Speech on a Matter of Public Concern**

> If an officer's speech addresses a matter that concerns the public, First Amendment protection is determined by balancing:
>
> 1.   the employee's interest in speaking out
> 2.   against the adverse effects of the speech on workplace efficiency.

---

[20]    Pickering v. Board of Education, *supra* note 6; Waters v. Churchill, *supra* note 4.

The degree of public concern surrounding an officer's speech affects the weight.[21] Officers disciplined for speech, nevertheless, generally face an uphill battle.[22] As one court explained, "[b]ecause police departments function as paramilitary organizations charged with maintaining public safety and order, they are given more latitude in their decisions regarding discipline and personnel regulations than an ordinary government employer."[23] As a result, courts are slow to second-guess police professionals about what is necessary for the proper functioning of a police department. The department's decision to discipline an officer for his or her speech is likely to stand if any of the following are present:

1. The officer made serious charges without an adequate investigation.[24]
2. The officer purported to act as a department spokesperson without authority.[25]

---

21  *See, e.g.*, Chappel v. Montgomery County Fire Protection Dist. No. 1, 131 F.3d 564 (6th Cir. 1997) (dismissal for disclosing misappropriation of public monies violated First Amendment); Solomon v. Royal Oak Township, 842 F.2d 862 (6th Cir. 1988) (dismissal for exposing corrupt practices of high-ranking police official violated First Amendment); Moore v. City of Kilgore, Tex., 877 F.2d 364 (5th Cir. 1989) (firefighter's statements to press about staff shortages protected by First Amendment).

22  *See, e.g.*, Kokkinis v. Ivkovich, 185 F.3d 840 (7th Cir. 1999) (noting that "[d]eference to the employer's judgment regarding the disruptive nature of an employee's speech is especially important in the context of law enforcement" because "there is a particularly urgent need for close teamwork among those involved in the 'high stakes' field of law enforcement. Speech that might not interfere with work in an environment less dependent on order, discipline, and esprit de corps could be debilitating to a police force."); Wagner v. City of Holyoke, 241 F. Supp. 2d 78 (D. Mass. 2003) ("[A] police department has a more significant interest than the typical government employer in regulating the speech activities of its employees in order to promote efficiency, foster loyalty and obedience to superior officers, maintain morale, and instill public confidence."); O'Donnell v. Barry, 148 F.3d 1126 (D.C. Cir. 1998) ("[B]ecause of the special degree of trust and discipline required in a police force, there may be a stronger governmental interest in regulating the speech of police officers than in regulating the speech of other governmental employees."); Stanley v. City of Dalton, Georgia, 219 F.3d 1280 (11th Cir. 2000) (recognizing strong interest in maintaining close working relationships, mutual respect, discipline, and trust in quasi-military organizations like police departments); Busby v. City of Orlando, 931 F.2d 764, 774 (11th Cir. 1991) (describing unique need for maintaining loyalty, discipline, and good working relationships "[i]n quasi-military organizations such as law enforcement agencies;" "comments concerning coworkers' performance of their duties and superior officers' integrity can directly interfere with the confidentiality, esprit de corps and efficient operation of the police department"); Egger v. Phillips, 710 F.2d 292 (7th Cir. 1983) ("Government law enforcement agencies . . . are indeed very similar to the military in terms of the need for direction, supervision, discipline, confidentiality, efficiency and esprit de corps. Thus, courts should defer, whenever possible consistent with the Constitution, to the superior expertise of law enforcement professionals in dealing with their respective personnel.").

23  Tindle v. Caudell, 56 F.3d 966, 971 (8th Cir. 1995). *See also* authorities *supra* note 22.

24  Pickering v. Board of Education, *supra* note 6, 391 U.S. at 574, 88 S. Ct. at 1737-38 (First Amendment does not protect false statements that are knowingly or recklessly made); Stanley v. City of Dalton, Georgia, *supra* note 22 (police department has a strong interest in preventing unfounded accusations made against superior officers); Chappel v. Montgomery County Fire Protection Dist. No. 1, 131 F.3d 564, 576 (6th Cir. 1997) (First Amendment protection unavailable when an officer knowingly or recklessly makes false statements).

25  *See, e.g.*, **Thomas v. Whalen, 51 F.3d 1285 (6th Cir. 1995)**; Moore v. City of Wynnewood, 57 F.3d 924 (10th Cir. 1995).

3.  The disclosure violated the department's confidentiality regulations.[26]
4.  The speech impaired close working relationships.[27]
5.  The speech undermined the authority of superiors.[28]
6.  The speech caused internal controversy or morale problems.[29]
7.  The speech eroded public confidence in the police department or tarnished its public image.[30]

---

[26]  Police departments normally have regulations prohibiting disclosure of the results of pending investigations and other confidential matters. *See* Jurgensen v. Fairfax County, 745 F.2d 868 (4th Cir. 1984) (upholding dismissal for releasing a confidential internal review report in violation of police confidentiality regulations); Lytle v. City of Haysville, 138 F.3d 857 (10 Cir. 1998) (upholding dismissal for speaking to news media and attorney for widow of shooting victim about confidential police investigation of the officer involved in the shooting); Ely v. Honnaker, 451 F. Supp. 16 (W.D. Va. 1977), *aff'd,* 588 F.2d 1348 (4th Cir. 1978) (upholding dismissal for discussing an ongoing investigation into a suspected prostitute ring with a television reporter before formal charges had been brought, in violation of department confidentiality rules).

[27]  *See, e.g.,* Kannisto v. City & County of San Francisco, 541 F.2d 841 (9th Cir. 1976), *cert. denied,* 430 U.S. 931, 97 S. Ct. 1552, 51 L. Ed. 2d 775 (1977) (upholding disciplinary measures imposed on a police lieutenant who, while addressing his subordinates during a morning inspection, described his immediate superior as an "unreasonable, contrary, vindictive individual," whose behavior was "unreasonable, belligerent, arrogant, contrary and unpleasant"); Cochran v. City of Los Angeles, 222 F.3d 1195 (9th Cir. 2000) (upholding disciplinary measures imposed for challenging superior's ability to make decisions free from racial and gender bias); Cochran v. City of Los Angeles, 222 F.3d 1195 (9th Cir. 2000) (observing that "employer's interest outweighs the employee's interest in speaking if the employee's speech impairs discipline by superiors or harmony among coworkers, has a detrimental impact on close working relationships for which personal loyalty and confidence are necessary, or impedes the performance of the speaker's duties or interferes with the regular operation of the enterprise"); Hosford v. State Personnel Bd., 74 Cal. App. 3d 302, 141 Cal. Rptr. 354 (1997) (upholding dismissal of patrol officer for insubordinate statements made to immediate superior).

[28]  *See, e.g.,* Kokkinis v. Ivkovich, 185 F.3d 840 (7th Cir. 1999) (affirming dismissal for making sensationalistic charges of impropriety against the police chief during a television news interview because it "could endanger the department's ability to perform effectively"); Campbell v. R.W. Towse, 99 F.3d 820 (7th Cir. 1997) (upholding suspension without pay of a police lieutenant for writing a letter to the chief of police criticizing a particular program the chief had initiated); Tyler v. City of Mountain Home, Ark., 72 F.3d 568 (8th Cir. 1995) (upholding disciplinary measures where officer violated chain of command in writing letter to another law enforcement agency). *See also* cases *supra* note 27.

[29]  *See, e.g.,* Waters v. Churchill, *supra* note 4 (affirming dismissal of nurse in public hospital for making comments critical of the department to a coworker during a dinner break); Greer v. Amesqua, 212 F.3d 358 (7th Cir. 2000) (city's interest in promoting efficiency outweighed firefighter's interest in his speech in form of news release accusing fire chief of favoring homosexuals and imposing overly lenient disciplinary action on female firefighter); Magri v. Giarrusso, 379 F. Supp. 353 (E.D. La. 1974) (upholding dismissal of police sergeant who, as head of the police union, made a public statement during a battle about pay raises in which he called the police superintendent a "coward" and a "liar" and demanded his resignation).

[30]  *See, e.g.,* Greer v. Amesqua, *supra* note 29 (affirming dismissal of firefighter who used a news release rather than internal procedures to complain about perceived favoritism toward gays and women, resulting in publication of a front-page newspaper story headlined, "Greer says fire chief plays gay games" that caused public embarrassment to the department); Shay-Castro v. New York City Police Dep't, 233 A.D.2d, 649 N.Y.S.2d 711 (1st Dep't 1996) (upholding termination of police officer for posing nude for a magazine in which she "used her position, uniform and police equipment, without authorization, for her personal commercial benefit, and actively promoted the commercial product, in a manner that was likely to hold the department up to public ridicule").

Whistle-blower speech is the one exception. Speech that exposes fraud, malfeasance, corruption, or wrongdoing in a police department is a matter of "utmost public concern"[31] and is entitled to protection even when it causes disruption in the workplace.[32]

### C. Political Activity and Patronage Practices

Many states have laws (called Hatch Acts) that prohibit government employees from taking an active role in political campaigns. The Supreme Court has upheld their constitutionality on the grounds that restrictions on partisan political activity foster impartial execution of the laws and ensure that the government workforce is not used to maintain powerful and corrupt political machines.[33]

Government employees, conversely, enjoy First Amendment protection against discharge because of party affiliation unless they occupy a policy-making position.[34] The age-old practice of cleaning house and restaffing government agencies with patronage appointments was declared unconstitutional in *Elrod v. Burns*[35] on the grounds that it interferes with a government employee's freedom of political beliefs and association. Political affiliation may not be used as a factor in hiring, transfer, or promotion decisions unless the job is a "policymaking position" in which the employee acts as an advisor or spokesperson for an elected official or is privy to confidential information, making party loyalty and shared ideological beliefs an appropriate requirement for the job.[36]

## § 11.3  Fourth Amendment Protection against Searches for Evidence of Work-Related Misconduct

Lovermore's second complaint—that his locker was searched without probable cause or a search warrant—also stands little chance of success. When the police department acts as a criminal investigator, the Fourth Amendment

---

[31] O'Donnell v. Yanchulis, 875 F.2d 1059 (3d Cir. 1989) (whistleblowing about malfeasance in a police department is of the "utmost public concern"); Brawner v. City of Richardson, Tex., 855 F.2d 187 (5th Cir. 1988) ("disclosure of misbehavior by public officials is a matter of public interest and therefore deserves the constitutional protection, especially when it concerns the operation of a police department"); Hughes v. Whitmer, 714 F.2d 1407, 1423 (8th Cir. 1983) ("[A]n employee's First Amendment interest is entitled to more weight where he is acting as a whistle-blower exposing government corruption.").

[32] *See* authorities *supra* notes 14, 21, and 31.

[33] United Public Workers of America v. Mitchell, 330 U.S. 75, 67 S. Ct. 556, 91 L. Ed. 754 (1947); United States Civil Service Commission v. National Assn. of Letter Carriers, 413 U.S. 548, 93 S. Ct. 2880, 37 L. Ed. 2d 796 (1973); Broadrick v. Oklahoma, 413 U.S. 601, 93 S. Ct. 2908, 37 L. Ed. 2d 830 (1973).

[34] Elrod v. Burns, 427 U.S. 347, 96 S. Ct. 2673, 49 L. Ed. 2d 547 (1976); Branti v. Finkel, 445 U.S. 507, 100 S. Ct. 1287, 63 L. Ed. 2d 574 (1980) (assistant public defender could not be terminated for his political allegiance).

[35] *Supra* note 34.

[36] Rutan v. Republican Party of Illinois, 497 U.S. 62, 110 S. Ct. 2729, 111 L. Ed. 2d 52 (1990).

generally requires probable cause and a search warrant. However, neither requirement applies when the police department acts in the role of an employer searching for evidence of suspected work-related misconduct.[37] In *O'Connor v. Ortega*,[38] the Supreme Court explained that public employees generally have a diminished expectation of privacy in their offices, desks, and file cabinets, because co-workers are frequently at liberty to enter their work spaces to retrieve needed reports, documents, and files and that insisting on cumbersome warrant procedures when the government investigates suspected employee wrongdoing would impede workplace efficiency.

## A. Constitutionality of Searching Desks, Lockers, File Cabinets, Computers, Squad Cars, etc. for Evidence of Work-Related Misconduct

A police officer must have a reasonable expectation of privacy in the area searched in order to challenge the existence of grounds for a search.[39] Even when such an expectation is present, the department is allowed to conduct a search whenever it has reasonable suspicion that the search will turn up evidence of work-related misconduct.[40] Putting these two requirements together, a police officer can successfully challenge a supervisory search for evidence of work-related misconduct only if: (1) the officer has a reasonable expectation of privacy in the location searched, and (2) the search is conducted without reasonable suspicion of job-related misconduct.

Figure 11.4
**Constitutionality of Workplace Searches**

> A supervisory search of an officer's desk, locker, file cabinet, computer, squad car, etc. for evidence of work-related misconduct violates an officer's Fourth Amendment rights only if:
>
> 1.  the officer has a reasonable expectation of privacy in the location searched, and
> 2.  the search is conducted without reasonable suspicion of work-related misconduct.

---

[37]  **O'Connor v. Ortega, 480 U.S. 709, 107 S. Ct. 1492, 94 L. Ed. 2d 714 (1987)**; Skinner v. Railway Labor Executives' Ass'n, 489 U.S. 602, 109 S. Ct. 1402, 103 L. Ed. 2d 639 (1989); *see also* 4 LAFAVE, SEARCH & SEIZURE § 10.3(d), at 487-488 (3d ed. 1996) (warrant requirement does not apply when department is engaged in internal investigation of work-related criminal conduct).

[38]  *Supra* note 37.

[39]  *Id.*; Rakas v. Illinois, 439 U.S. 128, 99 S. Ct. 421, 58 L. Ed. 2d 387 (1978); Gossmeyer v. McDonald, 128 F.3d 481 (7th Cir. 1997); State v. Nelson, 189 W. Va. 778, 434 S.E.2d 697 (1993).

[40]  **O'Connor v. Ortega**, *supra* note 37.

Police officers generally fare poorly on the first inquiry, making the second one unnecessary. No reasonable expectation of privacy is recommended in property issued for official use, such as desks, lockers, file cabinets, computers, and squad cars, unless the officer is entitled to exclusive dominion and control over them.[41] For example, an officer whose workstation is located in an open space accessible to co-workers or members of the public has no reasonable expectation of privacy in documents located on top of his or her desk or even documents located inside if others have keys and regularly enter the desk to retrieve correspondence, files, and reports.[42] The same holds true for an officer's locker; no reasonable expectation of privacy exists if the officer's supervisor has a master key or a copy of the combination and routinely enters to remove work-related materials.[43]

Police department regulations can also affect an officer's privacy expectations. Regulations, for example, commonly reserve the right to inspect lockers and squad cars at any time and for any reason. The retention of an unlimited right of inspection negates the existence of a reasonable expectation of privacy.[44] A Texas court recently held that a police officer lacked a constitutionally protected privacy interest in objects placed in the trunk of his patrol car because police department regulations reserved an unlimited right of inspection.[45]

---

[41]    *Id.* (reasonable expectation of privacy existed in contents of locked file cabinet in locked office provided for employee's exclusive use); United States v. Taketa, 923 F.2d 665 (9th Cir. 1991) (reasonable expectation of privacy existed in airport DEA agent's office where the office was provided for his exclusive use, was not open to the public, was not subject to regular inspection visits by DEA personnel, and no regulation provided for a right of inspection); United States v. Slanina, 283 F.3d 670 (5th Cir. 2002) (fire marshal had reasonable expectation of privacy in pornographic files stored on his work computer located in his officer where: (1) his office was private, (2) the door was kept locked, (3) access to his computer was protected by a password, and (4) city had no policy forbidding employees from storing personal information on city computers or warning them that their computer usage would be monitored.). *See also generally,* L. Camille Hebert, *Searches of Employer Property in Which Employees Have Interest,* 1 EMPL. PRIVACY LAW § 8:6 (2002).

[42]    **O'Connor v. Ortega,** *supra* note 37 ("Public employees' expectations of privacy in their offices, desks and file cabinets, like similar expectations of employees in the private sector, may be reduced by virtue of actual office practices and procedures. . ."); United States v. Simons, 206 F.3d 392 (4th Cir. 2000) (holding that in light of employer policy to inspect and monitor Internet activity, government employee had no reasonable expectation of privacy in files transferred from Internet); Sacramento County Deputy Sheriff's Ass'n v. County of Sacramento, 51 Cal. App.4th 1468, 59 Cal. Rptr. 2d 834 (1997) (jail employee did not have a reasonable expectation of privacy in office that was not assigned to his exclusive use and that had no lock on the door).

[43]    Shaffer v. Field, 339 F. Supp. 997 (C.D. Cal. 1972); Moore v. Constantine, 191 A.D.2d 769, 594 N.Y.S.2d 395 (1993).

[44]    American Postal Workers Union v. United States Postal Serv., 871 F.2d 556 (6th Cir. 1989) (concluding that employees lacked a reasonable expectation of privacy in lockers because regulations allowed for inspections); Los Angeles Police Protection League v. Gates, 579 F. Supp. 36, 44 (C.D. Cal. 1984) (same); People v. Rosa, 928 P.2d 1365 (Colo. Ct. App. 1996) (same); *but see* United States v. Speights, 557 F.2d 362 (3d Cir. 1977) (reasonable expectation of privacy existed in lockers where officers supplied their own locks and department regulations did not provide for inspections or searches).

[45]    State v. Stoddard, 909 S.W.2d 454 (Tex. Crim. App. 1994). *See also* Martin v. State, 686 A.2d 1130 (Md. Ct. App. 1996) (Defendant lacked reasonable expectation of privacy in police vehicle that he was authorized to use where department placed restrictions on vehicle's use; vehicle was subject to inspections by supervisor at any time; vehicle could be operated by common key and used by other officers if necessary; and defendant testified that he, in his supervisory capacity, believed he had right to enter and inspect vehicles similarly entrusted to other officers.).

An officer's personal belongings stand on a different footing. A constitutionally protected privacy interest exists in belongings brought into the workplace for an officer's personal use, such as lunch bags and purses.[46] As a result, a search of personal belongings requires reasonable suspicion that the search will turn up evidence that the officer is guilty of job-related misconduct.[47]

The lesser reasonable suspicion standard applies only to searches conducted for an administrative purpose. Police officers are not subject to a watered-down version of the Fourth Amendment when the police department conducts a criminal investigation.[48] In *Cerrone v. Cahill*,[49] an officer suspected of criminal wrongdoing was transported in a squad car to a second location where he was read his *Miranda* rights, informed that he was the target of a criminal investigation, and questioned for six hours. The court held that the traditional probable cause standard applied, even though the suspected wrongdoing was work-related, because the police were seeking evidence to build a criminal case.

The original purpose of the search determines whether the reasonable suspicion or probable cause standard applies. The reasonable suspicion standard applies when the search is conducted for an administrative purpose, even though the search turns up evidence that is later offered against the officer in a criminal prosecution.[50]

## B. Mandatory Drug Testing

Drugs abuse affects all levels of society. No one knows for certain how prevalent this problem is in the ranks of police departments, but considering the high stress levels associated with police work, there is no reason to assume that it is less pervasive here than elsewhere. Many police departments have drug testing programs. Requiring an officer to produce a urine sample for drug testing is considered a search.[51] Consequently, drug testing programs must satisfy Fourth Amendment standards of reasonableness. A police officer may be

---

[46] **O'Connor v. Ortega**, *supra* note 37 ("Even when an officer has a reasonable expectation of privacy, the department may always initiate a search if it has "reasonable grounds for suspecting that the search will turn up evidence that the employee is guilty of work-related misconduct, or that the search is necessary for a noninvestigatory work-related purpose."); United States v. Chandler, 197 F.3d 1198 (8th Cir. 1999).

[47] *See* cases *supra* note 46.

[48] United States v. Taketa, *supra* note 41 ("[W]here the search is conducted by the government employer to further a criminal investigation, the traditional requirements of probable cause and warrant are applicable."); United States v. Jones, 286 F.3d 1146 (9th Cir. 2002) (FBI's warrantless search of city employee's office violated Fourth Amendment where search was not a supervisory search for work-related purposes, but was instead conducted solely for law enforcement purposes).

[49] 84 F. Supp. 2d 330 (N.D.N.Y. 2000).

[50] *See, e.g.*, United States v. Simons, *supra* note 42.

[51] **Schmerber v. California, 384 U.S. 757, 87 S. Ct. 1826, 16 L. Ed. 2d 908 (1966)**; Skinner v. Railway Labor Executives' Ass'n, 489 U.S. 602, 109 S. Ct. 1402, 103 L. Ed. 2d 639 (1989); **National Treasury Employees Union v. Von Raab, 489 U.S. 656, 109 S. Ct. 1384, 103 L. Ed. 2d 685 (1989)**.

compelled to undergo drug testing only if: (1) the department has a reasonable suspicion that the particular officer is using drugs, or (2) the testing is conducted as part of a systematic, suspicionless drug screening program.

## 1. Drug Testing Based on Reasonable Suspicion

When the police department selectively singles out a particular officer to undergo drug testing, the Fourth Amendment demands reasonable suspicion of drug use.[52] Reasonable suspicion requires more than a rumor or a hunch; it can be based on a combination of factors, including deficient job performance, unexplained excessive absenteeism, apparent substance-related impairments, aberrant behavior, and financial difficulties.[53] Reasonable suspicion was found to exist where an officer was arrested for trespassing in a location frequented by drug dealers, failed to report the arrest as required by department regulations, and had excessive absenteeism.[54] On the other hand, it was not present where socializing with another officer suspected of drug use was the sole basis for the department's suspicion.[55]

## 2. Mandatory Testing Without Suspicion

Drug impairment can be present before an officer exhibits outward signs, making discovery through close supervision undependable. Because police officers carry weapons and drive high-speed vehicles, and momentary lapses of attention can cause fatal accidents, police departments have a special need to discover drug abuse before accidents happen. The Fourth Amendment allows searches to be conducted without particularized grounds for suspicion when the search serves a special need beyond the normal need for law enforcement.[56] This exception is known as a special needs exception. The special needs exception permits suspicionless drug testing of government employees who hold safety-sensitive positions, a category that includes police officers.[57]

---

[52]   Copeland v. Philadelphia Police Department, 840 F.2d 1139 (3d Cir. 1988), *cert. denied*, 490 U.S. 1004, 109 S. Ct. 1639, 104 L. Ed. 2d 153 (1989); Ford v. Dowd, 931 F.2d 1286 (8th Cir. 1991); Jackson v. Gates, 975 F.2d 648 (9th Cir. 1992); Nocera v. New York City Fire Commissioner, 921 F. Supp. 192 (S.D.N.Y. 1996). The suspected drug abuse does not have to involve conduct while on duty. *See* Palm Bay v. Bauman, 475 So. 2d 1322 (Fla. Dist. Ct. App. 1985) (testing for off-duty drug use justified by physical, mental, and psychological effects of drug use and on need to have police officers abide by the laws they enforce). The same is true for alcohol testing. Officers may be compelled to undergo alcohol testing based on reasonable suspicion of off-duty alcohol intoxication. *See, e.g.*, Grow v. City of Milwaukee, 84 F. Supp. 2d 990 (E.D. Wis. 2000) (off-duty police officer, encountered under circumstances in which intoxication could present a danger to public safety, may be compelled to undergo alcohol testing based on reasonable suspicion of intoxication).

[53]   Fraternal Order of Police Lodge No. 5 v. Tucker, 868 F.2d 74 (3d Cir. 1989); Copeland v. Philadelphia Police Department, *supra* note 52.

[54]   Nocera v. New York City Fire Commissioner, *supra* note 52. *See also* Felder v. Kelly, 210 A.D.2d 78, 619 N.Y.S.2d (1994).

[55]   Jackson v. Gates, *supra* note 52.

[56]   **National Treasury Employees Union v. Von Raab**, *supra* note 51.

[57]   *Id.*

As a result, police officers may be compelled to undergo drug testing, without individualized suspicion, when the testing is conducted as part of a systematic drug screening program.[58]

In order to be considered a systematic drug screening program, the selection process must be evenhanded and nondiscretionary.[59] Testing may be required at the time of employment; at scheduled periodic intervals; when applying for a promotion;[60] as part of regularly scheduled, routine medical exams;[61] after accidents;[62] after other triggering events;[63] or based on computerized random selection.[64]

## § 11.4   Fifth Amendment Protection against Self-Incrimination during Police Internal Affairs Investigations

When a police officer is suspected of misconduct, the police department internal affairs division will normally conduct an investigation into whether discipline is warranted. When the investigation involves matters that could lead to a criminal prosecution, there is a clash between the department's need for answers and the officer's Fifth Amendment privilege against self-incrimination. This section explores two related questions. First, can an officer be compelled, under a threat of job termination, to disclose information pertaining to criminal activity? And second, if an officer can be compelled to answer, can the officer's statement be used against him or her in a criminal prosecution?

The answer to both questions requires a brief review of Fifth Amendment protection against self-incrimination. The Fifth Amendment provides that "[n]o person . . . shall be compelled in any criminal case to be a witness against himself." The Fifth Amendment privilege against self-incrimination can be asserted during administrative proceedings, as well as judicial proceedings.[65] Conse-

---

[58]   *Id.*

[59]   *Id.*; National Federation of Federal Employees v. Cheney, 884 F.2d 603 (D.C. Cir. 1989), *cert. denied*, 493 U.S. 1056, 110 S. Ct. 864, 107 L. Ed. 2d 948 (1990); McCloskey v. Honolulu Police Dep't, 71 Haw. 568, 799 P.2d 953 (1990); New Jersey Transit PBA Local 304 v. New Jersey Transit Corp., 151 N.J. 531, 701 A.2d 1243 (1997).

[60]   **National Treasury Employees Union v. Von Raab**, *supra* note 51 (upholding Customs Service regulation requiring employees seeking transfer or promotions to certain Customs Service positions to submit to urinalysis).

[61]   Wrightsell v. Chicago, 678 F. Supp. 727 (N.D. Ill. 1988).

[62]   Skinner v. Railway Labor Executives Ass'n, *supra* note 51 (permitting suspicionless drug testing of railroad employees conducted pursuant to government regulations requiring testing of employees involved in major train accidents).

[63]   Delaraba v. Nassau County Police Department, 83 N.Y.2d 367, 632 N.E.2d 1251, 610 N.Y.S.2d 928 (1994).

[64]   *Id.*

[65]   Lefkowitz v. Turley, 414 U.S. 70, 77, 94 S. Ct. 316, 322, 38 L. Ed. 2d 274 (1973) ("The [Fifth] Amendment not only protects the individual against being involuntarily called as a witness against himself in a criminal prosecution but also privileges him not to answer official questions put to him in any other proceeding, civil or criminal, formal or informal, where the answers might incriminate him in future criminal proceedings.").

quently, police officers undergoing an internal affairs investigation are protected by the Fifth Amendment.

The police department, as an employer, nevertheless, has a right to demand that officers account for their official conduct. The spectacle of police officers taking the Fifth Amendment when called upon to account for their official conduct is singularly unappealing. As a result, statutes and departmental regulations often make an officer's refusal to answer questions relating to his or her official conduct grounds for automatic dismissal.[66] You may be wondering how, if the Fifth Amendment privilege against self-incrimination applies, an officer can be fired for refusing to answer questions that relate to criminal activity.

The answer lies in immunity, a concept that was covered in Chapter 7.[67] Officers can be compelled to answer questions pertaining to criminal activity provided they are granted immunity from use of compelled statements (and evidence derived from them) in a criminal prosecution. In fact, immunity automatically attaches when the police department compels an officer to answer potentially incriminating questions under the threat of job termination. This immunity is called *Garrity* immunity because it derives from *Garrity v. New Jersey*.[68] In *Garrity*, a police officer undergoing an internal investigation for "fixing" traffic tickets was told that he could invoke the Fifth Amendment, but that if he did so, he would be discharged. The officer disclosed incriminating information for which he was later prosecuted. The Supreme Court ruled that when an officer makes a statement under threat of dismissal for refusing to answer, the statement is compelled and cannot be used against the officer in a criminal prosecution. In a subsequent case,[69] the Court explained that the Fifth Amendment does not bar compulsion to extract self-incriminat-

---

[66] *See, e.g.*, New York Police Department Patrol Guide, Procedure 206-13 (Jan. 1, 2000) (warning officers that "if [they] refuse to testify or to answer questions relating to the performance of [their] official duties, [they] will be subject to departmental charges, which could result in [their] dismissal from the Police Department"); 1 Los Angeles Police Dep't Manual § 210.47 (2000) ("When police officers acquire knowledge of facts which will tend to incriminate any person, it is their duty to disclose such facts to their superiors and to testify freely concerning such facts when called upon to do so, even at the risk of self-incrimination. It is a violation of duty for police officers to refuse to disclose pertinent facts within their knowledge, and such neglect of duty can result in disciplinary action up to and including termination.") *quoted in* Steven D. Clymer, *Compelled Statements from Police Officers and Garrity Immunity*, 76 N.Y.U. L. Rev. 1309 at fn. 15 (2001).

[67] Testimony compelled under a grant of immunity is covered in § 7.3(C).

[68] 385 U.S. 493, 87 S. Ct. 616, 17 L. Ed. 2d 562 (1967) (Fifth Amendment prohibits use in subsequent criminal proceedings of statements obtained under threat of removal from office). For a discussion of "*Garrity* immunity," *see generally* Steven D. Clymer, *Compelled Statements from Police Officers and Garrity Immunity*, 76 N.Y.U. L. Rev. 1309 (2001); J. Michael McGuinness, *Representing Law Enforcement Officers in Personnel Disputes And Employment Litigation*, 77 AM. JUR. TRIALS 1, § 10 (2000); Kate E. Bloch, *Police Officers Accused of Crime: Prosecutorial and Fifth Amendment Risks Posed by Police-Elicited "Use Immunized" Statements*, 1992 U. Ill. L. Rev. 625 (1992). For cases applying "*Garrity* immunity," *see* United States v. Koon, 34 F.3d 1416 (9th Cir. 1994); United States. v. Vangates, 287 F.3d 1315 (11th Cir. 2002).

[69] Chavez v. Martinez, 538 U.S. 760, 123 S. Ct. 1994, 155 L. Ed. 2d 984 (2003) ("[G]overnments may penalize public employees . . . with loss of their jobs . . . to induce them to respond to relevant inquiries, so long as the answers elicited (and their fruits) are immunized from use in any criminal case against the speaker.").

ing statements. Rather, it bars the *courtroom use* of compelled statements in the criminal prosecution of the maker. However, no violation occurs if the statement is never used. Accordingly, the department may threaten an officer with dismissal to obtain information needed for an internal investigation.[70] However, the department is limited to making disciplinary use of the information; compelled information may not be used in a criminal prosecution.[71]

Officers undergoing internal affairs investigations may be tempted to deny the charges and lie. This, too, provides grounds for termination.[72]

## § 11.5    Fourteenth Amendment Protection for a Police Officer's Personal Liberty

Police department regulations impose significant restrictions on a police officer's liberty, both on and off the job. In fact, the profession is more highly regulated than any career outside the military. One court commented on this while discussing a 72-page manual of police department rules and regulations.[73] We have culled a few of the regulations mentioned in the opinion to provide a sampling of the range of subjects that police department regulations address:

- **Standard of Conduct.** Members and employees shall conduct their private and professional lives in such a manner as to avoid bringing the department into disrepute.

- **Debts—Incurring and Payment.** Members and employees shall pay all just debts and legal liabilities incurred by them.

- **Persons and Places of Bad Reputation.** Members and employees shall not frequent places of bad reputation, nor associate with persons of bad reputation, except as may be required in the course of police duty.

- **Liquor.** Employees of the department shall refrain from drinking intoxicating beverages for a period of at least four (4) hours before going on duty.

---

[70] **Lingler v. Fechko, 312 F.3d 237 (6th Cir. 2002)** (Fifth Amendment not violated by compelling officers to furnish potentially incriminating information as part of an internal affairs investigation where statement was not used against them in a criminal prosecution); **Wiley v. Mayor & City Council of Baltimore, 58 F.3d 773 (4th Cir. 1995)** (officers' Fifth Amendment rights were not violated when they were required as a condition of continued employment to take polygraph examination during an internal investigation into shooting incident, but were not asked to waive their Fifth Amendment privilege against self-incrimination and were never charged with any offense); Erwin v. Price, 778 F.2d 668 (11th Cir. 1986) (affirming dismissal of police officer who refused to answer specific questions about an alleged gun-pointing incident).

[71] *See, e.g.*, Driebel v. Milwaukee, 298 F.3d 622 fn. 8 (7th Cir. 2002); Riggins v. Walter, 279 F.3d 422, 431 (7th Cir. 1995) (per curiam); Confederation of Police v. Conlisk, 489 F.2d 891, 894 (7th Cir. 1973).

[72] LaChance v. Erickson, 522 U.S. 262, 118 S. Ct. 753, 130 L. Ed. 2d 695 (1998). *See also* United States v. Veal, 153 F.3d 1233 (11th Cir. 1998) (the Fifth Amendment does not protect an officer who makes false statements under oath during an internal investigation from a later criminal prosecution for perjury).

[73] Policemen's Benevolent Association of New Jersey, Local 318 v. Township of Washington, 850 F.2d 133 (3d Cir. 1988).

- **Smoking While On Duty.** Members shall not smoke on duty while in direct contact with the public nor when in uniform in public view, except that smoking is permitted in public view at mealtimes and while patrolling in police automobiles, at which times it shall be as inconspicuous as possible.

- **Grooming.** Hair shall be evenly trimmed at all times while on duty. The hair shall at no point extend downward over the shirt collar in normal posture. Sideburns shall not extend below the bottom of the ear. The maximum width at the bottom of the sideburns shall not exceed $1^3/_4$ inches. A clean-shaven appearance is required, except that mustaches are permitted. Mustaches shall be neatly trimmed and shall not extend more than $^1/_4$ inch beyond the corners of the mouth nor more than $^1/_4$ inch below the corners of the mouth. Remainder of the face shall be clean shaven.

- **Use of Derogatory Terms.** Members and employees shall neither speak disparagingly of any race or minority group, nor refer to them in insolent or insulting terms of speech, whether prisoners or otherwise.

The justification for heightened regulation is found in the unique service that police officers perform, a service that sets them apart from ordinary citizens and from civil servants in other branches of government. Courts often use the phrase "paramilitary organization" to explain why restrictions on a police officer's conduct are condoned that would not be condoned if imposed on employees in other branches of government service. The explanation goes as follows:

> Police officers are members of quasi-military organizations called upon for duty at all times, armed at almost all times, and exercising the most awesome and dangerous power that a democratic state possesses with respect to its residents—the power to use lawful force to arrest and detain them. The need in a democratic society for public confidence, respect and approbation of the public officials on whom the state confers that awesome power is significantly greater than the state's need to instill confidence in the integrity of [other employees].[74]

When a police officer is unable to find a constitutional basis for challenging a police department regulation under any specific Bill of Rights guarantee, the officer is likely to claim that the regulation violates substantive due process.[75] This theory is grounded in the Fourteenth Amendment, which prohibits the government from arbitrarily depriving citizens of their liberty. In challenging a regulation on this theory, the officer is alleging that the regulation is arbitrary and capricious. This theory rarely succeeds because the officer must convince the court that the regulation has no rational relationship to any legitimate interest of the police department as an employer.[76] The perception of police departments as paramilitary organizations makes this task difficult indeed.

---

[74] *Id.*
[75] Substantive due process is discussed in §§ 1.15(B) and 10.15.
[76] Kelley v. Johnson, 425 U.S. 238, 96 S. Ct. 1440, 47 L. Ed. 2d 708 (1976).

Police department regulations most frequently challenged are discussed below.

## A. Regulation of Height, Weight, Grooming, and Personal Appearance

No one seriously questions the authority of police departments to require police officers to wear uniforms and to be neat and clean in appearance. However, police department regulations often go beyond this and regulate height, weight, hairstyle, and other aspects of an officer's personal appearance.

In *Kelley v. Johnson*,[77] a Patrolmen's Benevolent Association lodged an unsuccessful attack on a police department grooming standard that prescribed style and length of hair and prohibited beards and goatees. The Supreme Court pointed to the fact that the overwhelming majority of police departments require officers to wear uniforms and regulate their appearance as evidence that those in charge of directing the operations of police department regard similarity in appearance as desirable. Whether the reason was to make police officers readily recognizable to the public or for the esprit de corps that similarity in appearance fosters did not matter—either justification was sufficient to defeat the plaintiff's claim that the regulation had no rational relationship to the department's interest as an employer.

Challenges to police department regulations establishing maximum weight restrictions have met the same fate.[78] Police departments have a legitimate interest in an officer's weight because obesity is likely to make it difficult for an officer to execute some of the more strenuous tasks that the job requires. Constitutional challenges to regulations establishing maximum weights have, therefore, failed.

Challenges to police department regulations establishing minimum height and weight, in contrast, often succeed—but not on constitutional grounds. Title VII of the Civil Rights Act of 1964 prohibits employers from discriminating against job applicants based on their race, color, religion, gender, or national origin.[79] Minimum height and weight requirements disproportionately disqualify women and members of certain minority groups from securing jobs as police officers. Requirements that have this effect are illegal under Title VII unless they measure traits that are necessary for the successful performance of the job.[80] Police departments have had difficulty sustaining minimum height and weight requirements.[81]

---

[77]    *Id.*
[78]    *See, e.g.*, Dade County v. Wolf, 274 So. 2d 584 (Fla. 1973), *cert. denied*, 414 U.S. 1116, 94 S. Ct. 849, 38 L. Ed. 2d 743 (1973); Gray v. City of Florissant, 588 S.W.2d 722 (Mo. 1979).
[79]    Title VII protection against employment discrimination is discussed in § 11.7 *infra.*
[80]    Evans, *Height, Weight and Physical Agility Requirements: Title VII and Public Safety Employment*, 8 J. Pol. Sci. & Admin. 414 (1980).
[81]    Dothard v. Rawlinson, 433 U.S. 321, 97 S. Ct. 2720, 53 L. Ed. 2d 786 (1977).

## B. Citizenship Requirements

A majority of states require police officers to be United States citizens. In *Foley v. Connelie*,[82] a resident alien, turned down for a position as a New York state trooper, challenged this requirement as a denial of equal protection of the laws. The Supreme Court disagreed. Pointing out that police officers are vested with broad discretion that operates "in the most sensitive areas of daily life," the Court held that it is legitimate for states to confine police employment to those whom it "may reasonably presume to be more familiar with and sympathetic to American traditions."

## C. Residency Requirements

Many jurisdictions also have residency rules, requiring police officers to live in the political subdivision in which they are employed. The job-relatedness of residency requirements was upheld in *McCarthy v. Philadelphia Civil Service Commission*[83] on the grounds that residing in the district improves an officer's job effectiveness by increasing an officer's knowledge of local geography, problems of the local community, and stake in its progress, and decreases problems of tardiness.

## D. Restrictions on Outside Employment

Police officers are generally prohibited from holding outside employment. Courts have shown little sympathy to suits challenging moonlighting restrictions, explaining that because police officers are required to make split-second decisions that tax their mental and physical capabilities to the limits, it is reasonable for police departments to insist that officers forego other employment that might lead to fatigue on the job.[84]

## E. Regulation of Smoking

As society has become more health-conscious, regulations banning smoking in the workplace are becoming increasingly common. In *Grusendorf v. City of Oklahoma City*,[85] a firefighter trainee unsuccessfully challenged a fire department regulation that prohibited firefighters from smoking cigarettes

---

[82]    435 U.S. 291, 98 S. Ct. 1067, 55 L. Ed. 2d 287 (1978).

[83]    424 U.S. 645, 96 S. Ct. 1154, 47 L. Ed. 2d 366 (1976).

[84]    Reichelderfer v. Ihrie, 59 F.2d 873 (D.C. Cir. 1932), *cert. denied*, 287 U.S. 631, 53 S. Ct. 82, 77 L. Ed. 2d 547 (1932); Hayes v. Civil Service Comm'n, 348 Ill. App. 346, 108 N.E.2d 505 (1952); Hopwood v. Paducah, 424 S.W.2d 134 (Ky. 1968); Isola v. Belmar, 112 A.2d 738 (N.J. 1955); Flood v. Kennedy, 12 N.Y.2d 345, 239 N.Y.S.2d 665, 190 N.E.2d 13 (1963). *But see* Firemen v. City of Crowley, 280 So. 2d 897 (La. 1973).

[85]    816 F.2d 539 (10th Cir. 1987).

either on or off duty for one year after being hired. The officer argued that this regulation impermissibly infringed on his Fourteenth Amendment liberty outside the workplace. The court disagreed. Noting that public safety employers have a legitimate interest in the health and fitness of employees, the court rejected the officer's claim that a total ban on smoking is arbitrary.

### F. Off-Duty Sexual Activity

Police departments regulations typically require police officers to conduct their private lives so as avoid bringing the department into disrepute.[86] When a police officer is disciplined for having an extramarital affair, the court must decide whether it is legitimate for a police department to delve into this aspect of an officer's private life. It is unquestionably legitimate when the officer's behavior has an adverse effect on the department.[87] Dismissal, for example, was upheld in a case in which a police chief's adulterous affair became front page news when he was sued for nonsupport of an illegitimate child.[88] Dismissals have also been upheld when the affair is with another officer or with the spouse of another officer because the conduct is likely to have an adverse effect on the department.[89] When an officer's private life has no repercussions in the workplace, case law is divided on whether an officer may be disciplined for having an illicit affair. Older cases treated police officers as role models, placed them on a moral pedestal, and punished them when they fell off.[90] However, a growing number of modern courts allow discipline for private sexual conduct only when the officer's conduct has an adverse effect on the department.[91]

---

[86]  See, e.g., Mercure v. Van Buren Township, 81 F. Supp. 2d 814 (E.D. Mich. 2000)

[87]  See, e.g., Fugate v. Phoenix Civil Service Board, 791 F.2d 736 (9th Cir. 1986) (affirming discharge for patronizing prostitutes).

[88]  Borough of Riegelsville v. Miller, 162 Pa. Commw. 654, 939 A.2d 1258 (1994).

[89]  Mercure v. Van Buren Township, supra note 86 (affirming dismissal for having affair with estranged wife of superior officer); City of Sherman v. Henry, 928 S.W.2d 464 (Tex. 1996) (same); Shawgo v. Spradlin, 701 F.2d 470, 483 (5th Cir. 1983) (upholding a police department's anti-cohabitation policy forbidding members of the department, especially those different in rank, to share an apartment or to cohabit).

[90]  Fabio v. Civil Service Commission of the City of Philadelphia, 30 Pa. Commw. 203, 373 A.2d 751 (1977), aff'd, 489 Pa. 309, 414 A.2d 82 (1980) (rejecting claim that police officer's constitutional rights were violated as a result of his dismissal for adultery; observing that police officers are held to a higher standard of conduct than other citizens).

[91]  Briggs v. North Muskegon Police Dep't, 563 F. Supp. 585 (W.D. Mich. 1983), aff'd mem., 746 F.2d 1475 (6th Cir. 1984), cert. denied, 473 U.S. 909, 105 S. Ct. 3535, 87 L. Ed. 2d 659 (1985) (married police officer's constitutional rights were violated when he was fired for living with a married woman who was not his wife); Thorne v. City of El Segundo, 726 F.2d 459 (9th Cir. 1983), cert. denied, 469 U.S. 979, 105 S. Ct. 380, 83 L. Ed. 2d 315 (1984) (female applicant's constitutional rights were violated when she was denied employment as a police officer because she had had an affair with a married police officer on the force); Reuter v. Skipper, 832 F. Supp. 1420 (D. Or. 1993) (female corrections officer could not be terminated for having relationship with ex-felon).

# § 11.6  Procedural Due Process in Police Disciplinary Actions

This section revisits Larry Lovermore's dispute with the Whosville Police Department. Lovermore's final complaint was that the Whosville Police Department deprived him of procedural due process by removing his name from the candidate list for promotion and subsequently firing him—both without a hearing. This complaint is rooted in the Fourteenth Amendment, which provides that no state shall deprive any person of life, liberty, or property without due process. Lovermore's due process right to a hearing will hinge on whether the Whosville Police Department's personnel actions deprived him of liberty or property. Only then would the Fourteenth Amendment entitle him to a hearing.[92]

## A.  "Property Interests"

A public employee's right to his or her job can constitute property for purposes of the Fourteenth Amendment.[93] However, to be considered property, the job must be one that cannot be taken away without *just cause*.[94] Just cause is a technical term that refers to relatively serious misconduct.[95] One author notes:

> Examples of reasons commonly establishing just cause include inadequate performance, sexual harassment, alcohol misuse, mistreatment of prisoners, and insubordination. Generally, the misconduct in issue must be substantial as opposed to something trivial. Insignificant or minor issues, such as isolated neglect of duty, excusable absence, even some rudeness have been held not to constitute just cause.[96]

Whether an officer's job is one that cannot be taken away without just cause is determined from sources outside the Fourteenth Amendment;[97] these sources include the terms of the officer's employment contract, police department personnel regulations, personnel handbooks, municipal ordinances, provisions of state law, and terms of collective bargaining agreements.[98] Officers

---

[92]  State statutes, local ordinances, department regulations, and collective bargaining agreements may also entitle a police officer to a hearing. These sources of hearing rights are beyond the scope of this chapter.

[93]  Board of Regents v. Roth, 408 U.S. 564, 92 S. Ct. 2701, 33 L. Ed. 2d 548 (1972) ("To have a property interest in a benefit, a person . . . must . . . have a legitimate claim of entitlement . . ."); Perry v. Sindermann, 408 U.S. 593, 92 S. Ct. 2694, 2698, 33 L. Ed. 2d 570 (1972) (same); Cleveland Bd. of Education v. Loudermill, 470 U.S. 532, 105 S. Ct.1487, 84 L. Ed. 2d 494 (1985) (classified civil service employee had property interest in continued employment because a state statute provided that such employees could not be dismissed except for certain specified reasons); Ciambriello v. County of Nassau, 292 F.3d 307 (2d Cir. 2002) (A police officer has a property interest in continued employment if the officer is guaranteed continued employment absent just cause for discharge).

[94]  *See* authorities *supra* note 93.

[95]  J. Michael McGuinness, *Representing Law Enforcement Officers in Personnel Disputes And Employment Litigation*, 77 AM. JUR. TRIALS 1, at § 15 (2000).

[96]  *Id.*

[97]  Bishop v. Wood, 426 U.S. 341, 344, 96 S. Ct. 2074, 2077, 48 L. Ed. 2d 684 (1976).

[98]  Bishop v. Wood, *supra* note 97; Golem v. Village of Put-In Bay, 222 F. Supp. 2d 924 (N. D. Ohio 2002).

who can be dismissed only for just cause are generally called permanent or tenured employees. This status is normally acquired only after satisfactory completion of a probationary period during which an officer can be dismissed for any reason.[99] Consequently, probationary or nontenured officers do not have property rights in their jobs.[100]

If Lovermore had tenure, the Fourteenth Amendment would entitle him to a hearing on whether grounds existed for his discharge, but not on whether grounds existed for removing his name from the candidate list.[101] A property right requires a legitimate claim of entitlement.[102] Because promotional decisions are normally discretionary, there is no property right in a promotion.[103] Accordingly, Lovermore was not entitled to a hearing to contest the removal of his name from the promotion list.

## B. Requirements of Procedural Due Process

A hearing provides a valuable safeguard against mistaken decisions. Officers who have a property right in their job may not be dismissed or demoted without receiving the following procedural rights: (1) notice of the charges; (2) a hearing before an impartial decisionmaker; (3) an opportunity to challenge the department's evidence; and (4) an opportunity to tell their version of the story and to present testimony.[104] While these rights must be provided at some point in the termination process, they need not be provided beforehand. Government employers are allowed to provide a truncated pretermination hearing, followed by a full evidentiary hearing afterward.[105]

---

[99]   Davis v. City of Chicago, 841 F.2d 186 (7th Cir. 1988); Fontano v. City of Chicago, 820 F.2d 213 (7th Cir. 1987).

[100]  See, e.g. Blanding v. Pennsylvania State Police,12 F.3d 1303 (3d Cir. 1993) (probationary officer did not have property right in continued employment); Pipkin v. Pennsylvania State Police, 693 A.2d 190 (Pa. 1997) (same).

[101]  Courts have uniformly rejected attempts to classify a police officer's expectation of promotion as a constitutionally protected property interest where the appointing authority has discretion to consider factors in addition to an applicant's test scores and ranking on an eligibility list. See, e.g., Meyer v. City of Joplin, 281 F.3d 759 (8th 2002) (sergeant had no constitutionally protected property interest in promotion to rank of lieutenant, even though he had highest score on competitive examination and was ranked as one of top three candidates, where personnel rules grant police chief discretion to consider subjective factors as well as competitive examination score); McMenemy v. City of Rochester, 241 F.3d 279 (2d Cir. 2001) (same); Nunez v. City of Los Angeles, 147 F.3d 867 (9th Cir. 1998) (same); Stuart v. Roache, 951 F.2d 446, 455 (1st Cir. 1991), cert. denied, 504 U.S. 913, 112 S. Ct. 1948, 118 L. Ed. 2d 553 (1992) (same); Olive v. City of Scottsdale, supra note 2 (same).

[102]  Board of Regents v. Roth, supra note 93; Nunez v. City of Los Angeles, supra note 101; McMenemy v. City of Rochester, supra note 101; Olive v. City of Scottsdale, supra note 2.

[103]  See authorities supra note 102.

[104]  Schweiker v. McClure, 456 U.S. 188, 102 S. Ct. 1665, 72 L. Ed. 2d 1 (1982); Brown v. Los Angeles, 102 Cal. App. 4th 155, 125 Cal. Rptr. 2d 474 (2002) ("At a minimum, an individual entitled to procedural due process should be accorded: written notice of the grounds for the disciplinary measures; disclosure of the evidence supporting the disciplinary grounds; the right to present witnesses and to confront adverse witnesses; the right to be represented by counsel; a fair and impartial decisionmaker; and a written statement from the fact finder listing the evidence relied upon and the reasons for the determination made.").

[105]  Cleveland Bd. of Edu. v. Loudermill, supra note 93.

The purpose of the pretermination hearing is to provide an initial check against mistaken decisions.[106] If a two-stage procedure is used, the officer is entitled at the pretermination stage to: (1) oral or written notice of the charges; (2) an explanation of the department's evidence; and (3) an opportunity to tell his or her side of the story.[107] The pretermination hearing does not have to be elaborate.[108] An adequate pretermination hearing, for example, was provided where a police lieutenant visited the hospital in which the officer was staying, showed him a copy of a citizen's complaint charging him with sexual misconduct, and asked him whether he wanted to respond.[109]

An officer who receives a truncated pretermination hearing must be given a more complete post-discharge hearing at which the four rights mentioned at the beginning of this section—formal notice of the charges, a hearing before an impartial decisionmaker, an opportunity to cross-examine the department's witnesses, and the right to present testimony—are provided.

## C. "Liberty Interest"

The Fourteenth Amendment also prohibits deprivations of "liberty" without due process. The term "liberty" encompasses a broad array of interests that include the right to pursue one's chosen occupation.[110] Although probationary officers lack a property right in their job, they have a liberty interest in their ability to take advantage of future employment opportunities.[111] This interest is infringed when a probationary officer is dismissed on the basis of "stigmatizing charges" that foreclose the officer's ability to obtain other employment in the law enforcement field. When this occurs, the officer is entitled to a "name clearing" hearing.[112]

Three conditions are necessary to be entitled to a name-clearing hearing. The charges must be: (1) false, (2) "stigmatizing," and (3) disclosed to the public.[113] To be considered "stigmatizing," the charges must impugn the officer's honesty or integrity[114] and not simply his or her professional competence

---

[106]   *Id.*

[107]   *Id.*

[108]   *Id.*

[109]   Buckner v. City of Highland Park, 901 F.2d 491 (6th Cir. 1990).

[110]   Paul v. Davis, 424 U.S. 693, 96 S. Ct. 1155, 47 L. Ed. 2d 405 (1976).

[111]   *See, e.g.*, Graham v. Johnson, 249 F. Supp. 2d 563 (E.D. Pa. 2003) (probationary police officer entitled to name-clearing hearing in order to refute charges of statutory sexual assault and corrupting the morals of a minor that led to termination of his employment).

[112]   Paul v. Davis, *supra* note 110; Palmer v. City of Monticello, 31 F.3d 1499, 1503 (10th Cir. 1994) (to establish claim of deprivation of liberty interest, plaintiff must prove "termination based on a publicized charge of sufficient opprobrium that would make plaintiff an unlikely candidate" for employment).

[113]   *See* cases *supra* note 112.

[114]   *See, e.g.*, Gibson v. Caruthersville School Dist. No. 8, 36 F.3d 768 (8th Cir. 2003) ("The requisite stigma has been found when the allegations involve 'dishonesty, immorality, criminality, racism, or the like.'"); Hade v. City of Fremont, 246 F. Supp. 2d 837 (N.D. Ohio 2003) (allegation of sexual improprieties).

or job performance.[115] As one court put it, the charges must brand the employee "with a badge of infamy." The requisite stigma exists when the charges involve lying,[116] dishonesty,[117] corruption,[118] misappropriation of property, taking bribes, racism, and the like.

Finally, there must be a public disclosure.[119] Placing a stigmatizing letter in a police officer's personnel file is not enough to entitle the officer to a name-clearing hearing.[120] Until there has been an actual disclosure, the officer lacks a remedy.[121] The requirement of a "public disclosure" does not mean that the department has to hold a press conference.[122] This requirement is satisfied by the official release of information to a prospective employer or to other persons outside the department, even if only to a few.[123]

The right to a name-clearing hearing is a limited remedy. The officer is entitled to a hearing in which to refute the charges, but not to challenge the personnel action taken on the basis of them. Because probationary officers are dismissible without cause, the only right they have when wrongfully dismissed is the right to clear their name.[124]

## § 11.7   Employment Discrimination Based on Race, Color, Religion, Gender, or National Origin

In 1964, Congress enacted a federal law that prohibits employment discrimination. The Equal Employment Opportunities Act of 1964,[125] better known as Title VII, makes it an unlawful employment practice for employers to refuse to hire, discharge, or otherwise to discriminate against any person

---

[115]  *See, e.g.*, Shands v. City of Kennett, 993 F.2d 1337 (8th Cir. 1992) (statement to television news reporter that officer was discharged for "acts of insubordination" not stigmatizing); Robinson v. City of Montomery City, 809 F.2d 1355 (8th Cir. 1987) (press release issued by city stating that chief of police was dismissed because of city's dissatisfaction with his performance not stigmatizing).

[116]  Cronin v. Town v. Amesbury, 895 F. Supp. 375 (D. Mass. 1995) (public statement that former police chief was terminated for lying about writing a pornographic letter was stigmatizing).

[117]  Palmer v. City of Monticello, 31 F.3d 1499 (10th Cir. 1994) (accusation that probationary officer had falsified speeding ticket was stigmatizing).

[118]  Rosenstein v. Dallas, 876 F.2d 392 (5th Cir. 1989) (charges that probationary officer made harassing and obscene telephone calls to fellow police officer was stigmatizing).

[119]  Olivieri v. Rodriguez, 944 F. Supp. 686 (N.D. Ill. 1996) (probationary officer terminated for sexual harassment was not entitled to a name-clearing hearing when there was no evidence that the information was disclosed outside the department).

[120]  Clark v. Maurer, 824 F.2d 565, 566 (7th Cir. 1987).

[121]  Olivieri v. Rodriguez, *supra* note 119.

[122]  Goss v. Lopez, 419 U.S. 565, 95 S. Ct. 729, 42 L. Ed. 2d 725 (1975).

[123]  Palmer v. City of Monticello, *supra* note 117 (charges for which officer was dismissed were discussed during a city council meeting attended by members of the public).

[124]  Board of Regents v. Roth, *supra* note 93, 408 U.S. at 573 n. 12, 92 S. Ct. at 2707 n. 12.

[125]  Civil Rights Act of 1964, § 701 *et seq.*, as amended, 42 U.S.C.A. § 2000e *et seq.* There are a vast array of federal, state, and local regulations that affect the employment relationship of police officers. Only a small handful of them are covered in this chapter. For an overview of the broad range of regulations, *see generally* James Baird & Ronald J. Kramer, *Municipal Personnel Practices*, MUNICIPAL LAW & PRACTICE IN ILLINOIS 10-1 (September, 2000); J. Michael McGuinness, *Representing Law Enforcement Officers in Personnel Disputes And Employment Litigation*, 77 AM. JUR. TRIALS 1 (2000).

because of the person's race, color, religion, gender, or national origin.[126] The employment practices of state and local governments were brought under Title VII in 1972. Since then, law enforcement agencies, long criticized for under-utilization of women and minorities, have repeatedly been called upon to defend Title VII discrimination suits. There are three different types of Title VII discrimination claims: (1) disparate treatment; (2) disparate impact; and (3) harassment.

## A. Disparate Treatment Discrimination

**Disparate treatment discrimination** occurs when one person is treated less favorably than others who are similarly situated because of race, color, religion, gender, or national origin.[127] Proof of a discriminatory intent is nec-essary to sue under this theory, but in certain situations, this intent will be inferred from the fact of differences in treatment.

To establish a Title VII disparate treatment claim, the plaintiff must prove that he or she: (1) belongs to a protected group; (2) was qualified and/or per-formed satisfactorily; (3) was subjected to adverse employment action; and (4) that similarly situated individuals received more favorable treatment.[128] Once a Title VII plaintiff establishes these things, there is a rebuttable presumption of discrimination, and the burden shifts to the employer to articulate a legiti-mate, nondiscriminatory reason for the allegedly biased treatment.[129] If the employer articulates a legitimate, nondiscriminatory reason for this treatment, the presumption of discrimination dissolves, and the employee then must demonstrate that the employer's nondiscriminatory explanation is pretextual (i.e., that the employer's explanation is untrue).[130] The employee may show this by proving either that the employer's explanation has no factual basis, was not the "real" reason, or was insufficient to justify the action taken.[131]

## B. Disparate Impact Discrimination

Most police departments have ceased practicing disparate treatment dis-crimination. However, compliance with Title VII requires more than this. In *Griggs v. Duke Power Company*,[132] the Supreme Court recognized a second theory, called **disparate impact discrimination**, which measurably increased

---

[126] Because sexual orientation is not the same thing as gender, Title VII does not cover employment dis-crimination based on sexual orientation. *See, e.g.*, De Santis v. Pacific Tel. & Tel. Co., 608 F.2d 327 (9th Cir. 1979); Holloway v. Arthur Andersen & Co., 566 F.2d 659 (9th Cir. 1977).

[127] International Bhd. of Teamsters v. United States, 431 U.S. 324, 335 n. 15, 97 S. Ct. 1843, 1854 n. 15, 52 L. Ed. 2d 396 (1977).

[128] McDonnell Douglas Corp. v. Green, 411 U.S. 792, 93 S. Ct. 1817, 36 L. Ed. 2d 668 (1973).

[129] *Id.*

[130] *Id.*

[131] *Id.*

[132] 401 U.S. 424, 91 S. Ct. 849, 28 L. Ed. 2d 158 (1971). The theory recognized in *Griggs* was subse-quently codified in Civil Rights Act of 1991, PUB L. NO. 102-166, § 3, 105 STAT. 1071, 1071 (1992).

the burdens of Title VII compliance. In *Griggs*, a private company used a professionally administered aptitude test to screen job applicants. Although the test was fair in form and was not employed with a discriminatory intent, it had the effect of disproportionately eliminating African-American applicants without being an accurate indicator of the knowledge, traits, or skills necessary for the job in question. Denouncing the use of this test as discriminatory, the Court declared:

> . . . [G]ood intent or absence of discriminatory intent does not redeem employment procedures or testing mechanisms that operate as "built-in headwinds" for minority groups and are unrelated to measuring job capability.

The form of discrimination recognized in *Griggs* is called *disparate impact* discrimination. Disparate impact discrimination occurs when an employer uses selection criteria that disproportionately eliminate members of a protected class without being valid predictors of the knowledge, skills, or traits necessary for the job. To establish a disparate impact discrimination claim, the plaintiff must demonstrate that the challenged selection requirement disproportionately eliminates members of a protected class (i.e., that they have significantly lower pass rates or are less likely to be hired or promoted than others to whom this requirement is applied). Once the plaintiff establishes this, there is a rebuttable presumption of discrimination and the burden shifts to the employer to justify its use of this selection requirement. Title VII does not prevent employers from attempting to ensure that persons hired or promoted are qualified for the job or from adopting appropriate screening devices to this end. What it requires is that when selection criteria disproportionately eliminate members of a protected class, the criteria be shown to be valid predictors of the knowledge, skills, or traits necessary for successful performance of the job.

The existence of statistically significant disparities in the representation of women and minorities in the ranks of police departments has made police departments sitting targets for disparate impact discrimination suits. Most police departments, for example, have minimum height, weight, strength, and agility qualifications. These qualifications unquestionably have a disparate impact on women and certain ethnic minorities and, consequently, are illegal under Title VII unless they can be shown, by professionally accepted methods, to be job-related.[133] In *Dothard v. Rawlinson*,[134] the Supreme Court threw out a five feet, two inches, 120-pound minimum height and weight requirement for the position of correctional officer because the corrections department was

---

[133]  Lanning v. Southeastern Pennsylvania Transportation Authority (SEPTA), 181 F.3d 487 (3d Cir. 1999) (aerobic fitness test requiring applicant to run 1.5 miles within 12 minutes, which disproportionately eliminated women applicants, held discriminatory when test was not shown, by professionally acceptable methods, to be significantly correlated with important elements of the job for which candidates are being evaluated); United States v. Commonwealth of Virginia, 620 F.2d 1018 (4th Cir. 1980) (requirement that state troopers be at least five feet nine inches tall and weigh at least 156 pounds, which effectively eliminated 98 percent of all women, violated Title VII when there was no showing of need for such requirement).

[134]  **433 U.S. 321, 97 S. Ct. 2720, 53 L. Ed. 2d 786 (1977).**

unable to establish this. While it may seem intuitively obvious that being at least five feet two inches and weighing at least 120 pounds or being able to do 25 situps or run an obstacle course in 25 seconds is necessary to have the physical strength and agility needed to be a police officer, courts do not take judicial notice of matters simply because they seem intuitively obvious to those who established the requirement. When hiring and promotional requirements are challenged, the department must able to prove, through professionally accepted methods, that the challenged selection criteria are predictive of or significantly correlated with important elements of the job in question. Police departments have frequently been forced to revise written entrance and promotional exams, restructure oral interviews, change methods of supervisory evaluations, and modify other selection criteria for lack of such proof. The disappointing record police departments have had in defending Title VII disparate impact discrimination suits highlights the need for police departments to hire qualified experts to conduct job analyses that identify important elements of work behavior for each position and to conduct validation studies designed to determine whether existing selection criteria are predictive of skills, traits, or knowledge necessary for effective performance of that particular job.

## C. Workplace Harassment

No workplace issue has recently received more public attention in recent years than sexual harassment. This issue has been continuously in the headlines since 1991, when Supreme Court Justice Clarence Thomas was accused of sexual harassment during Senate confirmation hearings, reaching higher yet when similar accusations were made against former president Bill Clinton.[135] The Equal Employment Opportunity Commission (EEOC), charged with the enforcement of Title VII, reports a dramatic increase in the number of sexual harassment complaints.

While Title VII condemns discrimination on the basis of "race, color, religion, gender, or national origin,"[136] it does not expressly mention sexual harassment. Nevertheless, sexual harassment has been recognized as a form of discrimination actionable under Title VII since the Supreme Court's 1986 decision in *Meritor Savings Bank v. Vinson*.[137] Title VII protects all employees from sexual harassment, regardless of their gender. Sexual harassment can occur when a man harasses a woman, a woman harasses a man,[138] or when either harass a person of the same sex.[139]

---

[135] Clinton v. Jones, 520 U.S. 681, 117 S. Ct. 1636, 137 L. Ed. 2d 945 (1997).

[136] Civil Rights Act of 1964, § 0703(a) (1), as amended, 42 U.S.C.A. § 2000e-2(a) (1) (1994).

[137] 477 U.S. 57, 106 S. Ct. 2399, 91 L. Ed. 2d 49 (1986).

[138] Shipbuilding & Dry Dock Co. v. EEOC, 462 U.S. 669, 103 S. Ct. 2622, 77 L. Ed. 2d 89 (1983).

[139] Oncale v. Sundowner Offshore Services, 523 U.S. 75, 118 S. Ct. 998, 140 L. Ed. 2d 201 (1998) Title VII protects same-sex victims as well as the opposite-sex victims against sexual harassment, but the harassment must be because of the person's sex. Harassment based on an employee's sexual orientation is not covered. *See, e.g.,* Simonton v. Runyon, 232 F.3d 33 (2d Cir. 2000) (Derogatory comments, hostile remarks, and jokes by coworkers based on employee's sexual orientation are not actionable under Title VII).

Most people have an idea (not always correct) about when conduct constitutes sexual harassment.[140] There are two distinct forms of sexual harassment recognized under Title VII: *quid pro quo* and *hostile work environment*.

### 1. Quid Pro Quo Sexual Harassment

Quid pro quo is a Latin phrase that means "this for that." **Quid pro quo sexual harassment** occurs when a superior threatens to take a negative action or to withhold a positive action unless a subordinate acquiesces in his or her sexual demands. Bluntly put, the superior tells the subordinate "put out or get out," or acts in ways that implicitly communicate this message. The threatened action can involve hiring, firing, promotions, work assignments, pay, vacations, travel, or any other tangible employment benefit.

### 2. Hostile Work Environment Sexual Harassment

**Hostile work environment sexual harassment** occurs when unwelcome sexual behavior becomes so pervasive or severe that it alters the conditions of a person's employment and creates a hostile, intimidating, abusive, or offensive work environment. The harassing behavior may be verbal, physical, or both, but to be actionable under Title VII, it must be: (1) unwelcome in the sense of not being invited or solicited; (2) regarded as offensive; and (3) so severe or pervasive as to create a hostile working environment. Factors that courts consider in deciding whether unwelcome sexual conduct has reached this level include: whether the conduct is verbal, physical, or both; whether the words or conduct are physically threatening or humiliating, or merely offensive; how often the acts are repeated; whether the conduct is perpetrated by a coworker or supervisor; whether other people join in the harassment; and whether the conduct unreasonably interferes with the employee's work performance.[141] Conduct does not have to be overtly sexual in order to constitute sexual harassment. Demeaning gender-related comments, sexual jokes, obscene graffiti, and the like are all considered acts of sexual harassment. In a recent Title VII sexual harassment claim brought against a police department by several female officers, the court said:

---

[140]    EEOC guidelines define sexual harassment, for purposes of Title VII, as follows:

> Unwelcome sexual advances, requests for sexual favours, and other verbal or physical conduct of a sexual nature constitutes sexual harassment when: (1) submission to such conduct is made either explicitly or implicitly a term or condition of an individual's employment, (2) submission to or rejection of such conduct by an individual is used as a basis for decisions affecting such individual, or (3) such conduct has the purpose or effect of unreasonably interfering with an individual's work performance or creating an intimidating, hostile, or offensive working environment. 29 C.F.R. § 1604.11(a) (1983).

> Subsections (1) and (2) describe quid pro quo sexual harassment. Subsection (3) addresses hostile work environment sexual harassment.

[141]    Harris v. Forklift Sys., Inc., 510 U.S. 17, 114 S. Ct. 367, 126 L. Ed. 2d 295 (1993).

[While] a police station need not be run like a day care center, it should not, however, have the ambience of a nineteenth century military barracks. We realize that it is unrealistic to hold an employer accountable for every isolated incident of sexism; however, we do not consider it an unfair burden on an employer of both genders to take measures to prevent an atmosphere of sexism to pervade the workplace. While Title VII does not require that an employer fire all "Archie Bunkers" in its employ, the law does require that an employer take prompt action to prevent such bigots from expressing their opinion in a way that abuses or offends their coworkers. By informing people that the expression of racist or sexist attitudes in public is unacceptable, people may eventually learn that such views are undesirable in private, as well. Thus, Title VII may advance the goal of eliminating prejudices and biases in our society.[142]

### 3. Police Department Liability for Sexual Harassment by Supervisors and Coworkers

Sexual harassers are not the only persons who can be held liable under Title VII. The police department can also be sued. The department's liability varies depending on the status of the harasser. When the harasser is a supervisor, the department can be held liable even though the department is unaware of the harassment.[143] If the plaintiff suffers a tangible job injury such as being discharged, demoted, or transferred to a less desirable position as a result of a supervisor's sexual harassment, the wrongdoer's actions are treated as the actions of the department and the department has no defense against liability.[144] If the plaintiff does not sustain tangible employment injury, the department may defend against liability by proving that it had a strong and effective mechanism for reporting and resolving complaints of sexual harassment that the plaintiff could have used to avoid further harassment and that he or she failed to take advantage of this mechanism. This is the only defense against liability for supervisory sexual harassment. Consequently, it is critical for police departments to formulate strong policies prohibiting sexual harassment, put grievance procedures in place, publicize them, and then follow through with prompt and thorough investigations of all complaints, and swift remedial action if the complaint is determined to be well-founded.

The department can also be sued for co-worker sexual harassment. However, a suit for co-worker sexual harassment requires proof that the harasser's supervisor knew or should have known of the harassment, but did nothing to stop it.[145] Here again, the existence of a well-publicized antiharassment policy and grievance procedures will provide a defense if the complaining employee fails to take advantage of it.

---

[142]  Andrews v. City of Philadelphia, 895 F.2d 1469, 1486 (3d Cir. 1990).
[143]  Faragher v. City of Boca Raton, 524 U.S. 775, 118 S. Ct. 2275, 141 L. Ed. 2d 662 (1998); Burlington Industries, Inc. v. Ellerth, 524 U.S. 742, 118 S. Ct. 2257, 141 L. Ed. 2d 633 (1998); Pennsylvania State Police v. Suders, ___ U.S. ___, 124 S. Ct. 2342, 159 L. Ed. 2d 204 (2004).
[144]  See cases supra note 143.
[145]  McKenzie v. Illinois Dept. of Transp., 92 F.3d 473, 480 (7th Cir. 1996); Yamaguchi v. United States Dept. of Air Force, 109 F.3d 1475, 1483 (9th Cir. 1997).

### 4. Racial, Ethnic, and Religious Harassment

Title VII's protection against workplace harassment is not limited to sexual harassment. In *Meritor Savings Bank v. Vinson*,[146] the Supreme Court declared that all employees have a "right to work in an environment free from discriminatory intimidation, ridicule, and insult" based on their race, color, religion, national origin, or sex. The requirements for racial, ethnic, or religious harassment are the same as for sexual harassment.[147] The harassment must be sufficiently severe or pervasive as to alter the conditions of the officer's employment and create a hostile, intimidating, or abusive working environment.[148] The fact that the officer is not present when racially derogatory remarks are made[149] or that they related to members of the officer's race rather than to the officer personally[150] does not preclude a finding of racial harassment. In *Ways v. City of Lincoln*,[151] an African-American police officer successfully sued his department for hostile work environment harassment. The officer proved that he had been subjected to repeated racial slurs and jokes, and that he complained, but nothing was done. The court ruled that when police department officials are aware of racial harassment and fail to investigate or take appropriate remedial action, the department is liable under Title VII.

## § 11.8  Equal Protection in the Police Workplace

The equal protection clause of the Fourteenth Amendment generally requires the government to treat citizens equally, without regard to their race or gender.[152] The Supreme Court has long struggled to reconcile this requirement with affirmative action.[153] Affirmative action refers to programs that give preferential treatment to individuals on the basis of race or gender. Title VII of the Civil Rights Act of 1964[154] neither requires nor prohibits affirmative action; affirmative action programs are voluntary.[155] However, when government agencies embark upon affirmative action, the program must comply with the equal protection clause.

---

[146]  *Supra* note 137.
[147]  Ways v. City of Lincoln, 871 F.2d 750 (8th Cir. 1989); Ross v. Douglas County, Nebraska, 234 F.3d 391 (8th Cir. 2000).
[148]  Harris v. Forklift Sys., Inc., *supra* note 141.
[149]  Schwapp v. Town of Avon, 118 F.3d 106 (2d Cir. 1997).
[150]  *Id.*
[151]  *Supra* note 147.
[152]  The equal protection clause was discussed in §§ 1.16 and 10.16.
[153]  *See generally*, Lara Hudgins, *Rethinking Affirmative Action in the 1990s: Tailoring the Cure to Remedy the Disease*, 47 BAYLOR. L. REV. 815 (1995); John Cocchi Day, Comment, *Retelling The Story of Affirmative Action: Reflections on a Decade of Federal Jurisprudence in The Public Workplace*, 89 CAL. L. REV. 59 (2001).
[154]  Title VII is covered in § 11.7 *supra*.
[155]  42 U.S.C. § 2000(e) (2) (j). (1994).

In the early years of affirmative action, the Supreme Court regarded prefer-ential treatment for females and minorities as "benign discrimination," because the government's purpose was to elevate their status, not to harm innocent males and nonminorities who were passed over for jobs or promotions.[156] More recently, the Supreme Court has come to appreciate that no discrimination seems benign to a person whose career is put on hold for someone else's benefit.[157]

After decades of litigation, consensus has now been reached on two matters. First, the government may not consider race or sex in making employment deci-sions unless this treatment is necessary to advance a compelling government interest.[158] And second, affirmative action programs may not be broader than necessary to address the need that justified initiating them.[159]

## A. Compelling Need for Affirmative Action

Only two interests have been accepted as sufficiently compelling to justify considering race and sex in police department employment decisions. The need to correct imbalances in the police department caused by the police depart-ment's own prior discriminatory employment practices is the most important.[160] If the Whosville Police Department has a documented history of discrimina-tion, then it can adopt an affirmative action plan and keep it in effect until the imbalances caused by its prior discrimination have been eradicated.[161] Eradica-tion takes time. The effects of prior discrimination can linger years after active discrimination has ceased.[162] In a recent federal case, the court approved out-of-rank promotions of several African American police officers to correct the effects of discrimination in the hiring of minorities that had occurred decades

---

[156]  Univ. of California Regents v. Bakke, 438 U.S. 265, 98 S. Ct. 2733, 57 L. Ed. 2d 750 (1978) (a public university may consider the race or ethnicity of an applicant for admission as one factor to be weighed against all others in the admissions process).

[157]  Adarand Constructors, Inc. v. Pena, 515 U.S. 200, 115 S. Ct. 2097, 132 L. Ed. 2d 158 (1995); City of Richmond v. J.A. Croson Co., 488 U.S. 469, 109 S. Ct. 706, 102 L. Ed. 2d 854 (1989) (plurality opin-ion); United States v. Paradise, 480 U.S. 149, 107 S. Ct. 1053, 94 L. Ed. 2d 203 (1987); Wygant v. Jack-son Board of Education, 476 U.S. 267, 106 S. Ct. 1842, 90 L. Ed. 2d 260 (1986). See also Reynolds v. City of Chicago, 296 F.3d 524 (7th Cir. 2002) ("Racial discrimination even of the 'affirmative action' sort, when practiced by a public agency and thus subject to the equal protection clause, requires proof, and not merely argument, that the agency had a compelling need to discriminate and that it went no fur-ther in discrimination than necessary to meet that need.").

[158]  See cases supra note 157.

[159]  Id.

[160]  Id. See also Reynolds v. City of Chicago, supra note 157 (affirmative action promotions of minority and female officers over higher-scoring Caucasian officers did not violate equal protection clause where past discrimination had depressed hiring of minority and female officers, leading to a deficit of minority and female officers in senior positions); Majeske v. City of Chicago, 218 F.3d 816, 823 (7th Cir. 2000), cert. denied, 531 U.S. 1079, 121 S. Ct. 779, 148 L. Ed. 2d 676 (2001) (holding that statis-tical evidence of disparity within a police department coupled with anecdotal evidence of discrimina-tion sufficiently establishes a compelling state interest that justifies an affirmative action plan).

[161]  See authorities supra notes 157, 160

[162]  See, e.g., Reynolds v. City of Chicago, supra note 157 (holding that the police department's discrimi-nation in hiring of blacks, leading to a deficit of blacks in senior positions, justified affirmative action promotions decades later); Cotter v. City of Boston, 323 F.3d 160 (1st Cir. 2003) (same).

before.[163] Discrimination at the entry level had limited the opportunities for minorities to move up through the ranks and racial disparities in the higher ranks of the police department were still present almost 30 years later. This justified the use of racial considerations in making promotional decisions.

The police department's operational need for diversity is the second interest that can justify considering sex and race in employment decisions. Police departments need the trust, respect, and confidence of the entire community in order to carry out their mission and this, in turn, requires a racially and sexually integrated police force.[164] In *Grutter v. Bollinger*,[165] the Supreme Court recognized promoting diversity as a compelling government interest in law school admissions. The Court stated:

> In order to cultivate a set of leaders with legitimacy in the eyes of the citizenry, it is necessary that the path to leadership be visibly open to talented and qualified individuals of every race and ethnicity. All members of our heterogeneous society must have confidence in the openness and integrity of the educational institutions that provide this training. As we have recognized, law schools "cannot be effective in isolation from the individuals and institutions with which the law interacts." Access to legal education (and thus the legal profession) must be inclusive of talented and qualified individuals of every race and ethnicity, so that all members of our heterogeneous society may participate in the educational institutions.[166]

---

[163]   Cotter v. City of Boston, *supra* note 162.

[164]   *See, e.g.*, Reynolds v. City of Chicago, *supra* note 157 (holding that affirmative-action promotion of Hispanic officer to rank of lieutenant over higher-scoring Caucasian officers was justified by operational need of police department for diversity among higher-level administrators); Patrolmen's Benevolent Ass'n of N.Y., Inc. v. City of N.Y., 310 F.3d 43, 52 (2d Cir. 2002) ("[A] law enforcement body's need to carry out its mission effectively, with a workforce that appears unbiased, is able to communicate with the public and is respected by the community it serves, may constitute a compelling state interest."); Wittmer v. Peters, 87 F.3d 916 (7th Cir. 1996) (finding operational need for promotion of black lieutenant in prison boot camp with 70% black inmates); Barhold v. Rodriguez, 863 F.2d 233, 238 (2d Cir. 1988) (holding that "a law enforcement body's need to carry out its mission effectively, with a workforce that appears unbiased, is able to communicate with the public and is respected by the community it serves" constitutes a compelling state interest for purpose of equal protection analysis); Talbert v. City of Richmond, 648 F.2d 925 (4th Cir. 1981) (decision to promote black police officer from rank of captain to major over higher-scoring white police officer did not violate equal protection where city took operational need for diversity in the police department's upper ranks into account.); Detroit Police Officers' Ass'n v. Young, 608 F.2d 671 (6th Cir. 1979) (recognizing operational needs of police department as a compelling interest for purposes of equal protection analysis). *See also* United States v. Paradise, *supra* note 157, 480 U.S. at 167 n. 18 (plurality opinion) (noting the argument that race-conscious hiring can be crucial to "restor[ing] community trust in the fairness of law enforcement and facilitat[ing] effective police service by encouraging citizen cooperation," but finding it unnecessary to decide whether operational needs constitute a compelling state interest, justifying the use of racial consideration in hiring and promotional decisions); Wygant v. Jackson Board of Education Wygant, *supra* note 157, 476 U.S., at 314, 106 S. Ct., at 1868 (Stevens, J., dissenting) ("[A]n integrated police force could develop a better relationship with the community and do a more effective job of maintaining law and order than a force composed only of white officers")

[165]   539 U.S. 306, 123 S. Ct. 2325, 156 L. Ed. 2d 304 (2003).

[166]   *Id.* at 332, 123 S. Ct. at 2341.

These observations apply with equal, if not greater, force to the staffing of police departments. At a time when charges of racially biased policing have emerged as one of the most critical and important issues facing police departments, a racially integrated police force has become an operational necessity. The Sixth Circuit Court of Appeals explained the operational needs justification for affirmative action in police personnel decisions with unusual clarity:[167]

> The argument that police need more minority officers is not simply that blacks communicate better with blacks or that a police department should cater to the public's desires. Rather, it is that effective crime prevention and solution depend heavily on the public support and cooperation which result only from public respect and confidence in the police. In short, the focus is not on the superior performance of minority officers, but on the public's perception of law enforcement officials and institutions.

The operational needs justification for affirmative action in police personnel decisions has been widely accepted by lower courts although the question has not yet been addressed by the Supreme Court.[168]

## B. Plan Adopted Is No Broader Than Necessary to Meet That Need

Affirmative action programs, even when justified, may not be broader than necessary to address the need.[169] While it is impossible to correct the effects of past discrimination without imposing some burdens on innocent people who are not responsible, these burdens must be kept to a minimum.

---

[167] Detroit Police Officers' Ass'n v. Young, *supra* note 164 at 695-696.

[168] *See* authorities *supra* note 164. *See also generally*, Nancy Love, Detroit Police Officers' Association v. Young: *The Operational Needs Justification for Affirmative Action in the Context of Public Employment*, 7 NAT'L BLACK L.J. 200 (1980-81) (describing the operational needs justification for affirmative action); Note, *Race as an Employment Qualification to Meet Police Department Operational Needs*, 54 N.Y.U. L. REV. 412 (1979) (same). Robert C. Diemer, Note, *Assuring the Public Interest in Equal Employment Opportunity after* Firefighters Local 1784 v. Stotts, 36 CASE W. RES. L. REV. 87 (1985) ("There are numerous substantiated examples of how police activity is directly affected by the racial mix of police departments. Racial makeup affects both the public's perception of the police and the department's own view of its constituent public. Race has been linked to the use of violence by police and to officer discretion. It has also been shown to be a substantial contributing factor in many race riots. Several studies have hypothesized that an integrated police department is crucial for effective crime prevention. Indeed, several cases suggest that the public interest demands integration. The modern urban public demands more than highly effective law enforcement for the improvement of police community relations. Once this threshold of mutual trust has been passed, police efficiency will increase as a greater percentage of crimes will be reported and correspondingly, investigations are pursued with greater vigor. Many police departments are thus attempting to implement their own affirmative action programs. It is undisputed that, as a body, the police have more day-to-day opportunities to interact with the public than any other government entity. Such interactions run the gamut of interpersonal communications. Yet, the fact that police discrimination is more potentially blatant and violent does not diminish the fact or effect of discrimination by other government employees.")

[169] *See, e.g.*, Grutter v. Bollinger, *supra* note 165; United States v. Paradise, *supra* note 157; Hiller v. County of Suffolk, 977 F. Supp. 202 (E.D.N.Y. 1997).

In *United States v. Paradise*,[170] the Supreme Court identified the following factors as relevant in deciding whether affirmative action plans that satisfy the compelling interest requirement comply with equal protection. First, the department must explore alternatives and assess them as inadequate before adopting the plan.[171] Second, the plan must be flexible. Preferences that treat race as a plus factor are more likely to be upheld than quotas that set aside a fixed number or percentage of jobs because quotas prevent non-minorities from competing for the jobs that have been set aside.[172] Third, the plan may not correct imbalances in the workforce by: (1) taking jobs away from people who already have them; (2) completely foreclosing advancement opportunities for people who are not members of a protected class; or (3) authorizing the hiring or promotion of unqualified candidates.[173] Finally, the plan must be temporary and must end when its remedial goals have been achieved. A racially balanced workforce may not be maintained through artificial means once the plan's goals are reached.[174]

## § 11.9  Summary

The constitutional provisions studied in earlier chapters often have a narrower application in the government workplace. The First Amendment, for example, protects a police officer's work-related speech only if: (1) the speech addresses a matter of public concern and (2) the officer's interest in speaking on this matter outweighs the department's interest in suppressing the speech to promote workplace efficiency.

The Fourth Amendment protects police officers against administrative searches for evidence of suspected rule violations only if: (1) they have a reasonable expectation of privacy in the location searched, and (2) the search is conducted without reasonable suspicion of work-related misconduct. Mandatory drug testing is considered a search, but is permitted if: (1) the department has a reasonable suspicion that an officer is abusing drugs; or (2) if the testing is conducted as part of a systematic drug-screening program.

The Fifth Amendment privilege against self-incrimination does not protect officers undergoing a police internal affairs investigation from being compelled, on threat of job termination, to account for their official conduct. However, incriminating statements obtained in this manner are treated as immunized testimony and may not be used against the officer in a criminal prosecution.

---

[170] *Supra* note 157.

[171] United States v. Paradise, *supra* note 157; City of Richmond v. J.A. Croson Co., *supra* note 157; Middleton v. City of Flint, Michigan, 93 F.3d 396 (6th Cir. 1966).

[172] United States v. Paradise *supra* note 157; Wygant v. Jackson Board of Education, *supra* note 157.

[173] *See* cases *supra* note 172.

[174] Detroit Police Officers Ass'n v. Young, 989 F.2d 225 (6th Cir. 1993) (holding that affirmative action plan was no longer valid when goal of 50 percent black sergeants had been virtually attained).

The job of police officer is more highly regulated than any career outside the military. Regulations that infringe on an officer's liberty are sometimes challenged as violating substantive due process. Substantive due process challenges rarely succeed because courts look upon police departments as paramilitary organizations and are reluctant to overturn their judgments about what is necessary for the successful operation of a police department. Challenges to regulations affecting a police officer's personal appearance and hairstyle, place of residence, off-duty employment, smoking habits and even private sexual behavior, have generally been unsuccessful.

The Fourteenth Amendment due process clause entitles police officers who have a property right in their job (i.e., who cannot be dismissed without just cause for removal) to notice of the charges and a hearing before an impartial decisionmaker before they may be dismissed or demoted. Officers, whether or not they have a property right in their job, are entitled to a due process "name clearing" hearing if stigmatizing charges are publicly made against them that could foreclose their ability to get another job in their chosen field.

The Equal Employment Opportunity Act, popularly known as Title VII, protects police officers against discrimination based on race, color, religion, gender, or national origin in hiring, promotion, discharge, and other employment decisions. Three different kinds of discrimination are recognized: (1) disparate treatment; (2) disparate impact; and (3) harassment. Disparate treatment discrimination occurs when one person is deliberately treated differently from others who are similarly situated because of his or her race, religion, color, gender, or national origin. Disparate impact discrimination occurs when an employer uses selection criteria that disproportionately eliminate members of a protected class without being valid predictors of traits, skills, or knowledge necessary for successful performance of the jobs for which the selection criteria are being used. Sexual harassment occurs when: (1) a supervisor threatens to take negative action or to withhold positive action unless a subordinate accedes to demands for sexual favors, or (2) when the sexual harassment is so pervasive or severe as to create a hostile work environment. Police departments are liable for sexual harassment committed by supervisors and also for harassment by co-workers if a supervisor is aware of the harassment and does nothing. Title VII also protects against workplace harassment based on race, religion, or ethnicity.

Efforts to increase representation by women and minorities on the police force have induced many police departments to adopt affirmative action programs. When race-conscious action is necessary, either to remedy the effects of the department's own prior discriminatory employment practices or to further the department's operational need for diversity, and the plan adopted is no broader than necessary to address this need, officers disadvantaged by the operation of the plan cannot complain. However, when either condition is lacking, unequal treatment based on race or gender violates the equal protection clause.

# Part II:
# Judicial Decisions and
# Statutes Relating To Part I

The judicial decisions in this part of the book have been selected to enhance understanding of the materials in Part I.

It is not enough to learn the decision or rule of law of a case. To fully appreciate the significance of a rule and to be capable of applying the rule intelligently, the reasoning of the court in reaching the decision must also be considered. Although a court decides only the case that is before it, the decision rendered would be of little use if it did not serve as a guideline for future cases in which similar factual patterns arise. Therefore, the facts are important, and careful attention must be paid to them in reading the cases.

Cases that follow have been selected either because of their importance as precedents or because of their "typicality." They interpret constitutional provisions and demonstrate the judicial processes followed when the United States Supreme Court or lower federal courts reach a decision involving a constitutional question. Due to space limitations, considerable editing has been necessary. For the reader who desires to acquire the full text of these cases, they are available in law schools and courthouse libraries.

# Part II: Table of Cases

# Cases Relating to Chapter 1

## History, Structure, and Content of the United States Constitution

**UNITED STATES**

**v.**

**LOPEZ**

**514 U.S. 549, 115 S. Ct. 1624, 131 L. Ed. 2d 626 (1995)**

*[Citations and footnotes omitted.]*

[Lopez, a 12th-grade student, was convicted of violating the Gun-Free School Zones Act, which made it a federal offense for any individual knowingly to possess a firearm in a school zone. The issue before the Supreme Court was whether Congress had the power to enact the Gun-Free School Zones Act under the Commerce Clause.]

Chief Justice REHNQUIST delivered the opinion of the Court.

* * *

. . . The Constitution creates a Federal Government of enumerated powers. As James Madison wrote, "[t]he powers delegated by the proposed Constitution to the federal government are few and defined. Those which are to remain in the State governments are numerous and indefinite." This constitutionally mandated division of authority "was adopted by the Framers to ensure protection of our fundamental liberties. Just as the separation and independence of the coordinate branches of the Federal Government serve to prevent the accumulation of excessive power in any one branch, a healthy balance of power between the States and the Federal Government will reduce the risk of tyranny and abuse from either front."

The Constitution delegates to Congress the power "[t]o regulate Commerce with foreign Nations, and among the several States, and with the Indian Tribes." . . .

* * *

. . . [W]e have identified three broad categories of activity that Congress may regulate under its commerce power. First, Congress may regulate the use of the channels of interstate commerce. "'[T]he authority of Congress to keep the channels of interstate commerce free from immoral and injurious uses has been frequently sustained, and is no longer open to question.'" Second, Congress is empowered to regulate and protect the instrumentalities of interstate commerce, or persons or things in interstate commerce, even though the threat may come only from intrastate activities. "[F]or example, the destruction of an aircraft or . . . thefts from interstate shipments. Finally, Congress' commerce authority includes the power to regulate those activities having a substantial relation to interstate commerce, i.e., those activities that substantially affect interstate commerce.

\* \* \*

We now turn to consider the power of Congress, in the light of this framework, to enact [The Gun-Free School Zones Act] 922(q). The first two categories of authority may be quickly disposed of: 922(q) is not a regulation of the use of the channels of interstate commerce, nor is it an attempt to prohibit the interstate transportation of a commodity through the channels of commerce; nor can 922(q) be justified as a regulation by which Congress has sought to protect an instrumentality of interstate commerce or a thing in interstate commerce. Thus, if 922(q) is to be sustained, it must be under the third category as a regulation of an activity that substantially affects interstate commerce.

First, we have upheld a wide variety of congressional Acts regulating intrastate economic activity where we have concluded that the activity substantially affected interstate commerce. Examples include the regulation of intrastate coal mining; intrastate extortionate credit transactions, restaurants utilizing substantial interstate supplies, inns and hotels catering to interstate guests, and production and consumption of home-grown wheat. These examples are by no means exhaustive, but the pattern is clear. Where economic activity substantially affects interstate commerce, legislation regulating that activity will be sustained.

\* \* \*

Section 922(q) is a criminal statute that by its terms has nothing to do with "commerce" or any sort of economic enterprise, however broadly one might define those terms. Section 922(q) is not an essential part of a larger regulation of economic activity, in which the regulatory scheme could be undercut unless the intrastate activity were regulated. It cannot, therefore, be sustained under our cases upholding regulations of activities that arise out of or are connected with a commercial transaction, which, viewed in the aggregate, substantially affects interstate commerce.

\* \* \*

. . . The possession of a gun in a local school zone is in no sense an economic activity that might, through repetition elsewhere, substantially affect any sort of interstate commerce. Respondent was a local student at a local school; there is no indication that he had recently moved in interstate commerce, and there is no requirement that his possession of the firearm have any concrete tie to interstate commerce.

To uphold the Government's contentions here, we would have to pile inference upon inference in a manner that would bid fair to convert congressional authority under the Commerce Clause to a general police power of the sort retained by the States. Admittedly, some of our prior cases have taken long steps down that road, giving great deference to congressional action. The broad language in these opinions has suggested the possibility of additional expansion, but we decline here to proceed any further. To do so would require us to conclude that the Constitution's enumeration of powers does not presuppose something not enumerated, and that there never will be a distinction between what is truly national and what is truly local. This we are unwilling to do.

For the foregoing reasons the judgment of the Court of Appeals is

Affirmed.

JUSTICE KENNEDY, with whom JUSTICE O'CONNOR joins, concurring.

* * *

Of the various structural elements in the Constitution, separation of powers, checks and balances, judicial review, and federalism, only concerning the last does there seem to be much uncertainty respecting the existence, and the content, of standards that allow the judiciary to play a significant role in maintaining the design contemplated by the Framers. Although the resolution of specific cases has proved difficult, we have derived from the Constitution workable standards to assist in preserving separation of powers and checks and balances. These standards are by now well accepted. Judicial review is also established beyond question, and though we may differ when applying its principles, its legitimacy is undoubted. Our role in preserving the federal balance seems more tenuous.

There is irony in this, because of the four structural elements in the Constitution just mentioned, federalism was the unique contribution of the Framers to political science and political theory. Though on the surface the idea may seem counterintuitive, it was the insight of the Framers that freedom was enhanced by the creation of two governments, not one. "In the compound republic of America, the power surrendered by the people is first divided between two distinct governments, and then the portion allotted to each subdivided among distinct and separate departments. Hence a double security arises to the rights of the people. The different governments will control each other, at the same time that each will be controlled by itself." . . .

The theory that two governments accord more liberty than one requires for its realization two distinct and discernable lines of political accountability: one between the citizens and the Federal Government; the second between the citizens and the States. . . . Were the Federal Government to take over the regulation of entire areas of traditional state concern, areas having nothing to do with the regulation of commercial activities, the boundaries between the spheres of federal and state authority would blur and political responsibility would become illusory. . . .

* * *

The statute before us upsets the federal balance to [the] degree that renders it an unconstitutional assertion of the commerce power, and our intervention is required. As the Chief Justice explains, unlike the earlier cases to come before the Court here neither the actors nor their conduct have a commercial character, and neither the purposes nor the design of the statute have an evident commercial nexus. The statute makes the simple possession of a gun within 1,000 feet of the grounds of the school a criminal offense. In a sense any conduct in this interdependent world of ours has an ultimate commercial origin or consequence, but we have not yet said the commerce power may reach so far. If Congress attempts that extension, then at the least we must inquire whether the exercise of national power seeks to intrude upon an area of traditional state concern.

An interference of these dimensions occurs here, for it is well established that education is a traditional concern of the States. The proximity to schools, including of course schools owned and operated by the States or their subdivisions, is the very premise for making the conduct criminal. In these circumstances, we have a particular duty to insure that the federal-state balance is not destroyed. . . .

While it is doubtful that any State, or indeed any reasonable person, would argue that it is wise policy to allow students to carry guns on school premises, considerable disagreement exists about how best to accomplish that goal. In this circumstance, the theory and utility of our federalism are revealed, for the States may perform their role as laboratories for experimentation to devise various solutions where the best solution is far from clear.

If a State or municipality determines that harsh criminal sanctions are necessary and wise to deter students from carrying guns on school premises, the reserved powers of the States are sufficient to enact those measures. Indeed, over 40 States already have criminal laws outlawing the possession of firearms on or near school grounds.

\* \* \*

The statute now before us forecloses the States from experimenting and exercising their own judgment in an area to which States lay claim by right of history and expertise, and it does so by regulating an activity beyond the realm of commerce in the ordinary and usual sense of that term. . . .

\* \* \*

. . . While the intrusion on state sovereignty may not be as severe in this instance as in some of our recent Tenth Amendment cases, the intrusion is nonetheless significant. Absent a stronger connection or identification with commercial concerns that are central to the Commerce Clause, that interference contradicts the federal balance the Framers designed and that this Court is obliged to enforce.

For these reasons, I join in the opinion and judgment of the Court.

## UNITED STATES

v.

## MORRISON

### 529 U.S. 598, 120 S. Ct. 1740, 146 L. Ed. 2d 658 (2000)

*[Citations and footnotes omitted]*

[Christy Brzonkala brought suit against three members of the Virginia Polytechnic Institute football team under the Violence Against Women Act, a statute that created a federal civil cause of action in favor of victims of gender-motivated crimes of violence. She alleged that the defendants had gang-raped her. The question before the Supreme Court was whether Congress had authority to enact this statute, either under the commerce clause or the Fourteenth Amendment, which forbids the states to deprive anyone of life, liberty, or property without due process of law.]

CHIEF JUSTICE REHNQUIST delivered the opinion of the Court.

Every law enacted by Congress must be based on one or more of its powers enumerated in the Constitution. . . . Congress explicitly identified the sources of federal authority on which it relied in enacting § 13981. It said that a "federal civil rights cause of action" is established "[p]ursuant to the affirmative power of Congress . . . under section 5 of the Fourteenth Amendment to the Constitution, as well as under section 8 of Article I of the Constitution." We address Congress' authority to enact this remedy under each of these constitutional provisions in turn.

Due respect for the decisions of a coordinate branch of Government demands that we invalidate a congressional enactment only upon a plain showing that Congress has exceeded its constitutional bounds. With this presumption of constitutionality in mind, we turn to the question whether § 13981 falls within Congress' power under Article I, § 8, of the Constitution. Brzonkala and the United States rely upon the third clause of the Article, which gives Congress power "[t]o regulate Commerce with foreign Nations, and among the several States, and with the Indian Tribes."

As we discussed at length in *Lopez*, our interpretation of the Commerce Clause has changed as our Nation has developed. We need not repeat that detailed review of the Commerce Clause's history here; it suffices to say that, in the years since *NLRB v. Jones & Laughlin Steel Corp.*, Congress has had considerably greater latitude in regulating conduct and transactions under the Commerce Clause than our previous case law permitted.

*Lopez* emphasized, however, that even under our modern, expansive interpretation of the Commerce Clause, Congress' regulatory authority is not without effective bounds.

"[E]ven [our] modern-era precedents which have expanded congressional power under the Commerce Clause confirm that this power is subject to outer limits. In *Jones & Laughlin Steel*, the Court warned that the scope of the interstate commerce power 'must be considered in the light of our dual system of government and may not be extended so as to embrace effects upon interstate commerce so indirect and remote that to embrace them, in view of our complex society, would effectually obliterate the distinction between what is national and what is local and create a completely centralized government.'"

As we observed in *Lopez*, modern Commerce Clause jurisprudence has "identified three broad categories of activity that Congress may regulate under its commerce power." "First, Congress may regulate the use of the channels of interstate commerce." "Second, Congress is empowered to regulate and protect the instrumentalities of interstate commerce, or persons or things in interstate commerce, even though the threat may come only from intrastate activities." "Finally, Congress' commerce authority includes the power to regulate those activities having a substantial relation to interstate commerce, . . . i.e., those activities that substantially affect interstate commerce."

Petitioners do not contend that these cases fall within either of the first two of these categories of Commerce Clause regulation. They seek to sustain § 13981 as a regulation of activity that substantially affects interstate commerce. Given § 13981's focus on gender-motivated violence wherever it occurs (rather than violence directed at the instrumentalities of interstate commerce, interstate markets, or things or persons in interstate commerce), we agree that this is the proper inquiry.

Since *Lopez* most recently canvassed and clarified our case law governing this third category of Commerce Clause regulation, it provides the proper framework for conducting the required analysis of § 13981. In *Lopez*, we held that the Gun-Free School Zones Act of 1990, which made it a federal crime to knowingly possess a firearm in a school zone, exceeded Congress' authority under the Commerce Clause. Several significant considerations contributed to our decision.

First, we observed that § 922(q) was "a criminal statute that by its terms has nothing to do with 'commerce' or any sort of economic enterprise, however broadly one might define those terms." Reviewing our case law, we noted that "we have upheld a wide variety of congressional Acts regulating intrastate economic activity where we have concluded that the activity substantially affected interstate commerce." Although we cited only a few examples, including *Wickard v. Filburn*, . . . we stated that the pattern of analysis is clear. "Where economic activity substantially affects interstate commerce, legislation regulating that activity will be sustained."

Both petitioners and Justice SOUTER's dissent downplay the role that the economic nature of the regulated activity plays in our Commerce Clause analysis. But a fair reading of *Lopez* shows that the noneconomic, criminal nature of the conduct at issue was central to our decision in that case. *Lopez*'s review of Commerce Clause case law demonstrates that in those cases where we have sustained federal regulation of intrastate activity based upon the activity's substantial effects on interstate commerce, the activity in question has been some sort of economic endeavor.

\* \* \*

Finally, our decision in *Lopez* rested in part on the fact that the link between gun possession and a substantial effect on interstate commerce was attenuated. The United States argued that the possession of guns may lead to violent crime, and that violent crime "can be expected to affect the functioning of the national economy in two ways. First, the costs of violent crime are substantial, and, through the mechanism of insurance, those costs are spread throughout the population. Second, violent crime reduces the willingness of individuals to travel to areas within the country that are perceived to be unsafe." The Government also argued that the presence of guns at schools poses a threat to the educational process, which in turn threatens to produce a less efficient and productive workforce, which will negatively affect national productivity and thus interstate commerce.

We rejected these "costs of crime" and "national productivity" arguments because they would permit Congress to "regulate not only all violent crime, but all activities that might lead to violent crime, regardless of how tenuously they relate to interstate commerce." We noted that, under this but-for reasoning:

> "Congress could regulate any activity that it found was related to the economic productivity of individual citizens: family law (including marriage, divorce, and child custody), for example. Under the[se] theories . . . it is difficult to perceive any limitation on federal power, even in areas such as criminal law enforcement or education where States historically have been sovereign. Thus, if we were to accept the Government's arguments, we are hard pressed to posit any activity by an individual that Congress is without power to regulate."

With these principles underlying our Commerce Clause jurisprudence as reference points, the proper resolution of the present cases is clear. Gender-motivated crimes of violence are not, in any sense of the phrase, economic activity. While we need not adopt a categorical rule against aggregating the effects of any noneconomic activity in order to decide these cases, thus far in our Nation's history our cases have upheld Commerce Clause regulation of intrastate activity only where that activity is economic in nature.

\* \* \*

We accordingly reject the argument that Congress may regulate noneconomic, violent criminal conduct based solely on that conduct's aggregate effect on interstate commerce. The Constitution requires a distinction between what is truly national and what is truly local.

In recognizing this fact we preserve one of the few principles that has been consistent since the Clause was adopted. The regulation and punishment of intrastate violence that is not directed at the instrumentalities, channels, or goods involved in interstate commerce has always been the province of the States. Indeed, we can think of no better example of the police power, which the Founders denied the National Government and reposed in the States, than the suppression of violent crime and vindication of its victims.

Because we conclude that the Commerce Clause does not provide Congress with authority to enact § 13981, we address petitioners' alternative argument that the section's civil remedy should be upheld as an exercise of Congress' remedial power under § 5 of the Fourteenth Amendment. As noted above, Congress expressly invoked the Fourteenth Amendment as a source of authority to enact § 13981.

The principles governing an analysis of congressional legislation under § 5 are well settled. Section 5 states that Congress may " 'enforce,' by 'appropriate legislation' the constitutional guarantee that no State shall deprive any person of 'life, liberty or property, without due process of law,' nor deny any person 'equal protection of the laws.'" . . .

\* \* \*

As our cases have established, state-sponsored gender discrimination violates equal protection unless it "'serves "important governmental objectives and . . . the discriminatory means employed" are "substantially related to the achievement of those objectives." However, the language and purpose of the Fourteenth Amendment place certain limitations on the manner in which Congress may attack discriminatory conduct. These limitations are necessary to prevent the Fourteenth Amendment from obliterating the Framers' carefully crafted balance of power between the States and the National Government. Foremost among these limitations is the time-honored principle that the Fourteenth Amendment, by its very terms, prohibits only state action. "[T]he principle has become firmly embedded in our constitutional law that the action inhibited by the first section of the Fourteenth Amendment is only such action as may fairly be said to be that of the States. That 'Amendment erects no shield against merely private conduct, however discriminatory or wrongful."

Shortly after the Fourteenth Amendment was adopted, we decided two cases interpreting the Amendment's provisions, *United States v. Harris*, and the Civil Rights Cases. In *Harris*, the Court considered a challenge to § 2 of the Civil Rights Act of 1871. That section sought to punish "private persons" for "conspiring to deprive any one of the equal protection of the laws enacted by the State." We concluded that this law exceeded Congress' § 5 power because the law was "directed exclusively against the action of private persons, without reference to the laws of the State, or their administration by her officers." In so doing, we reemphasized our statement from *Virginia v. Rives* that " 'these provisions of the Fourteenth Amendment have reference to State action exclusively, and not to any action of private individuals.'"

\* \* \*

For these reasons, we conclude that Congress' power under § 5 does not extend to the enactment of § 13981.

Petitioner Brzonkala's complaint alleges that she was the victim of a brutal assault. But Congress' effort in § 13981 to provide a federal civil remedy can be sustained neither under the

Commerce Clause nor under § 5 of the Fourteenth Amendment. If the allegations here are true, no civilized system of justice could fail to provide her a remedy for the conduct of respondent Morrison. But under our federal system that remedy must be provided by the Commonwealth of Virginia, and not by the United States. The judgment of the Court of Appeals is

Affirmed.

## McCULLOCH
### v.
## MARYLAND

### 17 U.S. (4 Wheat.) 316,
### 4 L. Ed. 579 (1819)

*[Citations and footnotes omitted]*

[In 1816, Congress enacted a law incorporating the Bank of the United States, which opened a branch in Baltimore. Two years later, the Maryland General Assembly passed a law levying a tax on all local banks that were not incorporated by the State of Maryland. The Bank of the United State refused to pay the tax and the case went the Supreme Court on two questions: (1) Did Congress have the constitutional authority to incorporate a bank? and (2) If so, may a state tax an instrument of the federal government?].

Mr. Chief Justice MARSHALL delivered the opinion of the Court.

\* \* \*

This government is acknowledged by all to be one of enumerated powers. The principle, that it can exercise only the powers granted to it, would seem too apparent, to have required to be enforced by all those arguments which its enlight-

ened friends, while it was depending before the people, found it necessary to urge. That principle is now universally admitted. But the question respecting the extent of the powers actually granted, is perpetually arising, and will probably continue to arise, as long as our system shall exist.

In discussing these questions, the conflicting powers of the general and State governments must be brought into view, and the supremacy of their respective laws, when they are in opposition, must be settled.

If any one proposition could command the universal assent of mankind, we might expect it would be this—that the government of the Union, though limited in its powers, is supreme within its sphere of action. This would seem to result necessarily from its nature. It is the government of all; its powers are delegated by all; it represents all, and acts for all. Though any one State may be willing to control its operations, no State is willing to allow others to control them. The nation, on those subjects on which it can act, must necessarily bind its component parts. But this question is not left to mere reason: the people have, in express terms, decided it, by saying, "this constitution, and the laws of the United States, which shall be made in pursuance thereof," "shall be the supreme law of the land," and by requiring that the members of the State legislatures, and the officers of the executive and judicial departments of the States, shall take the oath of fidelity to it.

The government of the United States, then, though limited in its powers, is supreme; and its laws, when made in pursuance of the constitution, form the supreme law of the land, "any thing in the constitution or laws of any State to the contrary notwithstanding."

Among the enumerated powers, we do not find that of establishing a bank or creating a corporation. But there is no phrase in the instrument which, like the articles of confederation, excludes incidental or implied powers; and which requires that every thing granted shall be expressly and minutely described. Even the 10th amendment, which was framed for the purpose of quieting the excessive jealousies which had been excited, omits the word "expressly," and declares only that the powers "not delegated to the United States, nor prohibited to the States, are reserved to the States or to the people;" thus leaving the question, whether the particular power which may become the subject of contest has been delegated to the one government, or prohibited to the other, to depend on a fair construction of the whole instrument. The men who drew and adopted this amendment had experienced the embarrassments resulting from the insertion of this word in the articles of confederation, and probably omitted it to avoid those embarrassments. A constitution, to contain an accurate detail of all the subdivisions of which its great powers will admit, and of all the means by which they may be carried into execution, would partake of the prolixity of a legal code, and could scarcely be embraced by the human mind. It would probably never be understood by the public. Its nature, therefore, requires, that only its great outlines should be marked, its important objects designated, and the minor ingredients which compose those objects be deduced from the nature of the objects themselves. That this idea was entertained by the framers of the American constitution, is not only to be inferred from the nature of the instrument, but from the language. Why else were some of the limitations, found in the ninth section of the 1st article, introduced? It is also, in some degree, warranted by their having omitted to use any restrictive term which might prevent its receiving a fair and just interpretation. In considering this question, then, we must

never forget, that it is a constitution we are expounding.

Although, among the enumerated powers of government, we do not find the word "bank" or "incorporation," we find the great powers to lay and collect taxes; to borrow money; to regulate commerce; to declare and conduct a war; and to raise and support armies and navies. The sword and the purse, all the external relations, and no inconsiderable portion of the industry of the nation, are entrusted to its government. . . . But it may with great reason be contended, that a government, entrusted with such ample powers, on the due execution of which the happiness and prosperity of the nation so vitally depends, must also be entrusted with ample means for their execution. The power being given, it is the interest of the nation to facilitate its execution. It can never be their interest, and cannot be presumed to have been their intention, to clog and embarrass its execution by withholding the most appropriate means. Throughout this vast republic, from the St. Croix to the Gulf of Mexico, from the Atlantic to the Pacific, revenue is to be collected and expended, armies are to be marched and supported. The exigencies of the nation may require that the treasure raised in the north should be transported to the south, that raised in the east conveyed to the west, or that this order should be reversed. Is that construction of the constitution to be preferred which would render these operations difficult, hazardous, and expensive? Can we adopt that construction, (unless the words imperiously require it,) which would impute to the framers of that instrument, when granting these powers for the public good, the intention of impeding their exercise by withholding a choice of means? If, indeed, such be the mandate of the constitution, we have only to obey; but that instrument does not profess to enumerate the means by which the powers it confers may be executed; nor does it prohibit the creation of a corporation, if the existence of such a being be essential to the beneficial exercise of those powers. It is, then, the subject of fair inquiry, how far such means may be employed.

\* \* \*

But the constitution of the United States has not left the right of Congress to employ the necessary means, for the execution of the powers conferred on the government, to general reasoning. To its enumeration of powers is added that of making "all laws which shall be necessary and proper, for carrying into execution the foregoing powers, and all other powers vested by this constitution, in the government of the United States, or in any department thereof."

\* \* \*

After the most deliberate consideration, it is the unanimous and decided opinion of this Court, that the act to incorporate the Bank of the United States is a law made in pursuance of the constitution, and is a part of the supreme law of the land.

\* \* \*

[The second part of the decision concerned the right of the State of Maryland to tax the Bank of the United States. The Court held that the tax was unconstitutional. The bank was an instrument of the federal government, created to assist the government in executing its constitutionally delegated powers. Allowing states to tax instrumentalities of the federal government would leave the federal government at the mercy of the states. If the states could tax one instrument employed by the government in the execution of its powers, they could tax any

and all others, including the mint, the mails, the judicial process, etc. This would enable the states to control and hinder the operations of the federal government. Because Article VI makes the Constitution and laws of the United States the supreme law of the land, state taxation of instruments of the federal government is unconstitutional.]

## PRINTZ
### v.
## UNITED STATES

### 521 U.S. 98, 117 S. Ct. 2365, 138 L. Ed. 2d 914 (1997)

*[Citations and footnotes omitted.]*

[In 1993, Congress enacted the Brady Handgun Violence Prevention Act, which required the Attorney General of the United States to establish a national system for instantly checking prospective handgun purchasers' backgrounds. As an interim measure, the law directed the "chief law enforcement officer" (CLEO) of each local jurisdiction to conduct background checks of would-be gun purchasers until such time as the national system became operative. A group of sheriffs for counties in Montana and Arizona sought to enjoin enforcement of this provision on the grounds that it was a violation of principles of federalism and state sovereignty for Congress to make state law enforcement officers administer federal programs.]

Justice SCALIA delivered the opinion of the Court.

\* \* \*

. . . [T]he Brady Act purports to direct state law enforcement officers to participate, albeit only temporarily, in the administration of a federally enacted regulatory scheme. Regulated firearms dealers are required to forward Brady Forms not to a federal officer or employee, but to the CLEOs, whose obligation to accept those forms is implicit in the duty imposed upon them to make "reasonable efforts" within five days to determine whether the sales reflected in the forms are lawful. . . .

The petitioners here object to being pressed into federal service, and contend that congressional action compelling state officers to execute federal laws is unconstitutional. Because there is no constitutional text speaking to this precise question, the answer to the CLEOs' challenge must be sought in historical understanding and practice, in the structure of the Constitution, and in the jurisprudence of this Court. . . .

* * *

It is incontestable that the Constitution established a system of "dual sovereignty." Although the States surrendered many of their powers to the new Federal Government, they retained "a residuary and inviolable sovereignty." This is reflected throughout the Constitution's text, including (to mention only a few examples) the prohibition on any involuntary reduction or combination of a State's territory, Art. IV, § 3; the Judicial Power Clause, Art. III, § 2, and the Privileges and Immunities Clause, Art. IV, § 2, which speak of the "Citizens" of the States; the amendment provision, Article V, which requires the votes of three-fourths of the States to amend the Constitution; and the Guarantee Clause, Art. IV, § 4, which "presupposes the continued existence of the states and . . . those means and instrumentalities which are the creation of their sovereign and reserved rights." Residual state sovereignty was also implicit, of course, in the Constitution's conferral upon Congress of not all governmental powers, but only discrete, enumerated ones, Art. I, § 8, which implication was rendered express by the Tenth Amendment's assertion that "[t]he powers not delegated to the United States by the Constitution, nor prohibited by it to the States, are reserved to the States respectively, or to the people."

The Framers' experience under the Articles of Confederation had persuaded them that using the States as the instruments of federal governance was both ineffectual and provocative of federal-state conflict. . . . [T]he Framers rejected the concept of a central government that would act upon and through the States, and instead designed a system in which the state and federal governments would exercise concurrent authority over the people—who were, in Hamilton's words, "the only proper objects of government." We have set forth the historical record in more detail elsewhere, and need not repeat it here. It suffices to repeat the conclusion: "The Framers explicitly chose a Constitution that confers upon Congress the power to regulate individuals, not States." The great innovation of this design was that "our citizens would have two political capacities, one state and one federal, each protected from incursion by the other"—"a legal system unprecedented in form and design, establishing two orders of government, each with its own direct relationship, its own privity, its own set of mutual rights and obligations to the people who sustain it and are governed by it." The Constitution thus contemplates that a State's government will represent and remain accountable to its own citizens. . . . As Madison expressed it: "[T]he local or municipal authorities form distinct and independent portions of the supremacy, no more subject, within their respective spheres, to the general authority than the general authority is subject to them, within its own sphere."

This separation of the two spheres is one of the Constitution's structural protections of liberty. "Just as the separation and independence of the coordinate branches of the Federal Government serve to prevent the accumulation of excessive power in any one branch, a healthy balance of power between the States and the Federal Government will reduce the risk of tyranny and abuse from either front." To quote Madison once again: "In the compound republic of America, the power surrendered by the people is first divided between two distinct governments, and then the portion allotted to each subdivided among distinct and separate departments. Hence a double security arises to the rights of the people. The different governments will control each other, at the same time that each will be controlled by itself." The power of the Federal Government would be augmented immeasurably if it were able to impress into its service—and at no cost to itself—the police officers of the 50 States.

We have thus far discussed the effect that federal control of state officers would have upon the first element of the "double security" alluded to by Madison: the division of power between State and Federal Governments. It would also have an effect upon the second element: the separation and equilibration of powers between the three branches of the Federal Government itself. The Constitution does not leave to speculation who is to administer the laws enacted by Congress; the President, it says, "shall take Care that the Laws be faithfully executed," Art. II, § 3, personally and through officers whom he appoints. . . . The Brady Act effectively transfers this responsibility to thousands of CLEOs in the 50 States, who are left to implement the program without meaningful Presidential control (if indeed meaningful Presidential control is possible without the power to appoint and remove). The

insistence of the Framers upon unity in the Federal Executive—to insure both vigor and accountability—is well known. That unity would be shattered, and the power of the President would be subject to reduction, if Congress could act as effectively without the President as with him, by simply requiring state officers to execute its laws.

The dissent of course resorts to . . . the Necessary and Proper Clause. It reasons that the power to regulate the sale of handguns under the Commerce Clause, coupled with the power to "make all Laws which shall be necessary and proper for carrying into Execution the foregoing Powers," Art. I, § 8, conclusively establishes the Brady Act's constitutional validity, because the Tenth Amendment imposes no limitations on the exercise of delegated powers but merely prohibits the exercise of powers "not delegated to the United States." What destroys the dissent's Necessary and Proper Clause argument, however, is not the Tenth Amendment but the Necessary and Proper Clause itself. When a "La[w] . . . for carrying into Execution" the Commerce Clause violates the principle of state sovereignty reflected in the various constitutional provisions we mentioned earlier, it is not a "La[w] . . . proper for carrying into Execution the Commerce Clause," and is thus, in the words of The Federalist, "merely [an] ac[t] of usurpation" which "deserve[s] to be treated as such." . . . "[E]ven where Congress has the authority under the Constitution to pass laws requiring or prohibiting certain acts, it lacks the power directly to compel the States to require or prohibit those acts. . . .

\* \* \*

We held in *New York* that Congress cannot compel the States to enact or enforce a federal regulatory program. Today we hold that Congress cannot circumvent that prohibition by conscripting the State's officers directly. The Federal Government may neither issue directives requiring the States to address particular problems, nor command the States' officers, or those of their political subdivisions, to administer or enforce a federal regulatory program. It matters not whether policymaking is involved, and no case-by-case weighing of the burdens or benefits is necessary; such commands are fundamentally incompatible with our constitutional system of dual sovereignty. Accordingly, the judgment of the Court of Appeals for the Ninth Circuit is reversed.

It is so ordered.

[Concurring and dissenting opinions omitted.]

## DeSHANEY
### v.
## WINNEBAGO COUNTY DEPARTMENT OF SOCIAL SERVICES

### 489 U.S. 189, 109 S. Ct. 998, 103 L. Ed. 2d 249 (1989)

*[Citations and footnotes omitted.]*

[Four-year-old Joshua DeShaney suffered permanent brain damage and mental retardation as a result of being severely beaten by his father. Social workers employed by the county department of social services had apparently received complaints that he was being abused, but took no steps to remove him from his father's custody. Joshua sued the county department of social welfare on the theory that the department's failure to remove him from his father's custody deprived him of liberty in violation of the Fourteenth Amendment. The issue before the Supreme Court was whether the Fourteenth Amendment imposes an affirmative duty on the states to provide protective services to citizens known to be at risk. We encourage you to study the Fourteenth Amendment, which you will find in the Appendix, before reading this opinion.]

Chief Justice REHNQUIST delivered the opinion of the Court.

### I

* * *

The Due Process Clause of the Fourteenth Amendment provides that "[n]o State shall . . . deprive any person of life, liberty, or property, without due process of law." Petitioners contend that the State deprived Joshua of his liberty interest in "free[dom] from . . . unjustified intrusions on personal security," by failing to provide him with adequate protection against his father's violence. The claim is one invoking the substantive rather than the procedural component of the Due Process Clause; petitioners do not claim that the State denied Joshua protection without according him appropriate procedural safeguards, but that it was categorically obligated to protect him in these circumstances.

But nothing in the language of the Due Process Clause itself requires the State to protect the life, liberty, and property of its citizens against invasion by private actors. The Clause is phrased as a limitation on the State's power to act, not as a guarantee of certain minimal levels of safety and security. It forbids the State itself to deprive individuals of life, liberty, or property without "due process of law," but its language cannot fairly be extended to impose an affirmative obligation on the State to ensure that those interests do not come to harm through other means. Nor does history support such an expansive reading of the constitutional text. Like its counterpart in the Fifth Amendment, the Due Process Clause of the Fourteenth Amendment was intended to prevent government "from abusing [its] power, or employing it as an instrument of oppression." Its purpose was to protect the people from the State, not to ensure that the State protected them from each other. The Framers were content to leave the extent of governmental obligation in the latter area to the democratic political processes.

Consistent with these principles, our cases have recognized that the Due Process Clauses generally confer no affirmative right to governmental aid, even where such aid may be necessary to secure life, liberty, or property interests of which the government itself may not deprive the individual. As we said in *Harris v. McRae*: "Although the liberty protected by the Due Process Clause affords protection against unwarranted government interference . . ., it does not confer an entitlement to such [governmental aid] as may be necessary to realize all the advantages of that freedom." If the Due Process Clause does not require the State to provide its citizens with particular protective services, it follows that the State cannot be held liable under the Clause for injuries that could have been averted had it chosen to provide them. As a general matter, then, we conclude that a State's failure to protect an individual against private violence simply does not constitute a violation of the Due Process Clause.

Petitioners contend, however, that even if the Due Process Clause imposes no affirmative obligation on the State to provide the general public with adequate protective services, such a duty may arise out of certain "special relationships" created or assumed by the State with respect to particular individuals. Petitioners argue that such a "special relationship" existed here because the State knew that Joshua faced a special danger of abuse at his father's hands, and specifically proclaimed, by word and by deed, its intention to protect him against that danger. Having actually undertaken to protect Joshua from this danger—which petitioners concede the State played no part in creating—the State acquired an affirmative "duty," enforceable through the Due Process Clause, to do so in a reasonably competent fashion. Its failure to discharge that duty, so the argument goes, was an abuse of governmental power that so "shocks the conscience," as to constitute a substantive due process violation.

We reject this argument. It is true that in certain limited circumstances the Constitution imposes upon the State affirmative duties of care and protection with respect to particular individuals. In *Estelle v. Gamble*, we recognized that the Eighth Amendment's prohibition against cruel and unusual punishment, made applicable to the States through the Fourteenth Amendment's Due Process Clause, requires the State to provide adequate medical care to incarcerated prisoners. We reasoned that because the prisoner is unable "by reason of the deprivation of his liberty [to] care for himself," it is only "just" that the State be required to care for him.

\* \* \*

. . . [W]hen the State takes a person into its custody and holds him there against his will, the Constitution imposes upon it a corresponding duty to assume some responsibility for his safety and general well-being. The rationale for this principle is simple enough: when the State by the affirmative exercise of its power so restrains an individual's liberty that it renders him unable to care for himself, and at the same time fails to provide for his basic human needs—e.g., food, clothing, shelter, medical care, and reasonable safety—it transgresses the substantive limits on state action set by the Eighth Amendment and the Due Process Clause. The affirmative duty to protect arises not from the State's knowledge of the individual's predicament or from its expressions of intent to help him, but from the limitation which it has imposed on his freedom to act on his own behalf. In the substantive due process analysis, it is the State's affirmative act of restraining the individual's freedom to act on his own behalf—through incarceration, institutionalization, or other similar restraint of personal liberty—which is the "deprivation of liberty" triggering the protections of the Due Process Clause, not its failure to act to protect his liberty interests against harms inflicted by other means.

The *Estelle-Youngberg* analysis simply has no applicability in the present case. Petitioners concede that the harms Joshua suffered occurred not while he was in the State's custody, but while he was in the custody of his natural father, who was in no sense a state actor. While the State may have been aware of the dangers that Joshua faced in the free world, it played no part in their creation, nor did it do anything to render him any more vulnerable to them. That the State once took temporary custody of Joshua does not alter the analysis, for when it returned him to his father's custody, it placed him in no worse position than that in which he would have been had it not acted at all; the State does not become the permanent guarantor of an individual's safety by having once offered him shelter. Under these circumstances, the State had no constitutional duty to protect Joshua.

\* \* \*

Affirmed.

**LAWRENCE**

**v.**

**TEXAS**

**539 U.S. 55, 123 S.Ct. 2472, 156 L. Ed. 2d 508 (2003)**

*[Citations and footnotes omitted.]*

[Houston police officers, responding to a hoax call about a weapons disturbance in John Lawrence's apartment, entered and saw Lawrence and Tyrone Garner, another adult male, engaging in homosexual conduct. They arrested both men and charged them with "deviate sexual intercourse," defined under Texas law as having "oral or anal sex, with a member of the same sex." Lawrence and Garner were both found guilty and appealed.]

JUSTICE KENNEDY delivered the opinion of the Court.

\* \* \*

We granted certiorari to consider three questions:

1. Whether Petitioners' criminal convictions under the Texas 'Homosexual Conduct' law—which criminalizes sexual intimacy by same-sex couples, but not identical behavior by different-sex couples—violate the Fourteenth Amendment guarantee of equal protection of laws?
2. Whether Petitioners' criminal convictions for adult consensual sexual intimacy in the home violate their vital interests in liberty and privacy protected by the Due Process Clause of the Fourteenth Amendment?
3. Whether *Bowers v. Hardwick* should be overruled?

\* \* \*

The facts in *Bowers* had some similarities to the instant case. A police officer, whose right to enter seems not to have been in question, observed Hardwick, in his own bedroom, engaging in intimate sexual conduct with another adult male. The conduct was in violation of a Georgia statute making it a criminal offense to engage in sodomy. One difference between the two cases is that the Georgia statute prohibited the conduct whether or not the participants were of the same sex, while the Texas statute, as we have seen, applies only to participants of the same sex. Hardwick was not prosecuted, but he brought an action in federal court to declare the state statute invalid. He alleged he was a practicing homosexual and that the criminal prohibition violated rights guaranteed to him by the Constitution. The Court, in an opinion by Justice White, sustained the Georgia law. . . .

The Court began its substantive discussion in *Bowers* as follows: "The issue presented is whether the Federal Constitution confers a fundamental right upon homosexuals to engage in sodomy and hence invalidates the laws of the many States that still make such conduct illegal and have done so for a very long time." That statement, we now conclude, discloses the Court's own failure to appreciate the extent of the liberty at stake. To say that the issue in *Bowers* was simply the right to engage in certain sexual conduct demeans the claim the individual put forward, just as it would demean a married couple were it to be said marriage is simply about the right to have sexual intercourse. The laws involved in *Bowers* and here are, to be sure, statutes that purport to do no more than prohibit a particular sexual act. Their penalties and purposes, though, have more far-reaching consequences, touching upon the most private human conduct, sexual behavior, and in the most private of places, the home. The statutes do seek to control a personal relationship that, whether or not entitled to formal recognition in the law, is within the liberty of persons to choose without being punished as criminals.

This, as a general rule, should counsel against attempts by the State, or a court, to define the meaning of the relationship or to set its boundaries absent injury to a person or abuse of an institution the law protects. It suffices for us to acknowledge that adults may choose to enter upon this relationship in the confines of their homes and their own private lives and still retain their dignity as free persons. When sexuality finds overt expression in intimate conduct with another person, the conduct can be but one element in a personal bond that is more enduring. The liberty protected by the Constitution allows homosexual persons the right to make this choice.

\* \* \*

It must be acknowledged, of course, that the Court in *Bowers* was making the broader point that for centuries there have been powerful voices to condemn homosexual conduct as immoral. The condemnation has been shaped by religious beliefs, conceptions of right and acceptable behavior, and respect for the traditional family. For many persons these are not trivial concerns but profound and deep convictions accepted as ethical and moral principles to which they aspire and which thus determine the course of their lives. These considerations do not answer the question before us, however. The issue is whether the majority may use the power of the State to enforce these views on the whole society through operation of the criminal law. "Our obligation is to define the liberty of all, not to mandate our own moral code."

. . . "[O]ur laws and traditions in the past half-century are of most relevance here. These references show an emerging awareness that liberty gives substantial protection to adult persons in deciding how to conduct their private lives in matters pertaining to sex. . . .

This emerging recognition should have been apparent when *Bowers* was decided. In 1955 the American Law Institute promulgated the Model Penal Code and made clear that it did not recommend or provide for "criminal penalties for consensual sexual relations conducted in private." It justified its decision on three grounds: (1) The prohibitions undermined respect for the law by penalizing conduct many people engaged in; (2) the statutes regulated private conduct not harmful to others; and (3) the laws were arbitrarily enforced and thus invited the danger of blackmail. In 1961 Illinois changed its laws to conform to the Model Penal Code. Other States soon followed.

* * *

. . . [T]he deficiencies in *Bowers* became even more apparent in the years following its announcement. The 25 States with laws prohibiting the relevant conduct referenced in the *Bowers* decision are reduced now to 13, of which 4 enforce their laws only against homosexual conduct. In those States where sodomy is still proscribed, whether for same-sex or heterosexual conduct, there is a pattern of nonenforcement with respect to consenting adults acting in private. The State of Texas admitted in 1994 that as of that date it had not prosecuted anyone under those circumstances.

Two principal cases decided after *Bowers* cast its holding into even more doubt. In *Planned Parenthood of Southeastern Pa. v. Casey,* the Court reaffirmed the substantive force of the liberty protected by the Due Process

Clause. The *Casey* decision again confirmed that our laws and tradition afford constitutional protection to personal decisions relating to marriage, procreation, contraception, family relationships, child rearing, and education. In explaining the respect the Constitution demands for the autonomy of the person in making these choices, we stated as follows:

> These matters, involving the most intimate and personal choices a person may make in a lifetime, choices central to personal dignity and autonomy, are central to the liberty protected by the Fourteenth Amendment. At the heart of liberty is the right to define one's own concept of existence, of meaning, of the universe, and of the mystery of human life. Beliefs about these matters could not define the attributes of personhood were they formed under compulsion of the State.

Persons in a homosexual relationship may seek autonomy for these purposes, just as heterosexual persons do. The decision in *Bowers* would deny them this right.

The second post-*Bowers* case of principal relevance is *Romer v. Evans*. There the Court struck down class-based legislation directed at homosexuals as a violation of the Equal Protection Clause. *Romer* invalidated an amendment to Colorado's constitution which named as a solitary class persons who were homosexuals, lesbians, or bisexual either by "orientation, conduct, practices or relationships," and deprived them of protection under state antidiscrimination laws. We concluded that the provision was "born of animosity toward the class of persons affected" and further that it had no rational relation to a legitimate governmental purpose.

As an alternative argument in this case, counsel for the petitioners and some *amici* contend that *Romer* provides the basis for declaring the Texas statute invalid under the Equal Protection Clause. That is a tenable argument, but we conclude the instant case requires us to address whether *Bowers* itself has continuing validity. Were we to hold the statute invalid under the Equal Protection Clause some might question whether a prohibition would be valid if drawn differently, say, to prohibit the conduct both between same-sex and different-sex participants.

Equality of treatment and the due process right to demand respect for conduct protected by the substantive guarantee of liberty are linked in important respects, and a decision on the latter point advances both interests. If protected conduct is made criminal and the law which does so remains unexamined for its substantive validity, its stigma might remain even if it were not enforceable as drawn for equal protection reasons. When homosexual conduct is made criminal by the law of the State, that declaration in and of itself is an invitation to subject homosexual persons to discrimination both in the public and in the private spheres. The central holding of *Bowers* has been brought in question by this case, and it should be addressed. Its continuance as precedent demeans the lives of homosexual persons.

The stigma this criminal statute imposes, moreover, is not trivial. The offense, to be sure, is but a class C misdemeanor, a minor offense in the Texas legal system. Still, it remains a criminal offense with all that imports for the dignity of the persons charged. The petitioners will bear on their record the history of their criminal convictions. Just this Term we rejected various challenges to state laws requiring the registration of sex offenders. We are advised that if Texas convicted an adult for private, consensual homosexual conduct under the statute here in question the convicted person would come within the registration laws of a least four States were he or she to be subject to their jurisdiction. This underscores the consequential nature of the punishment and the state-sponsored condemnation attendant to the criminal prohibition. Furthermore, the Texas criminal conviction carries with it the other collateral consequences always following a conviction, such as notations on job application forms, to mention but one example.

The foundations of *Bowers* have sustained serious erosion from our recent decisions in *Casey* and *Romer*. When our precedent has been thus weakened, criticism from other sources is of greater significance. In the United States criticism of *Bowers* has been substantial and continuing, disapproving of its reasoning in all respects, not just as to its historical assumptions. The courts of five different States have declined to follow it in interpreting provisions in their own state constitutions parallel to the Due Process Clause of the Fourteenth Amendment.

To the extent *Bowers* relied on values we share with a wider civilization, it should be noted that the reasoning and holding in *Bowers* have been rejected elsewhere. The European Court of Human Rights has followed not *Bowers* but its own decision in *Dudgeon v. United Kingdom*. Other nations, too, have taken action consistent with an affirmation of the protected right of homosexual adults to engage in intimate, consensual conduct. The right the petitioners seek in this case has been accepted as an integral part of human freedom in many other countries. There has been no showing that in this country the governmental interest in circumscribing personal choice is somehow more legitimate or urgent.

* * *

*Bowers* was not correct when it was decided, and it is not correct today. It ought not to remain binding precedent. *Bowers v. Hardwick* should be and now is overruled.

The present case does not involve minors. It does not involve persons who might be injured or coerced or who are situated in relationships where consent might not easily be refused. It does not involve public conduct or prostitution. It does not involve whether the government must give formal recognition to any relationship that homosexual persons seek to enter. The case does involve two adults who, with full and mutual consent from each other, engaged in sexual practices common to a homosexual lifestyle. The petitioners are entitled to respect for their private lives. The State cannot demean their existence or control their destiny by making their private sexual conduct a crime. Their right to liberty under the Due Process Clause gives them the full right to engage in their conduct without intervention of the government. "It is a promise of the Constitution that there is a realm of personal liberty which the government may not enter." The Texas statute furthers no legitimate state interest which can justify its intrusion into the personal and private life of the individual.

Had those who drew and ratified the Due Process Clauses of the Fifth Amendment or the Fourteenth Amendment known the components of liberty in its manifold possibilities, they might have been more specific. They did not presume to have this insight. They knew times can blind us to certain truths and later generations can see that laws once thought necessary and proper in fact serve only to oppress. As the Constitution endures, persons in every generation can invoke its principles in their own search for greater freedom.

The judgment of the Court of Appeals for the Texas Fourteenth District is reversed, and the case is remanded for further proceedings not inconsistent with this opinion.

It is so ordered.

## ALEXIS
## v.
## McDONALD'S RESTAURANTS OF MASSACHUSETTS, INC.

## 67 F.3d 341 (1st Cir. 1995)

*[Citations and footnotes omitted.]*

[Mrs. Alexis, an African-American, entered a McDonald's restaurant and placed her order at the service counter. When the order was improperly filled, a loud exchange followed, ending in the manager telling Mrs. Alexis and her family to take their food and leave. Upon her refusal, the manager summoned Michael Leporati, a uniformed police officer who was patrolling the neighborhood on foot, and told him that Mrs. Alexis had created an unwarranted disturbance. Without making further inquiry, Liporati proceeded to the dining area where she and her family were seated and told them that they would have to leave. When she denied causing a disturbance and asked Leporati to inquire of other customers about what had happened, he ignored her request and called for backup. When the backup arrived, Officer Leporati informed Mrs. Alexis that she was under arrest and, without asking her to get up, hauled her from the booth, handcuffed her hands behind her back, and dragged her out of the restaurant, ignoring her request to be allowed to walk out on her own. Upon reaching the squad car, he shoved her inside, ordering: "Get your ass in there." When her husband protested her treatment, Leporati responded, "You people have no rights. You better shut up your [expletive] mouth before I arrest you too."

Mrs. Alexis was charged with criminal trespass. Following her acquittal, she sued Officer Leporati for damages under 42 U.S.C. § 1983, claiming that he had violated her right to equal protection of the laws by arresting her and using excessive force against her because of her race. The district court granted Officer Leporati's motion for summary judgment and dismissed Mrs. Alexis' claim.]

CYR, Circuit Judge.

* * *

During the arrest, Sergeant Leporati stated to Mr. Alexis: "You people have no rights. You better shut up your . . . mouth before I arrest you too." Alexis insists that this statement betrayed a racial animus. * * *

A rational factfinder who credited this statement, as we must at summary judgment, reasonably could infer that Leporati harbored a racial animus * * *, especially since the record reflects that the only relevant behavior or physical characteristic—both apparent to Leporati and shared by the Alexis family—was their black skin. Indeed, a rational factfinder would be hard-pressed to glean a more plausible inference, particularly since Leporati has tendered no alternative interpretation supported by the present record. Viewed in context, therefore, the Leporati statement, tarring the entire family with the same brush—absent a scintilla of evidence that any member, with the possible exception of Alexis, had said or done anything remotely wrong or disorderly—cannot reasonably be presumed so innocent as to preclude a discriminatory animus.

* * *

Alexis claims that Leporati discriminated against her on the basis of her race, both in deciding to enforce the criminal trespass statute by effecting her immediate arrest, and by employing unreasonable force. Even assuming probable cause to arrest, she argues that Leporati would not have effected an immediate seizure of her person for so minor an infraction, nor used such excessive force, were it not for the color of her skin.

In order to avoid summary judgment on her Equal Protection Clause claim, Alexis had to tender competent evidence that a state actor intentionally discriminated against her because she belonged to a protected class. This she did. A rational factfinder, who credited Alexis's evidence of racial animus and excessive force, could conclude that Leporati resolved, on the basis of her race, to enforce the criminal trespass statute by effecting an immediate seizure of her person. Furthermore, a rational factfinder could conclude that, in electing to use excessive force to effect the violent seizure of Alexis's person and her forcible removal from the restaurant, Leporati was motivated by a discriminatory animus. We therefore hold, based on the present record, that the Equal Protection Clause claims under section 1983 are trialworthy.

* * *

## CONCLUSION

. . . The district court judgment entered in favor of Leporati on the . . . excessive force, and Equal Protection Clause claims is vacated, and these claims are remanded for further proceedings consistent with this opinion, . . .

SO ORDERED.

[Concurring and dissenting opinions omitted.]

# Cases Relating to Chapter 2

# Freedom of Speech

## NORWELL
### v.
## CITY OF CINCINNATI

### 414 U.S. 14, 94 S. Ct. 187, 38 L. Ed. 2d 170 (1973)

[Officer Johnson accosted Norwell, a 69-year-old immigrant, as he walked home from work, and asked him whether he lived in the neighborhood. When Norwell turned to walk away, Officer Johnson manually restrained him. Norwell threw Johnson off his arm and loudly protested "I don't tell you people anything." Johnson arrested Norwell for disorderly conduct under an ordinance that read: "No person shall wilfully conduct himself or herself in a noisy, boisterous, rude, insulting or other disorderly manner, with the intent to abuse or annoy any person."]

PER CURIAM.

* * *

Upon this record, we are convinced that petitioner was arrested and convicted merely because he verbally and negatively protested Officer Johnson's treatment of him. Surely, one is not to be punished for nonprovocatively voicing his objection to what he obviously felt was a highly questionable detention by a police officer. Regardless of what the motivation may have been behind the expression in this case, it is clear that there was no abusive language or fighting words. If there had been, we would have a different case.

The petition for certiorari is granted. The judgment is reversed.

## TEXAS
### v.
## JOHNSON

### 491 U.S. 397, 109 S. Ct. 2533, 105 L. Ed. 2d 342 (1989)

*[Citations and footnotes omitted.]*

[Johnson participated in a political protest demonstration in Dallas during the 1984 Republican National Convention. The demonstration ended in front of City Hall, where Johnson unfurled an American flag, doused it with kerosene, and set it on fire while the demonstrators chanted, "America, the red, white, and blue, we spit on you." No one was physically injured or threatened with injury, although several witnesses testified that they had been seriously offended by Johnson's behavior. Johnson was charged with and convicted of desecrating an American flag in violation of Tex. Penal Code Ann. § 42.09 (a)(3). The question before the Supreme Court was whether criminalizing flag burning violates the First Amendment.]

JUSTICE BRENNAN delivered the opinion of the Court.

* * *

The First Amendment literally forbids the abridgment only of "speech," but we have long recognized that its protection does not end at the spoken or written word. While we have rejected "the view that an apparently limitless variety of conduct can be labeled 'speech' whenever the person engaging in the conduct intends thereby to express an idea," we have acknowledged that conduct may be "sufficiently imbued with elements of communication to fall within the scope of the First and Fourteenth Amendments." In deciding whether particular conduct possesses sufficient communicative elements to bring the First Amendment into play, we have asked whether "[a]n intent to convey a particularized message was present, and [whether] the likelihood was great that the message would be understood by those who viewed it." Hence, we have recognized the expressive nature of students' wearing of black armbands to protest American military involvement in Vietnam; of a sit-in by blacks in a "whites only" area to protest segregation; of the wearing of American military uniforms in a dramatic presentation criticizing American military involvement in Vietnam; and of picketing about a wide variety of causes.

* * *

The State of Texas conceded for purposes of its oral argument in this case that Johnson's conduct was expressive conduct. . . . Johnson burned an American flag as part—indeed, as the culmina-

tion—of a political demonstration that coincided with the convening of the Republican Party and its renomination of Ronald Reagan for President. The expressive, overtly political nature of this conduct was both intentional and overwhelmingly apparent. At his trial, Johnson explained his reasons for burning the flag as follows: "The American Flag was burned as Ronald Reagan was being renominated as President. And a more powerful statement of symbolic speech, whether you agree with or not, couldn't have been made at that time. It's quite a just position [juxtaposition]. We had new patriotism and no patriotism." In these circumstances, Johnson's burning of the flag was conduct "sufficiently imbued with elements of communication to fall within the scope of the First and Fourteenth Amendments."

The Government generally has a freer hand in restricting expressive conduct than it has in restricting the written or spoken word. It may not, however, proscribe particular conduct *because* it has expressive elements. "[W]hat might be termed the more generalized guarantee of freedom of expression makes the communicative nature of conduct an inadequate *basis* for singling out that conduct for proscription. A law *directed* at the communicative nature of conduct must, like a law directed at speech itself, be justified by the substantial showing of need that the First Amendment requires." It is, in short, not simply the verbal or nonverbal nature of the expression, but the governmental interest at stake, that helps to determine whether a restriction on that expression is valid.

Thus, although we have recognized that where "'speech' and 'nonspeech' elements are combined in the same course of conduct, a sufficiently important governmental interest in regulating the nonspeech element can justify incidental limitations on First Amendment freedoms," we have limited the applicability of *O'Brien's* relatively lenient standard to those cases in which "the governmental interest is unrelated to the suppression of free expression." . . .

In order to decide whether *O'Brien's* test applies here, therefore, we must decide whether Texas has asserted an interest in support of Johnson's conviction that is unrelated to the suppression of expression. . . . The State offers two separate interests to justify this conviction: preventing breaches of the peace, and preserving the flag as a symbol of nationhood and national unity. We hold that the first interest is not implicated on this record and that the second is related to the suppression of expression.

Texas claims that its interest in preventing breaches of the peace justifies Johnson's conviction for flag desecration. However, no disturbance of the peace actually occurred or threatened to occur because of Johnson's burning of the flag. . . . The only evidence offered by the State at trial to show the reaction to Johnson's actions was the testimony of several persons who had been seriously offended by the flag-burning. The State's position, therefore, amounts to a claim that an audience that takes serious offense at particular expression is necessarily likely to disturb the peace and that the expression may be prohibited on this basis. Our precedents do not countenance such a presumption. On the contrary, they recognize that a principal "function of free speech under our system of government is to invite dispute. It may indeed best serve its high purpose when it induces a condition of unrest, creates dissatisfaction with conditions as they are, or even stirs people to anger." . . .

Thus, we have not permitted the Government to assume that every expression of a provocative idea will incite a riot, but have instead required careful consideration of the actual circumstances surrounding such expression, asking whether the expression "is directed to inciting or pro-

ducing imminent lawless action and is likely to incite or produce such action." To accept Texas' arguments that it need only demonstrate "the potential for a breach of the peace," and that every flag-burning necessarily possesses that potential, would be to eviscerate our holding in *Brandenburg*. This we decline to do.

Nor does Johnson's expressive conduct fall within that small class of "fighting words" that are "likely to provoke the average person to retaliation, and thereby cause a breach of the peace." No reasonable onlooker would have regarded Johnson's generalized expression of dissatisfaction with the policies of the Federal Government as a direct personal insult or an invitation to exchange fisticuffs.

We thus conclude that the State's interest in maintaining order is not implicated on these facts. The State need not worry that our holding will disable it from preserving the peace. We do not suggest that the First Amendment forbids a State to prevent "imminent lawless action." And, in fact, Texas already has a statute specifically prohibiting breaches of the peace, Tex. Penal Code Ann. § 42.01 (1989), which tends to confirm that Texas need not punish this flag desecration in order to keep the peace.

The State also asserts an interest in preserving the flag as a symbol of nationhood and national unity. In *Spence*, we acknowledged that the Government's interest in preserving the flag's special symbolic value "is directly related to expression in the context of activity" such as affixing a peace symbol to a flag. We are equally persuaded that this interest is related to expression in the case of Johnson's burning of the flag. The State, apparently, is concerned that such conduct will lead people to believe either that the flag does not stand for nationhood and national unity, but instead reflects other, less positive concepts, or that the concepts reflected in the flag do not in fact exist, that is, we do not enjoy unity as a Nation. These concerns blossom only when a person's treatment of the flag communicates some message, and thus are related "to the suppression of free expression" within the meaning of *O'Brien*. We are thus outside of *O'Brien's* test altogether.

It remains to consider whether the State's interest in preserving the flag as a symbol of nationhood and national unity justifies Johnson's conviction.

As in *Spence* "[w]e are confronted with a case of prosecution for the expression of an idea through activity," and "[a]ccordingly, we must examine with particular care the interests advanced by [petitioner] to support its prosecution." Johnson was not, we add, prosecuted for the expression of just any idea; he was prosecuted for his expression of dissatisfaction with the policies of this country, expression situated at the core of our First Amendment values.

\* \* \*

If there is a bedrock principle underlying the First Amendment, it is that the Government may not prohibit the expression of an idea simply because society finds the idea itself offensive or disagreeable.

We have not recognized an exception to this principle even where our flag has been involved. In *Street v. New York*, we held that a State may not criminally punish a person for uttering words critical of the flag. Rejecting the argument that the conviction could be sustained on the ground that Street had "failed to show the respect for our national symbol which may properly be demanded of every citizen," we concluded that "the constitutionally guaranteed 'freedom to be intellectually . . . diverse or even contrary,' and the 'right to differ as to things that touch the heart of the existing order,' encompass the freedom to express publicly one's opinions about our flag, including those opinions which are defiant or contemptuous." Nor may the Government, we have held, compel conduct that would evince respect for the flag. "To sustain the compulsory flag salute we are required to say that a Bill of Rights which guards the individual's right to speak his own mind, left it open to public authorities to compel him to utter what is not in his mind."

\* \* \*

In short, nothing in our precedents suggests that a State may foster its own view of the flag by prohibiting expressive conduct relating to it. To bring its argument outside our precedents, Texas attempts to convince us that even if its interest in preserving the flag's symbolic role does not allow it to prohibit words or some expressive conduct critical of the flag, it does permit it to forbid the outright destruction of the flag. The State's argument cannot depend here on the distinction between written or spoken words and nonverbal conduct. That distinction, we have shown, is of no moment where the nonverbal conduct is expressive, as it is here, and where the regulation of that conduct is related to expression, as it is here. In addition, both *Barnette* and *Spence* involved expressive conduct, not only verbal communication, and both found that conduct protected.

\* \* \*

We are fortified in today's conclusion by our conviction that forbidding criminal punishment for conduct such as Johnson's will not endanger the special role played by our flag or the feelings it inspires. . . .

We are tempted to say, in fact, that the flag's deservedly cherished place in our community will be strengthened, not weakened, by our holding today. Our decision is a reaffirmation of the principles of freedom and inclusiveness that the flag best reflects, and of the conviction that our toleration of criticism such as Johnson's is a sign and source of our strength. Indeed, one of the proudest images of our flag, the one immortalized in our own national anthem, is of the bombardment it survived at Fort McHenry. It is the Nation's resilience, not its rigidity, that Texas sees reflected in the flag—and it is that resilience that we reassert today.

The way to preserve the flag's special rule is not to punish those who feel differently about these matters. . . . We do not consecrate the flag by punishing its desecration, for in doing so we dilute the freedom that this cherished emblem represents.

Johnson was convicted for engaging in expressive conduct. The State's interest in preventing breaches of the peace does not support his conviction because Johnson's conduct did not threaten to disturb the peace. Nor does the State's interest in preserving the flag as a symbol of nationhood and national unity justify his criminal conviction for engaging in political expression. The judgment of the Texas Court of Criminal Appeals is therefore

*Affirmed.*

## SANDUL
## v.
## LARION

### 119 F.3d 1250 (6th Cir. 1997)

*[Citations and footnotes omitted.]*

[As the truck in which he was riding passed a group of abortion protesters at a high rate of speed, John Sandul leaned out, extended his middle finger to the group, and shouted "f——k you." The truck was then separated from the pro-testers by a line of traffic, a grassy median strip, and a sidewalk. Officer Larion, who witnessed this incident, pursued the truck and arrested Sandul for disorderly conduct. Sandul was acquitted and sued Officer Larion under 42 U.S.C. § 1983, for violating his First Amendment rights. The trial court dismissed Sandul's complaint and he appealed.]

NATHANIEL R. JONES, Circuit Judge.

\* \* \*

It is well-established that "absent a more particularized and compelling reason for its actions, [a] State may not, consistently with the First and Fourteenth Amendments, make the simple public display . . . of [a] four-letter expletive a criminal offense." In *Cohen [v. California]*, the words of individual expression were also "f—k you." The *Cohen* Court explained why such language is entitled to First Amendment protection although it appears to have little redeeming value:

[W]hile the particular four-letter word being litigated here is perhaps more distasteful than most others of its genre, it is nevertheless often true that one man's vulgarity is another's lyric. Indeed, we think it is largely because governmental officials cannot make principled distinctions in this area that the Constitution leaves matters of taste and style so largely to the individual.

Thus, the use of the "f-word" in and of itself is not criminal conduct.

First Amendment protection is very expansive. The only type of language that is denied First Amendment protection is "fighting words." *Chaplinsky [v. New Hampshire]* defined "fighting words" as:

548 CONSTITUTIONAL LAW

those which by their very utterance inflict injury or tend to incite an immediate breach of the peace. . . . [S]uch utterances are no essential part of any exposition of ideas, and are of such slight social value . . . that any benefit that may be derived from them is clearly outweighed by the social interest in order and morality.

The fighting words exception is very limited because it is inconsistent with the general principle of free speech recognized in our First Amendment jurisprudence. Fighting words are words that are likely to cause an average person to react thus causing a breach of the peace. They are words which an onlooker would consider a "direct personal insult or an invitation to exchange fisticuffs."

Sandul's words and actions do not rise to the level of fighting words. The actions were not likely to inflict injury or to incite an immediate breach of the peace. Sandul's vehicle was traveling at a high rate of speed on the opposite side of the street, a considerable distance away from the protesters to whom the language was directed. Sandul was in a moving vehicle; the entire incident was over in a matter of seconds. There is no evidence in the record that any abortion protester was offended, nor did anyone acknowledge Sandul's behavior with the exception of Officer Larion. There was no face-to-face contact between Sandul and the protestors. Thus, it is inconceivable that Sandul's fleeting actions and words would provoke the type of lawless action alluded to in *Chaplinsky*. Sandul's action was not fighting words and therefore was speech protected by the First Amendment.

\* \* \*

We conclude that Larion is not entitled to qualified immunity because his actions violated Sandul's clearly estab-

lished First Amendment rights of which a reasonable officer should have known. Accordingly, the judgment of the district court is REVERSED, and the case is REMANDED for further proceedings consistent with this opinion.

## BUFFKINS
v.
## CITY OF OMAHA

### 922 F.2d 465 (8th Cir. 1990)

*[Citations and footnotes omitted.]*

[On March 17, 1987, Omaha police received a tip that a black person arriving on a flight from Denver some time before 5:00 P.M. would be importing cocaine into the Omaha area. Officers Grigsby and Friend went to the airport to check out this tip. They noticed that Lu Ann Buffkins, the only black passenger to deplane on the 3:40 P.M. from Denver, was carrying a teddy bear with seams that appeared to have been resewn. They approached her, identified themselves as officers conducting a narcotics investigation, and asked her to bring her luggage and come with them to the security office to answer questions. She went, complaining that their conduct was racist and unconstitutional all along the way. The investigation in the security office turned up nothing and when the officers told Ms. Buffkins that she was free to go and to "have a nice day," she replied "I will have a nice day, asshole." The officers immediately arrested her for disorderly conduct.

Buffkins was acquitted and sued Grigsby and Friend under 42 U.S.C. § 1983 for violating her First Amendment rights by arresting her without cause to believe that her language constituted "fighting words." The jury returned a verdict in favor of the officers and Buffkins appealed.]

LAY, Chief Judge

\* \* \*

The Supreme Court held in *Chaplinsky v. New Hampshire* that "fighting words" are not protected speech under the First and Fourteenth Amendments. The *Chaplinsky* Court defines "fighting words" as words "which by their very utterance inflict injury or tend to incite an immediate breach of the peace." "Fighting words" are words that are "likely to cause an average addressee to fight.". . .

We conclude that the district court should have found as a matter of law that the officers did not have probable cause to arrest Buffkins for using "fighting words." There is no evidence that Buffkins' speech was an incitement to immediate lawless action. Neither arresting officer contended that Buffkins became violent or threatened violence. Moreover, both officers admitted that nobody outside the interview room heard Buffkins' comment. In addition, Buffkins' use of the word "asshole" could not reasonably have prompted a violent response from the arresting officers. In *Houston v. Hill*, the Supreme Court recognized that the "fighting words" doctrine may be limited in the case of communications addressed to properly trained police officers because police officers are expected to exercise greater restraint in their response than the average citizen. The *Houston* Court stated:

The First Amendment protects a significant amount of verbal criticism and challenge directed at police officers. . . . The freedom of individuals verbally to oppose or challenge police action without thereby risking arrest is one of the principal characteristics by which we distinguish a free nation from a police state.

\* \* \*

. . . We . . . hold that Buffkins' speech directed at the officers did not constitute "fighting words.". . .

# VIRGINIA
# v.
# BLACK

## 538 U.S. 343, 123 S. Ct. 1536, 155 L. Ed. 2d 535 (2003)

*[Citations and footnotes omitted]*

[Barry Black led a Ku Klux Klan rally, attended by 25 to 30 people, in an open field on private property. During the rally, the members took turns delivering hate speeches. At the conclusion of the rally, a 25- to 30-foot cross was set on fire. A sheriff who observed the rally from the side of the road arrested Black and charged him with violating a Virginia statute (§ 18.2-423) that made it unlawful to burn a cross with the intent to intimidate any person or group of persons. The statute further declared that the act of cross-burning was prima facie evidence of the existence of such intent. Black was convicted and appealed, arguing that the prima facie evidence provision rendered the statute unconstitutional.]

Justice O'CONNOR announced the judgment of the Court.

\* \* \*

To this day, regardless of whether the message is a political one or whether the message is also meant to intimidate, the burning of a cross is a "symbol of hate." And while cross burning sometimes carries no intimidating message, at other times the intimidating message is the only message conveyed. For example, when a cross burning is directed at a particular person not affiliated with the Klan, the burning cross often serves as a message of intimidation, designed to inspire in the victim a fear of bodily harm. Moreover, the history of violence associated with the Klan shows that the possibility of injury or death is not just hypothetical. The person who burns a cross directed at a particular person often is making a serious threat, meant to coerce the victim to comply with the Klan's wishes unless the victim is willing to risk the wrath of the Klan . . . In sum, while a burning cross does not inevitably convey a message of intimidation, often the cross burner intends that the recipients of the message fear for their lives. And when a cross burning is used to intimidate, few if any messages are more powerful.

The First Amendment, applicable to the States through the Fourteenth Amendment, provides that "Congress shall make no law . . . abridging the freedom of speech." The hallmark of the protection of free speech is to allow "free trade in ideas"—even ideas that the overwhelming majority of people might find distasteful or discomforting. Thus, the First Amendment "ordinarily" denies a State "the power to prohibit dissemination of social, economic and political doctrine which a vast majority of its citizens believes to be false and fraught with evil consequence." The First Amendment affords protection to symbolic or expressive conduct as well as to actual speech.

The protections afforded by the First Amendment, however, are not absolute, and we have long recognized that the government may regulate certain categories of expression consistent with the Constitution. The First Amendment permits "restrictions upon the content of speech in a few limited areas, which are 'of such slight social value as a step to truth that any benefit that may be derived from them is clearly outweighed by the social interest in order and morality.'"

Thus, for example, a State may punish those words "which by their very utterance inflict injury or tend to incite an immediate breach of the peace." We have consequently held that fighting words—"those personally abusive epithets which, when addressed to the ordinary citizen, are, as a matter of common knowledge, inherently likely to provoke violent reaction"—are generally proscribable under the First Amendment. Furthermore, "the constitutional guarantees of free speech and free press do not permit a State to forbid or proscribe advocacy of the use of force or of law violation except where such advocacy is directed to inciting or producing imminent lawless action and is likely to incite or produce such action." The First Amendment also permits a State to ban a "true threat."

"True threats" encompass those statements where the speaker means to communicate a serious expression of an intent to commit an act of unlawful violence to a particular individual or group of individuals. The speaker need not actually intend to carry out the threat. Rather, a prohibition on true threats "protect[s] individuals from the fear of violence" and "from the disruption that fear engenders," in addition to protecting people "from the possibility that the threatened violence will occur." Intimidation in the constitutionally proscribable sense of the word is a type of true threat, where a speaker directs a threat to a person or group of persons with the intent of placing the victim in fear of bodily harm or death. Respondents do not contest that some cross burnings fit within this meaning of intimidating speech, and rightly so. . . . [T]he history of cross burning in this country shows that cross burning is often intimidating, intended to create a pervasive fear in victims that they are a target of violence.

\* \* \*

As the history of cross burning indicates, a burning cross is not always intended to intimidate. Rather, sometimes the cross burning is a statement of ideology, a symbol of group solidarity. It is a ritual used at Klan gatherings, and it is used to represent the Klan itself. Thus, "[b]urning a cross at a political rally would almost certainly be protected expression." Indeed, occasionally a person who burns a cross does not intend to express either a statement of ideology or intimidation. Cross burnings have appeared in movies such as *Mississippi Burning*, and in plays such as the stage adaptation of Sir Walter Scott's *The Lady of the Lake*.

The prima facie provision makes no effort to distinguish among these different types of cross burnings. It does not distinguish between a cross burning done with the purpose of creating anger or resentment and a cross burning done with the purpose of threatening or intimidating a victim. It does not distinguish between a cross burning at a public rally or a cross burning on a neighbor's lawn. It does not treat the cross burning directed at an individual differently from the cross burning directed at a group of like-minded believers. It allows a jury to treat a cross burning on the property of another with the owner's acquiescence in the same manner as a cross burning on the property of another without the owner's permission. . . .

. . . The prima facie evidence provision in this case ignores all of the contextual factors that are necessary to decide whether a particular cross burning is intended to intimidate. The First Amendment does not permit such a shortcut.

For these reasons, the prima facie evidence provision . . . is unconstitutional on its face.

* * *

It is so ordered.

# HESS
## v.
# INDIANA

### 414 U.S. 105, 94 S. Ct. 326, 8 L. Ed. 2d 303 (1973)

*[Citations and footnotes omitted.]*

[The events leading to Hess' conviction began with an antiwar demonstration on the campus of Indiana University. In the course of the demonstration, approximately 100 to 150 of the demonstrators moved onto a public street and blocked the passage of vehicles. When the demonstrators did not respond to verbal directions from the sheriff to clear the street, the sheriff and his deputies began walking up the street, and the demonstrators in their path moved to the curbs on either side, joining a large number of spectators who had gathered. Hess was standing off the street as the sheriff passed him. The sheriff heard Hess utter the words "We'll take the fucking street later," or "We'll take the fucking street again." and immediately arrested him on disorderly conduct charges. Two witnesses who were in the immediate vicinity testified, apparently without contradiction, that they heard Hess' words and witnessed his arrest. They indicated that Hess did not appear to be exhorting the crowd to go back into the street, that he was facing the crowd and not the street when he uttered the statement, that his statement did not appear to be addressed to any particular person or group, and that his tone, although loud, was no louder than that of the other people in the area.]

PER CURIAM.

* * *

Indiana's disorderly conduct statute was applied in this case to punish only spoken words. It hardly needs repeating that "the constitutional guarantees of freedom of speech forbid the States to punish the use of words or language not within 'narrowly limited classes of speech.'" The words here did not fall within any of these "limited classes." In the first place, it is clear that the Indiana court specifically abjured any suggestion that Hess' words could be punished as obscene under *Roth v. United States* and its progeny. Indeed, after *Cohen v. California*, such a contention with regard to the language at issue would not be tenable. By the same token, any suggestion that Hess' speech amounted to "fighting words," could not withstand scrutiny. Even if under other circumstances this language could be regarded as a personal insult, the evidence is undisputed that Hess' statement was not directed to any person or group in particular. Although the sheriff testified that he was offended by the language, he also stated that he did not interpret the expression as being directed personally at him, and the evidence is clear that appellant had his back to the sheriff at the time. Thus, under our decisions, the State could not punish this speech as "fighting words."

. . . The Indiana Supreme Court placed primary reliance on the trial court's finding that Hess' statement "was intended to incite further lawless action on the part of the crowd in the vicinity of appellant and was likely to produce such action." At best, however, the statement could be taken as counsel for present moderation; at worst, it amounted to nothing more than advocacy of illegal action at some indefinite future time. This is not sufficient to permit the State to punish Hess' speech. Under our decisions, "the constitutional guarantees of free speech and free press do not permit a State to forbid or proscribe advocacy of the use of force or of law violation except where such advocacy is directed

to inciting or producing imminent lawless action and is likely to incite or produce such action." Since the uncontroverted evidence showed that Hess' statement was not directed to any person or group of persons, it cannot be said that he was advocating, in the normal sense, any action. And since there was no evidence, or rational inference from the import of the language, that his words were intended to produce, and likely to produce, imminent disorder, those words could not be punished by the State on the ground that they had "a 'tendency to lead to violence.'"

Accordingly, the motion to proceed in forma pauperis is granted and the judgment of the Supreme Court of Indiana is reversed.

*[Dissenting opinion omitted.]*

## INTERNATIONAL SOCIETY FOR KRISHNA CONSCIOUSNESS
### v.
### LEE

### 505 U.S. 672, 112 S. Ct. 2701, 120 L. Ed. 2d 541 (1992)

*[Citations and footnotes omitted)*

[International Society for Krishna Consciousness, Inc. (ISKCON) is a not-for-profit religious corporation whose members perform a ritual known as sankirtan. The ritual consists of going into public places, disseminating religious literature, and soliciting funds to support the religion. The primary purpose of this ritual is raising funds for the movement. The Port Authority, which owns and operates three major airports in the greater New York City area (John F. Kennedy International Airport, La Guardia Airport, and Newark International Airport) adopted a regulation forbidding solicitation of money or distribution of literature inside the terminals. ISKCON brought suit to have this regulation declared unconstitutional under the First Amendment.]

CHIEF JUSTICE REHNQUIST delivered the opinion of the Court.

In this case we consider whether an airport terminal operated by a public authority is a public forum and whether a regulation prohibiting solicitation in the interior of an airport terminal violates the First Amendment.

\* \* \*

It is uncontested that the solicitation at issue in this case is a form of speech protected under the First Amendment. But it is also well settled that the government need not permit all forms of speech on property that it owns and controls. Where the government is acting as a proprietor, managing its internal operations, rather than acting as lawmaker, its action will not be subjected to the heightened review to which its actions as a lawmaker may be subject. Thus, we have upheld a ban on political advertisements in city-operated transit vehicles, even though the city permitted other types of advertising on those vehicles. Similarly, we have permitted a school district to limit access to an internal mail system used to communicate with teachers employed by the district.

These cases reflect, either implicitly or explicitly, a "forum-based" approach for assessing restrictions that the government seeks to place on the use of its property. Under this approach, regulation of speech on government property that has traditionally been available for public expression is subject to the highest scrutiny. Such regulations survive only if they are narrowly drawn to achieve a compelling state interest. The second category of public property is the

designated public forum, property that the state has opened for expressive activity by part or all of the public. Regulation of such property is subject to the same limitations as that governing a traditional public forum. Finally, there is all remaining public property. Limitations on expressive activity conducted on this last category of property must survive only a much more limited review. The challenged regulation need only be reasonable and not an effort to suppress the speaker's activity due to disagreement with the speaker's view.

The parties do not disagree that this is the proper framework. Rather, they disagree whether the airport terminals are public fora or nonpublic fora. They also disagree whether the regulation survives the "reasonableness" review governing nonpublic fora, should that prove the appropriate category. Like the Court of Appeals, we conclude that the terminals are nonpublic fora and that the regulation reasonably limits solicitation.

The suggestion that the government has a high burden in justifying speech restrictions relating to traditional public fora made its first appearance in *Hague v. Committee for Industrial Organization*. Justice Roberts, concluding that individuals have a right to use "streets and parks for communication of views," reasoned that such a right flowed from the fact that "streets and parks . . . have immemorially been held in trust for the use of the public and, time out of mind, have been used for purposes of assembly, communicating thoughts between citizens, and discussing public questions." . . .

Our recent cases provide additional guidance on the characteristics of a public forum. In *Cornelius*, we noted that a traditional public forum is property that has "as a principal purpose . . . the free exchange of ideas." Moreover, consistent with the notion that the government— like other property owners—"has power to preserve the property under its control for the use to which it is lawfully dedicated," the government does not create a public forum by inaction. Nor is a public forum created "whenever members of the public are permitted freely to visit a place owned or operated by the Government." The decision to create a public forum must instead be made "by intentionally opening a nontraditional forum for public discourse." . . .

These precedents foreclose the conclusion that airport terminals are public fora. Reflecting the general growth of the air travel industry, airport terminals have only recently achieved their contemporary size and character. But given the lateness with which the modern air terminal has made its appearance, it hardly qualifies for the description of having "immemorially . . . time out of mind" been held in the public trust and used for purposes of expressive activity. . . . Thus, the tradition of airport activity does not demonstrate that airports have historically been made available for speech activity. Nor can we say that these particular terminals, or airport terminals generally, have been intentionally opened by their operators to such activity; the frequent and continuing litigation evidencing the operators' objections belies any such claim. . . .

* * *

[A]irports are commercial establishments funded by users fees and designed to make a regulated profit and where nearly all who visit do so for some travel related purpose. As commercial enterprises, airports must provide services attractive to the marketplace. In light of this, it cannot fairly be said that an airport terminal has as a principal purpose "promoting the free exchange of ideas." To the contrary, the record demonstrates that Port Authority management considers the purpose of the terminals to be the facilitation of passenger air travel, not the promotion of expression. Even if we look beyond the intent of the Port Authority to the manner in which the terminals have been operated, the terminals have never been dedicated (except under the threat of court order) to expression in the form sought to be exercised here: i.e., the solicitation of contributions and the distribution of literature.

The terminals here are far from atypical. Airport builders and managers focus their efforts on providing terminals that will contribute to efficient air travel. . . . Thus, we think that neither by tradition nor purpose can the terminals be described as satisfying the standards we have previously set out for identifying a public forum.

The restrictions here challenged, therefore, need only satisfy a requirement of reasonableness. We reiterate what we stated in *Kokinda*, the restriction "need only be reasonable; it need not be the most reasonable or the only reasonable limitation." We have no doubt that under this standard the prohibition on solicitation passes muster.

We have on many prior occasions noted the disruptive effect that solicitation may have on business. "Solicitation requires action by those who would respond: The individual solicited must decide whether or not to contribute (which itself might involve reading the solicitor's literature or hearing his pitch), and then, having decided to do so, reach for a wallet, search it for money, write a check, or produce a credit card. Passengers who wish to avoid the solicitor may have to alter their path, slowing both themselves and those around them. The result is that the normal flow of traffic is impeded. This is especially so in an airport, where air travelers, who are often weighted down by cumbersome baggage . . . may be hurrying to catch a plane or to arrange ground transportation. Delays may be particularly costly in this setting, as a flight missed by only a few minutes can result in hours' worth of subsequent inconvenience.

* * *

The inconveniences to passengers and the burdens on Port Authority officials flowing from solicitation activity may seem small, but viewed against the fact that pedestrian congestion is one of the greatest problems facing the three terminals, the Port Authority could reasonably worry that even such incremental effects would prove quite disruptive. Moreover, "the justification for the Rule should not be measured by the disorder that would result from granting an exemption solely to ISKCON." For if petitioner is given access, so too must other groups. "Obviously, there would be a much larger threat to the State's interest in crowd control if all other religious, nonreligious, and noncommercial organizations could likewise move freely. As a result, we conclude that the solicitation ban is reasonable. For the foregoing reasons, the judgment of the Court of Appeals sustaining the ban on solicitation in Port Authority terminals is

Affirmed.

## UNITED STATES
### v.
## GRACE

**461 U.S. 171, 103 S. Ct. 1702, 75 L. Ed. 2d 736 (1983)**

*[Citations and footnotes omitted.]*

[Around noon on March 17, 1980, Mary Grace entered the sidewalk in front of the Court and began to display a four-foot by two and one-half foot sign on which was inscribed the verbatim text of the First Amendment. A Court police officer approached Grace and informed her that she would have to go across the street if she wished to display the sign. Grace was informed that Title 40 § 13k of the United States Code prohibited her conduct and that if she did not cease she would be arrested. Grace left the grounds and filed suit seeking a declaratory judgment that the statute was unconstitutional and an injunction against its enforcement.]

JUSTICE WHITE delivered the opinion of the Court.

* * *

Section 13k prohibits two distinct activities: it is unlawful either "to parade, stand, or move in processions or assemblages in the Supreme Court Building or grounds," or "to display therein any flag, banner, or device designed or adapted to bring into public notice any party, organization, or movement." . . . Likewise, the controversy presented by appellees concerned their right to use the public sidewalks surrounding the Court building for the communicative activities they sought to carry out, and we shall address only whether the proscriptions of 13k are constitutional as applied to the public sidewalks.

* * *

The First Amendment provides that "Congress shall make no law . . . abridging the freedom of speech. . . ." There is no doubt that as a general matter peaceful picketing and leafletting are expressive activities involving "speech" protected by the First Amendment.

It is also true that "public places" historically associated with the free exercise of expressive activities, such as streets, sidewalks, and parks, are considered, without more, to be "public forums." In such places, the government's ability to permissibly restrict expressive conduct is very limited: the government may enforce reasonable time, place, and manner regulations as long as the restrictions "are content-neutral, are narrowly tailored to serve a significant government interest, and leave open ample alternative channels of communication." Additional restrictions such as an absolute prohibition on a particular type of expression will be upheld only if narrowly drawn to accomplish a compelling governmental interest.

\* \* \*

. . . The sidewalks comprising the outer boundaries of the Court grounds are indistinguishable from any other sidewalks in Washington, D.C., and we can discern no reason why they should be treated any differently. Sidewalks, of course, are among those areas of public property that traditionally have been held open to the public for expressive activities and are clearly within those areas of public property that may be considered, generally without further inquiry, to be public forum property. In this respect, the present case differs from *Greer v. Spock*. In *Greer*, the streets and sidewalks at issue were located within an enclosed military reservation, Fort Dix, N.J., and were thus separated from the streets and sidewalks of any municipality. That is not true of the sidewalks surrounding the Court. There is no separation, no fence, and no indication whatever to persons stepping from the street to the curb and sidewalks that serve as the perimeter of the Court grounds that they have entered some special type of enclave. . . . Traditional public forum property occupies a special position in terms of First Amendment protection and will not lose its historically recognized character for the reason that it abuts government property that has been dedicated to a use other than as a forum for public expression. Nor may

the government transform the character of the property by the expedient of including it within the statutory definition of what might be considered a nonpublic forum parcel of property. The public sidewalks forming the perimeter of the Supreme Court grounds, in our view, are public forums and should be treated as such for First Amendment purposes.

\* \* \*

We do not denigrate the necessity to protect persons and property or to maintain proper order and decorum within the Supreme Court grounds, but we do question whether a total ban on carrying a flag, banner, or device on the public sidewalks substantially serves these purposes. There is no suggestion, for example, that appellees' activities in any way obstructed the sidewalks or access to the building, threatened injury to any person or property, or in any way interfered with the orderly administration of the building or other parts of the grounds. As we have said, the building's perimeter sidewalks are indistinguishable from other public sidewalks in the city that are normally open to the conduct that is at issue here and that 13k forbids. A total ban on that conduct is no more necessary for the maintenance of peace and tranquility on the public sidewalks surrounding the building than on any other sidewalks in the city. Accordingly, 13k cannot be justified on this basis.

The United States offers another justification for 13k that deserves our attention. It is said that the federal courts represent an independent branch of the Government and that their decisionmaking processes are different from those of the other branches. Court decisions are made on the record before them and in accordance with the applicable law. The views of the parties and of others are to be presented by briefs and oral argument. Courts are not subject to lobbying, judges do not entertain visitors in their chambers for the purpose of urging that cases be resolved one way or another, and they do not and should not respond to parades, picketing, or pressure groups. Neither, the Government urges, should it appear to the public that the Supreme Court is subject to outside influence or that picketing or marching, singly or in groups, is an acceptable or proper way of appealing to or influencing the Supreme Court. Hence, we are asked to hold that Congress was quite justified in preventing the conduct in dispute here from occurring on the sidewalks at the edge of the Court grounds.

As was the case with the maintenance of law and order on the Court grounds, we do not discount the importance of this proffered purpose for 13k. But, again, we are unconvinced that the prohibitions of 13k that are at issue here sufficiently serve that purpose to sustain its validity insofar as the public sidewalks on the perimeter of the grounds are concerned. Those sidewalks are used by the public like other public sidewalks. There is nothing to indicate to the public that these sidewalks are part of the Supreme Court grounds or are in any way different from other public sidewalks in the city. We seriously doubt that the public would draw a different inference from a lone picketer carrying a sign on the sidewalks around the building than it would from a similar picket on the sidewalks across the street.

We thus perceive insufficient justification for 13k's prohibition of carrying signs, banners, or devices on the public sidewalks surrounding the building. We hold that under the First Amendment the section is unconstitutional as applied to those sidewalks. . . .

The judgment below is accordingly affirmed to the extent indicated by this opinion and is otherwise vacated.

So ordered.

# LOPER
## v.
## NEW YORK CITY POLICE DEPARTMENT

### 999 F.2d 699 (2d Cir. 1993)

*[Citations and footnotes omitted.]*

[The plaintiffs, a class of needy persons who beg on the public streets or in the public parks of New York City, brought an action seeking a declaratory judgment that N.Y. Penal Law § 240.35(1) violated the First Amendment and an injunction prohibiting the City Police from enforcing it. The statute provided: "A person is guilty of loitering when he . . . remains or wanders about in a public place for the purpose of begging." The trial court found for the plaintiffs and City Police appealed.]

MINER, Circuit Judge:

* * *

The City Police regard the challenged statute as an essential tool to address the evils associated with begging on the streets of New York City. They assert that beggars tend to congregate in certain areas and become more aggressive as they do so. Residents are intimidated and local businesses suffer accordingly. Panhandlers are said to station themselves in front of banks, bus stops, automated teller machines and parking lots and frequently engage in conduct described as "intimidating" and "coercive." Panhandlers have been known to block the sidewalk, follow people down the street and threaten those who do not give them money. It is said that they often make false and fraudulent representations to induce passers-by to part with their money. The City Police have begun to focus more attention on order maintenance activities in a program known as "community policing." They contend that it is vital to the program to have the statute available for the officers on the "beat" to deal with those who threaten and harass the citizenry through begging.

Although it is conceded that very few arrests are made and very few summonses are issued for begging alone, officers do make frequent use of the statute as authority to order beggars to "move on." The City Police advance the theory that panhandlers, unless stopped, tend to increase their aggressiveness and ultimately commit more serious crimes. According to this theory, what starts out as peaceful begging inevitably leads to the ruination of a neighborhood. It appears from the contentions of the City Police that only the challenged statute stands between safe streets and rampant crime in the city.

It is ludicrous, of course, to say that a statute that prohibits only loitering for the purpose of begging provides the only authority that is available to prevent and punish all the socially undesirable conduct incident to begging described by the City Police. There are, in fact, a number of New York statutes that proscribe conduct of the type that may accompany individual solicitations for money in the city streets. For example, the crime of harassment in the first degree is committed by one who follows another person in or about a public place or places or repeatedly commits acts that place the other person in reasonable fear of physical injury. If a panhandler, with intent to cause public inconvenience, annoyance or alarm, uses obscene or abusive language or obstructs pedestrian or vehicular traffic, he or she is guilty of disorderly conduct. A beggar who accosts a person in a public place with intent to defraud that person of money is guilty of fraudulent accosting. The crime of menacing in the third degree is committed by a panhandler who, by physical menace, intentionally places or attempts to place another person in fear of physical injury.

The distinction between the statutes referred to in the preceding paragraph and the challenged statute is that the former prohibit conduct and the latter prohibits speech as well as conduct of a communicative nature. Whether the challenged statute is consonant with the First Amendment is the subject of our inquiry. We do not write upon a clean slate as regards this inquiry, since the Supreme Court as well as this Court has addressed restrictions on the solicitation of money in public places.

* * *

. . . Despite government ownership, it is the nature of the forum that we must examine in order to determine the extent to which expressive activity may be regulated. It long has been settled that all forms of speech need not be permitted on property owned and controlled by a governmental entity.

* * *

The forum-based approach for First Amendment analysis subjects to the highest scrutiny the regulation of speech on government property traditionally available for public expression. Such property includes streets and parks, which are said to "have immemorially been held in trust for the use of the public and, time out of mind, have been used for purposes of assembly, communicating thoughts between citizens, and discussing public questions."

In these quintessential public forums, the government may not prohibit all communicative activity. For the State to enforce a content-based exclusion it must show that its regulation is necessary to serve a compelling state interest and that it is narrowly drawn to achieve that end. . . . The State may also enforce regulations of the time, place, and manner of expression which are content-neutral, are narrowly tailored to serve a significant government interest, and leave open ample alternative channels of communication.

* * *

. . . The regulation of expressive activity on public property neither traditionally available nor designated for that purpose is subject only to a limited review—the regulation must be reasonable and not designed to prohibit the activity merely because of disagreement with the views expressed. . . .

* * *

It cannot be gainsaid that begging implicates expressive conduct or communicative activity. . . .

* * *

. . . While we indicated in *Young* that begging does not always involve the transmission of a particularized social or political message, . . . begging frequently is accompanied by speech indicating the need for food, shelter, clothing, medical care or transportation. Even without particularized speech, however, the presence of an unkempt and disheveled person holding out his or her hand or a cup to receive a donation itself conveys a message of need for support and assistance. We see little difference between those who solicit for organized charities and those who solicit for themselves in regard to the message conveyed. The former are communicating the needs of others while the latter are communicating their personal needs. Both solicit the charity of others. The distinction is not a significant one for First Amendment purposes.

Having established that begging constitutes communicative activity of some sort and that, as far as this case is concerned, it is conducted in a traditional public forum, we next examine whether the statute at issue: (1) is necessary to serve a compelling state interest and is narrowly tailored to achieve that end; or (2) can be characterized as a regulation of the time, place and manner of expression that is content neutral, is narrowly tailored to serve significant government interests and leaves open alternate channels of communication.

First, it does not seem to us that any compelling state interest is served by excluding those who beg in a peaceful manner from communicating with their fellow citizens. Even if the state were considered to have a compelling interest in preventing the evils sometimes associated with begging, a statute that totally prohibits begging in all public places cannot be considered "narrowly tailored" to achieve that end. Because of the total prohibition, it is questionable whether the statute even can be said to "regulate" the time, place and manner of expression but even if it does, it is not content neutral because it prohibits all speech related to begging; it certainly is not narrowly tailored to serve any significant governmental interest, as previously noted, because of the total prohibition it commands; it does not leave open alternative channels of communication by which beggars can convey their messages of indigency.

* * *

. . . The New York statute does not square with the requirements of the First Amendment. The plaintiffs have demonstrated that they are entitled to the relief they seek.

The judgment appealed from is affirmed.

# Cases Relating to Chapter 3

# Authority to Detain and Arrest; Use of Force

UNITED STATES

v.

DRAYTON

536 U.S. 194, 122 S. Ct. 2105,
153 L. Ed. 2d 242 (2002)

*[Citations and footnotes omitted.]*

Christopher Drayton and Clifton Brown, Jr. were traveling on a Greyhound bus. When the bus made a scheduled stop in Tallahassee, Florida, Officers Hoover, Lang, and Blackburn of the Tallahassee Police Department boarded the bus as part of a routine drug and weapons interdiction effort. Once on board, Officer Hoover knelt beside the driver's seat, facing the rear of the bus where he could observe the passengers and ensure the safety of the two other officers without blocking the aisle or otherwise obstructing the bus exit. Officers Lang and Blackburn went to the rear of the bus. Blackburn remained there, facing forward while Lang worked his way toward the front of the bus, speaking with individual passengers about their travel plans.

Drayton and Brown were seated next to each other on the bus. Lang approached from the rear, leaned over Drayton's shoulder, held up his badge long enough for them to identify him as a police officer and then, with his face 12-to-18 inches away from Drayton's, said: "I'm

Investigator Lang with the Tallahassee Police Department. We're conducting bus interdiction [sic], attempting to deter drugs and illegal weapons being transported on the bus. Do you have any bags on the bus?"

When both men pointed to a green bag in the overhead luggage rack, Lang asked, "Do you mind if I check it?" Brown responded, "Go ahead." Lang handed the bag to Officer Blackburn to check. The bag contained no contraband.

Noticing that both men were wearing heavy jackets and baggy clothing despite the warm weather which, in Lang's experience, drug traffickers often do to conceal weapons or narcotics, Lang asked Brown if he had any weapons or drugs in his possession, stating: "Do you mind if I check your person?" Brown answered, "Sure," and cooperated by leaning up in his seat, pulling a cell phone out of his pocket, and opening up his jacket. Lang reached across Drayton and patted down Brown's jacket and pockets, including his waist area, sides, and upper thighs. In both thigh areas, Lang detected hard objects similar to drug packages detected on other occasions. Lang arrested and handcuffed Brown and Officer Hoover escorted him from the bus.

Lang then asked Drayton, "Mind if I check you?" Drayton responded by lifting his hands. Lang conducted a patdown and detected hard objects similar to those found on Brown. He placed Drayton under arrest. A further search revealed that Brown possessed three bundles containing 483 grams of cocaine. Drayton possessed two bundles containing 295 grams of cocaine.

Justice KENNEDY delivered the opinion of the Court.

\* \* \*

Law enforcement officers do not violate the Fourth Amendment's prohibition of unreasonable seizures merely by approaching individuals on the street or in other public places and putting questions to them if they are willing to listen. Even when law enforcement officers have no basis for suspecting a particular individual, they may pose questions, ask for identification, and request consent to search luggage—provided they do not induce cooperation by coercive means. If a reasonable person would feel free to terminate the encounter, then he or she has not been seized.

\* \* \*

[W]e conclude that the police did not seize respondents when they boarded the bus and began questioning passengers. The officers gave the passengers no reason to believe that they were required to answer the officers' questions. When Officer Lang approached respondents, he did not brandish a weapon or make any intimidating movements. He left the aisle free so that respondents could exit. He spoke to passengers one by one and in a polite, quiet voice. Nothing he said would suggest to a reasonable person that he or she was barred from leaving the bus or otherwise terminating the encounter.

There were ample grounds for the District Court to conclude that "everything that took place between Officer

Lang and [respondents] suggests that it was cooperative" and that there "was nothing coercive [or] confrontational" about the encounter. There was no application of force, no intimidating movement, no overwhelming show of force, no brandishing of weapons, no blocking of exits, no threat, no command, not even an authoritative tone of voice. It is beyond question that had this encounter occurred on the street, it would be constitutional. The fact that an encounter takes place on a bus does not on its own transform standard police questioning of citizens into an illegal seizure. Indeed, because many fellow passengers are present to witness officers' conduct, a reasonable person may feel even more secure in his or her decision not to cooperate with police on a bus than in other circumstances.

Respondents make much of the fact that Officer Lang displayed his badge. In *Florida v. Rodriguez,* however, the Court rejected the claim that the defendant was seized when an officer approached him in an airport, showed him his badge, and asked him to answer some questions. . . . Officers are often required to wear uniforms and in many circumstances this is cause for assurance, not discomfort. Much the same can be said for wearing sidearms. That most law enforcement officers are armed is a fact well known to the public. The presence of a holstered firearm thus is unlikely to contribute to the coerciveness of the encounter absent active brandishing of the weapon.

Officer Hoover's position at the front of the bus also does not tip the scale in respondents' favor. Hoover did nothing to intimidate passengers, and he said nothing to suggest that people could not exit and indeed he left the aisle clear. In *Delgado,* the Court determined there was no seizure even though several uniformed INS officers were stationed near the exits of the factory. The Court noted: "The presence of agents by the exits posed no reasonable threat of detention to these workers, . . . the mere possibility that they would be questioned if they sought to leave the buildings should not have resulted in any reasonable apprehension by any of them that they would be seized or detained in any meaningful way."

* * *

Drayton contends that even if Brown's cooperation with the officers was consensual, Drayton was seized because no reasonable person would feel free to terminate the encounter with the officers after Brown had been arrested. The Court of Appeals did not address this claim; and in any event the argument fails. The arrest of one person does not mean that everyone around him has been seized by police. If anything, Brown's arrest should have put Drayton on notice of the consequences of continuing the encounter by answering the officers' questions. Even after arresting Brown, Lang addressed Drayton in a polite manner and provided him with no indication that he was required to answer Lang's questions.

We turn now from the question whether respondents were seized to whether they were subjected to an unreasonable search, i.e., whether their consent to the suspicionless search was involuntary. In circumstances such as these, where the question of voluntariness pervades both the search and seizure inquiries, the respective analyses turn on very similar facts. And, as the facts above suggest, respondents' consent to the search of their luggage and their persons was voluntary. Nothing Officer Lang said indicated a command to consent to the search. Rather, when respondents informed Lang that they had a bag on the bus, he asked for their permission to check it. And when Lang requested to search Brown and Drayton's persons, he asked first if they objected,

thus indicating to a reasonable person that he or she was free to refuse. Even after arresting Brown, Lang provided Drayton with no indication that he was required to consent to a search. To the contrary, Lang asked for Drayton's permission to search him ("Mind if I check you?"), and Drayton agreed.

The Court has rejected in specific terms the suggestion that police officers must always inform citizens of their right to refuse when seeking permission to conduct a warrantless consent search. Nor do this Court's decisions suggest that . . . a presumption of invalidity attaches if a citizen consented without explicit notification that he or she was free to refuse to cooperate. Instead, the Court has repeated that the totality of the circumstances must control, without giving extra weight to the absence of this type of warning. Although Officer Lang did not inform respondents of their right to refuse the search, he did request permission to search, and the totality of the circumstances indicates that their consent was voluntary, so the searches were reasonable.

In a society based on law, the concept of agreement and consent should be given a weight and dignity of its own. Police officers act in full accord with the law when they ask citizens for consent. It reinforces the rule of law for the citizen to advise the police of his or her wishes and for the police to act in reliance on that understanding. When this exchange takes place, it dispels inferences of coercion.

We need not ask the alternative question whether, after the arrest of Brown, there were grounds for a *Terry* stop and frisk of Drayton, though this may have been the case. It was evident that Drayton and Brown were traveling together— Officer Lang observed the pair reboarding the bus together; they were each dressed in heavy, baggy clothes that were ill-suited for the day's warm temperatures; they were seated together on the bus; and they each claimed responsibility for the single piece of green carry-on luggage. Once Lang had identified Brown as carrying what he believed to be narcotics, he may have had reasonable suspicion to conduct a *Terry* stop and frisk on Drayton as well. That question, however, has not been presented to us. The fact the officers may have had reasonable suspicion does not prevent them from relying on a citizen's consent to the search. It would be a paradox, and one most puzzling to law enforcement officials and courts alike, were we to say, after holding that Brown's consent was voluntary, that Drayton's consent was ineffectual simply because the police at that point had more compelling grounds to detain him. After taking Brown into custody, the officers were entitled to continue to proceed on the basis of consent and to ask for Drayton's cooperation.

The judgment of the Court of Appeals is reversed, and the case is remanded for further proceedings consistent with this opinion.

*It is so ordered.*

[Dissenting opinion omitted.]

## CALIFORNIA
v.
## HODARI D.

**499 U.S. 621, 111 S. Ct. 1547, 113 L. Ed. 2d 290 (1991)**

*[Citations and footnotes omitted.]*

[Hodari, a juvenile, took off running as two police officers, rounding a corner, came into view. The officers gave chase. Hodari tossed away a small rock as he ran. A moment later, he was tackled. The rock Hodari discarded turned out to be crack cocaine. The California state court ruled that the rock should have been suppressed because Hodari was seized when the officers began chasing him. Because the officers lacked probable cause to believe that Hodari had committed a crime when the chase began, the seizure was illegal and that the rock should have been suppressed. The government appealed.]

JUSTICE SCALIA delivered the opinion of the Court.

* * *

As this case comes to us, the only issue presented is whether, at the time he dropped the drugs, Hodari had been "seized" within the meaning of the Fourth Amendment. If so, respondent argues, the drugs were the fruit of that seizure and the evidence concerning them was properly excluded. If not, the drugs were abandoned by Hodari and lawfully recovered by the police, and the evidence should have been admitted. . . .

We have long understood that the Fourth Amendment's protection against "unreasonable . . . seizures" includes seizure of the person. From the time of the founding to the present, the word "seizure" has meant a "taking possession." For most purposes at common law, the word connoted not merely grasping, or applying physical force to, the animate or inanimate object in question, but actually bringing it within physical control. . . .

* * *

. . . Hodari was untouched by Officer Pertoso at the time he discarded the cocaine. His defense relies instead upon the proposition that a seizure occurs "when the officer, by means of physical force or show of authority, has in some way restrained the liberty of a citizen." Hodari contends (and we accept as true for purposes of this decision) that Pertoso's pursuit qualified as a "show of authority" calling upon Hodari to halt. The narrow question before us is whether, with respect to a show of authority as with respect to application of physical force, a seizure occurs even though the subject does not yield. We hold that it does not.

The language of the Fourth Amendment, of course, cannot sustain respondent's contention. The word "seizure" readily bears the meaning of a laying on of hands or application of physical force to restrain movement, even when it is ultimately unsuccessful. ("She seized the purse-snatcher, but he broke out of her grasp.") It does not remotely apply, however, to the prospect of a policeman yelling "Stop, in the name of the law!" at a fleeing form that continues to flee. That is no seizure. Nor can the result respondent wishes to achieve be produced—indirectly, as it were—by suggesting that Pertoso's uncomplied-with show of authority was a common-law arrest, and then appealing to the principle that all common-law arrests are seizures. An arrest requires either physical force (as described above) or, where that is absent, submission to the assertion of authority.

Mere words will not constitute an arrest, while, on the other hand, no actual, physical touching is essential. The apparent inconsistency in the two parts of this statement is explained by the fact that an assertion of authority and purpose to arrest, followed by submission of the arrestee, constitutes an arrest. There can be no arrest without either touching or submission.

We do not think it desirable, even as a policy matter, to stretch the Fourth Amendment beyond its words and beyond the meaning of arrest, as respondent urges. Street pursuits always place the public at some risk, and compliance with police orders to stop should therefore be encouraged. Only a few of those orders, we must presume, will be without adequate basis, and since the addressee has no ready means of identifying the deficient ones, it almost invariably is the responsible course to comply. Unlawful orders will not be deterred, moreover, by sanctioning through the exclusionary rule those of them that are not obeyed. Since policemen do not command "Stop!" expecting to be ignored, or give chase hoping to be outrun, it fully suffices to apply the deterrent to their genuine, successful seizures.

* * *

In sum, assuming that Pertoso's pursuit in the present case constituted a "show of authority" enjoining Hodari to halt, since Hodari did not comply with that injunction, he was not seized until he was tackled. The cocaine abandoned while he was running was, in this case, not the fruit of a seizure, and his motion to exclude evidence of it was properly denied. We reverse the decision of the California Court of Appeal, and remand for further proceedings not inconsistent with this opinion.

It is so ordered.

## TERRY

### v.

## OHIO

### 392 U.S. 1, 88 S. Ct. 1868, 20 L. Ed. 2d 889 (1968)

*[Citations and footnotes omitted.]*

[Officer McFadden was patrolling in downtown Cleveland when his attention was attracted to two men standing on the corner. He observed one man leave the other, walk past some stores, pause for a moment to look in a store window, walk a short distance beyond, turn around and walk back, pausing to look in the same store window again before returning to his companion. He and his companion conferred briefly and then his companion went through the same series of motions. The two men alternated in repeating this ritual approximately five or six times each. A third man subsequently joined them. These observations caused Officer McFadden to suspect that the three men were casing the store, preparing for a robbery, and that they might have guns. He approached the three men, identified himself as a police officer, and asked for their names. When the men "mumbled something" in response to his inquiry, Officer McFadden grabbed one of them (Terry), spun him around, and patted down the outside of his clothing. Feeling a pistol in Terry's left breast pocket, Officer McFadden ordered all three men to enter Zucker's store. As they went in, he removed Terry's overcoat, retrieved a .38-caliber revolver from the pocket, and ordered all three men to face the wall with their hands raised. He proceeded to pat down the outer clothing of Chilton and Katz, the other two men. He discovered a revolver in the outer pocket of Chilton's overcoat, but no weapons were found on Katz. He testified that he only patted the men down to see whether they had weapons, and that he did not put his hands beneath the outer garments of either Terry or Chilton until he felt their guns. The trial court denied the defendants' motion to suppress the guns on the ground that Officer McFadden, on the basis of his experience, "had reasonable cause to believe that the defendants were conducting themselves suspiciously, and some interrogation should be made of their action."]

Mr. Chief Justice WARREN delivered the opinion of the Court.

This case presents serious questions concerning the role of the Fourth Amendment in the confrontation on the street between the citizen and the policeman investigating suspicious circumstances.

\* \* \*

. . . Unquestionably petitioner was entitled to the protection of the Fourth Amendment as he walked down the street in Cleveland. The question is whether in all the circumstances of this on-the-street encounter, his right to personal security was violated by an unreasonable search and seizure.

We would be less than candid if we did not acknowledge that this question thrusts to the fore difficult and troublesome issues regarding a sensitive area of police activity—issues which have never before been squarely presented to this Court. Reflective of the tensions involved are the practical and constitutional arguments pressed with great vigor on both sides of the public debate over the power of the police to 'stop and frisk'—as it is sometimes euphemistically termed—suspicious persons.

On the one hand, it is frequently argued that in dealing with the rapidly unfolding and often dangerous situations on city streets the police are in need of an escalating set of flexible responses, graduated in relation to the amount of information they possess. For this purpose it is urged that distinctions should be made between a "stop" and an "arrest" (or a "seizure" of a person), and between a "frisk" and a "search." Thus, it is argued, the police should be allowed to "stop" a person and detain him briefly for questioning upon suspicion that he may be connected with criminal activity. Upon suspicion that the person may be armed, the police should have the power to "frisk" him for weapons. If the "stop" and the "frisk" give rise to probable cause to believe that the suspect has committed a crime, then the police should be empowered to make a formal "arrest," and a full incident "search" of the person. This scheme is justified in part upon the notion that a 'stop' and a 'frisk' amount to a mere "minor inconvenience and petty indignity," which can properly be imposed upon the citizen in the interest of effective law enforcement on the basis of a police officer's suspicion.

On the other side the argument is made that the authority of the police must be strictly circumscribed by the law of arrest and search as it has developed to date in the traditional jurisprudence of the Fourth Amendment. It is contended with some force that there is not—and cannot be—a variety of police activity which does not depend solely upon the voluntary cooperation of the citizen and yet which stops short of an arrest based upon probable cause to make such an arrest. The heart of the Fourth Amendment, the argument runs, is a severe requirement of specific justification for any intrusion upon protected personal security, coupled with a highly developed system of judicial controls to enforce upon the agents of the State the commands of the Constitution. Acquiescence by the courts in the compulsion inherent in the field interrogation practices at issue here, it is urged, would constitute an abdication of judicial control

over, and indeed an encouragement of, substantial interference with liberty and personal security by police officers whose judgment is necessarily colored by their primary involvement in "the often competitive enterprise of ferreting out crime." This, it is argued, can only serve to exacerbate police-community tensions in the crowded centers of our Nation's cities.

In this context we approach the issues in this case mindful of the limitations of the judicial function in controlling the myriad daily situations in which policemen and citizens confront each other on the street. . . .

. . . Street encounters between citizens and police officers are incredibly rich in diversity. They range from wholly friendly exchanges of pleasantries or mutually useful information to hostile confrontations of armed men involving arrests, or injuries, or loss of life. Moreover, hostile confrontations are not all of a piece. Some of them begin in a friendly enough manner, only to take a different turn upon the injection of some unexpected element into the conversation. Encounters are initiated by the police for a wide variety of purposes, some of which are wholly unrelated to a desire to prosecute for crime. Doubtless some police "field interrogation" conduct violates the Fourth Amendment.

* * *

Our first task is to establish at what point in this encounter the Fourth Amendment becomes relevant. That is, we must decide whether and when Officer McFadden "seized" Terry and whether and when he conducted a "search." There is some suggestion in the use of such terms as "stop" and "frisk" that such police conduct is outside the purview of the Fourth Amendment because neither action rises to the level of a "search" or "seizure" within the meaning of the Constitution. We emphatically reject this notion. It is quite plain that the Fourth Amendment governs "seizures" of the person which do not eventuate in a trip to the station house and prosecution for crime— "arrests" in traditional terminology. It must be recognized that whenever a police officer accosts an individual and restrains his freedom to walk away, he has "seized" that person. And it is nothing less than sheer torture of the English language to suggest that a careful exploration of the outer surfaces of a person's clothing all over his or her body in an attempt to find weapons is not a "search." Moreover, it is simply fantastic to urge that such a procedure performed in public by a policeman while the citizen stands helpless, perhaps facing a wall with his hands raised, is a "petty indignity." It is a serious intrusion upon the sanctity of the person, which may inflict great indignity and arouse strong resentment, and it is not to be undertaken lightly.

* * *

We therefore reject the notions that the Fourth Amendment does not come into play at all as a limitation upon police conduct if the officers stop short of something called a "technical arrest" or a "full-blown search."

In this case there can be no question, then, that Officer McFadden "seized" petitioner and subjected him to a "search" when he took hold of him and patted down the outer surfaces of his clothing. We must decide whether at that point it was reasonable for Officer McFadden to have interfered with petitioner's personal security as he did. And in determining whether the seizure and search were "unreasonable" our inquiry is a dual one—whether the officer's action was justified at its inception, and whether it was reasonably related in

scope to the circumstances which justified the interference in the first place.

If this case involved police conduct subject to the Warrant Clause of the Fourth Amendment, we would have to ascertain whether "probable cause" existed to justify the search and seizure which took place. However, that is not the case. . . . Instead, the conduct involved in this case must be tested by the Fourth Amendment's general proscription against unreasonable searches and seizures.

. . . In order to assess the reasonableness of Officer McFadden's conduct as a general proposition, it is necessary "first to focus upon the governmental interest which allegedly justifies official intrusion upon the constitutionally protected interests of the private citizen," for there is "no ready test for determining reasonableness other than by balancing the need to search (or seize) against the invasion which the search (or seizure) entails." And in justifying the particular intrusion the police officer must be able to point to specific and articulable facts which, taken together with rational inferences from those facts, reasonably warrant that intrusion. . . . Anything less would invite intrusions upon constitutionally guaranteed rights based on nothing more substantial than inarticulate hunches, a result this Court has consistently refused to sanction. And simple "good faith on the part of the arresting officer is not enough." . . . If subjective good faith alone were the test, the protections of the Fourth Amendment would evaporate, and the people would be 'secure in their persons, houses, papers and effects,' only in the discretion of the police."

. . . One general interest is of course that of effective crime prevention and detection; it is this interest which underlies the recognition that a police officer may in appropriate circumstances and in an appropriate manner approach a person for purposes of investigating possibly criminal behavior even though there is no probable cause to make an arrest. It was this legitimate investigative function Officer McFadden was discharging when he decided to approach petitioner and his companions. He had observed Terry, Chilton, and Katz go through a series of acts, each of them perhaps innocent in itself, but which taken together warranted further investigation. There is nothing unusual in two men standing together on a street corner, perhaps waiting for someone. Nor is there anything suspicious about people in such circumstances strolling up and down the street, singly or in pairs. Store windows, moreover, are made to be looked in. But the story is quite different where, as here, two men hover about a street corner for an extended period of time, at the end of which it becomes apparent that they are not waiting for anyone or anything; where these men pace alternately along an identical route, pausing to stare in the same store window roughly 24 times; where each completion of this route is followed immediately by a conference between the two men on the corner; where they are joined in one of these conferences by a third man who leaves swiftly; and where the two men finally follow the third and rejoin him a couple of blocks away. It would have been poor police work indeed for an officer of 30 years' experience in the detection of thievery from stores in this same neighborhood to have failed to investigate this behavior further.

The crux of this case, however, is not the propriety of Officer McFadden's taking steps to investigate petitioner's suspicious behavior, but rather, whether there was justification for McFadden's invasion of Terry's personal security by searching him for weapons in the course of that investigation. We are now concerned with more than the governmental interest in investigating crime; in addi-

tion, there is the more immediate interest of the police officer in taking steps to assure himself that the person with whom he is dealing is not armed with a weapon that could unexpectedly and fatally be used against him. Certainly it would be unreasonable to require that police officers take unnecessary risks in the performance of their duties. American criminals have a long tradition of armed violence, and every year in this country many law enforcement officers are killed in the line of duty, and thousands more are wounded. Virtually all of these deaths and a substantial portion of the injuries are inflicted with guns and knives.

In view of these facts, we cannot blind ourselves to the need for law enforcement officers to protect themselves and other prospective victims of violence in situations where they may lack probable cause for an arrest. When an officer is justified in believing that the individual whose suspicious behavior he is investigating at close range is armed and presently dangerous to the officer or to others, it would appear to be clearly unreasonable to deny the officer the power to take necessary measures to determine whether the person is in fact carrying a weapon and to neutralize the threat of physical harm.

We must still consider, however, the nature and quality of the intrusion on individual rights which must be accepted if police officers are to be conceded the right to search for weapons in situations where probable cause to arrest for crime is lacking. Even a limited search of the outer clothing for weapons constitutes a severe, though brief, intrusion upon cherished personal security, and it must surely be an annoying, frightening, and perhaps humiliating experience. Petitioner contends that such an intrusion is permissible only incident to a lawful arrest, either for a crime involving the possession of weapons or for a crime the commission of which led the officer to investigate in the first place. However, this argument must be closely examined.

Petitioner does not argue that a police officer should refrain from making any investigation of suspicious circumstances until such time as he has probable cause to make an arrest; nor does he deny that police officers in properly discharging their investigative function may find themselves confronting persons who might well be armed and dangerous. Moreover, he does not say that an officer is always unjustified in searching a suspect to discover weapons. Rather, he says it is unreasonable for the policeman to take that step until such time as the situation evolves to a point where there is probable cause to make an arrest. When that point has been reached, petitioner would concede the officer's right to conduct a search of the suspect for weapons, fruits or instrumentalities of the crime, or "mere" evidence, incident to the arrest.

There are two weaknesses in this line of reasoning however. First, it fails to take account of traditional limitations upon the scope of searches, and thus recognizes no distinction in purpose, character, and extent between a search incident to an arrest and a limited search for weapons. The former, although justified in part by the acknowledged necessity to protect the arresting officer from assault with a concealed weapon is also justified on other grounds, and can therefore involve a relatively extensive exploration of the person. A search for weapons in the absence of probable cause arrest, however, must, like any other search, be strictly circumscribed by the exigencies which justify its initiation. Thus it must be limited to that which is necessary for the discovery of weapons which might be used to harm the officer or others nearby, and may realistically be characterized as something less than a "full" search, even though it remains a serious intrusion.

A second, and related, objection to petitioner's argument is that it assumes that the law of arrest has already worked out the balance between the particular interests involved here—the neutralization of danger to the policeman in the investigative circumstance and the sanctity of the individual. But this is not so. . . .

Our evaluation of the proper balance that has to be struck in this type of case leads us to conclude that there must be a narrowly drawn authority to permit a reasonable search for weapons for the protection of the police officer, where he has reason to believe that he is dealing with an armed and dangerous individual, regardless of whether he has probable cause to arrest the individual for a crime. The officer need not be absolutely certain that the individual is armed; the issue is whether a reasonably prudent man in the circumstances would be warranted in the belief that his safety or that of others was in danger. And in determining whether the officer acted reasonably in such circumstances, due weight must be given, not to his inchoate and unparticularized suspicion or "hunch," but to the specific reasonable inferences which he is entitled to draw from the facts in light of his experience.

* * *

The scope of the search in this case presents no serious problem in light of these standards. Officer McFadden patted down the outer clothing of petitioner and his two companions. He did not place his hands in their pockets or under the outer surface of their garments until he had felt weapons, and then he merely reached for and removed the guns. He never did invade Katz' person beyond the outer surfaces of his clothes, since he discovered nothing in his patdown which might have been a weapon. Officer McFadden confined his search strictly to what was minimally necessary to learn whether the men were armed and to disarm them once he discovered the weapons. He did not conduct a general exploratory search for whatever evidence of criminal activity he might find.

We conclude that the revolver seized from Terry was properly admitted in evidence against him. At the time he seized petitioner and searched him for weapons, Officer McFadden had reasonable grounds to believe that petitioner was armed and dangerous, and it was necessary for the protection of himself and others to take swift measures to discover the true facts and neutralize the threat of harm if it materialized. The policeman carefully restricted his search to what was appropriate to the discovery of the particular items which he sought. Each case of this sort will, of course, have to be decided on its own facts. We merely hold today that where a police officer observes unusual conduct which leads him reasonably to conclude in light of his experience that criminal activity may be afoot and that the persons with whom he is dealing may be armed and presently dangerous, where in the course of investigating this behavior he identifies himself as a policeman and makes reasonable inquiries, and where nothing in the initial stages of the encounter serves to dispel his reasonable fear for his own or others' safety, he is entitled for the protection of himself and others in the area to conduct a carefully limited search of the outer clothing of such persons in an attempt to discover weapons which might be used to assault him. Such a search is a reasonable search under the Fourth Amendment, and any weapons seized may properly be introduced in evidence against the person from whom they were taken.

Affirmed.

[Concurring and dissenting opinions have been omitted.]

# ILLINOIS
## v.
# WARDLOW

**528 U.S. 119, 120 S. Ct. 673, 145 L. Ed. 2d 570 (2000)**

*[Citations and footnotes omitted.]*

CHIEF JUSTICE REHNQUIST delivered the opinion of the Court.

\* \* \*

On September 9, 1995, Officers Nolan and Harvey were working as uniformed officers in the special operations section of the Chicago Police Department. The officers were driving the last car of a four-car caravan converging on an area known for heavy narcotics trafficking in order to investigate drug transactions. The officers were traveling together because they expected to find a crowd of people in the area, including lookouts and customers.

As the caravan passed 4035 West Van Buren, Officer Nolan observed respondent Wardlow standing next to the building holding an opaque bag. Respondent looked in the direction of the officers and fled. Nolan and Harvey turned their car southbound, watched him as he ran through the gangway and an alley, and eventually cornered him on the street. Nolan then exited his car and stopped respondent. He immediately conducted a protective pat-down search for weapons because in his experience it was common for there to be weapons in the near vicinity of narcotics transactions. During the frisk, Officer Nolan squeezed the bag respondent was carrying and felt a heavy, hard object similar to the shape of a gun. The officer then opened the bag and discovered a .38-caliber handgun with five live rounds of ammunition. The officers arrested Wardlow.

* * *

. . . An individual's presence in an area of expected criminal activity, standing alone, is not enough to support a reasonable, particularized suspicion that the person is committing a crime. But officers are not required to ignore the relevant characteristics of a location in determining whether the circumstances are sufficiently suspicious to warrant further investigation. Accordingly, we have previously noted the fact that the stop occurred in a "high crime area" among the relevant contextual considerations in a *Terry* analysis.

In this case, moreover, it was not merely respondent's presence in an area of heavy narcotics trafficking that aroused the officers' suspicion but his unprovoked flight upon noticing the police. Our cases have also recognized that nervous, evasive behavior is a pertinent factor in determining reasonable suspicion. Headlong flight—wherever it occurs—is the consummate act of evasion: it is not necessarily indicative of wrongdoing, but it is certainly suggestive of such. In reviewing the propriety of an officer's conduct, courts do not have available empirical studies dealing with inferences drawn from suspicious behavior, and we cannot reasonably demand scientific certainty from judges or law enforcement officers where none exists. Thus, the determination of reasonable suspicion must be based on commonsense judgments and inferences about human behavior. We conclude Officer Nolan was justified in suspecting that Wardlow was involved in criminal activity, and, therefore, in investigating further.

Such a holding is entirely consistent with our decision in Florida v. Royer, where we held that when an officer, without reasonable suspicion or probable cause, approaches an individual, the individual has a right to ignore the police

and go about his business. And any "refusal to cooperate, without more, does not furnish the minimal level of objective justification needed for a detention or seizure." But unprovoked flight is simply not a mere refusal to cooperate. Flight, by its very nature, is not "going about one's business"; in fact, it is just the opposite. Allowing officers confronted with such flight to stop the fugitive and investigate further is quite consistent with the individual's right to go about his business or to stay put and remain silent in the face of police questioning.

Respondent and *amici* also argue that there are innocent reasons for flight from police and that, therefore, flight is not necessarily indicative of ongoing criminal activity. This fact is undoubtedly true, but does not establish a violation of the Fourth Amendment. Even in *Terry*, the conduct justifying the stop was ambiguous and susceptible of an innocent explanation. The officer observed two individuals pacing back and forth in front of a store, peering into the window and periodically conferring. All of this conduct was by itself lawful, but it also suggested that the individuals were casing the store for a planned robbery. *Terry* recognized that the officers could detain the individuals to resolve the ambiguity.

In allowing such detentions, *Terry* accepts the risk that officers may stop innocent people. Indeed, the Fourth Amendment accepts that risk in connection with more drastic police action; persons arrested and detained on probable cause to believe they have committed a crime may turn out to be innocent. The *Terry* stop is a far more minimal intrusion, simply allowing the officer to briefly investigate further. If the officer does not learn facts rising to the level of probable cause, the individual must be allowed to go on his way. But in this case the officers found respondent in possession of a handgun, and arrested him for violation of an Illinois firearms statute. No question of the propriety of the arrest itself is before us.

The judgment of the Supreme Court of Illinois is reversed, and the cause is remanded for further proceedings not inconsistent with this opinion.

It is so ordered.

## FLORIDA
## v.
## J.L.

**529 U.S. 266, 120 S. Ct. 1375, 146 L. Ed. 2d 254 (2000)**

*[Citations and footnotes omitted.]*

Justice GINSBURG delivered the opinion of the Court.

The question presented in this case is whether an anonymous tip that a person is carrying a gun is, without more, sufficient to justify a police officer's stop and frisk of that person. We hold that it is not.

On October 13, 1995, an anonymous caller reported to the Miami-Dade Police that a young black male standing at a particular bus stop and wearing a plaid shirt was carrying a gun. So far as the record reveals, there is no audio recording of the tip, and nothing is known about the informant. Sometime after the police received the tip—the record does not say how long—two officers were instructed to respond. They arrived at the bus stop about six minutes later and saw three black males "just hanging out [there]." One of the three, respondent J.L., was wearing a plaid shirt. Apart from the tip, the officers had no reason to suspect any of the three of illegal conduct. The officers did not see a firearm, and J.L. made no threatening or otherwise unusual movements. One of the officers approached J.L., told him to put his hands up on the bus stop, frisked him, and seized a gun from J.L.'s pocket. The second officer frisked the other two individuals, against whom no allegations had been made, and found nothing.

J.L., who was at the time of the frisk "10 days shy of his 16th birth[day]," was charged under state law with carrying a concealed firearm without a license and possessing a firearm while under the age of 18. He moved to suppress the gun as the fruit of an unlawful search, and the trial court granted his motion. . . .

* * *

In the instant case, the officers' suspicion that J.L. was carrying a weapon arose not from any observations of their own but solely from a call made from an unknown location by an unknown caller. Unlike a tip from a known informant whose reputation can be assessed and who can be held responsible if her allegations turn out to be fabricated, "an anonymous tip alone seldom demonstrates the informant's basis of knowledge or veracity." As we have recognized, however, there are situations in which an anonymous tip, suitably corroborated, exhibits "sufficient indicia of reliability to provide reasonable suspicion to make the investigatory stop." The question we here confront is whether the tip pointing to J.L. had those indicia of reliability.

In *[Alabama v.] White*, the police received an anonymous tip asserting that a woman was carrying cocaine and predicting that she would leave an apartment building at a specified time, get into a car matching a particular description, and drive to a named motel. Standing alone, the tip would not have justified a *Terry* stop. Only after police observation showed that the informant had accurately predicted the woman's movements, we explained, did it become reasonable to think the tipster had inside knowledge about the suspect and therefore to credit his assertion about the cocaine. Although the Court held that the suspicion in *White* became reasonable after police surveillance, we regarded the case as borderline. Knowledge about a person's future movements indicates some familiarity with that person's affairs, but having such knowledge does not necessarily imply that the informant knows, in particular, whether that person is carrying hidden contraband. We accordingly classified *White* as a "close case."

The tip in the instant case lacked the moderate indicia of reliability present in *White* and essential to the Court's decision in that case. The anonymous call concerning J.L. provided no predictive information and therefore left the police without means to test the informant's knowledge or credibility. That the allegation about the gun turned out to be correct does not suggest that the officers, prior to the frisks, had a reasonable basis for suspecting J.L. of engaging in unlawful conduct: The reasonableness of official suspicion must be measured by what the officers knew before they conducted their search. All the police had to go on in this case was the bare report of an unknown, unaccountable informant who neither explained how he knew about the gun nor supplied any basis for believing he had inside information about J.L. If *White* was a close case on the reliability of anonymous tips, this one surely falls on the other side of the line.

Florida contends that the tip was reliable because its description of the suspect's visible attributes proved accurate: There really was a young black male wearing a plaid shirt at the bus stop. The United States as amicus curiae makes a similar argument, proposing that a stop and frisk should be permitted "when (1) an anonymous tip provides a description of a particular person at a particular

location illegally carrying a concealed firearm, (2) police promptly verify the pertinent details of the tip except the existence of the firearm, and (3) there are no factors that cast doubt on the reliability of the tip. . . ." These contentions misapprehend the reliability needed for a tip to justify a *Terry* stop.

An accurate description of a subject's readily observable location and appearance is of course reliable in this limited sense: It will help the police correctly identify the person whom the tipster means to accuse. Such a tip, however, does not show that the tipster has knowledge of concealed criminal activity. The reasonable suspicion here at issue requires that a tip be reliable in its assertion of illegality, not just in its tendency to identify a determinate person. Cf. 4 W. LaFave, *Search and Seizure* § 9.4(h), p. 213 (3d ed. 1996) (distinguishing reliability as to identification, which is often important in other criminal law contexts, from reliability as to the likelihood of criminal activity, which is central in anonymous-tip cases).

A second major argument advanced by Florida and the United States as amicus is, in essence, that the standard *Terry* analysis should be modified to license a "firearm exception." Under such an exception, a tip alleging an illegal gun would justify a stop and frisk even if the accusation would fail standard pre-search reliability testing. We decline to adopt this position.

Firearms are dangerous, and extraordinary dangers sometimes justify unusual precautions. Our decisions recognize the serious threat that armed criminals pose to public safety; *Terry's* rule, which permits protective police searches on the basis of reasonable suspicion rather than demanding that officers meet the higher standard of probable cause, responds to this very concern. But an automatic firearm exception to our established reliability analysis would rove too far. Such an exception would enable any person seeking to harass another to set in motion an intrusive, embarrassing police search of the targeted person simply by placing an anonymous call falsely reporting the target's unlawful carriage of a gun. Nor could one securely confine such an exception to allegations involving firearms. Several Courts of Appeals have held it per se foreseeable for people carrying significant amounts of illegal drugs to be carrying guns as well. If police officers may properly conduct *Terry* frisks on the basis of bare-boned tips about guns, it would be reasonable to maintain under the above-cited decisions that the police should similarly have discretion to frisk based on bare-boned tips about narcotics. As we clarified when we made indicia of reliability critical in Adams and White, the Fourth Amendment is not so easily satisfied.

The facts of this case do not require us to speculate about the circumstances under which the danger alleged in an anonymous tip might be so great as to justify a search even without a showing of reliability. We do not say, for example, that a report of a person carrying a bomb need bear the indicia of reliability we demand for a report of a person carrying a firearm before the police can constitutionally conduct a frisk. Nor do we hold that public safety officials in quarters where the reasonable expectation of Fourth Amendment privacy is diminished, such as airports and schools, cannot conduct protective searches on the basis of information insufficient to justify searches elsewhere.

Finally, the requirement that an anonymous tip bear standard indicia of reliability in order to justify a stop in no way diminishes a police officer's prerogative, in accord with *Terry*, to conduct a protective search of a person who has already been legitimately stopped. We

speak in today's decision only of cases in which the officer's authority to make the initial stop is at issue. In that context, we hold that an anonymous tip lacking indicia of reliability of the kind contemplated in *Adams* and *White* does not justify a stop and frisk whenever and however it alleges the illegal possession of a firearm.

The judgment of the Florida Supreme Court is affirmed.

It is so ordered.

## UNITED STATES
## v.
## PLACE

### 462 U.S. 696, 103 S. Ct. 2637, 77 L. Ed. 2d 110 (1983)

*[Citations and footnotes omitted.]*

[After receiving a tip that Place, a man fitting a drug courier profile, was en route on a plane from Miami to New York, two DEA agents waited at the arrival gate at LaGuardia Airport in New York. Place's behavior aroused the suspicion of the agents. After he had claimed his two bags and called a limousine, the agents decided to approach him. When Place refused to consent to a search of his luggage, one of the agents told him that they were going to take the luggage to a federal judge to try to obtain a search warrant and that Place was free to accompany them. Place declined, but obtained from one of the agents telephone numbers at which the agents could be reached. The agents then took the bags to Kennedy Airport, where they subjected the bags to a "sniff test" by a trained narcotics detection dog. The dog reacted positively to the smaller of the two bags but ambiguously to the larger bag. Approximately 90 minutes had elapsed since the seizure of respondent's luggage. Because it was late on a Friday afternoon, the agents retained the luggage until Monday morning, when they secured a search warrant from a magistrate for the smaller bag. Upon opening that bag, the agents discovered 1,125 grams of cocaine.]

JUSTICE O'CONNOR delivered the opinion of the Court.

This case presents the issue whether the Fourth Amendment prohibits law enforcement authorities from temporarily detaining personal luggage for exposure to a trained narcotics detection dog on the basis of reasonable suspicion that the luggage contains narcotics. Given the enforcement problems associated with the detection of narcotics trafficking and the minimal intrusion that a properly limited detention would entail, we conclude that the Fourth Amendment does not prohibit such a detention. On the facts of this case, however, we hold that the police conduct exceeded the bounds of a permissible investigative detention of the luggage.

* * *

At the outset, we must reject the Government's suggestion that the point at which probable cause for seizure of luggage from the person's presence becomes necessary is more distant than in the case of a *Terry* stop of the person himself. The premise of the Government's argument is that seizures of property are generally less intrusive than seizures of the person. While true in some circumstances, that premise is faulty on the facts we address in this case. The precise type of detention we confront here is seizure of personal luggage from the immediate possession of the suspect for the purpose of arranging exposure to a narcotics detection dog.

Particularly in the case of detention of luggage within the traveler's immediate possession, the police conduct intrudes on both the suspect's possessory interest in his luggage as well as his liberty interest in proceeding with his itinerary. The person whose luggage is detained is technically still free to continue his travels or carry out other personal activities pending release of the luggage. Moreover, he is not subjected to the coercive atmosphere of a custodial confinement or to the public indignity of being personally detained. Nevertheless, such a seizure can effectively restrain the person since he is subjected to the possible disruption of his travel plans in order to remain with his luggage or to arrange for its return. Therefore, when the police seize luggage from the suspect's custody, we think the limitations applicable to investigative detentions of the person should define the permissible scope of an investigative detention of the person's luggage on less than probable cause. Under this standard, it is clear that the police conduct here exceeded the permissible limits of a *Terry*-type investigative stop.

The length of the detention of respondent's luggage alone precludes the conclusion that the seizure was reasonable in the absence of probable cause. Although we have recognized the reasonableness of seizures longer than the momentary ones involved in *Terry*, *Adams*, and *Brignoni-Ponce*, the brevity of the invasion of the individual's Fourth Amendment interests is an important factor in determining whether the seizure is so minimally intrusive as to be justifiable on reasonable suspicion. Moreover, in assessing the effect of the length of the detention, we take into account whether the police diligently pursue their investigation. We note that here the New York agents knew the time of Place's scheduled arrival at La Guardia, had ample time to arrange for their additional investigation at that location, and thereby could have minimized the intrusion on respondent's Fourth Amendment interests. Thus, although we decline to adopt any outside time limitation for a permissible *Terry* stop, we have never approved a seizure of the person for the prolonged 90-minute period involved here and cannot do so on the facts presented by this case.

Although the 90-minute detention of respondent's luggage is sufficient to render the seizure unreasonable, the violation was exacerbated by the failure of the agents to accurately inform respondent of the place to which they were transporting his luggage, of the length of time he might be dispossessed, and of what arrangements would be made for return of the luggage if the investigation dispelled the suspicion. In short, we hold that the detention of respondent's luggage in this case went beyond the narrow authority possessed by police to detain briefly luggage reasonably suspected to contain narcotics.

* * *

. . . Consequently, the evidence obtained from the subsequent search of his luggage was inadmissible, and Place's conviction must be reversed. The judgment of the Court of Appeals, accordingly, is affirmed.

It is so ordered.

# HAYES
### v.
# FLORIDA

### 470 U.S. 811, 105 S. Ct. 1643, 84 L. Ed. 2d 705 (1985)

*[Citations and footnotes omitted.]*

[Police suspected the defendant of having committed a string of crimes and wanted a fingerprint sample to compare with those found at the crime scenes. They decided to visit the defendant's home to obtain his fingerprints or, if he was uncooperative, to arrest him. When he expressed reluctance to voluntarily accompany them to the station for fingerprinting, one of the investigators explained that they would therefore arrest him. The defendant stated that he would rather go voluntarily then be arrested. He was taken to the station house, where he was fingerprinted. When police determined that his prints matched those left at the scene of the crime, petitioner was placed under formal arrest.]

JUSTICE WHITE delivered the opinion of the Court.

The issue before us in this case is whether the Fourth Amendment to the Constitution of the United States, applicable to the States by virtue of the Fourteenth Amendment, was properly applied by the District Court of Appeal of Florida, Second District, to allow police to transport a suspect to the station house for fingerprinting, without his consent and without probable cause or prior judicial authorization.

* * *

. . . There is no doubt that at some point in the investigative process, police procedures can qualitatively and quantitatively be so intrusive with respect to a suspect's freedom of movement and privacy interests as to trigger the full protection of the Fourth and Fourteenth Amendments. And our view continues to be that the line is crossed when the police, without probable cause or a warrant, forcibly remove a person from his home or other place in which he is entitled to be and transport him to the police station, where he is detained, although briefly, for investigative purposes. We adhere to the view that such seizures, at least where not under judicial supervision, are sufficiently like arrests to invoke the traditional rule that arrests may constitutionally be made only on probable cause.

None of the foregoing implies that a brief detention in the field for the purpose of fingerprinting, where there is only reasonable suspicion not amounting to probable cause, is necessarily impermissible under the Fourth Amendment. In addressing the reach of a *Terry* stop in Adams v. Williams, we observed that "[a] brief stop of a suspicious individual, in order to determine his identity or to maintain the status quo momentarily while obtaining more information, may be most reasonable in light of the facts known to the officer at the time." Also, just this Term, we concluded that if there are articulable facts supporting a reasonable suspicion that a person has committed a criminal offense, that person may be stopped in order to identify him, to question him briefly, or to detain him briefly while attempting to obtain additional information. There is thus support in our cases for the view that the Fourth Amendment would permit seizures for the purpose of fingerprinting, if there is reasonable suspicion that the suspect has committed a criminal act, if there is a reasonable basis for believing that fingerprinting will establish or negate the suspect's connection with that crime, and if the procedure is carried out with

dispatch. Of course, neither reasonable suspicion nor probable cause would suffice to permit the officers to make a warrantless entry into a person's house for the purpose of obtaining fingerprint identification.

\* \* \*

[Concurring opinion omitted.]

## WHREN
### v.
## UNITED STATES

### 517 U.S. 806, 116 S. Ct. 1769, 135 L. Ed. 2d 89 (1996)

*[Citations and footnotes omitted.]*

[Officers were patrolling a "high drug area" of the city in an unmarked car. Their suspicions were aroused when they passed a dark Pathfinder truck with temporary license plates and youthful occupants waiting at a stop sign, the driver looking down into the lap of the passenger at his right. The truck remained stopped at the intersection for what seemed an unusually long time—more than 20 seconds. When the police car executed a U-turn in order to head back toward the truck, the Pathfinder turned suddenly to its right, without signaling, and sped off at an "unreasonable" speed. The policemen followed, and in a short while overtook the Pathfinder when it stopped behind other traffic at a red light. They pulled up alongside, and Officer Ephraim Soto stepped out and approached the driver's door, identifying himself as a police officer and directing the driver, petitioner Brown, to put the vehicle in park. When Soto drew up to the driver's window, he immediately observed two large plastic bags of what appeared to be crack cocaine in petitioner Whren's hands. Both were arrested, and quantities of several types of illegal drugs were retrieved from the vehicle.Petitioners challenged the legality of the stop and the resulting seizure of the drugs. They argued that the stop had not been justified by probable cause to believe, or even reasonable suspicion, that petitioners were engaged in illegal drug-dealing activity; and that Officer Soto's asserted ground for approaching the vehicle—to give the driver a warning concerning traffic violations—was pretextual. The District Court denied the suppression motion. Petitioners were convicted of the counts at issue here. The Court of Appeals affirmed the convictions, holding with respect to the suppression issue that, "regardless of whether a police officer subjectively believes that the occupants of an automobile may be engaging in some other illegal behavior, a traffic stop is permissible as long as a reasonable officer in the same circumstances could have stopped the car for the suspected traffic violation."]

Scalia, J., delivered the opinion for a unanimous Court.

* * *

. . . In this case we decide whether the temporary detention of a motorist who the police have probable cause to believe has committed a civil traffic violation is inconsistent with the Fourth Amendment's prohibition against unreasonable seizures unless a reasonable officer would have been motivated to stop the car by a desire to enforce the traffic laws.

* * *

The Fourth Amendment guarantees "[t]he right of the people to be secure in their persons, houses, papers, and effects, against unreasonable searches and seizures." Temporary detention of individuals during the stop of an automobile by the police, even if only for a brief period and for a limited purpose, constitutes a "seizure" of "persons" within the meaning of this provision. An automobile stop is thus subject to the constitutional imperative that it not be "unreasonable" under the circumstances. As a general matter, the decision to stop an automobile is reasonable where the police have probable cause to believe that a traffic violation has occurred.

Petitioners accept that Officer Soto had probable cause to believe that various provisions of the District of Columbia traffic code had been violated. They argue, however, that "in the unique context of civil traffic regulations" probable cause is not enough. Since, they contend, the use of automobiles is so heavily and minutely regulated that total compliance with traffic and safety rules is nearly impossible, a police officer will almost invariably be able to catch any given motorist in a technical violation. This creates the temptation to use traffic stops as a means of investigating other law violations, as to which no probable cause or even articulable suspicion exists. Petitioners, who are both black, further contend that police officers might decide which motorists to stop based on decidedly impermissible factors, such as the race of the car's occupants. To avoid this danger, they say, the Fourth Amendment test for traffic stops should be, not the normal one (applied by the Court of Appeals) of whether probable cause existed to justify the stop; but rather, whether a police officer, acting reasonably, would have made the stop for the reason given.

* * *

Petitioners urge as an extraordinary factor in this case that the "multitude of applicable traffic and equipment regulations" is so large and so difficult to obey perfectly that virtually everyone is guilty of violation, permitting the police to single out almost whomever they wish for a stop. But we are aware of no principle that would allow us to decide at what point a code of law becomes so expansive and so commonly violated that infraction itself can no longer be the ordinary measure of the lawfulness of enforcement. And even if we could identify such exorbitant codes, we do not know by what standard (or what right) we would decide, as petitioners would have us do, which particular provisions are sufficiently important to merit enforcement.

For the run-of-the-mine [sic] case, which this surely is, we think there is no realistic alternative to the traditional common-law rule that probable cause justifies a search and seizure.

Here the District Court found that the officers had probable cause to believe that petitioners had violated the traffic code. That rendered the stop reasonable under the Fourth Amendment, the evidence thereby discovered admissible, and the upholding of the convictions by the Court of Appeals for the District of Columbia Circuit correct.

Judgment affirmed.

## UNITED STATES
## v.
## KING

### 227 F.3d 732 (6th Cir. 2000)

[Kenneth King was charged with possession with intent to distribute cocaine within 1,000 feet of a schoolyard. The cocaine was found during the search of a basement in a two-family dwelling in which he resided. The search was conducted under the authority of a warrant. King filed a motion to suppress the cocaine on the grounds that affidavit submitted in support of the warrant was insufficient to establish probable cause to believe that illegal drugs would be found on the premises. The district court conducted a hearing and thereafter denied the motion to suppress. King was convicted and appealed. This case has been included because of its unusually clear discussion of the factors courts consider in evaluating whether probable cause for the issuance of a warrant has been established.]

CLAY, Circuit Judge.

* * *

The Fourth Amendment guarantees that "no Warrants shall issue, but upon probable cause, supported by Oath or affirmation." The warrant requirement serves to interpose between the police and an individual's personal privacy an orderly procedure involving "a neutral and detached magistrate[,]" who is responsible for making an "informed and deliberate determination" on the issue of probable cause. The warrant process thus avoids allowing the determination of probable cause to rest with the "zealous" actions of the police who are "engaged in the often competitive enterprise of ferreting out crime."

Probable cause is defined as "reasonable grounds for belief, supported by less than prima facie proof but more than mere suspicion," that "there is a fair probability that contraband or evidence of a crime will be found in a particular place." This determination does not lend itself to the application of "[r]igid legal rules," and no one decision may serve to provide a definitive basis upon which to rely inasmuch as "informant's tips, like all other clues and evidence . . . may vary greatly in the value and reliability." Rather, the probable cause standard is a "'practical non-technical conception . . . [wherein] we deal with probabilities . . .

[which are] the factual and practical considerations of everyday life on which reasonable and prudent men, not legal technicians, act.'" Stated otherwise, "probable cause is a fluid concept—turning on the assessment of probabilities in particular factual contexts—not readily, or even usefully, reduced to a neat set of legal rules. Informants' tips doubtless come in many shapes and sizes from many different types of persons. . . . Rigid legal rules are ill-suited to an area of such diversity. One simple rule will not cover every situation." As such, the issuing magistrate must apply a "totality of the circumstances" test to probable cause issues. This test requires the magistrate to "make a practical, common-sense decision whether, given all the circumstances set forth in the affidavit before him, including the 'veracity' and 'basis of knowledge' of persons supplying the hearsay information," probable cause exists.

The Supreme Court identified factors which, although not to be analyzed as "separate and independent requirements to be rigidly exacted in every case," should be weighed by a reviewing court in assessing the value that should be afforded to an informant's tip when determining whether a substantial basis for probable cause exists. These factors, which consist of the "veracity" or "reliability" as well as "basis of knowledge" of the tip, are relative where the strength of one factor may compensate for the deficiency of another. However, "the information presented must be sufficient to allow the official to independently determine probable cause; 'his action cannot be a mere ratification of the bare conclusions of others.'" "In order to ensure that such an abdication of the magistrate's duty does not occur, courts must continue to conscientiously review the sufficiency of affidavits on which warrants are issued." With these standards and cautionary instructions from

the Supreme Court in mind, we turn to the affidavit presented to the magistrate in this case to determine whether, under a totality of the circumstances, the affidavit was sufficient to establish probable cause for the warrant to issue.

The affidavit submitted to the court by Detective John Gannon of the Cleveland Police Department in support of the search warrant in question provided as follows:

Before me, a Judge of the Court of Common Pleas, Cuyahoga County, Ohio, personally appeared the undersigned Det. John Gannon, # 2452, who being first duly sworn, deposes and says that he is member of the Police Department of the City of Cleveland, in Cuyahoga County, Ohio, and that his training and experience include: twenty-six years experience with the Cleveland Police, with a current assignment to the Caribbean Gang Task Force; training in the recognition, production, and distribution of controlled substances; over one thousand arrests for drug-related offenses.

Affiant has good cause to believe that on the premises known as 1437 East 116th Street, Cleveland, Cuyahoga County, Ohio, and being more fully described as the downstairs unit in a two family, two and one half story, white wood sided dwelling with green trim, the numbers "1439," the address for the upstairs unit, clearly visible on the south side of the entrance door to the upstairs unit, the structure being located on the east side of East 116th Street, facing west, and in the vehicle described as 1980's model gray Chevrolet Cavalier, Ohio Temporary License Number K591513, there is now being kept, concealed, and possessed the following evidence of criminal offense: Cocaine, and other narcotic drugs, and/or controlled substances; instruments and paraphernalia used in taking or preparing drugs for sale, use, or shipment; records of illegal transactions including computers and computer files, articles of personal property, and papers tending to establish the identity of the persons in control of the premises; other contraband, including, but not limited to, money, communications equipment, motor vehicles, and weapons being illegally possessed therein; and/or any and all evidence pertaining to the violations of the laws of the State of Ohio, to wit:

1. Within the past twenty-four hours, affiant was contacted by another a confidential reliable informant concerning the delivery of a large quantity of crack cocaine to the above-described premises.

2. This information from confidential reliable informant (CRI) indicated that Kenneth King was trafficking in cocaine, and had crack cocaine at the above-described premises having been delivered to King by Antonio Cook within the past day.

3. CRI is made reliable in that CRI has given information to the law enforcement official which has led to the arrest and/or conviction of more than seventy individuals for violations of state and/or federal drug laws, as well as the confiscation of more than $100,000.00 and 5 kilograms of controlled substances.

4. CRI stated that King kept drugs at the above-described premises, giving a description of the premises, and King utilized the above-described vehicle for the purpose of making deliveries of smaller amounts of crack cocaine. Investigation revealed that the above-described address is listed in the records of the Ohio Bureau of Motor Vehicles as an address for vehicles registered to Kenneth King.

5. Affiant is also aware that Antonio Cook is a person known to members of the Task Force as a supplier of cocaine on the east side of Cleveland. Affiant also determined that King has a prior felony conviction for GSI and Aggravated Assault and has done prison time.

6. In the experience of affiant, narcotic drugs are frequently carried or concealed on people who are at locations where drugs are used, kept, or sold, and the size of useable quantities of drugs are small, making them easy to conceal on one's person.

7. Further, in the experience of affiant, persons who traffic in illegal drugs frequently keep records of illegal transactions, at times using computers for such records, and evidence of communications used in the furtherance of drug trafficking activity, including, but not limited to, pagers, cellular telephones, answering machines, and answering machine tapes.

8. Further, in the experience of the affiant, persons who traffic in illegal drugs frequently keep weapons, such as firearms, on or about their person or within their possession, for use against law enforcement officials, as well as other citizens.

9. Permitting a motor vehicle to be used in the commission of a felony drug abuse offense is a violation of R.C. 2925.13.

10. Affiant avers that it is urgently necessary that the above-mentioned premises be searched in the night sea-

son forthwith to prevent the above named property from being concealed or removed so as not to be found, and for the safety of the executing officers.

Defendant argues that the affidavit was insufficient to establish probable cause insofar as it fails to provide any basis as to the reliability or veracity of the confidential informant, and fails to indicate that Detective Gannon conducted an independent investigation to corroborate the informant's allegations. Defendant contends that Detective Gannon's verification of Defendant's address, via the Ohio Department of Motor Vehicles, as being that alleged by the informant as a place where drugs were being trafficked, was inadequate to corroborate the informant's claims. Defendant further contends that because the affidavit does not aver that the confidential informant observed drugs or paraphernalia on the premises of Defendant's home, corroboration by Detective Gannon was particularly necessary. We disagree with Defendant's claims, and believe that the affidavit in support of the search warrant was sufficient to establish probable cause that illegal drugs could be found on the premises inasmuch as the affidavit described the area to be searched with particularity, was based upon information provided by a known reliable informant, and was verified by Detective Gannon to the extent possible.

The affidavit described Defendant's residence with particularity as being "the downstairs unit in a two family, two and one half story, white wood sided dwelling with green trim, the numbers '1439,' the address for the upstairs unit, clearly visible on the south side of the entrance door to the upstairs unit, the structure being located on the east side of East 116th Street, facing west." The affidavit further described Defendant's vehicle used in the distribution of cocaine with particularity as a "1980's

model gray Chevrolet Cavalier, Ohio Temporary License Number K591513." The affidavit also indicated that in addition to describing the premises and the vehicle in such detail, the confidential reliable informant ("CRI") described the nature of alleged criminal activity in detail. For example, the CRI described the criminal activity as trafficking cocaine, and further stated that a large amount of cocaine had been delivered to the premises described in the affidavit twenty-four hours beforehand for the purposes of distribution. The CRI also stated that the large amount of cocaine had been delivered to the premises by Antonio Cook within the past day. The reliability of the informant was established in the affidavit by Detective Gannon's averments that the CRI had provided credible information in the past which had led to the arrest and/or conviction of "more than seventy individuals for violations of state and/or federal drug laws, as well as the confiscation of more than $100,000.00 and 5 kilograms of controlled substances." Moreover, the informant's tip was corroborated by Detective Gannon's own investigation. For example, the affidavit indicates that Detective Gannon verified with the Ohio Department of Motor Vehicles that the vehicle described by the informant was registered to Defendant and that the address provided by the informant was Defendant's address. Detective Gannon also verified that Defendant had a prior history of criminal offenses for which he had spent time in prison. Finally, Detective Gannon, as an experienced member of the task force established to ferret out drug-related crimes, averred that he was aware that Antonio Cook is a person known to members of the task force as a supplier of cocaine, which further supported the CRI's allegations.

When considering the above information under a totality of the circumstances, we conclude that the affidavit provided a "substantial basis" for the magistrate to believe that "there [was] a fair probability that contraband or evidence of a crime [would] be found in a particular place;" namely, Defendant's residence. Although the affidavit does not indicate that the CRI observed the delivery of a "large quantity of crack cocaine" to Defendant's residence firsthand, the affidavit does indicate that the CRI had provided accurate information in the past and that Antonio Cook, the individual alleged to have delivered the cocaine, was known to be a drug distributor. As a result, the lack of the firsthand observation is not fatal to the affidavit.

The affidavit in question is distinguishable from those cases where the affidavit was found to be insufficient to establish probable cause. For example, unlike in Weaver, where this Court held that the affidavit in support of the search warrant was insufficient to establish probable cause insofar as it presented no underlying factual circumstances to support the informant's knowledge, failed to indicate that the informant had provided information in the past, and failed to establish any independent police corroboration, the affidavit in the present case provides such detail. Similarly, in Leake, the affidavit was insufficient to establish probable cause in that the anonymous caller failed to provide the names of the individuals residing at the home where the marijuana was allegedly being grown, and failed to provide a date upon which the marijuana was allegedly seen; and the police failed to sufficiently corroborate the information. However, none of these insufficiencies [is] present here, even though the CRI did not observe the cocaine being delivered to Defendant's residence firsthand.

We therefore hold that the district court did not err in denying Defendant's motion to suppress the evidence, where the affidavit submitted in support of the warrant was rich in detail, was based upon a tip from a known and reliable informant, and was corroborated by independent police investigation.

* * *

PAYTON
v.
NEW YORK

445 U.S. 573, 100 S. Ct. 137
163 L. Ed. 2d 639 (1979)

[Citations and footnotes omitted.]

[The police went to Payton's home to arrest him. Although they had probable cause to believe that Payton committed a murder, they did not procure an arrest warrant or a search warrant. Once there, they used crowbars to pry their way into his house. Although Payton was nowhere to be found, police discovered an empty .30-caliber shell in plain view. A New York statute permitted police to enter homes without a warrant whenever necessary to make a felony arrest.]

Mr. Justice STEVENS delivered the opinion of the Court.

These appeals challenge the constitutionality of New York statutes that authorize police officers to enter a private residence without a warrant and with force, if necessary, to make a routine felony arrest.

* * *

Before addressing the narrow question presented by these appeals, we put to one side other related problems that are not presented today. Although it is arguable that the warrantless entry to effect Payton's arrest might have been justified by exigent circumstances, none of the New York courts relied on any such justification. The Court of Appeals majority treated both Payton's and Riddick's cases as involving routine arrests in which there was ample time to obtain a warrant, and we will do the same. Accordingly, we have no occasion to consider the sort of emergency or dangerous situation, described in our cases as "exigent circumstances," that would justify a warrantless entry into a home for the purpose of either arrest or search.

Nor do these cases raise any question concerning the authority of the police, without either a search or arrest warrant, to enter a third party's home to arrest a suspect. The police broke into Payton's apartment intending to arrest Payton. We also note that . . . it is [not] argued that the police lacked probable cause to believe that the suspect was at home when they entered. Finally, in both cases we are dealing with entries into homes made without the consent of any occupant. In *Payton*, the police used crowbars to break down the door. . . .

It is familiar history that indiscriminate searches and seizures conducted under the authority of "general warrants" were the immediate evils that motivated the framing and adoption of the Fourth Amendment. Indeed, as originally proposed in the House of Representatives, the draft contained only one clause, which directly imposed limitations on the issuance of warrants, but imposed no express restrictions on warrantless searches or seizures. As it was ultimately adopted, however, the Amendment contained two separate clauses, the first protecting the basic right to be free from unreasonable searches and seizures and the second requiring that warrants be particular and supported by probable cause. The Amendment provides:

The right of the people to be secure in their persons, houses, papers, and effects, against unreasonable searches

and seizures, shall not be violated, and no Warrants shall issue, but upon probable cause, supported by Oath or affirmation, and particularly describing the place to be searched, and the persons or things to be seized.

It is thus perfectly clear that the evil the Amendment was designed to prevent was broader than the abuse of a general warrant. Unreasonable searches or seizures conducted without any warrant at all are condemned by the plain language of the first clause of the Amendment. Almost a century ago the Court stated in resounding terms that the principles reflected in the Amendment "reached farther than the concrete form" of the specific cases that gave it birth, and "apply to all invasions on the part of the government and its employees of the sanctity of a man's home and the privacies of life." Without pausing to consider whether that broad language may require some qualification, it is sufficient to note that the warrantless arrest of a person is a species of seizure required by the Amendment to be reasonable. . . .

The simple language of the Amendment applies equally to seizures of persons and to seizures of property. Our analysis in this case may therefore properly commence with rules that have been well established in Fourth Amendment litigation involving tangible items. As the Court reiterated just a few years ago, the "physical entry of the home is the chief evil against which the wording of the Fourth Amendment is directed." And we have long adhered to the view that the warrant procedure minimizes the danger of needless intrusions of that sort.

It is a "basic principle of Fourth Amendment law" that searches and seizures inside a home without a warrant are presumptively unreasonable. Yet it is also well settled that objects such as weapons or contraband found in a public place may be seized by the police without a warrant. The seizure of property in plain view involves no invasion of privacy and is presumptively reasonable, assuming that there is probable cause to associate the property with criminal activity. . . .

As the late Judge Leventhal recognized, this distinction has equal force when the seizure of a person is involved. Writing on the constitutional issue now before us . . . , Judge Leventhal first noted the settled rule that warrantless arrests in public places are valid. He immediately recognized, however, that

> [a] greater burden is placed . . . on officials who enter a home or dwelling without consent. Freedom from intrusion into the home or dwelling is the archetype of the privacy protection secured by the Fourth Amendment.

His analysis of this question then focused on the long-settled premise that, absent exigent circumstances, a warrantless entry to search for weapons or contraband is unconstitutional even when a felony has been committed and there is probable cause to believe that incriminating evidence will be found within. He reasoned that the constitutional protection afforded to the individual's interest in the privacy of his own home is equally applicable to a warrantless entry for the purpose of arresting a resident of the house; for it is inherent in such an entry that a search for the suspect may be required before he can be apprehended. Judge Leventhal concluded that an entry to arrest and an entry to search for and to seize property implicate the same interest in preserving the privacy and the sanctity of the home, and justify the same level of constitutional protection.

\* \* \*

But the critical point is that any differences in the intrusiveness of entries to

search and entries to arrest are merely ones of degree rather than kind. The two intrusions share this fundamental characteristic: the breach of the entrance to an individual's home. The Fourth Amendment protects the individual's privacy in a variety of settings. In none is the zone of privacy more clearly defined than when bounded by the unambiguous physical dimensions of an individual's home—a zone that finds its roots in clear and specific constitutional terms: "The right of the people to be secure in their . . . houses . . . shall not be violated." That language unequivocally establishes the proposition that "[a]t the very core [of the Fourth Amendment] stands the right of a man to retreat into his own home and there be free from unreasonable governmental intrusion." In terms that apply equally to seizures of property and to seizures of persons, the Fourth Amendment has drawn a firm line at the entrance to the house. Absent exigent circumstances, that threshold may not reasonably be crossed without a warrant.

\* \* \*

Thus, our study of the relevant common law does not provide the same guidance that was present in Watson. Whereas the rule concerning the validity of an arrest in a public place was supported by cases directly in point and by the unanimous views of the commentators, we have found no direct authority supporting forcible entries into a home to make a routine arrest and the weight of the scholarly opinion is somewhat to the contrary. Indeed, the absence of any 17th- or 18th-century English cases directly in point, together with the unequivocal endorsement of the tenet that "a man's house is his castle," strongly suggests that the prevailing practice was not to make such arrests except in hot pursuit or when authorized by a warrant. In all events, the issue is not one that can be said to have been definitively settled by the common law at the time the Fourth Amendment was adopted.

\* \* \*

The parties have argued at some length about the practical consequences of a warrant requirement as a precondition to a felony arrest in the home. In the absence of any evidence that effective law enforcement has suffered in those States that already have such a requirement, we are inclined to view such arguments with skepticism. More fundamentally, however, such arguments of policy must give way to a constitutional command that we consider to be unequivocal. Finally, we note the State's suggestion that only a search warrant based on probable cause to believe the suspect is at home at a given time can adequately protect the privacy interests at stake, and since such a warrant requirement is manifestly impractical, there need be no warrant of any kind. We find this ingenious argument unpersuasive. It is true that an arrest warrant requirement may afford less protection than a search warrant requirement, but it will suffice to interpose the magistrate's determination of probable cause between the zealous officer and the citizen. If there is sufficient evidence of a citizen's participation in a felony to persuade a judicial officer that his arrest is justified, it is constitutionally reasonable to require him to open his doors to the officers of the law. Thus, for Fourth Amendment purposes, an arrest warrant founded on probable cause implicitly carries with it the limited authority to enter a dwelling in which the suspect lives when there is reason to believe the suspect is within.

Because no arrest warrant was obtained in either of these cases, the judgments must be reversed and the cases remanded to the New York Court of Appeals for further proceedings not inconsistent with this opinion.

It is so ordered.

[Concurring and dissenting opinions have been omitted.]

## TENNESSEE
v.
## GARNER

### 471 U.S. 1, 105 S. Ct. 1694, 85 L. Ed. 2d 1 (1985)

*[Citations and footnotes omitted.]*

[At about 10:45 p.m. on October 3, 1974, Memphis Police Officers Elton Hymon and Leslie Wright were dispatched to answer a "prowler inside call." Behind the house, Hymon saw someone run across the backyard. The fleeing suspect, who was appellee-respondent's decedent, Edward Garner, stopped at a 6-feet-high chain-link fence at the edge of the yard. With the aid of a flashlight, Hymon was able to see Garner's face and hands. He saw no sign of a weapon, and, although not certain, was "reasonably sure" and "figured" that Garner was unarmed. He thought Garner was 17 or 18 years old and about 5'5" or 5'7" tall. While Garner was crouched at the base of the fence, Hymon called out "police, halt" and took a few steps toward him. Garner then began to climb over the fence. Convinced that if Garner made it over the fence he would elude capture, Hymon shot him. The bullet hit Garner in the back of the head. Garner was taken by ambulance to a hospital, where he died on the operating table. Ten dollars and a purse taken from the house were found on his body. Both a Tennessee statute and departmental policy authorized Hymon to shoot under these circumstances. Garner's father brought a suit for damages against Hymon and the county claiming that the shooting violated his son's Fourth Amendment right to be free from unreasonable force.]

JUSTICE WHITE delivered the opinion of the Court.

This case requires us to determine the constitutionality of the use of deadly force to prevent the escape of an apparently unarmed suspected felon. We conclude that such force may not be used unless it is necessary to prevent the escape and the officer has probable cause to believe that the suspect poses a significant threat of death or serious physical injury to the officer or others.

* * *

Whenever an officer restrains the freedom of a person to walk away, he has seized that person. While it is not always clear just when minimal police interference becomes a seizure, there can be no question that apprehension by the use of deadly force is a seizure subject to the reasonableness requirement of the Fourth Amendment.

A police officer may arrest a person if he has probable cause to believe that person committed a crime. Petitioners and appellant argue that if this requirement is satisfied, the Fourth Amendment has nothing to say about how that seizure is made. This submission ignores the many cases in which this Court, by balancing the extent of the intrusion against the need for it, has examined the reasonableness of the manner in which a search or seizure is conducted. To determine the constitutionality of a seizure, "[w]e must balance the nature and quality of the intrusion on the individual's Fourth Amendment interests against the importance of the governmental interests

alleged to justify the intrusion." We have described "the balancing of competing interests" as "the key principle of the Fourth Amendment." Because one of the factors is the extent of the intrusion, it is plain that reasonableness depends on not only when a seizure is made, but also how it is carried out.

* * *

. . . [N]otwithstanding probable cause to seize a suspect, an officer may not always do so by killing him. The intrusiveness of a seizure by means of deadly force is unmatched. The suspect's fundamental interest in his own life need not be elaborated upon. The use of deadly force also frustrates the interest of the individual, and of society, in judicial determination of guilt and punishment. Against these interests are ranged governmental interests in effective law enforcement. It is argued that overall violence will be reduced by encouraging the peaceful submission of suspects who know that they may be shot if they flee. Effectiveness in making arrests requires the resort to deadly force, or at least the meaningful threat thereof. "Being able to arrest such individuals is a condition precedent to the state's entire system of law enforcement."

Without in any way disparaging the importance of these goals, we are not convinced that the use of deadly force is a sufficiently productive means of accomplishing them to justify the killing of nonviolent suspects. The use of deadly force is a self-defeating way of apprehending a suspect and so setting the criminal justice mechanism in motion. If successful, it guarantees that that mechanism will not be set in motion. And while the meaningful threat of deadly force might be thought to lead to the arrest of more live suspects by discouraging escape attempts, the presently available evidence does not support this thesis. The fact is that a majority of police departments in this country have forbidden the use of deadly force against nonviolent suspects. If those charged with the enforcement of the criminal law have abjured the use of deadly force in arresting nondangerous felons, there is a substantial basis for doubting that the use of such force is an essential attribute of the arrest power in all felony cases. Petitioners and appellant have not persuaded us that shooting nondangerous fleeing suspects is so vital as to outweigh the suspect's interest in his own life.

The use of deadly force to prevent the escape of all felony suspects, whatever the circumstances, is constitutionally unreasonable. It is not better that all felony suspects die than that they escape. Where the suspect poses no immediate threat to the officer and no threat to others, the harm resulting from failing to apprehend him does not justify the use of deadly force to do so. It is no doubt unfortunate when a suspect who is in sight escapes, but the fact that the police arrive a little late or are a little slower afoot does not always justify killing the suspect. A police officer may not seize an unarmed, nondangerous suspect by shooting him dead. The Tennessee statute is unconstitutional insofar as it authorizes the use of deadly force against such fleeing suspects.

It is not, however, unconstitutional on its face. Where the officer has probable cause to believe that the suspect poses a threat of serious physical harm, either to the officer or to others, it is not constitutionally unreasonable to prevent escape by using deadly force. Thus, if the suspect threatens the officer with a weapon or there is probable cause to believe that he has committed a crime involving the infliction or threatened infliction of serious physical harm, deadly force may be used if necessary to prevent escape, and if, where feasible, some warning has been given. . . .

* * *

Nor do we agree with petitioners and appellant that the rule we have adopted requires the police to make impossible, split-second evaluations of unknowable facts. We do not deny the practical difficulties of attempting to assess the suspect's dangerousness. However, similarly difficult judgments must be made by the police in equally uncertain circumstances. Nor is there any indication that in States that allow the use of deadly force only against dangerous suspects, supra, the standard has been difficult to apply or has led to a rash of litigation involving inappropriate second-guessing of police officers' split-second decisions. Moreover, the highly technical felony/misdemeanor distinction is equally, if not more, difficult to apply in the field. An officer is in no position to know, for example, the precise value of property stolen, or whether the crime was a first or second offense. Finally, as noted above, this claim must be viewed with suspicion in light of the similar self-imposed limitations of so many police departments.

* * *

. . . Officer Hymon could not reasonably have believed that Garner—young, slight, and unarmed—posed any threat. Indeed, Hymon never attempted to justify his actions on any basis other than the need to prevent an escape. The District Court stated in passing that "[t]he facts of this case did not indicate to Officer Hymon that Garner was 'non-dangerous.'" This conclusion is not explained, and seems to be based solely on the fact that Garner had broken into a house at night. However, the fact that Garner was a suspected burglar could not, without regard to the other circumstances, automatically justify the use of deadly force. Hymon did not have probable cause to believe that Garner, whom he correctly believed to be unarmed, posed any physical danger to himself or others.

The dissent argues that the shooting was justified by the fact that Officer Hymon had probable cause to believe that Garner had committed a nighttime burglary. While we agree that burglary is a serious crime, we cannot agree that it is so dangerous as automatically to justify the use of deadly force. The FBI classifies burglary as a "property" rather than a "violent" crime. Although the armed burglar would present a different situation, the fact that an unarmed suspect has broken into a dwelling at night does not automatically mean he is physically dangerous. This case demonstrates

as much. In fact, the available statistics demonstrate that burglaries only rarely involve physical violence. During the 10-year period from 1973-1982, only 3.8% of all burglaries involved violent crime.

\* \* \*

The judgment of the Court of Appeals is affirmed, and the case is remanded for further proceedings consistent with this opinion.

So ordered.

*[The dissenting opinion has been omitted.]*

# Cases Relating to Chapter 4

# Search and Seizure

## CALIFORNIA
## v.
## GREENWOOD

### 486 U.S. 35, 108 S. Ct. 1625, 100 L. Ed. 2d 30 (1988)

*[Citations and footnotes omitted.]*

[In early 1984, Investigator Jenny Stracner of the Laguna Beach Police Department received information indicating that respondent Greenwood might be engaged in narcotics trafficking. She asked the neighborhood's regular trash collector to pick up the plastic garbage bags that Greenwood had left on the curb in front of his house and to turn the bags over to her without mixing their contents with garbage from other houses. The trash collector cleaned his truck bin of other refuse, collected the garbage bags from the street in front of Greenwood's house, and turned the bags over to Stracner. She searched through the rubbish, found items indicative of narcotics use, and used this information to obtain a search warrant to search Greenwood's home. Narcotics and evidence of narcotics trafficking were found during the search. Greenwood was arrested and prosecuted for trafficking in narcotics.]

JUSTICE WHITE delivered the opinion of the Court.

The issue here is whether the Fourth Amendment prohibits the warrantless search and seizure of garbage left for collection outside the curtilage of a home. We conclude, in accordance with the vast majority of lower courts that have addressed the issue, that it does not.

\* \* \*

The warrantless search and seizure of the garbage bags left at the curb outside the Greenwood house would violate the Fourth Amendment only if respondents manifested a subjective expectation of privacy in their garbage that society accepts as objectively reasonable. Respondents do not disagree with this standard.

They assert, however, that they had, and exhibited, an expectation of privacy with respect to the trash that was searched by the police: The trash, which was placed on the street for collection at a fixed time, was contained in opaque plastic bags, which the garbage collector was expected to pick up, mingle with the trash of others, and deposit at the garbage dump. The trash was only temporarily on the street, and there was little likelihood that it would be inspected by anyone.

It may well be that respondents did not expect that the contents of their garbage bags would become known to the police or other members of the public. An expectation of privacy does not give rise to Fourth Amendment protection, however, unless society is prepared to accept that expectation as objectively reasonable.

Here, we conclude that respondents exposed their garbage to the public sufficiently to defeat their claim to Fourth Amendment protection. It is common knowledge that plastic garbage bags left on or at the side of a public street are readily accessible to animals, children, scavengers, snoops, and other members of the public. Moreover, respondents placed their refuse at the curb for the express purpose of conveying it to a third party, the trash collector, who might himself have sorted through respondents' trash or permitted others, such as the police, to do so. Accordingly, having deposited their garbage "in an area particularly suited for public inspection and, in a manner of speaking, public consumption, for the express purpose of having strangers take it," respondents could have had no reasonable expectation of privacy in the inculpatory items that they discarded.

Furthermore, as we have held, the police cannot reasonably be expected to avert their eyes from evidence of criminal activity that could have been observed by any member of the public. Hence, "[w]hat a person knowingly exposes to the public, even in his own home or office, is not a subject of Fourth Amendment protection." . . .

Similarly, we held in *California v. Ciraolo*, that the police were not required by the Fourth Amendment to obtain a warrant before conducting surveillance of the respondent's fenced backyard from a private plane flying at an altitude of 1,000 feet. We concluded that the respondent's expectation that his yard was protected from such surveillance was unreasonable because "[a]ny member of the public flying in this air-space who glanced down could have seen everything that these officers observed."

Our conclusion that society would not accept as reasonable respondents' claim to an expectation of privacy in trash left for collection in an area accessible to the public is reinforced by the unanimous rejection of similar claims by the Federal Courts of Appeals. . . .

* * *

We reject respondent Greenwood's alternative argument for affirmance: that his expectation of privacy in his garbage should be deemed reasonable as a matter of federal constitutional law because the warrantless search and seizure of his garbage was impermissible as a matter of California law. . . .

Individual States may surely construe their own constitutions as imposing more stringent constraints on police conduct than does the Federal Constitution. We have never intimated, however, that whether or not a search is reasonable within the meaning of the Fourth Amendment depends on the law of the particular State in which the search occurs. . . . Respondent's argument is no less than a suggestion that concepts of privacy under the laws of each State are to determine the reach of the Fourth Amendment. We do not accept this submission.

* * *

The judgment of the California Court of Appeal is therefore reversed, and this case is remanded for further proceedings not inconsistent with this opinion.

It is so ordered.

[Dissenting opinion omitted.]

## BOND

### v.

## UNITED STATES

**529 U.S. 334, 120 S. Ct. 1462,
146 L. Ed. 2d 365 (2000)**

*[Footnotes and citations omitted.]*

CHIEF JUSTICE REHNQUIST delivered the opinion of the Court.

This case presents the question whether a law enforcement officer's physical manipulation of a bus passenger's carry-on luggage violated the Fourth Amendment's proscription against unreasonable searches. We hold that it did.

Petitioner Steven Dewayne Bond was a passenger on a Greyhound bus that left California bound for Little Rock, Arkansas. The bus stopped, as it was required to do, at the permanent Border Patrol checkpoint in Sierra Blanca, Texas. Border Patrol Agent Cesar Cantu boarded the bus to check the immigration status of its passengers. After reaching the back of the bus, having satisfied himself that the passengers were lawfully in the United States, Agent Cantu began walking toward the front. Along the way, he squeezed the soft luggage which passengers had placed in the overhead storage space above the seats.

Petitioner was seated four or five rows from the back of the bus. As Agent Cantu inspected the luggage in the compartment above petitioner's seat, he squeezed a green canvas bag and noticed that it contained a "brick-like" object. Petitioner admitted that the bag was his and agreed to allow Agent Cantu to open it. Upon opening the bag, Agent Cantu discovered a "brick" of methamphetamine. The brick had been wrapped in duct tape until it was oval-shaped and then rolled in a pair of pants.

Petitioner was indicted for conspiracy to possess, and possession with intent to distribute, methamphetamine in violation of 84 Stat. 1260, 21 U.S.C. § 841(a)(1). He moved to suppress the drugs, arguing that Agent Cantu conducted an illegal search of his bag. Petitioner's motion was denied, and the District Court found him guilty on both counts and sentenced him to 57 months in prison. On appeal, he conceded that other passengers had access to his bag, but contended that Agent Cantu manipulated the bag in a way that other passengers would not. The Court of Appeals rejected this argument, stating that the fact that Agent Cantu's manipulation of petitioner's bag was calculated to detect contraband is irrelevant for Fourth Amendment purposes. Thus, the Court of Appeals affirmed the denial of the motion to suppress, holding that Agent Cantu's manipulation of the bag was not a search within the meaning of the Fourth Amendment. We granted certiorari and now reverse.

The Fourth Amendment provides that "[t]he right of the people to be secure in their persons, houses, papers, and effects, against unreasonable searches and seizures, shall not be violated . . . " A traveler's personal luggage is clearly an "effect" protected by the Amendment. Indeed, it is undisputed here that petitioner possessed a privacy interest in his bag.

But the Government asserts that by exposing his bag to the public, petitioner lost a reasonable expectation that his bag would not be physically manipulated. The Government relies on our decisions in *California v. Ciraolo* and *Florida v. Riley* for the proposition that matters open to public observation are not protected by the Fourth Amendment. In *Ciraolo*, we held that police observation of a backyard from a plane flying at an altitude of 1,000 feet did not violate a reasonable expectation of privacy. Similarly, in *Riley*, we relied on *Ciraolo* to hold that police observation of a greenhouse in a home's curtilage from a helicopter passing at an altitude of 400 feet did not violate the Fourth Amendment. We reasoned that the property was "not necessarily protected from inspection that involves no physical invasion," and determined that because any member of the public could have lawfully observed the defendants' property by flying overhead, the defendants' expectation of privacy was "not reasonable and not one 'that society is prepared to honor.'"

But *Ciraolo* and *Riley* are different from this case because they involved only visual, as opposed to tactile, observation. Physically invasive inspection is simply more intrusive than purely visual inspection. For example, in *Terry v. Ohio*, we stated that a "careful [tactile] exploration of the outer surfaces of a person's clothing all over his or her body" is a "serious intrusion upon the sanctity of the person, which may inflict great indignity and arouse strong resentment, and is not to be undertaken lightly." Although Agent Cantu did not "frisk" petitioner's person, he did conduct a probing tactile examination of petitioner's carry-on luggage. Obviously, petitioner's bag was not part of his person. But travelers are particularly concerned about their carry-on luggage; they generally use it to transport personal items that, for whatever reason, they prefer to keep close at hand.

Here, petitioner concedes that, by placing his bag in the overhead compartment, he could expect that it would be exposed to certain kinds of touching and handling. But petitioner argues that Agent Cantu's physical manipulation of his luggage "far exceeded the casual contact [petitioner] could have expected from other passengers." The Government counters that it did not.

Our Fourth Amendment analysis embraces two questions. First, we ask whether the individual, by his conduct, has exhibited an actual expectation of privacy; that is, whether he has shown that "he [sought] to preserve [something] as private." Here, petitioner sought to preserve privacy by using an opaque bag and placing that bag directly above his seat. Second, we inquire whether the individual's expectation of privacy is "one that society is prepared to recognize as reasonable." When a bus passenger places a bag in an overhead bin, he expects that other passengers or bus employees may move it for one reason or another. Thus, a bus passenger clearly expects that his bag may be handled. He does not expect that other passengers or bus employees will, as a matter of course, feel the bag in an exploratory manner. But this is exactly what the agent did here. We therefore hold that the agent's physical manipulation of petitioner's bag violated the Fourth Amendment.

The judgment of the Court of Appeals is affirmed.

## MAPP
### v.
## OHIO

**367 U.S. 643, 81 S. Ct. 1684, 6 L. Ed. 2d 1081 (1961)**

*[Citations and footnotes omitted.]*

[After receiving a tip that a man wanted for questioning in connection with a recent bombing was hiding out in Ms. Mapp's house, three Ohio State police officers went there, knocked on the door, and demanded entrance. Ms. Mapp refused to let them in without a search warrant. Three hours later, the officers returned, waiving a piece of paper which they claimed was a search warrant, but which they refused to let Ms. Mapp examine. When she tried to grab the paper, the officers twisted her hand, handcuffed her and forced their way into her house. They then proceeded to search the entire house, even looking through photo albums and private papers. Ms. Mapp was placed under arrest on obscenity charges after the police discovered lewd books in a trunk in the basement. No search warrant probably existed because none was produced at the trial. The trial court admitted the lewd books into evidence, ruling that even if the officers' search of Ms. Mapp's home had violated the Fourth Amendment, this evidence was admissible because the exclusionary rule was not binding on the states. Ms. Mapp was convicted of possessing obscene materials.]

MR. JUSTICE CLARK delivered the opinion of the Court.

* * *

. . . [I]n the year 1914 in the *Weeks* case, this Court "for the first time" held that "in a federal prosecution the Fourth Amendment barred the use of evidence secured through an illegal search and seizure." This Court has ever since required of federal law officers a strict adherence to that command which this Court has held to be a clear, specific, and constitutionally required—even if judicially implied—deterrent safeguard without insistence upon which the Fourth Amendment would have been reduced to a "form of words." It means, quite simply, that "conviction by means of unlawful seizures and enforced confessions . . . should find no sanction in the judgment of the courts . . . ," and that such evidence "should not be used at all."

* * *

In 1949, 35 years after *Weeks* was announced, this Court, in *Wolf v. Colorado*, again for the first time, discussed the effect of the Fourth Amendment upon the States through the operation of the Due Process Clause of the Fourteenth Amendment. It said: "We have no hesitation in saying that were a State affirmatively to sanction such police incursion into privacy it would run counter to the guaranty of the Fourteenth Amendment." Nevertheless, after declaring that the "security of one's privacy against arbitrary intrusion by the police" is "implicit in 'the concept of ordered liberty' and as such enforceable against the States through the Due Process Clause," and announcing that it "stoutly adhere[d]" to the *Weeks* decision, the Court decided that the *Weeks* exclusionary rule would not then be imposed upon the States as "an essential ingredient of the right.". . .

. . . While in 1949, prior to the *Wolf* case, almost two-thirds of the States were opposed to the use of the exclusionary rule, now, despite the *Wolf* case, more than half of those since passing upon it, by their own legislative or judicial decision, have wholly or partially adopted or adhered to the *Weeks* rule. Significantly, among those now following the rule is California, which, according to its highest court, was "compelled to reach that conclusion because other remedies have completely failed to secure compliance with the constitutional provisions . . ." The experience of California that such other remedies have been worthless and futile is buttressed by the experience of other States. The obvious futility of relegating the Fourth Amendment to the protection of other remedies has, moreover, been recognized by this Court since *Wolf*.

\* \* \*

The ignoble shortcut to conviction left open to the State tends to destroy the entire system of constitutional restraints on which the liberties of the people rest. Having once recognized that the right to privacy embodied in the Fourth Amendment is enforceable against the States, and that the right to be secure against rude invasions of privacy by state officers is, therefore, constitutional in origin, we can no longer permit that right to remain an empty promise. Because it is enforceable in the same manner and to like effect as other basic rights secured by the Due Process Clause, we can no longer permit it to be revocable at the whim of any police officer who, in the name of law enforcement itself, chooses to suspend its enjoyment. Our decision, founded on reason and truth, gives to the individual no more than that which the Constitution guarantees him, to the police officer no less than that to which honest law enforcement is entitled, and, to the courts, that judicial integrity so necessary in the true administration of justice.

The judgment of the Supreme Court of Ohio is reversed and the cause remanded for further proceedings not inconsistent with this opinion.

Reversed and remanded.

## FLIPPO
### v.
## WEST VIRGINIA

**528 U.S. 11, 120 S. Ct. 7, 145 L. Ed. 2d 16 (1999)**

*[Citations omitted.]*

[One night in 1996, petitioner and his wife were vacationing at a cabin in a state park. After petitioner called 911 to report that they had been attacked, the police arrived to find petitioner waiting outside the cabin, with injuries to his head and legs. After questioning him, an officer entered the building and found the body of petitioner's wife, with fatal head wounds. The officers closed off the area, took petitioner to the hospital, and searched the exterior and environs of the cabin for footprints or signs of forced entry. When a police photographer arrived at about 5:30 A.M., the officers reentered the building and proceeded to "process the crime scene." For more than 16 hours they took photographs, collected evidence, and searched the contents of the cabin. They found, among other things, a briefcase on a table, which they opened, in which they found and seized various photographs and negatives. The photographs included several taken of a man who appears to be taking off his jeans. He was later identified as Joel Boggess, a friend of petitioner and a member of the congregation of which petitioner was the minister. At petitioner's trial for murder, the prosecution sought to introduce the photographs as evidence of petitioner's relationship with Mr. Boggess in an attempt to establish that the victim's displeasure with this relationship was one of the reasons petitioner killed her. Petitioner sought to suppress the photographs on the grounds that the police did not obtain a warrant and that no exception to the warrant requirement justified the search and seizure.

The trial court denied the motion on the grounds that investigating officers, having secured, for investigative purposes, the homicide crime scene, were within the law in conducting a thorough investigation and examination of anything and everything found within the crime scene area.

PER CURIAM.

A warrantless search by the police is invalid unless it falls within one of the narrow and well-delineated exceptions to the warrant requirement, none of which the trial court invoked here. It simply found that after the homicide crime scene was secured for investigation, a search of "anything and everything found within the crime scene area" was "within the law."

This position squarely conflicts with *Mincey v. Arizona*, where we rejected the contention that there is a "murder scene exception" to the Warrant Clause of the Fourth Amendment. We noted that police may make warrantless entries onto premises if they reasonably believe a person is in need of immediate aid and may make prompt warrantless searches of a homicide scene for possible other victims or a killer on the premises, but we rejected any general "murder scene exception" as "inconsistent with the Fourth and Fourteenth Amendments— . . . the warrantless search of Mincey's apartment was not constitutionally permissible simply because a homicide had recently occurred there." Mincey controls here.

\* \* \*

The motion for leave to proceed in forma pauperis and the petition for a writ of certiorari are granted, the judgment of the West Virginia Supreme Court of Appeals is reversed, and the case is remanded for further proceedings not inconsistent with this opinion.

It is so ordered.

## UNITED STATES
## v.
## ROBINSON

### 414 U.S. 218, 94 S. Ct. 467, 38 L. Ed. 2d 427 (1973)

*[Citations and footnotes omitted.]*

[The defendant was arrested and taken into custody for driving without a license. Upon arresting him, the officer searched his person, his pockets and the contents and found, inside a crumpled cigarette pack, 14 gelatin capsules of white powder which he thought to be, and which later analysis proved to be, heroin. The lower court suppressed the evidence on the grounds that the search was unconstitutional because the officer lacked grounds to believe that the search would turn up weapons or evidence of the crime for which the defendant was arrested.]

MR. JUSTICE REHNQUIST delivered the opinion of the Court.

\* \* \*

It is well settled that a search incident to a lawful arrest is a traditional exception to the warrant requirement of the Fourth Amendment. This general exception has historically been formulated into two distinct propositions. The first is that a search may be made of the person of the arrestee by virtue of the lawful arrest. The second is that a search may be made of the area within the control of the arrestee.

\* \* \*

*Terry v. Ohio* did not involve an arrest for probable cause, and it made quite clear that the "protective frisk" for weapons which it approved might be conducted without probable cause. This Court's opinion explicitly recognized that there is a "distinction in purpose, character, and extent between a search incident to an arrest and a limited search for weapons."

"The former, although justified in part by the acknowledged necessity to protect the arresting officer from assault with a concealed weapon, is also justified on other grounds, and can therefore involve a relatively extensive exploration of the person. . . .

". . . An arrest is a wholly different kind of intrusion upon individual freedom from a limited search for weapons, and the interests each is designed to serve are likewise quite different. . . .

\* \* \*

The Court of Appeals in effect determined that the only reason supporting the authority for a full search incident to lawful arrest was the possibility of discovery of evidence or fruits. Concluding that there could be no evidence or fruits in the case of an offense such as that with which respondent was charged, it held that any protective search would have to be limited by the conditions laid down in Terry for a search upon less than probable cause to arrest. . . .

\* \* \*

. . . . The standards traditionally governing a search incident to lawful arrest are not, therefore, commuted to the stricter Terry standards by the absence of probable fruits or further evidence of the particular crime for which the arrest is made.

Nor are we inclined, on the basis of what seems to us to be a rather speculative judgment, to qualify the breadth of the general authority to search incident to a lawful custodial arrest on an assumption that persons arrested for the offense of driving while their licenses have been revoked are less likely to possess dangerous weapons than are those arrested for other crimes. It is scarcely open to doubt that the danger to an officer is far greater in the case of the extended exposure which follows the taking of a suspect into custody and transporting him to the police station than in the case of the relatively fleeting contact resulting from the typical Terry-type stop. This is an adequate basis for treating all custodial arrests alike for purposes of search justification.

. . . A police officer's determination as to how and where to search the person of a suspect whom he has arrested is necessarily a quick ad hoc judgment which the Fourth Amendment does not require to be broken down in each instance into an analysis of each step in the search. The authority to search the person incident to a lawful custodial arrest, while based upon the need to disarm and to discover evidence, does not depend on what a court may later decide was the probability in a particular arrest situation that weapons or evidence would in fact be found upon the person of the suspect. A custodial arrest of a suspect based on probable cause is a reasonable intrusion under the Fourth Amendment; that intrusion being lawful, a search incident to the arrest requires no additional justification. It is the fact of the lawful arrest which establishes the authority to search, and we hold that in the case of a lawful custodial arrest a full search of the person is not only an exception to the warrant requirement of the Fourth Amendment, but is also a "reasonable" search under that Amendment.

\* \* \*

The search of respondent's person conducted by Officer Jenks in this case and the seizure from him of the heroin, were permissible under established Fourth Amendment law. While thorough, the search partook of none of the extreme or patently abusive characteristics which were held to violate the Due Process Clause of the Fourteenth Amendment in *Rochin v. California.* Since it is the fact of custodial arrest which gives rise to the authority to search, it is of no moment that Jenks did not indicate any subjective fear of the respondent or that he did not himself suspect that respondent was armed. Having in the course of a lawful search come upon the crumpled package of cigarettes, he was entitled to inspect it; and when his inspection revealed the heroin capsules, he was entitled to seize them as "fruits, instrumentalities, or contraband" probative of criminal conduct. The judgment of the Court of Appeals holding otherwise is

Reversed.

[Concurring and dissenting opinions omitted.]

## CHIMEL
### v.
## CALIFORNIA

**395 U.S. 752, 89 S. Ct. 2034
23 L. Ed. 2d 685 (1969)**

*[Citations and footnotes omitted.]*

[The police, suspecting the defendant of having burglarized a coin shop, obtained a warrant for his arrest. They arrested him in his home and requested permission to conduct a search. When permission was refused, the officers informed the defendant that they would do so "on the basis of the lawful arrest." They proceeded to search his attic, garage, and various rooms in his house. In a drawer in his bedroom, the police discovered some of the stolen coins.]

MR. JUSTICE STEWART delivered the opinion of the Court.

This case raises basic questions concerning the permissible scope under the Fourth Amendment of a search incident to a lawful arrest . . .

\* \* \*

. . . *United States v. Rabinowitz* [is] the decision upon which California primarily relies in the case now before us. In *Rabinowitz*, federal authorities had been informed that the defendant was dealing in stamps bearing forged overprints. On the basis of that information they secured a warrant for his arrest, which they executed at his one-room business office. At the time of the arrest, the officers "searched the desk, safe, and file cabinets in the office for about an hour and a half, and seized 573 stamps with forged overprints. The stamps were admitted into evidence at the defendant's trial, and this Court affirmed his conviction, rejecting the contention that the warrantless search had been unlawful. The Court held that the search in its entirety fell within the principle giving law enforcement authorities "the right 'to search the place where the arrest is made in order to find and seize things connected with the crime . . .'" . . . The test, said the Court, "is not whether it is reasonable to procure a search warrant, but whether the search was reasonable." *Rabinowitz* has come to stand for the proposition, *inter alia*, that a warrantless search "incident to a lawful arrest" may generally extend to the area that is considered to be in the "possession" or under the "control" of the person arrested. And it was on the basis of that proposition that the California courts upheld the search of the petitioner's entire house in this case. That doctrine, however, at least in the broad sense in which it was applied by the California courts in this case, can withstand neither historical nor rational analysis . . .

\* \* \*

. . . When an arrest is made, it is reasonable for the arresting officer to search the person arrested in order to remove any weapons that the latter might seek to use in order to resist arrest or effect his escape. Otherwise, the officer's safety might well be endangered, and the arrest itself frustrated. In addition, it is entirely reasonable for the arresting officer to search for and seize any evidence on the arrestee's person in order to prevent its concealment or destruction. And the area into which an arrestee might reach in order to grab a weapon or evidentiary items must, of course, be governed by a like rule. A gun on a table or in a drawer in front of one who is arrested can be as dangerous to the arresting officer as one concealed in the clothing of the person arrested. There is ample justification, therefore, for a search of the arrestee's person and the area "within his immediate control"—construing that phrase to mean the area from within which he might gain possession of a weapon or destructible evidence.

There is no comparable justification, however, for routinely searching any room other than that in which an arrest occurs—or, for that matter, for searching through all the desk drawers or other closed or concealed areas in that room itself. Such searches, in the absence of

well-recognized exceptions, may be made only under the authority of a search warrant. The "adherence to judicial processes" mandated by the Fourth Amendment requires no less . . .

\* \* \*

Application of sound Fourth Amendment principles to the facts of this case produces a clear result. The search here went far beyond the petitioner's person and the area from within which he might have obtained either a weapon or something that could have been used as evidence against him. There was no constitutional justification, in the absence of a search warrant, for extending the search beyond that area. The scope of the search was, therefore, "unreasonable" under the Fourth and Fourteenth Amendments, and the petitioner's conviction cannot stand.

Reversed.

## WYOMING
## v.
## HOUGHTON

### 526 U.S. 559, 119 S. Ct. 1297, 143 L. Ed. 2d 748 (1999)

*[Citations and footnotes omitted.]*

In the early morning hours of July 23, 1995, a Wyoming Highway Patrol officer stopped an automobile for speeding and driving with a faulty brake light. There were three passengers in the front seat of the car: David Young (the driver), his girlfriend, and respondent. While questioning Young, the officer noticed a hypodermic syringe in Young's shirt pocket. He left the occupants under the supervision of two backup officers as he went to get gloves from his patrol car. Upon his return, he instructed Young to step out of the car and place the syringe on the hood. The officer then asked Young why he had a syringe; with refreshing candor, Young replied that he used it to take drugs.

At this point, the backup officers ordered the two female passengers out of the car and asked them for identification. Respondent falsely identified herself as "Sandra James" and stated that she did not have any identification. Meanwhile, in light of Young's admission, the officer searched the passenger compartment of the car for contraband. On the back seat, he found a purse, which respondent claimed as hers. He removed from the purse a wallet containing respondent's driver's license, identifying her properly as Sandra K. Houghton. When the officer asked her why she had lied about her name, she replied: "In case things went bad."

Continuing his search of the purse, the officer found a brown pouch and a black wallet-type container. Respondent denied that the former was hers, and claimed ignorance of how it came to be there; it was found to contain drug paraphernalia and a syringe with 60 ccs of methamphetamine. Respondent admitted ownership of the black container, which was also found to contain drug paraphernalia, and a syringe (which respondent acknowledged was hers) with 10 ccs of methamphetamine—an amount insufficient to support the felony conviction at issue in this case. The officer also found fresh needle-track marks on respondent's arms. He placed her under arrest.

The State of Wyoming charged respondent with felony possession of methamphetamine in a liquid amount greater than three-tenths of a gram. After a hearing, the trial court denied her motion to suppress all evidence obtained from the purse as the fruit of a violation of the Fourth and Fourteenth Amendments. The court held that the officer had probable cause to search the car for contraband, and, by extension, any containers therein that could hold such contraband. A jury convicted respondent as charged.

The Wyoming Supreme Court, by divided vote, reversed the conviction . . .

* * *

Justice SCALIA delivered the opinion of the Court.

This case presents the question whether police officers violate the Fourth Amendment when they search a passenger's personal belongings inside an automobile that they have probable cause to believe contains contraband.

* * *

It is uncontested in the present case that the police officers had probable cause to believe there were illegal drugs in the car. *Carroll v. United States* similarly involved the warrantless search of a car that law enforcement officials had probable cause to believe contained contraband—in that case, bootleg liquor. . . . [T]he Court held that "contraband goods concealed and illegally transported in an automobile or other vehicle may be searched for without a warrant" where probable cause exists.

. . . In *Ross*, we upheld as reasonable the warrantless search of a paper bag and leather pouch found in the trunk of the defendant's car by officers who had probable cause to believe that the trunk contained drugs. . . .

* * *

To be sure, there was no passenger in *Ross*, and it was not claimed that the package in the trunk belonged to anyone other than the driver. Even so, if the rule of law that *Ross* announced were limited to contents belonging to the driver, or contents other than those belonging to passengers, one would have expected that substantial limitation to be expressed. . . .

. . . [T]he analytical principle underlying the rule announced in *Ross* is fully consistent . . . with the balance of our Fourth Amendment jurisprudence. *Ross* concluded from the historical evidence that the permissible scope of a warrantless car search "is defined by the object of the search and the places in which there is probable cause to believe that it may be found." The same principle is reflected in an earlier case involving the constitutionality of a search warrant directed at premises belonging to one who is not suspected of any crime: "The critical element in a reasonable search is not that the owner of the property is suspected of crime but that there is reasonable cause to believe that the specific 'things' to be searched for and seized are located on the property to which entry is sought.". . .

In sum, neither *Ross* itself nor the historical evidence it relied upon admits of a distinction among packages or containers based on ownership. When there is probable cause to search for contraband in a car, it is reasonable for police officers—like customs officials in the Founding era—to examine packages and containers without a showing of individualized probable cause for each one. A passenger's personal belongings, just like the driver's belongings or containers attached to the car like a glove compartment, are "in" the car, and the officer has probable cause to search for contraband in the car.

Even if the historical evidence, as described by *Ross*, were thought to be equivocal, we would find that the balancing of the relative interests weighs decidedly in favor of allowing searches of a passenger's belongings. Passengers, no less than drivers, possess a reduced expectation of privacy with regard to the property that they transport in cars, which "travel public thoroughfares," "seldom serv[e] as . . . the repository of personal effects," are subjected to police stop and examination to enforce "pervasive" governmental controls "[a]s an everyday occurrence" and, finally, are exposed to traffic accidents that may render all their contents open to public scrutiny.

* * *

Whereas the passenger's privacy expectations are, as we have described, considerably diminished, the governmental interests at stake are substantial. Effective law enforcement would be appreciably impaired without the ability to search a passenger's personal belongings when there is reason to believe contraband or evidence of criminal wrongdoing is hidden in the car. As in all car-search cases, the "ready mobility" of an automobile creates a risk that the evidence or contraband will be permanently lost while a warrant is obtained. In addition, a car passenger . . . will often be engaged in a common enterprise with the driver, and have the same interest in concealing the fruits or the evidence of their wrongdoing. A criminal might be able to hide contraband in a passenger's belongings as readily as in other containers in the car—perhaps even surreptitiously, without the passenger's knowledge or permission. (This last possibility provided the basis for respondent's defense at trial; she testified that most of the seized contraband must have been placed in her purse by her traveling companions at one or another of various times, including the time she was "half asleep" in the car.)

. . . To require that the investigating officer have positive reason to believe that the passenger and driver were engaged in a common enterprise, or positive reason to believe that the driver had time and occasion to conceal the item in the passenger's belongings, surreptitiously or with friendly permission, is to impose requirements so seldom met that a "passenger's property" rule would dramatically reduce the ability to find and seize contraband and evidence of crime. . . . But once a "passenger's property" exception to car searches became widely known, one would expect passenger-confederates to claim everything as their own. And one would anticipate a bog of litigation—in the form of both civil lawsuits and motions to suppress in criminal trials—involving such questions as whether the officer should have believed a passenger's claim of ownership. . . . When balancing the competing interests, our determinations of "reasonableness" under the Fourth Amendment must take account of these practical realities. We think they militate in favor of the needs of law enforcement, and against a personal-privacy interest that is ordinarily weak.

* * *

We hold that police officers with probable cause to search a car may inspect passengers' belongings found in the car that are capable of concealing the object of the search. The judgment of the Wyoming Supreme Court is reversed.

It is so ordered.

## FLORIDA
## v.
## JIMENO

**500 U.S. 248, 111 S. Ct. 1801,
114 L. Ed. 2d 297 (1991)**

*[Footnotes and citations omitted.]*

[Officer Trujillo, believing that Jimeno might be involved in illegal drug traf-

ficking, followed Jimeno's car until he made a right turn at a red light without stopping, at which point he pulled Jimeno over to the side of the road, issued a traffic citation, and then asked for permission to search his car, stating that he had reason to believe that Jimeno was carrying narcotics in his car. Jimeno gave permission. Officer Trujillo then went to the passenger side, opened the door, and saw a folded, brown paper bag on the floorboard. He picked up the bag, opened it, and found a kilogram of cocaine inside. Jimeno was charged with possession with intent to distribute cocaine. Before trial, he moved to suppress the cocaine found in the bag on the ground that his consent to search the car did not extend to the closed paper bag inside of the car. The trial court granted the motion.]

Chief Justice REHNQUIST delivered the opinion of the Court.

In this case we decide whether a criminal suspect's Fourth Amendment right to be free from unreasonable searches is violated when, after he gives a police officer permission to search his automobile, the officer opens a closed container found within the car that might reasonably hold the object of the search. We find that it is not. The Fourth Amendment is satisfied when, under the circumstances, it is objectively reasonable for the officer to believe that the scope of the suspect's consent permitted him to open a particular container within the automobile.

* * *

The touchstone of the Fourth Amendment is reasonableness. The Fourth Amendment does not proscribe all state-initiated searches and seizures; it merely proscribes those which are unreasonable. Thus, we have long approved consensual searches because it is no doubt reasonable for the police to conduct a search once they have been permitted to do so. The standard for measuring the scope of a suspect's consent under the Fourth Amendment is that of "objective" reasonableness—what would the typical reasonable person have understood by the exchange between the officer and the suspect? The question before us, then, is whether it is reasonable for an officer to consider a suspect's general consent to a search of his car to include consent to examine a paper bag lying on the floor of the car. We think that it is.

The scope of a search is generally defined by its expressed object. In this case, the terms of the search's authorization were simple. Respondent granted Officer Trujillo permission to search his car, and did not place any explicit limitation on the scope of the search. Trujillo had informed respondent that he believed respondent was carrying narcotics, and that he would be looking for narcotics in the car. We think that it was objectively reasonable for the police to conclude that the general consent to search respondent's car included consent to search containers within that car which might bear drugs. A reasonable person may be expected to know that narcotics are generally carried in some form of container. Contraband goods rarely are strewn across the trunk or floor of a car. The authorization to search in this case, therefore, extended beyond the surfaces of the car's interior to the paper bag lying on the car's floor.

The facts of this case are therefore different from those in *State v. Wells*, on which the Supreme Court of Florida relied in affirming the suppression order on this case. There the Supreme Court of Florida held that consent to search the trunk of a car did not include authorization to pry open a locked briefcase found inside the trunk. It is very likely unreasonable to think that a suspect, by consenting to the search of his trunk, has

agreed to the breaking open of a locked briefcase within the trunk, but it is otherwise with respect to a closed paper bag.

Respondent argues, and the Florida trial court agreed with him, that if the police wish to search closed containers within a car they must separately request permission to search each container. But we see no basis for adding this sort of superstructure to the Fourth Amendment's basic test of objective reasonableness. A suspect may of course delimit as he chooses the scope of the search to which he consents. But if his consent would reasonably be understood to extend to a particular container, the Fourth Amendment provides no grounds for requiring a more explicit authorization. "[T]he community has a real interest in encouraging consent, for the resulting search may yield necessary evidence for the solution and prosecution of crime, evidence that may ensure that a wholly innocent person is not wrongly charged with a criminal offense."

The judgment of the Supreme Court of Florida is accordingly reversed, and the case remanded for further proceedings not inconsistent with this opinion.

It is so ordered.

## ARIZONA
## v.
## HICKS

### 480 U.S. 321, 107 S. Ct. 1149, 94 L. Ed. 2d 347 (1987)

*[Citations and footnotes omitted.]*

[A bullet was fired through the floor of respondent's apartment, striking and injuring a man in the apartment below. The police arrived and entered respondent's apartment to search for the shooter and the weapon. They found and seized three weapons, including a sawed-off rifle. While on the premises, one of the officers noticed some very expensive stereo equipment, which seemed out of place. Suspecting that the equipment was stolen, he turned the stereo around so he could read out the serial numbers to the radio operator. The operator checked the numbers and informed him that the equipment was stolen. The defendant was indicted and convicted of theft. The Arizona Court of Appeals, while conceding that the warrantless entry was justified by the exigent circumstances of the shooting, ruled that turning the stereo around to read the serial numbers resulted in an additional search, unrelated to the exigency, in violation of the Fourth Amendment, requiring that the fruits of this search be suppressed.]

Justice SCALIA delivered the opinion of the Court.

In *Coolidge v. New Hampshire*, we said that in certain circumstances a warrantless seizure by police of an item that comes within plain view during their lawful search of a private area may be reasonable under the Fourth Amendment. We granted certiorari in the present case to decide whether this "plain view" doctrine may be invoked when the police have less than probable cause to believe that the item in question is evidence of a crime or is contraband.

\* \* \*

As an initial matter, the State argues that Officer Nelson's actions constituted neither a "search" nor a "seizure" within the meaning of the Fourth Amendment. We agree that the mere recording of the serial numbers did not constitute a seizure. . . . [I]t did not "meaningfully interfere" with respondent's possessory interest in either the serial numbers or

the equipment, and therefore did not amount to a seizure.

Officer Nelson's moving of the equipment, however, did constitute a "search" separate and apart from the search for the shooter, victims, and weapons that was the lawful objective of his entry into the apartment. Merely inspecting those parts of the turntable that came into view during the latter search would not have constituted an independent search, because it would have produced no additional invasion of respondent's privacy interest. But taking action, unrelated to the objectives of the authorized intrusion, which exposed to view concealed portions of the apartment or its contents, did produce a new invasion of respondent's privacy unjustified by the exigent circumstance that validated the entry. This is why, contrary to Justice POWELL's suggestion, the "distinction between 'looking' at a suspicious object in plain view and 'moving' it even a few inches" is much more than trivial for purposes of the Fourth Amendment. It matters not that the search uncovered nothing of any great personal value to the respondent—serial numbers rather than (what might conceivably have been hidden behind or under the equipment) letters or photographs. A search is a search, even if it happens to disclose nothing but the bottom of a turntable.

The remaining question is whether the search was "reasonable" under the Fourth Amendment.

\* \* \*

. . . "It is well established that under certain circumstances the police may *seize* evidence in plain view without a warrant. Those circumstances include situations "[w]here the initial intrusion that brings the police within plain view of such [evidence] is supported . . . by one of the recognized exceptions to the warrant requirement," such as the exigent-circumstances intrusion here. It would be absurd to say that an object could lawfully be seized and taken from the premises, but could not be moved for closer examination. It is clear, therefore, that the search here was valid if the "plain view" doctrine would have sustained a seizure of the equipment.

There is no doubt it would have done so if Officer Nelson had probable cause to believe that the equipment was stolen. The State has conceded, however, that he had only a "reasonable suspicion," by which it means something less than probable cause. . . . We have not ruled on the question whether probable cause is required in order to invoke the "plain view" doctrine . . . We now hold that probable cause is required. To say otherwise would be to cut the "plain view" doctrine loose from its theoretical and practical moorings. The theory of that doctrine consists of extending to non-public places such as the home, where searches and seizures without a warrant are presumptively unreasonable, the police's longstanding authority to make warrantless seizures in public places of such objects as weapons and contraband. And the practical justification for that extension is the desirability of sparing police, whose viewing of the object in the course of a lawful search is as legitimate as it would have been in a public place, the inconvenience and the risk—to themselves or to preservation of the evidence—of going to obtain a warrant. Dispensing with the need for a warrant is worlds apart from permitting a lesser standard of *cause* for the seizure than a warrant would require, i.e., the standard of probable cause. No reason is apparent why an object should routinely be seizable on lesser grounds, during an unrelated search and seizure, than would have been needed to obtain a warrant for that same object if it had been known to be on the premises.

We do not say, of course, that a seizure can never be justified on less than probable cause. We have held that it can—where, for example, the seizure is minimally intrusive and operational necessities render it the only practicable means of detecting certain types of crime. . . . No special operational necessities are relied on here, however—but rather the mere fact that the items in question came lawfully within the officer's plain view. That alone cannot supplant the requirement of probable cause.

The same considerations preclude us from holding that, even though probable cause would have been necessary for a *seizure*, the *search* of objects in plain view that occurred here could be sustained on lesser grounds. A dwelling-place search, no less than a dwelling-place seizure, requires probable cause, and there is no reason in theory or practicality why application of the plain-view doctrine would supplant that requirement. Although the interest protected by the Fourth Amendment injunction against unreasonable searches is quite different from that protected by its injunction against unreasonable seizures, neither the one nor the other is of inferior worth or necessarily requires only lesser protection. We have not elsewhere drawn a categorical distinction between the two insofar as concerns the degree of justification needed to establish the reasonableness of police action, and we see no reason for a distinction in the particular circumstances before us here. Indeed, to treat searches more liberally would especially erode the plurality's warning in *Coolidge* that "the 'plain view' doctrine to be used to extend a general exploratory search from one object to another until something incriminating at last emerges." In short, whether legal authority to move the equipment could be found only as an inevitable concomitant of the authority to seize it, or also as a consequence of some independent power to search certain objects in plain view, probable cause to believe the equipment was stolen was required.

Justice O'CONNOR's dissent suggests that we uphold the action here on the ground that it was a "cursory inspection" rather than a "full-blown search," and could therefore be justified by reasonable suspicion instead of probable cause. As already noted, a truly cursory inspection—one that involves merely looking at what is already exposed to view, without disturbing it—is not a "search" for Fourth Amendment purposes, and therefore does not even require reasonable suspicion. We are unwilling to send police and judges into a new thicket of Fourth Amendment law, to seek a creature of uncertain description that is neither a plain-view inspection nor yet a "full-blown search." Nothing in the prior opinions of this Court supports such a distinction . . .

Justice POWELL's dissent reasonably asks what it is we would have had Officer Nelson do in these circumstances. . . . The answer depends, of course, upon whether he had probable cause to conduct a search, a question that was not preserved in this case. If he had, then he should have done precisely what he did. If not, then he should have followed up his suspicions, if possible, by means other than a search—just as he would have had to do if, while walking along the street, he had noticed the same suspicious stereo equipment sitting inside a house a few feet away from him, beneath an open window. It may well be that, in such circumstances, no effective means short of a search exist. But there is nothing new in the realization that the Constitution sometimes insulates the criminality of a few in order to protect the privacy of us all. Our disagreement with the dissenters pertains to where the proper balance should be struck; we

choose to adhere to the textual and traditional standard of probable cause.

The State contends that, even if Officer Nelson's search violated the Fourth Amendment, the court below should have admitted the evidence thus obtained under the "good faith" exception to the exclusionary rule. That was not the question on which certiorari was granted, and we decline to consider it.

For the reasons stated, the judgment of the Court of Appeals of Arizona is

*Affirmed.*

The concurring and dissenting opinions are not included.

\* \* \*

## UNITED STATES
## v.
## WEINBENDER

### 109 F.3d 1327 (8th Cir. 1997)

*[Citations and footnotes omitted.]*

[Police obtained a search warrant for Ralph Weinbender's home, listing items including: a bluish-gray windbreaker jacket; a dark pair of shorts, pockets in the front, one pocket in the rear; tannish Reebok shoes; and a ball hat with logo. Before the warrant was executed, the officers were advised that the defendant had several "hiding places" in his attic and basement in which the items listed in the warrant might be located. While executing the warrant, one of the officers entered a basement closet, removed a picture hanging on a wall and found a loose piece cut in the drywall. Upon removing the piece and shining a flashlight in, the officer discovered a homemade silencer sitting on an I-beam which the officer seized even though it was not listed in the warrant. Weinben-

der was prosecuted for unlawful possession of the silencer. After the trial court
denied his motion to suppress the
silencer, Weinbender entered a conditional plea of guilty and was sentence to
a term of imprisonment of 24 months.
This appeal followed.]

MONTGOMERY, District Judge.

* * *

A lawful search extends to all areas
and containers in which the object of the
search may be found. However, "[t]he
manner in which a warrant is executed is
always subject to judicial review to
ensure that it does not traverse the general Fourth Amendment proscription
against unreasonableness."

In this case, the search warrant authorized officers to search the entirety of
Weinbender's home for the specified
items. Moreover, the officers had been
informed that "hiding places," including
under the basement stairs, were utilized
by Weinbender. The space along the I-
beam was sufficiently large to permit any
of the listed items to be stored there. . . .

* * *

In light of the information possessed
by the searching officers, the relative
ease with which the officer removed the
drywall and the reasonable probability
of finding the sought-for items hidden
behind the drywall, the actions of Officer Schmit were reasonable.

Weinbender also argues that the
seizure of the homemade silencer was
not justified under the plain view doctrine. The plain view doctrine permits
law enforcement officers to "seize evidence without a warrant when (1) 'the
officer did not violate the Fourth
Amendment in arriving at the place from
which the evidence could be plainly

viewed,' (2) the object's incriminating
character is immediately apparent, and
(3) the officer has 'a lawful right of
access to the object itself.'"

In this case, the law enforcement officers gained access to Weinbender's residence under a properly issued warrant.
As indicated [above], since the items
listed in the warrant could have been
concealed along the I-beam, the officers
did not violate the Fourth Amendment
by visually searching that location. In
addition, to properly observe the items
secreted along the I-beam and to ensure
that no additional items were present
there, each item had to be removed.
Thus, Officer Schmit did not violate the
Fourth Amendment in removing the
items from their secret storage place
along the I-beam.

When Officer Schmit pulled the first
metal object from its resting spot along
the I-beam, he believed that it was a pipe
bomb. He later learned the object was
part of a homemade silencer. "The
'immediately apparent' requirement
means that officers must have 'probable
cause to associate the property with
criminal activity.'" "Probable cause
demands not that an officer be 'sure' or
'certain' but only that the facts available
to a reasonably cautious man would warrant a belief 'that certain items may be
contraband or stolen property or useful
as evidence of a crime.'"

Here, the incriminating character of
the object was immediately apparent to
Officer Schmit. The possession of either
a pipe bomb or a homemade silencer is
illegal. The fact that the item turned out
to be the silencer, instead of a pipe
bomb, did not vitiate the probable cause.
Thus, the seizure of the homemade
silencer was justified under the plain
view doctrine.

. . . Accordingly, we affirm the judgment of the district court.

## STATE
## v.
## WILSON

### 112 N.C. App. 777,
### 437 S.E.2d 387 (1993)

*[Citations and footnotes omitted.]*

[Officer Faulkenberry, after receiving an anonymous tip that drugs were being sold out of an apartment building in a known drug area, went to that location. When his squad car pulled up, the defendant started running. Officer Faulkenberry stopped the defendant and performed a protective weapons frisk. While doing this, he felt a lump in the defendant's breast pocket that he immediately believed to be crack cocaine. Upon retrieving a bag from the pocket, Faulkenberry discovered crack, as he had suspected.]

LEWIS, Judge

\* \* \*

There are two separate issues before this Court: (I) Whether Officer Faulkenberry had a reasonable suspicion to justify his stop of defendant, and (II) Whether Officer Faulkenberry's frisk of defendant was more intrusive than necessary.

\* \* \*

As to the first issue defendant argues that the facts of this case are identical to those in *State v. Fleming*, where this Court held that reasonable suspicion did not exist. We do not agree. In *Fleming* this Court stated that: ". . . A brief investigative stop of an individual must be based on specific and articulable facts as well as inferences from those facts, viewing the circumstances surrounding the seizure through the eyes of a reason-able cautious police officer on the scene, guided by his experience and training." This Court further held that there was no reasonable suspicion because the officers seized a defendant who had merely been standing in an open area between two apartment buildings and then chose to walk in a direction away from the officers. The Fleming Court determined that the officers had only a generalized suspicion based on the time, place and the fact that defendant was unfamiliar to the area, and that if a generalized suspicion was enough then innocent citizens could be subjected to unreasonable searches at an officer's whim.

In the present case we find that Officer Faulkenberry had much more than a generalized suspicion. Officer Faulkenberry was in the area because the police had received an anonymous phone call that individuals were dealing drugs at the apartment complex. Further, when the squad car pulled into the parking lot, defendant and several other individuals attempted to flee the scene. Officer Faulkenberry also testified that as a seven-year veteran of the force, it was his experience that weapons were frequently involved in drug transactions. We find that when these factors are considered as a whole and from the point of view of a reasonably cautious officer present on the scene, Officer Faulkenberry had reasonable suspicion to seize defendant and to perform a pat down search.

We next address the question of whether or not Officer Faulkenberry's search of defendant was more intrusive than was necessary to assure himself that defendant was not dangerous. Since the filing of the briefs in this case, the United States Supreme Court decided the factually similar case of *Minnesota v. Dickerson*. In *Dickerson*, a police officer stopped a suspect and performed a routine pat down search. Although the search revealed no weapons, the officer became curious about a small lump in the front pocket of the defendant's jacket. The officer testified "I examined it with my fingers and it slid and it felt to be a lump of crack cocaine in cellophane." Believing the lump to be cocaine the officer reached into defendant's pocket and retrieved a small cellophane bag, confirming his suspicion.

On appeal, the Supreme Court addressed the narrow question of whether or not an officer may seize non-threatening contraband detected during a pat down search. The Supreme Court held that such was permissible as long as the officer's search was within the bounds established by Terry v. Ohio. Supplying the rationale for its decision, the Supreme Court stated that:

> [i]f a police officer lawfully pats down a suspect's outer clothing and feels an object whose contour or mass makes its identity immediately apparent, there has been no invasion of the suspect's privacy beyond that already authorized by the officer's search for weapons; if the object is contraband, its warrantless seizure would be justified by the same practical considerations that inhere in the plain view context.

Applying this "plain feel" exception to the facts before it, the Supreme Court held that the officer's search was not authorized by *Terry* because the incriminating character of the lump in defendant's pocket was not immediately apparent because the officer had to slide it through his fingers and otherwise manipulate the lump to determine its incriminating character.

In the present matter Officer Faulkenberry testified that while performing his pat down search he felt a package or a lump in defendant's pocket and that he could tell there were smaller pieces within the lump. At first blush, the present matter appears indistinguishable from *Dickerson*. However, upon closer examination there are several critical differences between the case at bar and *Dickerson*. In both *Dickerson* and the case at bar, the officer testified that he felt a lump and opined that it was cocaine. However, in *Dickerson* there was additional testimony that the officer manipulated the contents of the defendant's pocket to form his opinion that the substance was cocaine, thus refuting any notion that the character of the contraband was immediately apparent to the officer. In the case at bar there is no such additional testimony that Officer Faulkenberry manipulated the contents of defendant's pocket or that he performed a search that was not permitted under Terry. The extent of Officer Faulkenberry's testimony was:

> As I was conducting the pat-down, I . . . started down the front and in his left breast pocket I felt a package or felt a lump. I could tell that there were small individual pieces inside of that lump and based on my past experience, I believed it to be a Controlled Substance, more than likely Crack.

Though Officer Faulkenberry's testimony sufficiently distinguishes this case from Dickerson, it still does not answer the ultimate question of whether the incriminating character of the lump in defendant's pocket was "immediately apparent." The resolution of this question is made difficult because the Supreme Court failed, for whatever reason, to provide a definition or a test for the phrase "immediately apparent." In fact, it has been suggested by one court that the "immediately apparent" test confuses "knowledge" and "suspicion" because an officer cannot truly verify the illegal character of a contraband substance without looking at it, and perhaps even testing it.

Since *Dickerson* was decided in June of this year, there have been several cases construing it. In *Ross*, the Southern District Court of Alabama held that the incriminating character of a matchbox found in the defendant's crotch during a lawful pat down was not immediately apparent because a matchbox is not contraband and it was irrelevant that the officer thought it contained cocaine. Similarly, in *United States v. Winter*, the Massachusetts District Court held that the "plain feel" rationale of *Dickerson* did not apply where the arresting officer repeatedly testified that he did not know the incriminating character of the contraband until he removed it. In contrast, the Wisconsin Court of Appeals upheld a trial court's denial of a motion to suppress in light of *Dickerson* when the arresting officer testified that he immediately recognized the incriminating character of a plastic bag found in defendant's waistband during a pat down search. The court reasoned that "given what the officer knew about the storage of cocaine, his conclusions about the character of the plastic baggie [were] reasonable." These cases clearly establish that the item seized must be contraband itself and that the officer must be aware of the incriminating character of the contraband before seizing such.

* * *

. . . [T]he above cases offer little more than case by case guidance and fall short of definitively answering the ultimate question of what is "immediately apparent." In resolving this question we are guided by search and seizure cases decided under the "plain view" exception to the Fourth Amendment, because the "immediately apparent" requirement is common to both the "plain view"

exception and the "plain feel" exception. In *State v. White*, our Supreme Court held that in the context of the "plain view" exception the term "immediately apparent" is "satisfied if the police have probable cause to believe that what they have come upon is evidence of criminal conduct." Given this statement we need only determine whether Officer Faulkenberry had probable cause to believe that the contraband he felt during his pat down search was cocaine. "Probable cause is a 'common sense, practical question' based on 'the factual and practical considerations of everyday life on which reasonable and prudent men, not legal technicians, act.'" "The standard to be met when considering whether probable cause exists is the totality of the circumstances." Based upon the fact that Officer Faulkenberry was called to the scene to investigate alleged drug dealings and because he had made prior drug arrests in his seven years of service, we find that upon using his tactile senses, he had probable cause to believe that the contraband in defendant's pocket was cocaine. We hold that Officer Faulkenberry's search was no more intrusive than necessary because the incriminating character of the contraband substance was "immediately apparent" to him. We also distinguish this case from *Dickerson* because Officer Faulkenberry was in the midst of a weapons search when he felt the contraband, whereas in *Dickerson* the officer had already convinced himself that defendant's pocket did not contain a weapon. We find that the facts of this case are distinguishable from those in *Dickerson* and affirm the trial court's denial of defendant's motion to suppress.

Affirmed.

# Cases Relating to Chapter 5

# Eavesdropping and Interception of Communications

## OLMSTEAD
### v.
## UNITED STATES

### 277 U.S. 438, 48 S. Ct. 564, 72 L. Ed. 944 (1928)

*[Citations and footnotes omitted.]*

[Olmstead was convicted of conspiring to violate the National Prohibition Act, based on evidence of private telephone conversations between him and others, intercepted by tapping his telephone line from a junction box located on a public street. The insertion was made without trespassing upon any property of the defendant. The wiretapping, which continued for many months, was conducted without probable cause or a warrant and in violation of local statutes. The trial court refused to suppress the conversations as the fruits of an illegal search. Olmstead was convicted and appealed the trial court's decision to admit the evidence.]

Mr. Chief Justice TAFT delivered the opinion of the Court.

\* \* \*

The Fourth Amendment provides:

The right of the people to be secure in their persons, houses, papers, and effects, against unreasonable searches and seizures, shall not be violated, and no warrants shall issue, but upon probable cause, supported by oath or affirmation, and particularly describing the place to be searched, and the persons or things to be seized.

\* \* \*

The amendment itself shows that the search is to be of material things—the person, the house, his papers, or his effects. The description of the warrant necessary to make the proceeding lawful is that it must specify the place to be searched and the person or things to be seized.

[In *Ex parte Jackson*, we held that the protection of the Fourth Amendment was applicable to sealed letters and packages in the mail, and that, consistently with it, such matter could only be opened and examined upon warrants issued on oath or affirmation particularly describing the thing to be seized.]

It is urged that the language of Mr. Justice Field in *Ex parte Jackson* . . . offers an analogy to the interpretation of the Fourth Amendment in respect of wire tapping. But the analogy fails. . . . It is plainly within the words of the amendment to say that the unlawful rifling by a government agent of a sealed letter is a search and seizure of the sender's papers or effects. The letter is a paper, an effect, and in the custody of a government that forbids carriage, except under its protection.

. . . The amendment does not forbid what was done here. There was no searching. There was no seizure. The evidence was secured by the use of the sense of hearing and that only. There was no entry of the houses or offices of the defendants. By the invention of the telephone 50 years ago, and its application for the purpose of extending communications, one can talk with another at a far distant place.

The language of the amendment cannot be extended and expanded to include telephone wires, reaching to the whole world from the defendant's house or office. The intervening wires are not part of his house or office, any more than are the highways along which they are stretched.

* * *

Congress may, of course, protect the secrecy of telephone messages by making them, when intercepted, inadmissible in evidence in federal criminal trials, by direct legislation, and thus depart from the common law of evidence. But the courts may not adopt such a policy by attributing an enlarged and unusual meaning to the Fourth Amendment. The reasonable view is that one who installs in his house a telephone instrument with connecting wires intends to project his voice to those quite outside, and that the wires beyond his house, and messages while passing over them, are not within the protection of the Fourth Amendment. Here those who intercepted the projected voices were not in the house of either party to the conversation.

Neither the cases we have cited nor any of the many federal decisions brought to our attention hold the Fourth Amend-

ment to have been violated as against a defendant, unless there has been an official search and seizure of his person or such a seizure of his papers or his tangible material effects or an actual physical invasion of his house 'or curtilage' for the purpose of making a seizure.

We think, therefore, that the wire tapping here disclosed did not amount to a search or seizure within the meaning of the Fourth Amendment.

What has been said disposes of the only question that comes within the terms of our order granting certiorari in these cases. But some of our number, departing from that order, have concluded that there is merit in the twofold objection, overruled in both courts below, that evidence obtained through intercepting of telephone messages by a government agent was inadmissible, because the mode of obtaining it was unethical and a misdemeanor under the law of Washington. . . .

* * *

Nor can we, without the sanction of congressional enactment, subscribe to the suggestion that the courts have a discretion to exclude evidence, the admission of which is not unconstitutional, because unethically secured. This would be at variance with the common-law doctrine generally supported by authority. There is no case that sustains, nor any recognized text-book that gives color to, such a view. Our general experience shows that much evidence has always been receivable, although not obtained by conformity to the highest ethics. The history of criminal trials shows numerous cases of prosecutions of oathbound conspiracies for murder, robbery, and other crimes, where officers of the law have disguised themselves and joined the organizations, taken the oaths, and given themselves every appearance of active members engaged in the promotion of crime for the purpose of securing evidence. Evidence secured by such means has always been received.

A standard which would forbid the reception of evidence, if obtained by other than nice ethical conduct by government officials, would make society suffer and give criminals greater immunity than has been known heretofore. In the absence of controlling legislation by Congress, those who realize the difficulties in bringing offenders to justice may well deem it wise that the exclusion of evidence should be confined to cases where rights under the Constitution would be violated by admitting it.

The statute of Washington, adopted in 1909, provides that:

Every person . . . who shall intercept, read or in any manner interrupt or delay the sending of a message over any telegraph or telephone line . . . shall be guilty of a misdemeanor.

This statute does not declare that evidence obtained by such interception shall be inadmissible, and by the common law, already referred to, it would not be. Whether the state of Washington may prosecute and punish federal officers violating this law, and those whose messages were intercepted may sue them civilly, is not before us. But clearly a statute, passed 20 years after the admission of the state into the Union, cannot affect the rules of evidence applicable in courts of the United States. . . .

* * *

AFFIRMED.

Mr. Justice BRANDEIS (dissenting).

. . . By objections seasonably made and persistently renewed, the defendants objected to the admission of the evidence obtained by wire tapping, on the ground that the government's wire tapping constituted an unreasonable search and seizure, in violation of the Fourth Amendment . . .

The government makes no attempt to defend the methods employed by its officers. Indeed, it concedes that, if wire tapping can be deemed a search and seizure within the Fourth Amendment, such wire tapping as was practiced in the case at bar was an unreasonable search and seizure, and that the evidence thus obtained was inadmissible. But it relies on the language of the amendment, and it claims that the protection given thereby cannot properly be held to include a telephone conversation.

* * *

When the Fourth and Fifth Amendments were adopted, 'the form that evil had theretofore taken' had been necessarily simple. . . . It could secure possession of his papers and other articles incident to his private life—a seizure effected, if need be, by breaking and entry. Protection against such invasion of 'the sanctities of a man's home and the privacies of life' was provided in the Fourth and Fifth Amendments by specific language. But 'time works changes, brings into existence new conditions and purposes.' Subtler and more far-reaching means of invading privacy have become available to the government. Discovery and invention have made it possible for the government, by means far more effective than stretching upon the rack, to obtain disclosure in court of what is whispered in the closet. Moreover, 'in the application of a Constitution, our contemplation cannot be only of what has been, but of what may be.' The progress of science in furnishing the government with means of espionage is not likely to stop with wire tapping. Ways may some day be developed by which the government, without removing papers from secret drawers, can reproduce them in court, and by which it will be enabled to expose to a jury the most intimate occurrences of the home. Advances in the psychic and related sciences may bring means of exploring unexpressed beliefs, thoughts and emotions. 'That places the liberty of every man in the hands of every petty officer' was said by James Otis of much lesser intrusions than these. To Lord Camden a far slighter intrusion seemed 'subversive of all the comforts of society.' Can it be that the Constitution affords no protection against such invasions of individual security?

A sufficient answer is found in *Boyd v. United States*, a case that will be remembered as long as civil liberty lives in the United States. This court there reviewed the history that lay behind the Fourth and Fifth Amendments. We said with reference to Lord Camden's judgment in *Entick v. Carrington*:

The principles laid down in this opinion affect the very essence of constitutional liberty and security. They reach farther than the concrete form of the case there before the court, with its adventitious circumstances; they apply to all invasions on the part of the government and its employee of the sanctities of a man's home and the privacies of life. It is not the breaking of his doors, and the rummaging of his drawers, that constitutes the essence of the offense; but it is the invasion of his indefeasible right of personal security, personal liberty and private property, where that right has never been forfeited by his conviction of some public offense—it is the invasion of this sacred right which underlies and constitutes the essence of Lord Camden's judgment. Breaking into a house and opening boxes and drawers are circumstances of aggravation; but any

forcible and compulsory extortion of a man's own testimony or of his private papers to be used as evidence of a crime or to forfeit his goods, is within the condemnation of that judgment. In this regard the Fourth and Fifth Amendments run almost into each other.

In *Ex parte Jackson*, it was held that a sealed letter intrusted to the mail is protected by the amendments. The mail is a public service furnished by the government. The telephone is a public service furnished by its authority. There is, in essence, no difference between the sealed letter and the private telephone message. As Judge Rudkin said below:

True, the one is visible, the other invisible; the one is tangible, the other intangible; the one is sealed, and the other unsealed; but these are distinctions without a difference.

The evil incident to invasion of the privacy of the telephone is far greater than that involved in tampering with the mails. Whenever a telephone line is tapped, the privacy of the persons at both ends of the line is invaded, and all conversations between them upon any subject, and although proper, confidential, and privileged, may be overheard. Moreover, the tapping of one man's telephone line involves the tapping of the telephone of every other person whom he may call, or who may call him. As a means of espionage, writs of assistance and general warrants are but puny instruments of tyranny and oppression when compared with wire tapping.

\* \* \*

. . . The makers of our Constitution undertook to secure conditions favorable to the pursuit of happiness. They recognized the significance of man's spiritual nature, of his feelings and of his intellect. They knew that only a part of the pain, pleasure and satisfactions of life are to be found in material things. They sought to protect Americans in their beliefs, their thoughts, their emotions and their sensations. They conferred, as against the government, the right to be let alone—the most comprehensive of rights and the right most valued by civilized men. To protect, that right, every unjustifiable intrusion by the government upon the privacy of the individual, whatever the means employed, must be deemed a violation of the Fourth Amendment. And the use, as evidence in a criminal proceeding, of facts ascertained by such intrusion must be deemed a violation of the Fifth.

Applying to the Fourth and Fifth Amendments the established rule of construction, the defendants' objections to the evidence obtained by wire tapping must, in my opinion, be sustained. It is, of course, immaterial where the physical connection with the telephone wires leading into the defendants' premises was made. And it is also immaterial that the intrusion was in aid of law enforcement. Experience should teach us to be most on our guard to protect liberty when the government's purposes are beneficent. Men born to freedom are naturally alert to repel invasion of their liberty by evil-minded rulers. The greatest dangers to liberty lurk in insidious encroachment by men of zeal, well-meaning but without understanding.

Independently of the constitutional question, I am of opinion that the judgment should be reversed. By the laws of Washington, wire tapping is a crime. To prove its case, the government was obliged to lay bare the crimes committed by its officers on its behalf. A federal court should not permit such a prosecution to continue.

\* \* \*

When these unlawful acts were committed they were crimes only of the officers individually. The government was innocent, in legal contemplation; for no federal official is authorized to commit a crime on its behalf. When the government, having full knowledge, sought, through the Department of Justice, to avail itself of the fruits of these acts in order to accomplish its own ends, it assumed moral responsibility for the officers' crimes. . . . [A]nd if this court should permit the government, by means of its officers' crimes, to effect its purpose of punishing the defendants, there would seem to be present all the elements of a ratification. If so, the government itself would become a lawbreaker.

\* \* \*

Decency, security, and liberty alike demand that government officials shall be subjected to the same rules of conduct that are commands to the citizen. In a government of laws, existence of the government will be imperiled if it fails to observe the law scrupulously. Our government is the potent, the omnipresent teacher. For good or for ill, it teaches the whole people by its example. Crime is contagious. If the government becomes a lawbreaker, it breeds contempt for law; it invites every man to become a law unto himself; it invites anarchy. To declare that in the administration of the criminal law the end justifies the means—to declare that the government may commit crimes in order to secure the conviction of a private criminal—would bring terrible retribution. Against that pernicious doctrine this court should resolutely set its face.

\* \* \*

## KATZ

v.

## UNITED STATES

### 389 U.S. 347, 88 S. Ct. 507, 19 L. Ed. 2d 576 (1967)

*[Citations and footnotes omitted.]*

[Katz, a bookie, was convicted of transmitting wagering information, based on evidence overheard by FBI agents who had attached a recording device to the exterior of a public telephone booth from which Katz habitually made his business calls. The agents were able to overhear Katz's portion of a telephone conversation without physically intruding into the booth. The conversation proved incriminating and the defendant was convicted of illegal wagering.]

MR. JUSTICE STEWART delivered the opinion of the Court.

* * *

Because of the misleading way the issues have been formulated, the parties have attached great significance to the characterization of the telephone booth from which the petitioner placed his calls. The petitioner has strenuously argued that the booth was a "constitutionally protected area." The Government has maintained with equal vigor that it was not. But this effort to decide whether or not a given "area," viewed in the abstract, is "constitutionally protected" deflects attention from the problem presented by this case. For the Fourth Amendment protects people, not places. What a person knowingly exposes to the public, even in his own home or office, is not a subject of Fourth Amendment protection. But what he seeks to preserve as private, even in an area accessible to the public, may be constitutionally protected.

The Government stresses the fact that the telephone booth from which the petitioner made his calls was constructed partly of glass, so that he was as visible after he entered it as he would have been if he had remained outside. But what he sought to exclude when he entered the booth was not the intruding eye—it was the uninvited ear. He did not shed his right to do so simply because he made his calls from a place where he might be seen. No less than an individual in a business office, in a friend's apartment, or in a taxicab, a person in a telephone booth may rely upon the protection of the Fourth Amendment. One who occupies it, shuts the door behind him, and pays the toll that permits him to place a call is surely entitled to assume that the words he utters into the mouthpiece will not be broadcast to the world. To read the Constitution more narrowly is to ignore the vital role that the public telephone has come to play in private communication.

The Government contends, however, that the activities of its agents in this case should not be tested by Fourth Amendment requirements, for the surveillance technique they employed involved no physical penetration of the telephone booth from which the petitioner placed his calls. It is true that the absence of such penetration was at one time thought to foreclose further Fourth Amendment inquiry for that Amendment was thought to limit only searches and seizures of tangible property. But "[t]he premise that property interests control the right of the Government to search and seize has been discredited." Thus, although a closely divided Court supposed in *Olmstead* that surveillance without any trespass and without the seizure of any material object fell outside the ambit of the Constitution, we have since departed from the narrow view on which that decision rested. Indeed, we have expressly held that the

Fourth Amendment governs not only the seizure of tangible items, but extends as well to the recording of oral statements, over-heard without any "technical trespass under . . . local property law." Once this much is acknowledged, and once it is recognized that the Fourth Amendment protects people—and not simply "areas"—against unreasonable searches and seizures, it becomes clear that the reach of that Amendment cannot turn upon the presence or absence of a physical intrusion into any given enclosure.

We conclude that the underpinnings of *Olmstead* and *Goldman* have been so eroded by our subsequent decisions that the "trespass" doctrine there enunciated can no longer be regarded as controlling. The Government's activities in electronically listening to and recording the petitioner's words violated the privacy upon which he justifiably relied while using the telephone booth and thus constituted a "search and seizure" within the meaning of the Fourth Amendment. The fact that the electronic device employed to achieve that end did not happen to penetrate the wall of the booth can have no constitutional significance.

The question remaining for decision, then, is whether the search and seizure conducted in this case complied with constitutional standards. In that regard, the Government's position is that its agents acted in an entirely defensible manner: They did not begin their electronic surveillance until investigation of the petitioner's activities had established a strong probability that he was using the telephone in question to transmit gambling information to persons in other States, in violation of federal law. Moreover, the surveillance was limited, both in scope and in duration, to the specific purpose of establishing the contents of the petitioner's unlawful telephonic communications. The agents confined their surveillance to the brief periods during which he used the telephone

booth, and they took great care to over-hear only the conversations of the petitioner himself.

Accepting this account of the Government's actions as accurate, it is clear that this surveillance was so narrowly circumscribed that a duly authorized magistrate, properly notified of the need for such investigation, specifically informed of the basis on which it was to proceed, and clearly apprised of the precise intrusion it would entail, could constitutionally have authorized, with appropriate safeguards, the very limited search and seizure that the Government asserts in fact took place. Only last Term we sustained the validity of such an authorization, holding that, under sufficiently "precise and discriminate circumstances," a federal court may empower government agents to employ a concealed electronic device "for the narrow and particularized purpose of ascertaining the truth of the . . . allegations" of a "detailed factual affidavit alleging the commission of a specific criminal offense." Discussing that holding, the Court in *Berger v. New York*, said that "the order authorizing the use of the electronic device" in Osborn "afforded similar protections to those . . . of conventional warrants authorizing the seizure of tangible evidence." Through those protections, "no greater invasion of privacy was permitted than was necessary under the circumstances." Here, too, a similar judicial order could have accommodated "the legitimate needs of law enforcement" by authorizing the carefully limited use of electronic surveillance.

* * *

. . . Wherever a man may be, he is entitled to know that he will remain free from unreasonable searches and seizures. The government agents here ignored "the procedure of antecedent justification . . . that is central to the Fourth Amendment," a procedure that we hold to be a constitutional precondition of the kind of electronic surveillance involved in this case. Because the surveillance here failed to meet that condition, and because it led to the petitioner's conviction, the judgment must be reversed.

It is so ordered.

[Concurring and dissenting opinions omitted.]

**UNITED STATES CODE
TITLE 18. CRIMES AND
CRIMINAL PROCEDURE**

**PART I—CRIMES**

**CHAPTER 119—WIRE AND
ELECTRONIC
COMMUNICATIONS
INTERCEPTION AND
INTERCEPTION OF ORAL
COMMUNICATIONS**

§ 2510. Definitions
§ 2511. Interception and disclosure of wire, oral, or electronic communications prohibited
§ 2512. Manufacture, distribution, possession, and advertising of wire, oral, or electronic communication intercepting devices prohibited [omitted]
§ 2513. Confiscation of wire, oral, or electronic communication intercepting devices [omitted]
§ 2514. Repealed. Pub.L. 91-452, Title II, s 227(a), Oct. 15, 1970, 84 Stat. 930
§ 2515. Prohibition of use as evidence of intercepted wire or oral communications
§ 2516. Authorization for interception of wire, oral, or electronic communications
§ 2517. Authorization for disclosure and use of intercepted wire, oral, or electronic communications
§ 2518. Procedure for interception of wire, oral, or electronic communications

§ 2519. Reports concerning intercepted wire, oral, or electronic communications
§ 2520. Recovery of civil damages authorized
§ 2521. Injunction against illegal interception [omitted]
§ 2522. Enforcement of the Communications Assistance for Law Enforcement Act

§ 2510. Definitions

As used in this chapter—

(1) "wire communication" means any aural transfer made in whole or in part through the use of facilities for the transmission of communications by the aid of wire, cable, or other like connection between the point of origin and the point of reception (including the use of such connection in a switching station) furnished or operated by any person engaged in providing or operating such facilities for the transmission of interstate or foreign communications or communications affecting interstate or foreign commerce;

(2) "oral communication" means any oral communication uttered by a person exhibiting an expectation that such communication is not subject to interception under circumstances justifying such expectation, but such term does not include any electronic communication;

(3) "State" means any State of the United States, the District of Columbia, the Commonwealth of Puerto Rico, and any territory or possession of the United States;

(4) "intercept" means the aural or other acquisition of the contents of any wire, electronic, or oral communication through the use of any electronic, mechanical, or other device.

(5) "electronic, mechanical, or other device" means any device or apparatus which can be used to intercept a wire, oral, or electronic communication other than—

(a) any telephone or telegraph instrument, equipment or facility, or any component thereof, (i) furnished to the subscriber or user by a provider of wire or electronic communication service in the ordinary course of its business and being used by the subscriber or user in the ordinary course of its business or furnished by such subscriber or user for connection to the facilities of such service and used in the ordinary course of its business; or (ii) being used by a provider of wire or electronic communication service in the ordinary course of its business, or by an investigative or law enforcement officer in the ordinary course of his duties;

(b) a hearing aid or similar device being used to correct subnormal hearing to not better than normal;

(6) "person" means any employee, or agent of the United States or any State or political subdivision thereof, and any individual, partnership, association, joint stock company, trust, or corporation;

(7) "Investigative or law enforcement officer" means any officer of the United States or of a State or political subdivision thereof, who is empowered by law to conduct investigations of or to make arrests for offenses enumerated in this chapter, and any attorney authorized by law to prosecute or participate in the prosecution of such offenses;

(8) "contents," when used with respect to any wire, oral, or electronic communication, includes any information concerning the substance, purport, or meaning of that communication;

(9) "Judge of competent jurisdiction" means—

(a) a judge of a United States district court or a United States court of appeals; and

(b) a judge of any court of general criminal jurisdiction of a State who is authorized by a statute of that State to enter orders authorizing interceptions of wire, oral, or electronic communications;

(10) "communication common carrier" has the meaning given that term in section 3 of the Communications Act of 1934;

(11) "aggrieved person" means a person who was a party to any intercepted wire, oral, or electronic communication or a person against whom the interception was directed;

(12) "electronic communication" means any transfer of signs, signals, writing, images, sounds, data, or intelligence of any nature transmitted in whole or in part by a wire, radio, electromagnetic, photoelectronic or photooptical system that affects interstate or foreign commerce, but does not include—

(A) any wire or oral communication;

(B) any communication made through a tone-only paging device;

(C) any communication from a tracking device (as defined in section 3117 of this title); or

(D) electronic funds transfer information stored by a financial institution in a communications system used for the electronic storage and transfer of funds;

(13) "user" means any person or entity who—

(A) uses an electronic communication service; and

(B) is duly authorized by the provider of such service to engage in such use;

(14) "electronic communications system" means any wire, radio, electromagnetic, photooptical or photoelectronic facilities for the transmission of wire or electronic communications, and any computer facilities or related electronic equipment for the electronic storage of such communications;

(15) "electronic communication service" means any service which provides to users thereof the ability to send or receive wire or electronic communications;

(16) "readily accessible to the general public" means, with respect to a radio communication, that such communication is not—

(A) scrambled or encrypted;

(B) transmitted using modulation techniques whose essential parameters have been withheld from the public with the intention of preserving the privacy of such communication;

(C) carried on a subcarrier or other signal subsidiary to a radio transmission;

(D) transmitted over a communication system provided by a common carrier, unless the communication is a tone only paging system communication; or

(E) transmitted on frequencies allocated under part 25, subpart D, E, or F of part 74, or part 94 of the Rules of the Federal Communications Commission, unless, in the case of a communication transmitted on a frequency allocated under part 74 that is not exclusively allocated to broadcast auxiliary services, the communication is a two-way voice communication by radio;

(17) "electronic storage" means—

(A) any temporary, intermediate storage of a wire or electronic communication incidental to the electronic transmission thereof; and

(B) any storage of such communication by an electronic communication service for purposes of backup protection of such communication;

(18) "aural transfer" means a transfer containing the human voice at any point between and including the point of origin and the point of reception;

(19) "foreign intelligence information," for purposes of section 2517(6) of this title, means—

(A) information, whether or not concerning a United States person, that relates to the ability of the United States to protect against—

(i) actual or potential attack or other grave hostile acts of a foreign power or an agent of a foreign power;

(ii) sabotage or international terrorism by a foreign power or an agent of a foreign power; or

(iii) clandestine intelligence activities by an intelligence service or network of a foreign power or by an agent of a foreign power; or

(B) information, whether or not concerning a United States person, with respect to a foreign power or foreign territory that relates to—

(i) the national defense or the security of the United States; or

(ii) the conduct of the foreign affairs of the United States;

(20) "protected computer" has the meaning set forth in section 1030; and

(21) "computer trespasser"—

(A) means a person who accesses a protected computer without authorization and thus has no reasonable expectation of privacy in any communication transmitted to, through, or from the protected computer; and

(B) does not include a person known by the owner or operator of the protected computer to have an existing contractual relationship with the owner or operator of the protected computer for access to all or part of the protected computer.

§ 2511. Interception and disclosure of wire, oral, or electronic communications prohibited

(1) Except as otherwise specifically provided in this chapter any person who—

(a) intentionally intercepts, endeavors to intercept, or procures any other person to intercept or endeavor to intercept, any wire, oral, or electronic communication;

(b) intentionally uses, endeavors to use, or procures any other person to use or endeavor to use any electronic, mechanical, or other device to intercept any oral communication when—

(i) such device is affixed to, or otherwise transmits a signal through, a wire, cable, or other like connection used in wire communication; or

(ii) such device transmits communications by radio, or interferes with the transmission of such communication; or

(iii) such person knows, or has reason to know, that such device or any component thereof has been sent through the mail or transported in interstate or foreign commerce; or

(iv) such use or endeavor to use (A) takes place on the premises of any business or other commercial establishment the operations of which affect interstate or foreign commerce; or (B) obtains or is for the purpose of obtaining information relating to the operations of any business or other commercial establishment the operations of which affect interstate or foreign commerce; or

(v) such person acts in the District of Columbia, the Commonwealth of Puerto Rico, or any territory or possession of the United States;

(c) intentionally discloses, or endeavors to disclose, to any other person the contents of any wire, oral, or electronic communication, knowing or having reason to know that the information was obtained through the interception of a wire, oral, or electronic communication in violation of this subsection;

(d) intentionally uses, or endeavors to use, the contents of any wire, oral, or electronic communication, knowing or having reason to know that the information was obtained through the interception of a wire, oral, or electronic communication in violation of this subsection; or

(e) (i) intentionally discloses, or endeavors to disclose, to any other person the contents of any wire, oral, or electronic communication, intercepted by means authorized by sections 2511(2)(a)(ii), 2511(2)(b)-(c), 2511(2)(e), 2516, and 2518 of this chapter, (ii) knowing or having reason to know that the information was obtained through the interception of such a communication in connection with a criminal investigation, (iii) having obtained or received the information in connection with a criminal investigation, and (iv) with intent to improperly obstruct, impede, or interfere with a duly authorized criminal investigation, shall be punished as provided in subsection (4) or shall be subject to suit as provided in subsection (5).

(2)(a)(i) It shall not be unlawful under this chapter for an operator of a switchboard, or an officer, employee, or agent of a provider of wire or electronic communication service, whose facilities are used in the transmission of a wire or electronic communication, to intercept, disclose, or use that communication in the normal course of his employment while engaged in any activity which is a necessary incident to the rendition of his service or to the protection of the rights or property of the provider of that service, except that a provider of wire communication service to the public shall not utilize service observing or random monitoring except for mechanical or service quality control checks.

(ii) Notwithstanding any other law, providers of wire or electronic communication service, their officers, employees, and agents, landlords, custodians, or other persons, are authorized to provide information, facilities, or technical assistance to persons authorized by law to intercept wire, oral, or electronic communications or to conduct electronic surveillance, as defined in section 101 of the Foreign Intelligence Surveillance Act of 1978, if such provider, its officers, employees, or agents, landlord, custodian, or other specified person, has been provided with—

(A) a court order directing such assistance signed by the authorizing judge, or

(B) a certification in writing by a person specified in section 2518(7) of this title or the Attorney General of the United States that no warrant or court order is required by law, that all statutory requirements have been met, and that the specified assistance is required, setting forth the period of time during which the provision of the information, facilities, or technical assistance is authorized and specifying the information, facilities, or technical assistance required. No provider of wire or electronic communication service, officer, employee, or agent thereof, or landlord, custodian, or other specified person shall disclose the existence of any interception or surveillance or the device used to accomplish the interception or surveillance with respect to which the person has been furnished a court order or certification under this chapter, except as may otherwise be required by legal process and then only after prior notification to the Attorney General or to the principal prosecuting attorney of a State or any political subdivision of a State, as may be appropriate. Any such disclosure shall render such person liable for the civil damages provided for in section 2520. No cause of action shall lie in any court against any provider of wire or electronic communication service, its officers, employees, or agents, landlord, custodian, or other specified person for providing information, facilities, or assistance in accordance with the terms of a court order, statutory authorization, or certification under this chapter.

(b) It shall not be unlawful under this chapter for an officer, employee, or agent of the Federal Communications Commission, in the normal course of his employment and in discharge of the monitoring responsibilities exercised by the Commission in the enforcement of chapter 5 of title 47 of the United States Code, to intercept a wire or electronic communication, or oral communication transmitted by radio, or to disclose or use the information thereby obtained.

(c) It shall not be unlawful under this chapter for a person acting under color of law to intercept a wire, oral, or electronic communication, where such person is a

party to the communication or one of the parties to the communication has given prior consent to such interception.

(d) It shall not be unlawful under this chapter for a person not acting under color of law to intercept a wire, oral, or electronic communication where such person is a party to the communication or where one of the parties to the communication has given prior consent to such interception unless such communication is intercepted for the purpose of committing any criminal or tortious act in violation of the Constitution or laws of the United States or of any State.

(e) Notwithstanding any other provision of this title or section 705 or 706 of the Communications Act of 1934, it shall not be unlawful for an officer, employee, or agent of the United States in the normal course of his official duty to conduct electronic surveillance, as defined in section 101 of the Foreign Intelligence Surveillance Act of 1978, as authorized by that Act.

(f) Nothing contained in this chapter or chapter 121 or 206 of this title, or section 705 of the Communications Act of 1934, shall be deemed to affect the acquisition by the United States Government of foreign intelligence information from international or foreign communications, or foreign intelligence activities conducted in accordance with otherwise applicable Federal law involving a foreign electronic communications system, utilizing a means other than electronic surveillance as defined in section 101 of the Foreign Intelligence Surveillance Act of 1978, and procedures in this chapter or chapter 121 and the Foreign Intelligence Surveillance Act of 1978 shall be the exclusive means by which electronic surveillance, as defined in section 101 of such Act, and the interception of domestic wire, oral, and electronic communications may be conducted.

(g) It shall not be unlawful under this chapter or chapter 121 of this title for any person—

(i) to intercept or access an electronic communication made through an electronic communication system that is configured so that such electronic communication is readily accessible to the general public;

(ii) to intercept any radio communication which is transmitted—

(I) by any station for the use of the general public, or that relates to ships, aircraft, vehicles, or persons in distress;

(II) by any governmental, law enforcement, civil defense, private land mobile, or public safety communications system, including police and fire, readily accessible to the general public;

(III) by a station operating on an authorized frequency within the bands allocated to the amateur, citizens band, or general mobile radio services; or

(IV) by any marine or aeronautical communications system;

(iii) to engage in any conduct which—

(I) is prohibited by section 633 of the Communications Act of 1934; or

(II) is excepted from the application of section 705(a) of the Communications Act of 1934 by section 705(b) of that Act;

(iv) to intercept any wire or electronic communication the transmission of which is causing harmful interference to any lawfully operating station or consumer electronic equipment, to the extent necessary to identify the source of such interference; or

(v) for other users of the same frequency to intercept any radio communication made through a system that utilizes frequencies monitored by individuals engaged in the provision or the use of such system, if such communication is not scrambled or encrypted.

(h) It shall not be unlawful under this chapter—

(i) to use a pen register or a trap and trace device (as those terms are defined for the purposes of chapter 206 (relating to pen registers and trap and trace devices) of this title); or

(ii) for a provider of electronic communication service to record the fact that a wire or electronic communication was initiated or completed in order to protect such provider, another provider furnishing service toward the completion of the wire or electronic communication, or a user of that service, from fraudulent, unlawful or abusive use of such service.

(i) It shall not be unlawful under this chapter for a person acting under color of law to intercept the wire or electronic communications of a computer trespasser transmitted to, through, or from the protected computer, if—

(I) the owner or operator of the protected computer authorizes the interception of the computer trespasser's communications on the protected computer;

(II) the person acting under color of law is lawfully engaged in an investigation;

(III) the person acting under color of law has reasonable grounds to believe that the contents of the computer trespasser's communications will be relevant to the investigation; and

(IV) such interception does not acquire communications other than those transmitted to or from the computer trespasser.

(3)(a) Except as provided in paragraph (b) of this subsection, a person or entity providing an electronic communication service to the public shall not intentionally divulge the contents of any communication (other than one to such person or entity, or an agent thereof) while in transmission on that service to any person or entity other than an addressee or intended recipient of such communication or an agent of such addressee or intended recipient.

(b) A person or entity providing electronic communication service to the public may divulge the contents of any such communication—

(i) as otherwise authorized in section 2511(2)(a) or 2517 of this title;

(ii) with the lawful consent of the originator or any addressee or intended recipient of such communication;

(iii) to a person employed or authorized, or whose facilities are used, to forward such communication to its destination; or

(iv) which were inadvertently obtained by the service provider and which appear to pertain to the commission of a crime, if such divulgence is made to a law enforcement agency.

(4)(a) Except as provided in paragraph (b) of this subsection or in subsection (5), whoever violates subsection (1) of this section shall be fined under this title or imprisoned not more than five years, or both.

(b) Conduct otherwise an offense under this subsection that consists of or relates to the interception of a satellite transmission that is not encrypted or scrambled and that is transmitted—

(i) to a broadcasting station for purposes of retransmission to the general public; or

(ii) as an audio subcarrier intended for redistribution to facilities open to the public, but not including data transmissions or telephone calls,

is not an offense under this subsection unless the conduct is for the purposes of direct or indirect commercial advantage or private financial gain.

(5)(a)(i) If the communication is—

(A) a private satellite video communication that is not scrambled or encrypted and the conduct in violation of this chapter is the private viewing of that communication and is not for a tortious or illegal purpose or for purposes of direct or indirect commercial advantage or private commercial gain; or

(B) a radio communication that is transmitted on frequencies allocated under subpart D of part 74 of the rules of the Federal Communications Commission that is not scrambled or encrypted and the conduct in violation of this chapter is not for a tortious or illegal purpose or for purposes of direct or indirect commercial advantage or private commercial gain, then the person who engages in such conduct shall be subject to suit by the Federal Government in a court of competent jurisdiction.

(ii) In an action under this subsection—

(A) if the violation of this chapter is a first offense for the person under paragraph (a) of subsection (4) and such person has not been found liable in a civil action under section 2520 of this title, the Federal Government shall be entitled to appropriate injunctive relief; and

(B) if the violation of this chapter is a second or subsequent offense under paragraph (a) of subsection (4) or such person has been found liable in any prior civil action under section 2520, the person shall be subject to a mandatory $500 civil fine.

(b) The court may use any means within its authority to enforce an injunction issued under paragraph (ii)(A), and shall impose a civil fine of not less than $500 for each violation of such an injunction.

§ 2515. Prohibition of use as evidence of intercepted wire or oral communications

Whenever any wire or oral communication has been intercepted, no part of the contents of such communication and no evidence derived therefrom may be received in evidence in any trial, hearing, or other proceeding in or before any court, grand jury, department, officer, agency, regulatory body, legislative committee, or other authority of the United States, a State, or a political subdivision thereof if the disclosure of that information would be in violation of this chapter.

§ 2516. Authorization for interception of wire, oral, or electronic communications

(1) The Attorney General, Deputy Attorney General, Associate Attorney General, or any Assistant Attorney General, any acting Assistant Attorney General, or any Deputy Assistant Attorney General or acting Deputy Assistant Attorney General in the Criminal Division specially designated by the Attorney General, may authorize an application to a Federal judge of competent jurisdiction for, and such judge may grant in conformity with section 2518 of this chapter an order authorizing or approving the interception of wire or oral communications by the Federal Bureau of Investigation, or a Federal agency having responsibility for the investigation of the offense as to which the application is made, when such interception may provide or has provided evidence of—
(a) any offense punishable by death or by imprisonment for more than one year under sections 2274 through 2277 of title 42 of the United States Code (relating to the enforcement of the Atomic Energy Act of 1954), section 2284 of title 42 of the United States Code (relating to sabotage of nuclear facilities or fuel), or under the following chapters of this title: chapter 37 (relating to espionage), chapter 105 (relating to sabotage), chapter 115 (relating to treason), chapter 102 (relating to riots) chapter 65 (relating to malicious mischief), chapter 111 (relating to destruction of vessels), or chapter 81 (relating to piracy);
(b) a violation of section 186 or section 501(c) of title 29, United States Code (dealing with restrictions on payments and loans to labor organizations), or any offense which involves murder, kidnapping, robbery, or extortion, and which is punishable under this title;
(c) any offense which is punishable under the following sections of this title: section 201 (bribery of public officials

and witnesses), section 215 (relating to bribery of bank officials), section 224 (bribery in sporting contests), subsection (d), (e), (f), (g), (h), or (i) of section 844 (unlawful use of explosives), section 1032 (relating to concealment of assets), section 1084 (transmission of wagering information), section 751 (relating to escape), section 1014 (relating to loans and credit applications generally; renewals and discounts), sections 1503, 1512, and 1513 (influencing or injuring an officer, juror, or witness generally), section 1510 (obstruction of criminal investigations), section 1511 (obstruction of State or local law enforcement), section 1751 (Presidential and Presidential staff assassination, kidnapping, and assault), section 1951 (interference with commerce by threats or violence), section 1952 (interstate and foreign travel or transportation in aid of racketeering enterprises), section 1958 (relating to use of interstate commerce facilities in the commission of murder for hire), section 1959 (relating to violent crimes in aid of racketeering activity), section 1954 (offer, acceptance, or solicitation to influence operations of employee benefit plan), section 1955 (prohibition of business enterprises of gambling), section 1956 (laundering of monetary instruments), section 1957 (relating to engaging in monetary transactions in property derived from specified unlawful activity), section 659 (theft from interstate shipment), section 664 (embezzlement from pension and welfare funds), section 1343 (fraud by wire, radio, or television), section 1344 (relating to bank fraud), sections 2251 and 2252 (sexual exploitation of children), sections 2312, 2313, 2314, and 2315 (interstate transportation of stolen property), section 2321 (relating to trafficking in certain motor vehicles or motor vehicle parts), section 1203 (relating to hostage taking), section 1029 (relating to fraud and related activity in connection with access devices), section 3146 (relating to penalty for failure to appear), section 3521(b)(3) (relating to witness relocation and assistance), section 32 (relating to destruction of aircraft or aircraft facilities), section 38 (relating to aircraft parts fraud), section 1963 (violations with respect to racketeer influenced and corrupt organizations), section 115 (relating to threatening or retaliating against a Federal official), section 1341 (relating to mail fraud), a felony violation of section 1030 (relating to computer fraud and abuse), section 351 (violations with respect to congressional, Cabinet, or Supreme Court assassinations, kidnapping, and assault), section 831 (relating to prohibited transactions involving nuclear materials), section 33 (relating to destruction of motor vehicles or motor vehicle facilities), section 175 (relating to biological weapons), section 1992 (relating to wrecking trains), a felony violation of section 1028 (relating to production of false identification documentation), section 1425 (relating to the procurement of citizenship or nationalization unlawfully), section 1426 (relating to the reproduction of naturalization or citizenship papers), section 1427 (relating to the sale of naturalization or citizenship papers), section 1541 (relating to passport issuance without authority), section 1542 (relating to false statements in passport applications), section 1543 (relating to forgery or false use of passports), section 1544 (relating to misuse of passports), or section 1546 (relating to fraud and misuse of visas, permits, and other documents);

(d) any offense involving counterfeiting punishable under section 471, 472, or 473 of this title;

(e) any offense involving fraud connected with a case under title 11 or the manufacture, importation, receiving, concealment, buying, selling, or otherwise dealing in narcotic drugs, marihuana, or other dangerous drugs, punishable under any law of the United States;

(f) any offense including extortionate credit transactions under sections 892, 893, or 894 of this title;

(g) a violation of section 5322 of title 31, United States Code (dealing with the reporting of currency transactions);

(h) any felony violation of sections 2511 and 2512 (relating to interception and disclosure of certain communications and to certain intercepting devices) of this title;

(I) any felony violation of chapter 71 (relating to obscenity) of this title;

(j) any violation of section 60123(b) (relating to destruction of a natural gas pipeline) or section 46502 (relating to aircraft piracy) of title 49;

(k) any criminal violation of section 2778 of title 22 (relating to the Arms Export Control Act);

(l) the location of any fugitive from justice from an offense described in this section;

(m) a violation of section 274, 277, or 278 of the Immigration and Nationality Act (8 U.S.C. 1324, 1327, or 1328) (relating to the smuggling of aliens);

(n) any felony violation of sections 922 and 924 of title 18, United States Code (relating to firearms);

(o) any violation of section 5861 of the Internal Revenue Code of 1986 (relating to firearms);

(p) a felony violation of section 1028 (relating to production of false identification documents), section 1542 (relating to false statements in passport applications), section 1546 (relating to fraud and misuse of visas, permits, and other documents) of this title or a violation of section 274, 277, or 278 of the Immigration and Nationality Act (relating to the smuggling of aliens);

(p) any conspiracy to commit any offense described in any subparagraph of this paragraph.

(q) any criminal violation of section 229 (relating to chemical weapons); or sections 2332, 2332a, 2332b, 2332d, 2332f, 2339A, 2339B, or 2339C of this title (relating to terrorism); or

(r) any conspiracy to commit any offense described in any subparagraph of this paragraph.

(2) The principal prosecuting attorney of any State, or the principal prosecuting attorney of any political subdivision thereof, if such attorney is authorized by a statute of that State to make application to a State court judge of competent jurisdiction for an order authorizing or approving the interception of wire, oral, or electronic communications, may apply to such judge for, and such judge may grant in conformity with section 2518 of this chapter and with the applicable State statute an order authorizing, or approving the interception of wire, oral, or electronic communications by investigative or law enforcement officers having responsibility for the investigation of the offense as to which the application is made, when such interception may provide or has provided evidence of the commission of the offense of murder, kidnapping, gambling, robbery, bribery, extortion, or dealing in narcotic drugs, marihuana or other dangerous drugs, or other crime dangerous to life, limb, or property, and punishable by imprisonment for more than one year, designated in any applicable State statute authorizing such interception, or any conspiracy to commit any of the foregoing offenses.

(3) Any attorney for the Government (as such term is defined for the purposes of the Federal Rules of Criminal Procedure) may authorize an application to a Federal judge of competent jurisdiction for, and such judge may grant, in conformity with section 2518 of this title, an order authorizing or approving the interception of electronic communications by an investigative or law enforcement officer having responsibility for the investigation of the offense as to which the application is made, when such interception may provide or has provided evidence of any Federal felony.

§ 2517. Authorization for disclosure and use of intercepted wire, oral, or electronic communications

(1) Any investigative or law enforcement officer who, by any means authorized by this chapter, has obtained knowledge of the contents of any wire, oral, or electronic communication, or evidence derived therefrom, may disclose such contents to another investigative or law enforcement officer to the extent that such disclosure is appropriate to the proper performance of the official duties of the officer making or receiving the disclosure.

(2) Any investigative or law enforcement officer who, by any means authorized by this chapter, has obtained knowledge of the contents of any wire, oral, or electronic communication or evidence derived therefrom may use such contents to the extent such use is appropriate to the proper performance of his official duties.

(3) Any person who has received, by any means authorized by this chapter, any information concerning a wire, oral, or electronic communication, or evidence derived therefrom intercepted in accordance with the provisions of this chapter may disclose the contents of that communication or such derivative evidence while giving testimony under oath or affirmation in any proceeding held under the authority of the United States or of any State or political subdivision thereof.

(4) No otherwise privileged wire, oral, or electronic communication intercepted in accordance with, or in violation of, the provisions of this chapter shall lose its privileged character.

(5) When an investigative or law enforcement officer, while engaged in intercepting wire, oral, or electronic communications in the manner authorized herein, intercepts wire, oral, or electronic communications relating to offenses other than those specified in the order of authorization or approval, the contents thereof, and evidence derived therefrom, may be disclosed or used as provided in subsections (1) and (2) of this section. Such contents and any evidence derived therefrom may be used under subsection (3) of this section when authorized or approved by a judge of competent jurisdiction where such judge finds on subsequent application that the contents were otherwise intercepted in accordance with the provisions of this chapter. Such application shall be made as soon as practicable.

(6) Any investigative or law enforcement officer, or attorney for the Government, who by any means authorized by this chapter, has obtained knowledge of the contents of any wire, oral, or electronic communication, or evidence derived therefrom, may disclose such contents to any other Federal law enforcement, intelligence, protective, immigration, national defense, or national security official to the extent that such contents include foreign intelligence or counterintelligence (as defined in section 3 of the National Security Act of 1947 (50 U.S.C. 401a)), or foreign intelligence information (as defined in subsection (19) of section 2510 of this title), to assist the official who is to receive that information in the performance of his official duties. Any Federal official who receives information pursuant to this provision may use that information only as necessary in the conduct of that person's official duties subject to any limitations on the unauthorized disclosure of such information.

(7) Any investigative or law enforcement officer, or other Federal official in carrying out official duties as such Federal official, who by any means authorized by this chapter, has obtained knowledge of the contents of any wire, oral, or electronic communication, or evidence derived therefrom, may disclose such contents or derivative evidence to a foreign investigative or law enforcement officer to the extent that such disclosure is appropriate to the proper performance of the official duties of the officer making or receiving the disclosure, and foreign investigative or law enforcement officers may use or disclose such contents or derivative evidence to the extent such use or disclosure is appropriate to the proper performance of their official duties.

(8) Any investigative or law enforcement officer, or other Federal official in carrying out official duties as such Federal official, who by any means authorized by this chapter, has obtained knowledge of the contents of any wire, oral, or electronic communication, or evidence derived therefrom, may disclose such contents or derivative evidence to any appropriate Federal, State, local, or foreign government official to the extent that such contents or derivative evidence reveals a threat of actual or potential attack or other grave hostile acts of a foreign power or an agent of a foreign power, domestic or international sabotage, domestic or international terrorism, or clandestine intelligence gathering activities by an intelligence service or network of a foreign power or by an agent of a foreign power, within the United States or elsewhere, for the purpose of preventing or responding to such a threat. Any official who receives information pursuant to this provision may use that information only as necessary in the conduct of that person's official duties subject to any limitations on the unauthorized disclosure of such information, and any State, local, or foreign official who receives information pur-

suant to this provision may use that information only consistent with such guidelines as the Attorney General and Director of Central Intelligence shall jointly issue.

§ 2518. Procedure for interception of wire, oral, or electronic communications

(1) Each application for an order authorizing or approving the interception of a wire, oral, or electronic communication under this chapter shall be made in writing upon oath or affirmation to a judge of competent jurisdiction and shall state the applicant's authority to make such application. Each application shall include the following information:

(a) the identity of the investigative or law enforcement officer making the application, and the officer authorizing the application;

(b) a full and complete statement of the facts and circumstances relied upon by the applicant, to justify his belief that an order should be issued, including (I) details as to the particular offense that has been, is being, or is about to be committed, (ii) except as provided in subsection (11), a particular description of the nature and location of the facilities from which or the place where the communication is to be intercepted, (iii) a particular description of the type of communications sought to be intercepted, (iv) the identity of the person, if known, committing the offense and whose communications are to be intercepted;

(c) a full and complete statement as to whether or not other investigative procedures have been tried and failed or why they reasonably appear to be unlikely to succeed if tried or to be too dangerous;

(d) a statement of the period of time for which the interception is required to be maintained. If the nature of the investigation is such that the authorization for interception should not automatically terminate when the described type of communication has been first obtained, a particular description of facts establishing probable cause to believe that additional communications of the same type will occur thereafter;

(e) a full and complete statement of the facts concerning all previous applications known to the individual authorizing and making the application, made to any judge for authorization to intercept, or for approval of interceptions of, wire, oral, or electronic communications involving any of the same persons, facilities or places specified in the application, and the action taken by the judge on each such application; and

(f) where the application is for the extension of an order, a statement setting forth the results thus far obtained from the interception, or a reasonable explanation of the failure to obtain such results.

(2) The judge may require the applicant to furnish additional testimony or documentary evidence in support of the application.

(3) Upon such application the judge may enter an ex parte order, as requested or as modified, authorizing or approving interception of wire, oral, or electronic communications within the territorial jurisdiction of the court in which the judge is sitting (and outside that jurisdiction but within the United States in the case of a mobile interception device authorized by a Federal court within such jurisdiction), if the judge determines on the basis of the facts submitted by the applicant that—

(a) there is probable cause for belief that an individual is committing, has committed, or is about to commit a particular offense enumerated in section 2516 of this chapter;

(b) there is probable cause for belief that particular communications concerning that offense will be obtained through such interception;

(c) normal investigative procedures have been tried and have failed or reasonably appear to be unlikely to succeed if tried or to be too dangerous;

(d) except as provided in subsection (11), there is probable cause for belief that the facilities from which, or the place where, the wire, oral, or electronic communications are to be intercepted are being used, or are about to be used, in connection with the commission of such offense, or are leased to, listed in the name of, or commonly used by such person.

(4) Each order authorizing or approving the interception of any wire, oral, or electronic communication under this chapter shall specify—

(a) the identity of the person, if known, whose communications are to be intercepted;

(b) the nature and location of the communications facilities as to which, or the place where, authority to intercept is granted;

(c) a particular description of the type of communication sought to be intercepted, and a statement of the particular offense to which it relates;

(d) the identity of the agency authorized to intercept the communications, and of the person authorizing the application; and

(e) the period of time during which such interception is authorized, including a statement as to whether or not the interception shall automatically terminate when the described communication has been first obtained.

An order authorizing the interception of a wire, oral, or electronic communication under this chapter shall, upon request of the applicant, direct that a provider of wire or electronic communication service, landlord, custodian or other person shall furnish the applicant forthwith all information, facilities, and technical assistance necessary to accomplish the interception unobtrusively and with a minimum of interference with the services that such service provider, landlord, custodian, or person is according the person whose communications are to be intercepted. Any provider of wire or electronic communication service, landlord, custodian or other person furnishing such facilities or technical assistance shall be compensated therefor by the applicant for reasonable expenses incurred in providing such facilities or assistance. Pursuant to section 2522 of this chapter, an order may also be issued to enforce the assistance capability and capacity requirements under the Communications Assistance for Law Enforcement Act.

(5) No order entered under this section may authorize or approve the interception of any wire, oral, or electronic communication for any period longer than is necessary to achieve the objective of the authorization, nor in any event longer than thirty days. Such thirty-day period begins on the earlier of the day on which the investigative or law enforcement officer first begins to conduct an interception under the order or ten days after the order is entered. Extensions of an order may be granted, but only upon application for an extension made in accordance with subsection (1) of this section and the court making the findings required by subsection (3) of this section. The period of extension shall be no longer than the authorizing judge deems necessary to achieve the purposes for which it was granted and in no event for longer than thirty days. Every order and extension thereof shall contain a provision that the authorization to intercept shall be executed as soon as practicable, shall be conducted in such a way as to minimize the interception of communications not otherwise subject to interception under this chapter, and must terminate upon attainment of the authorized objective, or in any event in thirty days. In the event the intercepted communication is in a code or foreign language, and an expert

in that foreign language or code is not reasonably available during the interception period, minimization may be accomplished as soon as practicable after such interception. An interception under this chapter may be conducted in whole or in part by Government personnel, or by an individual operating under a contract with the Government, acting under the supervision of an investigative or law enforcement officer authorized to conduct the interception.

(6) Whenever an order authorizing interception is entered pursuant to this chapter, the order may require reports to be made to the judge who issued the order showing what progress has been made toward achievement of the authorized objective and the need for continued interception. Such reports shall be made at such intervals as the judge may require.

(7) Notwithstanding any other provision of this chapter, any investigative or law enforcement officer, specially designated by the Attorney General, the Deputy Attorney General, the Associate Attorney General or by the principal prosecuting attorney of any State or subdivision thereof acting pursuant to a statute of that State, who reasonably determines that—

(a) an emergency situation exists that involves—

(I) immediate danger of death or serious physical injury to any person,

(ii) conspiratorial activities threatening the national security interest, or

(iii) conspiratorial activities characteristic of organized crime, that requires a wire, oral, or electronic communication to be intercepted before an order authorizing such interception can, with due diligence, be obtained, and

(b) there are grounds upon which an order could be entered under this chapter to authorize such interception, may intercept such wire, oral, or electronic communication if an application for an order approving the interception is made in accordance with this section within forty-eight hours after the interception has occurred, or begins to occur. In the absence of an order, such interception shall immediately terminate when the communication sought is obtained or when the application for the order is denied, whichever is earlier. In the event such application for approval is denied, or in any other case where the interception is terminated without an order having been issued, the contents of any wire, oral, or electronic communication intercepted shall be treated as having been obtained in violation of this chapter, and an inventory shall be served as provided for in subsection (d) of this section on the person named in the application.

(8) (a) The contents of any wire, oral, or electronic communication intercepted by any means authorized by this chapter shall, if possible, be recorded on tape or wire or other comparable device. The recording of the contents of any wire, oral, or electronic communication under this subsection shall be done in such way as will protect the recording from editing or other alterations. Immediately upon the expiration of the period of the order, or extensions thereof, such recordings shall be made available to the judge issuing such order and sealed under his directions. Custody of the recordings shall be wherever the judge orders. They shall not be destroyed except upon an order of the issuing or denying judge and in any event shall be kept for ten years. Duplicate recordings may be made for use or disclosure pursuant to the provisions of subsections (1) and (2) of section 2517 of this chapter for investigations. The presence of the seal provided for by this subsection, or a satisfactory explanation for the absence thereof, shall be a prerequisite for the use or disclosure of the contents of any wire, oral, or electronic communication

or evidence derived therefrom under subsection (3) of section 2517.

(b) Applications made and orders granted under this chapter shall be sealed by the judge. Custody of the applications and orders shall be wherever the judge directs. Such applications and orders shall be disclosed only upon a showing of good cause before a judge of competent jurisdiction and shall not be destroyed except on order of the issuing or denying judge, and in any event shall be kept for ten years.

(c) Any violation of the provisions of this subsection may be punished as contempt of the issuing or denying judge.

(d) Within a reasonable time but not later than ninety days after the filing of an application for an order of approval under section 2518(7)(b) which is denied or the termination of the period of an order or extensions thereof, the issuing or denying judge shall cause to be served, on the persons named in the order or the application, and such other parties to intercepted communications as the judge may determine in his discretion that is in the interest of justice, an inventory which shall include notice of—

(1) the fact of the entry of the order or the application;

(2) the date of the entry and the period of authorized, approved or disapproved interception, or the denial of the application; and

(3) the fact that during the period wire, oral, or electronic communications were or were not intercepted.

The judge, upon the filing of a motion, may in his discretion make available to such person or his counsel for inspection such portions of the intercepted communications, applications and orders as the judge determines to be in the interest of justice. On an ex parte showing of good cause to a judge of competent jurisdiction the serving of the inventory required by this subsection may be postponed.

(9) The contents of any wire, oral, or electronic communication intercepted pursuant to this chapter or evidence derived therefrom shall not be received in evidence or otherwise disclosed in any trial, hearing, or other proceeding in a Federal or State court unless each party, not less than ten days before the trial, hearing, or proceeding, has been furnished with a copy of the court order, and accompanying application, under which the interception was authorized or approved. This ten-day period may be waived by the judge if he finds that it was not possible to furnish the party with the above information ten days before the trial, hearing, or proceeding and that the party will not be prejudiced by the delay in receiving such information.

(10)(a) Any aggrieved person in any trial, hearing, or proceeding in or before any court, department, officer, agency, regulatory body, or other authority of the United States, a State, or a political subdivision thereof, may move to suppress the contents of any wire or oral communication intercepted pursuant to this chapter, or evidence derived therefrom, on the grounds that—(i) the communication was unlawfully intercepted;

(ii) the order of authorization or approval under which it was intercepted is insufficient on its face; or

(iii) the interception was not made in conformity with the order of authorization or approval.

Such motion shall be made before the trial, hearing, or proceeding unless there was no opportunity to make such motion or the person was not aware of the grounds of the motion. If the motion is granted, the contents of the intercepted wire or oral communication, or evidence derived therefrom, shall be treated as having been obtained in violation of this chapter. The judge, upon the filing of such motion by the aggrieved person, may in his discretion make available to the aggrieved person or his counsel for inspection such portions of the intercepted communication or evidence derived therefrom as the judge determines to be in the interests of justice.

(b) In addition to any other right to appeal, the United States shall have the right to appeal from an order granting a motion to suppress made under paragraph (a) of this subsection, or the denial of an application for an order of approval, if the United States attorney shall certify to the judge or other official granting such motion or denying such application that the appeal is not taken for purposes of delay. Such appeal shall be taken within thirty days after the date the order was entered and shall be diligently prosecuted.

(c) The remedies and sanctions described in this chapter with respect to the interception of electronic communications are the only judicial remedies and sanctions for nonconstitutional violations of this chapter involving such communications.

(11) The requirements of subsections (1)(b)(ii) and (3)(d) of this section relating to the specification of the facilities from which, or the place where, the communication is to be intercepted do not apply if—

(a) in the case of an application with respect to the interception of an oral communication—

(I) the application is by a Federal investigative or law enforcement officer and is approved by the Attorney General, the Deputy Attorney General, the Associate Attorney General, an Assistant Attorney General, or an acting Assistant Attorney General;

(ii) the application contains a full and complete statement as to why such specification is not practical and identifies the person committing the offense and whose communications are to be intercepted; and

(iii) the judge finds that such specification is not practical; and

(b) in the case of an application with respect to a wire or electronic communication—

(i) the application is by a Federal investigative or law enforcement officer and is approved by the Attorney General, the Deputy Attorney General, the Associate Attorney General, an Assistant Attorney General, or an acting Assistant Attorney General;

(ii) the application identifies the person believed to be committing the offense and whose communications are to be intercepted and the applicant makes a showing of a purpose, on the part of that person, to thwart interception by changing facilities; and

(iii) the judge finds that such purpose has been adequately shown.

(iv) the order authorizing or approving the interception is limited to interception only for such time as it is reasonable to presume that the person identified in the application is or was reasonably proximate to the instrument through which such communication will be or was transmitted.

(12) An interception of a communication under an order with respect to which the requirements of subsections (1)(b)(ii) and (3)(d) of this section do not apply by reason of subsection (11) shall not begin until the facilities from which, or the place where, the communication is to be intercepted is ascertained by the person implementing the interception order. A provider of wire or electronic communications service that has received an order as provided for in subsection (11)(b) may move the court to modify or quash the order on the ground that its assistance with respect to the interception cannot be performed in a timely or reasonable fashion. The court, upon notice to the government, shall decide such a motion expeditiously.

§ 2519. Reports concerning intercepted wire, oral, or electronic communications

(1) Within thirty days after the expiration of an order (or each extension thereof) entered under section 2518, or the denial of an order approving an interception, the issuing or denying judge shall report to the Administrative Office of the United States Courts—

(a) the fact that an order or extension was applied for;

(b) the kind of order or extension applied for (including whether or not the order was an order with respect to which the requirements of sections 2518(1)(b)(ii) and 2518(3)(d) of this title did not apply by reason of section 2518(11) of this title);

(c) the fact that the order or extension was granted as applied for, was modified, or was denied;

(d) the period of interceptions authorized by the order, and the number and duration of any extensions of the order;

(e) the offense specified in the order or application, or extension of an order;

(f) the identity of the applying investigative or law enforcement officer and agency making the application and the person authorizing the application; and

(g) the nature of the facilities from which or the place where communications were to be intercepted.

(2) In January of each year the Attorney General, an Assistant Attorney General specially designated by the Attorney General, or the principal prosecuting attorney of a State, or the principal prosecuting attorney for any political subdivision of a State, shall report to the Administrative Office of the United States Courts—

(a) the information required by paragraphs (a) through (g) of subsection (1) of this section with respect to each application for an order or extension made during the preceding calendar year;

(b) a general description of the interceptions made under such order or extension, including (I) the approximate nature and frequency of incriminating communications intercepted, (ii) the approximate nature and frequency of other communications intercepted, (iii) the approximate number of persons whose communications were intercepted, and (iv) the approximate nature, amount, and cost of the manpower and other resources used in the interceptions;

(c) the number of arrests resulting from interceptions made under such order or extension, and the offenses for which arrests were made;

(d) the number of trials resulting from such interceptions; (e) the number of motions to suppress made with respect to such interceptions, and the number granted or denied;

(f) the number of convictions resulting from such interceptions and the offenses for which the convictions were obtained and a general assessment of the importance of the interceptions; and

(g) the information required by paragraphs (b) through (f) of this subsection with respect to orders or extensions obtained in a preceding calendar year.

(3) In April of each year the Director of the Administrative Office of the United States Courts shall transmit to the Congress a full and complete report concerning the number of applications for orders authorizing or approving the interception of wire, oral, or electronic communications pursuant to this chapter and the number of orders and extensions granted or denied pursuant to this chapter during the preceding calendar year. Such report shall include a summary and analysis of the data required to be filed with the Administrative Office by subsections (1) and (2) of this section. The Director of the Administrative Office of the United States Courts is authorized to issue binding regulations dealing with

the content and form of the reports required to be filed by subsections (1) and (2) of this section.

§ 2520. Recovery of civil damages authorized

(a) In general.—Except as provided in section 2511(2)(a)(ii), any person whose wire, oral, or electronic communication is intercepted, disclosed, or intentionally used in violation of this chapter may in a civil action recover from the person or entity which engaged in that violation such relief as may be appropriate.

(b) Relief.—In an action under this section, appropriate relief includes—(1) such preliminary and other equitable or declaratory relief as may be appropriate;

(2) damages under subsection (c) and punitive damages in appropriate cases; and

(3) a reasonable attorney's fee and other litigation costs reasonably incurred.

(c) Computation of damages.—(1) In an action under this section, if the conduct in violation of this chapter is the private viewing of a private satellite video communication that is not scrambled or encrypted or if the communication is a radio communication that is transmitted on frequencies allocated under subpart D of part 74 of the rules of the Federal Communications Commission that is not scrambled or encrypted and the conduct is not for a tortuous or illegal purpose or for purposes of direct or indirect commercial advantage or private commercial gain, then the court shall assess damages as follows:

(A) If the person who engaged in that conduct has not previously been enjoined under section 2511(5) and has not been found liable in a prior civil action under this section, the court shall assess the greater of the sum of actual damages suffered by the plaintiff, or statutory damages of not less than $50 and not more than $500.

(B) If, on one prior occasion, the person who engaged in that conduct has been enjoined under section 2511(5) or has been found liable in a civil action under this section, the court shall assess the greater of the sum of actual damages suffered by the plaintiff, or statutory damages of not less than $100 and not more than $1000.

(2) In any other action under this section, the court may assess as damages whichever is the greater of—

(A) the sum of the actual damages suffered by the plaintiff and any profits made by the violator as a result of the violation; or

(B) statutory damages of whichever is the greater of $100 a day for each day of violation or $10,000.

(d) Defense.—A good faith reliance on—

(1) a court warrant or order, a grand jury subpoena, a legislative authorization, or a statutory authorization;

(2) a request of an investigative or law enforcement officer under section 2518(7) of this title; or

(3) a good faith determination that section 2511(3) of this title permitted the conduct complained of; is a complete defense against any civil or criminal action brought under this chapter or any other law.

(e) Limitation.—A civil action under this section may not be commenced later than two years after the date upon which the claimant first has a reasonable opportunity to discover the violation.

§ 2522. Enforcement of the Communications Assistance for Law Enforcement Act

(a) Enforcement by court issuing surveillance order.—If a court authorizing an interception under this chapter, a State statute, or the Foreign Intelligence Surveillance Act of 1978 (50 U.S.C. 1801 et seq.) or authorizing use of a pen register or a trap and trace device under chapter 206 or a State statute finds that a telecommunications carrier has failed to comply with the requirements of the Communications Assistance for Law Enforcement Act, the court may, in accordance with section 108 of such Act, direct that the carrier comply forthwith and may direct that a provider of support services to the carrier or the manufacturer of the carrier's transmission or switching equipment furnish forthwith modifications necessary for the carrier to comply.

(b) Enforcement upon application by Attorney General.—The Attorney General may, in a civil action in the appropriate United States district court, obtain an order, in accordance with section 108 of the Communications Assistance for Law Enforcement Act, directing that a telecommunications carrier, a manufacturer of telecommunications transmission or switching equipment, or a provider of telecommunications support services comply with such Act.

(c) Civil penalty.—

(1) In general.—A court issuing an order under this section against a telecommunications carrier, a manufacturer of telecommunications transmission or switching equipment, or a provider of telecommunications support services may impose a civil penalty of up to $10,000 per day for each day in violation after the issuance of the order or after such future date as the court may specify.

(2) Considerations.—In determining whether to impose a civil penalty and in determining its amount, the court shall take into account—(A) the nature, circumstances, and extent of the violation;

(B) the violator's ability to pay, the violator's good faith efforts to comply in a timely manner, any effect on the violator's ability to continue to do business, the degree of culpability, and the length

of any delay in undertaking efforts to comply; and

(C) such other matters as justice may require.

(d) Definitions.—As used in this section, the terms defined in section 102 of the Communications Assistance for Law Enforcement Act have the meanings provided, respectively, in such section.

## UNITED STATES
## v.
## LONGORIA

### 177 F.3d 1179 (10th Cir. 1999)

*[Citations and footnotes omitted.]*

[Federal agents, with the help of a confidential informant, conducted a lengthy investigation of a drug smuggling operation in which Mr. Longoria was suspected of being involved. The informant owned a tire shop in Kansas City at which Mr. Longoria and his co-defendants allegedly unloaded drug shipments and conducted drug transactions. Under FBI supervision, the informant surreptitiously recorded conversations occurring at the tire shop on video- and audiotape. The tapes not only captured conversations between Mr. Longoria and the informant, but also recorded Mr. Longoria conversing with his accomplices in the informant's presence. Based on these recordings and other information provided by the informant, a grand jury indicted Mr. Longoria and his co-defendants on various drug-related offenses. Longoria moved to suppress tapes recorded by the government's informant, arguing they violated Title III of the Omnibus Crime Control and Safe Street Act of 1968. The trial court denied this motion. Mr. Longoria pleaded guilty, was sentenced, and appealed.]

BRORBY, Circuit Judge.

\* \* \*                                    \* \* \*

Title III only regulates the interception of certain types of communications; and, in order to receive Title III's protections, the communication at issue must fall within the definitions set out in § 2510 of the Act. Oral communications protected by Title III are those communications "uttered by a person exhibiting an expectation that such communication is not subject to interception under circumstances justifying such expectation." The legislative history of Title III instructs that Congress intended this definition to parallel the "reasonable expectation of privacy test" articulated by the Supreme Court in *Katz v. United States*. Accordingly, for Title III to apply, the court must conclude: (1) the defendant had an actual, subjective expectation of privacy—i.e., that his communications were not subject to interception; and (2) the defendant's expectation is one society would objectively consider reasonable.

In this case, the government's informant overheard and recorded Mr. Longoria conversing with his co-defendants in Spanish—a language the informant did not understand. In his motion to suppress and on appeal, Mr. Longoria argues he knew the informant could not understand Spanish and, therefore, he had a reasonable expectation of privacy. As such, Mr. Longoria contends the conversations with his co-defendants in Spanish were "oral communications" within the meaning of Title III and the government's failure to obtain court approval prior to recording the conversations warrants suppression. The district court disagreed, finding Mr. Longoria had no reasonable expectation of privacy in his conversations in the presence of the informant. Without such an expectation, the court concluded the conversations were not oral communications protected by Title III and denied the motion to suppress.

As discussed above, to determine if the conversations at issue constitute "oral communications" under Title III, we must consider whether (1) Mr. Longoria had an actual, subjective expectation of privacy and (2) whether that expectation is one that society is willing to recognize as reasonable. The district court made no specific findings as to the first issue. Nevertheless, based on Mr. Longoria's undisputed assertion that he had such an expectation, we assume for the purposes of this appeal Mr. Longoria did have an actual, subjective expectation of privacy. Thus, the key issue remaining is whether or not Mr. Longoria's expectation that the confidential informant would not disclose the substance of his conversation is one which society would objectively consider reasonable. We do not believe it is.

The Supreme Court has recognized that "[w]hat a person knowingly exposes to the public, even in his own home or office, is not a subject of Fourth Amendment protection." If a person knowingly exposes statements to the "plain view of outsiders," such statements are not protected under the Fourth Amendment because the speaker has not exhibited an "intention to keep them to himself." As the Court noted, "'[t]he risk of being overheard . . . is . . . inherent in the conditions of human society. It is the kind of risk we necessarily assume whenever we speak.'"

This principle applies with equal force to statements knowingly exposed to government informants. In *Hoffa*, defendants knowingly conversed with and in front of a man they believed to be an trusted accomplice but who in fact was a government informant. The Court allowed the informant to testify to conversations he overheard, noting the Fourth Amendment offers no protection for "a wrongdoer's misplaced belief that a person to whom he voluntarily confides his wrongdoing will not reveal it." Thus, one contemplating illegal activities assumes the risk that his companions may be reporting to the police and has no reasonable expectation of privacy in conversations he knowingly exposes to them.

In this case, Mr. Longoria voluntarily entered the informant's tire shop and knowingly made incriminating statements in the informant's presence. Although the conversations occurred in a back room not accessible to the general public, it is clear Mr. Longoria spoke in a tone clearly audible by the informant. Because Mr. Longoria exposed his statements in such a manner, we conclude he had no reasonable expectation that the person in whose presence he conducts conversations will not reveal those conversations to others. He assumed the risk that the informant would reveal his incriminating statements to law enforcement. As such, the informant was free to report the contents of the conversations to the FBI and to testify regarding them.

We emphasize that "the Fourth Amendment protects people, not places." If a defendant such as Mr. Longoria knowingly exposes his conversations to accomplices, even in a room not accessible to the general public, his conversations are not subject to Fourth Amendment protection from disclosure by such accomplices.

Mr. Longoria argues he had a reasonable expectation of privacy because he spoke in Spanish. Essentially, Mr. Longoria contends he did not "knowingly expose" his conversations to the informant because he spoke in a language he believed the informant could not understand. However, we find no precedent recognizing expectations of privacy based on a listener's ability to comprehend a foreign language and decline to find such an expectation in this case for several reasons. First, comprehension is a malleable concept not easily measured

by either the defendant or the court. Attempting to delineate a standard based on subjective evaluations of linguistic capabilities would be unworkable to say the least. More important, we do not find such an expectation to be objectively reasonable. In our increasingly multilingual society, one exposing conversations to others must necessarily assume the risk his statements will be overheard and understood. Although Mr. Longoria contends he knew the informant could not understand Spanish, the informant very well may have concealed his ability to speak Spanish the same as he concealed the recording equipment and his allegiance with law enforcement. Mr. Longoria exposed his statements by speaking in a manner clearly audible by the informant. His hope that the informant would not fully understand the contents of the conversation is not an expectation "society is prepared to recognize as 'reasonable.'"

Having thus established that Mr. Longoria had no reasonable expectation of privacy in statements made in the informant's presence, the admissibility of tape recordings of the same conversations becomes apparent. In *White*, the Supreme Court held "[i]f the conduct and revelations of an agent operating without electronic equipment do not invade the defendant's constitutionally justifiable expectations of privacy, neither does a simultaneous recording of the same conversations made by the agent." The Court emphasized that one contemplating illegal activities assumes the risk that his companions will report to the police, either directly or via electronic recording. "If the law gives no protection to the wrongdoer whose trusted accomplice is or becomes a police agent, neither should it protect him when that same agent has recorded or transmitted the conversations which are later offered in evidence to prove the State's case."

Accordingly, Mr. Longoria had no reasonable expectation that his conversations would not be "subject to interception" by his accomplices. He assumed the risk that his conversations would be overheard and recorded by the informant. As such, the conversations were not "oral communications" protected by Title III and the district court property denied Mr. Longoria's motion to suppress. The order of the district court is AFFIRMED.


## UNITED STATES
## v.
## WILLOUGHBY

### 860 F.2d 15 (2d Cir. 1988)

*[Citations and footnotes omitted.]*


[Quintin, Montgomery, and Willoughby were convicted of bank robbery, based in part on a recorded telephone conversation between Quinton and Willoughby while Quintin was in jail awaiting trial. Quinton placed the call to Willoughby with notice that inmate calls made on institutional telephones were recorded.]


KEARSE, Circuit Judge:

\* \* \*

Title III generally prohibits the intentional interception of wire communications, including telephone conversations, in the absence of authorization by court order. The prohibition against interception does not apply, however, when "one of the parties to the communication has given prior consent to such interception." Such consent may be express or implied. In the prison setting, when the institution has advised inmates that their telephone calls will be monitored and has prominently posted a notice that their "use of institutional telephones

constitutes consent to this monitoring," the inmates' use of those telephones constitutes implied consent to the monitoring within the meaning of Title III.

In the present case, the record established that MCC had a policy and practice of automatically recording and randomly monitoring all inmate calls, other than those properly placed to an attorney, made on institutional telephones. Inmates received ample notice of this practice. First, they were advised of the practice at orientation lectures upon their arrival at MCC; Quintin attended such a lecture in March 1987. In addition, MCC posted above each telephone available to inmates a bilingual sign, the English version of which read:

### NOTICE

The Bureau of Prisons reserves the authority to monitor conversations on this telephone. Your use of institutional telephones constitutes consent to this monitoring. A properly placed telephone call to an attorney is not monitored.

In these circumstances the district court could properly find that Quintin impliedly consented to the monitoring and taping of his call to Willoughby.

Finally, Quintin was given a form that stated as follows:

The Bureau of Prisons reserves the authority to monitor (this includes recording) conversations on any telephone located within its institutions, said monitoring to be done to preserve the security and orderly management of the institution and to protect the public. An inmate's use of institutional telephones constitutes consent to this monitoring.

Just above a line for the signature of the inmate, the form included the statement, "I understand that telephone calls I make from institution telephones may be monitored and recorded." Quintin signed the form on March 5, 1987. This sufficed to support a finding that Quintin expressly consented to the taping. We conclude that the court properly rejected Quintin's Title III contention.

The court also properly rejected the Title III arguments made on behalf of Willoughby. Whether or not Willoughby himself consented to the interception, the consent of Quintin alone, as a party to the conversation, sufficed to avoid the prohibitions of Title III. 18 U.S.C. § 2511(2)(c) (interception not prohibited when "one" of the parties to the communication has consented).

\* \* \*

## CONCLUSION

The judgments of conviction are affirmed.

# KYLLO

v.

# UNITED STATES

**533 U.S. 527, 121 S. Ct. 2038, 150 L. Ed. 2d 94 (2001)**

*[Citations and footnotes omitted.]*

JUSTICE SCALIA delivered the opinion of the Court.

This case presents the question whether the use of a thermal-imaging device aimed at a private home from a public street to detect relative amounts of heat within the home constitutes a 'search' within the meaning of the Fourth Amendment.

In 1991 Agent William Elliott of the United States Department of the Interior came to suspect that marijuana was being grown in the home belonging to petitioner Danny Kyllo, part of a triplex on Rhododendron Drive in Florence, Oregon. Indoor marijuana growth typically requires high-intensity lamps. In order to determine whether an amount of heat was emanating from petitioner's home consistent with the use of such lamps, at 3:20 A.M. on January 16, 1992, Agent Elliott and Dan Haas used an Agema Thermovision 210 thermal imager to scan the triplex. Thermal imagers detect infrared radiation, which virtually all objects emit but which is not visible to the naked eye. The imager converts radiation into images based on relative warmth—black is cool, white is hot, shades of gray connote relative differences; in that respect, it operates somewhat like a video camera showing heat images. The scan of Kyllo's home took only a few minutes and was performed from the passenger seat of Agent Elliott's vehicle across the street from the front of the house and also from the street in back of the house. The scan showed that the roof over the garage and a side wall of petitioner's home were relatively hot compared to the rest of the home and substantially warmer than neighboring homes in the triplex. Agent Elliott concluded that petitioner was using halide lights to grow marijuana in his house, which indeed he was. Based on tips from informants, utility bills, and the thermal imaging, a Federal Magistrate Judge issued a warrant authorizing a search of petitioner's home, and the agents found an indoor growing operation involving more than 100 plants. Petitioner was indicted on one count of manufacturing marijuana, in violation of 21 U.S.C. §841(a)(1). He unsuccessfully moved to suppress the evidence seized from his home and then entered a conditional guilty plea.

\* \* \*

The present case involves officers on a public street engaged in more than naked-eye surveillance of a home. We have previously reserved judgment as to how much technological enhancement of ordinary perception from such a vantage point, if any, is too much. While we upheld enhanced aerial photography of an industrial complex in *Dow Chemical*, we noted that we found it important that this is not an area immediately adjacent to a private home, where privacy expectations are most heightened.

It would be foolish to contend that the degree of privacy secured to citizens by the Fourth Amendment has been entirely unaffected by the advance of technology. For example, as the cases discussed above make clear, the technology enabling human flight has exposed to public view (and hence, we have said, to official observation) uncovered portions of the house and its curtilage that once were private. The question we confront today is what limits there are upon this power of technology to shrink the realm of guaranteed privacy.

The *Katz* test—whether the individual has an expectation of privacy that society is prepared to recognize as reasonable—has often been criticized as circular, and hence subjective and unpredictable. While it may be difficult to refine *Katz* when the search of areas such as telephone booths, automobiles, or even the curtilage and uncovered portions of residences are at issue, in the case of the search of the interior of homes—the prototypical and hence most commonly litigated area of protected privacy—there is a ready criterion, with roots deep in the common law, of the minimal expectation of privacy that exists, and that is acknowledged to be reasonable. To withdraw protection of this minimum expectation would be to permit police technology to erode the privacy guaranteed by the Fourth Amendment. We think that obtaining by

sense-enhancing technology any information regarding the interior of the home that could not otherwise have been obtained without physical "intrusion into a constitutionally protected area," constitutes a search—at least where (as here) the technology in question is not in general public use. This assures preservation of that degree of privacy against government that existed when the Fourth Amendment was adopted. On the basis of this criterion, the information obtained by the thermal imager in this case was the product of a search.

The Government maintains, however, that the thermal imaging must be upheld because it detected "only heat radiating from the external surface of the house." The dissent makes this its leading point, contending that there is a fundamental difference between what it calls "off-the-wall" observations and "through-the-wall surveillance." But just as a thermal imager captures only heat emanating from a house, so also a powerful directional microphone picks up only sound emanating from a house—and a satellite capable of scanning from many miles away would pick up only visible light emanating from a house. We rejected such a mechanical interpretation of the Fourth Amendment in *Katz*, where the eavesdropping device picked up only sound waves that reached the exterior of the phone booth. Reversing that approach would leave the homeowner at the mercy of advancing technology— including imaging technology that could discern all human activity in the home. While the technology used in the present case was relatively crude, the rule we adopt must take account of more sophisticated systems that are already in use or in development . . .

The Government also contends that the thermal imaging was constitutional because it did not "detect private activities occurring in private areas." It points out that in *Dow Chemical* we observed that the enhanced aerial photography did not reveal any "intimate details." *Dow Chemical*, however, involved enhanced aerial photography of an industrial complex, which does not share the Fourth Amendment sanctity of the home. The Fourth Amendment's protection of the home has never been tied to measurement of the quality or quantity of information obtained. In *Silverman*, for example, we made clear that any physical invasion of the structure of the home, "by even a fraction of an inch," was too much, and there is certainly no exception to the warrant requirement for the officer who barely cracks open the front door and sees nothing but the nonintimate rug on the vestibule floor. In the home, our cases show, all details are intimate details, because the entire area is held safe from prying government eyes. Thus, in *Karo*, the only thing detected was a can of ether in the home; and in *Arizona v. Hicks*, the only thing detected by a physical search that went beyond what officers lawfully present could observe in "plain view" was the registration number of a phonograph turntable. These were intimate details because they were details of the home, just as was the detail of how warm—or even how relatively warm—Kyllo was heating his residence.

Limiting the prohibition of thermal imaging to "intimate details" would not only be wrong in principle; it would be impractical in application, failing to provide "a workable accommodation between the needs of law enforcement and the interests protected by the Fourth Amendment." To begin with, there is no necessary connection between the sophistication of the surveillance equipment and the "intimacy" of the details that it observes—which means that one cannot say (and the police cannot be assured) that use of the relatively crude equipment at issue here will always be lawful. The Agema Thermovision 210 might disclose, for example, at what hour each night the lady of the house takes her daily sauna and bath—a detail that many would consider "intimate"; and a much more sophisticated system might detect nothing more intimate than the fact that someone left a closet light on. We could not, in other words, develop a rule approving only that through-the-wall surveillance which identifies objects no smaller than 36 by 36 inches, but would have to develop a jurisprudence specifying which home activities are "intimate" and which are not. And even when (if ever) that jurisprudence were fully developed, no police officer would be able to know in advance whether his through-the-wall surveillance picks up "intimate" details—and thus would be unable to know in advance whether it is constitutional.

\* \* \*

We have said that the Fourth Amendment draws "a firm line at the entrance to the house." That line, we think, must be not only firm but also bright—which requires clear specification of those methods of surveillance that require a warrant. While it is certainly possible to conclude from the videotape of the thermal imaging that occurred in this case that no "significant" compromise of the homeowner's privacy has occurred, we must take the long view, from the original meaning of the Fourth Amendment forward. "The Fourth Amendment is to be construed in the light of what was deemed an unreasonable search and seizure when it was adopted, and in a manner which will conserve public interests as well as the interests and rights of individual citizens." Where, as here, the Government uses a device that is not in general public use, to explore details of the home that would previously have been unknowable without physical intrusion, the surveillance is a "search" and is presumptively unreasonable without a warrant.

Since we hold the Thermovision imaging to have been an unlawful search, it will remain for the District Court to determine whether, without the evidence it provided, the search warrant issued in this case was supported by probable cause—and if not, whether there is any other basis for supporting admission of the evidence that the search pursuant to the warrant produced.

The judgment of the Court of Appeals is reversed; the case is remanded for further proceedings consistent with this opinion.

It is so ordered.

## UNITED STATES

### v.

### McIVER

### 186 F.3d 1119 (9th Cir. 1999), cert. denied, 528 U.S. 1177, 120 S.Ct. 1210, 145 L. Ed. 2d 1111 (2000)

*[Citations and footnotes omitted.]*

[United States Forest Service law enforcement officers observed transplanted marijuana plants growing in the Sunday Creek area of the Kootenai National Forest. Because it was not feasible to station officers around the clock to learn the identity of the persons responsible for growing the plants, the decision was made to install motion-activated video cameras to photograph persons who approached the area where the plants were growing. Over the course of the next few weeks, two men and a white Toyota 4Runner truck were photographed in the vicinity of the plants on several occasions. On September 18, Special Agent Deist saw the Toyota 4Runner on Highway 93 near the Sunday Creek area and followed it to a Burlington Northern parking lot. The driver appeared to be the same person captured on the photographs at the Sunday Creek marijuana garden. Special Agent Deist traced the vehicle's registration and determined that it was registered to Christopher McIver.

Early on the morning of September 23, 1997, Special Agent Deist placed a magnetized tracking device on the undercarriage of the Toyota 4Runner while it was parked in McIver's driveway outside the curtilage of his residence. The device was a Birddog 300 electronic transmitter that sends a weak signal or a "beep" to an audio unit ("monitor") installed in the officer's vehicle. When the monitoring vehicle gets close to the transmitter, the signal received in the audio unit becomes stronger.

On October 2, 1997, a surveillance officer observed the Toyota 4Runner leave the residence, headed in the direction of Sunday Creek area. Special Agent Deist followed the vehicle to the Radnor Creek turn-off from Highway 93.

The video surveillance cameras photographed two persons harvesting the marijuana plants and stuffing them into shiny plastic bags. At 10:30 P.M., the monitor received a new signal from the Birddog 300 electronic tracking device indicating that the Toyota 4Runner was again moving. A few minutes later, Special Agent Deist observed the vehicle turn onto Highway 93 headed south and followed it. Meanwhile, Officer Young checked the marijuana plants in the Sunday Creek area and reported that several had been harvested. Special Agent Deist alerted Officer Stewart, who was on surveillance duty at the McIver/Eberle residence that the Toyota 4Runner appeared to be returning to that location.

From an alley opposite McIver/Eberle residence, Officer Stewart, using night vision equipment, observed McIver and Eberle drive up, park, and remove two large plastic bags from the back of the Toyota 4Runner and carry the bags into the house. The bags had stems protruding from them.

McIver and Eberle were subsequently arrested. The video surveillance and tracking evidence was introduced at their trial, along with other evidence, and they were convicted.]

ALARCON, Circuit Judge.

* * *

We discuss each of the issues raised by McIver and Eberle, and the facts pertinent thereto, under separate headings.

## A. Warrantless placement of unmanned surveillance cameras on national forest land

McIver and Eberle maintain that the placement of unmanned cameras in a remote area of a national forest without a search warrant violated their reasonable expectation of privacy. They cite no authority that supports this novel proposition.

McIver and Eberle were on public land in a national forest when they cultivated their marijuana garden. Thus, they knowingly exposed their illegal activities to any person who visited that area. McIver and Eberle conceded that the observation of the marijuana plants by the Forest Service officers did not violate their Fourth Amendment rights. Clearly, the Forest Service officers had a right to carry out their law enforcement duties in each area of the Kootenai National Forest. It is also beyond dispute that the Forest Service could have stationed officers to conduct a 24-hour surveillance of the marijuana garden.

McIver and Eberle argue that the use of an unmanned camera, as opposed to a camera operated by a Forest Service officer, constitutes an unreasonable search in violation of the Fourth Amendment. . . . We reject the notion that the visual observation of the site became

unconstitutional merely because law enforcement chose to use a more cost-effective "mechanical eye" to continue the surveillance. We conclude that while McIver and Eberle may have anticipated that cultivating marijuana in a remote area of a national forest would not be observed by law enforcement officers, they have failed to demonstrate that they had an objectively reasonable expectation of privacy in their cultivation of marijuana in an area open to the public. We are also persuaded that the use of photographic equipment to gather evidence that could be lawfully observed by a law enforcement officer does not violate the Fourth Amendment. The use of a motion activated camera under these circumstances appears to us to be a prudent and efficient use of modern technology.

* * *

## B. Legality of the warrantless placement of the electronic tracking devices on the Toyota 4Runner

McIver argues that the act of placing the electronic tracking devices on the undercarriage of the Toyota 4Runner constituted an unreasonable search and seizure. He does not contend that the officers infringed his Fourth Amendment rights by monitoring the beeper as the Toyota 4Runner traveled on the streets and highways. He forthrightly cites *United States v. Knotts* for the proposition that there is no reasonable expectation of privacy while on a public thoroughfare. Instead, he asserts that the district court erred in denying his motion to suppress "all evidence gathered as a result of the tracking devices."

McIver first maintains that a search warrant was required because the officers committed a trespass by placing the electronic tracking devices on the undercarriage of the Toyota 4Runner while it was parked in his driveway. McIver concedes that the Toyota 4Runner was outside the curtilage. The record shows that the driveway and the apron in front of the garage were open to observation from persons passing by. The driveway was not enclosed by a fence and a gate.

In *Oliver*, the Court stated that "only the curtilage, not the neighboring open fields, warrants the Fourth Amendment protections that attach to the home." . . . Assuming *arguendo* that the officers committed a trespass in walking into McIver's open driveway, he has failed to demonstrate that he had a legitimate expectation of privacy cognizable under the Fourth Amendment in this portion of his property.

Secondly, McIver contends that the mere placement of the electronic tracking devices on the undercarriage of the Toyota 4Runner was an illegal search and seizure. "We must first determine whether this can be considered a 'search' subject to the Fourth Amendment—did it infringe an expectation of privacy that society is prepared to consider reasonable?" In *New York v. Class*, the Court held that there is no reasonable expectation of privacy in the exterior of a car because "[t]he exterior of a car, of course, is thrust into the public eye, and thus to examine it does not constitute a 'search'." In *Class*, the officer's conduct in opening the door of the respondent's car to move papers that obscured the vehicle's identification number ("VIN") located on the dashboard was held not to violate the Fourth Amendment. The Court reasoned that "[t]he VIN's mandated visibility makes it more similar to the exterior of the car than to the trunk or glove compartment." Relying in part on the Supreme Court's opinion in *Class*, the Tenth Circuit held in *United States v. Rascon-Ortiz* that "[t]he undercarriage is part of the car's exterior, and as such, is not afforded a reasonable expectation of privacy." In *Rascon-Ortiz*, an officer

"knelt down and looked under the car with a flashlight." Here, rather than making a visual inspection of the undercarriage of the Toyota 4Runner, the officers placed the magnetized electronic devices on the vehicle's undercarriage. In determining whether the officer's conduct was a search, we must decide whether McIver has demonstrated that he intended to preserve the undercarriage of the Toyota 4Runner as private—free from warrantless governmental intrusion. McIver did not produce any evidence to show that he intended to shield the undercarriage of his Toyota 4Runner from inspection by others. Furthermore, in placing the electronic devices on the undercarriage of the Toyota 4Runner, the officers did not pry into a hidden or enclosed area.

At oral argument, McIver argued that the placing of the electronic devices on the undercarriage of the Toyota 4Runner was a seizure of the vehicle. This argument ignores the principle articulated by the Supreme Court in *United States v. Karo*. There, the Court wrote:

A "seizure" of property occurs when "there is some meaningful interference with an individual's possessory interests in that property." Although the can may have contained an unknown and unwanted foreign object, it cannot be said that anyone's possessory interest was interfered with in a meaningful way. At most, there was a technical trespass on the space occupied by the beeper. The existence of a physical trespass is only marginally relevant to the question of whether the Fourth Amendment has been violated, however, for an actual trespass is neither necessary nor sufficient to establish a constitutional violation.

McIver did not present any evidence that the placement of the magnetized tracking devices deprived him of dominion and control of his Toyota 4Runner, nor did he demonstrate that the presence of these objects caused any damage to the electronic components of the vehicle. Under these circumstances, we hold that no seizure occurred because the officers did not meaningfully interfere with McIver's possessory interest in the Toyota 4Runner.

* * *

AFFIRMED.

# Cases Relating to Chapter 6

# Interrogations and Confessions

## ARIZONA
## v.
## FULMINANTE

### 499 U.S. 279, 111 S. Ct. 1246, 113 L. Ed. 2d 302 (1991)

[Fulminante was suspected of molesting and murdering a child in Arizona. While he was imprisoned in Florida on an unrelated offense, he shared a cell with Sarivola, who unbeknownst to him was an FBI informant. Sarivola made repeated attempts to influence the defendant to confess to the murder, but the defendant repeatedly denied involvement. Word of the heinous murder spread within the jail community and other inmates began to threaten Fulminante. Sarivola told Fulminante that he could protect the him, but that Fulminante would first have to tell him the truth about the murder. Fulminante then admitted to killing the child. Arizona tried Fulminante for murder and the confession was offered into evidence.]

Justice White delivered the opinion of the court.

* * *

We deal first with the State's contention that the court below erred in holding Fulminante's confession to have been coerced. . . . [T]he Arizona Supreme Court stated that a "determination regarding the voluntariness of a confession . . . must be viewed in a totality of the circumstances," and under that standard plainly found that Fulminante's statement to Sarivola had been coerced.

In applying the totality of the circumstances test to determine that the confession to Sarivola was coerced, the Arizona Supreme Court focused on a number of relevant facts. First, the court noted that "because [Fulminante] was an alleged child murderer, he was in danger of physical harm at the hands of other inmates." In addition, Sarivola was aware that Fulminante had been receiving "'rough treatment from the guys.'" Using his knowledge of these threats, Sarivola offered to protect Fulminante in exchange for a confession to Jeneane's murder, and "[i]n response to Sarivola's offer of protection, [Fulminante] confessed." Agreeing with Fulminante that "Sarivola's promise was 'extremely coercive,'" the Arizona court declared: "[T]he confession was obtained as a direct result of extreme coercion and was tendered in the belief that the defendant's life was in jeopardy if he did not confess. This is a true coerced confession in every sense of the word."

* * *

Although the question is a close one, we agree with the Arizona Supreme Court's conclusion that Fulminante's confession was coerced. The Arizona Supreme Court found a credible threat of physical violence unless Fulminante confessed. Our cases have made clear that a finding of coercion need not depend upon actual violence by a government agent; a credible threat is sufficient. As we have said, "coercion can be mental as well as physical, and . . . the blood of the accused is not the only hallmark of an unconstitutional inquisition." As in *Payne*, where the Court found that a confession was coerced because the interrogating police officer had promised that if the accused confessed, the officer would protect the accused from an angry mob outside the jailhouse door, so too here, the Arizona Supreme Court found that it was fear of physical violence, absent protection from his friend (and Government agent) Sarivola, which motivated Fulminante to confess. Accepting the Arizona court's finding, permissible on this record, that there was a credible threat of physical violence, we agree with its conclusion that Fulminante's will was overborne in such a way as to render his confession the product of coercion.

\* \* \*

## UNITED STATES CODE

## TITLE 18. CRIMES AND CRIMINAL PROCEDURE

§ 3501. Admissibility of confessions

(a) In any criminal prosecution brought by the United States or by the District of Columbia, a confession, as defined in subsection (e) hereof, shall be admissible in evidence if it is voluntarily given. Before such confession is received in evidence, the trial judge shall, out of the presence of the jury, determine any issue as to voluntariness. If the trial judge determines that the confession was voluntarily made it shall be admitted in evidence and the trial judge shall permit the jury to hear relevant evidence on the issue of voluntariness and shall instruct the jury to give such weight to the confession as the jury feels it deserves under all the circumstances.

(b) The trial judge in determining the issue of voluntariness shall take into consideration all the circumstances surrounding the giving of the confession, including

(1) the time elapsing between arrest and arraignment of the defendant making the confession, if it was made after arrest and before arraignment,

(2) whether such defendant knew the nature of the offense with which he was charged or of which he was suspected at the time of making the confession,

(3) whether or not such defendant was advised or knew that he was not required to make any statement and that any such statement could be used against him,

(4) whether or not such defendant had been advised prior to questioning of his right to the assistance of counsel; and

(5) whether or not such defendant was without the assistance of counsel when questioned and when giving such confession.

The presence or absence of any of the above-mentioned factors to be taken into consideration by the judge need not be conclusive on the issue of voluntariness of the confession.

(c) In any criminal prosecution by the United States or by the District of Columbia, a confession made or given by a person who is a defendant therein, while such person was under arrest or other detention in the custody of any law-enforcement officer or law-enforcement agency, shall not be inadmissible solely because of delay in bringing such person before a magistrate or other officer empowered to commit persons charged with offenses against the laws of the United States or of the District of Columbia if such confession is found by the trial judge to have been made voluntarily and if the weight to be given the confession is left to the jury and if such confession was made or given by such person within six hours immediately following his arrest or other detention: Provided, That the time limitation contained in this subsection shall not apply in any case in which the delay in bringing such person before such magistrate or other officer beyond such six-hour period is found by the trial judge to be reasonable considering the means of transportation and the distance to be traveled to the nearest available such magistrate or other officer.

(d) Nothing contained in this section shall bar the admission in evidence of any confession made or given voluntarily by any person to any other person without interrogation by anyone, or at any time at which the person who made or gave such confession was not under arrest or other detention.

(e) As used in this section, the term "confession" means any confession of guilt of any criminal offense or any self-incriminating statement made or given orally or in writing.

## MIRANDA
## v.
## ARIZONA

### 384 U.S. 436, 86 S. Ct. 1602, 16 L. Ed. 2d 694 (1966)

[On March 13, 1963, Ernesto Miranda was arrested at his home and taken in custody to a Phoenix police station. He was there identified by the complaining witness. The police then took him to "Interrogation Room No. 2" of the detective bureau, where he was questioned by two police officers. The officers admitted at trial that Miranda was not advised that he had a right to have an attorney present. Two hours later, the officers emerged from the interrogation room with a written confession signed by Miranda. At the top of the statement was a typed paragraph stating that the confession was made voluntarily, without threats or promises of immunity and "with full knowledge of my legal rights, understanding any statement I make may be used against me."

At his trial before a jury, the written confession was admitted into evidence over the objection of defense counsel, and the officers testified to the prior oral confession made by Miranda during the interrogation. Miranda was found guilty of kidnapping and rape. He was sentenced to 20 to 30 years' imprisonment on each count, the sentences to run concurrently. On appeal, the Supreme Court of Arizona held that Miranda's constitutional rights were not violated in obtaining the confession and affirmed the conviction. In reaching its decision, the court emphasized heavily the fact that Miranda did not specifically request counsel.]

MR. CHIEF JUSTICE WARREN delivered the opinion of the Court.

The cases before us raise questions which go to the roots of our concepts of American criminal jurisprudence: the restraints society must observe consistent with the Federal Constitution in prosecuting individuals for crime. More specifically, we deal with the admissibility of statements obtained from an individual who is subjected to custodial police interrogation and the necessity for procedures which assure that the individual is accorded his privilege under the Fifth Amendment to the Constitution not to be compelled to incriminate himself.

We dealt with certain phases of this problem recently in *Escobedo v. Illinois*. . . .

\* \* \*

We start here, as we did in *Escobedo*, with the premise that our holding is not an innovation in our jurisprudence, but an application of principles long recognized and applied in other settings. We have undertaken a thorough re-examination of the *Escobedo* decision and the principles it announced, and we reaffirm it. That case was but an explication of basic rights that are enshrined in our Constitution—that "No person . . . shall be compelled in any criminal case to be a witness against himself," and that "the accused shall . . . have the Assistance of Counsel"—rights which were put in jeopardy in this case through official overbearing. These precious rights were fixed in our Constitution only after centuries of persecution and struggle. And in the words of Chief Justice Marshall, they were secured "for ages to come, and designed to approach immortality as nearly as human institutions can approach it."

\* \* \*

Our holding will be spelled out with some specificity in the pages which follow but briefly stated it is this: the prosecution may not use statements, whether exculpatory or inculpatory, stemming from custodial interrogation of the defendant unless it demonstrates the use of procedural safeguards effective to secure the privilege against self-incrimination. By custodial interrogation, we mean questioning initiated by law enforcement officers after a person has been taken into custody or otherwise deprived of his freedom of action in any significant way. As for the procedural safeguards to be employed, unless other fully effective means are devised to inform accused persons of their right of

silence and to assure a continuous opportunity to exercise it, the following measures are required. Prior to any questioning, the person must be warned that he has a right to remain silent, that any statement he does make may be used as evidence against him, and that he has a right to the presence of an attorney, either retained or appointed. The defendant may waive effectuation of these rights, provided the waiver is made voluntarily, knowingly and intelligently. If, however, he indicates in any manner and at any stage of the process that he wishes to consult with an attorney before speaking there can be no questioning. Likewise, if the individual is alone and indicates in any manner that he does not wish to be interrogated, the police may not question him. The mere fact that he may have answered some questions or volunteered some statements on his own does not deprive him of the right to refrain from answering any further inquiries until he has consulted with an attorney and thereafter consents to be questioned.

\* \* \*

An understanding of the nature and setting of this in-custody interrogation is essential to our decisions today. The difficulty in depicting what transpires at such interrogations stems from the fact that in this country they have largely taken place incommunicado. From extensive factual studies undertaken in the early 1930's, including the famous Wickersham Report to Congress by a Presidential Commission, it is clear that police violence and the "third degree" flourished at that time. In a series of cases decided by this Court long after these studies, the police resorted to physical brutality—beating, hanging, whipping—and to sustained and protracted questioning incommunicado in order to extort confessions. . . .

* * *

Again, we stress that the modern practice of in-custody interrogation is psychologically rather than physically oriented. As we have stated before. "Since *Chambers v. Florida*, this Court has recognized that coercion can be mental as well as physical, and that the blood of the accused is not the only hallmark of an unconstitutional inquisition." Interrogation still takes place in privacy. Privacy results in secrecy and this in turn results in a gap in our knowledge as to what in fact goes on in the interrogation rooms. A valuable source of information about present police practices, however, may be found in various police manuals and texts which document procedures employed with success in the past, and which recommend various other effective tactics. These texts are used by law enforcement agencies themselves as guides. It should be noted that these texts professedly present the most enlightened and effective means presently used to obtain statements through custodial interrogation. By considering these texts and other data, it is possible to describe procedures observed and noted around the country.

* * *

To highlight the isolation and unfamiliar surroundings, the manuals instruct the police to display an air of confidence in the suspect's guilt and from outward appearance to maintain only an interest in confirming certain details. The guilt of the subject is to be posited as a fact. The interrogator should direct his comments toward the reasons why the subject committed the act, rather than court failure by asking the subject whether he did it. Like other men, perhaps the subject has had a bad family life, had an unhappy childhood, had too much to drink, had an unrequited desire for women. The officers are instructed to minimize the moral seriousness of the offense, to cast blame on the victim or on society. These tactics are designed to put the subject in a psychological state where his story is but an elaboration of what the police purport to know already—that he is guilty. Explanations to the contrary are dismissed and discouraged.

The texts thus stress that the major qualities an interrogator should possess are patience and perseverance. One writer describes the efficacy of these characteristics in this manner:

"In the preceding paragraphs emphasis has been placed on kindness and stratagems. The investigator will, however, encounter many situations where the sheer weight of his personality will be the deciding factor. Where emotional appeals and tricks are employed to no avail, he must rely on an oppressive atmosphere of dogged persistence. He must interrogate steadily and without relent, leaving the subject no prospect of surcease. He must dominate his subject and overwhelm him with his inexorable will to obtain the truth. He should interrogate for a spell of several hours pausing only for the subject's necessities in acknowledgment of the need to avoid a charge of duress that can be technically substantiated. In a serious case, the interrogation may continue for days, with the required intervals for food and sleep, but with no respite from the atmosphere of domination. It is possible in this way to induce the subject to talk without resorting to duress or coercion. The method should be used only when the guilt of the subject appears highly probable."

The manuals suggest that the suspect be offered legal excuses for his actions in order to obtain an initial admission of guilt. Where there is a suspected revenge-killing, for example, the interrogator may say:

"Joe, you probably didn't go out looking for this fellow with the purpose of shooting him. My guess is, however, that you expected something from him and that's why you carried a gun—for your own protection. You knew him for what he was, no good. Then when you met him he probably started using foul, abusive language and he gave some indication that he was about to pull a gun on you, and that's when you had to act to save your own life. That's about it, isn't it, Joe?"

Having then obtained the admission of shooting, the interrogator is advised to refer to circumstantial evidence which negates the self-defense explanation. This should enable him to secure the entire story. One text notes that "Even if he fails to do so, the inconsistency between the subject's original denial of the shooting and his present admission of at least doing the shooting will serve to deprive him of a self-defense 'out' at the time of trial."

When the techniques described above prove unavailing, the texts recommend they be alternated with a show of some hostility. One ploy often used has been termed the "friendly-unfriendly" or the "Mutt and Jeff" act:

". . . In this technique, two agents are employed. Mutt, the relentless investigator, who knows the subject is guilty and is not going to waste any time. He's sent a dozen men away for this crime and he's going to send the subject away for the full term. Jeff, on the other hand, is obviously a kindhearted man. He has a family himself. He has a brother who was involved in a little scrape like this. He disapproves of

Mutt and his tactics and will arrange to get him off the case if the subject will cooperate. He can't hold Mutt off for very long. The subject would be wise to make a quick decision. The technique is applied by having both investigators present while Mutt acts out his role. Jeff may stand by quietly and demur at some of Mutt's tactics. When Jeff makes his plea for cooperation, Mutt is not present in the room."

The interrogators sometimes are instructed to induce a confession out of trickery. The technique here is quite effective in crimes which require identification or which run in series. In the identification situation, the interrogator may take a break in his questioning to place the subject among a group of men in a line-up. "The witness or complainant (previously coached, if necessary) studies the line-up and confidently points out the subject as the guilty party." Then the questioning resumes "as though there were now no doubt about the guilt of the subject." . . .

The manuals also contain instructions for police on how to handle the individual who refuses to discuss the matter entirely, or who asks for an attorney or relatives. The examiner is to concede him the right to remain silent. "This usually has a very undermining effect. First of all, he is disappointed in his expectation of an unfavorable reaction on the part of the interrogator. Secondly, a concession of this right to remain silent impresses the subject with the apparent fairness of his interrogator." After this psychological conditioning, however, the officer is told to point out the incriminating significance of the suspect's refusal to talk: "Joe, you have a right to remain silent. That's your privilege and I'm the last person in the world who'll try to take it away from you. If that's the way you want to leave this, O.K. But let me ask you this. Suppose you were in my shoes and I were in yours and you called me in to ask me about this and I told you, 'I don't want to answer any of your questions.' You'd think I had something to hide, and you'd probably be right in thinking that. That's exactly what I'll have to think about you, and so will everybody else. So let's sit here and talk this whole thing over."

Few will persist in their initial refusal to talk, it is said, if this monologue is employed correctly.

In the event that the subject wishes to speak to a relative or an attorney, the following advice is tendered: "(T)he interrogator should respond by suggesting that the subject first tell the truth to the interrogator himself rather than get anyone else involved in the matter. If the request is for an attorney, the interrogator may suggest that the subject save himself or his family the expense of any such professional service, particularly if he is innocent of the offense under investigation. The interrogator may also add, 'Joe, I'm only looking for the truth, and if you're telling the truth, that's it. You can handle this by yourself.'"

From these representative samples of interrogation techniques, the setting prescribed by the manuals and observed in practice becomes clear. In essence, it is this: "To be alone with the subject is essential to prevent distraction and to deprive him of any outside support. The aura of confidence in his guilt undermines his will to resist. He merely confirms the preconceived story the police seek to have him describe. Patience and persistence, at times relentless questioning, are employed. To obtain a confession, the interrogator must 'patiently maneuver himself or his quarry into a position from which the desired objective may be attained.'" When normal procedures fail to produce the needed result, the police may resort to deceptive stratagems such as giving false legal advice. It is important to keep the sub-

ject off balance, for example, by trading on his insecurity about himself or his surroundings. The police then persuade, trick, or cajole him out of exercising his constitutional rights.

\* \* \*

In the cases before us today, given this background, we concern ourselves primarily with this interrogation atmosphere and the evils it can bring. In No. 759, *Miranda v. Arizona*, the police arrested the defendant and took him to a special interrogation room where they secured a confession. . . .

In these cases, we might not find the defendants' statements to have been involuntary in traditional terms. Our concern for adequate safeguards to protect precious Fifth Amendment rights is, of course, not lessened in the slightest. In each of the cases, the defendant was thrust into an unfamiliar atmosphere and run through menacing police interrogation procedures. The potentiality for compulsion is forcefully apparent, for example, in *Miranda*, where the indigent Mexican defendant was a seriously disturbed individual with pronounced sexual fantasies. . . . To be sure, the records do not evince overt physical coercion or patent psychological ploys. The fact remains that in none of these cases did the officers undertake to afford appropriate safeguards at the outset of the interrogation to insure that the statements were truly the product of free choice.

It is obvious that such an interrogation environment is created for no purpose other than to subjugate the individual to the will of his examiner. This atmosphere carries its own badge of intimidation. To be sure, this is not physical intimidation, but it is equally destructive of human dignity. The current practice of incommunicado interrogation is at odds with one of our Nation's most cherished principles—that the individual may not be compelled to incriminate himself. Unless adequate protective devices are employed to dispel the compulsion inherent in custodial surroundings, no statement obtained from the defendant can truly be the product of his free choice.

* * *

Today, . . . there can be no doubt that the Fifth Amendment privilege is available outside of criminal court proceedings and serves to protect persons in all settings in which their freedom of action is curtailed in any significant way from being compelled to incriminate themselves. We have concluded that without proper safeguards the process of in-custody interrogation of persons suspected or accused of crime contains inherently compelling pressures which work to undermine the individual's will to resist and to compel him to speak where he would not otherwise do so freely. In order to combat these pressures and to permit a full opportunity to exercise the privilege against self-incrimination, the accused must be adequately and effectively apprised of his rights and the exercise of those rights must be fully honored.

. . . We encourage Congress and the States to continue their laudable search for increasingly effective ways of protecting the rights of the individual while promoting efficient enforcement of our criminal laws. However, unless we are shown other procedures which are at least as effective in apprising accused persons of their right of silence and in assuring a continuous opportunity to exercise it, the following safeguards must be observed.

At the outset, if a person in custody is to be subjected to interrogation, he must first be informed in clear and unequivocal terms that he has the right to remain silent. For those unaware of the privilege, the warning is needed simply to make them aware of it—the threshold requirement for an intelligent decision as to its exercise. More important, such a warning is an absolute prerequisite in overcoming the inherent pressures of the interrogation atmosphere. It is not just the subnormal or woefully ignorant who succumb to an interrogator's imprecations, whether implied or expressly stated, that the interrogation will continue until a confession is obtained or that silence in the face of accusation is itself damning and will bode ill when presented to a jury. Further, the warning will show the individual that his interrogators are prepared to recognize his privilege should he choose to exercise it.

The Fifth Amendment privilege is so fundamental to our system of constitutional rule and the expedient of giving an adequate warning as to the availability of the privilege so simple, we will not pause to inquire in individual cases whether the defendant was aware of his rights without a warning being given. Assessments of the knowledge the defendant possessed, based on information as to his age, education, intelligence, or prior contact with authorities, can never be more than speculation; a warning is a clear-cut fact. More important, whatever the background of the person interrogated, a warning at the time of the interrogation is indispensable to overcome its pressures and to insure that the individual knows he is free to exercise the privilege at that point in time.

The warning of the right to remain silent must be accompanied by the explanation that anything said can and will be used against the individual in court. This warning is needed in order to make him aware not only of the privilege, but also of the consequences of forgoing it. It is only through an awareness of these consequences that there can be any assurance of real understanding and intelligent exercise of the privilege. Moreover, this warning may serve to make the individual more acutely aware that he is faced with a phase of the adversary system that he is not in the presence of persons acting solely in his interest.

The circumstances surrounding in-custody interrogation can operate very quickly to overbear the will of one merely made aware of his privilege by his interrogators. Therefore, the right to have counsel present at the interrogation is indispensable to the protection of the Fifth Amendment privilege under the system we delineate today. Our aim is to assure that the individual's right to choose between silence and speech remains unfettered throughout the inter-rogation process. A once-stated warning, delivered by those who will conduct the interrogation, cannot itself suffice to that end among those who most require knowledge of their rights. A mere warn-ing given by the interrogators is not alone sufficient to accomplish that end. Prosecutors themselves claim that the admonishment of the right to remain silent without more "will benefit only the recidivist and the professional." Even preliminary advice given to the accused by his own attorney can be swiftly over-come by the secret interrogation process. Thus, the need for counsel to protect the Fifth Amendment privilege compre-hends not merely a right to consult with counsel prior to questioning, but also to have counsel present during any ques-tioning if the defendant so desires.

The presence of counsel at the interro-gation may serve several significant sub-sidiary functions as well. If the accused decides to talk to his interrogators, the assistance of counsel can mitigate the dangers of untrustworthiness. With a lawyer present the likelihood that the police will practice coercion is reduced, and if coercion is nevertheless exercised the lawyer can testify to it in court. The presence of a lawyer can also help to guarantee that the accused gives a fully accurate statement to the police and that the statement is rightly reported by the prosecution at trial.

An individual need not make a pre-interrogation request for a lawyer. While such request affirmatively secures his right to have one, his failure to ask for a lawyer does not constitute a waiver. No effective waiver of the right to counsel during interrogation can be recognized unless specifically made after the warn-ings we here delineate have been given. The accused who does not know his rights and therefore does not make a request may be the person who most needs counsel. . . .

* * *

Accordingly we hold that an individ-ual held for interrogation must be clear-ly informed that he has the right to con-sult with a lawyer and to have the lawyer with him during interrogation under the system for protecting the privilege we delineate today. As with the warnings of the right to remain silent and that any-thing stated can be used in evidence against him, this warning is an absolute prerequisite to interrogation. No amount of circumstantial evidence that the per-son may have been aware of this right will suffice to stand in its stead. Only through such a warning is there ascer-tainable assurance that the accused was aware of this right.

If an individual indicates that he wish-es the assistance of counsel before any interrogation occurs, the authorities can-not rationally ignore or deny his request on the basis that the individual does not have or cannot afford a retained attorney. The financial ability of the individual has no relationship to the scope of the rights involved here. The privilege against self-incrimination secured by the Constitution applies to all individuals.

The need for counsel in order to protect the privilege exists for the indigent as well as the affluent. In fact, were we to limit these constitutional rights to those who can retain an attorney, our decisions today would be of little significance. The cases before us as well as the vast majority of confession cases with which we have dealt in the past involve those unable to retain counsel. While authorities are not required to relieve the accused of his poverty, they have the obligation not to take advantage of indigence in the administration of justice. Denial of counsel to the indigent at the time of interrogation while allowing an attorney to those who can afford one would be no more supportable by reason or logic than the similar situation at trial and on appeal struck down in *Gideon v. Wainwright*.

In order fully to apprise a person interrogated of the extent of his rights under this system then, it is necessary to warn him not only that he has the right to consult with an attorney, but also that if he is indigent a lawyer will be appointed to represent him. Without this additional warning, the admonition of the right to consult with counsel would often be understood as meaning only that he can consult with a lawyer if he has one or has the funds to obtain one. The warning of a right to counsel would be hollow if not couched in terms that would convey to the indigent—the person most often subjected to interrogation—the knowledge that he too has a right to have counsel present. As with the warnings of the right to remain silent and of the general right to counsel, only by effective and express explanation to the indigent of this right can there be assurance that he was truly in a position to exercise it.

Once warnings have been given, the subsequent procedure is clear. If the individual indicates in any manner, at any time prior to or during questioning, that he wishes to remain silent, the interrogation must cease. At this point he has shown that he intends to exercise his Fifth Amendment privilege; any statement taken after the person invokes his privilege cannot be other than the product of compulsion, subtle or otherwise. Without the right to cut off questioning, the setting of in-custody interrogation operates on the individual to overcome free choice in producing a statement after the privilege has been once invoked. If the individual states that he wants an attorney, the interrogation must cease until an attorney is present. At that time, the individual must have an opportunity to confer with the attorney and to have him present during any subsequent questioning. If the individual cannot obtain an attorney and he indicates that he wants one before speaking to police, they must respect his decision to remain silent. This does not mean, as some have suggested, that each police station must have a "station house lawyer" present at all times to advise prisoners. It does mean, however, that if police propose to interrogate a person they must make known to him that he is entitled to a lawyer and that if he cannot afford one, a lawyer will be provided for him prior to any interrogation. If authorities conclude that they will not provide counsel during a reasonable period of time in which investigation in the field is carried out, they may refrain from doing so without violating the person's Fifth Amendment privilege so long as they do not question him during that time.

If the interrogation continues without the presence of an attorney and a statement is taken, a heavy burden rests on the government to demonstrate that the defendant knowingly and intelligently waived his privilege against self-incrimination and his right to retained or appointed counsel. This Court has always set high standards of proof for the waiver of constitutional rights, and we reassert these standards as applied to in-custody interrogation. Since the State is responsible for establishing the isolated circumstances under which the interrogation takes place and has the only means of making available corroborated evidence of warnings given during incommunicado interrogation, the burden is rightly on its shoulders.

An express statement that the individual is willing to make a statement and does not want an attorney followed closely by a statement could constitute a waiver. But a valid waiver will not be presumed simply from the silence of the accused after warnings are given or simply from the fact that a confession was in fact eventually obtained. A statement we made in *Carnley v. Cochran*, is applicable here: "Presuming waiver from a silent record is impermissible. The record must show, or there must be an allegation and evidence which show, that an accused was offered counsel but intelligently and understandingly rejected the offer. Anything less is not waiver." Moreover, where in-custody interrogation is involved, there is no room for the contention that the privilege is waived if the individual answers some questions or gives some information on his own prior to invoking his right to remain silent when interrogated.

Whatever the testimony of the authorities as to waiver of rights by an accused, the fact of lengthy interrogation or incommunicado incarceration before a statement is made is strong evidence that the accused did not validly waive his rights. In these circumstances the fact that the individual eventually made a statement is consistent with the conclusion that the compelling influence of the interrogation finally forced him to do so. It is inconsistent with any notion of a voluntary relinquishment of the privilege. Moreover, any evidence that the accused was threatened, tricked, or cajoled into a waiver will, of course, show that the defendant did not voluntarily waive his privilege. The requirement of warnings and waiver of rights is a fundamental with respect to the Fifth Amendment privilege and not simply a preliminary ritual to existing methods of interrogation.

The warnings required and the waiver necessary in accordance with our opinion today are, in the absence of a fully effective equivalent, prerequisites to the admissibility of any statement made by a defendant. No distinction can be drawn between statements which are direct confessions and statements which amount to "admissions" of part or all of an offense. The privilege against self-incrimination protects the individual from being compelled to incriminate himself in any manner; it does not distinguish degrees of incrimination. Similarly, for precisely the same reason, no distinction may be drawn between inculpatory statements and statements alleged to be merely "exculpatory." If a statement made were in fact truly exculpatory it would, of course, never be used by the prosecution. In fact, statements merely intended to be exculpatory by the defendant are often used to impeach his testimony at trial or to demonstrate untruths in the statement given under interrogation and thus to prove guilt by implication. These statements are incriminating in any meaningful sense of the word and may not be used without the full warnings and effective waiver required for any other statement. In *Escobedo* itself, the defendant fully intended his accusation of another as the slayer to be exculpatory as to himself.

The principles announced today deal with the protection which must be given to the privilege against self-incrimination when the individual is first subjected to police interrogation while in custody at the station or otherwise deprived of his freedom of action in any significant way. It is at this point that our adversary system of criminal proceedings commences, distinguishing itself at the outset from the inquisitorial system recognized in some countries. Under the system of warnings we delineate today or under any other system which may be devised and found effective, the safeguards to be erected about the privilege must come into play at this point.

Our decision is not intended to hamper the traditional function of police officers in investigating crime. When an individual is in custody on probable cause, the police may, of course, seek out evidence in the field to be used at trial against him. Such investigation may include inquiry of persons not under restraint. General on-the-scene questioning as to facts surrounding a crime or other general questioning of citizens in the fact-finding process is not affected by our holding. It is an act of responsible citizenship for individuals to give whatever information they may have to aid in law enforcement. In such situations the compelling atmosphere inherent in the process of in-custody interrogation is not necessarily present.

In dealing with statements obtained through interrogation, we do not purport to find all confessions inadmissible. Confessions remain a proper element in law enforcement. Any statement given freely and voluntarily without any compelling influences is, of course, admissible in evidence. The fundamental import of the privilege while an individual is in custody is not whether he is allowed to talk to the police without the benefit of warnings and counsel, but whether he can be interrogated. There is no requirement that police stop a person who enters a police station and states that he wishes to confess to a crime, or a person who calls the police to offer a confession or any other statement he desires to make. Volunteered statements of any kind are not barred by the Fifth Amendment and their admissibility is not affected by our holding today.

To summarize, we hold that when an individual is taken into custody or otherwise deprived of his freedom by the authorities in any significant way and is subjected to questioning, the privilege against self-incrimination is jeopardized. Procedural safeguards must be employed to protect the privilege and unless other fully effective means are adopted to notify the person of his right of silence and to assure that the exercise of the right will be scrupulously honored, the following measures are required. He must be warned prior to any questioning that he has the right to remain silent, that anything he says can be used against him in a court of law, that he has the right to the presence of an attorney, and that if he cannot afford an attorney one will be appointed for him prior to any questioning if he so desires. Opportunity to exercise these rights must be afforded to him throughout the interrogation. After such warnings have been given, and such opportunity afforded him, the individual may knowingly and intelligently waive these rights and agree to answer questions or make a statement. But unless and until such warnings and waiver are demonstrated by the prosecution at trial, no evidence obtained as a result of interrogation can be used against him.

\* \* \*

We turn now to these facts to consider the application to these cases of the constitutional principles discussed above. . . .

\* \* \*

. . . From the testimony of the officers and by the admission of respondent, it is clear that Miranda was not in any way apprised of his right to consult with an attorney and to have one present during the interrogation, nor was his right not to be compelled to incriminate himself effectively protected in any other manner. Without these warnings the statements were inadmissible. The mere fact that he signed a statement which contained a typed-in clause stating that he had "full knowledge" of his "legal rights" does not approach the knowing and intelligent waiver required to relinquish constitutional rights.

* * *

Therefore, in accordance with the foregoing, the judgments of the Supreme Court of Arizona in No. 759, of the New York Court of Appeals in No. 760, and of the Court of Appeals for the Ninth Circuit in No. 761 are reversed. . . .

It is so ordered.

# BERKEMER
# v.
# McCARTY

## 468 U.S. 420, 104 S. Ct. 3138, 82 L. Ed. 2d 317 (1985)

*[Citations and footnotes omitted.]*

[Trooper Williams pulled respondent's car over after observing him weaving in and out of traffic on an interstate highway. He asked respondent to get out of the car. Upon noticing that respondent was having difficulty standing, Trooper Williams decided to take him into custody, but did not inform him of this fact until after asking him whether he had been using intoxicants. Respondent replied that "he had consumed two beers and had smoked several joints of marijuana a short time before." Williams thereupon formally placed respondent under arrest and transported him in the patrol car to the Franklin County Jail. At no time did Williams administer *Miranda* warnings.]

JUSTICE MARSHALL delivered the opinion of the Court.

. . . [D]oes the roadside questioning of a motorist detained pursuant to a traffic stop constitute custodial interrogation for the purposes of the doctrine enunciated in *Miranda*?

* * *

. . . Respondent urges that it should, on the ground that *Miranda* by its terms applies whenever "a person has been taken into custody or otherwise deprived of his freedom of action in any significant way." Petitioner contends that a holding that every detained motorist must be advised of his rights before being questioned would constitute an unwarranted extension of the *Miranda* doctrine.

It must be acknowledged at the outset that a traffic stop significantly curtails the "freedom of action" of the driver and the passengers, if any, of the detained vehicle. Under the law of most States, it is a crime either to ignore a policeman's signal to stop one's car or, once having stopped, to drive away without permission. Certainly few motorists would feel free either to disobey a directive to pull over or to leave the scene of a traffic stop without being told they might do so. Partly for these reasons, we have long acknowledged that "stopping an automobile and detaining its occupants constitute a 'seizure' within the meaning of [the Fourth] Amendmen[t], even though the purpose of the stop is limited and the resulting detention quite brief."

However, we decline to accord talismanic power to the phrase in the *Miranda* opinion emphasized by respondent. Fidelity to the doctrine announced in *Miranda* requires that it be enforced strictly, but only in those types of situations in which the concerns that powered the decision are implicated. Thus, we must decide whether a traffic stop exerts upon a detained person pressures that sufficiently impair his free exercise of his privilege against self-incrimination to require that he be warned of his constitutional rights.

Two features of an ordinary traffic stop mitigate the danger that a person questioned will be induced "to speak where he would not otherwise do so freely," First, detention of a motorist pursuant to a traffic stop is presumptively temporary and brief. The vast majority of roadside detentions last only a few minutes. A motorist's expectations, when he sees a policeman's light flashing behind him, are that he will be obliged to spend a short period of time answering questions and waiting while the officer checks his license and registration, that he may then be given a citation, but that in the end he most likely will be allowed to continue on his way. In this respect, questioning incident to an ordinary traffic stop is quite different from stationhouse interrogation, which frequently is prolonged, and in which the detainee often is aware that questioning will continue until he provides his interrogators the answers they seek.

Second, circumstances associated with the typical traffic stop are not such that the motorist feels completely at the mercy of the police. To be sure, the aura of authority surrounding an armed, uniformed officer and the knowledge that the officer has some discretion in deciding whether to issue a citation, in combination, exert some pressure on the detainee to respond to questions. But other aspects of the situation substantially offset these forces. Perhaps most importantly, the typical traffic stop is public, at least to some degree. Passersby, on foot or in other cars, witness the interaction of officer and motorist. This exposure to public view both reduces the ability of an unscrupulous policeman to

use illegitimate means to elicit self-incriminating statements and diminishes the motorist's fear that, if he does not cooperate, he will be subjected to abuse. The fact that the detained motorist typically is confronted by only one or at most two policemen further mutes his sense of vulnerability. In short, the atmosphere surrounding an ordinary traffic stop is substantially less "police dominated" than that surrounding the kinds of interrogation at issue in Miranda itself.

In both of these respects, the usual traffic stop is more analogous to a so-called "*Terry* stop," than to a formal arrest. Under the Fourth Amendment, we have held, a policeman who lacks probable cause but whose "observations lead him reasonably to suspect" that a particular person has committed, is committing, or is about to commit a crime, may detain that person briefly in order to "investigate the circumstances that provoke suspicion." "[T]he stop and inquiry must be 'reasonably related in scope to the justification for their initiation.'" Typically, this means that the officer may ask the detainee a moderate number of questions to determine his identity and to try to obtain information confirming or dispelling the officer's suspicions. But the detainee is not obliged to respond. And, unless the detainee's answers provide the officer with probable cause to arrest him, he must then be released. The comparatively nonthreatening character of detentions of this sort explains the absence of any suggestion in our opinions that *Terry* stops are subject to the dictates of *Miranda*. The similarly noncoercive aspect of ordinary traffic stops prompts us to hold that persons temporarily detained pursuant to such stops are not "in custody" for the purposes of *Miranda*.

Respondent contends that to "exempt" traffic stops from the coverage of *Miranda* will open the way to widespread abuse. Policemen will simply delay formally arresting detained motorists, and will subject them to sustained and intimidating interrogation at the scene of their initial detention. . . .

We are confident that the state of affairs projected by respondent will not come to pass. It is settled that the safeguards prescribed by *Miranda* become applicable as soon as a suspect's freedom of action is curtailed to a "degree associated with formal arrest." If a motorist who has been detained pursuant to a traffic stop thereafter is subjected to treatment that renders him "in custody" for practical purposes, he will be entitled to the full panoply of protections prescribed by *Miranda*.

Admittedly, our adherence to the doctrine just recounted will mean that the police and lower courts will continue occasionally to have difficulty deciding exactly when a suspect has been taken into custody. Either a rule that *Miranda* applies to all traffic stops or a rule that a suspect need not be advised of his rights until he is formally placed under arrest would provide a clearer, more easily administered line. However, each of these two alternatives has drawbacks that make it unacceptable. The first would substantially impede the enforcement of the Nation's traffic laws—by compelling the police either to take the time to warn all detained motorists of their constitutional rights or to forgo use of self-incriminating statements made by those motorists—while doing little to protect citizens' Fifth Amendment rights. The second would enable the police to circumvent the constraints on custodial interrogations established by *Miranda*.

Turning to the case before us, we find nothing in the record that indicates that respondent should have been given *Miranda* warnings at any point prior to the time Trooper Williams placed him under arrest. For the reasons indicated above, we reject the contention that the initial stop of respondent's car, by itself, rendered him "in custody." And respondent has failed to demonstrate that, at any time between the initial stop and the arrest, he was subjected to restraints comparable to those associated with a formal arrest. Only a short period of time elapsed between the stop and the arrest. At no point during that interval was respondent informed that his detention would not be temporary. Although Trooper Williams apparently decided as soon as respondent stepped out of his car that respondent would be taken into custody and charged with a traffic offense, Williams never communicated his intention to respondent. A policeman's unarticulated plan has no bearing on the question whether a suspect was "in custody" at a particular time; the only relevant inquiry is how a reasonable man in the suspect's position would have understood his situation. Nor do other aspects of the interaction of Williams and respondent support the contention that respondent was exposed to "custodial interrogation" at the scene of the stop. From aught that appears in the stipulation of facts, a single police officer asked respondent a modest number of questions and requested him to perform a simple balancing test at a location visible to passing motorists. Treatment of this sort cannot fairly be characterized as the functional equivalent of formal arrest.

\* \* \*

Accordingly, the judgment of the Court of Appeals is

Affirmed.
[Concurring opinion omitted.]

## RHODE ISLAND

v.

## INNIS

### 446 U.S. 291, 100 S. Ct. 1682, 64 L. Ed. 2d 297 (1980)

*[Citations and footnotes omitted.]*

[A taxicab driver who was robbed by a man with a sawed-off shotgun identified Innis from a picture shown him by police. Shortly thereafter, a patrolman spotted Innis on the street, arrested him, and advised him of his *Miranda* rights. Innis stated that he understood his rights and wanted to speak with a lawyer. He was then placed in a squad car to be driven to the police station, accompanied by three officers who were instructed not to question him. While en route to the station, two of the officers engaged in a conversation between themselves concerning the missing shotgun. One of the officers stated that there were "a lot of handicapped children running around in this area" because a school for such children was located nearby, and "God forbid one of them might find a weapon with shells and they might hurt themselves." Innis interrupted the conversation, stating that the officers should turn the car around so he could show them where the gun was located. Upon returning to the scene of the arrest, Innis was again advised of his *Miranda* rights, replied that he understood his rights, but that he "wanted to get the gun out of the way because of the kids in the area in the school." He then led the police to the shotgun. The shotgun was used as evidence at his trial which resulted in a conviction.]

MR. JUSTICE STEWART delivered the opinion of the Court.

In *Miranda v. Arizona*, the Court held that, once a defendant in custody asks to speak with a lawyer, all interrogation must cease until a lawyer is present. . . .

In the present case, the parties are in agreement that Innis was fully informed of his Miranda rights and that he invoked his Miranda right to counsel when he told Captain Leyden that he wished to consult with a lawyer. It is also uncontested that Innis was "in custody" while being transported to the police station.

The issue, therefore, is whether the respondent was "interrogated" by the police officers in violation of the respondent's undisputed right under Miranda to remain silent until he had consulted with a lawyer. In resolving this issue, we first define the term "interrogation" under Miranda before turning to a consideration of the facts of this case.

The starting point for defining "interrogation" in this context is, of course, the Court's *Miranda* opinion. There the Court observed that "[b]y custodial interrogation, we mean questioning initiated by law enforcement officers after a person has been taken into custody or otherwise deprived of his freedom of action in any significant way." This passage and other references throughout the opinion to "questioning" might suggest that the *Miranda* rules were to apply only to those police interrogation practices that involve express questioning of a defendant while in custody.

We do not, however, construe the *Miranda* opinion so narrowly. The concern of the Court in *Miranda* was that the "interrogation environment" created by the interplay of interrogation and custody would "subjugate the individual to the will of his examiner" and thereby undermine the privilege against compulsory self-incrimination. The police practices that evoked this concern included several that did not involve express questioning. For example, one of the practices discussed in *Miranda* was the use of line-ups in which a coached witness would pick the defendant as the perpetrator. This was designed to establish that the defendant was in fact guilty as a predicate for further interrogation. . . . The Court in *Miranda* also included in its survey of interrogation practices the use of psychological ploys, such as to "posi[t]" "the guilt of the subject," to "minimize the moral seriousness of the offense," and "to cast blame on the victim or on the society." It is clear that these techniques of persuasion, no less than express questioning, were thought, in a custodial setting, to amount to interrogation.

This is not to say, however, that all statements obtained by the police after a person has been taken into custody are to be considered the product of interrogation. As the Court in *Miranda* noted:

Confessions remain a proper element in law enforcement. Any statement given freely and voluntarily without any compelling influences is, of course, admissible in evidence. The fundamental import of the privilege while an individual is in custody is not whether he is allowed to talk to the police without the benefit of warnings and counsel, but whether he can be interrogated. . . . Volunteered statements of any kind are not barred by the Fifth Amendment and their admissibility is not affected by our holding today.

It is clear therefore that the special procedural safeguards outlined in *Miranda* are required not where a suspect is simply taken into custody, but rather where a suspect in custody is subjected to interrogation. "Interrogation," as conceptualized in the *Miranda* opinion, must reflect a measure of compulsion above and beyond that inherent in custody itself. We conclude that the *Miranda* safeguards come into play whenever a person in custody is subjected to either express questioning or its functional equivalent. That is to say, the term "interrogation" under *Miranda* refers not only to express questioning, but also to any words or actions on the part of the police (other than those normally attendant to arrest and custody) that the police should know are reasonably likely to elicit an incriminating response from the suspect. The latter portion of this definition focuses primarily upon the perceptions of the suspect, rather than the intent of the police. This focus reflects the fact that the *Miranda* safeguards were designed to vest a suspect in custody with an added measure of protection against coercive police practices, without regard to objective proof of the underlying intent of the police. A practice that the police should know is reasonably likely to evoke an incriminating response from a suspect thus amounts to interrogation. But, since the police surely cannot be held accountable for the unforeseeable results of their words or actions, the definition of interrogation can extend only to words or actions on the part of police officers that they should have known were reasonably likely to elicit an incriminating response.

Turning to the facts of the present case, we conclude that the respondent was not "interrogated" within the meaning of *Miranda*. It is undisputed that the first prong of the definition of "interrogation" was not satisfied, for the conversation between Patrolmen Gleckman and McKenna included no express questioning of the respondent. Rather, that conversation was, at least in form, nothing more than a dialogue between the two officers to which no response from the respondent was invited.

Moreover, it cannot be fairly concluded that the respondent was subjected to the "functional equivalent" of questioning. It cannot be said, in short, that Patrolmen Gleckman and McKenna should have known that their conversation was reasonably likely to elicit an incriminating response from the respondent. There is nothing in the record to suggest that the officers were aware that the respondent was peculiarly susceptible to an appeal to his conscience concerning the safety of handicapped children. Nor is there anything in the record to suggest that the police knew that the respondent was unusually disoriented or upset at the time of his arrest.

The case thus boils down to whether, in the context of a brief conversation, the officers should have known that the respondent would suddenly be moved to make a self-incriminating response. Given the fact that the entire conversation appears to have consisted of no more than a few offhand remarks, we cannot say that the officers should have known that it was reasonably likely that Innis would so respond. This is not a case where the police carried on a lengthy harangue in the presence of the suspect. Nor does the record support the respondent's contention that, under the circumstances, the officers' comments were particularly "evocative." It is our view, therefore, that the respondent was not subjected by the police to words or actions that the police should have known were reasonably likely to elicit an incriminating response from him.

The Rhode Island Supreme Court erred, in short, in equating "subtle compulsion" with interrogation. That the officers' comments struck a responsive chord is readily apparent. Thus, it may be said, as the Rhode Island Supreme Court did say, that the respondent was subjected to "subtle compulsion." But that is not the end of the inquiry. It must also be established that a suspect's incriminating response was the product of words or actions on the part of the police that they should have known were reasonably likely to elicit an incriminating response. This was not established in the present case.

For the reasons stated, the judgment of the Supreme Court of Rhode Island is vacated, and the case is remanded to that court for further proceedings not inconsistent with this opinion.

It is so ordered.

[Concurring and dissenting opinions omitted.]

## PENNSYLVANIA
## v.
## MUNIZ

### 496 U.S. 582, 110 S. Ct. 2638, 110 L. Ed. 2d 528 (1990)

[This case is reproduced on p. 686.]

## BENSON
## v.
## STATE

### 698 So. 2d 333 (Fla. Dist. Ct. App. 1997)

*[Citations and footnotes omitted.]*

[When making an arrest for crack cocaine, police observed Benson place something in his mouth and start chewing. Believing Benson had swallowed the cocaine, and knowing that swallowing too much crack can be lethal, one of the officers asked Benson how much crack he had eaten. Benson replied that he had eaten one rock. Benson had not been Mirandized prior to this admission.]

PARIENTE, J.

The issue we address in this appeal is one of first impression in Florida: whether an exception to the *Miranda* rule may arise where a suspect is questioned by police in order to address a life-threatening medical emergency. The question in this case stemmed from the officer's objectively reasonable concern, based on his personal observations, over an immediate threat to defendant's health. Under these narrow circumstances, we find that the failure to administer *Miranda* warnings before asking defendant how much crack cocaine he had swallowed did not require suppression of defendant's inculpatory response. Accordingly, we affirm the trial court's denial of the motion to suppress.

\* \* \*

The state, while conceding that *Miranda* would otherwise apply, argues that the response should not be suppressed because the circumstances fall within the "public safety" exception to the *Miranda* rule set forth in *New York v. Quarles*. In *Quarles*, the defendant was arrested in a supermarket. Police believed that just before the arrest the defendant had discarded a loaded firearm inside the supermarket in a place where a third party could gain access. Without first administering the *Miranda* warnings, police questioned the defendant about the location of the gun. The defendant responded with an inculpatory statement. The Supreme Court concluded that the statement need not be suppressed:

We believe that this case presents a situation where concern for public safety must be paramount to adherence to the literal language of the prophylactic rules enunciated in *Miranda*.

\* \* \*

Recognizing that emergencies require split-second decisions, the Supreme Court declined to place officers . . . in the untenable position of having to con-

sider, often in a matter of seconds, whether it best serves society for them to ask the necessary questions without the *Miranda* warnings and render whatever probative evidence they uncover inadmissible, or for them to give the warnings in order to preserve the admissibility of evidence they might uncover but possibly damage or destroy their ability to . . . neutralize the volatile situation confronting them. [The Court ruled that when a life-threatening emergency arises, the need for answers to questions in a situation posing a threat to the public safety outweighs the need for the prophylactic rule protecting the Fifth Amendment's privilege against self-incrimination.]

. . . Since *Quarles*, however, several state and federal courts have addressed and applied the "public safety" exception to *Miranda* in a variety of circumstances, including concern for the safety of victims and police officers. . . . [T]he ninth circuit upheld the admission of the defendant's incriminating response because the "[officer's] question stemmed from an objectively reasonable need to protect himself from immediate danger."

\* \* \*

An analogous exception to the *Miranda* rule pertinent to the facts of this case is the rescue doctrine. . . .

\* \* \*

In *State v. Stevenson*, . . . a deputy observed the defendant place something in his mouth and also saw a rock of cocaine drop to the ground. After arresting the defendant, the deputy observed a white residue in the defendant's mouth. It appeared to the deputy that the defendant had chewed up rock cocaine.

Concerned with a possible overdose, the deputy immediately transported the defendant to a local hospital. The emergency room doctor stated that the defendant was at risk of acute myocardial infarction and hemorrhagic stroke. In response to questioning by the officer, the defendant initially denied ingesting any narcotics. However, when told about the risk of ingesting any controlled substances, "appellant reluctantly admitted he had swallowed six to eight pieces of rock cocaine."

The *Stevenson* court found that the deputy had a reasonable belief that the defendant had consumed cocaine because the deputy saw the defendant place his hand to his mouth, recovered the rock of cocaine that dropped as the defendant's hand went to his mouth, and observed white residue in his mouth. The deputy, aware that cardiac arrest and death can result from a cocaine overdose, testified he felt an "obligation and responsibility" to make sure that the defendant received treatment if he had consumed a dangerous amount of narcotics.

\* \* \*

The questioning in this case stemmed from an objectively reasonable concern over an immediate threat to defendant's health. The officers witnessed the defendant swallowing the contents of a film canister, which the officers reasonably believed contained cocaine. They did not know how much cocaine defendant swallowed, but if he had ingested too much, he could have overdosed. Detective Raulerson asked the question in response to an emergency situation which unfolded before his eyes. Objectively, it appears that his motive was to ascertain what defendant swallowed, not what he possessed.

Officers in such an emergency situation should not be placed in the untenable position of having to choose between having the response and any "fruits" of

the response excluded and potentially saving the defendant's life. Neither defendants nor society would benefit from the application of an inflexible rule under these narrow circumstances.

\* \* \*

. . . Most citizens would consider the police to be derelict in their duties if they administered the *Miranda* warnings before addressing a life-threatening situation. The right to remain silent would be of little practical value to a defendant who becomes comatose from a drug overdose while being read his *Miranda* rights.

# DAVIS
## v.
# UNITED STATES

### 512 U.S. 452, 114 S. Ct. 2350, 129 L. Ed. 2d 362 (1994)

*[Citations and footnotes omitted.]*

[On October 3, 1988, the body of a sailor, beaten to death with a pool cue, was found at the Charleston Naval Base. The investigation gradually focused on Davis. A month later, Davis was interviewed by the Naval Investigative Service. The agents advised Davis that he was a suspect in the killing, that he was not required to make a statement, that any statement could be used against him at a trial by court-martial, and that he was entitled to speak with an attorney and have an attorney present during questioning. Davis waived his rights to remain silent and to counsel, both orally and in writing. About an hour and a half into the interview, Davis said, "Maybe I should talk to a lawyer." When the agents inquired whether he wanted a lawyer, he responded that he did not. The interview continued for another hour, at which point Davis said, "I think I want a lawyer before I say anything else," at which point questioning ceased. A military judge denied Davis's motion to suppress statements made at the interview, holding that his mention of a lawyer during the interrogation was not a request for counsel. He was convicted of murder, and, ultimately, the Court of Military Appeals affirmed.]

JUSTICE O'CONNOR delivered the opinion of the Court.

In *Edwards v. Arizona*, we held that law enforcement officers must immediately cease questioning a suspect who has clearly asserted his right to have counsel present during custodial interrogation. In this case, we decide how law enforcement officers should respond when a suspect makes a reference to counsel that is insufficiently clear to invoke the Edwards prohibition on further questioning.

* * *

The right to counsel recognized in Miranda is sufficiently important to suspects in criminal investigations, we have held, that it "requir[es] the special protection of the knowing and intelligent waiver standard." If the suspect effectively waives his right to counsel after receiving the *Miranda* warnings, law enforcement officers are free to question him. But if a suspect requests counsel at any time during the interview, he is not subject to further questioning until a lawyer has been made available or the suspect himself reinitiates conversation. This "second layer of prophylaxis for the *Miranda* right to counsel," is "designed to prevent police from badgering a defendant into waiving his previously asserted *Miranda* rights," To that end, we

have held that a suspect who has invoked the right to counsel cannot be questioned regarding any offense unless an attorney is actually present. "It remains clear, however, that this prohibition on further questioning—like other aspects of *Miranda*—is not itself required by the Fifth Amendment's prohibition on coerced confessions, but is instead justified only by reference to its prophylactic purpose."

The applicability of the " 'rigid' prophylactic rule" of *Edwards* requires courts to "determine whether the accused actually invoked his right to counsel." To avoid difficulties of proof and to provide guidance to officers conducting interrogations, this is an objective inquiry. Invocation of the *Miranda* right to counsel "requires at a minimum, some statement that can reasonably be construed to be an expression of a desire for the assistance of an attorney." But if a suspect makes a reference to an attorney that is ambiguous or equivocal in that a reasonable officer, in light of the circumstances, would have understood only that the suspect might be invoking the right to counsel, our precedents do not require the cessation of questioning. ("The likelihood that a suspect would wish counsel to be present is not the test for applicability of *Edwards*").

Rather, the suspect must unambiguously request counsel. As we have observed, "a statement either is such an assertion of the right to counsel or it is not." Although a suspect need not "speak with the discrimination of an Oxford don," he must articulate his desire to have counsel present sufficiently clearly that a reasonable police officer, in the circumstances, would understand the statement to be a request for an attorney. If the statement fails to meet the requisite level of clarity, *Edwards* does not require that the officers stop questioning the suspect.

We decline petitioner's invitation to extend *Edwards* and require law enforcement officers to cease questioning immediately upon the making of an ambiguous or equivocal reference to an attorney. The rationale underlying *Edwards* is that the police must respect a suspect's wishes regarding his right to have an attorney present during custodial interrogation. But when the officers conducting the questioning reasonably do not know whether or not the suspect wants a lawyer, a rule requiring the immediate cessation of questioning "would transform the *Miranda* safeguards into wholly irrational obstacles to legitimate police investigative activity," because it would needlessly prevent the police from questioning a suspect in the absence of counsel even if the suspect did not wish to have a lawyer present. . . .

\* \* \*

. . . The Edwards rule—questioning must cease if the suspect asks for a lawyer—provides a bright line that can be applied by officers in the real world of investigation and interrogation without unduly hampering the gathering of information. But if we were to require questioning to cease if a suspect makes a statement that might be a request for an attorney, this clarity and ease of application would be lost. Police officers would be forced to make difficult judgment calls about whether the suspect in fact wants a lawyer even though he hasn't said so, with the threat of suppression if they guess wrong. We therefore hold that, after a knowing and voluntary waiver of the *Miranda* rights, law enforcement officers may continue questioning until and unless the suspect clearly requests an attorney.

Of course, when a suspect makes an ambiguous or equivocal statement, it will often be good police practice for the interviewing officers to clarify whether or not he actually wants an attorney. That was the procedure followed by the NIS agents in this case. Clarifying questions help protect the rights of the suspect by ensuring that he gets an attorney if he wants one, and will minimize the chance of a confession being suppressed due to subsequent judicial second-guessing as to the meaning of the suspect's statement regarding counsel. But we decline to adopt a rule requiring officers to ask clarifying questions. If the suspect's statement is not an unambiguous or unequivocal request for counsel, the officers have no obligation to stop questioning him.

\* \* \*

The courts below found that petitioner's remark to the NIS agents—"Maybe I should talk to a lawyer"—was not a request for counsel, and we see no reason to disturb that conclusion. The NIS agents therefore were not required to stop questioning petitioner, though it was entirely proper for them to clarify whether petitioner in fact wanted a lawyer. Because there is no ground for suppression of petitioner's statements, the judgment of the Court of Military Appeals is

Affirmed.

[Concurring opinions omitted.]

**MICHIGAN**

**v.**

**JACKSON**

**475 U.S. 625, 106 S. Ct. 1404,
89 L. Ed. 2d 631 (1986)**

*[Citations and footnotes omitted.]*

[Jackson was one of four participants in a murder for hire. He was arrested and arraigned on these charges. During the arraignment, Jackson requested that counsel be appointed for him. The police involved in his investigation were present at the arraignment. On the following morning, before Jackson had an opportunity to consult with counsel, two police officers, after advising Jackson of his Miranda rights, questioned him and obtained a statement from him to that he was the person who had shot the victim. Jackson was convicted, over objections to the admission of the confession in evidence. The Michigan Supreme Court ruled that Jackson's statement was improperly obtained in violation of his Sixth Amendment rights and should have been suppressed.]

JUSTICE STEVENS delivered the opinion of the Court.

In *Edwards v. Arizona*, we held that an accused person in custody who has "expressed his desire to deal with the police only through counsel, is not subject to further interrogation by the authorities until counsel has been made available to him, unless the accused himself initiates further communication, exchanges, or conversations with the police." . . .

\* \* \*

The question is not whether respondents had a right to counsel at their postar-

raignment, custodial interrogations. The existence of that right is clear. . . . The Sixth Amendment guarantee of the assistance of counsel also provides the right to counsel at postarraignment interrogations. The arraignment signals "the initiation of adversary judicial proceedings" and thus the attachment of the Sixth Amendment, thereafter, government efforts to elicit information from the accused, including interrogation, represent "critical stages" at which the Sixth Amendment applies. The question in these cases is whether respondents validly waived their right to counsel at the postarraignment custodial interrogations.

\* \* \*

. . . [a]fter a formal accusation has been made—and a person who had previously been just a "suspect" has become an "accused" within the meaning of the Sixth Amendment—the constitutional right to the assistance of counsel is of such importance that the police may no longer employ techniques for eliciting information from an uncounseled defendant that might have been entirely proper at an earlier stage of their investigation. Thus, the surreptitious employment of a cellmate, or the electronic surveillance of conversations with third parties, may violate the defendant's Sixth Amendment right to counsel even though the same methods of investigation might have been permissible before arraignment or indictment. . . .

\* \* \*

. . . [t]he State maintains that each of the respondents made a valid waiver of his Sixth Amendment rights by signing a postarraignment confession after again being advised of his constitutional rights. In *Edwards*, however, we rejected the notion that, after a suspect's request for counsel, advice of rights and acquiescence in police-initiated questioning could establish a valid waiver. We find no warrant for a different view under a Sixth Amendment analysis. Indeed, our rejection of the comparable argument in *Edwards* was based, in part, on our review of earlier Sixth Amendment cases. Just as written waivers are insufficient to justify police-initiated interrogations after the request for counsel in a Fifth Amendment analysis, so too they are insufficient to justify police-initiated interrogations after the request for counsel in a Sixth Amendment analysis.

*Edwards* is grounded in the understanding that "the assertion of the right to counsel [is] a significant event," and that "additional safeguards are necessary when the accused asks for counsel." We conclude that the assertion is no less significant, and the need for additional safeguards no less clear, when the request for counsel is made at an arraignment and when the basis for the claim is the Sixth Amendment. We thus hold that, if police initiate interrogation after a defendant's assertion, at an arraignment or similar proceeding, of his right to counsel, any waiver of the defendant's right to counsel for that police-initiated interrogation is invalid.

Although the *Edwards* decision itself rested on the Fifth Amendment and concerned a request for counsel made during custodial interrogation, the Michigan Supreme Court correctly perceived that the reasoning of that case applies with even greater force to these cases. The judgments are accordingly affirmed.

It is so ordered.

[Concurring and dissenting opinions omitted.]

# KUHLMANN
## v.
# WILSON

### 477 U.S. 436, 106 S. Ct. 2616, 91 L. Ed. 2d 364 (1986)

*[Citations and footnotes omitted.]*

[After his arraignment on charges arising from a 1970 robbery and murder in New York, the defendant was confined in a cell with a prisoner named Benny Lee, who had previously agreed to act as a police informant. Lee was instructed not to solicit any admissions, but only to listen to the defendant. The defendant first spoke to Lee, telling him the same story he had told the police. Lee advised him that this explanation "didn't sound too good," but the defendant did not alter his story. The defendant then received a visit from his brother, who mentioned that members of his family were upset because they believed that he murdered the dispatcher. After the visit, the defendant again described the crimes to Lee. The defendant now admitted that he and two other men, whom he never identified, had planned and carried out the robbery, and had murdered the dispatcher.]

JUSTICE POWELL announced the judgment of the Court and delivered the opinion of the Court with respect to Parts I, IV, and V, and an opinion with respect to Parts II and III in which THE CHIEF JUSTICE, JUSTICE REHNQUIST, and JUSTICE O'CONNOR join.

* * *

The decision in *Massiah* had its roots in two concurring opinions written in *Spano v. New York*. Following his indictment for first-degree murder, the defendant in *Spano* retained a lawyer and sur rendered to the authorities. Before leaving the defendant in police custody, counsel cautioned him not to respond to interrogation. The prosecutor and police questioned the defendant, persisting in the face of his repeated refusal to answer and his repeated request to speak with his lawyer. The lengthy interrogation involved improper police tactics, and the defendant ultimately confessed. Following a trial at which his confession was admitted in evidence, the defendant was convicted and sentenced to death. Agreeing with the Court that the confession was involuntary and thus improperly admitted in evidence under the Fourteenth Amendment, the concurring Justices also took the position that the defendant's right to counsel was violated by the secret interrogation. As Justice Stewart observed, an indicted person has the right to assistance of counsel throughout the proceedings against him. The defendant was denied that right when he was subjected to an "all-night inquisition," during which police ignored his repeated requests for his lawyer.

The Court in *Massiah* adopted the reasoning of the concurring opinions in *Spano* and held that, once a defendant's Sixth Amendment right to counsel has attached, he is denied that right when federal agents "deliberately elicit" incriminating statements from him in the absence of his lawyer. The Court adopted this test, rather than one that turned simply on whether the statements were obtained in an "interrogation," to protect accused persons from "'indirect and surreptitious interrogations as well as those conducted in the jailhouse. In this case, Massiah was more seriously imposed upon . . . because he did not even know that he was under interrogation by a government agent.'" Thus, the Court made clear that it was concerned with interrogation or investigative techniques that were equivalent to interrogation, and

that it so viewed the technique in issue in *Massiah*.

In *United States v. Henry*, the Court applied the *Massiah* test to incriminating statements made to a jailhouse informant. The Court of Appeals in that case found a violation of *Massiah* because the informant had engaged the defendant in conversations and "had developed a relationship of trust and confidence with [the defendant] such that [the defendant] revealed incriminating information." This Court affirmed, holding that the Court of Appeals reasonably concluded that the Government informant "deliberately used his position to secure incriminating information from [the defendant] when counsel was not present." Although the informant had not questioned the defendant, the informant had "stimulated" conversations with the defendant in order to "elicit" incriminating information. The Court emphasized that those facts, like the facts of *Massiah*, amounted to "'indirect and surreptitious interrogatio[n]'" of the defendant.

Earlier this Term, we applied the *Massiah* standard in a case involving incriminating statements made under circumstances substantially similar to the facts of *Massiah* itself. In *Maine v. Moulton*, the defendant made incriminating statements in a meeting with his accomplice, who had agreed to cooperate with the police. During that meeting, the accomplice, who wore a wire transmitter to record the conversation, discussed with the defendant the charges pending against him, repeatedly asked the defendant to remind him of the details of the crime, and encouraged the defendant to describe his plan for killing witnesses. The Court concluded that these investigatory techniques denied the defendant his right to counsel on the pending charges. Significantly, the Court emphasized that, because of the relationship between the defendant and the informant, the informant's engaging the defendant "in active conversation about their upcoming trial was certain to elicit" incriminating statements from the defendant. Thus, the informant's participation "in this conversation was 'the functional equivalent of interrogation.'"

As our recent examination of this Sixth Amendment issue in *Moulton* makes clear, the primary concern of the *Massiah* line of decisions is secret interrogation by investigatory techniques that are the equivalent of direct police interrogation. Since "the Sixth Amendment is not violated whenever—by luck or happenstance—the State obtains incriminating statements from the accused after the right to counsel has attached," a defendant does not make out a violation of that right simply by showing that an informant, either through prior arrangement or voluntarily, reported his incriminating statements to the police. Rather, the defendant must demonstrate that the police and their informant took some action, beyond merely listening, that was designed deliberately to elicit incriminating remarks.

\* \* \*

The state court found that Officer Cullen had instructed Lee only to listen to respondent for the purpose of determining the identities of the other participants in the robbery and murder. The police already had solid evidence of respondent's participation. The court further found that Lee followed those instructions, that he "at no time asked any questions" of respondent concerning the pending charges, and that he "only listened" to respondent's "spontaneous" and "unsolicited" statements. The only remark made by Lee that has any support in this record was his comment that respondent's initial version of his participation in the crimes "didn't sound too good." Without holding that any of the state court's findings were not entitled to

the presumption of correctness under 2254(d), the Court of Appeals focused on that one remark and gave a description of Lee's interaction with respondent that is completely at odds with the facts found by the trial court. In the Court of Appeals' view, "[s]ubtly and slowly, but surely, Lee's ongoing verbal intercourse with [respondent] served to exacerbate [respondent's] already troubled state of mind." After thus revising some of the trial court's findings, and ignoring other more relevant findings, the Court of Appeals concluded that the police "deliberately elicited" respondent's incriminating statements. This conclusion conflicts with the decision of every other state and federal judge who reviewed this record, and is clear error in light of the provisions and intent of 2254(d).

\* \* \*

It is so ordered.

[Concurring and dissenting opinions omitted.]

## MISSOURI
## v.
## SEIBERT

___ U.S. ___, 124 S. Ct. 2601,
159 L. Ed. 2d 643 (2004)

*[Citations and footnotes omitted.]*

Respondent Seibert feared charges of neglect when her son, afflicted with cerebral palsy, died in his sleep. She was present when two of her sons and their friends discussed burning her family's mobile home to conceal the circumstances of her son's death. Donald, an unrelated mentally ill 18-year-old living with the family, was left to die in the fire, in order to avoid the appearance that Seibert's son had been unattended.

Five days later, the police arrested Seibert, but did not read her her rights under *Miranda v. Arizona*. At the police station, Officer Hanrahan questioned her for 30 to 40 minutes, obtaining a confession that the plan was for Donald to die in the fire. He then gave her a 20-minute break, returned to give her *Miranda* warnings, and obtained a signed waiver. He resumed questioning, confronting Seibert with her prewarning statements and getting her to repeat the information. Seibert moved to suppress both her prewarning and postwarning statements. Hanrahan testified that he made a conscious decision to withhold *Miranda* warnings, question first, then give the warnings, and then repeat the question until he got the answer previously given. The District Court suppressed the prewarning statement but admitted the postwarning one, and Seibert was convicted of second-degree murder. . . .

SOUTER, J., announced the judgment of Court and delivered an opinion, in which STEVENS, GINSBURG, and BREYER, JJ., joined.

This case tests a police protocol for custodial interrogation that calls for giving no warnings of the rights to silence and counsel until interrogation has produced a confession. Although such a statement is generally inadmissible, since taken in violation of *Miranda v. Arizona*, the interrogating officer follows it with *Miranda* warnings and then leads the suspect to cover the same ground a second time. The question here is the admissibility of the repeated statement. Because this midstream recitation of warnings after interrogation and unwarned confession could not effectively comply with *Miranda*'s constitutional requirement, we hold that a statement repeated after a warning in such circumstances is inadmissible.

* * *

The technique of interrogating in successive, unwarned and warned phases raises a new challenge to *Miranda*. Although we have no statistics on the frequency of this practice, it is not confined to Rolla, Missouri. An officer of that police department testified that the strategy of withholding *Miranda* warnings until after interrogating and drawing out a confession was promoted not only by his own department, but by a national police training organization and other departments in which he had worked. . . .

When a confession so obtained is offered and challenged, attention must be paid to the conflicting objects of *Miranda* and question-first. *Miranda* addressed "interrogation practices . . . likely . . . to disable [an individual] from making a free and rational choice" about speaking and held that a suspect must be "adequately and effectively" advised of the choice the Constitution guarantees. The object of question-first is to render *Miranda* warnings ineffective by waiting for a particularly opportune time to give them, after the suspect has already confessed.

Just as "no talismanic incantation [is] required to satisfy [*Miranda*'s] strictures," it would be absurd to think that mere recitation of the litany suffices to satisfy *Miranda* in every conceivable circumstance. "The inquiry is simply whether the warnings reasonably 'conve[y] to [a suspect] his rights as required by *Miranda*.'" The threshold issue when interrogators question first and warn later is thus whether it would be reasonable to find that in these circumstances the warnings could function "effectively" as *Miranda* requires. Could the warnings effectively advise the suspect that he had a real choice about giving an admissible statement at that juncture? Could they reasonably convey that he could choose to stop talking even if he had talked earlier? For unless the warnings could place a suspect who has just been interrogated in a position to make such an informed choice, there is no practical justification for accepting the formal warnings as compliance with *Miranda*, or for treating the second stage of interrogation as distinct from the first, unwarned and inadmissible segment.

There is no doubt about the answer that proponents of question-first give to this question about the effectiveness of warnings given only after successful interrogation, and we think their answer is correct. By any objective measure, applied to circumstances exemplified here, it is likely that if the interrogators employ the technique of withholding warnings until after interrogation succeeds in eliciting a confession, the warnings will be ineffective in preparing the suspect for successive interrogation, close in time and similar in content. After all, the reason that question-first is catching on is as obvious as its manifest purpose, which is to get a confession the suspect would not make if he understood his rights at the outset; the sensible underlying assumption is that with one confession in hand before the warnings, the interrogator can count on getting its duplicate, with trifling additional trouble. Upon hearing warnings only in the aftermath of interrogation and just after making a confession, a suspect would hardly think he had a genuine right to remain silent, let alone persist in so believing once the police began to lead him over the same ground again. . . .

Missouri argues that a confession repeated at the end of an interrogation sequence envisioned in a question-first strategy is admissible on the authority of *Oregon v. Elstad*, but the argument disfigures that case. In *Elstad*, the police went to the young suspect's house to take him into custody on a charge of burglary.

Before the arrest, one officer spoke with the suspect's mother, while the other one joined the suspect in a "brief stop in the living room," where the officer said he "felt" the young man was involved in a burglary. The suspect acknowledged he had been at the scene. This Court noted that the pause in the living room "was not to interrogate the suspect but to notify his mother of the reason for his arrest," and described the incident as having "none of the earmarks of coercion." The Court, indeed, took care to mention that the officer's initial failure to warn was an "oversight" that "may have been the result of confusion as to whether the brief exchange qualified as 'custodial interrogation' or . . . may simply have reflected . . . reluctance to initiate an alarming police procedure before [an officer] had spoken with respondent's mother." At the outset of a later and systematic station house interrogation going well beyond the scope of the laconic prior admission, the suspect was given *Miranda* warnings and made a full confession. In holding the second statement admissible and voluntary, *Elstad* rejected the "cat out of the bag" theory that any short, earlier admission, obtained in arguably innocent neglect of *Miranda*, determined the character of the later, warned confession; on the facts of that case, the Court thought any causal connection between the first and second responses to the police was "speculative and attenuated." Although the *Elstad* Court expressed no explicit conclusion about either officer's state of mind, it is fair to read *Elstad* as treating the living room conversation as a good-faith *Miranda* mistake, not only open to correction by careful warnings before systematic questioning in that particular case, but posing no threat to warn-first practice generally.

\* \* \*

At the opposite extreme are the facts here, which by any objective measure reveal a police strategy adapted to undermine the *Miranda* warnings. The unwarned interrogation was conducted in the station house, and the questioning was systematic, exhaustive, and managed with psychological skill. When the police were finished there was little, if anything, of incriminating potential left unsaid. The warned phase of questioning proceeded after a pause of only 15 to 20 minutes, in the same place as the unwarned segment. When the same officer who had conducted the first phase recited the *Miranda* warnings, he said nothing to counter the probable misimpression that the advice that anything Seibert said could be used against her also applied to the details of the inculpatory statement previously elicited. In particular, the police did not advise that her prior statement could not be used. Nothing was said or done to dispel the oddity of warning about legal rights to silence and counsel right after the police had led her through a systematic interrogation, and any uncertainty on her part about a right to stop talking about matters previously discussed would only

have been aggravated by the way Officer Hanrahan set the scene by saying "we've been talking for a little while about what happened on Wednesday the twelfth, haven't we?" The impression that the further questioning was a mere continuation of the earlier questions and responses was fostered by references back to the confession already given. It would have been reasonable to regard the two sessions as parts of a continuum, in which it would have been unnatural to refuse to repeat at the second stage what had been said before. These circumstances must be seen as challenging the comprehensibility and efficacy of the *Miranda* warnings to the point that a reasonable person in the suspect's shoes would not have understood them to convey a message that she retained a choice about continuing to talk.

. . . Because the question-first tactic effectively threatens to thwart *Miranda's* purpose of reducing the risk that a coerced confession would be admitted, and because the facts here do not reasonably support a conclusion that the warnings given could have served their purpose, Seibert's postwarning statements are inadmissible. . . .

# Cases Relating to Chapter 7

# Compulsory Self-Incrimination

**UNITED STATES**

v.

**HUBBELL**

**530 U.S. 27, 120 S. Ct. 2037, 147 L. Ed. 2d 24 (2000)**

*[Citations and footnotes omitted.]*

[The Independent Counsel commenced an investigation of Webster Hubbell's involvement in the Whitewater Development Corporation to determine whether there was a violation of federal law. Hubbell was served with a subpoena duces tecum calling for the production of 11 categories of documents before a grand jury sitting in Little Rock, Arkansas. On November 19, he appeared before the grand jury and invoked his Fifth Amendment privilege against self-incrimination. In response to questioning by the prosecutor, respondent initially refused "to state whether there are documents within my possession, custody, or control responsive to the Subpoena." Thereafter, the prosecutor produced an order, which had previously been obtained from the District Court pursuant to 18 U.S.C. § 6003(a), directing him to respond to the subpoena and granting him immunity "to the extent allowed by law." Respondent then produced 13,120 pages of documents and records and responded to a series of questions that established that those were all of the documents in

his custody or control that were responsive to the commands in the subpoena, with the exception of a few documents he claimed were shielded by the attorney-client and attorney work-product privileges.

The contents of the documents produced by respondent provided the Independent Counsel with the information that led to this prosecution. On April 30, 1998, a grand jury in the District of Columbia returned a 10-count indictment charging respondent with various tax-related crimes and mail and wire fraud. . . .]

Justice STEVENS delivered the opinion of the Court.

\* \* \*

It is useful to preface our analysis of the constitutional issue with a restatement of certain propositions that are not in dispute. The term "privilege against self-incrimination" is not an entirely accurate description of a person's constitutional protection against being "compelled in any criminal case to be a witness against himself."

The word "witness" in the constitutional text limits the relevant category of compelled incriminating communications to those that are "testimonial" in character. As Justice Holmes observed, there is a significant difference between the use of compulsion to extort communications from a defendant and compelling a person to engage in conduct that may be incriminating. Thus, even though the act may provide incriminating evidence, a criminal suspect may be compelled to put on a shirt, to provide a blood sample or handwriting exemplar, or to make a recording of his voice. The act of exhibiting such physical characteristics is not the same as a sworn communication by a witness that relates either express or implied assertions of fact or belief. Similarly, the fact that incriminating evidence may be the byproduct of obedience to a regulatory requirement, such as filing an income tax return, maintaining required records, or reporting an accident, does not clothe such required conduct with the testimonial privilege.

More relevant to this case is the settled proposition that a person may be required to produce specific documents even though they contain incriminating assertions of fact or belief because the creation of those documents was not "compelled" within the meaning of the privilege. Our decision in *Fisher v. United States* dealt with summonses issued by the Internal Revenue Service (IRS) seeking working papers used in the preparation of tax returns. Because the papers had been voluntarily prepared prior to the issuance of the summonses, they could not be "said to contain compelled testimonial evidence, either of the taxpayers or of anyone else." Accordingly, the taxpayer could not "avoid compliance with the subpoena merely by asserting that the item of evidence which he is required to produce contains incriminating writing, whether his own or that of someone else." It is clear, therefore, that respondent Hubbell could not avoid compliance with the subpoena served on him merely because the demanded documents contained incriminating evidence,

whether written by others or voluntarily prepared by himself.

On the other hand, we have also made it clear that the act of producing documents in response to a subpoena may have a compelled testimonial aspect. We have held that "the act of production" itself may implicitly communicate "statements of fact." By "producing documents in compliance with a subpoena, the witness would admit that the papers existed, were in his possession or control, and were authentic." Moreover, as was true in this case, when the custodian of documents responds to a subpoena, he may be compelled to take the witness stand and answer questions designed to determine whether he has produced everything demanded by the subpoena. The answers to those questions, as well as the act of production itself, may certainly communicate information about the existence, custody, and authenticity of the documents. Whether the constitutional privilege protects the answers to such questions, or protects the act of production itself, is a question that is distinct from the question whether the unprotected contents of the documents themselves are incriminating.

Finally, the phrase "in any criminal case" in the text of the Fifth Amendment might have been read to limit its coverage to compelled testimony that is used against the defendant in the trial itself. It has, however, long been settled that its protection encompasses compelled statements that lead to the discovery of incriminating evidence even though the statements themselves are not incriminating and are not introduced into evidence. Thus, a half-century ago we held that a trial judge had erroneously rejected a defendant's claim of privilege on the ground that his answer to the pending question would not itself constitute evidence of the charged offense. As we explained: "The privilege afforded not only extends to answers that would in themselves support a conviction under a federal criminal statute but likewise embraces those which would furnish a link in the chain of evidence needed to prosecute the claimant for a federal crime." Compelled testimony that communicates information that may "lead to incriminating evidence" is privileged even if the information itself is not inculpatory. It is the Fifth Amendment's protection against the prosecutor's use of incriminating information derived directly or indirectly from the compelled testimony of the respondent that is of primary relevance in this case.

Acting pursuant to 18 U.S.C. § 6002, the District Court entered an order compelling respondent to produce "any and all documents" described in the grand jury subpoena and granting him "immunity to the extent allowed by law." . . .

* * *

The "compelled testimony" that is relevant in this case is not to be found in the contents of the documents produced in response to the subpoena. It is, rather, the testimony inherent in the act of producing those documents. The disagreement between the parties focuses entirely on the significance of that testimonial aspect.

* * *

It is apparent from the text of the subpoena itself that the prosecutor needed respondent's assistance both to identify potential sources of information and to produce those sources. Given the breadth of the description of the 11 categories of documents called for by the subpoena, the collection and production of the materials demanded was tantamount to answering a series of interrogatories asking a witness to disclose the existence and location of particular documents fitting certain broad descriptions. The assembly of literally hundreds of pages of material in response to a request for "any and all documents reflecting, referring, or relating to any direct or indirect sources of money or other things of value received by or provided to" an individual or members of his family during a 3-year period is the functional equivalent of the preparation of an answer to either a detailed written interrogatory or a series of oral questions at a discovery deposition. Entirely apart from the contents of the 13,120 pages of materials that respondent produced in this case, it is undeniable that providing a catalog of existing documents fitting within any of the 11 broadly worded subpoena categories could provide a prosecutor with a "lead to incriminating evidence," or "a link in the chain of evidence needed to prosecute."

. . . It is abundantly clear that the testimonial aspect of respondent's act of producing subpoenaed documents was the first step in a chain of evidence that led to this prosecution. The documents did not magically appear in the prosecutor's office like "manna from heaven." They arrived there only after respondent asserted his constitutional privilege, received a grant of immunity, and—under the compulsion of the District Court's order—took the mental and physical steps necessary to provide the prosecutor with an accurate inventory of the many sources of potentially incriminating evidence sought by the subpoena. It was only through respondent's truthful reply to the subpoena that the Government received the incriminating documents of which it made "substantial use . . . in the investigation that led to the indictment."

For these reasons, we cannot accept the Government's submission that respondent's immunity did not preclude its derivative use of the produced documents because its "possession of the documents [was] the fruit only of a simple physical act—the act of producing the documents." It was unquestionably necessary for respondent to make extensive use of "the contents of his own mind" in identifying the hundreds of documents responsive to the requests in the subpoena. The assembly of those documents was like telling an inquisitor the combination to a wall safe, not like being forced to surrender the key to a strongbox. The Government's anemic view of respondent's act of production as a mere physical act that is principally non-testimonial in character and can be entirely divorced from its "implicit" testimonial aspect so as to constitute a "legitimate, wholly independent source" (as required by *Kastigar*) for the documents produced simply fails to account for these realities.

In sum, we have no doubt that the constitutional privilege against self-incrimination protects the target of a grand jury investigation from being compelled to answer questions designed to elicit information about the existence of sources of potentially incriminating evidence. That constitutional privilege has the same application to the testimonial aspect of a response to a subpoena seeking discovery of those sources. . . .

\* \* \*

Given our conclusion that respondent's act of production had a testimonial aspect, at least with respect to the existence and location of the documents sought by the Government's subpoena, respondent could not be compelled to produce those documents without first receiving a grant of immunity under § 6003. As we construed § 6002 in *Kastigar*, such immunity is co-extensive with the constitutional privilege. *Kastigar* requires that respondent's motion to dis-

miss the indictment on immunity grounds be granted unless the Government proves that the evidence it used in obtaining the indictment and proposed to use at trial was derived from legitimate sources "wholly independent" of the testimonial aspect of respondent's immunized conduct in assembling and producing the documents described in the subpoena. . . .

Accordingly, the indictment against respondent must be dismissed. The judgment of the Court of Appeals is affirmed.

It is so ordered.

## SCHMERBER
### v.
## CALIFORNIA

### 384 U.S. 757, 86 S. Ct. 1826, 16 L. Ed. 2d 908 (1966)

[Police arrested Schmerber at the scene of an automobile accident for driving under the influence of intoxicating liquor (DUI). While he was at a hospital being treated for injuries sustained in the accident, one of the officers instructed a physician to withdraw a blood sample. Schmerber refused to consent, but a sample was taken anyway. The sample revealed a blood alcohol content in excess of the state's maximum for DUI. Schmerber moved to suppress the test results on several grounds, including that withdrawal of his blood and admission of the test results into evidence violated his Fifth Amendment privilege against self-incrimination and his Fourth Amendment right not to be subjected to unreasonable searches and seizures. Schmerber's motion to suppress was denied and he was convicted.]

MR. JUSTICE BRENNAN delivered the opinion of the Court.

* * *

*The Privilege Against*
*Self-Incrimination Claim*

It could not be denied that in requiring petitioner to submit to the withdrawal and chemical analysis of his blood the State compelled him to submit to an attempt to discover evidence that might be used to prosecute him for a criminal offense. He submitted only after the police officer rejected his objection and directed the physician to proceed. The officer's direction to the physician to administer the test over petitioner's objection constituted compulsion for the purposes of the privilege. The critical question, then, is whether petitioner was thus compelled 'to be a witness against himself.'

* * *

It is clear that the protection of the privilege reaches an accused's communications, whatever form they might take, and the compulsion of responses which are also communications, for example, compliance with a subpoena to produce one's papers. On the other hand, both federal and state courts have usually held that it offers no protection against compulsion to submit to fingerprinting, photographing, or measurements, to write or speak for identification, to appear in court, to stand, to assume a stance, to walk, or to make a particular gesture. The distinction which has emerged, often expressed in different ways, is that the privilege is a bar against compelling 'communications' or 'testimony,' but that compulsion which makes a suspect or accused the source of 'real or physical evidence' does not violate it.

* * *

. . . Not even a shadow of testimonial compulsion upon or enforced communication by the accused was involved either in the extraction or in the chemical analysis. Petitioner's testimonial capacities were in no way implicated; indeed, his participation, except as a donor, was irrelevant to the results of the test, which depend on chemical analysis and on that alone. Since the blood test evidence, although an incriminating product of compulsion, was neither petitioner's testimony nor evidence relating to some communicative act or writing by the petitioner, it was not inadmissible on privilege grounds.

* * *

*The Search and Seizure Claim*

In *Breithaupt*, as here, it was also contended that the chemical analysis should be excluded from evidence as the product of an unlawful search and seizure in violation of the Fourth and Fourteenth Amendments. The Court did not decide whether the extraction of blood in that case was unlawful, but rejected the claim on the basis of *Wolf v. People of State of Colorado*. That case had held that the Constitution did not require, in state prosecutions for state crimes, the exclusion of evidence obtained in violation of the Fourth Amendment's provisions. We have since overruled *Wolf* in that respect, holding in *Mapp v. Ohio* that the exclusionary rule adopted for federal prosecutions in *Weeks v. United States* must also be applied in criminal prosecutions in state courts. The question is squarely presented therefore, whether the chemical analysis introduced in evidence in this case should have been excluded as the product of an unconstitutional search and seizure.

The overriding function of the Fourth Amendment is to protect personal privacy and dignity against unwarranted intrusion by the State. In *Wolf* we recognized "(t)he security of one's privacy against arbitrary intrusion by the police" as being "at the core of the Fourth Amendment" and "basic to a free society." We reaffirmed that broad view of the Amendment's purpose in applying the federal exclusionary rule to the States in *Mapp*.

. . . But if compulsory administration of a blood test does not implicate the Fifth Amendment, it plainly involves the broadly conceived reach of a search and seizure under the Fourth Amendment. That Amendment expressly provides that "(t)he right of the people to be secure in their persons, houses, papers, and effects, against unreasonable searches and seizures, shall not be violated. . . ." (Emphasis added.) It could not reasonably be argued, and indeed respondent does not argue, that the administration of the blood test in this case was free of the constraints of the Fourth Amendment. Such testing procedures plainly constitute searches of "persons," and depend antecedently upon seizures of "persons," within the meaning of that Amendment.

Because we are dealing with intrusions into the human body rather than with state interferences with property relationships or private papers—"houses, papers, and effects"—we write on a clean slate. Limitations on the kinds of property which may be seized under warrant, as distinct from the procedures for search and the permissible scope of search, are not instructive in this context. We begin with the assumption that once the privilege against self-incrimination has been found not to bar compelled intrusions into the body for blood to be analyzed for alcohol content, the Fourth Amendment's proper function is to constrain, not against all intrusions as such, but against intrusions which are not justified in the circumstances, or which are made in an improper manner. In other words, the questions we must decide in

this case are whether the police were justified in requiring petitioner to submit to the blood test, and whether the means and procedures employed in taking his blood respected relevant Fourth Amendment standards of reasonableness.

In this case, as will often be true when charges of driving under the influence of alcohol are pressed, these questions arise in the context of an arrest made by an officer without a warrant. Here, there was plainly probable cause for the officer to arrest petitioner and charge him with driving an automobile while under the influence of intoxicating liquor. The police officer who arrived at the scene shortly after the accident smelled liquor on petitioner's breath, and testified that petitioner's eyes were "bloodshot, watery, sort of a glassy appearance." The officer saw petitioner again at the hospital, within two hours of the accident. There he noticed similar symptoms of drunkenness. He thereupon informed petitioner "that he was under arrest and that he was entitled to the services of an attorney, and that he could remain silent, and that anything that he told me would be used against him in evidence."

While early cases suggest that there is an unrestricted "right on the part of the government always recognized under English and American law, to search the person of the accused when legally arrested, to discover and seize the fruits or evidences of crime," the mere fact of a lawful arrest does not end our inquiry. The suggestion of these cases apparently rests on two factors—first, there may be more immediate danger of concealed weapons or of destruction of evidence under the direct control of the accused; second, once a search of the arrested person for weapons is permitted, it would be both impractical and unnecessary to enforcement of the Fourth Amendment's purpose to attempt to confine the search to those objects alone. Whatever the validity of these considerations in general, they have little applicability with respect to searches involving intrusions beyond the body's surface. The interests in human dignity and privacy which the Fourth Amendment protects forbid any such intrusions on the mere chance that desired evidence might be obtained. In the absence of a clear indication that in fact such evidence will be found, these fundamental human interests require law officers to suffer the risk that such evidence may disappear unless there is an immediate search.

Although the facts which established probable cause to arrest in this case also suggested the required relevance and likely success of a test of petitioner's blood for alcohol, the question remains whether the arresting officer was permitted to draw these inferences himself, or was required instead to procure a warrant before proceeding with the test. Search warrants are ordinarily required for searches of dwellings, and absent an emergency, no less could be required where intrusions into the human body are concerned. The requirement that a warrant be obtained is a requirement that inferences to support the search "be drawn by a neutral and detached magistrate instead of being judged by the officer engaged in the often competitive enterprise of ferreting out crime." The importance of informed, detached and deliberate determinations of the issue whether or not to invade another's body in search of evidence of guilt is indisputable and great.

The officer in the present case, however, might reasonably have believed that he was confronted with an emergency, in which the delay necessary to obtain a warrant, under the circumstances, threatened "the destruction of evidence." We are told that the percentage of alcohol in the blood begins to diminish shortly after drinking stops, as the body functions to eliminate it from the system. Particularly in a case such as this, where time had to be taken to bring the accused to a hospital and to investigate the scene of the accident, there was no time to seek out a magistrate and secure a warrant. Given these special facts, we conclude that the attempt to secure evidence of blood-alcohol content in this case was an appropriate incident to petitioner's arrest.

Similarly, we are satisfied that the test chosen to measure petitioner's blood-alcohol level was a reasonable one. Extraction of blood samples for testing is a highly effective means of determining the degree to which a person is under the influence of alcohol. Such tests are commonplace in these days of periodic physical examination and experience with them teaches that the quantity of blood extracted is minimal, and that for most people the procedure involves virtually no risk, trauma, or pain. Petitioner is not one of the few who on grounds of fear, concern for health, or religious scruple might prefer some other means of testing, such as the "Breathalyzer" test petitioner refused, see n. 9, supra. We need not decide whether such wishes would have to be respected.

Finally, the record shows that the test was performed in a reasonable manner. Petitioner's blood was taken by a physician in a hospital environment according to accepted medical practices. We are thus not presented with the serious questions which would arise if a search involving use of a medical technique, even of the most rudimentary sort, were made by other than medical personnel or in other than a medical environment— for example, if it were administered by police in the privacy of the stationhouse. To tolerate searches under these conditions might be to invite an unjustified element of personal risk of infection and pain.

We thus conclude that the present record shows no violation of petitioner's right under the Fourth and Fourteenth Amendments to be free of unreasonable searches and seizures. It bears repeating, however, that we reach this judgment only on the facts of the present record. The integrity of an individual's person is a cherished value of our society. That we today told that the Constitution does not forbid the States minor intrusions into an individual's body under stringently limited conditions in no way indicates that it permits more substantial intrusions, or intrusions under other conditions.

Affirmed.

### PENNSYLVANIA
### v.
### MUNIZ

**496 U.S. 582, 110 S. Ct. 2638, 110 L. Ed. 2d 528 (1990)**

*[Citations and footnotes omitted.]*

[A patrol officer, spotting Muniz's parked car on the shoulder of a highway, inquired whether he needed assistance, Muniz replied that he had stopped the car so he could urinate. The officer smelled alcohol on Muniz's breath and observed that Muniz's eyes were glazed and bloodshot and his face was flushed. The officer then directed Muniz to remain parked until his condition improved, and Muniz gave assurances that he would do so, but immediately drove off. After pursuing Muniz down the highway and pulling him over, the officer, without advising Muniz of his *Miranda* rights, asked him to perform two standard field sobriety tests: a "walk and turn" test and a "one leg stand" test. Muniz performed these tests poorly and informed the officer that he had failed the tests because he had been drinking.

Muniz was taken to a booking center where, as was the routine practice, he was told that his actions and voice would be videotaped. He then answered seven questions regarding his name, address, height, weight, eye color, date of birth, and current age, stumbling over two responses. The officer then asked Muniz to take a Breathalyzer test and explained that under the law his refusal to take the test would result in automatic suspension of his driver's license for one year. Muniz asked a number of questions about the law and then, commenting about his inebriated state, refused to take the breath test. At this point, Muniz was for the first time advised of his *Miranda* rights. The video and audio portions of the tape were admitted at trial over Muniz's objection that this evidence was procured in violation of his Fifth Amendment privilege against self-incrimination. Muniz was convicted and appealed.]

JUSTICE BRENNAN delivered the opinion of the Court.

We must decide in this case whether various incriminating utterances of a drunken-driving suspect, made while performing a series of sobriety tests, constitute testimonial responses to custodial interrogation for purposes of the Self-Incrimination Clause of the Fifth Amendment.

\* \* \*

The Self-Incrimination Clause of the Fifth Amendment provides that no "person . . . shall be compelled in any criminal case to be a witness against himself." Although the text does not delineate the ways in which a person might be made a "witness against himself, we have long held that the privilege does not protect a suspect from being compelled by the State to produce "real or physical evidence." Rather, the privilege "protects an accused only from being compelled to testify against himself, or otherwise provide the State with evidence of a testimonial or communicative nature." "[I]n order to be testimonial, an accused's communication must itself, explicitly or implicitly, relate a factual assertion or disclose information. Only then is a person compelled to be a 'witness' against himself."

\* \* \*

Because Muniz was not advised of his *Miranda* rights until after the videotaped proceedings at the booking center were completed, any verbal statements that were both testimonial in nature and elicited during custodial interrogation should have been suppressed. We focus first on Muniz's responses to the initial informational questions . . .

In the initial phase of the recorded proceedings, Officer Hosterman asked Muniz his name, address, height, weight, eye color, date of birth, current age, and the date of his sixth birthday. Both the delivery and content of Muniz's answers were incriminating. As the state court found, "Muniz's videotaped responses . . . certainly led the finder of fact to infer that his confusion and failure to speak clearly indicated a state of drunkenness that prohibited him from safely operating his vehicle." The Commonwealth argues, however, that admission of Muniz's answers to these questions does not contravene Fifth Amendment principles because Muniz's statement regarding his sixth birthday was not "testimonial" and his answers to the prior questions were not elicited by custodial interrogation. We consider these arguments in turn.

We agree with the Commonwealth's contention that Muniz's answers are not rendered inadmissible by *Miranda* merely because the slurred nature of his speech was incriminating. The physical inability to articulate words in a clear manner due to "the lack of muscular coordination of his tongue and mouth," is not itself a testimonial component of Muniz's responses to Officer Hosterman's introductory questions. In *Schmerber v. California*, we drew a distinction between "testimonial" and "real or physical evidence" for purposes of the privilege against self-incrimination. We noted that in *Holt v. United States*, Justice Holmes had written for the Court that "'[t]he prohibition of compelling a man in a criminal court to be witness against himself is a prohibition of the use of physical or moral compulsion to extort communications from him, not an exclusion of his body as evidence when it may be material.'" We also acknowledged that "both federal and state courts have usually held that it offers no protection against compulsion to submit to fingerprinting, photographing, or measurements, to write or speak for identification, to appear in court, to stand, to assume a stance, to walk, or to make a particular gesture." Embracing this view of the privilege's contours, we held that "the privilege is a bar against compelling 'communications' or 'testimony,' but that compulsion which makes a suspect or accused the source of 'real or physical evidence' does not violate it." Using this "helpful framework for analysis," we held that a person suspected of driving while intoxicated could be forced to provide a blood sample, because that sample was "real or physical evidence" outside the scope of the privilege and the sample was obtained in a manner by which "[p]etitioner's testimonial capacities were in no way implicated."

\* \* \*

We have since applied the distinction between "real or physical" and "testimonial" evidence in other contexts where the evidence could be produced only through some volitional act on the part of the suspect. In *United States v. Wade*, we held that a suspect could be compelled to participate in a lineup and to repeat a phrase provided by the police so that witnesses could view him and listen to his voice. We explained that requiring his presence and speech at a lineup reflected "compulsion of the accused to exhibit his physical characteristics, not compulsion to disclose any knowledge he might have." In *Gilbert v. California*, we held that a suspect could be compelled to provide a handwriting exemplar, explaining that such an exemplar, "in contrast to the content of what is written, like the voice or body itself, is an identifying physical characteristic outside [the privilege's] protection." And in *United States v. Dionisio*, we held that suspects could be compelled to read a transcript in order to provide a voice exemplar, explaining that the "voice recordings were to be used solely to measure the physical properties of the witnesses' voices, not for the testimonial or communicative content of what was to be said."

Under *Schmerber* and its progeny, we agree with the Commonwealth that any slurring of speech and other evidence of lack of muscular coordination revealed by Muniz's responses to Officer Hosterman's direct questions constitute nontestimonial components of those responses. Requiring a suspect to reveal the physical manner in which he articulates words, like requiring him to reveal the physical properties of the sound produced by his voice, does not, without more, compel him to provide a "testimonial" response for purposes of the privilege.

\* \* \*

We disagree with the Commonwealth's contention that Officer Hosterman's first seven questions regarding Muniz's name, address, height, weight, eye color, date of birth, and current age do not qualify as custodial interrogation as we defined the term in Innis, merely because the questions were not intended to elicit information for investigatory purposes. As explained above, the *Innis* test focuses primarily upon "the perspective of the suspect." We agree . . . however, that Muniz's answers to these first seven questions are nonetheless admissible because the questions fall within a "routine booking question" exception which exempts from *Miranda*'s coverage questions to secure the "'biographical data necessary to complete booking or pretrial services.'" The state court found that the first seven questions were "requested for record-keeping purposes only," and therefore the questions appear reasonably related to the police's administrative concerns. In this context, therefore, the first seven questions asked at the booking center fall outside the protections of *Miranda* and the answers thereto need not be suppressed.

\* \* \*

. . . [W]e conclude that *Miranda* does not require suppression of the statements Muniz made when asked to submit to a Breathalyzer examination. Officer Deyo read Muniz a prepared script explaining how the test worked, the nature of Pennsylvania's Implied Consent Law, and the legal consequences that would ensue should he refuse. Officer Deyo then asked Muniz whether he understood the nature of the test and the law and whether he would like to submit to the test. Muniz asked Officer Deyo several questions concerning the legal consequences of refusal, which Deyo answered directly, and Muniz then commented upon his state of inebriation. After offering to take the test only after waiting a couple of hours or drinking some water, Muniz ultimately refused.

We believe that Muniz's statements were not prompted by an interrogation within the meaning of *Miranda*, and therefore the absence of *Miranda* warnings does not require suppression of these statements at trial. As did Officer Hosterman when administering the three physical sobriety tests, Officer Deyo carefully limited her role to providing Muniz with relevant information about the Breathalyzer test and the Implied Consent Law. She questioned Muniz only as to whether he understood her instructions and wished to submit to the test. These limited and focused inquiries were necessarily "attendant to" the legitimate police procedure, and were not likely to be perceived as calling for any incriminating response.

. . . Accordingly, the court's judgment reversing Muniz's conviction is vacated, and the case is remanded for further proceedings not inconsistent with this opinion.

It is so ordered.

[Concurring and dissenting opinions omitted.]

STATE
v.
TAPP

353 So. 2d 265 (La. 1977)

*[Citations and footnotes omitted.]*

[Police officers were executing a search warrant for narcotics at a house on Lowerline Street in New Orleans, Louisiana. All they uncovered was some heroin residue on a syringe found in the refrigerator. While they were inside the house, Tapp, the defendant, entered the door. When he saw the police, the defendant placed a small, cellophane-wrapped packet into his mouth. Three officers set upon him and attempted to force the packet out of his mouth. The ensuing fight rolled onto the front porch, down the steps, and into the yard where two other officers joined the fight. One officer held his hands around defendant's throat in an effort to prevent him from swallowing the evidence. According to the officers, they pummeled defendant in the face and head with their fists, and called on defendant to "Spit it out!" According to defendant's uncontradicted testimony one officer eventually held defendant's nose in an effort to cut off his breathing. The officers estimated that the fight, which one of them described as "one hell of a fight," lasted 15 to 20 minutes. Eventually the five officers successfully caused defendant to spit up the packet, which was then apparently lodged near or at the top of his esophagus, and they arrested him for heroin possession. A search warrant issued for a second house based in part on that evidence. Within they discovered a large amount of heroin. Based on the search of the second house, the defendant was charged with possession with intent to distribute. The trial court refused to suppress the evidence and the defendant was convicted.]

CALOGERO, Justice

* * *

We assume for our present purposes that the officers reasonably believed that defendant was attempting to swallow contraband, and that they had a reasonable basis on which to arrest him for its possession. That finding does not end the matter, however, for we must still decide whether the force with which the officers garnered the questioned evidence constituted an unreasonable search and seizure under the fourth amendment, and whether the manner of seizure fell short of civilized standards of decency and fair play in derogation of the due process clause of the fifth and fourteenth amendments.

The seminal case articulating the standards for police use of force to extract physical evidence from the body of a nonconsenting suspect is *Rochin v. California*. In *Rochin*, police officers, following an anonymous tip, burst into defendant's apartment. Defendant picked up two capsules from a night stand and swallowed them. The Court described the events in this way: "A struggle ensued, in the course of which the three officers "'jumped upon him' and attempted to extract the capsules." When this effort failed, the officers took Rochin to a hospital where, against his will, his stomach was pumped. The two capsules were vomited up and defendant was convicted of their possession. The high court held, on due process grounds, that the evidence seized should have been excluded at trial:

> [W]e are compelled to conclude that the proceedings by which this conviction was obtained do more than offend some fastidious squeamishness or private sentimentalism about combating crime too energetically. This is conduct that shocks the conscience. Illegally breaking into the privacy of the petitioner, the struggle to open his mouth and remove what was there, the forcible extraction of his stomach's contents this course of proceeding by agents of government to obtain evidence is bound to offend even hardened sensibilities. They are methods too close to the rack and the screw to permit of constitutional differentiation."

\* \* \*

The decision in *Rochin*, which as indicated earlier was based entirely on due process grounds, can be compared to the same court's contrary result under the fourth amendment in *Schmerber v. California*. In that case, police arrested defendant at a hospital where he had been taken for treatment after an automobile accident. At police request, medical personnel took a blood sample from the defendant, without his consent and without a warrant. In approving this procedure, the court noted specifically that the officers proceeded in an accepted medical procedure and that the operation was performed in a reasonable manner without trauma or pain. Moreover, the court found an "emergency situation" in the highly evanescent nature of the evidence: "We are told that the percentage of alcohol in the blood begins to diminish shortly after drinking stops, as the body functions to eliminate it from the system. . . . [T]here was no time to seek out a magistrate and secure a warrant." The court emphasized that:

> [W]e reach this judgment only on the facts of the present record. The integrity of an individual's person is a cherished value of our society. That we today hold that the Constitution does not forbid the States minor intrusions into an individual's body under stringently limited conditions in no way indicates that it permits more substantial intrusions, or intrusions under other conditions.

We find that the forcible seizure of the evidence here is far closer to the facts in *Rochin* than those in *Schmerber*. The beating and choking of defendant Tapp is reminiscent of, if not more excessive than, the beating officers gave to defendant Rochin. The prolonged and brutal struggle to cause Tapp to disgorge the packet was excessive under the circumstances and thereby abused common conceptions of decency and civilized conduct. Although policemen can use reasonable force to attempt to prevent the swallowing of evidence, particularly when a search for evidence is underway pursuant to a warrant, police officers may not constitutionally beat and choke suspects in order to gain that evidence. In so doing, these officers used unreasonable force to recover the evidence, thus offending the fifth amendment guarantee of due process and causing the evidence so recovered to be inadmissible at defendant's trial.

The state urges us to adopt a rule it alleges is prevalent in some jurisdictions which would allow the choking of a suspect so as to recover physical evidence.

We do not find the legal principles in those cases different from those we here adopt. Those opinions recognize that the application of unreasonable force in the recovery of physical evidence offends due process, but find, on the facts there presented, that the force used was reasonable. In none of those cases was a suspect beaten at all, much less with the intensity of the beating administered to defendant Tapp.

In addition to the due process violation heretofore described, we also find that the search and seizure offended the fourth amendment. Unlike the situation in *Schmerber*, the extraction of this evidence was not the result of painless, medically approved procedures. Nor was there the need for speed in the gaining of evidence which the *Schmerber* court found persuasive. We see no evidence in the record (and indeed, the state does not so argue) that this material, if swallowed, would not have traveled through defendant's body without destruction of the evidence or harm to defendant. We hold that this was not the "minor intrusion into an individual's body under stringently limited conditions" approved in *Schmerber*, but rather a grievous, dangerous, painful and unjustifiable assault upon a human being in an effort to get physical evidence from inside his body. The evidence against him so obtained should not have been admitted at the trial

because it was gained in violation of the fourth amendment.

We find therefore that the seizure of the packet of heroin from defendant Tapp's throat exceeded the constitutional limitations of the fourth amendment requirement that safeguards the right to be free from unreasonable searches and seizures, and of the fifth and fourteenth amendments which assure individuals fair and humane treatment by law enforcement officers. Thus, the packet of heroin extracted from defendant's person should not have been admitted into evidence against him.

We turn now to the issue of the validity of the search warrant gained for the second residence, a warrant granted partially on the basis of the heroin seized from defendant's person.

The facts of these various searches bear repeating. Officers had gained a search warrant for defendant Tapp's residence on Lowerline Street because of an informer's tip. The application for that warrant gave no indication of any place other than the Lowerline address where defendant Tapp might have hidden his suspected contraband. The search of the Lowerline address was fruitless, except for a heroin residue on a single syringe admittedly not belonging to defendant. But police did recover five packets of heroin from Tapp's person in the unconstitutional manner already described. Police also interviewed defendant's children, ages 8 and 5, who had arrived at the house with Tapp. Although they indicated no criminal activity on Tapp's part, they did direct the officers to a nearby house from which they had come and indicated that their father owned this house also. The officers then applied for and received a warrant to search this Palmetto Street residence, a search which produced a large quantity of heroin. This warrant is based primarily upon the seizure of heroin from defendant's person, a seizure we have already found invalid under both the fourth and fifth amendments. The affidavit relies secondarily upon information gleaned from Tapp's small children that their father maintained another residence, but as previously explained, the children supplied no information relating to criminal activity. Thirdly, the affidavit relates that a reliable and confidential informant had stated that he had been present at the Lowerline Street address when defendant left "in order to procure additional amounts of heroin and exhibited a belief that the stash pad was in close proximity to Tapp's residence due to the fact that Tapp was absent for only a quarter of an hour before returning with the contraband." This informer tip offered no indication of the location of the surmised "stash pad," no personal observation or knowledge of the existence of a second residence, and, of course, no personal or recent observation of contraband at such a place. In summary, then, the warrant was issued on the basis of an unconstitutional seizure, innocent information from two children as to a particular address, and an uncorroborated hunch from an unidentified tipster that he "believed" that defendant Tapp might have a "stash pad" at an unknown location.

* * *

We hold that the illegally seized material tainted the warrant which depended on it, and that the independent portions of the warrant (the informant's hunch and the innocent address) do not offer a showing of probable cause upon which a person's privacy may be invaded.

For these reasons, we find that the affidavit in support of the search warrant issued for the Palmetto Street address is fatally deficient, and that the trial court therefore erred in denying relator's motion to suppress based on that deficiency.

Decree

For these reasons, defendant's convictions and sentences are reversed and the case remanded to the district court.

REVERSED AND REMANDED.

[Concurring opinion omitted.]

SANDERS, Chief Justice (dissenting).

In my opinion, the majority erroneously interprets the struggle between the officers and the defendant as one in which the officers' only goal was to extract the heroin from the defendant's mouth. The record clearly indicates that the police action was aimed at both preventing the defendant from effectuating his escape and seizing the contraband. As the police had two objectives, their action must be allocated between these objectives.

When the officers attempted to place the defendant under arrest, he immediately ran, placing the cellophane packet in his mouth. An officer attempted to grab him from the rear, but the defendant resisted. Other officers joined in the struggle. The defendant continued to resist, fighting and kicking the officers. In a stipulation by the State and defense, the officers admitted that they hit the defendant three times before he was subdued.

Louisiana Code of Criminal Procedure Article 220 provides:

A person shall submit peaceably to a lawful arrest. The person making a lawful arrest may use reasonable force to effect the arrest and detention, and also to overcome any resistance or threatened resistance of the person being arrested or detained.

Under this codal provision, I believe the officers' action in using force to effectuate the arrest justified.

Whether police action in extracting contraband from the defendant's person is unreasonable, uncivilized, or shocking depends upon the totality of the circumstances.

As I construe the record, the only police action that may be directly attributed to the seizure of the evidence is the police's choking the defendant and their order to expel the packet. The issue then becomes: is the choking and the command unreasonable, uncivilized, or shocking. I think not.

\* \* \*

It is common knowledge that narcotic offenders often try to swallow narcotics to defeat the law enforcement process. Law enforcement officers, of course, may adopt reasonable measures to retrieve the contraband. In the present case, the officers used a spoon to remove the particles of marijuana from the defendant's tongue. Under the circumstances, the action of the officers was neither cruel nor bizarre. As the United States Supreme Court observed in *Schmerber v. California*, the officers were confronted with an emergency that threatened the destruction of evidence.

Several courts in other jurisdictions have upheld similar seizures. State v. Young, 15 Wash. App. 581, 550 P.2d 689 (1976) (the officer "placed his hands on his throat, constricting his ability to swallow" and another officer pinched his nose to make the defendant breathe through his mouth and spit out the evidence); United States v. Harrison, 139 U.S. App. D.C. 266, 432 F.2d 1328 (1970) (the officer grabbed the defendant by the throat and made him expel the evidence); State v. Santos, 101 N.J. Super. 98, 243 A.2d 274 (1968) (the officers grabbed the defendant by the throat and tried to pry his mouth open); Espinoza v. United States, 278 F.2d 802 (5th Cir. 1960) (the officers choked the defendant and attempted "to pry open his mouth by placing pressure against his jaw and nose"); State v. O'Shea, 16 N.J. 1, 105 A.2d 833 (1954) (the officers struggled with the defendant and "forced him to disgorge the papers he was attempting to swallow").

Considering the facts of this case and the cited jurisprudence, I conclude that the record supports the trial court's ruling that the evidence was reasonably seized. Thus, I would affirm the denial of the motion to suppress.

For the reasons assigned, I respectfully dissent.

# Cases Relating to Chapter 8

# Assistance of Counsel

## GIDEON
### v.
## WAINWRIGHT

### 372 U.S. 335, 83 S. Ct. 792, 9 L. Ed. 2d 799 (1963)

[Gideon was charged in a Florida state court with having broken and entered a poolroom, an offense that was a felony under Florida law. Appearing in court without funds and without a lawyer, he asked the court to appoint counsel for him. The judge denied Gideon's request, advising him that under Florida law appointment of counsel was available only for defendants charged with a capital offense. Placed on trial before a jury, Gideon conducted his defense about as well as could be expected from a layperson. He made an opening statement to the jury, cross-examined the State's witnesses, presented witnesses in his own defense, declined to testify himself, and made a short closing argument emphasizing his innocence. The jury returned a verdict of guilty, and sentenced Gideon to serve five years in the state prison. The Florida Supreme Court denied Gideon's habeas corpus petition attacking his conviction and sentence on the ground that the trial court's refusal to appoint counsel for him denied him his constitutional rights.]

MR. JUSTICE BLACK delivered the opinion of the Court.

. . . Since 1942, when *Betts v. Brady* was decided by a divided Court, the problem of a defendant's federal constitutional right to counsel in a state court has been a continuing source of controversy and litigation in both state and federal courts. To give this problem another review here, we granted certiorari. Since Gideon was proceeding in forma pauperis, we appointed counsel to represent him and requested both sides to discuss in their briefs and oral arguments the following: "Should this Court's holding in *Betts v. Brady* be reconsidered?"

The facts upon which Betts claimed that he had been unconstitutionally denied the right to have counsel appointed to assist him are strikingly like the facts upon which Gideon here bases his federal constitutional claim. Betts was indicted for robbery in a Maryland state court. On arraignment, he told the trial judge of his lack of funds to hire a lawyer and asked the court to appoint one for him. Betts was advised that it was not the practice in that county to appoint counsel for indigent defendants except in murder and rape cases. He then pleaded not guilty, had witnesses summoned, cross-examined the State's witnesses, examined his own, and chose not to testify himself. He was found guilty by the judge, sitting without a jury, and sentenced to eight years in prison. Like Gideon, Betts sought release by habeas corpus, alleging that he had been denied the right to assistance of counsel in violation of the Fourteenth Amendment. Betts was denied any relief, and on review this Court affirmed. It was held that a refusal to appoint counsel for an indigent defendant charged with a felony did not necessarily violate the Due Process Clause of the Fourteenth Amendment, which for reasons given the Court deemed to be the only applicable federal constitutional provision. The Court said:

> Asserted denial [of due process] is to be tested by an appraisal of the totality of facts in a given case. That which may, in one setting, constitute a denial of fundamental fairness, shocking to the universal sense of justice, may, in other circumstances, and in the light of other considerations, fall short of such denial.

Treating due process as "a concept less rigid and more fluid than those envisaged in other specific and particular provisions of the Bill of Rights," the Court held that refusal to appoint counsel under the particular facts and circumstances in the *Betts* case was not so "offensive to the common and fundamental ideas of fairness" as to amount to a denial of due process. Since the facts and circumstances of the two cases are so nearly indistinguishable, we think the *Betts v. Brady* holding if left standing would require us to reject Gideon's claim that the Constitution guarantees him the assistance of counsel. Upon full reconsideration we conclude that *Betts v. Brady* should be overruled.

The Sixth Amendment provides, "In all criminal prosecutions, the accused shall enjoy the right . . . to have the Assistance of Counsel for his defence." We have construed this to mean that in federal courts counsel must be provided for defendants unable to employ counsel unless the right is competently and intelligently waived. Betts argued that this right is extended to indigent defendants in state courts by the Fourteenth Amendment. In response the Court stated that, while the Sixth Amendment laid down "no rule for the conduct of the States, the question recurs whether the constraint laid by the Amendment upon the national courts expresses a rule so fundamental and essential to a fair trial, and so, to due process of law, that it is made obligatory upon the States by the Fourteenth Amendment." In order to decide whether the Sixth Amendment's guarantee of counsel is of this fundamental nature, the Court in *Betts* set out and considered "relevant data on the subject . . . afforded by constitutional and statutory provisions subsisting in the colonies and the States prior to the inclusion of the Bill of Rights in the national Constitution, and in the constitutional, legislative, and judicial history of the States to the present date." On the basis of this historical data the Court concluded that "appointment of counsel is not a fundamental right, essential to a fair trial." It was for this reason the *Betts* Court refused to accept the contention that the Sixth Amendment's guarantee of counsel for indigent federal defendants was extended to or, in the words of that Court, "made obligatory upon the States by the Fourteenth Amendment." . . .

* * *

We accept *Betts v. Brady's* assumption, based as it was on our prior cases, that a provision of the Bill of Rights which is "fundamental and essential to a fair trial" is made obligatory upon the States by the Fourteenth Amendment. We think the Court in *Betts* was wrong, however, in concluding that the Sixth Amendment's guarantee of counsel is not one of these fundamental rights. Ten years before *Betts v. Brady*, this Court, after full consideration of all the historical data examined in *Betts*, had unequivocally declared that "the right to the aid of counsel is of this fundamental character." While the Court at the close of its *Powell* opinion did by its language, as this Court frequently does, limit its holding to the particular facts and circumstances of that case, its conclusions about the fundamental nature of the right to counsel are unmistakable. Several years later, in 1936, the Court reemphasized what it had said about the fundamental nature of the right to counsel in this language:

We concluded that certain fundamental rights, safeguarded by the first eight amendments against federal action, were also safeguarded against state action by the due process of law clause of the Fourteenth Amendment, and among them the fundamental right of the accused to the aid of counsel in a criminal prosecution."

And again in 1938 this Court said:

[The assistance of counsel] is one of the safeguards of the Sixth Amendment deemed necessary to insure fundamental human rights of life and liberty. . . . The Sixth Amendment stands as a constant admonition that if the constitutional safeguards it provides be lost, justice will not "still be done."

In light of these and many other prior decisions of this Court, it is not surprising that the *Betts* Court, when faced with the contention that "one charged with crime, who is unable to obtain counsel, must be furnished counsel by the State," conceded that "expressions in the opinions of this court lend color to the argument . . ." The fact is that in deciding as it did—that "appointment of counsel is not a fundamental right, essential to a fair trial"—the Court in *Betts v. Brady* made an abrupt break with its own well-considered precedents. In returning to these old precedents, sounder we believe than the new, we but restore constitutional principles established to achieve a fair system of justice. Not only these precedents but also reason and reflection require us to recognize that in our adversary system of criminal justice, any person haled into court, who is too poor to hire a lawyer, cannot be assured a fair trial unless counsel is provided for him. This seems to us to be an obvious truth. Governments, both state and federal, quite properly spend vast sums of money to establish machinery to try defendants accused of crime. Lawyers to prosecute are everywhere deemed essential to protect the public's interest in an orderly society. Similarly, there are few defendants charged with crime, few indeed, who fail to hire the best lawyers they can get to prepare and present their defenses. That government hires lawyers to prosecute and defendants who have the money hire lawyers to defend are the strongest indications of the widespread belief that lawyers in criminal courts are necessities, not luxuries. The right of one charged with crime to counsel may not be deemed fundamental and essential to fair trials in some countries, but it is in ours. From the very beginning, our state and national constitutions and laws have laid great emphasis on procedural and substantive safeguards designed to assure fair trials before impartial tribunals in which every defendant stands equal before the law. This noble ideal cannot be realized if the poor man charged with crime has to face his accusers without a lawyer to assist him. A defendant's need for a lawyer is nowhere better stated than in the moving words of Mr. Justice Sutherland in *Powell v. Alabama*:

The right to be heard would be, in many cases, of little avail if it did not comprehend the right to be heard by counsel. Even the intelligent and educated layman has small and sometimes no skill in the science of law. If charged with crime, he is incapable, generally, of determining for himself whether the indictment is good or bad. He is unfamiliar with the rules of evidence. Left without the aid of counsel he may be put on trial without a proper charge, and convicted upon incompetent evidence, or evidence irrelevant to the issue or otherwise inadmissible. He lacks both the skill and knowledge adequately to prepare his defense, even though he have a perfect one. He requires the guiding hand of counsel at every step in the proceedings against him. Without it, though he be not guilty, he faces the danger of conviction because he does not know how to establish his innocence.

The Court in *Betts v. Brady* departed from the sound wisdom upon which the Court's holding in *Powell v. Alabama* rested. Florida, supported by two other States, has asked that *Betts v. Brady* be left intact. Twenty-two States, as friends of the Court, argue that *Betts* was "an anachronism when handed down" and that it should now be overruled. We agree.

The judgment is reversed and the cause is remanded to the Supreme Court of Florida for further action not inconsistent with this opinion.

Reversed.

**STATE**

v.

**QUATTLEBAUM**

**338 S. C. 441, 527 S.E.2d 105 (2001)**

[Appellant voluntarily went to the sheriff's office for questioning concerning his involvement in an armed robbery and murder and agreed to take a polygraph examination. After the exam was administered, he was left alone in the polygraph room where he was joined by his attorney. Unbeknownst to either of them, their conversation was audio and videotaped by detectives in the presence of a deputy solicitor. This fact was not revealed to appellant or his attorneys for two years. The deputy solicitor who participated in the eavesdropping was an active participant in appellant's trial and gave the closing argument in the guilt phase. The jury convicted appellant and recommended a sentence of death. This appeal followed.]

BURNETT, Justice:

* * *

Appellant argues his Sixth Amendment right to counsel was violated and the solicitor's office should have been disqualified as a result. We agree.

The Sixth Amendment right to counsel protects the integrity of the adversarial system of criminal justice by ensuring that all persons accused of crimes have access to effective assistance of counsel for their defense. The right is grounded in "the presumed inability of a defendant to make informed choices about the preparation and conduct of his defense." Although the Sixth Amendment right to counsel is distinguishable from the attorney-client privilege, the two concepts overlap in many ways. The right to counsel would be meaningless without the protection of free and open communication between client and counsel. The United States Supreme Court has noted that "conferences between counsel and accused . . . sometimes partake of the inviolable character of the confessional."

\* \* \*

This is, fortunately, a case of first impression in South Carolina. Never before have we addressed a case involving deliberate prosecutorial intrusion into a privileged conversation between a criminal defendant and his attorney. Federal jurisprudence in this area is decidedly ambiguous, and we have found no precedent dealing with a prosecutor deliberately eavesdropping on an accused and his attorney.

In the 1950s and 1960s, when first faced with cases involving government eavesdropping on attorney-client conversations, federal courts refused to examine either the government's motives or the degree of prejudice to the defendant. Over time, the rule that began to emerge would have required either a showing of deliberate prosecutorial misconduct or prejudice, but not both.

In 1977, the United States Supreme Court appeared to alter this standard in *Weatherford v. Bursey. Weatherford* involved an informant/codefendant who attended meetings between Bursey and his attorney. The Supreme Court found no Sixth Amendment violation where there was no tainted evidence, no communication of defense strategy to the prosecution, and no purposeful intrusion by the government. The Court held that establishing a violation of a defendant's Sixth Amendment right to counsel requires a showing of "at least a realistic possibility" of prejudice.

Because the government interceptions in *Weatherford* were "unintended and undisclosed," the Court did not address whether the rule would be different in a case involving deliberate misconduct by the government. Nor did the Court decide who bears the burden of proving prejudice. . . .

*Weatherford* is inapplicable to the case *sub judice,* where a member of the prosecution team intentionally eavesdropped on a confidential defense conversation. We conclude, consistent with existing federal precedent, that a defendant must show either deliberate prosecutorial misconduct *or* prejudice to make out a violation of the Sixth Amendment, but not both. Deliberate prosecutorial misconduct raises an irrebuttable presumption of prejudice. The content of the protected communication is not relevant. The focus must be on the misconduct. In cases involving unintentional intrusions into the attorney-client relationship, the defendant must make a prima facie showing of prejudice to shift the burden to the prosecution to prove the defendant was not prejudiced.

Because a deputy solicitor of the Eleventh Circuit Solicitor's Office eavesdropped on a privileged conversation between appellant and his attorney, we reverse appellant's conviction and disqualify the Eleventh Circuit Solicitor's office from prosecuting appellant at his new trial.

Although we have disqualified the Eleventh Circuit Solicitor's Office from prosecuting appellant, we address appellant's second assertion because of its importance to judges, attorneys, criminal defendants, and indeed all citizens of this state. Every South Carolinian has a vital interest in the fair administration of justice. This Court bears the ultimate responsibility for maintaining judicial integrity and high standards of professional conduct among the members of the bar, and for protecting and defending the constitutional rights of the accused.

The integrity of the entire judicial system is called into question by conduct such as that engaged in by the deputy solicitor and investigating officers in this case. Prosecutors are ministers of justice and not merely advocates. A prosecutor has special responsibilities to do justice and is held to the highest standards of professional ethics. The participation at trial of a prosecutor who has eavesdropped on the accused and his attorney tarnishes us all. We will not tolerate deliberate prosecutorial misconduct which threatens rights fundamental to liberty and justice.

REVERSED

## UNITED STATES
## v.
## DOWNS

### 230 F.3d 272 (7th Cir. 2000)

DIANE P. WOOD, Circuit Judge.

\* \* \*

On March 31, 1999, a white male wearing sunglasses and a blue hat resembling those issued by the LaPrairie Mutual Insurance Company approached Denise Brown, the walk-up teller at Heritage Bank. He told Brown to remove all of the money from the drawer, but then, speaking in a low voice, he altered his instructions and indicated that he wanted only bundles and no $1 bills. Brown later said that she paid close attention to his mouth and lower face, because she was concerned that the robber might become agitated if she had difficulty understanding him. In the 50-some seconds she had to observe him, she also formed the impression that he was lightly unshaven, between 5'6" and 5'8" tall, about 150 pounds, and between 35 and 45 years old. The other teller on duty, Karen Jones, was serving drive-up customers and thus caught only a glimpse of the robber; her description of him was similar to Brown's.

The next day, someone gave Peoria police officers and FBI agents a tip that a woman named Kim Salzman could help them. Salzman was cooperative. She told the officers that the person in the surveillance video from the bank strongly resembled her brother, Randy Downs. Her statement, along with her account that Downs's gambling problems had led him to break into her printing business and steal a compressor in order to pawn it, increased the suspicions of the investigators. They decided to assemble a photo array and show it to both Brown and Jones. They did so, but neither was able positively to identify Downs as the robber from the pictures. Brown suggested that it would be more helpful to see people wearing hats and sunglasses.

Later that day, the officers interviewed Downs himself, first on a gambling boat and then later in a security office. The next day, they talked to Richard Downs, his father. The elder Mr. Downs told the officers that he had given Randy a hat from LaPrairie Mutual Insurance very similar to the one that appeared on the video. He also volunteered that when he had refused to loan Randy $2,000, Randy had responded "you leave me little choice." After this, the officers searched Randy's apartment, with his consent; they found nothing there.

On April 5, the officers held the line-up that is the focus of this appeal. On that day, they had finally arrested Downs and brought him to the police station. One officer telephoned Jones and asked her to come to the station, and he informed Jones that they had arrested someone. Another officer called Brown and asked her to come, but it is unclear whether or not she was told there had been an arrest. For the line-up, each person was given a LaPrairie Mutual hat and a pair of sunglasses. They entered the room *seriatim*; each man stepped in, walked around, and said "No, put the money in the envelope, hurry." Downs was the second to walk in. As the exhibits Downs later introduced make crystal clear, the other four all sported heavy moustaches; only Downs had no facial hair at all. Otherwise (but it is a big "otherwise"), they were similar in body build.

At the line-up, both Brown and Jones identified Downs as the robber. Jones was not very confident in her choice, describing her certainty as a seven out of ten, if ten meant absolutely sure. Brown, in contrast, jumped behind one of the detectives the minute she saw Downs enter the room, and exclaimed "Oh my God, that's him." She was crying and trembling, according to the testimony of another officer. Brown then viewed the last three line-up participants, and at the end reiterated that she was "positive" the robber was Downs, based on "the lower half of his face" and his "stocky upper body."

On July 1, 1999, the district court heard testimony on Downs's motion to suppress both the line-up and any in-court identification the government might want to elicit from Brown or Jones. The court concluded that the line-up was indeed too suggestive. It then decided that the Jones testimony would be so unreliable that both her line-up identification should be suppressed and she should be prevented from offering an in-court identification. With respect to Brown, the oral rulings and written record became somewhat confused. Orally, the court first indicated that the circumstances as a whole made Brown's identification reliable and thus admissible. Then, in response to a question from the prosecutor, the judge said that both women's line-up identifications would be suppressed. Later, however, in a written order the court ruled that Brown could be questioned about her line-up identification (and could give an in-court statement).

* * *

A ruling on a motion to suppress an identification, like many other matters in a criminal trial, presents the kind of mixed question of constitutional law and fact that the Supreme Court has instructed us to review *de novo*, but with due deference to findings of historical fact made by the district court.

On the merits, we conduct a two-step inquiry when we assess the admissibility of a line-up identification. First, we ask whether the line-up was unduly suggestive. If it was, then we look more closely to see if the totality of the circumstances nevertheless shows that the testimony was reliable. In this case, although the government has made a token effort to argue that the line-up was not unduly suggestive, we agree entirely with the district court that it was. Even a glance at the photographs of the men in the line-up, which appear as exhibits in the record, is enough to see why Downs jumps out from the others because of his lack of facial hair. We therefore turn immediately to the second question, whether Brown's testimony was reliable notwithstanding the problems with the line-up.

The reliability inquiry touches on five factors: (1) the opportunity of the witness to view the criminal at the time of the crime, (2) the witness's degree of attention, (3) the accuracy of the witness's prior description, (4) the level of certainty demonstrated by the witness at the confrontation, and (5) the length of time between the crime and the confrontation. All of these, in one way or another, support the reliability of Brown's identification. She could see the lower half of the robber's face, and this was the basis of her identification. At the time of the crime, she was very close to the robber, and she stated firmly that she was paying strict attention to what she saw. Although 50 seconds may not sound like much, under conditions of great stress they can pass quite slowly. The physical descriptions Brown had given of the robber were reasonably detailed and close to Brown's actual appearance. Brown's dramatic reaction when Downs walked into the room showed clearly that she was quite certain that Downs was the robber. Finally, five days between the incident and the line-up is not such a long span of time that memory lapses would be a problem.

Last is a point not mentioned in this particular five-factor test, but it gives us the opportunity both to note that these tests are principally useful as a guide to the inquiry at hand and that they are not intended to be straitjackets. Given the way this line-up was conducted, Brown had seen only one man (who had a moustache) before she saw Downs and emphatically identified him. She did not know then that the other three men would also have moustaches (or indeed that they would either resemble Downs or stand apart from him in any other way). This as well as the other evidence convinces us that Brown knew what she was talking about; her identification of Downs at the line-up was sufficiently reliable that the jury was entitled to learn about it, and there was no error in allowing her to identify him at trial.

In light of our conclusion that the flaws in the line-up did not require the suppression of Brown's testimony, we need not reach the government's alternative argument that any error in this respect was harmless. The judgment of the district court is

AFFIRMED.

# Cases Relating to Chapter 9

# Trial and Punishment

AMERICAN BAR ASSOCIATION
STANDARDS FOR CRIMINAL
JUSTICE (3rd. ed. 1992)

## Chapter 8 FAIR TRIAL and FREE PRESS

## STANDARD 8-1.1. EXTRAJUDICIAL STATEMENTS BY ATTORNEYS

(a) A lawyer should not make or authorize the making of an extrajudicial statement that a reasonable person would expect to be disseminated by means of public communication if the lawyer knows or reasonably should know that it will have a substantial likelihood of prejudicing a criminal proceeding.

(b) Statements relating to the following matters are ordinarily likely to have a substantial likelihood of prejudicing a criminal proceeding:

(1) the prior criminal record (including arrests, indictments, or other charges of crime) of a suspect or defendant;

(2) the character or reputation of a suspect or defendant;

(3) the opinion of the lawyer on the guilt of the defendant, the merits of the case or the merits of the evidence in the case;

(4) the existence or contents of any confession, admission, or statement given by the accused, or the refusal or failure of the accused to make a statement;

(5) the performance of any examinations or tests, or the accused's refusal or failure to submit to an examination or test, or the identity or nature of physical evidence expected to presented.

(6) the identity, expected testimony, criminal record or credibility of prospective witnesses;

(7) the possibility of a plea of guilty to the offense charged, or other disposition; and

(8) information which the lawyer knows or has reason to know would be inadmissible as evidence in a trial.

(c) Notwithstanding paragraphs (a) and (b), statements relating to the following matters may be made:

(1) the general nature of the charges against the accused, provided that there is included therein a statement explaining that the charge is merely an accusation and the defendant is presumed innocent until and unless proven guilty;

(2) the general nature of the defense to the charges or to other public accusations against the accused, including that the accused has no prior criminal record;

(3) the name, age, residence, occupation and family status of the accused;

(4) information necessary to aid in the apprehension of the accused or to warn the public of any dangers that may exist.

(5) a request for assistance in obtaining evidence;

(6) the existence of an investigation in progress, including the general length and scope of the investigation, the charge or defense involved, and the identity of the investigating officer or agency;

(7) the facts and circumstances of an arrest, including the time and place, and the identity of the arresting officer or agency;

(8) the identity of the victim, where the release of that information is not otherwise prohibited by law or would not be harmful to the victim;

(9) information contained within a public record, without further comment; and

(10) the scheduling or result of any stage in the judicial process;

(d) Nothing in this standard is intended to preclude the formulation or application of more restrictive rules relating to the release of information about juvenile offenders, to preclude the holding of hearings or the lawful issuance of reports by legislative, administrative, or investigative bodies, to preclude any lawyer from replying to charges of misconduct that are publicly made against him or her, or to preclude or inhibit any lawyer from making an otherwise permissible statement which serves to educate or inform the public concerning the operations of the criminal justice system.

## STANDARD 8-2.1. RELEASE OF INFORMATION BY LAW ENFORCEMENT AGENCIES

(a) The provisions of Standard 1.1 should be applicable to the release of information to the public by law enforcement officers and agencies.

(b) Law enforcement officers and agencies should not exercise their custodial authority over an accused individual in a manner that is likely to result in

either: (1) the deliberate exposure of a person in custody for the purpose of photographing or televising by representatives of the news media, or (2) the interviewing by representatives of the news media of a person in custody except upon request or consent by that person to an interview after being informed adequately of the right to consult with counsel and of the right to refuse to grant an interview.

(c) Nothing in this standard is intended to preclude any law enforcement officer or agency from replying to charges of misconduct that are publicly made against him or her from participating in any legislative, administrative, or investigative hearing, nor is the standard intended to supersede more restrictive rules governing the release of information concerning juvenile offenders.

## KYLES
### v.
## WHITLEY

### 514 U.S. 419, 115 S. Ct. 1555, 131 L. Ed. 2d 490 (1995)

*[Citations and footnotes omitted.]*

[An elderly woman was shot in the head and killed in a grocery store parking lot. The killer took her keys and drove away in her car. Since the police believed the killer might have driven his own car to the lot and left it there when he drove off in the victim's car, they recorded the license numbers of the cars remaining in the parking lots around the store. Kyles's car was not among these listed. Police also took descriptions from six eyewitnesses. Their descriptions of the killer's height, age, weight, build, and hair length differed significantly from each other and most bore little resemblance to Kyles.

The investigation did not focus on Kyles until an informant known as Beanie, who resembled the descriptions given by the witnesses, told police that the Kyles committed the crime. Kyles was indicted for first-degree murder. Before trial, Kyles's attorney filed a motion for disclosure by the prosecutor of any exculpatory or impeachment evidence. The prosecutor responded that there was none. The prosecutor, however, was unaware of the following items in the hands of the police because the prosecutor was never informed of these items: (1) contemporaneous descriptions given by the six eyewitnesses; (2) the computer print-out of license numbers of cars parked in the grocery store parking lot on the night of the murder; and (3) evidence linking Beanie to other crimes committed in the same parking lot, including an unrelated murder.

Kyles's first trial ended in a hung jury. At the second trial, the prosecution offered a blown-up photograph taken at the crime scene soon after the murder and argued that a poorly-discernible vehicle in the background belonged to Kyles. Kyles maintained his innocence. The defense's theory was that Kyles had been framed by Beanie. Kyles was convicted and sentenced to death.]

JUSTICE SOUTER delivered the opinion of the Court.

* * *

The prosecution's affirmative duty to disclose evidence favorable to a defendant can trace its origins to early 20th-century strictures against misrepresentation and is of course most prominently associated with this Court's decision in *Brady v. Maryland*. *Brady* held "that the suppression by the prosecution of evidence favorable to an accused upon request violates due process where the evidence is material either to guilt or to

punishment, irrespective of the good faith or bad faith of the prosecution.". . .

. . . [F]avorable evidence is material, and constitutional error results from its suppression by the government, "if there is a reasonable probability that, had the evidence been disclosed to the defense, the result of the proceeding would have been different."

* * *

While the definition of *Bagley* materiality in terms of the cumulative effect of suppression must accordingly be seen as leaving the government with a degree of discretion, it must also be understood as imposing a corresponding burden. On the one side, showing that the prosecution knew of an item of favorable evidence unknown to the defense does not amount to a *Brady* violation, without more. But the prosecution, which alone can know what is undisclosed, must be assigned the consequent responsibility to gauge the likely net effect of all such evidence and make disclosure when the point of "reasonable probability" is reached. This in turn means that the individual prosecutor has a duty to learn of any favorable evidence known to the others acting on the government's behalf in the case, including the police. But whether the prosecutor succeeds or fails in meeting this obligation (whether, that is, a failure to disclose is in good faith or bad faith), the prosecution's responsibility for failing to disclose known, favorable evidence rising to a material level of importance is inescapable.

The State of Louisiana would prefer an even more lenient rule. It pleads that some of the favorable evidence in issue here was not disclosed even to the prosecutor until after trial, and it suggested below that it should not be held accountable under *Bagley* and *Brady* for evidence known only to police investigators and not to the prosecutor. To accommodate the State in this manner would, however, amount to a serious change of course from the *Brady* line of cases. In the State's favor it may be said that no one doubts that police investigators sometimes fail to inform a prosecutor of all they know. But neither is there any serious doubt that "procedures and regulations can be established to carry [the prosecutor's] burden and to insure communication of all relevant information on each case to every lawyer who deals with it." Since, then, the prosecutor has the means to discharge the government's *Brady* responsibility if he will, any argument for excusing a prosecutor from disclosing what he does not happen to know about boils down to a plea to substitute the police for the prosecutor, and even for the courts themselves, as the final arbiters of the government's obligation to ensure fair trials.

\* \* \*

In this case, disclosure of the suppressed evidence to competent counsel would have made a different result reasonably probable.

As the District Court put it, "the essence of the State's case" was the testimony of eyewitnesses, who identified Kyles as Dye's killer. Disclosure of their statements would have resulted in a markedly weaker case for the prosecution and a markedly stronger one for the defense. To begin with, the value of two of those witnesses would have been substantially reduced or destroyed.

\* \* \*

Next to be considered is the prosecution's list of the cars in the Schwegmann's parking lot at mid-evening after the murder. . . . [I]t would have had some value as exculpation and impeachment, and it counts accordingly in determining whether *Bagley's* standard of materiality

is satisfied. On the police's assumption, argued to the jury, that the killer drove to the lot and left his car there during the heat of the investigation, the list without Kyles's registration would obviously have helped Kyles and would have had some value in countering an argument by the prosecution that a grainy enlargement of a photograph of the crime scene showed Kyles's car in the background. The list would also have shown that the police either knew that it was inconsistent with their informant's second and third statements (in which Beanie described retrieving Kyles's car after the time the list was compiled) or never even bothered to check the informant's story against known fact. Either way, the defense would have had further support for arguing that the police were irresponsible in relying on Beanie to tip them off to the location of evidence damaging to Kyles.

\* \* \*

[The State's obligation under *Brady* to disclose evidence favorable to the defense turns on the cumulative effect of all such evidence suppressed by the government. We hold that the prosecutor remains responsible for gauging that effect, regardless of any failure by the police to bring favorable evidence to the prosecutor's attention. Because the net effect of the evidence withheld by the State in this case raises a reasonable probability that its disclosure would have produced a different result, Kyles is entitled to a new trial.]

The judgment of the Court of Appeals is reversed, and the case is remanded for further proceedings consistent with this opinion.

It is so ordered.

[Concurring and dissenting opinions omitted.]

# PEOPLE
## v.
## WRIGHT

**658 N.E.2d 1009, 635 N.Y.S.2d
136 (N.Y. Ct. App. 1995)**

*[Citations and footnotes omitted.]*

[Defendant was charged with assaulting a man named Washington. Her defense was that she was trying to fend off an attempted rape. According to the defendant, the two of them had met at a bar and as she prepared to leave the bar she noticed that her jacket was missing. Washington told her that his friend had it and offered to call him, but not from the bar. Defendant agreed to let Washington call from her apartment. At her apartment, she showed Washington the phone in the living room, and went to the bedroom to hide her purse. While she was in the bedroom Washington entered naked and announced his intention to have sex with her. Fearing for her safety, she took a knife and injured him. According to Washington, the defendant invited him back to her apartment, allowed him to undress in her bedroom and then took out a knife and attacked him.

After the altercation, the defendant called police to her home. Investigating officer Walczak stated in his police report that he recovered a pair of boxer shorts, a shoe and a hat from defendant's apartment that night, and that these articles were located outside the bedroom, facts that substantiated the defendant's account. At trial, however, he testified that the shoe and boxer shorts were found inside the bedroom, and that the hat was discovered at the threshold to the bedroom, which supported Washington's account. Detective Keane, who took Washington's statement, recorded that Washington stated he undressed outside the bedroom, but at trial testified that he

could not remember whether Washington had said this.

The defendant was convicted and eventually moved to set aside her conviction after learning that Washington was an occasional informant for the police department. Defendant argued that the state's failure to disclose this information to the defense required a new trial because, among other reasons, the state should have disclosed the victim's status as a police informant.]

Chief Judge Kaye.

This case presents the question whether the People's failure to inform the defendant that the complainant had previously operated as an informant for the local police department violated defendant's right to due process. We conclude that the People were required to disclose this information pursuant to *Brady v. Maryland* and therefore reverse defendant's conviction.

* * *

In *Brady v. Maryland*, the Supreme Court held that the prosecution has an affirmative duty to disclose to the defense evidence in its possession that is both favorable to the defense and material to guilt or punishment. . . . [T]he failure to disclose *Brady* material violates a defendant's constitutional right to due process.

* * *

Manifestly, Washington's status as a police informant was evidence favorable to the defense here. Specifically, the reports prepared by Detective Keane and Officer Walczak confirmed defendant's claim that Washington was already undressed when he entered her bedroom. Nevertheless, at trial both officers supported Washington's version of events—

Walczak contradicted his report and testified that Washington's boxer shorts and shoe were discovered inside defendant's bedroom, and Keane could no longer recall whether Washington had stated that he entered defendant's bedroom without any clothing. Had defendant been armed with the knowledge that Washington was an informant for the same police department that employed Keane and Walczak, she could have presented the jury with a motive for them to favor Washington. Like evidence tending to affect credibility, evidence establishing such a motive for prosecution witnesses to corroborate the complainant falls within the ambit of the *Brady* rule. Additionally, that Washington had previously operated as a police informant would have provided the defense with an explanation for the decision by the police to disbelieve, and subsequently to arrest, defendant—who promptly notified 911 following the incident—as opposed to Washington.

The People's failure to disclose this favorable evidence to the defense requires reversal, however, only if the evidence was material. . . . [T]he undisclosed evidence must be deemed material because there is a reasonable probability that, had the evidence been disclosed to the defense, the result of the proceeding would have been different.

The outcome of this case turned on whether the jury believed Washington's account of an unprovoked attack or defendant's claim that Washington entered the bedroom naked planning to rape her. Whether Washington undressed inside or outside the bedroom constituted a critical issue in this close credibility contest. Washington's status as a police informant provided the defense with an explanation for Keane's and Walczak's switch to a version of the facts that supported Washington's contention that he undressed inside the bedroom. Tellingly, during deliberations the jury

focused on this aspect of Walczak's trial testimony—it asked for a readback of his testimony regarding where Washington's clothing was discovered.

Also of central importance to the defense in this case was the argument that Washington's reluctance to go to the hospital or the police after he was allegedly brutally victimized by defendant evidenced his consciousness of guilt and undermined his credibility. In summation, the prosecutor explained Washington's behavior by arguing that, because of his criminal record, Washington did not "expect justice from the system":

[M]aybe [Fred Washington] didn't want to go to the hospital because he's thinking the cops are going to think I did something wrong, this looks bad. You know, I didn't do anything but hey, the cops know me and maybe once a criminal, always a criminal, and you know, I didn't do anything, but hey, I've done things in the past. . . .

You know, I've been on the other side of the criminal justice system. I've been arrested and the cops aren't my friends (emphasis added).

Evidence that Washington had, in fact, provided the police with information on prior occasions would have effectively refuted the prosecutor's proffered justification for Washington's behavior. Indeed, had the jury been aware that Washington had a relationship with the local police, his efforts to circumvent police discovery might have appeared even more suspicious.

Under these circumstances, Washington's history as a police informant was both favorable and material to the defense, and the People's failure to disclose this information to the defense violated defendant's constitutional right to due process. The People's reliance in their opposition papers on the trial prosecutor's lack of personal knowledge regarding any instances in which Washington had operated as an informant is unavailing. The mandate of *Brady* extends beyond any particular prosecutor's actual knowledge. Furthermore, "the individual prosecutor has a duty to learn of any favorable evidence known to the others acting on the government's behalf in the case, including the police." The People therefore were not relieved of their obligation to turn over *Brady* material by the trial prosecutor's failure to discover that the police were in possession of exculpatory information.

In light of our conclusion that the People's nondisclosure of Washington's status as a police informant violated defendant's right to due process, we need not reach defendant's remaining contentions.

Accordingly, the order of the Appellate Division should be reversed and the indictment dismissed without prejudice to an application by the People for leave to resubmit the charge of assault in the second degree.

Order reversed, etc.

# ARIZONA
# v.
# YOUNGBLOOD

**488 U.S. 51, 109 S. Ct. 333, 102 L. Ed.2d 281 (1988)**

*[Citations and footnotes omitted.]*

[The victim, a 10-year-old boy, was abducted, molested, and sodomized by a middle-aged man. After the assault, he was taken to a hospital where a physician used a swab from a "sexual assault kit" to collect samples of the perpetrator's semen. The sample taken was insufficient for adequate testing. The police failed to refrigerate the boy's clothing, which also contained semen. As a result, police criminologists were unable to obtain information about the identity of the boy's assailant. The boy identified the respondent. Defense experts testified at the trial that respondent might have been completely exonerated by timely performance of tests on properly preserved semen samples. Respondent was convicted of child molestation, sexual assault, and kidnapping. The Arizona Court of Appeals reversed the conviction on the ground that the State had breached a constitutional duty to preserve the semen samples from the victim's body and clothing.]

Chief Justice REHNQUIST delivered the opinion of the Court.

\* \* \*

Decision of this case requires us to again consider "what might loosely be called the area of constitutionally-guaranteed access to evidence." In *Brady v. Maryland* we held "that the suppression by the prosecution of evidence favorable to the accused upon request violates due process where the evidence is material either to guilt or to punishment, irrespective of the good faith or bad faith of the prosecution." In *United States v. Agurs*, we held that the prosecution had a duty to disclose some evidence of this description even though no requests were made for it, but at the same time we rejected the notion that a "prosecutor has a constitutional duty routinely to deliver his entire file to defense counsel."

There is no question but that the State complied with *Brady* and *Agurs* here. The State disclosed relevant police reports to respondent, which contained information about the existence of the swab and the clothing, and the boy's examination at the hospital. The State provided respondent's expert with the laboratory reports and notes prepared by the police criminologist, and respondent's expert had access to the swab and to the clothing.

If respondent is to prevail on federal constitutional grounds, then, it must be because of some constitutional duty over and above that imposed by cases such as *Brady* and *Agurs*. Our most recent decision in this area of the law, *California v. Trombetta*, arose out of a drunk driving prosecution in which the State had introduced test results indicating the concentration of alcohol in the blood of two motorists. The defendants sought to suppress the test results on the ground that the State had failed to preserve the breath samples used in the test. We rejected this argument for several reasons: first, "the officers here were acting in 'good faith and in accord with their normal practice' "; second, in the light of the procedures actually used the chances that preserved samples would have exculpated the defendants were slim; and, third, even if the samples might have shown inaccuracy in the tests, the defendants had "alternative means of demonstrating their innocence." In the present case, the likelihood that the preserved materials would have enabled the defendant to exonerate himself appears to be greater than it was in *Trombetta*, but here, unlike in *Trombetta*, the State did not attempt to make any use of the materials in its own case in chief.

\* \* \*

The Due Process Clause of the Fourteenth Amendment, as interpreted in *Brady*, makes the good or bad faith of the State irrelevant when the State fails to disclose to the defendant material exculpatory evidence. But we think the Due Process Clause requires a different result when we deal with the failure of the State to preserve evidentiary material of which no more can be said than that it could have been subjected to tests, the results of which might have exonerated the defendant. Part of the reason for the difference in treatment is found in the observation made by the Court in *Trombetta* that "[w]henever potentially exculpatory evidence is permanently lost, courts face the treacherous task of divining the import of materials whose contents are unknown and, very often, disputed." Part of it stems from our unwillingness to read the "fundamental fairness" requirement of the Due Process Clause as imposing on the police an undifferentiated and absolute duty to retain and to preserve all material that might be of conceivable evidentiary significance in a particular prosecution. We think that requiring a defendant to show bad faith on the part of the police both limits the extent of the police's obligation to preserve evidence to reasonable bounds and confines it to that class of cases where the interests of justice most clearly require it, i.e., those cases in which the police themselves by their conduct indicate that the evidence could form a basis for exonerating the defendant. We therefore hold that unless a criminal defendant can show bad faith on the part of the police, failure to preserve potentially useful evidence does not constitute a denial of due process of law.

In this case, the police collected the rectal swab and clothing on the night of the crime: respondent was not taken into custody until six weeks later. The failure of the police to refrigerate the clothing and to perform tests on the semen samples can at worst be described as negligent. None of this information was concealed from respondent at trial, and the evidence—such as it was—was made available to respondent's expert who declined to perform any tests on the samples. The Arizona Court of Appeals noted in its opinion—and we agree—that there was no suggestion of bad faith on the part of the police. It follows, therefore, from what we have said, that there was no violation of the Due Process Clause.

The Arizona Court of Appeals also referred somewhat obliquely to the State's "inability to quantitatively test" certain semen samples with the newer P-30 test. If the court meant by this statement that the Due Process Clause is violated when the police fail to use a particular investigatory tool, we strongly disagree. The situation here is no different than a prosecution for drunk driving that rests on police observation alone; the defendant is free to argue to the finder of fact that a breathalyzer test might have been exculpatory, but the police do not have a constitutional duty to perform any particular tests.

The judgment of the Arizona Court of Appeals is reversed and the case remanded for further proceedings not inconsistent with this opinion.

Reversed.

## COKER

### v.

## GEORGIA

**433 U.S. 584, 97 S. Ct. 2861,
53 L. Ed. 2d 982 (1977)**

*[Citations and footnotes omitted.]*

[Coker was convicted of rape and sentenced to death by a Georgia jury. His conviction and sentence were affirmed by the Georgia Supreme Court. Coker appealed, claiming that the punishment of death for the crime of rape violates the Eighth Amendment, which prohibits "cruel and unusual punishments."]

MR. JUSTICE WHITE announced the judgment of the Court

\* \* \*

*Furman v. Georgia*, and the Court's decisions last Term in *Gregg v. Georgia* and others, make unnecessary the recanvassing of certain critical aspects of the controversy about the constitutionality of capital punishment. It is now settled that the death penalty is not invariably cruel and unusual punishment within the meaning of the Eighth Amendment; it is not inherently barbaric or an unacceptable mode of punishment for crime; neither is it always disproportionate to the crime for which it is imposed. It is also established that imposing capital punishment, at least for murder, in accordance with the procedures provided under the Georgia statutes saves the sentence from the infirmities which led the Court to invalidate the prior Georgia capital punishment statute in *Furman v. Georgia*.

In sustaining the imposition of the death penalty in *Gregg*, however, the Court firmly embraced the holdings and dicta from prior cases, *Furman v. Georgia, Robinson v. California, Trop v. Dulles*, and *Weems v. United States*, to the effect that the Eighth Amendment bars not only those punishments that are "barbaric" but also those that are "excessive" in relation to the crime committed. Under *Gregg*, a punishment is "excessive" and unconstitutional if it (1) makes no measurable contribution to acceptable goals of punishment and hence is nothing more than the purposeless and needless imposition of pain and suffering; or (2) is grossly out of proportion to the severity of the crime. A punishment might fail the test on either ground. Furthermore, these Eighth Amendment judgments should not be, or appear to be, merely the subjective views of individual Justices; judgment should be informed by objective factors to the maximum possible extent. To this end, attention must be given to the public attitudes concerning a particular sentence history and precedent, legislative attitudes, and the response of juries reflected in their sentencing decisions are to be consulted. In *Gregg*, after giving due regard to such sources, the Court's judgment was that the death penalty for deliberate murder was neither the purposeless imposition of severe punishment nor a punishment grossly disproportionate to the crime. But the Court reserved the question of the constitutionality of the death penalty when imposed for other crimes.

That question, with respect to rape of an adult woman, is now before us. We have concluded that a sentence of death is grossly disproportionate and excessive punishment for the crime of rape and is therefore forbidden by the Eighth Amendment as cruel and unusual punishment.

As advised by recent cases, we seek guidance in history and from the objective evidence of the country's present judgment concerning the acceptability of death as a penalty for rape of an adult woman. At no time in the last 50 years have a majority of the States authorized death as a punishment for rape. In 1925, 18 States, the District of Columbia, and the Federal Government authorized capital punishment for the rape of an adult female. By 1971 just prior to the decision in *Furman v. Georgia*, that number had declined, but not substantially, to 16 States plus the Federal Government. *Furman* then invalidated most of the capital punishment statutes in this country, including the rape statutes, because, among other reasons, of the manner in which the death penalty was imposed and utilized under those laws.

With their death penalty statutes for the most part invalidated, the States were faced with the choice of enacting modified capital punishment laws in an attempt to satisfy the requirements of *Furman* or of being satisfied with life imprisonment as the ultimate punishment for any offense. Thirty-five States

immediately reinstituted the death penalty for at least limited kinds of crime. This public judgment as to the acceptability of capital punishment, evidenced by the immediate, post-*Furman* legislative reaction in a large majority of the States, heavily influenced the Court to sustain the death penalty for murder in *Gregg v. Georgia*.

But if "the most marked indication of society's endorsement of the death penalty for murder is the legislative response to *Furman*," it should also be a telling datum that the public judgment with respect to rape, as reflected in the statutes providing the punishment for that crime, has been dramatically different. In reviving death penalty laws to satisfy *Furman's* mandate, none of the States that had not previously authorized death for rape chose to include rape among capital felonies. Of the 16 States in which rape had been a capital offense, only three provided the death penalty for rape of an adult woman in their revised statutes—Georgia, North Carolina, and Louisiana. In the latter two States, the death penalty was mandatory for those found guilty, and those laws were invalidated by *Woodson* and *Roberts*. When Louisiana and North Carolina, responding to those decisions, again revised their capital punishment laws, they re-enacted the death penalty for murder but not for rape; none of the seven other legislatures that to our knowledge have amended or replaced their death penalty statutes since July 2, 1976, including four States (in addition to Louisiana and North Carolina) that had authorized the death sentence for rape prior to 1972 and had reacted to *Furman* with mandatory statutes, included rape among the crimes for which death was an authorized punishment.

\* \* \*

It should be noted that Florida, Mississippi, and Tennessee also authorized the death penalty in some rape cases, but only where the victim was a child and the rapist an adult. The Tennessee statute has since been invalidated because the death sentence was mandatory. The upshot is that Georgia is the sole jurisdiction in the United States at the present time that authorizes a sentence of death when the rape victim is an adult woman, and only two other jurisdictions provide capital punishment when the victim is a child.

The current judgment with respect to the death penalty for rape is not wholly unanimous among state legislatures, but it obviously weighs very heavily on the side of rejecting capital punishment as a suitable penalty for raping an adult woman.

\* \* \*

These recent events evidencing the attitude of state legislatures . . . do not wholly determine this controversy, for the Constitution contemplates that in the end our own judgment will be brought to bear on the question of the acceptability of the death penalty under the Eighth Amendment. Nevertheless, the legislative rejection of capital punishment for rape strongly confirms our own judgment, which is that death is indeed a disproportionate penalty for the crime of raping an adult woman.

We do not discount the seriousness of rape as a crime. It is highly reprehensible, both in a moral sense and in its almost total contempt for the personal integrity and autonomy of the female victim and for the latter's privilege of choosing those with whom intimate relationships are to be established. Short of homicide, it is the "ultimate violation of self." . . .

\* \* \*

Rape is without doubt deserving of serious punishment; but in terms of moral depravity and of the injury to the person and to the public, it does not compare with murder, which does involve the unjustified taking of human life. Although it may be accompanied by another crime, rape by definition does not include the death of or even the serious injury to another person. The murderer kills; the rapist, if no more than that, does not. Life is over for the victim of the murderer; for the rape victim, life may not be nearly so happy as it was, but it is not over and normally is not beyond repair. We have the abiding conviction that the death penalty, which is "unique in its severity and irrevocability," is an excessive penalty for the rapist who, as such, does not take human life.

\* \* \*

. . . The judgment of the Georgia Supreme Court upholding the death sentence is reversed, and the case is remanded to that court for further proceedings not inconsistent with this opinion. So ordered.

[Concurring opinions omitted.]

# Cases Relating to Chapter 10

## Federal Criminal and Civil Remedies for Unconstitutional Conduct

**WILSON**

v.

**LAYNE**

**526 U.S. 603, 119 S. Ct. 1692, 143 L. Ed. 2d 818 (1999)**

*[Citations and footnotes omitted.]*

[Police officers invited a newspaper reporter and a photographer to accompany them while executing a warrant for Dominic Wilson's arrest. Unknown to the police, the address where they believed Dominic Wilson lived was actually the home of his parents, Charles and Geraldine Wilson. The officer and media representatives entered the Wilsons' home at around 6:45 A.M. The Wilsons were still in bed when they heard the noise and ran into the living room in their night clothes. Police performed a protective sweep, which revealed that Dominic Wilson was not there. The reporters observed and photographed the entire incident. The Wilsons subsequently sued the officers under 42 U.S.C. § 1983.]

Chief Justice REHNQUIST delivered the opinion of the Court.

\* \* \*

The reasons advanced by respondents, taken in their entirety, fall short of justifying the presence of media inside a home. We hold that it is a violation of the Fourth Amendment for police to bring members of the media or other third parties into a home during the execution of a warrant when the presence of the third parties in the home was not in aid of the execution of the warrant.

Since the police action in this case violated the petitioners' Fourth Amendment right, we now must decide whether this right was clearly established at the time of the search. As noted above, . . . government officials performing discretionary functions generally are granted a qualified immunity and are "shielded from liability for civil damages insofar as their conduct does not violate clearly established statutory or constitutional rights of which a reasonable person would have known." What this means in practice is that "whether an official protected by qualified immunity may be held personally liable for an allegedly unlawful official action generally turns on the 'objective legal reasonableness' of the action, assessed in light of the legal rules that were 'clearly established' at the time it was taken."

In *Anderson*, we explained that what "clearly established" means in this context depends largely "upon the level of generality at which the relevant 'legal rule' is to be established." "Clearly established" for purposes of qualified immunity means that "[t]he contours of the right must be sufficiently clear that a reasonable official would understand that what he is doing violates that right. This is not to say that an official action is protected by qualified immunity unless the very action in question has previously been held unlawful, but it is to say that in the light of pre-existing law the unlawfulness must be apparent."

It could plausibly be asserted that any violation of the Fourth Amendment is "clearly established," since it is clearly established that the protections of the Fourth Amendment apply to the actions of police. . . . However, as we explained in *Anderson*, the right allegedly violated must be defined at the appropriate level of specificity before a court can determine if it was clearly established. In this case, the appropriate question is the objective inquiry of whether a reasonable officer could have believed that bringing members of the media into a home during the execution of an arrest warrant was lawful, in light of clearly established law and the information the officers possessed.

We hold that it was not unreasonable for a police officer in April 1992 to have believed that bringing media observers along during the execution of an arrest warrant (even in a home) was lawful. First, the constitutional question presented by this case is by no means open and shut. The Fourth Amendment protects the rights of homeowners from entry without a warrant, but there was a warrant here. The question is whether the invitation to the media exceeded the scope of the search authorized by the warrant. Accurate media coverage of police activities serves an important public purpose, and it is not obvious from the general principles of the Fourth Amend-

ment that the conduct of the officers in this case violated the Amendment.

Second, although media ride-alongs of one sort or another had apparently become a common police practice, in 1992 there were no judicial opinions holding that this practice became unlawful when it entered a home. The only published decision directly on point was a state intermediate court decision which, though it did not engage in an extensive Fourth Amendment analysis, nonetheless held that such conduct was not unreasonable. From the federal courts, the parties have only identified two unpublished District Court decisions dealing with media entry into homes, each of which upheld the search on unorthodox non-Fourth Amendment right to privacy theories. These cases, of course, cannot "clearly establish" that media entry into homes during a police ride-along violates the Fourth Amendment.

At a slightly higher level of generality, petitioners point to *Bills v. Aseltine* in which the Court of Appeals for the Sixth Circuit held that there were material issues of fact precluding summary judgment on the question of whether police exceeded the scope of a search warrant by allowing a private security guard to participate in the search to identify stolen property other than that described in the warrant. *Bills*, which was decided a mere five weeks before the events of this case, did anticipate today's holding that police may not bring along third parties during an entry into a private home pursuant to a warrant for purposes unrelated to those justifying the warrant. However, we cannot say that even in light of *Bills*, the law on third-party entry into homes was clearly established in April 1992. Petitioners have not brought to our attention any cases of controlling authority in their jurisdiction at the time of the incident which clearly established the rule on which they seek to rely, nor have they identified a consensus of cases of persuasive authority such that a reasonable officer could not have believed that his actions were lawful.

Finally, important to our conclusion was the reliance by the United States marshals in this case on a Marshal's Service ride-along policy which explicitly contemplated that media who engaged in ride-alongs might enter private homes with their cameras as part of fugitive apprehension arrests. The Montgomery County Sheriff's Department also at this time had a ride-along program that did not expressly prohibit media entry into private homes. Such a policy, of course, could not make reasonable a belief that was contrary to a decided body of case law. But here the state of the law as to third parties accompanying police on home entries was at best undeveloped, and it was not unreasonable for law enforcement officers to look and rely on their formal ride-along policies.

Given such an undeveloped state of the law, the officers in this case cannot have been "expected to predict the future course of constitutional law." Between the time of the events of this case and today's decision, a split among the Federal Circuits in fact developed on the question whether media ride-alongs that enter homes subject the police to money damages. If judges thus disagree on a constitutional question, it is unfair to subject police to money damages for picking the losing side of the controversy.

For the foregoing reasons, the judgment of the Court of Appeals is affirmed.

It is so ordered.

# JOHNSON

## v.

# CANNON

### 947 F. Supp. 1567 (M.D. Fla. 1996)

*[Citations and footnotes omitted.]*

[On April 7, 1994, Deputy Armstrong, who was employed by Defendant Sheriff Cannon, stopped Johnson for traffic infraction, gave her two traffic citations, and asked her if she was "willing to negotiate the tickets." He threatened to arrest her and have her children removed to an HRS facility if she did not "negotiate" with him. Armstrong then proceeded to Johnson's residence, at which time he sexually assaulted Johnson. Johnson sued under 42 U.S.C. § 1983.]

KOVACHEVICH, District Judge

* * *

Only two allegations are required to state a cause of action under 42 U.S.C. § 1983. "First, the Plaintiff must allege that some person has deprived him of a federal right. Second, he must allege that the person who has deprived him of that right acted under color of state or territorial law."

Defendant Cannon argues that Deputy Armstrong was not acting under the color of law when the alleged misconduct occurred. "It is firmly established that a Defendant in a Section 1983 suit acts under color of state law when he abuses the position given to him by the State." "Generally, a public employee acts under color of state law while acting in his official capacity or while exercising his responsibilities pursuant to state law." According to the allegations in the Complaint, Armstrong abused the position of deputy which was given to him by the State. Johnson has alleged that

Armstrong's misconduct occurred while he was on duty, wearing his uniform, wearing his badge, carrying a gun, utilizing a marked police vehicle, and that Defendant Armstrong stopped her by use of his authority as a Sheriff's Deputy. The Complaint clearly alleges that Armstrong used the authority given to him by the State in order to deprive Johnson of her constitutional rights.

Defendant Cannon is correct in stating that all acts of state employees are not under color of state law, yet the alleged facts in the instant case demonstrate that Armstrong was acting under color of state law. . . . In the instant case, the alleged act occurred during the performance of Armstrong's job and in conjunction with the authority given to him as a result of his position as deputy. Action is taken under color of state law when it is made possible only because the wrongdoer is clothed with the authority of state law.

\* \* \*

## GRAHAM
### v.
## CONNOR

### 490 U.S. 386, 109 S. Ct. 1865, 104 L. Ed. 2d 443 (1989)

*[Citations and footnotes omitted.]*

[Graham, a diabetic who was having an insulin reaction, had a friend to drive him to a convenience store so that he could purchase orange juice to counteract it. Seeing a large number of people ahead of him, Graham hurriedly left the store and asked his friend to drive him home. Connor, a city police officer, observed Graham hastily enter and leave the store and became suspicious. He followed the car, stopped it and, ignoring Graham's attempts to explain, handcuffed him

while he investigated what happened in the store. Upon learning that nothing happened, he released Graham who filed suit under 42 U.S.C. § 1983, alleging that Connor had used excessive force in violation of his rights under the Fourteenth Amendment.]

Chief Justice REHNQUIST delivered the opinion of the Court.

This case requires us to decide what constitutional standard governs a free citizen's claim that law enforcement officials used excessive force in the course of making an arrest, investigatory stop, or other "seizure" of his person. We hold that such claims are properly analyzed under the Fourth Amendment's "objective reasonableness" standard, rather than under a substantive due process standard.

\* \* \*

. . . In addressing an excessive force claim brought under § 1983, analysis begins by identifying the specific constitutional right allegedly infringed by the challenged application of force. In most instances, that will be either the Fourth Amendment's prohibition against unreasonable seizures of the person, or the Eighth Amendment's ban on cruel and unusual punishments, which are the two primary sources of constitutional protection against physically abusive governmental conduct. The validity of the claim must then be judged by reference to the specific constitutional standard which governs that right, rather than to some generalized "excessive force" standard.

Where, as here, the excessive force claim arises in the context of an arrest or investigatory stop of a free citizen, it is most properly characterized as one invoking the protections of the Fourth Amendment, which guarantees citizens the right "to be secure in their persons . . . against unreasonable . . . seizures" of the person. This much is clear from our decision in *Tennessee v. Garner*. In *Garner*, we addressed a claim that the use of deadly force to apprehend a fleeing suspect who did not appear to be armed or otherwise dangerous violated the suspect's constitutional rights, notwithstanding the existence of probable cause to arrest. Though the complaint alleged violations of both the Fourth Amendment and the Due Process Clause, we analyzed the constitutionality of the challenged application of force solely by reference to the Fourth Amendment's prohibition against unreasonable seizures of the person, holding that the "reasonableness" of a particular seizure depends not only on *when* it is made, but also *how* it is carried out. Today we make explicit what was implicit in *Garner's* analysis and hold that *all* claims that law enforcement officers have used excessive force—deadly or not—in the course of an arrest, investigatory stop, or other "seizure" of a free citizen should be analyzed under the Fourth Amendment and its "reasonableness" standard, rather than under a "substantive due process" approach. Because the Fourth Amendment provides an explicit textual source of constitutional protection against this sort of physically intrusive governmental conduct, that Amendment, not the more generalized notion of "substantive due process," must be the guide for analyzing these claims.

Determining whether the force used to effect a particular seizure is "reasonable" under the Fourth Amendment requires a careful balancing of " 'the nature and quality of the intrusion on the individual's Fourth Amendment interests' " against the countervailing governmental interests at stake. Our Fourth Amendment jurisprudence has long recognized that the right to make an arrest or investigatory stop necessarily carries

with it the right to use some degree of physical coercion or threat thereof to effect it. Because "[t]he test of reasonableness under the Fourth Amendment is not capable of precise definition or mechanical application," however, its proper application requires careful attention to the facts and circumstances of each particular case, including the severity of the crime at issue, whether the suspect poses an immediate threat to the safety of the officers or others, and whether he is actively resisting arrest or attempting to evade arrest by flight.

The "reasonableness" of a particular use of force must be judged from the perspective of a reasonable officer on the scene, rather than with the 20/20 vision of hindsight. The Fourth Amendment is not violated by an arrest based on probable cause, even though the wrong person is arrested, nor by the mistaken execution of a valid search warrant on the wrong premises. With respect to a claim of excessive force, the same standard of reasonableness at the moment applies: "Not every push or shove, even if it may later seem unnecessary in the peace of a judge's chambers," violates the Fourth Amendment. The calculus of reasonableness must embody allowance for the fact that police officers are often forced to make split-second judgments—in circumstances that are tense, uncertain, and rapidly evolving—about the amount of force that is necessary in a particular situation.

As in other Fourth Amendment contexts, however, the "reasonableness" inquiry in an excessive force case is an objective one: the question is whether the officers' actions are "objectively reasonable" in light of the facts and circumstances confronting them, without regard to their underlying intent or motivation. An officer's evil intentions will not make a Fourth Amendment violation out of an objectively reasonable use of force; nor will an officer's good intentions make an objectively unreasonable use of force constitutional.

Because petitioner's excessive force claim is one arising under the Fourth Amendment, the Court of Appeals erred in analyzing it under the four-part *Johnson v. Glick* test. That test, which requires consideration of whether the individual officers acted in "good faith" or "maliciously and sadistically for the very purpose of causing harm," is incompatible with a proper Fourth Amendment analysis. We do not agree with the Court of Appeals' suggestion, that the "malicious and sadistic" inquiry is merely another way of describing conduct that is objectively unreasonable under the circumstances. Whatever the empirical correlations between "malicious and sadistic" behavior and objective unreasonableness may be, the fact remains that the "malicious and sadistic" factor puts in issue the subjective motivations of the individual officers, which our prior cases make clear has no bearing on whether a particular seizure is "unreasonable" under the Fourth Amendment. Nor do we agree with the Court of Appeals' conclusion that because the subjective motivations of the individual officers are of central importance in deciding whether force used against a convicted prisoner violates the Eighth Amendment, it cannot be reversible error to inquire into them in deciding whether force used against a suspect or arrestee violates the Fourth Amendment. Differing standards under the Fourth and Eighth Amendments are hardly surprising: the terms "cruel" and "punishment" clearly suggest some inquiry into subjective state of mind, whereas the term "unreasonable" does not. Moreover, the less protective Eighth Amendment standard applies "only after the State has complied with the constitutional guarantees traditionally associated with criminal prosecutions." The Fourth Amendment inquiry is one of "objective reasonableness" under the circumstances,

and subjective concepts like "malice" and "sadism" have no proper place in that inquiry.

Because the Court of Appeals reviewed the District court's ruling on the motion for directed verdict under an erroneous view of the governing substantive law, its judgment must be vacated and the case remanded to that court for reconsideration of that issue under the proper Fourth Amendment standard.

*It is so ordered.*

# VANN
## v.
## CITY OF NEW YORK

### 72 F.3d 1040 (2d Cir. 1995)

*[Citations and footnotes omitted.]*

[Walter Vann, while driving a bus on his regular route, collided with Officer Raul Morrison's personal vehicle. Morrison, who was then off-duty and out-of-uniform, got out of his car, identified himself as a police officer, drew his service revolver, and told Vann, "I should shoot you nigger and make sure you never drive a bus." Morrison proceeded to hit Vann in the head and face several times, threw him against a wall and against the bus several times, and handcuffed him. Morrison placed Vann under arrest and took him to the police station, where the precinct commander voided the arrest. As a result of Morrison's use of force, Vann was treated at a hospital for injuries to the head, face, and body. The injuries forced Vann to miss work for some seven weeks.

Prior to this incident, numerous complaints of violent behavior had been lodged against Morrison, both by civilians and by colleagues. Morrison had been disciplined several times, received a negative psychological evaluation, and had been placed on restricted duty. Approximately 21 months before the Vann incident, he was returned to active duty, following which he was involved in several additional incidents before assaulting Vann. These incidents included injuring a civilian by ramming him in the stomach with a nightstick, threatening to "beat the shit out" of another civilian, and assaulting and pointing his gun at a motorist while off-duty.

After his reinstatement, Morrison was not monitored by Psychological Services Unit ("PSU"), the unit responsible for evaluating employees who were experiencing psychological problems. The three new civilian complaints against Morrison were not communicated to PSU.

Vann sued the police department under § 1983, contending that the department's failure to monitor Morrison after his reinstatement to full-duty status was pursuant to a policy of deliberate indifference concerning police officers who had a known history of abusive conduct.

KEARSE, Circuit Judge:

* * *

In order to establish the liability of a municipality in an action under § 1983 for unconstitutional acts by a municipal employee below the policymaking level, a plaintiff must establish that the violation of his constitutional rights resulted from a municipal custom or policy. This does not mean that the plaintiff must show that the municipality had an explicitly stated rule or regulation. A § 1983 plaintiff injured by a police officer may establish the pertinent custom or policy by showing that the municipality, alerted to the possible use of excessive force by its police officers, exhibited deliberate indifference.

To prove such deliberate indifference, the plaintiff must show that the need for more or better supervision to protect against constitutional violations was obvious. An obvious need may be demonstrated through proof of repeated complaints of civil rights violations; deliberate indifference may be inferred if the complaints are followed by no meaningful attempt on the part of the municipality to investigate or to forestall further incidents. Deliberate indifference may also be shown through expert testimony that a practice condoned by the defendant municipality was "contrary to the practice of most police departments" and was "particularly dangerous" because it presented an unusually high risk that constitutional rights would be violated.

* * *

In the present case, Vann presented evidence of the Department's general methods of dealing with problem policemen and of its responses to past incidents involving Morrison. Taken in the light most favorable to Vann, the evidence of the Department's system for dealing with problem officers in the earlier stages of their difficulties highlights the paucity of its monitoring system after such officers were reinstated. The deposition testimony indicated that, after a problem officer was restored to full-duty status, the Department's supervisory units paid virtually no attention to the filing of new complaints against such officers even though such filings should have been red-flag warnings of possibly renewed and future misconduct. DAO (Department Advocate's Office), which monitored officers who were on disciplinary probation, was typically not informed by CPI, by precinct commanders, or by the CCRB as to the filing of civilian complaints. In any event, DAO, woefully understaffed for any significant monitoring function, was not concerned that officers they monitored were the subject of new civilian complaints. And the director of PSU, who acknowledged that the receipt of new complaints was significant for the evaluation of the likelihood that the problem officer would engage in future wrongful conduct, also testified that she "typically" did not tell the commanders to alert DAO or PSU to the receipt of such complaints.

With respect to Morrison in particular, PSU psychologists had early noted Morrison's personality disorder; they had noted thereafter that he did not respond productively to counseling and that he altered his attitude and behavior only in response to administrative discipline; they foresaw that if restored to full duty his problems might recur; and they suggested that if he engaged in further misconduct, he should be dismissed. Yet even while Morrison was on disciplinary probation, there was no mechanism for ensuring that DAO or PSU was alerted that within two months of his restoration to full-duty service the Department had begun to receive new complaints of his physical abuse of civilians. . . .

. . . [T]he three post-reinstatement complaints indicated that Morrison was acting in accordance with his established, and departmentally well known, tendency to escalate confrontations, inappropriately, to the point where he used force. In light of the Department's "systemic failure" to alert the supervisory units of the filing of new complaints against problem officers, and in the absence of any significant administrative response to Morrison's resumption of his abusive misconduct upon reinstatement, it was entirely foreseeable that Morrison would engage in misconduct yet again.

In sum, a rational jury could find that, where an officer had been identified by the police department as a "violence-prone" individual who had a personality disorder manifested by frequent quick-tempered demands for "respect," escalating into physical confrontations for which he always disavowed responsibili-

ty, the need to be alert for new civilian complaints filed after his reinstatement to full-duty status was obvious. The jury could also rationally find that the Department's election to staff DAO with the equivalent of just $1\frac{1}{4}$ employees to monitor 200 problem officers, together with the systematic lack of communication to the supervisory divisions of information with regard to new civilian complaints, including PSU's routine failure, despite its expertise, to instruct commanders to relay that information reflected a deliberate indifference on the part of the municipal defendants to the dangers posed by problem policemen who had been restored to full-duty service.

* * *

CONCLUSION

We have considered all of the municipal defendants' arguments in support of the judgment in their favor and have found them to be without merit. For the foregoing reasons, the judgment of the district court is vacated and the case is remanded.

# YANG
## v.
# HARDIN

### 37 F.3d 282 (7th Cir. 1994)

*[Citations and footnotes omitted.]*

[On January 8, 1991, at approximately 11:00 P.M., Mike Yang, co-owner of a south-side shoe store, received a call from his alarm company notifying him that the store had been burglarized. Yang called his brother, Myung, and an employee, Bob. The defendants, uniformed police officers employed by the Chicago Police Department, had already arrived at the store when Yang got there.

While Yang and his employee and brother busied themselves with repairing the shattered front display window, Officer Hardin prepared a police report by the front door of the store, adjacent to the broken window. Officer Brown entered the store to investigate. While inside the store looking for a board to repair the window, employee Bob noticed that Officer Brown was perusing the store in the manner of a shoplifter. Bob alerted Yang to this. As Officers Brown and Hardin began to leave, Yang noticed a bulge in Officer Brown's jacket. Believing that Officer Brown had stolen some merchandise, Yang approached the officer and requested that the merchandise be returned. At first, Officer Brown denied that he had taken any merchandise. But after a discussion that escalated into an argument, Officer Brown reached into his jacket and pulled out a pair of "L.A. Raiders" shorts and threw them at Yang. Officers Brown and Hardin then proceeded to enter their police car to drive away. When Yang followed, Officer Brown shoved Yang. Throughout the confrontation, Officer Hardin stood by the passenger door of the squad car. He did not speak or intervene in any manner despite Yang's repeated requests for Officer Hardin to call the police sergeant.

In an attempt to prevent Officer Brown from leaving, Yang held onto the driver's side door of the squad car to keep it open so that Officer Brown could not drive off. However, Officer Brown drove anyway, with the driver's side door ajar and Yang hanging onto the car. Officer Brown drove fast and recklessly in a zig-zagging pattern, braking and accelerating, in an attempt to throw Yang off. Officer Brown also repeatedly struck Yang in the ribs with his left elbow. Yang asserts that he was unable to let go of the car without being run over. Throughout the drive, Officer Hardin sat in the passenger seat. Officer Hardin did not say anything or in any way attempt to intervene. The squad car traveled, with Yang hanging on, more than two full city blocks until two men on the sidewalk saw what was happening and ran out to the street to stop the police car. Yang let go when the car stopped. Officer Brown then got out of the car and punched Yang in the face, knocking him to the ground. Officers Brown then got back in the police car and drove away.

Yang pressed criminal charges and both officers were convicted of felonies. He then sued both officers 42 U.S.C. § 1983. The trial judge found against Brown and ordered him to pay $229,658.10 in damages. However, the judge ruled that Officer Hardin was not liable for violating § 1983. Yang appealed.]

BAUER, Circuit Judge.

* * *

Liability under § 1983 requires proof of two essential elements: that the conduct complained of (1) "was committed by a person acting under color of state law" and (2) "deprived a person of rights, privileges, or immunities secured by the Constitution or laws of the United States." In the present case there is no dispute that Yang has proved the first element. The district court found that both Officers Brown and Hardin acted under color of state law. They were on duty, wearing Chicago police uniforms, driving a marked squad car and were investigating a crime when the incident occurred. The crux of this case is whether Officer Hardin's failure to intervene deprived Yang of his liberty rights under the Due Process Clause of the Fourteenth Amendment and his rights under the Fourth Amendment to be free from unreasonable seizure.

* * *

*Byrd v. Brishke* remains the seminal case in this circuit on the duty of an officer to intervene to prevent summary punishment. In *Brishke*, this court held that "one who is given a badge of authority of a police officer may not ignore the duty imposed by his office and fail to stop other officers who summarily punish a third person in his presence or otherwise within his knowledge." This responsibility to intervene applies equally to supervisory and nonsupervisory officers. An officer who is present and fails to intervene to prevent other law enforcement officers from infringing the constitutional rights of citizens is liable under § 1983 if that officer had reason to know: (1) that excessive force was being used, (2) that a citizen has been unjustifiably arrested, or (3) that any constitutional violation has been committed by a law enforcement official; and the officer had a realistic opportunity to intervene to prevent the harm from occurring.

The district court orally ruled in favor of Officer Hardin. The court found that the facts alleged by Yang did not demonstrate the availability of a reasonable time for Officer Hardin to intervene, or a reasonable likelihood of successful intervention. This finding is clearly erroneous. Although Yang's complaint fails to explicitly specify the existence of an opportunity for Officer Hardin to have intervened, the facts demonstrate several opportunities during which Hardin could have acted. At a minimum Officer Hardin could have called for a backup, called for help, or at least cautioned Officer Brown to stop. In fact, Officer Hardin should have arrested Officer Brown. . . .

\* \* \*

## MARTINEZ
## v.
## UNITED STATES

### 92 F. Supp. 2d 780 (N.D. Ill. 2000)

*[Citations and footnotes omitted.]*

[Martinez, a Hispanic former police trainee, sued the Village of Mount Prospect Police Department alleging that he was subjected to employment discrimination because of his national origin. As part of his proof that the Department was hostile to Hispanics, he introduced evidence that Hispanic members of the community were targeted to meet various arrest quotas, that Hispanic drivers received a disproportionately high percentage of traffic tickets as compared to their numbers in the community, and that supervisors encouraged police officers to target Hispanics for traffic and investigatory stops. The jury returned a verdict in Martinez's favor, awarding him $1,179,000 in damages. At the conclusion of the trial, the judge took the extraordinary action of entering an order that neither party requested. He enjoined the Village from directing police officers to focus law enforcement efforts on any person solely because of the person's national origin and asked the Justice Department to conduct an investigation to determine whether the civil rights of Hispanic members of the community were being violated.]

CASTILLO, District Judge.

\* \* \*

Our nation, throughout its history, has continually struggled with the issue of race. As we begin the twenty-first century, it is critical that our legal system assist in the elimination of all racial discrimination. We must constantly strive to ensure that race plays no role in the day-to-day operation of our justice system. These two lawsuits are reflective of some of the racial issues we must as a society address in our criminal justice system.

\* \* \*

. . . Racial profiling of any kind is anathema to our criminal justice system because it eviscerates the core integrity that is necessary to operate that system effectively in our diverse democracy. Many respected legal scholars have closely analyzed the critical societal problems caused by racial profiling.

Professor Cole of the Georgetown Law Center, for example, points out that double standards based on race, such as profiling, undermine law enforcement itself, because they breed resentment and alienation among minorities. . . . People who see the criminal justice system as fundamentally unfair will be less likely to cooperate with police, to testify as witnesses, to serve on juries, and to convict guilty defendants when they do serve. In addition, people who have lost respect for the law's legitimacy are more likely to break the law themselves. . . . Finally, the perception and reality of a fundamentally unfair criminal justice system contributes to broader racial divisions in society. If we cannot believe that our nation's law enforcement officers will enforce the law in a racially neutral manner, then we will be left with a society where members of the minority community always view the actions of any police officer with great suspicion. . . .

The reverse will also be true because racial profiling is a self-fulfilling prophecy. Officers that engage in profiling will necessarily come into contact with law-breaking members of minority communities far more frequently than with law-breaking whites and thus will view the actions of minority civilians with

a presumption of guilt. . . . Roberts, *Forward*, 89 J. CRIM. L. & CRIMINOLOGY at 818 ("[T]argeting Blacks for police surveillance results in higher rates of arrest, reinforcing the presumption of Black criminality. If police stopped and frisked whites as frequently as they do Blacks, white arrest rates would increase.").

\* \* \*

Racially stereotypic perceptions operate like a deadly cancer on our justice system. As Professor Kennedy accurately notes, "[t]aking race into account in a small, marginal, even infinitesimal amount still constitutes racial discrimination." Simply put, our country can ill afford to tolerate any form of racial profiling by any law enforcement agent because it threatens the notion of equal justice upon which our legal system is based. "Legitimacy is one of the law's most powerful tools, and when the law forfeits legitimacy, its only alternative is to rely on brute force." For many law-abiding citizens their only contact with the criminal justice system is via interaction with the police, predominantly during traffic stops. Any hint of racism in policing erodes the public support so necessary to law enforcement efforts. The reality is that very few innocent victims of racial profiling ever come forward with complaints. Instead, these victims simply retain vivid memories of their police encounter for future reference. The ultimate result of such erosion is all too often a series of questionable jury verdicts which are difficult to explain without resort to racial analysis or justification. Further, as Professor Cole aptly notes, "It is not surprising that virtually all the riots we have experienced in this country since World War II have been sparked by racially charged police-citizen encounters." Id. Thus, we must vigorously combat and abolish racial profiling wherever it may exist.

As racial profiling moves to the fore-front of the national consciousness, police departments, the federal government, and courts are beginning to address the invidi-ous effects of race profiling. Thus, for example, just last week a congressional subcommittee conducted hearings into the profiling issue. Recently, the New Jersey State Police resolved Justice Department charges of racial profiling by its officers by agreeing to extensive reform efforts and reporting requirements, and the Sec-ond Circuit Court of Appeals affirmed a jury verdict of $245,000 in favor of two African American youngsters and against police in a profiling case.

Similarly, courts across the country are recognizing claims based on police use of racial profiling. We believe this trend is a positive step toward eradicat-ing the ills of racial profiling and encouraging minority civilian support for necessary law enforcement efforts.

Against this background, the Court was initially concerned that the settle-ment agreements at issue did not contain any measures addressing the racial pro-filing evidence revealed during the Mar-tinez trial. Nevertheless, the Court is sat-isfied that the Village of Mount Prospect is moving in a positive direction to alle-viate even the appearance of racial pro-filing by its police force. On March 1, 2000, the Village announced measures to increase public trust in its Police Department similar to those contained in the New Jersey consent decree. For example, the Village has promised to enact a formal policy banning racial pro-filing, has eliminated ticket quotas for its officers, and will require officers to note the race of all drivers they stop. Additionally, the Village will create a computer database to track the racial and ethnic information collected by officers

making traffic stops and aggressively recruit minorities for its police force. Finally, the Village will create a human rights review board, made up of a village manager, a resident, and a clergy mem-ber, to monitor racial profiling com-plaints as well as the information generat-ed by the other reform efforts. These reform efforts should place Mount Prospect at the forefront of the local com-munities that are seeking to address both the perception and reality of racial profil-ing. The Court hopes that other commu-nities will follow Mount Prospect's courageous lead without the need for protracted and expensive litigation.

At the same time, Mount Prospect and other suburban communities should realize that the effort to eliminate both the perception and reality of racial pro-filing is a major undertaking. All aspects of Mount Prospect's announced mea-sures are critical. Recent national and local police incidents show that merely hiring minority police officers is not a sufficient stand-alone remedy to address this difficult problem. Indeed, as the Martinez lawsuit shows, making sure that hired minority officers succeed and are given opportunities in their respec-tive departments is an important second step. Diversity training classes, for both minority and non-minority officers, is a critical third step. Only through constant efforts to comprehend and appreciate our racial and ethnic differences can we effectively serve our diverse citizenry. Proactive monitoring of all these efforts, as well as collecting and analyzing all police stop data on the basis of race and ethnicity, is another key component of a true effort to combat racial profiling.

* * *

# Cases Relating to Chapter 11

# Constitutional and Civil Rights in the Government Workplace

## CONNICK
### v.
## MYERS

**461 U.S. 138, 103 S. Ct. 1684, 75 L. Ed. 2d 708 (1983)**

*[Citations and footnotes omitted.]*

[Sheila Myers was employed as an Assistant District Attorney in New Orleans for five and one-half years. She served at the pleasure of petitioner Harry Connick, the District Attorney for Orleans Parish. During this period, Myers competently performed her responsibilities of trying criminal cases.

In the early part of October, 1980, Myers was informed that she would be transferred to prosecute cases in a different section of the criminal court. Myers was strongly opposed to the proposed transfer and expressed her view to several of her supervisors, including Connick. Despite her objections, on October 6, Myers was notified that she was being transferred. That night Myers prepared a questionnaire soliciting the views of her fellow staff members concerning office transfer policy, office morale, the need for a grievance committee, the level of confidence in supervisors, and whether employees felt pressured to work in political campaigns. The following morning, Myers distributed the ques-

tionnaire to 15 assistant district attorneys. Shortly after noon, Connick was told that Myers was creating a "mini-insurrection" within the office and informed Myers that she was being terminated for refusal to accept the transfer. She was also told that her distribution of the questionnaire was considered an act of insubordination.

Myers sued, claiming that her discharge for circulating a questionnaire to co-workers violated her First Amendment rights. The issue before the Supreme Court was whether the First Amendment protects a government employee from discharge for circulating a questionnaire to co-workers enlisting their opinions about an internal office affair that had affected her.]

JUSTICE WHITE delivered the opinion of the Court.

\* \* \*

. . . We hold only that when a public employee speaks not as a citizen upon matters of public concern, but instead as an employee upon matters only of personal interest, absent the most unusual circumstances, a federal court is not the appropriate forum in which to review the wisdom of a personnel decision taken by a public agency allegedly in reaction to the employee's behavior. Our responsibility is to ensure that citizens are not deprived of fundamental rights by virtue of working for the government; this does not require a grant of immunity for employee grievances not afforded by the First Amendment to those who do not work for the State.

Whether an employee's speech addresses a matter of public concern must be determined by the content, form, and context of a given statement, as revealed by the whole record. In this case, with but one exception, the questions posed by Myers to her co-workers do not fall under the rubric of matters of "public concern." We view the questions pertaining to the confidence and trust that Myers' co-workers possess in various supervisors, the level of office morale, and the need for a grievance committee as mere extensions of Myers' dispute over her transfer to another section of the criminal court. . . . Myers did not seek to inform the public that the District Attorney's Office was not discharging its governmental responsibilities in the investigation and prosecution of criminal cases. Nor did Myers seek to bring to light actual or potential wrongdoing or breach of public trust on the part of Connick and others. . . .While discipline and morale in the workplace are related to an agency's efficient performance of its duties, the focus of Myers' questions is not to evaluate the performance of the office but rather to gather ammunition for another round of controversy with her superiors. These questions reflect one employee's dissatisfaction with a transfer and an attempt to turn that displeasure into a cause celebre.

To presume that all matters which transpire within a government office are of public concern would mean that virtually every remark—and certainly every criticism directed at a public official— would plant the seed of a constitutional case. While as a matter of good judgment, public officials should be recep-

tive to constructive criticism offered by their employees, the First Amendment does not require a public office to be run as a roundtable for employee complaints over internal office affairs.

\* \* \*

. . . When a government employee personally confronts his immediate superior, the employing agency's institutional efficiency may be threatened not only by the content of the employee's message but also by the manner, time, and place in which it is delivered. Here the questionnaire was prepared and distributed at the office; the manner of distribution required not only Myers to leave her work but others to do the same in order that the questionnaire be completed. . . .

\* \* \*

Myers' questionnaire . . . is most accurately characterized as an employee grievance concerning internal office policy. The limited First Amendment interest involved here does not require that Connick tolerate action which he reasonably believed would disrupt the office, undermine his authority, and destroy close working relationships. Myers' discharge therefore did not offend the First Amendment. . . .

Our holding today is grounded in our longstanding recognition that the First Amendment's primary aim is the full protection of speech upon issues of public concern, as well as the practical realities involved in the administration of a government office. Although today the balance is struck for the government, this is no defeat for the First Amendment. For it would indeed be a Pyrrhic victory for the great principles of free expression if the Amendment's safeguarding of a public employee's right, as a citizen, to participate in discussions concerning public affairs were confused with the attempt to constitutionalize the employee grievance that we see presented here. The judgment of the Court of Appeals is

Reversed.

[Dissenting opinion omitted.]

## THOMAS
## v.
## WHALEN

### 51 F.3d 1285 (6th Cir. 1995)

*[Citations and footnotes omitted.]*

[Lt. Harry Thomas is an outspoken opponent of gun control laws and an active member of the National Rifle Association. On several occasions, he attended rallies in Washington, D.C., sponsored by the NRA to protest the Brady Bill, during which he appeared at press conferences, introduced himself as a member of the Cincinnati police force, and wore his police badge on the breast pocket of civilian clothing. Thomas was disciplined for failing to request permission to attend these press conferences, as required by his department's regulations, for wearing his official insignia, and for introducing himself as a member of the Cincinnati Police Department. Thomas filed suit under § 1983, claiming that his First Amendment rights were violated.]

DAUGHTREY, Circuit Judge.

\* \* \*

The determination whether a public employer has properly discharged an employee for engaging in speech requires "a balance between the interests of the [employee], as a citizen, in commenting upon matters of public concern and the interest of the State, as an employer, in promoting the efficiency of the public services it performs through its employees." This balancing is necessary in order to accommodate the dual role of the public employer as a provider of public services and as a government entity operating under the constraints of the First Amendment. On the one hand, public employers are employers, concerned with the efficient function of their operations; review of every personnel decision made by a public employer could, in the long run, hamper the performance of public functions. On the other hand, "the threat of dismissal from public employment is . . . a potent means of inhibiting speech." Vigilance is necessary to ensure that public employers do not use authority over employees to silence discourse, not because it hampers public functions but simply because superiors disagree with the content of employees' speech. Thus, determining whether the defendants could rightfully take adverse employment action against Thomas on the basis of his speech (or, to put it differently, whether they violated Thomas's clearly established rights) is a two-step process.

The threshold inquiry is whether the speech that Thomas cites as the basis for defendants' actions "may be 'fairly characterized as constituting speech on a matter of public concern.'" The debate over the propriety of gun control legislation is, obviously, a matter of public concern.

We must next determine whether Thomas's interest in speaking freely is outweighed by a state interest in promoting the efficiency of public services. "The more central a matter of public concern the speech [or association] at issue, the stronger the employer's showing of counter-balancing governmental interest must be." . . .

In essence, Thomas claims that the defendants have restricted his speech in two ways. He has been ordered, when pursuing his NRA-type advocacy, (1) "not to appear in uniform, display any identification card, or display [his] Police Division badge", and (2) not to "represent or identify [him]self as a Lieutenant in the Cincinnati Police Division." He admits that his speech and activities have not otherwise been restricted. . . .

\* \* \*

A paramilitary law enforcement unit, such as the police, has many of the same interests as the military in regulating its employees' uniforms. . . .

\* \* \*

In *Detroit Fire Fighters*, the district court held that the City of Detroit could reasonably restrict the public appearance of uniformed firefighters to advocate the defeat of a proposed charter amendment, without running afoul of the First Amendment. In reaching its decision, the court noted that political neutrality on the part of a paramilitary organization such as the fire department outweighs the right of individual firefighters to appear in uniform in television advertisements advocating a position on a political issue. The same analysis is patently applicable to the issue of gun control, where guns represent a daily life-and-death issue for every police officer.

\* \* \*

. . . Thomas was advertising and invoking his experience not just as a police officer, but as a highly ranked member of the Cincinnati Police Division, in a manner that entangled the Division in a matter of national controversy. . . . The extra margin of credibility lent his cause by exploiting his affiliation does not outweigh the Cincinnati Police Division's interest in preserving the appearance of impartiality in areas closely related to its core mission.

\* \* \*

. . . "[I]t is not only important that the Government and its employees in fact avoid practicing political justice, but it is also critical that they appear to the public to be avoiding it, if confidence in the system of representative Government is not to be eroded to a disastrous extent.". . . These arguments seem particularly relevant when applied to police employment and gun control, and thus buttress our conclusion that Lt. Thomas did not have a clearly established right to invoke the name of the Cincinnati Police Division or display the police department's insignia in order to enhance his own credibility in advocating a political position.

## O'CONNOR
### v.
## ORTEGA

### 480 U.S. 709, 107 S. Ct. 1492, 94 L. Ed. 2d 714 (1987)

*[Citations and footnotes omitted.]*

[Dr. Magno Ortega, a physician and psychiatrist, held the position of Chief of Professional Education at Napa State Hospital (Hospital) for 17 years. As Chief of Professional Education, Dr. Ortega had primary responsibility for training young physicians in psychiatric residency programs. In July 1981, Hospital officials became concerned about possible improprieties in Dr. Ortega's management of the residency program. Hospital officials were concerned, in particular, with the charges that he had coerced residents into contributing to the purchase of a computer for his own personal use and that he had sexually harassed two female Hospital employees. Dr. Ortega was placed on administrative leave for the duration of investigation of these charges. While he was on leave, his office, desk, and file cabinets were searched a number of times for evidence for use against him in the administrative disciplinary proceedings. Following his dismissal, Dr. Ortega commenced action under 42 U.S.C. § 1983, alleging that the search of his office violated the Fourth Amendment.]

JUSTICE O'CONNOR announced the judgment of the Court and delivered an opinion in which THE CHIEF JUSTICE, JUSTICE WHITE, and JUSTICE POWELL join.

\* \* \*

. . . Searches and seizures by government employers or supervisors of the private property of their employees, . . . are subject to the restraints of the Fourth Amendment.

[This suit presents two issues concerning the scope of this protection. First, we must decide when a public employee has a reasonable expectation of privacy in his office, desk, and file cabinets at his place of work. Second, we must determine the appropriate Fourth Amendment standard for searches conducted by public employers of areas in which the employee is found to have a reasonable expectation of privacy.]

Within the workplace context, this Court has recognized that employees may have a reasonable expectation of privacy against intrusions by police. As with the expectation of privacy in one's home, such an expectation in one's place of work is "based upon societal expectations that have deep roots in the history of the Amendment.". . .

. . . The operational realities of the workplace, however, may make some employees' expectations of privacy

unreasonable when an intrusion is by a supervisor rather than a law enforcement official. Public employees' expectations of privacy in their offices, desks, and file cabinets, like similar expectations of employees in the private sector, may be reduced by virtue of actual office practices and procedures, or by legitimate regulation. . . . The employee's expectation of privacy must be assessed in the context of the employment relation. An office is seldom a private enclave free from entry by supervisors, other employees, and business and personal invitees. Instead, in many cases offices are continually entered by fellow employees and other visitors during the workday for conferences, consultations, and other work-related visits. Simply put, it is the nature of government offices that others—such as fellow employees, supervisors, consensual visitors, and the general public— may have frequent access to an individual's office. . . . [S]ome government offices may be so open to fellow employees or the public that no expectation of privacy is reasonable. Given the great variety of work environments in the public sector, the question whether an employee has a reasonable expectation of privacy must be addressed on a case-by-case basis.

\* \* \*

. . . [W]e recognize that the undisputed evidence suggests that Dr. Ortega had a reasonable expectation of privacy in his desk and file cabinets. The undisputed evidence discloses that Dr. Ortega did not share his desk or file cabinets with any other employees. Dr. Ortega had occupied the office for 17 years and he kept materials in his office, which included personal correspondence, medical files, correspondence from private patients unconnected to the Hospital, personal financial records, teaching aids and notes, and personal gifts and mementos. The files on physicians in residency training were kept outside Dr. Ortega's office. Indeed, the only items found by the investigators were apparently personal items . . .

* * *

Having determined that Dr. Ortega had a reasonable expectation of privacy in his office, . . . we must determine the appropriate standard of reasonableness applicable to the search. A determination of the standard of reasonableness applicable to a particular class of searches requires "balanc[ing] the nature and quality of the intrusion on the individual's Fourth Amendment interests against the importance of the governmental interests alleged to justify the intrusion." In the case of searches conducted by a public employer, we must balance the invasion of the employees' legitimate expectations of privacy against the government's need for supervision, control, and the efficient operation of the workplace.

* * *

The legitimate privacy interests of public employees in the private objects they bring to the workplace may be substantial. Against these privacy interests, however, must be balanced the realities of the workplace, which strongly suggest that a warrant requirement would be unworkable. While police, and even administrative enforcement personnel, conduct searches for the primary purpose of obtaining evidence for use in criminal or other enforcement proceedings, employers most frequently need to enter the offices and desks of their employees for legitimate work-related reasons wholly unrelated to illegal conduct. Employers and supervisors are

focused primarily on the need to complete the government agency's work in a prompt and efficient manner. An employer may have need for correspondence, or a file or report available only in an employee's office while the employee is away from the office. . . .

In our view, requiring an employer to obtain a warrant whenever the employer wished to enter an employee's office, desk, or file cabinets for a work-related purpose would seriously disrupt the routine conduct of business and would be unduly burdensome. . . . [T]he imposition of a warrant requirement would conflict with "the common-sense realization that government offices could not function if every employment decision became a constitutional matter."

* * *

. . . To ensure the efficient and proper operation of the agency, therefore, public employers must be given wide latitude to enter employee offices for work-related, noninvestigatory reasons.

. . . Even when employers conduct an investigation, they have an interest substantially different from "the normal need for law enforcement." Public employers have an interest in ensuring that their agencies operate in an effective and efficient manner, and the work of these agencies inevitably suffers from the inefficiency, incompetence, mismanagement, or other work-related misfeasance of its employees. . . . In our view, therefore, a probable cause requirement for searches of the type at issue here would impose intolerable burdens on public employers. The delay in correcting the employee misconduct caused by the need for probable cause rather than reasonable suspicion will be translated into tangible and often irreparable damage to the agency's work, and ultimately to the public interest. Additionally, while law enforcement officials are expected to "schoo[l] themselves in the niceties of probable cause," no such expectation is generally applicable to public employers, at least when the search is not used to gather evidence of a criminal offense. It is simply unrealistic to expect supervisors in most government agencies to learn the subtleties of the probable cause standard. As Justice Blackmun observed in T.L.O., "[a] teacher has neither the training nor the day-to-day experience in the complexities of probable cause that a law enforcement officer possesses, and is ill-equipped to make a quick judgment about the existence of probable cause." We believe that this observation is an equally apt description of the public employer and supervisors at the Hospital, and we conclude that a reasonableness standard will permit regulation of the employer's conduct "according to the dictates of reason and common sense."

[We conclude that public employer intrusions on the constitutionally protected privacy interests of government employees for noninvestigatory, work-related purposes, as well as for investigations of work-related misconduct, should be judged by the standard of reasonableness under all the circumstances.]

* * *

Ordinarily, a search of an employee's office by a supervisor will be "justified at its inception" when there are reasonable grounds for suspecting that the search will turn up evidence that the employee is guilty of work-related misconduct, or that the search is necessary for a noninvestigatory work-related purpose such as to retrieve a needed file. Because petitioners had an "individualized suspicion" of misconduct by Dr. Ortega, we need not decide whether individualized suspicion is an essential element of the standard of reasonableness that we adopt today. . . .

* * *

[Concurring and dissenting opinions omitted]

## NATIONAL TREASURY EMPLOYEES UNION
### v.
## VON RAAB

### 489 U.S. 656, 109 S. Ct. 1384, 103 L. Ed. 2d 685 (1989)

*[Citations and footnotes omitted.]*

[The United States Customs Service implemented a drug-screening program requiring employees who applied for promotion to positions involving interdiction of illegal drugs that required carrying firearms or handling classified materials to produce urine samples for chemical testing. A federal employees' union filed suit alleging that the drug-testing program violated the Fourth Amendment.]

Justice KENNEDY delivered the opinion of the Court.

We granted certiorari to decide whether it violates the Fourth Amendment for the United States Customs Service to require a urinalysis test from employees who seek transfer or promotion to certain positions.

* * *

In *Skinner v. Railway Labor Executives Assn.*, decided today, we held that federal regulations requiring employees of private railroads to produce urine samples for chemical testing implicate the Fourth Amendment, as those tests invade reasonable expectations of privacy. Our earlier cases have settled that the Fourth Amendment protects individuals from unreasonable searches conducted by the Government, even when the Government acts as an employer and, in view of our holding in *Railway Labor Executives* that urine tests are searches, it follows that the Custom Service's drug testing program must meet the reasonableness requirement of the Fourth Amendment.

While we have often emphasized, and reiterate today, that a search must be supported, as a general matter, by a warrant issued upon probable cause, our decision in *Railway Labor Executives* reaffirms the longstanding principle that neither a warrant nor probable cause, nor, indeed, any measure of individualized suspicion, is an indispensable component of reasonableness in every circumstance. As we note in *Railway Labor Executives*, our cases establish that where a Fourth Amendment intrusion serves special governmental needs, beyond the normal need for law enforcement, it is necessary to balance the individual's privacy expectations against the Government's interests to determine whether it is impractical to require a warrant or some level of individualized suspicion in the particular context.

It is clear that the Customs Service's drug testing program is not designed to serve the ordinary needs of law enforcement. Test results may not be used in a criminal prosecution of the employee without the employee's consent. The purposes of the program are to deter drug use among those eligible for promotion to sensitive positions within the Service and to prevent the promotion of drug users to those positions. These substantial interests, no less than the Government's concern for safe rail transportation at issue in *Railway Labor Executives*, present a special need that may justify departure from

the ordinary warrant and probable cause requirements.

\* \* \*

The Customs Service is our Nation's first line of defense against one of the greatest problems affecting the health and welfare of our population. We have adverted before to "the veritable national crisis in law enforcement caused by smuggling of illicit narcotics." . . .

Many of the Service's employees are often exposed to this criminal element and to the controlled substances they seek to smuggle into the country. The physical safety of these employees may be threatened, and many may be tempted not only by bribes from the traffickers with whom they deal, but also by their own access to vast sources of valuable contraband seized and controlled by the Service . . .

It is readily apparent that the Government has a compelling interest in ensuring that front-line interdiction personnel are physically fit, and have unimpeachable integrity and judgment. . . . This national interest in self-protection could be irreparably damaged if those charged with safeguarding it were, because of their own drug use, unsympathetic to their mission of interdicting narcotics. A drug user's indifference to the Service's basic mission or, even worse, his active complicity with the malefactors, can facilitate importation of sizable drug shipments or block apprehension of dangerous criminals. The public interest demands effective measures to bar drug users from positions directly involving the interdiction of illegal drugs.

The public interest likewise demands effective measures to prevent the promotion of drug users to positions that require the incumbent to carry a firearm, even if the incumbent is not engaged directly in the interdiction of drugs. Customs employees who may use deadly force plainly "discharge duties fraught with such risks of injury to others that even a momentary lapse of attention can have disastrous consequences." We agree with the Government that the public should not bear the risk that employees who may suffer from impaired perception and judgment will be promoted to positions where they may need to employ deadly force. Indeed, ensuring against the creation of this dangerous risk will itself further Fourth Amendment values, as the use of deadly force may violate the Fourth Amendment in certain circumstances.

Against these valid public interests we must weigh the interference with individual liberty that results from requiring these classes of employees to undergo a urine test. The interference with individual privacy that results from the collection of a urine sample for subsequent chemical analysis could be substantial in some circumstances. We have recognized, however, that the "operational realities of the workplace" may render entirely reasonable certain work-related intrusions by supervisors and co-workers that might be viewed as unreasonable in other contexts. While these operational realities will rarely affect an employee's expectations of privacy with respect to searches of his person, or of personal effects that the employee may bring to the workplace, it is plain that certain forms of public employment may diminish privacy expectations even with respect to such personal searches. Employees of the United States Mint, for example, should expect to be subject to certain routine personal searches when they leave the workplace every day. Similarly, those who join our military or intelligence services may not only be required to give what in other contexts might be viewed as extraordinary assurances of trustworthiness and probity, but also may expect intrusive inquiries into their physical fitness for those special positions. We think Customs employees who are directly involved in the interdiction of illegal drugs or who are required to carry firearms in the line of duty likewise have a diminished expectation of privacy in respect to the intrusions occasioned by a urine test. Unlike most private citizens or government employees in general, employees involved in drug interdiction reasonably should expect effective inquiry into their fitness and probity. Much the same is true of employees who are required to carry firearms. Because successful performance of their duties depends uniquely on their judgment and dexterity, these employees cannot reasonably expect to keep from the Service personal information that bears directly on their fitness. While reasonable tests designed to elicit this information doubtless infringe some privacy expectations, we do not believe these expectations outweigh the Government's compelling interests in safety and in the integrity of our borders.

* * *

In sum, we believe the Government has demonstrated that its compelling interests in safeguarding our borders and the public safety outweigh the privacy expectations of employees who seek to be promoted to positions that directly involve the interdiction of illegal drugs or that require the incumbent to carry a firearm. We hold that the testing of these employees is reasonable under the Fourth Amendment.

* * *

The judgment of the Court of Appeals for the Fifth Circuit is affirmed in part and vacated in part, and the case is remanded for further proceedings consistent with this opinion.

It is so ordered.

[Concurring and dissenting opinions omitted.]

**LINGLER**

v.

**FECHKO**

**312 F.3d 237 (6th Cir. 2002)**

DAVID A. NELSON, Circuit Judge

\* \* \*

On what must have been a slow day for crime in Seven Hills, Ohio, police officers James Lingler and Jeffrey Gezymalla, the plaintiffs in this civil rights action, decided to tidy up the station house. In the course of their housekeeping efforts the officers removed an old couch and some dilapidated chairs from a training room. The furniture was placed in a dumpster behind the building.

The chief of police, defendant John R. Fechko, had not authorized any such property disposal. When he found that the furniture was not in its usual place, he ordered a "full investigation." Suspicion soon fell on Officers Lingler and Gezymalla, whose daily activity logs made reference to "station cleanup."

Chief Fechko called Officer Gezymalla into his office and asked him to explain the log entry. The officer detailed his efforts to clean up the station house, including the discarding of the old furniture. Whether in earnest or in an attempt to "impress upon Officer Gezymalla the gravity of his actions," Chief Fechko observed that the disposal of the furniture could be considered theft of city property. In this connection the chief spoke of reading the officer his rights.

Chief Fechko next met with Officer Lingler, who responded in the negative to a question about knowledge of "possible theft, missing city property." When asked about the "station cleanup" entry on his activity log, Officer Lingler replied "oh, you mean the junk furniture." During this interview Officer Lingler said he wanted to have an attorney present if the investigation were criminal in nature.

Following these meetings, Chief Fechko ordered the officers to prepare detailed written statements concerning the station cleanup. The officers objected, and Officer Lingler again stated that he wanted a lawyer. Chief Fechko said that the matter was not criminal, and he ordered the men to turn in their statements by the end of their work shift.

The officers did so, producing statements that described the cleanup efforts generally but made no reference to the furniture. Because of what he viewed as a failure to comply with his order, the chief then initiated disciplinary proceedings against the officers. After consulting counsel, the officers submitted statements with detailed accounts of the station house cleanup and the removal of the furniture. At no stage, as far as the record discloses, was either officer required to waive his constitutional privilege against self-incrimination.

Although Chief Fechko recommended that the mayor suspend the officers for 30 days, no punishment of any kind was imposed. We are told that the chief also recommended the initiation of criminal proceedings, but that this recommendation was rejected as well. The officers were never prosecuted.

In due course the officers sued the chief in an Ohio court. The complaint asserted a claim under 42 U.S.C. § 1983 for violation of the constitutional privilege against self-incrimination. . . . The case was removed to the United States District Court for the Northern District of Ohio, where the chief moved for summary judgment. The district court granted the motion. . . . A final judgment thus having been entered, the officers perfected the present appeal.

To prevail on their first claim the officers would have to prove that the chief, while acting under color of state law, subjected them to the deprivation of a right secured by the Constitution or laws of the United States. See 42 U.S.C. § 1983. The right of which the officers

contend they were deprived is one arising from the Fifth Amendment prohibition (made applicable to the states by the
Fourteenth Amendment) against any
person being "compelled in any criminal
case to be a witness against himself." We
agree with the district court that the
chief did not violate this right.

By its terms, the Fifth Amendment
does not prohibit the act of compelling a
self-incriminating statement other than
for use in a criminal case. See . . .
*Mahoney v. Kesery*, ("the Fifth Amendment does not forbid the forcible extraction of information but only the use of
information so extracted as evidence in a
criminal case . . .").

The statements given by Officers Lingler and Gezymalla were not used against
them in any criminal case. Indeed, under
*Garrity v. New Jersey*, the statements
could not have been so used. See *Garrity*
(holding that the constitutional protection
against coerced statements "prohibits use
in subsequent criminal proceedings of
statements obtained under threat of
removal from office, and . . . it extends to
all, whether they are policemen or other
members of our body politic").

\* \* \*

. . . There is an important distinction . . .
between plaintiffs not on the public payroll—"private citizens who may claim a
generalized right to be free from compelled interrogation by the government"—and plaintiffs who are public
employees. Plaintiffs who wear the uniforms of police officers "can make no
tenable claim that a Fifth Amendment
violation occurred when the Police
Department merely exercised its legitimate right, as an employer, to question
them about matters narrowly relating to
their job performance."

AFFIRMED.

# KELLEY
## v.
# JOHNSON

**425 U.S. 238, 96 S. Ct. 1440,
47 L. Ed. 2d 708 (1976)**

*[Citations and footnotes omitted.]*

MR. JUSTICE REHNQUIST delivered the opinion of the Court.

\* \* \*

In 1971 respondent's predecessor,
individually and as president of the Suffolk County Patrolmen's Benevolent
Association, brought this action under
the Civil Rights Act of 1871, 42 U.S.C.
§1983, against petitioner's predecessor,
the Commissioner of the Suffolk County
Police Department. The Commissioner
had promulgated Order No. 71-1, which
established hair-grooming standards
applicable to male members of the
police force. The regulation was directed
at the style and length of hair, sideburns,
and mustaches; beards and goatees were
prohibited, except for medical reasons;
and wigs conforming to the regulation
could be worn for cosmetic reasons. The
regulation was attacked as violative of
respondent patrolman's right of free
expression under the First Amendment
and his guarantees of due process and
equal protection under the Fourteenth
Amendment, in that it was "not based
upon the generally accepted standard of
grooming in the community" and placed
"an undue restriction" upon his activities
therein.

\* \* \*

Respondent has sought the protection
of the Fourteenth Amendment, not as a
member of the citizenry at large, but on
the contrary as an employee of the police

department of Suffolk County, a subdivision of the State of New York. While the Court of Appeals made passing reference to this distinction, it was thereafter apparently ignored. We think, however, it is highly significant. In *Pickering v. Board of Education*, after noting that state employment may not be conditioned on the relinquishment of First Amendment rights, the Court stated that "[a]t the same time it cannot be gainsaid that the State has interests as an employer in regulating the speech of its employees that differ significantly from those it possesses in connection with regulation of the speech of the citizenry in general." More recently, we have sustained comprehensive and substantial restrictions upon activities of both federal and state employees lying at the core of the First Amendment. If such state regulations may survive challenges based on the explicit language of the First Amendment, there is surely even more room for restrictive regulations of state employees where the claim implicates only the more general contours of the substantive liberty interest protected by the Fourteenth Amendment.

The hair-length regulation here touches respondent as an employee of the county and, more particularly, as a policeman. Respondent's employer has, in accordance with its well-established duty to keep the peace, placed myriad demands upon the members of the police force, duties which have no counterpart with respect to the public at large. Respondent must wear a standard uniform, specific in each detail. When in uniform he must salute the flag. He may not take an active role in local political affairs by way of being a party delegate or contributing or soliciting political contributions. He may not smoke in public. All of these and other regulations of the Suffolk County Police Department infringe on respondent's freedom of choice in personal matters, and it was apparently the view of the Court of Appeals that the burden is on the State to prove a "genuine public need" for each and every one of these regulations.

This view was based upon the Court of Appeals' reasoning that the "unique judicial deference" accorded by the judiciary to regulation of members of the military was inapplicable because there was no historical or functional justification for the characterization of the police as "para-military." But the conclusion that such cases are inapposite, however correct, in no way detracts from the deference due Suffolk County's choice of an organizational structure for its police force. Here the county has chosen a mode of organization which it undoubtedly deems the most efficient in enabling its police to carry out the duties assigned to them under state and local law. Such a choice necessarily gives weight to the overall need for discipline, esprit de corps, and uniformity.

The county's choice of an organizational structure, therefore, does not depend for its constitutional validity on any doctrine of historical prescription. Nor, indeed, has respondent made any such claim. His argument does not challenge the constitutionality of the organizational structure, but merely asserts that the present hair-length regulation infringes his asserted liberty interest under the Fourteenth Amendment. We believe, however, that the hair-length regulation cannot be viewed in isolation, but must be rather considered in the context of the county's chosen mode of organization for its police force.

The promotion of safety of persons and property is unquestionably at the core of the State's police power, and virtually all state and local governments employ a uniformed police force to aid in the accomplishment of that purpose. Choice of organization, dress, and equipment for law enforcement personnel is a decision entitled to the same sort of presumption of legislative validity as are state choices designed to promote other aims within the cognizance of the State's police power. Having recognized in other contexts the wide latitude accorded the government in the "dispatch of its own internal affairs," we think Suffolk County's police regulations involved here are entitled to similar weight. Thus the question is not, as the Court of Appeals conceived it to be, whether the State can "establish" a "genuine public need" for the specific regulation. It is whether respondent can demonstrate that there is no rational connection between the regulation, based as it is on the county's method of organizing its police force, and the promotion of safety of persons and property.

We think the answer here is so clear that the District Court was quite right in the first instance to have dismissed respondent's complaint. Neither this Court, the Court of Appeals, nor the District Court is in a position to weigh the policy arguments in favor of and against a rule regulating hairstyles as a part of regulations governing a uniformed civilian service. The constitutional issue to be decided by these courts is whether petitioner's determination that such regulations should be enacted is so irrational that it may be branded "arbitrary," and therefore a deprivation of respondent's "liberty" interest in freedom to choose his own hairstyle. The overwhelming majority of state and local police of the present day are uniformed. This fact itself testifies to the recognition by those who direct those operations, and by the people of the States and localities who directly or indirectly

choose such persons, that similarity in appearance of police officers is desirable. This choice may be based on a desire to make police officers readily recognizable to the members of the public, or a desire for the esprit de corps which such similarity is felt to inculcate within the police force itself. Either one is a sufficiently rational justification for regulations so as to defeat respondent's claim based on the liberty guarantee of the Fourteenth Amendment.

The Court of Appeals relied on *Garrity v. New Jersey* and amicus in its brief in support of respondent elaborates an argument based on the language in *Garrity* that "policemen, like teachers and lawyers, are not relegated to a watered-down version of constitutional rights. *Garrity*, of course, involved the protections afforded by the Fifth Amendment to the United States Constitution as made applicable to the States by the Fourteenth Amendment. Certainly its language cannot be taken to suggest that the claim of a member of a uniformed civilian service based on the "liberty" interest protected by the Fourteenth Amendment must necessarily be treated for constitutional purposes the same as a similar claim by a member of the general public. The regulation challenged here did not violate any right guaranteed respondent by the Fourteenth Amendment to the United States Constitution, and the Court of Appeals was therefore wrong in reversing the District Court's original judgment dismissing the action. The judgment of the Court of Appeals is

Reversed.

[Concurring and dissenting opinions have been omitted.]

## EQUAL EMPLOYMENT OPPORTUNITIES ACT

### Pub. L. No. 88-352, Title VII § 703, July 1964

78 Stat. 253 et seq. Codified and amended, this Act appears as 42 U.S.C. § 2000e et seq.

Sec. 2000e-2(a). Employer practices
It shall be an unlawful employment practice for an employer—

(1) to fail or refuse to hire or to discharge any individual, or otherwise to discriminate against any individual with respect to his compensation, terms, conditions, or privileges of employment, because of such individual's race, color, religion, sex, or national origin; or

(2) to limit, segregate, or classify his employees or applicants for employment in any way which would deprive or tend to deprive any individual of employment opportunities or otherwise adversely affect his status as an employee, because of such individual's race, color, religion, sex, or national origin.

Sec. 2000e-2(h). Preferential treatment not to be granted on account of existing number or percentage imbalance

Nothing contained in this subchapter shall be interpreted to require any employer . . . subject to this subchapter to grant preferential treatment to any individual or to any group because of the race, color, religion, sex, or national origin of such individual or group on account of an imbalance which may exist with respect to the total number or percentage of persons of any race, color, religion, sex, or national origin employed by any employer . . .in comparison with the total number or percentage of persons of such race, color, religion, sex, or national origin in any community, State, section, or other area, or in the available work force in any community, State, section, or other area.

## DOTHARD
## v.
## RAWLINSON

### 433 U.S. 321, 97 S. Ct. 2720, 53 L. Ed. 2d 786 (1977)

*[Citations and footnotes omitted.]*

[Dianne Rawlinson, a 22-year-old college graduate with a major in correctional psychology, sought employment with the Alabama Board of Corrections as a prison guard, called in Alabama a "correctional counselor." A correctional counselor's primary duty was to maintain security and control of the inmates by continually supervising and observing their activities. To be eligible for consideration, an applicant had to possess a valid Alabama driver's license, a high school education or its equivalent, be free from physical defects, be between the ages of 20½ years and 45 years at the time of appointment, and fall between the minimum height and weight requirements of 5 feet 2 inches and 120 pounds, and the maximum of 6 feet 10 inches, and 300 pounds. Rawlinson was refused employment because she failed to meet the minimum 120-pound weight requirement. She filed suit challenging the statutory height and weight minima as violative of Title VII. She also challenged Regulation 204, which established gender criteria for "contact positions" in maximum-security institutions that required continual close physical proximity to inmates.]

MR. JUSTICE STEWART delivered the opinion of the Court.

* * *

In enacting Title VII, Congress required "the removal of artificial, arbitrary, and unnecessary barriers to employment when the barriers operate invidiously to discriminate on the basis of racial or other impermissible classification." The District Court found that the minimum statutory height and weight requirements that applicants for employment as correctional counselors must meet constitute the sort of arbitrary barrier to equal employment opportunity that Title VII forbids. The appellants assert that the District Court erred both in finding that the height and weight standards discriminate against women, and in its refusal to find that, even if they do, these standards are justified as "job related."

The gist of the claim that the statutory height and weight requirements discriminate against women does not involve an assertion of purposeful discriminatory motive. It is asserted, rather, that these facially neutral qualification standards work in fact disproportionately to exclude women from eligibility for employment by the Alabama Board of Corrections. We dealt in *Griggs v. Duke Power Co.* and *Albemarle Paper Co. v. Moody* with similar allegations that facially neutral employment standards disproportionately excluded Negroes from employment, and those cases guide our approach here.

Those cases make clear that to establish a prima facie case of discrimination, a plaintiff need only show that the facially neutral standards in question select applicants for hire in a significantly discriminatory pattern. Once it is thus shown that the employment standards are discriminatory in effect, the employer must meet "the burden of showing that any given requirement [has] . . . a manifest relationship to the employment in question." If the employer proves that the challenged requirements are job related, the plaintiff may then show that

other selection devices without a similar discriminatory effect would also "serve the employer's legitimate interest in 'efficient and trustworthy workmanship.' "

Although women 14 years of age or older compose 52.75% of the Alabama population and 36.89% of its total labor force, they hold only 12.9% of its correctional counselor positions. In considering the effect of the minimum height and weight standards on this disparity in rate of hiring between the sexes, the District Court found that the 5'2" requirement would operate to exclude 33.29% of the women in the United States between the ages of 18-79, while excluding only 1.28% of men between the same ages. The 120-pound weight restriction would exclude 22.29% of the women and 2.35% of the men in this age group. When the height and weight restrictions are combined, Alabama's statutory standards would exclude 41.13% of the female population while excluding less than 1% of the male population. Accordingly, the District Court found that Rawlinson had made out a prima facie case of unlawful sex discrimination.

\* \* \*

 . . . [W]e cannot say that the District Court was wrong in holding that the statutory height and weight standards had a discriminatory impact on women applicants. . . .

We turn, therefore, to the appellants' argument that they have rebutted the prima facie case of discrimination by showing that the height and weight requirements are job related. These requirements, they say, have a relationship to strength, a sufficient but unspecified amount of which is essential to effective job performance as a correctional counselor. In the District Court, however, the appellants produced no evidence correlating the height and weight requirements with the requisite amount of strength thought essential to good job performance. Indeed, they failed to offer evidence of any kind in specific justification of the statutory standards.

If the job-related quality that the appellants identify is bona fide, their purpose could be achieved by adopting and validating a test for applicants that measures strength directly. Such a test, fairly administered, would fully satisfy the standards of Title VII because it would be one that "measure[s] the person for the job and not the person in the abstract." But nothing in the present record even approaches such a measurement.

For the reasons we have discussed, the District Court was not in error in holding that Title VII of the Civil Rights Act of 1964, as amended, prohibits application of the statutory height and weight requirements to Rawlinson and the class she represents.

*III*

Unlike the statutory height and weight requirements, Regulation 204 explicitly discriminates against women on the basis of their sex. In defense of this overt discrimination, the appellants rely on § 703 (e) of Title VII, 42 U.S.C. § 2000e-2 (e), which permits sex-based discrimination "in those certain instances where . . . sex . . . is a bona fide occupational qualification reasonably necessary to the normal operation of that particular business or enterprise."

\* \* \*

We are persuaded—by the restrictive language of § 703 (e), the relevant legislative history, and the consistent interpretation of the Equal Employment Opportunity Commission—that the bfoq exception was in fact meant to be an extremely narrow exception to the general prohibition of discrimination on the basis of sex. In the particular factual circumstances of this case, however, we conclude that the District Court erred in rejecting the State's contention that Regulation 204 falls within the narrow ambit of the bfoq exception.

The environment in Alabama's penitentiaries is a peculiarly inhospitable one for human beings of whatever sex. Indeed, a Federal District Court has held that the conditions of confinement in the prisons of the State, characterized by "rampant violence" and a "jungle atmosphere," are constitutionally intolerable. The record in the present case shows that because of inadequate staff and facilities, no attempt is made in the four maximum-security male penitentiaries to classify or segregate inmates according to their offense or level of dangerousness—a procedure that, according to expert testimony, is essential to effective penological administration. Consequently, the estimated 20% of the male prisoners who are sex offenders are scattered throughout the penitentiaries' dormitory facilities.

In this environment of violence and disorganization, it would be an oversimplification to characterize Regulation 204 as an exercise in "romantic paternalism." In the usual case, the argument that a particular job is too dangerous for women may appropriately be met by the rejoinder that it is the purpose of Title VII to allow the individual woman to make that choice for herself. More is at stake in this case, however, than an individual woman's decision to weigh and accept the risks of employment in a "contact" position in a maximum-security male prison.

The essence of a correctional counselor's job is to maintain prison security. A woman's relative ability to maintain order in a male, maximum-security, unclassified penitentiary of the type Alabama now runs could be directly reduced by her womanhood. There is a basis in fact for expecting that sex offenders who have criminally assaulted women in the past would be moved to do so again if access to women were established within the prison. There would also be a real risk that other inmates, deprived of a normal heterosexual environment, would assault women guards because they were women. In a prison system where violence is the order of the day, where inmate access to guards is facilitated by dormitory living arrangements, where every institution is understaffed, and where a substantial portion of the inmate population is composed of sex offenders mixed at random with other prisoners, there are few visible deterrents to inmate assaults on women custodians.

Appellee Rawlinson's own expert testified that dormitory housing for aggressive inmates poses a greater security problem than single-cell lockups, and further testified that it would be unwise to use women as guards in a prison where even 10% of the inmates had been convicted of sex crimes and were not segregated from the other prisoners. The likelihood that inmates would assault a woman because she was a woman would pose a real threat not only to the victim of the assault but also to the basic control of the penitentiary and protection of its inmates and the other security personnel. The employee's very womanhood would thus directly undermine her capacity to provide the security that is the essence of a correctional counselor's responsibility.

There was substantial testimony from experts on both sides of this litigation that the use of women as guards in "contact" positions under the existing conditions in Alabama maximum-security male penitentiaries would pose a substantial security problem, directly linked to the sex of the prison guard. On the basis of that evidence, we conclude that the District Court was in error in ruling that being

male is not a bona fide occupational qualification for the job of correctional counselor in a "contact" position in an Alabama male maximum-security penitentiary.

The judgment is accordingly affirmed in part and reversed in part, and the case is remanded to the District Court for further proceedings consistent with this opinion.

It is so ordered.

[Concurring opinions have been omitted.]

## JONES
### v.
## CLINTON

**990 F. Supp. 657 (E.D. Ark. 1998)**

*[Citations and footnotes omitted.]*

[Paula Corbin Jones, a former Arkansas government employee, sued William Clinton, then President of the United States, under Title VII for an incident that allegedly occurred in a hotel suite in Little Rock, Arkansas, while the President was Governor of Arkansas. According to Ms. Jones' complaint, then-Governor Clinton was at the Excelsior Hotel on the day in question, delivering a speech at an official conference being sponsored by the Arkansas Industrial Development Commission (AIDC). The plaintiff was working at a conference registration desk when Trooper Danny Ferguson, the Governor's bodyguard, delivered a piece of paper to her with a four-digit number written on it, and said that the Governor would like to meet with her in this suite number. Thinking that it was an honor to be asked to meet the Governor and that it might lead to an enhanced employment opportunity, plaintiff states that she agreed to the meeting and that Ferguson escorted her to the floor of the hotel upon which the Governor's suite was located.

Plaintiff states that upon arriving at the suite and announcing herself, the Governor shook her hand, invited her in, and closed the door. She states that a few minutes of small talk ensued, which included the Governor asking her about her job and him mentioning that Dave Harrington, plaintiff's ultimate superior within the AIDC and a Clinton appointee, was his "good friend." Plaintiff states that the Governor then "unexpectedly reached over to [her], took her hand, and pulled her toward him, so that their bodies were close to each other." She states she removed her hand from his and retreated several feet, but that the Governor approached her again and, while saying, "I love the way your hair flows down your back" and "I love your curves," put his hand on her leg, started sliding it toward her pelvic area, and bent down to attempt to kiss her on the neck, all without her consent. Plaintiff states that she exclaimed, "What are you doing?," told the Governor that she was "not that kind of girl," and "escaped" from the Governor's reach "by walking away from him." She states she was extremely upset and confused and, not knowing what to do, attempted to distract the Governor by chatting about his wife. Plaintiff states that she sat down at the end of the sofa nearest the door, but that the Governor approached the sofa where she had taken a seat and, as he sat down, "lowered his trousers and underwear, exposed his penis (which was erect) and told [her] to 'kiss it.'" She states that she was "horrified" by this and that she "jumped up from the couch" and told the Governor that she had to go, saying something to the effect that she had to get back to the registration desk. Plaintiff states that the Governor, "while fondling his penis," said, "Well, I don't want to make you do anything you don't want to do," and then pulled up his pants and said, "If you get in trouble for leaving work, have Dave call me immediately and I'll take care of

it." She states that as she left the room (the door of which was not locked), the Governor "detained" her momentarily, "looked sternly" at her, and said, "You are smart. Let's keep this between ourselves."

Plaintiff states that the Governor's advances to her were unwelcome, that she never said or did anything to suggest to the Governor that she was willing to have sex with him, and that during the time they were together in the hotel suite, she resisted his advances although she was "stunned by them and intimidated by who he was." She states that when the Governor referred to Dave Harrington, she "understood that he was telling her that he had control over Mr. Harrington and over her job, and that he was willing to use that power." She states that from that point on, she was "very fearful" that her refusal to submit to the Governor's advances could damage her career and even jeopardize her employment.

Plaintiff states that when she left the hotel suite, she was in shock and upset but tried to maintain her composure. Plaintiff continued to work at AIDC following the alleged incident in the hotel suite. One of her duties was to deliver documents to and from the Office of the Governor, as well as other offices around the Arkansas State Capitol. She states that in June 1991, while performing these duties for the AIDC, she encountered Ferguson who told her that Mrs. Clinton was out of town often and that the Governor wanted her phone number and wanted to see her. Plaintiff states she refused to provide her phone number to Ferguson. She also states that she was "accosted" by the Governor in the Rotunda of the Arkansas State Capitol when he "draped his arm over her, pulled her close to him and held her tightly to his body," and said to his bodyguard, "Don't we make a beautiful couple: Beauty and the Beast?" Plaintiff additionally states that on an unspecified date, she was waiting in the Governor's outer office on a delivery run when the Governor entered the office, patted her on the shoulder, and in a "friendly fashion" said, "How are you doing, Paula?"

Plaintiff states that she continued to work at AIDC "even though she was in constant fear that the Governor would retaliate against her because she had refused to have sex with him." She states this fear prevented her from enjoying her job.

Plaintiff voluntarily terminated her employment with AIDC on February 20, 1993, in order to move to California with her husband, who had been transferred.]

Susan Webber Wright, UNITED STATES DISTRICT JUDGE.

[The court first considered the plaintiff's quid pro quo sexual harassment claim.]

To make a prima facie case of quid pro quo sexual harassment, this plaintiff must show, among other things, that her refusal to submit to unwelcome sexual advances or requests for sexual favors resulted in a tangible job detriment. "[A] supervisor's mere threat or promise of job-related harm or benefits in exchange for sexual favors does not constitute quid pro quo harassment. . . ."

* * *

. . . Indeed, it is undisputed that plaintiff received every merit increase and cost-of-living allowance for which she was eligible during her nearly two-year tenure with the AIDC and consistently received satisfactory job evaluations. . . .

* * *

In sum, the Court finds that a showing of a tangible job detriment or adverse employment action is an essential element of plaintiff's § 1983 quid pro quo sexual harassment claim and that plaintiff has not demonstrated any tangible job detriment or adverse employment action for her refusal to submit to the Governor's alleged advances. The President is therefore entitled to summary judgment on plaintiff's claim of quid pro quo sexual harassment.

The Court now turns to plaintiff's hostile work environment claim. Unlike quid pro quo sexual harassment, hostile work environment harassment arises when "sexual conduct has the purpose or effect of unreasonably interfering with an individual's work performance or creating an intimidating, hostile, or offensive working environment." . . . The behavior creating the hostile working environment need not be overtly sexual in nature, but it must be " 'unwelcome' in the sense that the employee did not solicit or invite it, and the employee regarded the conduct as undesirable or offensive." . . .

The President essentially argues that aside from the alleged incident at the Excelsior Hotel, plaintiff alleges only two other contacts with him, alleges only a few additional contacts with Ferguson, and contains conclusory claims that plaintiff's supervisors were rude. He argues that taken individually or as a whole, these contacts do not in any way constitute the kind of pervasive, intimidating, abusive conduct that courts require to establish a hostile work environment claim. The Court agrees.

In assessing the hostility of an environment, a court must look to the totality of the circumstances. Circumstances to be considered include "the frequency of the discriminatory conduct; its severity; whether it is physically threatening or humiliating, or a mere offensive utterance; and whether it unreasonably interferes with an employee's work performance." . . .

* * *

Plaintiff certainly has not shown under the totality of the circumstances that the alleged incident in the hotel and her additional encounters with Ferguson and the Governor were so severe or pervasive that it created an abusive working environment. She admits that she never missed a day of work following the alleged incident in the hotel, she continued to work at AIDC another nineteen months (leaving only because of her husband's job transfer), she continued to go on a daily basis to the Governor's Office to deliver items and never asked to be relieved of that duty, she never filed a formal complaint or told her supervisors of the incident while at AIDC, and she never consulted a psychiatrist, psychologist, or incurred medical bills as a result of the alleged incident. . . .

While the alleged incident in the hotel, if true, was certainly boorish and offensive, the Court has already found that the Governor's alleged conduct does not constitute sexual assault. This is thus not one of those exceptional cases in which a single incident of sexual harassment, such as an assault, was deemed sufficient to state a claim of hostile work environment sexual harassment. Cf. Crisonino v. New York City Housing Auth., 985 F. Supp. 385 (S.D.N.Y. 1997) (supervisor called plaintiff a "dumb bitch" and "shoved her so hard that she fell backward and hit the floor, sustaining injuries from which she has yet to fully recover").

Considering the totality of the circumstances, it simply cannot be said that the conduct to which plaintiff was allegedly subjected was frequent, severe, or physically threatening, and the Court finds that defendants' actions as shown by the record do not constitute the kind of sustained and nontrivial conduct necessary for a claim of hostile work environment. . . .

In sum, the Court finds that the record does not demonstrate conduct that was so severe or pervasive that it can be said to have altered the conditions of plaintiff's employment and created an abusive working environment. Accordingly, the President is entitled to summary judgment on plaintiff's claim of hostile work environment sexual harassment.

\* \* \*

# Part III:
# Appendix

# THE CONSTITUTION OF THE UNITED STATES OF AMERICA

We the People of the United States, in Order to form a more perfect Union, establish Justice, insure domestic Tranquillity, provide for the common defence, promote the general Welfare, and secure the Blessings of Liberty to ourselves and our Posterity, do ordain and establish this Constitution for the United States of America.

## ARTICLE I.

Section 1. All legislative Powers herein granted shall be vested in a Congress of the United States, which shall consist of a Senate and House of Representatives.

Section 2. The House of Representatives shall be composed of Members chosen every second Year by the People of the several States, and the Electors in each State shall have the Qualifications requisite for Electors of the most numerous Branch of the State Legislature.

No Person shall be a Representative who shall not have attained to the age of twenty five Years, and been seven Years a Citizen of the United States, and who shall not, when elected, be an Inhabitant of that State in which he shall be chosen.

Representatives and direct Taxes shall be apportioned among the several States which may be included within this Union, according to their respective Numbers, which shall be determined by adding to the whole Number of free Persons, including those bound to Service for a Term of Years, and excluding Indians not taxed, three fifths of all other Persons. The actual Enumeration shall be made within three Years after the first Meeting of the Congress of the United States, and within every subsequent Term of ten Years, in such Manner as they shall by Law direct. The Number of Representatives shall not exceed one for every thirty Thousand, but each State shall have at Least one Representative; and until such enumeration shall be made, the State of New Hampshire shall be entitled to chuse three, Massachusetts eight, Rhode-Island and Providence Plantations one, Connecticut five, New-York six, New Jersey four, Pennsylvania eight, Delaware one, Maryland six, Virginia ten, North Carolina five, South Carolina five, and Georgia three.

When vacancies happen in the Representation from any State, the Executive Authority thereof shall issue Writs of Election to fill such Vacancies.

The House of Representatives shall chuse their Speaker and other Officers; and shall have the sole Power of Impeachment.

Section 3. The Senate of the United States shall be composed of two Senators from each State, chosen by the Legislature thereof, for six Years; and each Senator shall have one Vote.

Immediately after they shall be assembled in Consequence of the first Election, they shall be divided as equally as may be into three Classes. The Seats of the Senators of the first Class shall be vacated at the Expiration of the second Year, of the second Class at the Expiration of the fourth Year, and of the third Class at the Expiration of the sixth Year, so that one third may be chosen every second Year; and if Vacancies happen by Resignation, or otherwise, during the Recess of the Legislature of any State, the Executive thereof may make temporary Appointments until the next Meeting of the Legislature, which shall then fill such Vacancies.

No Person shall be a Senator who shall not have attained to the Age of thirty Years, and been nine Years a Citizen of the United States, and who shall not, when elected, be an Inhabitant of that State for which he shall be chosen.

The Vice President of the United States shall be President of the Senate but shall have no Vote, unless they be equally divided.

The Senate shall chuse their other Officers, and also a President pro tempore, in the Absence of the Vice President, or when he shall exercise the Office of President of the United States.

The Senate shall have the sole Power to try all Impeachments. When sitting for that Purpose, they shall be on Oath or Affirmation. When the President of the United States is tried, the Chief Justice shall preside: And no Person shall be convicted without the Concurrence of two thirds of the Members present.

Judgment in Cases of Impeachment shall not extend further than to removal from Office, and disqualification to hold and enjoy any Office of honor, Trust or Profit under the United States: but the Party convicted shall nevertheless be liable and subject to Indictment, Trial, Judgment and Punishment, according to Law.

Section 4. The Times, Places and Manner of holding Elections for Senators and Representatives, shall be prescribed in each State by the Legislature thereof; but the Congress may at any time by Law make or alter such Regulations, except as to the Places of chusing Senators.

The Congress shall assemble at least once in every Year, and such Meeting shall be on the first Monday in December, unless they shall by Law appoint a different Day.

Section 5. Each House shall be the Judge of the Elections, Returns and Qualifications of its own Members, and a Majority of each shall constitute a Quorum to do Business; but a smaller Number may adjourn from day to day, and may be authorized to compel the Attendance of absent Members, in such Manner, and under such Penalties as each House may provide.

Each House may determine the Rules of its Proceedings, punish its Members for disorderly Behaviour, and, with the Concurrence of two thirds, expel a Member.

Each House shall keep a Journal of its Proceedings, and from time to time publish the same, excepting such Parts as may in their Judgment require Secrecy; and the Yeas and Nays of the Members of either House on any question shall, at the Desire of one fifth of those Present, be entered on the Journal.

Neither House, during the Session of Congress, shall, without the Consent of the other, adjourn for more than three days, nor to any other Place than that in which the two Houses shall be sitting.

Section 6. The Senators and Representatives shall receive a Compensation for their Services, to be ascertained by Law, and paid out of the Treasury of the United States. They shall in all Cases, except Treason, Felony and Breach of the Peace, be privileged from Arrest during their Attendance at the Session of their respective Houses, and in going to and returning from the same; and for any Speech or Debate in either House, they shall not be questioned in any other Place.

No Senator or Representative shall, during the Time for which he was elected, be appointed to any civil Office under the Authority of the United States, which shall have been created, or the Emoluments whereof shall have been encreased during such time; and no Person holding any Office under the United States, shall be a Member of either House during his Continuance in Office.

Section 7. All Bills for raising Revenue shall originate in the House of Representatives; but the Senate may propose or concur with amendments as on other Bills.

Every Bill which shall have passed the House of Representatives and the Senate, shall, before it become a law, be presented to the President of the United States: If he approve he shall sign it, but if not he shall return it, with his Objections to that House in which it shall have originated, who shall enter the Objections at large on their Journal, and proceed to reconsider it. If after such Reconsideration two thirds of that House shall agree to pass the Bill, it shall be sent, together with the Objections, to the other House, by which it shall likewise be reconsidered, and if approved by two thirds of that House, it shall become a Law. But in all such Cases the Votes of both Houses shall be determined by Yeas and Nays, and the Names of the Persons voting for and against the Bill shall be entered on the Journal of each House respectively. If any Bill shall not be returned by the President within ten Days (Sundays excepted) after it shall have been presented to him, the Same shall be a Law, in like Manner as if he had signed it, unless the Congress by their Adjournment prevent its Return, in which Case it shall not be a Law.

Every Order, Resolution, or Vote to which the Concurrence of the Senate and House of Representatives may be necessary (except on a question of Adjournment) shall be presented to the President of the United States; and before the Same shall take Effect, shall be approved by him, or being disapproved by him, shall be repassed by two thirds of the Senate and House of Representatives, according to the Rules and Limitations prescribed in the Case of a Bill.

Section 8. The Congress shall have Power To lay and collect Taxes, Duties, Imposts and Excises, to pay the Debts and provide for the common Defence and general Welfare of the United States; but all Duties, Imposts and Excises shall be uniform throughout the United States;

To borrow Money on the credit of the United States;

To regulate Commerce with foreign Nations, and among the several States, and with the Indian Tribes;

To establish an uniform Rule of Naturalization, and uniform Laws on the subject of Bankruptcies throughout the United States;

To coin Money, regulate the Value thereof, and of foreign Coin, and fix the Standard of Weights and Measures;

To provide for the Punishment of counterfeiting the Securities and current Coin of the United States;

To establish Post Offices and post Roads;

To promote the Progress of Science and useful Arts, by securing for limited Times to Authors and Inventors the exclusive Right to their respective Writings and Discoveries;

To constitute Tribunals inferior to the supreme Court;

To define and punish Piracies and Felonies committed on the high Seas, and Offences against the Law of Nations;

To declare War, grant Letters of Marque and Reprisal, and make Rules concerning Captures on Land and Water;

To raise and support Armies, but no Appropriation of Money to that Use shall be for a longer Term than two Years;

To provide and maintain a Navy;

To make Rules for the Government and Regulation of the land and naval Forces;

To provide for calling forth the Militia to execute the Laws of the Union, suppress Insurrections and repeal Invasions;

To provide for organizing, arming, and disciplining, the Militia, and for governing such Part of them as may be employed in the Service of the United States, reserving to the States respectively, the Appointment of the Officers, and the Authority of training the Militia according to the discipline prescribed by Congress;

To exercise exclusive Legislation in all Cases whatsoever, over such District (not exceeding ten Miles square) as may, by Cession of Particular States, and the Acceptance of Congress, become the Seat of the Government of the United States, and to exercise like Authority over all Places purchased by the Consent of the Legislature of the State in which the Same shall be, for the Erection of Forts, Magazines, Arsenals, dock-Yards and other needful Buildings;—And

To make all Laws which shall be necessary and proper for carrying into Execution the foregoing Powers and all other Powers vested by this Constitution in the Government of the United States, or in any Department or Officer thereof.

Section 9. The Migration or Importation of such Persons as any of the States now existing shall think proper to admit, shall not be prohibited by the Congress prior to the Year one thousand eight hundred and eight, but a Tax or duty may be imposed on such Importation, not exceeding ten dollars for each Person.

The Privilege of the Writ of Habeas Corpus shall not be suspended, unless when in Cases of Rebellion or Invasion the public Safety may require it.

No Bill of Attainder or ex post facto Law shall be passed.

No Capitation, or other direct, Tax shall be laid, unless in Proportion to the Census of Enumeration herein before directed to be taken.

No Tax or Duty shall be laid on Articles exported from any State.

No Preference shall be given by any Regulation of Commerce or Revenue to the Ports of one State over those of another: nor shall Vessels bound to, or from, one State, be obliged to enter, clear or pay Duties in another.

No Money shall be drawn from the Treasury, but in Consequence of Appropriations made by Law; and a regular Statement and Account of the Receipts and Expenditures of all public Money shall be published from time to time.

No Title of Nobility shall be granted by the United States: And no Person holding any Office of Profit or Trust under them, shall, without the Consent of the Congress, accept of any present, Emolument, Office, or Title, of any kind whatever, from any King, Prince or foreign State.

Section 10. No State shall enter into any Treaty, Alliance, or Confederation; grant Letters of Marque and Reprisal; coin Money; emit Bills of Credit; make any Thing but gold and silver Coin a Tender in Payment of Debts; pass any Bill of Attainder, ex post facto Law, or Law impairing the Obligation of Contracts, or grant any Title of Nobility.

No State shall, without the Consent of the Congress, lay any Imposts or Duties on Imports or Exports, except what may be absolutely necessary for executing it's inspection Laws: and the net Produce of all Duties and Imposts, laid by any State on Imports or Exports, shall be for the Use of the Treasury of the United States; and all such Laws shall be subject to the Revision and Control of the Congress.

No State shall, without the Consent of Congress, lay any Duty of Tonnage, keep Troops, or Ships of War in time of Peace, enter into any Agreement or Compact with another State, or with a foreign Power, or engage in War, unless actually invaded, or in such imminent Danger as will not admit of delay.

# ARTICLE II.

Section 1. The executive Power shall be vested in a President of the United States of America. He shall hold his Office during the Term of four Years, and, together with the Vice President, chosen for the same Term, be elected, as follows:

Each State shall appoint, in such Manner as the Legislature thereof may direct, a Number of Electors, equal to the whole Number of Senators and Representatives to which the State may be entitled in the Congress: but no Senator or Representative, or Person holding an Office of Trust or Profit under the United States, shall be appointed an Elector.

The Electors shall meet in their respective States, and vote by Ballot for two Persons, of whom one at least shall not be an Inhabitant of the same State with themselves. And they shall make a List of all the Persons voted for, and of the Number of Votes for each; which List they shall sign and certify, and transmit sealed to the Seat of the Government of the United States, directed to the President of the Senate. The President of the Senate shall, in the Presence of the Senate and House of Representatives, open all the Certificates, and the Votes shall then be counted. The Person having the greatest Number of Votes shall be the President, if such Number be a Majority of the whole Number of Electors appointed; and if there be more than one who have such Majority, and have an equal Number of Votes, then the House of Representatives shall immediately chuse by Ballot one of them for President; and if no Person have a Majority, then from the five highest on the List the said House shall in like Manner chuse the President. But in chusing the President, the Votes shall be taken by States, the Representatives from each State having one Vote; a quorum for this Purpose shall consist of a Member or Members from two thirds of the States, and a Majority of all the States shall be necessary to a Choice. In every Case, after the Choice of the President, the Person having the greatest Number of Votes of the Electors shall be the Vice President. But if there should remain two or more who have equal Votes, the Senate shall chuse from them by Ballot the Vice President.

The Congress may determine the Time of chusing the Electors, and the Day on which they shall give their Votes; which Day shall be the same throughout the United States.

No Person except a natural born Citizen, or a Citizen of the United States, at the time of the Adoption of this Constitution, shall be eligible to the Office of President; neither shall any person be eligible to that Office who shall not have attained to the Age of thirty five Years, and been fourteen Years a Resident within the United States.

In Case of the Removal of the President from Office, or of his Death, Resignation, or Inability to discharge the Powers and Duties of the said Office, the Same shall devolve on the Vice President, and the Congress may by Law provide for the Case of Removal, Death, Resignation or Inability, both of the President and Vice President, declaring what Officer shall then act as President, and such Officer shall act accordingly, until the Disability be removed, or a President shall be elected.

The President shall, at stated Times, receive for his Services, a Compensation, which shall neither be encreased nor diminished during the Period for which he shall have been elected, and he shall not receive within that Period any other Emolument from the United States, or any of them.

Before he enter on the Execution of his Office, he shall take the following Oath or Affirmation:—"I do solemnly swear (or affirm) that I will faithfully execute the Office of President of the United States, and will to the best of my Ability, preserve, protect and defend the Constitution of the United States."

Section 2. The President shall be Commander in Chief of the Army and Navy of the United States, and of the Militia of the several States, when called into the actual Service of the United States; he may require the Opinion, in writing, of the principal Officer in each of the executive Departments, upon any Subject relating to the Duties of their respective Offices, and he shall have Power to Grant Reprieves and Pardons for Offences against the United States, except in Cases of Impeachment.

He shall have Power, by and with the Advice and Consent of the Senate, to make Treaties, provided two thirds of the Senators present concur; and he shall nominate, and by and with the Advice and Consent of the Senate, shall appoint Ambassadors, other public Ministers and Consuls, Judges of the supreme Court, and all other Officers of the United States, whose Appointments are not herein otherwise provided for, and which shall be established by Law: but the Congress may by Law vest the Appointment of such inferior Officers, as they think proper, in the President alone, in the Courts of Law, or in the Heads of Departments.

The President shall have Power to fill up all Vacancies that may happen during the Recess of the Senate, by granting Commissions which shall expire at the End of their next Session.

Section 3. He shall from time to time give to the Congress Information on the State of the Union, and recommend to their Consideration such Measures as he shall judge necessary and expedient; he may, on extraordinary Occasions, convene both Houses, or either of them, and in Case of Disagreement between them, with Respect to the Time of Adjournment, he may adjourn them to such Time as he shall think proper; he shall receive Ambassadors and other public Ministers; he shall take Care that the Laws be faithfully executed, and shall Commission all the Officers of the United States.

Section 4. The President, Vice President and all Civil Officers of the United States, shall be removed from Office on Impeachment for and Conviction of, Treason, Bribery, or other high Crimes and Misdemeanors.

## ARTICLE III.

Section 1. The judicial Power of the United States, shall be vested in one supreme Court, and in such inferior Courts as the Congress may from time to time ordain and establish. The Judges, both of the supreme and inferior Courts, shall hold their Offices during good Behaviour, and shall, at stated Times, receive for their Services, a Compensation, which shall not be diminished during their Continuance in Office.

Section 2. The judicial Power shall extend to all Cases, in Law and Equity, arising under this Constitution, the Laws of the United States, and Treaties made, or which shall be made, under their Authority;—to all Cases affecting Ambassadors, other public ministers and Consuls;—to all Cases of admiralty and maritime Jurisdiction;—to

Controversies to which the United States shall be a Party;—to Controversies between two or more States;—between a State and Citizens of another State;—between Citizens of different States;—between Citizens of the same State claiming Lands under Grants of different States, and between a State, or the Citizens thereof, and foreign States, Citizens or Subjects.

In all Cases affecting Ambassadors, other public Ministers and Consuls, and those in which a State shall be Party, the supreme Court shall have original Jurisdiction. In all the other Cases before mentioned, the supreme Court shall have appellate Jurisdiction, both as to Law and Fact, with such Exceptions, and under such Regulations as the Congress shall make.

The Trial of all Crimes, except in Cases of Impeachment, shall be by Jury; and such Trial shall be held in the State where the said Crimes shall have been committed; but when not committed within any State, the Trial shall be at such Place or Places as the Congress may by Law have directed.

Section 3. Treason against the United States, shall consist only in levying War against them, or in adhering to their Enemies, giving them Aid and Comfort. No Person shall be convicted of Treason unless on the Testimony of two Witnesses to the same overt Act, or on Confession in open Court.

The Congress shall have Power to declare the Punishment of Treason, but no Attainder of Treason shall work Corruption of Blood, or Forfeiture except during the Life of the Person attainted.

# ARTICLE IV.

Section 1. Full Faith and Credit shall be given in each State to the public Acts, Records, and judicial Proceedings of every other State. And the Congress may by general Laws prescribe the Manner in which such Acts, Records and Proceedings shall be proved, and the Effect thereof.

Section 2. The Citizens of each State shall be entitled to all Privileges and Immunities of Citizens in the several States.

A Person charged in any State with Treason, Felony, or other Crime, who shall flee from Justice, and be found in another State, shall on Demand of the executive Authority of the State from which he fled, be delivered up, to be removed to the State having Jurisdiction of the Crime.

No Person held to Service or Labour in one State, under the Laws thereof, escaping into another, shall, in Consequence of any Law or Regulation therein, be discharged from such Service or Labour, but shall be delivered up on Claim of the Party to whom such Service or Labour may be due.

Section 3. New States may be admitted by the Congress into this Union; but no new State shall be formed or erected within the Jurisdiction of any other State; nor any State be formed by the Junction of two or more States, or Parts of States, without the Consent of the Legislatures of the States concerned as well as of the Congress.

The Congress shall have Power to dispose of and make all needful Rules and Regulations respecting the Territory or other Property belonging to the United States; and nothing in this Constitution shall be so construed as to Prejudice any Claims of the United States, or of any particular State.

Section 4. The United States shall guarantee to every State in this Union a Republican Form of Government, and shall protect each of them against Invasion; and on

Application of the Legislature, or of the Executive (when the Legislature cannot be convened) against domestic Violence.

# ARTICLE V.

The Congress, whenever two thirds of both Houses shall deem it necessary, shall propose Amendments to this Constitution, or, on the Application of the Legislatures of two thirds of the several States, shall call a Convention for proposing Amendments, which, in either Case, shall be valid to all Intents and Purposes, as Part of this Constitution, when ratified by the Legislatures of three fourths of the several States, or by Conventions in three fourths thereof, as the one or the other Mode of Ratification may be proposed by the Congress; Provided that no Amendment which may be made prior to the Year One thousand eight hundred and eight shall in any Manner affect the first and fourth Clauses in the Ninth Section of the first Article; and that no State, without its Consent, shall be deprived of its equal Suffrage in the Senate.

# ARTICLE VI.

All Debts contracted and Engagements entered into, before the Adoption of this Constitution, shall be as valid against the United States under this Constitution, as under the Confederation.

This Constitution, and the Laws of the United States which shall be made in Pursuance thereof; and all Treaties made, or which shall be made, under the Authority of the United States, shall be the supreme Law of the Land; and the Judges in every State shall be bound thereby, any Thing in the Constitution or Laws of any state to the Contrary notwithstanding.

The Senators and Representatives before mentioned, and the Members of the several State Legislatures, and all executive and judicial Officers, both of the United States and of the several States, shall be bound by Oath or Affirmation, to support this Constitution; but no religious Test shall ever be required as a Qualification to any Office or public Trust under the United States.

# ARTICLE VII.

The Ratification of the Conventions of nine States, shall be sufficient for the Establishment of this Constitution between the States so ratifying the same.

Done in Convention by the Unanimous Consent of the States present the Seventeenth Day of September in the Year of our Lord one thousand seven hundred and Eighty seven and of the Independence of the United States of America the Twelfth. In witness whereof We have hereunto subscribed our Names.

GO. WASHINGTON—*Presid't.*
*and deputy from Virginia*

| | | | |
|---|---|---|---|
| *New Hampshire* | JOHN LANGDON<br>NICHOLAS GILMAN | *Delaware* | GEO: READ<br>GUNNING BEDFORD JUN<br>JOHN DICKINSON<br>RICHARD BASSETT |
| *Massachusetts* | NATHANIEL GORHAM<br>RUFUS KING | | JACO: BROOM |
| *Connecticut* | WM. SAML. JOHNSON<br>ROGER SHERMAN | *Maryland* | JAMES MCHENRY<br>DAN OF ST THOS<br>JENIFER<br>DAN'L CARROLL |
| *New York* | ALEXANDER HAMILTON | *Virginia* | JOHN BLAIR<br>JAMES MADISON, JR. |
| *New Jersey* | WIL: LIVINGSTON<br>DAVID BREARLEY<br>WM. PATTERSON<br>JONA: DAYTON | *North Carolina* | WM. BLOUNT<br>RICHD DOBBS SPAIGHT<br>HU WILLIAMSON<br>J. RUTLEDGE |
| *Pennsylvania* | B FRANKLIN<br>THOMAS MIFFLIN<br>ROB'T MORRIS<br>GEO. CLYMER<br>THOS. FITZSIMONS<br>JARED INGERSOL<br>JAMES WILSON<br>GOUV MORRIS | *South Carolina* | J. RUTLEDGE<br>CHARLES COTESWORTH<br>PINCKNEY<br>CHARLES PINCKNEY<br>PIERCE BUTLER |
| | | *Georgia* | WILLIAM FEW<br>ABR BALDWIN |

Attest                                                                    WILLIAM JACKSON
                                                                                *Secretary*

Articles in addition to, and amendment of, the Constitution of the United States of America, proposed by Congress, and ratified by the several states, pursuant to the Fifth Article of the original Constitution

## AMENDMENT I

Congress shall make no law respecting an establishment of religion, or prohibiting the free exercise thereof; or abridging the freedom of speech, or of the press; or the right of the people peaceably to assemble, and to petition the Government for a redress of grievances.

## AMENDMENT II

A well regulated Militia, being necessary to the security of a free State, the right of the people to keep and bear Arms, shall not be infringed.

## AMENDMENT III

No Soldier shall, in time of peace be quartered in any house, without the consent of the Owner, nor in time of war, but in a manner to be prescribed by law.

## AMENDMENT IV

The right of the people to be secure in their persons, houses, papers, and effects, against unreasonable searches and seizures, shall not be violated, and no Warrants shall issue, but upon probable cause, supported by Oath or affirmation, and particularly describing the place to be searched, and the persons or things to be seized.

## AMENDMENT V

No person shall be held to answer for a capital, or otherwise infamous crime, unless on a presentment or indictment of a Grand Jury, except in cases arising in the land or naval forces, or in the Militia, when in actual service in time of War or public danger; nor shall any person be subject for the same offence to be twice put in jeopardy of life or limb; nor shall be compelled in any criminal case to be a witness against himself, nor be deprived of life, liberty, or property, without due process of law; nor shall private property be taken for public use, without just compensation.

## AMENDMENT VI

In all criminal prosecutions, the accused shall enjoy the right to a speedy and public trial, by an impartial jury of the State and district wherein the crime shall have been committed, which district shall have been previously ascertained by law, and to be informed of the nature and cause of the accusation; to be confronted with the witnesses against him; to have compulsory process for obtaining witnesses in his favor, and to have the Assistance of Counsel for his defence.

## AMENDMENT VII

In Suits at common law, where the value in controversy shall exceed twenty dollars, the right of trial by jury shall be preserved, and no fact tried by a jury, shall be otherwise re-examined in any Court of the United States, than according to the rules of the common law.

## AMENDMENT VIII

Excessive bail shall not be required, nor excessive fines imposed, nor cruel and unusual punishments inflicted.

## AMENDMENT IX

The enumeration in the Constitution, of certain rights, shall not be construed to deny or disparage others retained by the people.

## AMENDMENT X

The powers not delegated to the United States by the Constitution, nor prohibited by it to the States, are reserved to the States respectively, or to the people.

## AMENDMENT XI

The Judicial power of the United States shall not be construed to extend to any suit in law or equity, commenced or prosecuted against one of the United States by Citizens of another State, or by Citizens or Subjects of any Foreign State.

## AMENDMENT XII

The Electors shall meet in their respective states and vote by ballot for President and Vice-President, one of whom, at least, shall not be an inhabitant of the same state with themselves; they shall name in their ballots the person voted for as President, and in distinct ballots the person voted for as Vice-President, and they shall make distinct lists of all persons voted for as President, and of all persons voted for as Vice-President, and of the number of votes for each, which lists they shall sign and certify, and transmit sealed to the seat of the government of the United States, directed to the President of the Senate;—The President of the Senate shall, in the presence of the Senate and House of Representatives, open all the certificates and the votes shall then be counted;—The person having the greatest Number of votes for President, shall be the President, if such number be a majority of the whole number of Electors appointed; and if no person have such majority, then from the persons having the highest numbers not exceeding three on the list of those voted for as President, the House of Representatives shall choose immediately, by ballot, the President. But in choosing the President, the votes shall be taken by states, the representation from each state having one vote; a quorum for this purpose shall consist of a member or members from two-thirds of the states, and a majority of all the states shall be necessary to a choice. And if the House of Representatives shall not choose a President whenever the right of choice shall devolve upon them, before the fourth day of March next following, then the Vice-President shall act as President, as in the case of the death or other constitutional disability of the President.—The person having the greatest number of votes as Vice-President, shall be the Vice-President, if such number be a majority of the whole number of Electors appointed, and if no person have a majority, then from the two highest numbers on the list, the Senate shall choose the Vice-President; a quorum for the purpose shall consist of two-thirds of the whole number of Senators, and a majority of the whole number shall be necessary to a choice. But no person constitutionally ineligible to the office of President shall be eligible to that of Vice-President of the United States.

# AMENDMENT XIII

Section 1. Neither slavery nor involuntary servitude, except as a punishment for crime whereof the party shall have been duly convicted, shall exist within the United States, or any place subject to their jurisdiction.

Section 2. Congress shall have power to enforce this article by appropriate legislation.

# AMENDMENT XIV

Section 1. All persons born or naturalized in the United States and subject to the jurisdiction thereof, are citizens of the United States and of the State wherein they reside. No State shall make or enforce any law which shall abridge the privileges or immunities of citizens of the United States; nor shall any State deprive any person of life, liberty, or property, without due process of law; nor deny to any person within its jurisdiction the equal protection of the laws.

Section 2. Representatives shall be apportioned among the several States according to their respective numbers, counting the whole number of persons in each State, excluding Indians not taxed. But when the right to vote at any election for the choice of electors for President and Vice President of the United States, Representatives in Congress, the Executive and Judicial officers of a State, or the members of the Legislature thereof, is denied to any of the male inhabitants of such State, being twenty-one years of age, and citizens of the United States, or in any way abridged, except for participation in rebellion, or other crime, the basis of representation therein shall be reduced in the proportion which the number of such male citizens shall bear to the whole number of male citizens twenty-one years of age in such State.

Section 3. No person shall be a Senator or Representative in Congress, or elector of President and Vice President, or hold any office, civil or military, under the United States, or under any State, who, having previously taken an oath, as a member of Congress, or as an officer of the United States, or as a member of any State legislature, or as an executive or judicial officer of any State, to support the Constitution of the United States, shall have engaged in insurrection or rebellion against the same, or given aid or comfort to the enemies thereof. But Congress may by a vote of two-thirds of each House, remove such disability.

Section 4. The validity of the public debt of the United States, authorized by law, including debts incurred for payment of pensions and bounties for services in suppressing insurrection or rebellion, shall not be questioned. But neither the United States nor any State shall assume or pay any debt or obligation incurred in aid of insurrection or rebellion against the United States, or any claim for the loss or emancipation of any slave; but all such debts, obligations and claims shall be held illegal and void.

Section 5. The Congress shall have power to enforce, by appropriate legislation, the provisions of this article.

# AMENDMENT XV

Section 1. The right of citizens of the United States to vote shall not be denied or abridged by the United States or by any State on account of race, color, or previous condition of servitude.

Section 2. The Congress shall have power to enforce this article by appropriate legislation.

# AMENDMENT XVI

The Congress shall have power to lay and collect taxes on incomes, from whatever source derived, without apportionment among the several States, and without regard to any census or enumeration.

# AMENDMENT XVII

The Senate of the United States shall be composed of two Senators from each State, elected by the people thereof, for six years; and each Senator shall have one vote. The electors in each State shall have the qualifications requisite for electors of the most numerous branch of the State legislatures.

When vacancies happen in the representation of any State in the Senate, the executive authority of such State shall issue writs of election to fill such vacancies: *Provided*, That the legislature of any State may empower the executive thereof to make temporary appointments until the people fill the vacancies by election as the legislature may direct.

This amendment shall not be so construed as to affect the election or term of any Senator chosen before it becomes valid as part of the Constitution.

## AMENDMENT XVIII

Section 1. After one year from the ratification of this article the manufacture, sale, or transportation of intoxicating liquors within, the importation thereof into, or the exportation thereof from the United States and all territory subject to the jurisdiction thereof for beverage purposes is hereby prohibited.

Section 2. The Congress and the several States shall have concurrent power to enforce this article by appropriate legislation.

Section 3. This article shall be inoperative unless it shall have been ratified as an amendment to the Constitution by the legislatures of the several States, as provided in the Constitution, within seven years from the date of the submission hereof to the States by the Congress.

## AMENDMENT XIX

The right of citizens of the United States to vote shall not be denied or abridged by the United States or by any State on account of sex.

Congress shall have power to enforce this article by appropriate legislation.

## AMENDMENT XX

Section 1. The terms of the President and Vice President shall end at noon on the 20th day of January, and the terms of Senators and Representatives at noon on the 3d day of January, of the years in which such terms would have ended if this article had not been ratified; and the terms of their successors shall then begin.

Section 2. The Congress shall assemble at least once in every year, and such meeting shall begin at noon on the 3d day of January, unless they shall by law appoint a different day.

Section 3. If, at the time fixed for the beginning of the term of the President, the President elect shall have died, the Vice President elect shall become President. If a President shall not have been chosen before the time fixed for the beginning of his term, or if the President elect shall have failed to qualify, then the Vice President elect shall act as President until a President shall have qualified; and the Congress may by law provide for the case wherein neither a President elect nor a Vice President shall have qualified, declaring who shall then act as President, or the manner in which one who is to act shall be selected, and such person shall act accordingly until a President or Vice President shall have qualified.

Section 4. The Congress may by law provide for the case of the death of any of the persons from whom the House of Representatives may choose a President whenever the right of choice shall have devolved upon them, and for the case of the death of any of the persons from whom the Senate may choose a Vice President whenever the right of choice shall have devolved upon them.

Section 5. Sections 1 and 2 shall take effect on the 15th day of October following the ratification of this article.

Section 6. This article shall be inoperative unless it shall have been ratified as an amendment to the Constitution by the legislatures of three-fourths of the several States within seven years from the date of its submission.

# AMENDMENT XXI

Section 1. The eighteenth article of amendment to the Constitution of the United States is hereby repealed.

Section 2. The transportation or importation into any State, Territory, or Possession of the United States for delivery or use therein of intoxicating liquors, in violation of the laws thereof, is hereby prohibited.

Section 3. This article shall be inoperative unless it shall have been ratified as an amendment to the Constitution by conventions in the several States, as provided in the Constitution, within seven years from the date of the submission hereof to the States by the Congress.

# AMENDMENT XXII

Section 1. No person shall be elected to the office of the President more than twice, and no person who has held the office of President, or acted as President, for more than two years of a term to which some other person was elected President shall be elected to the office of the President more than once. But this Article shall not apply to any person holding the office of President, when this Article was proposed by the Congress, and shall not prevent any person who may be holding the office of President, or acting as President, during the term within which this Article becomes operative from holding the office of President or acting as President during the remainder of such term.

Section 2. This article shall be inoperative unless it shall have been ratified as an amendment to the Constitution by the legislatures of three-fourths of the several States within seven years from the date of its submission to the States by the Congress.

# AMENDMENT XXIII

Section 1. The District constituting the seat of Government of the United States shall appoint in such manner as Congress may direct:

A number of electors of President and Vice President equal to the whole number of Senators and Representatives in Congress to which the District would be entitled if it were a State, but in no event more than the least populous State; they shall be in addition to those appointed by the States, but they shall be considered, for the purposes of the election of President and Vice President, to be electors appointed by a State; and they shall meet in the District and perform such duties as provided by the twelfth article of amendment.

Section 2. The Congress shall have power to enforce this article by appropriate legislation.

# AMENDMENT XXIV

Section 1. The right of citizens of the United States to vote in any primary or other election for President or Vice President, for electors for President or Vice President, or for Senator or Representative in Congress, shall not be denied or abridged by the United States or any State by reason of failure to pay any poll tax or other tax.

Section 2. The Congress shall have power to enforce this article by appropriate legislation.

# AMENDMENT XXV

Section 1. In case of the removal of the President from office or of his death or resignation, the Vice President shall become President.

Section 2. Whenever there is a vacancy in the office of the Vice President, the President shall nominate a Vice President who shall take office upon confirmation by a majority vote of both Houses of Congress.

Section 3. Whenever the President transmits to the President pro tempore of the Senate and the Speaker of the House of Representatives his written declaration that he is unable to discharge the powers and duties of his office, and until he transmits to them a written declaration to the contrary, such powers and duties shall be discharged by the Vice President as Acting President.

Section 4. Whenever the Vice President and a majority of either the principal officers of the executive departments or of such other body as Congress may by law provide, transmit to the President pro tempore of the Senate and the Speaker of the House of Representatives their written declaration that the President is unable to discharge the powers and duties of his office, the Vice President shall immediately assume the powers and duties of the office as Acting President.

Thereafter, when the President transmits to the President pro tempore of the Senate and the Speaker of the House of Representatives has written declaration that no inability exists, he shall resume the powers and duties of his office unless the Vice President and a majority of either the principal officers of the executive department or of such other body as Congress may by law provide, transmit within four days to the President pro tempore of the Senate and the Speaker of the House of Representatives their written declaration that the President is unable to discharge the powers and duties of his office. Thereupon Congress shall decide the issue, assembling within forty-eight hours for that purpose if not in session. If the Congress, within twenty-one days after receipt of the latter written declaration, or, if Congress is not in session, within twenty-one days after Congress is required to assemble, determines by two-thirds vote of both Houses that the President is unable to discharge the powers and duties of his office, the Vice President shall continue to discharge the same as Acting President; otherwise, the President shall resume the powers and duties of his office.

# AMENDMENT XXVI

Section 1. The right of citizens of the United States, who are eighteen years of age or older, to vote shall not be denied or abridged by the United States or by any State on account of age.

Section 2. The Congress shall have power to enforce this article by appropriate legislation.

# AMENDMENT XXVII

No law, varying the compensation for the services of the Senators and Representatives, shall take effect, until an election of Representatives shall have intervened.

# Glossary

**Absolute immunity (from prosecution):** Court order compelling a witness who has invoked the Fifth Amendment privilege against self-incrimination to testify, but granting the witness immunity from prosecution for crimes revealed.

**Absolute immunity (from tort liability):** Complete exemption from civil liability for official acts, even when undertaken maliciously.

**Accused:** A person against whom formal charges have been lodged.

**Affidavit:** A written statement of facts, signed and sworn to before a person having authority to administer an oath.

**Aggravating circumstances:** Factors that must be present before the death penalty may be imposed on a defendant convicted of a capital crime. Also called aggravating factors.

**Appearance evidence:** Physical evidence derived from body characteristics that are routinely displayed to the public, such as one's physical appearance, voice, handwriting, and fingerprints.

**Appointed counsel:** An attorney provided by the government free of charge to an indigent person.

**Arraignment:** The defendant's initial appearance before a committing magistrate. During this appearance, the defendant is read the charges, informed of his or her right to counsel, and given an opportunity to request appointment of counsel. *See* formal charges.

**Arrest:** A seizure performed with the intent of making a formal arrest or one that lasts too long or is too invasive to be treated as an investigatory stop. *See* investigatory detention, investigatory stop, seizure, and *Terry* stop.

**Arrest warrant:** A written order of a court, made on behalf of the government, directing an officer to arrest a person and bring him or her before a magistrate.

**Bodily evidence:** Physical evidence derived from: (1) searching parts of a suspect's body not normally exposed to the public, (2) seizing biological materials, or (3) seizing foreign substances on or inside the body.

**Child pornography:** Works that visually depict real children engaged in sexual acts.

**Collateral estoppel:** Doctrine that bars relitigation of issues that have already been tried in a legal proceeding involving the same parties. Once a party places a matter in issue in a legal proceeding and the matter is resolved against him or her, he or she may not relitigate the same matter in any subsequent legal proceeding involving the same parties or others closely allied with them.

**Commercial speech:** Speech designed to arouse interest in a commercial transaction.

**Common law:** A body of legal principles that derives its authority from the decisions of courts rather than statutes; unwritten law.

**Confrontation:** Any pretrial event in which the prosecution or the police engage the accused for the purpose of gathering evidence or advancing the prosecution.

**Container:** Any receptacle that is capable of holding another object, such as luggage, boxes, bags, purses, briefcases, automobile glove compartments, etc.

**Contempt (of court):** Willful disobedience of court procedures or orders. Contempt of court is punishable by fines or imprisonment.

**Contraband:** Any property that it is unlawful to possess, such as illegal drugs, illegal weapons, and stolen property. *See* seizable evidence.

***Corpus delicti*:** The requirement that the prosecution put on proof, independent of a confession, that the crime charged was in fact committed by someone, before a confession may be introduced in evidence.

**Critical stage:** The accused is entitled to counsel during all critical stages in a criminal proceeding. To be considered a critical stage, the event must occur after the initiation of a prosecution and involve a confrontation between the accused and the government in which the lack of counsel may have a prejudicial effect on the outcome of the case (i.e., rights may be lost, defenses waived, or privileges not claimed).

**Curtilage:** The grounds and outbuildings immediately surrounding a dwelling, which are regularly used for domestic and family purposes, such as the yard and garage.

**Custodial interrogation:** Questioning or other actions initiated by a law enforcement officer, after a suspect has been taken into custody, that are designed to elicit an incriminating response from the suspect. *See* custody and investigative questioning.

**Custody:** The restraint of a suspect's liberty to the degree associated with a formal arrest. This determination is made from the point of view of a reasonable person in the suspect's position.

***De facto* arrest.** An arrest that occurs by operation of law when an investigatory detention last too long or is too invasive to be treated as an investigatory detention, resulting in a violation of the Fourth Amendment unless probable cause is present.

**Custody:** The restraint of a suspect's liberty to the degree associated with a formal arrest. This determination is made from the point of view of a reasonable person in the suspect's position.

***De minimis*:** Trivial; of no real consequence.

**Derivative evidence:** Evidence that is inadmissible because it derives from an illegal confession or other illegally obtained evidence.

**Detention:** A temporary, limited seizure made for the purpose of investigating suspicious circumstances; also called an investigatory stop or a *Terry* stop. *See* arrest, investigatory stop, seizure, and *Terry* stop.

**Device:** Any apparatus used to monitor or record an oral, wire, or electronic communication.

**Disparate impact discrimination:** A Title VII violation committed when an employer uses selection criteria that disproportionately eliminate members of a protected class without being valid predictors of the knowledge, skills, or traits necessary for successful performance of the job.

**Disparate treatment discrimination:** A Title VII violation committed when a person is deliberately treated unequally in employment matters because of race, sex, religion, color, or national origin.

**Eavesdropping:** Listening with the unaided ear to the conversations of others.

**Electronic communications:** Transmissions of matters other than human voice messages, such as written words, signs, signals, symbols, images, or other data, over telegraph or telex lines, between fax machines, between computers, etc.

**Elements (of a crime):** The acts, accompanying mental state, and consequences that constitute the statutory components of a crime.

**Exigent circumstances:** A situation that requires swift action to protect lives or safety, or to prevent destruction of evidence or escape.

**Expressive conduct:** Conduct that communicates a message—such as picketing, marching, distributing handbills, soliciting funds, using a bullhorn, or engaging in symbolic speech.

**Facially valid warrant:** A search warrant that appears regular on its face. To be regular on its face, the warrant must describe with particularity the place to be searched and the items to be seized.

**Felony:** A crime punishable by death or imprisonment for a term of one year or more. *See* misdemeanor.

**Fighting words:** Personally abusive and derogatory words spoken to another in a face-to-face encounter under circumstances that, as a matter of common knowledge, are inherently likely to provoke the other person into making an immediate violent response.

**Foreign intelligence information:** Information that relates to actual or potential attacks by foreign governments or their agents, foreign spying activity inside the United States, domestic activity of international terrorist organizations, and the national defense and security of the United States.

**Formal charges:** Depending on local procedures, formal charges may be initiated by an arraignment, preliminary hearing, indictment, or information. *See* arraignment, indictment, and information.

**Fresh pursuit:** The right of police officers to cross jurisdictional lines when they are in immediate, uninterrupted pursuit of a fleeing suspect.

**Frisk:** A limited weapons search conducted by patting down a suspect's outer clothing.

**Fruits (of a crime):** Tangible objects derived through or in consequence of the commission of a crime, such as stolen money or property or funds obtained from the sale of stolen property. *See* seizable evidence.

**Fruits (of an unconstitutional search or seizure):** Evidence uncovered during an unconstitutional search or seizure, plus any further evidence that is later derived from or discovered as a result of that evidence.

**Full search:** Search conducted to discover incriminating evidence.

**Grand jury:** A grand jury is a jury of inquiry empaneled to hear evidence presented by the prosecutor and decide whether the evidence is sufficient to hold the person for trial. If the evidence is deemed sufficient, the grand jury will return an indictment. *See* formal charges and indictment.

**Hate speech:** Speech that expresses contempt and loathing for others because of race, religion, ethnicity, sex, sexual orientation, or other vulnerable characteristics.

**Hostile work environment sexual harassment:** A Title VII violation that is committed by unwelcome verbal or physical conduct of a sexual nature, so severe or pervasive that it alters the conditions of the victim's employment and creates an intimidating, hostile, abusive, or offensive work environment.

**Hot pursuit:** The right of police officers to make a warrantless entry into a private residence or other protected area when they are in immediate, uninterrupted pursuit of a fleeing felon.

**Impoundment:** Occurs when police take custody of a person's property for reasons other than use as evidence. Examples include taking custody of an arrestee's belongings incident to jailing, towing an abandoned or illegally parked car to a police lot, etc.

**Indictment:** A formal written accusation made by a grand jury. *See* formal charges and information.

**Information:** A formal accusation or complaint, filed by the prosecutor, charging a person with a designated crime. It is used as a substitute for an indictment in certain classes of criminal cases. *See* formal charges and indictment.

**Inventory search:** A search conducted to make an inventory of property that police have taken into custody.

**Instrumentalities (of a crime):** Tools, vehicles, etc. used to commit a crime. *See* seizable evidence.

**Intensity of a search:** The thoroughness of the search activity that is permitted. Depending on the grounds for search authority, the permissible intensity can vary from a cursory inspection to a microscopic examination. The intensity of a search may be no greater than necessary to discover the items for which police have search authority.

**Interception:** Use of a device to monitor or record the contents of an oral, wire, or electronic communication.

**Interception order:** A judicial order, similar to a search warrant, that authorizes interception of a communication.

**Interrogation:** Questioning that is designed to elicit an incriminating response. Interrogation also includes actions that are the functional equivalent of a question, such as telling the suspect that an eyewitness has identified him or her. *See* custody, custodial interrogation, and investigative questioning.

**Investigative questioning:** Questioning of a suspect who is not in custody or charged with the crime to which the questions relate.

**Investigatory detention:** Temporary, limited seizure made for the purpose of investigating suspicious circumstances; also called an investigatory stop or a *Terry* stop. *See* arrest, investigatory stop, seizure, and *Terry* stop.

**Investigatory stop:** Temporary, limited seizure made for the purpose of investigating suspicious circumstances; also called an investigatory detention or a *Terry* stop. *See* arrest, investigatory detention, seizure, and *Terry* stop.

**Jury venire:** Group of potential jurors from which the trial jury is selected; also called "jury pool."

**Limited weapons search:** A search conducted to disarm a suspect and remove weapons so that an officer can conduct a traffic stop, *Terry* investigation, execute a search warrant, etc. without fear for personal safety. *See* frisk, pat-down, protective sweep.

**Lineup:** A police identification procedure in which a group of individuals with similar characteristics are exhibited, to determine whether the victim or an eyewitness can make an identification.

**Manual body cavity search:** A search of rectal or genital cavities that includes touching or probing.

**Mere evidence:** Evidence that links a suspect to a crime, other than the fruits or instrumentalities of the crime or contraband. Clothing worn during the crime is an example. *See* seizable evidence.

**Misdemeanor:** A crime less serious than a felony, punishable by a fine or a jail sentence, generally for a term of less than one year. *See* felony.

**Mitigating circumstances:** Factors that permit the sentencer to show mercy and withhold the death penalty for a crime for which the death penalty is authorized. Also called mitigating factors.

**Motion to dismiss:** A request made to a court in which a civil action is pending, to terminate the plaintiff's action without a trial.

**Nonpublic forum:** Government facilities reserved for the government's business uses.

**Obscenity:** Movies, books, literature, magazines, and other similar materials that appeal to the prurient interest, depict hard-core sexual acts in a patently offensive way, and lack serious literary, artistic, political, scientific, or other value.

**Oral communications:** Human voice communications that travel through the air by sound waves. Face-to-face conversations are the most common example. The communication must be spoken under circumstances in which the speaker has a reasonable expectation of noninterception in order to be protected by Title III.

**Panhandling:** Begging in a public place.

**Pat-down:** A weapons frisk that is performed by patting down the person's outer clothing; reasonable suspicion that the person is armed or may be dangerous is necessary to perform a pat-down search.

**Per se:** Necessarily; as a matter of course; in all cases.

**Petit jury:** A jury empaneled to decide whether an accused is guilty; also called a "trial jury."

**Photographic identification:** A pretrial identification procedure in which a group of photographs is shown to the victim or a witness to determine whether an identification can be made.

**Physical evidence:** Tangible evidence of a crime. Physical evidence includes everything except testimony.

**Plain view doctrine:** An exception to the warrant requirement that allows police to seize articles without a search warrant describing them if the officer comes across the article while conducting a lawful search and its incriminating nature is immediately apparent to the officer.

**Peremptory challenge:** The right to challenge and strike a potential juror without being required to give a reason. In most jurisdictions, each side has a specified number of peremptory challenges and, after using them, must establish cause, such as bias, for further challenges to witnesses.

**Prejudicial error:** An error committed during trial that is sufficiently serious that it furnishes grounds for a new trial, or for reversal on appeal. Also called reversible error.

**Pretextual traffic stop:** A stop made for a traffic violation in which the officer's real motive is to check a hunch about unrelated criminal activity.

**Privilege (evidentiary):** The right to withhold evidence that the government could otherwise compel.

**Probable cause (to arrest):** The degree of factual certainty needed to justify an arrest. Probable cause exists when an officer is aware of facts and circumstances sufficient to warrant a reasonable person in believing a crime has been committed and the person to be arrested committed it. Probable cause is sometimes referred to as reasonable grounds. *See* reasonable grounds.

**Probable cause (to search):** The degree of factual certainty needed for the issuance of a search warrant. Probable cause exists if a prudent person would conclude that specific objects linked to a crime will be found at a particular location.

**Probable cause (to seize):** The degree of factual certainty needed to seize an object as evidence. Probable cause to seize exists if a prudent person would conclude that the object in question is associated with criminal activity.

**Protective sweep:** Cursory visual inspection of closets and other spaces immediately adjoining the place of arrest in which persons posing a danger to the officer could be hiding; permitted whenever the police arrest someone inside a dwelling.

**Public forums by designation:** Property the government has deliberately set aside for speech uses by members of the public.

**Qualified immunity:** Immunity from liability for unconstitutional acts that a reasonable police officer would have believed were lawful.

*Quid pro quo* **sexual harassment:** A Title VII violation committed when the victim's submission to a supervisor's unwelcome sexual advances is explicitly or implicitly made a condition of receiving tangible job benefits or not suffering tangible job detriments.

**Racial profiling:** Any action taken during a traffic stop that is based upon racial or ethnic stereotypes and that has the effect of treating minority motorists differently from other motorists. Such actions include both the initial decision to pull the vehicle over and actions taken during the stop, such as ordering the occupants to step out of the vehicle, questioning them about drugs, making the decision to frisk, search, or request consent, summoning a drug-detection dog to the scene, etc.

**Reasonable expectation of privacy:** Factor that determines whether police activity constitutes a search or an interception. *See* search.

**Reasonable grounds:** An alternative expression for probable cause. *See* probable cause.

**Reasonable suspicion:** The level of suspicion needed for an investigatory stop. Reasonable suspicion exists when an officer can articulate and point to facts that, together with rational inferences that flow from them, would warrant a reasonable police officer in suspecting the person detained of committing, having committed, or being about to commit a crime. *See* probable cause and reasonable grounds.

**Retained counsel:** An attorney hired and paid for by the accused.

**"Same elements" test:** The test used in the federal courts and a majority of state courts to determine when prosecutions brought under different sections of the penal code represent the same offense. This test treats crimes defined under different sections of the penal code as distinct offenses for double jeopardy purposes so long as each statute requires proof of at least one distinct element.

**"Same transaction" test:** Test used in a minority of state courts to determine when prosecutions brought under different sections of the penal code represent the same offense for purposes of double jeopardy. This test treats all crimes committed as part of the same underlying transaction as a single offense for double jeopardy purposes.

**Scope (of a search):** Areas police have the authority to search. In searches under the authority of a search warrant, the scope of the search is determined by the warrant's description of the place to be searched.

**Search:** A search occurs when the police perform acts that intrude on a suspect's "reasonable expectation of privacy." A search can occur either by: (1) physically intruding into a constitutionally protected location or (2) technological invasions of privacy.

**Search warrant:** A written order, issued by a justice or magistrate, in the name of the state, authorizing an officer to search a specified location for described objects that constitute evidence of a crime or contraband.

**Seizable evidence:** Objects that police have probable cause to believe are connected to a crime. There are four categories: (1) the fruits of a crime, (2) instrumentalities used in its commission, (3) contraband, and (4) mere evidence.

**Seizure (of a person):** A seizure occurs when a suspect submits to a police officer's show of legal authority or the officer gains physical control over him or her. Seizures are separated into two classes—investigative stops and arrests—based on their scope and duration. *See* arrest, investigatory detention, investigatory stop, show of legal authority, and *Terry* stop.

**Seizure (of things):** A seizure occurs when police commit a meaningful interference with a suspect's possessory rights in property.

**Self-incrimination:** Declarations and declaratory acts, furnished or performed under government compulsion, that implicate a person in a crime.

**Sequester (a jury):** To isolate jurors from contact with the public during the course of a trial.

**Show of legal authority:** Police words or conduct that would induce a reasonable person to believe that he or she was not free to leave. *See* seizure.

**Showup:** An identification procedure in which police bring the suspect to the victim or a witness for identification.

**Sovereign:** The government of an independent nation or state.

**Statute of limitations:** A law prescribing the period following a crime during which the government must either bring charges or lose the right to prosecute.

**Strip search:** Compulsory disrobing followed by comprehensive, methodical visual examination of a suspect's naked body.

***Subpoena ad testificatum*:** Command by a court or legislative body to appear at a certain time and date and give testimony.

***Subpoena duces tecum*:** Command by a court or legislative body to produce designated documents, books, papers, records, or other things.

**Suspect:** Person whom the government believes committed a crime, but who has not yet been formally charged.

**Symbolic speech:** Mute conduct performed for the sake of communicating a message that is likely to be understood by those who view it.

***Terry* stop:** Temporary, limited seizure of a person made for the sake of investigating suspicious circumstances; also called an investigatory stop or investigatory detention. *See* arrest, investigatory stop, investigatory detention, and seizure.

**Testimony/testimonial evidence:** Statements elicited from a witness.

**Tort:** Legal wrong, other than a breach of contract, for which the court will provide a remedy in the form of damages.

**Traditional public forums:** Used in First Amendment analysis to refer to streets, sidewalks, and parks.

**Tribunal:** The factfinder at a trial; the petit jury functions as the factfinder in a jury trial and the judge functions as the factfinder in a bench trial.

**"Under color of" state law:** The misuse of power, possessed by virtue of state law, and made possible only because the wrongdoer is clothed with the authority of state law.

**Use immunity/derivative use immunity:** Court order compelling a witness who has invoked the Fifth Amendment privilege against self-incrimination to testify, but barring the government from using the testimony and evidence derived from it against the witness in a subsequent criminal prosecution.

**Voir dire:** A preliminary examination of a prospective juror, conducted by the court or counsel, to determine the prospective juror's qualifications and suitability for jury service.

**Voluntary encounter:** An investigative encounter in which a suspect's cooperation is voluntary.

**Vulgar speech:** Speech that is crude, coarse, profane, ribald, or patently offensive.

**Wire communications:** Human voice messages that are transmitted across a public communications network, such as a telephone call.

**Witness:** A person who is called to testify before a court or to provide answers to official questions.

# Table of Cases

*This list includes all cases cited in the text.*
*Cases in boldface type are printed in Part II of the text.*

# Index